Range Plant Handbook

Prepared by UNITED STATES
DEPARTMENT OF AGRICULTURE,
FOREST SERVICE

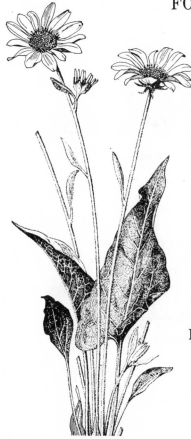

DOVER PUBLICATIONS, INC.
NEW YORK

Published in Canada by General Publishing Company, Ltd.,
30 Lesmill Road, Don Mills, Toronto, Ontario.

Published in the United Kingdom by Constable and Company, Ltd., 10 Orange Street, London WC2H 7EG.

This Dover edition, first published in 1988, is an unabridged republication of the work originally published by the United States Department of Agriculture, Forest Service (United States Government Printing Office), Washington, D.C., March 1937. Eighteen illustrations originally in color have been reproduced here in black and white.

Manufactured in the United States of America
Dover Publications, Inc., 31 East 2nd Street, Mineola, N.Y. 11501

Library of Congress Cataloging-in-Publication Data

Range plant handbook / prepared by United States Department of Agriculture, Forest Service.
     p.   cm.
    Reprint. Originally published: Washington : U.S. G.P.O. : For sale by the Supt. of Docs., 1937.
    Includes bibliographical references and index.
    ISBN 0-486-25783-5 (pbk.)
    1. Range plants—United States—Identification. I. United States. Forest Service.
SB193.3.U5R36   1988
633.2′00973—dc19   88-16992
                           CIP

UNITED STATES DEPARTMENT OF AGRICULTURE

Washington, D. C.   Issued March 1937

RANGE PLANT HANDBOOK

Prepared, under immediate supervision of W. A. DAYTON, *in charge Range Forage Investigations, Division of Range Research,* by THOMAS LOMMASSON, *Senior Range Examiner,* and BARRY C. PARK, *Assistant Range Examiner, Northern Region;* CHARLES A. KUTZLEB, *Assistant Forester, Rocky Mountain Region;* ODELL JULANDER, *Assistant Range Examiner, Southwestern Region;* ARNOLD R. STANDING, *Inspector of Grazing, Intermountain Region;* SELAR S. HUTCHINGS, *Assistant Forest Ecologist, Intermountain Forest and Range Experiment Station;* LLOYD W. SWIFT, *Associate Range Examiner, California Region;* EDWARD P. CLIFF, *Associate Range Examiner, Northern Pacific Region;* DORIS W. HAYES, *Assistant Forest Ecologist;* MIRIAM L. BOMHARD, *Botanist, Forest Service.* Technical review by W. R. CHAPLINE, *Chief, Division of Range Research;* R. R. HILL, *Assistant Chief, Division of Range Management;* LINCOLN ELLISON, *Associate Range Examiner, Northern Rocky Mountain Forest and Range Experiment Station, Forest Service.*[1]

CONTENTS [2]

INTRODUCTION

Repeated requests from field officers of the Forest Service for an accurate publication, readily consultable under field conditions, in as simple language as possible, which could be assembled as desired, and be easily revised, were the genesis of this loose-leaf range-plant handbook. Its intended audience is primarily busy field administrative men who are not specialists in botany; its chief purpose is twofold: (1) To evaluate for such persons, in as succinct, understandable, complete, and useful form as possible, the relative importance of some 300 or more of the outstanding "key" plants of western ranges as regards grazing, watershed protective cover, recreational, and other uses; and (2) to enable the ready field identification of these plants in order to insure the correlation of the proper management data with each species.

---

[1] Illustrations prepared by Leta Hughey, and, under her supervision, by Elnor L. Keplinger, Gene Walker, Margaret Austin, Hermione Dreja, Harold W. Sentiff, and Elsie L. Pomeroy.

[2] It will be noted that there are certain gaps in the symbols for the write-ups of individual genera and species included in this handbook. These gaps are explained in the introduction which follows.

I

Altogether, there are 728,000,000 acres of range lands in the West, inhabited naturally by over 1,200 genera and 10,000 species of flowering plants. The economic and social significance of this range vegetation challenges comprehension. While this handbook is chiefly representative of mountain ranges typical of the western national forests, many of the genera and species discussed occur also on the enormous areas of other and lower ranges.

Nearly every phase of range management is intimately associated with a knowledge of the range plants, their requirements, life history, and forage value. Proper grazing capacity of range lands, periods and degrees of use, and class of livestock to which a particular range is best suited are determined largely by the character and composition of the range vegetation and the life habits and values of the plants themselves. Indications of overgrazing cannot be properly interpreted by and frequently are not discernible to persons unfamiliar with the plant cover. Recognition of the important forage plants, combined with knowledge of the extent to which each can be properly grazed, are essential to proper range use. Range fencing and salting are undertaken chiefly because of local forage conditions. Poisonous plants, unless recognized and guarded against, menace the welfare of herds and flocks. Soil protection, soil erosion, and supply of water for domestic use, as well as for irrigation and hydroelectric power, are all intimately correlated with mountain range vegetative cover. Timber values are involved in numerous ways, as the composition, quantity, and quality of range vegetation frequently are closely associated with injuries to timber reproduction by domestic livestock, rodents, and other agencies, as well as with the harboring of insect pests and pathogenic organisms. Furthermore, the recreational importance of many localities is intimately interwoven with the beauty of the local flora or with its food value for local wildlife.

No book or group of publications provide this precise information required by the range administrator. Large sections of the western range country (e. g., Idaho and Arizona) are not treated, at present, in botanical manuals. In his identifications the field man must depend on fragmentary works, few of which are illustrated, usually either couched in unfamiliar technical phraseology or so generalized and inadequate as to be almost worthless for his purpose. For economic, ecological, and miscellaneous information he must search even farther and generally with less success.

For his convenience the range plant handbook employs a novel method whereby the technical, diagnostic parts of a plant are portrayed in a manner readily comprehensible by a person untrained in botany. To the right of each illustration are the key diagnostic characters. This arrangement enables the reader to grasp clearly the essential morphological characters of species.

This handbook presents 339 generic and specific write-ups incorporated with which, however, are notes on over 500 additional species. The main treatments include 98 grasses, 8 grasslike plants (chiefly sedges and rushes), 137 range weeds (nongrasslike herbs), and 96 browse plants. Because of the loose-leaf structure of this handbook, the text and illustrations are not paged.* Each plant discussion has its own symbol (G1, G2, etc., for grasses; GL1, GL2, etc., for grasslike plants; W1, W2, etc., for range weeds; and B1, B2, etc., for browse). Gaps which appear in the symbol sequences are by way of provision for the possible future inclusion of some 173 other plants of material range importance.

Sources

The information upon which the articles in this handbook are based was gleaned from both published and unpublished data of the Forest Service, as well as from many other sources. One very important source is the Forest Service range plant herbarium containing 80,000 annotated specimens, unquestionably the richest single storehouse of information on western montane vegetation. This herbarium is the result of a fairly systematic collection of annotated range plant specimens, by about 1,300 Forest Service officers, inaugurated by James T. Jardine as the first chief of range research in the Forest Service. Much of the annotated material with these specimens is the result of intensive field investigations by special grazing men both in administration and research. The specimens themselves have been identified

---

*A continuous pagination has been added to the Dover edition (1988) for the user's convenience. No changes have been made, however, in the table of Contents or the Index.

under the direction of Dr. Frederick V. Coville, Bureau of Plant Industry. The majority of the determinations, aside from grasses, have been made by the late Dr. E. L. Greene (1908–15) and Ivar Tidestrom (1915–35). Grasses have been identified by the late Prof. A. S. Hitchcock, Mrs. Agnes Chase, and assistants; the late Kenneth D. Mackenzie check-identified the sedges; Dr. Coville determined most of the rushes, currants, gooseberries, and blueberries; Dr. C. R. Ball, most of the willows; Dr. S. F. Blake, many composites; W. W. Eggleston and Dr. C. P. Smith, lupines; Dr. F. W. Pennell, numerous Scrophulariaceae; and the late Dr. C. V. Piper, many plants from eastern Oregon and Washington. Other Forest Service sources include a booklet of grass notes (1914)), Dr. Arthur W. Sampson's Important Range Plants (1917), and Dayton's Important Western Browse Plants (1931); also unpublished notes on upwards of 3,000 species, palatability tables developed by numerous range reconnaissance parties, and unpublished manuscripts on western range weeds ("forbs", or nongrasslike herbs) and on Southwestern range plants.

The more outstanding and most frequently consulted of over 400 publications, outside those of the Forest Service, used in connection with the preparation of this handbook include the following:

Coulter, Botany of Western Texas (1891–94).
Howell, A Flora of Northwest America (1897–1903).
Lyons, Plant Names Scientific and Popular (1900).
Rydberg, Catalogue of the Flora of Montana and the Yellowstone National Park (1900).
Blankinship, Native Economic Plants of Montana (1905).
Knight, Hepner, and Nelson, Wyoming Forage Plants and their Chemical Composition (4 papers, 1905–11).
Rydberg, Flora of Colorado (1905).
Piper, Flora of Washington (1906).
Coulter and Nelson, New Manual of Botany of the Central Rocky Mountains (1909).
Thornber, The Grazing Ranges of Arizona (1910).
Schneider, Pharmacal Plants and their Culture (1912).
Wooton and Standley, The Grasses and Grass-like Plants of New Mexico (1912).
Wooton and Standley, Flora of New Mexico (1915).
Rydberg, Flora of the Rocky Mountains and Adjacent Plains (1917).
Hitchcock, The Genera of Grasses of the United States, with Special Reference to the Economic Species (1920).
Standley, Trees and Shrubs of Mexico (1920–26).
Youngken, A Textbook of Pharmacognosy (1921).
Hadwen and Palmer, Reindeer in Alaska (1922).
Abrams, An Illustrated Flora of the Pacfic States (1923).
Jepson, A Manual of the Flowering Plants of California (1923–25).
Piper, Forage Plants and their Culture (1924).
Tidestrom, Flora of Utah and Nevada (1925).
Sampson and Chase, Range Grasses of California (1927).
Wilson, The Artificial Reseeding of New Mexico Ranges (1931).
Rydberg, Flora of the Prairies and Plains of Central North America (1932).
Bailey, The Standard Cyclopedia of Horticulture (1933).
Saunders, Western Wild Flowers and their Stories (1933).
Silveus, Texas Grasses (1933).
Stuhr, Manual of Pacific Coast Drug Plants (1933).

The grass nomenclature in the handbook is in accord with that of Hitchcock's Manual of Grasses of the United States (1935). For data on poisonous plants the copious literature of Pammel, Marsh, Chesnut, Clawson, Roe, Couch, Beath, Fleming, Glover, and other specialists was freely used.

Ethnobotanical notes on plants used by American Indians were obtained chiefly from the works of Chesnut, Coville, Geyer, Gilmore, Harrington, Havard, Palmer, Robbins, Russell, Standley, and Stevenson. Pellett's publications on American honey plants, outstanding in that field, have been freely drawn upon.

Palatability of Range Plants

The use of the term "palatability", as found in this publication, is in accordance with the usage of national-forest grazing surveys, and has been defined [3] as

the degree to which the herbage within easy reach of stock is grazed when a range is properly utilized under the best practicable range management. The percentage of the readily accessible herbage of a species that is grazed when the range is properly utilized determines the palatability of the species.

---

[3] United States Department of Agriculture, Forest Service. INSTRUCTIONS FOR GRAZING SURVEYS ON NATIONAL FORESTS. 40 pp., illus. (Mimeographed.) 1935.

Palatability applies to the growing season of the vegetation in which the species in question occurs and, in some cases, to the yearlong season. The following palatability tabulation has been followed in this work:

	Percent		*Percent*
Practically worthless	−5	Good	55 to 70
Poor	5 to 15	Very good	75 to 85
Fair	20 to 35	Excellent	90 and over
Fairly good	40 to 50		

There are numerous available records to the effect that species are grazed in greater degree than that shown in this handbook. Where investigation has shown that such records indicate overgrazing, they have been ignored or properly discounted.

Nomenclature

The scientific (Latin) nomenclature adopted is in accordance with that used in the Bureau of Plant Industry, U. S. Department of Agriculture. Readers who seek an introduction to Latin plant nomenclature should consult such works as Hitchcock's Descriptive Systematic Botany (1925), Swingle's A Textbook of Systematic Botany (1928), and Pool's Flowers and Flowering Plants (1929). Synonymous names are shown only so far as usage in the common western manuals is concerned. Latin plant names in quotation marks, followed by the phrase "not _____", indicate that the
Name of author
name is valid but misapplied to the plant under discussion.

There are obvious advantages in having the English nomenclature of important plants standardized, so far as that is now feasible. In this work the standard authorities of the Department of Agriculture have been consulted, namely, Sudworth's Check List of the Forest Trees of the United States, Their Names and Ranges; Standardized Plant Names, and the list of preferred plant names spellings in the Style Manual of the Government Printing Office. Some of the plants discussed in this publication have had no well-established or acceptable English name; this work attempts to correct that situation, and several new English plant names appear here for the first time in print.

Pronunciation

An attempt has been made in these articles to assist the reader in the pronunciation of scientific plant names by the insertion of accent marks. An excellent discussion of this subject, in simple language, appears in a book by Prof. L. H. Bailey[4] in the section Pronunciation (pp. 132–136, of the chapter entitled "The Names and the Words", *op. cit.*).

Broadly speaking, there is no single standard way of pronouncing scientific plant names. There are two general methods of pronouncing such names in this country: The English, and the continental European methods. The latter method (which attempts to restore, insofar as is possible, the original Latin pronunciation) has more world-wide use and is adopted here. There are three main rules of Latin pronunciation: (1) Words of two syllables are accented on the first syllable, thus: *Lō'tŭs, Phlē'ŭm, Pī'nŭs, Rō'sā, Rū'bŭs;* (2) Words of more than two syllables are accented on the next to the last syllable (penult) if that is long, thus: *Balsamorhī'zā, Cicū'tā, Solidā'gō, Zygadē'nŭs;* (3) The accent falls on the third syllable from the last (antepenult) if the penult is short, thus: *Amelān'chǐ-ĕr, Ē'phĕ-drā, Junī'pĕ-rŭs, Paeō'nǐ-ā.* Notes on Latin vowel quantities are available in any Latin grammar.

---

[4] Bailey, L. H. HOW PLANTS GET THEIR NAMES. 209 pp., illus. New York. 1933.

WHEATGRASSES

Agropy'ron spp.

The wheatgrasses form a genus of about 35 species widely distributed in temperate climates. Approximately two-thirds of these species occur in the Western States, with Colorado apparently their center of distribution. Wheatgrasses are erect perennials belonging to the barley tribe (Hordeae), a tribe of the greatest economic importance, as it includes such grains as wheat, rye, and barley, as well as many highly important range and meadow plants.

The wheatgrasses rank very high as range plants, especially in the western United States where they are widely distributed and often abundant. In general, sheep prefer the herbage of these grasses while the plants are still young and succulent, but also eagerly devour the seed heads of the unbearded or short-awned species. Practically all species are continuously palatable to cattle and horses and make excellent winter forage. In the Southwest, the wheatgrasses when young and tender are grazed slightly by deer, but when mature are spurned by these game animals. This probably holds true in other parts of the country. Elk graze the wheatgrasses to a somewhat greater degree than deer; buffalo or bison prefer certain species, usually bluebunch wheatgrass (*A. spicatum*), as winter forage. Slender wheatgrass (*A. pauciflorum*), a native species extensively grown as a hay crop, appears to have been the first native American grass to be cultivated. Crested wheatgrass (*A. cristatum*) introduced from Siberia, shows promise for revegetating depleted range lands in the cooler portions of the mountain and Great Plains States.

For many years botanists considered the wheatgrasses and wheat (*Triticum*) as belonging to the same genus, and the older species of *Agropyron* were originally placed under *Triticum*. No doubt the common name, wheatgrass, was applied because of the resemblance of many of the agropyrons to wheat. The scientific name (from Greek, *agros*, a field, and *pyros*, wheat) is another reminder of this close resemblance and relationship.

The heads (spikes) of wheatgrasses are commonly rather dense, erect, and either conspicuously bearded (awned), short-awned, or without awns, in general resembling the heads of wheat. Individual flower clusters (spikelets) are three- to many-flowered, without individual stalks (sessile), solitary or rarely in pairs at each joint of the somewhat zigzag axis (rachis) of the spike. The rachis, although jointed, does not break apart at these joints save in a few exceptional cases, and the lowest (2) spikelet bracts (glumes) remain attached to the stem after the seed falls. In the cases of three western species, rock wheatgrass (*A. saxicola*), spreading wheatgrass (*A. scribneri*), and Saunders wheatgrass (*A. saundersii*, syn. *Elymus saundersii*), however, the rachis tardily disarticulates. Such species show a transition toward the related squirreltails (*Sitanion* spp.). Rock wheatgrass and Saunders wheatgrass are also remarkable among wheatgrasses in that their spikelets often occur in pairs at the rachis joints and the glumes are somewhat bristlelike and prolonged into awns. In rock wheatgrass, a densely tufted perennial with thick heads up to 5 inches long, occurring sparsely on mountain slopes in Idaho, Oregon, Washington, and California, the awns are divergent, those of the glumes being from three-fourths of an inch to 2 inches long. In this species the lemmas, or outer flower bracts, bear divergent awns from about three-sixteenths to three-fourths of an inch long. In Saunders wheatgrass, a species locally distributed in western Colorado and eastern Utah, the purplish, erect heads are from about 3 to 6 inches long and the awns are straight. The awns of the lemmas are from three-eighths to nine-sixteenths of an inch long and those of the glumes are from three-fourths of an inch to 1½ inches long. Spreading wheatgrass is a densely tufted perennial with thick, bearded heads up to 3 inches long. It occurs typically on rocky slopes in the high mountains from Montana and Idaho to California and New Mexico and is relatively unimportant as a range forage plant.

Quackgrass (*A. repens*), a perennial, is native to Europe but widely distributed in the United States and is on the increase in the West. It is frequently a pernicious weed in many agricultural lands but is valuable as a range plant, and constitutes a good soil-binder for railway embankments and other cuts or slopes. It serves as a satisfactory hay plant for 2 or 3 years but then becomes sod bound. Quackgrass is rather coarse with bright yellowish green, scaly rootstocks which contain considerable sugar and triticin, a carbohydrate similar to inulin, valuable for treatment of kidney disorders.

Some species of wheatgrass, notably bluestem (*A. smithii*) and quackgrass, are often infected with ergot. This poisonous fungus replaces the "seeds" with black or purplish club-shaped bodies. If the infested heads are consumed by livestock, illness and possibly death result, although comparatively large dosages are required. The symptoms of ergotism naturally assume two forms: (1) The gangrenous form, and (2) the nervous, or spasmodic form. In the first there are coldness and anesthesia (lack of feeling) of the extremities, including the feet, ears, and tail of quadrupeds; the comb, tongue, and beak of birds—followed by the appearance of passive congestion, blebs (blisters), and dry gangrene in the vicinity of these parts, the hoofs and beak often dropping off. In the nervous, or spasmodic, form are seen toxic contraction of the flexor tendons of the limbs and anesthesia of the extremities; muscular trembling and general tetanic spasm, with opisthotonos (bending backward of the body), convulsions, and delirium. Death ensues, in both forms, from general exhaustion.[1]

---

[1] Pammel, L. H., A MANUAL OF POISONOUS PLANTS, CHIEFLY OF EASTERN NORTH AMERICA, WITH BRIEF NOTES ON ECONOMIC AND MEDICINAL PLANTS . . . 2 pts., illus. Cedar Rapids, Iowa. 1910–11.

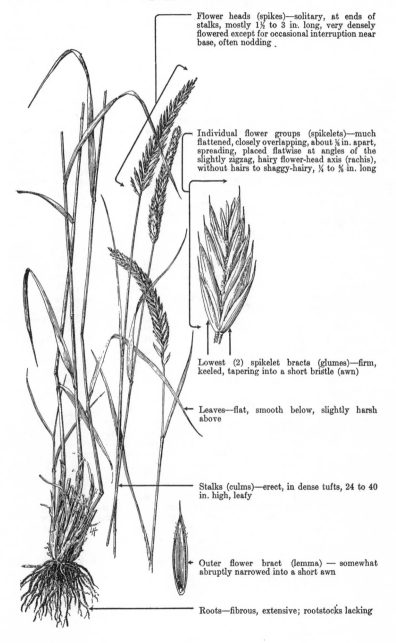

CRESTED WHEATGRASS

Agropy'ron crista'tum

Flower heads (spikes)—solitary, at ends of stalks, mostly 1½ to 3 in. long, very densely flowered except for occasional interruption near base, often nodding .

Individual flower groups (spikelets)—much flattened, closely overlapping, about ⅛ in. apart, spreading, placed flatwise at angles of the slightly zigzag, hairy flower-head axis (rachis), without hairs to shaggy-hairy, ¼ to ⅝ in. long

Lowest (2) spikelet bracts (glumes)—firm, keeled, tapering into a short bristle (awn)

Leaves—flat, smooth below, slightly harsh above

Stalks (culms)—erect, in dense tufts, 24 to 40 in. high, leafy

Outer flower bract (lemma) — somewhat abruptly narrowed into a short awn

Roots—fibrous, extensive; rootstocks lacking

3

As Westover[1] and others have pointed out, crested wheatgrass, a hardy, long-lived perennial bunchgrass, has been introduced into the United States from its native cold, dry plains of Siberia and Russia in an attempt to obtain a pasture and hay grass well suited to the severe growing conditions of our semiarid northern Great Plains and perhaps also useful for certain foothill and mountain range lands of the West. The species is a member of a genus noteworthy for palatability and nutritiousness and as range plants.

Crested wheatgrass is remarkable for its tolerance of extreme temperatures, particularly cold, and for very early spring growth. It naturally inhabits soils of a great variation in texture, ranging from sandy loam to heavy clay. Westover (*op. cit.*) has indicated that crested wheatgrass is especially well adapted to our northern Great Plains, and that it is considered "one of the most promising dry-land grasses for eastern Oregon and Washington and northeastern California." It is reported to give good results as a pasture crop in Colorado at altitudes of about 5,000 feet. It does not appear to be very promising for the southern part of the United States, except possibly at the higher altitudes of the mountain range country.

In recent range reseeding trials[2] only thin stands of crested wheatgrass were obtained at 7,400 feet elevation in the oak zone in central Utah and at 7,600 feet elevation in southwestern Colorado; and not more than a fair stand was obtained in the foothills of the Rocky Mountains in northern Colorado. In these localities smooth brome (*Bromus inermis*) proved somewhat better than crested wheatgrass. On the whole, the species seems better adapted for plains and lower foothills of the North, rather than for the South or for the higher foothills and mountain ranges generally, or where rainfall is appreciably in excess of about 17 inches per annum.

Crested wheatgrass is highly palatable to all classes of livestock and its hay compares favorably with that of the native bluestem (*A. smithii*) in palatability. At most stages of its growth, analyses thus far made appear to indicate that it has a somewhat higher protein content than either slender wheatgrass (*A. pauciflorum*) or smooth brome; and there is no doubt but that it is a highly nutritious species, whether in pasturage or hay. Its fine stems make excellent hay which cures quickly and well, and is readily eaten by all classes of livestock, horses being particularly fond of it. The best quality of hay is obtained if the grass is cut shortly after blooming. In the northern Great Plains, crested wheatgrass is used in combination with other grasses or legumes, which provide more feed during the hot weather when this wheatgrass is dormant. It starts growth earlier in the spring and, when moisture is available, continues to grow later in the fall than most of the other grasses with which it is grown, thus prolonging the grazing season. Westover (*op. cit.*) has called attention to the usefulness of this species for seeding rights-of-way along northern highways, where a permanent growth is needed to control coarse weeds, and for dry-land lawns, golf courses, and airports where finer turf grasses cannot be maintained.

Although crested wheatgrass is tender in the seedling stage and requires favorable conditions for germination and early growth, once established it is very resistant to both cold and drought. This characteristic seems to be correlated with its extensive root system, which permits storage of abundant food reserves as well as ready utilization of water when available. During hot, dry spells the grass becomes dormant but resumes growth with cooler weather and more favorable moisture conditions. It is a vigorous seeder, yields well, and the seeds ripen while the plants are still green. The seeds are about half as large as those of slender wheatgrass. Those of some plants have pronounced bristles (awns) while others are practically awnless. Awnless seed is preferable for planting. For further details respecting the use of this valuable species the reader is referred to United States Department of Agriculture Leaflet 104, above mentioned.

---

[1] Westover, H. L. CRESTED WHEATGRASS. U. S. Dept. Agr. Leaflet 104, 8 pp., illus. 1934.

[2] Forsling, C. L., and Dayton, W. A. ARTIFICIAL RESEEDING ON WESTERN MOUNTAIN RANGE LANDS. U. S. Dept. Agr. Circ. 178, 48 pp., illus. 1931.

THICKSPIKE WHEATGRASS

Agropy'ron dasystach'yum, syns. *A. dasystach'yum subvillo'sum, A. lanceola'-tum, A. subvillo'sum, A. yukonen'se*

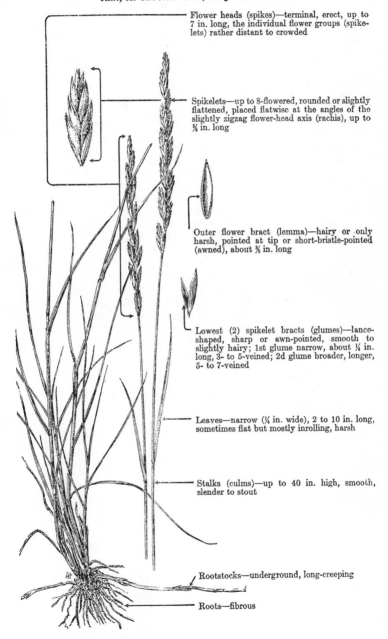

Flower heads (spikes)—terminal, erect, up to 7 in. long, the individual flower groups (spikelets) rather distant to crowded

Spikelets—up to 8-flowered, rounded or slightly flattened, placed flatwise at the angles of the slightly zigzag flower-head axis (rachis), up to ⅝ in. long

Outer flower bract (lemma)—hairy or only harsh, pointed at tip or short-bristle-pointed (awned), about ⅜ in. long

Lowest (2) spikelet bracts (glumes)—lance-shaped, sharp or awn-pointed, smooth to slightly hairy; 1st glume narrow, about ¼ in. long, 3- to 5-veined; 2d glume broader, longer, 5- to 7-veined

Leaves—narrow (¼ in. wide), 2 to 10 in. long, sometimes flat but mostly inrolling, harsh

Stalks (culms)—up to 40 in. high, smooth, slender to stout

Rootstocks—underground, long-creeping

Roots—fibrous

Thickspike wheatgrass, known also as downy, fuzzyhead, northern, small, thickstalk, and Yukon wheatgrass, is a somewhat turfed perennial with extensively creeping underground rootstocks. The species, as now understood by prevalent botanical opinion, has a wider range than most other wheatgrasses, occurring from Hudson Bay to Alaska, northeastern California, southern Colorado, Nebraska, and the shores of Lakes Superior, Michigan, and Huron. It prefers sandy soils, and is found on the lower dry plains in central Idaho and up to at least 10,000 feet elevation in the Wasatch Mountains. It also occurs on the drier hillsides, exposed flats and ridges, and on benchlands and well-drained meadows. The species seldom forms pure stands of any great extent although it is often dominant or even appears in practically pure stands over small local areas.

Although the fineness of its herbage and its characteristically low stature render thickspike wheatgrass more palatable to sheep than some of the other wheatgrasses of coarser habit, its tendency to become wiry as the season advances somewhat lowers this palatability. However, it furnishes at least fair forage for all classes of livestock, and is worthy of extensive reseeding trial on range lands.[1]

The long-creeping underground rootstocks of this wheatgrass enable it to withstand heavy grazing and considerable trampling. Once established, thickspike wheatgrass, if conservatively grazed, normally continue to spread and thicken their stand.

Sampson [2] has called attention to the fact that, on the higher ranges of the Wasatch Mountains of Utah, thickspike wheatgrass is the most common and typical of the turfed species of wheatgrass. The chief mass of its roots there is confined to the upper 8 inches of soil, but is so densely matted after the plants are well established that moisture percolation through them is exceedingly slow and the ingress of other plants with deeper root habits is prevented. The average maximum root depth of matured and well-developed, thickspike wheatgrass plants is about 15 inches.

---

[1] Forsling, C. L., and Dayton, W. A. ARTIFICIAL RESEEDING ON WESTERN MOUNTAIN RANGE LANDS. U. S. Dept. Agr. Circ. 178, 48 pp., illus. 1931.
[2] Sampson, A. W. PLANT SUCCESSION IN RELATION TO RANGE MANAGEMENT. U. S. Dept. Agr. Bull. 791, 76 pp., illus. 1919.

SLENDER WHEATGRASS

**Agropy'ron pauciflo'rum, syns. *A. pseudore'pens, A. te'nerum,*
"A. viola'ceum" [1]**

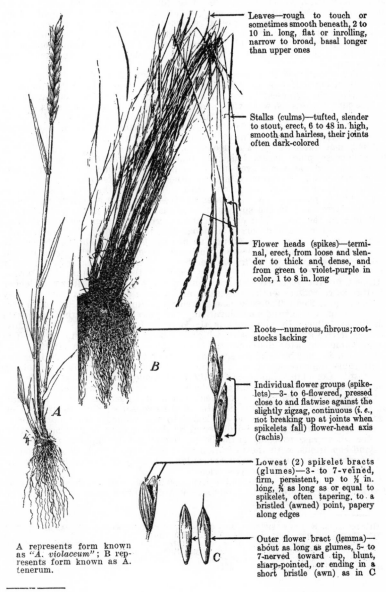

Leaves—rough to touch or sometimes smooth beneath, 2 to 10 in. long, flat or inrolling, narrow to broad, basal longer than upper ones

Stalks (culms)—tufted, slender to stout, erect, 6 to 48 in. high, smooth and hairless, their joints often dark-colored

Flower heads (spikes)—terminal, erect, from loose and slender to thick and dense, and from green to violet-purple in color, 1 to 8 in. long

Roots—numerous, fibrous; rootstocks lacking

Individual flower groups (spikelets)—3- to 6-flowered, pressed close to and flatwise against the slightly zigzag, continuous (*i. e.,* not breaking up at joints when spikelets fall) flower-head axis (rachis)

Lowest (2) spikelet bracts (glumes)—3- to 7-veined, firm, persistent, up to ½ in. long, ⅔ as long as or equal to spikelet, often tapering to a bristled (awned) point, papery along edges

Outer flower bract (lemma)—about as long as glumes, 5- to 7-nerved toward tip, blunt, sharp-pointed, or ending in a short bristle (awn) as in C

A represents form known as *"A. violaceum"*; B represents form known as A. tenerum.

---

[1] Of U. S. authors.

Until very recently this species has customarily been regarded as two separate species, viz, typical slender wheatgrass (*A. tenerum*) and violet wheatgrass (*A. violaceum* of U. S. authors, not (Hornem.) Lange)—one, the tall, slender form, usually found at lower elevations, having a narrow, mostly elongated, green flower head (spike), the individual flower groups (spikelets) separated; the other, the chunky, thick-stalked form, mostly subalpine, with a dense and pudgy, shortened, violet-hued spike, with plump, overlapping, and crowded spikelets. However, all possible intergradations between these two forms are known to occur. Moreover, true *A. violaceum* appears to be a wholly Old World wheatgrass, specifically distinct from the American grass called by that name. *A. pauciflorum* is an older name than *A. tenerum*, which is one of its synonyms. These considerations have led to the adoption of the nomenclatural change indicated.[2]

Slender wheatgrass is a perennial bunchgrass with erect, slender to stout stems from one-half foot to 4 feet high. It is the most widely distributed of our native wheatgrasses, ranging from Newfoundland to Alaska, and south to Missouri, Kansas, New Mexico, and California. The species makes its best growth in moderately moist, well-drained, light sandy-loam soils, but is somewhat tolerant of alkali, moderately drought-enduring, and is more common than any other wheatgrass in dry mountain meadows. It is typical of river bottoms, mountain valleys and meadows, and open timberlands up through the ponderosa pine, aspen, lodgepole pine, and Engelmann spruce belts to timber line and sometimes even up to the higher alpine meadow sites at about 12,000 feet elevation, especially in the southern part of its range.

Slender wheatgrass is one of the most palatable of the true wheatgrasses and is highly palatable to all classes of livestock; it is also very nutritious. Growth starts early in the spring, and the plants remain green and palatable until late in the fall. The entire plant is cropped throughout the growing season by both cattle and horses, although late in the season the flower stalks are not eaten so close to the ground as are the basal leaf blades. Sheep are fond of the flower and seed heads. The seed, when mixed with more succulent feed, produces hard, substantial fat on sheep. Slender wheatgrass is probably more widely distributed in native hay meadows than any other wheatgrass.

Except for the vegetative enlargement of the bunches by tillering, slender wheatgrass reproduces entirely by seed, and a large seed crop of good viability is usually produced. The seed is matured from June through September, depending upon the latitude or elevation. Commercial seed of this species is usually available. In fact, this is the only native wheatgrass, and almost the only native grass of any sort, which has been extensively cultivated. The forage value and wide distribution of this species, and the comparative ease with which it may be established, indicate that it has great possibilities for future range improvement if an adequate seed supply can be made available at low cost.[3] Complaint has occasionally been made that the use of slender wheatgrass in artificial reseeding of depleted range lands has been only moderately successful. Failure, in some cases at least, to get the seed in adequate contact with the soil explains certain of these unsatisfactory results. This seed is large and needs to be worked into the ground. This normally is effected on the range after seed dispersal by the trampling of grazing animals. Slender wheatgrass probably is the best perennial grass adaptable for western dry-land conditions, with the exception of smooth brome, and, in some places, crested wheatgrass. Slender wheatgrass is extensively cultivated in the northern Great Plains for hay and pasturage.[4]

Although it does not withstand heavy grazing as well as those species of wheatgrass which reproduce by rootstocks, it will endure a reasonable amount of grazing and trampling.

[2] Hitchcock, A. S. NEW SPECIES, AND CHANGES IN NOMENCLATURE, OF GRASSES OF THE UNITED STATES. Amer. Jour. Bot. 21(3) : 127–139, illus. 1934.
[3] Forsling, C. L., and Dayton, W. A. ARTIFICIAL RESEEDING ON WESTERN MOUNTAIN RANGE LANDS. U. S. Dept. Agr. Circ. 178, 48 pp., illus. 1931.
[4] Piper, C. V. CULTIVATED GRASSES OF SECONDARY IMPORTANCE. U. S. Dept. Agr. Farmers' Bull. 1433, 42 pp., illus. 1925.

BLUESTEM

Agropy'ron smi'thii, syn. *A. occidenta'lis*

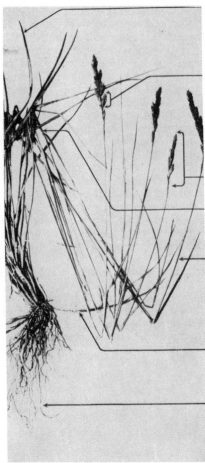

Leaves—4 to 8 in. long, rigid, upright, becoming inrolled, ridged, rough-margined and usually rough on back, otherwise smooth

Individual flower groups (spikelets)—7- to 13-flowered, usually solitary at each joint of zigzag flower-head axis (rachis), placed flatwise, flattened, spreading, crowded together on stem; rachis stiff-hairy along edges, not breaking up at maturity

Flower head (spike)—straight, and at top of stalk, 2 to 7 in. long, pale bluish color

Leaf sheaths—hairless, shorter than stalk internodes

Stalks (culms)—numerous, ridged, hairless

Rootstocks—pale gray or tawny, scaly, long-creeping, underground

Roots—fibrous

Lowest (2) spikelet bracts (glumes)—equal in length, narrow but broadened above the base, sharp, often beard- (awn-) pointed, rough along veins, from ½ to ⅔ as long as spikelet they partly enclose

Outer flower bract (lemma)—hard, hairless, awn-pointed at tip; inner flower bract (palea) shorter than lemma, stiff-hairy along edges

Bluestem, known as bluejoint in the Montana region and sometimes called Colorado bluestem, Smith bluejoint, and western wheatgrass, is one of the commonest and most abundant of the western wheatgrasses. It is a perennial from creeping rootstocks, and under the most favorable conditions may grow in dense patches or even form a compact sod. It occurs from southern Ontario and northern Minnesota west to British Columbia and south to west central California, western Texas, northwestern Arkansas, and Indiana. Bluestem grows in a great variety of soils and withstands drought well. It is best adapted to well-drained bottom lands, but is commonly found on open plains, hillsides, and benchlands. It is alkali-enduring and often occupies lands inhabited by few other grasses. It occurs in considerable abundance, and on adobe soils is often the dominant grass over large areas. In Montana this grass is often the first to appear in quantity on abandoned, dry farm lands.

Bluestem is one of the most valuable native forage plants of the West. It is an important constituent of numerous spring, summer, and early fall ranges. Despite the stiff leaves the plant rarely becomes sufficiently coarse and rank to prevent sheep from grazing it. Sheep are particularly fond of the heads. It cures well on the ground, makes very good winter forage and also yields excellent hay of high feeding value. The limited seed supply usually matures late but this handicap is offset by vigorous reproduction from rootstocks. The species has been tried experimentally under cultivation, with moderate success. Very little seed, however, is available commercially. Bluestem is rated as a choice forage plant for elk and deer.

The plants are covered with a bluish or whitish waxy bloom (glaucous); the erect, rigid stalks, 1 to 5 feet high, have enlarged joints darker in color than the rest of the stalk. The spikes are erect with unawned or awn-pointed spikelets rather close together.

BLUEBUNCH WHEATGRASS

Agropy'ron spica'tum

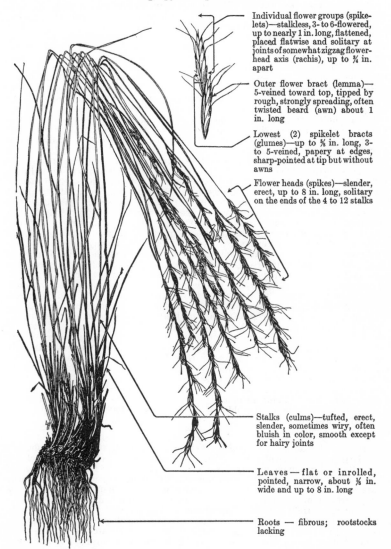

Individual flower groups (spikelets)—stalkless, 3- to 6-flowered, up to nearly 1 in. long, flattened, placed flatwise and solitary at joints of somewhat zigzag flowerhead axis (rachis), up to ¾ in. apart

Outer flower bract (lemma)—5-veined toward top, tipped by rough, strongly spreading, often twisted beard (awn) about 1 in. long

Lowest (2) spikelet bracts (glumes)—up to ⅝ in. long, 3- to 5-veined, papery at edges, sharp-pointed at tip but without awns

Flower heads (spikes)—slender, erect, up to 8 in. long, solitary on the ends of the 4 to 12 stalks

Stalks (culms)—tufted, erect, slender, sometimes wiry, often bluish in color, smooth except for hairy joints

Leaves — flat or inrolled, pointed, narrow, about ⅛ in. wide and up to 8 in. long

Roots — fibrous; rootstocks lacking

Bluebunch wheatgrass, also known as big bunchgrass, wire bunchgrass, western wheatgrass, and spiked wheatgrass, is a typical perennial bunchgrass, of bluish color, 1 to 4 feet high. The species is widely distributed, ranging from Alaska to northern California, New Mexico, and Montana. It is a distinctly drought-resistant grass and is found chiefly on dry soils in the open or in partial shade, seldom growing on wet soils and rarely in thick timber.

11

It is abundant in parts of Montana, Wyoming, Idaho, and eastern Oregon and Washington, often forming stands up to about a 60-percent ground cover.

Because of its extensive distribution, abundance—especially on sites too dry for most of the more palatable grasses and weeds—and its high palatability, bluebunch wheatgrass is one of the leading native western forages, and is a key species on many ranges. Where abundant it frequently constitutes the bulk of the spring, fall, and early winter range forage as well as a goodly part of the summer grass forage of ranges within the ponderous pine belt. The Northwest regards it as its most important indigenous grass. Its palatability is very good or even excellent for cattle, horses, and sheep, except where it has not been grazed for a year or two so that the old growth near the ground is rank and tough. Sheep then leave it for more tender herbage. This stem wiriness and the rather troublesome awns are the chief drawbacks of "bluebunch" as a forage plant. Its leafiness enables it to produce a large amount of forage per plant. The leafage remains green throughout the grazing season and is nutritious and palatable after growth ceases. At lower elevations, unless conditions are too dry, a fair amount of good seed matures but in the higher and drier portions of its range seed stalks are put forth irregularly and relatively late in the season and normally only a small amount of seed, of low viability, is produced.

Bluebunch wheatgrass withstands proper grazing well, but new plants are established entirely from seed and it is essential, if this species is to maintain itself, that opportunity be afforded for the early seed to mature. Deferred grazing works well with this species and the trampling by grazing animals after seed has fallen materially assists in planting the seed. On millions of acres of range land where unrestricted grazing has obtained "bluebunch" has succumbed to overstocking and too early grazing. It has practically disappeared from much of the wheatgrass-sagebrush type, where such abuse has prevailed, being largely replaced by such annuals as downy chess. Because of its great value as a forage plant successful effort is often made to increase this species on ranges where it naturally occurs, through observance of good range management principles, supplemented occasionally by artificial reseeding. Attempts to extend its range to other areas, however, have usually failed.

Bluebunch wheatgrass is a favorite forage species with elk, and is grazed extensively by them. On bison range in Montana it is not grazed in summer but is utilized as a winter feed. This natural selection permits "bluebunch" to seed and maintain itself on bison range.

Bluebunch wheatgrass has numerous, smooth, rather short leaves and slender, bearded heads 2 to 8 inches long. The spikelets are narrow, relatively long, erect or spreading, and placed rather far apart. The flowering scales (lemmas) are slightly longer than the glumes beneath them and bear conspicuous, typically stout beards (awns).

For a number of years the descriptions of *Agropyron spicatum* were thought by many botanists to apply to bluestem (*A. smithii*). As a consequence notes on *A. spicatum* in some of the older writings apply to bluestem rather than to bluebunch wheatgrass.

———————

Beardless wheatgrass (*A. inérme*, syn. *A. spicátum inérme*), sometimes called beardless (or awnless) bluebunch wheatgrass, is very closely related botanically to bluebunch wheatgrass and by many botanists is regarded as a variety of it. It is similar in appearance to "bluebunch" except that beardless wheatgrass, as both its English and scientific names imply, has no beards (awns). Its stems tend to be more slender and tufted and its leaves narrower and more tightly rolled than those of "bluebunch." It is not quite so widely distributed as bluebunch wheatgrass, ranging from British Columbia to Oregon, Utah, and western Montana, but has approximately the same habitat, and similar forage values except that *A. inerme* is generally less abundant than *A. spicatum*, and the absence of awns improves its palatability later in the season. However, in the Great Basin beardless wheatgrass is a very important range plant, known locally as Great Basin wheatgrass.

Toward the southern portion of its range, at least, beardless wheatgrass, as does its relative bluebunch wheatgrass, matures relatively early, drying up during the dry summer season. However, when the fall rains start these grasses green up promptly and provide excellent fall grazing.

BEARDED WHEATGRASS

Agropy'ron subsecun'dum, syns. *A. caninoi'des, "A. cani'num",*[1] *A. richardso'ni*

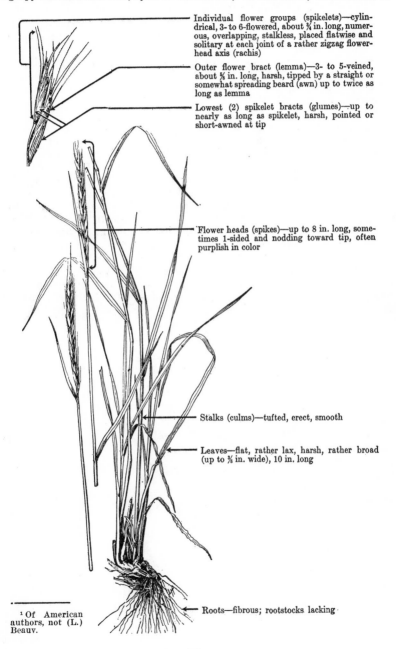

Individual flower groups (spikelets)—cylindrical, 3- to 6-flowered, about ¾ in. long, numerous, overlapping, stalkless, placed flatwise and solitary at each joint of a rather zigzag flowerhead axis (rachis)

Outer flower bract (lemma)—3- to 5-veined, about ⅝ in. long, harsh, tipped by a straight or somewhat spreading beard (awn) up to twice as long as lemma

Lowest (2) spikelet bracts (glumes)—up to nearly as long as spikelet, harsh, pointed or short-awned at tip

Flower heads (spikes)—up to 8 in. long, sometimes 1-sided and nodding toward tip, often purplish in color

Stalks (culms)—tufted, erect, smooth

Leaves—flat, rather lax, harsh, rather broad (up to ⅜ in. wide), 10 in. long

Roots—fibrous; rootstocks lacking

[1] Of American authors, not (L.) Beauv.

Bearded wheatgrass, known also as awned wheatgrass, dogtooth wheatgrass, and fibrous-rooted wheatgrass, is a smooth, slender and erect-stemmed, light green bunchgrass from 2 to 4 feet high. It is one of the five most widely distributed of our native western wheatgrasses, and ranges from Greenland to Alaska, California, and North Carolina. It occurs typically in light sandy soils in meadows, open grasslands, bottom lands, and on moist slopes, although often found scatteringly on dry hillsides, bench lands, and in partial shade in aspen and open coniferous timber or among shrubs. It is probably most common in Montana and Wyoming where it is sometimes locally abundant at elevations between 3,000 and 7,500 feet. In Colorado it has been collected at an elevation of 11,700 feet, indicating its wide altitudinal range.

Bearded wheatgrass is a valuable forage plant, highly palatable to all classes of livestock. The plants ordinarily produce an abundance of relatively soft leaves which are especially palatable. Naturally the bearded heads are not so palatable as those of the unbearded species. New plants, established entirely by seed, are ordinarily abundant, mature from August to October, and usually are of good quality. Bearded wheatgrass is fairly resistant to grazing and, if afforded reasonable opportunity, will maintain itself on the range. Because of its bunch habit of growth and the bearded heads, it is not so important a hay plant as certain other species of wheatgrass.

Until comparatively recently the European *Agropyron caninum* was thought to occur naturally in this country, but current agrostological opinion is that the American plant is a distinct species, *A. subsecundum.*

REDTOPS AND BENTGRASSES

Agros'tis spp.

Redtops and bentgrasses belong to the large redtop tribe (Agrostideae) of the grass family. The genus is composed of approximately 100 species which are widely distributed throughout the temperate and cool regions of the world, especially in the northern hemisphere. Some 25 to 30 species occur in the United States, with California and the Pacific Northwest as the center of distribution. The scientific name *Agrostis* is derived from the Greek word *agros*, meaning a field, and refers to the field habitat of many of the species. It is of interest that Agrostideae, the redtop tribe, and agrostology, the branch of botany dealing with grasses, take their names from the genus *Agrostis*.

The name, bentgrass, has been widely used for many species of *Agrostis*. It most fittingly applies, however, only to those species which actually have bent, trailing stems with a low, decumbent habit of growth. The true bentgrasses are usually turf-formers which reproduce by means of stolons as well as by underground rootstocks and seed. The characteristic reddish or purplish hue of the flower heads of many species, and especially of the common redtop (*A. alba*), gives rise to the name, redtop. This name is applicable to both tufted and sod-forming species which have erect and unbent stems, particularly if their heads are reddish or purplish. It seems preferable to use redtop, as a generic name for most of the native range species of *Agrostis*.

The redtops and bentgrasses are distributed throughout North America except in the extreme North. The use of a number of species as lawn, pasture, and hay grasses has greatly increased their distribution. Since the species of *Agrostis* thrive best in temperate or cool climates, they are of greatest importance in cultivation and on the range in the northern part of the United States and in the higher regions. Grasses of the *Agrostis* genus are typically moisture-loving plants. They thrive in wet or moist rich soils but are also capable of growing on drier situations. The native species occupy a great variety of sites, ranging from said dunes at sea level to alpine meadows above timber line. They occur largely in wet or moist, rich soils in meadows, grassy parks, along stream banks, in shaded woodlands and aspen stands, and are capable of growing in extremely wet situations, thriving even with their stems partially submerged in water during part of the season. However, some species often appear in drier situations, such as sagebrush and wheatgrass types, on open ridges and in waste places. The cultivated species also favor wet or moist habitats and are usually grown in meadows, but where they have escaped from cultivation they may be found in waste places and along ditch banks and roadsides. Several foreign species have become established on many range areas, probably mostly through artificial reseeding activities, and are now rather widely distributed on some of the ranges of the West. A number of species are able to grow where the soil is acid or lacking in lime and are used in meadows and lawns where bluegrass and other cultivated grasses do not thrive.

The genus furnishes a number of species that are extremely important forage plants either in cultivation or on the ranges in the West. In the range country the redtops are highly regarded as forage plants. The forage produced by this group of plants is usually rated as good to very good for cattle and horses and fairly good to very good for sheep. Several species having large, finely branched panicles are grazed readily before heading out but are avoided afterward. The redtops are choice elk feed, but are eaten only with slight relish by deer. Many of the individual species are scattered and do not occur in abundance except in restricted meadow and park areas. A few, however, are common and widespread range plants and make up an important component of the vegetation. Several of the more outstanding and typical species are deserving of mention.

The common redtop (*A. al'ba*), originally introduced from Europe but now extensively cultivated in this country for hay and as a meadow and pasture grass, is the most important species. It has been successfully used in the artificial reseeding of meadows on depleted range lands and has become firmly established and widespread on moist, favorable sites on many range areas.

Spike redtop (*A. exara'ta*) is one of the most important range species. It is a common tufted grass with a contracted, spikelike panicle and is found throughout the western portion of North America.

Winter redtop (*A. hiema'lis*), often called ticklegrass, is a bunchgrass with a finely branched, large, spreading panicle. It is distributed throughout the continent except in the far North and is one of the most common and widely distributed grasses on the western ranges. The above three species (redtop, spike redtop, and winter redtop) are perhaps the most common of all the species of *Agrostis* on western national forests.

Leafy redtop (*A. diegoen'sis*, syns. *A. folio'sa, A. pal'lens folio'sa*), often called thin grass, one of the most abundant of the native sod-forming species of *Agrostis*, is a moderately tall, fine-leaved grass with a narrow panicle. It is distributed from British Columbia to southern California, with an elevational range from sea level to about 7,500 feet. In general, its growth is rather scattered, but the forage production per plant is comparatively large. The herbage is relished by all classes of livestock, and the spreading rootstocks enable the plant to withstand extremely heavy grazing.

Alpine redtop (*A. ros'sae*), also known as Ross redtop, is an example of the low, delicate species which grow in high mountains. It is about 4 to 8 inches tall, and has fine, narrow panicles. This plant is confined to the alpine zone from British Columbia to central California and eastward to Colorado and Montana. It is regarded as fairly good to very good forage for all classes of livestock. Pygmy redtop (*A. hu'milis*), a related alpine species, ranging from British Columbia to Oregon and Colorado, is highly palatable to all classes of livestock. It is seldom over 6 inches high.

Idaho redtop (*A. idahoen'sis*) is a tufted grass resembling alpine redtop but is taller—up to 16 inches high—and has open, loosely spreading panicles. It is widely distributed, growing in mountain meadows from Washington to southern California and east to New Mexico and Montana. It furnishes fair to good forage for sheep and is good to very good for cattle and horses.

The typical bentgrasses usually reproduce vigorously by means of stolons, thus forming a dense turf which makes them ideal for use on lawns and golf greens. When used in pastures, they are highly resistant to damage from excessive trampling and grazing. In addition, they are exceptionally efficient soil-binding plants and are being used in reclaiming gullies in erosion-control work. Creeping bent (*A. palus'tris*), certain cultivated forms of which are known as carpet bent, is a characteristic representative of the cultivated bentgrasses. This plant is a native of Europe, and is now extensively cultivated in this country. It has dense spikelike panicles and long creeping stolons or runners which may attain a length of 4 feet in a single season. This species is most esteemed for the fine turf it produces, superior to practically all other temperate grasses. It is widely used for lawns and golf greens and is a poular and valuable pasture grass. On both the Atlantic and Pacific coasts it occurs in extensive seaside meadow areas which are used for both hay and pasture. This grass succeeds very well inland, especially where the soil is fairly moist.[1] It shows promise in the reseeding of meadows on western ranges and may be worthy of further experiments.[2]

The grasses of the *Agrostis* genus are usually low and delicate or moderately tall perennials (only three annuals occur in this country), with smooth, hairless, slender stalks and diverse habits of growth. The leaf blades are flat or inrolled and often rough to the touch; the leaf sheaths are usually channeled and rough. The flower heads (panicles) may be open with widely spreading, hairlike branches or contracted, very narrow and spikelike. The individual flower groups (spikelets) are very small, V-shaped and one-flowered, with the lowest two spikelet bracts (glumes) remaining attached after the seed has fallen. These glumes are about equal, sharp-pointed, and harsh on the keel. The outer flower bract (lemma) is usually shorter than the glumes, blunt-pointed, very thin, either beardless (awnless) or with a slender awn on the back. The inner flower bract (palea) is inconspicuous or lacking.

[1] Piper, C. V. CULTIVATED GRASSES OF SECONDARY IMPORTANCE. U. S. Dept. Agr. Farmers Bull. 1433, 42 pp., illus. 1925.
[2] Forsling, C. L., and Dayton, W. A. ARTIFICIAL RESEEDING ON WESTERN MOUNTAIN RANGE LANDS. U. S. Dept. Agr. Circ. 178, 48 pp., illus. 1931.

REDTOP

Agros'tis al'ba, syn. *"A. palus'tris"* [1]

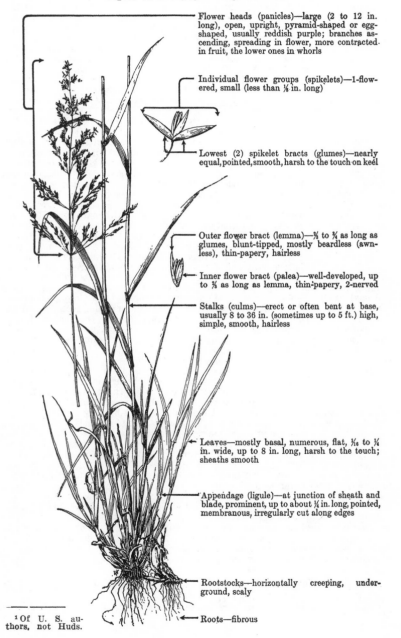

Flower heads (panicles)—large (2 to 12 in. long), open, upright, pyramid-shaped or egg-shaped, usually reddish purple; branches ascending, spreading in flower, more contracted in fruit, the lower ones in whorls

Individual flower groups (spikelets)—1-flowered, small (less than ⅛ in. long)

Lowest (2) spikelet bracts (glumes)—nearly equal, pointed, smooth, harsh to the touch on keel

Outer flower bract (lemma)—⅝ to ¾ as long as glumes, blunt-tipped, mostly beardless (awnless), thin-papery, hairless

Inner flower bract (palea)—well-developed, up to ⅔ as long as lemma, thin-papery, 2-nerved

Stalks (culms)—erect or often bent at base, usually 8 to 36 in. (sometimes up to 5 ft.) high, simple, smooth, hairless

Leaves—mostly basal, numerous, flat, 1/16 to ¼ in. wide, up to 8 in. long, harsh to the touch; sheaths smooth

Appendage (ligule)—at junction of sheath and blade, prominent, up to about ¼ in. long, pointed, membranous, irregularly cut along edges

Rootstocks—horizontally creeping, underground, scaly

Roots—fibrous

[1] Of U. S. authors, not Huds.

Redtop, so named because of the usual reddish hue of its characteristic pyramid-shaped panicles, is one of the most important perennial grasses in the United States. It was early introduced into the American colonies from Europe and is now widely distributed throughout most of North America, occurring from Alaska to Newfoundland, Florida, California, and Mexico.

Redtop is probably adapted to a wider range of climatic and soil conditions than any other cultivated grass, and succeeds well over most of the United States, except in the drier regions and the extreme South. This species is as resistant to cold as is timothy and withstands summer heat much better.[2] It is recognized as the best wet-land grass among the cultivated species, as it thrives on moist or wet soils and is able to grow vigorously in shallow ponds, which later become dry. It also grows well on acid soils so deficient in lime as to prohibit the growth of bluegrass and most other valuable grasses. If moisture is abundant, redtop does not show a marked preference for soil types though it grows best on rich, sandy, or clay loams. Although essentially adapted to grow on wet ground, redtop sometimes occurs on well-drained and rather infertile soils. This grass, however, is not tolerant to shade and seldom appears in dense timber or other shaded situations.[2] On the mountainous western ranges redtop usually occupies wet or moist meadows, parks, openings in the timber, stream banks, and moist canyon bottoms; it also occurs, to a less extent, on well-drained soils in sagebrush parks, open grasslands and cut-over and burned-over timber lands. It has escaped from cultivation in many places and is found along roadsides and in waste places. It ranges from sea level to about 10,000 feet, but commonly to about 8,000 feet.

Redtop has become firmly established on many ranges and is now widely distributed throughout the mountains of the West. Although cultivated pasture experiments have shown that cattle usually prefer all other cultivated grasses to redtop,[2] it is highly regarded as a range forage plant. Redtop is usually given a palatability rating of good to very good for cattle and horses, fairly good to good for sheep, and is regarded as highly satisfactory forage for elk. On moist sites the herbage of redtop usually remains green all summer and is cropped with relish throughout the grazing season. The vigorous intertwining rootstocks of this grass form a dense sod which binds the soil firmly and enables the plants to withstand excessive trampling and close grazing.

Redtop has proved a valuable plant for use in the artificial reseeding of the more favorable sites of western mountain range lands. On wet acid sites it gives better reseeding results than any other cultivated grass, but on drier sites other grasses are usually superior to redtop. Experiments in artificial reseeding conducted on national forest lands in the West since 1902[3] demonstrate that this grass should be used only in the reseeding of meadows at medium to high elevations, below timber line, on the interior range lands, and on range lands on the west coastal slope, where the annual precipitation exceeds 40 inches. On sites which are conducive to rapid growth and early establishment, from 8 to 10 pounds per acre of the extremely small seed should be sown to obtain a full stand. Soil treatment should be very shallow.[3]

Redtop is valuable for pasture, hay, and lawns. It is extensively raised as a meadow hay and pasture grass in the valleys of the West. The yields of redtop hay on wet lands are usually better than any other hay grass.[2] However, best results obtain when redtop is grown in mixture with other hay plants, particularly timothy and clover, as it matures at about the same time as timothy and will usually add materially to the yield of a timothy and clover hay crop.[4] This plant is a vigorous grower and will form a good turf in a short time, a characteristic which makes redtop valuable for use as a soil-binder in stopping and reclaiming gullies and for holding slopes and banks.

Cultivated redtop is extremely variable. The leaves may be very narrow or over one-fourth of an inch in width, dark bluish green or pale green in color; the rather open panicles vary from 2 up to 12 inches in length and from green to reddish or purplish in color; the running rootstocks may be abundant and vigorous or few or even lacking entirely.

[2] Piper, C. V. FORAGE PLANTS AND THEIR CULTURE. Rev., 671 pp., illus. New York. 1924.
[3] Forsling, C. L., and Dayton, W. A. ARTIFICIAL RESEEDING ON WESTERN MOUNTAIN RANGE LANDS. U. S. Dept. Agr. Circ. 178, 48 pp., illus. 1931.
[4] Piper, C. V. IMPORTANT CULTIVATED GRASSES. U. S. Dept. Agr. Farmers' Bull. 1254, 38 pp., illus. 1922.

SPIKE REDTOP

Agros'tis exara'ta

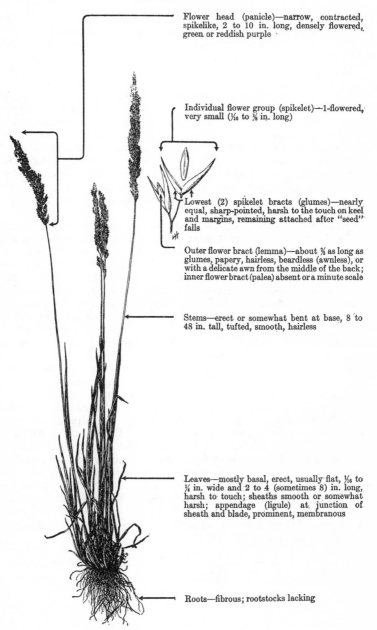

Flower head (panicle)—narrow, contracted, spikelike, 2 to 10 in. long, densely flowered, green or reddish purple

Individual flower group (spikelet)—1-flowered, very small (1/16 to 1/8 in. long)

Lowest (2) spikelet bracts (glumes)—nearly equal, sharp-pointed, harsh to the touch on keel and margins, remaining attached after "seed" falls

Outer flower bract (lemma)—about 5/6 as long as glumes, papery, hairless, beardless (awnless), or with a delicate awn from the middle of the back; inner flower bract (palea) absent or a minute scale

Stems—erect or somewhat bent at base, 8 to 48 in. tall, tufted, smooth, hairless

Leaves—mostly basal, erect, usually flat, 1/16 to 1/4 in. wide and 2 to 4 (sometimes 8) in. long, harsh to touch; sheaths smooth or somewhat harsh; appendage (ligule) at junction of sheath and blade, prominent, membranous

Roots—fibrous; rootstocks lacking

Spike redtop, so named because of its spikelike panicle, is also known as purple redtop and western redtop. This perennial bunch grass is one of the commonest and most valuable western species of redtop. Because it is exceedingly variable in size and form, this species has been the victim of extensive botanical emasculation and appears in various manuals as *A. ampla, A. asperifolia, A. densiflora, A. glomerata, A. grandis, A. inflata, A. microphylla,* and *A. scouleri.* The present trend among botanists, however, is to include all these under the one species, *A. exarata.*

This species is widely distributed in western North America, ranging from Alaska to southern California and Mexico, and eastward to western Texas, western Nebraska, and Manitoba. Its elevational range extends from about sea level on the Pacific Coast to approximately 10,500 feet in Colorado, Utah, New Mexico, and the southern portion of its range. This grass is a moisture-loving species but it is less exacting in its moisture requirements than some of the other redtops. It typically occurs in meadows, along streams, in moist parks, and in moist, semishaded woodlands and aspen stands. However, it also appears on drier situations, growing on moderately dry soils in association with wheatgrass, sagebrush, needlegrass, and oakbrush.

Spike redtop often occurs in abundance on the moister portions of the range, being especially common near the California seacoast, where it reaches its best development. In some localities this grass furnishes a large part of the forage.[1] The herbage remains green and succulent until late in the season and is grazed throughout the summer by all classes of livestock. Its forage value varies somewhat in different portions of the West. On the average, the palatability is considered to be good to very good for cattle and horses and from fair to good for sheep. Elk relish the herbage of this plant and deer use it to a slight extent. The period of flowering and seed dissemination varies with the altitudinal and latitudinal range of this plant. Under average conditions the seed ripens between the first week in August and the early part of September. The production of a moderate amount of seed having fair viability is characteristic.[2]

This grass varies in size and form according to its habitat, ranging from dwarf plants with small dense panicles in alpine situations to tall robust forms. Dwarf forms are generally awned with delicate prickles on the back of the lemmas. The plant described as *A. glomerata* is a low seacoast form with a compact panicle and often inflated sheaths; *A. microphylla* has dense, often interrupted panicles and well-developed awns; *A. grandis* is a robust form up to 60 inches tall with compact panicles and awnless lemmas; and *A. ampla,* another tall form, has somewhat open panicles and awned lemmas. The form originally described as *A. exarata* occupies an intermediate position in the range of variation.

---

[1] Dayton, W. A. SOME OUTSTANDING FORAGE GRASSES OF WESTERN CATTLE RANGES. Producer 9 (10) : [3]–7, illus. 1928.
[2] Sampson, A. W. NATIVE AMERICAN FORAGE PLANTS. 435 pp., illus. New York. 1924.

WINTER REDTOP

Agros'tis hiema'lis, syn. *A. sca'bra*

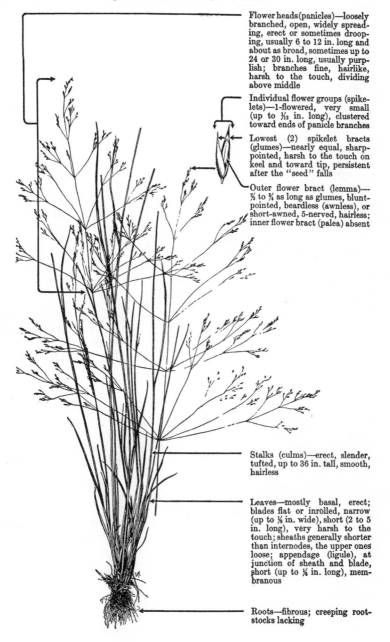

Flower heads (panicles)—loosely branched, open, widely spreading, erect or sometimes drooping, usually 6 to 12 in. long and about as broad, sometimes up to 24 or 30 in. long, usually purplish; branches fine, hairlike, harsh to the touch, dividing above middle

Individual flower groups (spikelets)—1-flowered, very small (up to ½ in. long), clustered toward ends of panicle branches

Lowest (2) spikelet bracts (glumes)—nearly equal, sharppointed, harsh to the touch on keel and toward tip, persistent after the "seed" falls

Outer flower bract (lemma)— ⅔ to ¾ as long as glumes, bluntpointed, beardless (awnless), or short-awned, 5-nerved, hairless; inner flower bract (palea) absent

Stalks (culms)—erect, slender, tufted, up to 36 in. tall, smooth, hairless

Leaves—mostly basal, erect; blades flat or inrolled, narrow (up to ⅛ in. wide), short (2 to 5 in. long), very harsh to the touch; sheaths generally shorter than internodes, the upper ones loose; appendage (ligule), at junction of sheath and blade, short (up to ⅙ in. long), membranous

Roots—fibrous; creeping rootstocks lacking

Winter redtop, a slender, fine-leaved open-ground species, is also called ticklegrass and hairgrass because of its large, open panicles with their widely spreading, hairlike branches. The name, winter redtop, is preferred because the other two names have been applied to other grasses. Ticklegrass is a term loosely applied to a number of grasses which have fine panicles; hairgrass is the generally recognized English name for plants of the *Deschampsia* genus. This species appears in some of the manuals as *A. hyemalis*.

This widely distributed grass occurs throughout most of North America, from the lower valleys, plains, and foothills to alpine situations, up to about 12,000 feet, and is especially characteristic of the cooler- and higher-range areas. The species is common in moist to wet meadows, along streams, in moist canyon bottoms, and dry to moist open woodlands and aspen stands. It thrives under a variety of moisture conditions, however, as it also appears in drier situations such as sagebrush parks, open well-drained grasslands, rocky scablands, burned-over areas, ponderosa pine stands, dry meadows, and sandy lowlands. Although usually scattered over the range, this grass sometimes grows in moderate abundance in restricted meadow and park areas, waste places, and in moist, denuded sites.

When young, winter redtop is readily grazed by all classes of livestock but, after heading out, it is utilized very little. The large, finely branched panicles are apparently objectionable to grazing animals and discourage the use of the fine, short leaves. The large ratio of seed-head to foliage prevents consideration of this grass as a really important forage plant despite the fact that it is a very common and widely distributed species. It is generally rated as one of the least palatable of the redtops but, considering its relatively high palatability during the early part of the season, this species merits a rating of fair to fairly good for sheep and fairly good to good for cattle and horses. However, on some range areas, particularly in Utah, Nevada, and Montana, this plant is regarded more highly and is rated up to very good for cattle and good for sheep. In Montana, elk have been observed eating winter redtop with moderate relish.

In the range country the flowering period is usually from July to September and the seed is ripened and shed during August and September. Hitchcock[1] reports that the broad seed-head sometimes breaks away from the plant at maturity and is blown by the wind as a tumbleweed. The purplish seed-heads are sometimes used in flower bouquets for decoration.

Alpine winter redtop (*A. hiema'lis gemina'ta*, syn. *A. gemina'ta*) is a variety which is confined to the alpine and sub-alpine zones from Alaska to California and Colorado. It is similar to winter redtop in appearance and palatability but is usually less than a foot high and has smaller and less diffuse panicles. The lemmas usually bear a straight, slender awn but are awnless in the more southern portions of its range. A taller, more robust form, *A. hiema'lis subre'pens*, is a variety sometimes recognized in the Southwest.

---

[1] Hitchcock, A. S. THE GENERA OF GRASSES OF THE UNITED STATES, WITH SPECIAL REFERENCE TO THE ECONOMIC SPECIES. U. S. Dept. Agr. Bill. 772, 307 pp., illus. 1920.

BEARDGRASSES

Andropo'gon spp., syns. *Schizachy'rium spp., Amphi'lophis spp.*

Andropogon is a large genus of perennial grasses which are widely distributed in the warmer parts of the world. In the United States, they are best represented in the Southeast, but species of this genus are found in all the Western States, except possibly Oregon and Washington. The genus is the namesake of the sorghum tribe (Andropogoneae) and is the largest in number of species (about 150) in this tribe although not the most important economically, as the sorghums and sugarcane belong to other genera of this tribe. The andropogons are abundant in the Plains States and the Southwest. Prairie beardgrass, or little bluestem (*A. scoparius*), is often the most abundant grass in the northern Plains States on dry sandy soils. In the southern Plains States some species, notably bluejoint turkeyfoot, or "big bluestem" (*A. furcatus*, syn. *A. provincialis*), frequently occur in dense stands and are cut for hay. In the Southwest the drought resistance of certain species increases their utility on arid ranges where they comprise a large proportion of the herbaceous plant growth.

The beardgrasses are palatable to livestock while young and tender but they become coarse and tough rather early in the summer and are little grazed during late summer and fall. The plants cure well, however, and are utilized by cattle and horses as winter forage. Silver beardgrass (*A. saccharoides*, syn. *A. argenteus*) has attractively conspicuous flower and seed clusters (inflorescences) and is grown as an ornamental.

Beardgrass is perhaps the most common name for this genus although certain species, like many other common range plants, have fairly well-established individual names, such as broomsedge (*A. virginicus*) and turkeyfoot (*A. hallii*). The name, beardgrass, is a rather literal interpretation of the scientific name *Andropogon*, which is derived from the Greek *andros* (man's) and *pogon* (beard), referring to the long white hairs which, in many species, occur in the heads.

Stems of the beardgrasses are solid or pithy (like cornstalks) differing in this respect from most other grasses which have hollow stems partitioned at the joints. Individual flower groups (spikelets) are in rather narrow, spikelike clusters (racemes), each stalk (culm) usually producing several racemes which are borne either singly, in twos or in groups of several to many. The raceme axis (rachis) is jointed and generally hairy with two spikelets at each joint in most species. One spikelet is without an individual stalk (sessile) and is seed-producing (fertile); the other is stalked, does not produce seed, and often consists of a single small bract.

Some authors state that vetiver, a mat-making fiber, and that citronella, cuscus, and certain other aromatic commercial oils are derived from various Old World species of *Andropogon*, but the best present-day botanical opinion is that such species are preferably placed in the related genera *Cymbopogon* and *Vetiveria*.

CANE BEARDGRASS

Andropo'gon barbino'dis, syns. "A. saccharoi'des",[1] Amphi'lophis bardino'dis

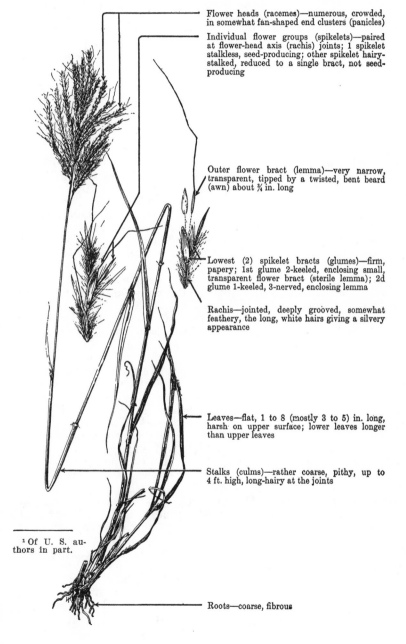

Flower heads (racemes)—numerous, crowded, in somewhat fan-shaped end clusters (panicles)

Individual flower groups (spikelets)—paired at flower-head axis (rachis) joints; 1 spikelet stalkless, seed-producing; other spikelet hairy-stalked, reduced to a single bract, not seed-producing

Outer flower bract (lemma)—very narrow, transparent, tipped by a twisted, bent beard (awn) about ¾ in. long

Lowest (2) spikelet bracts (glumes)—firm, papery; 1st glume 2-keeled, enclosing small, transparent flower bract (sterile lemma); 2d glume 1-keeled, 3-nerved, enclosing lemma

Rachis—jointed, deeply grooved, somewhat feathery, the long, white hairs giving a silvery appearance

Leaves—flat, 1 to 8 (mostly 3 to 5) in. long, harsh on upper surface; lower leaves longer than upper leaves

Stalks (culms)—rather coarse, pithy, up to 4 ft. high, long-hairy at the joints

[1] Of U. S. authors in part.

Roots—coarse, fibrous

Cane beardgrass is a perennial bunchgrass and one of the comparatively few common range grasses with solid or pithy stems. This species has been generally confused in the western botanical manuals with silver beardgrass (*A. saccharoides*); the "*A. saccharoides*" (syn. *A. saccharoides laguroides*), as listed in those works, largely include both true *A. saccharoides* and *A. barbinodis*. Cane beardgrass differs from silver beardgrass chiefly because its head is shorter, fan-shaped, rather than elongated, and the joints of its stems bear longer hairs. Other local names, such as Torrey beardgrass, big feathergrass, feather bluestem, and beargrass, are applied indiscriminately to these species, but silver beardgrass is the most commonly used name because of the silvery appearance of the heads. The specific name of cane beardgrass *barbinodis* is derived from the Latin *barba*, beard, and *nodus*, a joint, and refers to the conspicuously hairy joints of the stems.

Cane beardgrass occurs from Oklahoma to Arizona and Texas and south into Mexico; it is less widely distributed and more distinctly western than silver beardgrass, which ranges from Alabama to Missouri, Colorado, and California, and south into Mexico. Cane beardgrass is very important in the Southwest because it grows on very dry soils; in Arizona for example, it occurs on those areas of cindery soils where almost no other grasses thrive. It is also found on moderately dry soils in gullies and along the banks of dry washes and the like, but usually occurs scatteringly and seldom forms dense, pure stands. It extends upward to the woodland and ponderosa pine belts but is more common at lower elevations.

Most observers agree that cane beardgrass is fair to good forage while it is young, and that the mature growth, although mostly too rank and coarse to be of the highest value, is fair forage for cattle and horses and supplies considerable winter feed for these classes of livestock, although too coarse for sheep.

The species is very drought-resisting and hence is invaluable on certain southwestern ranges. It will grow where the annual precipitation is about 5 or 6 inches, when supplemented by occasional flooding incident to heavy summer showers. Its drought resistance and natural occurrence in well-drained soils, ditches, and gullies suggest its possible use in erosion-control work in dry areas.

Cane beardgrass is a robust species having coarse, usually straw-colored, pithy stems, often 4 feet high, with enlarged, hairy joints, or nodes. The head is rather short, about 3 to 5 inches long, long-exserted from the upper leaf sheath, and consists of from 7 to 10 branches (racemes) arranged in a somewhat fan-shaped, silvery-hairy, terminal cluster. The axis of the raceme is conspicuously jointed, a pair of spikelets being produced at each joint. One of these spikelets is stalkless and seed-producing, the outer flower bract (lemma) bearing a twisted and bent awn about three-fourths of an inch long. The other spikelet is on a short stalk and consists of a single bract. The leaves are usually flat, harsh on the upper surface, and frequently turn reddish in drying. The grass is a rather handsome one, when headed out, and it is of interest to note that certain varieties of its very close relative, silver beardgrass (*A. saccharoides*, syn. *A. argenteus*) are cultivated as ornamentals.

PRAIRIE BEARDGRASS

Andropo'gon scopa'rius, syn. *Schizachy'rium scopa'rium*

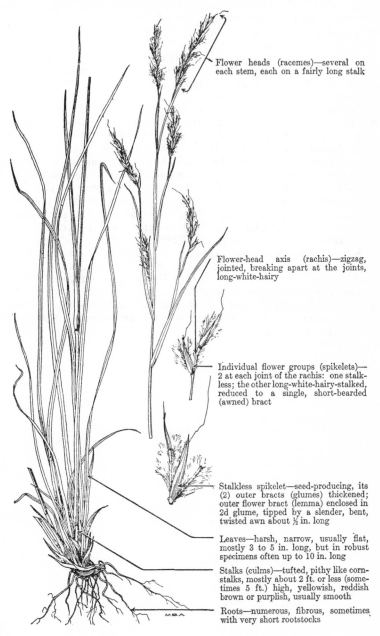

Flower heads (racemes)—several on each stem, each on a fairly long stalk

Flower-head axis (rachis)—zigzag, jointed, breaking apart at the joints, long-white-hairy

Individual flower groups (spikelets)— 2 at each joint of the rachis: one stalkless; the other long-white-hairy-stalked, reduced to a single, short-bearded (awned) bract

Stalkless spikelet—seed-producing, its (2) outer bracts (glumes) thickened; outer flower bract (lemma) enclosed in 2d glume, tipped by a slender, bent, twisted awn about ½ in. long

Leaves—harsh, narrow, usually flat, mostly 3 to 5 in. long, but in robust specimens often up to 10 in. long

Stalks (culms)—tufted, pithy like cornstalks, mostly about 2 ft. or less (sometimes 5 ft.) high, yellowish, reddish brown or purplish, usually smooth

Roots—numerous, fibrous, sometimes with very short rootstocks

Prairie beardgrass, known also as broom beardgrass, broomsedge, little bluestem, and small feathergrass, is a perennial bunchgrass, with hairy flower heads. The specific name, *scoparius*, from *scopa*, a broom, means a sweeper, and alludes to the resemblance of the bunches or tufts of stiff stems to a crude broom, although there appears to be no record of the plants being used in the construction of brooms. This species probably occurs in every State except Washington, Oregon, and California. In the Bad Lands and the Black Hills of South Dakota it is one of the most common grasses. It is a relatively low-altitude grass, seldom extending above the ponderosa-pine belt and is commonly found on dry, sandy, or gravelly soils.

Prairie beardgrass is chiefly grazed while young and tender. This is particularly true in the Southwest where the species is scattered over much of the woodland and ponderosa-pine types, supplying a large amount of forage. During the summer, after the plant is "in the boot", and before the seeds mature and the heads break up, prairie beardgrass is not grazed, probably because the bearded, hairy heads are unpalatable. After the tops fall, however, this bunchgrass makes fair forage for cattle and horses, but is somewhat too coarse and tough for sheep. Prairie beardgrass does not withstand grazing especially well and often is supplanted by the gramas or other species of the "short-grass" type on areas which are subject to heavy spring grazing. This species is often a satisfactory constituent of prairie hay if cut early. Prairie beardgrass was widely used for hay in early days, especially in the Southwest where it formerly was much more plentiful than at present. In some localities, notably in the sand-hill regions of Kansas and Nebraska, prairie beardgrass is often regarded as a pest species, worthless as forage for livestock.

THREE-AWNS

Ari'stida spp.

Three-awns, also commonly called needlegrasses, wiregrasses, and poverty grasses, constitute a large genus of the redtop tribe (Agrostideae) and are widely distributed throughout the Western States, being especially well represented in the Southwest. They grow chiefly on dry sandy soils and are common grasses on semidesert areas, on plains, and at lower elevations in the mountains.

Three-awns vary greatly in forage value in the different regions of the West. When mixed with the more palatable grasses, such as bluegrasses and fescues, they are usually ranked low even while green. In the Southwest they are often considered good spring and summer forage while green, before the seeds mature. Some species start growth early in the spring before most other grasses and are sometimes valuable as early forage. Some of the southwestern three-awns have two growing seasons: One in the spring, if moisture and other weather conditions are favorable, and another in the summer with the advent of summer rains. Under such conditions considerable green palatable forage is produced. The small annuals and a few perennial species produce but little leafage and are poor or worthless as forage. A large number of the perennial species, however, are leafy and produce considerable forage; such leafy perennials are more valuable range plants, particularly on spring ranges, than some observers, prejudiced by the prickly beards (awns) and wiry stems of three-awns, are willing to admit. Three-awns mature in summer or fall depending upon the time the summer rains begin, after which time they are of little value as forage. The leaves dry up and are unpalatable and the troublesome seeds (fruits) are avoided by grazing animals.

Three-awns are relatively short-lived and depend upon seed for reproduction. The seeds are well adapted for dissemination and in general the plants reproduce well. These grasses sometimes indicate, on areas where they are abundant, that the site is too poor for the growth of more desirable species, or they may be an indicator of range depletion or other disturbances.

A characteristic three-branched beard at the tip of the seed is the most outstanding feature by which the three-awns may be distinguished. The two lateral branches of the awn may be small (very small or absent in *A. orcuttiana*). The seed is hard, slender, and cyindrical with a sharp-pointed base covered with short, rather stiff hair. These barbed seeds often trouble grazing animals by working into their eyes, nostrils, and ears, and sometimes causing sore mouth. The individual flower groups (spikelets) are one-flowered (i. e., each seed or flower is borne singly) and the flowering head (panicle) is usually narrow but open and sometimes spreading. The two empty bracts (glumes) at the base of the spikelet are narrow and remain attached to the stem (pedicel) after the floret, or seed, has fallen.

ARIZONA THREE-AWN

Ari'stida arizo'nica

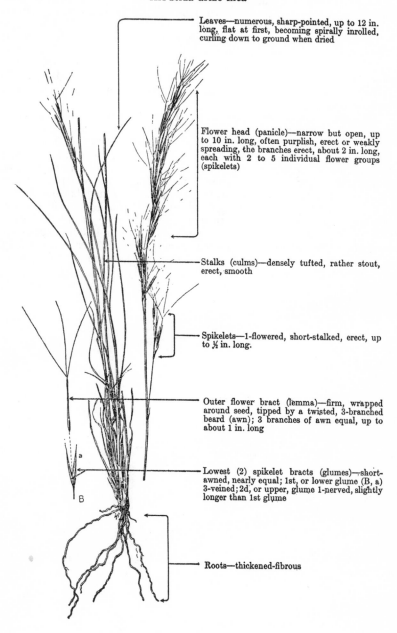

Leaves—numerous, sharp-pointed, up to 12 in. long, flat at first, becoming spirally inrolled, curling down to ground when dried

Flower head (panicle)—narrow but open, up to 10 in. long, often purplish, erect or weakly spreading, the branches erect, about 2 in. long, each with 2 to 5 individual flower groups (spikelets)

Stalks (culms)—densely tufted, rather stout, erect, smooth

Spikelets—1-flowered, short-stalked, erect, up to ½ in. long.

Outer flower bract (lemma)—firm, wrapped around seed, tipped by a twisted, 3-branched beard (awn); 3 branches of awn equal, up to about 1 in. long

Lowest (2) spikelet bracts (glumes)—short-awned, nearly equal; 1st, or lower glume (B, a) 3-veined; 2d, or upper, glume 1-nerved, slightly longer than 1st glume

Roots—thickened-fibrous

Arizona three-awn, often called curly three-awn and tall three-awn, is a stout, rather coarse, erect, perennial bunchgrass 1 to 2½ feet high, and is one of the largest of the three-awns. As the leaves become mature and start drying many of them roll up spirally giving the grass a curly appearance, from which the name "curly three-awn" has originated.

Arizona three-awn inhabits sandy-gravelly mesas and foothills at elevations up to 9,000 feet but mainly below 6,000 feet. It belongs mostly to the upper woodland and ponderosa pine types and occurs from western Texas to Arizona and south into northern Mexico. It is usually found in scattered bunches mixed with other grasses but sometimes is locally abundant.

This species is usually rated as good forage in the Southwest while green. It greens up and grows readily when spring moisture comes and, when conditions are favorable, will produce considerable succulent forage in early spring before most of the grasses have started growth. The main period of growth comes with the summer rains. When rains start early in these two periods this relatively large three-awn produces a considerable amount of green palatable forage which remains succulent for several months. If summer rains come late the seeds develop and mature rapidly and little succulent forage is produced. After maturity the seeds may be troublesome to grazing animals. The herbage dries at that time and is practically worthless as forage until winter or spring rains occur. Occasionally the species is sufficiently dense and large to be cut for hay.

POVERTY THREE-AWN

Ari'stida divarica'ta, syn. *A. pal'meri*

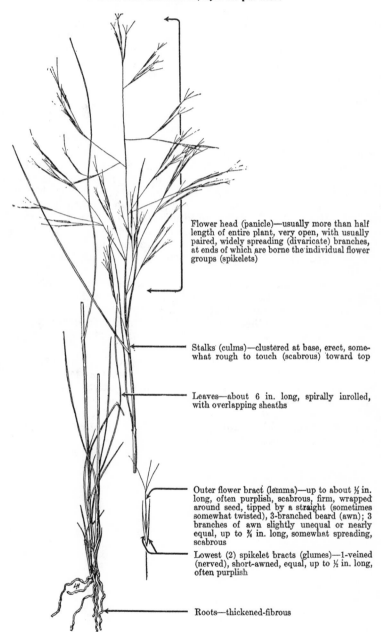

Flower head (panicle)—usually more than half length of entire plant, very open, with usually paired, widely spreading (divaricate) branches, at ends of which are borne the individual flower groups (spikelets)

Stalks (culms)—clustered at base, erect, somewhat rough to touch (scabrous) toward top

Leaves—about 6 in. long, spirally inrolled, with overlapping sheaths

Outer flower bract (lemma)—up to about ½ in. long, often purplish, scabrous, firm, wrapped around seed, tipped by a straight (sometimes somewhat twisted), 3-branched beard (awn); 3 branches of awn slightly unequal or nearly equal, up to ¾ in. long, somewhat spreading, scabrous

Lowest (2) spikelet bracts (glumes)—1-veined (nerved), short-awned, equal, up to ½ in. long, often purplish

Roots—thickened-fibrous

Poverty three-awn, also known as Texas poverty grass, Texas three-awn, and spreading three-awn, is a large, perennial, bunch-grass 1 to 3 feet high with leaves often as long as 6 inches. This grass is commonly found on "poverty" areas—dry deserts and foot-hills, but it sometimes grows in the mountains up to about 7,000 feet. It ranges from Kansas to southern California and south, through Mexico, into Central America. In Arizona and New Mexico it is largely found on the sandy areas toward the southern portions of the States. Usually it grows in scattered stands mixed with other grasses but sometimes is fairly abundant over localized areas.

Poverty three-awn is usually considered good forage in the South-west, especially for cattle and horses, while green and succulent, although in some sections it is given a low forage rating. It has two growing seasons when weather conditions are favorable. It makes early spring growth when moisture is abundant although its main growing season comes with the summer rains. If the summer rains come early poverty three-awn remains green for a month or more and produces considerable succulent forage. When, however, summer rains occur very late the seeds develop and mature rapidly and but little usable forage is produced. It becomes almost worth-less or even a menace to livestock when the troublesome awns appear. The plants green up mainly at the base and send up new shoots with the advent of winter and spring rains and make valuable forage at that time.

The specific name *divaricata* and the English name of spreading three-awn refer to the spreading branches of the flower head, or seed cluster. The common names involving the word "poverty" apply to the poor, rather sterile soils in which this grass typically occurs and possibly also to its poor forage value at the time of seed maturity.

Poverty three-awn is distinguished from most of the three-awns, when mature, by its widely branched seed head (panicle), which is often more than half the length of the entire plant. The branches of the panicle are rigid and straight and extend horizontally from the main stem; usually they are in pairs and bear seeds only out toward the ends. The panicle breaks off easily when mature and is blown about by the wind.

FENDLER THREE-AWN

Ari'stida fendleria'na

Flower head (panicle)—up to 5 in. long, narrow but open, with stiffly erect, short branches

Individual flower group (spikelet)—1-flowered, short-stalked, erect

Lowest (2) spikelet bracts (glumes)—sharp-pointed but without awns, 1-nerved, unequal in length; 1st, or lower glume half as long as 2d, or upper glume which is about ½ in. long

Outer flower bract (lemma)—firm, wrapped around "seed", ending below in a finely hairy base (callus), and tipped above by a long, 3-parted beard (awn); 3 awn divisions equal in length, up to 2 in. long, ascending

Stalks (culms)—densely tufted below, erect, often naked but sometimes with 1 or 2 very short stem leaves

Leaves—fine, crowded at base, forming a dense, curly cushion, inrolled, sharp-pointed, up to 2 or 3 in. long, having a ring of fine hairs where blade joins sheath

Roots—thickened-fibrous

Fendler three-awn, also called small triple-awn grass, is a small, tufted perennial 4 to 12 inches high. The species largely inhabits dry, sandy soils of deserts, plains, mesas, and foothills but sometimes is found in dry mountain parks up to 8,500 feet. It is a widely distributed species, occurring in the West from South Dakota and Montana to Texas and Lower California.

In the Southwest Fendler three-awn has fair forage value while green in spring and early summer. The volume of forage produced is small and it is inferior to most of the larger three-awn species for forage. In the Intermountain Region it is considered almost worthless, and stockmen sometimes call it "no-eat-um grass" because of its unpalatability. The seeds mature in midsummer or later, after which time it is practically worthless as forage and is occasionally a menace to grazing animals when the large three-branched beards (awns) appear. In some localities Fendler three-awn is abundant, although usually it occurs in scattered stands mixed with other grasses, weeds, and shrubs.

RED THREE-AWN

Ari'stida longise'ta [1]

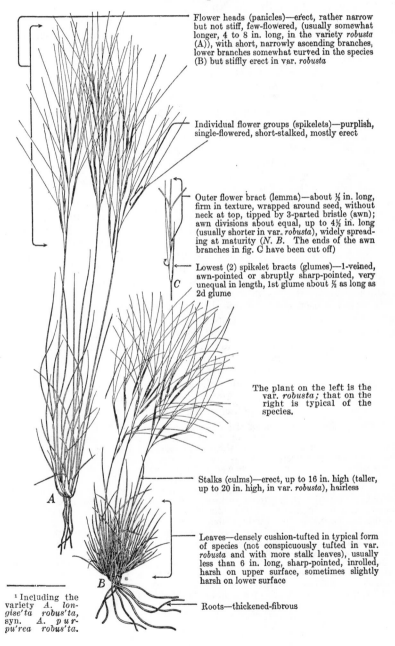

Flower heads (panicles)—erect, rather narrow but not stiff, few-flowered, (usually somewhat longer, 4 to 8 in. long, in the variety *robusta* (A)), with short, narrowly ascending branches, lower branches somewhat curved in the species (B) but stiffly erect in var. *robusta*

Individual flower groups (spikelets)—purplish, single-flowered, short-stalked, mostly erect

Outer flower bract (lemma)—about ½ in. long, firm in texture, wrapped around seed, without neck at top, tipped by 3-parted bristle (awn); awn divisions about equal, up to 4½ in. long (usually shorter in var. *robusta*), widely spreading at maturity (*N. B.* The ends of the awn branches in fig. C have been cut off)

Lowest (2) spikelet bracts (glumes)—1-veined, awn-pointed or abruptly sharp-pointed, very unequal in length, 1st glume about ½ as long as 2d glume

The plant on the left is the var. *robusta;* that on the right is typical of the species.

Stalks (culms)—erect, up to 16 in. high (taller, up to 20 in. high, in var. *robusta*), hairless

Leaves—densely cushion-tufted in typical form of species (not conspicuously tufted in var. *robusta* and with more stalk leaves), usually less than 6 in. long, sharp-pointed, inrolled, harsh on upper surface, sometimes slightly harsh on lower surface

Roots—thickened-fibrous

[1] Including the variety *A. lon-gise'ta robus'ta,* syn. *A. pur-pu'rea robus'ta.*

Red three-awn, also known as dogtown grass, long-awned needle-grass, prairie three-awn, longneedle three-awn, and wire needlegrass, is a perennial bunchgrass, and is perhaps the most easily recognized species of the genus. The outstanding mark of distinction of the species is the unusually long three-branched (trifid) beards (awns), which may be as long as 4½ inches. The variety *robusta*, as its name intimates, is typically more robust and taller; it has more leaves on the stalks, and has more stiffly erect branches in the seed head. However, there are numerous intergradations between typical forms of the species and the variety and, for that reason, they are here considered together.

Red three-awn ranges rather widely in the region west of the Mississippi River, especially in the Southwest. It is known to occur from Kansas to Montana, eastern Oregon, Arizona, western Texas, and south into Mexico. It has also been reported from Washington and southern British Columbia. Probably most of the more northern material is of the variety *robusta*. The species is common throughout New Mexico and Arizona at elevations below those of the ponderosa pine belt. It prefers the dry sandy soils on plains, mesas, and foothills, and is an aggressive invader of denuded areas, or of soils recently disturbed by burrowing animals, ploughing, or washing. Complaint has been registered against it on the ground that it supplants wheatgrass on the range [2] in Wyoming and elsewhere, but such a condition is almost certainly correlated with utilization of the wheatgrass so close that the plants are weakened to such an extent that they cannot successfully compete with species of inferior palatability.

There has been considerable difference of opinion among observers as to the forage value of this species. Some reports and publications indicate that it is practically worthless. However, the grass produces a considerable volume of fine leaves and deserves a higher rating than is frequently given it. According to Forest Service experience, red three-awn, when partially green, during the winter and spring months, rates at least fair in palatability both for cattle and sheep. This fact combined with its abundance qualify it as one of the most important species of the genus in New Mexico and Arizona.

Through the cooperation of the Bureau of Chemistry, United States Department of Agriculture, a series of monthly analyses was made for the Forest Service of the herbage of red three-awn over a 2-year period, 1917–18, the material being collected on the Jornada Experimental Range in southern New Mexico. The analyses showed a surprising amount of variation in the relative proportions of the chemical constituents, apparently somewhat correlated with fluctuations in rainfall. As contrasted with the valuable black grama, with which it is often associated, red three-awn proved rather uniformly higher in ash and lower in ether extract, its water and protein content almost identical, the crude fiber slightly higher, and the nitrogen-free extract slightly less. As far as such analyses may give a clue to feeding values this species would appear to be about as nutritious as is the better known black grama, on the whole, but more fluctuating.

Red three-awn is a vigorous seeder, its seed crop usually being plentiful. After maturity the seeds, with their long bristles (awns), often become a menace by getting into the eyes and nostrils of grazing animals, as well as penetrating the wool of sheep and lowering fleece values.

---

[2] Johnson, L. A DESTRUCTIVE RANGE GRASS. Producer 8 (8) : 18, illus. 1927.

SINGLE-AWN ARISTIDA

Aris'tida orcuttia'na, syn. *A. schiedea'na*

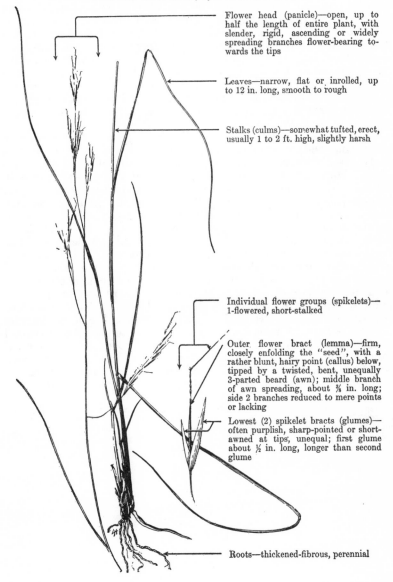

Flower head (panicle)—open, up to half the length of entire plant, with slender, rigid, ascending or widely spreading branches flower-bearing towards the tips

Leaves—narrow, flat or inrolled, up to 12 in. long, smooth to rough

Stalks (culms)—somewhat tufted, erect, usually 1 to 2 ft. high, slightly harsh

Individual flower groups (spikelets)—1-flowered, short-stalked

Outer flower bract (lemma)—firm, closely enfolding the "seed", with a rather blunt, hairy point (callus) below, tipped by a twisted, bent, unequally 3-parted beard (awn); middle branch of awn spreading, about ⅜ in. long; side 2 branches reduced to mere points or lacking

Lowest (2) spikelet bracts (glumes)—often purplish, sharp-pointed or short-awned at tips, unequal; first glume about ½ in. long, longer than second glume

Roots—thickened-fibrous, perennial

Single-awn aristida is a rather unusual member of the three-awn genus because the two lateral awns are very short or entirely lacking; hence the English name, single-awn aristida. The generic name comes from the Latin *arista*, a beard or awn, and refers to the bearded seeds of all members of this genus. This species ranges from western Texas through most of New Mexico, southern Arizona and into Mexico. It has also been reported from San Diego, Calif.[1] It grows on the dry mesas, plains, and foothills in open grassland, desert shrub and oak woodland types on rocky, gravelly, or especially, on sandy soils. This grass occasionally is locally abundant but is usually scattered, and frequently grows in association with poverty three-awn (*A. divaricata*), blue grama (*Bouteloua gracilis*), galleta (*Hilaria jamesii*), dropseeds (*Sporobolus* spp.), mesquites (*Prosopis* spp.), and scrub live oak (*Quercus turbinella*).

Single-awn aristida is one of the earliest grasses to green up in the spring and, when moisture is adequate, produces considerable early green forage, which is grazed readily by all classes of livestock. However, the main growing season of this grass comes with the advent of summer rains; while green, it is usually rated good in palatability. Its palatability decreases as the plant reaches maturity, and becomes very low after the foliage dries and the awns develop. On a seasonlong basis, it is commonly ranked as fairly good forage. Although the awned seeds of this species are not as troublesome (the awn being single) as those of most three-awn grasses, they are, nevertheless, avoided by grazing animals.

Single-awn aristida is a perennial bunch grass, commonly from 1 to 2 feet tall, with an upright, loosely flowered, often purplish panicle. Its single awn readily distinguishes this plant from other species of *Aristida*. It is frequently mistaken for a needlegrass (*Stipa*) because its awns are apparently single and somewhat twisted at the base, like those of the needlegrasses. Upon careful examination, however, the two often very short, lateral branches of the awn are discernible on at least a few of the seeds, a feature which distinguishes it at once from the needlegrasses.

---

[1] Jepson, W. L. A MANUAL OF THE FLOWERING PLANTS OF CALIFORNIA. 1,238 pp., illus. Berkeley, Calif. [1925.]

40

TALL OATGRASS

Arrhena'therum ela'tius

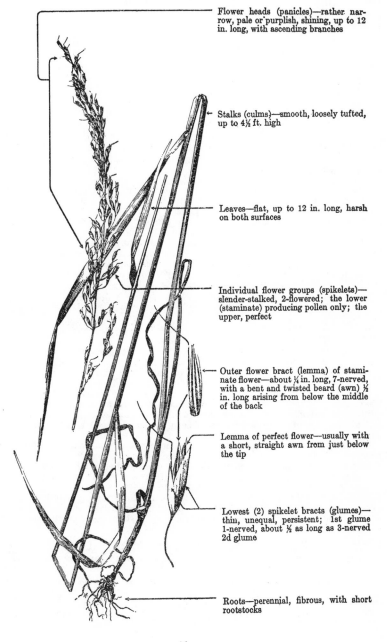

Flower heads (panicles)—rather narrow, pale or purplish, shining, up to 12 in. long, with ascending branches

Stalks (culms)—smooth, loosely tufted, up to 4½ ft. high

Leaves—flat, up to 12 in. long, harsh on both surfaces

Individual flower groups (spikelets)—slender-stalked, 2-flowered; the lower (staminate) producing pollen only; the upper, perfect

Outer flower bract (lemma) of staminate flower—about ¼ in. long, 7-nerved, with a bent and twisted beard (awn) ½ in. long arising from below the middle of the back

Lemma of perfect flower—usually with a short, straight awn from just below the tip

Lowest (2) spikelet bracts (glumes)—thin, unequal, persistent; 1st glume 1-nerved, about ½ as long as 3-nerved 2d glume

Roots—perennial, fibrous, with short rootstocks

Tall oatgrass, a leafy, tufted, perennial member of the oat tribe of the grass family (Gramineae), is a native of Europe. Originally introduced into the United States as a meadow grass it was more or less well established in New England and the Tennessee and Ohio Valleys as early as 1884. At that time it was known as evergreen grass, tall oatgrass, and meadow oatgrass. At the present time tall oatgrass is the well-established common name of this species and is particularly descriptive of this tall and oatlike plant. The scientific name is also suitable, the generic part being derived from Greek *arren*, masculine, and *ather*, awn, and the specific name from Latin *elatius*, taller. The Greek words of the generic name refer to the awn which is borne on the male flower of each spikelet, while the specific name, *elatius*, of course, refers to the habit of the plant being taller than that of most oat (*Avena*) plants.

Tall oatgrass has become naturalized in many places throughout the United States and is found along roadsides and in other waste places as an escape from cultivation. It has not, however, become established on the range to any extent.

This species, although inclined to be rather stemmy, is palatable to all classes of livestock, both while green and as winter forage. It ordinarily begins growth about two weeks earlier and remains green later in the fall than most native grasses with which it is associated on the range, thus materially extending the period during which succulent forage may be obtained by grazing animals. Livestock do not relish tall oatgrass when confined to it as an exclusive diet, but eat it freely in mixtures. When first introduced into the United States tall oatgrass was regarded very favorably as a meadow grass, especially in the South where it remains green practically yearlong and yields a large crop of good hay. Dr. Vasey [1] reports, in part:

It (tall oatgrass) is widely naturalized and well adapted to a great variety of soils (in Mississippi). On sandy or gravelly soils it succeeds admirably, growing 2 to 3 feet high. On rich dry uplands it grows from 5 to 7 feet high. It has an abundance of perennial, long, fibrous roots penetrating deeply in the soil, being therefore less affected by drought or cold, and enabled to yield a large quantity of foliage, winter and summer.

Tall oatgrass is one of the most drought-resistant of all cultivated grasses [2] and in recent years has received some attention as a possibly promising species for reseeding certain portions of the depleted grazing lands of the West. Vinall and Enlow [3] state that it is best suited to the Ohio Valley and the north Pacific coast regions and is better in a hay mixture than in pastures. They also state that it is suitable to any soil, except sand, and that for permanent pastures it is useful only in mixtures and should be sown in the fall at the rate of 20 to 25 pounds of seed per acre. Seed is available on the market and is not unduly expensive.

In the Southwest, experimental range seedings of tall oatgrass failed to produce satisfactory stands. In Montana, experimental seedings indicate that the species will prosper on moderately dry sites at lower elevations. It may prove to be a very valuable grass for that region, especially on winter elk range, as the tall stems project above the snow.

Forsling and Dayton [4] state that the species may have possibilities in the lower range country where satisfactory moisture conditions obtain, but results with it thus far are too meager to warrant other than experimental plantings.

[1] Vasey, G. THE AGRICULTURAL GRASSES AND FORAGE PLANTS OF THE UNITED STATES; AND SUCH FOREIGN KINDS AS HAVE BEEN INTRODUCED, WITH AN APPENDIX ON THE CHEMICAL COMPOSITION OF GRASSES, BY CLIFFORD RICHARDSON, AND A GLOSSARY OF TERMS USED IN DESCRIBING GRASSES. U. S. Dept. Agr., Div. Bot., Special Bull. [Unnumbered], rev., 148 pp., illus. 1889.
[2] Piper, C. V. FORAGE PLANTS AND THEIR CULTURE. Rev., 671 pp., illus. New York, 1924.
[3] Vinall, H. N., and Enlow, C. R. GRASSES AND LEGUMES FOR PERMANENT PASTURES. U. S. Dept. Agr., Bur. Plant Indus. [Unnumbered Pub.], 16 pp. 1934. [Mimeographed.]
[4] Forsling, C. L., and Dayton, W. A. ARTIFICIAL RESEEDING ON WESTERN MOUNTAIN RANGE LANDS. U. S. Dept. Agr. Circ. 178, 48 pp., illus. 1931.

WILD OAT

Ave'na fa'tua

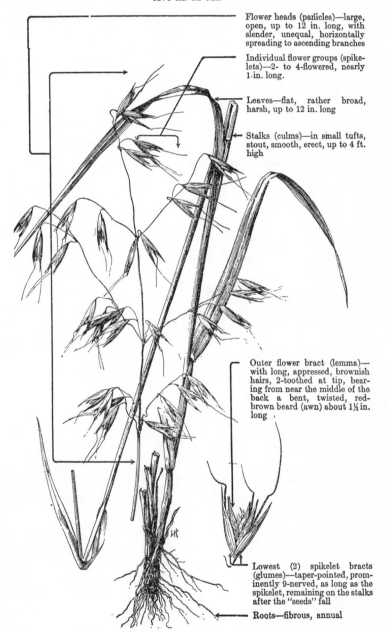

Flower heads (panicles)—large, open, up to 12 in. long, with slender, unequal, horizontally spreading to ascending branches

Individual flower groups (spikelets)—2- to 4-flowered, nearly 1-in. long.

Leaves—flat, rather broad, harsh, up to 12 in. long

Stalks (culms)—in small tufts, stout, smooth, erect, up to 4 ft. high

Outer flower bract (lemma)—with long, appressed, brownish hairs, 2-toothed at tip, bearing from near the middle of the back a bent, twisted, red-brown beard (awn) about 1½ in. long

Lowest (2) spikelet bracts (glumes)—taper-pointed, prominently 9-nerved, as long as the spikelet, remaining on the stalks after the "seeds" fall

Roots—fibrous, annual

Wild oat, an annual grass native to Europe, is widely naturalized in many parts of the United States, occurring along roadsides and in grain fields, and, to some extent, on the range, but only in California is it sufficiently well established to rank as an important range plant. This species is often the dominant plant in California valleys and foothills, growing in nearly pure stands over large areas and in a variety of soils. Although it occurs in pine stands, it is characteristic of open slopes. Wild oat was well established in California at a very early date, probably at the time the missions were established.

Today, many of the hills and valleys in California are clothed with a cover of wild oat, together with annual species of bromegrass and fescue. Clements [1] points out that, in a country with winter rainfall, the perennial grasses are especially susceptible to damage by overgrazing during the dry period from May to December. In fact, the original bunchgrass cover in the foothills of central and southern California was replaced largely by wild oat due to the long-continued overgrazing which began during the Spanish occupation and, at the present time, wild oat has come to simulate a climax type in many respects. However, in recent decades, it has suffered more and more from overgrazing, gradually being replaced by less palatable bromes and fescues.

Wild oat produces an abundance of forage and is highly palatable until the seeds are dropped and the herbage dies. It is a winter annual in California, its development being dependent upon the winter rains. With the advent of the fall rains in that State, much of the dried herbage is devoured with the new lush growth. Since wild oat is an annual, a seed crop must be matured and distributed each year if the plant is to be maintained on the range. In California a rapid growth of the grass is made in the spring, seed begins to ripen in May, and by the latter part of June the seed has largely fallen. Preliminary experiments have indicated that the species should be grazed lightly during the seed-production period from about mid-March to the last of June. After the seed has fallen the trampling of grazing animals assists in planting it. [2] This species is a good hay plant, and in some localities is regularly mowed for that purpose. Ordinarily, sufficient seed matures and shells out so that the grass maintains itself.

The seeds of wild oat, gathered by beating them into baskets, are consumed in large quantities by the Indians. The hairs and awns are singed off, and the seeds parched by tossing them about in shallow baskets with live coals. Finally, they are ground into a meal known as pinole. [3] Wild oat is also used by rustic anglers as an artificial fly. [4]

Smooth wild oat (*A. fatua glabrata*), a variety of wild oat, and slender oat (*A. barbata*), both annuals and natives of Europe, also occur in California. They are commonly associated with wild oat and are similar to it in palatability and productive capacity. Smooth wild oat differs from the others in having smooth rather than hairy lemmas. In slender oat the lemmas are clothed with red hairs and the teeth of the lemmas terminate in long bristles, but wild oat has brown, hairy lemmas and is without long bristles.

The generic name *Avena* is the classic Latin word for oat and was adopted for the genus by Linnaeus. Oat (*A. sativa*), the cereal, is one of the six species of *Avena*, two of which are native, that are found in the United States. Wild oat is the only range species sufficiently abundant to be of much importance.

Some believe that the domesticated species has been derived from wild oat by cultivation and selection, and that if neglected enough will revert into the wild species. There is no conclusive proof of this, however, although the two species are very closely related. Wild oat differs from oat chiefly in the long awns, longer flower heads, densely hairy instead of smooth lemmas, and in the fact that the grain readily fall from the glumes.

[1] Clements, F. E. THE RELICT METHOD IN DYNAMIC ECOLOGY. Jour. Ecology [London] 22(1) : 1–68, illus. 1934.
[2] Sampson, A. W., and Chase, A. RANGE GRASSES OF CALIFORNIA. Calif. Agr. Expt. Sta. Bull. 430, 94 pp., illus. 1927.
[3] Chesnut, V. K. PLANTS USED BY THE INDIANS OF MENDOCINO COUNTY, CALIFORNIA. U. S. Dept. Agr., Div. Bot., Contrib. U. S. Natl. Herbarium 7 : 295–422, illus. 1902.
[4] Sowerby, J. ENGLISH BOTANY; OR COLOURED FIGURES OF BRITISH PLANTS. Edited by J. T. B. Syme and Mrs. [P.] Lankester. Ed. 3, enl. and entirely rev., 12 v., illus. London. 1873–86.

PINE DROPSEED

Blepharoneu'ron tricho'lepis, syn. *Sporo'bolus tricho'lepis*

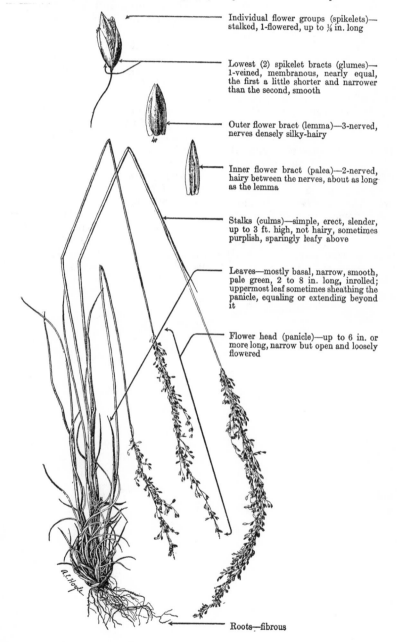

Individual flower groups (spikelets)— stalked, 1-flowered, up to ⅛ in. long

Lowest (2) spikelet bracts (glumes)— 1-veined, membranous, nearly equal, the first a little shorter and narrower than the second, smooth

Outer flower bract (lemma)—3-nerved, nerves densely silky-hairy

Inner flower bract (palea)—2-nerved, hairy between the nerves, about as long as the lemma

Stalks (culms)—simple, erect, slender, up to 3 ft. high, not hairy, sometimes purplish, sparingly leafy above

Leaves—mostly basal, narrow, smooth, pale green, 2 to 8 in. long, inrolled; uppermost leaf sometimes sheathing the panicle, equaling or extending beyond it

Flower head (panicle)—up to 6 in. or more long, narrow but open and loosely flowered

Roots—fibrous

Pine dropseed, also known as beadless pinegrass, beardless dropseed, and beardless bunchgrass, is a slender, erect, densely tufted, perennial bunchgrass with deep, fibrous roots, occuring in the mountains chiefly in open glades and parks or in open timber on moderately dry, rocky soils, in the ponderosa pine and lodgepole pine and spruce-fir zones from Colorado and Utah to Arizona and western Texas and south into Mexico. It is commonly associated with mountain and ring muhlies, junegrass, and with Sandberg and smooth bluegrasses, but generally comprises only a small portion of the stand. The palatability of pine dropseed, at least when young and tender, is very good for all classes of livestock—about equal to that of mountain muhly but somewhat lower than that of bluegrass and junegrass. Its stems and seed heads are either neglected or only slightly grazed during the latter part of the season. The leaves are abundant and sometimes attain a length of 8 inches but usually are considerably shorter and ordinarily not much forage per plant is produced. Pine dropseed is an important secondary species which will maintain itself normally on properly grazed ranges.

This grass gets its scientific name from the Greek, *blepharis*, eyelash, + *neuron*, nerve, and from *tricho*-, hair, + *lepis*, scale, both the generic and specific parts of the name referring to the hairiness of the three nerves of the lemma. It is the only species of this genus found in the United States. The stems are erect, densely tufted, often purplish, usually from 10 to 30 inches high; the flowering part, or inflorescence (panicle) head, is somewhat open and from 2 to 9 inches long; the spikelets are single-flowered and up to about one-eighth of an inch long.

GRAMAS

Boutelou'a spp.

The gramas which clothe thousands of square miles of the Great Plains and are the principal plants in the so-called buffalo grass or short grass association, grow exclusively in the Western Hemisphere.

The Spanish conquistadores, finding extensive areas of *Bouteloua* species in the tablelands of central Mexico, called them grama (literally, grass), probably because the flaglike spikes reminded them of the familiar related grama of Spain (what we call Bermuda grass). The name is now well established for the entire genus *Bouteloua*. Gramas occur in all the Western States except Washington and Oregon but are most abundant in the Southwest, especially in Arizona and New Mexico. They thrive chiefly on dry sites and at low elevations, and only rarely extend above the ponderosa pine zone. They also occur in greater or less abundance in the eastern foothills of the Rocky Mountains from southern Canada southward, in southern and eastern Utah, western Colorado, and in many of the warmer sections of California and the Intermountain Region.

In the Southwest the gramas are one of the mainstays of the range and furnish more forage than any rival plant at altitudes from the lowlands and dry mesas up to about 7,500 feet elevation. Most species are relished by all classes of livestock and withstand heavy grazing, and many of them rank as good to excellent forage plants. The gramas, however, produce very little spring forage; their main growth is chiefly dependent upon the amount of moisture available after the advent of warm, summer weather, and during drought years it may be practically negligible.

Certain species of gramas are easily distinguished from other common western range grasses by their characteristic (mostly few) flag-like spikes or seed clusters (as shown in the illustrations of black and blue gramas). Other species have an entirely different-looking inflorescence with many small flower clusters (spikes) as shown in the illustration of side-oats grama. In all gramas, the individual flower groups (spikelets) are small and single-flowered, with rudiments of one or more individual flowers (florets) above, arranged in two rows along one side of a more or less curved axis, forming spikes.

The gramas are excellent soil binders and aid materially in curbing erosion. They seldom form a complete sod but, in most of their habitats, grow typically in patches.

The genus was named by the illustrious Spanish botanist Mariano Lagasca (1776–1839) in honor of two contemporary Spanish gardeners, Claudio and Esteban Boutelou.

SPRUCETOP GRAMA

Boutelou'a chondrosioi'des

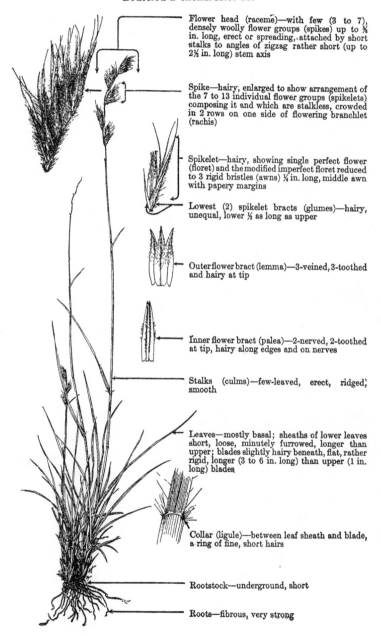

Flower head (raceme)—with few (3 to 7), densely woolly flower groups (spikes) up to ⅝ in. long, erect or spreading, attached by short stalks to angles of zigzag rather short (up to 2½ in. long) stem axis

Spike—hairy, enlarged to show arrangement of the 7 to 13 individual flower groups (spikelets) composing it and which are stalkless, crowded in 2 rows on one side of flowering branchlet (rachis)

Spikelet—hairy, showing single perfect flower (floret) and the modified imperfect floret reduced to 3 rigid bristles (awns) ¼ in. long, middle awn with papery margins

Lowest (2) spikelet bracts (glumes)—hairy, unequal, lower ½ as long as upper

Outer flower bract (lemma)—3-veined, 3-toothed and hairy at tip

Inner flower bract (palea)—2-nerved, 2-toothed at tip, hairy along edges and on nerves

Stalks (culms)—few-leaved, erect, ridged, smooth

Leaves—mostly basal; sheaths of lower leaves short, loose, minutely furrowed, longer than upper; blades slightly hairy beneath, flat, rather rigid, longer (3 to 6 in. long) than upper (1 in. long) blades

Collar (ligule)—between leaf sheath and blade, a ring of fine, short hairs

Rootstock—underground, short

Roots—fibrous, very strong

49

Sprucetop grama, esteemed as a very valuable grass wherever it occurs, is an erect mostly tufted perennial, usually attaining a height of about 15 to 18 inches but under the best growth conditions it may occasionally grow as high as 3 feet and almost form a turf.

This species is restricted to southern Arizona in the United States, its main range being in Mexico. In southern Arizona it occurs chiefly in the foothills and desert areas where it constitutes a large portion of the forage on some ranges, occasionally growing in nearly pure stands but more frequently in mixture with slender grama (*B. filiformis*), side-oats grama (*B. curtipendula*), false-mesquite (*Calliandra eriophylla*), and velvetpod mimosa, or Arizona rose (*Mimosa dysocarpa*).

While somewhat less palatable than the associated side-oats and slender gramas, sprucetop grama is grazed on some considerable scale, particularly during the summer growing season. The leaves, although short, are numerous so that the plants furnish considerable forage. This species cures very well on the ground and is valuable for late fall, winter, and spring use. In fact, sprucetop grama forms the backbone of some year-long ranges.

In order to promote maximum forage production this plant should be grazed conservatively during its period of rapid growth. Flower stalks are usually sent up in July and August and the seed is largely disseminated during September and October. This species has two methods of reproduction—by rootstocks and by seed. It is said to form a turf in parts of Mexico. It is drought-resistant and withstands grazing satisfactorily unless subjected to continued abuse.

Sprucetop grama has numerous slender, flat leaves and comparatively naked stems, each bearing commonly 3 to 7 woolly-bristly spikes. Its appearance varies considerably at different growth stages. The flowers, and later the seeds, are borne on the axis of the spike in two comb-teethlike rows, a characteristic of many gramas. This identifying feature disappears with the development of the rigid awns of the spikelets. Although this species resembles slender grama with which it is associated commonly, it is readily distinguishable from the latter by its woolly spikes. *Bouteloua eludens*, a species with no accepted common name, is often associated with *B. chondrosioides* and is difficult to separate from it botanically. This plant apparently is not so common on the range, though of about equal palatability.

The species is sometimes called woollyspike and Havard grama (the United States form of the species was originally known as *B. havardii*). It is of historical interest, as the illustrious Baron von Humboldt collected its type specimens in Mexico in the early nineteenth century.

SIDE-OATS GRAMA

Boutelou'a curtipen'dula

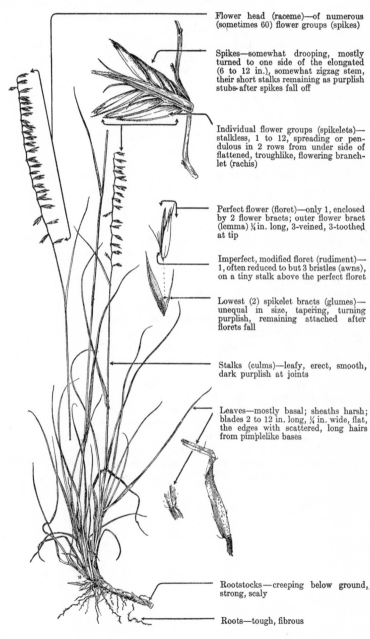

Flower head (raceme)—of numerous (sometimes 60) flower groups (spikes)

Spikes—somewhat drooping, mostly turned to one side of the elongated (6 to 12 in.), somewhat zigzag stem, their short stalks remaining as purplish stubs after spikes fall off

Individual flower groups (spikelets)—stalkless, 1 to 12, spreading or pendulous in 2 rows from under side of flattened, troughlike, flowering branchlet (rachis)

Perfect flower (floret)—only 1, enclosed by 2 flower bracts; outer flower bract (lemma) ¼ in. long, 3-veined, 3-toothed at tip

Imperfect, modified floret (rudiment)—1, often reduced to but 3 bristles (awns), on a tiny stalk above the perfect floret

Lowest (2) spikelet bracts (glumes)—unequal in size, tapering, turning purplish, remaining attached after florets fall

Stalks (culms)—leafy, erect, smooth, dark purplish at joints

Leaves—mostly basal; sheaths harsh; blades 2 to 12 in. long, ¼ in. wide, flat, the edges with scattered, long hairs from pimplelike bases

Rootstocks—creeping below ground, strong, scaly

Roots—tough, fibrous

Side-oats grama, also called tall grama, derives its common and specific names from the peculiar arrangement of the many spikes, commonly from 20 to 60, which hang pendent on one side of the stem. It is an erect perennial with coarse fibrous roots, strong, creeping rootstocks, wide flat leaves, and rather leafy stems from 1 to 4 feet high. Despite the presence of rootstocks its growth is typically tufted like the bunchgrasses.

This species is widely distributed from Connecticut and New Jersey to Tennessee and Alabama, and from Montana and Utah to California and Texas; also through Mexico south into South America. It occurs in Montana as a plains grass, growing usually in scattered stands in mixture with other grasses although occasionally occurring in some abundance on dry, rocky ridges. In the Southwest it is typically a grass of dry slopes, ridges, and rocky hillsides at elevations from 3,000 to 8,000 feet. In Arizona it makes its best growth on alluvial soils where it sometimes is rather abundant over limited areas.

Side-oats grama is a vigorous grower, produces a considerable volume of leafage per plant, and is a valuable forage species wherever sufficiently abundant. It is generally considered of high palatability while green and is consumed mainly during the growing season. It is recognized as both a good winter and summer forage although, as a winter feed, it is inferior to blue, black, or sprucetop grama. However, it is a valuable grass when used in mixture with these other gramas. The leaves are superior to the stems of the plant in palatability to the extent that the latter sometimes remain untouched even after all the leaves have been eaten. This species differs from some other important grasses in that it produces desirable green feed in the spring which is relished highly by livestock, if and when satisfactory spring rains occur.

The spikes of side-oats grama project from two sides of the flattened, zigzag axis but the delicate stems attaching the spikes often twist and bend so that those sharp-pointed parts extend over on the same side. When the flowers open, the showy, orange-red pollen sacs (anthers) give a very distinctive appearance to the flower head.

This species produces a fair amount of seed of rather low viability. It is propagated in the main by underground rootstocks. Where sufficiently abundant in the Southwest and Great Plains areas, it is occasionally cut for hay. Because of its size, vigorous growth, adaptability to varying growth conditions, and economic value, it appears to be the most promising grama for domestication.

BLACK GRAMA

Boutelou'a erio'poda

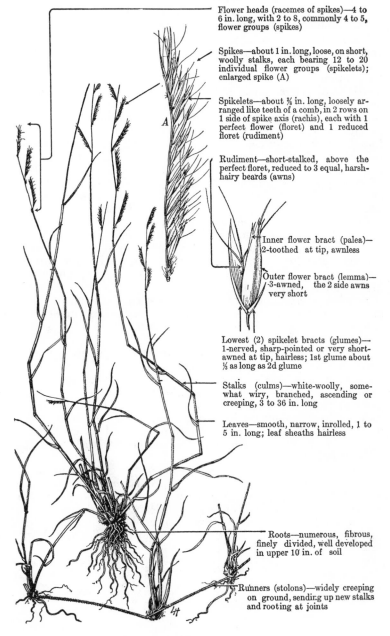

Flower heads (racemes of spikes)—4 to
6 in. long, with 2 to 8, commonly 4 to 5,
flower groups (spikes)

Spikes—about 1 in. long, loose, on short,
woolly stalks, each bearing 12 to 20
individual flower groups (spikelets);
enlarged spike (A)

Spikelets—about ⅜ in. long, loosely arranged like teeth of a comb, in 2 rows on
1 side of spike axis (rachis), each with 1
perfect flower (floret) and 1 reduced
floret (rudiment)

Rudiment—short-stalked, above the
perfect floret, reduced to 3 equal, harsh-
hairy beards (awns)

Inner flower bract (palea)—
2-toothed at tip, awnless

Outer flower bract (lemma)—
3-awned, the 2 side awns
very short

Lowest (2) spikelet bracts (glumes)—
1-nerved, sharp-pointed or very short-
awned at tip, hairless; 1st glume about
⅓ as long as 2d glume

Stalks (culms)—white-woolly, somewhat wiry, branched, ascending or
creeping, 3 to 36 in. long

Leaves—smooth, narrow, inrolled, 1 to
5 in. long; leaf sheaths hairless

Roots—numerous, fibrous,
finely divided, well developed
in upper 10 in. of soil

Runners (stolons)—widely creeping
on ground, sending up new stalks
and rooting at joints

Black grama, also called woolly-foot grama, is a tufted, long-lived perennial grass. Unlike most gramas it reproduces and spreads vegetatively by means of runners (stolons). Although Griffiths [1] states that it is occasionally an annual, under range conditions it is practically invariably a perennial. It is a key species on many Southwestern ranges of lower elevations and has been the subject of more intensive study than most native, western forage plants.

Black grama ranges from western Texas, through New Mexico and Arizona, south into Mexico. It is characteristically a lower-altitude grass, its main altitudinal range being from 3,500 to 5,500 feet, although it is occasionally found above 7,000 feet. It occurs mostly in open grasslands and on dry, gravelly or sandy soils. Originally it occurred almost as a pure type over extensive areas, and is still a dominant plant under favorable conditions. It occurs less commonly in the foothills, being very intolerant of shade, and is found but rarely on clay loams or adobe flats. It is very abundant in portions of the Rio Grande Valley of New Mexico where it occupies large stretches of the open, gently sloping country between the rugged upper foothills and the brushy areas of the lower foothills and mesas above the bottom lands. Here, in favorable years, it sometimes makes a crop heavy enough to be cut for hay.

Black grama is a choice forage grass, and was originally the mainstay of the range on numerous areas of the Southwest. It is highly palatable and nutritious both in summer and winter, and makes a valuable year-long range forage plant, especially for cattle. As Nelson [2] points out, the lower parts of the stems remain green during the milder winters, and clusters of leaves may start growth from some of the stem joints (nodes) in the spring. If it does not remain green, it cures well on the stalk and retains its nutritive value through the dry, spring period when other range forage is unpalatable or unavailable.

Although black grama can withstand recurrent grazing by livestock on heavily used ranges it spreads but little. Too heavy utilization seriously impairs its vigor and plants so weakened die out during drought periods. Campbell and Bomberger [3] point out that, in parts of the Southwest, black grama is subject to serious depletion as a result of drought or overgrazing, or both. In order to enable this valuable forage grass to maintain its stand its methods of reproduction and spreading must be considered when grazing the range.

Black grama maintains and increases the size of its stand in three different ways, viz (1), by seed production, (2) lateral spread by tillering, and (3) revegetation by stolons from old tufts. On the whole, black grama reproduces very little from seed. Its seed habits are unusually variable and are not dependable. During very favorable growing seasons a heavy crop of flower stalks and flowers is

[1] Griffiths, D. THE GRAMA GRASSES : BOUTELOUA AND RELATED GENERA. U. S. Natl. Mus., Contrib. U. S. Natl. Herbarium 14 : 343–444, illus. 1912.
[2] Nelson, Enoch W. THE INFLUENCE OF PRECIPITATION AND GRAZING UPON BLACK GRAMA GRASS RANGE. U. S. Dept. Agr. Tech. Bull. 409, 32 pp., illus. 1934.
[3] Campbell, R. S., and Bomberger, E. H. THE OCCURRENCE OF GUTIERREZIA SAROTHRAE ON BOUTELOUA ERIOPODA RANGES IN SOUTHERN NEW MEXICO. Ecology 15 : 49–61, illus. 1934.

produced although many of these do not mature their seed satisfactorily; even when well matured the seed has poor viability. During drought years practically no flowers or seed are produced. The
increase in area by tillering during a given growing season depends somewhat upon the intensity of the grazing and the density
of the existing vegetation, but chiefly upon the vigor built up in the
preceding year. For revegetation by stolons to be highly successful,
two successive favorable growing seasons are required, one for the
new sets to be produced and the second for the sets to become rooted
and established as individual plants. The number of stolons per tuft
varies from 1 to 9, but the number produced appears to have no
relation to the size of the tuft producing them. The chief value
of this method of revegetation is that it makes it possible for new
plants to be established at some distance from the parent plant and
this results in a greater area increase than would be possible from
tillering alone. In general, stolons are not so effective a means of
revegetation on grazed areas as is tillering nor are they as effective,
either in good or poor years, on grazed as on ungrazed areas. The
trampling of the grazing animals breaks off many of the stolons before the new sets can be established.

Based on quadrat experiments carried on in a 13-year study with
four different intensities of grazing use of black grama on the
Jornada Experimental Range in southern New Mexico, Nelson (*op.
cit.*) gives the following results:

Heavy overgrazing year after year has a fivefold effect upon the stand of
black grama: (1) The existing stand of black grama rapidly broke down and
eventually died; (2) natural revegetation was seriously handicapped and
reduced because of the low density and poor vigor of the old plants and
excessive trampling of new plants; (3) drought losses were intensified; (4)
competition from inferior perennial grasses and weeds increased; and (5)
a marked reduction appeared in the annual forage crop.

Overgrazing during the summer growing season, when the main growth of
black grama is made, reduces the height growth even in favorable growing
seasons, although not so severely as does heavy, yearlong overgrazing. If
this is repeated summer after summer the vigor of the plants is impaired and
no spread by tillering or establishment of new plants by stolons can occur even
in favorable growing periods.

Full use in the better years and slight overgrazing in dry years did not permit the full recovery of black grama from the losses suffered in drought
years, and the lateral spread of the tufts by tillering in the favorable growing years was not so effective as on the ungrazed or conservatively grazed
ranges. The average height growth in favorable growing years was only
slightly under that of the ungrazed years. In drought years, the species is
hindered from attaining its optimum condition. On the whole, this method
"prevents the maximum development of the black grama stand and permits
the inferior, associated grasses and other species to secure a foothold on the
more depleted black grama ranges."

Conservative grazing, i. e., grazing management on a sustained yield basis,
enables forage production of black grama to be maintained "as well as or
better than under complete protection from grazing." While revegetation by
stolons is not so extensive nor so effective under this method as is lateral
spread by tillering, a more even distribution of the smaller tufts over the
soil surface results, and the stand as a whole is not reduced. Without doubt,
conservative grazing is the most stable and productive system of grazing for
black grama.

In general appearance black grama somewhat resembles blue grama (*Bouteloua gracilis*). Black grama has an above-ground stoloniferous method of revegetation, a greater number (usually 4 or 5) of flaglike spikes in the flower head, conspicuous tufts of whitish, woolly hair at the bases of the loosely arranged spikelets, and jointed, branched, and densely woolly stems. Such characters contrast strongly with blue grama's underground rootstock method of spreading (which in the north results in a rough sod formation), its fewer (usually 1 to 3), erect (in age strongly curved) spikes, crowded spikelets (as many as 80 in some spikes), and its unbranched stems (except occasionally at base), and serve to distinguish these two very important gramas.

BLUE GRAMA

Boutelou'a gra'cilis, syn. *B. oligostach'ya*

Flower head (raceme)—upright, composed of usually 2 flower groups (spikes)

Spikes—¾ to 2 in. long, purplish, curved at maturity, composed of numerous, crowded, individual flower groups (spikelets) in 2 rows arranged like teeth of comb on one side of the axis (rachis); rachis not prolonged at end

Stalks (culms) —densely tufted at base, slender, unbranched above, smooth, erect, 6 to 36 in. high

Leaves—numerous, mostly basal, narrow, flat, smooth, 1 to 4 in. long, with a few, soft, white hairs at junction of blade and sheath

Roots—fibrous, spreading

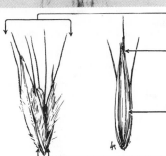

Spikelets—3-flowered; lowest flower perfect, stalkless; upper 2 flowers imperfect, stalked, hairy, reduced to bristles and scales

Outer flower bract (lemma) of perfect flower—3-nerved, 3-awned, hairy on the back

Inner flower bract (palea) of perfect flower—2-nerved, 2-toothed

Lowest (2) spikelet bracts (glumes)—unequal, somewhat hairy, bristle- (awn-) tipped

Blue grama, also known locally as white, red, or purple grama, though not quite as widely distributed as hairy and side-oats gramas, is, without doubt, the most common species of grama throughout the Western States and economically the most important species of the genus. It occurs from Wisconsin to Alberta, California, and Texas, extending southward, through Mexico, into South America. It is found in all the Western States except, possibly, Washington, Oregon, and Idaho, and is especially characteristic of the short grass areas of the Great Plains.

Blue grama varies considerably in growth habits and general appearance in different parts of its range. In the northern part, and under favorable moisture conditions, it tends to form a sod. Farther south on the Plains and other places where conditions are less favorable as a result of less rainfall or higher evaporation, it does not form so complete a cover but occurs in patches, and along the Mexican border at an elevation of about 5,000 feet it has more the appearance of a bunchgrass.[1] In the North the stems seldom reach a height of over 12 to 16 inches, sometimes being as low as 6 inches, but in the Southwest stems 2 to 2½ feet high are not uncommon.

Blue grama occurs on rather dry plains and foothills, as well as in the mountains in the woodland and ponderosa pine zones, inhabiting sandy or gravelly soils and also compact loams and gumbos. It is a quick-growing species and matures in about 60 to 70 days. Growth ordinarily does not start, or at least is very light, until after summer rains begin. The species is drought-resistant and has the ability to become dormant during drought periods in what would normally be the growing season. Subsequently, as soon as moisture becomes available, if temperatures are sufficient, it greens up and immediately resumes growth.

Generally, blue grama is rated as a choice forage species for all classes of livestock. It withstands grazing very well. On ranges suitable for fall and winter grazing it does best and yields greatest returns if it is grazed lightly in the summer during the period of rapid growth and is allowed to mature a crop, which, curing well on the ground, makes very good fall and winter forage. It forms a fairly good ground cover which gives it great soil-protective value. Its drawbacks as a range forage plant are that, over much of its range, it produces a relatively small crop and practically no green forage during spring and early summer at the time when succulent forage is especially desirable. However, it is a valuable forage plant for use at any time in the Southwest, where the spring growth of grasses is normally scanty.

Blue grama roots appear mainly in the upper 18 inches of soil, most of the roots being near the surface; consequently the grass is well adapted to situations where, because of a compact soil through which water percolates slowly, or because of light storms, much of the moisture during the growing season is confined to the surface 6 or 8 inches of soil. Under these conditions blue grama, and perhaps some of the other gramas also, forms the climax vegetative type. On many ranges, however, the grama or short grass type has come in as a result of heavy grazing, which has helped to eliminate the bunch grasses or tall grass which naturally occupy such areas. Studies on the Coconino Plateau by Hill and Talbot[2] show that blue grama, after long protection, gives way to some extent to the bunchgrasses where it is growing near the upper elevational limits of its range but, on the open range, easily holds its own under light grazing and withstands heavy grazing remarkably well. Even though grazing of this species by domestic livestock is carefully regulated, it is often subject to severe use by rodents. The seed habits of blue grama are weak and probably only in favorable years is a crop of good seed produced. However, this is offset to a considerable extent by the fact that the plants spread rather vigorously by tillering.

Typically each slender, erect, smooth stem of blue grama bears two spikes, but stems with one or three are not uncommon, and occasionally as many as six spikes will be found on a stem. The numerous leaves are mostly basal, from 1 to 4 inches long, rather narrow, flat, and smooth, and bear a few soft, white hairs at the junction of blade and sheath. The specific name *gracilis* refers to the slender, graceful habit of this species.

---

[1] Griffiths, D. THE GRAMA GRASSES : BOUTELOUA AND RELATED GENERA. U. S. Natl. Mus., Contrib. U. S. Natl. Herbarium 14 : 343–444, illus. 1912.

[2] Talbot, M. W., and Hill, R. R. PROGRESS REPORT ON RANGE STUDY PLOTS, COCONINO NATIONAL FOREST. 33 pp. 1923. [Unpublished ms.]

HAIRY GRAMA

Boutelou'a hirsu'ta

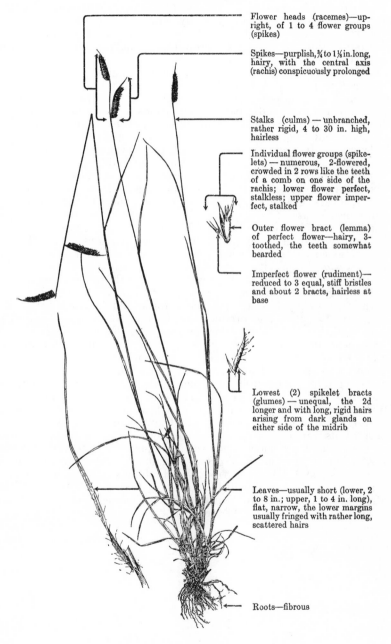

Flower heads (racemes)—upright, of 1 to 4 flower groups (spikes)

Spikes—purplish, ¾ to 1⅛ in. long, hairy, with the central axis (rachis) conspicuously prolonged

Stalks (culms) — unbranched, rather rigid, 4 to 30 in. high, hairless

Individual flower groups (spikelets) — numerous, 2-flowered, crowded in 2 rows like the teeth of a comb on one side of the rachis; lower flower perfect, stalkless; upper flower imperfect, stalked

Outer flower bract (lemma) of perfect flower—hairy, 3-toothed, the teeth somewhat bearded

Imperfect flower (rudiment)—reduced to 3 equal, stiff bristles and about 2 bracts, hairless at base

Lowest (2) spikelet bracts (glumes) — unequal, the 2d longer and with long, rigid hairs arising from dark glands on either side of the midrib

Leaves—usually short (lower, 2 to 8 in.; upper, 1 to 4 in. long), flat, narrow, the lower margins usually fringed with rather long, scattered hairs

Roots—fibrous

Hairy grama, an erect, rigid perennial, occurs from British Columbia to Illinois, Texas and California and south into Mexico; also, along the Gulf Coast, to the pinelands of peninsular Florida. It is one of the two or three most widely distributed species of grama. It is named *hirsuta* (hairy) because of the hairy spikes and because the margins of the leaves typically, although not invariably, bear rather long, scattered hairs. However, the chief distinguishing feature is that the spike axis projects as a naked point beyond the uppermost spikelet.

This grass occurs chiefly on dry, sandy and sandy loam soils, occasionally up to 8,000 feet, though rarely above elevations of 7,000 feet, and, in southern Arizona, attains most satisfactory development upon stable sandy loams at elevations between 4,000 and 6,000 feet. It is often associated with blue grama but is more drought-resistant and frequently grows at lower altitudes and on less favorable sites. It occurs over much of the Southwest, especially in southern Arizona, and is one of the outstanding grasses of that region, being seldom found in pure stands but often appearing abundantly in mixture with side-oats grama (*Bouteloua curtipendula*), slender grama (*B. filiformis*), other gramas (*Bouteloua* spp.), cane beardgrass (*Andropogon barbinodis*), mesquites (*Prosopis* spp.), and catclaw (*Acacia greggii*). Hairy grama is very abundant in the sandy soils along the more southern portions of the Texas-New Mexico State line where, with a few species of beardgrasses (*Andropogon* spp.), it constitutes about the only forage and, on the plateau of central Mexico, it grows in practically pure stands.[1]

Hairy grama has about the same palatability as blue grama, constituting very good forage especially for winter use, but ordinarily it is a smaller plant and produces less forage. It withstands grazing very well, but, like most other gramas, does better if it is grazed lightly during the summer growing period, leaving most of the crop, which cures very well on the ground, for use during fall, winter, and spring. Little growth is made until after the summer rains begin but, if precipitation then is adequate, the species matures rapidly. During exceptionally dry years this grass produces very little forage, although it withstands such droughts remarkably well.

Hairy grama is variable in size and appearance. In the northern part of its range this species usually has only one or two spikes on a stalk and has short rootstocks (rhizomes) which tend to form a sod, but in the South it grows in clumps, closely resembling a bunchgrass, and often has from two to four spikes on each culm. The spikes are often purplish and are ¾ to 1⅛ inches long. The leaves are flat and narrow, and are more numerous on the lower than on the upper portions of the stem.

---

[1] Griffiths, D. THE GRAMA GRASSES: BOUTELOUA AND RELATED GENERA. U. S. Natl. Mus., Contrib. U. S. Natl. Herb. 14 : 343–444, illus. 1912.

ROTHROCK GRAMA

Boutelou'a rothrock'ii

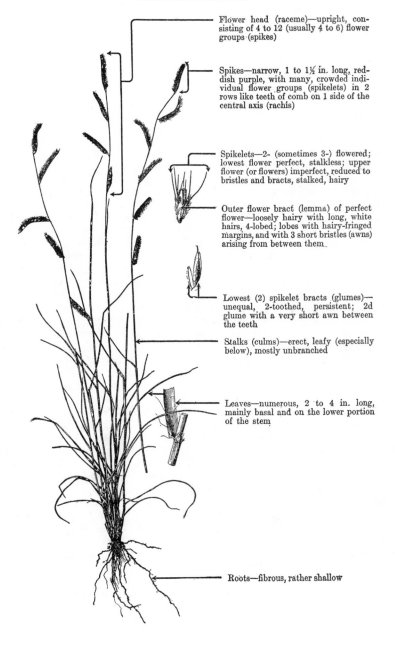

Flower head (raceme)—upright, consisting of 4 to 12 (usually 4 to 6) flower groups (spikes)

Spikes—narrow, 1 to 1½ in. long, reddish purple, with many, crowded individual flower groups (spikelets) in 2 rows like teeth of comb on 1 side of the central axis (rachis)

Spikelets—2- (sometimes 3-) flowered; lowest flower perfect, stalkless; upper flower (or flowers) imperfect, reduced to bristles and bracts, stalked, hairy

Outer flower bract (lemma) of perfect flower—loosely hairy with long, white hairs, 4-lobed; lobes with hairy-fringed margins, and with 3 short bristles (awns) arising from between them

Lowest (2) spikelet bracts (glumes)—unequal, 2-toothed, persistent; 2d glume with a very short awn between the teeth

Stalks (culms)—erect, leafy (especially below), mostly unbranched

Leaves—numerous, 2 to 4 in. long, mainly basal and on the lower portion of the stem

Roots—fibrous, rather shallow

Rothrock grama, also known as crowfoot grama and mesa grama, is a relatively short-lived perennial with a meager root system, commonly forming small tufts 1 to 3 inches in diameter. Its specific name commemorates Dr. Joseph Trimble Rothrock (1839–1923), an eminent botanist, explorer, and conservationist known as the Father of Pennsylvania Forestry. Rothrock grama occurs from southern Utah through Arizona and southern California into Mexico, but is of major importance in southern Arizona where it grows on the mesas and gentle open slopes of the foothills. Its main elevational range is between 1,800 and 5,500 feet, but it is occasionally found at either higher or lower elevations. At the lower altitudinal range this grass grows chiefly on the deeper soils and more moist situations, but at the upper elevations where more precipitation occurs it extends out over mesas and foothills in a wide variety of soils, varying from adobe to coarse gravelly or rocky sites. This species sometimes occurs in almost pure stands over large areas. It frequently grows in mixture with black grama (*Bouteloua eriopoda*), needle grama (*B. aristidoides*), side-oats grama (*B. curtipendula*), *Hilaria* spp., desert hackberry (*Celtis reticulata*), mesquites (*Prosopis* spp.), and catclaw (*Acacia greggii*).

The great abundance of Rothrock grama makes it an outstanding grass on some ranges. It varies from fair to good or even very good in palatability during the growing season but rates somewhat lower at other seasons of the year. This grass is highest in palatability and of maximum forage value during the summer growing season because it dries up quickly in the fall and does not cure as well on the range as do other common gramas. Rothrock grama, in contrast to most gramas, is a second-rate forage grass. Being short-lived and poorly rooted, it does not withstand heavy grazing satisfactorily, and rates as a so-called flash species, appearing or receding in accordance with climatic fluctuations. This characteristic behavior explains why Rothrock grama is sometimes mistaken for an annual grass. It decreases very noticeably during continued drought but, being a prolific seeder, reappears rapidly under favorable conditions.[1] Rothrock grama is sometimes cut for hay, yielding from 600 to 1,500 pounds an acre in favorable years on limited areas where it is particularly abundant. The early pioneers of southern Arizona are said to have used it rather extensively as hay.

The species bears a family resemblance to blue grama (*B. gracilis*), with which it is sometimes confused, although readily distinguishable from blue grama because of its growth in small bunches, rather than in turflike patches, and by its more numerous (from 4 to 12; commonly 4 to 6 on each stem) and somewhat finer flower spikes. These spikes frequently lend a reddish brown tint to the landscape, blending beautifully with the green of the open savanna woodland. The numerous slender leaves on the lower portion of the stems usually give the plant a leafy appearance, which also helps to distinguish it from blue grama.

---

[1] Thornber. J. J. THE GRAZING RANGES OF ARIZONA. Ariz. Agr. Expt. Sta. Bull. 65: [245]–360, illus. 1910.

BROMES

Bro'mus spp.

Brome is a large and very important genus, of the fescue-bluegrass tribe, found mostly in the North Temperate Zone. With very few exceptions the native western species are perennials, but about a dozen annuals, usually known as chess, or cheat, are naturalized on western ranges from the Old World. Another foreigner, the perennial smooth brome (*Bromus inermis*), has proven to be one of the most valuable species for reseeding certain western mountain ranges.[1] Bromes are robust grasses and generally make a moderately rank growth. The name "brome" comes from a Greek word meaning "food", and it is a fact that most species are eaten with relish by livestock at certain times or even throughout the growing season. A few bromes are valuable for hay. On the other hand, some of the annual bromes are highly undesirable weeds because of their invasion of agricultural lands. Some of these annuals have stiff prominent bristles (awns) that penetrate eye, nose, and mouth tissues, causing sores and blindness in livestock and game. Ripgut grass (*B. rigidus*), introduced from the Mediterranean region into California and contiguous States, is, when mature, a particularly serious menace because of its detached sharp-pointed florets and long, hard, spinelike awns.

Several characters help to distinguish bromes from other genera in the fescue tribe to which they belong. Leaf blades are characteristically flat and relatively broad with the edges of the leaf sheath grown together forming a tube. The seed heads (panicles) are seldom spikelike but usually more or less open and spreading. The lower glume, i. e., the lower of the two bracts at the base of the group (spikelet) of little flowers (florets), has 1 to 3 nerves and the upper, 3 to 9, usually 3 to 5. Backs of the florets are rounded in most species, but in others only on the lower part, whereas toward the top the midrib stands out like the keel on the bottom of a boat. The rather rigid outer seed husk (lemma) is notched at the tip, making two teeth between which the beard (awn) arises, and the veins (nerves) of the lemma converge at the apex.

---

[1] Forsling, C. L., and Dayton, W. A. ARTIFICIAL RESEEDING ON WESTERN MOUNTAIN RANGE LANDS. U. S. Dept. Agr. Circ. 178, 48 pp., illus. 1931.

BIG MOUNTAIN BROMES (CALIFORNIA BROME, BIG BROME, POLYANTHUS BROME)[1]

Bro'mus carina'tus, B. margina'tus, B. polyan'thus

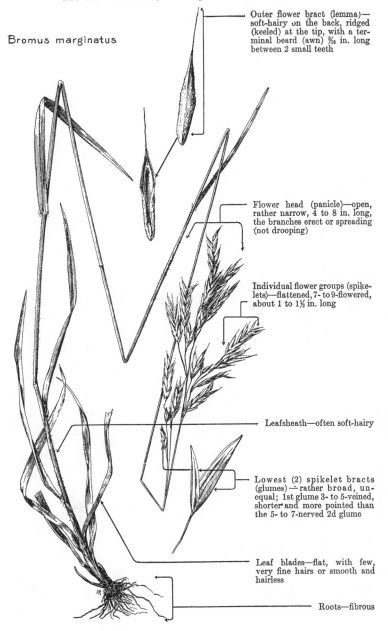

Bromus marginatus

Outer flower bract (lemma)—soft-hairy on the back, ridged (keeled) at the tip, with a terminal beard (awn) ³⁄₁₆ in. long between 2 small teeth

Flower head (panicle)—open, rather narrow, 4 to 8 in. long, the branches erect or spreading (not drooping)

Individual flower groups (spikelets)—flattened, 7- to 9-flowered, about 1 to 1½ in. long

Leafsheath—often soft-hairy

Lowest (2) spikelet bracts (glumes)—rather broad, unequal; 1st glume 3- to 5-veined, shorter and more pointed than the 5- to 7-nerved 2d glume

Leaf blades—flat, with few, very fine hairs or smooth and hairless

Roots—fibrous

Big mountain bromes are here considered to include three prominent bromes that are closely related and very similar in appearance, growth habits, and forage value. Of these three, big brome is very widely distributed in the range States but is particularly prevalent in Idaho, Washington, and Oregon; polyanthus brome prospers throughout the Rocky Mountains from Montana to Arizona and New Mexico; and California brome abounds on the Pacific slope, and is also at home in Montana, Arizona, and the Southwest; it is strikingly absent from the central Rocky Mountains. All three species grow in canyons, on grassy hillsides, and in the higher mountains at elevations up to 10,000 feet, although, on the Pacific Coast, California brome grows as low as 2,000 feet. They are common in the spruce and aspen zones and on the Pacific slope, and thrive well in the ponderosa pine type. They prefer rich, deep, moderately moist soil, but will also grow on rather poor, depleted soil, and fairly dry sites. They avoid dense shade. Ordinarily these three grasses grow in scattered bunches, but occasionally, as in the case of polyanthus brome in some localities, in the aspen zone of central and northern Utah, they make a fairly dense stand over large areas.

These robust, moderately coarse-stemmed short-lived, perennial bunchgrasses grow 1 to 4 feet high, or even higher under very favorable conditions. Their numerous rough leaves are about 6 to 12 or more inches long and one-fourth to three-eighths of an inch wide. The seed head (inflorescence) is ordinarily 4 to 9 inches long, with the groups (spikelets) of little flowers (florets) borne on erect (or ascending) branches.

These species rate among the best forage grasses on the western ranges. A deep, fibrous, spreading root system makes them fairly resistant to grazing and drought. The large leafy plants yield an abundance of forage which is relished by all classes of livestock during the growing season. At maturity the herbage becomes somewhat harsh and fibrous, especially in the case of California brome, and is then less palatable, particularly to sheep. Horses and sheep relish the nutritious seed heads. Lambs fatten rapidly and economically when an abundance of such seed heads is accessible. When grazed off early in the season these species produce a good aftermath of foliage that is devoured with relish even late in the autumn.

These three bromes depend on seed to reproduce, although the clumps stool out somewhat. Under proper management and normal growth conditions an abundance of good seed is produced and the range is adequately reseeded. Sometimes a smut (*Ustilago bromivora*) attacks the seed heads, but ordinarily it is not a serious menace on the ranges. Seeds of these species gathered on the ranges or grown in small mountain nurseries have been used with success in artificial reseeding.[2] As soon as a more adequate seed supply can be obtained a much wider use of these bromes for reseeding depleted mountain ranges should ensue. The big mountain bromes have been used to a limited extent in hay meadows and have yielded as high as 2 tons per acre on good soils.

Important technical characteristics identifying big mountain bromes include the spikelets 1 to 1½ inches long with 5 to 11 florets each about one-half inch long. The lower of the two glumes (bracts at the base of the spikelets) is about one-fourth and the upper about three-eighths inch long. The lemma (outer seed husk) has 7 to 9 nerves (veins).

The most salient characters distinguishing these three species from other perennial bromes (except *B. subvelutinus* which is easily recognizable by its hoary leaf blades covered with fine grayish-white hairs) are: Spikelets prominently flattened even when immature, the small awn (beard) about one-eighth to three-eighths inch long on the lemma, and the sharp ridging or keeling of the top of the lemma. California brome and big brome have fine hairs on the lemma, at least toward the top, and on the leaf sheaths and joints of the stems, whereas polyanthus brome is lacking in such hairs. California brome has a little longer awn than big brome, its inflorescence tends to be slightly more spreading and drooping, its foliage is often more harsh and hairy, and its leaf-blades tend to be narrower.

---

[1] Since this manuscript went to press, Hitchcock's "Manual of the Grasses of the United States" has appeared, raising serious question as to the specific validity of *Bromus marginatus* and *B. polyanthus*. There is now general agreement in the Forest Service to use the name "mountain brome" for *Bromus carinatus*, considering *B. marginatus* and *B. polyanthus* as synonyms.

[2] Forsling, C. L., and Dayton, W. A. ARTIFICIAL RESEEDING ON WESTERN MOUNTAIN RANGE LANDS. U. S. Dept. Agr. Circ. 178, 48 pp., illus. 1931.

RICHARDSON BROME

Bro'mus cilia'tus, syn. *B. richardso'ni*

Flower head (panicle)—4 to 12 in. long, open, nodding, with spreading and drooping branches

Outer flower bract (lemma)—about ½ in. long, broad, silky-hairy along the margins and lower part of the back but smooth near the tip, 5- to 7-veined (nerved), bearded (awned) from between a 2-pointed tip; awns usually about ⅛ in. long

Individual flower groups (spike-lets)—somewhat rounded, about 1¼ in. long, 5- to 12-flowered, at ends of slender, drooping stalks

Lowest (2) spikelet bracts (glumes)—smooth, unequal; 1st glume 1-nerved, ⅜ in. long; 2d glume 3-nerved, about ½ in. long

Stalks (culms)—tufted, 2 to 5 ft. tall, rather stout, leafy, erect, simple, often hairy at the joints

Leaves—rather pale green, up to ½ in. wide, flat, rough or harsh and sometimes hairy above; sheaths smooth to hairy

Roots—fibrous

Richardson brome is a characteristic representative of the group of perennial bromes which have nodding seed heads (panicles). The species is widespread, extending from Saskatchewan to Newfoundland, West Virginia, Tennessee, and westward to Texas and California.

Richardson brome is a perennial bunchgrass but is not so strongly tuft-forming as are some of the fescues with which it is associated. It has deep, extensive roots but no underground stems (rootstocks). This species occurs commonly in the aspen, spruce-fir, ponderosa pine, and lodgepole pine types in good, reasonably moist soil. It grows in shaded areas and in canyon bottoms and also on open slopes and in moist mountain parks, meadows, and valleys. Frequent associates include blue grama, pinegrass, various bluegrasses and wheatgrasses, oakbrush, and rabbitbrush.

Richardson brome ranks with the choicest forage grasses in palatability. It is relished by all classes of livestock, especially cattle and horses, until late in the season. Sheep like the maturing seed heads. Elk and deer also graze this grass. Although this brome is not so abundant generally as are some of the more prominent western grasses and seldom occurs in dense stands, yet, because of its local abundance and wide distribution, it supplies a large amount of forage.

In favorable sites Richardson brome grows up to about 4 feet high. Its stems are quite leafy, strong, but not coarse. The basal leaves are also plentiful. The leaf blades vary from 4 to 15 inches long, but commonly are 6 to 10 inches.

Porter brome (*B. ano'malus*, syn. *B. por'teri*), one of the commonest Rocky Mountain bromes, resembles Richardson brome in most respects. Its general range is the same except for the three Pacific Coast States where its occurrence is probably limited to California—the one range State where Richardson brome probably is not found.

The site requirements of Porter brome are essentially those of Richardson brome, except possibly that it prefers somewhat lower elevations. Their plant associates are about the same. Porter brome also is a forage plant of first rank for all classes of livestock. Preliminary reseeding experiments [1] in central Utah resulted in a fair stand, although results were not so successful as with the big mountain bromes.

The botanical differences between Richardson and Porter bromes are rather slight. In Porter brome the entire back of the outer flower bract (lemma) is densely silky-hairy; in Richardson brome this hairiness is restricted to the lemma margins and base. Richardson brome has but one vein (nerve) on the lower of the two spikelet bracts (glumes), while Porter brome has three. On an average Richardson brome seems to be about 6 inches taller than Porter brome, and has somewhat wider leaf blades.

---

[1] Forsling, C. L., and Dayton, W. A. ARTIFICIAL RESEEDING ON WESTERN MOUNTAIN RANGE LANDS. U. S. Dept. Agr. Circ. 178, 48 pp., illus. 1931.

SMOOTH BROME

Bro'mus iner'mis

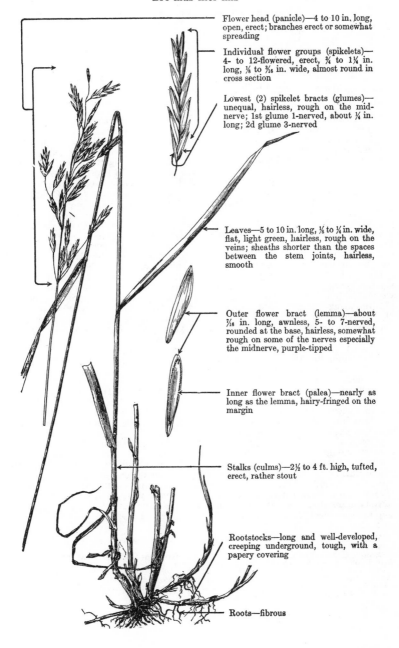

Flower head (panicle)—4 to 10 in. long, open, erect; branches erect or somewhat spreading

Individual flower groups (spikelets)— 4- to 12-flowered, erect, ¾ to 1¼ in. long, ⅛ to ³⁄₁₆ in. wide, almost round in cross section

Lowest (2) spikelet bracts (glumes)— unequal, hairless, rough on the midnerve; 1st glume 1-nerved, about ¼ in. long; 2d glume 3-nerved

Leaves—5 to 10 in. long, ⅛ to ¼ in. wide, flat, light green, hairless, rough on the veins; sheaths shorter than the spaces between the stem joints, hairless, smooth

Outer flower bract (lemma)—about ⁷⁄₁₆ in. long, awnless, 5- to 7-nerved, rounded at the base, hairless, somewhat rough on some of the nerves especially the midnerve, purple-tipped

Inner flower bract (palea)—nearly as long as the lemma, hairy-fringed on the margin

Stalks (culms)—2½ to 4 ft. high, tufted, erect, rather stout

Rootstocks—long and well-developed, creeping underground, tough, with a papery covering

Roots—fibrous

Smooth brome, often referred to as common brome, Hungarian brome, awnless brome, field brome, Austrian brome, and Russian brome, is a long-lived perennial grass with running rootstocks and is one of the most successful of cultivated, introduced species, being used extensively for pasture and forage crop plantings. The common name "smooth" refers to the hairless leaf sheaths and outer flower bracts. This imported grass has long been cultivated on the dry plains of Hungary and the Russian steppes. It was introduced into the United States about 1880 by the California Agricultural Experiment Station and has since been grown extensively as hay and pasturage from Alaska as far south as Tennessee, Kansas, and California.

Smooth brome grows best in regions of rather light rainfall and moderate summer temperatures. It is most popular in the Dakotas, Montana, and western Canada where it grows luxuriantly and produces an abundance of palatable and nutritious forage. This plant is one of the most palatable of all grasses, being relished by all classes of livestock especially during the spring and early summer. However, cattle and horses graze it more than sheep and goats.

This grass normally produces an abundance of viable seed except at the higher elevations where the seasons are too short for a seed crop. Commercial seed is produced in Canada and North Dakota, with yields ranging from 200 to 600 pounds per acre.[1] From 15 to 25 pounds of seed are sown per acre during the spring or late fall on well-prepared seed beds. Good stands are usually secured and, if grazed lightly the first year, they increase rapidly and form a complete sod the second or third year. Smooth brome is often one of the major constituents of many pasture mixtures, and is highly recommended for use in western Canada and the northwestern United States.[2]

Livestock do remarkably well on smooth brome hay, although it is considered more valuable for pasturage. It is frequently planted in mixture with alfalfa as these two forages ripen simultaneously; the brome expedites alfalfa curing and increases the value of the mixed hay. Hay yields vary from 1½ to 3¾ tons per acre. The crop is usually light the first year after planting, increases in tonnage the second year, and attains maximum production in the third season. Throughout its range, the crop usually is cut but once although in a few places two cuttings are secured.

Throughout its entire range, volunteer plants from the cultivated fields have gained sparse and scattered footholds on many of the mountain ranges, particularly in the semiarid regions of the West and Northwest. This species is frequently found at all elevations up to 9,000 feet. It will grow as high as 10,500 feet in central Utah but does not reseed at that elevation. It often makes a heavy growth of 2 feet or more on the deep, black clay loams of meadows and canyons but also thrives on the dry loose soils of the slopes and hills and succeeds fairly well on sandy soils.

Smooth brome is one of the best cultivated species introduced[3] into the western mountains. It has been widely used by the Forest Service in the artificial reseeding of mountain ranges and has proved well adapted for the rehabilitation of overgrazed, eroded, and burned-over[4] range lands. Good stands are usually obtained in fairly moist rather deep soils, where the species develops an extensive root system which frequently penetrates to depths of 5 feet or more, binds the soil firmly, and fortifies the plant to withstand grazing and unusual drought conditions.

[1] Piper, C. V. CULTIVATED GRASSES OF SECONDARY IMPORTANCE. U. S. Dept. Agr. Farmers' Bull. 1433, 42 pp., illus. 1925.
[2] Semple, A. T., Vinall, H. N., Enlow, C. R., and Woodward, T. E. A PASTURE HANDBOOK. U. S. Dept. Agr. Misc. Pub. 194, 89 pp., illus. 1934.
[3] Forsling, C. L., and Dayton, W. A. ARTIFICIAL RESEEDING ON WESTERN MOUNTAIN RANGE LANDS. U. S. Dept. Agr. Circ. 178, 48 pp., illus. 1931.
[4] Christ, J. H. RESEEDING BURNED-OVER LANDS IN NORTHERN IDAHO. Idaho Agr. Expt. Sta. Bull. 201, 28 pp., illus. 1934.

DOWNY CHESS

Bro'mus tecto'rum [1]

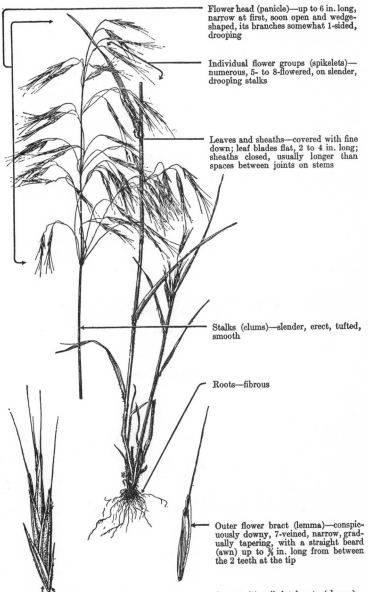

Flower head (panicle)—up to 6 in. long, narrow at first, soon open and wedge-shaped, its branches somewhat 1-sided, drooping

Individual flower groups (spikelets)—numerous, 5- to 8-flowered, on slender, drooping stalks

Leaves and sheaths—covered with fine down; leaf blades flat, 2 to 4 in. long; sheaths closed, usually longer than spaces between joints on stems

Stalks (clums)—slender, erect, tufted, smooth

Roots—fibrous

Outer flower bract (lemma)—conspicuously downy, 7-veined, narrow, gradually tapering, with a straight beard (awn) up to ⅜ in. long from between the 2 teeth at the tip

Lowest (2) spikelet bracts (glumes)—hairy, unequal in size; 1st, 1-nerved, shorter than the 3-nerved 2d glume

[1] Includes the variety *B. tecto'rum nu'dus,*

71

Downy chess, also known as downy brome, junegrass, and cheatgrass, attains a height up to about 2 feet and is either an annual or summer annual, meaning that the seeds often germinate in late summer or early fall allowing the plants to grow and stool out before winter sets in. The plant is introduced from Europe and has spread to a greater or less extent over portions of the 11 far western States except Arizona and New Mexico, occupying chiefly plains, foothills, and intermountain valleys. Thus far, in California, it is largely confined to the east side of the Sierras and the northeastern lava plateau region but is gradually extending westward. It has not yet reached coastal areas of Oregon and Washington. Downy chess does not grow in wet places and seldom appears at high elevations or in the more arid, western deserts. While its occupation of certain areas may be a result of continued past overgrazing and depletion of better forage plants, it does not expel established native species from the range nor prevent their return.

Downy chess is, comparatively, one of the less palatable species of the brome genus. Its short life, relatively sparse, hairy leafage, and high ratio of unpalatable seed heads all militate against its usefulness. On the other hand the species is so abundant locally that it supplies a considerable amount of forage, especially on many intermountain ranges, and particularly on many poorer sites where better plants do not occur. On several million acres in the intermountain country it comprises the bulk of early spring grazing for sheep, cattle, and horses. Thousands of sheep are lambed on downy chess. It is ready to graze early in March on the lower areas, and remains tender and palatable until about the middle of May when it begins to mature and turns reddish. A week or two later it dries completely and becomes straw-colored. On the higher foothills it is grazed from April to early June. In the late summer and early fall the less abundant but relished new growth appears. The livestock even consume some of the old herbage if it is saturated thoroughly by late season rains. At several-year intervals downy chess is attacked by a smut (*Ustilago bromivora*) which greatly reduces the stand temporarily on some areas although the grass reestablishes itself within a year or two. In the better areas, where grazing is properly regulated and fires are prevented, downy chess tends eventually to be largely replaced by more valuable and permanent, perennial species.

Although its roots are shallow and not extensive, downy chess is an important factor in erosion control where better plants do not occur. Both observation and experiments show that, if ungrazed and unburned, dense stands of downy chess will rather effectively hold the soil and check erosion.

When the plants are dry they increase the fire hazard on many areas. The sharp-pointed, bearded florets when about mature frequently injure animals that graze downy chess or consume its hay. These "seeds" either singly or in small wads work into the tongue and softer tissues of the mouth, causing sores and infection. The eyes are also sometimes affected. The encroachment of downy chess in orchards, gardens, and farms and its abundance in adjoining waste places make it a weed pest under those conditions.

Downy chess plants that stool have a bunchgrass appearance but there are also many single or few-stemmed individuals. The roots are fine, plentiful, and shallow. The slender stems grow 4 to 24 inches high. The flat, fairly numerous leaves are one-eighth to three-sixteenths of an inch wide. The panicle (seed head) is large, open, and drooping with the spikelets (groups of florets) borne on very slender branches. The florets are from three-eighths to one-half of an inch long, gradually tapering to a sharp point, and each has an untwisted beard (awn) from three-eighths to five-eighths of an inch long. In typical forms a soft down of fine, slender hairs covers the leaves and florets; the variety *nudus*, however, is distinguished by the fact that the florets are smooth and hairless.

The specific name *tectorum* means "of roofs" [Latin *tectum*, roof] and is reminiscent of the fact that in its original home in humid climates of the Old World this grass is a familiar denizen of thatched roofs of houses.

REEDGRASSES

Calamagros'tis spp.

The reedgrasses, perennial plants of the redtop tribe (Agrostideae), constitute a large genus of over 100 species distributed throughout the cool and temperate regions of the world. About 26 species occur in the United States, mostly in the western mountains, with the largest representation in the Northwest. The scientific name *Calamagrostis* is derived from the Greek and literally means reedgrass.

The western reedgrasses range from sea level on the Pacific coast to the high elevations in alpine and subalpine meadows. The moisture requirements of the different species vary considerably as their habitat ranges from wet acid sites to dry or saline situations. Many of the species occupy wet meadows, bogs, marshy areas, stream banks, and moist open woods; others are typically dry-land plants.

With the exception of bluejoint (*C. canadensis*) and pinegrass (*C. rubescens*), the members of this genus are generally scattered in occurrence and seldom appear in abundance over large range areas. The various species are usually classed as "fillers" or secondary forage plants. Considering the group as a whole, however, the reedgrasses are important on many ranges. The palatability to livestock varies considerably according to species; several are highly palatable to all livestock; others, particularly some of the dry-land plants, are distinctly inferior forage. But, on the whole, the reedgrasses are regarded as fair to good forage for all classes of livestock. They are grazed with moderate relish during the early part of the growing season but the herbage usually becomes tough and harsh as the season advances. Elk graze several of the species moderately and deer crop them to a slight extent.

Shorthair reedgrass (*C. brew'eri*), sometimes called Brewer reedgrass, is a low, densely tufted grass, 6 to 12 inches high, with a mass of fine, short foliage, slender stems, and open, few-flowered, purplish panicles. It grows in mountain meadows of the high Sierra Nevada Mountains of California. This is one of the most palatable of the reedgrasses and is eaten by all classes of livestock as well as by deer. Together with shorthair sedge (*Carex exserta*, syn. "*Carex filifolia*" in part) it makes up the highly valued, so-called shorthair ranges of the high Sierra Nevada.

Marsh reedgrass (*Calamagro'stis inexpan'sa*, syns. "*C. hyperbo'rea*" of United States authors, *C. hyperbo'rea america'na, C. hyperbo'rea elonga'ta*), a robust species growing up to 4 feet high from stout rootstocks, has a rather coarse spikelike panicle and firm, rather harsh, rigid leaves. It grows in meadows and marshes, extending from the plains to high mountains in all of the 11 far western States, as well as in the northeastern United States and throughout most of Canada. This species is fairly palatable to all classes of livestock but, due to its rank growth, is more readily grazed by cattle and horses than by sheep. It is not ordinarily abundant.

Plains reedgrass (*C. montanen'sis*) is an erect, dry-land species, up to 16 inches tall, with rigid stems, rough inrolled leaves, underground rootstocks, and narrow, purplish, or pale panicles. It grows on dry bench lands, flats, and hillsides of the sagebrush and wheat-grass types. Montana is about the center of distribution for this grass, which ranges from Saskatchewan and Alberta to South Da-kota, Utah, Idaho, and eastern Washington. This species is the only representative of this genus which has much range significance on the dry prairies and foothills. It is rated as poor to fair forage for sheep and up to fairly good for cattle and horses, being espe-cially relished in its younger stages. Plains reedgrass is sometimes confused with junegrass (*Koeleria cristata*), although the latter differs in lacking rootstocks, in having several-flowered spikelets, and in its hairiness of stem below the panicle.

Pacific reedgrass (*C. nutkaen'sis*, syn. *C. aleu'tica*) is a coarse, stemmy plant, attaining a maximum height of 5 feet, which has harsh blades 1 foot or more long and three-eighths of an inch wide, and narrow, loose panicles up to 12 inches long. This robust species grows in scattered stands in wet meadows, moist woods, brushlands, and sand dunes along the Pacific Coast from Alaska to central California. Cattle and horses graze the leafage until the seed is formed, after which it becomes harsh and tough and is little used. Sheep eat the herbage only in the spring.

Purple pinegrass (*C. purpuras'cens*), also known as purple reed-grass, is an erect, densely tufted grass up to 2½ feet tall, with dense, spikelike, pale, or often purplish flower heads (panicles), and rough, rather stiff leaves. It grows sparsely on subalpine open ridges, dry rocky hills, and dry woods, as well as in moist parks and meadows, from the arctic regions to California and Colorado. Early in the season, this grass is grazed readily by all classes of livestock but after midsummer only lightly or moderately by cattle and horses.

The species of the *Calamagrostis* genus are difficult to identify, due to the great variation of the individual species and to the ex-istence of series of integrading forms. They are usually moderately tall or robust perennial grasses with open or narrow panicles. The individual flower groups (spikelets) are small, and one-flowered. The lowest two spikelet bracts (glumes) are persistent, about equal, awnless, and pointed. The outer flower bract (lemma) is shorter and usually more delicate than the glumes, surrounded at the base by a tuft of hairs, and awned from the back, usually below the mid-dle, with a delicate, straight prickle or with a stouter, bent or twisted, exserted awn. The small, thin, and narrow inner flower bract (palea) is shorter than the lemma. Botanically, the reed-grasses are a somewhat artificial group, not sharply separable from the closely related redtops (*Agrostis* spp.). In general they are dis-tinguished by their tendency to have thicker or more wiry stems, and a coarser habit of growth; by the prolongation of the stalk of the spikelet (rachilla) as a hairy bristle behind the well-developed palea, and (in most cases), as stated above, by the tuft of hairs at the base of the lemma, which is typically shorter than the glumes. A few species of *Calamagrostis*, however, such as *C. breweri*, are small and delicate, and a few species of *Agrostis*, such as Alaska redtop (*A. aequival'vis*) have well-developed paleas, lemmas about as long as the glumes, the spikelet axis prolonged into a short rudiment, and the florets somewhat fuzzy at the base.

BLUEJOINT

Calamagros'tis canaden'sis

Stalks (culms)—2 to 5 ft. tall, erect, simple, usually smooth

Leaves—flat, harsh to the touch, up to 16 in. long and ⅜ in. wide, often drooping, pale green; sheaths shorter than spaces between joints on stalk

Flower head (panicle) — loosely branched, rather open especially at base, 4 to 8 in. long, usually nodding, purplish

Rootstocks—extensive, creeping underground

Roots—fibrous

Individual flower groups (spikelets)—1-flowered, small, ⅛ to ³⁄₁₆ in. long

Lowest (2) spikelet bracts (glumes)—persistent, about equal, taper-pointed, keeled, harsh on keel

Outer flower bract (lemma)—nearly as long as glumes, smooth, narrowed toward summit, ragged-tipped, awned just below the middle with a delicate, straight, inconspicuous prickle; base surrounded by a tuft of hairs about as long as lemma

Inner flower bract (palea)—shorter than the lemma, narrow, thin-papery

Bluejoint, also known in some localities as bluejoint reedgrass, meadow pinegrass, Canadian reedgrass, and marsh pinegrass, is the most common and widespread species of *Calamagrostis* in North America being first found in Canada. It is distributed from Labrador to Alaska and southward to California (in the south central Sierras), New Mexico, western Nebraska, Iowa, Michigan, and New Jersey, running southward, in the Allegheny and Appalachian Mountains, as far as western North Carolina. It thrives under cool climatic conditions, extending northward to the Arctic Circle, and, according to Hitchcock,[1] is the dominant grass in the interior of Alaska. Bluejoint is strictly a moisture-loving grass which grows typically in swamps, marshes, wet meadows and parks, along streams, and in moist canyon bottoms and semishaded woodlands. It extends from sea level in the North and Northwest to elevations of over 12,000 feet near the southern limit of its range in New Mexico and to over 11,000 feet in Colorado. On the western ranges, it is most common in the cool mountains at medium to high elevations where it is often very abundant on localized areas, sometimes forming dense pure stands.

The forage value of bluejoint varies considerably in different localities; it has been variously rated from poor to very good for all classes of livestock. The general tendency has been to give it a higher palatability rating than it actually deserves. Because of its wide distribution and abundance in many localities, however, this grass furnishes a large amount of forage. Under proper range management the average palatability of bluejoint is medium, or less, for all classes of livestock. The leafage is usually consumed with moderate relish by cattle and horses but, on account of its rank growth, is not closely grazed by sheep. The latter often eat the leaf blades but seldom graze the stems even in the forepart of the season. The herbage is most palatable when young and succulent, but the tendency of this grass to grow in wet habitats tends to prohibit its use by livestock, especially sheep, until late in the season when the leafage is more harsh and tough. This species is good elk feed and is grazed lightly by deer.

Bluejoint reproduces both vegetatively and by means of seed. In the Blue Mountains of Oregon, Sampson[2] observed that a large amount of seed of good viability was produced. Reproduction by rootstocks is prolific, stands in some localities becoming dense enough to be cut for hay. This species is an important source of wild hay from Wisconsin to North Dakota.[1]

Calamagrostis is a very difficult genus botanically, due to its great morphological variation and lack of stability, and bluejoint is no exception to this rule. Consequently its nomenclature is much confused in the books. *C. canadensis acuminata*, a variety based largely on its small spikelets and narrow, tapered (acuminate) glumes seems to intergrade completely with the species (*C. canadensis*). *C. blanda* (syn. *C. pallida* Vasey & Scribn., *not* C. Muell.), a Washington form, separated chiefly on its pale, flexuous panicle and rather long awn attached near the apex of the lemma, seems also to merge inseparably in *C. canadensis*. *C. cuprea* (syn. *C. inexpansa cuprea*) and *C. lactea* (syn. *C. langsdorfii lactea*) in the past have been more or less confused with *C. canadensis*. *C. cuprea* is now regarded as a synonym of *C. inexpansa*, and *C. lactea* is regarded as a rare, distinct species, known only from Mount Baker, Wash.

[1] Hitchcock, A. S. THE GENERA OF GRASSES OF THE UNITED STATES, WITH SPECIAL REFERENCE TO THE ECONOMIC SPECIES. U. S. Dept. Agr. Bull. 772, 307 pp., illus. 1920.
[2] Sampson, A. W. IMPORTANT RANGE PLANTS: THEIR LIFE HISTORY AND FORAGE VALUE. U. S. Dept. Agr. Bull. 545, 63 pp., illus. 1917.

PINEGRASS

Calamagros'tis rubes'cens, syns. *C. cusick'ii, C. luxu'rians, C. suksdor'fii, C. suksdor'fii luxu'rians*

Flower head (panicle)—narrow, dense, spike-like, 3 to 6 in. long, reddish or pale green, seldom produced under typical growing conditions

Stalks (culms)—slender, 16 to 40 in. high; flower stalks usually not produced except on plants growing in open sunlight

Individual flower groups (spikelets)—1-flowered, small, ⅛ to 3/16 in. long

Lowest (2) spikelet bracts (glumes) —persistent, about equal, taper-pointed, not strongly keeled, harsh to the touch

Outer flower bract (lemma)—nearly as long as glumes, smooth, thin, blunt at tip, surrounded at base by a tuft of short hairs about ⅓ as long as lemma, bristled (awned) on back near the base; awn delicate, bent and exserted at side of glume, shorter than the glumes; inner flower bract (palea) shorter than the lemma, narrow, thin-papery

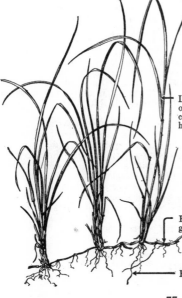

Leaves—mostly basal, flat or inrolled at tip only, 4 to 12 in. long, ascending with gracefully curved or drooping tips, harsh to the touch, hairless except on collar of sheaths

Rootstocks—extensive, creeping, underground, giving rise to numerous leaves along their length

Roots—fibrous

77

Pinegrass, so named because of its intimate association with ponderosa pine and lodgepole pine forests, is also occasionally called pine reedgrass and red reedgrass. The specific name *rubescens* is from the Latin and refers to the common reddish color of the flower heads and to the reddish hue which sometimes appears in the leafage, especially on the plants growing in open sunlight. This species is widely distributed from British Columbia and Manitoba southward to northern Colorado and central California. It ranges from sea level to elevations of about 10,000 feet but grows most luxuriantly at medium elevations beneath stands of ponderosa pine. It is also common on the floor of open to dense lodgepole pine forests, occurring in greatest abundance under the more open stands. Occasionally, this grass is also associated with aspen, larch, and open Douglas fir stands and occurs in openings both in and adjacent to the timbered areas. At the higher elevations, it is chiefly confined to the warmer southern and western exposures. Pinegrass is fairly drought-resistant and is able to thrive in well-drained situations where the soil is relatively dry during most of the summer. The strong, well-developed, creeping rootstocks of this grass produce a continuous, closely matted sod or turf, which enables it to become the dominant herbaceous plant over large range areas.

By virtue of its abundance, pinegrass is an important range plant in many localities, particularly in the ponderosa pine forests of the Northwest and the lodgepole pine stands of the northern Rocky Mountains. Much diversity of opinion exists regarding the forage value of pinegrass due, no doubt in large part, to its varying palatability at different times of the year. This plant is one of the least palatable of the more common range forage grasses, being classed in most localities as practically worthless to poor for sheep and poor to fair for cattle and horses. However, on some ranges it is rated up to fair for sheep and fairly good for cattle and horses. In the spring, when young and tender, pinegrass is grazed more readily than at any other time. As the season advances the tissues of the leaf blades become harsh and tough, and the grass is seldom eaten by any class of livestock if more succulent feed is available. In the fall of the year it is usually grazed again to a limited extent, since the leafage is apparently somewhat softened by the fall precipitation. It remains green late in the season, long after most of the other forage is dried up. Game animals crop pinegrass to a slight extent in the spring, and elks, especially, eat it again in the fall and winter until deep snows make it unavailable.

Both cattle and sheep can be forced to utilize this grass closely by holding them on pinegrass types by means of fencing or herding. However, such heavy use is ordinarily not to be recommended since it usually results in the overgrazing or elimination of highly palatable grasses as well as of the weed and browse species which grow in association with pinegrass. Although these more palatable associated species usually form a minor portion of the vegetative cover, they often make up a very important part of the usable forage. Consequently, the carrying capacity of pinegrass types is often lowered considerably by overgrazing, despite the fact that the stand of pinegrass itself is unharmed. Pinegrass turf is notoriously tough, as it stands up remarkably well under heavy grazing and severe trampling. It is especially valuable for watershed protection because of its effectiveness in binding and holding the soil against erosion.

This species reproduces vigorously by means of its rootstocks and, to a more limited extent, by seed. For the most part the plants consist of numerous flat, drooping leaves arising from the extensive system of underground rootstocks. Flowering stalks and heads are sparse, being seldom produced except on plants growing in the open or under full sunlight. However, the comparatively small amount of seed produced is usually high in fertility. In germination tests in the Blue Mountains of Oregon, Sampson[1] obtained results ranging from 58 to 98 percent. The seed-producing plants are usually somewhat tufted and erect, differing in appearance from the usual stemless, drooping-leaved form that grows under the shade of timber stands. The plants can usually be recognized by the ring of stiff short hairs at the junction of the sheath and blade.

[1] Sampson, A. W. IMPORTANT RANGE PLANTS : THEIR LIFE HISTORY AND FORAGE VALUE. U. S. Dept. Agr. Bull. 545, 63 pp., illus. 1917.

PRAIRIE SANDGRASS

Calamovil′fa longifo′lia

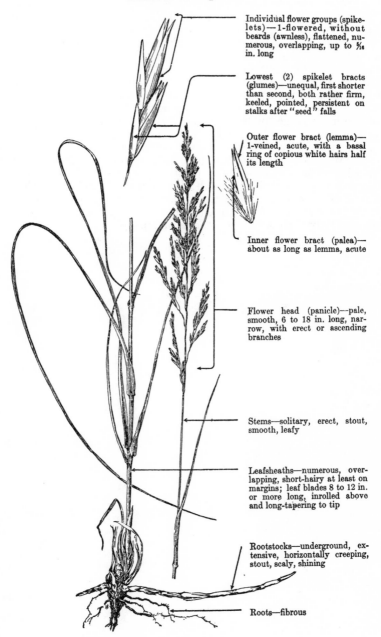

Individual flower groups (spikelets)—1-flowered, without beards (awnless), flattened, numerous, overlapping, up to ⁵⁄₁₆ in. long

Lowest (2) spikelet bracts (glumes)—unequal, first shorter than second, both rather firm, keeled, pointed, persistent on stalks after "seed" falls

Outer flower bract (lemma)—1-veined, acute, with a basal ring of copious white hairs half its length

Inner flower bract (palea)—about as long as lemma, acute

Flower head (panicle)—pale, smooth, 6 to 18 in. long, narrow, with erect or ascending branches

Stems—solitary, erect, stout, smooth, leafy

Leafsheaths—numerous, overlapping, short-hairy at least on margins; leaf blades 8 to 12 in. or more long, inrolled above and long-tapering to tip

Rootstocks—underground, extensive, horizontally creeping, stout, scaly, shining

Roots—fibrous

Prairie sandgrass, a tall, coarse, tough, perennial grass also known as sandreed, is a drought-resistant species which occurs chiefly in sandy soil (occasionally in heavy sterile soil) on plains and hills east of the Rocky Mountains from western Ontario to Saskatchewan, northeastern New Mexico, Kansas, and northern Indiana. It is the most widespread species of *Calamovilfa*, a genus of about four species restricted to North America. Grasses of this genus are perennials with horizontal rootstocks and single-flowered spikelets, belonging to the red-top tribe (Agrostideae) of grasses. Prairie sandgrass is of relatively inferior palatability and of little use during the growing season; however, it produces a considerable amount of forage which cures on the ground and is an important source of winter cattle feed. It abounds on some areas which support but few other forage plants. It is also cut for hay. Its rootstock system peculiarly adapts it for binding loose, sandy soils.

The rigid leafy stems are from 2 to 6 feet high. The leaves taper to a long, slender, inrolled (involute) point and have crowded sheaths. The glumes or two lowest empty bracts of the individual flower groups (spikelets), are shorter than the "floret", i. e., the solitary flower, composed of essential floral organs (stamen and pistil) with the lemma and the bract opposite it (palea). The grain is permanently inclosed by its lemma and palea.

OATGRASSES

Dantho'nia spp., syn. *Merathrep'ta spp.*

The North American representatives of *Danthonia*, of which seven species are now recognized by the more conservative botanists as occurring in the United States, are all perennial bunchgrasses. Six of these species are found in the western States. Other species, both of annuals and perennials, are abundant and widely distributed in warm and temperate regions in other parts of the world, especially in South Africa and Australia, where the genus is very important. Danthonia belongs to the oat tribe of grasses (Aveneae) and was named for Etienne Danthoine, a French botanist of the eighteenth century. It is a bit unfortunate that the common name, oatgrass, has become so firmly intrenched in western range usage for this genus, as the western species show no great resemblance to oats (*Avena* spp.) and the name, tall oatgrass, is well established for a species in another genus, *Arrenatherum elatius*.

All western danthonias, except poverty oatgrass (*D. spicata*, syn. *D. thermalis*), are at least fairly palatable to livestock. Poverty oatgrass can be recognized at any time of the year by its short, very curly leaves. It is well named, as it is an excellent indicator of poor soil and also is worthless as forage; no living thing, except perhaps meadow mice, will eat it unless forced to do so. Flatstem oatgrass (*D. compressa*) is chiefly an eastern species and not important in the West. Parry oatgrass (*D. parryi*) is of scattered occurrence and hence often unimportant as a range plant but may be abundant locally. One-spike oatgrass (*D. unispicata*), California oatgrass (*D. californica*), and timber oatgrass (*D. intermedia*) are sometimes locally abundant and of greater or less importance as range plants.

The individual flower groups, or spikelets, are about 4- to 10-flowered in the western species of oatgrass, with the lowest (2) spikelet bracts (glumes) much longer than the outer flowering bracts (lemmas), and commonly as long as the spikelet. The lemmas are 2-toothed and bear a stiff, bent, usually twisted beard (awn) from between the teeth. All the western species have large, hidden, self-fertilizing spikelets (cleistogenes) at the lower joints of the stems and enclosed by the leaf sheaths. These spikelets mature seed, and the stems commonly break off at the joints where the spikelets are borne.

CALIFORNIA OATGRASS

Dantho'nia califor'nica, syns. *D. america'na, Merathrep'ia califor'nica*

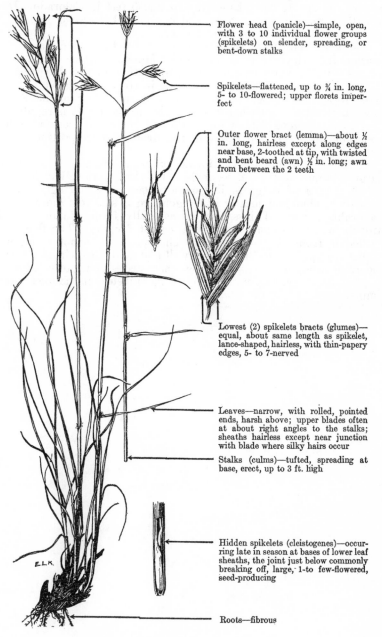

Flower head (panicle)—simple, open, with 3 to 10 individual flower groups (spikelets) on slender, spreading, or bent-down stalks

Spikelets—flattened, up to ¾ in. long, 5- to 10-flowered; upper florets imperfect

Outer flower bract (lemma)—about ½ in. long, hairless except along edges near base, 2-toothed at tip, with twisted and bent beard (awn) ½ in. long; awn from between the 2 teeth

Lowest (2) spikelets bracts (glumes)—equal, about same length as spikelet, lance-shaped, hairless, with thin-papery edges, 5- to 7-nerved

Leaves—narrow, with rolled, pointed ends, harsh above; upper blades often at about right angles to the stalks; sheaths hairless except near junction with blade where silky hairs occur

Stalks (culms)—tufted, spreading at base, erect, up to 3 ft. high

Hidden spikelets (cleistogenes)—occurring late in season at bases of lower leaf sheaths, the joint just below commonly breaking off, large, 1-to few-flowered, seed-producing

Roots—fibrous

California oatgrass is a fairly tall, rather leafy perennial which typically grows in small tufts. It ranges from British Columbia to Montana, Colorado, and California and occurs in both dry and moist soils on hillsides, benches, and in canyons of the ponderosa pine, aspen, and spruce belts, ascending to 10,000 feet in Colorado. It is usually typical of open parks, and meadows, but also is present in partial shade in open stands of timber.

The specimens from the Pacific coast are taller and have finer leafage than those from Colorado and Montana, which perhaps accounts for the variation in the forage rating in the two sections. While immature, California oatgrass is considered good to very good forage for cattle and horses in California, Oregon, and Washington, although somewhat less palatable to sheep. It is reputed as fair to fairly good forage for cattle and horses and somewhat less palatable to sheep and goats in the drier, eastern portion of its range.

Individual plants of California oatgrass produce a relatively large amount of forage, as it is a tall leafy grass, but like the other species of oatgrass it generally occurs scatteringly. It is sometimes abundant locally in Oregon and is said to form a sod in favorable places. This species occasionally forms stands in California which are dense enough to be cut for hay. The flowering period is from May to August. The species does not produce a copious supply of seed but stools well and is able to withstand considerable heavy grazing. Like the other species of western oatgrass, it produces large, hidden, self-fertilizing spikelets at the lower stem joints.

TIMBER OATGRASS

Dantho'nia interme'dia, syns. *D. cusick'ii, D. interme'dia cusick'ii,*
Merathrep'ta interme'dia

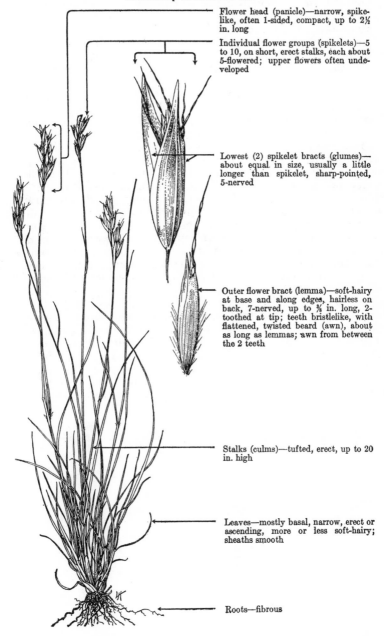

Flower head (panicle)—narrow, spike-like, often 1-sided, compact, up to 2½ in. long

Individual flower groups (spikelets)—5 to 10, on short, erect stalks, each about 5-flowered; upper flowers often undeveloped

Lowest (2) spikelet bracts (glumes)—about equal in size, usually a little longer than spikelet, sharp-pointed, 5-nerved

Outer flower bract (lemma)—soft-hairy at base and along edges, hairless on back, 7-nerved, up to ⅜ in. long, 2-toothed at tip; teeth bristlelike, with flattened, twisted beard (awn), about as long as lemmas; awn from between the 2 teeth

Stalks (culms)—tufted, erect, up to 20 in. high

Leaves—mostly basal, narrow, erect or ascending, more or less soft-hairy; sheaths smooth

Roots—fibrous

Timber oatgrass, the most common and widespread of the western species of *Danthonia*, is a shallow-rooted perennial ranging from Quebec to British Columbia, California, and New Mexico. It usually grows in well-defined tufts, but under certain conditions the plants spread over small areas, so that the bunch habit of growth is obscured. Timber oatgrass is typically a mountain species occurring chiefly in the spruce and alpine belts, but often extending downward to the ponderosa pine and oakbrush types. At the higher altitudes it occurs mostly in the open, in moist parks and meadows, but toward the lower limits of its altitudinal range is more common in the shade of open coniferous timber and under aspen and oak. It normally occurs scatteringly but occasionally is locally abundant.

Timber oatgrass is regarded as good to very good forage for all classes of livestock in Montana, parts of Utah, and the Northwest. It is also well regarded for spring forage in most other parts of its range—probably because it greens up before many other plants begin growth. In some localities timber oatgrass is little grazed and probably should rate, at best, only as fair forage. It apparently withstands grazing very well, often being the dominant grass on badly depleted ranges. However, this may not denote ability to withstand grazing, but may indicate that timber oatgrass has a relatively low palatability and actually is not grazed to the same degree as associated species of reputedly comparable palatability.

Plants of timber oatgrass stool well and usually produce an abundance of basal leaves. The stems are comparatively low, with a few short upper leaves and compact, one-sided heads (panicles) of about 5 to 10 spikelets. The young heads have a distinct purplish tinge, due to the purple color of the large glumes. With age, however, the purple color disappears and the glumes become brown and papery. Flowering occurs during July and August. The small seed crop is disseminated during August and September. This species, like the other western oatgrasses, produces large self-fertilizing spikelets (cleistogenes) hidden at the lower stem joints. These spikelets, which mature seed, are enclosed by the leaf sheaths, and the stems break off commonly at the joints where the spikelets are borne.

TUFTED HAIRGRASS

Deschamp'sia caespito'sa, syn. *Ai'ra caespito'sa*

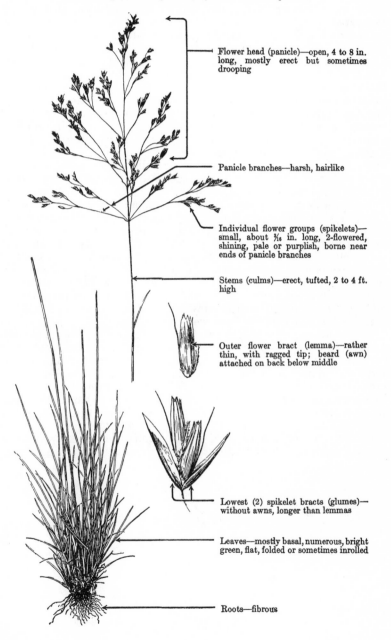

Flower head (panicle)—open, 4 to 8 in. long, mostly erect but sometimes drooping

Panicle branches—harsh, hairlike

Individual flower groups (spikelets)—small, about ⅛ in. long, 2-flowered, shining, pale or purplish, borne near ends of panicle branches

Stems (culms)—erect, tufted, 2 to 4 ft. high

Outer flower bract (lemma)—rather thin, with ragged tip; beard (awn) attached on back below middle

Lowest (2) spikelet bracts (glumes)—without awns, longer than lemmas

Leaves—mostly basal, numerous, bright green, flat, folded or sometimes inrolled

Roots—fibrous

Tufted hairgrass is a perennial bunchgrass found in the mountains in all of the Western States and is one of the most widely distributed of the western range grasses. It occurs chiefly in the spruce-fir belt and above timberline. In well-watered parks and meadows it often grows in nearly pure stands which, on the more favorable sites, form a nearly complete ground cover. On drier, less favorable sites it commonly grows in rather open stands in mixture with sedges, trisetum, false-strawberry (*Sibbaldia procumbens*), and other plants. It distinctly prefers the open and practically never is found in dense shade, although it is common in partial shade among willows and in open timber.

Tufted hairgrass belongs to the oat tribe (Aveneae) of grasses, and its individual flower clusters (spikelets), although very much smaller, resemble those of cultivated oat. It grows in compact bunches with the stems usually erect, 2 to 4 feet high. The leaves, growing mostly from near the base of the plant, are bright green and either flat, folded, or sometimes inrolled. The foliage is abundant and varies in texture from rather fine to moderately coarse, depending chiefly on site conditions.

This grass withstands fairly close grazing and is usually relished by all classes of livestock. Sometimes under the most favorable conditions it grows so luxuriantly that sheep especially and, to some extent, cattle and horses will graze it only slightly. It is sometimes cut for hay. The flowering period extends from July to September and a large amount of good seed is produced and disseminated during August and September. New plants are established entirely from seed, and sufficient seed should be permitted to mature to provide the necessary replacements, although tufted hairgrass plants stool out very well.

About five species of hairgrass are recognized by the more conservative botanists as occurring in the western United States; of these, tufted hairgrass is the most common and widespread. Dorsal awns and glumes longer than the lemmas, shown in the illustration, are characteristic of the oat tribe. The awns are very fine and hairlike, attached near the base of and slightly longer than the lemmas, which have broad, toothed (erose) tips. Spikelets are two-flowered, small, shining, and often purplish; in *D. caespitosa* they are borne near the ends of the slender, rough panicle branches, which are usually more or less spreading.

WILD-RYES

E'lymus spp.

Elymus is a fairly large genus of rather tall grasses of the North Temperate Zone with more species in the western United States than in any other region. With the exception of one introduced annual, the western species are wholly perennial; most of them are bunchgrasses; several form turf by means of underground rootstocks. Wild-ryes are widely distributed in the West, occurring from the lower semidesert areas to the aspen and spruce belts. Some species typically occur in the open in bottomlands and meadows and others in grasslands, brush types, and woodlands.

Generally speaking, the foliage of wild-ryes is harsh and is only moderately palatable to livestock. Furthermore, the flower heads (spikes) of many species are bristly or bearded (awned) and are not relished. Some species are widely distributed and fairly abundant, at least locally, so that the genus, although probably of secondary importance, supplies much forage for livestock on the western ranges. One species, Medusa-head (*E. caput-medusae*), an imported annual which now occurs on the Pacific coast, is practically worthless as forage. The smaller, softer-leaved species as typified by blue wild-rye (*E. glaucus*) are fairly good forage for cattle and horses during the forepart of the season. After the heads form the plants are not relished. The large, coarse species, such as giant wild-rye (*E. condensatus*), are less palatable and are grazed for only a short period in the spring. However, they are of considerable value in some localities as winter forage for cattle and horses. The wild-ryes are not very palatable to sheep, although when young and tender they are often grazed by this class of livestock.

The flower heads of wild-rye are usually erect, rather densely flowered, with a jointed main axis (rachis) which usually does not break up. In at least one species, however, Macoun wild-rye (*E. macounii*) the rachis disarticulates, showing a transition to the genus *Sitanion*. Individual flower groups (spikelets) are typically in pairs at each joint of the rachis, but in some species there may be three or more and in others only one, the latter being a transition to the wheatgrasses (*Agropyron* spp.). In the single-spikeletted wild-ryes the lowest (2) spikelet bracts (glumes) are more or less awl-like, while in the wheatgrasses the glumes are of a broader type. Blue wild-rye is the most common and widely distributed species of the group which has two spikelets at the rachis joints. Giant wild-rye is easily the outstanding member of the genus, because of its large size and habit of growing in enormous bunches. Its spikelets occur in groups of 3 to 6, the heads completely or nearly awnless. This species is widely distributed and formerly was very abundant in bottomlands in Nevada, but has been largely destroyed by overgrazing, except on protected areas utilized as hay lands.

Among the turf-forming species, beardless wild-rye (*E. triticoides*), a blue-green perennial with long rootstocks, and with spikelets in groups of 1 to 3, is common throughout the West and is fairly abundant along the Humboldt River in Nevada, often in association with giant wild-rye. This species is frequently cut for hay and is superior to giant wild-rye for this purpose. It resembles bluestem (*Agropyron smithii*) somewhat but is usually more robust. This species produces an abundance of seed and was used as meal, or pinole, by the Indians. Such utilization was so common that the whites often referred to *E. triticoides* as squawgrass.[1]

Wild-ryes are thus named because of their resemblance to cultivated rye (*Secale cereale*). They are also called ryegrasses and lymegrasses. Their scientific name is derived from the Greek *elumos*, which was an ancient name for a kind of grain. The wild-rye genus belongs to the barley tribe of grasses (Hordeae) which, among others, includes the wheatgrasses and several of the grains such as rye, barley, and wheat. Western wild-ryes are not cultivated on any extensive scale, although a few species are cut for hay when they occur in natural stands of sufficient size and density.

Many species of wild-rye, including two of the common western species, Canada wild-rye (*E. canadensis*) and giant wild-rye are susceptible to infestation by ergot, a fungous disease. It is possible that all species of wild-rye will contract this disease which most commonly occurs on rye. This fungous growth infects the heads of the grasses and replaces the seed with black or purplish club-shaped bodies. Ergot contains several poisonous compounds and, if infected grasses are consumed by livestock, illness and death may result. Most such cases of livestock poisoning in the United States result from wild-rye ergot.[2] Losses probably occur on the range in which the responsibility of this poison is not recognized.

---

[1] Chesnut, V. K. PLANTS USED BY THE INDIANS OF MENDOCINO COUNTY, CALIFORNIA. U. S. Dept. Agr., Div. Bot., Contrib. U. S. Natl. Herbarium 7 : 295–422, illus. 1902.

[2] Pammel, L. H. A MANUAL OF POISONOUS PLANTS CHIEFLY OF EASTERN NORTH AMERICA, WITH BRIEF NOTES ON ECONOMIC AND MEDICINAL PLANTS . . . 2 pts., illus. Cedar Rapids, Iowa. 1910–1911.

GIANT WILD-RYE

E'lymus condensa'tus

Flower head (spike)—erect, up to 1 ft. long, often compound and interrupted below; axis (rachis) joined but not breaking apart

Stalks (culms)—in large, dense tufts, up to 12 ft. high and ½ in. thick, ridged, smooth below, harsh above

Leaves—flat or somewhat inrolled, as much as ¾ in. wide and 2 ft. long, harsh at least above; sheaths smooth

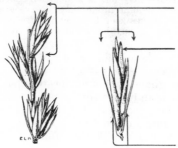

Individual flower groups (spikelets)— 2 to 6 at each rachis joint, 3- to 6- flowered, stalkless

Outer flower bract (lemma)—sharp- pointed or sometimes bristle- (awn-) pointed

Lowest (2) spikelet bracts (glumes)– narrow, awl-shaped, bristle-pointed, about as long as the lemma

91

Giant wild-rye is appropriately named; it is the largest of our native wild-ryes and perhaps the largest grass commonly found on western ranges. It is a coarse, robust plant with stems up to 12 feet high and growing in large bunches, often several feet in diameter, from short, thick, knotted, perennial rootstocks. This species occurs in all the far Western States except New Mexico, ranging from British Columbia and Saskatchewan to Nebraska, Arizona, and California. It is fairly abundant in the Northwest, in southwestern Wyoming, and in parts of Utah, Nevada, and California. This bunchgrass usually grows in moist or wet saline situations in bottomlands, along stream and ditch banks, and in gullies and canyons. It is also found in moderately dry, rich soils, not uncommonly associated with wheatgrass and sagebrush.

Giant wild-rye is grazed to some extent while young, but soon becomes coarse and tough and is not utilized as summer forage, if more palatable feed is available. However, the plants produce an enormous amount of forage and, where allowed to stand, provide a considerable amount of winter feed for cattle and horses. Formerly, this species was very important as a winter forage plant in parts of Nevada, but overgrazing, especially during the spring months, when growth was starting, has greatly reduced or eliminated it. It has been almost entirely replaced on many such areas by a species of dropseed which is practically unpalatable. In Nevada giant wild-rye formerly occurred chiefly in the valley bottoms often in large patches several miles in extent. The pioneer cattlemen established ranches in many of these bottoms, utilizing the wild-rye for hay. It still thrives on many fields which were fenced and protected for hay production. Old time freighters report that they never carried hay for their oxen but turned them loose at evening in patches of this grass, which were so extensive, tall, and dense that the beasts were often lost for several days. Today the grass cover is so scanty on some of those same areas which have been seriously overgrazed that cattle are easily visible across the entire area.

Prof. F. Lamson-Scribner made observations on Montana grasses in 1883 and is quoted by Dr. Vasey [1] as follows:

Elymus condensatus, or wild-rye grass * * * grows along streams and rivers often covering extensive areas. It is valued chiefly as a winter forage plant. It yields a great bulk of coarse hay but is seldom harvested. Where growing in fields of blue-joint the blue-joint is cut and the rye grass is left standing. If cut before flowering it makes good hay, but if left until it comes into flower it is not only too hard for hay but is too hard to cut except with a bush scythe.

In Oregon and Washington, where giant wild-rye occurs in considerable abundance, this species is extensively cut for hay and, if mowed early, provides fair roughage. It is moderately palatable to cattle and horses in California and the Northwest, except during the fall, when it becomes very hard and dry. After the winter rains begin it softens and is again grazed. Giant wild-rye rates as an inferior forage species, insofar as palatability and nutritive qual-

---

[1] Vasey, G. THE AGRICULTURAL GRASSES OF THE UNITED STATES. U. S. Dept. Agr. Rept. 32 : 1–115, illus. 1884.

ities are concerned, because of its coarseness and its relatively high ash and crude fiber content. The following chemical analysis compares the composition of giant wild-rye with the average 67 common western range grasses: [2]

	Giant wild-rye	Average composition, 67 grasses
Ash	9. 81	7. 48
Ether extract	1. 13	2. 05
Crude fiber	40. 82	35. 92
Crude protein	9. 09	8. 02
Nitrogen-free extract	39. 15	46. 53

Ergot (*Claviceps purpurea*), a black fungous growth which infests the heads of certain grasses, replacing the grains with the black or purple club-shaped bodies of the fungus, has been observed on the heads of giant wild-rye in the vicinity of the Colville National Forest, Wash., and probably occurs on this grass in other localities. If ergot-infested grasses are consumed, losses may result, although comparatively large doses of the poison must be consumed in a comparatively short time to cause trouble, as chronic poisoning through the ingestion of small amounts of ergot over a period of time are very rare. The symptoms of ergotism naturally assume two forms: (1) the gangrenous form, and (2) the nervous, or spasmodic form. In the first there are coldness and anesthesia (lack of feeling) of the extremities, including the feet, ears, and tail of quadrupeds; the comb, tongue, and beak of birds—followed by the appearance of passive congestion, blebs (blisters), dry gangrene in the vicinity of these parts, and often the dropping off of hoofs and beak. In the nervous, or spasmodic form are seen toxic contraction of the flexor tendons of the limbs and anesthesia of the extremities; muscular trembling and general tetanic spasm, with opisthotonos (bending backward of the body), convulsions, and delirium. Death ensues in both forms from general exhaustion.[3]

Giant wild-rye has an extensive root system from short, thick, perennial rootstocks and is a valuable soil binder for ditch banks, railway embankments, and the like. The seeds were used as food by many tribes of Indians.

---

[2] Knight, H. G., Hepner, F. E., and Nelson, A. WYOMING FORAGE PLANTS AND THEIR CHEMICAL COMPOSITION. — STUDIES NO. 4. Wyo. Agr. Expt. Sta. Bull. 87, 152 pp., illus. 1911.
[3] Pammel, L. H. A MANUAL OF POISONOUS PLANTS CHIEFLY OF EASTERN NORTH AMERICA, WITH BRIEF NOTES ON ECONOMIC AND MEDICINAL PLANTS. . . 2 pts., illus. Cedar Rapids, Iowa. 1910–11.

BLUE WILD-RYE

E'lymus glau'cus

Leaves—broad, thin, flat or inrolled, usually harsh, sometimes smooth beneath, up to 12 in. long

Flower heads (spikes)—narrow, erect, up to 8 in. long, long-exserted from the upper leaf sheath; axis (rachis) jointed but not separating at the joints

Stalks (culms)—usually somewhat tufted, smooth, up to 5 ft. high

Roots—fibrous, perennial

Individual flower groups (spikelets)—2 (rarely 3) at each rachis joint, stalkless, 2- to 6-flowered

Lowest (2) spikelet bracts (glumes)—narrow, distinctly 3- or 4-nerved to base, broadened above the base, rigid, bristle-(awn-) pointed, persistent

Outer flower bract (lemma)—shorter than glumes, often white-margined, mostly harsh near the tip, tapering to a slender, straight, harsh, ascending beard (awn) about ¾ in. long

Blue wild-rye, also known as smooth, mountain, or western wild-rye, or ryegrass, is a pale green or bluish white, perennial bunch-grass, commonly growing in small tufts of only a few stems. The name, ryegrass, is best restricted to species of the genus *Lolium*, on account of their long usage in cultivation. The species occurs from Alaska south to California and east to New Mexico, Missouri, and the Great Lakes. It ranges from near sea-level on the Pacific coast to elevations of more than 10,000 feet in Colorado and is the most widely distributed and common species of wild-rye found in the Western States. It is probably most abundant in woodlands of the central Rocky Mountain region, but is not uncommon in open parks and is frequently associated with sagebrush and other shrubs. This grass is a characteristic and sometimes fairly abundant species on old burns and cut-over areas, and, in the Northwest, in open fir stands and along streams under alder and maple. It favors mod-erately moist soils and, while sometimes abundant in local areas, it rarely ever occurs in pure stands, usually being intermixed with a variety of grass and weed species such as bromegrasses, bluegrasses, meadow barley, cinquefoil, strawberry, yarrow, asters, and wild-daisies. Although characteristic of moist sites, blue wild-rye with-stands drought remarkably well. In drought tests it did not wilt beyond recovery in most cases until the soil moisture was reduced to 7.5 percent.[1]

Although blue wild-rye produces rather coarse forage, it is grazed during the forepart of the season by cattle and horses and, to a less extent, by sheep. Livestock, however, do not relish the bearded seed clusters. Blue wild-rye has strong seed habits and, when grazing is restricted, responds quickly on areas depleted by over-grazing which are naturally adapted to its production. Although it has a fairly well-developed root system, this plant does not withstand continued heavy grazing especially well. It appears to be wholly dependent on seed for reproduction and probably should be regarded as a valuable secondary species to be encouraged only on areas where more desirable plants cannot be produced.

Blue wild-rye is typically glaucous, i. e., covered with a whitish or bluish bloom, to which fact the specific name *glaucus* refers.

---

[1] Sampson, A. W. IMPORTANT RANGE PLANTS : THEIR LIFE HISTORY AND FORAGE VALUE. U. S. Dept. Agr. Bull. 545, 63 pp., illus. 1917.

FESCUES

Festu'ca spp.

The large and widespread fescue genus is well represented in the West, both annual and perennial species being found in almost every locality. The perennials are mostly bunchgrasses and some of them rank among the best forage plants, both in farm pastures and meadows as well as on the range. The annuals are sometimes so abundant in waste places and so aggressive in extending their residence where unwelcome as to be pests. These annuals often inhabit compacted soils, and several have invaded range areas, mostly in the foothills, which have been overgrazed. Here they supply more or less early forage and provide a measure of soil protection in the absence of better plants.

As a rule, fescue species have abundant leaves which are largely basal and fairly fine. Fescues do not have a notched or two-toothed apex on the outer seed husk (lemma), which distinguishes them from the bromes. The lemma is pointed or bearded (awned), and the five ribs (nerves) converge at the apex. The back of the lemma is rounded except that toward the summit the midrib (nerve) sticks out like the keel on the bottom of a boat. In fescues, the backs of the bracts (glumes) at the base of the groups (spikelets) of flowers, or florets, are keeled. The Latin word *festuca* means a stalk or straw.

The fescue tribe (*Festuceae*), to which fescues, bromes, and bluegrasses belong, is one of the largest in the entire grass family, and from a range standpoint is one of the most important. It includes some of the outstanding pasture and hay grasses of the world. Several characters in combination distinguish this tribe: The flower cluster (inflorescence) is branched and compound (a panicle) but may be open, narrow, or so compact as to approach the appearance of being without branches and spikelike. There is always more than one floret, usually several, in a group (spikelet). If the outer seed husk (lemma) of the florets has a beard (awn), it is straight and attached at the apex, except that in a few cases the apex is notched, and the beard, if present, is attached at the base of the notch or just below. The two bracts (glumes) at the base of the spikelet are shorter than the first floret and usually remain on the branch after the seeds have matured and become detached.

ARIZONA FESCUE

Festu'ca arizo'nica, syn. *F. ovi'na arizo'nica*

Flower head (panicle)—narrow, 3 to 5½ in. long, with alternate, rough, erect branches

Stalks (culms) densely tufted from a perennial base, 4 in. to 3 ft. high, slender and curved at base

Leaves—mostly basal, very numerous, 6 to 12 in. long, rough, stiff, slender, inrolled, appearing almost round; basal sheaths about 4 in. long, becoming flattened in age

Outer flower bract (lemma)—about ¼ in. long, thick, tapering, obscurely 5-nerved, with short bristle (awn) about ⅟₁₆ in. long

Individual flower groups (spikelets)—4- to 6-flowered, erect, linear-lance-shaped, about ½ in. long

Lowest (2) spikelet bracts (glumes)—unequal; 1st, 1- to 3-nerved, shorter than the 3- to 5-nerved 2d glume

Arizona fescue, often called pinegrass or mountain bunchgrass, is a dense, tufted, perennial bunchgrass distributed from southern Colorado westward to southern Nevada and south to New Mexico and Arizona. Typically, it is a mountain species, growing at elevations from 6,000 to 10,000 feet, and is very abundant throughout the open ponderosa pine types, on slopes, mesas, and in open parks, chiefly in southern Colorado, New Mexico, and Arizona. Apparently it is rare in Utah. Although Arizona fescue is usually associated with blue grama, mountain muhly, pine dropseed, and cinquefoil, it frequently occurs in almost pure stands with the bunches only a few inches apart. It commonly inhabits dry, shallow, clay loams but grows well on sandy, gravelly or rocky soils, occasionally occurring in shaded places of better, moist sites.

Although not as palatable as many other range grasses, Arizona fescue is particularly important because of its abundance and, on many ranges, furnishes much of the forage. It is eaten by all classes of livestock, but is more readily grazed by cattle and horses than by sheep. In the Southwest this grass resumes growth in the spring, but its principal growth is made during the summer rainy season. It grows slowly and the forage produced has a relatively low water content. However, it is more palatable during this season than at any other time. When mature, the leaves become somewhat tough and are not eaten so readily during late summer as are those of blue grama and other more tender forage plants. The numerous fine but fibrous leaves, which remain green until late fall, furnish good forage for cattle and horses, but are eaten readily by sheep only during scarcity of better forage. Arizona fescue is not particularly resistant to grazing and even moderately close grazing tends to reduce the cover. It suffers from severe usage and, when overgrazed, is often replaced by blue grama. Near the upper altitudinal limits for blue grama, however, Arizona fescue tends to increase its stand under total protection or even light grazing at the expense of blue grama.

On Arizona fescue ranges occurring in the ponderosa-pine types in the Southwest, heavy grazing during periods when the forage is dry and water scarce has resulted in serious damage to the timber reproduction.[1] In the results of an investigation, as yet unpublished, C. K. Cooperrider, of the Southwestern Forest and Range Experiment Station, United States Forest Service, points out that the greatest damage usually occurs in the dry period of late spring and early summer before a vigorous, lush growth of the grass has been made. This damage is accentuated on poorly watered and heavily stocked range. Most of the damage can be eliminated by proper range and livestock management. Care should be taken that the ranges are not overstocked, especially in the dry late spring and early summer period, and that uniform distribution is secured. Ample water should be provided at all seasons, particularly during the dry periods. Within many ponderosa-pine areas, especially where Arizona fescue occurs in dense stands, the pine reproduction appears to be handicapped.[2] While the tufts favor germination and survival of the seedlings, and also afford early protection against grazing, their subsequent development is impeded, and heavy mortality may result from competition between seedlings and grass for soil moisture. However, the heavy losses of young ponderosa-pine seedlings on Arizona fescue ranges are apt to occur where the natural grass cover is decimated. Its extensive root system enables Arizona fescue to withstand both drought and trampling fairly well. Although this grass does not form a sod, yet its deep and abundant fibrous roots and the more or less dense spreading leafage tend to reduce run-off and thus impede erosion.

Although Arizona fescue produces an abundance of viable seed, artificial reseeding experiments with it on mountain ranges in the West[3] have not been very successful. Sowings were made in 1913 on the Coconino Plateau in northern Arizona, but although many seedlings resulted and attained average height, most of them subsequently succumbed and failed to maintain the stand. The seedlings which matured produced but little seed.

[1] Hill, R. R. EFFECTS OF GRAZING UPON WESTERN YELLOW PINE REPRODUCTION IN THE NATIONAL FORESTS OF ARIZONA AND NEW MEXICO. U. S. Dept. Agr. Bull. 580, 27 pp., illus. 1917.
[2] Pearson, G. A. NATURAL REPRODUCTION OF WESTERN YELLOW PINE IN THE SOUTHWEST. U. S. Dept. Agr. Bull. 1105, 143 pp., illus. 1923.
[3] Forsling, C. L., and Dayton, W. A. ARTIFICIAL RESEEDING ON WESTERN MOUNTAIN RANGE LANDS. U. S. Dept. Agr. Circ. 178, 48 pp., illus. 1931.

IDAHO FESCUE

Festu'ca idahoen'sis, syns. *F. ingra'ta, F. ovi'na ingra'ta*

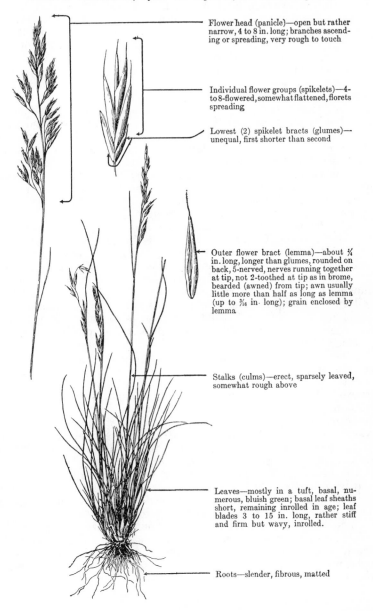

Flower head (panicle)—open but rather narrow, 4 to 8 in. long; branches ascending or spreading, very rough to touch

Individual flower groups (spikelets)—4- to 8-flowered, somewhat flattened, florets spreading

Lowest (2) spikelet bracts (glumes)—unequal, first shorter than second

Outer flower bract (lemma)—about ¼ in. long, longer than glumes, rounded on back, 5-nerved, nerves running together at tip, not 2-toothed at tip as in brome, bearded (awned) from tip; awn usually little more than half as long as lemma (up to ³⁄₁₆ in. long); grain enclosed by lemma

Stalks (culms)—erect, sparsely leaved, somewhat rough above

Leaves—mostly in a tuft, basal, numerous, bluish green; basal leaf sheaths short, remaining inrolled in age; leaf blades 3 to 15 in. long, rather stiff and firm but wavy, inrolled.

Roots—slender, fibrous, matted

Idaho fescue, sometimes called blue bunchgrass, is a densely tufted, perennial bunchgrass 1 to 3 feet high, and is one of the most common and widely distributed grasses in the 11 far Western States. However, it is either rare or does not occur in the southern portions of California, Nevada, and Arizona. Naturally with such a wide range in distribution, Idaho fescue occupies very diversified habitats. Forest Service collections show altitudinal variations from 800 feet in Oregon to 12,000 feet in Colorado. Though it may be found at any elevation between these extremes, it is most prevalent from about 5,000 to 8,000 feet in Montana, 7,000 to 10,000 feet in Utah and Colorado, and from 3,000 to 7,000 feet in California and the Northwest. It grows on all exposures and under a wide variety of soil conditions—from clay to rocky, shallow to deep, and moist to dry—but is most common in fairly dry, well-drained, moderately deep, sandy or gravelly loams. Exposed benchlands, hillsides and ridges, parks, meadows, woodlands, and open ponderosa and lodgepole pine stands are common habitats. Its frequent associates include wheatgrass, bluegrass, brome, geranium, yarrow, and sagebrush. A Forest Service officer has noted in the mountains of Wyoming, that Idaho fescue seems to be replaced by needlegrass (*Stipa*) as moisture decreased or overgrazing increased.

Idaho fescue is abundant and sometimes the dominant plant on extensive areas. It usually ranks with the choicest forage plants, and in Montana and possibly elsewhere is, everything considered, probably the best forage grass. However, it may not quite merit first rank in palatability in some sections. It produces a fair amount of seed of comparatively high viability and maintains itself well on the range if given a reasonable opportunity. Idaho fescue excels many of its associated forage species in ability to withstand heavy grazing and trampling, although it will succumb to continued grazing abuse. All classes of livestock relish it in the spring, as well as later in the season where it grows on north slopes or in cooler, moister sites and where the herbage remains tender. Under such conditions it is often grazed more closely than other associated grasses. As the season advances the plants tend to become somewhat tough and harsh, and less succulent, with a proportionate decrease in palatability for sheep, especially ewes and lambs; to some extent this is true for horses and cattle also. However, if more inviting forage is not available, livestock will graze this species throughout the season and thrive. Moreover, the plant cures well on the ground and makes a good or very good fall forage, being readily grazed by all classes of livestock until late in the season, while it also produces a good aftermath which is much relished. When accessible it is also a good forage for winter use.

Idaho fescue has numerous stems. The fine, narrow leaves have a bluish green color which accounts for the name "blue bunchgrass." Dried, stubby, straw-colored herbage from previous years usually contributes to the compactness of the bunch and is generally characteristic.

SHEEP FESCUE

Festu'ca ovi'na, syn. *F. saximonta'na*

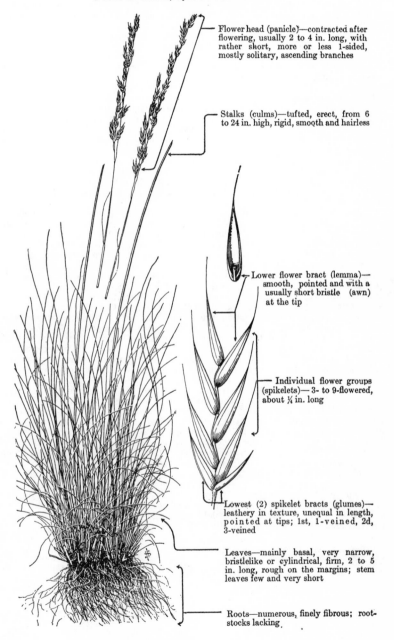

Flower head (panicle)—contracted after flowering, usually 2 to 4 in. long, with rather short, more or less 1-sided, mostly solitary, ascending branches

Stalks (culms)—tufted, erect, from 6 to 24 in. high, rigid, smooth and hairless

Lower flower bract (lemma)—smooth, pointed and with a usually short bristle (awn) at the tip

Individual flower groups (spikelets)— 3- to 9-flowered, about ¼ in. long

Lowest (2) spikelet bracts (glumes)—leathery in texture, unequal in length, pointed at tips; 1st, 1-veined, 2d, 3-veined

Leaves—mainly basal, very narrow, bristlelike or cylindrical, firm, 2 to 5 in. long, rough on the margins; stem leaves few and very short

Roots—numerous, finely fibrous; rootstocks lacking

Sheep fescue, a perennial and, under range conditions, a typical bunch grass, is not only a valuable range forage species but also an important cultivated pasture plant. The name sheep fescue is a literal translation of the scientific name for this grass, and is most appropriate, since its large volume of fine leaves is much relished by sheep.

Hitchcock[1] states that the typical Old World form of sheep fescue, as described by the great Swedish botanist, Linnaeus, "is the representative of a large group of varieties or closely allied species in Europe." The grass is very widely distributed, being native in the northern hemisphere of the Old World, and apparently in the New World as well. It exists in several varieties or forms in the Western States. Some of these variations (accorded specific or varietal rank by some botanists) resemble sheep fescue so closely that it is difficult to distinguish them from the species and, if such forms are included in its range, sheep fescue may be considered as occurring in all the 11 far Western States. Sheep fescue, although widely distributed, is abundant only locally. It is one of the dominant grasses in the Beartooth Mountains in Montana, on the Powell Plateau in Utah, and in similar localities at the higher altitudes, from 7,000 to 11,000 feet, in Colorado. In eastern Oregon, however, its altitudinal range descends to at least as low as 3,500 feet. Open hillsides, benchlands, parks, meadows, open woodlands, and lightly timbered areas are common habitats; dry, sandy, gravelly, or rocky soils seem to be preferred, although this grass is also found on the finer and moister clay soils, or occasionally even in marshy areas. It often grows in association with other bunchgrasses and with such browse as rabbitbrush and sagebrush, and with such herbs as asters and geraniums.

Sheep fescue is a valuable forage grass for all classes of livestock. It is one of the first range grasses to green up and be ready for grazing in early spring, and it is especially palatable at that time. Its very numerous, fine leaves remain green and comparatively tender until late in the fall, and its value as forage continues until that time. Its extensive root system makes it fairly resistant to drought and trampling; the absence of underground stems, however, and its lack of strong seed habits make difficult, if not impossible, the maintenance of good stands under excessive grazing.

Reseeding experiments with sheep fescue on mountain ranges in the western United States[2] have not been very promising. It is, however, frequently cultivated as a pasture or lawn grass, and succeeds better than many other grasses where the soil is sandy or gravelly and rather poor. It tends to be more bunchy than is desirable when grown alone, but in mixture with other grasses it helps to make a durable ground cover. As a pasture grass it is adapted to about the same general climatic conditions as Kentucky bluegrass (*Poa pratensis*), and can be grown as far north as agriculture is practiced.

The very fine, inrolled, very numerous and mostly basal leaves of sheep fescue are bluish green when fresh, but the stubbed-off dried leaves of former years tend to remain and together make up a very characteristic and compact tuft from 2 to 7 inches high. The smooth, slender stalks extend up above this basal clump, usually being from 7 to 16 inches tall, though they occasionally attain a height as great as 2 feet. Except for being smaller, and with rather shorter and more conspicuously basal leaves, sheep fescue is similar in appearance to Idaho fescue (*F. idahoensis*). Hard fescue (*F. ovina durius'cula,* syn. *F. durius'cula*), a variety of sheep fescue, is sometimes cultivated as a pasture grass in this country. As its name indicates, its leaves tend to be somewhat tougher than those of sheep fescue.

Sheep fescue flowers from June to September, and disseminates its seed from August to October. Since there are no underground stems (rootstocks, or rhizomes), reproduction is solely by seed. There is some vegetative enlargement of the bunches by tillering.

[1] Hitchcock, A. S. THE GENERA OF GRASSES OF THE UNITED STATES, WITH SPECIAL REFERENCE TO THE ECONOMIC SPECIES. U. S. Dept. Agr. Bull. 772, 307 pp., illus. 1920.
[2] Forsling, C. L., and Dayton, W. A. ARTIFICIAL RESEEDING ON WESTERN MOUNTAIN RANGE LANDS. U. S. Dept. Agr. Circ. 178, 48 pp., illus. 1931.

BUFFALO BUNCHGRASS

Festu'ca scabrel'la, syns. *F. campes'tris, F. hal'lii*

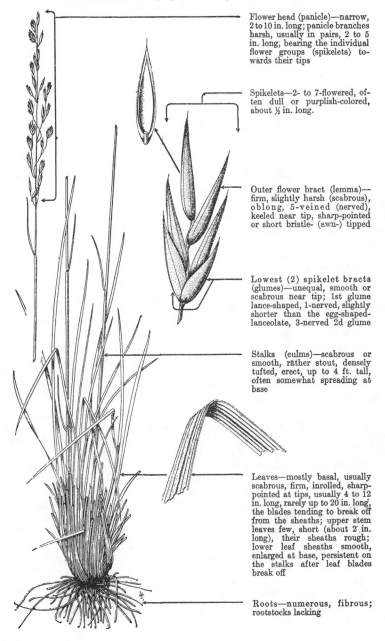

Flower head (panicle)—narrow, 2 to 10 in. long; panicle branches harsh, usually in pairs, 2 to 5 in. long; bearing the individual flower groups (spikelets) towards their tips

Spikelets—2- to 7-flowered, often dull or purplish-colored, about ½ in. long.

Outer flower bract (lemma)—firm, slightly harsh (scabrous), oblong, 5-veined (nerved), keeled near tip, sharp-pointed or short bristle- (awn-) tipped

Lowest (2) spikelet bracts (glumes)—unequal, smooth or scabrous near tip; 1st glume lance-shaped, 1-nerved, slightly shorter than the egg-shaped-lanceolate, 3-nerved 2d glume

Stalks (culms)—scabrous or smooth, rather stout, densely tufted, erect, up to 4 ft. tall, often somewhat spreading at base

Leaves—mostly basal, usually scabrous, firm, inrolled, sharp-pointed at tips, usually 4 to 12 in. long, rarely up to 20 in. long, the blades tending to break off from the sheaths; upper stem leaves few, short (about 2 in. long), their sheaths rough; lower leaf sheaths smooth, enlarged at base, persistent on the stalks after leaf blades break off

Roots—numerous, fibrous; rootstocks lacking

Buffalo bunchgrass is an erect, tufted, perennial bunchgrass from 1 to 4 feet high. The name buffalo bunchgrass refers to the fact that buffalo were fond of this grass, and also to its bunch habit of growth. It is also called big buffalo bunchgrass and rough fescue; the latter name alludes to the rough (scabrous) leaves and stalks, as does also the Latin specific name *scabrella*. In Montana it is sometimes known as great bunchgrass because it grows in large tussocks averaging 12 to 14 inches, sometimes becoming as much as 2 feet in diameter.

This is a widely distributed species, ranging across Canada from Newfoundland and Quebec to Yukon and British Columbia, and, in the United States, from Washington and Oregon to North Dakota and northern Michigan. With perhaps three exceptions, Colorado material hitherto referred to this species seems to be Thurber fescue (*Festuca thurberi*). It is one of the principal grasses in Montana and northern Idaho, and is also important in eastern Oregon and Washington. It is rarely reported from California. Prairies, open, sunny, hill and mountain slopes up to 10,000 feet elevation, rocky cliffs, and dry, open woods are its most frequent habitats, especially on dry, deep, sandy loam soils. Often it is so abundant locally as to form one of the chief features of the landscape; in extensive mountain park areas it may grow to the exclusion of other grasses.

Buffalo bunchgrass produces a large amount of forage of high palatability and is especially relished by horses and cattle; it is somewhat too hard a grass for sheep. On summer range it is highly valued for horses and cattle, and on winter ranges is considered one of the best grasses, as it cures well on the stalk and retains its nutritive properties all winter. On the lower ranges the small amount of snow held against the strong winds in the center of the grass bunches serves both to moisten and soften the herbage, and, in a measure, is a substitute for water for the livestock. This grass on the higher ranges, continuously covered by winter snow, greens up faster in the spring and appears to be better relished by livestock than when growing on the lower winter ranges.

The large tussock habit of growth makes buffalo bunchgrass difficult to mow with a machine, but, because it makes such excellent hay for horses, it is often cut in large quantities. Being a bunchgrass and devoid of underground stems (rootstocks) it never forms a turf and is unable to withstand trampling as well as some of the sod-forming grasses. The high palatability of both the leaves and stalks in many instances has resulted in cropping to the ground line. Such excessive volume utilization has decreased the abundance of this valuable species so that now it is not so prevalent as it once was, but has been replaced by other grasses, some of which, as, for example, Idaho fescue and some of the bluegrasses, are also highly palatable; often, however, the replacement is by inferior species.

Buffalo bunchgrass presents a very characteristic appearance with its large tufts of prominently ridged (striate) leaves and its noticeably bluish cast. Flowers are produced during June and July and seed is disseminated during August and September. Reproduction is solely by seed.

THURBER FESCUE

Festu'ca thur'beri

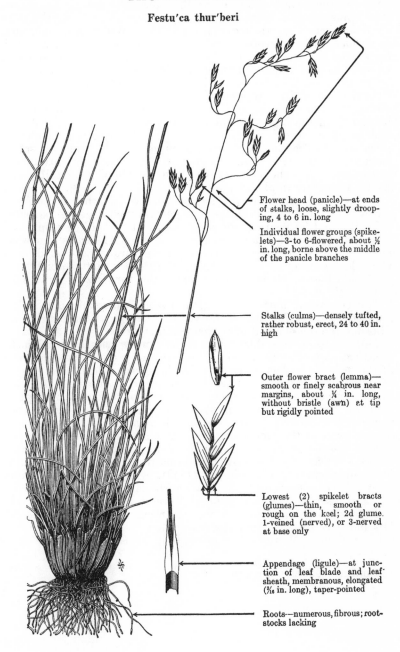

Flower head (panicle)—at ends of stalks, loose, slightly drooping, 4 to 6 in. long

Individual flower groups (spikelets)—3- to 6-flowered, about ½ in. long, borne above the middle of the panicle branches

Stalks (culms)—densely tufted, rather robust, erect, 24 to 40 in. high

Outer flower bract (lemma)—smooth or finely scabrous near margins, about ¼ in. long, without bristle (awn) at tip but rigidly pointed

Lowest (2) spikelet bracts (glumes)—thin, smooth or rough on the keel; 2d glume 1-veined (nerved), or 3-nerved at base only

Appendage (ligule)—at junction of leaf blade and leaf sheath, membranous, elongated (3/16 in. long), taper-pointed

Roots—numerous, fibrous; rootstocks lacking

Thurber fescue is a robust, densely tufted, perennial bunchgrass, growing up to a little over 3 feet tall, in rather large bunches. Prof. Aven Nelson [1] states that, in southwestern Wyoming, this handsome, bluegrasslike plant forms "large compact sods on the edge of the thickets along the mountain streams." While under optimum conditions, such as Professor Nelson describes, this grass may grow thickly enough to simulate a sod, its lack of underground stems (rootstocks) precludes it from being a truly turf-forming species.

The range of Thurber fescue is more restricted than that of most western fescues, its distribution apparently being limited to Wyoming, Colorado, Utah, and northern New Mexico. Its common habitat is in the higher mountains at elevations up to 12,000 feet, and in open parks, open stands of spruce, aspen, and ponderosa pine, on hillsides and ridges, and in meadows. It prefers a sandy loam soil, although it is able to grow in the heavier clay loams. It is common throughout its range, is often abundant locally, and sometimes occurs in almost pure stands.

Although reports as to the forage value of Thurber fescue vary somewhat in different localities, it is generally conceded to be better for cattle and horses than for sheep and goats. A large number of leaves are produced, but the roughness of the leaf blades somewhat impairs the palatability for sheep. In general, it is rated as a valuable forage grass for all classes of livestock, but especially for cattle and horses. It is palatable and usable for grazing until snow in the fall.

Thurber fescue flowers in July and seed is disseminated during August. Except for the vegetative enlargement of the bunches by tillering, the sole method of reproduction is by seed.

Thurber fescue resembles the more northern species, buffalo bunchgrass (*F. scabrella*) rather closely in habit of growth and roughness of the leaves. In fact, some botanists have regarded it as a variety of buffalo bunchgrass, under the name *F. scabrella vaseyana*. Certain others hold it to be a synonym of buffalo bunchgrass. Thurber fescue is perhaps most readily distinguished by its conspicuously elongated (nearly one-fourth of an inch long) ligule or papery bract at the junction of leaf blade and leaf sheath.

This species is named in honor of its discoverer, Dr. George Thurber (1821–90), botanist, quartermaster of the United States-Mexican Boundary Commission (1850), who collected the plants on which Dr. Gray's book Plantae Thurberianae is based. Thurber was professor of botany and horticulture at Michigan Agricultural College 1859–63, and editor of the American Agriculturist 1863–90. His influence on American agricultural education and research has been profound. Many western plants bear his name.

[1] Nelson, A. THE RED DESERT OF WYOMING AND ITS FORAGE RESOURCES. U. S. Dept. Agr., Div. Agrost. Bull. 13, 72 pp., illus. 1898.

GREEN FESCUE

Festu'ca viri'dula

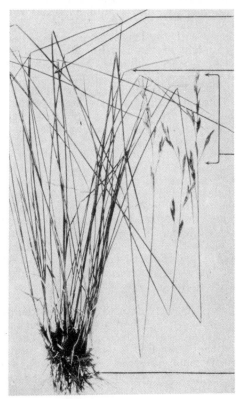

Stalks (culms)—densely tufted but easily separated, erect, 1 to 3½ ft. high, rather slender, round, smooth, slightly thickened at the base

Leaves—mostly basal numerous, light green, soft, erect, narrow, smooth, loosely folded or slightly inrolled, ½ as long as the stalks; collar (ligule) at junction of blade and sheath, a ring of short hairs

Flower head (panicle)—4 to 6 in. long, open; branches erect, becoming spreading, each with a slight padlike swelling (pulvinus) at point of attachment to rachis

Roots—perennial, coarse, deep, spreading

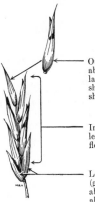

Outer flower bract (lemma)—about ⅜ in. long, narrowly lance-shaped, nearly smooth, shining, indistinctly 5-nerved, sharp-pointed

Individual flower groups (spikelets)—pale or purplish, 3- to 6-flowered, about ½ in. long

Lowest (2) spikelet bracts (glumes)—unequal; 1st glume about ¼ in. long; 2d glume about ½ longer than 1st

Every mountainous part of the West has its particular breed of mountain bunchgrass; thus, green fescue is the mountain bunchgrass of the Blue Mountain country of northeastern Oregon and southeastern Washington. Lambs fed on these ranges are famous for condition and the high market prices they command. Few sights are more pleasing to the eye than high knolls and ridges covered with a fine stand of green fescue. The rich green hue of the foliage contrasts strikingly with the bright bluish-purple heads.

Green fescue—distinctly a plant of the Northwest—ranges from British Columbia to Alberta, western Montana, Nevada, and central California, growing typically within the spruce-fir belt near timberline, mostly above 6,000 feet, although a few specimens have been collected as low as 5,000 feet. Although not widely distributed, it is often abundant on the better drained soils of plateaus, slopes, ridges, parks, and glades and in mountain meadows where it inhabits deep, sandy, gravelly, or clayey loams.

Throughout its range, green fescue furnishes an abundance of very palatable and nutritious feed. More recent palatability studies on the Wenatchee National Forest in central Washington show that this grass is relished by all classes of livestock throughout the entire grazing season, although sheep, which graze the leafage of this plant more than that of most other grasses, tend to discriminate against it during the late fall. Green fescue is very nutritious; chemical analyses indicate that it ranks with the wheatgrasses in food value and, when mature, with timothy hay in nutritiousness.[1] Green fescue has been reduced measurably on many ranges in Oregon and Washington because of its high palatability. Attention was directed toward depleted green fescue ranges on the Wallowa National Forest. in northeastern Oregon, during the early days of the Forest Service, and a scientific investigation followed.[2] The practical application to range management of the principles thus evolved on the Wallowa National Forest marked the beginning of the deferred and rotation grazing systems on western national forests.

Green fescue grows typically in densely tufted bunches, but even in very dense stands does not make a complete cover, and usually the tufts are intermixed with many other forage plants. This bunchgrass produces numerous coarse extensive roots which bind the surface soil and often penetrate to a depth of 3 feet, or more. These deep, matted roots form effective impediments against erosion and enable the plants to survive more or less protracted droughts. Green fescue, a dense, tufted perennial with an abundance of soft, long-folded or inrolled leaves, grows in tussocks of from 3 to 12 inches in diameter and attains heights of from 1 to 3½ feet. The panicles are from 4 to 6 inches long and somewhat open. Spikelets are three- to six-flowered, pale or purplish in color. This grass produces an abundance of seed, but Sampson[1] has found that the viability is low; the average germination for laboratory tests was 12.2 percent, although field trials gave a much higher percentage. Preliminary range reseeding experiments with green fescue in the Wasatch Mountain region have been failures.[3]

[1] Sampson, A. W. IMPORTANT RANGE PLANTS : THEIR LIFE HISTORY AND FORAGE VALUE. U. S. Dept. Agr. Bull. 545, 63 pp., illus. 1917.
[2] Sampson, A. W. NATURAL REVEGETATION OF RANGE LANDS BASED UPON GROWTH REQUIREMENTS AND LIFE HISTORY OF THE VEGETATION. Jour. Agr. Research [U. S.] 3: 93–148, illus. 1914.
[3] Forsling, C. L., and Dayton, W. A. ARTIFICIAL RESEEDING ON WESTERN MOUNTAIN RANGE LANDS. U. S. Dept. Agr. Circ. 178, 48 pp., illus. 1931.

G67

FOWL MANNAGRASS

Glyce'ria stria'ta, syns. *G. nerva'ta, Panicula'ria nerva'ta, P. ri'gida*

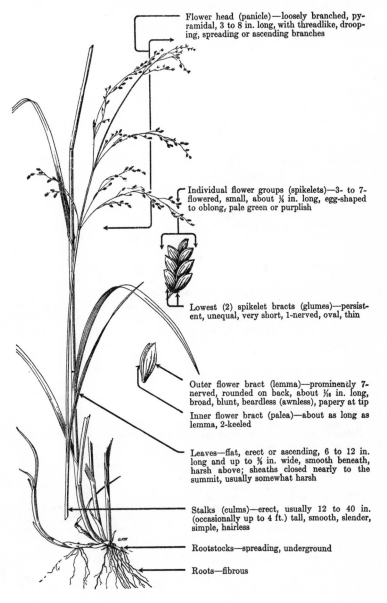

Flower head (panicle)—loosely branched, pyramidal, 3 to 8 in. long, with threadlike, drooping, spreading or ascending branches

Individual flower groups (spikelets)—3- to 7-flowered, small, about ⅛ in. long, egg-shaped to oblong, pale green or purplish

Lowest (2) spikelet bracts (glumes)—persistent, unequal, very short, 1-nerved, oval, thin

Outer flower bract (lemma)—prominently 7-nerved, rounded on back, about 1/16 in. long, broad, blunt, beardless (awnless), papery at tip

Inner flower bract (palea)—about as long as lemma, 2-keeled

Leaves—flat, erect or ascending, 6 to 12 in. long and up to ⅜ in. wide, smooth beneath, harsh above; sheaths closed nearly to the summit, usually somewhat harsh

Stalks (culms)—erect, usually 12 to 40 in. (occasionally up to 4 ft.) tall, smooth, slender, simple, hairless

Rootstocks—spreading, underground

Roots—fibrous

111

Fowl mannagrass, also locally known as nerved mannagrass, and tall meadowgrass, is a moderately tall, often tufted perennial grass of the fescue tribe (*Festuceae*). It is one of the most abundant and widespread of about 16 species of mannagrass which occur in the United States and fairly typical of the group in forage value.

Fowl mannagrass is distributed from Newfoundland to British Columbia, south to California, Mexico, and Florida, and has an elevational range of from near sea level to about 10,000 feet. This species is confined almost entirely to sites where moisture is abundant; it grows typically along stream banks and in and around wet meadows, marshes, and swamps. This grass is tolerant of shade and often occurs in seeps and boggy places under stands of aspen and coniferous timber. Although it sometimes grows pure in small patches, this grass ordinarily is intermixed scatteringly with other meadow grasses, sedges, and rushes, and supplies only a limited amount of forage.

The succulent herbage of fowl mannagrass is eaten by all classes of grazing animals and is usually rated as good to very good for cattle and horses, and fairly good for sheep. Livestock, especially sheep, do not graze in the excessively wet situations where this grass often grows. Accordingly, its value for forage is highest in the late summer when the leafage is less succulent and the sites somewhat drier. Cattle and horses consume both the flower stalks and leafage; sheep usually eat only the leaves. This grass is also grazed readily by elk but is used to only a slight extent by deer.

Some chemical analyses have disclosed traces of hydrocyanic acid in fowl mannagrass and, in fact, some cases of cattle poisoning have been ascribed to it.[1] Scientific evidence that the plants contain enough of the poison to kill livestock is lacking, however. In fact, experience on the national forest ranges demonstrates that the mannagrasses are good forage plants and can ordinarily be grazed without harmful results. The seed matures from July to the forepart of September and is dropped as soon as it ripens. In the Blue Mountains of Oregon, Sampson[2] found the germinative power of the seed to be relatively high and observed that natural reproduction was generally good.

The name mannagrass originated in Europe where, particularly in Germany and Poland, the seeds of several species of *Glyceria* are used in soups and gruels or ground into meal.[3][4]

The grains of our native American species are extremely small and have no economic use except possibly as food for birds. The generic name *Glyceria* is from the Greek (*glukeros*, sweet) and refers to the taste of the grain. The specific names *striata* and *nervata* refer to the (seven) prominent parallel nerves on the backs of the outer flower bracts (*lemmas*).

Tall mannagrass (*G. ela'ta*, syns. *Panicula'ria ela'ta*, *P. nerva'ta ela'ta*) is one of the most common and most valuable of the western species of mannagrass. This species is very similar to fowl mannagrass in general appearance, habitat requirements, and forage value. However, it is a more robust plant, has broader leaves, and grows from 3 to about 6½ feet tall. It ranges from British Columbia and Montana to Wyoming, New Mexico, and California.

[1] Alsberg, C. L., and Black, O. F. CONCERNING THE DISTRIBUTION OF CYANOGEN IN GRASSES, ESPECIALLY IN THE GENERA PANICULARIA OR GLYCERIA AND TRIDENS OR SIEGLINGIA. Jour. Biol. Chem. 21 : 601–[610]. 1915.
[2] Sampson, A. W. IMPORTANT RANGE PLANTS: THEIR LIFE HISTORY AND FORAGE VALUE. U. S. Dept. Agr. Bull. 545, 63 pp., illus. 1917.
[3] Francis, M. E. THE BOOK OF GRASSES. 351 pp., illus. Garden City, N. Y. 1912.
[4] Archer, T. C. POPULAR ECONOMIC BOTANY. 359 pp., illus. London. 1853.

HILARIAS

Hila'ria spp., syn. *Pleura'phis spp.*

Individual names are applied to each species of *Hilaria* but the genus as a whole has had no common name, so the scientific name is usually employed. This genus was named in honor of Auguste de Saint-Hilaire, an early French naturalist. There are four species of *Hilaria*, all perennials, in the United States, distributed from Wyoming to Nevada, southern California, central Texas, and south into Mexico. These grasses are all semidesert and desert plants, growing principally on arid plains, mesas, and foothills, often in association with gramas (*Bouteloua* spp.), three-awns (*Aristida* spp.), dropseeds (*Sporobolus* spp.), and mesquites (*Prosopis* spp.). They occur on a wide variety of soils—from clay adobe flats to gravelly or rocky ridges. Some authors prefer to divide these grasses into two genera, leaving only one species, curly-mesquite (*H. belangeri*, syn. "*H. cenchroides*" of United States authors), which has stolons and glandular glumes, in *Hilaria*, and classing the others, which have rootstocks and nonglandular glumes, in the genus *Pleuraphis*. The best current botanical opinion, however, unites the two groups into one genus.

Because of their abundance, ability to withstand heavy grazing and prolonged drought, and the fairly large volume of forage which some species produce, the hilarias are important grasses on many ranges of the Southwest. Their strong creeping rootstocks or stolons make them invaluable as soil binders.

Hilarias have narrow, flat, or inrolled leaves, and solid (pithy, as cornstalks), tufted, somewhat wiry or woody stems which are usually bent at the base and branched. The spikes are very distinctive, resembling somewhat those of the wild-ryes (*Elymus* spp.) and wheatgrasses (*Agropyron* spp.), but are readily recognized by their broad, papery glumes, which make the entire spike appear somewhat chaffy and papery. The spikelets are borne in close, stemless clusters alternately arranged on a zigzag main stem (rachis). Each cluster comprises three spikelets—the center one seed-producing, one-flowered, and the outer two not seed-producing and two-flowered. The entire cluster falls at maturity, leaving the rachis naked.

CURLY-MESQUITE

Hila'ria belan'geri, syn. "*H. cenchroi'des*" [1]

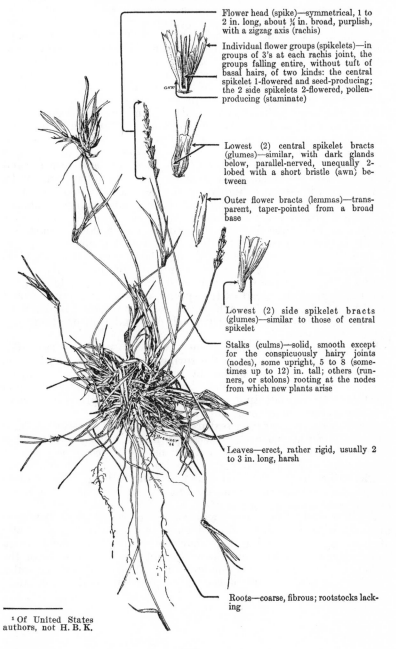

Flower head (spike)—symmetrical, 1 to 2 in. long, about ¼ in. broad, purplish, with a zigzag axis (rachis)

Individual flower groups (spikelets)—in groups of 3's at each rachis joint, the groups falling entire, without tuft of basal hairs, of two kinds: the central spikelet 1-flowered and seed-producing; the 2 side spikelets 2-flowered, pollen-producing (staminate)

Lowest (2) central spikelet bracts (glumes)—similar, with dark glands below, parallel-nerved, unequally 2-lobed with a short bristle (awn) between

Outer flower bracts (lemmas)—transparent, taper-pointed from a broad base

Lowest (2) side spikelet bracts (glumes)—similar to those of central spikelet

Stalks (culms)—solid, smooth except for the conspicuously hairy joints (nodes), some upright, 5 to 8 (sometimes up to 12) in. tall; others (runners, or stolons) rooting at the nodes from which new plants arise

Leaves—erect, rather rigid, usually 2 to 3 in. long, harsh

Roots—coarse, fibrous; rootstocks lacking

[1] Of United States authors, not **H. B. K.**

115

Curly-mesquite, sometimes called southwestern buffalo grass because of its similarity in growth to the true buffalo grass (*Buchloë dactyloides*), is identifiable at some distance because it forms light green patches. It is distinguishable from the other hilarias by the slender, wiry, creeping stolons which produce a close, firm sod in favorable soil. *Hilaria belangeri* perpetuates the name of Charles M. Belánger, a French naturalist and explorer of the nineteenth century. This grass occurs from central Texas to Arizona and south to Central America. It is most abundant on the plains of Texas and Mexico and also grows on a considerable scale in southwestern New Mexico and southern Arizona. Curly-mesquite develops small or fairly large patches on plains, mesas, and foothills in the grass and open woodland types and is found on dry, deep clay to gravelly or rocky soils at elevations of 3,500 to 5,500 feet. However, the species occasionally grows in scattered clumps on rocky slopes. Gramas (*Bouteloua* spp.), three awns (*Aristida* spp.), beardgrasses (*Andropogon* spp.), mesquites (*Prosopis* spp.), and catclaw and other acacias (*Acacia* spp.) are common associates of curly-mesquite.

This grass is esteemed highly for forage wherever it occurs, as it is one of the first to start spring growth, responds readily to summer rains, and produces a fair amount of forage despite its small size. Curly-mesquite cures well on the ground and is highly palatable to all classes of livestock for both winter and summer use. It is unusually resistant to extended drought and also withstands close grazing, as is shown by its increase on many of the heavily grazed ranges of the Southwest. Although the innumerable stolons facilitate the aggressive spread of the species, this valuable grass should be protected during its growth period for best results. Its habit of forming a sod makes it a very good soil binder in checking and preventing erosion.

Under favorable conditions curly-mesquite produces two seed crops—a minor production in the spring when moisture is adequate, followed in late summer or fall by the major seed output resulting from the summer rains. The species, however, depends chiefly upon its stolons for reproduction, as the natural seed supply is insufficient for satisfactory maintenance of the stands.

Curly-mesquite is of finer texture than the other species of *Hilaria* and has numerous, narrow, rather rigid leaves, usually 2 to 4 inches long, as well as a few upright, leafy stems 4 to 12 (commonly 5 to 8) inches high which are hairy at the nodes. The purplish spikes are single, rather loosely flowered, and 1 to 2 inches long. The clusters of spikelets lack the conspicuously long tuft of basal hairs characteristic of most other species of *Hilaria*.

Until recently this species was commonly confused in botanical manuals with *H. cenchroides*, which is now regarded as a wholly Mexican species differing from curly-mesquite in having a thick spike, darker spikelets, and the rachis internodes shorter than the spikelets. In contrast, curly-mesquite has a relatively slender spike, pale spikelets, and rachis internodes about as long as the spikelets.

GALLETA

Hila'ria jame'sii, syn. *Pleura'phis jame'sii*

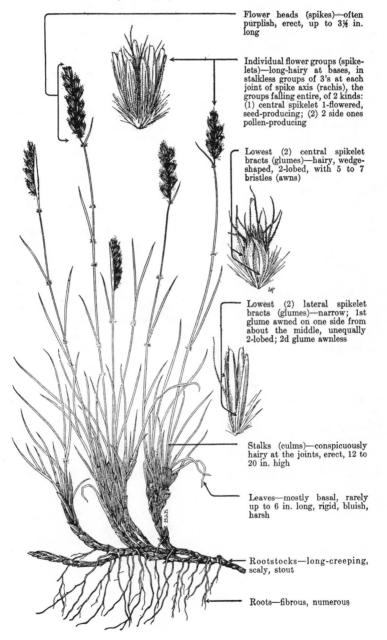

Flower heads (spikes)—often purplish, erect, up to 3½ in. long

Individual flower groups (spikelets)—long-hairy at bases, in stalkless groups of 3's at each joint of spike axis (rachis), the groups falling entire, of 2 kinds: (1) central spikelet 1-flowered, seed-producing; (2) 2 side ones pollen-producing

Lowest (2) central spikelet bracts (glumes)—hairy, wedge-shaped, 2-lobed, with 5 to 7 bristles (awns)

Lowest (2) lateral spikelet bracts (glumes)—narrow; 1st glume awned on one side from about the middle, unequally 2-lobed; 2d glume awnless

Stalks (culms)—conspicuously hairy at the joints, erect, 12 to 20 in. high

Leaves—mostly basal, rarely up to 6 in. long, rigid, bluish, harsh

Rootstocks—long-creeping, scaly, stout

Roots—fibrous, numerous

117

Galleta, sometimes and unfortunately referred to in older literature as black grama, is an erect perennial. It grows on mesas, plains, and deserts from Wyoming and Nevada to California, western Texas, and south into Mexico, but is probably most common in New Mexico and Arizona. In Utah, Wyoming, Colorado, and Nevada the species occurs chiefly in scattered stands, usually in association with blue grama in the sagebrush zone. In the Southwest it is abundant over extensive areas in the upper plains and in the lower limits of the ponderosa pine belt at elevations from 5,000 to 7,000 feet in the mountains. Wooton and Standley [1] state that galleta grass is by far the most abundant and characteristic plant on the plains in the northwestern corner of New Mexico, where it often forms practically pure stands which cover many miles of terrain.

The abundance of galleta and its capacity for heavy forage production make it a very important species on many southwestern ranges. Wooton and Standley (*op. cit.*) regard it as probably the second most valuable range grass of New Mexico. It is of highest palatability (up to good or very good) during the summer rainy growing season, and has the reputation among stockmen of being nutritious for all classes of livestock. Its maximum use at this period is desirable. Unless green and succulent its palatability is low or negligible. After growth ceases the rather harsh foliage soon becomes dry and tough and is of little or no interest to livestock. Range animals reject it during late fall and winter unless more palatable species are scanty or unavailable. Wooton and Standley [2] call attention to the local reputation of galleta for fattening horses. The tough, woody rootstocks, sometimes as much as 6 feet long, are its surest means of reproduction, fortify it against trampling and heavy grazing, and increase its effectiveness as a soil binder. The species is very drought-resistant and maintains itself satisfactorily on arid ranges. It is not easily killed by overstocking.

Although the galleta plants have strong, scaly rootstocks, they usually grow in bunches and it is only under very favorable conditions that these bunches grow sufficiently close together to approximate a sod. The numerous, narrow, rather wiry leaves are dull green. The flower head (spike) has a fine, hairy, chaffy appearance, often purplish at first and fading to almost white at maturity.

---

[1] Wooton, E. O., and Standley, P. C. FLORA OF NEW MEXICO. U. S. Natl. Mus., Contrib. U. S. Natl. Herbarium 19, 794 pp. 1915.
[2] Wooton, E. O., and Standley, P. C. THE GRASSES AND GRASS-LIKE PLANTS OF NEW MEXICO. N. Mex. Agr. Expt. Sta. Bull. 81, [176] pp., illus. 1912.

TOBOSA

Hila′ria mu′tica, syn. *Pleura′phis mu′tica*

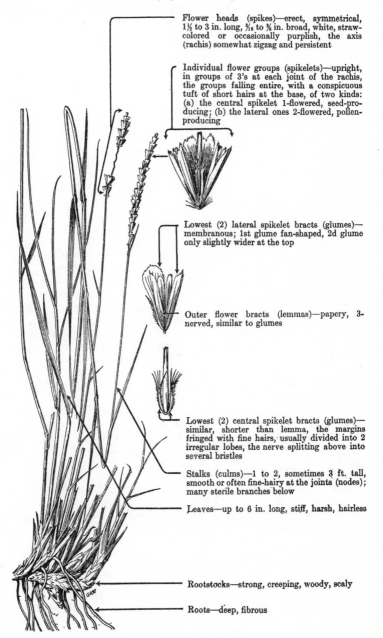

Flower heads (spikes)—erect, symmetrical, 1½ to 3 in. long, $\frac{3}{16}$ to $\frac{3}{8}$ in. broad, white, straw-colored or occasionally purplish, the axis (rachis) somewhat zigzag and persistent

Individual flower groups (spikelets)—upright, in groups of 3's at each joint of the rachis, the groups falling entire, with a conspicuous tuft of short hairs at the base, of two kinds: (a) the central spikelet 1-flowered, seed-producing; (b) the lateral ones 2-flowered, pollen-producing

Lowest (2) lateral spikelet bracts (glumes)—membranous; 1st glume fan-shaped, 2d glume only slightly wider at the top

Outer flower bracts (lemmas)—papery, 3-nerved, similar to glumes

Lowest (2) central spikelet bracts (glumes)—similar, shorter than lemma, the margins fringed with fine hairs, usually divided into 2 irregular lobes, the nerve splitting above into several bristles

Stalks (culms)—1 to 2, sometimes 3 ft. tall, smooth or often fine-hairy at the joints (nodes); many sterile branches below

Leaves—up to 6 in. long, stiff, harsh, hairless

Rootstocks—strong, creeping, woody, scaly

Roots—deep, fibrous

Tobosa is an erect perennial very similar in general appearance to galleta (*H. jamesii*). It ranges from western Texas to Arizona and south into Mexico. It grows most abundantly in the southern part of New Mexico and Arizona on the finer, somewhat compact soils on open flats, swales, and depressions and, to some extent, on similar soils in the foothills. It occurs more sparsely on sandy or gravelly soils, mainly at elevations between 3,000 and 5,000 feet. This grass is very common on areas subject to flooding in the rainy season, where it attains its best development; it is considered the climax vegetation in certain adobe clay depressions and swales.[1] Under such conditions, it may form a pure stand of coarse sod grass over areas as large as 1 or 2 acres. On the dry sites tobosa grass occurs in scattered stands in large tufts and is fairly resistant to drought although it suffers more during extended periods of dry weather and is slower in recovering from such a setback than are many of its associates. Although preferring areas subject to flooding, tobosa is one of the first grasses to die when submerged for periods of several months. It is also intolerant of shifting sands.[1]

Burrograss (*Scleropogon brevifolius*) and either alkali sacaton (*Sporobolus airoides*) or sacaton (*S. wrightii*) are common associates of tobosa on adobe clay soils. On sandy clay or gravelly clay loams, tobosa is often the most important forage species growing in association with blackbrush (*Flourensia cernua*), black grama (*Bouteloua eriopoda*), side-oats grama (*B. curtipendula*), dropseeds (*Sporobolus* spp.), and muhly grasses (*Muhlenbergia* spp.).

Tobosa is good in palatability when it is green and succulent, especially for cattle and horses. The species withstands grazing very well during the summer rainy season when its main growth occurs. Tobosa range should be grazed at that time as its grazing capacity is then maximum. Campbell [1] states that "it may be grazed up to 60 percent of its herbage production each summer without injury or without materially hindering the succession on adjacent areas supporting lower stages." Tobosa may be utilized to some extent in the fall but is of little value as winter forage because the stems and leaves soon become so dry and tough after growth ceases that livestock pass it by if other feed is available. Tobosa range, adjoining black grama range, affords a good combination, as the former may be grazed during the growing season, which facilitates deferred grazing on the black grama range. Such management enables these plants to produce the maximum volume of forage before being grazed.

Tobosa produces a fair amount of seed of moderate viability, and is not an aggressive seeder on the range. The strong rootstocks, although slow in spreading, provide the surest means of reproduction and make the plant resistant to trampling and a very valuable soil binder.

---

[1] Campbell, R. S. PLANT SUCCESSION AND GRAZING CAPACITY ON CLAY SOILS IN SOUTHERN NEW MEXICO. Jour. Agr. Research [U. S.] 43 : 1027–1051. 1931.

BARLEYS

Hor'deum spp.

The barleys are annual, biennial, or perennial bunchgrasses with dense, bearded or bristly heads (spikes). The fact that the axis (rachis) of the spike is jointed and readily breaks apart at the joints at maturity or on drying is almost a unique feature, the squirreltails (*Sitanion* spp.) and a few species of wheatgrasses (*Agropyron* spp.) being the only others among the common western range grasses with similar characteristics.

Hordeum is the ancient Latin name for barley (*H. vulgare*), which is the most important member of the genus and has been cultivated since prehistoric times. It is the most important cereal of northern countries and is extensively used for food where other grains are not sufficiently hardy. However, it is chiefly important as a livestock feed and for brewing beer. Pearl barley (*H. aegiceras*) is another member of the genus which is also cultivated. None of the native western species have been domesticated. Foxtail barley (*H. jubatum*) is a considerable detriment to western agriculture, as it is a weed species occurring in considerable abundance in hay and grain fields. The grain of this species is used for food by the Shoshone Indians of Oregon.

In the West, *Hordeum* is represented by eight indigenous species, most of which are perennials. In addition, five annual species have been naturalized, including common barley and pearl barley sometimes seen on the range as volunteers from cultivated fields. The introduced species are more common on the Pacific coast. Barleys in the West extend from lower elevations to well up into the spruce belt. Generally they prefer open sites such as meadows, grasslands, and parks, although some species appear in brush types and in woodlands. Several species are widely distributed, but as a rule are found in local patches and are not generally scattered over the range. Foxtail barley, however, is not only widely distributed but occurs in abundance.

The native barleys are fair to fairly good forage for all classes of livestock for spring and early summer, but are little grazed after the heads are well developed. Some species resume growth when the fall rains begin, and as they green up considerably and the troublesome heads have then largely disappeared, are important as fall and winter forage. On the whole, however, the barleys are distinctly inferior range grasses.

Individual flower groups (spikelets) in the native western species are one-flowered, occur in groups of three at each joint of the rachis, the center one being stalkless and seed producing, the lateral ones on short stalks and usually not seed producing. The lowest (2) spikelet bracts (glumes) are bristlelike, and the outer flower bract (lemma) is usually awned in the fertile floret, and in the sterile spikelet often reduced to a bristle.

FOXTAIL BARLEY

Hor'deum juba'tum

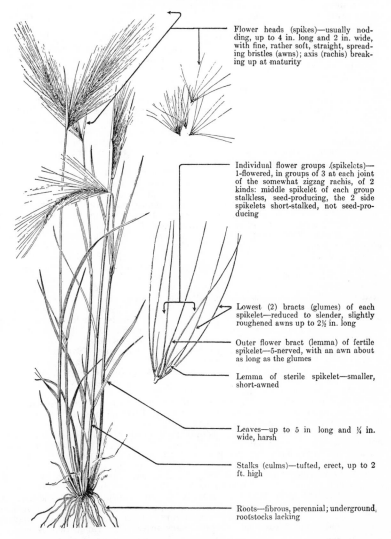

Flower heads (spikes)—usually nodding, up to 4 in. long and 2 in. wide, with fine, rather soft, straight, spreading bristles (awns); axis (rachis) breaking up at maturity

Individual flower groups (spikelets)—1-flowered, in groups of 3 at each joint of the somewhat zigzag rachis, of 2 kinds: middle spikelet of each group stalkless, seed-producing, the 2 side spikelets short-stalked, not seed-producing

Lowest (2) bracts (glumes) of each spikelet—reduced to slender, slightly roughened awns up to 2½ in. long

Outer flower bract (lemma) of fertile spikelet—5-nerved, with an awn about as long as the glumes

Lemma of sterile spikelet—smaller, short-awned

Leaves—up to 5 in long and ¼ in. wide, harsh

Stalks (culms)—tufted, erect, up to 2 ft. high

Roots—fibrous, perennial; underground rootstocks lacking

Foxtail barley, commonly known as foxtail or squirreltail barley and squirreltail grass, is a pestiferous perennial, from 8 to 30 inches high, growing in well-defined tufts or bunches. Indigenous in the Western States, the plant is now widely distributed from Alaska to Laborador, New Jersey, Texas, and California, growing more commonly at lower elevations on the plains and in the lower foothills, chiefly in grass types in moist saline and dry soils but also extending upward to subalpine elevations in the spruce belt. It is very common throughout the West, especially along roadsides and other waste places as well as in grain and hay fields. Its abundance in Montana in the early days is evidenced by Dr. Vasey,[1] who, in 1884, stated,

Hordeum jubatum, or foxtail grass, is common on the low lands (of Montana) especially where there is moisture. It is looked upon as one of the worst of weeds. Its presence with other grasses destroys their value entirely for hay.

The species is still common in Montana, although not so evident on the range as in grain and hay fields, probably because these fields now occupy the sites naturally suited to this grass.

While young, foxtail barley is palatable to livestock and, up to the time when heads develop, is fair to fairly good forage for cattle and horses and fair for sheep. After the heads form the plants are not grazed. When dry, even though immature, the bearded heads are very troublesome because they break apart readily, sections of the rachis remaining as sharp points on the spikelets which, with the stiff awns, become imbedded in the mouth tissues and sometimes in the nostrils and eyes of livestock and game animals that consume such forage. In California, foxtail barley is grazed slightly by deer, while the blades are young and tender. In Montana and in the Jackson Hole country of Wyoming the species is grazed readily by elk as winter forage and, when fed as hay, the foliage may be entirely consumed in spite of the awns. Such utilization, however, may reflect the near-starvation conditions which often prevail on those elk ranges.

Unquestionably foxtail barley is very harmful to all kinds of grazing animals, particularly to elk, deer, and antelope when the seed heads have dried. Rush,[2][3] for example, reports that when such game animals eat the seed heads the "awns stick into the soft tissues of the mouth" and, subsequently, continue to work into the tissues. Infection in these injuries causes necrotic sores and a disease known as necrotic stomatitis or calf diphtheria, which, in turn, finally attacks the bones and causes an abnormal enlargement (exostosis) as well as lumpy jaw and pus-forming abscesses.

Mr. O. J. Murie diagnosed necrotic stomatitis in 70 of 193 post-mortems of elk in the Jackson Hole country during the winter of 1928–29 and ascribed the mechanical injury which caused the disease to the awns of foxtail barley.[3] Hay containing an appreciable amount of the dry heads of this species is also very injurious to horses, especially when manger-fed, as the animals have little chance to avoid eating the foxtail heads. The sharp points and stiff awns become imbedded in their gums or collect between their lips and gums, causing foul-smelling abscesses. Cattle are injured to a less extent than horses, as the mucous membrane of their mouths is thicker and less easily penetrated by the awns and sharp head parts of this grass. Experienced sheepmen avoid foxtail-infested hay because the dry heads quickly cause sore mouths. Some stockmen maintain that hay infested with foxtail barley can be fed without danger during wet weather when the awns are somewhat softened by moisture. Furthermore, they assert that if such hay is fed liberally so that livestock are not forced to eat the foxtail barley heads, little injury will normally result even in dry weather. However, Fleming and Peterson[4] advise that lambing ewes should not be fed "foxtail" hay.

Once established, foxtail barley is difficult to eradicate. It is a prolific seeder, and the heads or their parts with the seed are blown about by the wind and transported in the hair of grazing animals; thus the species quickly invades all suitable areas. Seeding plowable meadows and pastures, after thorough cultivation, to a grass which will quickly form a dense stand should be effective in reducing the amount of foxtail barley. On the range, where cultivation is seldom practical, conservative grazing which will facilitate the reestablishment of the native, palatable perennial grasses is probably the most feasible method of reducing the "foxtail." Artificial reseeding of badly depleted areas to aggressive but palatable grasses may be necessary to expedite range improvement.

---

[1] VASEY, G. THE AGRICULTURAL GRASSES OF THE UNITED STATES. U. S. Dept. Agr. Rept. 32:1–115, illus. 1884.
[2] RUSH, W. M. NORTHERN YELLOWSTONE ELK STUDY. 131 pp., illus. Missoula, Mont. 1932.
[3] RUSH, W. M. FOXTAIL GRASS IS KILLING ELK. Mont. Wild Life 3(7) : 10–11, illus. 1930.
[4] FLEMING, C. E., and PETERSON, N. F. DON'T FEED FOX-TAIL HAY TO LAMBING EWES! Nev. Agr. Expt. Sta. Bull. 97, 18 pp., illus. 1919.

MEADOW BARLEY

Hor'deum nodo'sum

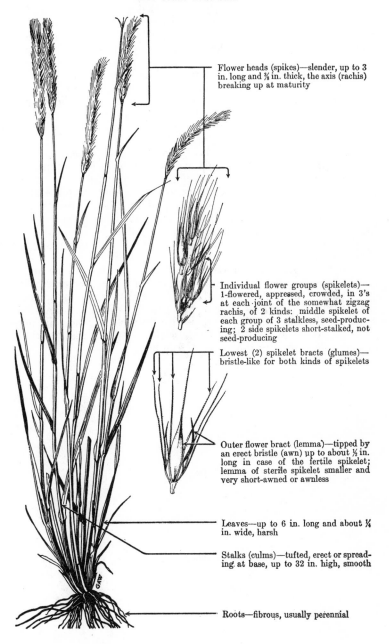

Flower heads (spikes)—slender, up to 3 in. long and ⅜ in. thick, the axis (rachis) breaking up at maturity

Individual flower groups (spikelets)—1-flowered, appressed, crowded, in 3's at each joint of the somewhat zigzag rachis, of 2 kinds: middle spikelet of each group of 3 stalkless, seed-producing; 2 side spikelets short-stalked, not seed-producing

Lowest (2) spikelet bracts (glumes)—bristle-like for both kinds of spikelets

Outer flower bract (lemma)—tipped by an erect bristle (awn) up to about ½ in. long in case of the fertile spikelet; lemma of sterile spikelet smaller and very short-awned or awnless

Leaves—up to 6 in. long and about ¼ in. wide, harsh

Stalks (culms)—tufted, erect or spreading at base, up to 32 in. high, smooth

Roots—fibrous, usually perennial

Meadow barley, often known as foxtail, is a fairly tall, leafy bunchgrass, which is perennial over most of its range but is sometimes annual in the South. In the United States it ranges from Minnesota and Indiana to Texas, California, and Washington, but the species also extends northward to Alaska and occurs in temperate Europe to Asia. This grass is found chiefly in moist soils along streams and in poorly drained meadows and parks, from the plains and foothills upward to the aspen and spruce belts, but typically attains its best development on sunny, open exposures where it often occurs in small, nearly pure stands. It is very common, however, in partial shade as among shrubs and in open aspen stands.

Before the heads are produced, meadow barley is fairly good to good forage for all classes of livestock. However, after the heads form it is not relished and, since heads develop comparatively early in the season, this plant is grazed for only a relatively short time. On favorable sites this species produces considerable foliage but, because of its localized occurrence and relatively low palatibility at maturity, it generally is of secondary importance as a range forage plant. Meadow barley tends to increase and replace the more palatable plants in moist meadows and in other sites favorable to its growth, especially if such areas are somewhat overgrazed. This increase evidently takes place because meadow barley is lightly utilized and is allowed to mature seed, while the other species are closely cropped.

This bunchgrass often occupies poorly drained areas in native hay meadows, generally to the exclusion of other species. Although these patches are usually small, meadow barley yields about as much hay as the other grasses customarily grown in such meadows, and its bristly spikes apparently do not injure livetock. Hence, the presence of meadow barley—unlike foxtail barley—neither reduces the yield nor seriously impairs the value of the hay.

JUNEGRASS

Koele'ria crista'ta

Flower head (panicle)—narrow, spikelike, 1 to 7 in. long, somewhat tapering at both ends, often interrupted near base

Stalks (culms)—slender, tufted, erect, 1 to 2½ ft. high, hairless except for very fine hairs just below panicle

Leaves—mostly basal, numerous, rather narrow, flat or with inrolled edges, 1½ to 5 in. long; hairiness rather variable

Roots—fibrous, perennial; rootstocks lacking

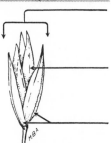

Individual flower groups (spikelets)—2- to 5-flowered, numerous, crowded, shining, pale, less than ¼ in. long, without beards or bristles (awns)

Outer flower bract (lemma)—narrow, lance-shaped, sharp-pointed, obscurely 5-nerved; inner flower bract (palea) tissue-papery, 2-toothed, 2-keeled

Lowest (2) spikelet bracts (glumes)—similar to lemmas, but thicker, about equal, persistent, 1st glume 1-nerved, narrower than 3-nerved 2d glume

Junegrass, also known as mountain junegrass, prairie junegrass, and koeleria, is a perennial bunchgrass and the only species of *Koeleria* native to western North America. It ranges from southern Ontario to British Columbia and southward to Texas, California, and Washington; it also occurs in Europe and Asia. Although june-grass rarely forms pure stands and, as a rule, occurs sparsely on the higher ranges, it is one of the most common and widely dis-tributed of the western grasses, extending over a wide altitudinal range and growing on a variety of dry to moist soils. Throughout the sagebrush, ponderosa pine, lodgepole pine, aspen, and to some extent, the spruce belts, this species is often an important forage member of the sagebrush, mixed grass, weed, and open timber types.

In general, junegrass is fairly good to good forage and is relished early in the season by all classes of livestock, but sheep do not graze the stalks after seed maturity. In some localities it is considered very good to excellent forage, but it is doubtful if it is ever as palat-able as certain bluegrasses and other leading forage species. June-grass is a comparatively low-growing species and, while leaves are generally produced in abundance, they are relatively short and mostly basal, so that the species does not yield a large amount of forage per plant.

This grass flowers during June and July and seed is disseminated from July to September. The seed is of low viability, but the nor-mally abundant crop counterbalances this low germination to a con-siderable degree. The plants also stool well on areas where compe-tition with other species is not too keen. Junegrass matures rela-tively early over much of its range, which probably explains why it is able to withstand considerable grazing, and yet maintain itself in a fairly satisfactory condition on closely utilized ranges.

Junegrass is variable in appearance throughout its wide range. It bears some resemblance to certain species of bluegrass (*Poa* spp.). The bluegrasses usually have folded leaves with blunt, boat-shaped tips, and the stalks below the flower heads are free of hairs. In junegrass, on the other hand, the leaves are usually flat or inrolled and sharp-pointed, and there are fine hairs on the stalks just below the flower heads. Ordinarily also junegrass flowers and matures somewhat earlier than those species of bluegrasses with which it is likely to be confused.

Plains reedgrass (*Calamagrostis montanensis*) and spike trisetum (*Trisetum spicatum*) are sometimes mistaken for junegrass. The reedgrass bears a sharp-pointed, stiff leaf just below the head, which feature is lacking in mountain junegrass. The heads of spike trise-tum are awned, whereas those of junegrass are awnless.

KOELERIAS (Koele'ria spp.)

Koeleria includes about 15 species of annual or perennial grasses occurring in the temperate regions of both hemispheres. While it has been placed by some botanists in the fescue tribe (Festuceae), most authorities prefer to place it in the oat tribe of grasses (Aveneae), since its glumes are relatively long and it has the other characters of this tribe except for the fact that the dorsal awns typical of the oat tribe are lacking. Junegrass is the only repre-sentative of the genus native to the Western States. One other species, *K. phleoides*, an annual native to Europe, has become established in western Florida and Alabama and in California and Oregon.

The genus was named for G. Ludwig Koeler (1764–1807), a German botanist, one of the first to make a special study of grasses, by Christian Persoon (1755–1837), father of the science of plant diseases (phytopathology).

WOLFTAIL

Lycu'rus phleoi'des

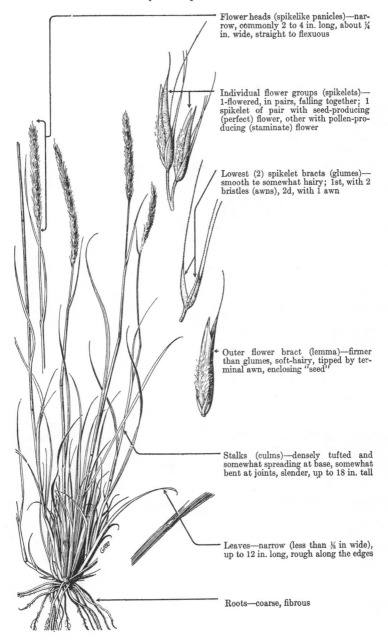

Flower heads (spikelike panicles)—narrow, commonly 2 to 4 in. long, about ¼ in. wide, straight to flexuous

Individual flower groups (spikelets)—1-flowered, in pairs, falling together; 1 spikelet of pair with seed-producing (perfect) flower, other with pollen-producing (staminate) flower

Lowest (2) spikelet bracts (glumes)—smooth to somewhat hairy; 1st, with 2 bristles (awns), 2d, with 1 awn

Outer flower bract (lemma)—firmer than glumes, soft-hairy, tipped by terminal awn, enclosing "seed"

Stalks (culms)—densely tufted and somewhat spreading at base, somewhat bent at joints, slender, up to 18 in. tall

Leaves—narrow (less than ⅛ in wide), up to 12 in. long, rough along the edges

Roots—coarse, fibrous

Wolftail, also known as Texas timothy, is a grayish green, perennial bunchgrass which gets its common name from the timothy-like panicle that resembles the tail of a wolf. The generic name *Lycurus* is from two Greek words meaning wolftail, and the specific name *phleoides* refers to the resemblance of this plant to timothy (*Phleum*). A member of the redtop tribe (*Agrostideae*), it is the only representative of this small genus in the United States. It inhabits western Texas, New Mexico, and Arizona, and extends southward into Mexico. It is very common in New Mexico and Arizona on mesas and sidehills of the woodland and ponderosa pine zones at elevations from 4,000 to 8,000 feet. It usually occurs in very scattered stands, but occasionally is fairly abundant, growing on dry, rocky, open hillsides, in mixture with other grasses, weeds, and shrubs. This grass grows on a wide variety of soils and exposures but seems to thrive best on sandy or gravelly loams of open grasslands and in dry canyon bottoms. Some of its common associates are the gramas (*Bouteloua* spp.), junegrass (*Koeleria cristata*), mountain muhly (*Muhlenbergia montana*), and oaks (*Quercus* spp.). Wolftail sometimes extends down into the mesquite (*Prosopis* spp.) and catclaw (*Acacia greggii*) zone.

In general, about 45 to 75 percent of the herbage of wolftail is grazed when the range is properly utilized. It is usually considered a good or very good forage grass. Its main growing season comes with the advent of summer rains. The foliage cures well on the range, and the semiperennial stems green up quickly and produce new growth in the spring when palatability of wolftail is highest. On closely grazed ranges it is likely to be utilized yearlong but, on conservatively grazed range in mixture with other grasses, it is grazed lightly in summer and winter and fairly heavily in the spring when it resumes growth.

Wolftail can be readily distinguished from timothy by the more conspicuous awns of its spikelets which give the slender lead-colored panicle a hairy appearance. The panicle is also less dense and not so rigid and erect as that of timothy. Wolftail is occasionally confused with spike muhly (*Muhlenbergia wrightii*), but may be distinguished from the latter by its more bristly, wolftail-like panicle. The spikelets of wolftail are borne in pairs and fall together entire, leaving the axis of the panicle (rachis) naked. On the other hand, the spikelets of spike muhly are borne singly and the glumes remain attached after the seeds fall. Furthermore, spike muhly may be distinguished by its rootstocks (rhizomes), which are lacking in wolftail. Wolftail usually flowers in July and August and the seeds are disseminated during late September and through October.

ONIONGRASS

Me'lica bulbo'sa, syn. *M. bel'la*

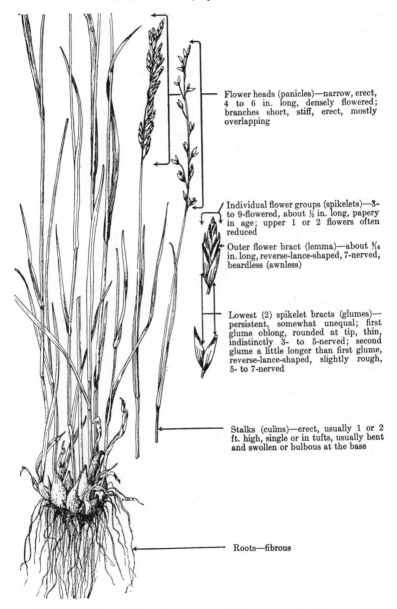

Flower heads (panicles)—narrow, erect, 4 to 6 in. long, densely flowered; branches short, stiff, erect, mostly overlapping

Individual flower groups (spikelets)—3- to 9-flowered, about ½ in. long, papery in age; upper 1 or 2 flowers often reduced

Outer flower bract (lemma)—about ⁵⁄₁₆ in. long, reverse-lance-shaped, 7-nerved, beardless (awnless)

Lowest (2) spikelet bracts (glumes)—persistent, somewhat unequal; first glume oblong, rounded at tip, thin, indistinctly 3- to 5-nerved; second glume a little longer than first glume, reverse-lance-shaped, slightly rough, 5- to 7-nerved

Stalks (culms)—erect, usually 1 or 2 ft. high, single or in tufts, usually bent and swollen or bulbous at the base

Roots—fibrous

Oniongrass, often called purple melic, is a rather tall perennial, with the base of the stalks frequently enlarged or swollen into a bulblike growth. The common name oniongrass, as well as the specific name *bulbosa*, refer to this basal enlargement. This grass is widely distributed, from British Columbia and Alberta southward to Colorado, and westward to California. Recently, it has also been definitely reported from western Texas; very possibly it occurs in northern Arizona and New Mexico, although no specimens have yet been collected in those States. Although growing most luxuriantly in the ponderosa pine and spruce-fir zones, this species flourishes from sea level to an elevation of 10,000 feet.

This grass usually grows sparingly in mixed grass, weed or brush types, being but rarely abundant and probably never occurring as the predominating species. It is commonly associated with big sagebrush, needlegrasses, bromegrasses, lupines, and aspen. Oniongrass inhabits open sagebrush types, open timber stands, and meadows, most of which are exposed to full or moderate sunlight. It thrives best on moist, rich, sandy or clay loams of meadows and also in dense aspen and moderately dense coniferous timber. This plant also does well on the better drained slopes and open sagebrush areas. Fairly drought-resistant, it often exists on dry, shallow soils during rather protracted periods of dry weather.

Oniongrass is very palatable to all classes of livestock as well as to elk and deer. The herbage is relished during the spring and summer, but in the fall the leafage becomes harsh and is not as closely cropped. This grass rates as good to excellent forage for cattle and horses and good for sheep and elk, being also grazed lightly by deer. Horses are especially fond of the seed heads and flower stalks. Although oniongrass is widely distributed and ranks with the bluegrasses and wheatgrasses in palatability, its scattered growth limits its importance as a forage species.

This grass produces a relatively small crop of poor seed. Seeds tested by Sampson[1] in 1908 germinated only 4 percent; those tested the previous year failed completely. Apparently, oniongrass is but poorly adapted for the revegetation of depleted ranges. The seed usually matures during the latter part of August, but this varies considerably with seasons and altitudinal range. Oniongrass grows in small, loose clumps consisting of a few slender stems. A single clump may produce several "bulbs" which appear in clusters similar to small onions. The foliage, however, is rather scant. The narrow panicles are from 4 to 6 inches long; the spikelets are few, purplish tinged and often somewhat showy, this being emphasized in the specific name *bella* (a Latin word meaning "pretty") of the synonym. The spikelets and panicle branches are erect; the lemmas, awnless. The roots are fibrous and well developed.

---

[1] Sampson, A. W. IMPORTANT RANGE PLANTS : THEIR LIFE HISTORY AND FORAGE VALUE. U. S. Dept. Agr. Bull. 545, 63 pp., illus. 1917.

MELICGRASSES AND ONIONGRASSES

Me'lica spp.

The melicgrasses, known individually as melics, a group of perennials belonging to the fescue tribe (*Festuceae*), are closely related to the bluegrasses, bromegrasses, and fescues. *Melica*, an old Italian and late Latin name for sorghum, is probably a derivative of the Greek *meli* (honey), *melikērion* (honeycomb), and *mēlikos* (melic, i. e., lyric, or "sweet-singing" poetry). The name, no doubt, refers to the sweet juice or sirup which the ancient Greeks, so the story goes, obtained from one of the Old World species. Linnaeus later applied the name to this genus of grasses. About 60 species of melicgrasses are widely distributed throughout the temperate regions of the world; 17 occur in the United States, with the center of distribution in California, where 13 species appear.

The melicgrasses grow at all elevations from sea level up to 10,000 feet, throughout mountain meadows, parks, timbered areas, and brushlands. They usually grow scatteringly in mixed grass-weed types, being commonly associated with bromegrasses, wheatgrasses, sedges, pentstemons, mountain-dandelions and bluebells. These species are seldom abundant and probably never become dominant in any association. Some of the melicgrasses are widely distributed; others occur rather locally. Oniongrass (*M. bulbosa*) is probably the most widely distributed of the western species. Yosemite oniongrass (*M. inflata*) has a very narrow range, occurring only in California. Although most species prefer the more moist and fertile soils of the slopes and timbered areas, some are found on the drier, infertile, open side hills, and a few occur even on moist meadows or along stream banks.

California melic (*M. imperfec'ta*) extends from central California to Lower California and perhaps also into western Arizona, growing from sea level to elevations of 6,500 feet. Although its favored home is the open foothills in pine and chaparral types, this plant also thrives on moist shaded sites, and is occasionally fairly abundant on shallow, infertile soils. In California this species produces a greater amount of forage than any other melicgrass.[2] It is rated as good to excellent forage for all classes of livestock. Horses and cattle crop the leafage season long and are especially fond of the flower stalks and heads, but sheep usually do not graze the foliage much until late fall. This plant has strong seed habits, producing a relatively large quantity of fertile seed.

Most melicgrasses are of secondary importance as forage species since they occur only scatteringly on the range. However, the herbage of most species is relished by all classes of livestock, as well as by elk, and deer often crop these grasses lightly. Several species, including oniongrass, showy oniongrass, or melic (*M. spectabilis*), and little oniongrass (*M. fugax*), rank as good to excellent forage for cattle and horses, and good for sheep and elk. Oniongrass and

---

[2] Sampson, A. W., and Chase, A. RANGE GRASSES OF CALIFORNIA. Calif. Agr. Expt. Sta. Bull. 430, 94 pp., illus. 1927.

showy oniongrass are probably the two most important range forage species of this genus in the West, being more widespread and usually somewhat more abundant than their sister species.

These perennial grasses are only moderately resistant to drought but withstand grazing fairly well. They usually produce limited amounts of rather large seed. Many of the melicgrasses, such as the native three-flower melic (*M. nitens*) and Porter melic (*M. porteri*), are rather ornamental, with large and handsome panicles, which wave back and forth in the wind; their spikelets are large, often lustrous, and richly colored. The melicgrasses usually grow in dense or loose clumps, with simple stalks. The rather large, two- to several-flowered, tawny or purplish spikelets characteristically bear from one to three sterile flowers in the form of empty, club-shaped lemmas more or less rolled up within each other. The glumes are large, unequal, papery, with thin transparent margins and three to five, usually prominent nerves. The lemmas may be either membranous or firm but have thin, translucent edges, and are either awnless or else awned from between the forked apex. This group of plants is distinguished from its allied genera by the thin, transparent (scarious) margins of the glumes and lemmas, the closed leaf sheaths, and the hooded or club-shaped sterile lemmas. The awned species of *Melica* closely resemble some species of *Bromus*.

MUHLY GRASSES

Muhlenber'gia spp., syn. *Epicam'pes spp.*

The large genus of the redtop tribe (Agrostideae) includes numerous perennial and a small number of annual grasses widely distributed in both Americas and parts of Asia. It is especially typical of the Mexican plateau and of the Southwestern States, where it is represented by more species than any other grass genus. With very few exceptions, species of this genus do not grow in pure stands over extensive areas but are usually scattered over a wide variety of types and soils. Their altitudinal distribution extends from low deserts to high subalpine parks and timbered areas. In this country they are important in the Southwest, the southern parts of Nevada and Utah, and in southern and central Colorado, where several species often occur in some abundance. Over the remainder of the western rangeland the muhly grasses occur sparsely and but few species are of economic importance.

The palatability of the muhly grasses varies greatly with the different species. Bush muhly (*M. porteri*), at one time a very abundant species of the Southwest, is so highly palatable year-long that it has been largely killed out by overuse. Spike muhly (*M. wrightii*) is one of the choice grasses wherever it occurs but is rather limited in abundance. Mountain muhly (*M. montana*) is fairly good forage and abounds on many southwestern mountain ranges to the extent that it rates as one of the most important local forage species. Many other perennial species are small, produce but little foliage and are only fair forage. The annuals are poor or almost worthless as forage. Muhlies are chiefly valuable for spring and summer use because the palatability of most species decreases greatly as the plants attain maturity.

The roots of a Mexican species (*M. macroura*, syn. *Epicampes macroura*), known as Mexican broomroot or Mexican whisk, are used in making brushes and are exported from Vera Cruz to Europe for this purpose.[1] After the roots are cut for brush making the tops are thrown away, and an experimental study has shown that the dried leaves and stems (straw) of this grass offer promising possibilities in the manufacture of paper.[2]

Several rather fine distinctions separate these grasses from their close relatives. They have small, one-flowered spikelets (*i. e.*, each flower and "seed" is borne singly). The narrow outer flower scale (lemma) closely envelops the grain and is 3- to 5-nerved, firm and sharp-pointed or tipped with a fine beard (awn). This awn, when present, is securely attached but not twisted. The lowest two-flower bracts (glumes) are usually shorter or about equal to the lemma (awned tips longer in *M. racemosa*) and remain attached to the stem after the seed falls. Some of the muhly grasses are often confused with species of dropseed (*Sporobolus*), ricegrass (*Oryzopsis*),

---

[1] Lamson-Scribner, F. ECONOMIC GRASSES. U. S. Dept. Agr., Div. Agrost. Bull. 14, rev., 85 pp., illus. 1900.
[2] Brand, C. J., and Merrill, J. L. ZACATON AS A PAPER-MAKING MATERIAL. U. S. Dept. Agr. Bull. 309, 28 pp., illus. 1915.

and certain needlegrasses (*Stipa*). They may be distinguished from dropseeds by their "seeds", which are closely enfolded by the firm outer flower scales (lemma and palea). The "seeds" of dropseeds, on the other hand, are free from the lemmas and paleas and loose within the outer "seed" coats (pericarps). Also the lemmas of the muhly grasses have short bristles (awns) or are sharp-pointed while the lemmas of dropseeds are awnless and blunt. Ricegrasses have a rather large, firm, hardened "seed" with an awn which readily falls from the "seed" when nature, separating at a joint at the apex of the lemma. Needlegrasses may be readily distinguished from the muhly grasses by their twisted and usually bent awns and by the pointed bearded base (callus) of the "seed."

The genus commemorates Rev. Dr. Gotthilf Heinrich Ernst Muhlenberg (1753–1815), an American clergyman and botanist, who wrote the first treatise on American grasses. Dr. Muhlenberg was a member of an unusually distinguished Pennsylvania family. His father, H. M. Mühlenberg, was the founder of the Lutheran Church in this country. His brother, Gen. J. P. G. Muhlenberg was second in command to Lafayette at the siege of Yorktown and is celebrated in American history for doffing his ecclesiastical garb in the pulpit, at the outset of the Revolution, revealing his colonel's uniform underneath and marching off to battle with nearly 300 members of his congregation. Another brother, F. A. C. Muhlenberg, was the first Speaker of the United States House of Representatives.

MOUNTAIN MUHLY

Muhlenber'gia montan'a, syns. *"M. gra'cilis"*,[1] *M. tri'flda*

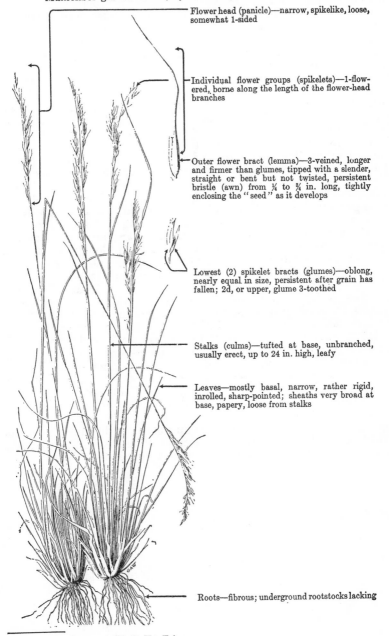

Flower head (panicle)—narrow, spikelike, loose, somewhat 1-sided

Individual flower groups (spikelets)—1-flowered, borne along the length of the flower-head branches

Outer flower bract (lemma)—3-veined, longer and firmer than glumes, tipped with a slender, straight or bent but not twisted, persistent bristle (awn) from ¼ to ¾ in. long, tightly enclosing the "seed" as it develops

Lowest (2) spikelet bracts (glumes)—oblong, nearly equal in size, persistent after grain has fallen; 2d, or upper, glume 3-toothed

Stalks (culms)—tufted at base, unbranched, usually erect, up to 24 in. high, leafy

Leaves—mostly basal, narrow, rather rigid, inrolled, sharp-pointed; sheaths very broad at base, papery, loose from stalks

Roots—fibrous; underground rootstocks lacking

---

[1] Of U. S. authors, not (H. B. K.) Trin.

Mountain muhly, also known as mountain bunchgrass and pine bunchgrass, is a bright green, perennial grass growing in very dense bunches, commonly 4 to 12 inches in diameter. It ranges from Wyoming to California and western Texas and south into Mexico.

The common habitat of this bunchgrass is under open ponderosa pine and in dry parks, parklike draws, and open hillsides of the ponderosa pine and spruce-fir belts, where it sometimes grows abundantly and becomes the dominant herbaceous plant. Its main altitudinal distribution is between about 7,000 and 10,000 feet, although it sometimes grows even higher, and not infrequently also at considerably lower elevations where moisture and temperature conditions are propitious for its growth. This species occurs on all slopes. Its soil preferences are varied, from dry adobe clays to black loams, but it is especially characteristic of gravelly or sandy loams. Mountain muhly apparently thrives on soils of both granitic and limestone formation. It is often associated with pine dropseed (*Blepharoneuron tricholepis*), Arizona fescue (*Festuca arizonica*), blue grama (*Bouteloua gracilis*), needlegrasses (*Stipa* spp.), and wild-daisies (*Erigeron* spp.).

In general, the palatability of mountain muhly is fairly good, but it is grazed chiefly while the foliage is young and succulent. The leaves become rather less tender at maturity and are not relished as much as some of the better grasses. If grazed closely, it retains a fairly high palatability throughout the growing season. All classes of livestock graze it freely if more palatable species are not available. The large volume of foliage produced enhances its value. Because of its great abundance this grass is the most important species in the higher ponderosa pine types in many areas of the Southwest and Colorado.

Mountain muhly is a long-lived grass, with rhizomelike roots well adapted to withstand grazing. An abundance of seed is produced and since, because of the awns, the seed heads are not generally eaten by livestock, satisfactory reproduction is favored. The usual flowering period is July and August, though the plants occasionally head out before the middle of June. Seed is usually disseminated by the end of October, or the period may begin as early as August or extend into November. Mountain muhly is easily distinguished from other muhlenbergias upon close examination since it is the only native muhly with a three-toothed second glume.

BUSH MUHLY

Muhlenber'gia por'teri

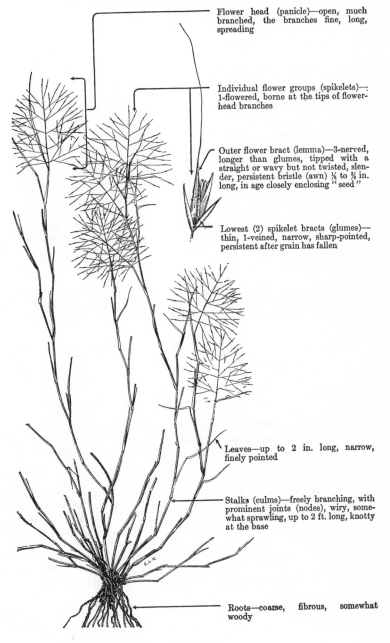

Flower head (panicle)—open, much branched, the branches fine, long, spreading

Individual flower groups (spikelets)—: 1-flowered, borne at the tips of flower-head branches

Outer flower bract (lemma)—3-nerved, longer than glumes, tipped with a straight or wavy but not twisted, slender, persistent bristle (awn) ⅛ to ⅜ in. long, in age closely enclosing "seed"

Lowest (2) spikelet bracts (glumes)— thin, 1-veined, narrow, sharp-pointed, persistent after grain has fallen

Leaves—up to 2 in. long, narrow, finely pointed

Stalks (culms)—freely branching, with prominent joints (nodes), wiry, somewhat sprawling, up to 2 ft. long, knotty at the base

Roots—coarse, fibrous, somewhat woody

Bush muhly, a perennial, also known as bush grass, has a variety of other local names. It is frequently called black grama in grazing literature, although it is neither a grama nor a close relative of the grama grasses. The names bush muhly and bush grass allude to its characteristic habit of growing under the protection of shrubs. It is sometimes called mesquite grass because of its occurrence under mesquite. Still another name is hoe grass, arising from the fact that when it was plentiful early pioneers hoed it for horse feed.

Bush muhly occurs from Colorado to California and Texas and south into Mexico. It is a desert plant, inhabiting the dry mesas and foothills under mesquite (*Prosopis* spp.), catclaw (*Acacia greggii*), Wright buckwheatbrush (*Eriogonum wrightii*), cactus, and other shrubs. Although, at least nowadays, characteristically a "brush grass" because of heavy grazing, it occasionally grows in the open, especially on ungrazed areas. In Arizona and New Mexico it occurs in the lower plains and foothills below 5,000 feet, but in Colorado it is occasionally found as high as 6,500 feet.

This grass is highly palatable to all classes of livestock. It remains green most of the year (yearlong, if sufficient moisture is available) which makes it especially palatable in the winter and before the summer rains start when other grasses are dry. Studies on the Santa Rita experimental range, southern Arizona, indicate that, on conservatively grazed ranges, bush muhly is utilized chiefly between December 1 and July 1; on heavily grazed range, however, it is eagerly sought yearlong. Cattle will force their way into the brush to graze it. It is now found only in scattered stands and almost entirely under partial protection of shrubs, but according to early pioneers it was formerly one of the most abundant and important grasses of southern Arizona and New Mexico.[1] Prof. Thornber states:

The early settlers stoutly maintain that in the pioneer days of stock ranching in southern Arizona black grama (*i. e., Muhlenbergia porteri*) and crowfoot grama were the all important mesa grasses; and that the former species grew in such abundance among shrubs and mesquite, and to some extent in the open, that with a few minutes work one could gather enough to feed a team of horses overnight. They also state that it disappeared rapidly as the country filled up with stock.

It is increasing slowly on some conservatively used ranges but is easily killed out by heavy grazing and lacks the necessary vigor and aggressiveness to cope successfully with present-day range conditions and requirements.

Bush muhly is a perennial, with many weak, much branched, leafy stems. When ungrazed it sometimes forms a tangled, leafy mass 1 to 3 feet high and 1½ to 3 feet in diameter, with the lower parts of the slender stems resting on the ground. The stems are partly perennial and do not die down entirely during the winter, and new spring growth starts from near the base of the previous year's stems. It is, therefore, a grass undershrub. The stems are often bent at the joints, knotty at the base, and support a fine, many-branched, usually loosely drooping, purplish panicle 2 to 4 inches long.

---

[1] Thornber, J. J. THE GRAZING RANGES OF ARIZONA. Ariz. Agr. Expt. Sta. Bull. 65: [245]–360, illus. 1910.

MAT MUHLY

Muhlenber'gia squarro'sa, syn. *M. richardso'nis*

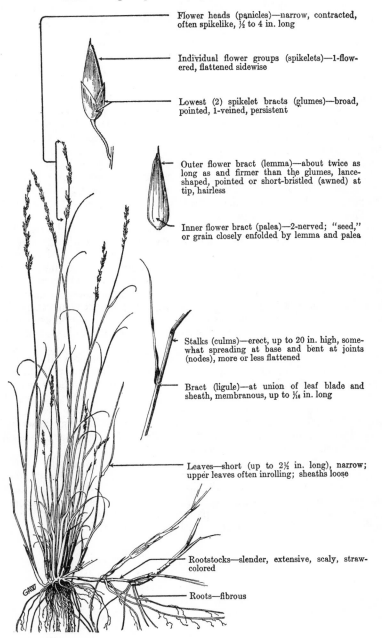

Flower heads (panicles)—narrow, contracted, often spikelike, ½ to 4 in. long

Individual flower groups (spikelets)—1-flowered, flattened sidewise

Lowest (2) spikelet bracts (glumes)—broad, pointed, 1-veined, persistent

Outer flower bract (lemma)—about twice as long as and firmer than the glumes, lance-shaped, pointed or short-bristled (awned) at tip, hairless

Inner flower bract (palea)—2-nerved; "seed," or grain closely enfolded by lemma and palea

Stalks (culms)—erect, up to 20 in. high, somewhat spreading at base and bent at joints (nodes), more or less flattened

Bract (ligule)—at union of leaf blade and sheath, membranous, up to ⅟₁₆ in. long

Leaves—short (up to 2½ in. long), narrow; upper leaves often inrolling; sheaths loose

Rootstocks—slender, extensive, scaly, straw-colored

Roots—fibrous

Mat muhly is usually a low, dull-green, perennial grass growing in scattered, dense carpetlike or matlike patches. The specific name *squarrosa* refers to the squarrose (*i. e.*, crowded, rigid, and somewhat spreading) leaves. It occurs in all of the 11 far-western range States. This species is widely known as dwarf muhly but the name mat muhly is preferable, especially in view of the Standardized Plant Names rule to restrict the word "dwarf" to horticultural varieties or forms dwarfed by plant breeders. Through the central Rockies and southward mat muhly is typically a small grass growing in dry meadows, parks, and open flats in the ponderosa pine, lodgepole pine, and spruce-fir belts, occasionally extending down into the sagebrush flats. Needlegrasses (*Stipa* spp.), bluegrasses (*Poa* spp.), mountain muhly (*Muhlenbergia montana*), western yarrow (*Achillea lanulosa*), pussytoes (*Antennaria* spp.), and cinquefoils (*Potentilla* spp.) are common associates. In Montana and the Northwest ic usually grows much more luxuriantly and occurs from the grass plains up to the high meadows and grasslands at elevations up to 10,000 feet or somewhat higher, associated with other grasses, sedges, and weeds. Although it occasionally grows on coarse rocky soils, it is usually restricted to the better sandy, gravelly, or clay loams. It also occurs to some extent on alkaline soils.

Mat muhly is usually found in scattered patches and is seldom sufficiently abundant in any one locality to be of great importance. Mat muhly withstands heavy grazing well because of its sod-forming habit. Ordinarily, the plant is rather stemmy in its southern range and produces only a small amount of foliage which, while young, is eaten readily by livestock but becomes less palatable at maturity. It is rated as good to very good forage in its northern range for cattle and horses and fairly good for sheep. On the Northern Plains it cures well on the ground and is grazed freely by all classes of livestock, especially during winter.

In Colorado mat muhly is sometimes abundant on heavily grazed bottomlands where gully erosion has lowered the water table and impaired soil fertility to such an extent that the sites have become unfavorable for the bluegrasses and other grasses which formerly occupied those areas. In such cases, mat muhly is a useful soil binder, although inferior to the previous cover. The usual flowering period of mat muhly is July and August and the seeds are disseminated mainly in August and September.

Mat muhly has fine creeping rootstocks and many inrolled, basal and stem leaves one-half to 2½ inches long. The numerous stems are wiry, commonly bent at the joints (especially the basal joints) and are usually 3 to 8 inches long, although sometimes as long as 16 or rarely 24 inches. The panicle is narrow and about 2 to 4 inches long—sometimes shorter, with very few flowers.

RING MUHLY

Muhlenber'gia tor'reyi, syn. *M. gracil'lima*

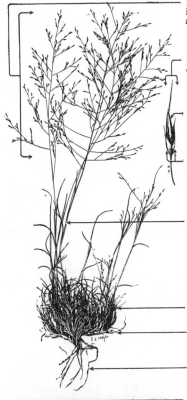

Flower head (panicle)—open, with long, spreading, very slender branches; ultimate branches single

Individual flower groups (spikelets)—1-flowered, somewhat flattened

Outer flower bract (lemma)—firm, tipped by slender bristle (awn) about ⅛ in. long; "seed" (caryopsis) closely enfolded by lemma, firm but not hard, not cylindrical

Lowest (2) spikelet bracts (glumes)—shorter than lemma, unequal, persistent; 2d glume longer, awn-pointed

Stalks (culms)—somewhat spreading and branched at base, slender, rigid, erect, up to 20 in. high, simple above

Leaves—mostly basal, up to 4 in. long, strongly curved, densely matted, inrolled, finely pointed

Rootstocks—slender, creeping, perennial

Roots—fibrous, perennial

Growth habit—showing characteristic ring formation

Ring muhly, also called ring grass, and ticklegrass, get it common names from its unusual and characteristic growth habit. As each tuft enlarges, the center dies, leaving a border of tufted grass 2 to 4 inches wide which forms a ring 6 to 18 inches (sometimes a few feet) in diameter. The species occurs from Colorado and Kansas to Texas and Arizona, being most abundant in New Mexico, Arizona, and southwestern Colorado. It grows mainly on plains and mesas in the woodland and ponderosa pine zones at elevations of 4,000 to 8,500 feet, but may ascend to 10,000 feet. This grass apparently prefers sandy or clay loams, although it occurs on coarse gravelly or rocky sites and will even grow on soils somewhat impregnated with gypsum. Blue grama (*Bouteloua gracilis*), three-awns (*Aristida* spp.), snakeweeds (*Gutierrezia* spp.), and miscellaneous weeds are common associates of ring muhly.

The abundance of ring muhly on some ranges of Colorado, New Mexico, and Arizona, coupled with the fair palatability of the plant while young and succulent make it of considerable importance. It sometimes comes in abundantly on overgrazed range as the more palatable plants are killed out and also in dogtown areas. Under such conditions, it is regarded as an indicator of range deterioration or soil disturbance—an indicator easily identified because of its ring formation. In the absence of a satisfactory stand of the better grasses ring muhly may partially substitute as a protective soil cover until the more desirable species are reestablished. Range management on ring muhly areas should favor the rehabilitation of the better species since ring muhly produces only a small volume of rather wiry foliage per plant and its season of usefulness as forage is short, the leaves becoming somewhat tough and unpalatable at maturity. After midsummer the plant is rated as poor forage. The seed, which usually matures by August, is produced in abundance and, as the fruiting heads are unpalatable, is ordinarily left to mature and to extend the stand.

Ring muhly leaves are 1 to 4 inches long and form dense, somewhat curly tufts. The stems are slender, erect, usually dark, and about 4 to 20 inches high. The panicle is 2 to 9 inches long, open and spreading, and brownish purple, with numerous "seeds" on very fine, wavy branches. The "seeds" are purplish, one-sixteenth to one-eighth of an inch long, and tipped with a very fine awn as long or even twice as long as the "seeds."

SPIKE MUHLY

Muhlenber'gia wrigh'tii

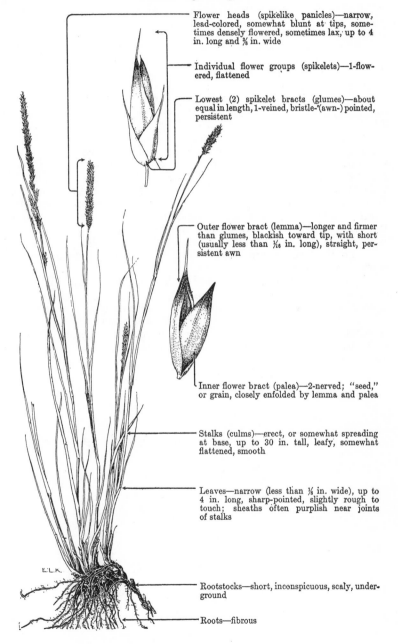

Flower heads (spikelike panicles)—narrow, lead-colored, somewhat blunt at tips, sometimes densely flowered, sometimes lax, up to 4 in. long and ⅜ in. wide

Individual flower groups (spikelets)—1-flowered, flattened

Lowest (2) spikelet bracts (glumes)—about equal in length, 1-veined, bristle-(awn-) pointed, persistent

Outer flower bract (lemma)—longer and firmer than glumes, blackish toward tip, with short (usually less than ¹⁄₁₆ in. long), straight, persistent awn

Inner flower bract (palea)—2-nerved; "seed," or grain, closely enfolded by lemma and palea

Stalks (culms)—erect, or somewhat spreading at base, up to 30 in. tall, leafy, somewhat flattened, smooth

Leaves—narrow (less than ⅛ in. wide), up to 4 in. long, sharp-pointed, slightly rough to touch; sheaths often purplish near joints of stalks

Rootstocks—short, inconspicuous, scaly, underground

Roots—fibrous

145

Spike muhly, a tufted perennial grass, is also known as timothy-like muhly, Wright (or black) muhly, black-timothy, wild-timothy, and deergrass. It occurs in southwestern Colorado, Arizona, New Mexico, and Mexico. This species grows scatteringly through browse, woodland, and ponderosa pine types at elevations ranging from about 5,500 to 9,000 feet, but is more common and abundant in semidry meadows, parks, and flats in the upper woodland and ponderosa pine zones. It is adapted to widely varying moisture conditions, being found near springs and in moist depressions as well as on dry rocky ridges. It occurs on all slopes with soil preferences ranging from moist clay to gravelly or rocky sites, but is more characteristic of sandy or clay loams. Mountain muhly (*M. montana*), side-oats grama (*Bouteloua curtipendula*), blue grama (*B. gracilis*), and pine dropseed (*Blepharoneuron tricholepis*) are among its most common associates.

Spike muhly is relished by all classes of livestock and is one of the most palatable members of its genus. It produces a fairly large amount of foliage which is grazed freely. Although it is abundant only on small localized areas, this species is common throughout the Southwest and, in the aggregate, produces a considerable amount of forage. The short rootstocks provide a limited means of reproduction and aid materially in perpetuating the species. Seed, however, is the chief means of reproduction and should be allowed to mature occasionally. Spike muhly is valued for its soil-binding qualities, especially on untimbered sites.

The common names spike muhly, timothy-like muhly, black-timothy, and wild-timothy have originated from the characteristic flower head, which resembles the head of timothy somewhat although it is darker, and does not usually form a continuous cylinder, but is often broken and with the short branches sometimes slightly spreading. The stems are somewhat flattened, usually erect, and form a noticeably stiff stubble.

INDIAN RICEGRASS

Oryzop'sis hymenoi'des, syns. *O. cuspida'ta, Erioco'ma cuspida'ta, E. hymenoi'des*

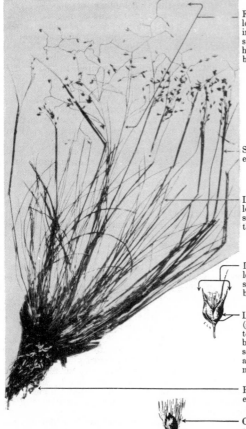

Flower head (panicle)—very loose, 6 to 12 in. long; branches in pairs, widely and stiffly spreading; ultimate branchlets hairlike, slightly zigzag or wavy, bending in opposite directions

Stalks (culms)—1 to 2 ft. tall, erect, rigid, tufted

Leaves—slender, 6 to 15 in. long, flat or inrolled, stiff, smooth or somewhat harsh to the touch, very numerous

Individual flower groups (spikelets)—1-flowered, solitary at slightly enlarged ends of forked branchlets

Lowest (2) spikelet bracts (glumes)—persistent, equal ¼ to ⅜ in. long, broad, rounded on back, with long, taper-pointed, somewhat spreading tips, thin and papery, 3- or 5-nerved, minutely downy

Roots—fibrous, numerous, deep, extensive

Outer flower bract (lemma)—about ½ as long as glumes, firm, hardened, broadly oval, bearded (awned) at tip, almost black at maturity, densely hairy; hairs erect, white, silky, exceeding lemmas; awn simple, straight, up to ¼ in. long, breaking off at maturity; inner flower bract (palea) enclosed by edges of lemma

Indian ricegrass is one of the most important forage grasses on the western desert and semidesert ranges. This hardy, densely tufted perennial is also commonly known as Indian mountain-rice, and is locally called Indian millet, sandgrass, sandrice, and silkygrass. It belongs to the redtop tribe (Agrostideae) and is the only one of about 13 species of *Oryzopsis* in the United States to occur in sufficient abundance and wide distribution on the western ranges to be of outstanding importance.

147

Indian ricegrass is widely distributed over the Western States, ranging from British Columbia southward on the east side of the Cascade and Sierra Nevada Mountains to southern California, and Mexico, and eastward to Texas, the Dakotas, and Manitoba. This species is one of the most drought-enduring of the native range grasses. It characteristically grows on dry sandy soils, sometimes even in sand dunes; hence the local name sandgrass. This grass reaches its highest development from the low-lying desert ranges up through the piñon-juniper belt where it grows in association with black sagebrush (*Artemisia nova*), blue grama (*Bouteloua gracilis*), galleta (*Hilaria jamesii*), and species of wheatgrass, needlegrass, and three-awn. It is also commonly associated with the two shrubby species, winterfat (*Eurotia lanata*) and shadscale (*Atriplex confertifolia*), which indicates that it is at least moderately tolerant to alkaline conditions. This species is not confined to desert ranges, however, as it also appears scatteringly on the higher grassy plains, in the wheatgrass or sagebrush types on the foothills, exposed ridges, and dry sandy or rocky mountain slopes. It has been collected at elevations ranging up to about 10,000 feet in Colorado, Utah, and New Mexico. At these higher elevations it almost invariably occurs on dry, open, southerly exposures under full sunlight.

This grass formerly grew abundantly over many of the desert ranges in the West. It sometimes formed almost pure stands and old-timers tell how this and associated grasses grew like fields of grain and furnished excellent grazing throughout the winter. The early freighters found that Indian ricegrass was the prevalent grass of the desert region of western Utah and valued it highly as a forage plant. Over much of its range Indian ricegrass has largely disappeared in the wake of destructive grazing but dead rootcrowns of this grass found on the winter ranges give evidence of its former profusion. At the present time, Indian ricegrass grows in abundance on some areas which have been ungrazed or conservatively grazed because of inaccessibility to livestock or because of their remoteness from watering places. It is now one of the commonest and most important grasses on some of the semidesert lands in the Columbia Basin in eastern Washington where it is locally called Quincy grass.

On winter range areas, Indian ricegrass is highly palatable to all classes of livestock, being rated as good to very good for sheep as well as for cattle and horses. The individual plants produce an abundance of herbage which cures exceptionally well on the stalk and is very nutritious. The plump seeds are likewise high in food value and are sought after by grazing animals. Stockmen regard this plant highly as a winter feed and seek out the prized areas upon which it grows. They call it a "warm feed" because of its high value for sustaining livestock during severe winter weather. Growth begins early in the spring and the tender green leafage is eagerly eaten by livestock during the early part of the growing season. Indian ricegrass is of only minor importance on the mountainous summer ranges. This is due to its scattered occurrence, relative scarcity, and the fact that it is usually not eaten so readily on mountain grazing lands as on the arid winter ranges. On the former it is generally rated as fairly good to very good for cattle and horses, and poor to fairly good for sheep.

This species produces an abundance of plump, oval seeds which supposedly resemble the seeds of common rice. This resemblance explains both the common name and the generic name *Oryzopsis*, which is taken from the Greek words *oruza*, rice, and *opsis*, appearance. The nutritious seeds of this species were formerly one of the food staples of many western Indians; hence the common name, Indian ricegrass. Indians ground the seeds into meal or flour which was made into bread. This food was held in high esteem by the Zuñi Indians of New Mexico who ate the ground seeds alone or mixed them with cornmeal. They gathered large amounts of the seed for winter provisions especially when their farm crops failed.[1]

---

[1] Stevenson, M. C. ETHNOBOTANY OF THE ZUÑI INDIANS. U. S. Bur. Amer. Ethnol. Ann. Rept. (1908–9) 30 : 33–102, illus. 1915.

PANICGRASSES

Pa′nicum spp.

Panicum, the largest of all grass genera, includes approximately 500 species, distributed chiefly in the warmer regions of both hemispheres. Hitchcock and Chase[1] list 157 species and 5 varieties as occurring in the United States, with the center of distribution in the Southeast. Although about 30 species grow in the 11 far Western States only 1 species, cushion witchgrass (*P. barbipulvina′tum*), occurs in all the Western States. The panic grasses are more typical of the warmer parts of the West, with approximately 17 species occurring in both Arizona and New Mexico, and 13 in California. The number of species found in the other Western States is considerably less, Utah having seven; Nevada, six; Colorado, five; Idaho, Montana, Oregon, and Washington, four each; and Wyoming, three.

In the range country, the panicgrasses are more common and abundant in the Southwest, where they are of material importance as range plants, although abundantly only in local areas. The panicgrasses vary in palatability from practically worthless to good or even, in some instances, very good. In general, the larger species become coarse and tough as they approach maturity, and are chiefly valuable as spring and early summer forage, while the growth is still succulent and tender. The palatability of the western species, as a whole, probably averages fair to fairly good for cattle and horses, and poor to fair for sheep and goats, at least for spring and early summer use.

The panic grasses belong to the millet tribe (*Paniceae*), *Panicum* being the Latin name for millet. For the most part, members of the *Panicum* genus are easily recognized, as the stalks of the individual flower group (spikelets) are jointed below the lower two spikelet bracts (glumes), so that the entire spikelet falls intact. Furthermore, the glumes are usually very unequal, the lower one being generally about half as long as the second. However, in some species, the lower glume is minute and, in a very few instances, is nearly as long as the second glume. The spikelets usually appear to be one-flowered, but actually are two-flowered, as in addition to an upper seed-producing flower, a more or less rudimentary flower consisting of a bract, known as the sterile lemma, also occurs and often encloses a male flower. The sterile lemma is generally about as long as the upper glume. The leaves are mostly flat, frequently hairy, and often have broad, heart-shaped bases, although this feature is variable. The heads vary from broad and open to narrow and spikelike panicles or (more rarely) are spikelike racemes. Some of the panic grasses merit special discussion.

A recent importation from Australia (*P. antidota′le*), which looks something like Johnson grass, is palatable, and will thrive under almost drought conditions. The plant is still in the experimental stage, but looks very promising, especially in connection with erosion-control work in the Southwest.[2]

Maidencane (*P. digitarioi′des*, syn. *P. wal′teri*), native from Delaware to Florida and Texas, is used extensively in the southeastern United States as a binder along railway embankments. An aquatic or semiaquatic with extensively creeping rootstocks, it sometimes becomes a pest in cultivated lands.

Guinea grass (*P. max′imum*), a native of Africa, is one of the most famous of all tropical grasses. This long-lived perennial was early introduced into the West Indies, incidentally with the slave trade. Piper[3] reports that it was introduced as early as 1756 into Jamaica and even then called Guinea grass. In the United States it is adapted for cultivation only to a narrow strip, extending from Florida to southern California. It has become naturalized in some localities, especially in Florida. It probably has little potential value as a western range grass. Under irrigation, in the warmer parts of the Southwest and California, Guinea grass probably would be a valuable forage crop, as six to eight cuttings a year of excellent hay can be made.

[1] Hitchcock, A. S., and Chase, A. THE NORTH AMERICAN SPECIES OF PANICUM. U. S. Natl. Mus., Contrib. U. S. Natl. Herbarium 15, 396 pp., illus. 1910.
[2] Anonymous. FOREST SERVICE NURSERY GROWS UNUSUAL PLANTS. U. S. Dept. Agr. Clip Sheet 878 : 2. 1935.
[3] Piper, C. V. CULTIVATED GRASSES OF SECONDARY IMPORTANCE. U. S. Dept. Agr. Farmers' Bull. 1433, 42 pp., illus. 1925.

Proso (*P. milia'ceum*), also called broomcorn millet and hog millet, is considered the type species of the genus, and is believed to have been the first cereal cultivated by man. Although not a range grass, proso is an excellent soiling crop, yields fair forage, and the grain is good poultry and hog feed.[4]

Para grass (*P. purpuras'cens*, syn. *P. barbino'de*), a perennial, probably native to South America, is cultivated in Florida, and is coming into increasing prominence in Texas and the Gulf Coast region, usually being propagated by runner cuttings. It is adaptable to moist places where the temperature does not drop below about 18° F., makes good hay and pasture, and is especially valuable for planting pond margins and in soils which are too wet for the cultivation of other crops.[5] Its possibilities of use in the far West, however, seem to be limited to wet sites and those where irrigation is available.

Among the panicgrasses native to the western range States, bulb panicgrass (*P. bulbo'sum*) and vine-mesquite (*P. obtu'sum*) are probably the most important and are discussed in detail elsewhere in this handbook. The eight species noted below are probably the most outstanding of the others.

Arizona panicgrass (*P. arizo'nicum*), an annual from 8 to 24 inches tall, with branching stems bent at the base and frequently rooting at the joints, occurs from Florida to Texas, Mexico, and southern California. The leaves are rounded at the base, hairless on both surfaces and rough beneath. This species has good palatability and occurs in sufficient abundance in Arizona to be of some local importance.

Cushion witchgrass (*P. barbipulvina'tum*) and witchgrass (*P. capilla're*) are very similar annuals, the former being more common in the West. Cushion witchgrass tends to be smaller, but otherwise is much like witchgrass, which is a variable species from 8 to 32 inches high, with large, open, purplish heads partially included in the upper leaf sheath until maturity. At maturity, the numerous fine branches of the heads are widely spreading, and bear long-stalked spikelets near their ends. The entire head of the plant commonly breaks off and is rolled about by the wind. Witchgrass is widely distributed in the East and central United States and occurs in Montana, Colorado, and California, possibly as an extension of its range. These two annuals have about the same palatability and are practically worthless to poor forage after the heads develop. In the spring, before the heads develop, these grasses generally rate as poor to fair or possibly fairly good forage, although in some localities, especially in the Southwest, they occupy somewhat higher rank.

Pacific panicgrass (*P. paci'ficum*), the commonest species of the genus in California, occurs on sandy shores and slopes and in moist crevices in rocks. It ranges northward to Oregon, Washington, and Idaho. During springtime, this perennial has erect, light-green stems, but, by autumn, the stems become prostrate-spreading and repeatedly branched from the upper and middle stem joints. This species is probably of at least fair palatability, although usually of negligible forage value, because of its limited occurrence.

Scribner panicgrass (*P. scribneria'num*), a widely distributed perennial, commonest in the Mississippi Valley, but ranging from Maine to Washington and from the District of Columbia through Tennessee, Arkansas, and Texas to California, is a palatable and nutritious grass but seldom is sufficiently abundant to be of importance on the western ranges.

Switchgrass (*P. virga'tum*) occurs in every State east of the Mississippi River and westward to southern Manitoba, southern Saskatchewan, eastern Montana, eastern Nevada, Arizona, and western Texas, and southward, through Mexico, to Central America. This grass is common and productive, especially on sandy, loose soils, in the Central States. It is occasionally cultivated both for pasture and hay but is more valuable as hay. In the Southwest switchgrass occurs mainly along stream banks, in moist valleys, canyons, moist uplands, and near tanks and pools but is seldom common in the mountains. Northward it has the reputation of producing but few leaves and is too rare to be of much importance as a range plant. This species, although palatable when young, is practically worthless as forage at maturity when the stems become hard. It is an erect, often purplish tinged perennial, from 2 to 5 feet high, with numerous, scaly, creeping rootstocks, and is an excellent soil binder.

---

[4] Martin, J. H. PROSO, OR HOG MILLET. U. S. Dept. Agr. Farmers' Bull. 1162, 15 pp., illus. 1920.
[5] Piper, C. V. IMPORTANT CULTIVATED GRASSES. U. S. Dept. Agr. Farmers' Bull. 1254, 38 pp., illus. 1922.

BULB PANICGRASS

Pa'nicum bulbo'sum

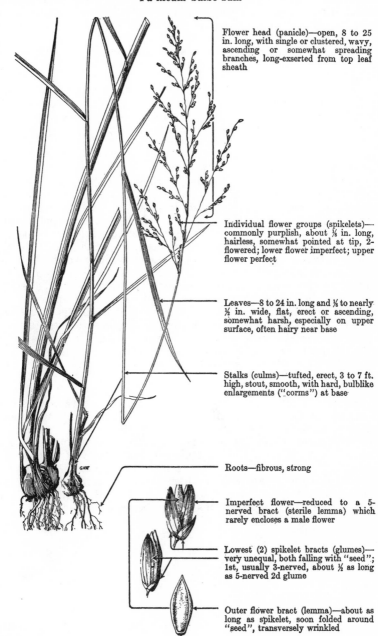

Flower head (panicle)—open, 8 to 25 in. long, with single or clustered, wavy, ascending or somewhat spreading branches, long-exserted from top leaf sheath

Individual flower groups (spikelets)—commonly purplish, about ⅛ in. long, hairless, somewhat pointed at tip, 2-flowered; lower flower imperfect; upper flower perfect

Leaves—8 to 24 in. long and ⅛ to nearly ½ in. wide, flat, erect or ascending, somewhat harsh, especially on upper surface, often hairy near base

Stalks (culms)—tufted, erect, 3 to 7 ft. high, stout, smooth, with hard, bulblike enlargements ("corms") at base

Roots—fibrous, strong

Imperfect flower—reduced to a 5-nerved bract (sterile lemma) which rarely encloses a male flower

Lowest (2) spikelet bracts (glumes)—very unequal, both falling with "seed"; 1st, usually 3-nerved, about ½ as long as 5-nerved 2d glume

Outer flower bract (lemma)—about as long as spikelet, soon folded around "seed", transversely wrinkled

Bulb panicgrass, thus named from the hard, bulblike enlargements, or corms at the bases of the stems, is one of the common perennial panicgrasses of the Southwest, occurring typically in moist canyons and valleys and in cultivated fields from Arizona and New Mexico to western Texas and Mexico. It is found chiefly in the upper woodland and ponderosa pine belts and, while usually of scattered occurrence, is at times locally abundant.

On the Coronado National Forest in southern Arizona where this species occurs extensively in pure stands, the grass ranks as good forage, being grazed by cattle and horses from July to December. Generally, it is considered fairly good to good forage for all classes of livestock during the spring and early summer while the growth is still young and tender. Toward fall, however, it becomes coarse and tough, and is little grazed. In localities where bulb panicgrass grows in dense stands it is sometimes cut for hay. The hay is of good quality although bulky and light in weight. The species flourishes and produces valuable hay crops even on alkaline soils. It is one of the few hay plants which yield well on such soils.

Bulb panicgrass is, unfortunately, sometimes known as alkali sacaton, and because of that fact is probably sometimes confused with true alkali sacaton (*Sporobolus airoides*). Although bulb panicgrass is commonly a taller, coarser grass than alkali sacaton and has longer heads and wider leaves, size is not always the acceptable distinction between the two because the smaller specimens of bulb panicgrass are not so large as the sizable forms of alkali sacaton. Bulb panicgrass, however, is readily recognizable by the cormlike swellings at the base of the hollow stems, and because the spikelets fall from the stems intact. Alkali sacaton shows no swellings at the base of its pithy stems, and the glumes of the spikelets are persistent, remaining after the seed falls. Moreover, in bulb panicgrass the spikelets include a well developed sterile lemma, and hence are two-flowered, whereas the spikelets of all *Sporobolus* species are one-flowered.

A variety of this species, little bulb panicgrass (*P. bulbosum minus*, syn. *P. bulbosum sciaphilum*), occurs along river banks and in ravines of mesas and similar situations in the Rocky Mountains and Sierra Madre Mountains from New Mexico and Arizona to central Mexico. It is a smaller plant than the species, commonly less than 3 feet high, with smaller spikelets, narrower leaf blades, and smaller corms at the base of the stems. The corms are usually not over one-quarter of an inch in diameter and commonly many together attached at the base to a rootstock. Its palatability is about the same as that of typical forms of the species.

VINE-MESQUITE

Pa'nicum obtu'sum

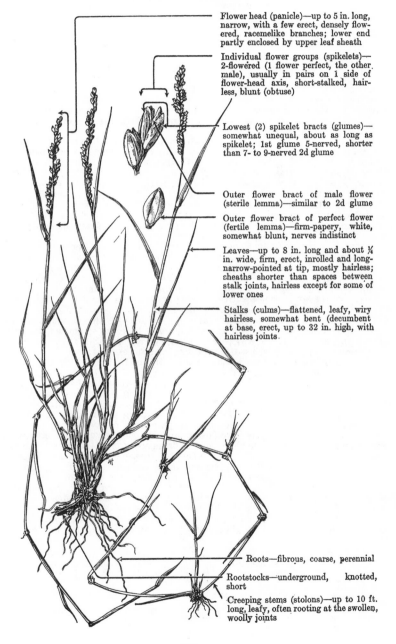

Flower head (panicle)—up to 5 in. long, narrow, with a few erect, densely flowered, racemelike branches; lower end partly enclosed by upper leaf sheath

Individual flower groups (spikelets)—2-flowered (1 flower perfect, the other male), usually in pairs on 1 side of flower-head axis, short-stalked, hairless, blunt (obtuse)

Lowest (2) spikelet bracts (glumes)—somewhat unequal, about as long as spikelet; 1st glume 5-nerved, shorter than 7- to 9-nerved 2d glume

Outer flower bract of male flower (sterile lemma)—similar to 2d glume

Outer flower bract of perfect flower (fertile lemma)—firm-papery, white, somewhat blunt, nerves indistinct

Leaves—up to 8 in. long and about ¼ in. wide, firm, erect, inrolled and long-narrow-pointed at tip, mostly hairless; sheaths shorter than spaces between stalk joints, hairless except for some of lower ones

Stalks (culms)—flattened, leafy, wiry hairless, somewhat bent (decumbent at base, erect, up to 32 in. high, with hairless joints.

Roots—fibrous, coarse, perennial

Rootstocks—underground, knotted, short

Creeping stems (stolons)—up to 10 ft. long, leafy, often rooting at the swollen, woolly joints

153

Vine-mesquite is unusual among western range grasses in that it produces creeping stems, or stolons, which sometimes are 10 feet long. It is also known, especially in Texas, as grapevine-mesquite and, in the Southwest, as vine panic-grass. Other local names are ricegrass, vine grass, and wire grass. *Obtusum* is the Latin for blunt, referring to the rounded spikelets; hence this species is sometimes known as blunt panicgrass.

This perennial occurs from western Missouri and southern Colorado south to Arizona, Texas, and Mexico. It is found typically in sandy or gravelly soil, chiefly in moist sites along stream and ditch banks, both in the open and in the shade of trees and shrubs. Vine-mesquite extends upward into the pon-derosa-pine belt, but is more common at lower altitudes. This grass requires warmth and is best adapted to a fine, compact soil but needs more moisture than is usually available in the greater part of the Southwest.

The species varies considerably in the amount and character of the leafage produced, which has resulted in rather conflicting reports about its forage value. Texans often report that livestock will not eat vine-mesquite if other forage is available. On the other hand, most Arizona and New Mexico ob-servers agree that it is fair to fairly good forage for all classes of livestock, at least while it is green and tender, although some New Mexico investigators speak of it as not uncommonly a weedy encroacher in pastures and fields and as not very good feed, though stock eat it when it is green and tender or when there is nothing better available.[1] The plant is readily established from seed, which is produced in abundance and ordinarily disseminated during July, August, and a part of September. Viability of the seed is generally low.[2][3] It also reproduces by means of long above-ground stolons as well as by short underground rootstocks. Because of its excellent soil-binding qualities and prolific reproduction system, the species seems to offer sufficient promise to warrant more extensive experiments in its cultivation.

Recent investigations by Hendricks[4] of the Southwestern Forest and Range Experiment Station, United States Forest Service, indicate that vine-mesquite, because it spreads rapidly by means of its stolons, or runners, and forms a dense mat of vegetation, is well adapted to assist in the control of soil erosion in the Southwest, especially in arroyos, gullies, and bottomlands. If already present on the area, conservative grazing will permit the natural extension of vine-mesquite, as well as other grasses, to form the necessary protective cover. Hendricks finds that transplants of seedlings of vine-mesquite usually result successfully if made at the beginning of either the spring or fall rainy season in years of average or better than average rainfall. Sod containing vine-mesquite may also be used to establish spots in critical areas.

Botanically, vine-mesquite is, at least so far as United States species are concerned, a unique species of *Panicum*, because of its long-creeping stems, with their swollen, woolly joints, the joints of the erect stems being quite hair-less, and also because of its glumes, which are nearly as long as the spikelets and only slightly unequal. The flower heads are usually partially enclosed in the upper leaf sheath and consist of a few, one-sided, spikelike densely flowered racemes. The spikelets occur in pairs, one on a shorter stem than the other, and are usually two-flowered, only one flower producing seed. The lemma of the fertile flower is white, firm-papery, and indistinctly nerved, which probably explains why the plant is sometimes known as ricegrass. Most species of panicgrass lack creeping stems, and have very unequal glumes which, as a rule, are conspicuously shorter than the spikelets. The only known species which at all closely resembles vine-mesquite is *P. repandum* of Brazil. However, Savannah panicgrass (*P. gymnocarpon*), which occurs in wet sites from Texas to Florida, is similar to vine-mesquite in that its stems are decumbent, root at the joints, and are often widely creeping. The fruit of vine-mesquite is almost one-eighth of an inch long and is not notably exposed at maturity.

[1] Wooton, E. O., and Standley, P. C. THE GRASSES AND GRASS-LIKE PLANTS OF NEW MEXICO. N. Mex. Agr. Expt. Sta. Bull. 81, [176] pp., illus. 1912.
[2] Jackson, C. V. SEED GERMINATION IN CERTAIN NEW MEXICO RANGE GRASSES. Bot. Gaz. 86 : 270–294, illus. 1928.
[3] Wilson, C. P. THE ARTIFICIAL RESEEDING OF NEW MEXICO RANGES. N. Mex. Agr. Expt. Sta. Bull. 189, 37 pp., illus. 1931.
[4] Hendricks, B. A. VINE-MESQUITE FOR EROSION CONTROL ON SOUTHWESTERN RANGES. U. S. Dept. Agr. Leaflet 114, 8 pp., illus. 1936.

ALPINE TIMOTHY

Phlo'um alpi'num

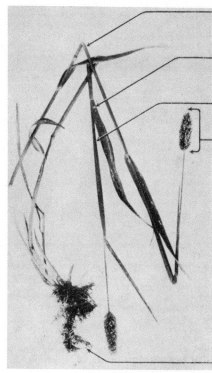

Stalks (culms)—erect, 6 to 24 in. tall, simple, smooth, hairless, not swollen but often bending or somewhat creeping at base

Leaves—flat, short (up to 6 in. long), up to ⅜ in. wide, smooth on under surface, harsh to the touch above; lower leaves usually longer than upper ones

Leaf sheaths—usually shorter than space between joints of stem; upper ones inflated

Flower head (panicle)—dense, spike-like, egg-shaped or oblong, short (½ to 2 in. long), 1½ to 3 times as long as wide, usually purplish

Roots—fibrous

Individual flower group (spikelet)—1-flowered, small, somewhat flattened

Lowest (2) spikelet bracts (glumes)—persistent, usually equal, about ⅛ in. long, thin, hairy-fringed on keel, abruptly bristled (awned) from slanting summit; awns up to ⅛ in. long

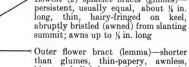

Outer flower bract (lemma)—shorter than glumes, thin-papery, awnless, blunt and slightly toothed on summit, 3- to 5-nerved

Inner flower bract (palea)—nearly as long as lemma, narrow, thin-papery

Alpine timothy, also known as mountain timothy and wild timothy, is the only species of *Phleum* known to be native to North America. It is a small sister species of the well-known cultivated timothy (*P. pratense*) which was supposedly introduced into this country from Europe. The genus belongs to the redtop tribe (Agrostideae) and consists of about 10 annual and perennial grasses of the Temperate and Arctic regions of the world. Alpine timothy is widely distributed throughout the cooler and higher portions of North America, ranging from Alaska and Labrador southward to New Hampshire, northern Michigan, South Dakota, New Mexico, and southern California. It also occurs in Mexico, Chile, Patagonia, and in northern Europe and Asia.

As the common name and the specific name *alpinum* imply, this species grows principally in alpine and subalpine situations, although it also extends down through the spruce-fir zone and into the aspen zone. Alpine timothy also occurs at sea level in Alaska and along the Northwest coast where the cool sea breezes produce a climate simulating that of alpine regions. It is a moisture-loving plant, as is suggested by the generic name *Phleum*, which is derived from *phleos*, an old Greek name for some kind of water plant or reed. Some authorities [1] believe that the Greek *phleos* was the cattail (*Typha*), and that Linnaeus, Latinizing it to *Phleum*, applied it to the timothies because of the natural habitat and the cattaillike spikes. This species characteristically grows in moist or wet mountain meadows, parks, along stream banks, in swales, around springs, and in the rich muck of bogs and marshes. It also appears on relatively well-drained soils on grassy slopes, in weed and aspen types, dry meadows, and occasionally in moist sagebrush parks. This grass is usually associated with other moisture-loving plants such as bluegrasses, bistort, clovers, hairgrass, meadow sedges and rushes, redtops, and willows. The stands are often dense and almost pure, but in many localities this species occurs scatteringly and forms only a minor portion of the range vegetation.

Alpine timothy is relished by all classes of livestock and is usually given a palatability rating of good to very good for cattle and horses, and fairly good to good for sheep. It is highly palatable to elk and is one of the grasses eaten most readily by deer. The plants produce a fair amount of nutritious foliage, which usually remains green and succulent throughout the summer and is especially valuable as a late feed. Stockmen consider it a washy feed during the early part of the season when it is young and very succulent. In some localities sheep make little early use of this grass as they avoid the excessively wet situations where it often occurs. However, as the season advances the soils usually become drier, and the plants, being less succulent, are then grazed with unusual relish. Alpine timothy is able to withstand heavy trampling fairly well, as it reproduces by means of shoots from its decumbent base as well as by seed.[2] The fertility of the seed crop, which usually ripens during August and September, is considerably above the average of typical subalpine herbaceous plants. Sampson's tests of alpine timothy seed in northeastern Oregon [3] gave an average germination of 69.5 percent.

Alpine timothy is often confused with the common cultivated timothy. The two species have somewhat the same general appearance, but alpine timothy is a much smaller plant. It ranges from 6 inches to 2 feet in height; has a short, egg-shaped or oblong flower head about one and one-half to three times as long as broad, and short leaves. The leaf sheaths are usually shorter than the space between the joints (internodes) on the stem and the upper sheaths are inflated. In contrast, cultivated timothy is a tall plant, usually 2 to 6 feet high, with elongated cylindrical flower heads up to 8 inches long, and leaves up to 13 inches in length; the leaf sheaths are often longer than the internodes and are usually not inflated. Furthermore, the awns on the glumes of alpine timothy are up to one-eighth of an inch long, or about twice the length of the awns of timothy, giving the flower heads a bristly appearance. The stems of alpine timothy are not swollen at the base but are often bent or decumbent; on the other hand, timothy stems are distinctly swollen or bulblike at the base.

---

[1] Stebler, F. G., and Schröter, C. THE BEST FORAGE PLANTS FULLY DESCRIBED AND FIGURED. . . . Transl. by A. N. McAlpine. 171 pp., illus. London. 1889.
[2] Sampson, A. W., and Chase, A. RANGE GRASSES OF CALIFORNIA. Calif. Agr. Expt. Sta. Bull. 430, 94 pp., illus. 1927.
[3] Sampson, A. W. IMPORTANT RANGE PLANTS : THEIR LIFE HISTORY AND FORAGE VALUE. U. S. Dept. Agr. Bull. 545, 63 pp., illus. 1917.

TIMOTHY

Phle'um praten'se

Leaf sheaths—often longer than spaces between joints of stem; upper ones usually not inflated

Leaves—flat, 3 to 13 in. long, up to ⅜ in. wide, usually somewhat harsh to the touch.

Flower head (panicle)—dense, spike-like, narrowly cylindrical, 1 to 6 or sometimes 8 in. long, erect

Stalks (culms)—tufted, erect, usually 2 to 4 ft. high, from a swollen or bulblike base, simple, smooth, hairless

Roots—fibrous, without creeping root-stocks

Individual flower group (spikelet)—1-flowered, small, somewhat flattened

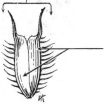

Lowest (2) spikelet bracts (glumes)—persistent, usually equal, up to ³⁄₁₆ in. long, thin, hairy-fringed on keel, abruptly bristled (awned) from slanting summit; awn short, about ¹⁄₃₂ in. long, ess than ½ length of glume

Inner flower bract (palea)—about as long as lemma, narrow, thin-papery

Outer flower bract (lemma)—about ½ as long as glumes, thin-papery, awnless, blunt and slightly toothed on summit, 3- to 5-nerved

Timothy is by far the most important perennial grass cultivated in North America. It is best known because of its extremely widespread use for hay, but also merits recognition as a very important forage plant on the western ranges. Whether it is native to parts of the North American continent is still somewhat in controversy, although the preponderance of belief is that timothy was presumably accidentally introduced into America in early colonial times from Europe. All authorities, however, seem to be agreed that it was first cultivated on this continent; that it bears an American name (timothy), and that it was introduced into the Old World as a cultivated plant from this country. Dr. Jared Eliot (1685–1763) writes in his Essay on Field Husbandry in New England that a man named Timothy Herd had collected seed of this grass and cultivated it there as early as 1747 and that, from him, it had come to be known as Herd's grass. In a letter to Eliot, dated July 16, 1747, Benjamin Franklin states that Herd grass seed received proved to be mere timothy. This appears to be the earliest record of the name timothy, which supposedly refers to Timothy Hansen, who was responsible for the introduction of this grass into Maryland, Virginia, and the Carolinas.[1][2] This plant is now known all over the world as timothy. The specific name *pratense* is Latin and refers to the meadow habitat of this species.

Timothy is now distributed throughout most of North America, as well as in Europe, Asia, and other temperate regions of the world. It is well adapted to cool, humid habitats and does best in the northern half of the United States and southward in the mountains. Its southern limit of successful culture practically coincides with the northern limit of cotton culture.[3] This species thrives fairly well along the Alaskan coast, produces satisfactorily, and survives the winters practically up to the Arctic circle. Timothy will grow under a wide diversity of site conditions but grows best on well-drained but moist clay or loam soils. It has become firmly established on many ranges and is now widely distributed throughout the mountains of the west, thriving best at medium elevations but growing successfully up to about 10,500 feet in Colorado. In the range country this grass usually grows in moist meadows, weedy or grassy parks, along stream banks, in moist canyon bottoms, open grassy slopes, woodlands, openings in the timber, and along roadsides and trails.

This plant has given better all-around results in the artificial reseeding of western mountain range lands than any other species. Experiments [4] have shown that it can be successfully and profitably used in reseeding inland range lands where the soil is moist and the growing season of sufficient duration for seed production. It is also suitable for reseeding cutover, burned-over, and overgrazed mountain ranges on the west coastal slope where the annual precipi-

[1] Piper, C. V. FORAGE PLANTS AND THEIR CULTURE. Rev., 671 pp., illus. New York. 1924.
[2] Stebler, F. G., and Schröter, C. THE BEST FORAGE PLANTS FULLY DESCRIBED AND FIGURED. . . . Transl. by A. N. McAlpine. 171 pp., illus. London. 1889.
[3] Piper, C. V. IMPORTANT CULTIVATED GRASSES. U. S. Dept. Agr. Farmers' Bull. 1254, 38 pp., illus. 1922.
[4] Forsling, C. L., and Dayton, W. A. ARTIFICIAL RESEEDING ON WESTERN MOUNTAIN RANGE LANDS. U. S. Dept. Agr. Circ. 178, 48 pp., illus. 1931.

tation exceeds 40 inches per year. Timothy can usually be introduced at a lower cost than any of the other highly desirable species because the seed is inexpensive compared with that of most other cultivated forage plants. Eight to fifteen pounds of seed per acre is required to produce a good stand. It seldom, if ever, pays to sow less than 8 pounds per acre on the range, since seed can usually be obtained for 5 to 15 cents a pound. This grass is especially valuable for reseeding, with such a slow-starting perennial as Kentucky bluegrass.[4]

Timothy becomes established by the second year after seeding and, because of its usual luxuriant growth, produces a great abundance of nutritious forage. The herbage is highly palatable to all classes of livestock, being rated as very good for cattle and horses and good for sheep. Elk consume the plants with relish and deer sometimes crop them lightly. This plant stands up very well if properly grazed but is not resistant to heavy grazing, as the "bulbs" are easily injured by close pasturing and heavy trampling. Timothy is known to have held up for 12 years or longer on good range lands, but ordinarily the stands tend to die out in about 6 or 7 years. In localities where fertile seed is produced the stands usually maintain themselves satisfactorily and the seed is often carried by livestock, wind, and other agencies to adjoining areas. At the higher elevations where the growing season is too short for viable seed to mature, this species does not revegetate naturally. However, on such sites where timothy may become readily established, the low cost of seed justifies its use in artificial reseeding.

Timothy is an outstanding crop plant in this country, with an annual value running into hundreds of millions of dollars. Piper[3] states that "the extent of its culture is four times as great as that of all other hay grasses combined and equal to that of all other hay plants, including clover and alfalfa." Timothy hay is the standard for all grass hay sold on the market. It has a rather high palatability combined with a moderate nutritive value, and because of its slight laxative effect it is practically impossible to injure an animal by overfeeding. It is especially valued for horse feed but is considered inferior to alfalfa and clover for fattening stock or feeding dairy cows.

The bulk of timothy hay grown in the United States is produced in the northeastern portion of the country, the region extending west to the Missouri River and southward to Missouri and Virginia. This grass is, however, also widely grown for hay in the West. In most western localities irrigation is necessary for successful production, although it is grown without irrigation in some of the moister valleys and on the northwest coast. This plant is especially popular in some of the high mountain valleys too cool for the most successful growing of alfalfa. It is often sown in mixture with red or alsike clover, redtop, and, in some localities, with alfalfa. The mixed hay generally yields better and has a higher feeding value for cattle and sheep than timothy alone.

Timothy alone is not well adapted to permanent pastures but is very useful in mixture with longer-lived pasture grasses. It often forms an important element in temporary pastures; timothy hay meadows are usually grazed in the fall after the hay is harvested and frequently again in the spring.

In addition to timothy, two other introduced species of *Phleum* occur in America. They are *P. grae'cum* and *P. bellar'di*, unimportant and little known annuals found in this country only at a few seaports on dumping grounds for ballast. Alpine timothy (*P. alpi'num*), the only species known to be native to America, and which also occurs in Europe and Asia, is discussed separately in this handbook.

BLUEGRASSES

Po'a spp.

The bluegrasses compose one of the largest, most important economically, and most taxonomically difficult genera of the grass family (Gramineae). Under the type basis of botanical nomenclature it becomes the type of the grass family to which it gives the name Poaceae, used in many of the botanical manuals. The bluegrasses belong to the immense fescue tribe (Festuceae), which includes the bromegrasses, fescues, melic grasses, orchard grass, and numerous other well-known genera. The name *poa* is a Greek word for grass, or any plant used as fodder by domestic livestock. The common name bluegrass refers to the characteristic blue-green color of the foliage of many species of *Poa* and perhaps was first applied to the species now called Canada bluegrass (*P. compressa*). The bluegrasses are often called speargrasses, and sometimes also pinegrasses and greengrasses. In England they are called meadowgrasses, because they are important constituents of most meadow pastures.

The bluegrass genus is easily the largest and one of the most widely distributed groups of western range grasses. On a conservative basis about 65 species of *Poa* occur on western range lands, and between about 150 and 200 species grow throughout the world, particularly in the temperate and cooler regions. Save only in the hotter and drier climates, almost wherever grasses grow, from the seashore to the highest limit of vegetation on the loftiest peaks, from the Arctic to the Antarctic, the genus *Poa* is represented.[1]

Bluegrasses are widely distributed throughout the United States, the majority occurring in the mountainous regions of the northern and western sections of the country. All but three or four of them are perennials. Bluegrasses are relatively unimportant in the Southwest, because the climate is too dry and the winds too desiccating, except in the higher mountains, to permit them to grow successfully. While most of the species occurring in the United States are native, a few have been introduced and cultivated for pasturage and lawns, thus greatly extending their range. Especially prominent among these foreign species are Kentucky bluegrass (*P. pratensis*) and Canada bluegrass, which have been planted extensively in Canada and the northern half of the United States as far west as Missouri and Iowa and, to a more limited extent, in the mountainous regions of the South and West. These two cultivated species have spread aggressively and are now common along ditch banks, in meadows, along roadsides, and are even moderately abundant on some of the western ranges. Native species of bluegrass are often the most important forage grasses of many of the cooler and moister western ranges. They occur in a great variety of sites, from sand dunes to mountain meadows. The majority, however, favor rich, moist, well-drained soils and are characteristic of meadows, grassy parks along stream banks, in shaded woodlands, and in open sage-

---

[1] Lamson-Scribner, F. ECONOMIC GRASSES. U. S. Dept. Agr., Div. Agrost. Bull. 14, rev., 85 pp., illus. 1900.

brush and wheatgrass types. A few species occur on the drier, in-fertile, open side hills, ridges, and waste places. Several species of bluegrass, including Kentucky bluegrass and Canada bluegrass, are used for reseeding depleted range lands. These two species are also very effective for checking erosion, as they grow and spread rapidly and form a continuous sod.

The bluegrasses are primarily valued for pasturage, although a few species are cut for hay. With a few exceptions they are all relished by both wild game and domesticated livestock. They rank among the most palatable of all range grasses, many of them being rated as excellent for cattle, horses, sheep, and elk. Such turf-form-ing species as Kentucky bluegrass, Canada bluegrass, Wheeler blue-grass (*P. nervosa*, syn. *P. wheeleri*), and Texas bluegrass (*P. arachnifera*) are well adapted for pasture and lawns. Of these, Kentucky bluegrass and Canada bluegrass are by far the most im-portant. These two grasses are major components of most lawn and pasture grass mixtures except in the far South. They grow luxuriantly in humid regions or where ample moisture is supplied, readily forming a dense sod cover. Their foliage is dark bluish green, and very attractive. Many of the native bluegrasses, such as muttongrass (*P. fendleriana*), Nevada bluegrass (*P. nevadensis*), Canby bluegrass (*P. canbyi*), pine bluegrass (*P. scabrella*, syn. *P. buckleyana*), Sandberg bluegrass (*P. secunda*, syn *P. sandbergii*), Wheeler bluegrass, and the introduced wood bluegrass (*P. nemor-alis*), are important range plants because they furnish an abundance of tender and nutritious forage.

Poa is distinguished from other genera in the fescue tribe by the following characters: spikelets—small, awnless; lemmas—with heavy midnerve like the keel of a boat, not bifid at the tip, often hairy or cobwebby at the base; glumes—one- to three-nerved, entire; leaf blades flat or folded, with boat-shaped tips.

CANADA BLUEGRASS

Po'a compres'sa

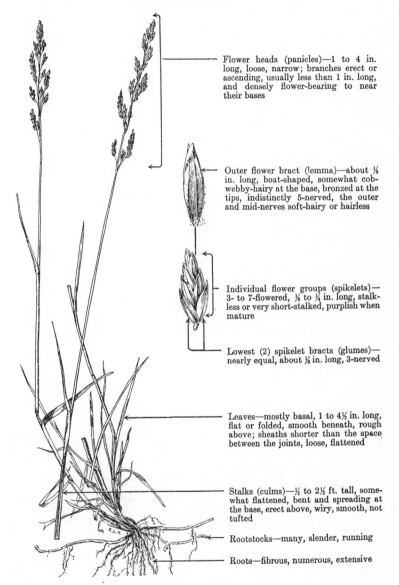

Flower heads (panicles)—1 to 4 in. long, loose, narrow; branches erect or ascending, usually less than 1 in. long, and densely flower-bearing to near their bases

Outer flower bract (lemma)—about ⅛ in. long, boat-shaped, somewhat cobwebby-hairy at the base, bronzed at the tips, indistinctly 5-nerved, the outer and mid-nerves soft-hairy or hairless

Individual flower groups (spikelets)— 3- to 7-flowered, ⅛ to ¼ in. long, stalkless or very short-stalked, purplish when mature

Lowest (2) spikelet bracts (glumes)— nearly equal, about ⅛ in. long, 3-nerved

Leaves—mostly basal, 1 to 4½ in. long, flat or folded, smooth beneath, rough above; sheaths shorter than the space between the joints, loose, flattened

Stalks (culms)—½ to 2½ ft. tall, somewhat flattened, bent and spreading at the base, erect above, wiry, smooth, not tufted

Rootstocks—many, slender, running

Roots—fibrous, numerous, extensive

This hardy perennial grass is generally designated throughout the United States and Canada as Canada bluegrass, although it has numerous local names, including English bluegrass, flat-stemmed grass, wiregrass, and Virginia bluegrass. Canada bluegrass is a rather appropriate name for the following reasons: (1) Some of the first botanical collections of the species in North America were made near Quebec; (2) the species appears to have first attained outstanding commercial importance in Canada; (3) it is most abundant in the Great Lakes region and particularly in the area bordering their northern shores, more especially southern Ontario; (4) probably the chief centers of commercial production of Canada bluegrass seed are in Ontario and Quebec. Because of its characteristic, dark blue-green foliage, this was perhaps the first of the poas to be called bluegrass. The Latin specific name *compressa* refers to the flattened (compressed) appearance of the stems (culms) and leaf sheaths.

Canada bluegrass is distributed widely throughout the cooler regions of North America, from Newfoundland and British Columbia southward to Georgia and California. However, insofar as its United States range is concerned, this grass is most common and abundant in that sector extending from New England to West Virginia and Ohio, and westward to Indiana and Missouri. Since being introduced into the Pacific Northwest, it has increased measurably and is now fairly common in many places.

In the southern United States, particularly the Southwest, Canada bluegrass occurs in the higher mountains, and on irrigated lawns and pastures where abundant moisture is supplied artificially. Throughout the entire western range country this grass occurs sparsely in the mountain meadows, parks, and along dry stream banks, but occasionally is abundant on sites where it has been seeded. It is very persistent, when once established, and will do better than Kentucky bluegrass on the poorer and drier sites.[1]

Although the former conception was that Canada bluegrass is native to America, most authorities now agree that it was introduced from the Old World, where it is indigenous.

Canada bluegrass grows better than any other grass commonly cultivated in the cooler parts of this country on stiff clay soils of low fertility, does well on gravelly areas, and even grows sparsely on sandy soils. This grass often occurs in pure, dense stands on the sides of highway and railroad cuts, and on eroded areas whose subsoil has been exposed. However, on the better top soils, this grass cannot cope with Kentucky bluegrass and other grasses, which frequently abound on such areas. Kentucky bluegrass and Canada bluegrass do not, as a rule, grow naturally intermixed in the sod, though they are often associated in neighboring but separated patches. Canada bluegrass reaches its greatest perfection and grows most luxuriantly in southern Ontario and western New York on glacial soils derived from sand, stone, and clay.

The lush foliage of Canada bluegrass is highly relished by all classes of livestock, and is also grazed to a considerable extent by elk. It is also cropped lightly by deer, especially during the spring and early summer when the foliage is tender and succulent. The species rates as choice forage for cattle and horses, and from good to very good for sheep. Although not so palatable as Kentucky bluegrass, it is highly nutritious. Sampson[2] states that "extensive chemical analysis and some feeding tests indicate that Canada bluegrass is nutritious though probably of somewhat less food value than Kentucky bluegrass because the former contains more crude fiber, only part of which is digestible." Canada bluegrass rates as much better pasturage if it is grazed and not allowed to become overly mature, as livestock eat the younger foliage with greater avidity. It withstands close use, is resistant to heavy trampling, and recuperates rapidly after severe grazing.

This grass is extensively used on the poorer soils, especially in the northeastern States and Canada, as pasturage, as hay, for lawns and golf courses.[3][4] However, it does not form so dense a sod or develop such a rich, uniform, dark green color as Kentucky bluegrass. Experimental range reseeding tests indicate that this species has potential value for reseeding certain depleted or badly eroded areas where precipitation is adequate and temperatures are cool.

[1] Forsling, C. L., and Dayton, W. A. ARTIFICIAL RESEEDING ON WESTERN MOUNTAIN RANGE LANDS. U. S. Dept. Agr. Circ. 178, 48 pp., illus. 1931.
[2] Sampson, A. W. BLUEGRASSES WITH A DISCUSSION OF CHEMICAL ANALYSIS. Natl. Wool Grower 6 (10) : 23–25, illus. 1916.
[3] Oakley, R. A. CANADA BLUEGRASS: ITS CULTURE AND USES. U. S. Dept. Agr. Farmers' Bull. 402, 20 pp., illus. 1910.
[4] Piper, C. V. IMPORTANT CULTIVATED GRASSES. U. S. Dept. Agr. Farmers' Bull. 1254, 38 pp., illus. 1922.

MUTTONGRASS

Po'a fendleria'na, syns. *P. brevipanicula'ta, P. longipeduncula'ta, P. scabrius'cula*

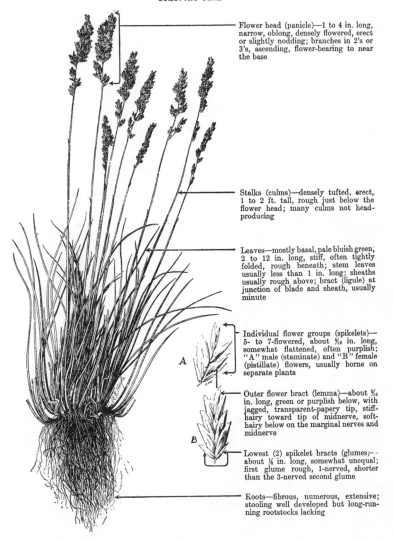

Flower head (panicle)—1 to 4 in. long, narrow, oblong, densely flowered, erect or slightly nodding; branches in 2's or 3's, ascending, flower-bearing to near the base

Stalks (culms)—densely tufted, erect, 1 to 2 ft. tall, rough just below the flower head; many culms not head-producing

Leaves—mostly basal, pale bluish green; 2 to 12 in. long, stiff, often tightly folded, rough beneath; stem leaves usually less than 1 in. long; sheaths usually rough above; bract (ligule) at junction of blade and sheath, usually minute

A

Individual flower groups (spikelets)— 5- to 7-flowered, about $\frac{5}{16}$ in. long, somewhat flattened, often purplish; "A" male (staminate) and "B" female (pistillate) flowers, usually borne on separate plants

Outer flower bract (lemma)—about $\frac{3}{16}$ in. long, green or purplish below, with jagged, transparent-papery tip, stiff-hairy toward tip of midnerve, soft-hairy below on the marginal nerves and midnerve

B

Lowest (2) spikelet bracts (glumes)—about $\frac{1}{8}$ in. long, somewhat unequal; first glume rough, 1-nerved, shorter than the 3-nerved second glume

Roots—fibrous, numerous, extensive; stooling well developed but long-running rootstocks lacking

Muttongrass, also called Fendler bluegrass and mutton bluegrass, is one of the most widely distributed and important of native blue-grasses. In fact, throughout the central Rocky Mountains it ranks among the 20 most important range grasses. The common name muttongrass is very appropriate, as it is one of the most nutritious forage plants in New Mexico and Arizona, being prized for fattening sheep. Its specific name *fendleriana* is in honor of August Fendler (1813–83).

This species ranges from southeastern British Columbia to Manitoba, western South Dakota, Colorado, western Texas, northern Mexico, California, and Idaho. It has been reported from eastern Washington, but the record is very doubtful. In New Mexico and other parts of the Southwest this tufted perennial is probably the only native species of bluegrass sufficiently abundant to be of much range value. In the southern parts of its range this bunchgrass usually grows at higher elevations, but does not appear on the lower slopes and mesas, where the summers are too hot and dry for bluegrasses. However, throughout its more northerly range it frequently occurs on the foothills and lower slopes, usually intermixed with needle-grasses, bromes, pentstemons, sagebrush, and sedges.

Muttongrass grows typically from the piñon-juniper belt, through the ponderosa pine and aspen types, to the Engelmann spruce-lodgepole pine zone, and reaches a maximum elevation of about 7,000 feet in Montana and Idaho, 10,000 feet in Utah, and 12,000 feet in Colorado. It appears chiefly on ridges and slopes and in open timbered areas and well-drained parks and meadows. Although this grass grows most commonly on well-drained, rich clay loams, it also inhabits drier, less fertile, shallow, gravelly or sandy soils on open hillsides, where it frequently becomes abundant. This species, like Sandberg bluegrass (*Poa secunda*, syn. *P. sandbergii*) is one of the most drought-resistant of the bluegrasses and, because of its deep fibrous root system, it frequently is an effective barrier against erosion. Germination tests have shown that the seeds of muttongrass are of low viability, which doubtless partly accounts for its failure thus far in artificial range reseeding experiments.[1]

This bluegrass, which starts growth during the warm days of late winter and early spring, is ready for grazing in advance of most other range forage plants. During early spring, it is particularly relished by all classes of domestic livestock. It rates as excellent forage for cattle and horses, and good for sheep, elk, and deer, despite that its palatability decreases somewhat at maturity, when the foliage becomes rather harsh and dry. Cattle and horses relish the plant and sheep eat considerable quantities throughout the entire summer. During the fall both cattle and horses eat the air-cured foliage, more tender and succulent forage being scarce.

Muttongrass, a perennial, is strictly a bunchgrass, varying from small tufts composed of a few stalks to dense tussocks a foot or more in diameter. The species is unusual among range grasses in that the male and female spikelets are generally borne on separate plants (dioecious). However, the female spikelets have only minute, non-functioning stamens. Muttongrass has no underground rootstocks, although the stems are often bent and more or less prostrate at the base, frequently resembling a short rootstock. This stooling characteristic governs the size of the individual tufts and facilitates reproduction and spread. This grass flowers from April to June, and matures seed from May to July, depending upon the locality and elevation.

[1] Forsling, C. L., and Dayton, W. A. ARTIFICIAL RESEEDING ON WESTERN MOUNTAIN RANGE LANDS. U. S. Dept. Agr. Circ. 178, 48 pp., illus. 1931.

NEVADA BLUEGRASS

Po'a nevaden'sis

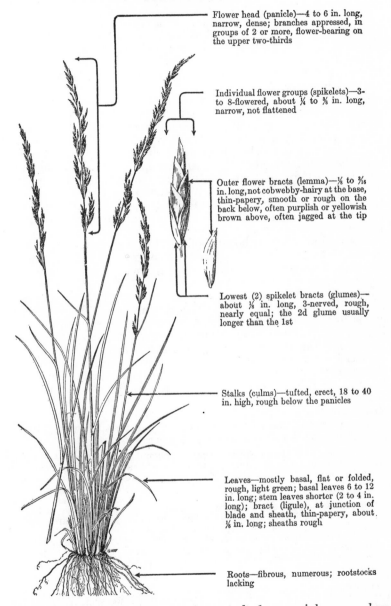

Flower head (panicle)—4 to 6 in. long, narrow, dense; branches appressed, in groups of 2 or more, flower-bearing on the upper two-thirds

Individual flower groups (spikelets)—3- to 8-flowered, about ¼ to ⅜ in. long, narrow, not flattened

Outer flower bracts (lemma)—⅛ to ³/₁₆ in. long, not cobwebby-hairy at the base, thin-papery, smooth or rough on the back below, often purplish or yellowish brown above, often jagged at the tip

Lowest (2) spikelet bracts (glumes)—about ⅛ in. long, 3-nerved, rough, nearly equal; the 2d glume usually longer than the 1st

Stalks (culms)—tufted, erect, 18 to 40 in. high, rough below the panicles

Leaves—mostly basal, flat or folded, rough, light green; basal leaves 6 to 12 in. long; stem leaves shorter (2 to 4 in. long); bract (ligule), at junction of blade and sheath, thin-papery, about ⅛ in. long; sheaths rough

Roots—fibrous, numerous; rootstocks lacking

Nevada bluegrass, a rather handsome tufted perennial, grows characteristically in small bunches, but seldom forms large tussocks. It is a widely distributed and important species throughout most of the range country, except in the Southwest. The grass is distributed along the east side of the Cascade and Sierra Nevada Mountains, from British Columbia southward to the Mohave Desert and east to Colorado, western South Dakota, and Montana.

The species occurs throughout an unusually wide elevational range, being found from several hundred feet above sea level in Washington and Oregon to as high as 11,000 feet in the central Colorado mountains. It is distributed on plains, dry meadows, and open hillsides, but seems to prefer the open woods of the slopes and foothills. Frequently, however, it is found along partially shaded stream banks and creek bottoms. In Washington and Oregon it appears not uncommonly in irrigated fields and meadows mixed with other grasses, where it occasionally establishes such a good stand as to produce a fair crop of hay. Although Nevada bluegrass grows luxuriantly and densely on the rich soils of moist situations, it is most common and widely distributed on the drier sites, growing on relatively infertile, loose, sandy, or loamy soils. Frequently it is a characteristic plant of the better scablands of Washington and Oregon and is often a conspicuous opponent of the sagebrush type, occurring in association with other grasses and such weeds as western yarrow, cinquefoil, lupine, and pentstemon.

Nevada bluegrass, although seldom abundant, is plentiful enough to furnish considerable forage throughout its range. This grass, one of the first to resume growth in the spring, is very palatable and highly relished by both game animals and domesticated livestock during the spring and early summer. At that time the plant is cropped closely by livestock. The palatability is somewhat lower at maturity, when the stalks and leaves become slightly tough, although cattle and horses continue to eat it throughout the summer. In the fall the air-dried foliage is grazed eagerly by all classes of livestock. No doubt the scarcity of more succulent and tender forage at that time, coupled with the softening of the dried leaves by the fall rains, enhances this late usage. In general, this grass rates as excellent forage for cattle and horses, good to excellent for sheep, good for elk, and fair to good for deer. Nevada bluegrass forage, when air-dried, is equal to timothy in feeding value, although the amount produced is somewhat meager.[1]

This grass, with the possible exception of Sandberg bluegrass (*P. secunda*, syn. *P. sandbergii*), is probably the most drought-enduring of the bluegrasses. Remarkably deep, extensive, and fibrous roots enable this plant to grow on rather dry sites and to endure extended droughts. Although drought-resistant, this grass succumbs to heavy grazing and trampling and hence has been killed out or reduced appreciably on many of the western ranges, because of intensive utilization. Nevada bluegrass begins flowering in May and matures an abundance of seed from July to September. The seed has fair viability and, if allowed to disseminate, will germinate eventually and grow on favorable sites.

Nevada bluegrass lacks the ability of Kentucky bluegrass to spread by underground rootstocks, and its vegetative reproduction by stooling is not pronounced.

[1] Knight, H. G., Hepner, F. E., and Nelson, A. WYOMING FORAGE PLANTS AND THEIR CHEMICAL COMPOSITION—STUDIES NO. 3. Wyo. Agr. Expt. Sta. Bull. 76, 119 pp., illus. 1908.

KENTUCKY BLUEGRASS

Po'a praten'sis

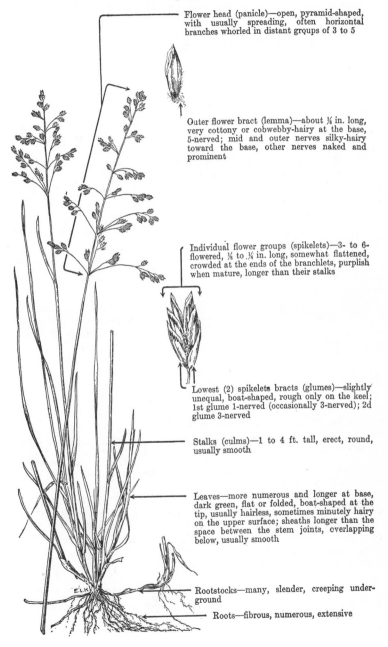

Flower head (panicle)—open, pyramid-shaped, with usually spreading, often horizontal branches whorled in distant groups of 3 to 5

Outer flower bract (lemma)—about ⅛ in. long, very cottony or cobwebby-hairy at the base, 5-nerved; mid and outer nerves silky-hairy toward the base, other nerves naked and prominent

Individual flower groups (spikelets)—3- to 6-flowered, ⅛ to ¼ in. long, somewhat flattened, crowded at the ends of the branchlets, purplish when mature, longer than their stalks

Lowest (2) spikelets bracts (glumes)—slightly unequal, boat-shaped, rough only on the keel; 1st glume 1-nerved (occasionally 3-nerved); 2d glume 3-nerved

Stalks (culms)—1 to 4 ft. tall, erect, round, usually smooth

Leaves—more numerous and longer at base, dark green, flat or folded, boat-shaped at the tip, usually hairless, sometimes minutely hairy on the upper surface; sheaths longer than the space between the stem joints, overlapping below, usually smooth

Rootstocks—many, slender, creeping underground

Roots—fibrous, numerous, extensive

169

Kentucky bluegrass, with the exception of timothy, is the most important perennial grass cultivated in North America, being particularly popular as a pasture and meadow grass; in fact, it is often referred to as "the king of the pasture lands." This plant is known by numerous common or local names, including lawn grass, speargrass, junegrass, and greensward. In England, where it abounds, the species is usually called meadow grass. Because of its abundance and luxuriant growth, throughout Kentucky, and especially near Lexington, "the city of the bluegrass", this species is most generally known as Kentucky bluegrass. The name bluegrass appears to have been first applied to Canada bluegrass (*P. compressa*), because of its characteristic bluish green foliage. Subsequently the entire *Poa* genus won recognition as bluegrasses.

The common belief that Kentucky bluegrass is indigenous in the United States probably is erroneous. Some agrostologists believe that certain bluegrass forms unquestionably native in the northern and cooler parts of North America may be varieties or subspecies of Kentucky bluegrass. Possibly this is true, although the present tendency is to regard such forms as distinct, though related species. According to Carrier and Bort [1] the first American record of what we now call Kentucky bluegrass emanated from William Penn who, in 1685, made an experimental sowing of the seed, obtained from England, in his courtyard. Penn wrote:

It grew very thick but I ordered it to be fed (grazed) being in the nature of a grass plot on purpose to see if the roots lay firm and though it had been mere sand cast off of the cellar but a year before the seed took much root and held and fed like old English ground.

Carrier and Bort (*op. cit.*) further record that in the same year (1685) Thomas Budd also advised farmers to sow English grass seed on well-drained low grounds, and the June notes in the New England Almanac for 1730 urge farmers to "cut your English grass seed." Various other references have been made to planting English grass seed. These observations, authorities agree, doubtless referred to what we now call Kentucky bluegrass.

The indications are that Kentucky bluegrass probably had not become widely distributed in Pennsylvania by 1749, since Kalm (as quoted by Pinkerton [2]) wrote as follows:

This country does not afford any green pastures like the Swedish ones; the woods are the places where the cattle must collect their food * * *. The trees stand far asunder; out the ground between them is not covered with green sods; for there are but few kinds of grasses in the woods, and they stand single and scattered.

This vivid description indicates that Kentucky bluegrass, if present, was certainly not abundant. The rich limestone soil of Kentucky, Virginia, and Pennsylvania provided an ideal habitat, and this grass spread rapidly over this humid region, especially on abandoned and cleared lands. In many places the species became so abundant and aggressive that it was considered a pest.

[1] Carrier, L., and Bort, K. S. THE HISTORY OF KENTUCKY BLUEGRASS AND WHITE CLOVER IN THE UNITED STATES. Jour. Amer. Soc. Agron. 8 : 256–266. 1916.
[2] Pinkerton, J. A GENERAL COLLECTION OF THE BEST AND MOST INTERESTING VOYAGES AND TRAVELS IN VARIOUS PARTS OF AMERICA. 4 v., illus. London, 1819.

Indians referred to it as "white man's foot grass"; they believed that, wherever the white man trod, this grass later grew as enduring markers of his footprints. The invasion and expansion of Kentucky bluegrass were so marked and rapid that early Kentucky pioneers, including James Nourse (in 1775), Daniel Boone (in 1784), and Imlay (in 1792), wrote about the abundance of grass meadows similar to those of Europe. At present most authorities agree that Kentucky bluegrass, like timothy and other of our cultivated grasses, was introduced into the country from the Old World, where it is native throughout Europe, northern Asia, and in the mountains of Algeria and Morocco.

Kentucky bluegrass is now widely distributed throughout most of North America north of Mexico, except in the warmer and desert areas. It is well adapted to the more humid and cooler temperate regions and grows most abundantly from Kentucky to Missouri northward to Alaska and Labrador. It also thrives in more arid regions where ample soil moisture is supplied. In the central Rocky Mountains it sometimes grows abundantly in the valleys but is seldom abundant in the mountains, although often common on localized areas, and is found at elevations up to as high as 10,000 feet. It occurs sparingly on favorable sites in the Southwest; and in California, where the summers are hot, is confined to the cool mountainous regions.

Kentucky bluegrass will grow on a wide diversity of sites, but it thrives best on well-drained loams or clay loams which are preeminently rich in humus. It is outstandingly abundant on the rich limestone soils of the historic bluegrass regions of Kentucky and Virginia, where the grass frequently attains such density as to crowd out all other species. Consequently experts formerly thought that Kentucky bluegrass required an abundance of lime. However, recent investigations of the United States Department of Agriculture at Arlington Farm, Va., show that application of lime to soils deficient in that chemical material had little or no effect on bluegrass growth. Kentucky bluegrass is frequently found on wet soils, but, unlike redtop, it does not thrive on acid soils and it cannot survive on water-logged sites. In the West this grass ordinarily inhabits the richer mountainous soils and moister sites, often occurring in meadows, along water courses, and in the more or less open and semishaded benchlands.

Kentucky bluegrass usually produces an abundance of nutritious forage and lush herbage which are highly palatable to all classes of livestock as well as to elk and deer. It rates as very good for cattle and horses, good for sheep and elk, and is one of the better forage grasses for deer. These game animals freely graze the tender leafage during the spring, immediately after growth begins, when the leaves are young and succulent. If moisture supply is ample and the temperature does not rise above 90° F., the foliage remains green and palatable throughout the summer. Kentucky bluegrass sod is unusually resistant to heavy utilization, being able not only to maintain itself but to increase the stand even on heavily trampled areas where the plants are cropped closely.

Kentucky bluegrass is especially adapted for use in the northern half of the United States. Southward to the Gulf of Mexico it is often grown in limited amounts but does not endure the prolonged summer heat and drought as well as do Bermuda grass (*Cynodon dactylon*), creeping bent (*Agrostis palustris*), carpet grass (*Axonopus compressus*), and certain other grasses. In the southern portions of the United States it often wilts and turns brown during the hot, dry summer months. However, after appearing dead, it frequently recovers rapidly during rains or when the cooler temperatures of autumn arrive. Throughout its range Kentucky bluegrass comes in voluntarily and occupies lands suited to its growth. It even aggressively invades irrigated timothy hay lands and reduces both the quantity and quality of the resultant mixed hay. This invasion is so marked that the timothy hay growers often class the grass as a major weed. Approximately 90 percent of the Kentucky bluegrass pastures in America are volunteer stands. Throughout much of its range this grass often dominates both fencerows and roadsides.

The species produces an abundance of high-quality seed. Commercial seed comes largely from the Kentucky bluegrass region of Kentucky and the Virginias, although recently Missouri and southern Iowa have gained some prominence as additional supply sources. Missouri, with approximately 8,000,-000 acres of Kentucky bluegrass, reaps an annual grazing income of about $24,000,000 from her excellent pastures and also harvests some $500,000 worth of seed.[3] The crop usually is harvested between about June 10 and 15 and often yields as high as 15 to 25 bushels per acre. The seed, as a rule, is especially viable and not uncommonly germinates from 55 to 75 percent.

By virtue of its strong seeding habits and its vigor in forming sod, Kentucky bluegrass is strikingly suitable for erosion control, especially within the northern part of the United States and in the western mountains. In the West, where moisture and fertility conditions are satisfactory, Kentucky bluegrass will effectively bind the soil of slopes, and the species is being used on a considerable scale in erosion control. Uhland[4] found Kentucky bluegrass very effective for checking erosion in Missouri.

Frequently this species has been used in reseeding depleted western range lands and good results have been secured, especially on fertile limestone soils.[5] Initial growth is slow, but ultimately good forage stands usually result on mountain areas, not too warm or too acid, where the annual precipitation averages over 20 inches. Kentucky bluegrass becomes established by the second year and eventually produces a sod and an abundance of nutritious forage. This grass is advisable for planting with early-starting species such as timothy, Italian ryegrass (*Lolium multiflorum*), and clover. The chief retardents which limit its use are the high cost of seed and the slowness of the species in establishing a satisfactory stand. However, its permanence, heavy production of nutritious forage, and ability to withstand severe trampling and grazing probably more than counterbalance these disadvantages.

Kentucky bluegrass, a dense turf and sod-forming plant, produces an abundance of slender, creeping rootstocks and a profusion of deep fibrous roots which often penetrate the soil to a depth of 3 to 4 feet. The numerous stalks (culms) grow from 1 to 4 feet high. These are somewhat tufted, smooth, and round. The leaves are mostly basal, smooth, soft, flat or folded, dark green, and succulent. The open panicle is pyramid-shaped; the lower branches longest, the upper ones successively shorter toward the peak.

[3] King, B. M. KENTUCKY BLUEGRASS IN MISSOURI. Mo. Agr. Expt. Sta. Circ. 155, 11 pp., illus. 1927.
[4] Uhland, R. E. CONTROLLING SMALL GULLIES BY BLUEGRASS SOD. U. S. Dept. Agr. Leaflet 82, 4 pp., illus. 1931.
[5] Forsling, C. L., and Dayton, W. A. ARTIFICIAL RESEEDING ON WESTERN MOUNTAIN RANGE LANDS. U. S. Dept. Agr. Circ. 178, 48 pp., illus. 1931.

SANDBERG BLUEGRASS

Po'a secun'da, syns. "*P. buckleya'na*",[1] *P. incur'va, P. sandber'gii*"

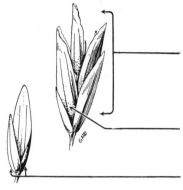

Individual flower groups (spikelets)—short (about ¼ in. long), 2- to 4-flowered, often purplish, borne above middle of branches

Outer flower bract (lemma)—not cobwebby-hairy at base but with very fine, curled hairs on lower part, linear-oblong, 5-nerved, with papery, blunt tip

Lowest (2) spikelet bracts (glumes)—lance-shaped, somewhat pointed; 1st glume 1-veined; 2d glume 2-veined

Flower head (panicle)—very narrow (not more than 1 in. wide even when flowers are open), up to 4 in. long, with ascending branches; lower branches unequal in length and arranged in groups of 2 or 3

Stalks (culms)—densely tufted or only 1 or 2, smooth, delicate, slender, nearly naked (with usually only 1 or 2 short stem leaves), erect, 6 to 30 in. high but averaging only about 12 in.

Leaves—mostly in a short basal tuft and somewhat curly at maturity, 2 to 6 in. long; blades very narrow, short, soft, and usually folded lengthwise as if by hinges; sheaths smooth

Roots—fibrous; creeping rootstocks lacking

[1] Of some authors, in part.

Sandberg bluegrass, also called little bluegrass, is a perennial and strictly a bunchgrass, growing variously in small tufts of but one or two stalks (culms) or in compact tussocks nearly a foot across. It is a widely distributed and important species in most of the western range country, except in the Southwest, where it occurs but sparsely and only in the northern part. It ranks among the six most important range grasses in Colorado, Oregon, and Washington.

Sandberg bluegrass grows throughout an unusually wide altitudinal range, being found at elevations as low as 1,000 feet in Washington and as high as 12,000 feet in the mountains of northern New Mexico. It grows in semidesert areas, in foothills, on grassy slopes and ridge tops, and in open timber and well-drained parks. In addition to other grasses, such weeds as yarrow and pentstemon, and such browse as sagebrush and rabbitbrush, are its frequent associates. Although Sandberg bluegrass will grow luxuriously in rich clay loam, it usually inhabits inferior shallow soils; it is often the most common and characteristic grass on scablands and on dry, rocky, or sandy soils.

It is one of the most drought-resistant of the bluegrasses and, on large areas of western semidesert hill range of the public domain, overgrazing has killed out most of the bunchgrasses except Sandberg bluegrass. This is due to the fact that its deeply penetrating masses of coarse, fibrous roots enable it to withstand trampling unusually well; also it has the ability to make its growth, produce its flowers, and mature its seeds early in the season while moisture is still available. Moreover, its season-long palatability is slightly less than that of some of the choicer grasses with which it grows.

Sandberg bluegrass is one of the first plants ready to graze in the spring, and the entire plant is very palatable and readily grazed by all classes of livestock in the spring and early summer. When mature its palatability is somewhat lowered, but cattle and horses continue to graze it to some extent throughout the summer. In the fall, when air-cured, the leaf blades are again eagerly grazed by all classes of livestock.

The leaves of Sandberg bluegrass are narrow, numerous, and mostly in a curly basal tuft. The stalks (culms) are rather delicate and, except for one or two short leaves, are naked. The flower heads (panicles, or inflorescence) are narrow and compact, not exceeding an inch in width even while blossoming. Unlike its relative, Kentucky bluegrass, it has no hair along the veins (nerves) of its flowers (florets), nor a tuft of cobwebby hairs at the base of the lower floret bracts (lemmas). It does, however, have fine crisp hairs on the lower part of the lemma backs. Sandberg bluegrass does not have underground stems (rhizomes, or rootstocks) and, except for the vegetative increase in the size of the tufts, it must rely solely on seed for reproduction. A fair seed crop, unfortunately of low viability, is produced in the high mountains and, even at the lower elevations, seed viability of the species is only fair. Sandberg bluegrass much resembles, and is often mistaken for, the closely related pine bluegrass (*P. scabrella*), though it is somewhat smaller, softer, and smoother than pine bluegrass.

BOTTLEBRUSH SQUIRRELTAIL

Sita'nion hys'trix

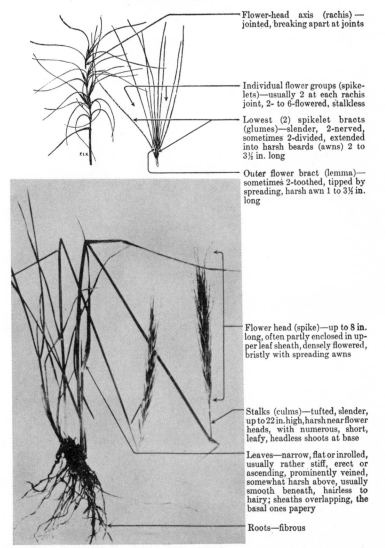

Flower-head axis (rachis) — jointed, breaking apart at joints

Individual flower groups (spikelets)—usually 2 at each rachis joint, 2- to 6-flowered, stalkless

Lowest (2) spikelet bracts (glumes)—slender, 2-nerved, sometimes 2-divided, extended into harsh beards (awns) 2 to 3½ in. long

Outer flower bract (lemma)—sometimes 2-toothed, tipped by spreading, harsh awn 1 to 3½ in. long

Flower head (spike)—up to 8 in. long, often partly enclosed in upper leaf sheath, densely flowered, bristly with spreading awns

Stalks (culms)—tufted, slender, up to 22 in. high, harsh near flower heads, with numerous, short, leafy, headless shoots at base

Leaves—narrow, flat or inrolled, usually rather stiff, erect or ascending, prominently veined, somewhat harsh above, usually smooth beneath, hairless to hairy; sheaths overlapping, the basal ones papery

Roots—fibrous

Bottlebrush squirreltail, sometimes called bristle grass, bushtail, and foxtail is a bright green, bristly headed, perennial bunch grass. The specific name *hystrix* (Greek, meaning porcupine) was given to this species primarily because of its resemblance to the bottlebrush grasses (*Hystrix* spp.). Bottlebrush squirreltail is very variable and has been separated by some botanists into numerous "species." This differentiation has been based on such characters as size, coarseness, or slenderness of stems; length and shape (flat or inrolled) of the leaves; absence or presence, amount and kind of hairs on the leaves and sheaths; the number of shoots produced by the plants; presence of one (as contrasted with two) fertile spikelets at each joint of the rachis, and relative length of the awns as compared with the lemma. These characters so intergrade that the best current agrostological opinion prefers to regard the following as synonyms of *S. hystrix: S. basalticola, S. brevifolium, S. californicum, S. ciliatum, S. cinereum, S. elymoides, S. glabrum, S. insulare, S. latifolium, S. longifolium, S. marginatum, S. minus, S. molle, S. montanum, S. pubiflorum, S. rigidum, S. strigosum,* and *S. velutinum.* Under this larger concept, the range of this species extends from eastern Washington to South Dakota, Missouri, Kansas, Texas, and California. Bottlebrush squirreltail grows chiefly on dry, gravelly soils or in saline situations and is fairly common—in some localities common—on hillsides and alkaline flats in grass, weed, and brush types. Occasionally it is abundant on small local areas, but is mainly of scattered occurrence.

The palatability of bottlebrush squirreltail varies somewhat according to locality and season of the year. In general, it is fair, fairly good, or occasionally good cattle forage and fair sheep forage for spring and early summer use before the heads develop. In the mountains of Arizona, Utah, and Nevada it ordinarily is grazed more freely than further north or in California. The bristly spikes are objectionable to livestock and, when present, the plant is little grazed. It tends to green up measurably with the advent of the fall rains and, if the objectionable heads have fallen, it is again grazed, use then largely depending upon the amount of other forage available. For example, in the desert regions of Utah and Nevada it classes as good fall and winter forage. On the Boise and Sawtooth National Forests of south central Idaho bottlebrush squirreltail is usually stunted, stemmy, and few-leaved, and better forage plants are associated with it.

SQUIRRELTAILS (Sita'nion spp.)

Sitanion is a small, western North American genus of three species of perennial bunchgrasses, according to conservative, present-day opinion. By far the most common and widely distributed of these species is bottlebrush squirreltail discussed in the foregoing paragraphs. Big squirreltail (*S. jubatum*), which is now considered to include *S. breviaristatum, S. multisetum,* and *S. villosum,* of the botanical manuals, ranges from Washington and California eastward to Idaho and New Mexico and is typical of dry, rocky soils, chiefly in the mountains. This is also a variable species, but ordinarily is the most robust member of the genus and has longer, thicker spikes and longer awns than the other species. It is distinguished from bottlebrush squirreltail by its glumes, which are divided into 3 to 12 long-awned lobes, those of bottlebrush squirreltail being entire or sometimes two-divided.

Hansen squirreltail (*S. han'seni*), including *S. anomalum, S. planifolium,* and *S. rubescens,* the other member of the genus, is typically a west coast species ranging from Washington to California, but also occurring inland to Idaho and Nevada. This species has three-nerved glumes, either entire or once or twice divided, which distinguishes it from bottlebrush squirreltail and its two-nerved glumes. Both big squirreltail and Hansen squirreltail have practically the same palatability as bottlebrush squirreltail but ordinarily are less common and hence less important.

The generic name *Sitanion* is derived from an ancient Greek plant name *sitanias* used by Theophratus (third century, B. C.) to designate some plant, perhaps buckwheat—from a stem word *sitos,* meaning grain, or food. Foxtail barley (*Hordeum jubatum*) is the only common western range grass which closely resembles the squirreltails. The heads of foxtail barley, however, are somewhat more delicate, with smaller spikelets and finer awns than those of squirreltail. Furthermore, the awns of squirreltails are very rough, while when mature the awns of the glumes are bent and stand out at right angles to the axis of the head, being strikingly different from those of foxtail barley, which, although spreading, are scarcely bent. The three spikelets at each joint of the rachis of foxtail barley, with the central spikelet the only fertile one, is a positive distinction, as the squirreltails never have more than two spikelets at each rachis joint, those spikelets invariably being fertile and several-flowered.

DROPSEEDS

Sporo'bolus spp.

The dropseeds, a large genus of the redtop tribe (Agrostideae), containing about 36 species in the United States, are chiefly perennials, but a few species are annuals. Both the common and scientific names of the genus refer to the prompt dropping of the seed as it ripens (Greek *spora*, seed, and *ballein*, to cast forth).

These plants grow mainly at lower elevations on desert, semi-desert, and plains. They are especially common in the Southwest and form a very important part of the forage on the lower ranges.

Most of the dropseeds are bunchgrasses, but a few of the perennial species, such as Mississippi dropseed, or rushgrass (*S. macrus*) and seashore dropseed, or rushgrass (*S. virginicus*), have creeping rootstocks (rhizomes). Practically all of the dropseeds produce an abundance of fairly viable long-lived seed, but the seed coats of most species are almost impervious to water and, when used in artificial reseeding, should be scarified for best results. Jackson[1] found that scratching or pricking the seed coats of *Sporobolus* seeds hastened germination greatly. Soaking affected the seed coat but little, and shaking in sand, even for 9 hours, had little effect. Alkali sacaton was the only dropseed tested which did not require puncturing the seed coat for good germination.

The large number of range dropseeds, their wide distribution, and the local abundance of several species give this genus a rather high forage rating, especially in the Southwest. Many of the dropseeds are good-sized, leafy grasses, and produce a large volume of forage. In general these plants are fairly palatable, although the foliage of most species tends to be rather too coarse to rank with that of some of the choice range grasses. However, black dropseed (*S. interruptus*) is an exceptionally good species, highly relished by livestock, and on some ranges sand dropseed (*S. cryptandrus*) is rated as very good forage. A few species are so coarse and harsh that they are of little value as forage except while young. The palatability of dropseeds is greatest while the plants are young and succulent, but, as they cure well on the ground, the perennial species which do not become too harsh when mature furnish good winter forage. Some dropseeds are important on certain ranges because they thrive on dry, alkaline soils where other grasses will not grow. The few annual species of dropseed on our western ranges are unimportant as forage plants. They are small, low in palatability, and their abundance, depending upon the variation in climatic conditions, is very uncertain. Even during favorable years their forage production is very low.

The flower heads (panicles) of the dropseeds are either spreading or spikelike. The small flowers and "seeds" are borne singly on a slender stem (in one-flowered spikelets), the "seeds" falling readily, leaving the empty lowest two flower bracts (glumes) attached to the

---

[1] Jackson, C. V. SEED GERMINATION IN CERTAIN NEW MEXICO RANGE GRASSES. Bot. Gaz. 86 : 270–294, illus. 1928.

stem. The dropseeds resemble some species of redtop (*Agrostis*) and muhly grass (*Muhlenbergia*), but are distinguishable from such species by the fruit. The one-nerved, awnless, thin, shining outer flower bract (lemma) is usually longer than (or at least as long as) the usually unequal glumes, and loosely encloses the grain until maturity, at which times the grain is allowed to fall free. In *Muhlenbergia* the lemma closely envelops the grain and is awned (sometimes only sharp-pointed). In *Agrostis* the glumes are nearly equal and are longer than the lemma. The stalks in many species of *Sporobolus* are solid (pithy, like cornstalks), which feature, though not common for the entire genus, may aid in distinguishing those species from redtops and many muhly grasses. Canfield [2] found that 74 percent of the grasses on the Jornada experimental range, in southern New Mexico, where the dropseeds are well represented, have solid stems and states that—

The solid stem is characteristic of the grasses which are apparently best able to survive under the semiarid conditions of the Jornada region * * *. Hollow stemmed grasses have not the ability to withstand the long dry periods.

He further suggests that the solid stem may be an index as to the suitability of grasses for introduction into semiarid regions.

---

[2] Canfield, R. H. STEM STRUCTURES OF GRASSES ON THE JORNADA EXPERIMENTAL RANGE. Bot. Gaz. 95(4) : 636–648, illus. 1934.

ALKALI SACATON

Sporo'bolus airoi'des

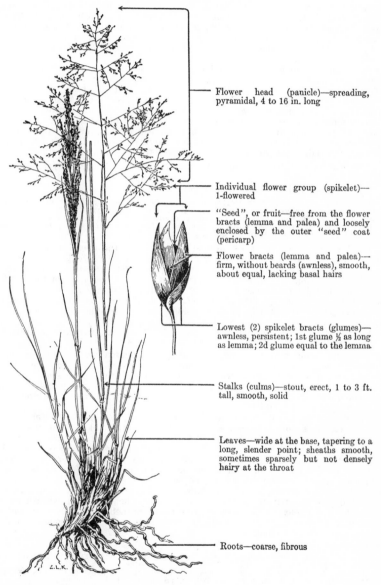

Flower head (panicle)—spreading, pyramidal, 4 to 16 in. long

Individual flower group (spikelet)— 1-flowered

"Seed", or fruit—free from the flower bracts (lemma and palea) and loosely enclosed by the outer "seed" coat (pericarp)

Flower bracts (lemma and palea)— firm, without beards (awnless), smooth, about equal, lacking basal hairs

Lowest (2) spikelet bracts (glumes)— awnless, persistent; 1st glume ½ as long as lemma; 2d glume equal to the lemma

Stalks (culms)—stout, erect, 1 to 3 ft. tall, smooth, solid

Leaves—wide at the base, tapering to a long, slender point; sheaths smooth, sometimes sparsely but not densely hairy at the throat

Roots—coarse, fibrous

Alkali sacaton, also known as bigplume bunchgrass, finetop saltgrass, and hairgrass dropseed, is a robust, perennial grass, widely distributed from Washington to South Dakota, western Texas, and California, and south into Mexico. Throughout its northern range this grass grows very scatteringly and is of little importance, but in the Southwest it occurs in sufficient abundance to be of considerable importance as a forage plant. Its most common habitat is the lower, slightly moist, alkaline flats where it frequently develops in almost pure stands. Although this species will endure much alkali, it is not restricted to alkaline soils but grows on rocky sites, open plains, valleys, and bottom lands, and is common in scattered stands along drainages in the desert and semi-desert areas. It abounds on some of the lower, open plains of New Mexico and Arizona and, not infrequently, occurs along the roadsides and fences of cultivated areas. Other species of *Sporobolus*, tobosa (*Hilaria mutica*), galleta (*H. jamesii*), and side-oats grama (*Bouteloua curtipendula*) are commonly associated with alkali sacaton.

An abundance of herbage is produced by this species, which is eaten freely by cattle and horses and, in the absence of more palatable forage, is often utilized closely. To obtain the maximum use of alkali sacaton, it should be grazed during the growing season, because the foliage becomes coarse, tough, and unpalatable as it matures and does not provide good winter forage, although it has some value at that time if there is a dearth of other forage. In some parts of the Southwest, where moisture is adequate to produce a good cover, patches of alkali sacaton are fenced for pasture and, if the species is kept closely cropped, it affords good grazing. Wooton and Standley[1] state:

It is said to be detrimental to sheep at certain stages of its development, causing them to bloat.

Griffiths, Bidwell, and Goodrich[2] report:

In the Pecos Valley of New Mexico injury has been done to cattle by allowing them to graze upon this grass at certain seasons of the year. It is the opinion of close observers, however, that the grass was not at fault, but that the injury was done by the soluble salts of the soil, these salts, by creeping up the grass stems during moist weather and by being eaten along with the grass, produce the deleterious effects.

In this connection, it is of interest to note that the chemical analyses of alkali sacaton[2] show a conspicuously high mineral (ash) content.

This species is typically a bunchgrass but, in moist sites, the plants develop extensive stooling, which measurably facilitates the perpetuation of the species, and increases its resistance to grazing. Alkali sacaton produces an abundant supply of exceptionally long-lived seed, which enable this species to extend its stand rather vigorously on favorable areas. According to Campbell:[3]

Its seeds remain viable for several years, because of the hard, waxy seed coats. Seeds collected in 1925 and tested that year showed only 77 percent germination, whereas 100 percent germination was obtained from the same sample a year later.

Jackson[4] found that the seed coats of alkali sacaton were more permeable than the seed coats of the other four southwestern species of *Sporobolus* tested, and was the only one which did not require pricking or scarifying the seed coats to expedite satisfactory germination. This species withstands the encroachment of shifting sand better than most of its grass associates, and is a very good soil binder.

Alkali sacaton has deep, coarse roots, and often pronounced stooling, which sometimes gives the appearance of short, thick rootstocks. The stems are smooth, solid, stout, leafy, 1 to 3 feet high, are spreading at the base and grow in dense bunches commonly from 8 to 12 inches in diameter. On the more favorable sites, when not overgrazed, it may sometimes form a uniform cover approaching a sod. The numerous basal leaves are up to 18 inches long and about one-eighth of an inch wide at the base and taper to long, slender, inrolled points. The leaf blades are smooth beneath but rough above, with the sheaths sparsely hairy at the throat. The upper leaf sheath sometimes loosely encloses the base of the much branched and usually widely spreading panicle. Alkali sacaton is similar to sacaton, although smaller and less coarse throughout.

[1] Wooton, E. O., and Standley, P. C. THE GRASSES AND GRASS-LIKE PLANTS OF NEW MEXICO. N. Mex. Agr. Expt. Sta. Bull. 81, [176] pp., illus. 1912.
[2] Griffiths, D., Bidwell, G. L., and Goodrich, C. E. NATIVE PASTURE GRASSES OF THE UNITED STATES. U. S. Dept. Agr. Bull. 201, 52 pp., illus. 1915.
[3] Campbell, R. S. PLANT SUCCESSION AND GRAZING CAPACITY ON CLAY SOILS IN SOUTHERN NEW MEXICO. Jour. Agr. Research [U. S.] 43 : 1027–1051, illus. 1931.
[4] Jackson, C. V. SEED GERMINATION IN CERTAIN NEW MEXICO RANGE GRASSES. Bot. Gaz. 86 : 270–294, illus. 1928.

SAND DROPSEED

Sporo'bolus cryptan'drus

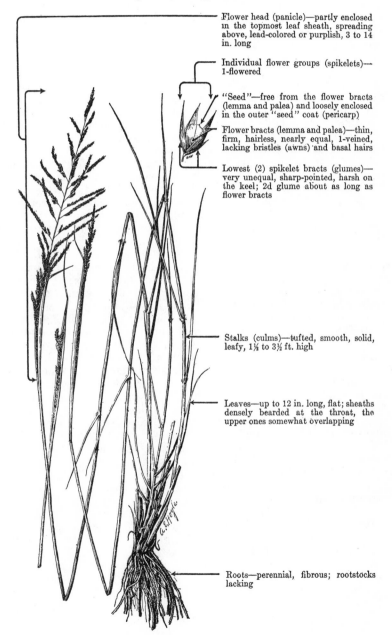

Flower head (panicle)—partly enclosed in the topmost leaf sheath, spreading above, lead-colored or purplish, 3 to 14 in. long

Individual flower groups (spikelets)—1-flowered

"Seed"—free from the flower bracts (lemma and palea) and loosely enclosed in the outer "seed" coat (pericarp)

Flower bracts (lemma and palea)—thin, firm, hairless, nearly equal, 1-veined, lacking bristles (awns) and basal hairs

Lowest (2) spikelet bracts (glumes)—very unequal, sharp-pointed, harsh on the keel; 2d glume about as long as flower bracts

Stalks (culms)—tufted, smooth, solid, leafy, 1½ to 3½ ft. high

Leaves—up to 12 in. long, flat; sheaths densely bearded at the throat, the upper ones somewhat overlapping

Roots—perennial, fibrous; rootstocks lacking

Sand dropseed, a tufted perennial, is widely distributed, occurring from Maine to Washington, Arizona, Mexico, Texas, and North Carolina. Although this species is common in all the western range States, except California, it is most important in the Southwest and in certain parts of the Snake, Salmon, and Clearwater river drainages in Idaho and Oregon. It most commonly appears at lower elevations and, as the common name implies, on sandy soils; it also grows on dry coarse soils up to an elevation of 8,000 feet. In its northern range sand dropseed occurs scatteringly with downy chess (*Bromus tectorum*), bluebunch wheatgrass (*Agropyron spicatum*), and Idaho fescue (*Festuca idahoensis*), and grows sparsely in the sagebrush type on plains and foothills and in canyons throughout the Great Basin. However, on sandy plains, mesas, and foothills in the woodland and ponderosa pine belts, it is common and is frequently associated in the Southwest with oaks, side-oats, and other gramas, muhly grasses, and beardgrasses (*Andropogon* spp.).

Sand dropseed produces a fairly large amount of foliage which is palatable to all classes of livestock. Its palatability, depending upon the association in which it occurs, is rated from fair to good on properly grazed range in the Southwest, but in Idaho this perennial is considered very good. In many places this species has been killed out on overgrazed range because of continued close cropping. The herbage cures rather well on the ground and furnishes fair to fairly good winter forage. This plant is a prolific seeder and, when protected or grazed properly, tends to increase on depleted range.

On the Nezperce National Forest, Idaho, sand dropseed occurs as scattered bunches or in large patches within heavy stands of downy chess and is rapidly replacing that less desirable species according to careful observers. The seeds, which mature in late summer or early fall, are produced in abundance and are remarkably long-lived, as shown by Goss [1] who found that the seed of sand dropseed had, in some samples, a high germination after having been buried in pots at 42 inches below the ground surface for 20 years. The highest germination out of 6 samples was 74.5 percent and the average of the 6 samples was about 26 percent. This was the highest germination secured from the 22 grasses used in the experiment. The seed coat of sand dropseed is very hard, and scarifying the seed before planting results in better germination.

Sand dropseed has erect or sometimes spreading, leafy, solid (pithy, like cornstalks) stems, often spreading at the base. The uppermost leaf sheaths partially, often almost entirely, enclose the panicle. The portion of the panicle not enclosed is somewhat spreading and open but is usually rather narrow. The panicle branches are densely flowered, often in pairs and sometimes hairy at the axils. The spikelets are less than one-eighth of an inch long, lead-colored, with unequal glumes—one about as long as the lemma and the other about half as long. Often after maturity a large amount of seed will be found in the enveloping leaf sheath.

---

[1] Goss, W. L. THE VITALITY OF BURIED SEEDS. Jour. Agr. Research [U. S.] 29 : 349–362. 1924.

BLACK DROPSEED

Sporo'bolus interrup'tus

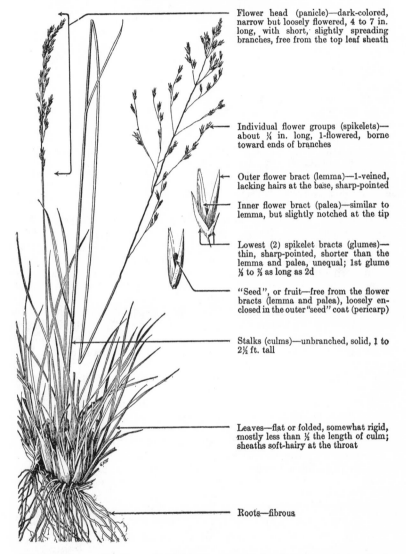

Flower head (panicle)—dark-colored, narrow but loosely flowered, 4 to 7 in. long, with short, slightly spreading branches, free from the top leaf sheath

Individual flower groups (spikelets)—about ¼ in. long, 1-flowered, borne toward ends of branches

Outer flower bract (lemma)—1-veined, lacking hairs at the base, sharp-pointed

Inner flower bract (palea)—similar to lemma, but slightly notched at the tip

Lowest (2) spikelet bracts (glumes)—thin, sharp-pointed, shorter than the lemma and palea, unequal; 1st glume ⅛ to ⅝ as long as 2d

"Seed", or fruit—free from the flower bracts (lemma and palea), loosely enclosed in the outer "seed" coat (pericarp)

Stalks (culms)—unbranched, solid, 1 to 2½ ft. tall

Leaves—flat or folded, somewhat rigid, mostly less than ½ the length of culm; sheaths soft-hairy at the throat

Roots—fibrous

Black dropseed, also called black sporobolus because of its dark-colored panicle, is an erect, densely tufted perennial with bright, light green foliage. This species is limited in distribution to Arizona and grows on thinly wooded areas, open parks and hillsides chiefly in the ponderosa pine and upper woodland belt of the Colorado Plateau south of Flagstaff, and in the White Mountains.

Although preferring the better loam soils on comparatively level sites, black dropseed also grows on a wide variety of soils—from clayey to somewhat rocky, and is not uncommon on moderately steep slopes at elevations of from 6,000 to 8,000 feet. It sometimes occurs abundantly over rather extensive areas in nearly pure stands, or else associated with other grasses, particularly blue grama (*Bouteloua gracilis*), fescues (*Festuca* spp.), bluestem (*Agropyron smithii*), and mountain muhly (*Muhlenbergia montana*).

This plant is one of the most palatable grasses of the Southwest and is a key species on ranges where it occurs in sufficient abundance to be of importance. It is always grazed closely and is preferred to any of its associates. Black dropseed produces a fairly large volume of foliage which greens up early and retains its palatability throughout the grazing season. Talbot and Hill [1] report:

Black sporobolus * * * showed a net gain of almost as much under overgrazing as under fence, indicating its high resistance to heavy grazing. * * * The data are meager—and the tendencies seem puzzling at first glance, but by the aid of wider observations it is believed that the same rule will probably apply to this grass as to blue grama, i. e., it will thrive under proper intensity of grazing and resist overgrazing in marked degree, but can be killed out by long continued overgrazing.

When not grazed too closely, black dropseed produces a large amount of viable seed which assists in the satisfactory reproduction of the species. Management should be such as to encourage the spread of this valuable grass. Reseeding experiments are now being made with black dropseed to increase its abundance and extend its range. These plantings are giving some promise of success, but the cost of seed collection is rather high.

Black dropseed can usually be distinguished from other dropseeds by its rather narrow, brownish, lead-colored panicle, its bright, light green foliage, and by the spikelets which are exceptionally large for a dropseed, being about one-fourth of an inch long. The panicle branches are short, alternate, and densely flowered near the tips but bare along the lower portions. With the autumn frosts, the foliage fades to a yellowish green color.

There has been considerable difference in opinion in the literature as to whether this grass possesses rootstocks. The fact that it forms a sod over small areas has led to the common belief that rootstocks are present. Actually, however, the plant does not have rootstocks, and the sod-forming habit is made possible by exceptionally pronounced stooling. The repeated development of new shoots from the base of the culms gives the appearance of short stout rootstocks.

In an unpublished note regarding this species, R. R. Hill, assistant chief of range management, United States Forest Service, states:

Black sporobolus is, in my judgment, the best grass that grows within its limited range; the most palatable season-long to all classes of livestock; very resistant to drought and grazing and capable of spreading vegetatively (I believe it has possibilities as a lawn grass). It greens up early and remains so continuously until late in the season. It richly deserves extensive experimentation.

---

[1] Talbot, M. W., and Hill, R. R. PROGRESS REPORT ON RANGE STUDY PLOTS, COCONINO NATIONAL FOREST. 33 pp. 1923. [Unpublished ms.]

SIXWEEKS DROPSEED

Sporo'bolus microsper'mus, syn. *S. confu'sus*

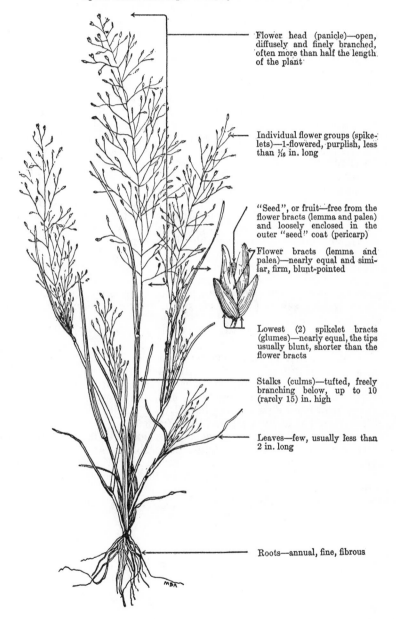

Flower head (panicle)—open, diffusely and finely branched, often more than half the length of the plant

Individual flower groups (spikelets)—1-flowered, purplish, less than ⅟₁₆ in. long

"Seed", or fruit—free from the flower bracts (lemma and palea) and loosely enclosed in the outer "seed" coat (pericarp)

Flower bracts (lemma and palea)—nearly equal and similar, firm, blunt-pointed

Lowest (2) spikelet bracts (glumes)—nearly equal, the tips usually blunt, shorter than the flower bracts

Stalks (culms)—tufted, freely branching below, up to 10 (rarely 15) in. high

Leaves—few, usually less than 2 in. long

Roots—annual, fine, fibrous

Sixweeks dropseed, also called tufted annual dropseed and six-weeks sporobolus, is one of the few annual species of *Sporobolus* and it is the only common and abundant one of our western ranges. This delicate grass grows in small, few-leaved tufts which often appear as fine, bushy masses of panicles. The specific name *microspermus*, meaning small seed (*micros*, small; *sperma*, seed), is aptly chosen for this grass. The common phrase sixweeks is often applied, especially in the Southwest, to short-lived annual plants whose growth period, from germination to dissemination and death, usually occupies only about 6 weeks or so.

Sixweeks dropseed is widely distributed, occurring from Washington to Montana, western Texas, and California, and south into Mexico, but is most common and abundant in the Southwest. It varies widely in habitat but is very common along the edges of streams and in moist places in the woodland and ponderosa pine belts, and sometimes at higher elevations. In the Southwest it occurs sporadically on a wide variety of soils and sites, but is commonest on moist, sandy, gravelly, or clayey loam soils in sheltered places and rocky cliffs at elevations from 3,000 to 9,500 feet.

The abundance of this annual, as is the case with most annuals, depends largely upon climatic conditions and the extent of depletion of the normal plant cover. It produces a very plentiful supply of seed when conditions are favorable and, when summer rains are adequate, it springs up abundantly in open sites and on bare ground. At times it comes in thickly on open, overgrazed areas during favorable growing seasons. Sixweeks dropseed is often associated with weeds and other annual grasses and also occurs sparsely with sedges (*Carex* spp.), gramas (*Bouteloua* spp.), hilarias (*Hilaria* spp.), and other perennial grasses.

Although sixweeks dropseed is worthy of mention here chiefly because of its commonness and local abundance, its forage value is slight or distinctly minor. The larger plants may be grazed to some extent but, because of its very small size, sparse leafage, and bushy panicles, it is ordinarily unattractive to grazing animals. If grazed early in the season it may furnish a small amount of fair forage in the absence of more palatable plants.

This grass has a few narrow leaves from 1 to 2½ inches long, and several to many slender, often poorly developed stems 2 to 10 inches high; occasionally, however, under favorable conditions, relatively luxuriant growth, as much as 15 inches high, may occur. The panicles are spreading, with many very fine branches, and are often more than half the length of the entire plant. Frequently, the upper two-thirds of the plant is a fine, loose mass of flowers or seeds.

SACATON

Sporo'bolus wrigh'tii

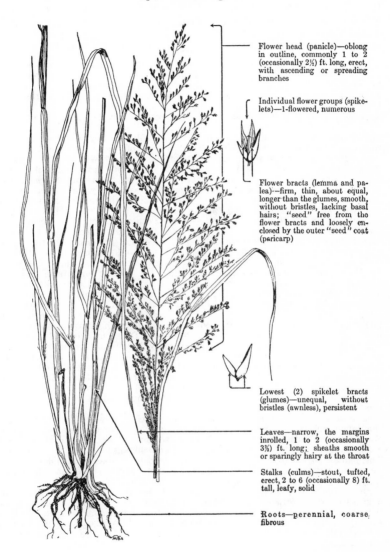

Flower head (panicle)—oblong in outline, commonly 1 to 2 (occasionally 2½) ft. long, erect, with ascending or spreading branches

Individual flower groups (spikelets)—1-flowered, numerous

Flower bracts (lemma and palea)—firm, thin, about equal, longer than the glumes, smooth, without bristles, lacking basal hairs; "seed" free from the flower bracts and loosely enclosed by the outer "seed" coat (pericarp)

Lowest (2) spikelet bracts (glumes)—unequal, without bristles (awnless), persistent

Leaves—narrow, the margins inrolled, 1 to 2 (occasionally 3⅔) ft. long; sheaths smooth or sparingly hairy at the throat

Stalks (culms)—stout, tufted, erect, 2 to 6 (occasionally 8) ft. tall, leafy, solid

Roots—perennial, coarse, fibrous

Sacaton is an exceptionally robust perennial bunchgrass, occurring from Arizona to western Texas and south into Mexico, mainly on low, alluvial flats, bottomlands, and arroyos subject to flooding. In such locations it is sometimes abundant. Unlike its relative, alkali sacaton (*S. airoides*), this species will not grow on soils which are highly impregnated with alkali and it is more exacting in its water requirements, although fairly drought-resistant after becoming established. Griffiths, Bidwell, and Goodrich [1] state:

In former times it (i. e., sacaton) was a beautiful, characteristic species of the river bottoms of the Southwest, forming dense growths 6 and even 8 feet in height, through which it was difficult to ride on horseback * * * As near as can be judged, it made a quite uniform stand over portions of the Santa Cruz bottoms in southern Arizona in early days, but of late years it grows almost invariably in large tussocks and at present there is very little of it left.

The young shoots of sacaton are highly relished early in the season by cattle and horses. Their popularity declines measurably as they become coarse and tough with maturity. Stockmen sometimes burn off the coarse, dead stems in late winter to increase the accessibility of the early growth for livestock. A large volume of herbage is produced which cures well and constitutes fairly good winter forage, despite its coarseness. If cut at the right time and cured properly, sacaton furnishes good, nutritious hay, especially for horses, as indicated by the relatively high protein and carbohydrate content shown in the following analysis made in the Bureau of Chemistry and Soils, United States Department of Agriculture: [1] Ash, 8.53 percent; ether extract, 1.70 percent; crude fiber, 32.27 percent; nitrogen-free extract, 47.93 percent; pentosans, a form of carbohydrates, 25.89 percent; protein, 9.57 percent. The analyses were made of air-dry material cut 4 inches above ground at the flowering period.

Sacaton is promising for cultivation on restricted areas which depend on floodwater for moisture and which are otherwise too dry for alfalfa and other more desirable crops. [2] This grass is a long-lived plant and produces an abundance of viable seed, which sprouts readily under proper moisture conditions. Thornber,[3] in a reseeding experiment with sacaton during a favorable year, secured practically no growth on areas receiving only the annual rainfall, although good stands of sacaton seedlings resulted on the lower adjacent areas that were occasionally flooded with storm water. On many areas where sacaton was once fairly abundant it now occurs sparsely, because of overgrazing. Under heavy grazing trails are trampled through stands of sacaton and tussocks are formed. When overgrazing is continued, rain and floodwater cut the trails deeper and deeper until the tussocks are finally left high and dry and eventually die. Russell [4] states that until sacaton was exterminated from the river banks, where most of their villages are located, the Pima Indian women made hair brushes from the roots of this grass.

Sacaton is similar to alkali sacaton, with which it is sometimes confused on the range, but typically is a much larger and coarser grass, growing in dense clumps, often forming hummocks 1 to 2 feet in diameter, with exceptionally robust leafy stalks 2 to 6 (commonly 5 and occasionally as much as 8) feet tall. The panicle of sacaton is generally 1 to 2 feet long, somewhat oblong-shaped, and densely flowered, while the panicle of alkali sacaton is commonly 4 to 16 inches long, pyramidal-shaped, and less densely flowered.

Sacaton is a Mexican name which appears to be derived from the word *zacate*, a grass or grass forage. The ending *on* gives it the meaning, a coarse grass, which is aptly applied to this species. There is a town named Sacaton, in Pinal County, Ariz., which appears to be named after this grass, although there is a small village of the same name in Spain of which it may be a namesake.

[1] Griffiths, D., Bidwell, G. L., and Goodrich, C. E. NATIVE PASTURE GRASSES OF THE UNITED STATES. U. S. Dept. Agr. Bull. 201, 52 pp., illus. 1915.
[2] Wooton, E. O., and Standley, P. C. THE GRASSES AND GRASS-LIKE PLANTS OF NEW MEXICO. N. Mex. Agr. Expt. Sta. Bull. 81: [176] pp., illus. 1912.
[3] Thornber, J. J. THE GRAZING RANGES OF ARIZONA. Ariz. Agr. Expt. Sta. Bull. 65: [245]–360, illus. 1910.
[4] Russell, F. THE PIMA INDIANS. Bur. Amer. Ethnol. Ann. Rept. (1904–05) 26: 3–[390], illus. 1908.

NEEDLEGRASSES

Sti'pa spp.

Needlegrasses are chiefly perennial bunchgrasses and are of world-wide distribution in temperate regions, mainly on plains and steppes. The genus belongs to the redtop tribe (*Agrostideae*) and includes a large number of species (about 100), of which about 30 (all perennials) occur in the West. The scientific name *Stipa* is from the Greek word *stupē* (tow, the coarse part of flax), referring to the feathery beards (awns) of some species. A number of our range species of *Stipa*, such as sleepygrass and needle-and-thread, have individual names, but most of them are called needlegrasses. The name porcupinegrass is sometimes applied to the whole genus but is best restricted to those species (particularly *S. spartea*) which have very large, coarse, and quill-like awns. A few species have conspicuously feathery (plumose) awns and are called feathergrasses; some of these are cultivated as ornamentals.

The needlegrasses are widely distributed over the Western States from the Great Plains to the Pacific coast but are most common and abundant in the Great Basin and in the Southwest. They also extend north into Canada and south into Chile. The number of species increases from north to south, the approximate distribution being as follows: Alaska, 1 species; Washington, 8; Utah and Nevada, 18, and Arizona, New Mexico, and California, about 15 each.

Taken as a group, the needlegrasses rank fairly high as forage plants on our western ranges. Their foliage tends to be somewhat wiry and occasionally coarse, especially when mature, lessening the palatability to some extent. On the other hand, their foliage usually remains green over a long growing period and cures well on the ground, making the needlegrasses valuable for late fall and winter grazing. Moreover, their abundance, wide distribution, and leafiness enhance their value. Most of them are prolific seeders, have deep, fibrous roots, and withstand grazing well.

The seeds are mechanically injurious to grazing animals. They sometimes work into the tissues of the mouth and tongue and also into the ears and nose of livestock and game animals, causing considerable trouble. Some of the Old World species of *Stipa* are poisonous and produce a narcotic effect upon grazing animals. Thus far only one of our native range species, sleepygrass (*S. robusta*, syn. *S. vaseyi*), has been found to be poisonous. Knowledge of the genus is not sufficiently complete to warrant the assumption that other western species are wholly free from narcotic properties, although there now appears to be no reason for suspecting any except sleepygrass. A European species, *S. tenacissima*, together with *Lygeum spartum*, make up the esparto of commerce, used in the manufacture chiefly of paper, and also of cordage, coarse cloth, shoes, and baskets.[1]

---

[1] Lamson-Scribner, F. ECONOMIC GRASSES. U. S. Dept. Agr., Div. Agrost. Bull. 14, rev., 85 pp., illus. 1900.

Needlegrasses have narrow or inrolled leaves and usually narrow, but open, occasionally spreading flower heads (panicles). The most outstanding feature by which the needlegrasses may be distinguished is the long, single beard (awn) which is twisted, bent, and, though securely attached at the tip of the "seed", has a distinct line of union. The "seeds" are hard, slender, and cylindrical (not plump as in rice-grass (*Oryzopsis* spp.)), and have a sharp-pointed base (callus) covered with fine, rather stiff, short hairs. This sharp point, with the accompanying hairs, aids effectively in planting and burying the seed. The process of self-planting is furthered by the long awn which reacts readily to moisture, untwisting when wet and twisting again when dry, thus screwing the seeds into the soil. Each seed is borne in a separate spikelet end singly on a slender stem (pedicel); the two spikelet bracts (glumes) are very thin, of about equal length, and remain attached to the stem after the seed has fallen.

SUBALPINE NEEDLEGRASS

Sti'pa columbia'na, syn. *S. mi'nor*

Flower head (panicle)—narrow, spike-like, often purplish, up to 8 in. long, not enclosed in leaf sheath when mature

Individual flower groups (spikelets)—1-flowered, short-stalked

Stalks (culms)—tufted, erect, up to 32 in. (or as much as 40 in. in var. *nelsoni*) high, with few, often purplish joints (nodes)

Leaves—flat or sometimes inrolled when dry, hairless; sheaths hairless; collar (ligule) at junction of blade and sheath very short

Lowest (2) spikelet bracts (glumes)—about ⅜ in. long, narrow, tapering to a fine point, persistent after "seed" falls

Outer flower bract (lemma)—firm, about ¼ in. long, evenly covered with short, soft hairs throughout, tipped with a securely attached beard (awn); awn twice-bent, twisted below, ½ to 1½ (usually ¾ to 1) in. long, not at all feathery

"Seed" (caryopsis)—hard, cylindrical, with sharp-pointed, bearded base (callus), closely enfolded by the lemma

Roots—fibrous

191

Subalpine needlegrass, also called Columbia needlegrass, and small mountain porcupinegrass or hairgrass, is one of the fine-leaved, slender-stemmed needle-grasses. This species grows in all 11 western range States, having the central Rocky Mountain as its center of distribution. This grass inhabits dry soils in canyons, and on open hillsides, mountain parks and plains. It is common from the upper sagebrush and woodland types to the dry, open parks and hill-sides at subalpine elevations, and is often associated with lanceleaf yellow-brush (*Chrysothamnus lanceolatus*), bluegrasses (*Poa* spp.), western yarrow (*Achillea lanulosa*), and other grasses and weeds.

Although the palatability of this needlegrass, under different conditions, varies from fair to very good, it is usually good forage for all classes of livestock. Cattle and horses, as a rule, graze it a little more closely than do sheep. On some ranges, especially where a shortage of highly palatable forage exists, subalpine needlegrass is grazed very closely. The fairly large amount of fine leafage produced remains green throughout the growing season and sometimes even until snow falls, thereby increasing the palatability of this grass to cattle and horses. The plant is particularly palatable in the spring and early summer.

At the limits of its range, subalpine needlegrass grows mainly in scattered stands, but through the central Rocky Mountains it is abundant over large areas and is a valuable forage plant for spring use on lambing grounds as well as for cattle and horses. Subalpine needlegrass often occurs abundantly on ranges where wheatgrass and bluegrass have been killed out by excessive use. It is considered a valuable replacement plant under such conditions. This grass is among the last of the fairly good grasses to disappear from the range under serious overgrazing and is among the first to reappear with the im-provement of badly depleted areas. Subalpine needlegrass withstands heavy grazing by sheep in the central Rockies because its "seeds", although not trouble-some, are usually left to mature. However, in the Southwest, where this grass occurs rather scatteringly and with less palatable species, it is sometimes cropped so closely that seed maturity is prevented and, under such use, it is rather easily killed out.

Sampson[1] lists subalpine needlegrass as one of the most important and valu-able species of his so-called porcupinegrass-yellowbrush consociation (mixed grass and weed stage), in the Intermountain Region. He states that the cover of small mountain porcupinegrass (i. e., *S. columbiana*) and yellowbrush (*Chrysothamnus lanceolatus*) next to the wheatgrass consociation, constitutes the highest and most stable forage type. Accordingly where conditions become unfavorable to the maintenance of the wheatgrass cover but not so adverse as drastically to change the fertility and available water content of the soil, porcupinegrass (i. e., *S. columbiana*) and yellowbrush soon gain dominion.

Subalpine needlegrass is a variable species, and has been divided by some authors into two or more species. The best current authorities now recognize only one variety, *S. columbiana nelsoni*. This variety differs chiefly in its larger size (up to 40 inches tall), broader culm blades, and larger, denser panicle.

In Montana, spike oat (*Avena hookeri*) is sometimes confused on the range with sub-alpine needlegrass because of a general similarity in appearance. They may be readily distinguished, as the spikelets of spike oat are two- to several-flowered, the glumes are longer than the florets, and the awn, though twisted and bent, is attached to the back of the lemma.

Letterman needlegrass (*S. letterma'ni*) is very similar to subalpine needlegrass botani-cally and economically, and it is often difficult to distinguish between the two in the field. The distribution of the two species is about the same, but Letterman needlegrass is less abundant at the northern and southern extremities of their range and does not extend to as high altitudes. Letterman needlegrass, however, is not uncommon in the spruce-fir zone, extends down into the sagebrush area, and is an abundant and valuable plant on many ranges.

The forage value of Letterman needlegrass is usually rated approximately equal to that of subalpine needlegrass, varying from fair to very good. However, being a little smaller and more delicate, some observers rate it slightly higher than its close relative.

Letterman needlegrass differs from subalpine needlegrass in being somewhat smaller (8 to 24 inches high), with very narrow, tightly inrolled leaves, 2 to 8 inches long, form-ing a rather crowded tuft at the base of the slender, wiry culms. The panicles are usually shorter and fewer-flowered, the seeds slightly smaller, and the glumes slender, thin, and prominently nerved on the back.

---

[1] Sampson, A. W. PLANT SUCCESSION IN RELATION TO RANGE MANAGEMENT. U. S. Dept. Agr. Bull. 791, 76 pp., illus. 1919.

NEEDLE-AND-THREAD

Sti'pa coma'ta

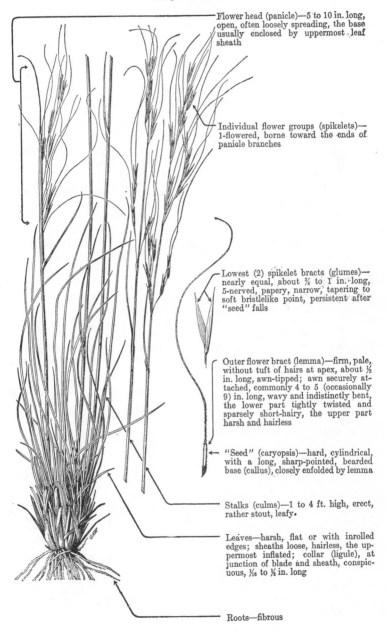

Flower head (panicle)—5 to 10 in. long, open, often loosely spreading, the base usually enclosed by uppermost leaf sheath

Individual flower groups (spikelets)— 1-flowered, borne toward the ends of panicle branches

Lowest (2) spikelet bracts (glumes)— nearly equal, about ¾ to 1 in. long, 5-nerved, papery, narrow, tapering to soft bristlelike point, persistent after "seed" falls

Outer flower bract (lemma)—firm, pale, without tuft of hairs at apex, about ½ in. long, awn-tipped; awn securely attached, commonly 4 to 5 (occasionally 9) in. long, wavy and indistinctly bent, the lower part tightly twisted and sparsely short-hairy, the upper part harsh and hairless

"Seed" (caryopsis)—hard, cylindrical, with a long, sharp-pointed, bearded base (callus), closely enfolded by lemma

Stalks (culms)—1 to 4 ft. high, erect, rather stout, leafy.

Leaves—harsh, flat or with inrolled edges; sheaths loose, hairless, the uppermost inflated; collar (ligule), at junction of blade and sheath, conspicuous, ⅟₁₆ to ⅛ in. long

Roots—fibrous

Needle-and-thread, an erect leafy bunchgrass, 1 to 4 feet high, is so named because of its most distinguishing feature, the exceptionally long, twisted, and tapering beards (awns) which suggest a threaded sewing needle. The specific name *comata*, from the Latin *coma*, head of hair, also refers to the effect of a tangled head of these awns. The plant is also called long-awned porcupinegrass, common or western needlegrass, sandgrass, and silkgrass. This grass is very widely distributed over the Western States and the Great Plains and also occurs in the upper valley of the Yukon. It is common on dry, sandy, or gravelly plains, mesas, and foothills and sometimes extends into the mountains up to elevations between 4,000 and 8,500 feet. It commonly occurs in the sagebrush, juniper-piñon, and ponderosa pine types of the Rocky Mountains and on semidesert plains and foothills of the Southwest.

The forage value of needle-and-thread varies in different regions, at different seasons, and with varied plant associates. In the Southwest and California, it is rated very high during the early season before the beards (awns) develop, and again after the seeds are dropped. This grass is valuable because it begins growth early in the spring when other grasses are dry. Furthermore, it greens up and produces new growth in summer and fall with the advent of sufficient precipitation. In some sections of the Southwest and California, it is grazed so closely that its extermination threatens because of deficient seed production. An abundance of leafage is produced which remains green during most of the grazing season, cures rather well and often is closely eaten on winter ranges. It is cut for hay in parts of eastern Wyoming, the Dakotas, and Nebraska where it rates as very good forage. When found in mixture with an abundance of choice forage, it is considered only fairly good spring and fall feed, as compared with other grasses, because of its coarseness and the tendency of the leaves to toughen rather early. If grazing occurs while the "seeds" are mature and before they are dropped, they may be mechanically injurious, especially to sheep.

This species is a deep-rooted bunchgrass which depends upon seed for reproduction. Although it does not reproduce readily on the drier ranges and is rather easily killed out by overuse, in the more favorable areas it usually reproduces very well and satisfactorily withstands heavy grazing in spring and fall when the plants are allowed to mature seed during the summer.

The basal leaf blades of needle-and-thread are narrow, usually inrolled, and 3 to 12 inches long; the stem leaves are shorter and broader. The uppermost leaf sheath is elongated and loosely encloses the base of the panicle. The panicle is 5 to 10 inches long, loosely spreading, with one-flowered spikelets (i. e., each flower or seed is borne singly) out near the ends of long branches. The "seeds" are about three-eights of an inch in length, tipped with a slender awn commonly 4 to 5, but occasionally as much as 9, inches long. The lower part of the awn, below the bend, is tightly twisted and has some very fine soft hairs. The upper part is rough to the touch, nearly straight or only slightly twisted, and tapers gradually to a fine point. Seed matures in midsummer and drops in late summer or early fall.

New Mexican feathergrass (*S. neomexicána*), also known as New Mexican needlegrass and porcupinegrass, is very closely related to needle-and-thread both botanically and economically, differing from it mainly in having a distinctly feathery awn (beard). This species is found from Colorado and Utah to California and western Texas. It was originally known from New Mexico, to which its English and scientific names refer.

WESTERN NEEDLEGRASS

Sti'pa occidenta'lis, syn. *S. oregonen'sis*

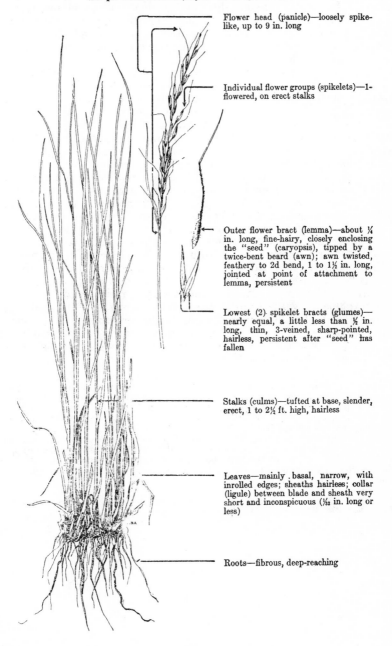

Flower head (panicle)—loosely spike-like, up to 9 in. long

Individual flower groups (spikelets)—1-flowered, on erect stalks

Outer flower bract (lemma)—about ¼ in. long, fine-hairy, closely enclosing the "seed" (caryopsis), tipped by a twice-bent beard (awn); awn twisted, feathery to 2d bend, 1 to 1½ in. long, jointed at point of attachment to lemma, persistent

Lowest (2) spikelet bracts (glumes)—nearly equal, a little less than ½ in. long, thin, 3-veined, sharp-pointed, hairless, persistent after "seed" has fallen

Stalks (culms)—tufted at base, slender, erect, 1 to 2½ ft. high, hairless

Leaves—mainly basal, narrow, with inrolled edges; sheaths hairless; collar (ligule) between blade and sheath very short and inconspicuous (¹⁄₃₂ in. long or less)

Roots—fibrous, deep-reaching

195

Western needlegrass, often called western porcupinegrass, grows from about 1 to 2½ feet high in fairly small clumps and, as the names (both scientific and common) imply, is a western species ranging from Washington, Oregon, and Idaho to Wyoming and California. It usually inhabits dry, well-drained soil on plains, ridges and in open, timber types, extending from the upper foothills into the higher mountains. It usually occurs in scattered clumps but sometimes forms the most conspicuous vegetation on restricted areas of open hillsides and ridgetops.

Like many of the needlegrasses, this species starts growth early, is slow in maturing, and remains green until late in the season—usually until fall. It produces a fairly large amount of leafage which is usually of good, although not choice, palatability for all classes of livestock. Its highest palatability is in the spring and early summer while the plants are young and succulent. As the species matures, the leaves become somewhat tough for sheep but are still grazed to some extent even after that condition develops. The value of western needlegrass as forage is relatively higher in the fall than in midsummer because it remains green after most of the grasses have dried up. Although the seeds apparently are not injurious, grazing animals avoid them when they begin to mature. Livestock, especially sheep, sometimes graze the leaves closely, leaving the stems untouched. Since a good share of the seed, which is usually of fair viability, is left to mature, reproduction is commonly fairly good, although this species is not so aggressive as some of the other needlegrasses. Western needlegrass has a spreading and deeply penetrating root system which makes it resistant to trampling and capable of withstanding considerable drought. "Its seedlings develop somewhat deeper roots than do the majority of the species, and because of this fact they have thrived during dry periods in certain places where other species able to exist in soils of slightly lower water content have died." [1]

This grass has numerous narrow, inrolled leaves crowded at the base. Although mostly basal, a few leaves also occur on the slender stems. The leaf sheaths are not hairy. The panicle is loose but narrow, almost spikelike, and about 4 to 8 inches long. The "seed", covered with soft hairs, is tipped with an awn 1 to 1½ inches long, twice bent, and also covered with hairs which make it feathery to the second bend. This species closely resembles Thurber needlegrass (*S. thurberiana*) but the leaves of western needlegrass are not so rough, the "seeds" are smaller, and the small bractlike appendage (ligule) attached at the junction of the leaf blade and sheath is but a minute membrane. In Thurber needlegrass, this ligule is conspicuous, being about one-eighth to one-fourth of an inch long.

[1] Sampson, A. W. IMPORTANT RANGE PLANTS: THEIR LIFE HISTORY AND FORAGE VALUE. U. S. Dept. Agr. Bull. 545, 63 pp., illus. 1917.

CALIFORNIA NEEDLEGRASS

Sti'pa pul'chra, syn. "*S. seti'gera*"[1]

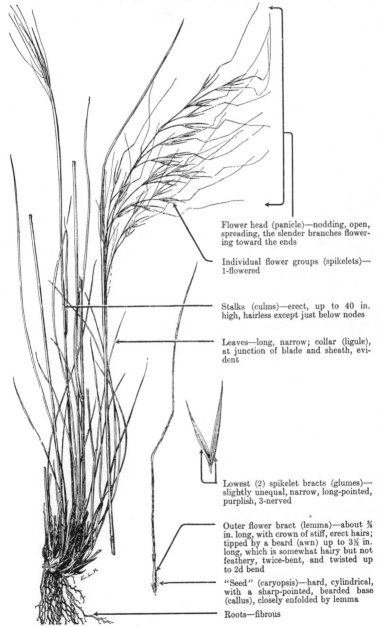

Flower head (panicle)—nodding, open, spreading, the slender branches flowering toward the ends

Individual flower groups (spikelets)—1-flowered

Stalks (culms)—erect, up to 40 in. high, hairless except just below nodes

Leaves—long, narrow; collar (ligule), at junction of blade and sheath, evident

Lowest (2) spikelet bracts (glumes)—slightly unequal, narrow, long-pointed, purplish, 3-nerved

Outer flower bract (lemma)—about ⅜ in. long, with crown of stiff, erect hairs; tipped by a beard (awn) up to 3½ in. long, which is somewhat hairy but not feathery, twice-bent, and twisted up to 2d bend

"Seed" (caryopsis)—hard, cylindrical, with a sharp-pointed, bearded base (callus), closely enfolded by lemma

Roots—fibrous

[1] Of United States authors, not Presl.

California needlegrass, a conspicuously awned grass, is sometimes called purple needlegrass, nodding needlegrass, southwestern porcupinegrass, and beargrass. It is chiefly a California species, commonly found on the warmer, open, well-drained flats and on sparsely timbered foothills and valleys at altitudes varying usually from about sea level to 5,500 feet. It is most abundant in the coast ranges of central California and extends south into Lower California, occurring but sparsely in northern California.

This species ranks high in forage value, being palatable to all classes of livestock, and particularly to cattle and horses. In some parts of California it is regarded as one of the most valuable grasses. Although its palatability is highest in the spring, it is grazed throughout the summer by cattle and horses and to some extent by sheep. It produces a large amount of comparatively fine leafage which remains green long after its commonly associated annuals have dried up. This plant also cures well on the ground. The seeds mature in early summer, after which the awns may be somewhat troublesome to sheep. When not grazed down during the summer, the species provides very good fall and winter forage.

California needlegrass is one of the most abundant needlegrasses in California. It is believed to have been formerly even more plentiful and one of the main grasses of the original bunchgrass cover in central California. It depends chiefly upon seed for reproduction and on many ranges has been largely killed out by being grazed so closely that seed could not mature. Under conservative use, California needlegrass reproduces well and will replace the annual grasses if given a chance.

California needlegrass has numerous slender rough stems 24 to 40 inches high, often ascending at an angle (not erect) from a tuft of long, slender, basal leaves. The panicle is commonly one-third to one-half the length of the stems, has slender, loosely spreading branches and, as a common name of the plant implies, has a distinctly nodding habit. The glumes are purplish, three-nerved, narrow, and long-tapering. The awns (beards) are 2 to $3\frac{1}{2}$ inches long, twisted, and twice-bent; the portion of the awn between the first and second bend is relatively short and the last segment is slender, tapering, and slightly curved.

SLEEPYGRASS

Sti'pa robus'ta, syn. *S. va'seyi*

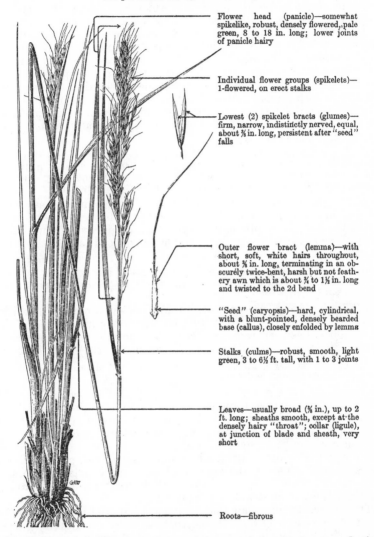

Flower head (panicle)—somewhat spikelike, robust, densely flowered, pale green, 8 to 18 in. long; lower joints of panicle hairy

Individual flower groups (spikelets)—1-flowered, on erect stalks

Lowest (2) spikelet bracts (glumes)—firm, narrow, indistinctly nerved, equal, about ⅜ in. long, persistent after "seed" falls

Outer flower bract (lemma)—with short, soft, white hairs throughout, about ⅜ in. long, terminating in an obscurely twice-bent, harsh but not feathery awn which is about ¾ to 1¼ in. long and twisted to the 2d bend

"Seed" (caryopsis)—hard, cylindrical, with a blunt-pointed, densely bearded base (callus), closely enfolded by lemma

Stalks (culms)—robust, smooth, light green, 3 to 6½ ft. tall, with 1 to 3 joints

Leaves—usually broad (⅜ in.), up to 2 ft. long; sheaths smooth, except at the densely hairy "throat"; collar (ligule), at junction of blade and sheath, very short

Roots—fibrous

Sleepygrass, so called because of its narcotic or sleep-producing effect upon livestock, is also known as Vasey needlegrass and robust porcupinegrass. It is a coarse, leafy, bright green grass which grows in thick bunches. The species, which usually is present in scattered stands and sometimes occurs over fairly large areas, is commonly found in open canyons or hillsides, and in parklike draws of timbered mountains at elevations between 5,000 and 9,000 feet.

Although its precise range is unknown it is typically a southwestern plant, and is known to occur in Colorado, western Texas, New Mexico, Arizona, and Mexico; it also occurs on San Nicolás Island, off the southern California coast.

Although Old World and South American species of *Stipa* are poisonous to domestic livestock, yet, so far as is known, sleepygrass is the only species in the United States known to be poisonous to livestock. While scientific analyses have thus far failed to uncover any poisonous principles in sleepygrass, its narcotic effect has long been recorded by many credible authorities. It is reported chiefly as affecting horses, but also causes sleepiness in cattle and sheep, and interferes with animal locomotion somewhat as does loco poisoning. The narcotic influence is usually only temporary but, in some cases, has been reported to last 48 hours and occasionally to be fatal.[1] Marsh and Clawson [2] report:

The grass has been shown by experimental feedings to produce a narcotic effect on horses. * * * While it may produce profound slumber, it does not cause death. Cattle showed no effect from the plant, and sheep, although slightly affected, did not show the typical symptoms of drowsiness.

The degree of narcotism depends upon the amount of grass eaten, which, in turn, is no doubt influenced by the scarcity of more palatable forage. Apparently sleepygrass produces different effects in different localities under similar conditions and utilization. Marsh and Clawson (*op. cit.*) state that

definite cases of sleepygrass poisoning have been reported from only two general localities, the Sacramento and the Sierra Blanca Mountains in Otero and Lincoln Counties, New Mexico.

On the other hand, in various New Mexico and Colorado localities this grass is eaten by livestock without any apparent narcotic effect.[1] Although it has been reported [1] that sleepygrass loses its poisonous properties when dried, Marsh and Clawson (*op. cit.*) state that

the green and the dry plant are about equally toxic if allowance is made for the loss of moisture in the dry plant.

Crawford [3] calls attention to some species of *Stipa* on the high plateaus of Argentine Republic which contain a glucoside which, when split up, yields hydrocyanic acid. He suggests the possibility that some North American species, particularly sleepygrass, may also on occasion yield hydrocyanic acid.

Sleepygrass is low in palatability but is sometimes grazed closely by cattle and horses in the absence of other more palatable forage. Wooton and Standley (*op. cit.*) state that animals brought into the region will consume it unless restrained.

This species produces an abundant supply of seed which results in satisfactory reproduction. It sometimes spreads over heavily grazed ranges after the better grasses have succumbed, but is not aggressive when in direct competition with them under controlled grazing.

[1] Wooton, E. O., and Standley, P. C. FLORA OF NEW MEXICO. U. S. Natl. Mus., Contrib. U. S. Natl. Herbarium 19, 794 pp. 1915.
[2] Marsh, C. D., and Clawson, A. B. SLEEPY GRASS (STIPA VASEYI) AS A STOCK-POISONING PLANT. U. S. Dept. Agr. Tech. Bull. 114, 20 pp., illus. 1929.
[3] Crawford, A. C. NOTES, MAINLY BIBLIOGRAPHICAL, ON TWO AMERICAN PLANTS—SLEEPY GRASS AND CREOSOTE BUSH. Pharm. Rev. 26 : 230–235. 1908.

GREEN NEEDLEGRASS

Sti'pa viri'dula

Flower head (panicle)—narrow, somewhat spikelike, greenish, 4 to 8 in. long

Individual flower groups (spikelets)—1-flowered, numerous from near the base of the erect flower-head branches

Lowest (2) spikelet bracts (glumes)—equal, ¼ to ⅜ in. long, thin, papery, tapering to slender point, with 3 prominent, green veins

Leaves—mainly basal, with somewhat hairy, inrolled margins, 4 to 12 in. long; upper leaves broader, sometimes flat; sheaths smooth, hairy at the throat and on margins

Stalks (culms)—mostly smooth, erect, up to 3½ (usually 2 to 3) ft. high

Outer flower bract (lemma)—evenly and sparingly soft-hairy, about ⁵⁄₁₆ in. long, tipped with a securely attached bristle (awn) which is ¾ to 1¼ in. long, twice bent, twisted to the second bend, and harsh but not feathery

"Seed" (caryopsis)—hard and cylindrical with a rather blunt-pointed, white-bearded base (callus), closely enfolded by lemma

Roots—fibrous

Green needlegrass, a perennial bunchgrass, is sometimes called green porcupinegrass and feather bunchgrass. The specific name *viridula* is a diminutive of the Latin word *viridis*, meaning green, and refers, as does the accepted common name, to the rather uniform bright green color of both herbage and flower heads. This species ranges from British Columbia to Minnesota, Kansas, New Mexico, Arizona, Nevada, and eastern Washington. It does not occur in California and perhaps is also absent from Oregon. Apparently it is more common in Montana, Wyoming, and Colorado than in the other western range States. It inhabits plains and foothills at fairly low elevations and is common on mountain meadowlands and open hillsides up to 9,000 feet in Wyoming and Montana. At the southern limit of its range, the species occurs in dry, open parks and canyons through the timbered mountains, chiefly in the ponderosa pine belt.

Green needlegrass is usually regarded as good forage, being one of the first grasses of its associations to start spring growth and remaining green until late in the season, thus supplying succulent forage over a long period. In general, this bunchgrass seems to be more palatable to cattle and horses than to sheep because sheep feed upon it chiefly in the spring and early summer, whereas cattle and horses graze it rather freely season-long. This species is sometimes regarded as more palatable to cattle and horses than are certain of the smaller needlegrasses. Although the sharp-pointed mature "seeds", or fruits, of this grass annoy grazing animals to some extent, especially sheep, they are not known to cause serious injury. They are usually avoided by livestock, being left to mature and replenish the stand. Although not abundant over large areas, green needlegrass supplies a fair amount of forage on many ranges in mixture with other grasses. It is also an important constituent of hay on some grass meadows of Montana.[1] This grass flowers from May to August, and the seeds are disseminated from July to September, depending upon climatic conditions.

Green needlegrass is a rather coarse, conspicuously fine-awned bunchgrass growing 1½ to 3 feet high or occasionally taller. The leaves are mainly basal, inrolled, about one-third to one-half as long as the stems and hairy at the junction of the blade and sheath. The stem leaves are somewhat shorter. The greenish panicle is 4 to 8 inches long, narrow, loosely spikelike, and rather densely flowered. The awn is commonly three-quarters to 1¼ inches long, slender, twice-bent, twisted to the second bend, and is not feathery. The two nearly equal glumes are thin with three prominent green nerves. The species closely resembles sleepygrass (*S. robusta*)— in fact, some authors regard sleepygrass as a variety of it—but green needlegrass is smaller, less robust throughout, and is mainly a northern grass, whereas sleepygrass occurs principally in the Southwest.

---

[1] Office of Grazing Studies, Forest Service. NOTES ON NATIONAL FOREST RANGE PLANTS, PART 1, GRASSES. 224 pp. 1914.

ARIZONA COTTONGRASS

Tricha'chne califor'nica, syn. *Valo'ta sacchara'ta*

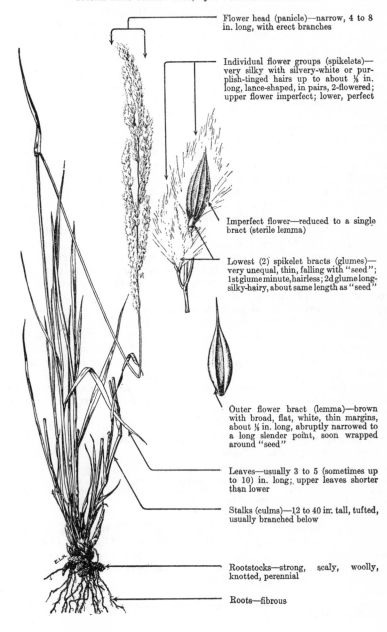

Flower head (panicle)—narrow, 4 to 8 in. long, with erect branches

Individual flower groups (spikelets)—very silky with silvery-white or purplish-tinged hairs up to about ⅛ in. long, lance-shaped, in pairs, 2-flowered; upper flower imperfect; lower, perfect

Imperfect flower—reduced to a single bract (sterile lemma)

Lowest (2) spikelet bracts (glumes)—very unequal, thin, falling with "seed"; 1st glume minute, hairless; 2d glume long-silky-hairy, about same length as "seed"

Outer flower bract (lemma)—brown with broad, flat, white, thin margins, about ⅛ in. long, abruptly narrowed to a long slender point, soon wrapped around "seed"

Leaves—usually 3 to 5 (sometimes up to 10) in. long; upper leaves shorter than lower

Stalks (culms)—12 to 40 in. tall, tufted, usually branched below

Rootstocks—strong, scaly, woolly, knotted, perennial

Roots—fibrous

Arizona cottongrass, a coarse, leafy perennial also called cotton-top, silky panicgrass, sugargrass, and small feathergrass, is a member of a small genus of the millet tribe (Paniceae), and is the only common species of the genus on the western ranges. Most of its common names originate from the silky-cottony appearance of the panicle. The generic name *Trichachne* is from the Greek *trich*, hair, and *achne*, chaff, referring to the hairy second glume and sterile lemma. This species, common on the deserts and foothills of southern New Mexico and Arizona in the woodland and semidesert types, occurs from Colorado to central Texas and Arizona and south into Mexico. It was originally described from Lower California, a fact imperfectly alluded to in the specific name *californica*. There is no record of its occurrence in California proper. It frequently is present on rocky ridges and along the edge of fields, as well as under cactus and other shrubs. Although seldom growing in extensive stands, this grass commonly constitutes from 2 to 5 percent of the ground cover in association with gramas (*Bouteloua* spp.), three-awns (*Aristida* spp.), and cane beardgrass (*Andropogon barbinodis*). This plant responds quickly to spring and summer rains, makes rapid growth and thus, although scattered, provides a considerable amount of highly palatable green forage at an earlier date than most of its associates. However, its season of maximum palatability is short, as the foliage becomes rather hard and tough when the plant stops growing. Consequently, its palatability decreases until the plant greens up again the following spring. The foliage cures on the ground and, generally speaking, the species ranks as both a good winter and summer grass although its winter use depends largely on the presence of more palatable forage. On conservatively grazed range Arizona cottongrass is utilized chiefly while green. It is, however, also a valuable grass in combination with the slower growing grama grasses, its common associates, as livestock will concentrate on young Arizona cottongrass and thus give the other grasses a better chance to develop. Propagation by rootstocks aids in the perpetuation and maintenance of this species under arid conditions and heavy grazing. Although a good seed crop is usually produced, the plant is not an aggressive spreader.

While reseeding tests have not yet given good results on the open range this species is believed to have good possibilities under favorable conditions. Wilson [1] states:

Of all the native range forage plant seeds tested at the experiment station, this has given the best germination. One sample of *Valota saccharata* (*i. e.*, *Trichachne californica*) seed tested in October 1930, a little over 10 years after maturity, gave a germination of 92 percent. A percentage of 70 to 85 percent for this species is not uncommon.

Arizona cottongrass has slender, erect stems 12 to 40 inches high, arising from strong, woolly, knotted rootstocks. The most outstanding character is the slender, silky-cottony panicle with its lance-shaped spikelets which grow in pairs and are covered with long, silky white (occasionally purplish) hairs.

---

[1] Wilson, C. P. THE ARTIFICIAL RESEEDING OF NEW MEXICO RANGES. N. Mex. Agr. Expt. Sta. Bull. 189, 37 pp., illus. 1931.

SPIKE TRISETUM

Trise'tum spica'tum, syn. *T. subspica'tum*

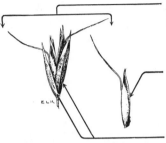

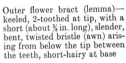

Individual flower groups (spikelets)—small, numerous, crowded, usually 2-flowered

Outer flower bract (lemma)—keeled, 2-toothed at tip, with a short (about ⅜ in. long), slender, bent, twisted bristle (awn) arising from below the tip between the teeth, short-hairy at base

Lowest (2) spikelet bracts (glumes)—somewhat unequal, persistent, without awns; 1st glume 1-nerved; 2d glume broader, 3-nerved

Flower heads (panicles)—dense, spikelike, erect, greenish or purplish, shining, 1 to 6 in. long

Leaves—flat or inrolled in age, rather narrow, about 2 to 6 in. long, usually more or less hairy; sheaths hairy

Stalks (culms)—densely tufted, erect, hairless to downy-hairy, up to 20 in. high

Roots—fibrous, perennial

Spike trisetum is a densely tufted perennial grass, which varies considerably in general appearance. However, it is easily recognized by its spikelike heads to which the fine, bent awns give a fuzzy appearance. Specimens from alpine situations are usually short, with thick stems and heads and densely hairy stems and leaves, in decided contrast to the taller, often nearly hairless plant, with slender stems and heads, of the lower altitudes.

This species is widely distributed in the mountainous regions of North America, Europe, and Australia and occurs in all the Western States, where it is typical of open, moist, alpine, and subalpine sites. However, it has a wide altitudinal range, and also occurs on dry soils, and in varying degrees of shade, among shrubs, aspen, open spruce, lodgepole pine, and ponderosa pine. It grows at elevations of from 7,500 feet to 13,000 feet in Colorado and extends down to an altitude of 6,000 feet in Utah. Spike trisetum ranges between 5,000 and 10,000 feet in California, and between 2,500 and 7,000 feet in Washington and Oregon. This grass is a common constituent of old burns and cut-over lands, but practically never occurs in dense, pure stands. However, from the standpoint of wide and general distribution over the western mountain ranges, spike trisetum ranks among the first four or five grass species.

The palatability of spike trisetum varies markedly in different regions, it being regarded as good to very good forage in the Northwest, where it is classed as somewhat more palatable to cattle and horses than to sheep. In California, where it is common in the higher mountains, it is relished by livestock, little being left even on areas not pastured until in the autumn.[1] In the Rocky Mountains from Montana southward this forage rates as fairly good to good for cattle and horses, and poor to fairly good for sheep. Growth begins early in the spring, and the plants remain green late in the fall. Presumably the grass is more readily grazed early in the season before the heads develop, and again in the fall after most other species are dry. Ordinarily, only a relatively limited amount of seed of low viability is produced. Dr. Sampson,[2] in his bulletin on range plants from which the illustration accompanying this article was taken, states that in the Blue Mountains region of northeastern Oregon seeds of this species ordinarily do not begin to ripen before about August 25, and generally are not all matured before inclement weather prevents further development. As a result, viable seed are produced only on the earliest flowering stalks and, in the tests made, had a very low germination percent. "In 1907 the seed crop averaged 11 percent germination, and in 1909 28 percent." The plants, however, stool well and are resistant to trampling and considerable close grazing.

TRISETUMS (Trise'tum spp.)

Trisetum is a genus of perennial or rarely annual grasses, widely distributed in the temperate and cooler or mountain regions of both the Northern and Southern Hemispheres. The name is derived from Latin *tri*, three, and *setum*, bristle, alluding to the three bristles (awns), which are borne on the outer flower bracts (lemmas) of many species. The awns of some species are very short and are hidden by the bracts of the spikelet; by some authors, those species are considered a distinct genus *Graphephorum*. The only common species of this type in the western United States is Wolf trisetum (*Trise'tum wolf'ii*, syns. *T. brande'gei, Graphe'phorum mu'ticum*).

The species of trisetum found in the Western States have similar palatability and are all fairly good to good forage, although somewhat less palatable to sheep than to cattle and horses.

Trisetums belong to the oat tribe of grasses (Aveneae). The leaves are usually flat, and the flower heads are narrow and spikelike or somewhat open, with numerous, small, three- to five-flowered individual flower groups (spikelets). The lowest (2) spikelet bracts (glumes) are unequal, sharp-pointed, and without awns, the second glume commonly being longer than the lowest lemma of each spikelet. Generally, the lemmas are short-hairy at the base, two-toothed at apex, and bear short, straight awns or longer, bent, and twisted awns from the back below the tip and between the teeth. The teeth of the lemma are themselves also frequently elongated into awns.

---

[1] Sampson, A. W., and Chase, A. RANGE GRASSES OF CALIFORNIA. Calif. Agr. Expt. Sta. Bull. 430, 94 pp., illus. 1927.

[2] Sampson, A. W. IMPORTANT RANGE PLANTS: THEIR LIFE HISTORY AND FORAGE VALUE. U. S. Dept. Agr. Bull. 545, 63 pp., illus. 1917.

SEDGES
Ca'rex spp.

The sedges vie with the groundsels (*Senecio* spp.) for the honor of being the largest genus of flowering plants in the world. It is true that more species of hawkweeds (*Hieracium* spp.) have been described than for any other plant genus, but, on a conservative nomenclatural basis, there is little question but that *Carex* and *Senecio* outrank all others. Sedges are herbs of world-wide distribution, occurring on all continents, especially in temperate climates. On western ranges they lead all other genera in number of species.

As a group, these plants resemble the grasses somewhat, having flat, grasslike leaves, and, frequently, similar growth habits. On this account the members of the genus *Carex*, as well as other genera of the sedge family (Cyperaceae) and the rushes (Juncaceae), are commonly referred to as grasslike plants. The sedges, however, have a number of characteristics which distinguish them definitely from other genera. For example, they are perennial by rootstocks, have solid, unjointed, and usually three-angled stems, mostly basal, closed sheaths, and leaves arranged in three ranks corresponding to the angles of the stem. The flowers are small, solitary in the axils of scales, without floral parts (perianth), and are always aggregated into a spike or spikes at or near the end or upper third of the stem. The grasses (Gramineae) growing on the ranges have cylindrical, jointed, and mostly hollow stems and the sheaths of the 2-ranked leaves are split or open. The flowers, however, are similar morphologically, being small, irregular, and subtended by a scale (glume); the fruit (achene) is dry and one-seeded.

The differences between the sedges and the rushes, however, are not always so obvious as these fundamental distinctions between the sedges and grasses. The stems of the rushes may be simple or branched, spongy-pithed or hollow, and naked or leafy. The leaves likewise vary, being round, flattened, or flat. The significant and constant difference is in the flowers, which, although brownish, and somewhat sedgelike in aspect, are lilylike in structure. They have a floral envelope (perianth) composed of six glumelike and regular segments. The stamens are six or sometime three, and the fruit is a three-celled capsule containing many small seeds.

The form of the aerial growth of a sedge depends largely on the character of its root system. Such a species as ovalhead sedge (*C. festivel'la*), which has very short rootstocks, produces stems and leaves at very short intervals, becomes tufted and looks much like a bunchgrass. Others, like the Douglas sedge (*C. dougla'sii*), have running rootstocks, from which a single group of stems and leaves arise at intervals of several inches, with each one having the appearance of a separate plant. Either type may develop a sodlike cover in dense stands, such as threadleaf sedge (*C. filifo'lia*) produces on dry sites, a condition particularly common in sedge meadows.

Sedge leaves are usually rather long, thin, and narrow. Some species, such as threadleaf sedge and its allies, have very fine, threadlike foliage, and a few species, typified by the eastern white-bear sedge (*C. albursi'na*, syn. *C. laxiflora latifolia*), have leaves up to 1½ inches wide. The leaves of most species on the western ranges, however, are less than one-fourth of an inch wide. In general, the dryland species have very fine, dull, or brownish-green foliage; the moist-soil species characteristically possess thin, bright green leaves less than one-fourth of an inch wide; and the wet, swampy, or bog-inhabiting species, broad, long, tough, brownish-green leaves.

The stems, of course, vary in height and size with the various species. A few of the more robust, western, wet-site sedges commonly attain a height of 3 feet or more, but most species range from 8 to 20 inches in height. The dryland species in the West, however, are principally less than 8 inches high. The stems may or may not be leafy, but when leafy the upper leaves become bract-like and subtend the flower heads, or spikes. The flower cluster in its simplest form, as in threadleaf sedge, consists of one terminal spike. In ovalhead sedge and similar species several spikes are closely aggregated into a head which has the general appearance of one large terminal spike. Other sedges, as beaked sedge (*C. rostra'ta*) and Nebraska sedge (*C. nebrasken'sis*), have two types of spikes: (1) terminal, relatively small, staminate or male, and (2) lower, axillary, larger and pistillate, or female. In many species, as in threadleaf sedge, both male and female flowers are borne in the same spike, with the male flowers uppermost, but in many others the female flowers are in the upper half of the spike.

The individual flowers are small, inconspicuous, and relatively simple in structure. Each flower, whether male or female, is sub-tended by a small scale, which corresponds to the glume of the grass flower. Although these scales are small, their variations in length, shape, color, and other characteristics are used frequently in botanical keys to separate species. The male flowers, with three or sometimes two stamens, are little used in species differentiations, as botanical keys are based largely on the character of the female flower, especially the mature fruit. The female flowers terminate in two or three threadlike stigmas. The often three-angled seed, which is an achene, is enclosed in a saclike body called the peri-gynium. The length, shape, and character of the surface, margins, and beak of the perigynium are all commonly used in botanical keys to separate major groups as well as species.

The popular impression that sedges are plants which occur exclusively in moist and wet situations lacks verity. Some species, notably elk sedge (*C. gey'eri*), grow on well-drained and dry slopes, and in timber. Threadleaf sedge and similar species commonly form dense and extensive, sodlike areas on open and dry plains, benches, and flats. Other species, such as Douglas sedge, inhabit meadow borders and other semimoist soils, and frequently form a distinct zone between the dryland vegetation and the wet meadow or other moist-soil types.

Sedges are usually adaptable to soils of various origins, provided they are moderately fertile and moisture conditions are favorable. Ordinarily, however, these plants are limited wholly to soils of neutral or acid reaction. Frequently, the extremely wet, highly organic soils of bogs and swamps are distinctly acid. Sedges are sometimes important in soil formation, especially on very boggy or wet sites, where the ungrazed and rank growth accumulates year after year. Many of the organic and peatlike mountain meadows and lake shore soils have been developed largely in that manner.

Despite that most sedges grow in full sunlight, there are various examples, both in dry and moist situations, of species which are shade enduring. The elevational range of *Carex* is probably as great as for any plant genus, species occurring from near sea level to the highest extension of flowering plants above timberline.

A common tendency exists to underrate the forage value of sedges on the western ranges. This is due, in part, to the difficulty of identifying the numerous species of sedges, and also to the fact that many species are mistaken for grasses, as may be noted in the erroneous use of such common names as hairgrass for threadleaf sedge and elkgrass for elk sedge. A common practice, even among technically trained men, is to group the sedges in one to several large classes according to leaf width or moisture requirements, but without regard to taxonomic relationships. Such treatment is convenient and often desirable, but has the obvious tendency to perpetuate inaccurate generalities. Furthermore, under such conditions, the characteristics and forage value of individual species are not accurately observed or recorded.

The discussions of several species of *Carex* in this handbook emphasize some of the forage and habitat variations within the genus. Elk sedge is representative of a small group of slope- and timber-inhabiting species, which ordinarily start growth early and remain green until fall and, although grazed season-long, are usually most valuable as spring and fall feed. The small-leaved, rather low, dry land species represented by threadleaf sedge, the similar short-hair sedge (*C. exser′ta*) and other species are often abundant and provide an important source of forage on many ranges. They start growth early and ordinarily mature before midsummer, and hence are most palatable in the spring. However, depending on local conditions, their use in certain cases may be either seasonlong or chiefly in the fall. The moist-meadow species, such as ovalhead sedge, are probably the most palatable of the genus, usually providing fine, green, and comparatively tender foliage, which remains succulent until fall, and is relished by sheep and even more so by cattle. Some of the wet-site species, including Nebraska sedge and the like, are generally good forage for cattle, but ordinarily are located in situations too wet for sheep. The more robust, large-leaved, and wet-site sedges, as beaked sedge, are of low palatability to sheep, and only fair forage for cattle. Because of favorable moisture conditions, they generally remain green longer than most range plants, and also show a marked tendency to produce replacement growth when grazed, which is relished by livestock especially after midsummer. This recurrent harvesting improves, as a rule, the palatability of the species.

The sedges, such as Douglas and Nebraska sedge, which commonly reproduce by rootstocks, withstand close use unusually well. Their strong root systems are well adapted to supply water and nutrients, as well as to hold the plant in position and to bind the soil. Seed production is obviously unnecessary for the maintenance of such species. The tufted, bunchlike species, characterized by threadleaf and ovalhead sedges, do not resist close use as well. Although the fibrous feeding roots are numerous and long, they do not bind the soil compactly unless the individual plants are so numerous as to be crowded. Seed production is probably at least occasionally necessary for satisfactory reproduction of the species in this group, although the very short rootstocks increase the size of the parent plant and, under proper management practices, should maintain the stand satisfactorily during the life of the parent plants.

Sedges are frequently important to wildlife. In Alaska they supply forage during both summer and winter for reindeer.[1] Elk graze sedges rather freely, especially on the summer ranges at higher altitudes, and they are also generally grazed by moose. In most localities deer, apparently, do not utilize sedges very much.[2]

Various species of moist- and wet-meadow sedges comprise a large percentage of the hay crop in such western areas as the agricultural mountain valleys, where livestock are winter fed. Although natural in most of the hay meadows, the sedges have, in many instances, increased greatly as a result of overirrigation. Conversely, on some swampy lands drainage has sometimes resulted in their replacement by grasses. Most species cure well and make a palatable hay, but, because of their light weight and short, smooth leaves and stems, are more difficult to handle than grain hays. Experimental work indicates that sedges deteriorate less than grasses as a result of late cutting.[3] They also show a less rapid decline in protein content than the common, associated, and introduced bluegrasses and bromes. Another interesting discovery is that the nutritional value of sedges, at least so far as crude protein and nitrogen-free extract (carbohydrates) are concerned, apparently increases with altitude more than is the case with grasses. Comparative chemical analyses of various species of *Carex* and of grasses show that their nutritive properties are similar in most cases, the sedges tending to produce less crude fiber and ash and more crude protein and nitrogen-free extract.[4][5]

Sedges are generally very effective in soil protection. The dense stands, both on dry and moist sites, prevent erosion and soil loss. The intertwining of the rootstocks and roots on meadows and swampy areas is usually so complex and thick that it resists even the passage of a shovel. This matlike layer, unless undermined, as from a gulley head or side, will usually protect and build up the soil and prevent washing.

The Indians formerly used sedge roots in basketry production.[6]

[1] Hadwen, S., and Palmer, L. J. REINDEER IN ALASKA. U. S. Dept. Agr. Bull. 1089, 74 pp., illus. 1922.
[2] Dixon, J. S. A STUDY OF THE LIFE HISTORY AND FOOD HABITS OF MULE DEER IN CALIFORNIA. PART 2, FOOD HABITS. Calif. Fish and Game 20(4) : [315]–354, illus. 1934.
[3] Roberts, E. N. WYOMING FORAGE PLANTS AND THEIR CHEMICAL COMPOSITION ; STUDIES NO. 7. EFFECT OF ALTITUDE, SEASONAL VARIATIONS, AND SHADING EXPERIMENTS. Wyo. Agr. Expt. Sta. Bull. 146, 89 pp., illus. 1926.
[4] Knight, H. G., Hepner, F. E., and Nelson, A. WYOMING FORAGE PLANTS AND THEIR CHEMICAL COMPOSITION ; STUDIES (NO. 2. Wyo. Agr. Expt. Sta. Bull. 70, 75 pp., illus. 1906.
[5] Knight, H. G., Hepner, F. E., and Nelson, A. WYOMING FORAGE PLANTS AND THEIR CHEMICAL COMPOSITION ; STUDIES NO. 3. Wyo. Agr. Expt. Sta. Bull. 76, 119 pp., illus. 1908.
[6] Merrill, R. E. PLANTS USED IN BASKETRY BY THE CALIFORNIA INDIANS. Calif. Univ. Pubs., Amer. Archeol. and Ethnol. 20 : 215–242, illus. 1923.

OVALHEAD SEDGE

Ca'rex festivel'la, syn. *"C. fes'tiva"* [1]

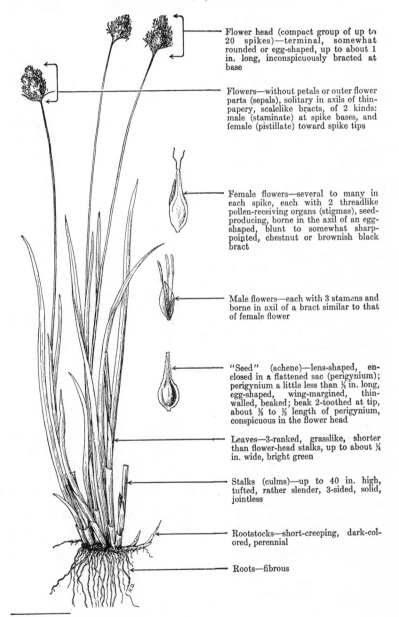

Flower head (compact group of up to 20 spikes)—terminal, somewhat rounded or egg-shaped, up to about 1 in. long, inconspicuously bracted at base

Flowers—without petals or outer flower parts (sepals), solitary in axils of thin-papery, scalelike bracts, of 2 kinds: male (staminate) at spike bases, and female (pistillate) toward spike tips

Female flowers—several to many in each spike, each with 2 threadlike pollen-receiving organs (stigmas), seed-producing, borne in the axil of an egg-shaped, blunt to somewhat sharp-pointed, chestnut or brownish black bract

Male flowers—each with 3 stamens and borne in axil of a bract similar to that of female flower

"Seed" (achene)—lens-shaped, enclosed in a flattened sac (perigynium); perigynium a little less than ¼ in. long, egg-shaped, wing-margined, thin-walled, beaked; beak 2-toothed at tip, about ⅓ to ½ length of perigynium, conspicuous in the flower head

Leaves—3-ranked, grasslike, shorter than flower-head stalks, up to about ¼ in. wide, bright green

Stalks (culms)—up to 40 in. high, tufted, rather slender, 3-sided, solid, jointless

Rootstocks—short-creeping, dark-colored, perennial

Roots—fibrous

[1] Of western United States authors, not Dewey.

Ovalhead sedge, a rather common, tufted, and green-leaved sedge, which occurs from Alberta to New Mexico and westward to Arizona, the Sierra Nevadas of California, eastern Oregon and British Columbia, is one of the most important forage sedges in the western mountains. It grows in moist situations but not in shallow water or swamps. This species prefers such sites as meadows and springy slopes, especially at higher elevations, growing on usually deep, loamy soils in the meadows, but it is also common on shallow and rocky soils on slopes and about springs. Occasionally, this sedge even grows in rock crevices, if the moisture supply is adequate. Where it appears to be growing in bogs and swampy areas, a closer examination usually shows that the sedge really is confined to elevated and moist areas such as hummocks and on the sides of rocks and logs. It normally grows in the full sunlight, although fair stands sometimes occur in the shade. The elevational range is great because of the wide distribution of this plant. Strange to say, in the Northwest and Canada this species grows within several hundred feet of sea level, yet in the southern Rockies it occurs at timberline (12,000 feet). Although sometimes abundant in the meadows of the ponderosa pine belt, it is most common in the high mountain meadows between the upper edge of that belt and timberline.

In general, ovalhead sedge is classed as fairly good for sheep and good to very good for cattle, although its palatability apparently varies widely with locality. It has relatively fine and tender, bright-green leafage which normally remains green until fall. It is usually entirely available to both sheep and cattle, growing on moist but solid soils, a feature particularly important to sheepmen, whose flocks and bands intuitively avoid wet and miry range. Although often abundant, this sedge does not ordinarily grow in pure stands, the tufted individuals usually being well-distributed among various other sedges and such grasses as bluegrasses and redtops.

Ovalhead sedge will not withstand close use. It has a tufted or bunch habit of growth, because of its very short rootstocks which increase the size of the parent plant but do not, as a rule, extend far enough to produce new plants. As a result, reproduction is almost wholly from seed (achenes); if this plant is grazed so closely that seed production is prevented, the stand soon succumbs. Overgrazing, leading to the ultimate destruction of the grasses and serious range depletion, gradually reduces the vitality of the clumps of this sedge until eventually they die. This sedge is frequently an important constituent of the meadow hays harvested in the mountain valleys for winter feeding, because it cures well, is light but bulky, and is eaten readily.

Ovalhead sedge is a member of a large group of closely related sedges (*Ovales* section), including *C. abrupta*, *C. ebenea*, *C. festiva*, and *C. microptera*. On the range many of these species are so similar in form, color, and habitat that few grazing men are able to distinguish between them. Even some botanists maintain that the slight differences in the fruit and other characters which separate these forms are doubtfully sufficient to warrant the recognition of many of them at least as separate species.

THREADLEAF SEDGE

Ca'rex filifo'lia, syn. *C. oreo'charis*

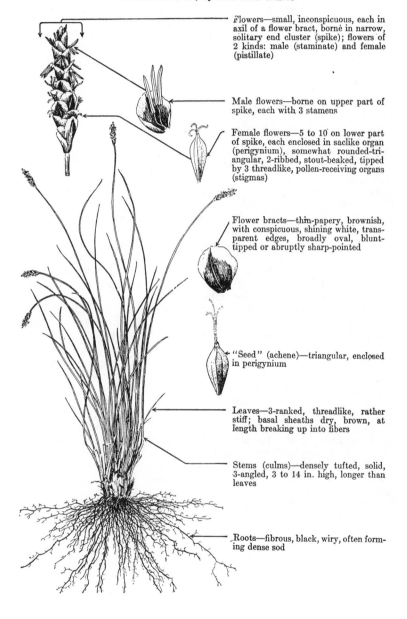

Flowers—small, inconspicuous, each in axil of a flower bract, borne in narrow, solitary end cluster (spike); flowers of 2 kinds: male (staminate) and female (pistillate)

Male flowers—borne on upper part of spike, each with 3 stamens

Female flowers—5 to 10 on lower part of spike, each enclosed in saclike organ (perigynium), somewhat rounded-triangular, 2-ribbed, stout-beaked, tipped by 3 threadlike, pollen-receiving organs (stigmas)

Flower bracts—thin-papery, brownish, with conspicuous, shining white, transparent edges, broadly oval, blunt-tipped or abruptly sharp-pointed

"Seed" (achene)—triangular, enclosed in perigynium

Leaves—3-ranked, threadlike, rather stiff; basal sheaths dry, brown, at length breaking up into fibers

Stems (culms)—densely tufted, solid, 3-angled, 3 to 14 in. high, longer than leaves

Roots—fibrous, black, wiry, often forming dense sod

213

Threadleaf sedge, sometimes called niggerwool, hair sedge, and shorthair sedge, is a small grasslike plant of the sedge family (Cyperaceae). The name shorthair sedge is perhaps preferably applied to the closely related Pacific species, *C. exserta.* The specific name *filifolia* refers to the fine, threadlike leaves characteristic of this plant. This sedge has a wide range from Yukon Territory to Saskatchewan, Texas, and California. It is found at elevations of from 3,000 feet up to nearly 12,000 feet and is typically a dryland sedge, occurring in great abundance on the dry soils of open prairies and rolling grasslands. On its favorite sites this plant occasionally forms almost pure stands, but usually is intermixed thoroughly with a variety of grasses. In the mountains this sedge is seen most commonly on dry open ridges, but it also occurs in open timber types and, at the higher elevations, sometimes grows in rather moist meadows. Threadleaf sedge is common on the east slopes of the ponderosa pine type of California, growing on the open, rather dry sandy flats, and in the gently rolling, open forest. The Oregon ground squirrel (*Citellus oregonus*) builds its furrows in northeastern California in the threadleaf sedge stands on sandy flats.

Threadleaf sedge not only withstands grazing well but is also considerably drought-resistant. In portions of the western Great Plains this sedge is considered invaluable in the prevention of erosion, especially wind erosion. Its many, black, fibrous roots are very tough and wiry and form a heavy sod which is highly resistant to heavy trampling. Even after the individual plants die their roots remain intact for many years and continue to hold the soil against the onslaughts of destructive run-off.

In general, the forage value of this sedge on the mountain ranges in the West varies from fair to fairly good for sheep, cattle, and horses, often being somewhat more valuable for sheep. Threadleaf sedge, shorthair sedge, and Brewer reedgrass (*Calamagrostis breweri*) compose the famous shorthair range of the high Sierra Nevada Mountains in California. On some of the dry open grassland ranges threadleaf sedge takes position as one of the best sedges, being of particular value early in the season and at that time rates in palatability from good to very good for sheep, cattle, and horses.

Shorthair sedge (*C. exser'ta*) is very difficult to distinguish from threadleaf sedge, and for all practical range purposes it is not necessary to separate the two. Shorthair sedge has a somewhat limited range, occurring only in southern Oregon and California. It grows on the same or similar sites as threadleaf sedge and is of equal palatability.

ELK SEDGE

Ca'rex gey'eri

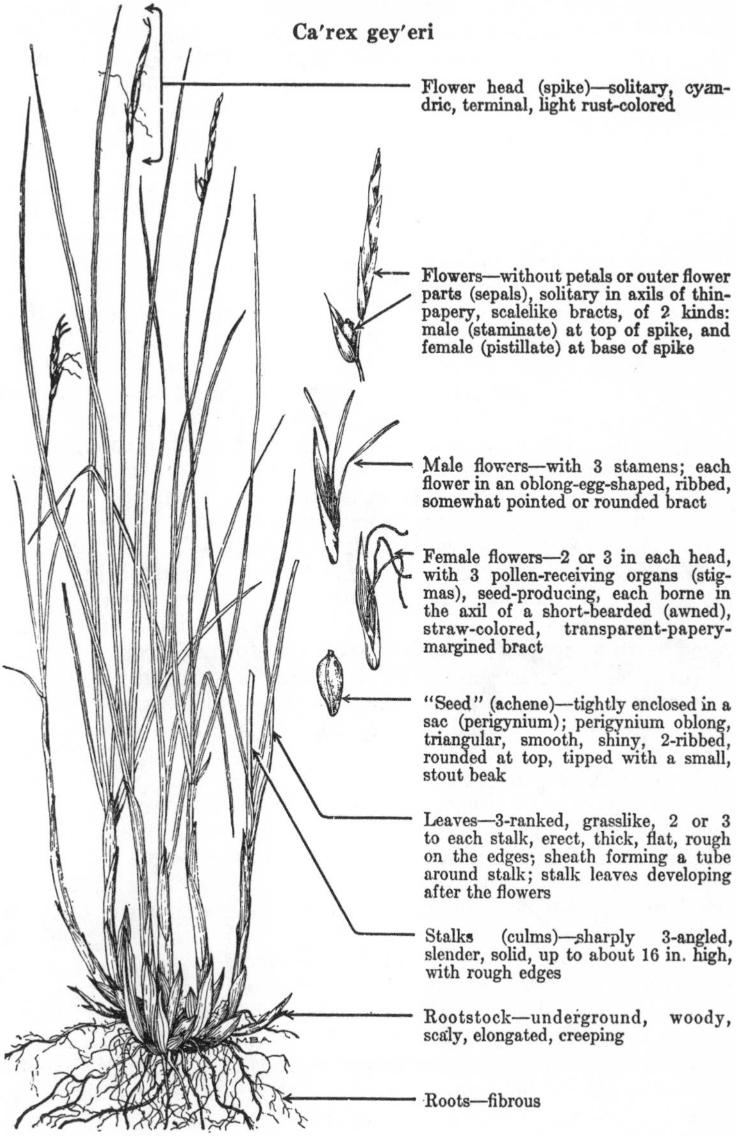

Flower head (spike)—solitary, cyandric, terminal, light rust-colored

Flowers—without petals or outer flower parts (sepals), solitary in axils of thin-papery, scalelike bracts, of 2 kinds: male (staminate) at top of spike, and female (pistillate) at base of spike

Male flowers—with 3 stamens; each flower in an oblong-egg-shaped, ribbed, somewhat pointed or rounded bract

Female flowers—2 or 3 in each head, with 3 pollen-receiving organs (stigmas), seed-producing, each borne in the axil of a short-bearded (awned), straw-colored, transparent-papery-margined bract

"Seed" (achene)—tightly enclosed in a sac (perigynium); perigynium oblong, triangular, smooth, shiny, 2-ribbed, rounded at top, tipped with a small, stout beak

Leaves—3-ranked, grasslike, 2 or 3 to each stalk, erect, thick, flat, rough on the edges; sheath forming a tube around stalk; stalk leaves developing after the flowers

Stalks (culms)—sharply 3-angled, slender, solid, up to about 16 in. high, with rough edges

Rootstock—underground, woody, scaly, elongated, creeping

Roots—fibrous

Elk sedge, sometimes known as Geyer sedge, pine sedge, or unfortunately pinegrass and elkgrass, is a grasslike plant belonging to the sedge family (Cyperaceae) This sedge is the most abundant of the comparatively few dry-land sedges, ranging from British Columbia to Montana, Colorado, Utah, and northern California. It occurs in a variety of sites on well-drained sandy, gravelly, or rocky soils at elevations of from about 1,000 up to 10,000 feet. Although most prominent on exposed hillsides, it grows well on open grass-lands and open timber types and sometimes also in fairly dense timber. This species, on parts of its range, appears typically in open ponderosa pine and lodgepole pine stands, frequently being inter-mixed with pinegrass (*Calamagrostis rubescens*). It commonly forms a heavy sod in almost pure stands on open hillsides and burns, which it readily invades.

Elk sedge withstands grazing exceptionally well, because it reproduces from woody, elongated, creeping rootstocks, forming dense, almost inseparable tufts. This plant is very drought-resist-ant, being close to the van among sedges in ability to withstand adverse moisture conditions.[1]

It abounds over much of its range and is one of the earliest forage plants on the lower ranges. Early in the season this foliage is eaten to some extent on most ranges when the leaves are relatively tender, although livestock prefer other forage, if such is available. The forage value of elk sedge for domestic livestock varies greatly, because it is considered worthless on many ranges, although, due to its abundance, early appearance, and its ability to remain green the entire season its average palatability rating is from poor to fair for sheep and from fair to fairly good for cattle and horses. In parts of the Pacific Northwest, where elk sedge occurs in great abundance, it is considered a valuable forage plant, with a palatability of from fair to good for sheep and from fairly good to very good for cattle and horses. In this same region, where elk sedge is found inter-mixed with pinegrass, livestock seek the former species but reject the pinegrass. Sheep, apparently, graze elk sedge more readily on those ranges where the more palatable weeds and browse species are rather deficient. The palatability for elk is fair to good but some-what lower for deer.

Elk sedge and pinegrass are sometimes confused, perhaps because they grow in similar sites and have somewhat similar leaves. When flower or seed heads are in evidence, the sedge, with its short, narrow, cylindrical, terminal, brownish flower cluster borne on 3-angled, pithy stems, is not readily mistaken for the grass with its 3 to 6 inch long, spikelike, reddish or pale green heads borne on hollow, round stems. It is rather characteristic of pinegrass, especially when growing in timber, rarely to produce flower heads, and, of course flower heads of the sedge are usually undeveloped in the spring and may largely disappear later in the season. However, the leaves of elk sedge are 3-ranked, erect, thick and rough on the edges, whereas those of pinegrass are mostly gracefully drooping, harsh or rough on both surfaces, and with a ring of stiff hairs at the collar (junction of blade and sheath).

---

[1] Sampson, A. W. IMPORTANT RANGE PLANTS: THEIR LIFE HISTORY AND FORAGE VALUE. U. S. Dept. Agr. Bull. 545, 63 pp., illus. 1917.

NEBRASKA SEDGE

Ca'rex nebrasken'sis

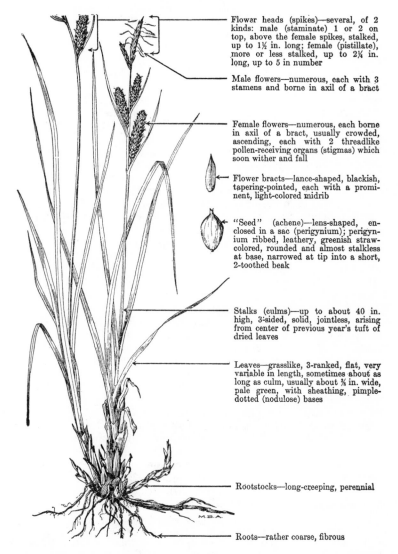

Flower heads (spikes)—several, of 2 kinds: male (staminate) 1 or 2 on top, above the female spikes, stalked, up to 1½ in. long; female (pistillate), more or less stalked, up to 2¼ in. long, up to 5 in number

Male flowers—numerous, each with 3 stamens and borne in axil of a bract

Female flowers—numerous, each borne in axil of a bract, usually crowded, ascending, each with 2 threadlike pollen-receiving organs (stigmas) which soon wither and fall

Flower bracts—lance-shaped, blackish, tapering-pointed, each with a prominent, light-colored midrib

"Seed" (achene)—lens-shaped, enclosed in a sac (perigynium); perigynium ribbed, leathery, greenish straw-colored, rounded and almost stalkless at base, narrowed at tip into a short, 2-toothed beak

Stalks (culms)—up to about 40 in. high, 3-sided, solid, jointless, arising from center of previous year's tuft of dried leaves

Leaves—grasslike, 3-ranked, flat, very variable in length, sometimes about as long as culm, usually about ⅜ in. wide, pale green, with sheathing, pimple-dotted (nodulose) bases

Rootstocks—long-creeping, perennial

Roots—rather coarse, fibrous

Nebraska sedge, one of the commonest western sedges inhabiting wet situations, ranges from South Dakota and Kansas to New Mexico, California, and British Columbia. Although this species is more important in the States west of Nebraska, it is called Nebraska sedge and *Carex nebraskensis* because the first specimens of it appear to have been collected in what is now that State. It occurs on the plains of Nebraska and contiguous States, and up to an elevation of 10,000 feet in Colorado and the southern Sierras of California. Nebraska sedge is found in favorable locations throughout the sagebrush and piñon belts but is, perhaps, most common in the ponderosa pine belt in mountainous regions. It is apparently not common in the coastal mountains of the Pacific States.

Throughout its range this sedge occurs exclusively in such wet sites as along slow streams, near springs, in shallow, swampy areas, and wet meadows. In the wet sedge meadows of the mountains it is frequently one of the dominant plants. After midsummer it is sometimes seen in places that are apparently dry, although invariably these locations are wet in the spring and early summer and probably are subirrigated during the rest of the season. It sometimes grows in wet gravelly soils, but generally inhabits water-deposited loams or highly organic, often peatlike, marshy soils.

The palatability of Nebraska sedge varies with the amount and distribution of palatable grasses and other plants associated with it, with the season of the year, and with the amount of moisture in the soil. As a rule, it is poor to fair forage for sheep and fairly good to good or occasionally very good for cattle. In general, the absolute palatability is perhaps greatest in the spring and early summer when the foliage and stems are tender, but this is affected by the factors mentioned above. Sheep sometimes make heavy use of the green foliage when it is readily available. Generally, however, the sites where this sedge grows are too wet for sheep until fall, when the mature foliage is coarse and of low palatability. Unless the soil is too boggy, cattle readily graze the moist areas where Nebraska sedge grows. However, if sufficient palatable grass and weeds are available, cattle often will avoid extensive wet sedge meadows containing Nebraska sedge and related species until after midsummer. In such cases, and on properly stocked range, the subsequent late summer and fall use of Nebraska sedge by cattle is usually such that satisfactory utilization is secured. A very different condition frequently obtains on cattle ranges and even sheep ranges, where sedge meadows provide but a small percentage of the forage. On such ranges livestock will often concentrate on the Nebraska sedge areas and utilize them so closely that the leaves are grazed almost to the ground and the production of stems and flowers is prevented. Despite such close use, this species, because of its strong root system and the prerequisite favorable moisture conditions, continues to send out new growth throughout the growing season. Its strongly developed rootstocks, from which new plants arise, make it particularly well adapted to withstand abusive grazing.

Nebraska sedge is commonly an important component of native meadow hay, particularly in the lower mountain valleys, where a large volume of natural and irrigated meadow hay for winter livestock feeding is harvested annually. In some sections, overirrigation has suppressed the grasses and greatly encouraged this and other sedges. Nebraska sedge hay cures well, but is not easily handled, being bulky and difficult to fork. Chemical analyses furnish evidence that, although this hay contains less than half as much crude protein as alfalfa, it yet ranks high in potential nutritive properties.[1]

[1] Knight, H. G., Hepner, F. E., and Nelson, A. WYOMING FORAGE PLANTS AND THEIR CHEMICAL COMPOSITION—STUDIES NO. 2. Wyo. Agr. Expt. Sta. Bull. 70, 75 pp., illus. 1906.

MILLET WOODRUSH

Juncoi'des parviflo'rum, syn. *Lu'zula parviflo'ra*

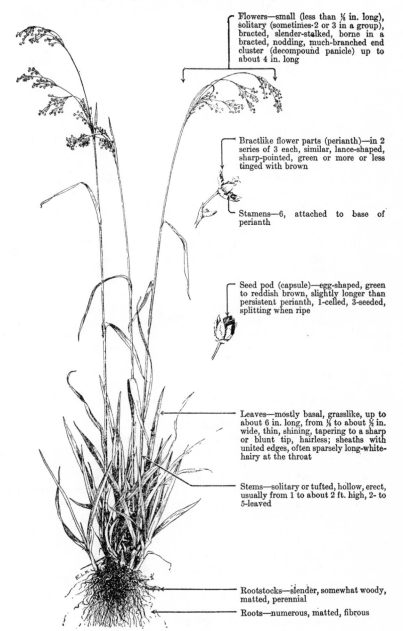

Flowers—small (less than ⅛ in. long), solitary (sometimes 2 or 3 in a group), bracted, slender-stalked, borne in a bracted, nodding, much-branched end cluster (decompound panicle) up to about 4 in. long

Bractlike flower parts (perianth)—in 2 series of 3 each, similar, lance-shaped, sharp-pointed, green or more or less tinged with brown

Stamens—6, attached to base of perianth

Seed pod (capsule)—egg-shaped, green to reddish brown, slightly longer than persistent perianth, 1-celled, 3-seeded, splitting when ripe

Leaves—mostly basal, grasslike, up to about 6 in. long, from ⅛ to about ½ in. wide, thin, shining, tapering to a sharp or blunt tip, hairless; sheaths with united edges, often sparsely long-white-hairy at the throat

Stems—solitary or tufted, hollow, erect, usually from 1 to about 2 ft. high, 2- to 5-leaved

Rootstocks—slender, somewhat woody, matted, perennial

Roots—numerous, matted, fibrous

219

Millet woodrush, one of the most common members of this moderately large genus of perennial, grasslike plants, is widely distributed in Europe and Asia as well as in North America. It grows in low woods and on open mountain slopes from Alaska to Labrador, south to New York, Minnesota, New Mexico, and California, occurring through the mountains of the 11 far Western States. The specific name *parviflorum* means "small-flowered", and the plant is sometimes called "small-flowered woodrush." However, since this species was originally described in 1791, several other west-American species, such as Piper woodrush (*J. pi'peri*) and Donner woodrush (*J. subconges'tum*), with even smaller flowers, have been collected and described. People without botanical training frequently mistake *J. parviflorum* for a *Panicum* (the grass genus to which broomcorn millet—the original "millet", *P. miliaceum*, oldest of cultivated cereals—belongs); it has a rather milletlike head, and the English name millet woodrush is here suggested as appropriate.

The altitudinal range of millet woodrush in the Western States is extensive. In the coastal region from Alaska as far south as Washington, at least, it descends to sea level. In the interior its range is largely restricted to the moist, high mountains up to about 6,000 feet in California, 6,500 feet in Washington and Oregon, 7,500 feet in Idaho, 8,500 feet in Montana, 10,500 feet in Utah and Nevada, and 12,000 feet or over in Colorado and New Mexico. Although seldom abundant, except perhaps in the coastal region of the Northwest, it is usually a common and characteristic plant of meadows, moist woods, and bogs. Its favorite sites are wet, highly organic, oozy soils, such as around seeps and the like, ·and where it is a common associate of tufted hairgrass (*Deschampsia caespitosa*) in moist meadows and other areas. Millet woodrush apparently does equally well under all light conditions, from full sunlight to rather dense shade. Distribution of this species is usually governed by favorable moisture conditions.

The forage value of millet woodrush on summer ranges is usually regarded as poor to fair for sheep and fair to fairly good, or occasionally good, for cattle. In general, its utilization tends to increase somewhat as the grazing season advances, due largely to the greater consumption of its more palatable grass associates during the spring and summer and to the partial drying of the areas its occupies. Frequently this plant is not available to livestock because of its occurrence in soft, miry areas, which range livestock intuitively avoid. In other instances, although the species is readily available in some parks and meadows, it is not utilized due to the isolation and nonuse of those areas. Even where the range is rather closely grazed, millet woodrush is often only slightly utilized. The reason for this local neglect, where it occurs, is obscure, as this species has the abundant succulent leafiness characteristic of a good forage plant. The individual plants of millet woodrush, though normally scattered, commonly form a several-stemmed, densely leafy tuft from the slender rootstocks (this species is less accurately referred to in some manuals as "stoloniferous") in simulation of the better range bunchgrasses. Furthermore, the foliage is still green and tender when most of the associated plants have matured.

WOODRUSHES

Juncoi'des spp., syn. *Lu'zula spp.*

The woodrushes, with the rushes (*Juncus* spp.), comprise the North American representatives of the rush family (Juncaceae) whose members are chiefly distinguished from the sedge family (Cyperaceae) and the grass family (Gramineae) by their regular, perfect flowers composed of six similar perianth segments, usually three or six stamens, and a three- to many-seeded fruit (capsule). Although small and dull-colored (greenish or brownish), the flowers are essentially lilylike in structure. The woodrushes, although similar to the rushes in many respects, differ chiefly in that the leaves are softer and flatter than in *Juncus* and not infrequently are hairy, the leaf sheaths are closed, the stems are hollow and conspicuously leafy, and the capsules are one-celled and one- or three-seeded. The stems of true rushes (Junci) are often leafless or, when leafy, the leaf sheaths are open, and the capsules are one- or three-celled and contain several to many seeds. In contrast to the soft, flat, grasslike leaf blades of the woodrushes, those of the rushes are usually stiff and may be flat, round, or channeled. *Juncoides* is composed of approximately 65 widely distributed species, with about 12 native to the western range States. The common name woodrush was applied to this genus because of its resemblance to the true rushes, and its frequent habit of growing in wooded areas. The generic name *Juncoides* is of Greek origin and means "like *Juncus*." Under the International Code of nomenclature, generic names with the *-oides* suffix are rejected under the theory that they are of doubtful scientific propriety. Hence, under that Code, the next oldest name, *Luzula* is adopted for this genus. The U. S. Department of Agriculture, under the leadership of Dr. Frederick V. Coville, the foremost living American student of Juncaceae, has accepted the American Code name *Juncoides* for these plants.

The other species of woodrush growing in the West are similar in many ways to millet woodrush. They generally inhabit moist to wet situations, either in the open or shade, with the exception that Piper and Donner woodrushes are largely limited to drier, sandy, or gravelly soils. Although the forage value of the individual species varies considerably, the palatability of the group as a whole is similar to that of millet woodrush, and they are seldom grazed as much as might be expected, considering their desirable and luscious-looking foliage.

Two other species, common on the western ranges, deserve mention. Field woodrush (*J. campes'tre*), sometimes called common woodrush and timber woodrush, is one of the most important, occurring, as it does, in the mountains and colder regions almost throughout North America, as well as in Europe and Asia. Like millet woodrush, it is common, but not abundant, in moist and wet situations both in open meadows and in the shade of willows and timber; it occasionally even grows in drier habitats. The stems of field woodrush are densely tufted and from 4 to 16 (occasionally 20) inches in height, with 2 to 4 stem leaves. The leaf blades are from 3 to 6 inches long, flat, and taper to a blunt tip; they are sparingly hairy, especially when young, and are densely hairy at the throat. The flowers are borne in rather dense, oblong clusters on the stalks of the usually loosely branched inflorescence, which spreads but does not nod. The entire inflorescence is subtended by several bracts, the largest of which is leaflike, often surpassing the inflorescence in length. In general, this species is probably utilized more than millet woodrush, because it appears to be somewhat more palatable and also is more likely to occur in areas grazed by both cattle and sheep. A. A. Hansen[1] mentions a case of sickness and loss among cattle and horses pastured in a Pennsylvania area where a third of the herbage was composed of this species. He states that no poisonous plants could be found, and that an autopsy showed a large accumulation of the "seeds" of this plant in the digestive tracts of the dead animals. "The verdict of the veterinarian was that death was due to eating the stalks and indigestible fruits of the woodrush, which so clogged the alimentary tract that food could not pass through."

Spike woodrush (*J. spica'tum*), which grows mainly in the spruce and alpine belts throughout the western mountains, has its dense, stalkless flower clusters aggregated into a nodding, spikelike inflorescence. It occurs widely in North America, ranging from Alaska to California, New Mexico, Colorado, and Montana, and, in the East, from the Arctic regions south to New Hampshire and New York. It is also native to the Old World. This species is commonly 4 to 16 inches in height with the stems closely tufted, although the individual plants are relatively small as rootstocks are lacking. The leaves are erect, narrow, often inrolled, and mostly less than 4 inches long. This plant prefers moist, sandy loams and is often associated with tufted hairgrass, bluegrasses, and aspen. Its palatability is moderate, about the same as that of millet woodrush, although, as it produces less herbage, its forage value is also less.

---

[1] Hansen, A. A. MECHANICAL INJURIES CAUSED BY WEEDS AND OTHER PLANTS. Ind. Acad. Sci. Proc. (1924) 34 : 229–254, illus. 1925.

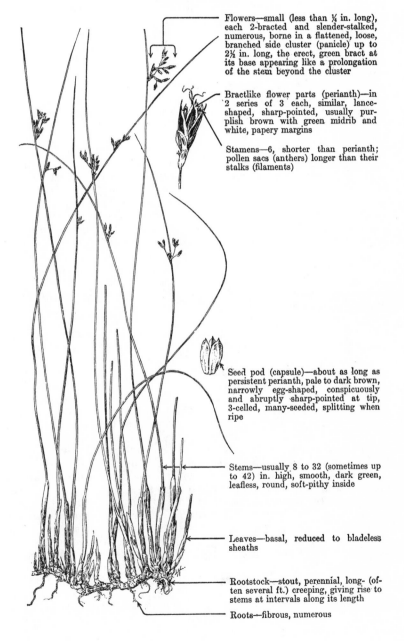

WIRE RUSH

Jun'cus bal'ticus

Flowers—small (less than ¼ in. long), each 2-bracted and slender-stalked, numerous, borne in a flattened, loose, branched side cluster (panicle) up to 2½ in. long, the erect, green bract at its base appearing like a prolongation of the stem beyond the cluster

Bractlike flower parts (perianth)—in 2 series of 3 each, similar, lance-shaped, sharp-pointed, usually pur-plish brown with green midrib and white, papery margins

Stamens—6, shorter than perianth; pollen sacs (anthers) longer than their stalks (filaments)

Seed pod (capsule)—about as long as persistent perianth, pale to dark brown, narrowly egg-shaped, conspicuously and abruptly sharp-pointed at tip, 3-celled, many-seeded, splitting when ripe

Stems—usually 8 to 32 (sometimes up to 42) in. high, smooth, dark green, leafless, round, soft-pithy inside

Leaves—basal, reduced to bladeless sheaths

Rootstock—stout, perennial, long- (often several ft.) creeping, giving rise to stems at intervals along its length

Roots—fibrous, numerous

Wire rush, one of the more common species of *Juncus*, and generally known in the western range States as wiregrass, is very widely distributed in both Europe and Asia as well as in North America, where it occurs from Newfoundland and Labrador to Alaska, California, New Mexico, Nebraska, Missouri, and Pennsylvania. The distinguished German botanist Carl L. Willdenow (1765–1812) appears to have named this plant *Juncus balticus* because of its commonness along the German shore bordering the Baltic Sea. Baltic rush, a translation of the scientific name, is sometimes used as the common name.

As indicated by its extensive distribution, wire rush occurs under a wide variety of environmental conditions and consists of a number of races or forms. It appears near sea level, through the valleys and deserts and almost to timberline in the mountains, growing on a variety of soil types. This species prefers moist or wet, deep, organic, meadow soils, where it usually appears in association with various sedges, bluegrasses, and willows, or sometimes occurs in pure stands. It is frequently common in shallow ponds or in other wet sites, where the water may stand until midsummer or longer, but is also occasionally found in rather dry situations such as sage flats and dry meadows. The plant grows on soils which are either shallow or gravelly, or a combination of both types if the moisture supply is ample, but the dry-site soils it inhabits are usually deep and fertile. The wet mountain meadows, bogs, and other cold, organic soils on which wire rush grows are often high acid, although this species also appears in soils that are alkaline or neutral. However, the densest and most vigorous growth apparently results on neutral or slightly acid soils.

The forage value of wire rush depends on a number of factors, such as stage of maturity, density of stand, and intensity of use. The wiriness of the mature stems, which are rather tough even when young, is so characteristic that the frequently used common name, wiregrass, is appropriate although, of course, Baltic rush is not a true grass. Its stems are so tough that they often pull free from the rootstocks when livestock, especially cattle, are tugging to nip them off. As might be expected, the palatability of this species is greatest in the spring, and gradually decreases as the stems become increasingly tough and mature.

On most ranges, wire rush is used advantageously by livestock if it composes less than 20 percent of the plant cover and is well distributed amidst other forage plants. Possibly, some of this use may be unintentional, wire rush being eaten along with the other forage plants. Under these conditions, it is usually rated as good for cattle and fairly good for sheep. Utilization normally decreases as the density of this species increases, until ultimately any area composed of 80 percent or more is very likely to be avoided, unless that area is small or the range overstocked. On ranges where the meadow type constitutes but a small portion of the forage, wire rush is usually closely grazed season-long, especially by cattle. Sometimes, patches of this species, which would be poor forage on the open range, are grazed closely when in pastures. This is particularly true in certain valleys where livestock are wintered.

Ordinarily, wire rush remains green all summer, even on such seemingly dry situations as flats and eroded meadows, but this probably results because of little competition with other species and the ability of its deep root system to obtain ample moisture. On some sites, however, this plant customarily matures by midsummer. This is particularly true of certain meadows which are extremely wet in the spring but later become exceedingly dry. Naturally, the palatability is greatest while the plant is green; in fact, under most range conditions, the forage is practically worthless after attaining maturity, when it turns brown.

Wire rush withstands close use longer than most forage plants, because of its strongly developed system of underground stems. In addition to numerous and extensive fibrous roots, it has thick, strong, long-creeping rootstocks from which leaf-bearing (aerial) stems arise at frequent intervals. As long as these rootstocks remain vigorous and continue to elongate and send up new leafy shoots, the production of seed is not necessary to maintain the stand. Under continued cropping and where the moisture supply is at all favorable, wire rush produces new growth throughout the growing season. Ordinarily, this process may continue for many years before the plant finally loses its vigor and dies.

Its ability to withstand close use often makes this species invaluable in soil protection, as it is one of the last plants of the original meadow association to disappear on overgrazed and eroded areas. Where dense, the numerous rootstocks and roots compose a matlike layer, which protects the surface soil very effectively. Unless this mat is undercut, as by a gulley, or its strength decreased through death of the plants, it will ordinarily protect the meadow soil against destructive erosion for an indefinite period.

Wire rush is probably one of the most common rushes occurring in the meadow hays of the Western States.[1][2] It is usually intermingled with sedges and grasses, but sometimes, particularly on wet or overirrigated areas, it may form the bulk of the harvest. Ordinarily, it cures well as a green-colored hay, which frequently is much more palatable than the herbage of the living plant in pasture or on the range. Chemical analysis[2] seems to indicate that wire rush ranks high in potential nutritive value, and is similar to timothy and alfalfa in proportions of nitrogen-free extract and crude fiber. It is definitely superior to timothy in crude protein content, but alfalfa excels wire rush in crude protein by about 3 percent.

Many of the American Indian tribes used the wiry stems of wire rush in manufacturing various articles. The Klamath Indians of Oregon,[3] and the White Mountain Apaches of the Arizona Plateau,[4]

[1] Griffiths, D. FORAGE CONDITIONS AND PROBLEMS IN EASTERN WASHINGTON, EASTERN OREGON, NORTHEASTERN CALIFORNIA, AND NORTHWESTERN NEVADA. U. S. Dept. Agr., Bur. Plant Indus. Bull. 38, 52 pp., illus. 1903.
[2] Knight, H. G., Hepner, F. E., and Nelson, A. WYOMING FORAGE PLANTS AND THEIR CHEMICAL COMPOSITION—STUDIES NO. 2. Wyo. Agr. Expt. Sta. Bull. 70, 75 pp., illus. 1906.
[3] Coville, F. V. NOTES ON THE PLANTS USED BY THE KLAMATH INDIANS OF OREGON. U. S. Dept. Agr., Div. Bot., Contrib. U. S. Natl. Herbarium 5 : 87–108. 1897.
[4] Coville, F. V. In Mason, O. T. ABORIGINAL AMERICAN BASKETRY : STUDIES IN A TEXTILE ART WITHOUT MACHINERY. U. S. Natl. Mus. Rept. 1901–1902 : 171–548, illus. 1904.

for example, made baskets and mats from the stems of this plant. Because of its abundance, it was often used by the Indian children, when learning to weave.

RUSHES

Jun'cus spp.

Juncus, the largest genus (about 215 species) of the rush family (Juncaceae), is of world-wide distribution, being most abundant in the North Temperate Zone. *Juncus*, the classical name for the rush, is derived from the Latin *jungo* (meaning join, or bind) and refers to the use of these plants as a binder in matting and basketry. The rushes are grasslike, usually perennial plants, which chiefly occur in swamps or other wet places. The typically unbranched and hairless stems are either scapelike, with all the leaves basal, or else bear some leaves on the stem. The leaf sheaths, when present, are open; the leaf blades are stiff, with free margins as in the grasses, and are rounded, channeled, or flat and, in some species, are conspicuously cross-partitioned. The clustered flowers are perfect and, though small and homely, essentially lilylike in form; their perianth parts (referred to as sepals and petals by some authors) are greenish or brown and often chaffy, and are in an outer and inner series of three each. The fruit is a one- to three-celled capsule containing from several to many small cinnamon-colored seeds often with tailed appendages.

Wire rush is representative of the group of species with an apparently lateral flower cluster, subtended by a leaf (involucral bract), which appears to be a direct prolongation of the main stem that otherwise is leafless. Rocky Mountain rush (*J. saximonta'nus*), occurring from Alberta to British Columbia, California, and New Mexico, is a good example of those range rushes which have a terminal flower cluster whose inflorescence leaf does not resemble a continuation of the main stem or, if so, is conspicuously channeled on the upper side.

In general, the palatability of the more tender species of range rushes ranks as fair to good or occasionally very good for cattle, and as fair or fairly good for sheep. The highest utilization of rushes, as a rule, is obtained with the fine-leaved, meadow type species, especially when growing mixed with other plants rather than in pure stand.

SEASIDE ARROWGRASS

Triglo'chin mari'tima, syn. *T. mari'tima de'bilis*

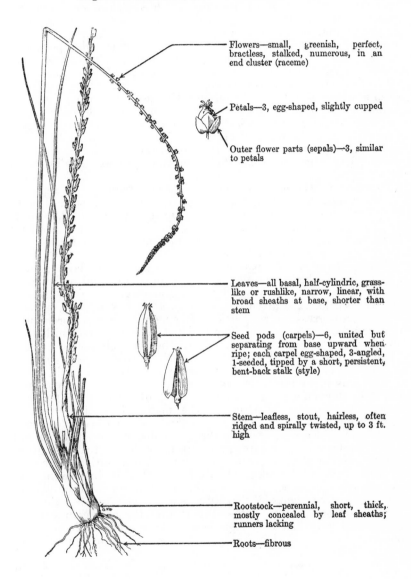

Flowers—small, greenish, perfect, bractless, stalked, numerous, in an end cluster (raceme)

Petals—3, egg-shaped, slightly cupped

Outer flower parts (sepals)—3, similar to petals

Leaves—all basal, half-cylindric, grass-like or rushlike, narrow, linear, with broad sheaths at base, shorter than stem

Seed pods (carpels)—6, united but separating from base upward when ripe; each carpel egg-shaped, 3-angled, 1-seeded, tipped by a short, persistent, bent-back stalk (style)

Stem—leafless, stout, hairless, often ridged and spirally twisted, up to 3 ft. high

Rootstock—perennial, short, thick, mostly concealed by leaf sheaths; runners lacking

Roots—fibrous

Seaside arrowgrass is a perennial herb of the arrowgrass family (Scheuchzeriaceae, syn. Juncaginaceae). Unfortunately, the common name arrowgrass is not entirely appropriate; the plant, while somewhat grasslike, is not, of course, a true grass; moreover, marsh arrowgrass (*T. palustris*) is the only North American species of this genus which has arrow-shaped fruits. To correct this, it has been suggested that podgrass be adopted as the English name for *Triglochin*, *T. maritima* to be known as shore (or seaside) podgrass, and *T. palustris* as arrow podgrass or arrowpod. The generic name is derived from the Greek words *tri*, three, and *glochin*, point, and refers to the three points of the ripe fruit of marsh arrowgrass. The specific name *maritima*, a Latin adjective meaning belonging to or found in the sea, refers to the frequent seashore habitat of this plant. In North America the species occurs in salt marshes near the coast from Alaska to Lower California and Mexico, and from Labrador to New Jersey; it also grows in the interior and across the continent, particularly from the Great Plains westward, in wet alkaline soils, along sloughs, and in wet meadows and seeps. It is also widely distributed in Europe, Asia, and northern Africa. It is replaced by *T. striata* in the Southeastern States. In the western United States this plant occurs from sea level up to elevations of 8,000 feet. It grows in clumps or small patches and is often found covering large areas, particularly in low-lying meadows utilized for hay, as, for example, in Utah and Wyoming.

Seaside arrowgrass is poisonous to cattle and sheep; large annual losses of cattle have been due to this plant. Deer and other game animals are sometimes killed by eating arrowgrass. Heavy losses of livestock have occurred on meadows after hay harvest, because seaside arrowgrass revives quickly after mowing, is more prominent than the second growth of the associated grasses, and furnishes an abundance of saline and succulent, though poisonous, forage.[1] Chemical analysis of this plant shows a high common salt content; lack of salt on the range would naturally lead livestock to the selection of this plant for their requirements.[2] Moreover, it frequently lacks the flowering stalks, and its clusters of leaves are often mistaken for wiregrass.[2] Although the matter is controversial, it seems prudent to avoid, as far as practical, the use of seaside arrowgrass in hay. Fleming *et al.*[3] in 1920 presented evidence that cut and dried plants of seaside arrowgrass are more deadly than the green plants. Marsh *et al.*[1] reported in 1929 that the air-dried plant used in the experimental work gradually lost most of its toxicity in drying, and they drew the conclusion that stock losses result only from eating the green plant and that there is no danger from hay containing arrowgrass. They further report that the people in Goshen, Utah, who have had long experience with the effect of the plant on cattle, state that they have never known cases of poisoning to

[1] Marsh, C. D., Clawson, A. B., and Roe, G. C. ARROW GRASS (TRIGLOCHIN MARITIMA) AS A STOCK-POISONING PLANT. U. S. Dept. Agr. Tech. Bull. 113, 15 pp., illus. 1929.

[2] Beath, O. A., Draize, J. H., and Gilbert, C. S. PLANTS POISONOUS TO LIVESTOCK. Wyo. Agr. Exp. Sta. Bull 200, 84 pp., illus. 1934.

[3] Fleming, C. E., Peterson, N. F., Miller, M. R., Wright, L. H., and Louck, R. C. ARROWGRASS, A NEW STOCK-POISONING PLANT (TRIGLOCHIN MARITIMA). Nev. Agr. Expt. Sta. Bull. 98, 22 pp., illus. 1920.

result from eating the plant in hay. In 1933 Beath *et al.*[4] found that the poison resides chiefly in the leaves; that the drying of the plant results in the loss of varying amounts of HCN, but that this is partly counterbalanced by the fact that the acid is more readily and completely released than in the green plant; that frosted, wilted, and stunted plants are less toxic than normal growth, and that, for some unknown reason, air-dried samples cured in hay differ materially in their retention of toxicity.

Beath *et al.*[4] regard this plant as the most rapidly acting poisonous species found on the western stock ranges. Hydrocyanic acid is the active poisonous principle. To produce poisoning, the toxic dose must be eaten in a short period of time. The sickness comes on very quickly, lasts a comparatively short time, and in cases of recovery seems to have no permanent effect.[1] The usual symptoms of poisoning by seaside arrowgrass are typical of hydrocyanic acid poisoning in general, *i. e.*, brief stimulation followed by depression and paralysis. Colic often occurs accompanied by stupor, difficult breathing, and frequent convulsions. Death results directly from respiratory paralysis, and frequently the heart continues to beat after breathing has ceased.[5]

Remedies for cyanide poisoning are as yet in the experimental stages. Recent experiments have shown that injections of a combination of sodium nitrite and sodium thiosulphate are effective in the treatment of cattle and sheep poisoned by arrowgrass.[6] However, death in most cases occurs so quickly that there is little opportunity to apply remedial measures. Certain feeds, such as alfalfa hay and linseed cake, seem to retard the production of hydrocyanic acid in the animals' stomachs and may prevent poisoning. The best way to prevent losses is not to pasture livestock on meadows containing an abundance of the plant and to refrain from cutting arrowgrass for hay.

Seaside arrowgrass is apparently poisonous throughout its entire growth period. Differences of opinion among stockmen about the poisonous properties of this species are no doubt largely attributable to the latent factors which increase or decrease the potential amount of hydrocyanic acid in the various plants. Hydrocyanic acid does not actually occur in any appreciable quantity in healthy growing plants, but two chemical substances are present, which, though not poisonous individually, combine to form hydrocyanic acid.[6] The amount of potential hydrocyanic acid in the various plants capable of producing hydrocyanic acid poisoning varies with the stage of growth and climatic and soil conditions; the damaging effects of drought, frost, trampling, or mowing tend to stimulate the formation of the poison in the plants.[6]

[4] Beath, O. A., Draize, J. H., and Eppson, H. F.   ARROW GRASS—CHEMICAL AND PHYSIO-
LOGICAL CONSIDERATIONS.   Wyo. Agr. Expt. Sta. Bull. 193, 36 pp., illus.   1933.
[5] Couch, J. F.   POISONING OF LIVESTOCK BY PLANTS THAT PRODUCE HYDROCYANIC ACID.
U. S. Dept. Agr. Leaflet 88, 4 pp.   1932.
[6] Bunyea, H., Couch, J. F., and Clawson, A. B.   THE NITRITE-THIOSULPHATE COMBINA-
TION AS A REMEDY FOR CYANIDE POISONING IN SHEEP.   Jour. Wash. Acad. Sci. 24(12) :
528–532.   1934.

Seaside arrowgrass has an oblong or ovoid fruit consisting of 6 carpels. The Klamath Indians called this plant gil-len-a. They ate the parched seeds and sometimes used them as a substitute for coffee.[7]

Triglochin is a small genus of herbs widely distributed in subarctic and temperate regions of the Northern Hemisphere and in northern Africa, growing mostly along seashores and in brackish or marshy places. In addition to seaside arrowgrass, two other species occur in the United States. All three are poisonous, but seaside arrowgrass, because of its abundance, is most important in the West. These species are perennial herbs with long, narrow, grasslike or rushlike leaves which sheath the base of the plants. The greenish or yellowish green flowers, individually small and inconspicuous, are borne on a leafless stalk in a long, spikelike raceme.

Marsh arrowgrass (*T. palus'tris*) occurs in brackish marshes, bogs, and alkaline meadows from Alaska to Washington and from Greenland to New Brunswick and New York; it is found inland along the St. John and St. Lawrence Rivers, about the Great Lakes, and in the Rocky Mountain region. It also occurs in South America, Europe, and Asia. It is the type species of the genus, the generic name *Triglochin* referring to the characteristic three narrow seed pods with taper-pointed tips.

Ridged arrowgrass (*T. stria'ta*) has only three flower (perianth) parts and three anthers (instead of six); its fruit is globular, consisting of three carpels, each ribbed on the back. This species has a more restricted range in the United States than the other two species, occurring in salt marshes in two widely separated strips: In the East, from Maryland to Florida and Louisiana, and, in California, from Mendocino County to Santa Barbara. It is also found in Mexico and in South America.

---

[7] Coville, F. V. NOTES ON THE PLANTS USED BY THE KLAMATH INDIANS OF OREGON. U. S. Dept. Agr., Div. Bot., Contrib. U. S. Natl. Herbarium 5: 87–108. 1897.

WESTERN YARROW

Achille'a lanulo'sa, syn. *A. millefo'lium lanulo'sa*

Flower heads—small, numerous, stalked, in compact, branched, terminal, flattened or round-topped clusters (panicles or compound cymes) 2 to 4 in. across

Bracts—in a series (involucre) surrounding base of flower heads, greenish with pale brown or straw-colored papery margins, overlapping in 3 or 4 rows, outer and lower ones much shorter than inner and upper ones

Outside (ray) flowers of the heads—broadly strap-shaped, white, petal-like, few, spreading, seed-producing

Center (disk) flowers of the heads—small, numerous, yellow, tubular, perfect, seed-producing, inner ones partly enclosed at base by membranous chaffy bracts (paleae)

Stems—densely white-woolly (lanulose), somewhat furrowed, unbranched, erect, up to 3 ft. high

Leaves—tansylike, lanulose, narrowly lance-shaped in outline, much divided and subdivided into very fine, narrow, crowded, ultimate divisions; upper leaves stalkless

Rootstocks—underground, extensive

Roots—numerous, fibrous

"Seeds" (achenes)—hairless, margined, oblong or reversely egg-shaped, without bristles or scales (pappus) at tips

Western yarrow, also called milfoil, wild-tansy, and woolly yarrow, is a strong-scented, occasionally turf-forming, perennial herb of the mayweed-tansy-sagebrush tribe (Anthemideae) of the huge aster, or composite family (Asteraceae, or Compositae). Its generic name *Achillea* is in honor of the legendary Greek hero Achilles, who is credited with first using yarrow to cure wounds; the specific name *lanulosa* is a diminutive of the Latin adjective for woolly (from *lana*, wool) and refers to the fine, dense, silky-woolly hairs which cover the plant and give it a somewhat grayish appearance.

Western yarrow is one of the most widely distributed and abundant herbaceous species in the 11 far western States. Its range includes large areas in southern Canada from British Columbia to Manitoba, a few of the Lake States, and all the States west of North Dakota and south into Mexico.

This species prospers in a great variety of habitats, such as sagebrush areas, canyon bottoms, glades, roadsides, and vacant lots. It is also prevalent in brushlands, aspen, and open timber, but avoids dense shade. It is comparatively drought-resistant and flourishes in the sandy and gravelly loam soils of open flats, parks, and dry meadows. The plants usually grow somewhat scatteringly, seldom forming pure stands on areas larger than a few square rods. In places where the natural plant cover has been but slightly or not at all disturbed, western yarrow occurs only sparsely, but it is one of the plants that invades readily and increases conspicuously when overgrazing makes growing conditions unfavorable for more palatable and less resistant species.

The forage value of western yarrow varies greatly with different localities and with different plant associates. On many ranges all classes of livestock graze this plant moderately throughout the season. Sheep (and sometimes cattle) often evince a fondness for the flower heads of western yarrow. They do not relish the stems when these parts become somewhat woody late in the season, although they occasionally graze the dried leaves. The species rates from poor to, rarely, good in palatability for sheep and from unpalatable to fair, seldom fairly good, for cattle. Its chief value for sheep appears to be in Nevada and New Mexico, although ranking as fairly good in parts of Utah and Arizona. It appears to be most valuable for cattle in parts of Colorado, Wyoming, Arizona, and New Mexico. In California it is usually regarded as poor or worthless. Horses graze it much less than do cattle. Deer, as a rule, eat western yarrow very sparingly, but on the Kaibab Plateau the species is regarded as fair mule-deer forage.

Sampson,[1] in his plant succession studies on high summer range in central Utah, shows that, when this type of range is undisturbed, its climax vegetation is made up of wheatgrasses. With overgrazing, however, this cover changes to a somewhat less stable mixed grass and weed type, the porcupinegrass-yellowbrush consociation. He reports further that when conditions unfavorable to growth are sufficiently prolonged gradually to destroy the porcupinegrass-yellowbrush cover, but not such as seriously to change the condition of the soil, shallow-rooted perennial weeds of the second weed stage, notably "blue foxglove" (*Pentstemon procerus*), "sweet sage" (*Artemisia discolor*), and yarrow (*Achillea lanulosa*), are the natural successors. Western yarrow is thus definitely placed by Sampson as one of the three perennial weeds that, under certain definite conditions of overgrazing, tend to dominate these high summer ranges. Under such conditions, local abundance of western yarrow would be an indicator of continued past overstocking and excessive utilization.

[1] Sampson, A. W. PLANT SUCCESSION IN RELATION TO RANGE MANAGEMENT. U. S. Dept. Agr. Bull. 791, 76 pp., illus. 1919.

On account of its extensive underground system of rootstocks, Forsling [2] reports the use of western yarrow, as well as of sweet sage, as a soil binder in certain types of erosion control on the Wasatch Plateau in central Utah. When such plants are started near the edges of small gullies, their rootstocks soon spread down in all directions across the depressions and serve to catch particles of sediment from water flowing past them, thus forming small alluvial fans and checking surface run-off.

In addition to this vegetative propagation by rootstocks or rhizomes, western yarrow also has fairly strong seed habits. It produces flowers practically throughout the summer, beginning as early as May or as late as September in the higher mountains; subsequently there is, in the case of the early-flowering plants, a long period of seed production. The late-flowering plants, however, often are unable to set seed.

The leaves of western yarrow are mostly basal, often forming rosettes. These lower leaves are stalked and are from 2 to 8 inches long, but the unpaired (alternate) stem leaves become increasingly shorter up the stem and are either stalkless (sessile) or nearly so. The dense flower clusters at the ends of the stems are somewhat flattened or convex like the top of a derby hat. What appear to be individual flowers are really flower heads, consisting of a group of flowers (both ray and disk flowers) attached to a common base (receptacle), and closely surrounded by a series (involucre) of small bracts (phyllaries) that overlap like shingles.

Common yarrow (*Achille'a millefo'lium*), a native of the Old World, is a widely distributed weed in the eastern part of the United States and in portions of the West. It is a taller, smoother, and greener plant than western yarrow, and has long been used for medicinal purposes. Its flowers are markedly aromatic and its leaves possess astringent properties. It is very probable that western yarrow (which is so closely related to common yarrow that some botanists consider it merely a variety of the former, and not a separate species) could be put to similar medicinal uses. Indians are said to have employed western yarrow as a mild laxative.

---

[2] Forsling, C. L.   A STUDY OF THE INFLUENCE OF HERBACEOUS PLANT COVER ON SURFACE RUN-OFF AND SOIL EROSION IN RELATION TO GRAZING ON THE WASATCH PLATEAU IN UTAH. U. S. Dept. Agr. Tech. Bull. 220, 72 pp., illus.   1931.

MONKSHOODS

Aconi'tum spp.

Monkshoods compose a fairly large genus of perennial herbs of the buttercup family (Ranunculaceae), being principally natives of the mountainous regions of the North Temperate Zone. Other common names used for the genus are aconite and wolfbane; the latter name, however, is perhaps best restricted [1] to the Old World *A. lycoctonum*, and aconite to the cultivated drug plant, *A. napellus*. *Aconitum* is the classical name for these plants. The genus is better represented in the Old World, and widely varying opinions exist about the number of species, as many as 70 species being recognized by some botanists. Probably about 15 species occur in the United States, Canada, and Alaska, each of the western range States having one or more species. The Intermountain region, with 6 species, is the center of distribution in this country.

In the West, monkshoods grow chiefly in the mountains, usually singly or in small patches, and seldom occur in great abundance over large areas. They appear commonly in moist open woods, along creeks, in meadows and grasslands, often extending into the higher mountains where the growing season is short. Their habitat is similar to that of larkspurs, with which they are often confused. Although widely distributed, monkshoods are seldom, if ever, sufficiently abundant to attain major importance on the range. They constitute fair feed for sheep, poor for cattle, and are but rarely grazed by horses. Although technically poisonous, the monkshoods probably never cause livestock fatalities, or even sickness on the range.[2] The most poisonous part of these plants is the root, usually inaccessible and unattractive to livestock. The seeds are also poisonous. The root of wolfbane (*A. lycoctonum*), cultivated in this country as an ornamental, has been extensively employed in the Old World to destroy wolves and other predators.

The important drug aconite, an arterial and nervous sedative, used in the treatment of sciatica and other neuralgias and in various other disorders, is commercially obtained from the roots of the Old World plant of similar name, *A. napellus*,[3] which is also the species of *Aconitum* most commonly cultivated in the United States as an ornamental. The chief active principle of this drug is the alkaloid *aconitine* ($C_{34}H_{47}O_{11}N$), a powerful poison. Apparently true aconitine is known only from *A. napellus*, similar alkaloids (previously called aconitine) derived from other monkshoods proving to be somewhat different chemically. McNair reports that the various aconitines have been separated only from members of the genus

[1] American Joint Committee on Horticultural Nomenclature. STANDARDIZED PLANT NAMES. Prepared by F. L. Olmsted, F. V. Coville, and H. P. Kelsey. 546 pp. Salem, Mass. 1923.
[2] Marsh, C. D. STOCK-POISONING PLANTS OF THE RANGE. U. S. Dept. Agr. Bull. 1245, rev., 75 pp., illus. 1929. Supersedes Bull. 575.
[3] Wood, H. C., Remington, J. P., Sadtler, S. P., assisted by Lyons, A. B., and Wood, H. C., Jr. THE DISPENSATORY OF THE UNITED STATES OF AMERICA, BY DR. GEO. B. WOOD AND DR. FRANKLIN BACHE. Ed. 19, thoroughly rev. and largely rewritten . . . 1,947 pp. Philadelphia and London. 1907.

Aconitum. *Aconitum* is noteworthy in giving a new chemical species of aconitine for each new botanical species analyzed, although all the aconitines are apparently closely related.[4] These plants should not be planted in or near kitchen gardens or in children's gardens,[5] as their roots, leaves, and sometimes the flowers may cause poisoning.

The roots or underground parts of monkshoods show considerable variation and, in collecting the plants, these parts should always be represented.[6][7] The roots of all western monkshoods are perennial, many are clustered, and most of them tuberous. The pithy or solid, often slender stems are frequently solitary, 1 to 6 feet tall, and vary greatly in leafiness and hairiness. The leaves are alternate, palmately lobed or divided, the lower ones long-stalked, and the upper ones somewhat reduced in size and short-stalked. The showy and ornamental flowers, which appear from mid to late summer, are wholly unlike those of any other plant in our flora, and are readily identifiable by the peculiar helmet-shaped hood formed by the large upper sepal. The fancied resemblance of the flower to the hood which a monk commonly wears is the origin of the English name, monkshood. The flowers occur in short, few-flowered or long and many-flowered, branched clusters, and are characteristically deep blue, although they may vary from violet to white. Frequently, the seed pods (follicles) in the lower part of the cluster have matured their seed while the upper flowers are still in blossom. Monkshoods are reproduced by root division as well as from seed.

These plants are attractive, hardy perennials much used for borders and mass formations in horticultural plantings because of their showy flowers and effective foliage.

The western species of monkshood, when not in bloom, may be confused with tall species of larkspur (*Delphinium* spp.) with which they are frequently associated, because of the similarity of the leaves and the somewhat analogous growth habits. Differentiation between the destructive, poisonous larkspurs and the (from a range standpoint) harmless monkshoods is not especially difficult, as the latter have solid or pithy stems in contrast to the hollow stems of the larkspurs. Furthermore, the roots of western monkshoods are short, clustered, somewhat fleshy, and tuberlike with short, yellowish rootlets, whereas the tall larkspurs have long, dark-colored, fibrous roots from well-developed, tough, somewhat woody root crowns. When the plants are in bloom, the irregular flowers of monkshood with the hoodlike upper sepal are so distinctive as to be readily recognizable; the spurred flowers of the larkspurs are also unmistakable.

Early in the season, before the stems develop, the western monkshoods may be confused with the species of wild geranium, or cranesbill (*Geranium* spp.) as the leaves are very similar, but ordinarily the crushed foliage of the latter has the characteristic geranium odor.

[4] McNair, J. B. THE EVOLUTIONARY STATUS OF PLANT FAMILIES IN RELATION TO SOME CHEMICAL PROPERTIES. Amer. Jour. Bot. 21 : 427–452, illus. 1934.
[5] Bailey, L. H. THE STANDARD CYCLOPEDIA OF HORTICULTURE . . . New ed., 3 v., illus. New York and London. 1933.
[6] Reichenbach, H. T. L. MONOGRAPHIA GENERIS ACONITI ICONIBUS OMNIUM SPECIERUM COLORATIS ILLUSTRATA LATINE ET GERMANICE ELABORATA. 100 pp., illus. Leipzig. 1820.
[7] Reichenbach, H. G. L. NEUE BEARBEITUNG DER ARTEN DER GATTUNG ACONITUM, UND EINIGER DELPHINIEN. [146] pp., illus. Leipzig. 1823–1827.

COLUMBIA MONKSHOOD

Aconi'tum columbia'num, syn. *A. pa'tens*

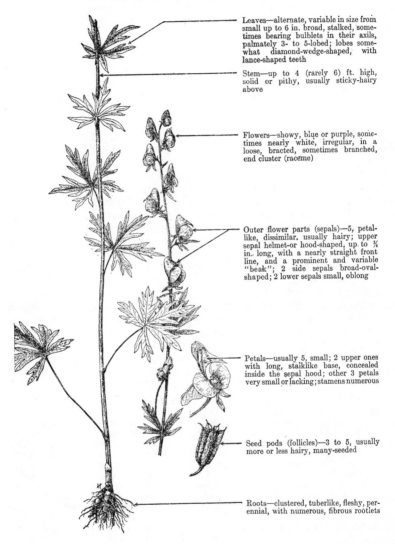

Leaves—alternate, variable in size from small up to 6 in. broad, stalked, sometimes bearing bulblets in their axils, palmately 3- to 5-lobed; lobes somewhat diamond-wedge-shaped, with lance-shaped teeth

Stem—up to 4 (rarely 6) ft. high, solid or pithy, usually sticky-hairy above

Flowers—showy, blue or purple, sometimes nearly white, irregular, in a loose, bracted, sometimes branched, end cluster (raceme)

Outer flower parts (sepals)—5, petal-like, dissimilar, usually hairy; upper sepal helmet-or hood-shaped, up. to ¾ in. long, with a nearly straight front line, and a prominent and variable "beak"; 2 side sepals broad-oval-shaped; 2 lower sepals small, oblong

Petals—usually 5, small; 2 upper ones with long, stalklike base, concealed inside the sepal hood; other 3 petals very small or lacking; stamens numerous

Seed pods (follicles)—3 to 5, usually more or less hairy, many-seeded

Roots—clustered, tuberlike, fleshy, perennial, with numerous, fibrous rootlets

Columbia monkshood is representative of the western species of *Aconitum* both in appearance and palatability and is the most common and widely distributed species of this genus in the West. It is a tall, perennial herb inhabiting all of the eleven western range States and occurs from British Columbia to California, New Mexico, and Montana. The common and specific names refer to the Columbia River, the first botanical description of this species resulting from a plant collected on the Columbia River near Walla Walla, Wash., about 1834. Columbia monkshood prefers moist, shady sites along streams and around springs in the foothills and mountains at elevations of from approximately 1,000 to 12,000 feet, but it is most frequent at the higher elevations. It grows in a great variety of weed, grass, and timber types, is common in aspen and among willows, and occurs frequently in moist mountain meadows. This plant is seldom, if ever, the dominant species in areas it inhabits, though it not infrequently grows in small, dense patches. It flourishes in deep, moist, sandy or clayey loams, especially if rich in humus.

Columbia monkshood, while recognized as potentially poisonous to cattle,[1] is very rarely, if ever, consumed by such animals in sufficient quantities under range conditions to cause losses. The use of this species varies considerably in different parts of the West. In California, the Southwest, the Intermountain Region, and Idaho, cattle seldom touch it, and sheep usually either ignore it or merely pick off some of the leaves and tops. In the northern Rocky Mountains, from Montana to Colorado, its utilization seems to be greater, sometimes being considered of fair palatability for cattle and fairly good for sheep. The greatest range use of the species ordinarily occurs on summer ranges of the Northwest where sheep frequently utilize from 70 to 80 percent of the herbage, and cattle between about 30 and 60 percent. From an investigation conducted by Beath [2] it would appear that Columbia monkshood is not a highly toxic species and would not make a satisfactory substitute for the Old World *A. napellus* as a source of the important drug, aconite. Beath found *A. columbianum* less than 0.5 percent as active as *A. napellus.*

Columbia monkshood is an erect, stout, single-stemmed plant, from 2 to occasionally 6 feet in height, the stem being solid or pithy within. This species has not as yet come into general use as an ornamental, although it is fully as handsome as a number of its sister species commonly grown for horticultural purposes.

The distinctive hooded flowers of all the monkshoods facilitate easy recognition. When not in flower, however, they are very likely to be confused with the tall larkspurs (*Delphinium* spp.), the leaves in many instances being almost identical; the same holds true in the case of the wild geraniums, or cranesbills (*Geranium* spp.). Columbia monkshood is frequently associated with tall larkspurs, which are responsible for heavy cattle losses in the West. In some localities, such as certain parts of Yellowstone Park, Columbia monkshood grows in great abundance whereas larkspurs are comparatively rare; in other places, such as the region between Yellowstone Lake and the Grand Canyon, the larkspurs are very abundant and Columbia monkshood is infrequent.[1] Inasmuch as the tall larkspurs are very poisonous, especially in the spring and fall, whereas Columbia monkshood, though possessing poisonous properties, seems to be negligible as a cause of range cattle losses, it is of great importance to learn to distinguish these plants in the field. Methods of recognizing these genera are discussed under the generic notes.

---

[1] Marsh, C. D. STOCK-POISONING PLANTS OF THE RANGE. U. S. Dept. Agr. Bull. 1245, rev., 75 pp., illus. 1929. Supersedes Bull. 575.
[2] Beath, O. A. EXTRACTS OF ACONITUM COLUMBIANUM. Jour. Amer. Pharm. Assoc. 15: 265–266. 1926.

ACTINEAS AND RUBBERWEEDS

Acti'nea spp.

Actinea is a fairly large American genus of annual, biennial, or perennial herbs belonging to the sneezeweed tribe (Helenieae) of the aster, or composite family (Asteraceae, or Compositae). Representatives of the genus occur in all the Western States except possibly Washington, ranging from the Sierra Nevada and Cascade Mountains to southern Alberta, Saskatchewan, the Dakotas, western Kansas, and Texas, to South America. In the United States, these plants appear chiefly on dry, open sites and on rocky slopes from the plains and western deserts to the ponderosa pine belt in the mountains. Some species occur at higher elevations with a few above timber line. The genus is best developed, both from the standpoint of abundance and maximum number of species, from central Colorado southward through western Texas and the Southwest.

Approximately 40 species and at least 6 definite varieties of *Actinea* occur in the Western States. The genus name is derived from the Greek *aktis* or *aktinos*, a ray, referring to the petallike, marginal ray flowers of the head. The small to comparatively large flower heads somewhat resemble those of sunflowers; the ray flowers, present in most species, are yellow. Probably the most reliable technical characters which distinguish this genus from other members of the Compositae are the 5 (sometimes 6 to 12), thin-papery, often sharp-pointed, scales (pappus), which crown the top-shaped, mostly five-angled, hairy body of the seedlike fruits (achenes); the close overlapping (rather than spreading) of the two- or three-rowed bracts (involucre) at the base of the flower head, and the absence of chaffy bracts between the individual flowers (*i. e.*, the "receptacle" is naked). The genus is a complex one, displaying a degree of variation which has led many authorities to separate it into a number of segregated genera. Actineas may be silky-hairy, woolly, or hairless (glabrous). Many of the species are without true stems, the leaves being basal, and the flower heads solitary on leafless stalks (scapes); others are leafy-stemmed, with alternate leaves, and numerous, clustered flower heads. The leaves may be entire-margined or variously cleft and divided; some are glandular-dotted.

In addition to *Actinea*, "*Actinella*" of American authors (not Pers.), *Hymenoxys* (syn. *Picradenia*), *Macdougalia, Rydbergia,* and *Tetraneuris* have been used as generic names, and one or more of these generic names are recognized in most of the current manuals, depending upon the conception of the various authors as to the segregation of the groups involved. However, Dr. S. F. Blake, an outstanding expert in Compositae in the Bureau of Plant Industry, United States Department of Agriculture, has advised the Forest Service that species occurring in Mexico show that these segregated groups, or genera, intergrade and, therefore, should, in his opinion, be considered as belonging to the one genus, *Actinea*. Recognition of the characters which distinguish these segregated groups, or genera, is helpful in understanding the genus as a whole, especially in discriminating between poisonous and nonpoisonous species.

Those actineas which belong to the *Hymenox'ys* (syn. *Picrade'nia*) section are generally known as rubberweeds. They can hardly be considered as palatable to domestic livestock, being consumed only under starvation conditions or when little or no other feed is available. The whole rubberweed group should be regarded with suspicion since bitter rubberweed (*A. odora'ta*, syn. *H. odorata*), locally known as bitterweed and limonillo, and pingüe (*A. richardso'ni*, syn. *H. floribun'da*), often called Colorado rubberweed, abundant over large areas, are poisonous to livestock, causing large losses, especially of sheep. (See W7.) Rubberweeds have erect, often branched, frequently somewhat hairy, leafy stems with the gland-dotted leaves commonly cut into many narrow divisions. The few to numerous, stalked flower heads, having three-lobed, petallike ray flowers, are relatively small, but showy; the bracts of the involucre of the flower head are in two series, the outer being firm and more or less united at the base.

The sole representative of the *Macdouga'lia* section in the United States, viz. *A. bigelo'vii* (syn. *M. bigelovii*), found in the mountains of New Mexico and Arizona, is probably negligible as forage. It is a loosely woolly, tufted, perennial herb, with slender, almost naked (scapelike) stems from a woody base, each stem having a single flower head. The linear, mainly undivided leaves are principally basal.

The rydbergias (section *Rydber'gia*), named in honor of the late Dr. Per Axel Rydberg, an eminent American botanist, include two species of low, alpine, woolly perennials with very large, showy flower heads having long, narrow, three-toothed ray flowers. The bracts of their involucres are distinct, in three rows, and densely woolly. The leaves, mostly parted or divided into narrow lobes, are crowded at the base on the simple, often chunky root crown, and scattered on the stout, short flowering stems. The seedlike fruits (achenes) are surmounted by a sort of brush (pappus) of five whitish, opaque, bristlelike scales (paleae). These plants (*A. brande'gei*, syn. *R. brandegei; A. grandiflo'ra*, syn. *R. grandiflora*) occur on the higher summits of certain sectors of the Rocky Mountains, the former apparently being confined to Colorado and New Mexico, while *A. grandiflora* ranges from Montana to Utah and New Mexico. Sheep on high summer range sometimes pick off the heads and nibble at the leaves, but the species are not important forage. Their showiness commends them to wildflower fans, and some day they will doubtless take their place among cultivated alpines.

The United States species of the *Tetraneu'ris* (syn. *Actinel'la* in part) section, some of which are known as tallowweeds, are rather small plants of distinctive appearance. Although widely distributed and fairly common, they are usually not a dominant feature of the vegetation on most of the western ranges. In the Southwest, however, they are sometimes locally abundant, the flower heads of a number of the species reputedly being good sheep and goat forage; local sheepmen in central and western Texas claim that these plants produce a good hard fat both on lambs and sheep.[1] These species also are grazed on some scale by cattle and probably by game animals. This group includes both perennial and annual herbs; the majority of the western range species have a persistent, often branched root crown (caudex) from which arise the basal, entire-margined, often gland-dotted leaves (rarely, some of them lobed), and a long, usually leafless stalk bearing a solitary, rather large flower head. These plants are more or less soft- or silky-hairy throughout; the presence of conspicuous, woolly hairs at the base of the leaf cluster is very characteristic of many of the species, and aids their identification when not in bloom. A few species have leafy, more or less branched stems with several to many flowers on slender flower stalks. The bright yellow ray flowers are inclined to persist, turning pale with age; they are not widened at the three-toothed apex, and are marked by four parallel, simple nerves (whence the name *Tetraneuris*, literally four-nerved). The thin, herbaceous involucral bracts of the flower head, all distinct and much alike, closely overlap in two rows. The nearly colorless pappus scales crowning the seedlike fruits (achenes) have a strong midrib, which is sometimes extended into a sharp point (awn).

---

[1] Bentley, H. L. A REPORT UPON THE GRASSES AND FORAGE PLANTS OF CENTRAL TEXAS. U. S. Dept. Agr., Div. Agrost. Bull. 10, 38 pp., illus. 1898.

STEMLESS ACTINEA

Acti'nea acau'lis, syns. *Actinel'la acau'lis, Tetraneu'ris acau'lis*

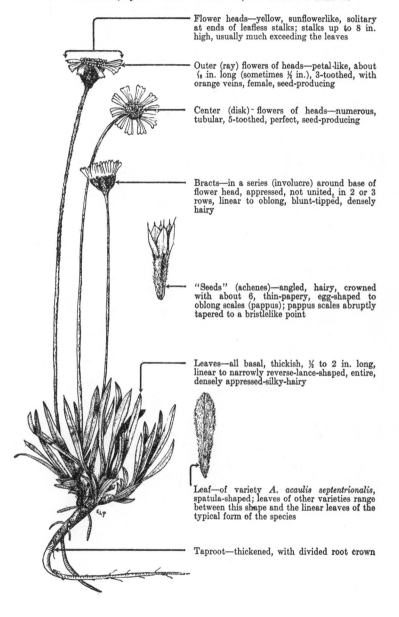

Flower heads—yellow, sunflowerlike, solitary at ends of leafless stalks; stalks up to 8 in. high, usually much exceeding the leaves

Outer (ray) flowers of heads—petal-like, about ⅛ in. long (sometimes ½ in.), 3-toothed, with orange veins, female, seed-producing

Center (disk) flowers of heads—numerous, tubular, 5-toothed, perfect, seed-producing

Bracts—in a series (involucre) around base of flower head, appressed, not united, in 2 or 3 rows, linear to oblong, blunt-tipped, densely hairy

"Seeds" (achenes)—angled, hairy, crowned with about 6, thin-papery, egg-shaped to oblong scales (pappus); pappus scales abruptly tapered to a bristlelike point

Leaves—all basal, thickish, ½ to 2 in. long, linear to narrowly reverse-lance-shaped, entire, densely appressed-silky-hairy

Leaf—of variety *A. acaulis septentrionalis,* spatula-shaped; leaves of other varieties range between this shape and the linear leaves of the typical form of the species

Taproot—thickened, with divided root crown

Stemless actinea is a relatively small, hairy, bitter, aromatic perennial, without true stems. This species has not acquired a well-established common name but is known by a great variety of (and often misapplied) local names, such as cloth-of-gold, golden-daisy, golden-head Indian-tobacco, ironweed, rayflower, rosinweed, and yellow-aster. The specific name *acaulis* is from the Greek prefix *a-*, signifying "not", and *kaulos*, stem, hence stemless actinea is suggested as an appropriate common name for the species despite that several others in this genus lack true stems. Stemless actinea is distributed from North Dakota to Idaho and south to southeastern California and Texas. It is found chiefly on dry soils and usually extends in grass and brush types from the plains to above timberline. This weed is abundant in South Dakota but elsewhere is largely scattered.

Stemless actinea is selected for special discussion in this handbook chiefly because of its commonness and wide distribution in the range country and because it is typical of one of the two larger groups into which the genus *Actinea* is divided. Opinions differ about the palatability of this species. Some observers report that it is fairly palatable to both sheep and cattle, yet others claim that it has a low to zero palatability for all classes of livestock. Its true palatability probably lies between these two extremes, with a tendency toward the lower value, as the disagreeably bitter flavor of stemless actinea's herbage is not conducive to high palatability. On the whole, this weed rates as a poor forage species both because of low palatability and limited herbage production. The flower heads of its relative, fineleaf actinea (*A. linearifolia*, syn. *Tetraneuris linearifolia*), known in the Southwest as tallowweed, are reputed by many Texas sheepmen to produce a good, hard fat on lambs.

The taproots of stemless actinea generally divide and produce several root crowns, each bearing a number of linear to reverse-lance-shaped, rather blunt, appressed-hairy leaves and a single flower stalk. The flowers are yellow with the ray flowers rather broad, three-toothed, and showing orange veins. Stemless actinea is a variable species with numerous, closely related, and more or less intergrading varieties or forms. Thus stemless actinea (*A. acaulis*), Arizona actinea (*A. acaulis arizonica*, syn. *Tetraneuris arizonica*), woolly actinea (*A. acaulis lanigera*, syns. *Actinella lanata* Nutt., 1841, not *A. lanata* Pursh, 1814, *Tetraneuris lanata*, *T. lanigera*), northern actinea (*A. acaulis septentrionalis*, syn. *Tetraneuris septentrionalis*), and sagebrush actinea (*A. acaulis simplex*, syns. *Actinella epunctata*, *A. simplex*, *Tetraneuris epunctata*, *T. simplex*) are all very similar, differing mainly in the width and hairiness of the leaves, the height of the flower stalks, and the shape of the involucral bracts and scales (pappus) of the fruits ("seeds"). Extremely hairy leaves indicate that the plant belongs either to the species *acaulis* or is one of the varieties *lanigera* or *septentrionalis*. The leaf shapes of these three intergrade, typical forms of the species having the narrowest leaves and the variety *septentrionalis* the widest, but the leaf shapes vary, and different forms of the varieties *lanigera* and *septentrionalis* may have leaves shaped identically like those of the typical form of the species. However, if the hairs are appressed, it is the typical form of *acaulis;* if spreading and woolly, the variety *lanigera;* and, if velvety, the variety *septentrionalis*. The leaves of the varieties *arizonica* and *simplex* are nearly hairless and are similar in shape, but the ray flowers of *simplex* have orange veins, in contrast to the lack of such coloration in *arizonica*. The varieties, with the exception of northern actinea, which extends into Canada, have a more or less restricted occurrence within the range of the species. They are probably similar in palatability, and in certain places are more abundant than the typical form of the species.

PINGÜE

Acti'nea richardso'ni

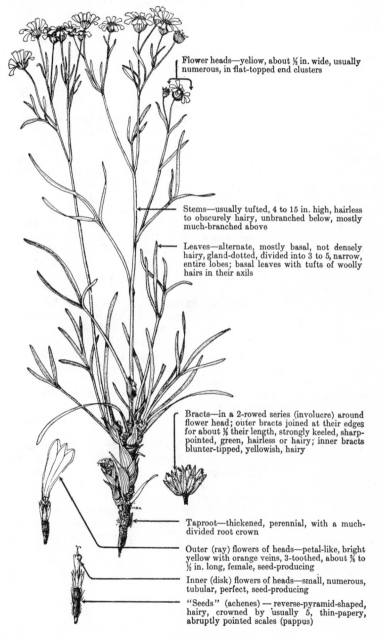

Flower heads—yellow, about ½ in. wide, usually numerous, in flat-topped end clusters

Stems—usually tufted, 4 to 15 in. high, hairless to obscurely hairy, unbranched below, mostly much-branched above

Leaves—alternate, mostly basal, not densely hairy, gland-dotted, divided into 3 to 5, narrow, entire lobes; basal leaves with tufts of woolly hairs in their axils

Bracts—in a 2-rowed series (involucre) around flower head; outer bracts joined at their edges for about ½ their length, strongly keeled, sharp-pointed, green, hairless or hairy; inner bracts blunter-tipped, yellowish, hairy

Taproot—thickened, perennial, with a much-divided root crown

Outer (ray) flowers of heads—petal-like, bright yellow with orange veins, 3-toothed, about ⅜ to ½ in. long, female, seed-producing

Inner (disk) flowers of heads—small, numerous, tubular, perfect, seed-producing

"Seeds" (achenes) — reverse-pyramid-shaped, hairy, crowned by usually 5, thin-papery, abruptly pointed scales (pappus)

Pingüe, also known as Colorado rubberweed or rubberweed, is a green, leafy, tufted, perennial with sunflowerlike heads. Unfortunately, this plant has been the subject of numerous christenings and goes under a variety of aliases in the manuals, including *Actinel'la richardso'ni*, *Hymenox'ys richardso'ni*, *H. floribun'da*, *Picrade'nia richardso'ni*, and *P. floribun'da*. Furthermore, one form of the plant has been considered a variety under the name *H. richardso'ni floribun'da*, and others as distinct species under the names *H. macran'tha* (syn *Picrade'nia macran'tha*) and *H. pu'mila* (syn. *Picrade'nia pu'mila*), but conservative botanists consider that the variations which these names represent are too slight, inconstant, and intergrading to justify specific or even varietal rank. Except for the list of conserved names recognized by the International Code both codes of botanical nomenclature recognize the oldest tenable name as the one to be accepted. *Actinea*, the oldest generic name, was published in 1803. *Richardsoni*, the oldest tenable specific name, was first published under *Picradenia richardsoni* in 1834 and, since recent studies indicate that those plants formerly regarded as composing the genera *Hymenoxys* (syn. *Picradenia*) and "*Actinella*" of American authors belong in the same genus, the oldest tenable name for pingüe would be *Actinea richardsoni*.

This plant was first collected in Saskatchewan by Dr. John Richardson (1787–1865) and was named *Picradenia richardsoni* in his honor by the celebrated British botanist Sir W. J. Hooker (1785–1865). Hooker refers to Dr. Richardson as a naturalist of two separate expeditions to the Polar Seas, by whom a great portion of the more rare and interesting plants that ornament this volume (Flora Boreali Americana) were collected. This botanical classic, dedicated by Hooker to Dr. Richardson and Sir John Franklin, was published in London serially from 1829 to 1840; its two volumes are now considered worthy of a place among the rare books in the Library of Congress. Pingüe, pronounced peeng'gway, the widely established and generally used common name of this species, is a Spanish word meaning oily, referring, undoubtedly, to the oily, resinous leaves. However, the names rubberweed and Colorado rubberweed are also appropriate as the plant contains rubber latex [1] and grows abundantly over large areas in central and southern Colorado.

This perennial is distributed, chiefly on dry, sandy, or gravelly soils, from Saskatchewan and Alberta to Texas, Arizona, eastern California, and eastern Oregon. The species occurs from the sagebrush belt upward to the spruce belt mostly in full sunlight on sites where it is relatively free from competition.

Pingüe, under normal conditions, has practically a zero palatability for all classes of livestock, although under starvation conditions it is grazed by sheep and goats, and to some extent by cattle, despite

---

[1] Cockerell, T. D. A. THE NORTH AMERICAN SPECIES OF HYMENOXYS. Bull. Torrey Bot. Club 31 : 461–509, illus. 1904.

that the species is poisonous to sheep, possibly also to goats and cattle. Marsh [2] reports:

Experimental work has proved that the plant is poisonous to sheep, but it has been found difficult, under corral conditions, to make them eat it.

At one time the livestock losses attributed to this plant were thought due to accumulation of rubber latex in the stomachs and intestines of the animals. In certain sections of the Southwest pingüe plants are infested with grubs, especially in the roots, crown, and stem bases, and sheepmen are often firmly convinced that their sheep losses are caused by these grubs. Investigations by the late Dr. C. D. Marsh, of the Bureau of Animal Industry, United States Department of Agriculture, have proved that some toxic compound in the plant causes the fatalities.[2] Symptoms of poisoning by pingüe are similar to those evidenced in cases of poisoning by bitter rubberweed (*Actinea odorata*) and are given in the discussion of that species which follows. Severe cases usually result fatally as there are no known medicinal remedies.

Undoubtedly pingüe has increased considerably on many of the western ranges due to heavy grazing which has reduced or eliminated the more palatable plants. Ordinarily, it is not sufficiently grazed to cause injury except during shortage of other forage. Hence, losses are more prevalent in late winter, early spring, and at other times either before palatable forage has started or when it is practically exhausted, especially on heavily used ranges. Losses may also occur when very hungry animals are liberated in areas where pingüe predominates, as the hungry animals seeking a quick fill may consume a large amount of pingüe in a comparatively short time.

Pingüe grows from thick taproots, which usually divide into a number of root crowns, each of which produces a more or less branched, leafy stem from 4 to 15 inches high. The root crowns are generally enlarged, bear the old leaf bases of the previous season's growth and a copious supply of white or tawny, woolly hairs. The leaves are mostly divided into three to five very narrow lobes. The flower heads are generally numerous; the ray flowers, about three-eighths to one-half of an inch long, are bright yellow with orange veins.

Bitter rubberweed (*Acti'nea odora'ta*, syns. *Hymenox'ys odora'ta, H. multiflo'ra*), known locally as bitterweed and limonillo, occurs from western Kansas to Arizona, western Texas, and south into Mexico. It has also been reported from southern California, but that is in dispute.

During recent years, bitter rubberweed has caused heavy sheep losses in Texas, especially in the Edwards Plateau, and this has led

---

[2] Marsh, C. D. STOCK-POISONING PLANTS OF THE RANGE. U. S. Dept. Agr. Bull. 1245, rev., 75 pp., illus. 1929. Supersedes Bull. 575.

to extensive experimental studies of the plant.[3] Clawson[4] reports that death may result fairly rapidly if a sheep consumes 1.3 percent or more of its own weight of the green plant. Even where a sheep consumes as little as 0.1 percent of its weight of this plant daily, the animal usually becomes ill in about 44 days. If larger daily doses are eaten, illness will result in a shorter time. The symptoms of bitter rubberweed poisoning are very similar in both acute and chronic cases and consist of salivation, nausea, vomiting, depression, and weakness. Early in the spring, this aromatic, somewhat lemon-scented annual, which is more increasingly abundant in its range each year, is often the only green forage available over large areas and, while normally very unpalatable, is grazed measurably at that time. If sheep are grazed on areas where bitter rubberweed abounds and other forage is lacking, losses are sure to occur as no effective medicinal treatment has been discovered.

[3] Hardy, W. T., Cory, V. L., Schmidt, H., and Dameron, W. H. BITTERWEED POISONING IN SHEEP. Tex. Agr. Expt. Sta. Bull. 433, 18 pp., illus. 1931.
[4] Clawson, A. B. A PRELIMINARY REPORT ON THE POISONOUS EFFECTS OF BITTER RUBBER WEED (ACTINEA ODORATA) ON SHEEP. Jour. Agr. Research [U. S.] 43: 693–701, illus. 1931.

NETTLELEAF HORSEMINT

Aga'stache urticifo'lia

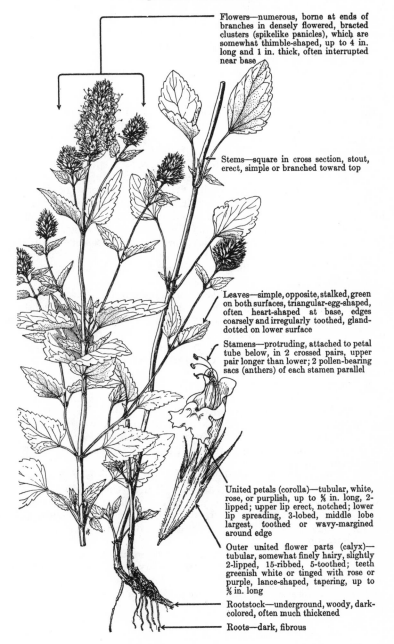

Flowers—numerous, borne at ends of branches in densely flowered, bracted clusters (spikelike panicles), which are somewhat thimble-shaped, up to 4 in. long and 1 in. thick, often interrupted near base

Stems—square in cross section, stout, erect, simple or branched toward top

Leaves—simple, opposite, stalked, green on both surfaces, triangular-egg-shaped, often heart-shaped at base, edges coarsely and irregularly toothed, gland-dotted on lower surface

Stamens—protruding, attached to petal tube below, in 2 crossed pairs, upper pair longer than lower; 2 pollen-bearing sacs (anthers) of each stamen parallel

United petals (corolla)—tubular, white, rose, or purplish, up to ⅝ in. long, 2-lipped; upper lip erect, notched; lower lip spreading, 3-lobed, middle lobe largest, toothed or wavy-margined around edge

Outer united flower parts (calyx)—tubular, somewhat finely hairy, slightly 2-lipped, 15-ribbed, 5-toothed; teeth greenish white or tinged with rose or purple, lance-shaped, tapering, up to ⅜ in. long

Rootstock—underground, woody, dark-colored, often much thickened

Roots—dark, fibrous

Nettleleaf horsemint, a tall, coarse, fragrant herb, up to 5 feet high, perennial from rootstocks, is the most important western forage species in the mint family. It grows in the mountains from western Montana to eastern Washington, California, and New Mexico. Nettleleaf horsemint occurs chiefly in the ponderosa pine, aspen, and spruce-fir belts in moist to somewhat dry, gravelly clay, clay loam, sandy loam, and gravelly loam soils in meadows, brushlands, open hillsides, glades, parks, and open stands of timber. Very commonly associated species are bromes, bluebells, lupines, geraniums, snowberry, and chokecherry. Usually it grows in scattered stands, rarely in dense stands, although sometimes it is fairly abundant in moist, rich soil in the aspen zone.

Livestock graze the plant until the flower parts begin to drop. Later in the summer only the foliage is eaten; but as the younger leaves remain green for some time after seed maturity, nettleleaf horsemint is preferred in the fall to a number of other valuable forage species. While all classes of livestock graze this species more or less, it is eaten chiefly by sheep. Cattle graze it moderately, horses slightly. For sheep its palatability varies from fair to very good, largely depending on associated species (principally the presence or absence of choice forage species), location, and season of use. In general, its palatability is greater in the drier portions of its range, in southern Idaho, Utah, Nevada, and the lava beds of northeastern California, than, for example, in northern Idaho and the Sierra Nevada in California. It is usually of greater value in browse, larkspur, and many weed types than in the better grass associations.

The flowers of nettleleaf horsemint bloom but a few days. The seed matures late in August. The seed supply produced is relatively small per plant and germination tests have shown that only about one-fourth of the seed is fertile (viable). Under proper range management sufficient plants tend to mature seed, satisfactory reproduction is fostered, and vegetative increase is attained in the individual clumps.

A number of segregates of this species have been proposed, including *Agastache greenei*, *A. montana*, *A. neomexicana*, and *A. pallidiflora*, based largely upon slight differences in color, shape, and length of the calyx teeth. For practical purposes, however, these are regarded in this treatment as synonyms of *A. urticifolia*; in fact, some of the more conservative botanists prefer to regard these as forms of one variable species, *A. urticifolia*.

The root system of nettleleaf horsemint is deep and extensive. The slightly furrowed stems are purplish at the base and, like all mints, are square in cross section. The numerous leaves are more or less tapering at the apex, green on both sides, and hairless (glabrous). They vary in size from quite small to 2½ inches wide and 3½ inches long.

The name *Agastache* is from the Greek *agan* (much) and *stachys* (a head of grain, or a spike) and refers to the large and often numerous spikes of flowers which the plants bear. The species name *urticifolia* refers to the resemblance of the leaves to those of nettle (*Urtica*).

SMOOTH MOUNTAIN-DANDELION

Ago'seris glau'ca, syn. *Tro'ximon glau'cum*

Flower head—solitary, large, at end of an unbranched, elongated, leafless stalk

Bracts—in a several-rowed series around base of flower head, commonly about ¾ in. high; lower row sometimes soft-hairy, never stiff-glandular-hairy

Leaves—all basal, shorter than leafless stalk, lance-shaped to narrowly reverse-lance-shaped, entire to toothed or lobed around edges, from ¼ to 1¼ in. wide, hairless, with waxy bloom (glaucous)

Seed head—mature, bristles expanded and seed ready for dissemination

Taproot—thickened, perennial, often with a somewhat branched root crown

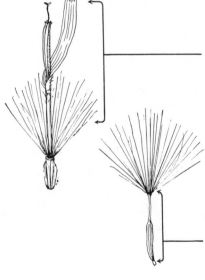

Flowers—yellow, often turning rose or purple in age, all strap-shaped, 5-toothed at tips

"Seeds" (achenes)—smooth, 10-ribbed, with beak about ½ as long as body, tipped by crown of whitish, persistent bristles (pappus)

Smooth mountain-dandelion and its several varieties are perennial herbs and are common members of a large genus of weeds belonging to the chicory tribe of the sunflower family (Compositae). They have a very wide distribution, appearing in all the 11 far-western States.

The smooth mountain-dandelions are most common in open and weedy sites in the ponderosa pine belt, although they are also common above and below this area. They are very adaptable, growing under nearly all variations of soil and moisture. Generally, they are most abundant on moderately dry flats and meadows. Their long taproots and good reproductive powers enable them to survive on disturbed, eroded, and drained meadows. Sagebrush and mules-ears are frequently associated with the smooth mountain-dandelions on slopes and dry flats, and wild-daisies, clovers, and the common dandelion in meadows.

Usually the smooth mountain-dandelions are slightly to moderately grazed by cattle and horses, but on overgrazed ranges and where stock concentrate the use is often much greater. Sheep are very fond of them and often graze each plant several times, especially under favorable growing conditions when the leaves remain green throughout the summer. Although common on the ranges, they are seldom abundant in any one place except locally where they have largely replaced the original vegetation. Close and continuous utilization by sheep may tend to kill them out, but on cattle ranges they may increase, especially on meadows, to the point where they may become undesirable.

The smooth mountain-dandelions have strong and often deep taproots. The leaves are all basal, and vary in shape from linear and grasslike to divided and dandelion-like, although most often they are narrowly lance-shaped and only slightly toothed. The leaves are from 4 to 12 inches long, usually slender and sparsely toothed and, as the common name, smooth, and specific name *glauca* suggest, they are smooth and covered with a bluish-white, waxy bloom. The stems are leafless and unbranched, bearing a large head of bright yellow, strap-shaped flowers, which turn purple in age. There frequently are several very short branches, or stems, of the root crown, each of which may produce one to several separate flower stalks from 4 to 20 inches high. The bracts enclosing the flower heads are in several rows and fit closely over one another like the shingles of a roof. The many, fine, and white (never feathery), bristles (pappus) are attached to the summit of the "seed" beak.

MOUNTAIN-DANDELIONS (Ago'seris spp., syn. *Tro'ximon spp.*)

The mountain-dandelions compose a large genus represented by over 30 species in the western States. The western species, except for one annual (*A. heterophylla*), are similar to smooth mountain-dandelion in that they are milky-juiced perennials with strong, deep taproots, often with short branched root crowns. The leaves vary in size, but are arranged in a basal tuft and sometimes are dandelionlike in form. These features, coupled with the close botanical relationship to the dandelion (*Leontodon taraxacum*) and the characteristic occurrence of these plants in mountainous areas, have given rise to the common name, mountain-dandelion, for the genus. Differences within the genus are not especially great, and a knowledge of smooth mountain-dandelion will usually enable one to recognize the other members of the genus. Most of the characters of mountain-dandelion species emphasized in the botanical keys are of a sort not readily observable in the field, such as shape, length, and surface covering of the bracts, or phyllaries, of the involucre, and length and shape of the seed and its beak.

Mountain-dandelions are sometimes confused with closely related genera, notably the dandelion and with the smaller species of hawksbeard (*Crepis*). The dandelion has many similar characteristics, such as basal leaves and slender, leafless flower stalks (scapes) terminating in a single flower head. Distinguishing characteristics are found in the leaves, involucre, and "seed" (achene). The dandelion tends to have more numerous, deep green leaves with a characteristic "runcinate" lobing; the bracts of the involucre subtending the flower head are not "shingled" but are in one main series with a short outer and lower row of down-bent bracts; the "seeds" are spinulose at the top. Hawksbeards are usually more easily distinguished, as most of them have branched and leafy stems that usually terminate in several flower heads. Mountain-dandelions often have soft woolly hairs near the base of their flower heads, never stiff glandular hairs as many hawksbeards do.

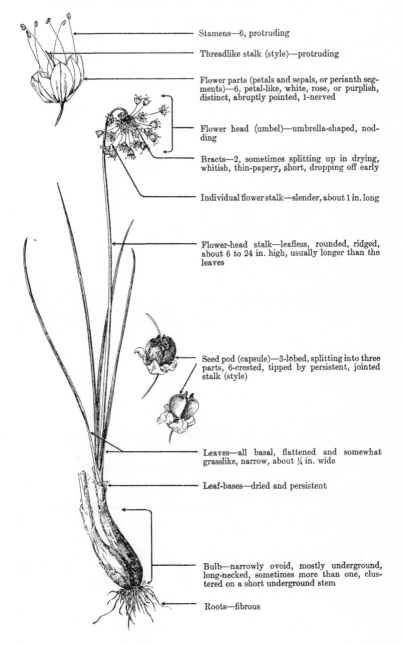

NODDING ONION

Al'lium cer'nuum, syns. *A. neomexica'num, A. recurva'tum*

Stamens—6, protruding

Threadlike stalk (style)—protruding

Flower parts (petals and sepals, or perianth segments)—6, petal-like, white, rose, or purplish, distinct, abruptly pointed, 1-nerved

Flower head (umbel)—umbrella-shaped, nodding

Bracts—2, sometimes splitting up in drying, whitish, thin-papery, short, dropping off early

Individual flower stalk—slender, about 1 in. long

Flower-head stalk—leafless, rounded, ridged, about 6 to 24 in. high, usually longer than the leaves

Seed pod (capsule)—3-lobed, splitting into three parts, 6-crested, tipped by persistent, jointed stalk (style)

Leaves—all basal, flattened and somewhat grasslike, narrow, about ¼ in. wide

Leaf-bases—dried and persistent

Bulb—narrowly ovoid, mostly underground, long-necked, sometimes more than one, clustered on a short underground stem

Roots—fibrous

Nodding onion, a perennial herb with characteristic onionlike odor and taste, is probably the most widespread and familiar of wild onions and is, therefore, selected to illustrate the genus. Its range extends from Saskatchewan to Colorado and Washington.

ONIONS (*Al'lium spp.*)

Onions are well-known perennials of the lily family, with nearly 76 species native to the West. They are found throughout the United States, being especially common in California. Ordinarily they grow in moist places on the plains, in the foothills, and meadows, as well as in woodlands and thickets.

Allium is the ancient Latin name of garlic, and onions are most readily recognized by their distinct onionlike or garliclike odor and taste. It has been shown that this is due "to an essential oil that is specific for each species." [1] Another distinguishing characteristic of these plants is their growth from solid or layered bulbs with the crown encircled by flat or cylindrical and sometimes tapering leaves. The flowers, borne in solitary, slightly rounded clusters on the end of a leafless stalk from 2 inches to 3½ feet high, vary in color from pinkish or purplish to white. Each petal has a purplish or pink middle line. Whitish, paperlike scales occur where the flower stems branch from the end of the stalk. Onions are prolific seeders and often grow in very dense patches on favorable soils.

Range onions, which usually are succulent and often abundant, are highly palatable to cattle and sheep. The different species vary considerably in size and amount of herbage. Some small species spring up quickly after the snow melts but wither and blow away with the coming of dry summer weather. A few species, especially the introduced ones, remain green during the season. Onions are an important and valuable forage genus, except for horses, which only occasionally consume them. This genus furnishes green, succulent herbage early in the spring, when it is eaten readily by cattle and sheep. Some stockmen make the mistake of turning their livestock onto the range in order to utilize onions before the main crop of forage plants have developed sufficiently to justify grazing. Such a practice is injurious to the more permanent vegetation on which proper seasonal use of the range should be based. Onions are objectionable for dairy cows unless grazed judiciously, because the volatile oils in these plants flavor the milk. Elk in Yellowstone Park and elsewhere feed extensively on onions, especially in spring. Bears dig up and eat the bulbs. Indians also utilized these bulbs as a source of food.

A number of familiar cultivated plants belong to the onion genus, including the garden onion (*Allium cepa*), shallot or scallions (*A. ascalonicum*), leek (*A. porrum*), and chives (*A. schoenoprasum*), as well as the ornamental, yellow-flowered moly, or lily leek (*A. moly*), of the flower gardens.

For centuries a medicinal oil has been commercially extracted from the cultivated garlic (*A. sativum*),[2] being used medicinally in several forms of bronchitis and for nervous diseases of young children, and acts as a general mild stimulant. The bruised bulbs are also used as a poultice in the treatment of catarrhal pneumonia. Canada garlic (*A. canadense*), which occurs from Maine to Colorado, is of equal value for medicinal purposes.

[1] Platenius, H. D. A METHOD FOR ESTIMATING THE VOLATILE SULPHUR CONTENT AND PUNGENCY OF ONIONS. Journ. Agr. Research [U. S.] 51 (9) : 847–853, illus. 1935.
[2] Wood, H. C., Remington, J. P., and Sadtler, S. P., assisted by Lyons, A. B., and Wood, H. C., Jr. THE DISPENSATORY OF THE UNITED STATES OF AMERICA, BY DR. GEO. B. WOOD AND DR. FRANKLIN BACHE. Ed. 19, thoroughly rev. and largely rewritten. . . . 1947 pp. Philadelphia and London, 1907.

TUBER STARWORT

Alsi'ne jamesia'na, syns. *A. curtis'ii, Stella'ria jamesia'na*

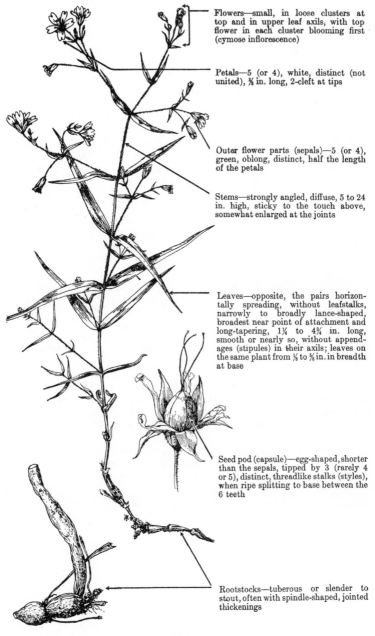

Flowers—small, in loose clusters at top and in upper leaf axils, with top flower in each cluster blooming first (cymose inflorescence)

Petals—5 (or 4), white, distinct (not united), ⅜ in. long, 2-cleft at tips

Outer flower parts (sepals)—5 (or 4), green, oblong, distinct, half the length of the petals

Stems—strongly angled, diffuse, 5 to 24 in. high, sticky to the touch above, somewhat enlarged at the joints

Leaves—opposite, the pairs horizontally spreading, without leafstalks, narrowly to broadly lance-shaped, broadest near point of attachment and long-tapering, 1¼ to 4¾ in. long, smooth or nearly so, without appendages (stipules) in their axils; leaves on the same plant from ⅛ to ⅝ in. in breadth at base

Seed pod (capsule)—egg-shaped, shorter than the sepals, tipped by 3 (rarely 4 or 5), distinct, threadlike stalks (styles), when ripe splitting to base between the 6 teeth

Rootstocks—tuberous or slender to stout, often with spindle-shaped, jointed thickenings

Tuber starwort, known also as starweed and mountain chickweed, is a sticky-hairy herb, perennial from thickened, starchy, often jointed rootstocks. It ranges, chiefly in moist sites, from the woodland and ponderosa pine to the aspen and spruce belts, from Wyoming to Washington, California, and western Texas. In the Rocky Mountains and Intermountain Region it occurs from about 4,500 to 10,000 feet above sea level, but in the Northwest it is found at 1,500 feet. Although occurring in a great variety of soils, it is more likely to grow on sandy or gravelly loams than in clayey soils. It is common among shrubs and in the aspen type.

Tuber starwort rates mention largely because of its wide distribution, commonness, and conspicuousness when in flower. The flowers are cropped by grazing animals, and the herbage is fair in palatability, or occasionally fairly good for sheep, and poor to fair for cattle. This variation depends chiefly on freshness of foliage and presence in quantity of more palatable associates. Sometimes tuber starwort is rather heavily grazed by sheep and cattle, but such extreme use is associated with overgrazing and other abnormal conditions. The amount of forage produced per plant is small despite that this is one of the largest plants in the genus. The tuberous rootstocks are edible and, when fresh and fleshy, are quite palatable; they were an important source of food among the Indians. These rootstocks enable the species to propagate vegetatively, as well as from seed.

STARWORTS AND CHICKWEEDS

(Alsi'ne spp., syn. *Stella'ria spp.*)

The starworts and chickweeds compose a genus of annual or perennial herbs with opposite leaves, white flowers, and often weak and spreading stems. Common chickweed (*A. media*, syn. *Stellaria media*), one of the best-known weeds in gardens and other cultivated ground, occasionally occurs on the range but is rather rare. Starworts and chickweeds are common and are found on a wide variety of sites; however, the majority of the species occur in moist or wet places, and for the most part are small, sparse in stand, and relatively unimportant as range plants. In palatability they are generally considered fair cattle forage and fairly good sheep forage.

The flowers in this genus consist of usually 5 (sometimes 4) separate sepals, 4 or 5 white, notched petals (lacking in some species), 10 or fewer stamens, and a single pistil with usually 3 styles. The capsules, or fruits, open nearly to the base by twice as many valves as there are styles. The stamens and petals are inserted around the margin of a disk under the stalkless (sessile) ovary.

PEARL EVERLASTING

Ana′phalis margarita′cea [1]

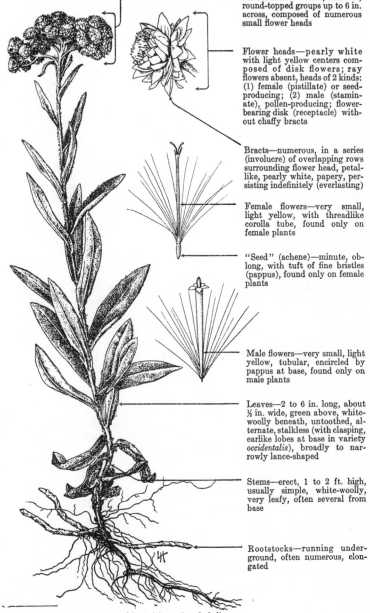

Flower cluster—close, terminal, round-topped groups up to 6 in. across, composed of numerous small flower heads

Flower heads—pearly white with light yellow centers composed of disk flowers; ray flowers absent, heads of 2 kinds: (1) female (pistillate) or seed-producing; (2) male (staminate), pollen-producing; flower-bearing disk (receptacle) without chaffy bracts

Bracts—numerous, in a series (involucre) of overlapping rows surrounding flower head, petal-like, pearly white, papery, persisting indefinitely (everlasting)

Female flowers—very small, light yellow, with threadlike corolla tube, found only on female plants

"Seed" (achene)—minute, oblong, with tuft of fine bristles (pappus), found only on female plants

Male flowers—very small, light yellow, tubular, encircled by pappus at base, found only on male plants

Leaves—2 to 6 in. long, about ½ in. wide, green above, white-woolly beneath, untoothed, alternate, stalkless (with clasping, earlike lobes at base in variety *occidentalis*), broadly to narrowly lance-shaped

Stems—erect, 1 to 2 ft. high, usually simple, white-woolly, very leafy, often several from base

Rootstocks—running underground, often numerous, elongated

[1] Including the varieties *occidenta′lis* and *subalpi′na*.

Pearl everlasting, a bunched or loosely tufted perennial herb of the aster family, also called pearly everlasting, cudweed, Indian-tobacco, and life everlasting, is often confused with the related pussytoes (*Antennaria* spp.), plants which also produce everlasting flowers. The most obviously distinguishing characters are as follows: pearl everlasting does not have the above-ground creeping stems (stolons) or the tufts of basal leaves which are characteristic of most of the pussytoes; the stem leaves of the pussytoes are usually few and often small, those of pearl everlasting are numerous and equal.

Anaphalis margaritacea, including its varieties, is the only species of the genus of any range importance. The distribution of the species, as given in the botanical manuals, is very wide, ranging from Newfoundland to North Carolina, Kansas, California, and Alaska. It is native also in northern Asia and is said to be naturalized in Europe. As far as the western range country is concerned, however, pearl everlasting is represented almost entirely by the two varieties, *occidentalis* and *subalpina*. The variety *occidentalis* ranges from California to Washington and perhaps to Alaska, at low and medium elevations; it is found chiefly in the mountains of California and Oregon. The variety *subalpina* (often given specific rank under the name *A. subalpina* in western manuals) is, as its name indicates, more typical of higher mountain elevations and occurs in all the 11 far-western States. The name *A. margaritacea*, as used in western botanical literature, undoubtedly refers in large part to the variety *subalpina*.

Very frequently pearl everlasting is found growing in dense stands in burned-over and cut-over areas; in the Northwest it is one of the most vigorous invaders of such areas, owing to the circle or tuft of very fine straight hairs (pappus) which carries the "seed" long distances. The widely creeping underground rootstocks and fibrous, spreading root system qualify pearl everlasting to increase rapidly after becoming established. The plants also occur on shaded hillsides, semidry slopes, openings in timber stands, banks of streams, and in parks, mountain meadows, and basins.

Although pearl everlasting produces numerous leaves on its stems and is often abundant, it is not an important forage plant, perhaps because the herbage is often so densely woolly. The slightly musky odor of the flowers may also be a factor in rendering it unpalatable. As a rule, livestock do not eat the plant unless forced to do so by a scarcity of more palatable forage. Occasionally, however, even under proper stocking and use, sheep will turn to pearl everlasting and crop it lightly to fairly.

The most characteristic feature of pearl everlasting is its numerous little but attractive, rounded, pearly flower heads, which are borne in close, roundish clusters at the tops of the stems. The conspicuous white portion of the flower heads is made up of numerous overlapping white, papery bracts which look like petals. These bracts (phyllaries), called collectively the involucre, surround a small, light yellow or buff-colored center composed of numerous small tubular flowers set upon a smooth base (receptacle). When the flowers are young these centers are hardly noticeable, but as they get older the white bracts spread out and the centers become darker and increase in size and prominence. Only about one-half of the flower heads are capable of producing seed because the male (pollen bearing) and the female (seed producing) flowers grow on different flower heads. Sometimes a few perfect flowers, containing both male and female parts, are borne in the center of the female (pistillate) flower heads; these look much like the female flowers but are usually sterile.

GLOBE ANE'MONE

Anemo'ne hudsonia'na, syns. *A. globo'sa,* "*A. multi'fida*"[1]

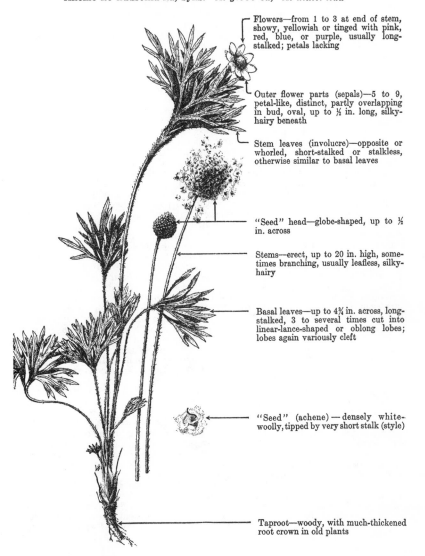

Flowers—from 1 to 3 at end of stem, showy, yellowish or tinged with pink, red, blue, or purple, usually long-stalked; petals lacking

Outer flower parts (sepals)—5 to 9, petal-like, distinct, partly overlapping in bud, oval, up to ½ in. long, silky-hairy beneath

Stem leaves (involucre)—opposite or whorled, short-stalked or stalkless, otherwise similar to basal leaves

"Seed" head—globe-shaped, up to ½ in. across

Stems—erect, up to 20 in. high, sometimes branching, usually leafless, silky-hairy

Basal leaves—up to 4¾ in. across, long-stalked, 3 to several times cut into linear-lance-shaped or oblong lobes; lobes again variously cleft

"Seed" (achene) — densely white-woolly, tipped by very short stalk (style)

Taproot—woody, with much-thickened root crown in old plants

Globe anemone, thus designated because of its globe-shaped seed head, is a perennial herb of the buttercup family (Ranunculaceae) and is a common and representative range species of this genus. It ranges from Alaska to New Brunswick, New England, New Mexico, and California and is the most abundant anemone throughout the Western States, from the low open valleys (4,000

---

[1] Of United States authors, not Poir.

feet) up to timberline (12,000 feet). Globe anemone occurs in a variety of soils on rather dry to moist sites and prefers sunny situations, but occasionally appears in open timber stands. The flowers vary in color from deep rose pink or red to purple, greenish yellow, white, and, sometimes, even bluish tinged. This anemone does not occur in dense stands, but is often abundant. It is generally more conspicuous in fruit because the numerous white-woolly "seeds" are borne at the top of the flower stalk in rounded, globe-shaped heads, which, when loosened by the wind, resemble balls of cotton. As forage, globe anemone is unimportant, being practically worthless for all classes of livestock. In some regions it is slightly palatable to sheep, and it is probably eaten to some extent by deer and elk.

ANEMONES (Anemo'ne spp.)

The Greek name for these flowers comes from *anemos* (wind), presumably because they supposedly opened at the command of the first mild breezes of spring, as the English name, windflower, suggests.[2] Anemones, of which about 85 species occur in the temperate and mountainous regions of the world, are well represented in the West where they flourish on moist and well-drained soils from near timberline on the mountains to the lower elevations in the foothills and valleys, in both open and shaded situations.

Some species constitute fair forage for sheep, deer, and elk, but, in the main, the anemones are practically worthless for cattle and only poor for sheep. Ordinarily, they are insignificant for forage purposes, largely because the more succulent species appear early and then quickly desiccate.

The flowers of some anemones are produced very early, with the first advent of spring, adding their bright colors to the rather drab landscape of the season. They are rather hardy, perennial herbs, various species being cultivated because of their beautiful, showy flowers and, in several cases, for their striking foliage as well. Very few of the commonly cultivated species are native to the western United States, although candle anemone (*A. cylindrica*) and meadow anemone (*A. canadensis*) are common garden species extending into the West.

Several species of anemone, in common with many other members of the buttercup family, are known to contain anemonin, a poison which affects powerfully the central nervous system. This poisonous substance occurs in the European wood anemone (*A. nemorosa*) and probably occurs in the closely related American wood anemone (*A. quinquefolia*) and in many other species. These plants are known to contain poisonous substances,[3] although there is no authentic record, apparently, of any cases of poisoning from them in the United States. However, it is reported that European wood anemone has caused illness of cattle in Europe.[4]

Anemonin is one of the active principles of the drug pulsatilla, which is the dried herbage of species of pasqueflowers (*Pulsatilla* spp.), which are closely related to the anemones and by many authors placed in the anemone genus. Some species of anemone were used by the Romans as a treatment for malarial fevers; American Indians used anemone roots in the treatment of wounds and attributed to them mystical healing powers.[5]

The western species are perennials with rootstocks or tuberous roots, from which stalks 3 to 30 inches high, arise. These stalks are bare except for two or three very irregular, deeply cut leaves (the involucre) close to the flowers or part way up the stalk. The flowers are borne at the ends of the branches and may occur singly or in curved or flat clusters, those at the center being the first to blossom. Only the outer series of petal-like flower parts (sepals), which vary in color from purple to white, are present in *Anemone*. The roughly cylindrical seed head is usually rounded or elongated and, when ripe, the "seeds" (achenes) are often densely hairy, giving the head a cottony appearance.

[2] Skinner, C. M. MYTHS AND LEGENDS OF FLOWERS, TREES, FRUITS, AND PLANTS IN ALL AGES AND IN ALL CLIMES. [302] pp. illus. Philadelphia and London. [1925.]
[3] Long, H. C. PLANTS POISONOUS TO LIVESTOCK. 119 pp., illus. Cambridge. 1917.
[4] Wood, H. C., Remington, J. P., and Sadtler, S. P., assisted by Lyons, A. B., and Wood, H. C., Jr. THE DISPENSATORY OF THE UNITED STATES OF AMERICA, BY DR. GEO. B. WOOD AND DR. FRANKLIN BACHE. Ed. 19, thoroughly rev. and largely rewritten. . . 1,947 pp. Philadelphia and London. 1907.
[5] Gilmore, M. R. USES OF PLANTS BY THE INDIANS OF THE MISSOURI RIVER REGION. U. S. Bur. Amer. Ethnol. Rept. (1911–12) 33 : 45–154, illus. 1919. (Reprinted, 1919).

LY'ALL ANGEL'ICA

Ange'lica lyal'lii

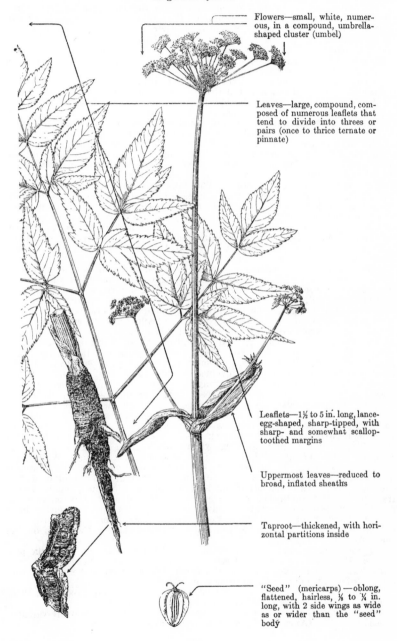

Flowers—small, white, numerous, in a compound, umbrella-shaped cluster (umbel)

Leaves—large, compound, composed of numerous leaflets that tend to divide into threes or pairs (once to thrice ternate or pinnate)

Leaflets—1½ to 5 in. long, lance-egg-shaped, sharp-tipped, with sharp- and somewhat scallop-toothed margins

Uppermost leaves—reduced to broad, inflated sheaths

Taproot—thickened, with horizontal partitions inside

"Seed" (mericarps)—oblong, flattened, hairless, ⅛ to ¼ in. long, with 2 side wings as wide as or wider than the "seed" body

The angelicas, also commonly but loosely called wildparsnips, are perennial herbs of the carrot family. Lyall angelica, named after Dr. David Lyall, who discovered the species while on the International Boundary Survey (1858 to 1860) between the United States and Canada, is probably the most widely distributed of the 19 species of *Angelica* native to the West.

Lyall angelica grows in the mountains from British Columbia to northern California, Utah, and western Montana. It is most frequently associated with sedges, willows, alders, aspen, bluebells, cow-parsnip, false-hellebore, and other moisture-loving plants at elevations varying from 1,500 to 8,500 feet. Its favorite habitats are moist, fertile lands, such as mountain meadows, canyon bottoms, and stream banks, moist shady woodlands, and about springs and seeps. It is seldom or never found growing in dry situations.

Lyall angelica is an erect plant, 2 to 5 feet tall, the stems of which are unusually thick, hollow, and practically free from hair. The sturdy taproot is fleshy in the smaller plants, but tends to become woody and hollow with age, frequently then showing horizontal partitions, which often cause it to be mistaken for the more commonly chambered root of waterhemlock. When bruised, angelica roots give off a strong aromatic odor, pleasant to most people.

Like most of the other angelicas, this species is a prized forage plant, highly palatable to sheep, moderately so or good for cattle, and is eaten readily by deer and elk. It does not ordinarily occur in dense stands or make up much of the plant cover, but in many localities it occurs in fair to moderate abundance and furnishes considerable forage. The individual plants, moreover, are large and produce an abundance of tender leafage and edible stems which generally remain green throughout the summer grazing season. All portions of the plants above ground are grazed. The large taproot not only anchors the plant in the ground, but serves so well as a storehouse for food material that the species is very resistant to overgrazing and trampling, unless long continued. As a rule the flowers are borne in July and August and the seeds are ripened from the middle of August to early October.

Angelicas are often mistaken for the extremely poisonous waterhemlocks (*Cicuta* spp.), and it is important that the range manager should be able to distinguish between these plants. The outstanding differences are as follows: *Cicuta* grows with its feet in the water, usually in much wetter places than *Angelica*. The leaves of the two are similar, but in general *Angelica* leaves tend to be larger and are more compound, the leaflets usually more numerous. These leaflets are oval, with irregularly toothed edges, as compared to the narrow leaflets with evenly toothed (serrate) edges of waterhemlock. Water-hemlocks are always wholly free from hairs, whereas angelicas, even when smooth, often show some hairs, especially in the tops (inflorescence). Water-hemlocks have small bracts (involucels) subtending the secondary flower clusters (umbellets); these are always inconspicuous and frequently quite absent in *Angelica*. The fruit or "seeds" are very different; Angelicas have flattened, winged seeds one-eighth to one-fourth of an inch long. Waterhem-lock seeds are round or egg-shaped, about three-sixteenths of an inch long or smaller, and ribbed with numerous equal ribs. In the past the presence of transverse partitions in the rootstock has been considered by many to be an infallible means of differentiating waterhemlock from angelicas and other harmless plants of similar growth. This, however, is a fallacy. While such partitions are, it is true, so frequently present as to be characteristic of water-hemlocks, they are by no means unknown in angelicas and certain other umbel-lifers as well. Waterhemlock roots have a disagreeable, musty odor in con-trast to the pleasant aroma of the angelicas. The flowers of waterhemlocks usually have prominent sepals or calyx teeth, while the angelicas either have no calyx teeth or very small ones. For a further description, with illustrations, of features distinguishing angelicas and waterhemlocks see the notes on the genus *Cicuta* (W52).

The angelicas reproduce largely from seed, of which they can be prolific pro-ducers. However, some of the species are able to propagate vegetatively from rootstocks or underground stems (rhizomes), which, when broken away from the parent plant, may give rise to new individuals.

The angelicas have long been noted for their medicinal properties. The Indians use the roots as remedies and also as good luck charms.

Angelica archangelica, a European species, is a source of several valuable drugs and an oil (Angelica oil) used in certain French liqueurs.

ROSE PUSSYTOES

Antenna'ria ro'sea, syns. *A. imbrica'ta, A. dioi'ca ro'sea*

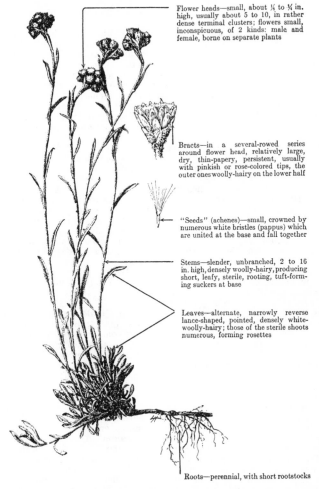

Flower heads—small, about ⅛ to ¼ in. high, usually about 5 to 10, in rather dense terminal clusters; flowers small, inconspicuous, of 2 kinds: male and female, borne on separate plants

Bracts—in a several-rowed series around flower head, relatively large, dry, thin-papery, persistent, usually with pinkish or rose-colored tips, the outer ones woolly-hairy on the lower half

"Seeds" (achenes)—small, crowned by numerous white bristles (pappus) which are united at the base and fall together

Stems—slender, unbranched, 2 to 16 in. high, densely woolly-hairy, producing short, leafy, sterile, rooting, tuft-forming suckers at base

Leaves—alternate, narrowly reverse lance-shaped, pointed, densely white-woolly-hairy; those of the sterile shoots numerous, forming rosettes

Roots—perennial, with short rootstocks

Rose pussytoes is a woolly perennial which often forms mats or tufts of considerable size. It ranges from Alaska to California, New Mexico, and South Dakota, extending from the plains upward to the spruce belt. It typically occurs in grass types of parks and meadows and on hillsides and benches in from dry to moderately moist soils. Normally, rose pussytoes is not abundant but, on ranges where the plant cover has been materially reduced as a result of excessive grazing, this species may form an appreciable part of the vegetation.

The flowers of rose pussytoes are cropped by sheep, but otherwise the species is practically worthless as forage. The plants are able to withstand considerable trampling and reproduce vegetatively both by rootstocks and rooting stems (stolons) and, since they are not weakened by excessive cropping, tend to increase on overgrazed ranges.

Rose pussytoes may be distinguished from all the other species of *Antennaria* by the following characters: The flower heads are arranged in dense clusters at the top of stems which far exceed the group of basal leaves in height; the bracts at the base of the flower head are rose colored, and the leaves are narrowly reverse lance-shaped.

PUSSYTOES (Antenna'ria spp.)

Pussytoes, often known as catsfoot, catspaws, and everlasting, is a genus of woolly, perennial herbs well represented in the West where about 50 species occur. The genus is a member of the everlasting tribe (Gnaphalieae) of the large aster, or composite, family (Asteraceae or Compositae). Everlasting is the common name used popularly in the West for these plants and has been applied, undoubtedly, because of the resemblance of the pussytoes to the true everlastings, which include the French immortelles (genera *Helipterum* and *Helichrysum* of Africa and Australia). The bracts of the flower heads in these genera, as well as of the related genera *Ammobium* and *Anaphalis*, are persistent and often white or brightly colored, hence, in popular understanding, the flowers are "everlasting". The pussytoes are found, to a greater or less extent, on nearly all the western ranges, but, as a rule, are not especially abundant. However, on severely overgrazed ranges, they are sometimes abundant and, though rarely, may even be the dominant herbaceous plants.

Except for the fact that their flower heads are sometimes cropped by sheep, most of the pussytoes are practically worthless as forage. This is particularly true of the rosette-forming species with the flower heads in rather dense clusters, as typified by rose pussytoes. A few species having basal rosettes of leaves but with the flower heads somewhat scattered along the stem and with the upper surfaces of the leaves free of hairs, are grazed slightly more than the species of the rose pussytoes type. Raceme pussytoes (*A. racemosa*) is characteristic of such species. Certain other relatively tall species, such as showy pussytoes (*A. pulcherrima*), in which the basal rosettes of leaves are absent, have their herbage cropped to some extent but probably are never better than fair forage. The somewhat higher palatability of these species may be due to the fact that they are taller, with the larger leaves borne on the stems so that the foliage is more easily available to grazing animals.

In this genus the sexes are distinct, male and female flowers being borne on separate plants. The seed-producing, or female plants, are much more common than the pollen-producing, or male plants. In some species viable seed is produced without pollination. Both the male and female flowers are very small and are borne in heads having the appearance of a single flower. The flowers also bear a copious supply of white bristles (pappus) which, in the female flowers, are united at the base and fall from the "seed" together. The pappus of the male flowers is sometimes barbed or has somewhat knoblike tips and the fancied resemblance of these bristles to the antennae of certain insects suggested the generic name *Antennaria*. The comparatively large, several-rowed bracts enveloping the small flower heads are the most conspicuous part of the flower heads; they usually have white, brown, pink, or rose-colored tips. These bracts persist long after the true flowers have completed their growth and fallen. The leaves are alternate, entire, and rather narrow, varying in the different species from linear to spatula-shaped. The stems, the lower half of the flower head bracts, and at least the lower surface of the leaves are densely hairy.

The only common range plants with which the pussytoes are likely to be confused are pearl everlasting (*Anaphalis margaritacea* and its varieties), the cudweeds (*Gnaphalium* spp.), and those species of eriogonum (*Eriogonum* spp.) whose basal leaves form rosettes or mats. Pearl everlasting and the cudweeds are close relatives of pussytoes and have small flower heads with conspicuous, white or colored persistent bracts. Basal leaves are lacking in pearl everlasting, and the stems are very leafy, but the stems of pussytoes are seldom very leafy and in most species rosettes of basal leaves are present. The cudweeds also lack the rosettes of basal leaves and ordinarily have multibranched stems; the stems of pussytoes usually are unbranched. Although the flowers of the eriogonums are small and are borne in bracted clusters, the bracts are neither brightly colored nor persistent, the flower clusters of most species are umbrella-shaped and the stems, or flower stalks, are mostly leafless or with few leaves.

262

SPREADING DOGBANE

Apo'cynum androsaemifo'lium

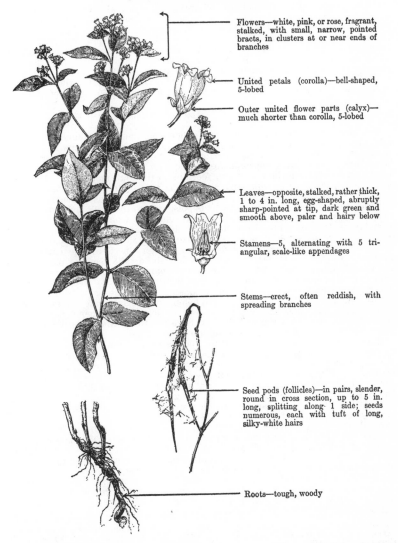

Flowers—white, pink, or rose, fragrant, stalked, with small, narrow, pointed bracts, in clusters at or near ends of branches

United petals (corolla)—bell-shaped, 5-lobed

Outer united flower parts (calyx)—much shorter than corolla, 5-lobed

Leaves—opposite, stalked, rather thick, 1 to 4 in. long, egg-shaped, abruptly sharp-pointed at tip, dark green and smooth above, paler and hairy below

Stamens—5, alternating with 5 triangular, scale-like appendages

Stems—erect, often reddish, with spreading branches

Seed pods (follicles)—in pairs, slender, round in cross section, up to 5 in. long, splitting along 1 side; seeds numerous, each with tuft of long, silky-white hairs

Roots—tough, woody

Spreading dogbane, a perennial herb containing a sticky, milky juice, belongs to the dogbane family (Apocynaceae) and is widely distributed, but not abundant, over most of the United States, as well as in parts of Alaska and Canada. It ranges from Nova Scotia to Alaska, and south to California, Texas, and Georgia, from sea level or fairly low elevations on the plains up to 11,000 feet in the mountains, growing in open timber stands and brushy areas, but appearing in greatest abundance on rather dry, exposed sites. Frequently, it forms dense stands on abandoned homesteads and over-utilized areas, and is common near the borders of thickets, fields, and fence rows. The specific name *androsaemifolium* apparently refers to the general similarity in size and shape of its leaves to those of tutsan, or sweet-amber (*Hypericum androsaemum*, syn. *Androsaemum officinale*), a cultivated, aromatic, Old World shrub belonging to the St. Johnswort genus.

This species is the botanical type of *Apocynum* and is also very representative of the western range dogbanes. It possesses little forage value, rating as worthless to fair for sheep and worthless for cattle and horses. The fragrant flowers attract bees, and in dry, interior regions with poor soils are particularly esteemed as sources of nectar.[1] The almost colorless resultant honey has an excellent flavor, considered by some experts as superior to that of fireweed honey.[1] Spreading dogbane blooms for an unusually long period, and hence is available when other honey plants have disappeared.[2] Local florists distribute spreading dogbane as a hardy border plant; it grows well in dry, open places.

DOGBANES (Apo′cynum spp.)

The dogbanes, commonly known as Indian-hemp[3] and Canadian-hemp, are a small genus of perennial herbs which occur chiefly throughout the North Temperate Zone. They are widely distributed in North America, especially in the temperate regions, with approximately 10 species native to the West, and generally occurring from the plains and foothills to the high mountains. Dogbanes are common on river bottoms and hillsides as well as in open woods, thickets, and fields. Dogbanes are always listed by toxicologists as poisonous plants, but the prevalent belief that the genus is poisonous to livestock lacks substantiation—largely due to the fact that domestic animals usually avoid them—presumably because of their bitter, milky, rubber-containing juice.

The generic name *Apocynum* is Latinized from the Greek *apokunon* (*apo*, from, off, or away from, + *kunōn*, dogs), a name used by the early Greek medical writer, Dioscorides Pedanius, to describe a milkweedlike plant. Both the generic name *Apocynum* and the common name dogbane allude to the idea that the plant is obnoxious to the canine family and, hence, keeps dogs away. These plants have a tough, fibrous bark, and are sources of a substitute for hemp, which explains the name, Indian-hemp, frequently applied to members of this genus. The bark fiber of both spreading dogbane and hemp dogbane (*A. canna′binum*) provided the principal cordage for the western aborigines;[4] the latter species was apparently superior for that purpose.

Hemp dogbane is another important species of dogbane growing extensively in the United States, frequently in the same situations as spreading dogbane. It ranges from New Brunswick and Ontario to British Columbia and south to California, Texas, and Florida, but does not occur in Alaska nor extend as far north in Canada as spreading dogbane. It grows chiefly in gravelly or sandy soil on moist ground, especially along streams, and also in open woods and thickets. Hemp dogbane is an erect species, from 2 to 4 feet tall, having usually ascending, leafy branches; the stems are smooth and often slightly covered with a waxy bloom (glaucescent). The greenish white or flesh-colored flowers are borne in dense, round-topped clusters (cymes). This species is the source of a valuable cardiac stimulant and diuretic, which is useful in the treatment of cardiac dropsy and chronic Bright's disease.[5] That drug causes violent vomiting and sometimes purging if given in very large doses; however, no serious case of poisoning attributable to this plant has been recorded.[5] Although somewhat similar to hemp dogbane in medicinal properties, spreading dogbane is considered inferior and is not now used officially.

---

[1] Pellett, F. C. AMERICAN HONEY PLANTS TOGETHER WITH THOSE WHICH ARE OF SPECIAL VALUE TO THE BEEKEEPER AS SOURCES OF POLLEN. Ed. 3, rev. and enl., 419 pp., illus. Hamilton, Ill. 1930.

[2] Clements, E. S. FLOWERS OF COAST AND SIERRA. 226 pp., illus. New York. 1928.

[3] Not to be confused with the narcotic, true Indian hemp, or hasheesh (*Cannabis indica*).

[4] Blankinship, J. W. NATIVE ECONOMIC PLANTS OF MONTANA. Mont. Agr. Expt. Sta. Bull. 56, 36 pp. 1905.

[5] Wood, H. C., Remington, J. P., and Sadtler, S. P., assisted by Lyons, A. B., and Wood, H. C., Jr. THE DISPENSATORY OF THE UNITED STATES OF AMERICA, BY DR. GEO. B. WOOD AND DR. FRANKLIN BACHE. Ed. 19, thoroughly rev. and largely rewritten . . . 1,947 pp. Philadelphia and London. 1907.

COLUMBINES

Aquile'gia spp.

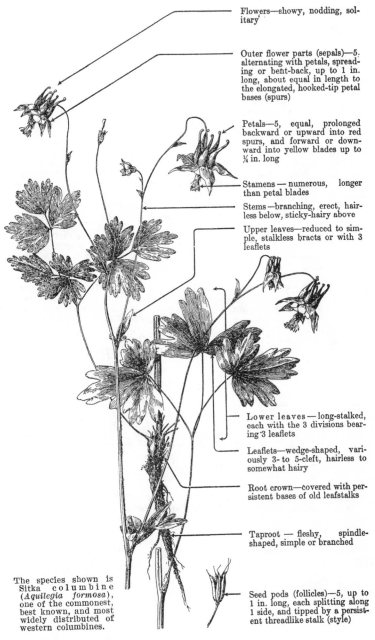

Flowers—showy, nodding, solitary

Outer flower parts (sepals)—5, alternating with petals, spreading or bent-back, up to 1 in. long, about equal in length to the elongated, hooked-tip petal bases (spurs)

Petals—5, equal, prolonged backward or upward into red spurs, and forward or downward into yellow blades up to ¼ in. long

Stamens — numerous, longer than petal blades

Stems—branching, erect, hairless below, sticky-hairy above

Upper leaves—reduced to simple, stalkless bracts or with 3 leaflets

Lower leaves — long-stalked, each with the 3 divisions bearing 3 leaflets

Leaflets—wedge-shaped, variously 3- to 5-cleft, hairless to somewhat hairy

Root crown—covered with persistent bases of old leafstalks

Taproot — fleshy, spindle-shaped, simple or branched

The species shown is Sitka columbine (*Aquilegia formosa*), one of the commonest, best known, and most widely distributed of western columbines.

Seed pods (follicles)—5, up to 1 in. long, each splitting along 1 side, and tipped by a persistent threadlike stalk (style)

Columbines, among the most beautiful native western plants, have varicolored flowers of unusual shape, belong to the buttercup family, and are native of both the Old World and North America. The name columbine is derived from the Latin for dove or pigeon (genus *Columba*), because of the fancied resemblance of the spurs to a circle of doves or pigeons on a perch. The generic name *Aquilegia* is associated with an imagined similarity of the spurs to the claws of an eagle (*aquila*). The great majority of the 30 species of columbine native in the United States and Alaska occur in the western range States; a few species are confined to the Eastern States. The columbine merits particular mention as an appropriate candidate for the national flower. The red, white, or blue flowers are handsome and the foliage graceful. At least one native species grows in each State.

As forage plants, columbines, though often large and leafy and sometimes abundant locally, are of but secondary importance. They rate in palatability as fair for sheep, poor for cattle, and practically worthless for horses. They are rather delicate plants and are likely to succumb if the range is depleted by overstocking, or other abuse, so that domestic livestock, especially sheep, graze them more closely than normal use would permit, particularly if seeding is prevented. Due to past mismanagement, columbines have been greatly reduced on sheep ranges in Colorado where formerly they were plentiful.

Columbines usually grow in moist situations such as shady stream banks, meadows, aspen groves, and open woods from the lower foothills to the high mountains. Some species appear on high, exposed rocky ridges and in sheltered canyons, seldom in pure stands, but more characteristically scattered.

These plants are perennial herbs from slender to stout, mostly perpendicular, often branched taproots. They vary in height from a few inches to about 5 feet, and produce mostly large leaves compounded in threes, each ultimate branch bearing three leaflets the edges of which are irregularly toothed. The strikingly ornate flowers have five petals, each with a long hollow spur extending backward from the frontal, leaflike blade which forms a part of the flower face. The stamens are numerous and indefinite in number. The five pods (follicles) each contain numerous seeds and are tipped with a slender bristle.

American columbine (*A. canaden'sis*), an attractive red-flowered, eastern species, which barely extends to the eastern borders of the range country, was of unique value to certain Indian tribes [1] as a love charm and medicine.

Colorado columbine (*A. coeru'lea*), a species with large and very handsome, blue and white flowers which bloom from June to August, is the State flower of Colorado and is protected by State law.

Sitka columbine (*A. formo'sa*), the species illustrated on the other side of this sheet, is a perennial herb, 3 or occasionally 4 feet high, which ranges from Alaska to northern California, New Mexico, and Montana, but also occurs in Siberia. The plant is found in the Sitka spruce type in Alaska, near sea level, at elevations from 1,000 to 7,500 feet in the Pacific States, and from 3,500 to 10,000 feet in the Rocky Mountain States. It is a common species in the aspen type and in openings in the lodgepole type, but it may be present in a great variety of soils and sites, sometimes being associated with sagebrush, ponderosa and Jeffrey pines, Douglas fir, and white fir. It is especially at home along stream banks, about seeps, springs, and ponds, in meadows, canyon bottoms, and on moist wooded mountain slopes, particularly in loamy soils. The species blossoms from late May or early June to August. In forage value Sitka columbine varies from worthless to fair or sometimes fairly good, sheep relishing it more than cattle. It is one of the most common, abundant, and widely distributed of the western columbines.

European columbine (A. *vulga'ris*), a frequently cultivated blue-flowered species naturalized in this country, has produced symptoms in the lower animals very similar to the extreme prostration caused by aconite.[2]

---

[1] Gilmore, M. R. USES OF PLANTS BY THE INDIANS OF THE MISSOURI RIVER REGION. U. S. Bur. Amer. Ethnol. Ann. Rept. (1911–12)33 : 45–154, illus. 1919. (Reprinted 1919).

[2] Wood, H. C., Remington, J. P., and Sadtler, S. P., assisted by Lyons, A. B., and Wood, H. C., Jr. THE DISPENSATORY OF THE UNITED STATES OF AMERICA, BY DR. GEO. B. WOOD AND DR. FRANKLIN BACHE. Ed. 19, thoroughly rev. and largely rewritten . . . 1,947 pp. Philadelphia and London. 1907.

MOUNTAIN ROCKCRESS

A'rabis drummon'dii, syn. *A. oxyphyl'la*

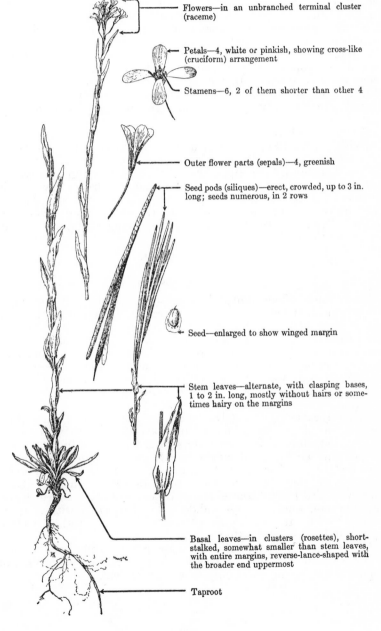

Flowers—in an unbranched terminal cluster (raceme)

Petals—4, white or pinkish, showing cross-like (cruciform) arrangement

Stamens—6, 2 of them shorter than other 4

Outer flower parts (sepals)—4, greenish

Seed pods (siliques)—erect, crowded, up to 3 in. long; seeds numerous, in 2 rows

Seed—enlarged to show winged margin

Stem leaves—alternate, with clasping bases, 1 to 2 in. long, mostly without hairs or sometimes hairy on the margins

Basal leaves—in clusters (rosettes), short-stalked, somewhat smaller than stem leaves, with entire margins, reverse-lance-shaped with the broader end uppermost

Taproot

This biennial (rarely perennial) is perhaps the most widespread and common native species of the rockcresses and has been selected to illustrate the genus. It is found in the 11 far-western States, as well as in many of the eastern States and in southern Canada, and grows in a wide variety of soils, and in moist to wet sites. It is more common in open grass and weed types but occurs also in shrub, woodland, and timber types, although seldom in dense shade. Generally, it occurs scatteringly but is abundant in some localities, especially on areas where the perennial grasses have largely been destroyed by overgrazing. Its forage value varies considerably, doubtless because of different conditions of abundance, habitat, size, and presence of more valuable species. In the main, where better plants are available, it is usually of low value but occasionally is reported as being grazed rather readily by sheep and even cattle, especially on overgrazed ranges.

Mountain rockcress develops a strong taproot. One to several unbranched stems, 10 to 32 inches high, grow up from a basal rosette of relatively narrow leaves which are narrowed toward the base rather than toward the tip. The stem leaves taper gradually to a pointed tip, and are somewhat larger than the basal leaves. The clusters of white or pinkish flowers are usually small and the seed pods are erect in a rather compact cluster. Sometimes the plants are slightly hairy toward the base, the hairs being horizontal and attached at the middle.

ROCKCRESSES

(A'rabis spp.)

Rockcresses include annual, biennial, or perenial weeds and are of world-wide distribution. There are more than 80 species in the western United States. This genus belongs to the mustard family (Brassicaceae). Many authors use Cruciferae as the name of this plant family, a name derived from the Latin *crux*, cross, and *fero*, bear, referring to the crosslike arrangement of the petals—a very marked characteristic of this family. These plants, even if not in flower, can often be recognized by the pungent or acrid taste of leaf or stem.

In the rockcress genus (*Arabis*, from Arabia) flowers are white, pink, or purple, rarely yellowish, and have the distinctive mustard-family characters of four separate sepals, four separate petals, and six stamens (pollen-producing organs), two of which are shorter than the others. The pistils (seed-producing organs of the flowers) mature into long, narrow, flattened pods, with numerous seeds usually in two rows. Leaves are entire or toothed; the stem leaves are alternate, almost always stalkless, and frequently with clasping bases. Usually there is a fairly dense cluster (rosette) of stalked leaves at the base of the stems.

In the aggregate the rockcresses are usually considered of low forage value but under some conditions, especially on overgrazed or depleted ranges, may be readily taken if succulent.

BALLHEAD SANDWORT

Arena'ria conges'ta

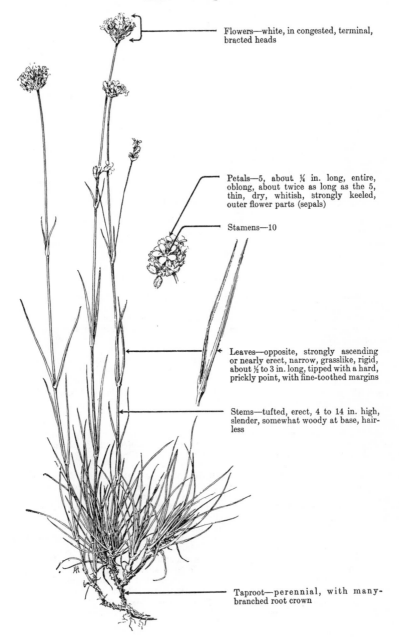

Flowers—white, in congested, terminal, bracted heads

Petals—5, about ¼ in. long, entire, oblong, about twice as long as the 5, thin, dry, whitish, strongly keeled, outer flower parts (sepals)

Stamens—10

Leaves—opposite, strongly ascending or nearly erect, narrow, grasslike, rigid, about ½ to 3 in. long, tipped with a hard, prickly point, with fine-toothed margins

Stems—tufted, erect, 4 to 14 in. high, slender, somewhat woody at base, hairless

Taproot—perennial, with many-branched root crown

269

Ballhead sandwort is a tufted perennial weed with opposite, stiff, sharp-pointed, grasslike or needlelike leaves. This species lacks a well-established, distinctive common name and ballhead sandwort is suggested, ballhead being a rather liberal interpretation of the specific name *congesta* which appropriately refers to the aggregation of the flowers into dense clusters, *congestus* (*-a, -um*) being a Latin adjective meaning congested or heaped together. Ballhead sandwort is distributed in the mountains from Montana and Colorado to California and Washington, occurring mostly between 5,000 and 10,000 feet, although found at both lower and higher altitudes. It grows on a wide variety of soils from deep, rich, moist loams to dry gravels, in grass, weed, sagebrush, aspen, ponderosa pine, lodgepole pine, and other vegetative types. Although a common plant on many of the Western ranges, it is not abundant, as a rule, and occurs scatteringly in mixture with other plants.

The palatability of ballhead sandwort varies considerably, especially in different localities and with the season of the year, and appears to be highest in those localities where it occurs most abundantly. While the growth is young and tender, the palatability of this species, in Montana, is fairly good for cattle and good for sheep; in Wyoming and Colorado it is fairly good for cattle but only fair for sheep; in the Southwest, only fair for both classes of livestock; in California and the Northwest, poor for sheep and practically worthless for cattle; and, in Utah, southern Idaho, and Nevada, it is apparently worthless.

The small, white flowers of this species grow in dense clusters at the tops of the stems. The narrow, rigid, light-green leaves are produced mostly at the base of the plants, while the stems bear three to four pairs of leaves rather distantly spaced, the uppermost pair being much smaller than the others. The flowers of the compact, headlike clusters are subtended by small, egg-shaped, papery-margined bracts. The five sepals are thin, dry and faintly three-nerved, and about one-half as long as the oblong petals. The seed-producing organ (ovary) develops into a three-celled capsule which opens by three two-cleft valves, releasing the numerous minute seeds.

SANDWORTS (Arena′ria spp.)

Sandworts are annual or perennial weeds, having opposite leaves and small, white flowers, borne in open or contracted terminal clusters or, less frequently, solitary in the leaf axils. The genus belongs to the chickweed family (Alsinaceae), which many botanists regard as a tribe or subfamily of the pink family (Silenaceae, or Caryophyllaceae). The generic name is derived from the Latin *arenarius*, belonging to sand, and refers to the characteristic habitat of many of the species. The Latin word *arena* means sand, or figuratively, since the Romans sprinkled sand on the fields used for gladiatorial contests to absorb the blood, the word came to mean any place of combat. The common name, sandwort, also implies a plant or weed of sandy places, wort being a Middle English word (Anglo-Saxon *wyrt*) meaning herb. Sandworts, widely distributed throughout the West, are most common on rather dry, sandy, or gravelly soils but are also found on moderately moist, rich loams. The sandworts are common on the western ranges, occurring from the plains and foothills to well above timber line in the mountains but, as a rule, are scattered among other plants and not abundant in any one place.

The sandworts, as a class, average from poor to fair in palatability for all classes of livestock, although in Utah, Nevada, southern Idaho, California, and the Northwest they are generally considered practically worthless to, at best, poor forage. The palatability of the sandworts undoubtedly varies not only for the different species but also for the same species in different localities and at different times of the year. In general, the palatability is highest in spring and in localities where the plants are most abundant.

Of the western sandworts the only annual species is thymeleaf sandwort (*A. serpyllifolia*), a cosmopolitan, introduced weed with egg-shaped, distinctly three-nerved leaves, and with the petals shorter than the sepals. Most of the perennial species are readily recognizable by their opposite, grasslike, or pine-needlelike leaves, but a few species have leaves of a broader type. The single ovary bears three threadlike styles and develops into a three-celled globular or oblong fruiting capsule opening by means of three two-cleft valves to discharge the numerous seeds.

270

ARNICAS

Ar'nica spp.

Arnica is a genus of perennial herbs of the composite (aster or sunflower) family, represented in the West by about 37 species. The arnicas occur throughout the mountains of the Western States, being much less common in the Southwest than in other sections. They occupy a wide variety of sites; some species are fairly drought-resistant while others grow best in wet or marshy areas. Taken as a whole, the favorite habitat of plants of this genus is moist shady woodlands or coniferous timber stands at moderate to high elevations.

In general, the arnicas are considered unimportant as forage plants, though their forage value is a matter for local determination, as it varies greatly with the species, the locality, and the presence and abundance of more palatable associates. Most arnicas are worthless or low, and, at best, only fair in palatability. Some species, however, are regarded locally as being moderately to highly palatable, especially for sheep. The flower heads are the portion of the plant most readily eaten.

The generic name *Arnica* appears to have been invented by the great Swedish botanist, Linnaeus (1707–78), possibly as a corruption of the old plant name *Ptarmica*. The medicinal arnica of commerce, which is used popularly in the treatment of bruises, sprains, rheumatic pains, and other ailments, is obtained from the flower heads and rootstocks of the European species, *Arnica montana*. It is with this medicinal product that the word arnica is most familiarly associated. Because of the similarity in appearance, odor, and taste, close botanical relationship, and use by the Indians, there is reason for believing that some of our native western arnicas may possess medicinal properties similar to those of the European species.

One of the most outstanding things about the plants of this genus is the typical opposite (paired) arrangement of the leaves although rarely the upper leaves are alternate. The erect stems are 6 inches to 2 feet high. One or more large sunflowerlike flower heads with showy yellow petal-like parts (ray flowers) are borne at the summit of the stems. Several species, of which rayless arnica, often called Parry arnica (*A. parryi*), is the most common, have no petals (ray flowers). The center, or disk portion of the flower head, is made up of numerous small, tubular flowers set upon a common, smooth (not chaffy but sometimes hairy) flattened base (receptacle). The involucre (circle of bracts around the flower head) is composed of oblong-lance-shaped to linear bracts (phyllaries). The seedlike fruits (achenes) are slender, somewhat spindle-shaped, and crowned with a circle or tuft of numerous, rigid, white, or grayish-tawny hairs.

HEARTLEAF ARNICA

Ar'nica cordifo'lia

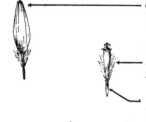

Outside (ray) flowers of head—petal-like, 7 to 13, about 1 in. long, toothed at tip, seed-bearing (pistillate)

Center (disk) flowers of head—numerous, small, yellow, tubular, perfect

"Seed" (achene)—narrow, 5- to 10-ribbed, hairy, the tip encircled by a ring of fine white bristles (pappus) which are rough to touch or with tiny barbs

Flower heads—usually solitary, sometimes several, showy, pale yellow, stalked, erect in bud

Bracts—in a series (involucre) surrounding base of flower head, green, about ¾ in. high, equal, usually in a single row, densely soft-hairy especially at base

Leaves—opposite; lowest pair rather long-stalked, usually distinctly heart-shaped, and coarsely toothed; stem leaves 2 to 4 pairs, egg-shaped or broadly lance-shaped and usually somewhat heart-shaped at base; uppermost leaves reduced, without stalks, narrower than lower ones

Stem—erect, somewhat sticky-hairy

Rootstock—underground, slender, creeping

Heartleaf arnica, a very common plant, is a perennial herb 6 to 24 inches high, growing from fibrous roots and underground rootstocks, and is undoubtedly the most widespread and abundant species of its genus in the West. It ranges from British Columbia to northern New Mexico and California. In the Pacific Northwest it occurs mostly on the east side of the Cascades. It grows at elevations ranging from around 1,000 feet in the ponderosa-pine stands of the Northwest to about 11,000 feet in the mountains of Colorado and Utah. Heartleaf arnica grows almost exclusively in moist, rich, shady woodlands and timbered areas. It thrives in aspen, lodgepole pine, and open Douglas fir stands and in moist humus soils of spruce-fir woods, often becoming abundant and forming almost pure stands. It is sometimes found growing amidst grasses and weeds within or around timbered areas.

Heartleaf arnica is included in this handbook chiefly because of its wide distribution, abundance, and showiness. It is not an important forage plant, its palatability for grazing animals usually being low. In many localities it is but rarely grazed. When grazed, usually only the flowers are consumed, although occasionally some of the leaves are also eaten. Sheep utilize this species more readily than do other classes of livestock.

The English name, heartleaf arnica, and the Latin species name, *cordifolia* (*cordis*=of the heart; *folia*=leaves), are descriptive of the most outstanding feature of this species. The basal and lower leaves are almost always heart-shaped. While this character is reasonably constant, it cannot always be used as an absolute means of identification, because there is some variation in the shape of the leaves; they may be broadly heart-shaped or kidney-shaped, rounded, or ovate. The lower stem leaves are 1 to 3 inches long and stalked (petioled); the upper stem leaves are usually smaller, stalkless, and broadly lance-shaped or diamond-shaped. The large yellow flower heads are often over 2 inches wide.

HOARY ARNICA
Ar'nica folio'sa inca'na, syns. *A. ca'na, A. inca'na* [1]

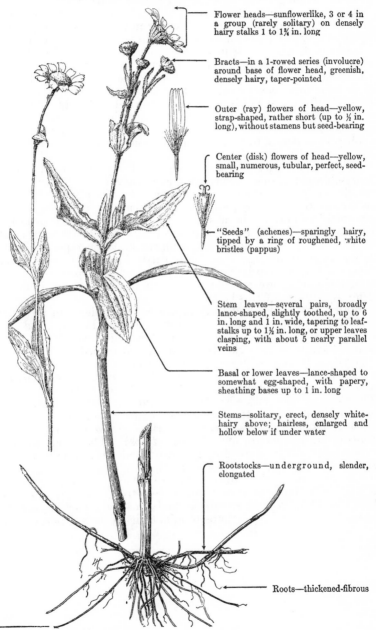

Flower heads—sunflowerlike, 3 or 4 in a group (rarely solitary) on densely hairy stalks 1 to 1¾ in. long

Bracts—in a 1-rowed series (involucre) around base of flower head, greenish, densely hairy, taper-pointed

Outer (ray) flowers of head—yellow, strap-shaped, rather short (up to ½ in. long), without stamens but seed-bearing

Center (disk) flowers of head—yellow, small, numerous, tubular, perfect, seed-bearing

"Seeds" (achenes)—sparingly hairy, tipped by a ring of roughened, white bristles (pappus)

Stem leaves—several pairs, broadly lance-shaped, slightly toothed, up to 6 in. long and 1 in. wide, tapering to leaf-stalks up to 1½ in. long, or upper leaves clasping, with about 5 nearly parallel veins

Basal or lower leaves—lance-shaped to somewhat egg-shaped, with papery, sheathing bases up to 1 in. long

Stems—solitary, erect, densely white-hairy above; hairless, enlarged and hollow below if under water

Rootstocks—underground, slender, elongated

Roots—thickened-fibrous

[1] (A. Gray) Greene, not Pursh.

Hoary arnica, also called water arnica, is a variety of leafy arnica (*A. foliosa*). Both the species and its variety *incana* are leafy-stemmed (the specific name, *foliosa*, means leafy) perennials, 8 to 24 inches high, growing from long-running rootstocks.

Hoary arnica occurs mostly in wet flats or meadows and often grows in the shallow waters of lakes or in the beds of former pools. In extremely wet places it makes a rank growth, sometimes reaching 2½ feet high, and the stems become thick and hollow. Hoary arnica is probably most common in California, where it often grows in abundance in mountain meadows. It is also occasionally found in drier situations, such as sagebrush-weed types. It ranges northward from California to Washington and eastward to Montana and Colorado. Leafy arnica (the species) grows in moist situations in canyon bottoms, open meadows, and parks, and under scattered timber at moderate to high elevations from Alaska to northern New Mexico and Utah.

Neither the variety nor the species is of any particular value for forage, although sheep sometimes graze leafy arnica lightly, at least the flower heads. Hoary arnica often grows in places wetter than sheep care to enter. Moreover, in most places its palatability is low or worthless but, in the absence of better feed, it may sometimes be grazed moderately by sheep or even cattle. Deer are said to eat it when it is dry. Occasionally, California stockmen report this plant as poisonous to livestock, especially cattle, because of losses suffered from grazing areas surrounding alkali ponds and pools. It should be understood, however, that there is no reliable substantiating evidence in support of this belief.

Both hoary arnica and leafy arnica are variable as to leaf shape, and the kind and amount of hairiness, and they also intergrade more or less with each other. Perhaps this variability explains why these plants have been so variously described and named in the different manuals. Hoary arnica appears in western botanical literature under at least four different names, *Arnica cana*, *A. denudata canescens*, *A. foliosa incana*, and *A. incana* (A. Gray) Greene (N. B.—The older *A. incana* Pursh refers to a different plant). Leafy arnica appears in western botanical manuals under at least seven different names, *A. celsa*, *A. chamissonis* in part, *A. denudata*, *A. foliosa*, *A. ocreata*, *A. rhizomata*, and *A. tomentulosa*. The stems of hoary arnica are usually more densely haired and white-woolly than are those of leafy arnica. Hoary arnica grows partly submerged in water more often than does leafy arnica, and when growing thus the lower part of the stem becomes free from hair (glabrate) and both the underground rootstocks and the lower part of the stem become hollow inside, perhaps to admit air to the submerged parts.

BROADLEAF ARNICA

Ar'nica latifo'lia, syn. *A. vento'rum*

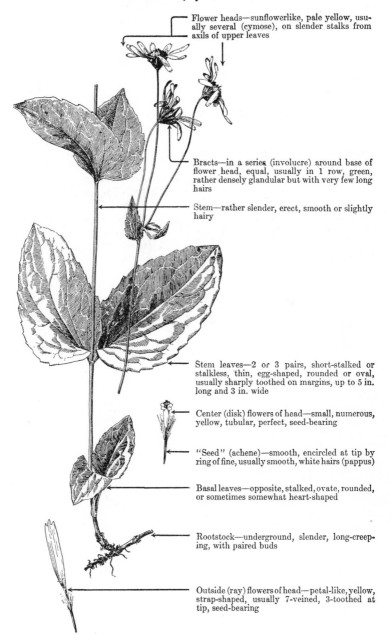

Flower heads—sunflowerlike, pale yellow, usually several (cymose), on slender stalks from axils of upper leaves

Bracts—in a series (involucre) around base of flower head, equal, usually in 1 row, green, rather densely glandular but with very few long hairs

Stem—rather slender, erect, smooth or slightly hairy

Stem leaves—2 or 3 pairs, short-stalked or stalkless, thin, egg-shaped, rounded or oval, usually sharply toothed on margins, up to 5 in. long and 3 in. wide

Center (disk) flowers of head—small, numerous, yellow, tubular, perfect, seed-bearing

"Seed" (achene)—smooth, encircled at tip by ring of fine, usually smooth, white hairs (pappus)

Basal leaves—opposite, stalked, ovate, rounded, or sometimes somewhat heart-shaped

Rootstock—underground, slender, long-creeping, with paired buds

Outside (ray) flowers of head—petal-like, yellow, strap-shaped, usually 7-veined, 3-toothed at tip, seed-bearing

Broadleaf arnica, a perennial herb from 8 to 18 inches tall, is one of the most abundant and widespread of the western arnicas. The species is distributed from Alaska and Alberta to Oregon, Utah, and Colorado. This plant occurs mostly in moist, shady, timbered areas such as aspen, lodgepole pine, Douglas fir, and spruce-fir stands, but it is also common in mountain meadows, shaded parks, and similar places. It grows at elevations varying from about 2,000 feet in the humid forests of the Northwest to about 9,000 feet further inland. In some localities it is the dominant species and may limitedly be found in almost pure stands.

Like most of the other arnicas, this species is rather low in forage value. Generally it is not relished, particularly by any class of livestock. In some localities it is grazed to a limited extent by sheep and cattle, the flower heads being eaten more readily than other portions of the plant.

Broadleaf arnica grows from fibrous roots and running rootstocks (underground stems). The leaves are broad (*latifolia* means broad leaves), and bright green. The lower leaves are usually 1 to 2½ inches long but sometimes from 3 to 5 inches long and 2 to 3 inches broad. The leaves, stems, and circle of bracts around the base of the flower head (involucre) are smooth or nearly free from hair, differing in this respect from heartleaf arnica with which the species is sometimes confused. From 1 to 5 showy, bright-yellow, sunflowerlike flower heads are borne on each stem.

CUDWEED SAGEWORT
Artemi'sia gnaphalo'des [1]

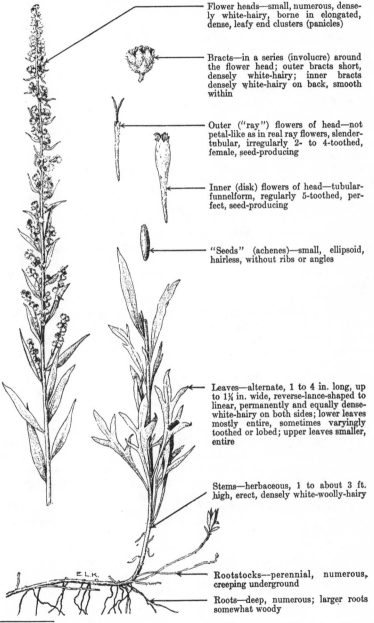

Flower heads—small, numerous, densely white-hairy, borne in elongated, dense, leafy end clusters (panicles)

Bracts—in a series (involucre) around the flower head; outer bracts short, densely white-hairy; inner bracts densely white-hairy on back, smooth within

Outer ("ray") flowers of head—not petal-like as in real ray flowers, slender-tubular, irregularly 2- to 4-toothed, female, seed-producing

Inner (disk) flowers of head—tubular-funnelform, regularly 5-toothed, perfect, seed-producing

"Seeds" (achenes)—small, ellipsoid, hairless, without ribs or angles

Leaves—alternate, 1 to 4 in. long, up to 1¼ in. wide, reverse-lance-shaped to linear, permanently and equally dense-white-hairy on both sides; lower leaves mostly entire, sometimes varyingly toothed or lobed; upper leaves smaller, entire

Stems—herbaceous, 1 to about 3 ft. high, erect, densely white-woolly-hairy

Rootstocks—perennial, numerous, creeping underground

Roots—deep, numerous; larger roots somewhat woody

---

[1] Synonyms: *A. al'bula, A, britto'nii, A. diversifo'lia, A. purshia'na, A. rhizo'mata, A. vulga'ris gnaphalo'des.*

Cudweed sagewort, also known as mugwort, a herbaceous perennial from a woody or shrubby base, is one of the most common and widely distributed of the herbaceous species of *Artemisia*. The specific name *gnaphalodes* means like Gnaphalium, and refers to the resemblance of this plant's soft-wooly leaves to those of cudweed (*Gnaphalium*). This species ranges from Ontario and Michigan to Missouri, Texas, Mexico, California, British Columbia, and Saskatchewan, and has also become naturalized in Pennsylvania and at various places along the Atlantic seaboard from Quebec to Delaware. It is most common on the plains and prairies as a conspicuous component of mixed grass-weed types, associated with fringed sagebrush, false tarragon, needlegrasses, blue grama, and muhly grasses. Throughout the West, this species grows typically in open grass-weed types from the big sagebrush and piñon-juniper to the ponderosa pine and aspen zones.

In southeastern Montana, cudweed sagewort is common and frequently abundant on open slopes and foothills mixed with grasses and weeds at elevations of about 2,800 feet. In the Wasatch Mountains of Utah, it has been found as high as 10,000 feet, in association with alpine weeds. The species also grows freely on rocky, sandy, or gravelly loams of open ridges, slopes, and mesas at moderate elevations, in association with wheatgrasses, mountain-dandelions, and western yarrow. It usually grows as scattered individuals or in small, distinctly matlike patches. However, on a few ranges, it becomes abundant and conspicuous, although seldom found in dense, extensive stands. It prefers open, sun-drenched sites, but occasionally grows in moderate shade.

Although widely distributed, this species, because of inferior palatability and general lack of abundance, usually does not have much forage value, although occasionally grazed by cattle and sheep, as well as by deer and elk. The palatability of this plant varies appreciably in different sections, being highest in the South, and decreasing in the North. In Montana, where this plant is often abundant, the palatability is rated as from worthless to fair for sheep and worthless to poor for cattle; elk and deer eat but small amounts of the leafage. On mixed grass-weed types at Mandan, N. Dak., where cudweed sagewort occurs scatteringly, cattle nibble the foliage, but with noticeably less relish than the grasses.[2] Farther south, particularly in southern Utah and Colorado, and in New Mexico, this species is sometimes a rather valuable forage, especially on spring-fall and winter ranges, rating as fair or fairly good for sheep, fair for cattle, and poor for deer and elk.

Cudweed sagewort has been an important plant in the primitive pharmacopoeia, as well as in the rituals and religious ceremonies of some of the Indian tribes.[3]

---

[2] Sarvis, J. T. EFFECT OF DIFFERENT SYSTEMS AND INTENSITIES OF GRAZING UPON THE NATIVE VEGETATION AT THE NORTHERN GREAT PLAINS FIELD STATION. U. S. Dept. Agr. Bull. 1170, 46 pp., illus. 1923.
[3] Gilmore, M. R. USES OF PLANTS BY THE INDIANS OF THE MISSOURI RIVER REGION. U. S. Bur. Amer. Ethnol. Rept. (1911–12) 33 : 45–154, illus. 1919.

HORSETAIL MILKWEED

Ascle'pias galioi'des

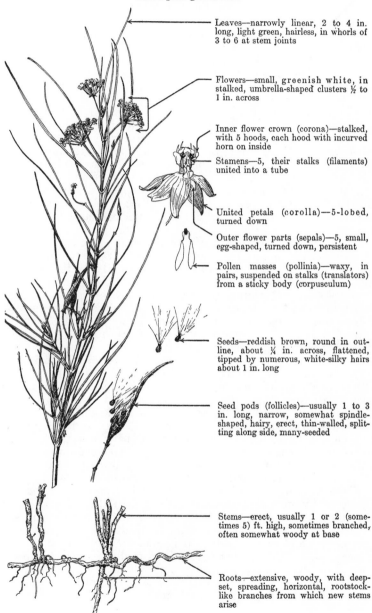

Leaves—narrowly linear, 2 to 4 in. long, light green, hairless, in whorls of 3 to 6 at stem joints

Flowers—small, greenish white, in stalked, umbrella-shaped clusters ½ to 1 in. across

Inner flower crown (corona)—stalked, with 5 hoods, each hood with incurved horn on inside

Stamens—5, their stalks (filaments) united into a tube

United petals (corolla)—5-lobed, turned down

Outer flower parts (sepals)—5, small, egg-shaped, turned down, persistent

Pollen masses (pollinia)—waxy, in pairs, suspended on stalks (translators) from a sticky body (corpusculum)

Seeds—reddish brown, round in outline, about ¼ in. across, flattened, tipped by numerous, white-silky hairs about 1 in. long

Seed pods (follicles)—usually 1 to 3 in. long, narrow, somewhat spindle-shaped, hairy, erect, thin-walled, splitting along side, many-seeded

Stems—erect, usually 1 or 2 (sometimes 5) ft. high, sometimes branched, often somewhat woody at base

Roots—extensive, woody, with deep-set, spreading, horizontal, rootstock-like branches from which new stems arise

Horsetail milkweed, also known as bedstraw milkweed and whorled milkweed, and locally as beeweed, a poisonous perennial herb, ranks among those plants most deadly to range livestock, especially sheep. *Asclepias* is the Latinized form for *asklepias*, an old plant name of uncertain identity used by the Greek medical writer, Dioscorides Pedanius; the word is evidently related to Aesculapius (Greek, *Asklepios*), tutelary god of medicine, and doubtless refers to the plant's putative virtues as a drug. Tournefort and, later, Linnaeus adopted *Asclepias* as generic name for the milkweeds. The specific name *galioides* means like *Galium*, and alludes to the fact that the whorled leaves of this milkweed suggest those of some bedstraw (*Galium*). The English name, horsetail milkweed, recalls the vegetative resemblance of the plant to some horsetail (*Equisetum*) and to the characteristic milky sap which exudes from the wounds when the plant is injured. This species ranges from Kansas to central Utah and south to west Texas, Arizona, and into Mexico, being most common and abundant in the United States in Arizona, New Mexico, and southern Colorado. It has been reported as flourishing and causing losses near Fallon, Nev.,[1] but the broader-leaved Mexican whorled milkweed (*A. mexicana*), another of the group of milkweeds with whorled (verticillate) leaves, may have been mistaken for it.

Horsetail milkweed grows commonly on dry plains and foothills at elevations ranging from 4,000 to about 8,000 feet. In the foothills of Colorado and New Mexico it apparently prefers the draws, and usually grows along watercourses. It inhabits sandy, clayey, or gravelly soils and ordinarily appears on such overgrazed ranges as bedgrounds and trails, or wherever the vegetative cover is broken. The plants are usually scattered on these areas, and seldom form extensive patches. Occasionally this dangerous plant occurs in hay fields, although that thicker vegetative cover discourages its extensive spread or prolific seed production, as essentially it is a sun-loving species. Unfortunately, the growth of this milkweed is notably stimulated by cultivation, new plants readily growing from very small root fragments. Irrigation ditches also help to spread the species by carrying the seeds considerable distances to places where the ditchbanks, with their loose soil, furnish ideal conditions for germination and establishment of new infestation centers. Fence rows, abandoned orchards, and broken or fallow fields also have proved sites favorable for horsetail milkweed to grow luxuriantly, spread rapidly, and form dense, extensive stands.

Wherever horsetail milkweed occurs, it is a possible menace to all classes of livestock, but fortunately its palatability is zero and it is not eaten except during scarcity of other feed. Cattle and sheep, when cropping this plant by mistake in mouthfuls of mixed herbage, may often be observed to discard it immediately because of its unpleasant taste. Death has resulted from feeding alfalfa hay infested with whorled milkweed to hungry, poorly nourished animals; the well-fed, vigorous livestock will nose out and reject the milkweed plants from the roughage. May[1] states: "It is very obvious, then,

---

[1] May, W. L. WHORLED MILKWEED, THE WORST STOCK-POISONING PLANT IN COLORADO. Colo. Agr. Expt. Sta. Bull. 255, 39 pp., illus. 1920.

that the only conditions under which poisoning from this plant may occur are those where the stock are very hungry and there is an absolute lack of other feed." Thus, the greatest losses have resulted along trails or driveways and on depleted bedgrounds, pastures, and ranges where the livestock were forced to eat the plant, due to lack of other forage.

Horsetail milkweed is so virulent that relatively small quantities may cause severe sickness, or even death. Marsh [2] states that 5½ pounds of the green vegetation ordinarily is sufficient to kill a 1,000-pound steer; 1½ pounds, a 1,000-pound horse; and 2¼ ounces, an average-sized sheep. The plant is, therefore, most toxic to sheep, less so to horses, and considerably less poisonous to cattle; with largest losses among sheep. Poisoning of horses seldom happens, as those animals are very discriminatory concerning their feed. Occasionally reports, probably authentic, are heard that this species has caused goat losses. The plant appears to remain rather uniformly toxic during the entire season; the leaves are much more virulently poisonous than the stems. Chemical analyses show that horsetail milkweed contains several poisonous substances, but the symptoms of range poisoning are believed due to a resinlike substance which can be extracted from the plant by use of cold alcohol.[3]

Animals poisoned by horsetail milkweed display very characteristic symptoms, such as loss of muscular control from about 2½ to 21 hours after grazing the plant. Affected animals stagger and wobble, especially in the hind legs, soon fall, and make strenuous but futile efforts to rise. In severe cases violent spasms follow, in which the prostrate animal outstretched on one side throws its head back and forth, and makes running movements with its legs. Under range conditions, the animals have even been observed beating their heads violently upon the ground.[3] Marsh and coworkers (*op. cit.*) further report that the poisoned animals bloat markedly, abdominal gas accumulating rapidly; the respiration is labored, and the pulse is both rapid and weak. In fatal cases, the spasms decrease in intensity before death, which results from respiratory paralysis. Body temperatures sometimes increase to over 110° F. during the sickness. Post-mortem examinations indicate that the outstanding effects of horsetail milkweed poison, besides the accumulation of gas, include lesions of the kidneys and central nervous system.[3] The poison apparently is not cumulative, since sickness or death do not result unless sufficient herbage either to prove toxic or kill the animal is eaten at one time. This plant, in certain far-western poisonous-plant literature, has been mistakenly referred to the more eastern, whorled milkweed (*A. verticillata*); the latter is a species of the Atlantic Plains and the Mississippi Valley, and apparently does not grow in the Rocky Mountains or farther west.

---

[2] Marsh, C. D. PLANTS POISONOUS TO SHEEP. III. THE WHORLED MILKWEED. Natl. Wool Grower 18 (10) : 25–26, illus. 1928.
[3] Marsh, C. D., Clawson, A. B., Couch, J. F., and Eggleston, W. W. THE WHORLED MILKWEED (ASCLEPIAS GALIOIDES) AS A POISONOUS PLANT. U. S. Dept. Agr. Bull. 800, 40 pp., illus. 1920.

Effective antidotes for horsetail milkweed poison have neither been discovered nor developed; hence, prevention is the only control. Areas heavily infested with horsetail milkweed should not be grazed. Wherever practicable this plant should be eradicated from hay fields and pastures and other grazing lands. The prolific seeding habit of this species, together with its ability to grow from even small pieces of root, make it difficult either to control or eradicate the pest. However, mowing and burning the plant secures temporary protection and also tends to reduce seed distribution. The most satisfactory method of eradication on tillable land [4] is to plow or grub areas infested with horsetail milkweed early in August, just before the plants seed. This should be followed by another grubbing or plowing when the green shoots appear in September. Artificial reseeding offers promise as an aid in controlling reinfestation of areas from which this plant has been eradicated. Where the plant occurs on ditchbanks, along fencerows, or on rocky hillsides, either grubbing or spraying with sodium arsenite are very effective. However, since sodium arsenite is extremely poisonous, livestock should be prohibited from areas sprayed with this chemical until the following season.

Horsetail milkweed has gained recognition as a possible source of commercial rubber, the leaves of the plant containing as much as 5.2 percent of rubber according to Hall and Long.[5]

As is characteristic of its genus, horsetail milkweed is admirably adapted to insect pollination. The five stamens are united by their stalks into a tube which surrounds the pollen-receiving organ (stigma). The paired pollen masses (pollinia) are waxy and pear-shaped, and each pollen mass is suspended on a short, slender stalk (translator) from a stick body (corpusculum) located on the stigma between adjacent stamens. These corpuscula are connected by translators to the pollen masses of the two adjacent pollen sacs (anthers). The pollinating insect in crawling over the stigma gets one or more of these corpuscula stuck to its feet and thus carries away the two attached pollen masses to the next flower visited. Doubtless the local name beeweed resulted from the numbers of bees present during the pollination period. The seeds are well fitted for wind dissemination, being numerous, light in weight, and crowned by a tuft of long, silky white hairs; however, they are also often water-borne for considerable distances, especially along irrigation ditches.

[4] May, W. L. CONTROL OF THE WHORLED MILKWEED IN COLORADO. Colo. Agr. Expt. Sta. Bull. 285, 24 pp., illus. 1923.
[5] Hall, H. M., and Long, F. L. RUBBER-CONTENT OF NORTH AMERICAN PLANTS. Carnegie Inst. Wash. Pub. 313, 66 pp., illus. 1921.

MEXICAN WHORLED MILKWEED

Ascle'pias mexica'na

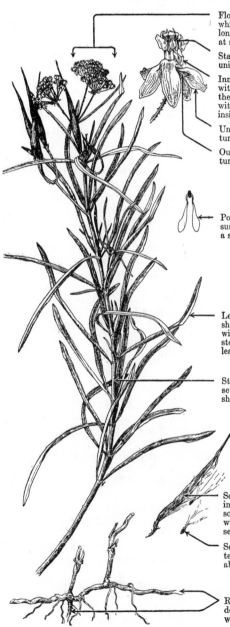

Flowers—small, numerous, greenish white or purplish, soft-short-hairy, in long-stalked, umbrella-shaped clusters at stem ends or in leaf axils

Stamens—5, their stalks (filaments) united into a tube

Inner flower crown (corona)—stalked, with 5 erect hoods; hoods shorter than the pollen sacs (anthers), each hood with horn projecting beyond it on inside

United petals (corolla)—5-lobed; lobes turned down after flower opens

Outer flower parts (sepals)—5, small, turned down, persistent

Pollen masses (pollinia)—waxy, paired, suspended on stalks (translators) from a sticky body (corpusculum)

Leaves—linear or narrowly lance-shaped, 2 to 6 in. long and up to ½ in. wide, hairless, in whorls of 3 to 6 at stem joints or uppermost and lower leaves opposite

Stems—woody at the base, solitary or several, erect, 1 to about 6 ft. high, short-soft-hairy above

Seed pods (follicles)—up to about 4 in. long, narrow (about ¼ in. thick), somewhat spindle-shaped, erect, thin-walled, splitting down the side, many-seeded

Seeds—reddish brown, egg-shaped, flattened, with tuft of silky, white hairs about 1¼ in. long at tip

Roots—deep, woody, extensive, with deep, horizontal, rootstocklike branches which give rise to new stems

Mexican whorled milkweed, a perennial herb often called narrow-leaf milkweed, is poisonous to livestock, having, in particular, caused serious sheep losses. The Latin specific name *mexicana*, as well as the Mexican of the English name, allude to the fact that the plant was first collected in Mexico; whorled refers to the arrangement of most of the leaves in circles (whorls) of 3 to 6 at the stem joints. Milkweed is a reminder of the milky juice which exudes from wounds of this and other plants of the milkweed family (Asclepiadaceae), when injured. This species is confined to western North America, where it ranges from southern Mexico northward through California to Washington, western Idaho, Utah, and western Arizona. It is most abundant in California and Nevada. Rather extensive patches grow practically throughout California, but chiefly in the dry ground of valleys and foothills, except along the coast in the northern part.

Mexican whorled milkweed often develops in small colonies on dry plains and foothills and may occur at altitudes up to 6,000 feet, although it usually appears at much lower elevations. It demands an open, sunny site; once established the deep-set and extensive root system enables this species to withstand extensive drought. However, it makes a more luxuriant growth and spreads faster in such moist situations as along watercourses, where shade is not excessive.

This plant usually inhabits sandy, rocky, clayey or gravelly soils, and frequently attains abundance on bedgrounds and newly disturbed or eroded areas, where the original cover has been depleted. It spreads rapidly, extending its range by invasions into disturbed soil areas along irrigation ditches, streams, roadsides, and fencerows, as well as into pastures, washes, and on abandoned agricultural land, where it frequently develops dense, extensive stands. Occasionally, this herb also occurs in hayfields and meadows, and either lowers the hay grade materially or makes the contaminated crop worthless or even dangerous. This obtains because Mexican whorled milkweed, in drying, loses some of its disagreeable taste, but not its poisonous properties, and is rather readily eaten in hay.

Animals grazed where Mexican whorled milkweed is intermixed with good forage, spurn it until the other feed is utilized. Although, as above intimated, most reported fatalities have been among sheep, some cattle losses have occurred, but practically no mortality has resulted among horses. The maximum sheep losses have been experienced along sheep trails or on bedding areas, and in overgrazed pastures and fields where the animals were forced to eat this plant due to the scarcity of better forage. While losses are usually few and scattered, occasionally almost entire bands have been wiped out at one time.

Although Mexican whorled milkweed is very poisonous, it is not nearly as serious a menace as its sister species, horsetail milkweed (*A. galioi'des*), being only one-fourth as toxic—in fact, the amount required for a lethal dose is six times as much.[1] Investigations [1][2] indicate that ordinarily about 1½ to 2½ pounds of green material

[1] Marsh, C. D., and Clawson, A. B. THE MEXICAN WHORLED MILKWEED (ASCLEPIAS MEXICANA) AS A POISONOUS PLANT. U. S. Dept. Agr. Bull. 969, 16 pp., illus. 1921.
[2] Fleming, C. E., and Peterson, N. F., assisted by Miller, M. R., Vawter, L. R., and Wright, L. H. THE NARROW-LEAVED MILKWEED (ASCLEPIAS MEXICANA) AND THE BROAD-LEAVED OR SHOWY MILKWEED (ASCLEPIAS SPECIOSA) PLANTS POISONOUS TO LIVESTOCK IN NEVADA. Nev. Agr. Expt. Sta. Bull. 99, 32 pp., illus. 1920.

of Mexican whorled milkweed is sufficient to kill a 100-pound sheep. Fleming and coauthors [2] state that amounts of 5 pounds or more apiece may reasonably be expected to kill yearling calves, and Marsh and Clawson [1] report that, due to the similarity in effects of Mexican whorled and horsetail milkweeds, it is fair to conclude that the former is poisonous also to horses.

Chemical analyses [2] indicate that the plant contains several poisonous substances, but the symptoms appearing in range poisoning are probably attributable to a black, resinlike substance which can be extracted from Mexican whorled milkweed with alcohol.

The symptoms of poisoning are somewhat similar to, but usually less severe than, those caused by horsetail milkweed. Sheep become sick in from about 5 to 14 hours after grazing this poisonous species, are generally depressed, refuse to eat, lack muscular coordination, and walk with an unsteady, wobbly gait with paralysis usually most marked in the hind legs.[1][2] In fatal cases the affected animal soon falls, unable to rise. The pulse is fast and weak, and the breathing is labored. Spasms are present but usually are neither so marked nor as violent as those produced by horsetail milkweed. No perceptible elevation of temperature may occur [1] or the temperature may rise during the spasms, the maximum being reached at the time of death.[2] The poisoned animals are often salivated and bloated. No effective antidote is available. Since Mexican whorled milkweed is easily recognized, livestock should be debarred from heavily infested areas. Whenever feasible, the plant should be eradicated from valuable pastures, fields, and hay lands, although its prolific seeding habit and ability to grow from even very small pieces of deep-seated, horizontal root make such eradication both difficult and costly. The most efficient control—similar to that used in the overthrow of horsetail milkweed in such areas—probably would be to plow or grub the plants early in August before seed maturity, repeating the process when the green shoots begin to appear in September. In some cases it is advisable to remove these pestiferous plants from fencerows, roadsides, ditchbanks, and rocky soils to prevent their serving as breeding centers for seed which would later infest agricultural, range, pasture, or hay lands.

Despite that it is poisonous to livestock, this species has several possible economic uses. Analyses by Hall and Long [3] indicate its potentialities as a source of commercial rubber, as much as 4.8 percent of rubber having been obtained from latex in the leaves. These authors also state:

> The largest plants are always found in moderately alkaline soil and are often associated with such halophytes as *Sporobolus airoides* and *Distichlis spicata*. These facts suggest that the proper place for the cultivation of the plant on a large scale would be the vast expanses of territory in the San Joaquin Valley of California and the valleys of western Nevada which are now uncultivated either because of alkaline conditions or the lack of water for irrigation.

---

[3] Hall, H. M., and Long, F. L. RUBBER-CONTENT OF NORTH AMERICAN PLANTS. Carnegie Inst. Wash. Pub. 313, 66 pp., illus. 1921.

Mexican whorled milkweed is insect-pollinated in a manner similar to that described in detail in the horsetail-milkweed discussion in this handbook. The waxy, paired pollen masses (pollinia) attached by stalks (translators) to a small, sticky body (corpusculum) on the stigma, become stuck to the legs of bees and other insects and are thus carried from one flower to another.

ASTERS

As'ter spp.

Aster, taking its name from the Greek, *aster*, a star, referring to the rayed flower heads, is a large (at least 250 species), chiefly North American genus of principally perennial, or occasionally annual or biennial plants, with a large representation in the West. Including the section of spiny asters and goldilocks (genera *Leucosyris* and *Linosyris* of some authors), the woody asters (genus *Xylorrhiza* of some authors) and the genera *Brachyactis, Doellingeria, Eremiastrum, Eucephalus, Herrickia, Ionactis, Leucelene, Machaeranthera, Oreostemma,* and *Unamia* of some authors, at least 150 species occur in the Western States. Of these, the spiny aster group (about 3 species) and the woody asters (approximately 10 species) are more or less woody, varying from scarcely more than herbs with a woody root and crown to true shrubs or undershrubs. The remainder of the western species are herbaceous plants, either with rootstocks or with taproots and a more or less well defined root crown. Asters are universally distributed in the Western States and occur in practically all soils and in all types from the desert and semidesert regions at low elevations to well above timberline. These species seldom appear in pure stands but, taking the western ranges as a whole, are so common and generally distributed that they form a considerable part of the plant cover.

The spiny and woody asters have a zero to very low palatability, so that if sheep or other livestock crop them on any scale it is a sure indication of improper range conditions.[1]

The smaller species of herbaceous asters, especially those with numerous small flower heads and the upper leaves distinctly smaller than the basal, are usually practically worthless to, at best, poor forage. They are seldom cropped by cattle and but slightly by sheep. These species have strong reproductive powers and frequently become abundant on overgrazed ranges. The taller species, with larger flower heads and leafy stems, are generally more palatable—some of the better species being considered fair to good forage for sheep and goats and fair forage for cattle. Horses rarely graze any of the asters. Observations of elk on the Lewis and Clark Forest in Montana have disclosed that a number of the larger asters are good fall and winter forage for these game animals and are also grazed in the spring and summer before heads are developed. Deer, however, have not been noticed to graze asters in that locality.

Among the asters one of the woody species, Parry aster (*A. parryi*, syn. *Xylorrhiza parryi*), often known as woody aster, is unusual in that it is known to poison sheep. A very closely related species, alkali aster (*A. glabriusculus*, syn. *Xylorrhiza glabriuscula*), ranging from Wyoming to northern Utah, is also under strong suspicion.[1] The range of Parry aster is, so far as known, confined to Wyoming, but it may also occur in northern Colorado. It is found only at the

---

[1] Dayton, W. A. IMPORTANT WESTERN BROWSE PLANTS. U. S. Dept. Agr. Misc. Pub. 101, 214 pp., illus. 1931.

lower elevations upon gumbo-clay soils, usually on gentle slopes or sometimes on ridges. Parry aster has a large woody taproot more or less branched at the surface of the ground. From these woody root crowns spring a number of leafy, woolly-hairy stems about 4 to 6 inches high which produce, usually during June, several daisy-like flower heads. The white, petallike ray flowers are about three-eighths of an inch long, and the narrow, spatula-shaped, hairy, alternate leaves are about 1 to 2 inches long. Parry aster has caused very heavy sheep losses in Wyoming, chiefly during the spring and early summer. Probably losses are greater during that period because the mature plants contain much less of the toxic principle and are less attractive to grazing animals. Apparently only a small amount of Parry aster is required to produce fatal results in sheep, but ordinarily this plant is not grazed except under conditions of extreme hunger or when there is a shortage of other forage. The toxic principle of Parry aster has been isolated, but its exact nature has not been determined.[2] There are no known medicinal remedies. Some observations indicate that Parry aster, which frequently occurs on selenium-bearing soils, may absorb enough of this element to be toxic to cattle.[3]

Asters belong to the immense aster, or composite family (Asteraceae, or Compositae). The flowers are small and borne in dense clusters, or heads, having the appearance of a single flower and commonly are produced from late July to late September. Flowers are of two kinds: (1) Those in the center of the heads (disk flowers), with yellow, tubular corollas which often turn reddish or purplish in drying, and (2) those at the edge of the heads (ray flowers) with strap-shaped and petallike, white, pink, blue, or purple corollas. The ray flowers are usually in one row, not very numerous, and their corollas are comparatively broad. The enlarged end of the stalk (receptacle), which bears the flowers, is flat. Heads are normally borne on leafy stalks and are surrounded at the base by several rows of strongly graduated, overlapping, somewhat herbaceous bracts. Numerous slender, white or tawny bristles are borne on top of each "seed" (achene) in both the disk and the ray flowers. The leaves are alternate, with entire or toothed margins.

The most common plants with which the asters are likely to be confused are the wild-daisies (*Erigeron* spp.). However, wild-daisy heads are usually fewer (often one to three) and generally borne on partially leafless stalks, the ray flowers are slender and generally numerous, and the disk flowers do not noticeably change color in drying. Furthermore, the involucral bracts are in fewer (mostly one or two) rows, usually looser, but slightly overlapping, and are nearly equal in length.

Asters are often grown as ornamentals, and a large number of well-recognized species and horticultural varieties are now available through commercial nurserymen. At least three of these species are native to the West. Rock aster (*A. alpinus*), an alpine species ranging from Alaska to Colorado and occurring in Europe and Asia, is a rather low plant with single stems arising from a somewhat woody root crown. Under natural conditions the ray flowers are white. This species, one of the hardy asters of nurserymen, is especially suitable for rock gardens, and about 17 named horticultural varieties of it have been developed. Smooth aster (*A. laevis*), a late blooming species with blue ray flowers and a stout, smooth stem often covered with a bluish waxy substance (glaucous), is native in the Rocky Mountains from British Columbia to New Mexico and eastward to Ontario, Maine, and Georgia. Wreath aster (*A. multiflorus*), a rather low, much-branched species with white ray flowers, occurs naturally east of the Rocky Mountains.

[2] Beath, O. A. CHEMICAL AND PHARMACOLOGICAL EXAMINATION OF THE WOODY ASTER. Wyo. Agr. Expt. Sta. Bull. 123: [40]–66, illus. 1920.
[3] Hill, J. A. [REPORT OF THE] CHEMISTRY DEPARTMENT. Wyo. Agr. Expt. Sta. Rept. 43: 14–16. 1933.

SHOWY ASTER

As'ter conspi'cuus

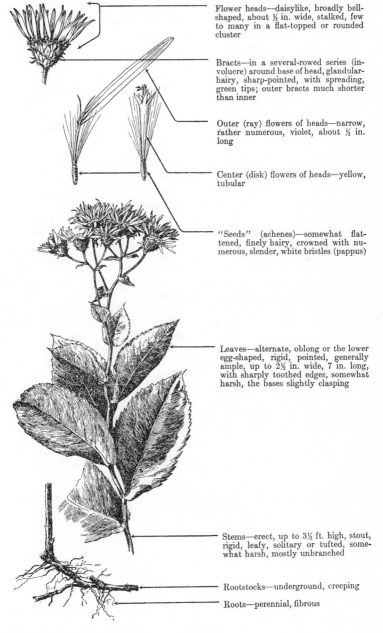

Flower heads—daisylike, broadly bell-shaped, about ½ in. wide, stalked, few to many in a flat-topped or rounded cluster

Bracts—in a several-rowed series (involucre) around base of head, glandular-hairy, sharp-pointed, with spreading, green tips; outer bracts much shorter than inner

Outer (ray) flowers of heads—narrow, rather numerous, violet, about ½ in. long

Center (disk) flowers of heads—yellow, tubular

"Seeds" (achenes)—somewhat flattened, finely hairy, crowned with numerous, slender, white bristles (pappus)

Leaves—alternate, oblong or the lower egg-shaped, rigid, pointed, generally ample, up to 2½ in. wide, 7 in. long, with sharply toothed edges, somewhat harsh, the bases slightly clasping

Stems—erect, up to 3½ ft. high, stout, rigid, leafy, solitary or tufted, somewhat harsh, mostly unbranched

Rootstocks—underground, creeping

Roots—perennial, fibrous

Showy aster, sometimes known as purple aster, although the ray flowers are violet rather than purple, is a perennial which starts blooming about the middle of July and continues until late September, or even later if weather conditions permit. The specific name *conspicuus*, Latin for conspicuous, or remarkable, is appropriate for this species, which produces its rather large yellow and violet flower heads at a time when but few other wild flowers add color to the green and brown hues of the wooded hillsides. It ranges from British Columbia to Oregon, Wyoming, South Dakota, and Saskatchewan. It occurs in considerable abundance on the east slope of the Cascade Mountains, but apparently does not grow in Washington and Oregon west of the Cascade Mountains, although it has been reported from Vancouver Island. Showy aster is confined chiefly to the ponderosa pine and lodgepole pine belts. It may be common and sometimes fairly abundant in aspen and open coniferous timber, especially in lodgepole pine, and also occurs sparsely in moist parks and old burns.

This species is generally rated as fairly good to good sheep and goat forage and as fair to fairly good cattle forage. Like practically all other asters, it is seldom grazed by horses. It is a fairly large, leafy plant occurring rather abundantly and produces a considerable amount of forage. Showy aster constitutes unusually good fall and winter elk forage, and the new leaves are grazed by those animals in spring. The species is especially important on fall and winter elk ranges in Idaho and Montana. Showy aster is not aggressive and does not tend to crowd out its associates to any great extent, although considerable seed is produced and new plants also develop from the stout, underground rootstocks.

Stems of this species are erect, up to 3½ feet high, rigid, and leafy. The leaves are relatively large and numerous, often 7 inches long and 2½ inches wide, with sharply toothed margins. The stem leaves are without leafstalks, their bases often partly clasping the stem. The leaves of the middle part of the stem are usually the largest. The flower heads are borne on short-branched, glandular stalks in a rounded or flat-topped cluster. The yellow disk flowers turn purplish in drying. The green-tipped involucral bracts are in about five rows, the outer ones being much shorter than the inner.

ENGELMANN ASTER

As'ter engelman'ni, syn. *Euce'phalus engelman'ni*

Flower heads—about ½ in. high, hemispherical, usually several on each stem,
arising from the upper leaf axils

Bracts—in a 5-rowed series (involucre)
around base of head, usually purple-
tinged, with hairy-fringed margins, the
outer ones shorter than the inner

Outer (ray) flowers of heads—white,
pinkish, or purple, 5 to 10, female, about
½ in. long

Center (disk) flowers of heads—small,
numerous, yellow, tubular, turning
brownish in drying

"Seeds" (achenes)—oblong, flattened,
more or less hairy, becoming hairless in
age, crowned with numerous tawny
bristles (pappus)

Leaves—alternate, mostly broadly
lance-shaped, 2 to 4 in. long, usually
sharp-pointed, stalkless, rather thin
with prominent midrib, generally hairless, somewhat bluish-waxy-coated, the
margins sometimes with a few fine
teeth

Stems—robust, up to 5 ft. high, solitary
or tufted, often branched toward the
top, hairless to somewhat fine-hairy

Rootstocks—creeping, underground,
perennial

Roots—fibrous

Engelmann aster, a tall, leafy perennial with underground running rootstocks, ranges from British Columbia to northern California and eastward to Colorado and Montana. It usually occurs in loam soils which may vary from a clay loam to a gravelly or even a rocky loam. It is not critical in its moisture requirements and is found on both moderately moist and fairly dry soils. It occurs in a variety of types, namely, in grass and weed mixtures, among shrubs, in aspen, and in open coniferous timber, probably reaching its best development in rich, moist soils in scattered aspen. Being a mountain plant, this species seldom occurs below an elevation of 3,000 feet in the Cascade Mountains of Washington and Oregon. In the Rocky Mountains its elevational range is from about 6,000 to 10,000 feet. This aster is fairly common and in some places is locally abundant, although it seldom constitutes more than a small part of the herbaceous plant growth.

There is some difference of opinion as to the palatability of Engelmann aster. There is general agreement, however, that it is one of the most palatable of the asters and, as it is rather widely distributed and fairly common, it is a rather valuable weed species. Engelmann aster is reputedly good sheep and cattle feed in parts of Utah and good sheep forage in parts of Wyoming. Generally throughout the rest of its range it rates as fairly good forage for sheep and goats, fair for cattle, but practically worthless for horses. All observers agree that before the buds develop it is good spring forage for elk, and that it also has value for fall and winter use. Some observers state that it is good deer and wild-goat feed, while others maintain that deer seldom graze this or any other species of aster.

Engelmann aster, one of many plants named for Dr. George Engelmann (1809–84), a celebrated American botanist, is a rather robust species with leafy stems either solitary or in small tufts. The basal leaves and the stem leaves are nearly equal in size, are relatively thin, with a prominent midrib, and of a pale green, somewhat yellowish color. The larger leaves often have a few small teeth along the margins. The stems often bear as many as 20 or more rather large heads, although stems with only 1 or 2 heads are not uncommon. The petallike ray flowers, mostly about 10 on each head, vary from white or pinkish to purple. Rocky Mountain specimens tend to produce white or pinkish ray flowers, whereas California specimens usually have darker-colored rays. The commonly reddish or purple-edged involucral bracts are in five rows, the outer ones being shorter than the inner.

This species, like many other asters, starts blooming about the middle of July and continues until late September. Seeds begin to mature about the 1st of September, and are produced as long as the weather permits. An abundance of seed is produced, and the plants also spread by means of the strong rootstocks. However, Engelmann aster is not an especially aggressive species; and while it maintains itself very well on grazed ranges, it does not tend to become overly abundant.

THICKSTEM ASTER

As'ter integrifo'lius, syn. *A. amplexifo'lius*

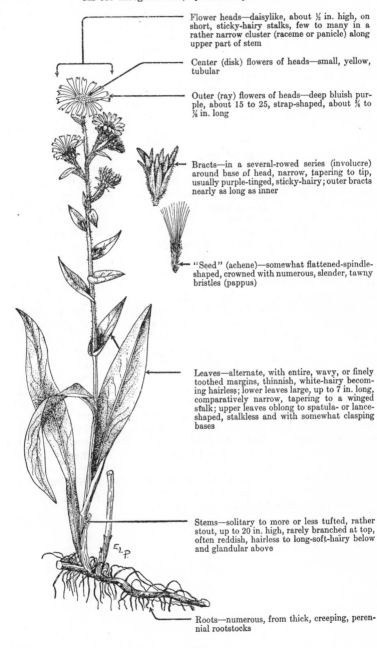

Flower heads—daisylike, about ½ in. high, on short, sticky-hairy stalks, few to many in a rather narrow cluster (raceme or panicle) along upper part of stem

Center (disk) flowers of heads—small, yellow, tubular

Outer (ray) flowers of heads—deep bluish purple, about 15 to 25, strap-shaped, about ⅜ to ⅞ in. long

Bracts—in a several-rowed series (involucre) around base of head, narrow, tapering to tip, usually purple-tinged, sticky-hairy; outer bracts nearly as long as inner

"Seed" (achene)—somewhat flattened-spindle-shaped, crowned with numerous, slender, tawny bristles (pappus)

Leaves—alternate, with entire, wavy, or finely toothed margins, thinnish, white-hairy becoming hairless; lower leaves large, up to 7 in. long, comparatively narrow, tapering to a winged stalk; upper leaves oblong to spatula- or lance-shaped, stalkless and with somewhat clasping bases

Stems—solitary to more or less tufted, rather stout, up to 20 in. high, rarely branched at top, often reddish, hairless to long-soft-hairy below and glandular above

Roots—numerous, from thick, creeping, perennial rootstocks

295

Thickstem aster is a leafy weed of the composite, or aster family (Compositae, or Asteraceae), with one or several stems growing from thick, creeping, perennial rootstocks. The name *integrifolius* is a Latin adjective compounded from *integer* (*-ra, -rum*), whole or entire (hence, untoothed) and *folium*, leaf. Thickstem aster is confined chiefly to the mountains from Washington and Montana to Colorado and California. It occurs mostly at elevations above 5,000 feet in the Rocky and Sierra Nevada Mountains and at somewhat lower elevations in the Cascade Mountains of Washington and Oregon. It prefers moist loam or often somewhat gravelly soils, being most abundant in meadows and parks along the edges of timber but also appearing in open timber and woodlands and to some extent in sagebrush types. This weed is often associated with goldenrod, lupine, yarrow, bromegrass, fescue, willow, and sagebrush. Although fairly common throughout its range and relatively abundant in some localities, this plant is principally scattered in its distribution.

Throughout its more northerly range, thickstem aster is especially prized as a fall elk weed; moreover in many parts of this region it is fair or fairly good sheep feed. Elsewhere it is, at best, only fair forage for sheep and goats, poor for cattle, and practically worthless for horses. It may be valuable as forage for elk and possibly also for deer over much of its range. In California, where this species is fairly common, it is considered poor forage even for sheep. Hence extensive utilization of this plant on California sheep ranges is a probable warning of overgrazing and range depletion.

The stems of thickstem aster are usually from about 8 to 20 inches tall and grow in small tufts, usually several arising from a stout often branched rootstock, although sometimes the bunches are considerably larger. The stems are often reddish, are usually more or less hairy toward the base and glandular-hairy or sticky toward the top. The lower leaves are large, comparatively narrow, and decidedly variable in shape, in some plants being broadest toward the tip and in others toward the base. The basal leaves taper into a winged stalk (petiole), but the stem leaves, which are smaller than the basal ones, are without stalks, their bases more or less clasping the stem. The plants start flowering about the middle of July and continue until early fall, the several short-stalked flower heads, about 1 inch across and one-half of an inch high, being borne in a rather narrow cluster toward the top of the stem. The petal-like ray-flowers are deep bluish purple, and the involucres and stems of the heads are glandular. The involucral bracts are rather loosely arranged in three or four rows, the outer ones being nearly as long as the usually purple-tinged inner ones.

TIMBER POISONVETCH

Astra′galus convalla′rius [1]

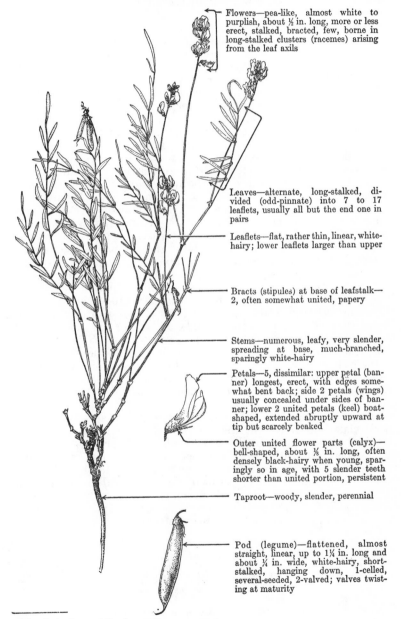

Flowers—pea-like, almost white to purplish, about ½ in. long, more or less erect, stalked, bracted, few, borne in long-stalked clusters (racemes) arising from the leaf axils

Leaves—alternate, long-stalked, divided (odd-pinnate) into 7 to 17 leaflets, usually all but the end one in pairs

Leaflets—flat, rather thin, linear, white-hairy; lower leaflets larger than upper

Bracts (stipules) at base of leafstalk—2, often somewhat united, papery

Stems—numerous, leafy, very slender, spreading at base, much-branched, sparingly white-hairy

Petals—5, dissimilar: upper petal (banner) longest, erect, with edges somewhat bent back; side 2 petals (wings) usually concealed under sides of banner; lower 2 united petals (keel) boat-shaped, extended abruptly upward at tip but scarcely beaked

Outer united flower parts (calyx)—bell-shaped, about ⅙ in. long, often densely black-hairy when young, sparingly so in age, with 5 slender teeth shorter than united portion, persistent

Taproot—woody, slender, perennial

Pod (legume)—flattened, almost straight, linear, up to 1¼ in. long and about ¼ in. wide, white-hairy, short-stalked, hanging down, 1-celled, several-seeded, 2-valved; valves twisting at maturity

[1] See footnote on following page.

Timber poisonvetch, also called greenvetch, timber milkvetch, and timber loco, a perennial herb of great practical and scientific interest, is poisonous in many areas and responsible for heavy losses of cattle, sheep, and horses, but in other areas is grazed without injurious results. This species, a member of the large loco-poisonvetch-milkvetch (*Astragalus*) genus of the pea family (Leguminosae), is related to the well-known poisonous crazyweed, or "stemless loco" (*Oxytropis lambertii*). A considerable number of species in the large *Astragalus* genus are recognized as poisonous to livestock; those which cause locoism are known as locos, or locoweeds; other toxic species, called poisonvetches, produce entirely different symptoms; still other species, called milkvetches, are innocuous. Accurate information concerning the great majority of range *Astragali* is lacking. Until recently timber poisonvetch was usually regarded as harmless; hence the name "milkvetch", so commonly used for this species, was not inappropriate; in fact, in many localities this plant is considered to be an excellent and nutritious forage species. The late Dr. E. L. Greene (1842–1915), at one time botanist for the Forest Service, is the author of the name *convallarius*, but did not explain it. Perhaps it was because of some imagined similarity of the racemes of this plant to those of lily-of-the-valley (*Convallaria*).

Timber poisonvetch, so far as is now known, ranges from southeastern British Columbia and eastern Washington to Montana and south to northern Arizona and Colorado; it probably also occurs in eastern Nevada and northern New Mexico. The plant grows typically on mountain slopes from the oakbrush and ponderosa pine belts to the upper reaches of the spruce zone. In British Columbia it is found at elevations of from about 2,000 to 4,500 feet and in Wyoming between 6,000 and 8,000 feet. It often grows on moist, timbered slopes, in open aspen stands, and along the edges of parks and meadows, thriving on many of these sites, and frequently being conspicuous amidst the plant cover. Although the species grows best on the rich, clayey, sandy, or gravelly loam soils of somewhat shaded sites, it often occurs scatteringly in open, drier sagebrush types. This plant seldom forms pure stands, but usually grows in mixed grass-weed types.

Timber poisonvetch, unlike many poisonous plants, is palatable to all classes of livestock; the delicacy of its leaves and stems undoubtedly enhances the readiness with which it is cropped. On many ranges sheep and cattle frequently eat measurable quantities without injurious effects; sheep on certain areas prefer it to any other feed. Beath and co-workers,[2] as a result of their chemical analyses of timber poisonvetch, state "the crude protein content is * * * above that of alfalfa." Potentially the plant would rank as highly nutritious, an opinion endorsed by many stockmen.

---

[1] The complex synonymy of this plant includes: *A. campestris* (Nutt.) A. Gray (1865), based on *Homalobus campestris* Nutt. (1838), not *A. campestris* L. (1753); *H. salidae; H. tenuifolius; Phaca convallaria; A. decumbens convallarius; A. serotinus campestris.* There are several other very similar *Astragali, e. g., A. decumbens, A. divergens, A. hylophilus, A. palliseri, A. serotinus,* and *A. strigosus,* which seem more or less to intergrade with *A. convallarius* and with each other, and which some authors have regarded as varieties of *A. convallarius.* Further study of this important and variable group of species is needed to establish definitely the specific limitations and precise geographic ranges.

[2] Beath, O. A., Draize, J. H., and Eppson, H. F. THREE POISONOUS VETCHES. Wyo. Agr. Expt. Sta. Bull. 189, 23 pp., illus. 1932.

In Wyoming, Beath and co-workers,[2][3] and Bruce[4] in British Columbia, have reported on the poisonous properties of timber poisonvetch and have contributed most of the available information concerning the effects of this plant upon livestock. In the case of sheep and cattle, females suckling their young are by far the most susceptible; ordinarily the death rate in horses is not high, although in certain cases losses of from 10 to 40 percent or more have occurred. However, horses once affected can never stand much work afterward. The greatest losses obtain among animals which are newcomers to the ranges; in time, however, they seem to develop partial (but never complete) immunity to the poison. Livestock suffer most from this disease during dry seasons, and the majority of range losses attributable to the plant are intimately connected with shortage of other forage. The toxic period of timber poisonvetch is not definitely known. Although a few livestock losses have occurred in its earlier stages of growth, most poisonings have developed during its flowering or seeding periods; after maturing and drying up it has been eaten without apparent injury.[4]

There is an extensive local lingo for the cumulative symptoms caused by timber poisonvetch, including such terms as alkali disease, blind staggers, cracker-heel, knocking disease, mountain fever, roaring disease, timber paralysis, and timber trouble. However, the first two names are not limited to poisoning caused by timber poisonvetch.

The disease may be chronic, as commonly in Wyoming,[2] lasting from several months to several years, or it may be acute, the symptoms appearing within a few days, and being rather quickly fatal. In the chronic cases symptoms are varied and often difficult to recognize. They include general sluggishness and inactivity, weakness, defective nutrition, often depraved appetite, impaired vision, tendency to wander aimlessly, and varying degrees of paralysis, especially in the hind legs.

In acute cases one or more such characteristic symptoms are noticeable, as sudden attacks in which the heart beats very rapidly and spasmodically; impairment of vision (blind staggers); muscle incoordination which causes the animal to knock its heels together in walking (knocking disease), or paralysis beginning in the hind legs, with a tendency to spread to other parts; difficult breathing, often accompanied by a wheezing or roaring (roaring disease). In addition there may be drooling, loss of voice, anemia, and a dangerous decline in body temperature. In fatal cases death ordinarily results from respiratory paralysis or from heart failure and may occur within a few days after the first symptoms appear. Autopsy reveals an enlarged and flabby heart with thin walls; the liver, lungs, spleen, and various parts of the digestive tract are usually congested; there may be some nerve degeneration, especially of the vagus nerve.

[3] Beath, O. A., Draize, J. H., and Gilbert, C. S. PLANTS POISONOUS TO LIVESTOCK. Wyo. Agr. Expt. Sta. Bull. 200, 84 pp., illus. 1934.
[4] Bruce, E. A. ASTRAGALUS CAMPESTRIS AND OTHER STOCK POISONING PLANTS OF BRITISH COLUMBIA. Canada Dept. Agr. Bull. 88, 44 pp., illus. 1927.

No specific antidote for the disease caused by timber poisonvetch has yet been discovered or developed; hence the problem is one of prevention. Livestock should be debarred from areas which are heavily infested with this plant, especially where previous fatalities have occurred. Animal newcomers to a range where this plant abounds should be carefully watched to prevent their consumption of excessive quantities of timber poisonvetch; areas on which it occurs should be grazed lightly.

The exact chemical nature of the toxin in this plant is unknown. Beath and co-workers [3] indicate that "stock poisoned by this plant exhibit symptoms suggestive of metallic poisoning. Ash analysis of the plant reveals the presence of comparatively large amounts of tin." The "trace" of selenium which those investigators obtained in their analysis is perhaps even more significant. It is possible that timber poisonvetch, like the closely related two-groove poisonvetch (*A. bisulcatus*) and several other plant species reported by Beath and co-workers,[5] may also be selenium-bearing when grown on certain soils. Several indications, at least, point that way: (1) As a result of the high protein content of timber poisonvetch, there is the possibility of its absorbing sulphur in large quantities; hence, if Hurd-Karrer's assumption of substitution of selenium for sulphur in certain synthesized plant compounds [6][7] is correct, then timber poisonvetch might reasonably be supposed to absorb considerable quantities of selenium if that element is present and available to the plant in the soil in which it grows; (2) the fact that Byers [8] reports that analyses of Bridger and Wasatch shales from Uinta County, Wyo., reveal no toxic amount of selenium, may explain why Beath and co-workers [2] failed to obtain symptoms of poisoning after feeding large quantities of timber poisonvetch to sheep on a range in that county; (3) the symptoms caused by timber poisonvetch and the autopsy results are similar to those of animals poisoned by small doses of the sodium salt of selenious acid; [5] (4) the increased losses of livestock from timber poisonvetch during seasons of insufficient rainfall agrees with the known fact that many of the selenium compounds are water-soluble and, therefore, would not leach out of the surface soil, as might reasonably be expected, during periods of normal or sufficient rainfall.

To sum up: Timber poisonvetch is a peculiar and important range plant, of value for forage under certain conditions and, under certain other (as yet undetermined) conditions, virulently poisonous. Further study of its occurrence, plant associates, and the conditions under which it is poisonous to livestock is essential.

[5] Beath, O. A., Draize, J. H. Eppson, H. F., Gilbert, C. S., and McCreary, O. C. CERTAIN POISONOUS PLANTS OF WYOMING ACTIVATED BY SELENIUM AND THEIR ASSOCIATION WITH RESPECT TO SOIL TYPES. Jour. Amer. Pharm. Assoc. 23(2) : 94–97. 1934.
[6] Hurd-Karrer, A. M. SELENIUM INJURY TO WHEAT PLANTS AND ITS INHIBITION BY SULPHUR. Jour. Agr. Research [U. S] 49(4) : 343–357, illus. 1934.
[7] Hurd-Karrer, A. M. FACTORS AFFECTING THE ABSORPTION OF SELENIUM FROM SOILS BY PLANTS. Jour. Agr. Research [U. S.] 50(5) : 413–427, illus. 1935.
[8] Byers, H. G. SELENIUM OCCURRENCE IN CERTAIN SOILS IN THE UNITED STATES WITH A DISCUSSION OF RELATED TOPICS. U. S. Dept. Agr. Tech. Bull. 482, 48 pp., illus. 1935.

WOOLLY LOCO

Astra'galus mollis'simus

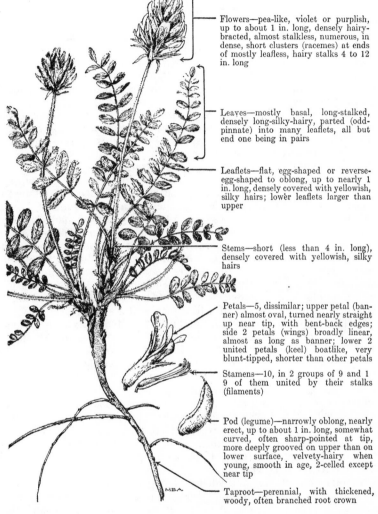

Flowers—pea-like, violet or purplish, up to about 1 in. long, densely hairy-bracted, almost stalkless, numerous, in dense, short clusters (racemes) at ends of mostly leafless, hairy stalks 4 to 12 in. long

Leaves—mostly basal, long-stalked, densely long-silky-hairy, parted (odd-pinnate) into many leaflets, all but end one being in pairs

Leaflets—flat, egg-shaped or reverse-egg-shaped to oblong, up to nearly 1 in. long, densely covered with yellowish, silky hairs; lower leaflets larger than upper

Stems—short (less than 4 in. long), densely covered with yellowish, silky hairs

Petals—5, dissimilar; upper petal (banner) almost oval, turned nearly straight up near tip, with bent-back edges; side 2 petals (wings) broadly linear, almost as long as banner; lower 2 united petals (keel) boatlike, very blunt-tipped, shorter than other petals

Stamens—10, in 2 groups of 9 and 1 9 of them united by their stalks (filaments)

Pod (legume)—narrowly oblong, nearly erect, up to about 1 in. long, somewhat curved, often sharp-pointed at tip, more deeply grooved on upper than on lower surface, velvety-hairy when young, smooth in age, 2-celled except near tip

Taproot—perennial, with thickened, woody, often branched root crown

Woolly loco, sometimes called purple, stemmed, Texas, and true loco, is a low, tufted, perennial herb poisonous to livestock. The common name woolly is very appropriate because the plant is densely covered with long, close (appressed), yellowish hairs. Loco is a Spanish word, meaning foolish or crazy, and refers to the extraordinary effects which these plants produce on the animals that consume them. The word was first applied by the Spaniards and Mexicans to a disease common among the horses, cattle, and sheep of the Southwest. The term "loco", as a definite common plant name, appears to have been first applied to *Astragalus mollissimus* in western Texas, where that plant was suspected of causing the disease known as locoism in livestock, inducing craziness or stupefaction. Subsequently, a large number of plants, chiefly of the genera *Astragalus* and *Oxytropis*, have, at one time or another, been called loco, because of their poisonous effects on domestic animals. Although the early Spaniards seemingly recognized the disease and symptoms, they were evidently unfamiliar with the fact that the disease was caused by woolly loco, because they named *Astragalus mollissimus* garbanzilla from its resemblance to the chickpea, Spanish "garbano" (*Cicer arietinum*), which is used in Spain as food. The application of the term "loco" to *Astragalus mollissimus* is no doubt relatively recent.

The fact that woolly loco is poisonous has made the plant the subject of considerable scientific study; consequently, its range is known with noteworthy precision. It extends throughout the southern plains region, being confined to the southwestern portion of South Dakota, extreme southeastern Wyoming, the western half of Nebraska, Kansas and Oklahoma, eastern Colorado, eastern Arizona, New Mexico, northern Texas, and south into Mexico. The species is most abundant in New Mexico and the Panhandle region of Texas.

Woolly loco typically grows on the breezy, sun-drenched slopes of the plains and prairies at elevations of from 4,000 to 6,000 feet above sea level, occurring usually in small scattered patches, but occasionally forming a moderate cover several acres in extent. It prefers the heavy, clayey soils of the depressions and grows commonly on heavy, sandy, or gravelly soils of the lower slopes, but seldom appears on ridges or elevated sites. Under favorable conditions, it frequently attains a height of 1 to 2 feet, and a spread of 2 feet.

Woolly loco is relatively unpalatable to all classes of livestock. Under ordinary conditions, cattle will not eat the plant except in dire hunger and neither horses nor sheep will partake readily of the foliage except when forced to do so by the scarcity of better and more succulent forage. However, Marsh et al.[1] state:

It has been demonstrated that the so-called loco disease of the Plains is not simply a matter of starvation, as many have supposed, though it is also clear that when other feed is abundant very few horses will eat loco.

If animals once begin to eat woolly loco, they are likely to form a habit similar to the drug habit, or narcotic craving in man, and when they become accustomed to graze the plant, they often consume great quantities with special avidity. Frequently, all livestock, but particularly horses, develop such a strong appetite for the herbage, that they cannot be induced to feed upon any other forage as long as woolly loco is available. Animals which continually consume this poisonous pest usually become locoed and finally die.

Woolly loco is one of the first range plants to become green in the spring. During the early growing season, the species is especially dangerous and constitutes a serious menace, because very little other succulent forage is then available. Throughout the late spring and

[1] Marsh, C. D., Clawson, A. B., and Eggleston, W. W. THE LOCO-WEED DISEASE. U. S. Dept. Agr. Farmers' Bull. 1054, rev., 26 pp., illus. 1929.

summer, the poisoning hazard is lessened since succulent grasses and other forage are more likely to be present. This plant remains green through the late fall and winter when it again is readily eaten, especially by horses.

Livestock losses are largely confined to horses on ranges where woolly loco is the only poisonous plant. However, occasional cattle and sheep losses are attributed to this pest. Losses are much less among animals native to the range than they are among newcomers to the range. Generally, the finer breeds of horses and cattle are much more susceptible to loco than the usual range breeds, grades, cross-breeds, or scrubs. This is true also of sheep, since losses are more likely to occur among such breeds as Hampshires and Southdowns than with Rambouillets and Merinos.[2]

Losses of horses have been especially heavy in Texas and Arizona, while the major cattle fatalities have occurred in Colorado. A peculiar feature about loco poisoning is that death usually does not occur immediately from a single feeding, but comes only after continued and comparatively heavy use of the plant. However, this species frequently exerts a more pronounced effect on horses than any other loco, so that heavy losses sometimes occur in a short time. In many cases, several weeks or months may elapse before the animal is observed to be affected. Initial symptoms of poisoning include in horses a general depression; the animal becomes dull and inclined to laziness, loses weight, and often looks poor and scrawny. As the disease develops, the symptoms become more evident. The animal is generally weak, walks with an irregular gait, drags its feet, particularly the hind ones, and exhibits an apparent lack of muscular control and coordination. The optical nerves are evidently affected, because the animal usually mistakes small objects for large ones, often steps high over the slightest obstruction and leaps over small depressions, as if they were big ditches. The disease apparently causes near-sightedness, since a badly locoed horse often fails to notice any objects except those within close range. In fact, a person can approach within a few feet of a locoed horse without detection. Then, unexpectedly, the animal will rear backwards and often fall upon the ground. The diseased beast drinks with a chewing movement of the jaws, shies violently at imaginary objects, cannot be backed readily and, if started forward, will travel at the same gait until stopped by some obstruction.[2] During the later stages of the disease, the horse loses flesh and its coat becomes rough.

Locoed cattle display symptoms very much like those of similarly affected horses, but the symptoms of sheep are not so marked, although the animals soon evince weakness. They fall frequently, and rise only with great difficulty. The animals usually die of starvation; post-mortem examinations almost invariably reveal accumulations of coagulated serum in various parts of the body. These concentrations are most pronounced around the heart and along the

---

[2] Marsh, C. D. THE LOCO-WEED DISEASE. U. S. Dept. Agr. Farmers' Bull. 380, 16 pp. 1909.

spinal cord. The nervous system is amply supplied with blood, and occasionally blood clots are found on the brain. The walls of the stomach and intestines are often inflamed, and ulcers at the pyloric end of the stomach are common in horses.[1]

Woolly loco affects not only livestock but is also known to result in death to bees and prairie dogs. In Arizona, New Mexico, and Texas where this plant is abundant large losses of bees have resulted. These losses are more pronounced during dry seasons when sweetclover and alfalfa flowers are scant and the desert flora furnishes a large share of the nectar. In several places, losses are so severe that beekeepers are forced to move their apiaries from infested areas. Prairie dogs which eat the foliage of woolly loco become stupefied and lazy, exhibiting many symptoms of locoism.

Detailed and exhaustive chemical analysis indicates that the plant contains a number of complex poisonous substances. From early analyses in which barium compounds were found in loco material[3] it was concluded that loco disease was, at least occasionally, caused by barium or its compounds, largely because that metal produces a definite physiological reaction in animals similar, in some respects, to those caused by loco. Later investigations,[4] however, tended to disprove the theory that barium is responsible for the toxicity of loco to range livestock. The amounts of barium present in loco extracts—barely more than traces—were insufficient to cause death; in fact, many other plants, not poisonous to livestock, contain similar amounts of barium. Barium occurs in an almost insoluble form in dried loco plants; and extracts from these plants usually contain sufficient salts of calcium, potassium, and metals other than barium to account for death.[4]

Although no specific remedy for loco poisoning has been discovered, affected animals should be removed from the infested ranges and fed a nutritious ration such as alfalfa and grain.[2] All animals chronically locoed are usually constipated, hence food and medicine should be administered to relieve this condition.[1] Alfalfa and oil meal is a very common laxative mixture which is used frequently to allay distress caused by locoism. Marsh et al.[1] recommend that, where the constipation is severe, drenching with Epsom salts is often efficacious. Cures if effected are slow, often requiring several months. They state that cures among horses may be hastened if daily doses of arsenic in the form of Fowler's solution are administered, the doses being from 15 to 20 cubic centimeters (4–6 drams). In the case of cattle these authors[1] recommend injections of small doses (usually not more than three- or four-twentieths of a grain) of strychnine to expedite recovery. Large animals may be given as much as one-half a grain, the maximum dose, although, in some cases, that is entirely too much. As a class, locos appear to have long-lived seed and no method of cheap and easy eradication of them has thus far been developed. Continuous grubbing, especially in horse pastures, tends to reduce the stand and thus allay danger.

[3] Crawford, A. C. BARIUM, A CAUSE OF THE LOCO-WEED DISEASE. U. S. Dept. Agr., Bur. Plant Indus. Bull. 129, 87 pp., illus. 1908.
[4] Marsh, C. D., Alsberg, C. L., and Black, O. F. THE RELATION OF BARIUM TO THE LOCO-WEED DISEASE. U. S. Dept. Agr., Bur. Plant Indus. Bull. 246, 67 pp., illus. 1912.

HOOKER BALSAMROOT

Balsamorhi'za hoo'keri, syn. *B. balsamorhi'za*[1]

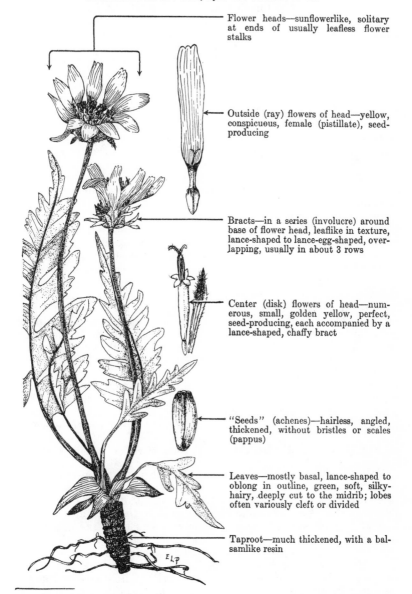

Flower heads—sunflowerlike, solitary at ends of usually leafless flower stalks

Outside (ray) flowers of head—yellow, conspicuous, female (pistillate), seed-producing

Bracts—in a series (involucre) around base of flower head, leaflike in texture, lance-shaped to lance-egg-shaped, over-lapping, usually in about 3 rows

Center (disk) flowers of head—numerous, small, golden yellow, perfect, seed-producing, each accompanied by a lance-shaped, chaffy bract

"Seeds" (achenes)—hairless, angled, thickened, without bristles or scales (pappus)

Leaves—mostly basal, lance-shaped to oblong in outline, green, soft, silky-hairy, deeply cut to the midrib; lobes often variously cleft or divided

Taproot—much thickened, with a balsamlike resin

---

[1] *Balsamorhiza balsamorhiza* (Hook.) Heller is the oldest combination under *Balsamorhiza* for this species but, being a duplicating binomial, is now rejected for the next oldest name, *B. hookeri* Nutt.

Hooker balsamroot, also known as cutleaf balsamroot and cutleaf sunflower, was named in honor of Dr. William J. Hooker (1785–1865), the very distinguished British botanist who first described this plant as well as the genus *Balsamorhiza* itself. Hooker balsamroot ranges from California and Nevada to Washington and Idaho. It grows on dry open flats and hillsides, rocky scabland areas, and gravelly banks within the sagebrush, juniper, and ponderosa pine belts up to elevations of about 5,500 feet.

As a forage plant, Hooker balsamroot is of relatively minor importance but is worthy of mention as being more or less typical of the four or five species of cleft-leaved balsamroots. Its distribution is not uniform, and usually the stand is sparse. Sometimes these plants are conspicuous in small isolated patches on hard-packed clay flats and on overgrazed or depleted areas. They are among the first plants to produce leaves and flowers in the spring and are probably of some value on the spring ranges, where they have been reported as being from worthless to good in palatability for all classes of livestock. Cattle, horses, and sheep usually graze the leafage lightly and often eat the flowers. Usually the plants become dry and worthless by midsummer.

Both the generic name *Balsamorhiza* (*balsamon*=balsam; *rhiza*=root) and the common name balsamroot refer to the thickened, resinous taproots common to all the western species. These roots have a thin corky bark and a fibrous yellowish center, and were once used by the Indians for food. The blades of the leaves are roughly arrowhead-shaped but are cleft to the midrib into numerous shaggy segments. The dull-green to silvery-gray leaves are covered with short hairs, are 6 to 12 inches long, and somewhat suggest those of the common dandelion in habit of growth. They are all basal and grow in the form of a flattened rosette or sometimes in a more erect tuft. The flower stalks, sometimes over a foot tall, are usually leafless, and each one bears a single sunflowerlike blossom. These flower heads are 1½ to 2½ inches across and consist of yellow ray flowers and a deep golden-colored disk made up of numerous small flowers grouped upon a common, chaffy, slightly convex, or flattened base. The involucre, a series of elongated, pointed, leafy bracts, underneath the flower head, varies from slightly hairy to white woolly.

CUTLEAF BALSAMROOT (Balsamorhi′za macrophyl′la)

Cutleaf balsamroot, known also as cleft-leaf balsamroot, a rank growing species, is the largest plant of this genus. Its stalked (petiolate) leaves, which grow in clumps to a height of 2 feet or more, are large, as the specific name *macrophylla* (*macro*=long; *phylla*=leaves) intimates, rich green in color, and slashed to the midrib into many lobes with hairy edges. The yellow blossoms are large and showy. This plant grows in scattered stands from Nevada and Utah through Wyoming to Montana, in the sagebrush, oakbrush, and ponderosa pine belts, and even in the aspen belt. The leaves and flowers are eaten by all classes of livestock with fair to moderate relish.

ARROWLEAF BALSAMROOT

Balsamorhi'za sagitta'ta

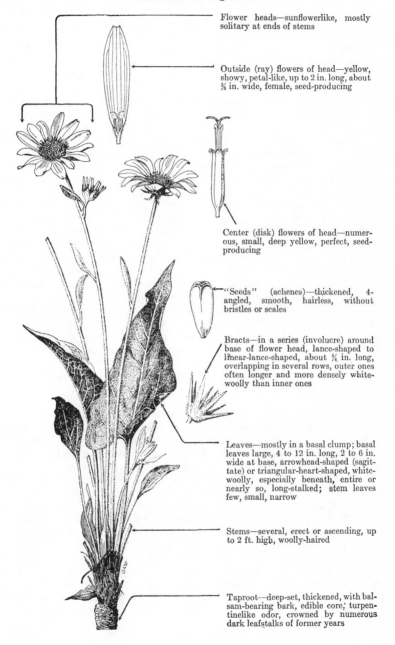

Flower heads—sunflowerlike, mostly solitary at ends of stems

Outside (ray) flowers of head—yellow, showy, petal-like, up to 2 in. long, about ⅜ in. wide, female, seed-producing

Center (disk) flowers of head—numerous, small, deep yellow, perfect, seed-producing

"Seeds" (achenes)—thickened, 4-angled, smooth, hairless, without bristles or scales

Bracts—in a series (involucre) around base of flower head, lance-shaped to linear-lance-shaped, about ¾ in. long, overlapping in several rows, outer ones often longer and more densely white-woolly than inner ones

Leaves—mostly in a basal clump; basal leaves large, 4 to 12 in. long, 2 to 6 in. wide at base, arrowhead-shaped (sagittate) or triangular-heart-shaped, white-woolly, especially beneath, entire or nearly so, long-stalked; stem leaves few, small, narrow

Stems—several, erect or ascending, up to 2 ft. high, woolly-haired

Taproot—deep-set, thickened, with balsam-bearing bark, edible core, turpentinelike odor, crowned by numerous dark leafstalks of former years

Arrowleaf balsamroot, a tufted perennial of the sunflower family, gets both its English and scientific name from its thick, resinous (balsamlike) roots (*rhiza*, root) and its arrowhead-shaped (sagittate) leaves. It is also known simply as balsamroot and is locally called sunflower, graydock, and breadroot. This plant is by far the most important, abundant, and widespread of about eleven species of *Balsamorhiza* which occur in the Western States.

Arrowleaf balsamroot is found from the Sierras of California northward, along the east side of the Cascade Mountains into British Columbia and eastward to Saskatchewan, South Dakota, and Colorado. It extends from the plains and valleys to elevations of about 9,000 feet, being common and abundant throughout most of its range. On many extensive foothill and low mountain ranges it is one of the dominant weed species, sometimes growing in almost pure stands and commonly making up a large portion of the plant cover. It grows on well-drained soils and open, fairly dry situations such as southerly exposures, open ridges, and parks throughout the sagebrush, oakbrush, and ponderosa pine types and also occurs on open, sunny slopes in the Douglas fir and aspen belts.

Arrowleaf balsamroot begins growth and produces its flowers early in the season. On ranges where the plant is common, it is useful as a familiar and reliable indicator of range readiness. Generally the range is ready for grazing when the majority of the plants are in full flower. Arrowleaf balsamroot is an important forage plant, especially valuable on the spring ranges. This plant is usually of fair palatability for all classes of livestock. In some localities both cattle and sheep graze it closely even where other palatable forage is abundant. The flowers are especially palatable but all portions of the plant except the coarser stalks are eaten. Horses like this weed and are especially fond of the flowers. The plants are eaten throughout the grazing season but are usually much more palatable during the spring and early summer than later when they become tough and dry. Deer and elk eat freely of the green leafage. It may well be that they also crop the heads; observations on this point are needed.

Ordinarily the seed of arrowleaf balsamroot ripens and the leaves dry up during midsummer, but on moist sites and at the higher elevations this does not occur until late summer. The dry leafage is eaten lightly by horses, cattle, sheep, and by foraging game animals, especially in the fall when moistened by the early rains and snows.

Reproduction is accomplished entirely by seed which is normally produced in fairly large quantities. This weed is not very aggressive in reproducing itself on grazed ranges, probably because the seeds are low in viability and the grazing of the flowers by livestock materially reduces the chances for production of a satisfactory seed crop. In some localities the seed crop is periodically destroyed by insects. The strong, deep, perennial root system enables arrowleaf balsamroot to withstand heavy trampling and close grazing fairly well. Under proper range management it should maintain and increase itself satisfactorily. The root often becomes several inches in diameter and reaches depths of several to many feet.

BISTORT

Bistor'ta bistortoi'des, syn. *Poly'gonum bistortoi'des*

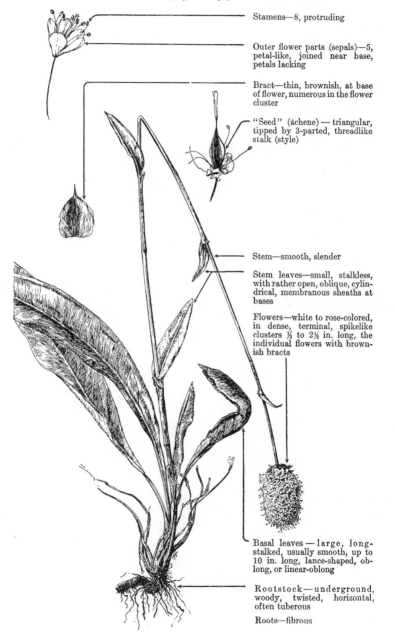

Stamens—8, protruding

Outer flower parts (sepals)—5, petal-like, joined near base, petals lacking

Bract—thin, brownish, at base of flower, numerous in the flower cluster

"Seed" (áchene) — triangular, tipped by 3-parted, threadlike stalk (style)

Stem—smooth, slender

Stem leaves—small, stalkless, with rather open, oblique, cylindrical, membranous sheaths at bases

Flowers—white to rose-colored, in dense, terminal, spikelike clusters ½ to 2½ in. long, the individual flowers with brownish bracts

Basal leaves — large, long-stalked, usually smooth, up to 10 in. long, lance-shaped, oblong, or linear-oblong

Rootstock—underground, woody, twisted, horizontal, often tuberous

Roots—fibrous

Bistort, also called American bistort, knotweed, and (though inappropriately) alpine smartweed, is a perennial herb of the buckwheat family, and attains a height of about 10 to 28 inches. It is widely distributed, ranging from Montana to British Columbia and Alaska, and southward to California and New Mexico. It grows in the mountains in wet meadows, swamps, around seeps, in moist openings in the timber and in high, moist mountain parks. It is most typically a plant of subalpine sites (Hudsonian Zone) but it also occurs in meadows at lower elevations, extending down into the ponderosa pine (Transition Zone). In many localities it grows only as scattered individuals and does not make up any appreciable part of the plant cover whereas in some restricted meadow and park areas it occurs in great abundance, occasionally being one of the dominant plants.

Bistort is eaten by both cattle and sheep along with the grasses and weeds found in its habitat. The palatability varies in different localities; in some places it is regarded as being worthless as forage while in others it is eaten readily, especially by sheep. On the average, this plant is considered to be low to fair for cattle and fair to fairly good for sheep. Deer and elk eat the foliage and stems to a slight extent.

SEGO-LILY

Calochor'tus nuttal'lii

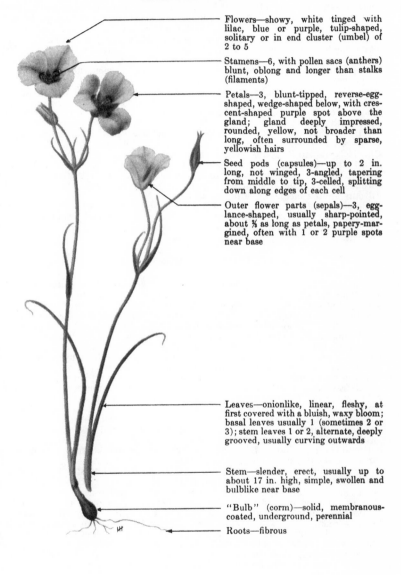

Flowers—showy, white tinged with lilac, blue or purple, tulip-shaped, solitary or in end cluster (umbel) of 2 to 5

Stamens—6, with pollen sacs (anthers) blunt, oblong and longer than stalks (filaments)

Petals—3, blunt-tipped, reverse-egg-shaped, wedge-shaped below, with crescent-shaped purple spot above the gland; gland deeply impressed, rounded, yellow, not broader than long, often surrounded by sparse, yellowish hairs

Seed pods (capsules)—up to 2 in. long, not winged, 3-angled, tapering from middle to tip, 3-celled, splitting down along edges of each cell

Outer flower parts (sepals)—3, egg-lance-shaped, usually sharp-pointed, about ⅔ as long as petals, papery-margined, often with 1 or 2 purple spots near base

Leaves—onionlike, linear, fleshy, at first covered with a bluish, waxy bloom; basal leaves usually 1 (sometimes 2 or 3); stem leaves 1 or 2, alternate, deeply grooved, usually curving outwards

Stem—slender, erect, usually up to about 17 in. high, simple, swollen and bulblike near base

"Bulb" (corm)—solid, membranous-coated, underground, perennial

Roots—fibrous

Sego-lily, sometimes erroneously spelled sago-lily, is a perennial herb of the lily family. The Latin specific name commemorates Thomas Nuttall, the original discoverer of the plant, who accompanied the Wyeth expedition to the Pacific coast in 1834. The common name sego-lily was adopted from the Indian name for the plant. It ranges from Montana to Oregon, California, and New Mexico. Sego-lily is one of the most conspicuous and beautiful early-blooming flowers of the semidesert and is unusually abundant in Utah, where it often occurs in large, fairly dense stands. This charming and useful plant has been dignified by legislative choice as the State flower of Utah. Sego-lily thrives on rather dry, sandy soils on the open sagebrush foothills and valleys, as well as in open ponderosa pine stands at moderate elevations.

On most ranges, sego-lily is of relatively little importance for forage, as it consists chiefly of flower stalks with but few leaves, which dry up quickly. Ordinarily, it ranks from poor to fair in palatability for both sheep and cattle, and is worthless for horses. In some localities, however, it rates as good in palatability for sheep.

The bulblike roots of sego-lily were deemed a great delicacy by the western Indians. This species figured prominently in the history of the Mormon Church.[1] When Brigham Young and his little band of followers emigrated into Salt Lake Valley in 1847, food was very scarce. It is reported that when the Mormon pioneers in Utah faced famine conditions in 1848–49 due to the inroads of crickets, drought, and frost on their grain fields, the sego-lily was an outstanding means of tiding them over.[2]

Before the flowers appear, the leaves of sego-lily are often confused with those of deathcamas (*Zygadenus* spp.), but may be readily distinguished by the rounded troughlike cross section of their U-shaped leaves, as opposed to the sharply V-shaped leaf of deathcamas.

MARIPOSAS (Calochor'tus spp.)

Mariposas, often called mariposa-lilies and mariposa-tulips, are perennials and rank among the most attractive flowers of the lily family (Liliaceae). This genus may be looked upon as the representative in the Western Hemisphere of the closely related tulips (*Tulipa*). The species of *Calochortus* are not native to the eastern United States, ranging only from Nebraska west to the Pacific, north into Canada, and south to Mexico. There are about 40 to 50 species of mariposa in the West, being particularly abundant in California and Oregon; they occur from the dry, open prairies and foothills up to the higher, moist, and shady alpine woods and meadows.

These plants dry up shortly after blossoming. However, early in the season, when fresh and succulent, their forage is of good palatability for sheep and fair for cattle. Horses, however, as a rule, eat these plants only through accident or necessity. Other species of mariposas besides sego-lily were used for food by the Indians and early settlers, although not so extensively. The bulbous roots of mariposas are eaten by pocket gophers and other rodents, which gather and store them for winter use.

Credit is due David Douglas, the eminent Scotch botanical explorer, as pioneer popularizer of the mariposas, especially for ornamental gardening. He discovered several species and introduced them into England. The mariposas are usually divided into three groups: (1) The typical mariposas with large, bowl-like or tulip-shaped flowers; (2) the star mariposas with wide, open, smaller flowers; and (3) the globe mariposas with nodding, globular flowers.

Mariposas usually have branched, more or less leafy stems with husk-coated, bulblike roots with a few, basal, narrow, somewhat grasslike leaves. The usually several, showy flowers are borne at the top of the flower stalks and are white, yellow-lilac, or bluish colored, or often a mixture of several of these colors, with a gland at the base of each petal. In some of the smaller species, the petals are quite hairy on the inside and are commonly and appropriately called cats-ears.

[1] Saunders, C. F. WESTERN WILD FLOWERS AND THEIR STORIES. 320 pp., illus. Garden City, N. Y. 1933.
[2] Bennion, D. EVER EAT SEGO LILY ROOTS? The Deseret News, sec. 3, pt. V. (Mar. 23) 1935.

YAMPA

Ca'rum gaird'neri, syn. *Ate'nia gaird'neri*

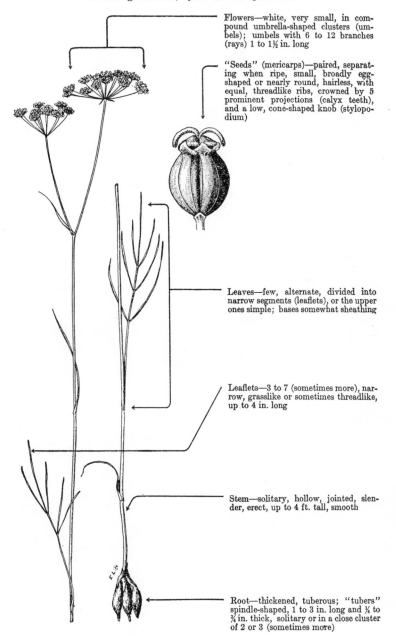

Flowers—white, very small, in compound umbrella-shaped clusters (umbels); umbels with 6 to 12 branches (rays) 1 to 1½ in. long

"Seeds" (mericarps)—paired, separating when ripe, small, broadly egg-shaped or nearly round, hairless, with equal, threadlike ribs, crowned by 5 prominent projections (calyx teeth), and a low, cone-shaped knob (stylopodium)

Leaves—few, alternate, divided into narrow segments (leaflets), or the upper ones simple; bases somewhat sheathing

Leaflets—3 to 7 (sometimes more), narrow, grasslike or sometimes threadlike, up to 4 in. long

Stem—solitary, hollow, jointed, slender, erect, up to 4 ft. tall, smooth

Root—thickened, tuberous; "tubers" spindle-shaped, 1 to 3 in. long and ¼ to ¾ in. thick, solitary or in a close cluster of 2 or 3 (sometimes more)

Yampa, a smooth, slender, erect perennial plant of the carrot or parsnip family (Umbelliferae), is also known as squawroot, wildcaraway, breadroot, Queen-Annes-lace, and Indian-potato. It is the best known of the several closely related species of *Carum* native to the West and is a sister species of the Old World caraway (*C. carvi*) which produces the caraway seed of commerce, sometimes observed on western range lands as an occasional (and probably short-lived) escape from cultivation. Yampa is an Indian name and was used in naming the Yampa River and the town of Yampa in Colorado. The name, *Carum*, is commonly held to be derived from Caria, an ancient country of western Asia Minor. The Carians were a seafaring people and perhaps introduced caraway into commerce. The species name, *gairdneri*, commemorates Dr. Meredith Gairdner, a surgeon of the Hudson Bay Co. who collected plants around Fort Vancouver, Wash., prior to 1840.

This weed is widely distributed throughout the western States, occurring from British Columbia and Washington south to California and eastward to New Mexico, Colorado, and the Black Hills of South Dakota. It grows on moderately moist soils in open, weedy parks within stands of aspen, ponderosa pine, and Douglas fir, in moist meadows, and in drier, more open situations within the sagebrush and wheatgrass types. It is found in the company of such plants as geranium, Idaho fescue, low larkspur, lupine, mules-ears, sedges, and yarrow. The elevations at which this plant is found vary from slightly above sea level along the Columbia River to about 9,000 feet in Montana and perhaps higher toward the southern limits of its range.

Yampa is not usually abundant on the range but occasionally occurs in small rather thick stands, and in some moist mountain meadows becomes very abundant. It is widely distributed, fair to high in palatability and furnishes an appreciable amount of feed on many western ranges. Because of the sparseness of the leafage, the individual plant does not produce very much forage. The forage which is produced, however, is of good quality. Both cattle and sheep readily eat the flowers, seeds, leaves, and sometimes a large portion of the stems. Yampa reproduces from seed as well as from tubers which break away from the parent plants to form new individuals.

From the standpoint of Indian lore, yampa is an extremely interesting plant. The tubers have a sweet, nutty, creamlike flavor and were formerly eaten extensively by the Indians, but now are little used. Piper [1] recognized yampa as the best food plant of the Northwestern Indians. Although the Klamath Indians originally called the plant kash, contemporary members of the tribe and white men know it as ipo, sometimes pronounced epa, apo, or apau. Klamath Indians say that the word ipo comes from the south and was the Shasta's tribal name for the plant. However, it is probably not of Shastan origin, but a corruption of the Spanish-Californian apio, meaning celery (*Apium* sp.), which members of the caraway genus somewhat resemble in appearance and flavor. The plant is valued by the Snake, Gosiute, and Ute tribes also, and is known to them as yampa. Sacajawea, the famous woman guide, counselor and interpreter for Lewis and Clark, appears to have been the first person to introduce this plant to the whites under that name. This Indian woman is said to have been exceptionally well versed in the uses of wild foods.[2] Capt. John C. Frémont ate the yampa as a vegetable with wild duck, and declared it to be the finest of all Indian roots. The roots were cleaned by placing them in baskets in running water where squaws trod them with bare feet to remove the dark outer skin and make them smooth and clean. They were then boiled or prepared as the Indians cooked other vegetables.[2] The roots were also eaten raw, ground into flour and made into bread, or used with other roots and seeds to make a meal or gruel. The seeds have an aromatic caraway flavor and were used to season other foods.

Yampa roots are fleshy and tuberous, growing up to 3 inches long and three-fourths of an inch thick, and resemble tiny sweetpotatoes. They grow at the base of the stem singly, in pairs or in groups of three or more. The stems are solitary, smooth, slender and sometimes branched, one-eighth to one-fourth of an inch in diameter and 1 to 4 feet in height.

[1] Piper, C. V. FLORA OF THE STATE OF WASHINGTON. U. S. Natl. Mus., Contrib. U. S. Natl. Herbarium 11, 637 pp., illus. 1906.
[2] Haskin, L. L. A FRONTIER FOOD, IPO, OR YAMPA, SUSTAINED THE PIONEERS. Nature Mag. 14 : 171–172, illus. 1929.

WYOMING PAINTBRUSH

Castille'ja linariaefo'lia, syn. *C. af'finis linariaefo'lia*

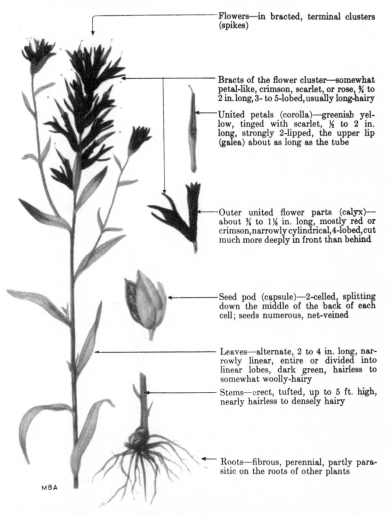

Flowers—in bracted, terminal clusters (spikes)

Bracts of the flower cluster—somewhat petal-like, crimson, scarlet, or rose, ¾ to 2 in. long, 3- to 5-lobed, usually long-hairy

United petals (corolla)—greenish yellow, tinged with scarlet, ½ to 2 in. long, strongly 2-lipped, the upper lip (galea) about as long as the tube

Outer united flower parts (calyx)—about ¾ to 1⅛ in. long, mostly red or crimson, narrowly cylindrical, 4-lobed, cut much more deeply in front than behind

Seed pod (capsule)—2-celled, splitting down the middle of the back of each cell; seeds numerous, net-veined

Leaves—alternate, 2 to 4 in. long, narrowly linear, entire or divided into linear lobes, dark green, hairless to somewhat woolly-hairy

Stems—erect, tufted, up to 5 ft. high, nearly hairless to densely hairy

Roots—fibrous, perennial, partly parasitic on the roots of other plants

MBA

Wyoming paintbrush, a tufted perennial with red, rose, or crimson flower clusters and narrow leaves, was selected in 1917 by the Wyoming Legislature as the State flower of that Commonwealth. This species is known most commonly as Indian paintbrush or narrowleaf paintbrush; the former name is untenable, as it is the accepted common name for *C. coccinea*, an eastern species which does not occur in Wyoming. Narrowleaf paintbrush is not a distinctive name in a genus of typically narrow-leaved species. Furthermore, it is not a literal translation of the specific name *linariaefolia*, which alludes to the resemblance of the leaves to those of the common bastard toadflax, or butter-and-eggs (*Linaria*). Since the species has been selected as the State flower of Wyoming it seems eminently fitting that it be christened with the English name Wyoming paintbrush.

This species is widely distributed, ranging from British Columbia to Wyoming, New Mexico, and California, and south into Mexico. It is one of the more common species of *Castilleja*, although generally not abundant. It occurs chiefly on dry or moderately dry soils, and often in rocky places, mostly in sagebrush, aspen, and open-pine types.

Wyoming paintbrush is one of the more palatable species of *Castilleja* but its value varies in different localities. It rates as fairly good cattle forage and good sheep forage in Colorado and Wyoming; poor for cattle and fair for sheep over the remainder of the range country except the Southwest where, in general, it is practically worthless for cattle and poor for sheep. However, in certain sections of the Southwest, especially on the Kaibab Forest in northern Arizona, it is rated as fair cattle forage and good sheep forage and also as good deer forage.

Wyoming paintbrush is variable, the bracts of the flower clusters being red, rose, or crimson, usually three-lobed and three-nerved. The corolla is greenish yellow tinged with scarlet, and is very unequally two-lipped, the upper lobe, or galea being prolonged and enclosing the four stamens which are arranged in two pairs of unequal length. The two pollen sacs (anthers) of each stamen are unequal, the outer one attached to its stalk (filament) by its middle, the other hanging from its attached upper end. The dark green leaves are narrow and entire or dissected into narrow lobes and vary from nearly hairless to somewhat woolly-hairy. The stems are usually tufted and either branched or unbranched.

PAINTBRUSHES AND PAINTED-CUPS (Castille′ja spp.)

Castilleja is a member of the figwort family (Scrophulariaceae). Many genera of this family include species with striking flowers; the widely cultivated snapdragons (*Antirrhinum* spp.) probably being the most familiar. The paintbrushes compose a fairly large, chiefly western North American genus of about 50 species of annual or perennial herbs, most of which are partially parasitic on the roots of other plants. The genus was named in 1781 by Dr. José Celestino Mutis (1732–1808), an eminent Spanish-Colombian physician and botanist, who came to America in 1760 and founded the botanical garden at Bogotá, where he died. Mutis collected the type species of *Castilleja* in New Granada (now Colombia), naming the genus in honor of his now rather obscure botanical contemporary, Domingo Castillejo, of Cadiz. Many botanists prefer to spell the generic name *Castilleia*, that form being more in accord with classic Latin traditions. Species of *Castilleja*, especially the reddish hued ones, are generally known as paintbrush or Indian paintbrush in the West, although the preferred book name seems to be painted-cup. The paintbrushes and painted-cups, although common, are never particularly abundant, always grow in association with other species, and compose but a small part of the plant cover. They occur from the lower elevations to above timberline in a wide variety of vegetative types.

This genus varies considerably in palatability. Some species are practically worthless as forage plants and are not grazed by either domestic livestock or game animals. Other species are fairly good cattle forage and good forage for sheep, deer, and elk, at least in certain regions. Insufficient information is available regarding the palatability of the individual species of this genus and, accordingly, direct observation will be necessary to determine the actual value of the plants in any given locality. In general, however, the castillejas are not abundant and are of secondary importance as range plants.

Paintbrushes and painted-cups are distinctive in that the flowers appear in terminal leafy spikes, being borne in the axils of usually large, brightly colored bracts, which are generally more conspicuous and showy than the flowers. In this particular, the paintbrushes resemble the closely related owlclover genus, *Orthocarpus*. The bracts are entire or 4- to 5-cleft, and are colored various shades of yellow, pink, red, or purple, or are green with the tips and margins of those colors. The outer flower parts (sepals) are united to form a narrowly cylindrical calyx, which is usually of the same color as the bracts in that particular species. The corollas are strongly 2-lipped with the upper lip much prolonged, enclosing the 4 stamens. The leaves are alternate, stalkless, entire or toothed, or divided into narrow lobes. The stems are usually somewhat tufted and either branched or unbranched.

FIREWEED

Chamaene'rion angustifo'lium, syns. *Epilo'bium angustifo'lium, E. spica'tum*

Leaves—up to 8 in. long, narrowly lance-shaped, alternate, stalkless or nearly so, green above, pale and veiny beneath, the edges entire; veins united near margin of leaf to form network

Stems—erect, up to 9 ft. high

Petals—4, purple or rose-colored, large (up to ¾ in. long), broadly reverse-egg-shaped

Outer flower parts (sepals)—4, often pink or purplish, somewhat hairy, united below into a very short tube, attached to top of seed-producing organ (inferior ovary)

Stamens—8, purple, 4 alternate ones longer than the other 4

Pollen-receiving organ (stigma)—4-lobed

Flower clusters—elongated, each flower stalked and with a small slender bract; buds drooping but flowers and fruit erect

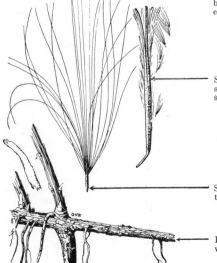

Seed pods (capsules)—up to 3 in. long, stalked, very narrow, 4-sided, 4-celled, splitting by 4 valves

Seeds—numerous, small, each with a tuft of fine, silky, white hairs

Rootstock—extensive, underground, with buds which give rise to new stems

Fireweed, a perennial herb of the evening-primrose family, ordinarily attains a height of from 2 to 6 feet, averaging about 3 or 3½ feet, although under the most favorable conditions, and in humid climates, it may grow as tall as 9 feet. Its common name, fireweed, is most appropriate, since the plant flourishes in especial abundance on newly burned-off forest lands. The name blooming sally is also often applied, especially when it is grown as an ornamental. In common with species of the closely related genus *Epilobium* (in which, in fact, many botanists place it) it is also called willowherb and willowweed, inasmuch as the leaves and the masses of small silky-haired seeds are suggestive of the foliage and cottony seeds, respectively, of willows. The growth of fireweed is not restricted to burns; it also occurs in openings in timbered and wooded areas, around cultivated fields, and along streams, roadsides, and irrigation ditches.

Fireweed has an enormous distribution. It extends across the North American continent from Labrador to Alaska and south into California, New Mexico, and North Carolina. It also grows in Europe and Asia. Its altitudinal range is likewise great, extending from near sea level in the East and in Alaska and the Northwest to an elevation of 11,000 feet in the Rocky Mountains. It is moderately drought-resistant and may grow on relatively dry sites as well as in moist situations, and on coarse gravelly soils as well as in deep loam.

Fireweed is undoubtedly one of the most important range forage weeds, and is the most valuable member of the evening-primrose family from the range standpoint. Its palatability varies from fair to good or occasionally, especially in Utah and parts of Idaho, very good for sheep, and from worthless to fair, averaging poor, for cattle. It is grazed to some extent by horses, deer, and elk. All portions of the plant are eaten when young, but as the season advances the stems become woody and tough, and only the flowers and leaves are grazed. Growth begins early in the season and, since the plants do not mature until late, palatable forage is usually produced throughout the summer grazing season.

From his studies in the Northwest, the late Douglas C. Ingram [1] concluded:

When other feed is available, fireweed is readily eaten at any stage of its growth, although 4 years' experience on the Columbia National Forest indicates that its most palatable stage is at full bloom. When it is the principal feed, sheep become restless and unmanageable, craving a change in diet.

An interesting point in connection with the grazing of this plant is the effect of early grazing in apparently stimulating the plant to put forth growth of palatable sprouts which form a supply for fall use. Although there is no definite proof for the belief, it may be that the early grazing stimulates the development of the latent rootstock buds which under ordinary conditions might not develop until the following year. The ultimate effect is a lowering of vitality and hastening of the life processes, resulting in smaller stems and a lower height growth the ensuing year, and finally in a shorter life cycle.

Since this plant is one of those which materially increase the inflammability of cut-over lands, the effect of grazing in suppressing and eliminating it is of particular importance.

[1] Ingram, D. C. VEGETATIVE CHANGES AND GRAZING USE ON DOUGLAS FIR CUT-OVER LAND. Jour. Agr. Research [U. S.] 43 : 387–417, illus. 1931.

The production of flower stalks and seeds continues for an unusually long period. The lower flowers appear early in the summer and are the first to unfold; as the season advances, there is a gradual succession in flowering toward the top of the cluster (raceme). The uppermost flowers are usually still in bud or in full bloom while the lower ones have developed mature seedpods (capsules), or even mature seeds, so that flowering continues in some localities for about 3 months, from about June to August. Fireweed produces a great abundance of seed which usually matures from mid-July to late September. When fully ripe, the long slender seedpods split into four divisions and liberate a great number of very small seeds, each provided with a tuft of silky hairs which enables them to be carried far and wide by the wind, a light breeze being sufficient. During the period of greatest seed dissemination in areas where fireweed is common, the air is filled with the light, cottony seeds, which are soon widely distributed. But few cut-over and burned-over areas escape their invasion. The seeds find ideal lodgement in new burns where the ashes apparently stimulate germination and growth, but their viability is evidently not very high, Sampson [2] having found that in 1908 and 1909 it averaged 21.5 percent in the Blue Mountains of Oregon. The seeds produced early in the season were from 10 to 12 percent higher in viability than those maturing later.

Fireweed is quickly established and usually forms a cover within two seasons which overtops or even excludes other plants and shrubs. Notwithstanding its great seed-producing capacity, this species soon appears to propagate mainly from underground rootstocks which bud along their length and send up new stems. Ingram (*op. cit.*) found that a definite rootstock is formed the first season, during which time it grows 4 to 6 feet in extent, and the above-ground part of the plant usually becomes 2 to 3 feet tall. The new growth above ground and the older portion of the rootstock die each succeeding year. In one instance, a 4-year-old rootstock was traced for a distance of 20 feet and about 56 undeveloped buds were counted along it, although the average number is probably less.

Ingram concluded that the ability of this plant to withstand competition is probably limited because, with the advent of shrubby species as reforestation proceeds, conditions become too unfavorable for its continued growth. It subsequently declines in quantity and size until, after 8 to 12 years, it comprises but a minor part of the vegetation.

Fireweed is well known as a nectar-producer, and bees and other insects are attracted by its flowers. In the coastal regions of Oregon and Washington apiarists follow the logging operations, moving every 5 to 7 years to newer cut-over areas where fireweed is most abundant.

[2] Sampson, A. W. IMPORTANT RANGE PLANTS : THEIR LIFE HISTORY AND FORAGE VALUE. U. S. Dept. Agr. Bull. 545, 63 pp., illus. 1917.

HAIRY GOLDEN-ASTER

Chrysop'sis villo'sa, syns. *C. a'rida, C. asprel'la, C. ba'keri, C. but'leri*

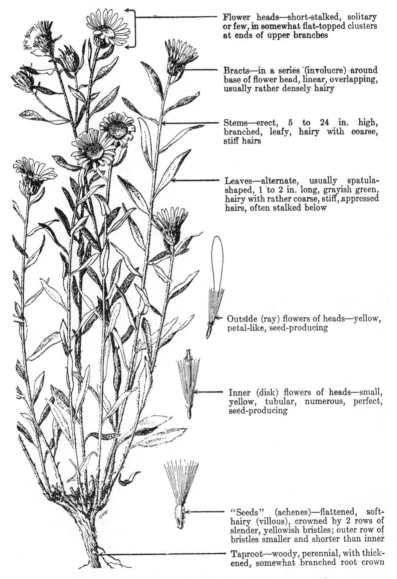

Flower heads—short-stalked, solitary or few, in somewhat flat-topped clusters at ends of upper branches

Bracts—in a series (involucre) around base of flower head, linear, overlapping, usually rather densely hairy

Stems—erect, 5 to 24 in. high, branched, leafy, hairy with coarse, stiff hairs

Leaves—alternate, usually spatula-shaped, 1 to 2 in. long, grayish green, hairy with rather coarse, stiff, appressed hairs, often stalked below

Outside (ray) flowers of heads—yellow, petal-like, seed-producing

Inner (disk) flowers of heads—small, yellow, tubular, numerous, perfect, seed-producing

"Seeds" (achenes)—flattened, soft-hairy (villous), crowned by 2 rows of slender, yellowish bristles; outer row of bristles smaller and shorter than inner

Taproot—woody, perennial, with thickened, somewhat branched root crown

Hairy golden-aster, a perennial herb of the composite, or aster, family (Compositae), is an abundant and highly characteristic western species of this small North American genus. It is common on the dry plains and foothill ranges from Manitoba and Minnesota to Texas, New Mexico, California, and British Columbia. This plant usually occurs on dry, sandy, or rocky soils from fairly low to medium elevations, but is sometimes found in open, drier sites of the higher mountains between altitudes of about 8,000 and 12,000 feet. Hairy golden-aster is notably resistant to drought and intense light and heat. Both the common and specific names allude to the white hairs (some stiff, others soft) which cover the plant, *villosa* being a Latin adjective which means soft, shaggy, hairy.

Because its leaves are rather harsh and the stems woody, this species is not particularly palatable to livestock; in fact, it usually is considered practically worthless, although on some of the desert ranges it has a fair palatability for sheep. This quite variable plant, which has several named forms, is used in ornamental borders.

GOLDEN-ASTERS (Chrysop'sis spp.)

Golden-asters compose a relatively small genus of possibly 30 or more species of herbaceous plants native to North America. Representatives of this genus occur practically throughout the United States and even extend into Mexico. This genus was christened *Chrysopsis* because of its yellow flowers, the name being derived from the Greek *chrysos*, golden, and *opsis*, aspect. The flowers resemble those of asters (*Aster* spp.), but are superficially distinguished by the golden tint of the outer flowers (rays) of the head, whence the common name, golden-aster.

In the West, these plants thrive on dry, frequently sandy, or rocky sites in full sunlight, from the low plains and hills to near timberline in the mountains. The strong, deep taproots of golden-asters sometimes penetrate the soil to a depth of over 8 feet [1] and facilitate their existence in dry places. Because of this fact, coupled with their ability to grow on the poorer, dry soils, they are locally valuable as soil binders. Although frequently abundant, these species never occur in pure stands. On some of the poor semidesert areas of the West, these plants are fair forage for sheep but, under more normal range conditions, are usually classed as worthless for all classes of livestock.

The western golden-asters are perennials (occasionally biennials or annuals) with a persistent, woody base. As a rule, both stems and leaves are conspicuously hairy or woolly, varying from soft-silky to stiff-bristly or sometimes both soft and stiff hairs occur in combination on the same plant; a few species are hairless or glandular-resinous. The alternate leaves are mostly without stalks (sessile), entire-edged, and noticeably hairy. The medium-sized, showy, golden-yellow flower heads, usually having many ray flowers (rarely rayless), are borne singly or in somewhat elongated clusters; the more or less bell-shaped cup of the flower head (involucre) comprises several series of narrow, overlapping bracts. The double arrangement of hairs (pappus) crowning the flattened, hairy body of the seedlike fruits (achenes) is characteristic of the genus.

[1] Weaver, J. E. THE ECOLOGICAL RELATIONS OF ROOTS. Carnegie Inst. Wash. Pub. 286, 128 pp., illus. 1919.

WATERHEMLOCKS

Cicu'ta spp.

Waterhemlocks are, without doubt, the most virulently poisonous flowering plants native to the United States; in fact, they are, perhaps, the most toxic of all higher plants growing in temperate regions of the world, dealing death among both human beings (especially children) and livestock. The several species are known locally as beaverpoison, (spotted) cowbane, musquashroot, poison- or spotted-hemlock, and snakeweed. In the West, they are often, but mistakenly, called parsnips, poisonparsnips, or wildparsnips. The common name, waterhemlock, originates from the wet sites of these plants and, simultaneously, distinguishes this group from the notorious, closely related poison-hemlock (*Co'nium*), also belonging to the large carrot, or parsnip family (Umbelliferae). The suffix "hemlock" refers to the deadly, Old World, poison-hemlock, or "hemlock" (*Conium maculatum*)—now, unfortunately, naturalized in parts of our western range country. It is noteworthy, in this connection, that, historically, *Conium maculatum* is the true hemlock, a name later usurped by our American tree genus *Tsuga*. Konrad Gesner, a herbalist of the 16th century, was probably the first to distinguish between *Conium* and the related, toxic, Old World waterhemlock (*Cicuta virosa*), which he called *Cicuta aquatica*.[1]

Cicuta is a small, chiefly North American genus of about eleven species; *C. virosa* is the only one native to Europe and Asia. The waterhemlocks, widely distributed on this continent from New Brunswick and Nova Scotia to Alaska, California, and Florida, and south into Mexico, occur along streams, in swamps, ditches, wet meadows, and boggy places, and in fresh, brackish, or saline marshes in probably every State of the Union. Conservatively speaking, six or possibly seven valid species are found in the West, although many more have been described. The western waterhemlocks usually occur almost from sea level to medium elevations, though occasionally observed at altitudes above 9,000 feet in Colorado and New Mexico.

It is quite possible that the species of waterhemlock are equally toxic. However, experimental data and other evidence of poisonings and their symptoms are largely concerned with the European species and with four American members: California waterhemlock (*C. califor'nica*), spotted waterhemlock (*C. macula'ta*), western waterhemlock (*C. occidenta'lis*), and tuber waterhemlock (*C. va'gans*).[1] Most fatalities reported, both for human beings and animals, are directly attributable to eating the roots, admittedly the most toxic parts. All American species coincide in having some part or parts of the underground portion elongated and decidedly thickened or tuberous; clusters of fleshy roots are characteristic of many of the waterhemlocks. Unfortunately, however, these underground parts are sometimes mistaken for those of edible plants. The young shoots are also generally recognized as very toxic. The basal part of the leaves of young plants is more virulent than the green blade, and, without doubt, the leaves of older plants are less poisonous than those of earlier growth.[2] Whether the toxicity of the aerial parts decreases with advancing maturity is a matter of dispute.[1][2][3]

Most livestock losses and deaths of human beings, due to these plants, occur in the spring. The young shoots are then eagerly devoured, providing tasty, succulent herbage when good forage is unavailable; at that time, greater likelihood also exists of the roots being pulled up easily from the loose, wet soil where they grow. These underground parts, though evidently very toxic at all times, appear to be particularly dangerous in the spring and in the fall, the greater stored food concentration at those periods seemingly being accompanied by an increase in the poisonous principle.

[1] Marsh, C. D., Clawson, A. B., and Marsh, H. CICUTA, OR WATER HEMLOCK. U. S. Dept. Agr. Bull. 69, 27 pp., illus. 1914.
[2] Chesnut, V. K., and Wilcox, E. V. THE STOCK-POISONING PLANTS OF MONTANA: A PRELIMINARY REPORT. U. S. Dept. Agr., Div. Bot. Bull. 26, 150 pp., illus. 1901.
[3] Pammel, L. H. A MANUAL OF POISONOUS PLANTS CHIEFLY OF EASTERN NORTH AMERICA, WITH BRIEF NOTES ON ECONOMIC AND MEDICINAL PLANTS . . . 2 pts., illus. Cedar Rapids, Iowa. 1910–11.

The roots, upon being cut or bruised, exude an oily, yellowish or reddish aromatic fluid. Cicutoxin, a bitter, disagreeable-tasting, amorphous, resinous substance, resides in the stems and leaves, but mainly occurs in the roots; it is violently poisonous, producing most of the symptoms characteristic of waterhemlock-poisoning. This toxic principle has a powerful and direct effect upon the central nervous system and secondarily influences the activity of the heart and respiratory organs. Even a very small piece of root will usually cause death in a short time. Waterhemlocks are probably not only toxic to all classes of livestock, but to warm-blooded animals in general. Although apparently no goat fatalities have been reported, evidence is lacking that these animals are immune to the poison.[1] The maximum losses have occurred among cattle and sheep; mortality of horses and hogs is also common.

The sequence in symptoms of waterhemlock poisoning is very characteristic and readily recognized. In man they include nausea, dizziness, abdominal pains, weakened pulse, arching of the back (opisthotonos), and other extreme muscular contractions, violent convulsions, and eventual death from exhaustion. In animals the symptoms are uneasiness, frothing at the mouth, severe pain, muscular twitchings, a weak, intermittent, and rapid pulse, and dilation of the pupils (eyes). If the dose is fatal, death comes from exhaustion due to severe muscular convulsions.[1][2][3] Death may occur within 15 minutes after the first symptoms or, where the first symptoms come in less rapid sequence, within 2 or 3 hours. The poison acts so quickly that usually it is impossible to save the animal. The toxic dose for cattle has been roughly estimated by Hedrick (in Pammel[3]) as a piece of root the size of a walnut. There is no known antidote, but in man the use of emetics has been effective. Bruce[4] writes that credit for the recovery of an animal treated with opiates, among other substances, to control the convulsions, is probably attributable to the small amount of poison consumed and not to the remedies.

Prevention is the only effective control. Hand-pulling is often the simplest method if pieces of the root are not left behind; grubbing or fencing also have their place. All eradicated roots should be carefully burned, as they are deadly even when dry.[5] Plowing or clearing new land may expose the deadly roots along waterways. Reports persist, probably based on fact, that losses have resulted from contamination of springs and small seeps by water-hemlock roots crushed under the hoofs of animals. However, this danger has probably been exaggerated, particularly as the poisonous principle is only slightly soluble in cold water.[1]

Members of the genus *Cicuta* are rather similar in appearance; for practical purposes, ability to identify the genus is essential, though it is hardly necessary to distinguish the species. Unfortunately, waterhemlocks and other members of the umbellifer family are often confused on the range. Such related plants as angelicas (*Ange'lica* spp.), sweetroots (*Osmorhi'za* spp.), and woollyhead-parsnip (*Sphenoscia'dium capitella'tum*) are harmless and good forage; moreover, they also occur in moist sites. The waterhemlocks are chiefly stout, coarse herbs with smooth, simple, or branched stems, occasionally as high as 10 feet, having fairly large, compound leaves, which are divided one or more times into usually even- and sharp-toothed leaflets. Tuber waterhemlock has a distinctive growth habit, with straggling, almost reclining, branches arising from the base of the plant; the other western species are erect. According to the late Dr. E. L. Greene,[6] the entire plant, including the underground parts, dies after flowering. The underground parts, located fairly near the ground level, are so distinctive that keys for specific recognition have been based upon them. Some American species have a short rootcrown, around which are clustered a group of elongated, fleshy-fibrous or tuberlike roots usually with an additional cluster or tuft of slender or thickened accessory roots; others have an enlarged rootstock, bearing fibrous roots on the under side. California waterhemlock has a freely branching rootstock, the branches close-jointed and enlarged at the ends with fibrous roots at the joints.[6] Published statements to the contrary, the presence of cross-partitions in the rootcrown, rootstocks, and ·

[1][2][3] See footnotes on preceding page.
[4] Bruce, E. A. ASTRAGALUS CAMPESTRIS AND OTHER STOCK POISONING PLANTS OF BRITISH COLUMBIA. Canada Dept. Agr. Bull. 88, 44 pp., illus. 1927.
[5] Lawrence, W. E. THE PRINCIPAL STOCK-POISONING PLANTS OF OREGON. Oreg. Agr. Expt. Sta. Bull. 187, 42 pp., illus. 1922.
[6] Greene, E. L. VEGETATIVE CHARACTERS OF THE SPECIES OF CICUTA. Pittonia 2 : 1–11. [1889.]

roots, although important, does not afford an infallible means of distinguishing waterhemlocks from nonpoisonous genera. In fact, some angelicas have similarly prominent cross-partitions. During spring, when maximum danger of poisoning obtains, the partitions are often not clearly discernible;[4] they are often absent or very indistinct in the younger roots. The small, white flowers of waterhemlocks are borne in compound, umbrellalike clusters (umbels) without bracts, or only a few, at the base of the rays of the entire cluster, but usually having some small, slender bractlets at the base of the stalks (pedicels) of each secondary cluster (umbellets). The flowers have five broad petals with incurved tips; the five pointed, toothlike outer flower parts (calyx lobes) are fairly prominent. The hairless, ribbed, oblong or ovoid, seedlike fruits are slightly flattened; a single oil tube is conspicuous in the intervals between the ribs. One species, bulbous waterhemlock (*C. bulbi'fera*), ranging from Nova Scotia and Maryland to Nebraska and Idaho, produces clustered bulblets in the axils of the upper, reduced leaves. Most species begin to bloom in June or July.

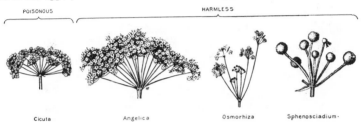

POISONOUS   HARMLESS

Cicuta   Angelica   Osmorhiza   Sphenosciadium·

FIGURE 1.—Flower cluster, or umbel (diagrammatic) of waterhemlock as contrasted with those of the harmless angelica, sweetroot, and woollyhead-parsnip.

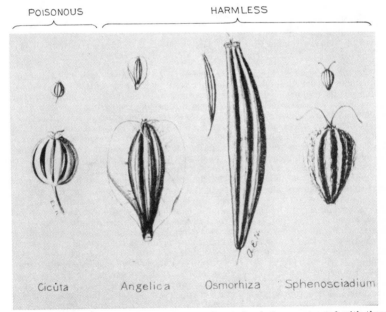

POISONOUS   HARMLESS

Cicúta   Angelica   Osmorhiza   Sphenosciadium

FIGURE 2.—Fruits, or "seeds" (diagrammatic) of waterhemlock as contrasted with those of the harmless angelica, sweetroot, and woollyhead-parsnip.

[4] See footnote on preceding page.

Figure 1 shows the relatively small flower clusters, in proportion to the size of *Cicuta* as compared with the larger flower clusters of *Angelica;* both bracts and bractlets are usually absent from the flower clusters in *Angelica*, but bractlets are usually present in *Cicuta*. The sweetroots (*Osmorhiza* spp.) have slender, irregular, few-rayed flower clusters; they, as well as the entire plant, emanate a sweet, aniselike odor. Incidentally, when once recognized, all three genera can be separated by odor alone from *Cicuta*, which is the least pleasant. *Sphenosciadium* has ball-like, cottony flower heads in a regular umbel.

Figure 2 illustrates the easily recognized character of the seedlike fruits of these genera. *Cicuta* has small, ribbed, wingless, rounded, oval or oblong, hairless fruits, up to about three-sixteenths of an inch long. *Angelica* fruits are flattened, broad-winged, and average about three-sixteenths to one-fourth of an inch long. The fruits of *Sphenosciadium* are hairy, ribbed below, and winged above; those of *Osmorhiza* are unmistakable, being elongated, somewhat club-shaped, narrowly ribbed, hairless or bristly and often tipped with a short beak.

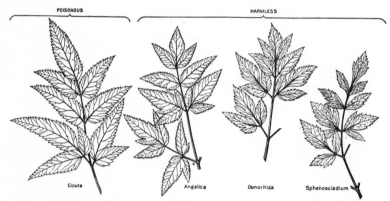

FIGURE 3.—Leaves (diagrammatic) of waterhemlock as contrasted with those of the harmless angelica, sweetroot, and woollyhead-parsnip.

Figure 3 illustrates the general character of the leaves with the venation of the leaflets shown in detail. Although attention has been called in various diagrams or discussions of the eastern spotted waterhemlock (*C. macula'ta*) and of western waterhemlock to the termination of the primary veins in the notches of the leaflets, Bomhard[7] has recently reported that the difference in the venation of the leaflets of *Cicuta* and *Angelica* is a practical aid in distinguishing these two genera, without the use of a hand lens, both afield and in the herbarium. The venation is usually more prominent on the under side of the leaflets in both genera. In *Angelica*, the primary veins, emanating from the midrib of the leaflets, proceed toward the middle of the apex of the teeth, as is usual in most toothed leaves. In the species of *Cicuta*, with one exception, the primary veins are directed toward the notches between the teeth. When the veins apparently end directly in the notches (*e. g.*, spotted waterhemlock, western waterhemlock, etc.), this diagnostic character is easily recognized; in most cases, however, it is the general trend of the veins (or their main forks) *in the direction of the notches* which must be noted since, just before reaching the notch, they deviate somewhat, or bend, sliding alongside a margin of the tooth but scarcely proceeding directly toward the middle of the tooth itself. California waterhemlock, the one exception, is a distinctive species, readily identifiable by other means. This venation method of separating the poisonous waterhemlocks from the nonpoisonous angelicas merits further testing, to determine its usefulness and accuracy, by first examining the leaflets of these plants when in flower or fruit and easily and accurately identifiable.

---

[7] Bomhard, M. L. LEAF VENATION AS A MEANS OF DISTINGUISHING CICUTA FROM ANGELICA. Jour. Wash. Acad. Sci. 26 (3) : 102–107, illus. 1936.

WESTERN WATERHEMLOCK

Cicu'ta occidenta'lis

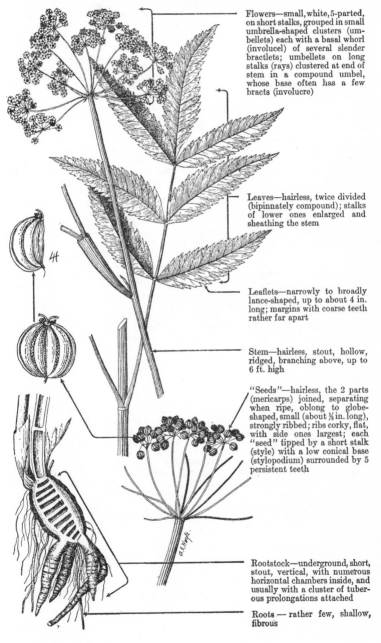

Flowers—small, white, 5-parted, on short stalks, grouped in small umbrella-shaped clusters (umbellets) each with a basal whorl (involucel) of several slender bractlets; umbellets on long stalks (rays) clustered at end of stem in a compound umbel, whose base often has a few bracts (involucre)

Leaves—hairless, twice divided (bipinnately compound); stalks of lower ones enlarged and sheathing the stem

Leaflets—narrowly to broadly lance-shaped, up to about 4 in. long; margins with coarse teeth rather far apart

Stem—hairless, stout, hollow, ridged, branching above, up to 6 ft. high

"Seeds"—hairless, the 2 parts (mericarps) joined, separating when ripe, oblong to globe-shaped, small (about ⅛ in. long), strongly ribbed; ribs corky, flat, with side ones largest; each "seed" tipped by a short stalk (style) with a low conical base (stylopodium) surrounded by 5 persistent teeth

Rootstock—underground, short, stout, vertical, with numerous horizontal chambers inside, and usually with a cluster of tuberous prolongations attached

Roots — rather few, shallow, fibrous

Western waterhemlock, also called cowbane, poisonhemlock, and poisonparsnip, is an extremely dangerous, poisonous plant of the carrot or parsnip family (Umbelliferae). It is a coarse, perennial marsh herb, which has a characteristic short, nearly erect, root crown, partitioned within, and bearing a cluster of elongated, coarse, fleshy roots. The stout, erect stem is 2½ to 6 feet high.

Western waterhemlock is the commonest and most widespread of the western species of waterhemlock, and ranges from South Dakota to New Mexico, California, British Columbia, and Alaska. South Dakota marks the eastern limit of western waterhemlock and, at the same time, the western limit of spotted waterhemlock (*C. macula'ta*), a more slender, essentially eastern species. In some of the important reference literature on range plants, *C. maculata* and *C. occidentalis* are not distinguished. Western waterhemlock is a moisture-loving plant, and commonly grows in marshes, swamps, wet meadows, along streams, irrigation ditches, and similar places. It occurs in the plains, foothills, and mountains up to elevations of about 9,000 feet. Ordinarily the plants have a scattered distribution, although in certain restricted areas they may be found growing in dense stands.

This plant, as well as other species of *Cicuta*, has not only killed large numbers of livestock, especially cattle and sheep, but has also resulted in fatalities among human beings. The root crown and other underground portions of the plant are the most poisonous parts. A small piece of root, which may easily be pulled up by a grazing animal, especially in the spring, is sufficient to cause sudden and violent death, the older root parts being the most toxic. The stems and leaves of the young shoots may poison livestock early in the season, but are not so dangerous in the summer and autumn. The dried seeds and older tops probably are not a source of danger.[1]

The high percentage of fatalities in western waterhemlock-poisoning cases indicates the need for efficient prevention. Livestock should be protected from the danger of eating waterhemlock by appropriate measures—herding, fencing, grubbing, etc., as the individual case may indicate. If the area of infestation is not too extensive, the most practical control is to eradicate the plants by grubbing. The plants thus removed should be burned as soon as possible before livestock have access to them.[2] The restricted habitat and ordinary relative scarcity of the plants in a given location facilitate this manual method of extermination. It is especially desirable to eliminate waterhemlock from the vicinity of water holes where livestock congregate regularly and are liable to eat the plant. It is often reported, although definite proof is lacking, that death has resulted from the contamination of water by the hoof-bruised roots of the western waterhemlock.

Both root crown and roots have a strong, disagreeable, musky odor, and when broken exude an acrid, yellowish fluid, which contains the poisonous principle.

Tuber waterhemlock (*C. vágans*), a species very closely related to western waterhemlock and sometimes called Oregon waterhemlock, has a more restricted range, occurring from British Columbia to Montana and south into northern California and central Idaho. It also occupies marshes and other wet places, mostly within the ponderosa pine belt, is virulently poisonous, and is the species of waterhemlock most frequently illustrated in the various publications concerning poisonous range plants. Its herbage has a bluish or purplish tinge, the stems are branched from the base, and are weaker than those of western waterhemlock; its large fleshy rootstocks (rhizomes) are horizontal and often occur partly above ground. The small, ribbed "seeds" of this species are rounded as contrasted with the more nearly egg-shaped or ellipsoidal fruits of the western waterhemlock.

---

[1] Marsh, C. D. STOCK-POISONING PLANTS OF THE RANGE. U. S. Dept. Agr. Bull. 1245, rev., 75 pp., illus. 1929. Supersedes Bull. 575. *See also* Marsh, C. D., Clawson, A. B., and Marsh, H. CICUTA, OR WATER HEMLOCK. U. S. Dept. Agr. Bull. 69, 27 pp., illus. 1914.

[2] Fleming, C. E., Peterson, N. F., Miller, M. R., Wright, L. H., and Louck, R. C. THE POISON PARSNIP OF WATER HEMLOCK (CICUTA OCCIDENTALIS), A PLANT DEADLY TO LIVESTOCK IN NEVADA. Nev. Agr. Expt. Sta. Bull. 100, 23 pp., illus. 1920.

BISCUITROOTS

Cogswel'lia spp., syns. *Loma'tium spp., Peuce'danum spp.*

Biscuitroots are perennial herbs and constitute a large rather variable genus of the carrot or parsnip family (Umbelliferae), consisting of about 66 species and belonging to the drier regions of western North America. The plants are also known locally as hogfennel, prairiefennel, whiskbroom-parsley, wildcarrot, wildparsley, and by the generic name, *Cogswellia.* Moreover, certain species, such as cous (*C. cous* and close allies), have individual names, and other species with large, fleshy, edible roots are often called Indianroot.

As a group the biscuitroots are perhaps the commonest and most widely distributed of all umbelliferous plants on the western ranges. They occur in all of the Western States but have a much smaller representation in Arizona and New Mexico than elsewhere. Biscuitroots are very common in most sections but are generally scattered and not abundant in any one place. They occur from slightly above sea level in the Columbia basin of the Northwest to elevations of about 10,000 feet in Utah and Wyoming. They grow in open or semi-open situations in the valleys and on hillsides from the piñon-juniper and sagebrush zones through the ponderosa pine and into the aspen belt. Many of the biscuitroots thrive under full sunlight and on well-drained soils, scablands, dry rocky mountain sides, open slopes, and exposed ridges; others abound in wet or semiwet areas, such as flats or depressions temporarily saturated by melting snows. Their common companions include sagebrush, wheatgrasses, arrowleaf balsamroot, bluegrasses, geraniums, lupines, mountain-dandelions, and yarrow.

These herbs are among the first plants to bloom in the spring. In making their extremely early growth and development they utilize the soil moisture left by melting snows. Except at the higher elevations, they mature their seeds and dry up by early summer. The plants of this genus reproduce mostly from seed, but species having tuberlike or bulblike roots also propagate vegetatively by means of the "tubers" which break away from the parent plants.

Because of their early growth and maturity, the biscuitroots are of appreciable value for forage only on ranges which are grazed in the spring and early summer. When at all abundant on such ranges, many of these plants generally rate as valuable forage weeds. The leaves, flowers, and green seeds of most of the species are eaten readily by sheep, and the leafage of several species is utilized even after drying. The palatability among the different species ranges from poor to good for cattle but is usually poor for horses. Deer, elk, and antelope are known to relish several species of *Cogswellia*, and it is probable that all the species are palatable to these game animals.

Many biscuitroots were important food plants of the Indians. The leafage of some species was eaten for greens, and the roots were used as a vegetable, eaten raw, baked, or roasted, or dried and ground into flour for bread; hence the name biscuitroot. Cous, above referred to, also known as cousroot and biscuitroot, and some of its close relatives, was one of the leading foods of the Northwestern Indians.[1] The fresh roots have a parsnip-like flavor, but, on drying, become brittle and white, with a somewhat celery-like taste. The dry root is readily ground into flour.

The root systems of biscuitroots are of two main types: (1) deep-set, elongated, often spindle-shaped, somewhat woody taproots or (2) fleshy, tuberlike, or bulblike roots of greatly varying shape. Some species have rounded and others elongated roots; in still others the roots are pinched or constricted to form a beadlike chain or string of "tubers." Most of the species have very short stems or are stemless except for the flower stalks which, in the majority of cases, are low (4 to 12 inches high), slender, unbranched, and leafless or nearly so; there are, however, many exceptions. The leaves and stems of several species make rank growth, sometimes attaining a height of 30 inches. *C. nudicaulis* and *C. platyphylla* are examples of species which have rather stout flower stalks with swollen or club-shaped tops where the flower clusters (umbels) begin. Individual plants of several species can be found which have somewhat branched leafy stems or flower stalks. As above intimated the leaves of most species are chiefly or wholly basal; i. e., they arise from the root crown or from the short, compressed stem. The stalks of these basal leaves are flattened or broadly dilated at the base. The leaves are always compound (divided into segments) with few to many divisions and, in the different species, are extremely variable in size and shape. In many species the leaves are cut up into very fine divisions and in general resemble parsley leaves; others with broader segments have fernlike leaves; some, such as nineleaf biscuitroot (*C. triternata*), have their leaves divided into long, narrow, grasslike lobes, and others, such as *C. nudicaulis* and *C. platyphylla*, have leaves with broad, egg-shaped, heart-shaped, or wedge-shaped divisions, sometimes $1\frac{1}{2}$ to 2 inches wide.

The flowers are usually yellow, in some species white, and occasionally purple. They are borne in umbrella-shaped clusters (umbels) of various sizes. In many species these umbels are characteristically irregular or lop-sided. In practically all species the hub or axis of the main umbel is without a circle of leaflike bracts (involucre), but it is characteristic of this genus that the secondary, small, flower clusters within the main umbel (umbellets) are usually encircled by a whorl of leafy bractlets (involucels). It is also characteristic that the sepals, or calyx teeth, are wanting or (very rarely) just visible. The fruits, or seeds, are strongly flattened, free from hairs and bristles and have thin, usually conspicuous side wings, equal thread-like ribs on the back, flattened faces, and lack prominent appendages (stylopodia) at the summit. The seeds grow in pairs, attached face to face by their side wings until maturity, and vary considerably in size and shape in the different species, from almost round to oblong in outline, and ranging from about one-eighth of an inch to 1 inch in length.

---

[1] Blankinship, J. W. NATIVE ECONOMIC PLANTS OF MONTANA. Mont. Agr. Expt. Sta. Bull. 56, 36 pp. 1905.

NINELEAF BISCUITROOT

Cogswel'lia triterna'ta, syns. *C. sim'plex, Loma'tium sim'plex, L. triterna'tum*

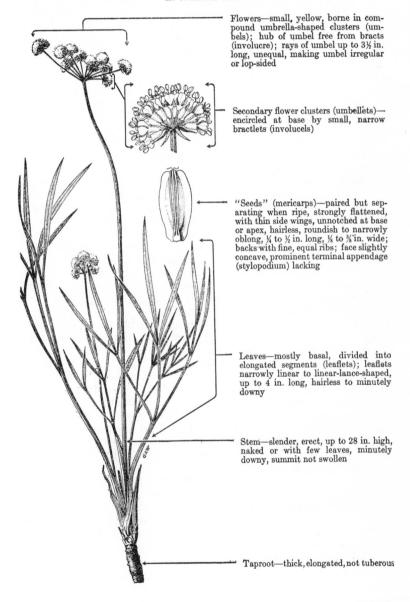

Flowers—small, yellow, borne in compound umbrella-shaped clusters (umbels); hub of umbel free from bracts (involucre); rays of umbel up to 3½ in. long, unequal, making umbel irregular or lop-sided

Secondary flower clusters (umbellets)—encircled at base by small, narrow bractlets (involucels)

"Seeds" (mericarps)—paired but separating when ripe, strongly flattened, with thin side wings, unnotched at base or apex, hairless, roundish to narrowly oblong, ¼ to ½ in. long, ⅛ to ⅜ in. wide; backs with fine, equal ribs; face slightly concave, prominent terminal appendage (stylopodium) lacking

Leaves—mostly basal, divided into elongated segments (leaflets); leaflets narrowly linear to linear-lance-shaped, up to 4 in. long, hairless to minutely downy

Stem—slender, erect, up to 28 in. high, naked or with few leaves, minutely downy, summit not swollen

Taproot—thick, elongated, not tuberous

Nineleaf biscuitroot has been selected for discussion because it is one of the most common and widespread species of the *Cogswellia* genus and is reasonably typical of the plants in this large and variable group. Because of its general appearance and its membership in the carrot, or parsnip family (Umbelliferae), it has been locally called wildcarrot, wildparsley, wildparsnip, and hogfennel. These names are undesirable, however, because they are loosely used for a large number of other umbelliferous plants. On the other hand, nineleaf biscuitroot, the common name adopted above, is distinctive, appropriate, and also fairly descriptive of the specific name, *triternata*, which means arranged in three times three, referring to the leaves, which are often divided into three main divisions, each of which is again divided into usually three or more long, narrow lobes. The roots of this and other species of *Cogswellia* are edible and were once used extensively as food by the Indians. They were eaten raw, or cooked as a vegetable, or diced and ground into flour for bread. This use of the plants gave rise to the name, biscuitroot, which is in common usage in many localities in the West.

Nineleaf biscuitroot is distributed from British Columbia to northeastern California, Colorado, and Alberta. It is typically a plant of the plains, foothills, and lower mountains, although occasionally it extends to higher altitudes, having been collected from dry open slopes at elevations of 9,500 feet in Utah and 10,000 feet in Wyoming. This species grows in well-drained or dry, rocky soils on the sunny open slopes, dry parks, and flats, open ridges and under open stands of timber through the sagebrush, piñon and ponderosa pine belts. It grows scatteringly in mixture with various other drought-resistant plants such as arrowleaf balsamroot, wheatgrass, sagebrush, oakbrush, and bitterbrush.

Nineleaf biscuitroot is one of the most valuable forage species in the *Cogswellia* genus. It is a rank-growing plant, sometimes attaining a height of 28 inches, and therefore produces more forage than many of the lower-growing biscuitroots. The plant is eaten by livestock and game animals throughout its range, being fair to very good for sheep and poor to fairly good for cattle. In the Northwest it is prized greatly because of its high palatability for both cattle and sheep. Unfortunately nineleaf biscuitroot is seldom abundant enough to form an important part of the plant cover. This plant begins growth early in the season and usually matures its seed and dries up by early summer; consequently it is of value for forage mainly on the spring ranges.

Most of the botanical manuals listing this plant separate it into two species: *Cogswellia triternata* and *C. simplex* (syn. *C. platycarpa*), which are very similar in appearance, differing chiefly in the shape of the seeds and the width of their wings, the wider-winged forms being placed in *C. simplex*. Since a complete series of intergrades exists wherever a line of division is drawn, the best present-day opinion is to combine both forms into one species under the oldest name *G. triternata*.

TAPERTIP HAWKSBEARD

Cre'pis acumina'ta

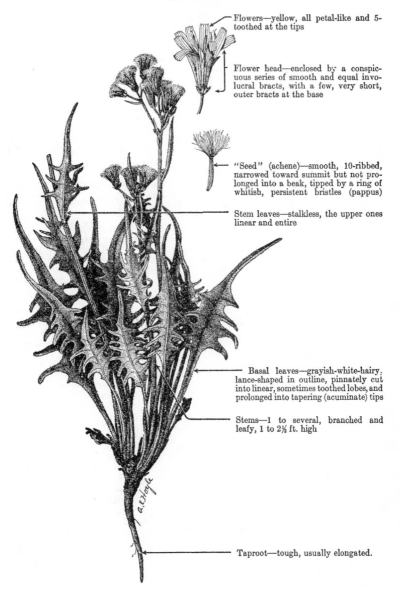

Flowers—yellow, all petal-like and 5-toothed at the tips

Flower head—enclosed by a conspicuous series of smooth and equal involucral bracts, with a few, very short, outer bracts at the base

"Seed" (achene)—smooth, 10-ribbed, narrowed toward summit but not prolonged into a beak, tipped by a ring of whitish, persistent bristles (pappus)

Stem leaves—stalkless, the upper ones linear and entire

Basal leaves—grayish-white-hairy, lance-shaped in outline, pinnately cut into linear, sometimes toothed lobes, and prolonged into tapering (acuminate) tips

Stems—1 to several, branched and leafy, 1 to 2½ ft. high

Taproot—tough, usually elongated.

Tapertip hawksbeard belongs to the chicory tribe (Cichorieae) of the large aster, or sunflower family (Compositae) and, like the other members of the genus, has yellow flowers with an involucre of a single series of long, sepallike phyllaries, and many-ribbed "seeds" (achenes), having the pappus of numerous soft, white bristles. It is a perennial, milky juiced herb, 1 to 2½ feet high.

Tapertip hawksbeard is the most common member of the genus and occurs in the foothills and mountains from British Columbia and Alberta to Colorado and California. It most commonly grows in well-drained, frequently stony soils on open slopes and hillsides in the ponderosa pine, piñon-juniper, and sagebrush belts. Commonly associated plants are eriogonums, lupines, Sandberg bluegrass, wheatgrasses, and arrowleaf balsamroot.

Although widespread, tapertip hawksbeard is seldom abundant and rarely provides a large part of the ground cover or forage. It is most palatable in the spring and early summer before the herbage matures and dries. Normally it is of low palatability to horses, fair for cattle, and good to excellent for sheep. In fact, overgrazing by sheep over a period of years has practically eliminated it from many western ranges.

Both the common name, tapertip hawksbeard, and the specific name, *acuminata*, refer to the conspicuously prolonged character of the leaves.

Gray hawksbeard (*C. interme'dia*) should be mentioned with tapertip hawksbeard, to which it is so closely related that it is sometimes considered a variety. The main distinguishing feature between the two is the gray covering of fine soft hairs which clothes the herbage of the former and accounts for its common name, gray hawksbeard. It inhabits much the same range and similar conditions of soil and moisture as does tapertip hawksbeard. Furthermore, grazing animals apparently do not show a preference in their use of these two species.

HAWKSBEARDS (Cre'pis spp.)

The 20 or more species of hawksbeards in the West vary considerably in height and in the size and shape of the leaves and the hairy character of their herbage, but, in general, the more common and widely distributed species are much alike. As a genus, they are most easily distinguished from the dandelions (*Leontodon* spp.) and mountain-dandelions (*Agoseris* spp.) by their branched and leafy stems. The hawksbeards differ from the hawkweeds (*Hieracium* spp.) chiefly in that the latter are usually rough-hairy, more slender-stemmed, and with darker, somewhat brownish-colored pappus bristles. The common name, hawksbeard, refers to a fancied resemblance of the copious hairs of the "seed" pappus to the bristles at the side of a hawk's beak.

Several species deserve mention, notably *C. nana*, *C. occidentalis*, *C. monticola*, and *C. runcinata*. These species do not, as yet, have well-established English names. *C. nana*, syn. *Youngia nana*, is unusual in the genus in that it is only 1 to 4 inches in height and tufted. Although rare, small, and confined to high altitudes in the Western States, there is reason to believe that it may be a valuable feed for game in Canada and Alaska. *C. occidentalis* is perhaps the most common species in the mountains of California; it has practically the same wide range as *C. intermedia* but extends into Arizona. It is similar to gray hawksbeard in color and, in fact, is called gray hawksbeard by some authors but, under field conditions, *C. occidentalis* is about half as tall as *C. intermedia* and deeper gray in color. *C. monticola*, a somewhat coarse species, is apparently limited to the mountains of northern California and southern Oregon. It is distinct from the other members of the genus, because the herbage is covered with long, brown, and glandular-bristly hairs. *C. runcinata*, common in the mountain valleys of the Rockies, differs from the other common species in having few, frequently entire, smooth leaves, and slender stems, bearing relatively few flowers. It is found in moist places, or even in standing water.

From a range use standpoint, the hawksbeards, as a group, resemble tapertip hawksbeard, occurring on open sites on well-drained soils, in the foothill and mountain areas. Sheep are fond of practically all species to the point of overgrazing.

Dr. E. B. Babcock, professor of genetics at the University of California, has shown that this genus consists of about 250 species, and is a natural group with its center of origin in south central Asia.[1][2]

[1] Babcock, E. B., and Navashin, M. THE GENUS CREPIS. Bibliog. Genetica 6 : 1–90, illus. 1930.
[2] Babcock, E. B., and Cameron, D. R. CHROMOSOMES AND PHYLOGENY IN CREPIS. II, THE RELATIONSHIPS OF ONE HUNDRED EIGHT SPECIES. Calif. Univ. Pubs., Agr. Sci. 6 (11) : 287–324, illus. 1934.

LARKSPURS

Delphi'nium spp.

The native larkspurs are perennial, while those naturalized from the Old World are annual. Some 60 native and 2 naturalized species of larkspur occur on western ranges. Throughout the West this genus is one of the best known members of the buttercup, or crowfoot, family (Ranunculaceae) because some species are poisonous and responsible for severe losses of cattle. Larkspurs are widespread, one or more species occurring in every western State, Alaska, and the Provinces of Canada. Larkspurs are common in the foothills and mountains in the Western States, chiefly occurring in well-drained loamy soil in mountain parks, grasslands, sagebrush areas, and in clumps of aspen or in partial shade of other trees. The generic name *Delphinium* is the Latin form for *delphinion*, a word used by the old Greek botanist Dioscorides for larkspur.

Many larkspurs are known to be poisonous to cattle, but it is questionable whether all species are poisonous under range conditions. However, as Marsh, Clawson, and Marsh [1] have pointed out, it is the safest policy to regard them all as suspicious pending full knowledge concerning them. Horses and sheep have been poisoned by forced feeding with certain species of larkspur but, under range conditions, horses usually avoid these plants while sheep eat them without injury. The greatest loss of cattle occurs during the early spring and summer, because larkspur produces an abundance of forage in advance of other plants and begins growth on the higher summer ranges soon after the snow melts. This group creates a serious problem in managing cattle on the range, because so many larkspurs are poisonous both before and after blooming. Under range conditions sheep are seldom poisoned by larkspur, and it is common for sheep to utilize larkspur areas. The palatability for sheep is considered good.

In the treatment of poisoned animals beneficial results usually are obtained by injecting a solution of 1 grain physostigmin salicylate, 2 grains pilocarpin hydrochloride, and ½ grain of strychnine sulphate, with a hypodermic syringe, preferably in the shoulder.[1] The above amount dissolved in approximately 1 tablespoon of water is the proper dose for an animal weighing 500 to 600 pounds. The formula should be doubled for an animal of 1,000 pounds. The syringe used in administering blackleg vaccine will serve.

Numerous larkspur-eradication projects have been conducted in the West, particularly with Barbey larkspur (*D. barbeyi*) and Sierra larkspur (*D. glaucum*). Eradication has been attempted both by grubbing and chemical means. In grubbing larkspur special care must be exercised to assure that all plants, including the seedlings and other small specimens, are dug. It is imperative that enough of the root system be removed to prevent the remnant from sprouting. This infers grubbing every larkspur plant discernible and

---

[1] Marsh, C. D., Clawson, A. B., and Marsh, H. LARKSPUR OR "POISON WEED." U. S. Dept. Agr. Farmers' Bull. 988, rev., 13 pp., illus. 1934. Supersedes Bull. 531.

removing the roots to a depth of not less than 8 inches, including all side roots as well as the base of the plant. Workmen must make sure that no roots fall back into the hole and that all dirt is shaken from the roots grubbed to prevent posible regrowth.

It is outstandingly important to burn all plants after removal to prevent their consumption by cattle. Regardless of the care exercised in digging Barbey and other larkspurs, it is always necessary to go over the area the following year to remove any plants which have been missed. Usually a second follow-up is necessary to eradicate plants developing from seed stored from previous seasons.[2]

Chemical eradication has thus far proved very effective in Montana, but only partly successful in Utah. In general, chemical eradication of larkspur is much more expensive than grubbing. The chemicals used are relatively costly, and heavy applications are needed to kill plants possessing such heavy deepset root systems as those of most tall larkspurs. If the plants are merely weakened they almost invariably recover unless the work is repeated. Although continued research with chemicals in larkspur eradication is justified, for the present, hand grubbing is the most practical method of eliminating small stands of these plants from the range.

Spraying with sodium chlorate in neutral, acid, or alkaline solutions of 2½ percent or more and upwards during the active growing period of larkspur is effective. However, it is risky to use this chemical because of its inflammability and toxicity in quantity to livestock. A salty taste increases its attractiveness and encourages consumption of treated plants. Calcium chlorate, while less effective than sodium chlorate, has also been successfully used in chemical eradication of larkspur and has the advantages of being neither poisonous nor inflammable. These soluble chemicals are readily applied, kill both tops and roots of the poisonous plants and thus prevent sprouting. The addition of a little whale-oil soap or glycerine facilitates the uniform distribution and retention of the solution upon the leaf surfaces.

Larkspurs may be bunched, leafy, and conspicuous or low, single-stemmed, and few-branched, and may vary in height from a few inches to 7 feet. In general, the species may be grouped, for practical purposes, in two divisions: Tall larkspurs and low larkspurs. The stalks arise from long and woody or from short and thick roots, being hollow, and often rather stout, with the alternate leaves hairy, smooth, or covered with a bluish-white coating like that of a grape or plum. The leaves often resemble those of maple or currant. The leaf divisions extend from the tip of the leaf stem like a human hand with outstretched fingers. During the spring, before the plants blossom, it is difficult to distinguish between the leaves of larkspur, monkshood and geranium. Larkspur flowers are usually colored various shades of violet, blue, and purple, although white-flowered forms occur in nearly all species, with a few species having red flowers.

[2]Aldous, A. E. ERADICATING TALL LARKSPUR ON CATTLE RANGES IN THE NATIONAL FORESTS. U. S. Dept. Agr. Farmers' Bull. 826, 23 pp., illus. 1917.

BARBEY LARKSPUR

Delphi'nium bar'beyi, syn. *D. subalpi'num*

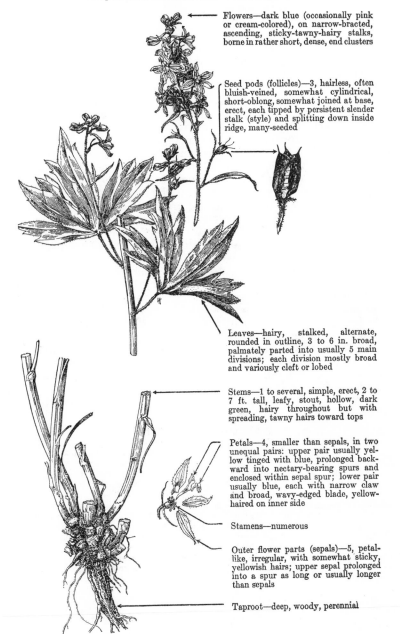

Flowers—dark blue (occasionally pink or cream-colored), on narrow-bracted, ascending, sticky-tawny-hairy stalks, borne in rather short, dense, end clusters

Seed pods (follicles)—3, hairless, often bluish-veined, somewhat cylindrical, short-oblong, somewhat joined at base, erect, each tipped by persistent slender stalk (style) and splitting down inside ridge, many-seeded

Leaves—hairy, stalked, alternate, rounded in outline, 3 to 6 in. broad, palmately parted into usually 5 main divisions; each division mostly broad and variously cleft or lobed

Stems—1 to several, simple, erect, 2 to 7 ft. tall, leafy, stout, hollow, dark green, hairy throughout but with spreading, tawny hairs toward tops

Petals—4, smaller than sepals, in two unequal pairs: upper pair usually yellow tinged with blue, prolonged backward into nectary-bearing spurs and enclosed within sepal spur; lower pair usually blue, each with narrow claw and broad, wavy-edged blade, yellow-haired on inner side

Stamens—numerous

Outer flower parts (sepals)—5, petal-like, irregular, with somewhat sticky, yellowish hairs; upper sepal prolonged into a spur as long or usually longer than sepals

Taproot—deep, woody, perennial

Barbey larkspur, a perennial herb, is one of the most characteristic, abundant, and widely distributed of the tall larkspurs. It is typically a plant of the higher mountains, ranging mostly from about 8,000 feet up to timber line, but occasionally as low as 6,000 feet toward the northwestern limits of its range. The species appears to be confined to four States: Wyoming, Colorado, Utah, and Idaho. Large patches of this tall larkspur may be found growing abundantly in canyons and on moist, well-drained soils. Probably the most serious cattle losses from tall-larkspur poisoning throughout its known western range is caused by Barbey larkspur, and the species has been the basis of much experimental work as representative of tall-larkspur poisoning.

The stored food in the large and deep woody taproot of this and other tall larkspurs facilitates the rapid growth of leafy stems early in the spring before many edible but harmless plants have made an appreciable start. Growth of as much as 1 to 2 feet in May has been reported, but the rapidity of development varies greatly according to the altitude and moisture and temperature conditions. The large leaves are more poisonous than the stems and are most toxic when the plants are starting spring growth. Their poisonous properties decrease when the flowers and seeds mature in July and August. In fact, cattle often graze the palatable green leaves that persist after the plant has seeded without harmful effect.[1] The seeds of this species are very poisonous and have occasionally caused some losses. Although the roots also contain the toxic principles, their woodiness, and deep underground habit of growth render them practically inaccessible to cattle. Barbey larkspur does not die down after setting seed; the leaves remain palatable until killed by frost.

Although Barbey larkspur, if eaten in sufficiently large quantities and within a comparatively short time, may cause sheep poisoning, range fatalities seldom, if ever, occur, except possibly under badly overgrazed or other very abnormal conditions. Horses may be poisoned experimentally by this species but, under range conditions, this class of livestock apparently never eats enough of this larkspur to be injured. In most instances infested ranges may be used with safety for pasturage of sheep and horses.

Although it is easy to distinguish Barbey larkspur after it blossoms because no other plant in its habitat has similar flowers, these plants, in the early stages of leaf and stem growth, are often confused with sticky geranium (*Geranium viscosissimum*), a harmless, widely distributed and common range plant, and also with monkshoods, particularly Columbia monkshood (*Aconitum columbianum*). The leaves of sticky geranium are mostly basal and long-stalked—those that do occur on the stem being paired—while the leaves of Barbey larkspur all come from the stem, are not paired, and are shorter-stalked. The leaves of monkshood are very similar in shape, size, and arrangement to those of Barbey larkspur, but are somewhat shorter-stalked; the stems of monkshood are pithy as a rule, while those of larkspur are usually hollow; the roots of monkshood are tuberous and often clustered near the soil surface, while those of Barbey larkspur are enlarged, woody, and deep; the well-developed hood of the monkshood flower and the marked spur of the larkspur are very distinctive.

[1] Marsh, C. D., Clawson, A. B., and Marsh, H. LARKSPUR OR "POISON WEED." U. S. Dept. Agr. Farmers' Bull. 988, rev., 13 pp., illus. 1934. Supersedes Bull. 531.
Clawson, A. B. ADDITIONAL INFORMATION CONCERNING LARKSPUR POISONING. U. S. Dept. Agr., Supplement to Farmers' Bull. 988, 2 pp. 1933.

LOW LARKSPUR

Delphi'nium bi'color

Flowers—dark blue or purplish (rarely white), usually few, large and showy, irregular, stalked; lower flower stalks elongated, borne in end clusters (racemes)

Sepals—petal-like, dark blue or purplish, egg-lance-shaped, sharp-pointed or tapering; upper sepal spurred, up to ¾ in. long

Petals—in 2 pairs; upper pair white or yellowish, veined with blue, prolonged backwards into a spur, enclosed in the spurred sepal; lower pair cleft, usually blue, with a tuft of hairs near the middle; stamens numerous

Leaves—alternate, finely hairy, round in outline, deeply parted into narrow, linear or linear-oblong, blunt-tipped segments; upper stem leaves smaller

Stem—up to 20 in. high, hollow, few-leaved, hairy, sometimes sticky-hairy above

Roots—thick, woody, elongate, often clustered

Seed pods (follicles)—erect or curving, 3 to 5, more or less sticky-hairy; each tipped by persistent, threadlike stalk (style), splitting down along inside ridge

Low larkspur, which resembles spring larkspur (*D. menziesii*), is a small, perennial, poisonous larkspur with rather large, showy flowers. It occurs on medium dry to moist sites on the plains, and in the mountains at elevations of from about 3,000 to 9,000 feet, from British Columbia to Montana, South Dakota, Colorado, Nevada, and Oregon. This plant, which seeks the full sunlight, is one of the earliest-appearing wild flowers, frequently blooming at the edge of snow banks in the mountains.

On many ranges, low larkspur is relatively abundant and during the early spring forms a very conspicuous part of the vegetation. As all parts of the plant are quite toxic to cattle, its extensive use results in some losses of that class of livestock, especially in Montana, where the species is rather plentiful. Under range conditions, apparently it is not poisonous to sheep;[1] in fact, the plant is usually considered fairly good forage for such animals. Fortunately, cattle losses are easily preventable by prohibiting entry of those animals to infested ranges until low larkspur, which matures early, has dried up, or until more palatable forage is available.

Being one of the most beautiful of the American larkspurs,[2] this species is frequently cultivated as an ornamental. The flowers are dark blue or purplish, although the two, small, upper petals are white or pale yellow streaked with blue, hence the specific name *bicolor*, two-colored. Early settlers in the West commonly used the seeds of this larkspur as poison baits in exterminating lice and other vermin.

---

[1] Marsh, C. D., Clawson, A. B., and Marsh H. LARKSPUR POISONING OF LIVE STOCK. U. S. Dept. Agr. Bull. 365, 91 pp., illus. 1916.
[2] Marsh, C. D., Clawson, A. B., and Marsh, H. LARKSPUR OR "POISON WEED." U. S. Dept. Agr. Farmers' Bull. 988, rev., 13 pp., illus. 1934. Supersedes Bull. 531.

SIERRA LARKSPUR

Delphi'nium glau'cum, syn. *D. scopulo'rum glau'cum*

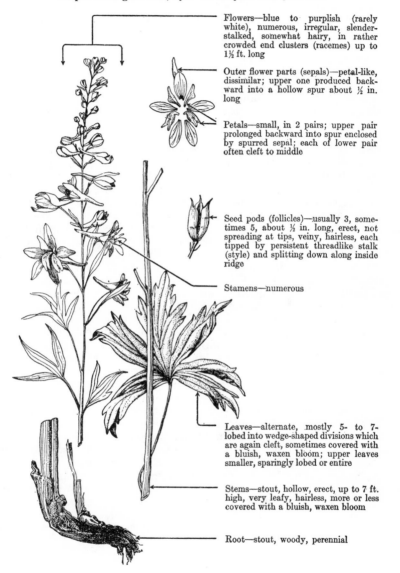

Flowers—blue to purplish (rarely white), numerous, irregular, slender-stalked, somewhat hairy, in rather crowded end clusters (racemes) up to 1½ ft. long

Outer flower parts (sepals)—petal-like, dissimilar; upper one produced backward into a hollow spur about ½ in. long

Petals—small, in 2 pairs; upper pair prolonged backward into spur enclosed by spurred sepal; each of lower pair often cleft to middle

Seed pods (follicles)—usually 3, sometimes 5, about ½ in. long, erect, not spreading at tips, veiny, hairless, each tipped by persistent threadlike stalk (style) and splitting down along inside ridge

Stamens—numerous

Leaves—alternate, mostly 5- to 7-lobed into wedge-shaped divisions which are again cleft, sometimes covered with a bluish, waxen bloom; upper leaves smaller, sparingly lobed or entire

Stems—stout, hollow, erect, up to 7 ft. high, very leafy, hairless, more or less covered with a bluish, waxen bloom

Root—stout, woody, perennial

Sierra larkspur is a tall poisonous perennial herb of the buttercup family (Ranunculaceae). The specific name is derived from the Greek word *glaucon*, meaning bluish, and refers to the bluish, waxy bloom which usually covers the herbage of this plant. The species is commonly found in the mountains of California to western Nevada and northward to the Yukon River. This larkspur, typically a plant of the high elevations (6,000 to 9,000 feet), is found in a variety of sites, but prefers rich, moist, shaded soils, along streams and in alpine meadows.

Sierra larkspur is poisonous to cattle and horses, but apparently is not injurious to sheep. Although all parts of the young plants, except perhaps the flowers, are poisonous, these toxic properties disappear subsequent to the blooming stage and maturity. Unfortunately, cattle relish California larkspur in the early spring, when the young and succulent plants are particularly toxic and other forage is scarce. Accordingly, the practical method of preventing losses is to prohibit this class of livestock from grazing infested areas until late summer, when this larkspur is no longer harmful.

The early symptoms of poisoning are similar to those produced by deathcamas—the animal's muscles stiffen and the gait becomes irregular; later, the front legs give way, and the animal falls, usually with muscles quivering. The animal kicks violently before death ensues. Poisoned animals become constipated, but usually recover if this condition is relieved. Bloating occurs in some cases. When the poisoning is sufficiently severe to produce fatal results, death ordinarily follows in a very short time.[1] In the treatment of larkspur poisoning, the animal's head is kept higher than the body and all unnecessary exercise prohibited. An injection, with a hypodermic syringe, is made of the following solution: 1 grain physostigmin salicylate; 2 grains pilocarpin hydrochlorid; ½ grain strychnin sulfate. This formula would apply to an animal weighing 500 or 600 pounds. For a large animal of 1,000 pounds the dose should be doubled. For further details concerning this formula the genus notes for *Delphinium* (W58) should be consulted.

Sierra larkspur is one of the so-called tall larkspurs. It is a large and showy plant, commonly from 2½ to 7 feet in height. The flowers are characteristically a deep purplish blue, and the ultimate leaf divisions are markedly jagged and sharp. The large lower leaves, as much as 6 inches across, are 5- to 7-lobed and somewhat resemble a maple or currant leaf. This species can be distinguished from the other tall larkspurs by the fact that the seed pods are hairless, and the hairless leaves and stems are usually covered with a whitish or bluish waxen bloom which easily rubs off.

---

[1] Marsh, C. D., Clawson, A. B., and Marsh, H. LARKSPUR OR "POISON WEED." U. S. Dept. Agr. Farmers' Bull. 988, rev., 13 pp., illus. 1934. Supersedes Bull. 531.

SPRING LARKSPUR

Delphi'nium menzie'sii, syns. *D. nelso'nii, D. pineto'rum*

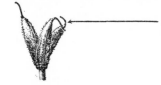

Seed pods (follicles)—3, smooth to hairy, about ½ to ¾ in. long, oblong-cylindrical, somewhat joined at base but recurving and widely spreading at tips, each splitting from tip downward along inside ridge, many-seeded, tipped by persistent short stalk (style)

Flowers—showy, dark blue or purplish, irregular, hairy, sometimes somewhat sticky, each on a slender, ascending or spreading, bracted stalk, in 2- to several-flowered, elongating end clusters (racemes)

Outer flower parts (sepals)—5, petal-like, irregular, ½ to ¾ in. long, spatula-shaped, oblong, the upper one prolonged into a slightly curved spur about equal in length to the sepals

Petals—4, small, pale to brownish yellow with conspicuous, dark purplish veins, in 2 unequal pairs; the upper pair prolonged into spurlike, nectar-bearing appendages, and enclosed in the spurred sepal; lower pair clawed, with rounded, slightly cleft blade about ⅛ in. long

Stamens—numerous

Stems—slender, erect but bending easily, usually less than 1 ft. (rarely 2 ft.) high, sparingly leafy, usually branching at base, the branches widely spreading

Leaves—alternate, somewhat rounded or kidney-shaped in outline, palmately 3- to 5-parted and each of these divisions variously cleft or lobed, smooth or hairy; lower leaves larger and longer-stalked than upper ones

Root—tuberous, clustered, perennial

343

Spring larkspur, a perennial herb, probably the most widely distributed of the low larkspurs, ranges from British Columbia to extreme northern California, New Mexico, and Montana. Its most abundant growth is probably in Colorado and Utah, though it is very common in Idaho, Montana, Oregon, Wyoming, and New Mexico. It is typically a plant of the mountains, growing at altitudes from 1,000 feet or so in northwestern California and in the northern and northwestern parts of its range up to elevations at least as high as 10,500 feet in the Rocky Mountains, especially the more southern portion. The species grows in numerous associations, in aspen, openings in lodgepole pine, and in the sagebrush, oakbrush, and ponderosa pine belts, but is especially characteristic of open grass-weed-brush areas. Frequent associates are lupines, bluegrasses, wheatgrasses, and rabbitbrushes. It inhabits a variety of soils—dry to moist, shallow and sandy, gravelly, or rocky, to deep rich loams or heavy clays.

Spring larkspur causes heavy losses of cattle on the spring and early summer ranges. This poisonous species is probably the most destructive of the low larkspurs. It is widely distributed, occurs in dense masses, grows in a variety of soils, and is readily grazed. Most of the United States Department of Agriculture experiments with low larkspur have been concerned with this species.[1] The formula of the recommended remedy and the methods of its use are presented in detail in the genus notes (W58).

No known losses of sheep or horses have occurred on the range from spring larkspur poisoning. This species is more palatable to sheep than to cattle and is sometimes grazed rather extensively by both classes of livestock when little other feed is available. Sheep generally prefer grasses and other weeds to the low larkspurs, and on some ranges in Idaho and Nevada spring larkspur is regarded as unpalatable to livestock. Due to the early seeding and subsequent dying down of spring larkspur on the range, it is usually safe to graze cattle after the first of July on areas which produce large quantities of this species, unless normal plant development is delayed by unfavorable weather or other conditions.

Although low larkspurs are somewhat similar in appearance to tall larkspurs, their solitary stalks and low growth distinguish them from the tall larkspurs. The leaves of low larkspurs are few in number and are more finely dissected than those of most tall larkspurs. As the common name spring larkspur indicates, this plant starts growth early, sending up a single, short (rarely 2 feet high), sparingly leafy stem with usually clustered, tuberous roots; the stalk generally branches somewhat near its base. The showy, dark blue or purplish (rarely white) flowers open in May or early June; seed forms in late June or early July, varying with the elevation or seasonal and site conditions. After seeding, the plant dries up and disappears.

---

[1] Marsh, C. D., Clawson, A. B., and Marsh, H. LARKSPUR OR "POISON WEED". U. S. Dept. Agr. Farmers' Bull. 988, rev., 13 pp., illus. 1934. Supersedes Bull. 531.

DUNCECAP LARKSPUR

Delphi'nium occidenta'le, syns. *D. abieto'rum, D. cuculla'tum*

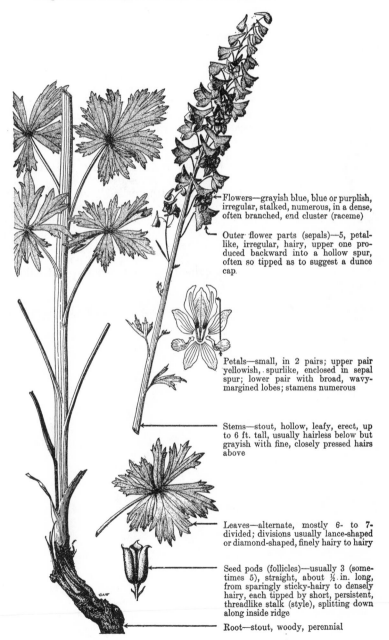

Flowers—grayish blue, blue or purplish, irregular, stalked, numerous, in a dense, often branched, end cluster (raceme)

Outer flower parts (sepals)—5, petal-like, irregular, hairy, upper one produced backward into a hollow spur, often so tipped as to suggest a dunce cap.

Petals—small, in 2 pairs; upper pair yellowish, spurlike, enclosed in sepal spur; lower pair with broad, wavy-margined lobes; stamens numerous

Stems—stout, hollow, leafy, erect, up to 6 ft. tall, usually hairless below but grayish with fine, closely pressed hairs above

Leaves—alternate, mostly 6- to 7-divided; divisions usually lance-shaped or diamond-shaped, finely hairy to hairy

Seed pods (follicles)—usually 3 (sometimes 5), straight, about ½ in. long, from sparingly sticky-hairy to densely hairy, each tipped by short, persistent, threadlike stalk (style), splitting down along inside ridge

Root—stout, woody, perennial

Duncecap larkspur is a tall perennial herb of the buttercup family (Ranunculaceae). The specific name *occidentale* is Latin for western, referring to the range of this plant. It is found in the higher mountains (5,000 to 11,500 feet) in all of the 11 far-western States except California, Arizona, and New Mexico. Duncecap larkspur grows in a variety of soils but prefers the richer loam soils in moist situations. This herb flourishes on both open and shaded sites and is common in aspen patches.

Recent experiments have demonstrated that this species is poisonous and is responsible for most of the deaths of cattle by larkspur in Montana.[1] While experiments have not definitely shown that this is true of larkspurs generally, and further study is necessary, the wisest range management must assume meanwhile that all species of larkspur, when abundant, are dangerous on cattle range. In the treatment of animals poisoned by larkspur the formula as given in the larkspur genus write-up (W58) should be used.

On the whole, duncecap larkspur resembles other tall larkspurs. It is commonly 3 to 6 feet high, with leaves divided somewhat as a maple or currant leaf. It may be distinguished from Barbey larkspur by the white, mildewy appearance of the upper part of the stalk, due to the presence of close-lying hairs upon the part, as contrasted with the tawny, stick hairs which stand straight out on the stems of Barbey larkspur. The seed pods are usually densely hairy, whereas those of *barbeyi* are hairless. The spur is pointed and resembles a duncecap, which explains the common name. The flowers are grayish blue when in full bloom.

---

[1] Marsh, C. D. STOCK-POISONING PLANTS OF THE RANGE. U. S. Dept. Agr. Bull. 1245, rev., 75 pp., illus. 1929. Supersedes Bull. 575.

WILD-DAISIES

Eri'geron spp., syn. *Lep'tilon spp.*

Erigeron, a member of the aster tribe of the composite family (Compositae), is a large genus of annual, biennial, or perennial herbs with numerous small flowers in heads which have the appearance of a single flower. Plants of this genus are commonly known as fleabanes, daisies, and erigerons; the source of the name fleabane is from the supposed value of some species as flea repellants. Presumably, when burned, at least some species of *Erigeron* were objectionable to insects; formerly bunches of the plants were hung in rural cottages for the purpose of excluding insects. However, the true fleabanes are European plants of other related genera, especially *Pulicaria* and *Conyza*. Daisy (or English daisy) is the accepted common name of the frequently cultivated, Old World plant, *Bellis perennis*, and, moreover, is popularly and rather loosely applied not only to species of *Erigeron*, but to asters (*Aster* spp.), oxeye daisy (*Chrysanthemum leucanthemum*), and other plants with similar flower heads. In the West, daisy is almost universally used for species of *Erigeron* and, although the English generic name wild-daisy is not entirely satisfactory, it seems much preferable, at least from the range standpoint, to the rather inappropriate fleabane, even though that name is widely used in the East and in the horticultural trade. *Erigeron*, an old Greek plant name used by Dioscorides and Theophrastus, reputedly was applied originally to some species of groundsel (*Senecio*).

This genus is widely distributed in temperate and mountainous regions and is particularly well represented in the western United States, where probably more than 100 species occur, Colorado being the center of distribution. The wild-daisies occur in nearly all kinds of soils and in practically all plant types throughout the West.

The palatability of the wild-daisies varies from practically worthless to about fair or, in some instances, good. They are more palatable to sheep and goats than to cattle, but are practically worthless for horses. Generally, those species with very hairy foliage are less palatable than the hairless species, and presumably are cropped to a greater extent on ranges where the forage is predominantly browse or grass, especially if such areas are used by sheep. Deer and elk also crop the wild-daisies. However, the majority of these plants are poor forage species, actually being nothing more than "weeds" and occupy space which, preferably, should be utilized by more palatable plants. Wild-daisies have undoubtedly increased on many areas which have been severely overgrazed.

The flower heads of wild-daisies are generally composed of center (disk) flowers with yellow tubular corollas, which do not change to purple, and usually numerous, petallike outer (ray) flowers with pink, bluish, purplish, or white, narrow, strap-shaped corollas. The ray flowers are rarely yellow or orange and in a few species are entirely absent. The flower heads are usually borne on leafless stalks. The bracts surrounding the base of the flower heads are mostly in two rows (sometimes one or three), not herbaceous, nearly equal in length, rather loose, and only slightly overlapping. The stems are leafy; the leaves alternate and entire, toothed, lobed, or divided. The fruits, or "seeds" (achenes) are usually flattened, mostly two-nerved, and crowned by slender white bristles.

Many species of western range plants, particularly asters, are sometimes confused with the wild-daisies, the flower heads of asters being similar to those of wild-daisies. In asters, however, the flower stalks tend to be somewhat coarser, less naked, and more leafy at the top than those of the wild-daisies; their disk flowers turn reddish or brownish in drying, and their heads are generally somewhat more numerous. Moreover, the bracts surrounding the base of aster flower heads are usually in rows, strongly graduated, overlapping, somewhat herbaceous, and rather numerous and the petallike, marginal, strap-shaped flowers (rays, or ligules) are much broader and fewer than in typical species of *Erigeron*. In view of these differences, most asters and wild-daisies are easily distinguished from each other but, in a few cases, it is sometimes necessary to examine the tips (stigmas) of the threadlike stalks (styles) of the seed-producing organ (ovary) and the brush of hairs (pappus) on the tips of the seedlike fruits for additional confirmation of identity. The stigmas in *Aster* tend to be narrow and sharp-pointed, rather than broad and blunt, as in *Erigeron*. The pappus on *Aster* fruits is simple and copious; that of *Erigeron* is often double (with a short outer series) and is more scanty and fragile.

Many of the wild-daisies bear attractive flower heads and several species are grown as ornamentals both at home and abroad. At least two of these species, Oregon wild-daisy (*E. specio'sus*), and smooth-wild-daisy (*E. glabel'lus*), are native to the West. Oregon wild-daisy has more or less woody stems from 12 to 24 inches high, with narrowly reverse-lance-shaped, stalkless stem leaves almost to the top, and fairly large heads of violet ray flowers. Smooth wild-daisy is a perennial with stems from 6 to 20 inches high, narrow leaves, and one to three large heads with violet-purple or white ray flowers. Various other western species are cultivated.

Some of the wild-daisies reputedly have remarkable medicinal properties and are under suspicion as poisonous to livestock. Outstanding among these species is horseweed (*E. canaden'sis*, syn. *Lep'tilon canaden'se*), so called probably because of its common occurrence in horse pastures. It is also known as Canada fleabane and, for some unknown reason, is often misnamed scabious. This annual is native to the eastern United States and is now diffused almost universally. The drug obtained from this plant physiologically produces smarting of the eyes, soreness of the throat, aching of the extremities, and prostration. It is reputed to be a diuretic, tonic, and astringent, being especially valuable in cases of chronic diarrhea, and in parturitional hemorrhage. The species is a bristly-hairy plant with erect, wandlike stems 4 to 12 inches high; it has linear, entire stem leaves; lobed basal leaves; and numerous small flower heads with very short, inconspicuous ray flowers. Annual wild-daisy (*E. an'nuus*) and Philadelphia wild-daisy, misnamed sweet scabious (*E. philadel'phicus*), both native and widely distributed in the eastern United States, are other wild-daisies with similar properties. "These plants were well known to the northern Indians by the name of Cocash or Squaw-weed, as emmenagogues and diuretics." [1]

[1] Good, P. P. FAMILY FLORA AND MATERIA MEDICA BOTANICA. . . 2 v., illus. Elizabethtown, N. J. 1845.

TRAILING WILD-DAISY

Eri'geron flagella'ris

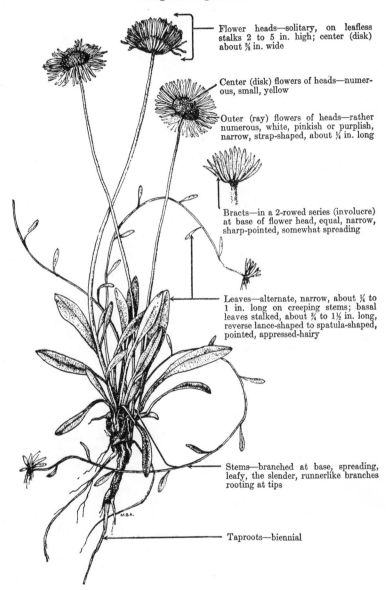

Flower heads—solitary, on leafless stalks 2 to 5 in. high; center (disk) about ⅜ in. wide

Center (disk) flowers of heads—numerous, small, yellow

Outer (ray) flowers of heads—rather numerous, white, pinkish or purplish, narrow, strap-shaped, about ¼ in. long

Bracts—in a 2-rowed series (involucre) at base of flower head, equal, narrow, sharp-pointed, somewhat spreading

Leaves—alternate, narrow, about ¼ to 1 in. long on creeping stems; basal leaves stalked, about ¾ to 1½ in. long, reverse lance-shaped to spatula-shaped, pointed, appressed-hairy

Stems—branched at base, spreading, leafy, the slender, runnerlike branches rooting at tips

Taproots—biennial

Trailing wild-daisy, sometimes known as trailing fleabane and, most commonly, as vine daisy or trailing daisy, is a small biennial with prostrate creeping stems which root at the tips. The specific name *flagellaris* is from the Latin *flagellum*, meaning a whip, or a whiplike shoot or branch of a plant, and refers to the long, slender, runnerlike stems. Trailing wild-daisy ranges from Montana to South Dakota, New Mexico, Arizona, and Mexico, and is typically a mountain species, occurring chiefly in the ponderosa pine, aspen, and spruce belts. It grows in a wide variety of (mostly rather dry) soils, including heavy clays, rich loams, and sandy or gravelly soils, both in the open and in moderately dense shade of brush and timber types. Trailing wild-daisy, together with bluestem (*Agropyron smithii*) and a small rabbitbrush (*Chrysothamnus* sp.), often make up the sparse cover in the adobe soils of southwestern Colorado.

Trailing wild-daisy is important on many of the western ranges, particularly in the Southwest, because of its abundance. It is sometimes considered fair forage for sheep and deer and poor to fair for cattle. However, it is a small plant with the stems and leaves borne close to the ground so that but little of the foliage is easily available to grazing animals.

Trailing wild-daisy is one of the range plants best adapted to grow on poor soils and, because it produces an abundance of seed and reproduces vigorously by means of creeping stems, it is able quickly to invade and revegetate depleted areas. This species is generally comparatively lightly grazed except on very closely utilized ranges, and its strong reproductive powers apparently enable it readily to replace the more palatable plants as they are destroyed by excessive grazing. Consequently, where trailing wild-daisy is abundant, consideration should be given to the possibility that the range has been severely overgrazed and the better cover depleted.

Only a few of the American species of *Erigeron* produce runners similar to those of trailing wild-daisy. Creeping wild-daisy (*E. repens*), a species having broadly reverse-egg-shaped to broadly spatula-shaped, toothed or lobed leaves, occurs in Texas and Mexico. Early wild-daisy (*E. vernus*), an eastern species producing short offsets or stolons and several flower heads on each stem, grows in wet soils from Virginia to Florida and Louisiana. Two species, hoary wild-daisy (*E. senilis*) and shorn wild-daisy (*E. tonsus*), are reported only from New Mexico and may be merely forms of *flagellaris*, the main differences being in the width and hairiness of the leaves and the size of the flower heads. *E. tonsus* is nearly hairless with small heads and *E. senilis* is very hairy and has blunt, reverse-egg-shaped to reverse-lance-shaped leaves. Sprawling wild-daisy (*E. nudiflorus*, syn. *E. commixtus*), a species very similar to trailing wild-daisy, occurs from Colorado to Nevada, Arizona, and Texas and south into Mexico. This densely hairy species has narrowly reverse-lance-shaped to spatula-shaped, entire or somewhat lobed basal leaves, and narrowly linear to reverse-lance-shaped stem leaves. The stems are branched at the base, but often are initially erect, the spreading branches being produced later. The flower heads are solitary, three-eighths of an inch wide at base, and have numerous white or pink ray flowers. Little information is available concerning the abundance and palatability of these close relatives, but it is probable that in low palatability and aggressive tendencies they resemble the trailing wild-daisy.

ROCKY MOUNTAIN WILD-DAISY

Eri'geron macran'thus

Flower heads—rather large, usually several, borne in a somewhat flat-topped cluster, on stalks from the upper leaf axils

Outer (ray) flowers of heads—numerous, narrow, strap-shaped, about ½ in. long, lilac to bluish purple

Bracts—in a 2-rowed series (involucre) around base of flower head, narrow, about equal, finely glandular

Center (disk) flowers of heads—numerous, yellow, tubular

"Seed" (achene)—flat, 2-nerved, crowned by numerous, slender, white bristles (pappus); outer bristles often somewhat scale-like

Stems—leafy, hairless or sparingly hairy above, up to 32, in. high

Leaves—alternate, entire, conspicuously long-hairy on the margin, 3-nerved, dull green; basal leaves stalked, reverse-lance-shaped, 2 to 4 in. long; stem leaves oval to narrowly lance-shaped, long-pointed, stalkless, the lower ones nearly as large as basal leaves, the upper ones reduced, chiefly egg-shaped

Rootstock—short, underground

Roots—perennial

351

Rocky Mountain wild-daisy is a somewhat tufted perennial with erect, leafy stems and daisylike flower heads with lilac or bluish purple ray flowers. The specific name *macranthus*, derived from the Greek *macros*, long (hence, loosely, large), and *anthos*, flower, refers to the relatively large flower heads of this species. Rocky Mountain wild-daisy, as the name implies, occurs chiefly in the mountains from British Columbia to Oregon, Arizona, New Mexico, South Dakota, and Alberta. This species is found mainly in the upper ponderosa pine, aspen, lodgepole pine, and spruce belts in parks, meadows, and burns and in the sagebrush and aspen types, but also occurs in cut-over and other open timber stands, although usually it does not grow in dense shade. It is a common weed in the better, moderately moist soils and is frequently locally abundant.

The palatability of Rocky Mountain wild-daisy apparently varies in different localities. In Wyoming, Colorado, Montana, and parts of Idaho, where this species is most abundant, it usually rates as poor cattle forage and fair to fairly good for sheep. Elsewhere it is considered practically worthless as cattle forage and only poor forage for sheep. Under normal conditions, horses practically never crop this plant. Deer and elk graze it somewhat, but it probably is only an incidental item in the forage they graze. However, since it is relatively tall and leafy, and is very common and sometimes locally abundant on the mountain ranges, the species, undoubtedly, supplies a considerable amount of forage despite its low palatability.

Although it bears a general resemblance to certain sister species of *Erigeron*, as well as to some of the asters (*Aster* spp.), Rocky Mountain wild-daisy is usually easy to identify if careful attention is paid to its species characters. The one to several flower heads are borne in somewhat flat-topped clusters on comparatively short stalks arising from the upper leaf axils. The central portion of the head (disk) is about five-eighths of an inch wide and is composed of flowers with tubular yellow corollas. The border of the head is formed of numerous flowers with very narrow, lilac to bluish purple, strap-shaped corollas about one-half of an inch long. The bracts surrounding the base of the flower heads are in two rows, somewhat spreading, narrow, about equal in length, and finely glandular but not hairy. The stems are erect and unbranched, solitary or tufted, and usually very leafy. The leaves are alternate, entire, conspicuously long-hairy on the margins, distinctly three-nerved, and dull green in color. The basal leaves are about 2 to 4 inches long, reverse-lance-shaped, and stalked; the stem leaves are oval to narrowly lance-shaped, stalkless, the lower ones being nearly as large as the basal leaves. This handsome plant is hardy and has proved to be very satisfactory in ornamental cultivation.

ERIOGONUMS

Erio'gonum spp.

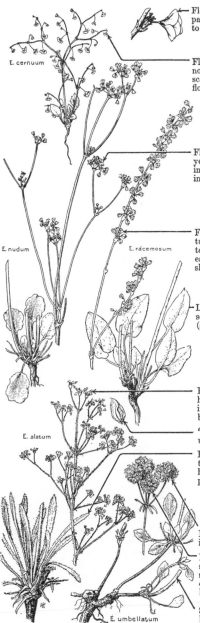

Flowers—small, with 6 petal-like outer flower parts (calyx) but without petals, stalked, few to many in a cuplike structure (involucre)

NODDING ERIOGONUM (*E. cernuum*)

Flowers—white or pink, hairless, borne in nodding-stalked, bell-shaped, 5-lobed involucres scattered along the repeatedly 2- or 3-forked flowering branches; plant an annual

BARESTEM ERIOGONUM (*E. nudum*)

Flowers—usually white, sometimes rose or yellow, in stalkless, erect, cylindric, 5-toothed involucres clustered at ends or forks of flowering branches; leaves all basal; plant perennial

REDROOT ERIOGONUM (*E. racemosum*)

Flowers—pink or white, in stalkless, erect, tubular-bell-shaped, 5-toothed involucres scattered (racemose) along the flowering branches; each involucre with 3 scalelike, united bractlets sheathing it

Leaves—basal, long-stalked, elliptic or oblong, sometimes heart-shaped, densely woolly-hairy (at least beneath); plant perennial

WING ERIOGONUM (*E. alatum*)

Flowers—greenish or yellowish, in stalked, hairy, top-shaped, erectly 5-toothed involucres in small groups (cymes) borne in large, open, branched clusters (panicles)

"Seeds" (achenes)—winged (alate), hairless, up to about ¼ in. long

Leaves—mostly basal, tufted, somewhat spatula-shaped, up to about 4 in. long, bristly-hairy on upper surface and on midrib beneath; plant perennial

SULPHUR ERIOGONUM (*E. umbellatum*)

Flowers—sulphur yellow, with calyx narrowed into a long, stalklike base

Involucres—long-stalked, usually 3 to 9, top-shaped, with 8 bent-back lobes, in an umbrella-shaped cluster (simple umbel), with a whorl of small, linear or reverse-egg-shaped, leaflike bracts at its base

Stems—erect, leafless, from a branching, woody base; plant perennial

E. cernuum

E. nudum

E. racemosum

E. alatum

E. umbellatum

Eriogonums constitute a large, exclusively North American genus belonging to the buckwheat family (Polygonaceae). On a conservative basis at least 175 species of *Eriogonum* occur in the western United States, the group ranking among the three largest genera of range plants. The buckwheat family also includes the well-known knotweeds (*Polygonum* spp.), docks (*Rumex* spp.), and such commonly cultivated plants as rhubarb (*Rheum rhaponticum*) and buckwheat (*Fagopyrum esculentum*). Although sometimes known as wildbuckwheats, the eriogonums do not strikingly resemble their buckwheat cousin, except for their three-angled achenes.

Growth habit within the genus is variable. The species may be frail annuals, herbaceous perennials, part shrubs, or genuine shrubs. Practically all species have well-developed taproots; some of the part shrubs have spreading or prostrate stems, which tend to root at the joints or near the ends. The herbaceous eriogonums frequently have but one main stem, which may be either simple or branched, and with or without leaves. Those species inclined to be shrubby usually have several stems, but often the flower-bearing portions are herbaceous, erect, and leafless (scapelike). The leaves are simple and entire, and in many herbaceous species are basal, but they may also occur alternately or in whorls on the stems; they are short-white-woolly in many species, but are dark green and hairless in some, at least on the upper surface. The individual flowers, mostly borne on tiny stalklets, are perfect, typically small, and usually occur in groups of several flowers, more or less protruding from a four- to eight-toothed flower-cluster cup (involucre). Although true petals are lacking, the more or less united outer flower parts (calyx, or perianth) are colored, petallike, six-parted or cleft and are persistent around the single, usually three-angled "seed" (achene); there are nine stamens. The flower clusters may be borne in heads, in stalked, umbrella-shaped groups (umbels), or scattered along the flowering branches, or at the ends of scapelike stems.

The eriogonums appear at practically all elevations, from sea level to above timber line. However, throughout their range they are plants of essentially dry situations, preferring rocky, sandy, and well-drained soils in regions of moderate or low rainfall, and can even withstand long and dry summers. They almost invariably grow in exposed, sunny, and warm sites, even when associated with brush, coniferous, or other woodland types. The genus is perhaps most abundantly represented in the foothill areas, especially those bordering the deserts of the Intermountain region.

As a group the eriogonums are inferior forage plants. Their use is limited largely to spring and fall or winter. In the spring the new growth, especially in the herbaceous species, is somewhat succulent, so that livestock tend to crop it, or to nip off the flower heads as they develop. Because of the absence of more palatable forage during the fall or winter, the somewhat shrubby species are at least slightly grazed. Taken as a whole, the eriogonums, so far as their herbage is concerned, probably average from worthless to poor for cattle, and from poor to fair for sheep. Livestock, however, particularly sheep, are fond of the flowering tops and frequently pick these off and ignore the rest.

The eriogonums seldom form extensive patches or become the dominant vegetation, but are characteristically scattered with greater or less frequency among associated plants; exceptions to this rule include the local concentration of some annual species on depleted areas.

A number of species, by reason of wide distribution, local frequency, or some other factor, rate special mention. Nodding eriogonum (*E. cer'nuum*), for example, is often common in waste places and overgrazed areas on the plains, foothills, and in canyons upward to the spruce belt. It ranges from Alberta and Saskatchewan, to Nebraska, Kansas, New Mexico, California, and Oregon. This annual usually grows from 6 to 12 inches high, and is much branched, especially above. The small white or pinkish flowers are borne in numerous, characteristically nodding, stalked clusters scattered along the branches of the inflorescence. This species is negligible as a forage plant.

Desert-trumpet (*E. infla'tum*), sometimes called Indianpipe weed, is another interesting annual, which ranges from Colorado and New Mexico to California, and is common along washes and on mesas and desert areas. As the specific name *inflatum* suggests, the tubular stems, naked except for the basal leaves, are inflated and trumpetlike near their ends, and somewhat resemble a cigarette holder. After the terminal, diffusely branched inflorescences fall off (often as units) and are blown away, the remaining stems whiten and tend to separate at the joints into pieces, which, when strewn over the ground, have given rise to the book name cigaretteplant, sometimes applied to this species.

Broom eriogonum (*E. vimi'neum*) has several wiry stems much branched above; the branches have a broomlike appearance, being borne rather stiffly erect. The stalkless, rose-colored, or yellowish flower clusters are scattered. Nowhere throughout its range, from Washington and Idaho to Utah, Arizona, and California, is this annual at all important as a forage plant.

Sorrell eriogonum (*E. polycla'don*) is a densely white-woolly annual with erect, many-branched stems from about 12 to 20 inches high. Its numerous, bright rose pink flowers, rather suggestive of sorrel, are borne in slender, one-sided racemes. It occurs scatteringly in dry, open, sandy, or gravelly plains and foothills from western Texas to Arizona, and has a little local utility as a sheep and cattle weed. Bidwell and Wooton [1] have published a chemical analysis of this plant.

The perennial eriogonums can be roughly arranged in three groups: (1) herbaceous, (2) partly shrubby, and (3) shrubs. Those species in the first group usually have stout taproots, a basal rosette of leaves, and annually produce herbaceous stems during a relatively short period in the spring, when moisture conditions are favorable. A number of the species in this group are common and widely distributed in the range country.

Wing eriogonum (*E. ala'tum*), a large, rather coarse, hairy weed with an erect, more or less leafy main stem, usually from 12 to about 40 inches high, and a much-branched (paniculate) inflorescence, is distributed from southern Wyoming to Nebraska, Texas, Arizona, and Utah. It prefers dry, sandy soils in open situations, occurring scatteringly among sagebrush and other dry-site plants from the foothills upward to the spruce belt. Where sufficiently abundant this is a fair species on southwestern goat and sheep ranges.

Rush eriogonum (*E. ela'tum*), so called because of its rushlike, almost leafless stems, is another rather tall, perennial, herbaceous eriogonum, sometimes attaining a height of about 3 feet. The common name catsfoot is frequently applied to this plant on account of its rounded clusters of whitish flowers borne prinicipally at the ends of the repeatedly three-forked flowering branches. The erect, long-stalked, basal leaves, especially on the more robust individuals, sometimes strikingly resemble those of a small arrowleaf balsamroot (*Balsamorhiza sagittata*). Rush eriogonum prefers the drier, rather rocky sites. Although widely distributed and common—it occurs from Washington to Idaho, Nevada, and California—it lacks forage importance.

Barestem eriogonum (*E. nu'dum*), sometimes called tibinagua, varies greatly in aspect and characters; at least nine of its varieties have been published. Typically, it has tall, slender, hairless stems, with basal leaves arising from a short woody root crown. The slender-stalked leaves are densely short-white-woolly beneath, but soon become hairless on the upper surface, or nearly so. The flowers are usually white, but sometimes are rose-colored or yellow, and are borne in clusters on a repeatedly two- or three-forked inflorescence. Barestem eriogonum grows scatteringly throughout the dry hills, valley flats, and mountain slopes from Washington to California and Nevada; a peculiar form, tentatively identified as this species, has been collected on the Weiser National Forest, west central Idaho. The young, succulent stems are palatable but, later in the season, livestock but rarely display any interest in them.

Redroot eriogonum (*E. racemo'sum*) is a white-woolly herb with one or more stoutish stems, usually from 8 to 32 inches high, arising from a thick, red-colored, woody taproot. Stalkless, close-pressed groups of white or pink flowers are borne in one-sided, spikelike clusters (cymes). The petal-like flower lobes (perianth) enlarge as the seed develops. Redroot eriogonum grows scatteringly on dry plains, in canyons, and on mountain slopes of the sagebrush belt upward to the spruce belt, from Colorado to Texas, Arizona, and Nevada. It is hardly important as a forage plant, although deer on the Kaibab National Forest, northern Arizona, have been reported as eating the stalks.

Three species of low, more or less cushionlike, eriogonums woody at the base may be mentioned because of their wide distribution and abundance:

[1] Bidwell, G. L., and Wooton, E. O. SALTBUSHES AND THEIR ALLIES IN THE UNITED STATES. U. S. Dept. Agr. Bull. 1345, 40 pp., illus. 1925.

James eriogonum (*E. jame'sii*), known locally as antelope sage, ground chaparral, ground eriogonum, and redroot, ranges from Kansas and Colorado to Arizona, Texas, and south into northern Mexico. Although its base is woody and somewhat branched, it is not so conspicuously cushionlike in appearance as the other two species mentioned immediately below, on account of the spreading stems and the repeatedly and irregularly forked, erect flower stalks with their leafy nodes. The long-stalked, spatula-shaped or oblong, mostly basal leaves are green and sparingly woolly-hairy above and densely gray-woolly-hairy beneath. Probably the most characteristic feature of this species is the repeatedly and irregularly branching (proliferating) habit of the headlike clusters of whitish or pale yellowish flowers which often become somewhat pink in age. In general, James eriogonum is almost worthless as forage.

Cushion eriogonum (*E. ovalifo'lium*), sometimes called ovalleaf eriogonum or silver plant, ranges from British Columbia and Alberta southward to New Mexico, Arizona, and California, and prefers exposed, rather rocky sites on plains and slopes from the sagebrush to the spruce belts. The color of the flowers varies from whitish or yellowish to pink, rose, wine-red, or even purplish; these color differences have been considered by some botanists as deserving varietal, or even specific, rank. The low cushion of leaves from the short, closely branched, woody caudex, and the numerous, rather short and slender scapelike flower stalks with their single, headlike flower clusters, constitute the characteristic growth habit of the species. Although cushion eriogonum is cropped to some extent by sheep and goats as good winter feed and on some exposed sites is a valuable ground cover, it is generally very sparse.

Piper eriogonum (*E. pi'peri*) is a northwestern species, ranging on high open, sunny sites from Washington and Oregon to Montana and northwestern Wyoming. It resembles yellow eriogonum (*E. fla'vum*) of the Rocky Mountains, differing mainly in its taller flower stalks and long-soft-hairy rather than woolly-hairy leaves. The woody, short-branched, cushionlike root crown is covered by long-stalked, erect leaves and numerous, slender flower stalks often 8 to 10 inches in height, which give the plant a herbaceous aspect. The greenish yellow hairy flowers, often tipped with scarlet in age, are borne in an equally five- to eight-rayed headlike umbel, subtended by a whorl of small leaves. Piper eriogonum is practically worthless as forage, and has become conspicuously abundant on certain badly depleted ranges in the Blue Mountains.

The partly shrubby species are divided more or less roughly into two types: (1) those with short, woody-branched root crown or stem bases that form dense leafy mats from which the erect flower stalks arise, and (2) those with spreading and woody stems, along which, particularly at the ends, are short, woody, upright leafy branches, whence the herbaceous flower stalks are produced. This second group of part shrubs is more important from a range standpoint than the first. Its members are very numerous, widely distributed in the range country, and are of low palatability.

Wyeth eriogonum (*E. heracleoi'des*), also called Indian-tobacco, was first collected about a hundred years ago by Nathaniel B. Wyeth, an American traveler and trader. The specific name *heracleoides* doubtless refers to a fancied resemblance of the large, umbrella-shaped clusters of yellowish flowers to those of the cowparsnip (*Heracleum lanatum*). Wyeth eriogonum is a much-branched plant, attaining a height of about 20 inches, with spreading, rather woody stems from which upright, more or less herbaceous stalks arise that bear a whorl of leaves near their middle. A rather dense covering of woolly hairs gives it a somewhat grayish appearance. It prefers the dry slopes of the ponderosa pine, aspen, and spruce belts, and is often associated with sagebrush and lanceleaf yellowbrush. Throughout its range, from British Columbia, Montana, and Wyoming to Utah and Nevada, this species is scattered and common, but seldom abundant and has little or no forage value.

Sulphur eriogonum (*E. umbella'tum*), a variable species of which numerous varieties have been proposed, has a wide range, extending from Montana, Wyoming, and Colorado west to the Pacific Coast States. It prefers open, dry situations in the valleys and on the mountain sides upward to the subalpine belt, but is seldom abundant. Typically it has showy, sulphur-yellow flowers in several-rayed, umbrella-like flower clusters subtended by a whorl of leaves. The rather bare (scapelike), herbaceous flower stalks arise from a branched, woody base which is tufted with leaves at the nodes.

Some of the representative shrub species of *Eriogonum* are treated briefly in connection with the discussion of Wright buckwheatbrush (B75).

ALFILERIA

Ero'dium cicuta'rium

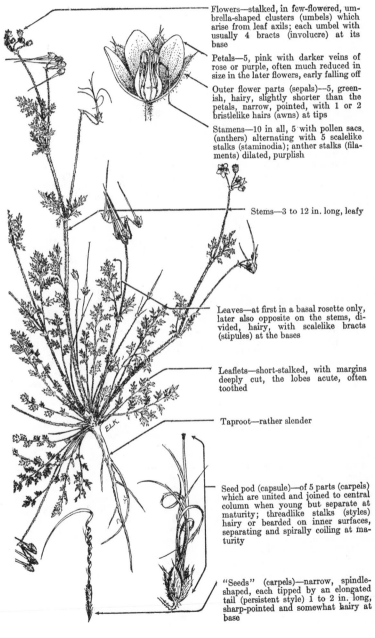

Flowers—stalked, in few-flowered, umbrella-shaped clusters (umbels) which arise from leaf axils; each umbel with usually 4 bracts (involucre) at its base

Petals—5, pink with darker veins of rose or purple, often much reduced in size in the later flowers, early falling off

Outer flower parts (sepals)—5, greenish, hairy, slightly shorter than the petals, narrow, pointed, with 1 or 2 bristlelike hairs (awns) at tips

Stamens—10 in all, 5 with pollen sacs (anthers) alternating with 5 scalelike stalks (staminodia); anther stalks (filaments) dilated, purplish

Stems—3 to 12 in. long, leafy

Leaves—at first in a basal rosette only, later also opposite on the stems, divided, hairy, with scalelike bracts (stipules) at the bases

Leaflets—short-stalked, with margins deeply cut, the lobes acute, often toothed

Taproot—rather slender

Seed pod (capsule)—of 5 parts (carpels) which are united and joined to central column when young but separate at maturity; threadlike stalks (styles) hairy or bearded on inner surfaces, separating and spirally coiling at maturity

"Seeds" (carpels)—narrow, spindle-shaped, each tipped by an elongated tail (persistent style) 1 to 2 in. long, sharp-pointed and somewhat hairy at base

Alfileria, also known as alfilerilla, filaree or redstem filaree, heronbill, pin-clover, pingrass, and storksbill, is an annual herb of the geranium family (Geraniaceae). This family is represented in the United States by two genera, *Geranium* and *Erodium*, both of which are easily recognized by their distinctive, beaked fruiting structures. In *Erodium* the hairy tails on the "seeds" (carpels) become spirally twisted and form a remarkable device of great importance in planting the sharp-pointed "seeds" effectively, since they unwind when moistened (hygroscopic motion), thus boring into the ground and firmly anchoring the seed. This species is a somewhat hairy weed of the rosette type, but it sometimes forms clumps. It is considerably branched from the base, and the reddish-colored stems are low and spreading or somewhat ascending. The name, *Erodium*, is from the Greek word, *erodios* (a heron). Alfileria is derived from the Spanish word *alfiler* meaning a pin. The name alfileria, sometimes spelled alfilaria, is now most often pronounced al-fill-ear'-ree-ah.

This plant is a native of Europe and has been introduced into the New World from the Mediterranean region, which is its original home. It is now well established in southern Canada and most of the United States, especially in the warmer areas, and extends into Mexico. It is common in all of the western range States and thrives particularly well in so-called desert ranges of Arizona and in the valleys and foothills of California, where it probably reaches its maximum growth in this country. The plant appears to have been introduced into the Southwest by the Spanish Conquistadores and later to have invaded other portions of the North American continent from that region. It occurs from the desert up to the aspen belt, but is most common in semiarid valleys and canyons and on the plains, mesas, and foothills of the piñon-juniper type (Upper Sonoran Zone). It grows well in sandy soils and often occurs on waste land and denuded areas. That the species is an aggressive invader, which spreads very rapidly, is indicated by the wide distribution which it has achieved since its introduction into this country.

Alfileria furnishes choice spring forage for all classes of livestock and is also relished by deer and possibly by other game animals. It makes a very vigorous growth early in the spring and is one of the very first plants to begin development at that time. In the most arid portions of its range it matures rapidly, dries up readily, and soon disappears. It also supplies winter forage, since it often begins to grow in the Southwest after the fall rains and may remain green all winter, if the season is mild, and it may even achieve some growth during the warm periods. Thornber [1] indicates that alfileria is perhaps the most valuable species of the group of winter annuals in Arizona, where the dried and discolored stems are often eaten by livestock until the beginning of the summer rains, when other forage becomes available. Together with Indianwheat (*Plantago*) it is one of the outstanding sheep weeds on desert lambing grounds about Phoenix, Ariz.

Over much of its range, alfileria occurs as a small, rather scattered plant and, under such conditions, produces but little forage. However, on favorable areas in the Southwestern States and California and, to some extent, elsewhere, it produces in the aggregate a large amount of herbage. On such ranges, where it grows in abundance, it often provides a large portion of the spring forage over extensive areas. It tends to hug the ground closely on heavily grazed range and thus somewhat protects itself by becoming less readily accessible. It evidences a marked ability to reproduce and maintain itself, and even succeeds in spreading on arid lands in spite of heavy grazing. This aggressiveness, coupled with its palatability and nutritive value, make alfileria a highly esteemed forage plant on many ranges.

The flowering period—usually from February to May—varies considerably, depending upon the region and the amount and distribution of seasonal rainfall. As a rule the seeds germinate in the fall or winter. Sampson [2] found that the germination of alfileria seed is high when collected in the late fall, but low when collected in the early summer and that, in artificial reseeding with the species, some preliminary soil treatment is necessary.

---

[1] Thornber, J. J. THE GRAZING RANGES OF ARIZONA. Ariz. Agr. Expt. Sta. Bull. 65: [245]–360, illus. 1910.
[2] Sampson, A. W. COLLECTION AND SOWING OF ALFILARIA SEED. U. S. Dept. Agr., Rev. Forest Serv. Invest. 2: 14–17. 1913.

CALIFORNIA-POPPY

Eschschol'tzia califor'nica

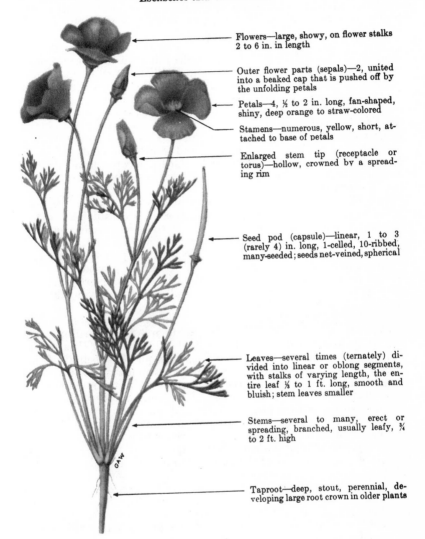

Flowers—large, showy, on flower stalks 2 to 6 in. in length

Outer flower parts (sepals)—2, united into a beaked cap that is pushed off by the unfolding petals

Petals—4, ½ to 2 in. long, fan-shaped, shiny, deep orange to straw-colored

Stamens—numerous, yellow, short, attached to base of petals

Enlarged stem tip (receptacle or torus)—hollow, crowned by a spreading rim

Seed pod (capsule)—linear, 1 to 3 (rarely 4) in. long, 1-celled, 10-ribbed, many-seeded; seeds net-veined, spherical

Leaves—several times (ternately) divided into linear or oblong segments, with stalks of varying length, the entire leaf ⅓ to 1 ft. long, smooth and bluish; stem leaves smaller

Stems—several to many, erect or spreading, branched, usually leafy, ¾ to 2 ft. high

Taproot—deep, stout, perennial, developing large root crown in older plants

California-poppy has attracted wide attention because of its abundance and great beauty. Much has been written about its charm, and many legends bear testimony to the fascination it has exercised on those who know it in its native haunts. Californians selected it for their State flower in 1890, thus making it the first generally accepted State flower in the Union. The early Spanish inhabitants called it copa de ora (cup of gold), and legend explains that the orange petals, turning to gold, filled the soil with the precious metal so eagerly sought for by the Forty-niners. The large, beautiful flowers unfold only in the full sunlight; when the plants are abundant the whole landscape may be gilded by their intense color. The species easily ranks among the most attractive native plants of the Pacific coast. Originally, it occurred from the lower Columbia River country to Lower California, in Mexico, and east to Arizona, but attained its best development and greatest abundance in the foothills and valleys of California. Garden escapes have increased its range so that it now appears, at least occasionally, in most of the Western States.

This species most commonly grows in patches or extensive fields, but always in the full sunlight. It occurs in a considerable variety of soils, provided they are porous or that there is sufficient slope for surplus moisture to drain away. Common sites are idle grain fields, railroad rights-of-way, and dry washes, but the plant becomes especially abundant on low, open, unused, or lightly grazed hills. The species is generally limited to low elevations, seldom growing naturally above 2,500 feet in California and occurring below the ponderosa pine belt throughout its natural range.

The foliage of California-poppy is not very palatable to livestock; it is rated as poor forage for cattle and fair for sheep. This deficiency in forage value appears to be due to some disagreeable taste, as otherwise the foliage has desirable qualities, being soft and juicy and remaining green long after the common associated plants have matured. It seems to have a higher palatability as a silage. In one study of plants harvested in full bloom, the cured silage was wet and slimy, with a pleasant odor and was eaten readily by cattle.[1] Livestock losses have been reported as due to California-poppy, although the toxic effect has not been verified by experimental feeding. The close relationship of this species to the opium poppy (*Papaver somniferum*) of the Old World doubtless explains, in part, why the former is sometimes suspected to be poisonous.

California-poppy is cultivated extensively as an ornamental, usually as a hardy annual, in most temperate climates and has now become naturalized in Europe, Australia, and elsewhere. The large, showy flowers and attractive bluish green foliage adapt this species for border plantings. In its native habitat, the bright, highly colored blossoms are extensively gathered for home decoration. The Indians are reputed to have used it as a food, boiling or roasting the foliage and then rinsing in water before eating. The Spanish-Americans prized as a hair oil a concoction made by boiling the

<hr/>

[1] Westover, H. L. SILAGE PALATABILITY TESTS. Jour. Amer. Soc. Agron. 26(2): 106–116. 1934.

leaves in olive oil, straining and adding perfume.[2] The foliage yields a drug that has some use as a harmless substitute for morphine to relieve headache and insomnia. This species, however, does not contain opium, although it does apparently produce a small amount of morphine.[3]

A very variable plant, California-poppy has been the subject of considerable taxonomic study. The species *E. columbiana* and *E. douglasii* of Oregon and Washington, for example, are sometimes considered variations of *E. californica*. In California, the apparent difference of various geographic races largely disappeared when they were grown under identical conditions.[4] In the Sacramento and San Joaquin Valleys, one variety (*E. californica crocea*) has two seasonal phases:[4] In the spring the stems are numerous and erect, the flowers are large and deep orange, and the receptacle ring very pronounced; in the summer the stems are fewer and more spreading, the buds much shorter and not long-pointed, the flowers small, pale or straw-colored, and the receptacle ring much reduced.

The individual plants of California-poppy are fairly compact, having many leaves and numerous stems. The foliage contains a colorless juice, but the juice of the roots may sometimes be reddish. The flowers appear in the spring, although, as mentioned previously, some varieties (as *crocea*) bloom again in the summer or fall.

GOLDPOPPIES

Eschschol'tzia spp.

The goldpoppies, a western North American genus of the poppy family (Papaveraceae), are annual or perennial herbs with watery, bitter juice. All the species resemble California-poppy in having stalked (petioled), ternately divided leaves, 2 sepals united into a cap, which is pushed off by the 4 unfolding, shiny and orange or straw-colored petals, and elongated, many-seeded capsules. The species are most abundant in California. The genus was named by the eminent German author, traveler, and botanist, Adelbert von Chamisso, in honor of his friend and co-worker, Dr. J. F. Eschscholtz, who was his companion during the Kotzebue scientific expedition around the world, visiting California in 1816.

As a group goldpoppies inhabit well-drained, sunny slopes, in the foothills and valleys and desert areas below the ponderosa pine belt.

Several species, notably *E. mexicana* and *E. glyptosperma*, occur in the desert areas, growing in the sagebrush and creosotebush (*Covillea*) belts in the Intermountain and Southwest regions. These species, however, are relatively unimportant on the range, being of

---

[2] Smith, E. E. THE GOLDEN POPPY. 231 pp., illus. Palo Alto, Calif. 1902.
[3] Wood, H. C., Remington, J. P., and Sadtler, S. P., assisted by Lyons, A. B., and Wood, H. C., Jr. THE DISPENSATORY OF THE UNITED STATES OF AMERICA, BY DR. GEO. B. WOOD AND DR. FRANKLIN BACHE. Ed. 19, thoroughly rev. and largely rewritten . . . 1,749 pp. Philadelphia and London. 1907.
[4] Jepson, W. L. A MANUAL OF THE FLOWERING PLANTS OF CALIFORNIA. 1,238 pp., illus. Berkeley, Calif. [1925.]

sparse or local distribution. Of the various species California-poppy is the most important, being the largest and the only one of the genus that grows in such profusion as sometimes to dominate the landscape with its gaudy color.

The members of this genus do not yield opium. This drug is derived from the juice of the opium poppy, which is extensively cultivated in the Old World.

BLUELEAF STRAWBERRY

Fraga'ria glau'ca, syn. *F. ova'lis glau'ca*

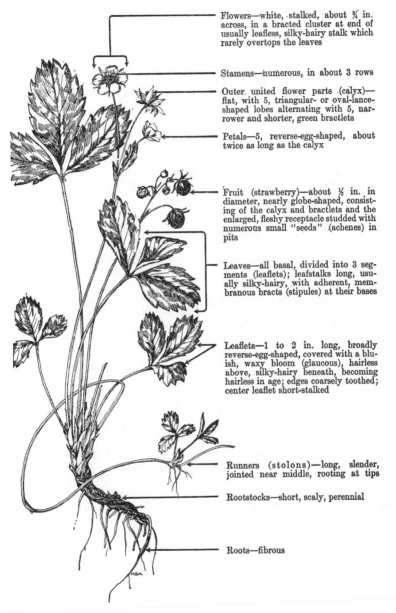

Flowers—white, stalked, about ¾ in. across, in a bracted cluster at end of usually leafless, silky-hairy stalk which rarely overtops the leaves

Stamens—numerous, in about 3 rows

Outer united flower parts (calyx)—flat, with 5, triangular- or oval-lance-shaped lobes alternating with 5, narrower and shorter, green bractlets

Petals—5, reverse-egg-shaped, about twice as long as the calyx

Fruit (strawberry)—about ½ in. in diameter, nearly globe-shaped, consisting of the calyx and bractlets and the enlarged, fleshy receptacle studded with numerous small "seeds" (achenes) in pits

Leaves—all basal, divided into 3 segments (leaflets); leafstalks long, usually silky-hairy, with adherent, membranous bracts (stipules) at their bases

Leaflets—1 to 2 in. long, broadly reverse-egg-shaped, covered with a bluish, waxy bloom (glaucous), hairless above, silky-hairy beneath, becoming hairless in age; edges coarsely toothed; center leaflet short-stalked

Runners (stolons)—long, slender, jointed near middle, rooting at tips

Rootstocks—short, scaly, perennial

Roots—fibrous

Blueleaf strawberry, one of the most common and widespread of the native western strawberries, may properly be considered as representative of the genus *Fragaria* in the West. The common name blueleaf and the specific name *glauca* both refer to the bluish white, waxy bloom on the lower surface of the leaves. This strawberry appears from Alaska and the District of Mackenzie south to Nevada, Arizona, New Mexico, and South Dakota. It occurs at altitudes between 3,000 and 8,000 feet in Montana, but in Colorado, principally from about 8,000 to 11,500 feet. Blueleaf strawberry thrives on dry to moist, sandy or clayey loam soils in the open woods, aspen groves, and meadows of the foothills and mountains, especially in canyons of the aspen and spruce belts. It is never very abundant and usually occurs as scattered individuals, although occasionally growing in small patches on satisfactory sites.

This species possesses but little forage value, having a palatability of from practically worthless to poor, or occasionally fair, for sheep and is practically worthless for cattle. The fruit frequently attains fair size and is of good flavor, being eaten readily by birds and various small rodents. It is unimportant for human consumption, seldom producing enough berries in any one patch to provide much fruit at one time.

STRAWBERRIES (Fraga'ria spp.)

The genus *Fragaria* belongs to the rose family (*Rosaceae*). Strawberries are low, apparently stemless, perennial herbs with underground, scaly rootstocks; they also have runners, which root at the tips, producing new plants. The generally rather numerous, basal leaves are composed of three, usually toothed leaflets; the rather long leafstalks (petioles) are sheathed at the base by a pair of membranous bracts (stipules). The flowers are white, rarely reddish, borne in flat-topped clusters on usually leafless stems (scapes), the central flowers being the first to blossom. The numerous, short, seed-producing organs (pistils) are borne on a cone-shaped, fleshy receptacle. The pistils, ripening into small, hard "seeds" (achenes), persist on the receptacle, which becomes pulpy and enlarged to form the familiar, edible "berry".

Strawberries are native in Europe, northern Asia, North America, and the cooler portions of India and South America. They extend from the low plains to alpine elevations in the high mountains, both in open, sunny situations and in the shade of brush and timber. Some 150 species have been described; actually, however, the genus probably includes less than 50 conservatively valid species. Leading authorities [1] report about 27 species in North America, of which approximately 11 are found on western ranges. The fact that these plants cross freely and produce mostly perfect hybrids, must be considered in estimating the accurate number of true species.

The generic name *Fragaria* comes from the Latin *fragum*, strawberry, a word derived from *fragrans*, fragrant, alluding to the attractive odor of the fruit. The origin of the common name strawberry is somewhat obscure; many authorities derive it from the An-

---

[1] Rydberg, P. A. ROSACEAE (PARS). North Amer. Flora 22: 293–388. 1908.

glo-Saxon *streawberige* (*streaw*, straw, and *berige*, berry), which, in turn, they say is so named from the resemblance of the plant runners to straws. Some authors (more plausibly) state that the Anglo-Saxon name means stray berry, because the runners cause the plants to stray from their original location.[2] The statement often heard, that strawberries are so named from being strawed to keep the berries clean is a fallacy, as the name of these plants obviously far antedates their cultivation.

These species are relatively unimportant as forage, generally rating as practically worthless or poor; they are grazed to a limited extent by livestock, except horses. Certain species, however, rank in some localities as fair in palatability for sheep and cattle, deer and elk. The fruits are relished by birds and rodents. The Indians have long esteemed these berries as a delicacy; in fact, most persons find time to linger for a few minutes in any patch of ripe wild strawberries to partake of the small but very appetizing fruits. In the words of quaint old Dr. Boteler (as quoted by Izaak Walton in his Compleat Angler), "Doubtless God could have made a better berry, but doubtless God never did."

The records fail to show that strawberries were cultivated by the Romans, who knew these plants exclusively as wild fruit. Strawberries were cultivated in France as early as the fourteenth century,[2] [3] but it was not until the sixteenth century that frequent mention is made of this table delicacy by various European writers, who refer both to the wild fruits and to those cultivated in gardens.[4] The Flemish botanist, de l'Obel (1538–1616), after whom our plant genus *Lobelia* is named, was apparently the first to give a distinct name to a cultivated variety of strawberry when, in 1576, he designated a variety of the Hautbois strawberry (*F. moscha'ta*, syn. *F. ela'tior*), having a large pale-colored berry, as Le Chapiron (or, later, Chapiton).[4] The early American colonists were much impressed by the abundance as well as the large size and sweet, agreeable flavor of the wild Virginia strawberry (*F. virginia'na*), which was superior to any of the three native European species; Virginia strawberry was forthwith introduced into England, where it became widely known and was improved under cultivation. In the meantime, the large, firm-fruited Chiloë strawberry (*F. chiloen'sis*), a native of the Pacific coast from Alaska to Chile, was introduced into France from Chile in 1712 by a French officer named Frezier. Strawberry culture was not begun in North America on any scale until about 1800, because of the abundant supply of appetizing wild berries. There were, however, collections in private gardens of English-improved varieties of Virginia strawberry, Chiloë strawberry, the "pine" strawberry (*F. ananas'sa*, syn. *F. grandiflo'ra*), and the native European species, *i. e.*, alpine strawberry (*F. ves'ca*), often

² Robbins, W. W., and Ramaley, F. PLANTS USEFUL TO MAN. 428 pp., illus. Philadelphia. 1933.
³ Fletcher, S. W. THE STRAWBERRY IN NORTH AMERICA: HISTORY, ORIGIN, BOTANY, AND BREEDING. 234 pp., illus. New York. 1917.
⁴ Sturtevant, E. L. NOTES ON THE HISTORY OF THE STRAWBERRY. Mass. Hort. Soc. Trans. (1888), Pt. 1: 191–204. 1888.

called wood strawberry, and the Hautbois strawberry, all of which had been introduced from Europe.[3]

The exact origin of our present garden strawberries is unknown, although the general opinion is that they are hybrids from the Virginia and Chiloë strawberries.[5] [6] The pine strawberry, progenitor of our modern strawberry, which first appeared in Europe about 1750, apparently was a hybrid of these two species.[3] [5] Recent genetical research[5] strongly indicates that neither the alpine nor the Hautbois strawberry played a part in the development of the garden type, despite that the alpine strawberry became naturalized in this country at an early date. It is notable, however, that the Hovey strawberry (parentage uncertain), originating in Boston in 1834, was the first named variety of any fruit produced in North America by systematic plant breeding.[3]

Strawberry breeding, designed to improve the flavor and shipping quality, and to develop strains adapted to a particular climate, has been carried on rather extensively, especially in recent years. The United States Department of Agriculture has sponsored much of this work; Government specialists have been experimenting with strawberries since 1920 in Maryland, North Carolina, and Oregon.[6] [7] Thousands of hybrid seedlings have been produced as a result of the use of both wild and cultivated varieties of strawberries as experimental (parent) stock. The wild stock included some 75 collections of native strawberries of the West made by national forest officers, working in cooperation with the Division of Range Research of the United States Forest Service. As a result of this intensive breeding work seven new and superior varieties of strawberries were selected and introduced to the trade by 1925.[6]

---

[3] See footnote on preceding page.
[5] Mangelsdorf, A. J. ORIGIN OF THE GARDEN STRAWBERRY. Jour. Heredity 18 : 177–184, illus. 1927.
[6] Darrow, G. M., Waldo, G. F., Schuster, C. E., and Pickett, B. S. TWELVE YEARS OF STRAWBERRY BREEDING . . . Jour. Heredity 25 (11) : 451–462, illus. 1934.
[7] Darrow, G. M., Waldo, G. F., and Schuster, C. E. TWELVE YEARS OF STRAWBERRY BREEDING. Jour. Heredity 24 : 391–402, illus. 1933.

NORTHERN BEDSTRAW

Ga'lium borea'le

Flowers—white, small (about ⅛ in. wide), numerous, stalked, borne in branched, showy end clusters (compound cymes)

Threadlike stalks (styles)—2-branched, tipping seed-producing organ (ovary), with knob-like ends (stigmas)

United petals (corolla)—wheel-shaped, with 4 spreading lobes; outer flower parts (sepals) lacking

Stamens—4, alternating with corolla lobes

Seed pod (capsule)—globular, about ¹⁄₁₆ in. in diameter, 2-celled, 2-seeded, somewhat stiff-hairy to smooth, dry and separating into 2 parts when mature

Stems—erect, up to about 2½ ft. high, 4-angled, usually rough on the angles but otherwise hairless, arising from underground, perennial, slender, woody rootstocks

Leaves—opposite but alternating with 2 leaf-like bracts (stipules), thus appearing as whorls of 4, linear to broadly lance-shaped, about ½ to 2 in. long, distinctly 3-veined, thick, blunt-tipped

Northern bedstraw is an erect, leafy perennial with 4-angled stems and numerous small white flowers. It takes its specific name from the Latin *borealis* (-e), northern. This is a widely distributed species which occurs in all the Western States, ranging in North America from Alaska to Quebec, New Jersey, Missouri, New Mexico, and California. It also occurs in Europe and northern Asia. Although usually scattered, it is of general occurrence from the plains and foothills to an elevation of 10,000 feet in the mountains of Colorado and New Mexico. It is typical in grass and weed types of parks, in brush types, in aspen and, to some extent, in open coniferous timber.

It favors moderately moist, rich loam soils, but is found on a wide variety of dry to moist soils.

This species is common and often forms an appreciable part of the plant cover, although not occurring in pure stands. It is practically worthless as forage for cattle and horses, and is only fair forage for sheep and goats which generally crop only the flowers and leaves. It is one of the species that is likely to increase on ranges which are somewhat overgrazed.

This species grows from perennial rootstocks normally producing numerous, leafy, sterile shoots as well as a number of flowering stems. The leaves appear to be in whorls of four, but actually are in pairs (opposite), each pair being accompanied by two bracts (stipules) which are similar to the leaves. Northern bedstraw forms attractive and conspicuous white bunches when in full bloom and is sometimes grown as an ornamental, especially in rock gardens.

BEDSTRAWS

Ga'lium spp.

The bedstraws, which belong to the very large madder family (*Rubiaceae*), compose a genus of anual or perennial herbs or woody perennials widely distributed throughout temperate regions. The majority of the madder family, including all the more important economic genera, such as coffee (*Coffea* spp.) and the Peruvian-bark trees (*Cinchona* spp.) from which quinine is obtained, are tropical trees, shrubs, and vines. Some authorities state that the generic name *Galium* is derived from the Greek *galion*, bedstraw; others claim that the word *galium* is derived from the Greek word for milk, *gala*, since certain species were used to curdle milk. Bedstraw is probably the most common name for species of *Galium*, but some species are known as cleavers (from *cleave*, to adhere closely).

Approximately 43 species and 9 varieties of bedstraw are indigenous in the West, about 9 species being undershrubby or shrubby, the rest often weak and trailing herbs.[1] In addition, several herbaceous species have been naturalized from the Old World. Bedstraws occur on a wide variety of soils and in practically all types from the lower elevations to above timberline, but probably are most common in grass, weed, and brush types. These plants, especially the smaller herbaceous species, are very common and make up an appreciable part of the plant cover on many western ranges, although they do not, as a rule, occur in dense stands to the exclusion of other plants.

The shrubby species of bedstraws usually have coarse, woody stems, small, thick, often pricklelike leaves, and are practically worthless as forage plants. Although the palatability varies with the different species and regions, the herbaceous species, in general, are of fair palatability to sheep and goats and of low to zero palatability to cattle and horses. Bedstraws like many of the relatively unpalatable range plants tend to increase, to a certain extent, on overgrazed ranges.

Several species of bedstraws were formerly used as medicinal plants. Goosegrass bedstraw (*G. aparine*), an annual common in North America, Europe, and Asia, and usually called goosegrass from its use as food for geese, was probably the most generally used in medicine. The roots of dye bedstraw (*G. tinctorium*) were used by the Indians in the preparation of red and yellow dyes. The roots of white bedstraw (*G. mollugo*) yield a purple dye.

The bedstraws all have four-angled (square) stems apparently with whorls of four to eight (sometimes only two) leaves at the joints. Actually the leaves are in pairs (opposite) or in whorls of threes or fours, accompanied by two, three, or four bracts (stipules) which are similar to the leaves. The flowers are small, usually less than one-fourth of an inch wide, white or greenish-white, yellowish, or purplish. Outer flower parts (sepals) are lacking and the corolla is wheel-shaped, consisting usually of four spreading lobes. The stems and fruits of many species are beset with hooked hairs. Some species are "dioecious", i. e., the male (pollen-producing) and female (seed-producing) flowers are borne on separate plants; or male, female, and perfect flowers may occur on the same plant.

---

[1] Dayton, W. A. IMPORTANT WESTERN BROWSE PLANTS. U. S. Dept. Agr. Misc. Pub. 101, 214 pp., illus. 1931.

WESTERN FRINGED GENTIAN

Gentia'na el'egans, syn. *Anthopo'gon el'egans*

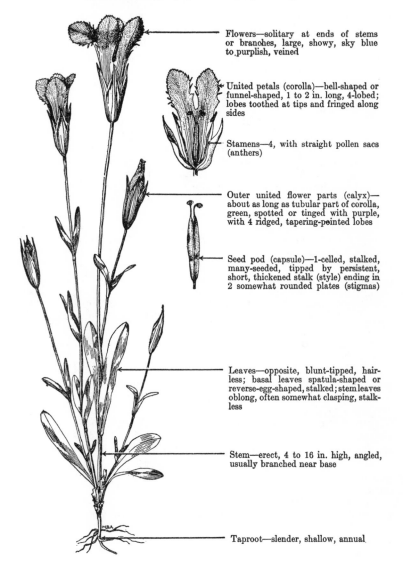

Flowers—solitary at ends of stems or branches, large, showy, sky blue to purplish, veined

United petals (corolla)—bell-shaped or funnel-shaped, 1 to 2 in. long, 4-lobed; lobes toothed at tips and fringed along sides

Stamens—4, with straight pollen sacs (anthers)

Outer united flower parts (calyx)—about as long as tubular part of corolla, green, spotted or tinged with purple, with 4 ridged, tapering-pointed lobes

Seed pod (capsule)—1-celled, stalked, many-seeded, tipped by persistent, short, thickened stalk (style) ending in 2 somewhat rounded plates (stigmas)

Leaves—opposite, blunt-tipped, hairless; basal leaves spatula-shaped or reverse-egg-shaped, stalked; stem leaves oblong, often somewhat clasping, stalkless

Stem—erect, 4 to 16 in. high, angled, usually branched near base

Taproot—slender, shallow, annual

Although feather gentian has been suggested as a desirable common name for this species, to avoid possible confusion with the fringed gentian (*G. crinita*) of the East, *Gentiana elegans* is always known as fringed gentian in the West, and it seems desirable to continue use of the latter name, though adding some modifying word, such as western, to distinguish it from its more advertised eastern cousin. Western fringed gentian, sometimes called Rocky Mountain fringed gentian, an annual herb of the gentian family (Gentianaceae), is one of the commonest of the range gentians and one of the most beautiful of western wild flowers. The specific name *elegans* is a Latin adjective meaning elegant (literally, elect, or choice). This species grows in the mountains at elevations of from about 6,000 to 13,000 feet, ranging from the Mackenzie River in northwestern Canada southward to Arizona and New Mexico. It prefers rich, moist, loam soils on open or partially shaded sites, being commonly associated with rushes and sedges. Western fringed gentian produces its handsome showy flowers chiefly during July and August. It occurs most commonly in the wet alpine and subalpine meadows of the higher mountains, and sometimes grows in such profusion that its gorgeous blue flowers emblazon wide stretches of landscape in almost ultramarine glory.

The gentians as a group—this species is no exception—are relatively low in palatability, being seldom better than poor cattle forage and fair sheep feed. However, western fringed gentian, which is so common on the higher ranges where sheep usually graze, furnishes considerable feed, although fundamentally not a good forage plant. In its native habitat, this plant possesses a high aesthetic value. It is particularly abundant in Yellowstone National Park and lends picturesque beauty to that playground. Being a plant of the higher elevations, it is not adapted to cultivation at the lower altitudes, where flower gardens customarily are located, and hence is apparently unknown to the horticultural trade. This species is probably the commonest and best known of those annual western gentians which have their flower parts in fours and the corolla lobes more or less fringed—the fringed gentians (section, subgenus or genus *Anthopogon*).

Unfortunately, the taxonomy of this gentian is greatly confused. In early American botanical manuals the species was misidentified as the Old World *G. serrata*—an error still perpetuated by some authors. Rydberg[1] states that *G. elegans* A. Nels. (1898) is a synonym of the older *G. thermalis* O. Kuntze (1891), a species based on depauperate material growing about hot springs. *G. thermalis* may, therefore, be the correct name for this species but, for the time being, it seems desirable to adhere to present usage in the Bureau of Plant Industry, United States Department of Agriculture.

---

[1] Rydberg, P. A. FLORA OF THE ROCKY MOUNTAINS AND ADJACENT PLAINS . . . 1,110 pp. New York. 1917.

GENTIANS (Gentia'na spp.)

In 1719 A. D. *Gentiana* was adopted as the generic name of this group of plants by the distinguished French botanist Tournefort (the father of plant genera). The name, however, is very old and according to Dioscorides, a Greek medical writer of the first century, B. C., commemorates Gentius, a king of Illyria in southern Europe (*circ.* 180–167 B. C.), reputedly the discoverer of the medicinal value of gentian (*i. e.*, the officinal yellow gentian (*G. lutea*) of Europe, a well-known drug plant). This large genus of annual, biennial, and perennial herbs of the gentian family (Gentianaceae) is native to the cooler portions of the earth—largely in mountainous regions and northern and north temperate areas. It is represented in every far western State, where about 36 species occur. In addition, about 11 other gentians are indigenous in the region from Alaska to British Columbia and Manitoba, and 4 other eastern species reach the edge of the range country at their western limits. Gentians characteristically grow in meadows and other moist, open sites in the mountains, although some species occur in the lower foothills or, farther north, near sea level.

Apparently correlated with their intense bitter flavor, gentians have a comparatively low palatability—mostly poor for cattle and poor to fair for sheep. Although horses seldom eat them, certain species provide fair feed for deer and elk. Some species are abundant, especially on the high summer sheep ranges, and supply considerable forage. Some observers believe that, despite their rather low palatability, gentians, because of their tonic and stomachic qualities, have a distinct value in the range menu of domestic livestock. This is a matter which merits scientific investigation.

Certain gentians, particularly yellow gentian, have long been famed for their medicinal qualities; many of the complex preparations handed down by the Greeks and Arabs contain gentian among other ingredients. Simple bitters or tonics made from gentian apparently are beneficial in all cases of digestive debility or where a general tonic is required and have proved useful in the treatment of malaria and various other diseases.[2] Gentian preparations have a somewhat sweet though bitter flavor and, if taken in overly large amounts, are likely to cause nausea. The roots of yellow gentian, relatively rich in sugar, are frequently fermented and distilled; the resultant liqueur is said to be used as a popular beverage in the Alps. The official preparations in this country include the extract, infusion, or tincture obtained from the roots of yellow gentian, although several other species have analogous properties.[2] A number of authorities have expressed the opinion that American gentians merit chemical study as possible substitutes for the Old World *G. lutea* and for other purposes.

---

[2] Wood, H. C., Remington, J. P., and Sadtler, S. P., assisted by Lyons, A. B., and Wood, H. C., Jr. THE DISPENSATORY OF THE UNITED STATES OF AMERICA, BY DR. GEO. B. WOOD AND DR. FRANKLIN BACHE. Ed. 19, thoroughly rev. and largely rewritten . . . 1,947 pp. Philadelphia and London. 1907.

The gentians have opposite (occasionally whorled), often clasping leaves, and attractive flowers with bell- or funnel-shaped, four- or five-lobed corollas, which are blue, violet-purple, greenish, yellow, red, or white. The characteristic hue of the American species is "gentian blue" and this is one of the reasons advanced by some American botanists for placing our native species in other genera— *Amarella, Anthopogon, Chondrophylla,* and *Dasystephana*—the botanical type of *Gentiana* being the Old World *G. lutea,* with yellow flowers.

Although the gentians are difficult to start, when once established, the perennials, at least, last indefinitely; many of the species rate the effort required to grow them.[3] Unfortunately, the fringed gentian (*G. crinita*), one of the most beautiful members of the genus, has not been successfully domesticated.[3] In fact, this eastern species is threatened with extinction as a result of the thoughtlessness of countless "nature lovers" who pick the beautiful blossoms at every opportunity. This is the fringed gentian that the poet Bryant, in his well-known ode of that name, described as "colored with the heaven's own blue."

The eastern and western fringed gentians are representative of those species whose flowers open in the morning and close at eventide. In other species, the flowers open only slightly, and the unique flowers of the closed gentian have been the theme of various poems. Legends concerning gentians are numerous, bizzare, and intriguing. One quaint and interesting tale seeks to explain why the flowers of some gentians open and close whereas those of other species remain closed. The story originally is, all gentian flowers were closed, until once when the fairy queen, unable to reach home, entreated a gentian to open its flower and allow her to spend the night therein. In gratitude for this hospitality, the fairy queen informed the gentian that, subsequently, she and all her children would open each morning.[4] During the reign of King Ladislas in Hungary, according to another gentian legend, the people were ravaged by a plague. The king, in despair, going into the field prayed that an arrow shot at random would be directed to some plant which would serve as an effective remedy. The arrow which he then shot pierced the root of a gentian. From that time forward, gentian roots used as a medicine supposedly effected wondrous cures.[5]

---

[3] Bailey, L. H. THE STANDARD CYCLOPEDIA OF HORTICULTURE . . . New ed., 3 v., illus. New York and London. 1933.
[4] Clements, E. S. FLOWERS OF COAST AND SIERRA. 226 pp., illus. New York. 1928.
[5] Skinner, C. M. MYTHS AND LEGENDS OF FLOWERS, TREES, FRUITS, AND PLANTS IN ALL AGES AND IN ALL CLIMES. [302] pp., illus. Philadelphia and London. [1925.]

GERANIUMS

Gera'nium spp.

Geraniums are perennial, annual, or occasionally biennial herbs and derive their name from the Greek word for crane (*geranos*), because of the fancied resemblance of the long fruit-bearing (styles) protruding from the center of the flower to that of a crane. There are approximately 16 species of geranium, almost wholly perennial, occurring natively on western ranges, and about five annual species naturalized from Europe according to conservative botanists. A few other species occur in Alaska. Geraniums are widely distributed and well known both in North America and in the Old World. There are at least several species of the genus in each of the 11 far-western States.

The common potted geraniums belong to the related South African genus *Pelargonium*. Therefore, the English name cranesbill has been designated in Standardized Plant Names as the approved name for members of the genus *Geranium*. Historically the name geranium applies to this genus, and these plants are universally known as geraniums both in the range country and in the literature of range plants. Standardized Plant Names approves the name wild geranium for one species of the genus (*G. maculatum*).

Geraniums occur up to elevations of at least 10,000 feet in drier mountain meadows and parks, in open timber where the ground is damp, and in the grasslands of plains and foothills. These plants usually prefer a rich loam with partial shade, growing as scattered individuals or in patches but seldom occur in pure stands.

Geraniums are of only moderate forage value, varying from fair to good in the central Rocky Mountains and Northwest, and fair in the Southwest. They are of more value for sheep than for cattle. Sheep frequently consume most of the herbage in the spring but later eat only the flowers or nibble the leaves. Cattle eat only the more tender herbage. Game, especially deer, graze both the flowers and the leaves. Some observers consider geraniums of greatest value during the latter part of the grazing season but this is probably due to the consumption of the herbage of the grasses and more palatable weeds as the season advances, which tends to concentrate grazing on the less palatable species. Geraniums customarily produce sufficient seed to maintain their stands. Nature has provided these plants with springlike mechanisms which effectively distribute the ripened seeds.

Certain geraniums are used for medicinal purposes, principally as astringents. Such utilization dates back to the Indians.[1] The native, spotted geranium (*G. maculatum*), often called wild geranium, which is frequently cultivated, furnishes a popular remedy for diarrhea, chronic dysentery, certain throat ailments, and other purposes. The annual, herb robert (*G. robertianum*), which grows

[1] Wood, H. C., Remington, J. P., and Sadtler, S. P., assisted by Lyons, A. B., and Woods, H. C., Jr. THE DISPENSATORY OF THE UNITED STATES OF AMERICA, BY DR. GEO. B. WOOD AND DR. FRANKLIN BACHE. Ed. 19, thoroughly revised and largely rewritten . . . 1,947 pp. Philadelphia and London. 1907.

wild both in Europe and in the United States, is popularly used for fever, hemorrhage, jaundice, and as a gargle. This solution is prepared by boiling the herbage.

Geraniums are readily recognized by their distinctive odor when the leaves are crushed, and by their peculiar fruiting structure which resembles a Maypole. Each section (carpel) of the five-lobed seedpod (capsule) separates elastically at maturity from the base to the beaked apex as it gradually curls upwards and outwards, thus expelling its solitary seed from the pouchlike covering which remains attached to each carpel strip. The flowers open from late spring until mid-to-late summer. The time of blossoming varies with the elevation, beginning earliest at the lower elevations. The flowers are borne either singly or in loose, flat or somewhat rounded clusters, and vary in color from deep purple to violet, pink and almost white, the five petals commonly being marked by pink or purplish lines.

The various species differ considerably in habit of growth. The stems occur singly or there may be several from the base; in some species they are erect, varying from 4 to 36 inches in height; in other species the stems extend along the ground with only the growing tip erect, or are produced in large tufts. The perennial species often develop a stout, vertical, woody root crown which may be branched or unbranched. The leaves may be either basal, arising directly from the root crown or may be placed opposite each other at the swollen joints of the plant stem. The leaves of geranium are parted somewhat like a human hand, being often confused early in the season with those of larkspurs and monkshoods. In addition to their peculiar odor and fruit, already referred to, geraniums are also readily distinguished by the two small leaflike outgrowths (stipules) arising from the base of the leafstalks where they join the stem. Larkspurs and monkshoods do not have stipules, and their leaves are alternate on the stem. The stems, leaves, leafstalks, flower stalks, and portions of the inflorescence of geraniums are usually provided with simple, often sticky hairs.

STICKY GERANIUM

Gera'nium viscosis'simum, syns. *G. inci'sum, G. orega'num, G. strigo'sum*

"Seed pods" (carpels)—5, each 1-seeded and tipped by a long, persistent stalk (style); the 5 styles grown together below and to the elongated central column from which they separate at maturity by simply recoiling

Flowers—rather large, showy, purple or rose-colored, rarely white, borne on branched, hairy, leafy-bracted stalks at ends of stems

Petals—5, up to nearly 1 in. long, broadly reverse-heart-shaped, usually conspicuously veined, densely bearded within at their bases

Stamens—10, joined together in a tube by their stalks, with glands at their bases; 5 of them longer than the other 5

Outer flower parts (sepals)—5, greenish or somewhat purplish, sometimes with papery edges, sticky-hairy, abruptly narrowed into a short, stout awn at the tip

Leaves—more or less hairy, mostly basal and long-stalked; stem leaves opposite, smaller and shorter-stalked than the basal leaves, rounded in outline, palmately 5-lobed, each lobe again deeply cleft, sometimes bearing bulblets in their axils, and with bracts (stipules) at base

Stems—stout, often forked, up to 3 ft. high, soft-hairy

Root crown—stout, woody, sometimes branched near top, covered with old leafstalk and stem bases

Sticky geranium, a coarse, leafy, branched perennial herb from 1 to 3 feet tall, is so named because it is practically covered with glandular hairs which make it sticky to the touch (viscid). It is perhaps the best known of the western geraniums since it is widely distributed throughout the West, ranging from British Columbia and Saskatchewan to California and Colorado, but apparently it does not extend into Arizona and New Mexico. Specimens have been collected throughout a wide altitudinal range as low as 750 feet above sea level in Oregon and up to 10,000 feet in Utah. The plant is most abundant in parks and glades of the foothills and mountains at elevations of between 5,000 and 8,000 feet.

This plant grows in abundance and is conspicuous on many forest ranges especially in the Intermountain region, but seldom occurs in pure stands. Sticky geranium is characteristic of open situations, being frequently associated with wheatgrasses, fescues, bluegrasses, lupines, paintbrushes, and yarrow and is also found intermixed with shrubs and in open woods, especially aspen. It rarely occurs under conifer timber. The species is not restricted to any particular type of soil, usually occurring on a fairly moist, either gravelly or sandy loam. It occasionally appears on drier granitic soils and on heavy clayey loams.

Sticky geranium is an important forage plant because of its abundance and leafiness, its palatability being only fair or fairly good or occasionally good for sheep and worthless or poor to fair for cattle. Any higher estimates of the species are largely based on overgrazed conditions. Horses rarely eat it. Practically the entire plant may be consumed in the spring but later in the season only the flowers and more tender herbage are eaten. This herb withstands grazing very well, due chiefly to the large reserve of food stored in its thick, vertical rootstock, which anchors the plant firmly in the ground and prevents pulling by grazing animals. The flowers appear in June and July, the fruits in August and September. After seed production, the leaves usually dry up and are then practically worthless as forage.

Sticky geranium has large, rather thick leaves, borne on long leaf-stalks, which are nearly round in outline and deeply and fingerwise cut into three or five divisions, which are again sharply cleft. Due to the similarity of the leaves, sticky geranium is sometimes mistaken for a larkspur, especially before flowering begins. Hence, it has occasionally and erroneously been considered as poisonous.

The related Richardson geranium (*G. richardsónii*) is also widely distributed over the same range in the West, except that it extends farther southwest, and is common in parts of Arizona and New Mexico, where sticky geranium is unknown. The growth requirements and sites of these two geraniums are similar. They apparently hybridize in the high mountain ranges of the Wasatch, and possibly elsewhere. Richardson geranium is slenderer, has hairs tipped by purple glands, especially on the upper part of the plant, and bears white flowers with pink or roseate veins. The palatabilities of Richardson and sticky geraniums are about equal but may vary in different localities. In the Southwest, Richardson geranium is rated as worthless to poor for cattle, poor to fair for sheep, and fair for deer.

CURLYCUP GUMWEED

Grinde'lia squarro'sa

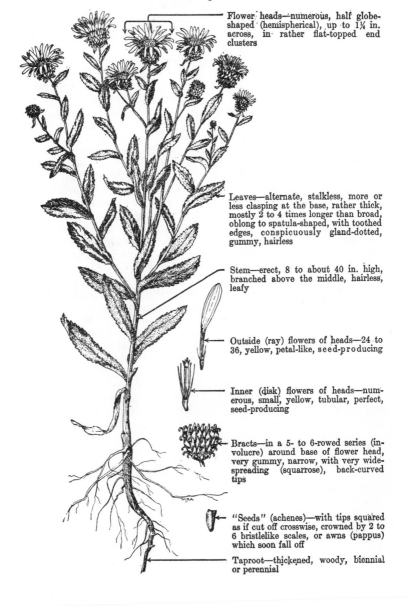

Flower heads—numerous, half globe-shaped (hemispherical), up to 1¼ in. across, in rather flat-topped end clusters

Leaves—alternate, stalkless, more or less clasping at the base, rather thick, mostly 2 to 4 times longer than broad, oblong to spatula-shaped, with toothed edges, conspicuously gland-dotted, gummy, hairless

Stem—erect, 8 to about 40 in. high, branched above the middle, hairless, leafy

Outside (ray) flowers of heads—24 to 36, yellow, petal-like, seed-producing

Inner (disk) flowers of heads—numerous, small, yellow, tubular, perfect, seed-producing

Bracts—in a 5- to 6-rowed series (involucre) around base of flower head, very gummy, narrow, with very wide-spreading (squarrose), back-curved tips

"Seeds" (achenes)—with tips squared as if cut off crosswise, crowned by 2 to 6 bristlelike scales, or awns (pappus) which soon fall off

Taproot—thickened, woody, biennial or perennial

Curlycup gumweed is a biennial (in cultivation, sometimes perennial [1]) herb of the sunflower, or aster family (Compositae). The name gumweed alludes to the sticky, resinous character of the plant, the flower heads being particularly gummy, especially when in bud. The specific name *squarrosa* refers to the widely spreading (squarrose), often down-curving, bracts (involucre) of the flower head.

Primarily a plant of the drier prairie soils, this species rather commonly inhabits plains and foothills from Manitoba and Minnesota to Missouri, Texas, Arizona, Nevada, Idaho, and Saskatchewan; it possibly extends into Mexico. In the long-narrow-leaved variety *G. squarro'sa serrula'ta* (syn. *G. serrula'ta*) it occurs naturally in parts of southern California. Curlycup gumweed is an aggressive plant, and its range is extending as it is steadily invading areas bordering the States mentioned. It is reported as being abundant locally in northeastern California and to have been collected in Oregon and Washington; it is now found in northeastern Michigan, Indiana, and Illinois, being widely naturalized along roadsides, railroad banks, and in fields of the eastern United States and Canada. The species appears up to about 9,000 feet in Colorado and New Mexico. It usually occurs on the drier, rocky, gravelly or sandy soils, being qualified to survive where moisture is limited. This herb also grows on deeper, sandy, or clayey loams and is characteristic of wastelands and overgrazed areas, often densely inhabiting old fields, eroded hill- and road-sides where the surface soil has been disturbed. Curlycup gumweed was first collected on the open prairies along the banks of the Missouri River by Captain Meriwether Lewis of the Lewis and Clark expedition (1804–06).

Curlycup gumweed has little forage value and is unpalatable to livestock, although sheep occasionally crop the flower heads on poor, overgrazed ranges. The leaves and flowering tops of this species and of the closely related shore gumweed (*G. robus'ta*), of California, are the official source of fluid extract of grindelia, a valuable antispasmodic, also used because of its stimulating effect upon the mucous membrane in the treatment of chronic bronchitis and asthma.[2] It is also used as a tonic. Curlycup gumweed is one of several species of *Grindelia* employed in the treatment of poison-oak and poison-ivy inflammation.[3] Honeybees favor this plant as a source of nectar, although the honey is reputedly inferior in flavor. Beekeepers also claim that it candies too quickly to be desirable in the comb. In fact, this nectar tends to coagulate so rapidly that it candies in the sacks of the bees unless they hurry to the hive immediately after gathering the material.[4][5]

[1] Steyermark, J. A. STUDIES IN GRINDELIA. II. A MONOGRAPH OF THE NORTH AMERICAN SPECIES OF THE GENUS GRINDELIA. Ann. Mo. Bot. Gard. 21: 227–230, 433–608, illus. 1934.

[2] Wood, H. C., Remington, J. P., and Sadtler, S. P., assisted by Lyons, A. B., and Wood, H. C., Jr. THE DISPENSATORY OF THE UNITED STATES OF AMERICA, BY DR. GEO. B. WOOD AND DR. FRANKLIN BACHE. Ed. 19, thoroughly rev. and largely rewritten . . . 1,947 pp. Philadelphia and London. 1907.

[3] Stuhr, E. T. MANUAL OF PACIFIC COAST DRUG PLANTS . . . 189 pp., illus. Lancaster, Pa. 1933.

[4] Clements, E. S. FLOWERS OF COAST AND SIERRA. 226 pp., illus. New York. 1928.

[5] Pellett, F. C. AMERICAN HONEY PLANTS TOGETHER WITH THOSE WHICH ARE OF SPECIAL VALUE TO THE BEEKEEPER AS SOURCES OF POLLEN. Ed. 3, rev. and enl., 419 pp., illus. Hamilton, Ill. 1930.

GUMWEEDS

Grinde'lia spp.

Gumweeds compose a moderate-sized group of coarse, annual, biennial, or perennial herbs, sometimes woody at the base, native to western North and South America, and particularly well represented in the United States west of the Mississippi. *Grindelia* is a very homogeneous group of plants, easily distinguished by clear-cut characters. However, as is the case with certain other well-marked and distinctive genera (*e. g., Rubus, Salix, Viola*), considerable variation and instability within the genus itself makes specific boundaries difficult.[1] Although the species total has long been estimated at 25 or 30, the genus in its entirety has not been carefully studied; recent intensive study, both in North and South America, indicates that the number of species is probably greater than has hitherto been supposed. The eminent German botanist, Karl Ludwig Willdenow, named this genus in honor of David Hieronymus Grindel (1776–1836), a Russian professor and botanical author. The resinous character of many species has given rise to the common names, gumweeds, gumplants, and rosinweeds; the flower heads usually exude the most of this medicinal resin.[2][3]

These plants grow on a variety of sites at medium elevations. Many species prefer dry, rocky, or gravelly situations, often appearing along water courses; some invade roadsides, embankments, and waste ground; still others inhabit saline or marshy sites, or grow on alkaline or limy soils. Despite moderate abundance in some regions gumweeds possess little forage value and are relatively unpalatable to all classes of livestock; presumably even goats refuse to eat them. Local abundance of gumweeds is often an indication of depletion, due to severe and prolonged overgrazing; the plants frequently form dense stands on abused and abandoned dry-farming areas.

Some species of gumweed were used by the Indians and early western settlers as a tonic and blood purifier.[6] The Indians also used the resinous buds in the treatment of asthma and bronchitis.[4] Fluid extract of grindelia, an official drug, is obtained from the flowering tops and leaves of two species (either separately or in mixture) of this genus, curlycup gumweed, and shore gumweed. These plants are extremely hardy; some species are cultivated for their ornamental yellow flowers.

Gumweeds have simple or branched stems, sometimes much-branched from the base. The rather stiff, undivided leaves are alternate, with sessile or partly clasping bases, or the lower leaves may be short-stalked; they are commonly toothed on the margins, hairless or occasionally hairy, and usually gland-dotted, sometimes shining because of the resinous covering; the herbage exudes a pleasant, balsamlike odor. The rather large flower heads are solitary or

---

[1][2][3][4] See footnotes on preceding page.
[6] Chesnut, V. K. PLANTS USED BY THE INDIANS OF MENDOCINO COUNTY, CALIFORNIA. U. S. Dept. Agr., Div. Bot., Contrib. U. S. Natl. Herbarium 7 : 295–422, illus. 1902.

borne in end-clusters. The western species commonly have conspicuous yellow petallike parts (ray flowers), but some species of the genus have none, the flower heads being rayless (discoid). The flower head cup (involucre), composed of four to eight series of frequently sharp-pointed bracts, is probably the most distinctive character of the gumweeds; these bracts overlap closely and may be erect, widely spreading, or curved downward. The inner bracts, at least, are gland-dotted and the involucral cups of the budding flower heads are often completely filled with a gummy exudation.

ROCKY MOUNTAIN SWEETVETCH

Hedy'sarum pabula're

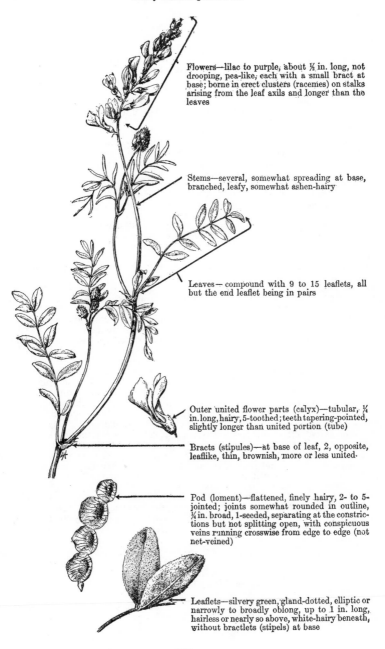

Flowers—lilac to purple, about ½ in. long, not drooping, pea-like, each with a small bract at base; borne in erect clusters (racemes) on stalks arising from the leaf axils and longer than the leaves

Stems—several, somewhat spreading at base, branched, leafy, somewhat ashen-hairy

Leaves— compound with 9 to 15 leaflets, all but the end leaflet being in pairs

Outer united flower parts (calyx)—tubular, ¼ in. long, hairy, 5-toothed; teeth tapering-pointed, slightly longer than united portion (tube)

Bracts (stipules)—at base of leaf, 2, opposite, leaflike, thin, brownish, more or less united.

Pod (loment)—flattened, finely hairy, 2- to 5-jointed; joints somewhat rounded in outline, ¼ in. broad, 1-seeded, separating at the constrictions but not splitting open, with conspicuous veins running crosswise from edge to edge (not net-veined)

Leaflets—silvery green, gland-dotted, elliptic or narrowly to broadly oblong, up to 1 in. long, hairless or nearly so above, white-hairy beneath, without bractlets (stipels) at base

Rocky Mountain sweetvetch is a perennial herb of the pea family and superficially resembles certain locos, peavines, and vetches. It has a stout, tough, deep taproot and a somewhat woody root crown from which grow several fairly leafy, branching stems from 6 to 30 inches long. Some of the stems are rather erect and others extend out laterally along or near the ground a few inches before curving upward.

The name *Hedysarum* is from the two Greek words *hedys* (sweet) and *aroma* (a spice or sweet herb; whence our English word aroma, meaning pleasant odor)—apparently referring to the fragrant flowers and sweet-tasting herbage of some species. "Jointpod" is sometimes applied as a common name, because of the peculiar jointed pods (loments). Depending on the species concept of the individual botanist, about 9 to 11 species of sweetvetch occur in the West, ranging from Alaska to the Dakotas, New Mexico, Nevada, and Oregon. The genus apparently does not occur in California and Arizona.

Rocky Mountain sweetvetch is one of the most widespread and abundant of these species and is selected here as illustrative and characteristic of the genus *Hedysarum* from a range standpoint. It ranges from Montana to Utah and New Mexico and is the only species of *Hedysarum* occurring in New Mexico. Generally, it is scattered sparsely but is limitedly abundant on a few localized areas. Rocky Mountain sweetvetch grows mostly on dry, open, or lightly shaded areas in the sagebrush, oakbrush, ponderosa pine, and aspen belts at elevations from 4,000 to 10,000 feet.

Some observers have reported Rocky Mountain sweetvetch to be of low palatability, but almost certainly they have confused it with loco. Of course, the association of sweetvetch with abundant and very choice grasses will doubtless reduce its consumption by livestock.[1] It is of interest to note that Prof. Aven Nelson, in describing this species,[1] states that it "is reputed an excellent forage plant", and the scientific name he applied to the species (*pabulare*)[2] reflects this viewpoint. Moreover, this appears to be the species which Prof. Nelson formerly called "*H. mackenzii*" and which he states is greatly relished by livestock, of frequent occurrence, locally abundant, and an important source of forage in the Red Desert of Wyoming.[3]

Utah sweetvetch (*H. utahen'se*) is very similar to Rocky Mountain sweetvetch, very closely related to it, and probably intergrades with it. *Hedysarum utahense* differs chiefly in its flowers, which are more rose-purple and have a little longer calyx. Utah sweetvetch is limited to Utah and eastern Idaho, but is there locally abundant. Forest Service technicians report it as moderately to well used on Utah ranges, by both sheep and cattle, although intensive use of the species is related to close grazing of the range. Artificial reseeding trials made with Utah sweetvetch in its native habitat by the Intermountain Forest and Range Experiment Station have thus far failed.

Sweetvetch species, as a rule, are grazed by all classes of domestic livestock. Their strong, woody, deep taproots get sustenance from a large soil area and render the plants resistant to abuse. The peculiar, easily broken, jointed pods are conducive to seed dispersal, on which reproduction of the plants is necessarily dependent. Reports of these plants holding their own, or even increasing, on overgrazed range are doubtless correlated, in part, with these root and fruit characters, and probably also with less resistant qualities of associated palatable species. The plants are frequently confused with locoweeds by observers, but the gland-dotted leaves (apparent when held to the light), the squared effect of the flower tips, and above all the characteristic pods clearly distinguish *Hedysarum* from *Astragalus*.

In parts of southern Italy, Algeria, Spain, and other portions of the Mediterranean region a native species of sweetvetch called "sulla" (*H. coronarium*) is a very important cultivated forage plant, locally having about the same status as alfalfa does in this country.

[1] Nelson, A. THE GENUS HEDYSARUM IN THE ROCKY MOUNTAINS. Biol. Soc. Wash. Proc. 15 : 183–186. 1902.
[2] Latin *pabularis, –e*, fit for fodder (*pabulum*).
[3] Nelson, A. THE RED DESERT OF WYOMING AND ITS FORAGE RESOURCES. U. S. Dept. Agr., Div. Agrost. Bull. 13, 72 pp., illus. 1898.

ORANGE SNEEZEWEED

Hele′nium hoope′sii, syn. *Dugal′dia hoope′sii*

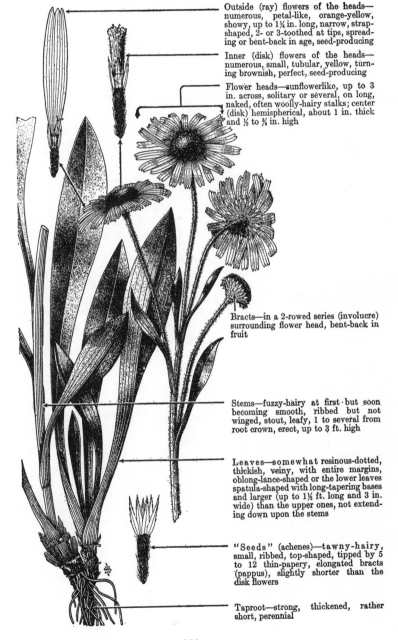

Outside (ray) flowers of the heads—numerous, petal-like, orange-yellow, showy, up to 1¼ in. long, narrow, strap-shaped, 2- or 3-toothed at tips, spreading or bent-back in age, seed-producing

Inner (disk) flowers of the heads—numerous, small, tubular, yellow, turning brownish, perfect, seed-producing

Flower heads—sunflowerlike, up to 3 in. across, solitary or several, on long, naked, often woolly-hairy stalks; center (disk) hemispherical, about 1 in. thick and ½ to ¾ in. high

Bracts—in a 2-rowed series (involucre) surrounding flower head, bent-back in fruit

Stems—fuzzy-hairy at first · but soon becoming smooth, ribbed but not winged, stout, leafy, 1 to several from root crown, erect, up to 3 ft. high

Leaves—somewhat resinous-dotted, thickish, veiny, with entire margins, oblong-lance-shaped or the lower leaves spatula-shaped with long-tapering bases and larger (up to 1½ ft. long and 3 in. wide) than the upper ones, not extending down upon the stems

"Seeds" (achenes)—tawny-hairy, small, ribbed, top-shaped, tipped by 5 to 12 thin-papery, elongated bracts (pappus), slightly shorter than the disk flowers

Taproot—strong, thickened, rather short, perennial

Orange sneezeweed, sometimes also called Hoopes sneezeweed, owls-claws, sunflower, western sneezeweed, and yellowweed, is a perennial herb of the sneezeweed tribe (Helenieae) of the immense aster, or composite family (Asteraceae, or Compositae). It is one of the important western poisonous plants and sometimes proves a very serious handicap to profitable range sheep raising, especially in Utah.

Helenium is Latinized from the Greek word *helenion*, an old plant name possibly referring to this genus or, more likely, to the related, cultivated elecampane (*Inula helenium*). The ancient plant helenion is said by some to have been named in honor of the famous Helen of Troy, wife of Menelaus, King of Sparta, and whose abduction by Paris "fired a thousand ships and burnt the topless towers of Ilion." Others state that the plant commemorates another outstanding figure of the Trojan War, the warrior-seer Helenus, son of Priam and Hecuba, by whose advice the Greeks built the celebrated wooden horse whereby they entered the walls of Troy (Ilium, or Ilion) and captured it. The name of the species is in honor of its first collector, Thomas Hoopes.

Orange sneezeweed extends from eastern Oregon to western Montana and southward to New Mexico and California. Although its altitudinal range is from 5,000 to 12,500 feet, or from the ponderosa pine belt to well above timberline, it most frequently occurs between elevations of about 7,000 and 10,500 feet. It prefers moist, well-drained soils on sunny slopes of the aspen and spruce-fir belts, but it also thrives in open parks, mountain meadows, and along streambanks or near colonies of willows. Where the range is properly managed and normal vegetative conditions obtain the species typically occurs in small, scattered patches. On range subjected by overgrazing and overstocking to prolonged soil and cover deterioration this aggressive invader may be locally abundant and even the dominant species on extensive areas.

Wherever good forage plants are plentiful orange sneezeweed is so low in palatability as to be scarcely grazed, with the occasional exception of young plants, which are sometimes moderately grazed by sheep. It is, however, grazed by all classes of livestock when palatable plants are lacking, and this situation makes it a source of danger. The entire plant is poisonous, at least to sheep, at all seasons, but since the effects of the poison are cumulative a single or even several feedings usually have no noticeable effect, if the animal has not previously grazed it. Sheep that graze orange sneezeweed to any great extent, however, eventually become sick and are often so seriously affected that death results. Although experiments[1] have shown that orange sneezeweed is proportionately as poisonous to cattle as it is to sheep and occasional instances of the death of cattle have been directly attributed to it, there is little danger of cattle losses under range conditions, due to the greater bodily size of cattle

[1] Marsh, C. D., Clawson, A. B., Couch, J. F., and Marsh, H. WESTERN SNEEZEWEED (HELENIUM HOOPESII) AS A POISONOUS PLANT. U. S. Dept. Agr. Bull. 947, 46 pp., illus. 1921. *See also* Marsh, C. D. STOCK-POISONING PLANTS OF THE RANGE. U. S. Dept. Agr. Bull. 1245, rev., 75 pp., illus. 1929. Supersedes Bull. 575.

and their lesser inclination to graze weeds, and sneezeweed in particular. Horses are rarely, if ever, poisoned by this plant.

Nausea, which is often the only symptom of orange sneezeweed poisoning noticed by herders on the range, has given rise to the name of the "spewing or vomiting sickness" of which sheep are the usual victims. Other accompanying symptoms may include depression, weakness, salivation, bloating, and diarrhea. Inasmuch as the poison acts slowly, animals suffering from having eaten orange sneezeweed have generally grazed the plant over an extended period of time. It has been the common observation of people who handle sheep in Utah that when a band of sheep is introduced to a sneezeweed range comparatively few cases of poisoning occur the first year, with more the second, and still more the third, the effects of the feeding continuing over from year to year. The results of experiments carried out by Marsh, Clawson, et al., *op. cit.*, show that the effects of the poisoning "may be permanent; that sheep once affected by this plant are likely to succumb more quickly to a succeeding feeding, and, even if they apparently recover, are likely to prove worthless." Sheep may even die on the winter range from the effects of having grazed orange sneezeweed during the previous summer.

The losses in Utah have been greatly reduced by removing the sheep from sneezeweed-infested range when they show symptoms of poisoning and driving them to lower brush range until their condition is improved; they are then returned to the sneezeweed range until the poisoning symptoms recur when the process is repeated. This is but a temporary expedient and does not effect a real cure. It is obviously advisable to prohibit, if possible, the ingress of livestock to ranges infested with this poisonous plant and also to encourage the restoration of the range by proper management which, though a slow process, is apparently the only sure means of lessening the spread of orange sneezeweed. Marsh, Clawson, et al., in the work referred to, report that grubbing the plants has been found to be too costly a method of exterminating them from the range and cutting with a scythe seems to stimulate rather than prevent growth. Orange sneezeweed presents a serious problem on the range, since it is a vigorous grower, spreads rapidly, produces seeds in abundance, and propagates prolifically from the underground parts.

This species has a stout, woody taproot only a few inches long which develops into a crown, whereby the plant enlarges vegetatively, and there are also numerous, slender, fibrous roots. Orange sneezeweed has a strong tendency to develop adventitious buds on these parts. Clumps of leafy stems sometimes as large as one foot in diameter arise from the older plants. The stems, although sometimes unbranched and bearing only one flower head, are usually branched near the top into a few sparsely leaved stems several inches long, each terminated by a large, orange-yellow flower head. The pale to dark green, parallel-veined leaves show a gradual transition in size and shape from the base to the top of the plant. Both the stems and the leaves are inclined to be hairy or woolly when young, but later lose the hairs (become glabrous). The greenish, leaflike bracts (phyllaries) that encircle the flower head are in two rows and, at maturity, curve outward at their tips, a characteristic which has given rise to a Navaho name for the plant, meaning owl's claws.

LITTLE-SUNFLOWER

Helianthel'la uniflo'ra

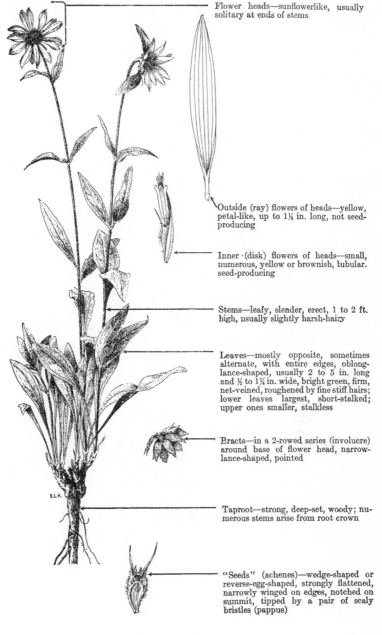

Flower heads—sunflowerlike, usually solitary at ends of stems

Outside (ray) flowers of heads—yellow, petal-like, up to 1⅛ in. long, not seed-producing

Inner (disk) flowers of heads—small, numerous, yellow or brownish, tubular, seed-producing

Stems—leafy, slender, erect, 1 to 2 ft. high, usually slightly harsh-hairy

Leaves—mostly opposite, sometimes alternate, with entire edges, oblong-lance-shaped, usually 2 to 5 in. long and ½ to 1¼ in. wide, bright green, firm, net-veined, roughened by fine stiff hairs; lower leaves largest, short-stalked; upper ones smaller, stalkless

Bracts—in a 2-rowed series (involucre) around base of flower head, narrow-lance-shaped, pointed

Taproot—strong, deep-set, woody; numerous stems arise from root crown

"Seeds" (achenes)—wedge-shaped or reverse-egg-shaped, strongly flattened, narrowly winged on edges, notched on summit, tipped by a pair of scaly bristles (pappus)

387

Little-sunflower, a perennial herb belonging to the sunflower tribe of the aster family (Compositae), is closely related to the common sunflowers (*Helianthus* spp.). It is one of the most important forage plants of the *Helianthella* genus, which is represented in the West by about nine species, all similar in appearance and palatability. The scientific name of this species is very descriptive. In the generic name the diminutive suffix *-ella* signifies that it is a small *Helianthus*, or sunflower (from the Greek, *helios*, sun; *anthos*, flower); hence the common name, little-sunflower. The specific name *uniflora*, meaning one flower, refers to the usually solitary flower head. The names one-flowered sunflower and single-flowered helianthella are also sometimes used for this species.

Little-sunflower ranges from Montana to eastern Oregon and south to Nevada, Arizona, and New Mexico. It occurs at medium to high elevations and may be found up to 10,000 feet in Utah. It grows on moderately rich soils in wheat-grass and weed types, on open exposures within the oakbrush, ponderosa pine, and aspen types and extends into the spruce-fir zone. Among its most common associates are arrowleaf balsamroot, lupine, yarrow, Idaho fescue, mules-ears, geranium, and snowberry. This plant usually grows in mixture with other plants, and rarely, if ever, occurs in pure stands. It sometimes grows in abundance in dense patches but as a rule is scattered.

Little-sunflower apparently does not occur in California, but the genus is represented in that State by other species of *Helianthella*. The most common of these is *H. californica*, which is very similar to little-sunflower but of less importance as a forage plant. In Oregon little-sunflower grows on the eastern side only of the Cascade Mountains, and there appears to be no authentic record of its occurrence in Washington. However, a closely related northwestern species, *H. douglasii*, is sometimes mistaken for it, the two species being very similar in appearance and forage value. *H. douglasii*, which differs mainly in being more hairy-stemmed and having thinner leaves, is common in eastern Oregon and Washington and extends northward to British Columbia and eastward into western Wyoming and Montana.

In some sections little-sunflower provides considerable forage. The leafage, flowers, and more tender portions of the stems are eaten by all classes of grazing animals, being fair to very good in palatability for sheep and only slightly less palatable for cattle. The flower heads are eaten with unusual relish. The foliage is utilized by all classes of grazing animals during the summer but after drying in the fall is grazed to a less extent by livestock and game. The strong woody taproot enables this plant to stand up unusually well under heavy grazing and trampling. Reproduction is from seed only. The seed usually ripens during August and is shed soon after maturity.

The helianthellas are often confused with some of the common sunflowers (*Helianthus* spp.), but can be distinguished by the "seeds" (achenes), which are strongly compressed, narrowly winged along the edges, notched on top and tipped with a pair of scaly awns. On the other hand, the "seeds" of the common sunflowers are 4-angled and thickened and are neither winged, strongly flattened, nor notched. The helianthellas are also sometimes confused with *Viguiera multiflora* which differs, however, in having numerous flowers, dark green foliage, thickened "seeds", and in being smaller and more slender-stemmed. The stems of little-sunflower are 1 to 2 feet high and grow in rather loose bunches of 20 to 30 from a tough woody root crown. The lower leaves are largest and have short stems (petioles); the upper ones are stemless and tend to get smaller toward the top, the topmost sometimes being very small. The yellow flower heads are large (up to 2¾ inches across) and usually one borne solitary on the stem though occasionally the stems branch into two or more stalks, each bearing a single flower. The individual flowers of the flower head are set among firm-papery bracts (paleae) on the common seed-bearing disk (receptacle). The circle of bracts (involucre) below the flower head is somewhat rigid and hairy especially on the edges.

COW-PARSNIP

Heracle'um lana'tum

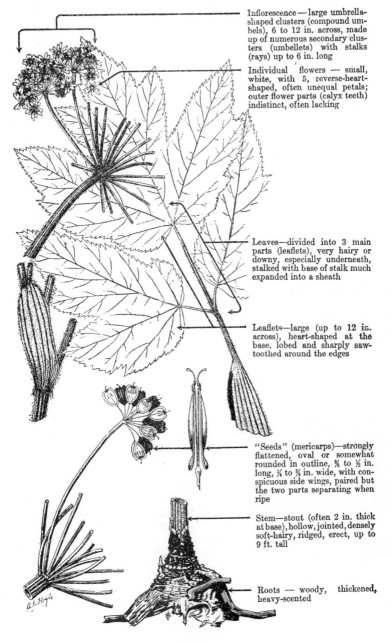

Inflorescence — large umbrella-shaped clusters (compound umbels), 6 to 12 in. across, made up of numerous secondary clusters (umbellets) with stalks (rays) up to 6 in. long

Individual flowers — small, white, with 5, reverse-heart-shaped, often unequal petals; outer flower parts (calyx teeth) indistinct, often lacking

Leaves—divided into 3 main parts (leaflets), very hairy or downy, especially underneath, stalked with base of stalk much expanded into a sheath

Leaflets—large (up to 12 in. across), heart-shaped at the base, lobed and sharply saw-toothed around the edges

"Seeds" (mericarps)—strongly flattened, oval or somewhat rounded in outline, ⅜ to ½ in. long, ¼ to ⅜ in. wide, with conspicuous side wings, paired but the two parts separating when ripe

Stem—stout (often 2 in. thick at base), hollow, jointed, densely soft-hairy, ridged, erect, up to 9 ft. tall

Roots — woody, thickened, heavy-scented

Cow-parsnip is a leafy-stemmed, perennial herb, 3 to 9 feet tall, one of the largest in the carrot or parsnip family (Umbelliferae). It is also frequently called cow-cabbage and wild-pieplant. Swine are fond of the plant—which explains the name hogweed sometimes used. It is a common and unusually widespread plant, growing from Labrador, Newfoundland, New England, and Ontario to Alaska southward to North Carolina, Texas, New Mexico, and California.

Cow-parsnip is very widely distributed through the more moist range lands of the West. It is a typical moisture-loving plant which thrives best under conditions of semishade and grows chiefly on rich loamy soils along stream banks, on wet bottoms, in open woodlands, shrub types, and meadow areas. Its common associates are willows, alders, sedges, false-hellebore, and other water-loving plants. Frequently it grows in scattered groups on moist, northern, or well-shaded hillsides in aspen stands and similar places. Its altitudinal range extends from slightly above sea level to about 10,000 feet.

Cow-parsnip is highly palatable to all classes of livestock, being relished by cattle, sheep, and goats, especially in the earlier stages of its growth. The large tender leaves, flowers, and green seeds are eaten first, and frequently the large juicy stems are consumed nearly to the ground. In many places of scattering occurrence it is becoming extinct because the livestock seek it in preference to more abundant forage. Although cow-parsnip seldom grows in dense stands, it frequently produces a plentiful supply of excellent forage owing to its large size and abundant leafage. The foliage remains green and palatable throughout the summer. Reproduction is entirely from seed.

The tender leaf and flower stalks of cow-parsnip, being sweet and aromatic, are sought by certain Indians for green food before the flowers have expanded in the spring and early summer. Formerly the Indians used the thick basal parts of the stems as a salt substitute. The early Spaniards are reported to have used a medicine, compounded from the roots, in the treatment of rheumatism.

Because of its vigor and great size cow-parsnip was given the generic name, *Heracleum*, in honor of Heracles (Greek for Hercules). The species name *lanatum* means woolly or hairy, and refers to the fine silky hairs usually found on the plants, especially on the upper portions. This is the only species of *Heracleum* native to North America.

The roots of cow-parsnip are thick, woody, and aromatic. The hollow, jointed stems are very stout, often being about 2 inches thick at the base. The leaves are compound and each is divided into three large, rather thin leaflets which are usually very hairy or downy underneath. Each leaflet has an individual stalk (petiole) and, to the casual observer, looks like a large simple leaf. Because of their form, they remind one of rhubarb or pieplant leaves. The small white flowers grow in large, showy umbrella-shaped clusters (umbels) 6 to 12 inches broad. Blossoming usually occurs during July and August. "Seeds" are borne in rather large quantities and usually ripen during September; they are oval, strongly flattened, somewhat hairy, and have conspicuous side wings.

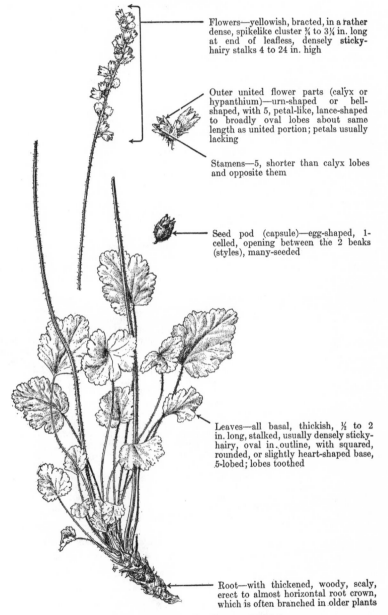

ALUMROOTS

Heu'chera spp.

Flowers—yellowish, bracted, in a rather dense, spikelike cluster ¾ to 3¼ in. long at end of leafless, densely sticky-hairy stalks 4 to 24 in. high

Outer united flower parts (calyx or hypanthium)—urn-shaped or bell-shaped, with 5, petal-like, lance-shaped to broadly oval lobes about same length as united portion; petals usually lacking

Stamens—5, shorter than calyx lobes and opposite them

Seed pod (capsule)—egg-shaped, 1-celled, opening between the 2 beaks (styles), many-seeded

Leaves—all basal, thickish, ½ to 2 in. long, stalked, usually densely sticky-hairy, oval in outline, with squared, rounded, or slightly heart-shaped base, 5-lobed; lobes toothed

Root—with thickened, woody, scaly, erect to almost horizontal root crown, which is often branched in older plants

Ovalleaf alumroot (*Heuchera ovulifo'lia*).

The genus *Heuchera*, named by Linnaeus in honor of Johann Heinrich von Heucher (1677–1747), professor of botany in Wittenberg, Germany, is an exclusively North American group, ranging from the Arctic regions to Mexico. About 80 species, all perennial herbs, are known; of these, at least 30 species occur in the western range country; about 12 others are confined to the Eastern States. Alumroots, blossoming as they do before hot, dry weather begins, prefer steep, rocky hillsides, that are moist in the early spring. They frequently occur in sheltered crevices of cliffs, apparently growing upon solid rocks. These plants rank among the first perennial vegetation to inhabit rock slides. Nearly all alumroots have strong, deep, vertical, taprootlike rootstocks which anchor them securely in the soil and fortify them against both drought and cold. The group is an exceptionally hardy one, and their leaves often persist throughout the winter. These plants are called alumroots because of the alumlike taste of the rootstocks; some species are locally prized on account of their astringent properties.

Alumroots are seldom abundant and frequently grow in places inaccessible to livestock; they are seldom eaten, however, probably due to the stinging astringency of the herbage. The rootstock of American alumroot (*H. america'na*), an eastern species, is the source of the drug *heuchera*, an astringent and antiseptic, formerly official in medicine. It was used by the Indians as a powder in the treatment of sores, wounds, ulcers, and as a base for cancer powders.[1] Analysis [2] has shown that tannin is present in this drug. Holm [1] also reports that hunters in Montana use the rootstocks of three native western alumroots, *i. e.*, rough alumroot (*H. his'pida*), roundleaf alumroot (*H. cylin'drica*) and littleleaf alumroot (*H. parvifo'lia*), as astringents, and particularly as a remedy for the diarrhea caused by drinking alkali water. Some pharmacologists believe that our American alumroots justify thorough study from the chemical and pharmaceutical standpoints.[3] [4]

A few alumroots are known horticulturally, being grown chiefly in rock gardens. Coralbells (*H. sangui'nea*), a very showy, red-flowered species growing on shaded cliffs in Arizona, New Mexico, and Mexico, is probably the most widely cultivated species, the source of a number of named horticultural varieties.[5]

The leaves of alumroots are usually long-stalked, more or less heart-shaped, shallow-lobed with toothed edges, and are mostly basal, or reduced and alternate when they occur on the stems bearing the flower clusters. The small, white, yellowish, greenish, purplish, or red, bell-shaped flowers are borne in loose, delicate clusters (panicles) on a slender or stout stalk. The five petals vary in length as compared with the five sepals or occasionally are lacking; they are often less conspicuous than the sepals and calyx tube (hypanthium), which are usually colored. The five slender-stalked stamens are inserted with the petals on the calyx tube, which is attached to the lower portion of the seed-producing organ (ovary). The dry, one-celled, two-beaked fruit (capsule) separates into two halves at maturity.

Ovalleaf alumroot (*Heuchera ovalifolia*), a more or less tufted perennial herb with oval leaves, is representative of the range species of this genus. It occurs from southern British Columbia and southern Alberta to Colorado, Nevada, and northern California, being especially characteristic of the aspen, spruce, and alpine belts but occasionally appearing at elevations of less than 2,000 feet in Washington. The plant prefers dry, sunny sites, growing commonly among the cliffs and rocks of the foothills and mountains; sometimes, however, it develops as scattered individuals on the better soils of open grass or weed types.

Although rather widely distributed, ovalleaf alumroot is not very abundant and has practically negligible livestock value. Deer and elk sometimes eat the plant, and sheep occasionally nibble at the flowers.

[1] Holm, T. MEDICINAL PLANTS OF NORTH AMERICA. 65—HEUCHERA AMERICANA L. Merck's Rept. 21 : 267–269, illus. 1912.

[2] Peacock, J. C., and Peacock, B. L. DeG. FURTHER STUDY OF THE TANNIN OF HEUCHERA AMERICANA, LINNE. Jour. Amer. Pharm. Assoc. 16 : 729–737. 1927.

[3] Schneider, A. PHARMACAL PLANTS AND THEIR CULTURE. Calif. State Bd. Forestry Bull. 2, 175 pp. 1912.

[4] Stuhr, E. T. MANUAL OF PACIFIC COAST DRUG PLANTS . . . 189 pp., illus. Lancaster, Pa. 1933.

[5] Bailey, L. H. THE STANDARD CYCLOPEDIA OF HORTICULTURE . . . New ed., 3 v., illus. New York and London, 1933.

WHITE HAWKWEED

Hiera'cium albiflo'rum

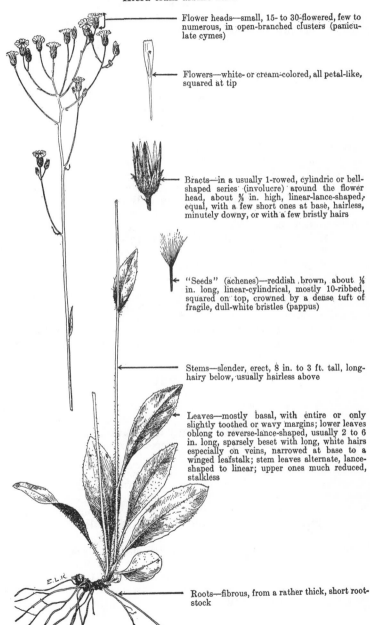

Flower heads—small, 15- to 30-flowered, few to numerous, in open-branched clusters (paniculate cymes)

Flowers—white- or cream-colored, all petal-like, squared at tip

Bracts—in a usually 1-rowed, cylindric or bell-shaped series (involucre) around the flower head, about ⅜ in. high, linear-lance-shaped, equal, with a few short ones at base, hairless, minutely downy, or with a few bristly hairs

"Seeds" (achenes)—reddish brown, about ⅛ in. long, linear-cylindrical, mostly 10-ribbed, squared on top, crowned by a dense tuft of fragile, dull-white bristles (pappus)

Stems—slender, erect, 8 in. to 3 ft. tall, long-hairy below, usually hairless above

Leaves—mostly basal, with entire or only slightly toothed or wavy margins; lower leaves oblong to reverse-lance-shaped, usually 2 to 6 in. long, sparsely beset with long, white hairs especially on veins, narrowed at base to a winged leafstalk; stem leaves alternate, lance-shaped to linear; upper ones much reduced, stalkless

Roots—fibrous, from a rather thick, short rootstock

393

White hawkweed, also known as white-flowered hawkweed and white woollyweed, is one of the most widely distributed and economically important western species of *Hieracium*. It is rather typical in general appearance and forage value of most of the 25 or more species which occur on the western ranges, but is the only native species which has white flowers. The Latin specific name is an adjective meaning white-flowered (derived from *albus*, white, and *flos*, flower); both it and the English name refer to the distinctive white flowers.

White hawkweed is distributed from Alaska to British Columbia and Saskatchewan, and south to Colorado and California. It grows in dry to moderately moist, open wooded slopes in the foothills and mountains, ranging from a few hundred feet above sea level in California and the Northwest to over 9,500 feet in the Rocky Mountains. This species occurs most commonly under the shade of ponderosa-pine and lodgepole-pine stands, but also grows in old burns, cut-over lands, Douglas fir, and spruce-fir forests and, to a slight extent, in open grass and weed types.

Unfortunately, white hawkweed almost invariably grows sparsely scattered over the range, making up only a very small part of the total ground cover and, on that account, is usually classed as a filler. Where found, it is a valuable range weed as it is palatable to all classes of livestock, usually rating good to very good for sheep, fair to fairly good for cattle, and fair for horses. Deer and elk also graze this weed with relish from the time it first appears until it dries up in the fall.

Apparently, white hawkweed is unable to withstand continued heavy grazing, as it is gradually disappearing from some of the closely utilized western sheep ranges. Reproduction occurs entirely from seed, but on most ranges relatively few seedlings are in evidence even under the most favorable conditions, indicating that the seeding habits of this species are weak.

HAWKWEEDS (Hiera′cium spp.)

The hawkweeds are members of the chicory tribe (Cichorieae) of the composite family (Compositae). A number of those range species which are conspicuously shaggy-hairy are usually called woollyweeds. Many of the Old World species are conspicuously variable and have attracted the attention of students of mutation. As a result over 6,800 species of *Hieracium* have been described, making it, apparently, the world's largest genus of flowering plants. However, a conservative estimate of the actual number of species is probably about 400. Hawkweeds are distributed throughout the north temperate regions of the world and in the Andes Mountains of South America, with the greatest number occurring in Europe and northern Asia. Only a relatively few species are native to the United States, of which approximately 25 species grow on the ranges of the West. The generic name *Hieracium* is derived from the Greek word *hierax*, a hawk—hence the common name, hawkweed. According to ancient legends, hawks sharpened their eyesight by using the sap of these plants.

Hawkweeds are widely distributed in the Western States. They grow most abundantly in woodlands, open timberlands, moderately dry open habitats or, in the case of a few species, in moist meadows and parks. Practically all of the species are grazed closely by sheep and goats, and are also fair forage for cattle and horses. A number of species are utilized readily by game animals. Ordinarily, the hawkweeds occur sparsely throughout the western grazing lands and are usually of minor importance in any given locality. Several of the most characteristic and more valuable western species merit special mention.

Woollyweed (*H. scou'leri*, syns. *H. gris'eum*, *H. alberti'num*), a yellow-flowered plant with its foliage, stems, and involucres densely covered with long, soft, white hairs, is one of the most important range species. It grows typically on dry, open grass and weed types and under open ponderosa pine timber, ranging from British Columbia and Alberta to Wyoming, Utah, and California. Woollyweed is highly palatable to sheep, but only fair for cattle. Although usually scattered in occurrence, it is sometimes fairly abundant in localized range areas.

Houndstongue hawkweed (*H. cynoglossoi'des*), a species resembling woollyweed but less hairy, is distributed over dry, grassy hillsides, benchlands, and open woods, from British Columbia and Montana to Wyoming and California. It is one of the most important hawkweeds in the Northwest; all parts of the plant are grazed closely by sheep, and with moderate relish by cattle. It is a yellow-flowered species, from 1 to 2 feet high; the lower leaves are rather hairy, but the upper ones, the upper part of the stem, and the bracts of the involucre are usually only sparingly hairy or often hairless.

Slender hawkweed (*H. gra'cile*), a small, slender, moisture-loving species, characteristically grows in mountain meadows, alpine parks, along streams, and in damp places of open woods or old burns. It is distributed from Alaska to Alberta, New Mexico, and California, but, like most of the other hawkweeds, is seldom abundant. When sufficiently abundant and accessible, it is regarded as a valuable weed. It is highly palatable to sheep and is grazed to some extent by cattle. Slender hawkweed is a relatively low plant, usually 4 to 12 inches high; the leaves are mostly basal, hairless or nearly so; the stems are slender, naked or few-leaved, hairless or minutely woolly; its yellow flowers are in rather small flower heads, and the involucres ordinarily are densely covered with black hairs.

Several of the hawkweeds are serious pests in the Eastern States, the leading one being orange hawkweed (*H. auranti'acum*), which has become one of the most troublesome weeds ever introduced into America. The handsome, orange-red flower heads have led to its use in ornamental plantings. Several other species are used in rock gardens, wild-flower gardens, and borders. Shaggy hawkweed (*H. villo'sum*), an Old World species, has proved particularly desirable for ornamental purposes.

The hawkweeds are hairy, glandular, or sometimes smooth perennial herbs with alternate or basal, entire, or merely slightly toothed or wavy-margined leaves, and one to many flower heads of yellow, orange, red, pinkish, or sometimes white flowers. All of the individual flowers of each head are set on a flat, naked, common base (receptacle), and each has a strap-shaped (ligulate) corolla, which is squared and five-toothed at the summit. The involucres are cylindrical or bell-shaped, with the principal bracts in one to three series, the outer ones usually being smaller than the others. The "seeds" (achenes) are columnar or cylindric, mostly 10-ribbed, not tapering toward the apex but squared on top, and are crowned with long tufts of fragile, stiffish, tawny, brownish or dull white bristles (pappus). The hawkweeds are closely related to the hawkbeards (*Crepis* spp.), and some of the species of the two genera are often confused. They can be readily distinguished, however, since most of the hawkbeards have toothed or deeply cleft leaves, their "seeds" are narrowed both at the top and base, and the copious tufts of hairs crowning the "seeds" are soft and white. In the hawkbeards the bracts of the involucre are thickened at the base or on the midrib, and the foliage is either hairless or densely woolly, whereas hawkweeds have unthickened bracts and the foliage tends to be rough-hairy.

BALLHEAD WATERLEAF

Hydrophyl'lum capita'tum

Leaves—mostly basal, long-stalked, 4 to 12 in. long, hairy, darker green above than below, divided into 5 to 7 main lobes; lobes 1 to 2 in. long, oblong to egg-shaped or reverse-egg-shaped, blunt or abruptly sharp-tipped, sometimes 2- or 3-cleft or again lobed

Flowers—violet-blue, in dense, ball-shaped (capitate) clusters; flower-cluster stalk (peduncle) shorter than the leafstalks

Threadlike stalk (style)—2-cleft, equaling the stamens

Outer flower parts (sepals)—5, linear-oblong, about ⅔ as long as united petals (corolla), united at base, very hairy

Corolla—bell-shaped, 5-lobed, ¼ to ⅜ in. long

Stamens—5, protruding; stalks (filaments) long, threadlike, hairy at the middle

Roots—fleshy, fibrous

397

Ballhead waterleaf is also known as cats-breeches, ragged-breeches, bear-cabbage, and simply as waterleaf. It is a low, perennial herb with attractive ball-shaped clusters of violet-blue flowers; deeply-lobed, long-stalked, hairy leaves; short, indistinct stems; and numerous, fleshy roots clustered on a short, underground rootstock. The genus *Hydrophyllum*, which gives the waterleaf family (*Hydrophyllaceae*) its name, is strictly American and consists of approximately a dozen species. Ballhead waterleaf is the most common and abundant of the seven or eight species of waterleaf which occur on the western ranges and is fairly representative of the group in general appearance and forage value. The name waterleaf is a literal translation of *Hydrophyllum*, derived from the Greek *hydro-*, water, and *phyllon*, leaf. This name has a practical significance, as the foliage of the plants in this genus contains a high percentage of water and hence is termed washy feed by the western stockman. Ballhead waterleaf gets its Latin and English specific names from its distinctive ball-shaped (capitate) flower heads.

Ballhead waterleaf ranges from British Columbia and Montana to Colorado, and central California; it does not occur west of the Cascade Mountains in the Northwest. This herb extends from the low valleys and foothills up to the aspen and spruce belts, being most common at medium elevations. It most typically occupies fertile, semishaded sites in or bordering woodlands, open stands of aspen and ponderosa pine, in canyon bottoms, and on brushy hillsides. However, it is not uncommon in weed or grass types of open slopes exposed to full sunlight. Ballhead waterleaf is one of the spring plant pioneers, as it appears with the first warm days of the season and makes its growth while the soil is still moist from the receding snows.

This species has been used as an indicator of either range readiness or lack of readiness. Ordinarily, the principal forage plants are not ready for grazing until after ballhead waterleaf passes the flowering stage. Since this plant matures its seed, dries up, and disappears from most ranges early in the grazing season, it is usually of little value for forage. However, on some spring range areas and lambing grounds, it is readily grazed by all classes of livestock, and constitutes an important part of the early forage crop. On such areas, its palatability ranks as fairly good to very good for sheep, and fair for cattle. Deer and elk, after a winter diet of browse and dried herbage, welcome the appearance of this succulent herb and graze it with relish.

The young, tender shoots of this plant, as well as of several other species of waterleaf, are often eaten by both Indians and white men. They provide excellent greens, especially if gathered before flowering; the western Indians sometimes eat them raw.

Western waterleaf (*H. occidenta'le*), also known as squawlettuce, because of its use for food by the Indians, ranges from Oregon to California and western Nevada. It is locally important on spring-range areas in eastern California, where it grows in abundance and ranks as fairly good forage for cattle and very good for sheep. This species closely resembles ballhead waterleaf in appearance and habitat, but is a taller plant, usually 5 to 15 inches high but sometimes attaining a height of 24 inches; its clusters of violet purple to white flowers are borne on long stalks, and its leaves are divided into 7 to 15 sharp-pointed lobes, which may be further lobed or divided.

Whiteface waterleaf (*H. al'bifrons*), a rank-growing, white-flowered species, is an important forage plant in some localities in the Northwest, where it ranges from British Columbia to Washington and Idaho. It grows in dense patches in high mountain parks and meadows, as well as scatteringly along shady stream banks and in or near willow and alder thickets at lower elevations. The succulent foliage is grazed with relish by livestock, especially sheep, during the forepart of the summer grazing season. It produces washy forage lacking in substance, however, and usually dries up early, practically disappearing from the range by midsummer.

COMMON ST.JOHNSWORT

Hype'ricum perfora'tum

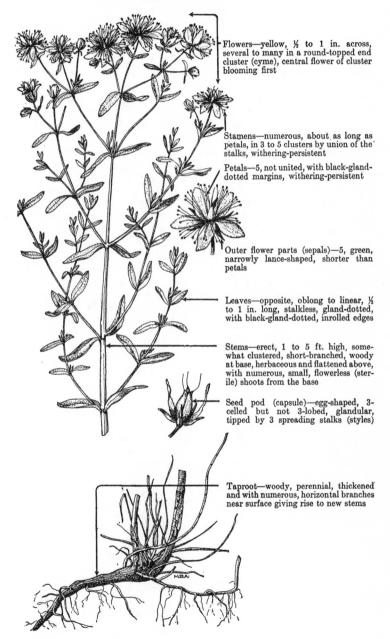

Flowers—yellow, ½ to 1 in. across, several to many in a round-topped end cluster (cyme), central flower of cluster blooming first

Stamens—numerous, about as long as petals, in 3 to 5 clusters by union of the stalks, withering-persistent

Petals—5, not united, with black-gland-dotted margins, withering-persistent

Outer flower parts (sepals)—5, green, narrowly lance-shaped, shorter than petals

Leaves—opposite, oblong to linear, ½ to 1 in. long, stalkless, gland-dotted, with black-gland-dotted, inrolled edges

Stems—erect, 1 to 5 ft. high, somewhat clustered, short-branched, woody at base, herbaceous and flattened above, with numerous, small, flowerless (sterile) shoots from the base

Seed pod (capsule)—egg-shaped, 3-celled but not 3-lobed, glandular, tipped by 3 spreading stalks (styles)

Taproot—woody, perennial, thickened and with numerous, horizontal branches near surface giving rise to new stems

Common St.Johnswort is a very aggressive, moderately poisonous range weed pest introduced from Europe—first reported in New England about 1800, and growing on the Pacific coast since 1900. It does not seem to be regarded as a very serious weed pest throughout the Middle West and East, but is firmly established and spreading in the Pacific Coast States, especially in northern California. It occurs less extensively in Montana, Idaho, and Utah, although, at present, also increasing its range in these States. The common name St.Johnswort has come from the Old World, where according to legend it bloomed on June 24, St. John the Baptist's Day.[1] This species is commonly known in California and Oregon as Klamath weed, as the original infestation came from the Klamath River country near the Oregon line.

This species usually establishes itself on eroded pastures and abandoned or poorly cultivated fields, although it also becomes abundant on adjoining deep and fertile soils. It prefers full sunshine on well-drained slopes and never grows satisfactorily in shaded areas, or where the soil remains moist. This plant flourishes at low elevations and probably does not occur above the ponderosa-pine belt in any of the western States. Since this weed usually grows in pastures and fields, its associates include such grasses as annual fescues, wild oats, and bromes as well as perennials like needlegrass and bluegrass. However, once well established it forms dense patches or even extensive fields, and dominates the soil to the exclusion of practically all other herbaceous vegetation. The mature plants are woody and, as a rule, unpalatable; the young spring shoots, however, furnish fair forage for goats, and are sometimes grazed lightly by sheep and cattle. The weed is heavily grazed only where animals are forced to consume it and, under such starvation conditions, sickness and losses are most likely to ensue.

Common St.Johnswort has long been recognized as a poisonous plant, although it is toxic only to white or unpigmented animals. This curious situation is probably due to some fluorescent substance in the plant which exerts harmful effects when absorbed by white-skinned animals that are subsequently exposed to full light.[2] Apparently all parts of the plant are toxic; well-bred and young animals react most readily to the poison. Marsh and Clawson's[3] feeding experiments show that cattle are more susceptible than sheep. Briefly, these investigators ascertained that the consumption of green foliage equivalent to 4 percent of the animal's weight poisoned sheep, but as little as 1 percent was toxic to cattle, with 5 percent probably fatal. Sensitiveness varies with individual animals, as some are not poisoned by repeated dosages, yet others sicken in a few hours and continue to show symptoms even a month after the feeding of this weed is discontinued. The first symptoms are increased pulse, temperature, respiration, and general uneasiness, probably caused by intense skin irritation. Later, blisters and a

[1] Bailey, W. W. ST.JOHNSWORT. Amer. Bot. 15(3) : 68–70. 1909.
[2] Rogers, T. B. ON THE ACTION OF ST.JOHN'S WORT AS A SENSITIZING AGENT FOR NON-PIGMENTED SKIN. Amer. Vet. Rev. 46 : 145–162, illus. 1914.
[3] Marsh, C. D., and Clawson, A. B. TOXIC EFFECT OF ST.JOHNSWORT (HYPERICUM PERFORATUM) ON CATTLE AND SHEEP. U. S. Dept. Agr. Tech. Bull. 202, 24 pp., illus. 1930.

scabby condition usually develop over the face and ears, but sometimes over the back and sides. Sick animals soon lose weight and in severe cases become blind, develop sore mouths, and may even die from malnutrition. Obviously, the poisonous effects of common St.Johnswort are largely cumulative and result in lower market prices and in curtailed wool quality and yield.

In northern California common St.Johnswort is such a common pest that its eradication is a major problem. Sampson and Parker [4] found such mechanical controls as digging, mowing, covering with opaque material, and flooding practical only on small areas. Burning not only endangered other property values but extended the stands of common St.Johnswort, both by regrowth of the old plant from root crowns and underground runners and through increased germination of the heated seeds. A 15-percent solution of sodium chlorate applied as a fine spray during the spring or late summer appears to be the most effective means thus far developed for eradicating a stand of common St.Johnswort. Sodium chlorate, however, is expensive and must be used with care. Clothing and other organic matter spattered with any of the evaporated solution are highly inflammable and explosive. The two California investigators mentioned believe that systematic goat grazing—the weed is fairly palatable and only mildly poisonous to goats—would probably help control common St.Johnswort.

Common St.Johnswort blooms throughout the spring and early summer, the blossoms forming a mass of yellow wherever the plants form large patches. Later the flowers wilt, the leaves, stems, and seed pods become brown, and the whole colony acquires an unkempt, weedy appearance. The leaves are interesting, as they are speckled with glands resembling perforations, which accounts for the specific name *perforatum*.

ST.JOHNSWORTS (Hype'ricum spp.)

Hypericum is a large genus of over 200 species widely distributed in the temperate and subtropical regions, especially of the northern hemisphere, although there are probably less than six species native to the Western States. They are herbs or shrubs, with opposite, stemless, or short-petioled and gland-dotted leaves, mostly yellow flowers of five equal petals and sepals, numerous, more or less united stamens, and 3- to 5-celled capsules. One annual, trailing St.Johnswort (*H. anagalloi'des*), is from 2 to 7 inches high and forms small mats in very wet places in the mountains from British Columbia to California and Montana. Scouler St.Johnswort (*H. scou'leri*), a native perennial, is smaller than common St.Johnswort, although similar in form and site requirements, but can be readily distinguished by the absence of sterile shoots. It occurs from British Columbia to Montana, Colorado, and California.

---

[4] Sampson, A. W., and Parker, K. W. ST. JOHNSWORT ON RANGE LANDS OF CALIFORNIA. Calif. Agr. Expt. Sta. Bull. 503, 48 pp, illus. 1930.

A large and handsome shrubby species of the East, golden St. Johnswort (*H. au'reum*), is cultivated as an ornamental. All of the species are probably poisonous to livestock. Hypericum red, a well-known extract from this genus (specifically *H. perforatum*), is a red, resinous substance formerly used extensively in the treatment of wounds.

THICKET STICKSEED

Lap'pula floribun'da

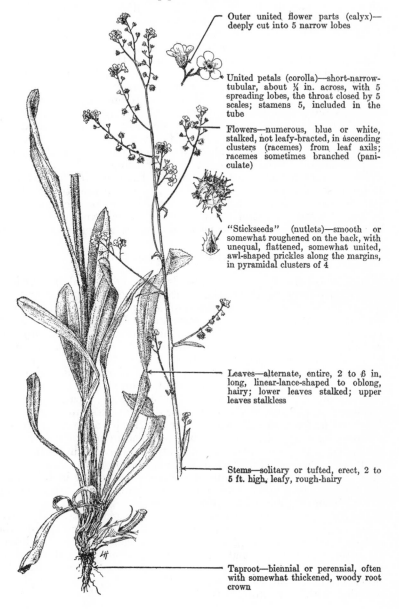

Outer united flower parts (calyx)—deeply cut into 5 narrow lobes

United petals (corolla)—short-narrow-tubular, about ¼ in. across, with 5 spreading lobes, the throat closed by 5 scales; stamens 5, included in the tube

Flowers—numerous, blue or white, stalked, not leafy-bracted, in ascending clusters (racemes) from leaf axils; racemes sometimes branched (paniculate)

"Stickseeds" (nutlets)—smooth or somewhat roughened on the back, with unequal, flattened, somewhat united, awl-shaped prickles along the margins, in pyramidal clusters of 4

Leaves—alternate, entire, 2 to 6 in. long, linear-lance-shaped to oblong, hairy; lower leaves stalked; upper leaves stalkless

Stems—solitary or tufted, erect, 2 to 5 ft. high, leafy, rough-hairy

Taproot—biennial or perennial, often with somewhat thickened, woody root crown

Thicket stickseed, a fairly tall, leafy, biennial or perennial weed, with burlike fruits, is a moderately common and fairly widely distributed species, ranging from western Ontario to British Columbia, California, New Mexico, and Minnesota. It is distributed from the plains and foothills to the spruce zone, although more common at the lower elevations and in the ponderosa pine zone. It grows in from moderately moist to rather dry soils, and generally occurs most abundantly in thickets and among bushes and in such waste places as roadsides and neglected dooryards. However, although generally scattered, it is common on the range and occurs in grass-weed, sagebrush, aspen and, to some extent, open conifer types.

This species, probably because of the rough-hairy character of its stems and leaves and on account of the prickly fruits, is generally poor forage for cattle and only fair for sheep. In a few localities, it ranks as fair cattle forage and fairly good sheep forage. On the range it is often most abundant where more palatable vegetation has been depleted as a result of overgrazing.

The flowers, which are blue or white, have usually formed fruit at the base of the cluster, while those at the top are still in bloom. The flowers are numerous, a fact to which the specific name *floribunda* (literally, abounding in flowers) refers, and the plant in bloom is rather showy. This species ordinarily flowers from June to August.

STICKSEEDS (Lap′pula spp.)

Stickseeds, also known as burseeds, sticktights, and beggarticks, thus named because the burlike nutlets cling to clothing and the fur of animals, compose a genus of about 40 species of annuals, biennials, or perennials mostly native in the North Temperate Zone. This genus is a member of the borage family (Boraginaceae) and gets its name *Lappula*, meaning a little bur, from the Latin, *lappa*, a bur. The stickseeds are widely distributed in the West, but usually are abundant only in such waste places as along roads and fences and in abandoned fields. They are of common occurrence on the range, however, and often increase on overgrazed areas.

Generally, the stickseeds are practically worthless to poor forage for cattle and horses and poor to fair for sheep and goats, although occasionally they may rate somewhat higher in palatability. As a rule, stickseeds are not abundant and are of secondary importance.

Stickseeds are often pest weeds in fields and pastures. Their seeds, which cling tightly to clothing and become entangled in the manes and tails of cattle and horses and in the wool of sheep, are annoying to both men and animals.

The seed-producing organ (ovary) of this genus is deeply four-lobed and develops into four nutlets with barbed prickles on the margins or back. The plants are usually rough-hairy; the leaves are alternate, narrow, and entire; and the small, regular flowers are blue or white. The five-lobed corollas have a very short tube, closed at the throat by five scales. The five stamens are short and included within the corolla tube.

ROCKY MOUNTAIN IRIS

I'ris missourien'sis

Flowers—large, showy, pale blue or purplish with darker veins, variegated, from 2 papery, dilated, rarely separated bracts, each flower on a stalk up to 2 in. long

Outer flower parts (sepals)—3, colored, petal-like, broad, dilated, spreading or bent back, long-clawed, up to 2½ in. long

Petals—3, ascending, narrower than sepals, up to 2 in. long, alternating with sepals and united with them below to form the perianth tube

Appendages (styles)—at tip of seed-producing organ, colored, petal-like, 3-cleft at apex, opposite to and arching over the 3 stamens, almost completely united at base with perianth tube

Seed pod (capsule)—below perianth tube, oblong, 2¼ in. long and ¾ in. wide, many-seeded, 3-celled, 6-ridged, splitting down from the top along the middle back of each cell

Stems—6 to 40 in. high, leafless or nearly so, usually 2-flowered, slender, round

Leaves—mostly basal, 2-ranked, shorter than the stems, flat, sword-shaped, about ½ in. wide, with parallel veins

Roots—thickened, fibrous, perennial, from stout, underground, dark-fibrous-coated rootstocks

Rocky Mountain iris is a perennial herb, with large, attractive, blue flowers on long succulent stalks from thickened, dark, fibrous-coated, underground rootstocks. It occurs from North Dakota to New Mexico, southern California, and British Columbia and is the only species of *Iris* indigenous to the far Western States except for the three Pacific States, where other species are found. It appears chiefly in bottomlands or moist situations, in meadows and parks, at elevations upward to 10,000 feet. It generally grows in small clumps or patches but, under favorable conditions, may occur in dense, nearly pure stands of considerable size. It also frequently grows in such sites as gravelly hillsides which dry out during the summer.

Rocky Mountain iris is worthless as a forage plant but, when its stand is increasing, it may be an indicator of overgrazing, as its robust underground rootstocks enable it to withstand trampling and to spread rather rapidly when other vegetation is weakened. This species, when once extensively established, greatly retards the revegetation of the range by more palatable plants. It is a good soil binder, but ordinarily grows in moist soils which are potentially capable of supporting other plants of equal soil-holding qualities and of greater forage value.

This species flowers from May to July, depending on latitude and elevation. If moisture is available the plants remain green throughout the summer, otherwise they dry up in midsummer after the seed matures.

IRISES (I'ris spp.)

Iris is a large genus of herbaceous plants of north temperate regions, well known because of their attractive blossoms. Other common names are flag, flag-lily, snake-lily, and water-flag. A great variety and number of species occur in the southeastern United States, but the genus is rather poorly represented in the Western States, where only nine native species occur, eight of which grow exclusively in the Pacific Coast States. Generally, irises are found in moist to wet sites, or in situations where plenty of moisture is present early in the season during the main growth period, despite that such sites subsequently become very dry. However, the distribution of irises in the West is spotted rather than general, although these species frequently are so abundant on favorable sites that they form nearly pure stands.

Irises are worthless as forage plants. They are sometimes important obstacles to range improvement, in that they tend to increase on overgrazed areas adapted to their growth, and when once established greatly retard the regeneration of palatable forage species.

The genus is of considerable importance commercially, as many species are grown extensively as ornamentals. The American Iris Society has recognized some 2,300 named commercial varieties and hybrids which have been developed through intensive cultivation.[1]

The Indians formerly used the tough, flexible fibers from the leaf margins of certain species, such as Oregon iris (*I. tenax*), in making strong twine for snares and nets. They also used the rhizome, or "root" of blueflag iris (*I. versicolor*), the most widespread species in the eastern United States, as a remedy for stomach disorders, and are reputed to have grown this plant for its medicinal value.[2] Both Indians and whites used this species as an alterative, diuretic, and purgative (*op. cit.*). An extract of the root was also used as a remedy for dropsy and is listed as an official drug in the United States Dispensatory.[3] The rhizome in the fresh state possesses considerable potency as a cathartic and emetic. It has no odor, but the taste is acrid and nauseous. An analysis of the roots of this species disclosed that the principal compounds are yellow oil, isophthalic acid, salicylic acid, tannin, sugar, and resins containing fatty acids.[4] The rhizomes of Florentina iris (*I. germanica*, syn. *I. florentina*) and of sweet iris (*I. pallida*) are used in the preparation of orrisroot, which is imported chiefly from Leghorn, a province in Italy. This product is used in medicine, as a sachet powder, for dry shampoos, and for cleaning teeth.

[1] American Joint Committee on Horticultural Nomenclature. STANDARDIZED PLANT NAMES . . . Prepared by F. L. Olmsted, F. V. Coville, and H. P. Kelsey. 546 pp. Salem, Mass. 1923.
[2] Henkel, A. AMERICAN ROOT DRUGS. U. S. Dept. Agr., Bur. Plant Indus. Bull. 107, 80 pp., illus. 1907.
[3] Remington, J. P., Wood, H. C., Jr., Sadtler, S. P., LaWall, C. H., Kraemer, H., and Anderson, J. F. THE DISPENSATORY OF THE UNITED STATES OF AMERICA, by Dr. Geo. B. Wood and Dr. Franklin Bache. Ed. 20, thoroughly rev. and largely rewritten . . . 2,010 pp. Philadelphia and London. 1918.
[4] Power, F. B., and Salway, A. H. THE CONSTITUENTS OF THE RHIZOME OF IRIS VERSICOLOR. Amer. Jour. Pharm. 83 : 1–14. 1911.

ASPEN PEAVINE

La'thyrus leucan'thus

Flowers—white, yellowish or yellow, in 2- to many-flowered clusters (racemes) arising from axils of middle leaves, with 5 dissimilar petals forming a pea-like bloom about ½ in. long

Upper petal (banner)—broader than others

2 middle petals—usually shorter than upper one

2 lowest petals (keel)—united, boatlike, curved

Stamens—10, in 2 groups of 9 and 1, enclosed in the keel, their threadlike stalks united into a tube which is squarely cut across the top

Outer united flower parts (calyx)—about ½ as long as petals, green, deeply 5-toothed, the lower teeth somewhat longer than upper

A. Stalk (style)—of seed-producing organ (ovary), flattened toward the tip, with white hairs along only one side. B. Illustrates the style of the very similar vetches (*Vicia* spp.)

Leaves—alternate, divided, stalked; midrib extended into a tendril, often much reduced

Leaflets—2 to 4 pairs (rarely more), oval, up to 2 in. long, hairless, veiny, abruptly sharp-pointed

Leaflike bracts (stipules)—2, at base of leafstalks, each shaped like half an arrowhead, about ½ as long as leaflets

Stems—more or less 4-sided, usually erect, sometimes trailing

Rootstocks—underground, slender, somewhat spreading

Taproot—slender, somewhat woody at top

Pod (legume)—hanging, broadest toward tip

407

Aspen peavine is a delicate, trailing, or climbing perennial herb with the graceful, pealike, rather sweet-smelling blossoms so characteristic of many members of the pea family (Leguminosae, or Fabaceae). This species is confined to the Rocky Mountains, ranging from southern Idaho to Wyoming, New Mexico, and Arizona. It is a plant of the higher elevations and occurs in greatest abundance in the upper aspen and spruce belts. Its preferred habitat is the rich, moist soils of aspen groves where it often makes up a large part of the undergrowth. This herb seldom grows in stands dense enough to exclude other species and is commonly associated with American vetch (*Vicia americana*), asters (*Aster* spp.), blue wild-rye (*Elymus glaucus*), cinquefoils (*Potentilla* spp.), wild-daisies (*Erigeron* spp.), and yarrows (*Achillea* spp.). The specific name, *leucanthus*, is a Greek word meaning white-flowered.

Opinions differ as to the palatability of aspen peavine. Some observers state that it is nearly if not quite as palatable as American vetch, which is one of the best range weeds; others maintain that it is almost worthless as a forage plant. Probably its true value lies somewhere between these extremes. Ordinarily, sheep and cattle as well as goats graze aspen peavine readily, although in Utah and southern Idaho sheep usually do not graze it much until after the first frost. Horses graze it in the fall after the pods are mature and quickly put on good, hard fat when a plentiful supply of this plant is available. Deer and elk also forage aspen peavine.

PEAVINES (La'thyrus spp.)

The peavines constitute a genus comprising mostly smooth, weak-stemmed, trailing, or climbing plants with divided (even-pinnately compound) leaves. All the native western species are perennials. The best known member of the genus is undoubtedly the cultivated sweetpea (*L. odoratus*). This annual, originally a native of Sicily, is widely cultivated for its delicately odorous, variegated blossoms. At present at least 65 named and well-recognized varieties have been developed through intensive cultivation and selection.

The genus is well represented in the West and, although no one species ranges over the entire region, several species occur in each State—California, Oregon, and Washington having the largest number. Peavines occur from near sea level on the Pacific coast to above timber line in the Rocky Mountains, but are most abundant at medium elevations. They are found in moist, rich soils and on dry scablands, in open exposures in grass and weed types, among shrubs, and in the shade of coniferous and broadleaf timber, being most typical of open aspen areas.

Peavines vary considerably in palatability. Generally the trailing or climbing species with tendrils on the leaves are more palatable than the erect-stemmed species and are usually at least fair to good forage for cattle, sheep, and goats. The erect-stemmed species probably are not better than poor to fair forage and in Utah, southern Idaho, and the Southwest the palatability of most species of *Lathyrus* appears to be low. Horses ordinarily graze peavines only in the fall after the pods are well matured. Among the more palatable species are cream peavine (*L. ochroleucus*), marsh peavine (*L. palustris*), sulphur peavine (*L. sulphureus*), and bush peavine (*L. eucosmus*); some of medium palatablity are Nuttall peavine (*L. nuttallii*), fewflower peavine (*L. pauciflorus*), Arizona peavine (*L. arizonicus*), and aspen peavine (*L. leucanthus*); and some of less than average palatability are Sandberg peavine (*L. bijugatus sandbergii*, syn. *L. sandbergii*) and thickleaf peavine (*L. coriaceus*). All species of peavine are of value for forage chiefly during the summer and fall, as they do not cure well but dry up and largely disappear after the first heavy frosts. Some species have extensive root systems with horizontal rootstocks and are able to withstand considerable heavy grazing.

The pealike blossoms, divided (even-pinnately compound) leaves usually terminated by a tendril or this reduced to a tip or small appendage, and the frequently four-sided, weak stems will serve to distinguish the peavines from most other range plants except the very similar vetches (*Vicia* spp.).

DANDELION

Leon′todon tara′xacum, syns. *Tara′xacum dens-leo′nis, T. officina′le, T. tara′xacum*

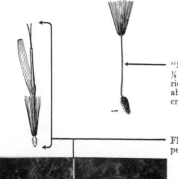

"Seeds" (achenes)—green to brownish yellow, ⅛ in. long, spindle-shaped, each ridged, the ridges with tiny spines near tops, tapering above into a beak ⅜ in. long; beak tipped by a crown of fine, brownish or white hairs (pappus)

Flowers—all strap-shaped, bright golden-yellow, perfect and seed-bearing

Flower stalks—1 to several, 2 to 16 in. high, round in cross section, hollow, each ending in a single flower head

Bracts (involucre)—surrounding flower head, about ½ in. high, narrow or narrowly lance-shaped, green with white-papery margins, usually in 2 rows, outer row early bent back, inner enclosing immature flower head, but spreading or reflexing when flowers fully open

Leaves—up to 12 in. long, in a basal rosette from a stout, perennial taproot, oblong or spatula-shaped in outline, ragged-toothed to coarsely and pinnately lobed with the pointed lobe tips pointing toward base of plant

Dandelion, probably the best known and most widespread weed in the world, grows on a wide variety of soils but prefers moist soils or, at least, those that remain moist until midsummer. Hence it is found commonly on the range in weedy meadows, along open stream banks and to a less degree on moist, open slopes, in stands of aspen and lodgepole pine. A typical location for dandelion is the gully-drained soils of eroded meadows.

Dandelion provides good forage on the range and is often regarded as an important forage plant. It is readily eaten by all classes of livestock, being especially relished by sheep. It is one of the first plants to begin growth in the spring and when the herbage is removed, as in grazing, it continues growth and retains its succulence until fall if moisture conditions are favorable. The leaves may be upright, or if the plant cover is unusually dense or the growth rank, they may be spreading. Under intensive grazing and denuded soil conditions, dandelion plants usually cling to the ground, which prevents complete use of the foliage. Because of its strong, deep taproot, dandelion is able to withstand trampling and heavy use.

The presence of dandelion on the range may or may not indicate overgrazed conditions, and therefore its classification as an indicator of overgrazing must be carefully qualified. It occurs frequently in protected pastures and similar locations which support a normally undisturbed plant cover of weeds and grasses, indicative of satisfactory growing conditions. It also occurs on sites where the normal plant cover has been depleted as a result of overgrazing or less favorable moisture conditions due to abnormal drainage, trampling, and drought.

The dandelion is a pest in lawns, etc. It is outstandingly aggressive and persistent because of its deep and stout taproot, many leaves, and abundant, widely scattered seed. The fact that it is found from sea level almost to timber line indicates its adaptability to a great variety of conditions, especially with regard to temperature and length of growing period.

The dandelion is a good honey plant in the more humid parts of the country, its copious blooms being the source of large quantities of nectar and pollen, although their season of production is often short.[1][2] Dandelion has long been cultivated for greens, the more delicate early growth of the wild plants being used for that purpose. Its bitter root is used medicinally as a tonic, and liver stimulant.[3][4]

From an evolutionary standpoint dandelion is of great interest; its deep perennial taproot, milky juice, leaf rosettes, immense vitality, aggressiveness, and intense efficiency in the production and dissemination of seed enable it to withstand extreme variations in growth conditions, as reflected by its cosmopolitan distribution. Many botanists consider it the most specialized of plants and place it at the evolutionary summit of the plant kingdom.

The leaves of dandelion are wholly basal. Its flowers are generally produced in the spring and summer and, under favorable conditions, throughout the year. Dandelion leaves are oblong, divided into a number of opposite lobes with curved tips pointing toward the base of the plant. The flower stalk—each plant has one or more—terminates in a single flower head. The bracts, which in the bud enclose the flower head, are double-rowed, both rows subsequently folding under the base of the head, the outer row before flowering and the inner row shortly after the petals are lost.

The scientific name *Leontodon* and the common name dandelion both signify lion's tooth, in reference to the peculiarly jagged leaf edges.

[1] Pellett, F. C. AMERICAN HONEY PLANTS, TOGETHER WITH THOSE WHICH ARE OF SPECIAL VALUE TO THE BEEKEEPER AS SOURCES OF POLLEN. Ed. 3, rev. and enl., 419 pp., illus. Hamilton, Ill. 1930.
[2] Vansell, G. H. NECTAR AND POLLEN PLANTS OF CALIFORNIA. Calif. Agr. Expt. Sta. Bull. 517. [60] pp. 1931.
[3] Lyons, A. B. PLANT NAMES SCIENTIFIC AND POPULAR . . . Ed. 2, thoroughly rev. and enl., 630 pp. Detroit. 1907.
[4] Sievers, A. F. AMERICAN MEDICINAL PLANTS OF COMMERCIAL IMPORTANCE. U. S. Dept. Agr. Misc. Pub. 77, 74 pp., illus. 1930.

CARROTLEAF

Leptotae'nia multi'fida, syn. *L. dissec'ta multi'fida*

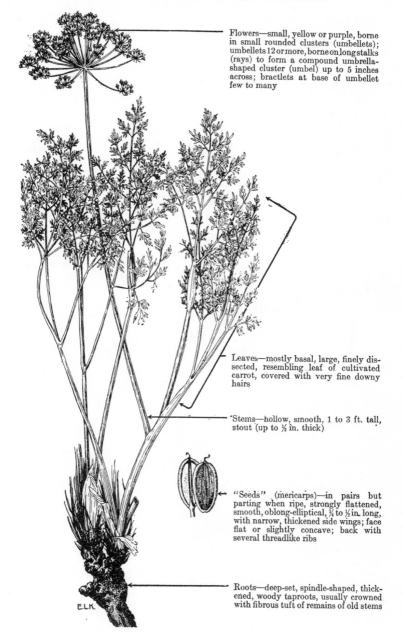

Flowers—small, yellow or purple, borne in small rounded clusters (umbellets); umbellets 12 or more, borne on long stalks (rays) to form a compound umbrella-shaped cluster (umbel) up to 5 inches across; bractlets at base of umbellet few to many

Leaves—mostly basal, large, finely dissected, resembling leaf of cultivated carrot, covered with very fine downy hairs

Stems—hollow, smooth, 1 to 3 ft. tall, stout (up to ½ in. thick)

"Seeds" (mericarps)—in pairs but parting when ripe, strongly flattened, smooth, oblong-elliptical, ¼ to ½ in. long, with narrow, thickened side wings; face flat or slightly concave; back with several threadlike ribs

Roots—deep-set, spindle-shaped, thickened, woody taproots, usually crowned with fibrous tuft of remains of old stems

E.L.K.

Carrotleaf, frequently called wildcarrot, Indian-balsam, wildcelery, wild-parsley, and wildparsnip, is a moderately tall, stout perennial herb of the carrot family (Umbelliferae). This is the most common, abundant, and wide-spread of about 12 species of *Leptotaenia* which grow in the West, and is more or less typical of the group in appearance, habitat, and forage value.

Carrotleaf grows from Alberta to western Wyoming, New Mexico, California, and British Columbia. It is typically a plant of the foothills and open lower mountain slopes, but ranges from the piñon-juniper, through the ponderosa pine, to the aspen belt, occurring in the plains and valleys and extending into the mountains up to elevations of about 9,000 feet. The species usually grows on dry, gravelly, or rocky soils, but occasionally is found in more or less shaded places and in rich, sandy bottom loams. It occurs most commonly and makes its best growth, however, on warm, open exposures. Plants with which it is usually associated include arrowleaf balsamroot, sagebrush, lupine, and wheatgrass. Ordinarily its growth is scattered, but it is abundant and one of the dominant spring plants on some localized areas.

Carrotleaf, like most other species of its genus, is valuable for forage only in the spring and early summer. Growth starts early, soon after the snow disappears. The plants utilize the early spring soil moisture in making their development. The flowers are produced in April and May and the plants dry up soon after the seeds mature in June and July. When dry, the plants become hard and brittle and are worthless for forage. The herbage, while green, is highly palatable to all classes of livestock. Sheep, in particular, seek the plants and often eat them down to the ground. Palatability ratings of this plant are from fair to good or very good for sheep, and poor to good for cattle. Reports are occasionally made, and have even appeared in print, that this plant is suspected of being poisonous. No scientific evidence whatever appears to exist to support this viewpoint; but, on the contrary, the experience of the Forest Service is that, under range conditions, it is harmless and a good forage plant. It seems likely that the bad reputation of some of its relatives, such as the poisonous waterhemlocks, have been saddled upon it. In preliminary trials, which have been made to use carrotleaf in artificial range reseeding, it has become established from the original seeding, but thus far has failed to reproduce.[1]

Carrotleaf has parsniplike roots which are characteristically crowned with tufts of the coarse, fibrous remains of old stems. These strong, deep-set aromatic taproots fortify the plants against loss from heavy grazing. The leaves are mostly basal but occasionally arise from a short, branched stem or from the flower stalks. The stalks, which bear the flower clusters, usually extend above the general level of the leaves and are 1 to 3 feet tall and as much as one-half of an inch in diameter. They are hollow and smooth, and sometimes have a purplish tinge. The fruits or "seeds" are produced in fairly large quantities and are grouped in tufts on short stalks (pedicels) one-fourth to seven-eighths of an inch long at the ends of the main branches (rays) of the umbel. The leptotaenias can easily be distinguished from other western umbellifers by their strongly flattened smooth "seeds". These are shaped like ordinary squash seeds, although somewhat smaller, being from one-fourth to one-half of an inch long and about half as wide. The edges are bordered by narrow but thick corky wings. One face of the "seed" is flat or slightly dished (concave) and has a distinct rib or scar down the middle. The other face is slightly rounded and bears several threadlike ribs. The name *Leptotaenia* is from the Greek (*leptos*, slender; *tainia*, a band) and refers to these threadlike ribs on the "seeds." The specific name *multifida* is descriptive of the much-divided (multifid) leaves which, with their numerous fine segments, strongly suggest those of the cultivated carrot.

The resinous balsamic roots of leptotaenias were extensively used, after roasting, as food by the Indians. When dried and powdered or grated these parts were also used as medicine, especially for sores.[2]

---

[1] Forsling, C. L., and Dayton, W. A. ARTIFICIAL RESEEDING ON WESTERN MOUNTAIN RANGE LANDS. U. S. Dept. Agr. Circ. 178, 48 pp., illus. 1931.
[2] Teit, J. A., and Steedman, E. V. ETHNOBOTANY OF THE THOMPSON INDIANS OF BRITISH COLUMBIA. U. S. Bur. Amer. Ethnol. Ann. Rept. 45: 441–522. 1930.

BITTERROOT

Lewi'sia redivi'va

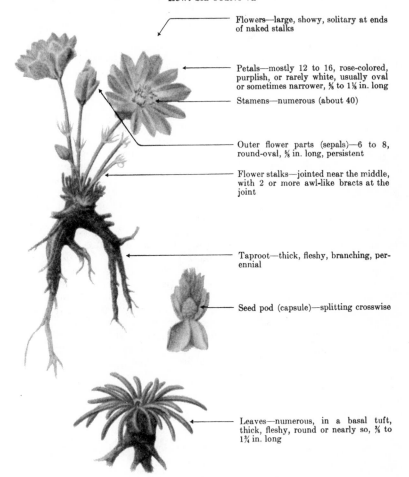

Flowers—large, showy, solitary at ends of naked stalks

Petals—mostly 12 to 16, rose-colored, purplish, or rarely white, usually oval or sometimes narrower, ⅝ to 1⅛ in. long

Stamens—numerous (about 40)

Outer flower parts (sepals)—6 to 8, round-oval, ⅜ in. long, persistent

Flower stalks—jointed near the middle, with 2 or more awl-like bracts at the joint

Taproot—thick, fleshy, branching, perennial

Seed pod (capsule)—splitting crosswise

Leaves—numerous, in a basal tuft, thick, fleshy, round or nearly so, ⅜ to 1¾ in. long

Bitterroot, a member of the portulaca family, is a smooth, low-growing, succulent perennial herb, which bears large, conspicuous, and attractive blossoms during the spring. The old settlers, translating the vernacular names of the Indians, called the plant bitterroot because of the bitter taste of the roots. These plants were given the scientific name *Lewisia* in honor of the illustrious Capt. Meriwether Lewis, of the Lewis and Clark exploring expedition into the Northwest. Although the species occurs from British Columbia to New Mexico and California, it is best known in Montana, where it is the State flower and where the Bitterroot Mountains, the Bitterroot Valley, and the Bitterroot National Forest are named in its honor. Bitterroot is occasionally known as redhead Louisa. It was called spatlum by the Flatheads and konah by the Snakes.

Bitterroot plants are small and the leaves dry up and vanish as soon as the flowers appear. The species has no forage significance. The roots, which formerly were important in the dietary of the Indians, are still used to a considerable extent. The early explorer Geyer wrote:[1] "The root is dug during flower-time, when the cuticle is easily removed; by that it acquires a white colour, is brittle, and by transportation broken to small pieces. Before boiling, it is steeped in water, which makes it swell, and after boiling it becomes five to six times larger in size; resembling a jelly like substance. As it is so small a root, it requires much labour to gather a sack, which commands generally the price of a good horse. Indians from the lower regions trade in this root by handfuls, paying a high price." And Granville Stuart states:[2] "It is very nutritious, but has an exceedingly bitter taste, hence its name. I never could eat it, unless very hungry, but many of the mountaineers are very fond of it."

Bitterroot grows on gravelly benches, river bars, and prairies at lower elevations and on stony slopes and open ridges at high elevations in the mountains, its thick fleshy taproot creeping down and anchoring in the crevices of the rocks. The fleshy, cylindrical, sometimes club-shaped leaves form basal tufts whence arise the short, leafless, jointed flower stalks. The black and shiny seeds are borne in a capsule which splits into an upper and lower part.

---

[1] Geyer, C. A. NOTES ON THE VEGETATION AND GENERAL CHARACTER OF THE MISSOURI AND OREGON TERRITORIES, MADE DURING A BOTANICAL JOURNEY FROM THE STATE OF MISSOURI, ACROSS THE SOUTH-PASS OF THE ROCKY MOUNTAINS, TO THE PACIFIC, DURING THE YEARS 1843 AND 1844. Jour. Bot. [London] 5 : 285–310. 1846.
[2] Stuart, G. MONTANA AS IT IS; BEING A GENERAL DESCRIPTION OF ITS RESOURCES, BOTH MINERAL AND AGRICULTURAL, INCLUDING A COMPLETE DESCRIPTION OF THE FACE OF THE COUNTRY, ITS CLIMATE, ETC. . . . 175 pp. New York. 1865.

LOVEROOTS

Ligus'ticum spp.

The loveroots, known commonly as wildcelery, lovage, osha, wild-parsley, and ligusticum, are smooth perennial herbs of the carrot, or parsnip, family (Umbelliferae). They are known as chuchupate in the Southwest, and two Rocky Mountain species are called cough-roots because of their medicinal uses. *Ligusticum* occurs chiefly in the Northern Hemisphere. With perhaps two or three exceptions, all the North American species are confined to the western part of the continent and about 18 species occur on the mountain ranges of the West.

Loveroots grow at elevations ranging from slightly above sea level in the humid forests of the Pacific Northwest to about 12,000 feet in Colorado and the Southwest. They are typically plants of the higher elevations and are found throughout the mountains of all the Western States. They grow in scattered stands in the rich moist soils of shady woodlands, marshes, meadows, along stream banks, and in alpine or subalpine parks. Although plants of this genus often appear in drier situations on the sandy, gravelly, or rocky soils of moderately dry meadows and hillsides, they prefer the more moist and fertile sites. The loveroots are commonly asso-ciated with bluegrasses, bromegrasses, columbine, cow-parsnip, false-hellebore, sedges, larkspurs, willows, and other species inhabiting the better soils or glades.

Sampson,[1] in his studies in the Blue Mountains of Oregon, found that the water requirements of Oregon loveroot (*L. oreganum*), which is described as typical of the majority of the more palatable species, were somewhat higher than most of its associates. The plant wilts usually beyond recovery in a soil whose water content is reduced to a point between 8 and 9.5 percent. That investigator also disclosed that the plants had weak seeding habits, the seed being low in viability. In 1907 and the two following seasons he obtained germinations of 2.6 and 11.5 percent, respectively. Oregon loveroot, and especially in its fruiting parts, is very sensitive to frost, which may partially explain the low viability of the seed, as frosts in the early fall are rather frequent in the high mountains where the plant occurs. Reproduction occurs sparingly on the range, even on allot-ments in process of reseeding under deferred grazing. Since the loveroots have taproot systems and do not regenerate vegetatively from running rootstocks, they depend entirely upon seed for repro-duction and are probably not capable of forming pure or nearly pure stands even under the most favorable conditions. However, they are sufficiently abundant in some small scattered areas to form a very important part of the palatable vegetation.

Most of the loveroots are highly palatable to all classes of live-stock. Sheep, especially, are fond of the herbage; cattle will eat a high percentage, and horses also often show a liking for it. Several

---

[1] Sampson, A. W. IMPORTANT RANGE PLANTS : THEIR LIFE HISTORY AND FORAGE VALUE. U. S. Dept. Agr. Bull. 545, 63 pp., illus. 1917.

species of loveroot are highly palatable to deer and elk, and it is very probable that all species are eaten readily by game animals. The plants remain green and palatable until the first heavy frosts, when they lose their foliage and become dry and brittle, and are practically worthless as forage.

The roots of a number of these plants are used for digestive ailments and as a tonic, and are considered valuable in the treatment of coughs and colds. An eastern species, Canada loveroot (*L. canadense*), sometimes called American lovage, is employed extensively for flavoring tobacco. Several Old World species are cooked as potherbs.

The loveroots grow from aromatic, deepset, stout, woody, and sometimes branched taproots. The blackish, hairlike fibrous remnant of old leaves forms a conspicuous tuft upon the older root crowns. Loveroots can also be readily recognized by the very distinctive, sharp, strong, warm, and somewhat celerylike flavor of the roots. This flavor cannot be described adequately in words but, once experienced, is recognized as highly distinctive. The stems are hollow, generally slender and smooth, and quite variable in size. Several species are slender plants and grow from 8 inches to 2 feet tall; others attain a height of 3 feet, with some individuals growing up to 4 feet or more. The stout stems of the larger plants are often from one-half to three-fourths of an inch in diameter. The leaves are usually large, and mostly basal, very few growing on the main stalk. In all species the leaves are divided into many segments which vary considerably in shape and size among the different species. The segments in some species are long, fine, and linear, and resemble those of carrot leaves, while others are broader, like the divisions of fern leaves. Several species have leaves which suggest those of celery.

Loveroot flowers are white or pinkish and are borne in rather large, many-rayed, umbrella-shaped clusters (umbels), 2 to 5 inches broad, which are usually free from bracts or leaflike appendages. The loveroots can be distinguished from other plants of the carrot family by their fruits or "seeds". These "seeds" are not strongly flattened but are shaped like an elongated egg, are tipped with conspicuous conical beaks (stylopodia), and have prominent equal ribs. The "seeds" are rather small, being one-eighth to five-sixteenths of an inch long.

FERNLEAF LOVEROOT

Ligus'ticum filici'num

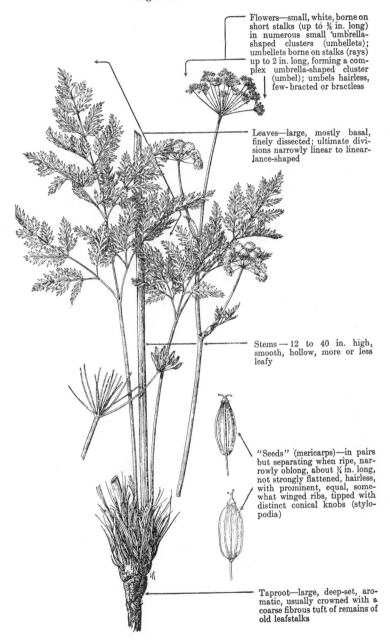

Flowers—small, white, borne on short stalks (up to ⅜ in. long) in numerous small umbrella-shaped clusters (umbellets); umbellets borne on stalks (rays) up to 2 in. long, forming a complex umbrella-shaped cluster (umbel); umbels hairless, few-bracted or bractless

Leaves—large, mostly basal, finely dissected; ultimate divisions narrowly linear to linear-lance-shaped

Stems—12 to 40 in. high, smooth, hollow, more or less leafy

"Seeds" (mericarps)—in pairs but separating when ripe, narrowly oblong, about ¼ in. long, not strongly flattened, hairless, with prominent, equal, somewhat winged ribs, tipped with distinct conical knobs (stylopodia)

Taproot—large, deep-set, aromatic, usually crowned with a coarse fibrous tuft of remains of old leafstalks

Fernleaf loveroot, also called fernleaf lovage, osha, wildcelery, and wildparsnip, is one of the most abundant of the western love-roots. It ranges from Idaho and western Montana to Colorado and Utah. It grows in the mountains at moderate to high elevations, extending through the ponderosa pine, aspen, and spruce belts to elevations of approximately 10,000 feet. Like its sister species, this plant prefers moist, fertile soils in grassy parks, meadows, and shady woods, but is also found on drier well-drained soils on the open hillsides.

Throughout its range fernleaf loveroot is highly prized as a forage plant because of its high palatability. It is an excellent sheep weed, ranks fair to good in palatability for cattle, is also grazed by game animals and to a limited extent by horses. It usually remains green throughout the summer months and is relished as much late in the season as early in the summer. This plant seldom is abundant in any one place and, due to its high palatability but relative scarcity, is often referred to as an ice cream plant.

Fernleaf loveroot is a stout herb, 12 to 40 inches tall, with an abundance of large, finely dissected leaves, whose fernlike character is referred to in the specific name *filicinum*, which is derived from the Latin word *filix*, fern. The main stalk of the plant is thick, hollow, and somewhat leafy. The small white flowers are borne in large, compound umbels, often 4 and 5 inches broad. The fruits, or "seeds", grow in pairs but separate when ripe. They are narrowly oblong with prominent equal ribs, are smooth, without spines or bristles, and have flat or slightly dished inner surfaces where they face each other.

Porter loveroot (*L. por'teri*), also called osha and chuchupate, may be regarded as a more southern and coarser-leaved sister species of fernleaf loveroot, to which it is very closely related and similar in forage value and general appearance. It is usually a stouter plant and differs mainly in that the ultimate leaf segments are con-spicuously broader, being lance-shaped to ovate-lance-shaped as con-trasted with the linear leaf divisions of fernleaf loveroot.

Porter loveroot is the most important *Ligusticum* in the central Rocky Mountain and southwestern regions. It ranges from Wyo-ming to New Mexico, Arizona, and Utah. The habitat and alti-tudinal range are similar to those of fernleaf loveroot. In the moun-tains of New Mexico it grows to elevations of over 11,000 feet. In Colorado it is a common and highly valued component of the vege-tation under aspen stands, as well as in weed types of old subalpine spruce burns.

The aromatic roots of both this species and fernleaf loveroot have a pleasant warm taste and are used in the treatment of coughs, colds, stomach disorders, and other ailments. In the drug trade they are sold under the names of Colorado or Rocky Mountain coughroot and osha.

PRAIRIE FLAX

Li'num lewi'sii

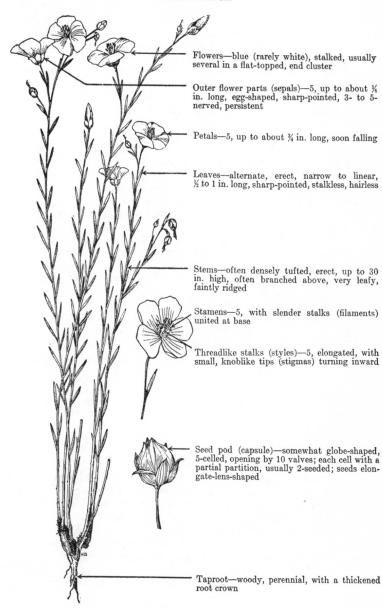

Flowers—blue (rarely white), stalked, usually several in a flat-topped, end cluster

Outer flower parts (sepals)—5, up to about ¼ in. long, egg-shaped, sharp-pointed, 3- to 5-nerved, persistent

Petals—5, up to about ¾ in. long, soon falling

Leaves—alternate, erect, narrow to linear, ½ to 1 in. long, sharp-pointed, stalkless, hairless

Stems—often densely tufted, erect, up to 30 in. high, often branched above, very leafy, faintly ridged

Stamens—5, with slender stalks (filaments) united at base

Threadlike stalks (styles)—5, elongated, with small, knoblike tips (stigmas) turning inward

Seed pod (capsule)—somewhat globe-shaped, 5-celled, opening by 10 valves; each cell with a partial partition, usually 2-seeded; seeds elongate-lens-shaped

Taproot—woody, perennial, with a thickened root crown

Near the Continental Divide in Montana, Capt. Meriwether Lewis, of the famous Lewis and Clark expedition, found, one day, blue fields of a wild flax which particularly interested him, because the plant had perennial roots. This flax proved to be a new species and was named *Linum lewisii* by Frederick Pursh, the distinguished botanist (1774–1820), in honor of its first collector. Prairie flax is a native western North American species, which is widely distributed from Manitoba to Alaska and southward to California, Texas, and Mexico. Although common over the prairies and foothills, where it often forms dense stands, it also grows in the coniferous timber types of the mountains and occasionally occurs as high as 10,000 feet in Colorado and the Southwest. The "common blue flowering flax" to which Frémont [1] so frequently alludes, in describing western floral landscapes, is almost certainly *Linum lewisii*.

Over most of its range, prairie flax ranks as worthless, poor, or, when young and tender in the spring, occasionally fair forage. In certain regions of intensive use, particularly in parts of Montana, Wyoming, and adjacent eastern Idaho, Colorado, and the Modoc areas of northeastern California, it sometimes rates as fair for cattle and fairly good for sheep. Such utilization, however, is largely correlated with an inferior stand of palatable grasses and weeds. Although at least one native American flax species has positively been involved in livestock losses, apparently no definite suspicion of poisonous properties has fastened on prairie flax. Analysis by the Bureau of Chemistry and Soils, of *Linum lewisii* material, from the Gila National Forest, New Mexico, failed to demonstrate the presence of hydrocyanic acid or other toxic substance.

Prairie flax was an important fiber plant among the western Indians. Today, it merits cultivation as an ornamental, even if not needed for cordage and similar purposes. In describing its use by the Klamath Indians, Dr. Coville [2] writes:

The stems produce a remarkably strong fine fiber which is made into strings and cords. These are employed in certain parts of baskets and mats, in the meshes of snowshoes, and in the weaving of fish nets. . . . The plant grows in openings of yellow-pine forests and in the upper altitudes of the sage plains, and could doubtless be propagated successfully in such areas without irrigation. It deserves careful experiment as a source of commercial fiber.

FLAXES

Li'num spp.

Linum, a genus of annual or perennial herbs of the relatively small flax family (*Linaceae*), consists of between about 90 and 100 species, growing in the temperate and warm regions of both hemispheres. Approximately one-fourth of these species occur in the United States. Linen thread, manufactured from the cultivated, Old World flax (*L. usitatis'simum*), is the most important vegetable fiber from the standpoints of long-continued and widespread usage. Its use in Asia and Europe dates back to the dawn of history, an antiquity which is partly evidenced by the similarity of its nomenclature, at

[1] Frémont, J. C. REPORT OF THE EXPLORING EXPEDITION TO OREGON AND NORTH CALIFORNIA, IN THE YEARS 1843–'44. U. S. H. Doc. 166 : [103]–294, illus. 1845.
[2] Coville, F. V. NOTES ON THE PLANTS USED BY THE KLAMATH INDIANS OF OREGON. U. S. Dept. Agr., Div. Bot., Contrib. U. S. Natl. Herbarium 5 : 87–108. 1897.

least in European languages. Thus, Greek *linon*, Latin *linum*, Anglo-Saxon *linen*, German *leinen*, and Swedish *linne* all refer to flax, or the genus *Linum*. Our English words "line" (literally, linen thread), "linen", and "linseed" are derived, of course, from the same etymological stem.

Flaxes are common on sunny sites in the West, from the grass-lands of the plains to the high mountains, and occur on well-drained to dry soils. They are, as a class, low in forage value, and rate from worthless to fair in palatability for sheep, somewhat lower for cattle, and are seldom touched by horses. The yellow-flowered range flaxes having terminal, headlike (capitate) stigmas, and glandular sepals (genus *Cathartoli'num* of some authors) may, on further study, prove as a group to be more or less poisonous. Several of them are under suspicion. One of these species, New Mexican flax (*Linum neomexica'num*, syn. *C. neomexica'num*), sometimes known by the misleading name yellow pine flax, which grows in New Mex-ico, Arizona, and Mexico, is definitely cataloged among the plants dangerous to livestock. The first intimation that New Mexican flax is poisonous developed in 1912, when Supervisor Roscoe G. Willson reported the deaths of some horses on the Tonto National Forest, Arizona, apparently due to this plant. The Bureau of Chemistry and Soils was unable to detect poisonous compounds in this species from analysis of material submitted in 1914 from that forest. In his report on the analysis, Dr. C. A. Alsberg, then chief of the Bureau, stated: "Species of *Linum* develop cyanogenetic glucosides during the early stages of their growth, and it is quite likely that poisonous substances occur in the New Mexican flax prior to the fruiting period." Subsequent research [3] has definitely located a toxic substance in this species, tentatively named "linotoxin." This poison, although slow in action, is fatal if large enough quantities are eaten under stipulated conditions.[3] Chesnut [4] indicates that stiffstem flax (*L. ri'gidum*, syn. *C. ri'gidum*), a southwestern species, has poisoned sheep in the Pecos Valley, Texas. Linseed cake, the byproduct which remains after linseed oil is extracted from the seeds of cultivated flax (*L. usitatis'simum*), is manufactured into livestock feed. When fed in concentration to hogs and cattle, scours and other digestive disturbances and sometimes even deaths have resulted.[5]

Flaxseed contains about 40 percent linseed oil, which is used exten-sively in paint and varnish production.[6] Linoleum and cork carpet are made by compressing a mixture of ground cork and linseed oil upon canvas. After the oil has been extracted from flaxseed the

[3] Eggleston, W. W., Black, O. F., and Kelly, J. W. LINUM NEOMEXICANUM (YELLOW PINE FLAX) AND ONE OF ITS POISONOUS CONSTITUENTS. Jour. Agr. Research [U. S.] 41: 715–718, illus. 1930.
[4] Chesnut, V. K. PRELIMINARY CATALOG OF PLANTS POISONOUS TO STOCK. U. S. Dept. Agr., Bur. Anim. Indus. Ann. Rept. (1898) 15 : 387–420, illus. 1899.
[5] Pammel, L. H. A MANUAL OF POISONOUS PLANTS CHIEFLY OF EASTERN NORTH AMERICA, WITH BRIEF NOTES ON ECONOMIC AND MEDICINAL PLANTS . . . 2 pts., illus. Cedar Rapids, Iowa. 1910–11.
[6] Robbins, W. W., and Ramaley, F. PLANTS USEFUL TO MAN. 428 pp., illus. Phila-delphia. 1933.

residue is pressed into cakes or ground into linseed meal for livestock. Flaxseed is also employed in the manufacture of a variety of breakfast cereals. The threshed straw is used in upholstering furniture and for the insulation of cold-storage plants, refrigerator cars, and ice boxes.

Flaxseed, an official drug, has long been used for medicinal purposes. It has an oily taste, and the seed coats contain a mucilaginous substance. Linseed tea, a mixture of licorice root and flaxseed, is used in the treatment of coughs and to allay irritation and inflammation of the mucous membranes. Poultices made by boiling linseed meal are useful as a counterirritant for the relief of pain and where there is deep-seated inflammation. These poultices are also used efficaciously in the treatment of boils and ulcers. Linseed oil, in combination with an equal quantity of lime water, forms carron oil, an excellent and popular application for scalds and burns.

Flaxes are easily cultivated, many species being valued as ornamentals. Most species, however, lose their petals soon after blooming. One European species, perennial flax (*L. peren'ne*), blooms in the morning, the petals fall before noon, and new flowers blossom again the next day. Our native flaxes constitute an inviting field of scientific research. Various species are handsome plants when in full bloom and deserve painstaking horticultural study. Flaxes are sometimes shrubby at the base and have many narrow, small, alternate (rarely opposite) leaves. The white, blue, yellow, or red flowers are usually in flat-topped or slightly curve-topped clusters.

DEERVETCHES
Lo'tus spp.

The deervetches (*Lotus* spp.), members of the pea family, are in the main perennial or annual herbs, although some are semi-shrubby with stems which do not die down entirely each year. Varying in size from small, semiprostrate to upright plants 4 feet in height, they are distributed throughout the West from the low-lying deserts to the spruce-fir belts of the higher mountains but are largely natives of California, where 29 species occur. As regards habit, western deervetches subdivide broadly into two groups: (1) Mostly low plants, with small, whitish, somewhat woolly leaves, examples being birdsfoot deervetch, or "Spanish clover" (*L. americanus*), Douglas deervetch (*L. douglasii*), and foothill deervetch (*L. humistratus*); (2) darker green, upright, and mostly tall species, usually with rather conspicuous flowers, of which big deervetch (*L. crassifolius*) and stream deervetch (*L. oblongifolius*) are typical representatives. Members of the first group are usually found on dry, well-drained soils, while species of the second group generally inhabit more moist situations and as a rule are somewhat higher in palatability. Desert deervetch (*L. argensis*), a very good forage species common in the semidesert and chaparral browse ranges of Arizona and locally in southeastern California, is representative of those species whose stems do not die down entirely each year.

The forage value of different species of *Lotus* ranges from very low to high. Most of the range species usually occur in scattered stands making up a rather small percentage of the vegetation.

Lotus is a large and variable genus of world-wide distribution. Some American botanists place all the native species in the genus *Hosackia* and regard *Lotus* as a strictly Old World genus. Other botanists prefer to divide these plants into five genera: *Acmispon, Anisolotus, Hosackia, Lotus,* and *Syrmatium*. The Bureau of Plant Industry, United States Department of Agriculture, customarily places all these diverse deervetches in the one genus *Lotus*. That usage is followed here.

The most distinctive characters of this genus are: Leaves entirely without dotted glands, mostly pinnately compound, as in our common sweetpea but without tendrils and with usually three to many (but sometimes only one or two) smooth-edged (entire) leaflets; flowers pealike, from yellow to nearly white, often marked with rose, red, or purple, and usually borne in umbrella-shaped clusters (umbels) but sometimes singly or in heads; stamens 10, in 2 sets (diadelphous), 1 stamen by itself, and 9 united at base. The pod is a narrow, straight or curved, often flattened, one to many-seeded legume. The halves of the pod (valves) at maturity often twist spirally and expel the seeds with considerable force.

Deervetches are known by a variety of local names including deerclover, deerpea, and deerweed. The "three-leaved" (trifoliolate) species are frequently called trefoil, but historically that is a name which belongs to the clover genus (*Trifolium*).

RED-AND-YELLOW-PEA

Lo'tus wright'ii, syn. *Anisolo'tus wright'ii*

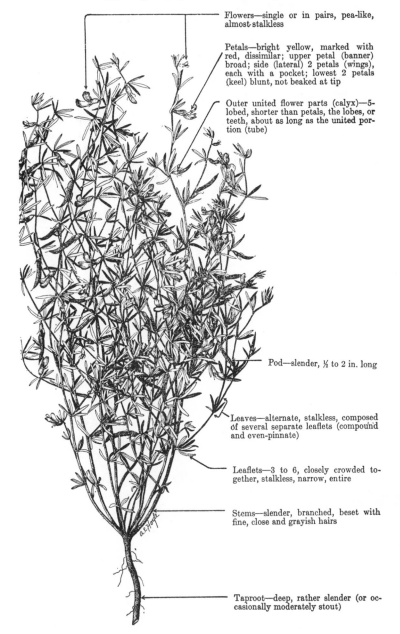

Flowers—single or in pairs, pea-like, almost stalkless

Petals—bright yellow, marked with red, dissimilar; upper petal (banner) broad; side (lateral) 2 petals (wings), each with a pocket; lowest 2 petals (keel) blunt, not beaked at tip

Outer united flower parts (calyx)—5-lobed, shorter than petals, the lobes, or teeth, about as long as the united portion (tube)

Pod—slender, ½ to 2 in. long

Leaves—alternate, stalkless, composed of several separate leaflets (compound and even-pinnate)

Leaflets—3 to 6, closely crowded together, stalkless, narrow, entire

Stems—slender, branched, beset with fine, close and grayish hairs

Taproot—deep, rather slender (or occasionally moderately stout)

425

This small perennial herb, with its dark green, bushy, fine-leaved herbage and bright yellow and red flowers, is found scatteringly from southern Utah and southern Colorado through New Mexico and Arizona, on sandy, gravelly, or clay soils, in dry parks, open ridges, or in open stands of timber. It ranges in altitude from the upper woodland type up through the ponderosa pine and into the lower spruce-fir belt. When plentiful, red-and-yellow-pea is often a range plant of considerable importance—at least in the Southwest, where its palatability averages high for all classes of livestock, but especially for sheep. In southern Colorado and Utah it is not so extensively grazed. It grows commonly only 4 to 12 inches tall; the leaves, though small, are delicate and numerous. Being a legume, its proportion of nitrogenous matter is relatively high; it appears to be particularly appetizing during the latter part of the growing season, when the pods are formed. Deer and probably other herbivorous wild life graze it readily. The deep woody taproot draws moisture and food material from considerable depths, assisting the plant to withstand drought and abuse; even so, however, the species is disappearing from a number of overgrazed Southwestern ranges.

LUPINES

Lupi'nus spp.

Lupines compose one of the largest, commonest, most widespread, and characteristic genera of western plants, and are familiar to most persons interested in the vegetation of their region. The genus, which belongs to the woadwaxen tribe (Genisteae) of the pea, or legume, family, and is closely related to rattlebox (*Crotalaria*), broom (*Cytisus*), and gorse (*Ulex*), is found throughout the world but is probably best developed in the Western States, where numerous species occur in each State. Lupines are characteristic of temperate and warm climates, but two species occur in Alaska. The species occupy a wide variety of sites, extending from the plains, prairies, and foothills to the stream courses, canyons, brush areas, grasslands, and meadows of the mountains. They are most conspicuous in full bloom and mass formation over large areas during the spring and early summer. These plants have many common names, including blue-bean, bluebonnet, blue-pea, quakerbonnts, wild-alfalfa, wildbean, and wolfbean, although lupine (often spelled and pronounced lupin) is, doubtless, the name in most popular use. The generic name *Lupinus* is the classic Latin word for these plants and is evidently associated with the Latin word for wolf (*lupus*); some say that lupines were so called because they were thought to rob the soil of its fertility.

Many lupines have the reputation of being poisonous, at least so far as the seed is concerned. Certain species are deadly to sheep and, to a lesser degree, to cattle. Cases of horse poisoning from these plants are infrequent. Further experimental work is required to ascertain which, if any, species are harmless. Therefore the safest procedure is to utilize lupine ranges only when other feed is abundant, and especially when the lupines are not in fruit.

The majority of reported cases of lupine poisoning have resulted from eating the seeds and pods, although serious losses have occurred when the young plants of certain species have been taken in quantity. Unpublished researches by A. B. Clawson indicate that all parts of some species are poisonous. The poisonous effects of many lupines are influenced by wet weather. Heavy losses have resulted when sheep grazed lupines after a rainstorm; fatalities also occur when hungry sheep are unloaded from cars and allowed to graze lupine freely. In other cases sheep frequently graze over extensive areas of these plants without injury. Comprehensive and accurate information is needed concerning the poisonous properties of the common species of lupine before definite management of lupine ranges can be recommended. Cattle seldom eat lupines unless good grass is scant, but horses often prefer them to other forage. Lupines also furnish fairly good forage for elk.

Typical lupine poisoning, at least in sheep, is characterized by labored breathing, excitement, snoring, convulsions, and occasionally frothing at the mouth. The animals run about in a frenzy and butt against any opposing object. The action of the poison is not cumulative, and usually no ill effects obtain where the animals consume only small amounts.[1]

Being handsome plants, many of the lupines are cultivated as ornamentals; a number of the western species are particularly popular for that purpose. Lupine, under the name bluebonnet, is the State flower of Texas. Various species of lupine, including *L. albus* and *L. tremis*, have been cultivated since ancient times in Italy, Greece, Egypt, and generally throughout the Mediterranean region as forage and soiling plants. Formerly the seeds were used as food for the poor, being boiled to remove the bitter taste. This is the same plant called the sad lupine (*tristis lupinus*) by the poet Virgil.

The majority of lupines are perennial herbs, although many are annuals and a relatively few species are shrubs. Lupine species range in height from about 2½ inches to 10 feet. They are smooth or hairy, usually branching, and have alternate, mostly long-stemmed leaves without glands. The bracts (stipules) at the bases of the leaf-stems are narrow. Typically the leaves of lupines are compound and divided into from 4 to 17 fingerlike leaflets. In a few lupines, however, particularly of the Southeastern States, the leaves are simple, being reduced to a solitary, mostly evergreen leaflet. In several other species the leaves are cloverlike, with three leaflets (trifoliolate). Lupine leaves have long been noted for their "sleep movements", the leaflets folding up in various fashions, usually during the middle of the day. The pealike flowers are, generally, blue, bluish, or purplish; in some species, however, the flowers are white, yellow, reddish, or of a mixture of colors. The flowers often grow in circles around the upper stalk and are borne in usually long, showy clusters. The floral cup (calyx) is two-lipped, the upper "lip" two-lobed, the three lobes of the lower "lip" united. The sides of the topmost petal are bent backward; the two lowest, conjoined petals are curved inward and often fringed-hairy above. The 10 stamens are fused together into one group and their pollen-sacs (anthers) are of two sorts: alternately large and small. The fruit is a 2-valved, flattened, 2- to 12-seeded pod (legume).

Because of their fingerlike leaves, without tendrils, and their characteristically upright (never twining or vinelike) habit, lupines may always be readily distinguished from peavines (*Lathyrus* spp.) and vetches (*Vicia* spp.). Goldenpeas (*Thermopsis* spp.) may be distinguished by their three-leafletted leaves with big leafy stipules, their trailing rootstocks, usually brilliant yellow flowers, and separated stamens. The conspicuous glands of the herbage, and often the starchy tubers, in the "pomme-de-prairie" genus *Psoralea* immediately set those plants apart from lupines. True clovers (*Trifolium* spp.) differ from lupines in the typically three-leafletted leaves with toothed leaflets, the flowers massed in a dense, mostly rounded head, and in the diminutive pods.

---

[1] Marsh, C. D., Clawson, A. B., and Marsh, H. LUPINES AS POISONOUS PLANTS. U. S. Dept. Agr. Bull. 405, 45 pp., illus. 1916.
Marsh, C. D. STOCK-POISONING PLANTS OF THE RANGE. U. S. Dept. Agr. Bull. 1245. rev., 75 pp., illus. 1929. Supersedes Bull. 575.

TAILCUP LUPINE

Lupi′nus cauda′tus, syns. *L. argenti′nus, L. gree′nei, L. monti′genus,*
L. oreo′philus

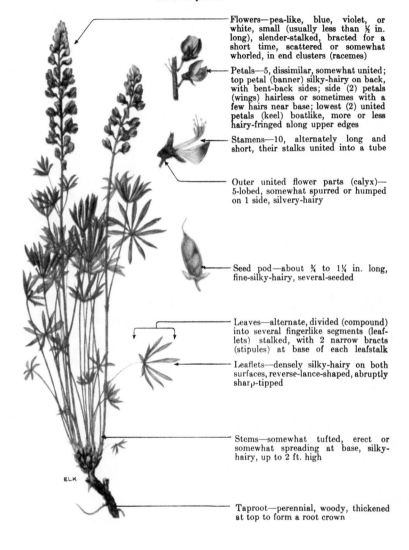

Flowers—pea-like, blue, violet, or white, small (usually less than ½ in. long), slender-stalked, bracted for a short time, scattered or somewhat whorled, in end clusters (racemes)

Petals—5, dissimilar, somewhat united; top petal (banner) silky-hairy on back, with bent-back sides; side (2) petals (wings) hairless or sometimes with a few hairs near base; lowest (2) united petals (keel) boatlike, more or less hairy-fringed along upper edges

Stamens—10, alternately long and short, their stalks united into a tube

Outer united flower parts (calyx)—5-lobed, somewhat spurred or humped on 1 side, silvery-hairy

Seed pod—about ¾ to 1¼ in. long, fine-silky-hairy, several-seeded

Leaves—alternate, divided (compound) into several fingerlike segments (leaflets) stalked, with 2 narrow bracts (stipules) at base of each leafstalk

Leaflets—densely silky-hairy on both surfaces, reverse-lance-shaped, abruptly sharp-tipped

Stems—somewhat tufted, erect or somewhat spreading at base, silky-hairy, up to 2 ft. high

Taproot—perennial, woody, thickened at top to form a root crown

ELK

429

Tailcup lupine, sometimes called silver lupine, is a perennial herb of the pea family (Leguminosae). The specific name is a Latin word meaning tailed (from *cauda*, tail), and alludes to the short prolongation backward of the upper part of the calyx, or outer floral cup; hence the common name, tailcup lupine. This plant ranges from Washington and Oregon (east of the Cascades) to California (chiefly, if not entirely, east of the Sierra Nevada Mountains), Nevada, Colorado, and Idaho. It may possibly also inhabit Arizona, New Mexico, and Montana, although it is not now definitely known as occurring in those States. It grows chiefly between elevations of about 3,000 and 8,500 feet, characteristically appearing in rather dry, well-drained soils from the sagebrush type up to open coniferous timber stands. It is one of the common lupines in the ponderosa pine belt, growing chiefly in parks and openings where, especially in California, it is often associated with Idaho fescue (*Festuca idahoensis*) and bitterbrush (*Purshia tridentata*). Tailcup lupine is fairly common over much of its range and often is locally abundant.

This species is one of the more palatable kinds of lupine; cattle and horses, on the average, utilize about 30 percent of the herbage, and sheep and goats about 50 to 60 percent. This relatively high use is unfortunate because the plant is particularly poisonous to cattle and horses, as well as somewhat toxic to sheep.[1] In this respect it is almost unique among the lupines, only one other species (and that a very closely related one), looseflower lupine (*L. laxiflo'rus*), being identified definitely as seriously poisonous to cattle and horses. Tailcup lupine may also be poisonous to game animals, although deer graze it rather freely, and no authentic reports of deer losses attributable to it have been received.

Clawson[1] reports that cattle poisoned by tailcup lupine show symptoms similar to those caused by larkspur, especially the general weakness and muscular trembling, followed by convulsions and prostration. Horses poisoned by this plant act as if they have colic; sheep appear very nervous and excitable. The species may be dangerous even when associated with an abundance of harmless, palatable plants easily available to livestock; losses, however, are more likely to occur and be more severe if other palatable vegetation is scarce. Comprehensive experimentation is needed for a complete determination of the poisonous properties of this plant.

Although the lupines as a group are well known, many species are so similar in appearance that it is extremely difficult to distinguish between them unless one has a wide knowledge of the genus and considerable botanical training. However, the following characters taken together will usually identify tailcup lupine: The stems, about 8 inches to 2 feet high, are densely appressed-silky- or satiny-hairy; at least some of the lower leaves are long-stalked; the abruptly sharp-pointed leaflets (characteristically about 7 to 9) vary in number from 5 to 11 or more, and are densely silky-hairy on both surfaces; the outer flower part (calyx) is somewhat spurred or humped on one side and densely hairy; the upper petal (banner) is hairy on the back.

---

[1] Clawson, A. B. TWO LUPINES SHOWN TO BE POISONOUS TO LIVESTOCK. U. S. Dept. Agr. Off. Rec. 10(9) : 71. 1931.

Looseflower lupine, the other species known to have poisonous properties similar to those of tailcup lupine, is also a perennial with rather long, scattered flower clusters. The stems of looseflower lupine, up to 28 inches in height, are hairy, but scarcely silky; the 7 to 13 leaflets are sparsely hairy or hairless above; the calyx is distinctly spurred, with often only the lower lobes green, the upper lobes forming a rather broad lip, much shorter than the lower lip, and often fully exposed; the petals vary from blue or lilac to yellowish or white; the upper petal (banner) is long-clawed; the 2 side petals (wings) are somewhat hairy outside near the upper and outer angle. Otherwise the plant is similar to tailcup lupine. Looseflower lupine ranges from British Columbia to Montana, Colorado, Arizona, and eastern California. Like tailcup lupine, it is fairly palatable and has caused some losses of cattle and horses in parts of Wyoming, Washington, and Oregon.[1] It is well known, of course, that the seeds and pods of a number of range lupines are very poisonous to sheep.[2]

---

[1] See footnote on preceding page.
[2] Marsh, C D., Clawson, A. B., and Marsh, H. LUPINES AS POISONOUS PLANTS. U. S. Dept. Agr. Bull. 405, 45 pp., illus. 1916.

CALIFORNIA BUR-CLOVER

Medica'go his'pida, syn. *M. denticula'ta*

Flowers—small (less than ⅙ in. long), pea-like, yellow, usually 2 to 5 in a slender-stalked cluster; stalk as long as or longer than the leaflets

Bracts (stipules)—at base of leafstalks, finely toothed

Leaves—alternate, stalked, divided (pinnately compound) into 3 segments (leaflets)

Leaflets—reverse-heart-shaped, mostly less than ¾ in. long, without splotches, the upper edges wavy and short-toothed from extension of the veins

"Bur" (pod)—2 to 3 times spirally twisted, prominently veined, several-seeded, with ridged edges bearing a double row of hooked or curved spines

Stems—several from the base, spreading and prostrate but with ends ascending, 6 to 24 in. long

Taproot—annual, occasionally with a somewhat thickened root crown

California bur-clover, sometimes called toothed bur-clover, a yellow-flowered annual, is one of the few western examples of an aggressive and valuable introduced forage plant. A native of Europe, it was probably introduced into southern California by the Spanish explorers and is very abundant in that State. Its ability to spread is illustrated by the fact that this species now grows vigorously in most regions of mild climate. In North America it extends from Nova Scotia to Florida, throughout the South and Southwest, inland, to Nebraska, south into Mexico, and on the Pacific coast northward to Washington.

In California, this species is a winter annual; the seeds germinate after the fall rains and the plant matures at the end of the rainy period in May or June. In the Southwest and inland it makes most of its growth in the spring, but in the moist South and East, under normal conditions, it grows throughout the spring and summer. This species inhabits practically all soils, such as sands, stony loams, and adobe, provided they are moist, but not wet. All exposures are invaded, and it does well under light conditions varying from full sunlight to heavy shade. However, it is a plant of the valleys and low foothills, occurring only as scattered individuals in the ponderosa pine belt of the Western States. In the Southwest and on the Pacific coast it is commonly associated with annual weeds and grasses. In California, the plant may occur in pure stands, but more often is associated with other winter annuals, such as bromegrasses, wild oats, and various species of alfileria.

California bur-clover is one of the most valuable annual forage plants on the Pacific coast,[1] even though the green foliage has a somewhat bitter taste. Once accustomed to this peculiar taste, all classes of livestock, except horses and mules, eat it greedily, especially when it is maturing.[2] At this time it is very nutritious and, where abundant, often serves as a finishing feed for lambs. However, excessive use of the green, dew-coated foliage sometimes causes bloat in livestock unaccustomed to grazing it regularly. Because of the abundant and nutritious burs, this species provides a summer and fall feed superior to that of other common annuals; sheep especially, seek the fallen burs. This close use is probably most common after the spiny burs have been softened by the fall rains. However, during summer, the burs accumulate in the wool as numerous mats which decrease the value of the clip.

Chemical analyses indicate that California bur-clover is very similar to alfalfa in forage value, and definitely superior to the former's common annual range associates, especially in protein and phosphorus content.[3] Like other forage plants, bur-clover loses nutritive value by excessive exposure to moisture and light after it cures on the range, although the burs are not appreciably affected.[4] Leaching and bleaching reduce the digestibility of all nutrients except crude fiber, and the loss of soluble constituents causes decreased palatability.

California bur-clover is a common constituent of wild hay, especially in California, although the cutting is limited to sites where it is upright due to its own abundance or the density of other plants. Bur-clover is invaluable as a cover crop or green manure [2] both in western orchards and throughout the Cotton Belt. It is especially

[1] Jepson, W. L. A MANUAL OF THE FLOWERING PLANTS OF CALIFORNIA. 1,238 pp., illus. Berkeley, Calif. [1925.]
[2] Piper, C. V. BUR CLOVER. U. S. Dept. Agr. Farmers' Bull. 693, 14 pp., illus. 1915.
[3] Hart, G. H., Guilbert, H. R., and Goss, H. SEASONAL CHANGES IN THE CHEMICAL COMPOSITION OF RANGE FORAGE AND THEIR RELATION TO NUTRITION OF ANIMALS. Calif. Agr. Expt. Sta. Bull. 543, 62 pp., illus. 1932.
[4] Guilbert, H. R., and Mead, S. W. THE DIGESTIBILITY OF BUR CLOVER AS AFFECTED BY EXPOSURE TO SUNLIGHT AND RAIN. Hilgardia 6: 1–12. 1931.

satisfactory for such purposes because of its rapid, dense growth and its ability as a legume to increase the available nitrogen supply in the soil. Frequently, in the case of new plantings, it is necessary to inoculate the seed with the fixation bacteria. This plant has considerable promise for range reseeding at the lower elevations where mild winters are the rule.[5] It is not essential to prepare a seedbed, although some minor preparation is desirable. The seed should be freed from the burs and sown just before the fall rains. Seed is usually obtainable as it is a common impurity in grains, and also is salvaged from wool wastes.[6]

California bur-clover clearly shows its close relationship to alfalfa (*M. sativa*), having much the aspect of a small and prostrate alfalfa, except for its small yellow flowers and numerous spiny burs. The burs and the three-foliolate, cloverlike leaves are aptly described in the common name bur-clover. The specific name *hispida* refers to the bristly or spiny character of the pods, or burs.

MEDICKS

Medica′go spp.

The medicks, consisting of about 50 species native to Europe, Asia, and Africa, comprise a very important genus of the pea, or legume family (Fabaceae, or Leguminosae). Alfalfa (*M. sativa*), the type species, often known in the Old World as lucerne, snailclover, and purple medick, is one of the most valuable of all forage plants, being extensively grown in the temperate climates of all continents. As the generic name intimates, the original home of *Medicago* is reported to have been ancient Media (now largely in what is known as Azerbaijan, Irak, and northwestern Persia). It appears to have been first cultivated in that part of the world and to have been introduced into early cultivation in Greece as a result of the Medo-Persian invasions. Alfalfa compares favorably with timothy as a cultivated forage plant in North America, but so far reseeding experiments on the ranges have generally proven unsuccessful. None of the present varieties seem hardy enough to withstand the very severe climatic fluctuations characteristic of western mountain ranges; however, it is by no means impossible that new and more suitable strains will eventually be developed.

The eight or more species of *Medicago* in North America were all introduced from Europe; four of these are very important and widely distributed forage plants. Alfalfa is a perennial with blue flowers; the others are annuals and yellow-flowered. Spotted medick (*M. arabica*) is similar to California bur-clover in that its pods are spiny and burlike, but, as the common name indicates, the leaves have a

[5] Forsling, C. L., and Dayton, W. A. ARTIFICIAL RESEEDING ON WESTERN MOUNTAIN RANGE LANDS. U. S. Dept. Agr. Circ. 178, 48 pp., illus. 1931.
[6] McKee, R., and Ricker, P. L. NONPERENNIAL MEDICAGOS : THE AGRONOMIC VALUE AND BOTANICAL RELATIONSHIP OF THE SPECIES. U. S. Dept. Agr., Bur. Plant Indus. Bull. 267, 38 pp., illus. 1913.

conspicuous dark spot, or spots, near the center of each leaflet. It is similar to California bur-clover in palatability and growth requirements, but is not as common or widely distributed. Black medick (*M. lupulina*) differs from the other two important annuals chiefly in that its burs are one-seeded, spineless, and merely curved, rather than twisted or coiled. This species is widely distributed in North America, and extends into higher elevations than the other annual species. It is highly regarded as a forage plant and sometimes is called nonesuch, indicative of its superior value.

WHITE SWEETCLOVER

Melilo'tus al'ba

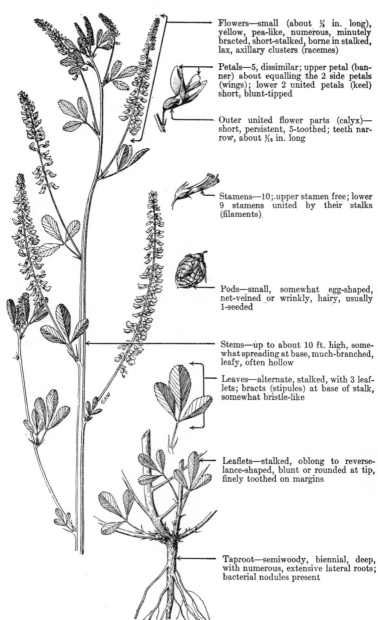

Flowers—small (about ¼ in. long), yellow, pea-like, numerous, minutely bracted, short-stalked, borne in stalked, lax, axillary clusters (racemes)

Petals—5, dissimilar; upper petal (banner) about equalling the 2 side petals (wings); lower 2 united petals (keel) short, blunt-tipped

Outer united flower parts (calyx)—short, persistent, 5-toothed; teeth narrow, about ¹⁄₁₆ in. long

Stamens—10; upper stamen free; lower 9 stamens united by their stalks (filaments).

Pods—small, somewhat egg-shaped, net-veined or wrinkly, hairy, usually 1-seeded

Stems—up to about 10 ft. high, somewhat spreading at base, much-branched, leafy, often hollow

Leaves—alternate, stalked, with 3 leaflets; bracts (stipules) at base of stalk, somewhat bristle-like

Leaflets—stalked, oblong to reverse-lance-shaped, blunt or rounded at tip, finely toothed on margins

Taproot—semiwoody, biennial, deep, with numerous, extensive lateral roots; bacterial nodules present

White sweetclover, known also as bee-clover, honeyclover, galy-gumber, and as Bokhara, Siberian, and white melilot, is a robust biennial herb belonging to the pea family (*Leguminosae*). In this immense family it is classified in the clover tribe (*Trifolieae*), sandwiched between the true clovers (*Trifolium*) and the alfalfa genus (*Medicago*).

White sweetclover is native to the temperate regions of Europe and Asia as far east as Tibet.[1][2] Its first authentic record in the United States was in 1739,[1][3] when Dr. John Clayton collected this plant in Virginia. However, its actual cultivation in this country dates from 1856, when Prof. Henry Tutwiler of Green Springs Academy, Ala., established a stand with seed obtained from Chile. White sweetclover has attained the status of a major farm crop in the United States and Canada only since about 1900.

Indications are that white sweetclover might do well, where soil and precipitation conditions are favorable,[4] for reseeding certain abandoned farmlands which should revert to range, in the Pacific Northwest, western Montana, and limitedly elsewhere. Good results were obtained from planting this species on burned-over forest lands near Sandpoint, Idaho,[5] at elevations of from 2,000 to 2,500 feet, where the annual precipitation averages over 20 inches; it was one of the few forages studied which increased in density from year to year. Unlike many grasses, white sweetclover does not cure on the stem for fall and winter grazing. On experimentally reseeded range areas in Utah and Oregon having about 20 inches of rainfall a good stand was secured, but it failed to reestablish itself and in from 3 to 5 years the stand was practically gone.

Growing on a wide variety of farm soils, from cemented clays and gravels to poor sands, white sweetclover exhibits much latitude in physical site requirements. However, it will not succeed on acid soils, unless limed, or on very wet soils.[1][6] It can be grown on both the adobe and granitic soils of the Pacific coast as well as on heavy black hardpan, prairie loams, newly exposed heavy clays, and on the poor, infertile soils of abandoned farms in the more humid areas. The species grows luxuriantly on fertile, well-drained, limy soils, and also flourishes on lands with a shallow water table, that are unsuitable for alfalfa production. It is one of the most alkali-resistant of our economic crops, being so tolerant as to survive on strongly alkaline bottom seepage.[3]

White sweetclover is adapted for cultivation in a wide variety of climatic conditions and can be grown under greater environmental extremes than any of the true cultivated clovers. If the stand is comparatively dense, it very seldom winter-kills. Although heavy damage resulted in Montana during an unusually severe winter

[1] Coe, H. S. SWEET CLOVER: GROWING THE CROP. U. S. Dept. Agr. Farmers' Bull. 797, 35 pp., illus. 1917.
[2] Westgate, J. M., and Vinall, H. N. SWEET CLOVER. U. S. Dept. Agr. Farmers' Bull. 485, 39 pp., illus. 1912.
[3] Piper, C. V. FORAGE PLANTS AND THEIR CULTURE. Rev., 671 pp., illus. New York. 1924.
[4] Forsling C. L., and Dayton, W. A. ARTIFICIAL RESEEDING ON WESTERN MOUNTAIN RANGE LANDS. U. S. Dept. Agr. Circ. 178, 48 pp., illus. 1931.
[5] Christ, J. H. RESEEDING BURNED-OVER LANDS IN NORTHERN IDAHO. Idaho Agr. Expt. Sta. Bull. 201, 28 pp., illus. 1934.
[6] Pieters, A. J. SWEET CLOVER. U. S. Dept. Agr. Leaflet 23, 8 pp., illus. [1928.]

where white sweetclover was seeded in 3-foot rows, no loss occurred on closely drilled plots. Coe [1] reports: "Apparently neither the high temperatures of the South nor the cold winters of the North severely affect the plants, provided there is sufficient moisture in the soil." It is drought-resistive [1][3] and often grows satisfactorily on areas too dry for alfalfa. Hulbert [7] states: "It is grown in Idaho on high, dry land where the rainfall is too light to produce other crops successfully." In sites where it is well adapted, this plant often resists the invasion of other vegetation for a long time. [5] Willoughby and Wells [8] report that, in Kansas, "it rapidly adds organic matter and nitrogen to thin soils and is an excellent crop for preventing washing on rolling land."

The early unpopularity of white sweetclover, which caused farmers to indict it as worthless, resulted from the distaste of livestock for the plant, probably because of its high content of bitter coumarin. This bitterness, although less pronounced when the plants are young and succulent, becomes obnoxious as they mature and become more woody. Livestock, however, can be taught early in the spring to relish the young plants; once the animals become accustomed to the flavor of the lush foliage, they eat it with considerable avidity. Chemical analyses appear to indicate that this plant may potentially be as nutritious as alfalfa, either for pasturage or hay. Coe [9] reports that lambs, in experimental tests, made slightly greater daily gains on alfalfa. He adds: "Each year in the Middle West and Northwest many cattle that bring high prices are being fed with no other roughage than sweetclover hay." Steers fattened on such pasturage customarily command top prices when sold. This plant also provides excellent forage for dairy cows; its regular use increases live weight gains and milk flow. It is also useful as horse pasturage. Its early spring growth is a particularly outstanding feature; it produces good pasturage before other such crops have commenced growth. [2][10]

When cut and cured properly the forage makes a nutritious and palatable hay. The first hay crop is leafy and relatively fine-stemmed; normally, the second hay crop is rather coarse and unpalatable, unless cut before the flower buds appear. [9] In nonirrigated areas, a nurse crop decreases the second year's hay yield. [7] On the fertile northern and western soils, where two cuttings are usually harvested the second season, the first crop has yielded from 1½ to 3 tons and the second crop from three-fourths to 1½ tons per acre. [9] In many places the first cutting occurs before the plants flower; the second crop is then allowed to mature seed. Cropping method depends on utilization and whether the plant is seeded alone or with a nurse crop. Sweetclover ensilage has also gained some popularity, being fed to

---

[1][2][3][5] See footnotes on preceding page.
[7] Hulbert, H. W. SWEET CLOVER: GROWING AND HANDLING THE CROP IN IDAHO. Idaho Agr. Expt. Sta. Bull. 147, 20 pp., illus. 1927.
[8] Willoughby, L. E., and Wells, E. B. SWEET CLOVER IN KANSAS. Kan. Agr. Col. Ext. Bull. 45, rev., 18 pp., illus. 1926.
[9] Coe, H. S. SWEET CLOVER: UTILIZATION. U. S. Dept. Agr. Farmers' Bull. 820, 32 pp., illus. 1917.
[10] McKee, C. GROWING AND USING SWEET CLOVER IN MONTANA. Mont. Agr. Expt. Sta. Circ. 118, 31 pp., illus. 1923.

all classes of livestock. The first crop of the second season may be cut with a grain binder for ensilage and the second crop harvested for seed. If not cut until in full bloom, a yield of from 10 to 12 tons per acre sometimes results, although usually the plants are killed by such treatment.[9] Hulbert[7] states that the cases of livestock poisoning from sweetclover hay, reported from Canada, Colorado, Minnesota, and the Dakotas, were due to the use of moldy hay or silage, but were not attributable to any inherent poisonous property of the plants. Experiments in feeding moldy hay to calves at the North Dakota Experiment Station resulted fatally within 40 days. Relatively few authentic cases of bloat caused by white sweetclover have been reported.[9]

This species of sweetclover is outstanding as a soil improver. It not only makes good growth in soils deficient in humus, but its extensive, large, and succulent taproots penetrate deeply beyond the normal plow line, break up the subsoil, and thus facilitate aeration and drainage. In addition, after the death of the plants, the rapid decay of the roots, together with stubble plowed under as green manure, add much nitrogenous matter to the soil. Numerous experiments conclusively prove that production increases result from either 2- or 3-year rotations with white sweetclover. In this respect, at least, it is superior to both alfalfa and the lupines. Being a biennial, it is especially well adapted to short rotations.

The utilization of this species as a honey plant dates from remote antiquity. American beekeepers have long recognized its value as a honey plant; in fact, its early distribution and use were based largely on its nectar content. Maximum production occurs in the hot, dry climate of the plains region where yields as high as 200 pounds of commercial honey per colony are obtained. In the West, the mixed nectar obtained from clover and alfalfa plants produces a high-grade honey. Both observations and experiments in North Dakota[11] demonstrate that honeybees increase the yield of sweetclover seed over 100 percent.

Among the common causes of failure in growing white sweetclover are: Acid soil, a high percentage of hard seeds, improper preparation of the seedbed (it should be firm, with a thin cover of loose soil), and lack of inoculation. Soil inoculation is necessary unless alfalfa, one of the sweetclovers, or other nitrogen-fixing crop has previously been produced on that tract. Inoculation is accomplished either by the transfer of soil from a sweetclover field or by treating the seed with pure cultures of bacteria. Growing white sweetclover with a nurse crop is advisable on weedy land or where there is sufficient moisture for two crops but, in the dry-farming regions of the West, it is preferable to grow white sweetclover alone.[6][7] On irrigated land, this sweetclover is usually seeded with oats, barley, or wheat as a nurse crop.[10]

———

For brief generic notes on *Melilotus*, see W124.

———

[6][7][9][10] See footnotes on preceding pages.
[11] Shepperd, J. H. SWEET CLOVER: EXPERIMENTS IN PASTURING. N. Dak. Agr. Expt. Sta. Bull. 211, [57] pp., illus. 1927.

YELLOW SWEETCLOVER

Melilo'tus officina'lis

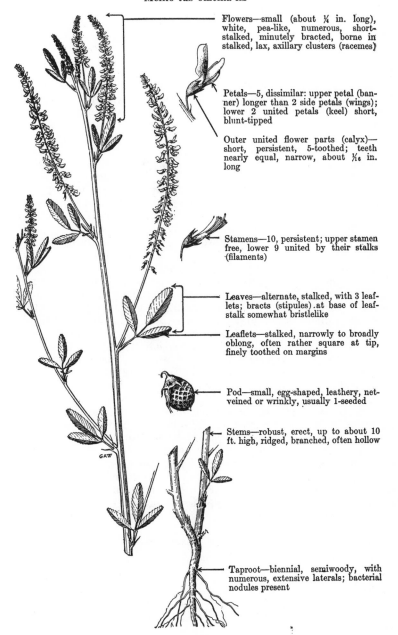

Flowers—small (about ¼ in. long), white, pea-like, numerous, short-stalked, minutely bracted, borne in stalked, lax, axillary clusters (racemes)

Petals—5, dissimilar: upper petal (banner) longer than 2 side petals (wings); lower 2 united petals (keel) short, blunt-tipped

Outer united flower parts (calyx)—short, persistent, 5-toothed; teeth nearly equal, narrow, about ⅟₁₆ in. long

Stamens—10, persistent; upper stamen free, lower 9 united by their stalks (filaments)

Leaves—alternate, stalked, with 3 leaflets; bracts (stipules) at base of leafstalk somewhat bristlelike

Leaflets—stalked, narrowly to broadly oblong, often rather square at tip, finely toothed on margins

Pod—small, egg-shaped, leathery, net-veined or wrinkly, usually 1-seeded

Stems—robust, erect, up to about 10 ft. high, ridged, branched, often hollow

Taproot—biennial, semiwoody, with numerous, extensive laterals; bacterial nodules present

GAW

Yellow sweetclover, also known as biennial yellow sweetclover and yellow melilot, is native to Europe and Asia but now widely naturalized in North America. It is a large herbaceous biennial closely resembling white sweetclover although not so tall and with a more spreading habit of growth. Its common name comes from the cloverlike leaves and fragrant yellow flowers; its blossoms yield a sweet nectar that is especially attractive to honeybees. The specific name *officinalis* arises from the use of its dried leaves and flowering tops in pharmacy; the plant, like other members of this genus, contains coumarin (a vanilla substitute) and melilotic acid.[1]

This sweetclover has spread throughout the United States and the southern half of Canada; it is almost as widely distributed as white sweetclover but only rarely is as abundant.[2] Yellow sweetclover is even less common than white sweetclover on the mountain ranges of the West, but occurs sparsely at the lower elevations along streams. This species has been cultivated both for pasture and hay and, in many farming areas where it has escaped from cultivation, now is a common and prolific weed. The plant has established itself abundantly in semihumid or humid areas on abandoned farms, eroded hillsides, and along fence rows, railroads, and highways; it also inhabits many such infertile sites as cuts and barrow pits, where the surface soil has been removed.

Yellow sweetclover makes more rapid growth, maturing from one to two weeks earlier, and produces more seed than white sweetclover.[3] Its resistance to heavy use, aggressiveness, greater tolerance to heat and drought, and its ready adaptability to poorer soils are desirable characteristics. The species is even less exacting than white sweetclover in soil and climatic requirements, being, among other things, more drought-resistant and winter-hardy. It is better qualified to succeed in dry weather and, for this reason, may be more effective than white sweetclover in soil-improvement projects in areas where it is adapted. Yellow sweetclover is preferable for pasturage in the western mountain sections, since, unlike white sweetclover, it matures seed even under moderately heavy utilization. Its lower, more spreading growth insures production of some flower heads fairly close to the ground. If the stand is pastured, the lower flowers are not usually cropped by grazing animals but are left to reseed naturally; consequently, the yellow biennial maintains a permanent stand from year to year.[4][5] This species has not been used extensively in reseeding depleted ranges; potentially, however, it may prove valuable for that purpose.[3] Although white sweetclover alone was used in reseeding experiments on burned-over land at Sandpoint, Idaho, probably the yellow-flowered species would be even better able to withstand intensive cropping by livestock.[6] It is equally important

[1] Youngken, H. W. A TEXT BOOK OF PHARMACOGNOSY. 538 pp., illus. Philadelphia. 1921.
[2] Piper, C. V. FORAGE PLANTS AND THEIR CULTURE. Rev., 671 pp., illus. New York. 1924.
[3] Forsling, C. L., and Dayton, W. A. ARTIFICIAL RESEEDING ON WESTERN MOUNTAIN RANGE LANDS. U. S. Dept. Agr. Circ. 178, 48 pp., illus. 1931.
[4] McKee, C. GROWING AND USING SWEET CLOVER IN MONTANA. Mont. Agr. Expt. Sta. Circ. 118, 31 pp., illus. 1923.
[5] Hulbert, H. W. SWEET CLOVER: GROWING AND HANDLING THE CROP IN IDAHO. Idaho Agr. Expt. Sta. Bull. 147, 20 pp., illus. 1927.
[6] Christ, J. H. RESEEDING BURNED-OVER LANDS IN NORTHERN IDAHO. Idaho Agr. Expt. Sta. Bull. 201, 28 pp., illus. 1934.

as a nectar source, since it blooms earlier, and may be used to supplement white sweetclover in bee pastures.[7]

Because of its withstanding heavy usage and its production of seed close to the ground, yellow sweetclover sometimes becomes objectionable in mixed meadows, increasing too much at the expense of other desirable species.[7][8] However, these characteristics may be advantageous when a permanent pasture is desired as, for example, on a badly depleted area. White sweetclover eclipses its yellow-flowered relative in acreage throughout the United States, largely because of its greater yield. Yellow sweetclover is less popular for hay than its white sister, which commonly yields 1 ton more hay per acre,[5] although the former is better liked in some places because of its fine stems, which make a superior hay. Like the other species of sweetclover, yellow sweetclover is an excellent plant, where it can be grown, for improving soils because of the nitrogen-fixing bacteria in the root-nodules and because the roots decay rapidly after the death of the plant, thus adding humus to the soil. Yellow sweetclover, however, is inferior in this respect to the white-flowered biennial because of its smaller root growth.[9] The mature seeds of yellow sweetclover are distinguished from those of white sweetclover by their dark greenish yellow color and the purple flecks.

In addition to *M. officinalis*, two other yellow-flowered species of *Melilotus* are in cultivation. Annual yellow sweetclover (*M. in'dica*), also known as sourclover and King Island melilot, a native of Eurasia found on ballast and waste places along the Atlantic seaboard and Gulf Coast of North America, and locally in the interior, has become an abundant weed in farming areas of California and the Southwest. Wooton and Standley[10] report that no weed is more common in alfalfa fields of New Mexico. It is a winter annual, averaging 1½ to 3 feet in height, and has been extensively grown in California as a green manure crop in the citrus orchards.[2] The species is useful for pasturage and hay in the warmer sections of the United States but useless in the North. Daghestan sweetclover (*M. suave'olens*) is a yellow-flowered biennial resembling white sweetclover in growth habit. It has recently been introduced into America and is showing promise in the Dakotas and Minnesota.[2]

The sweetclovers, sometimes called melilots, include approximately 20 to 25 species of annual or biennial herbs native in Europe, Asia, and Africa but now widely distributed throughout the temperate and subtropical regions. Some species are valuable forage plants and have attained importance under cultivation; others are merely

---

[2][5] See footnotes on preceding page.
[7] Westgate, J. M., and Vinall, H. N. SWEET CLOVER. U. S. Dept. Agr. Farmers' Bull. 485, 39 pp., illus. 1912.
[8] Clark, S. P. SWEET CLOVER IN ARIZONA. Ariz. Agr. Expt. Sta. Circ. 34, 7 pp. 1921.
[9] Coe, H. S. SWEET CLOVER: GROWING THE CROP. U. S. Dept. Agr. Farmers' Bull. 797, 35 pp., illus. 1917.
[10] Wooton. E. O., and Standley, P. C. FLORA OF NEW MEXICO. U. S. Natl. Mus., Contrib. U. S. Natl. Herbarium 19, 794 pp. 1915.

aggressive weeds. Although at least four species and one variety of sweetclover are cultivated in the United States, white sweetclover and yellow sweetclover are by far the most important and in recent years have attained popularity as hay and forage plants. The high coumarin content, which gives the herbage a bitter taste, is characteristic of the genus, although livestock may be taught to relish the two most widely cultivated species if pastured thereon early in the season. Prolonged exposure to sunlight causes most of the coumarin to volatilize; consequently the cured hay loses much of its bitter taste. There is probably a promising field for the development of more drought-resistant sweetclover strains better adapted to range conditions, finer-textured, less bitter tasting, and of improved yield.

Hubam sweetclover (*M. al'ba an'nua*), often called Hubam clover or annual white sweetclover, an annual form of white sweetclover, has recently aroused considerable interest among experimental plant breeders, largely because of its variability and numerous strains. It is a rank-growing, late-maturing variety which yields seed the first year sown. Although inferior to the typical form of the species because producing, in general, less forage and because its slender root and annual habit are not so conducive to soil improvement, it is a particularly valuable honey plant, its late blooms prolonging the sweetclover nectar season. It is possible that sufficiently drought-resistant and aggressive strains may yet be developed to give this variety local value for artificial reseeding of badly depleted and eroded range areas where a quick-growing, luxuriant, soil-improving ground cover is needed, pending eventual establishment of perennial species.

The generic name *Melilotus* is the Latinized form of an old Greek plant name, used by Aristotle and Theophrastus, which probably refers to a true sweetclover; *melilotus*, in turn, doubtless comes from the Greek *meli*, honey, and *lotŏs*, a kind of wild clover, or trefoil, used as feed by horses in the meadows about Sparta and Troy.

PENARD MINT

Men'tha penar'di

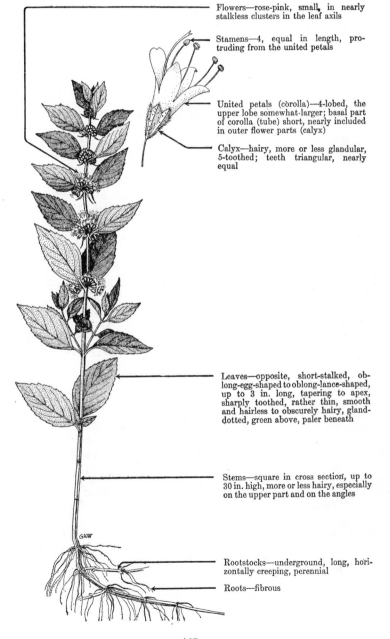

Flowers—rose-pink, small, in nearly stalkless clusters in the leaf axils

Stamens—4, equal in length, protruding from the united petals

United petals (corolla)—4-lobed, the upper lobe somewhat larger; basal part of corolla (tube) short, nearly included in outer flower parts (calyx)

Calyx—hairy, more or less glandular, 5-toothed; teeth triangular, nearly equal

Leaves—opposite, short-stalked, oblong-egg-shaped to oblong-lance-shaped, up to 3 in. long, tapering to apex, sharply toothed, rather thin, smooth and hairless to obscurely hairy, gland-dotted, green above, paler beneath

Stems—square in cross section, up to 30 in. high, more or less hairy, especially on the upper part and on the angles

Rootstocks—underground, long, horizontally creeping, perennial

Roots—fibrous

445

Penard mint is an aromatic perennial having a somewhat penny-royallike odor, small, rose-pink flowers in axillary whorls, opposite leaves, and 4-angled stems. Unfortunately, this common western mint is disguised in botanical literature under a variety of aliases. Some botanists prefer to regard it as a smooth, short-leafstalked, native variety of the introduced, Old World field mint (*M. arven'sis*) and call it *M. arven'sis penar'di* (syn. *M. arven'sis glabra'ta*). Others regard it as a smooth, broader-leaved variety of the native Canada mint (*M. canaden'sis*, syns. *M. borea'lis*, *M. canaden'sis borea'lis*) and call it *M. canaden'sis glabra'ta*. Some ultraconservative botanists prefer to merge it in either the European *M. arven'sis* or in the American *M. canaden'sis*. Still others, of a more radical school of thought, prefer to separate *M. penar'di* itself into additional species, including *M. gla'brior*, *M. occidenta'lis*, and *M. rubel'la*. This confusion of names has resulted because some of the mints hybridize readily, producing intergrading forms, which are extremely difficult to classify.

Penard mint, named for E. Penard, a Swiss botanist who collected plants in the Western States in the 1890's, ranges from British Columbia to Saskatchewan, Nebraska, New Mexico, and California, occurring chiefly in wet or, at least, moist soils along streams, around springs and seeps, and in similar situations. It characteristically grows among bushes and probably is most abundant in the ponderosa-pine belt, although it occurs from the desert-shrub belt to the spruce-fir. Generally, Penard mint occurs scatteringly, although locally it is common or even abundant. On the bulk of the western ranges, however, its scarcity relegates this species to an unimportant place among range plants.

The palatability of Penard mint undoubtedly varies somewhat, as it is rated from fair to fairly good for cattle and from fair to good for sheep. The bulk of opinion, however, designates this species as seldom better than fair forage for cattle, sheep, and goats. It is practically worthless as horse forage, and probably is of negligible value as game feed.

MINTS (Men'tha spp.)

The mints constitute a genus of aromatic perennial herbs having opposite leaves, four-angled stems, and numerous, relatively small flowers in dense axillary or terminal clusters. Some of the species hybridize freely, producing numerous intergrading forms, which has caused much confusion about names and considerable doubt as to the number of species. On a conservative nomenclatural basis there are approximately 30 species, all natives of the Northern Hemisphere. Including the native and naturalized species, approximately 15 species occur in the United States, with probably not more than 4 native to the West. The genus belongs to the mint family (Menthaceae) and derives its name from the Greek, *minthe*, the name applied by the Greek philosopher Theophrastus to one of these plants. *Minthe* was the name of a nymph, fabled to have been changed into a mint plant by Proserpine.

The mints typically grow in wet or moist places, and are most common at medium elevations in the West. These plants are abundant and important locally on the western ranges. The western species are probably comparable to Penard mint in palatability.

Peppermint (*M. piperi'ta*), the source of the oil of peppermint of commerce, is undoubtedly the most important member of the genus. It is a perennial herb with branched, smooth stems; lance-shaped, pointed, sharply toothed, mostly stalked, gland-dotted leaves; and thick, terminal flower clusters (spikes) of purple (rarely white) flowers. It is a native of Europe and is now widely naturalized in the United States, especially the East, having been introduced into cultivation in this country more than 100 years ago.[1] Considerable acreage in the United States, the principal producing country, is devoted to the commercial growing of peppermint, the average annual production of oil being approximately 500,000 pounds.[1] Peppermint oil enters into numerous medicinal products, but its chief use is for flavoring candies, chewing gum, and tooth paste. There is also a limited use of the dried herbage of peppermint in medicine.[2]

Spearmint (*M. spica'ta*, syn. *M. vi'ridis*), a species very similar to peppermint except that the leaves are usually stalkless, and the flower clusters are narrow and interrupted, is also grown commercially for the essential oil, oil of spearmint, which it yields. This plant is a native of Europe and Asia but is now naturalized in the United States even more widely than peppermint, probably because spearmint is commonly grown as a culinary herb in home gardens, being prized for making mint jelly, mint tea, for flavoring lamb sauce, and for mint juleps. The chief commercial use of oil of spearmint is for flavoring chewing gum, the average annual production of oil in the United States being approximately 50,000 pounds.[1]

The antiseptic drug, menthol, widely used in medicinal products is an ingredient of the oils of peppermint and spearmint and is manufactured from them to some extent.[3] However, the chief source of menthol is the Japanese mint (*M. arven'sis piperas'cens*) which is extensively grown in Japan, but, as yet, its commercial cultivation in this country is limited.[1]

[1] Sievers, A. F. PEPPERMINT AND SPEARMINT AS FARM CROPS. U. S. Dept. Agr. Farmers' Bull. 1555, 26 pp., illus. 1929.
[2] Sievers, A. F. AMERICAN MEDICINAL PLANTS OF COMMERCIAL IMPORTANCE. U. S. Dept. Agr. Misc. Pub. 77, 74 pp., illus. 1930.
[3] Wood, H. C., Remington, J. P., and Sadtler, S. P., assisted by Lyons, A. B., and Wood, H. C., Jr. THE DISPENSATORY OF THE UNITED STATES OF AMERICA, BY DR. GEO. B. WOOD AND DR. FRANKLIN BACHE. Ed. 19, thoroughly rev. and largely rewritten . . . 1.947 pp. Philadelphia and London. 1907.

BLUEBELLS

Merten'sia spp.

Bluebells, sometimes called lungworts and languid-ladies, are well-known perennial herbs of the borage family. They are natives of the Northern Hemisphere, ranging from the shores of the Arctic southward, in North America, to Alabama, New Mexico, and California. The genus is best developed in the Far West, where between 35 and 65 species occur, depending on the opinion of the individual botanist. These plants grow in moist, usually rich soils, in prairies, meadows, parks, along streams, and in scattered timber in the mountains, generally in partial shade. Some valley and foothill species blossom in the spring, while the higher mountain species bloom during the summer months. The name *Mertensia* is in honor of Franz Karl Mertens (1764–1831), a German botanist.

Some species of bluebells are sparsely distributed; others grow in large clumps, especially in mountain meadows, and often on old bedgrounds and burns. The larger species are choice sheep feed and, because of their succulence, are particularly valuable for growing lambs and flushing ewes. Bluebells are good feed for cattle in some localities, but in most regions these plants have little value for that class of livestock. Horses rarely eat these plants. The natural tendency of sheep, and to some extent cattle, is to graze the more important species of bluebells so intensively that new plants are produced chiefly from the strong rootstocks. If reproduction by seed is prevented for an extended period by overutilization, the plants will decrease appreciably and may ultimately disappear.

These herbs have stems 4 to 60 inches high, produced from stout, thickened roots or rootstocks, and in some species the roots are rather tuberlike; their herbage is usually smooth, sometimes with a few fine hairs, and is often beset with a bluish waxen bloom as occurs on a cabbage leaf or the skin of a plum. The leaves are alternate, without teeth or indentations. The somewhat bell-like, blue or purple (rarely white), nodding, mostly bractless flowers are borne in showy terminal clusters and are five-lobed at the end; the floral cup (calyx) at the base of the flower is deeply five-cleft and persists in fruit. The fruit consists of four small "seeds" (nutlets), wrinkled at maturity, and attached obliquely near their bases to a somewhat convex or flattened receptacle, the scar of attachment being small and inconspicuous. Bluebells are sometimes confused with pentstemons, but are readily distinguishable from the latter by their alternate leaves and regular, bell-mouthed flowers, as opposed to the opposite leaves and two-lipped flowers of the pentstemons.

MOUNTAIN BLUEBELLS

Merten'sia cilia'ta, syns. *M. polyphyl'la,* *"M. sibi'rica"* [1]

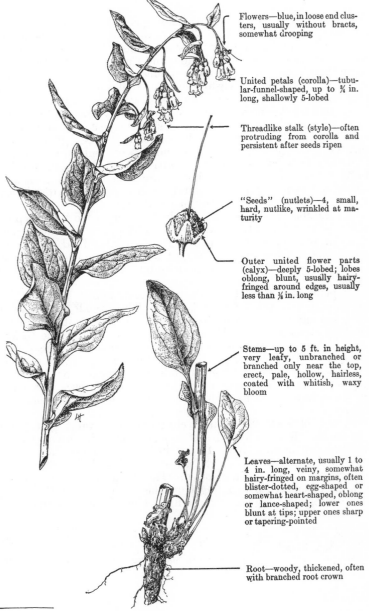

Flowers—blue, in loose end clusters, usually without bracts, somewhat drooping

United petals (corolla)—tubular-funnel-shaped, up to ¾ in. long, shallowly 5-lobed

Threadlike stalk (style)—often protruding from corolla and persistent after seeds ripen

"Seeds" (nutlets)—4, small, hard, nutlike, wrinkled at maturity

Outer united flower parts (calyx)—deeply 5-lobed; lobes oblong, blunt, usually hairy-fringed around edges, usually less than ⅛ in. long

Stems—up to 5 ft. in height, very leafy, unbranched or branched only near the top, erect, pale, hollow, hairless, coated with whitish, waxy bloom

Leaves—alternate, usually 1 to 4 in. long, veiny, somewhat hairy-fringed on margins, often blister-dotted, egg-shaped or somewhat heart-shaped, oblong or lance-shaped; lower ones blunt at tips; upper ones sharp or tapering-pointed

Root—woody, thickened, often with branched root crown

[1] See footnote on following page.

Mountain bluebells, one of the large species of its genus, is a tall, leafy perennial herb of the borage family (Boraginaceae). It is so named because it usually occurs in the mountains and has blue, bell-shaped flowers. The Latin specific name *ciliata* is derived from the word *cilium* (eyelid) and refers to the eyelashlike hairs along the edges of the leaves.

Mountain bluebells is a very variable species and its exact range is in dispute, largely owing to differences of opinion among botanists.[1] *M. ciliata* is found only in the western United States, from western Montana to eastern Oregon, Nevada, and Colorado, but extending to California in the variety *stomatechoides* (syn. *M. stomatechoides*) and as far northwest as Washington and Idaho in the variety *longipedunculata* (syns. *M. ambigua* and *M. denticulata*, at least in part). The altitudinal range varies from approximately 5,000 to 12,000 feet. This species prefers sheltered, moist situations such as high alpine meadows. It often occurs on rich loam soils, but also grows well on sandy or gravelly loams if an abundance of moisture is present, although it appears occasionally on drier soils. Mountain bluebells usually grows in clumps or in almost pure stands in local areas along streams and near springs, frequently associated with willow, baneberry (*Actaea*), butterweed, and monkeyflower.

The palatability of mountain bluebells is very good for sheep and goats and fair for cattle and horses. Sheep eat the entire plant because it is leafy and succulent. Deer are also fond of it. The flowers appear from June to August and the fruits in September; after the seeds mature the plant dries up and is then worthless as forage.

This plant is a favorite of the rockrabbit, known as pika, little chief hare or cony (*Ochotona princeps*). These small rodents of the higher mountains simulate the activities of the professional hay farmer by cutting off the plants, spreading them out on the rocks to dry, and then storing them away in piles in sheltered places under the rocks for food during the long winter season. E. W. Nelson[2] states that these piles of forage, including grasses and many herbaceous plants, often contain as much as one bushel each. The porcupine also grazes the succulent herbage of mountain bluebells with great relish.

Mountain bluebells has usually clustered stems varying in height up to about 5 feet. The hairless or somewhat hairy leaves vary in size; they are usually from 1 to 4 inches, but sometimes up to 7 inches in length and, as a rule, are hairy-fringed (ciliate) around the edges, and often blister-dotted. The threadlike stalks (styles), which are often seen protruding from the blossoms when the flowers are in full bloom, may also remain until after the nutlets ripen.

---

[1] Some American authors have considered *M. ciliata* synonymous with *M. sibirica* (L.) Don, which would include Siberia in its range, and possibly Alaska. The best present-day botanical opinion, however, regards *M. sibirica* as a species wholly confined to Siberia and absent from North America.

[2] Nelson, Edward W. SMALLER MAMMALS OF NORTH AMERICA. Natl. Geogr. Mag. 33(5) : [371]–493, illus. 1918.

TALL BLUEBELLS

Merten'sia leonar'di, syn. *M. sampso'nii*

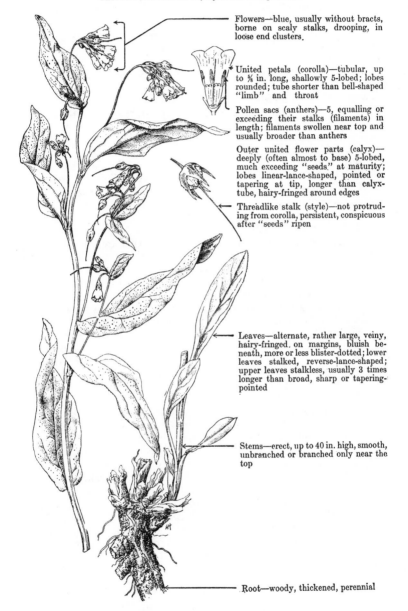

Flowers—blue, usually without bracts, borne on scaly stalks, drooping, in loose end clusters.

United petals (corolla)—tubular, up to ⅝ in. long, shallowly 5-lobed; lobes rounded; tube shorter than bell-shaped "limb" and throat

Pollen sacs (anthers)—5, equalling or exceeding their stalks (filaments) in length; filaments swollen near top and usually broader than anthers

Outer united flower parts (calyx)— deeply (often almost to base) 5-lobed, much exceeding "seeds" at maturity; lobes linear-lance-shaped, pointed or tapering at tip, longer than calyx-tube, hairy-fringed around edges

Threadlike stalk (style)—not protruding from corolla, persistent, conspicuous after "seeds" ripen

Leaves—alternate, rather large, veiny, hairy-fringed on margins, bluish beneath, more or less blister-dotted; lower leaves stalked, reverse-lance-shaped; upper leaves stalkless, usually 3 times longer than broad, sharp or tapering-pointed

Stems—erect, up to 40 in. high, smooth, unbranched or branched only near the top

Root—woody, thickened, perennial

453

Tall bluebells, a rather robust, leafy perennial herb of the borage family (Boraginaceae), is one of the most important forage weeds in the Intermountain region. It has a limited range, occurring mainly in Utah, although also found to some extent in Idaho and Nevada. This plant grows characteristically in the cooler mountains at elevations of from 6,000 to 11,000 feet, in rather large clumps in scattered stands with such other herbaceous plants as geranium, yarrow, and bromegrasses. It is abundant on fairly moist or well-drained soils in aspen stands, but also appears in partial shade along streams and in canyon bottoms from the ponderosa pine to the Engelmann spruce belt. The type specimen of this bluebells was collected in Mill Creek Canyon, Utah, by F. E. Leonard in 1884, and was named in his honor by the late Dr. Rydberg in 1909.

Individual plants produce an abundance of succulent forage and have a palatability of from good to very good for sheep and goats and fairly good for cattle. Deer and elk also relish this species. Tall bluebells is eaten readily throughout the growing season, as the herbage remains green and succulent until killed by frost. Sheep consume the entire plant, but cattle usually eat only the flowers and leaves. On many of the mountain ranges in Utah this forage is one of the choice feeds for fattening lambs.

The large bunches of tall bluebells, crowned with clusters of bright blue, bell-shaped flowers, add a distinctive beauty to the mountain flora. Tall bluebells is very similar to mountain bluebells (*M. ciliata*) and, since the two plants are separated on the basis of rather slight botanical differences, they are difficult to distinguish in the field. However, the calyx lobes of mountain bluebells are blunt-tipped (obtuse), of a narrow (linear) type, and only about 2 mm. ($\frac{1}{12}$ inch) long, whereas those of tall bluebells are broader (lanceolate), sharp-tipped, and about 4 mm. ($\frac{1}{6}$ inch) long. The united petals (corollas) of tall bluebells tend to be somewhat larger and longer than those of mountain bluebells.

In 1913 Tidestrom, at that time unaware of the existence of the earlier *M. leonardi* Rydb., published a high-range, Wasatch Mountain species of this genus under the name *M. sampsonii*, in honor of its collector, Dr. A. W. Sampson. Somewhat later, in 1925 [1] Tidestrom believed that *M. sampsonii* was perhaps only a form of *M. leonardi*, though keying it out from *leonardi* on its smaller flowers (about one-half of an inch long) and rather more deeply cleft calyx. However, field studies of the Forest Service have demonstrated that it is impossible to separate *leonardi* and *sampsonii* on the range, and Tidestrom in more recent identification work for the Forest Service has remanded *sampsonii* to synonymy. Sampson [2] states that this form, Sampson bluebells, begins growth early in the season and remains green until killing frosts, so that there is a long period of palatability; he further states that many Utah sheep growers depend largely on the plant to fatten their lambs for market, reserving bluebells areas for the finishing period.

[1] Tidestrom, I. FLORA OF UTAH AND NEVADA. U. S. Natl. Mus., Contrib. U. S. Natl. Herbarium 25, 665 pp., illus. 1925.
[2] Sampson, A. W. NATIVE AMERICAN FORAGE PLANTS. 435 pp., illus. New York. 1924.

SMALL BLUEBELLS

Merten'sia pulchel'la

Flowers—crowded, in end clusters

United petals (corolla)—5-lobed, rose red in bud, turning to sky blue when fully opened, tubular-funnel-shaped, from ⅜ to ¾ in. long; tube up to about 3 times as long as outer flower parts

Outer flower parts (sepals)—5, united near base, oblong-lance-shaped, sharp-pointed, minutely toothed on margins, persistent

Leaves—alternate, ¾ to 4 in. long, green, thickish, egg-shaped, minutely warty above, smooth beneath, with rough margins

Stems—erect, 3 to 8 in. high, smooth, solitary or several to many, from black, tuberous-thickened, often clustered roots

Small bluebells, a perennial herb of the borage family (Boraginaceae), is so called because of its low growth and blue, bell-shaped flowers. The specific name is derived from the Latin *pulchellus*, a diminutive word for pretty. The name is very appropriate because small bluebells, with its dense clusters of flowers, deep sky-blue at maturity, is one of the most beautiful of western mountain plants. The occurrence of small bluebells is limited to southern British Columbia, Washington, Oregon, Idaho, and western Montana, except that it extends into extreme northern California (Modoc National Forest) in the variety *glauca*. It is the common low bluebells of this northwestern area. The altitudinal range varies from 2,000 feet above sea level up to 8,000 feet. The species characteristically grows on mountain slopes, in sandy, clayey, and gravelly loam soils, scattered among grasses and weeds, but never growing in pure stands.

Small bluebells is not so palatable as most of the larger and more leafy species of *Mertensia*, being only fairly good for sheep and goats and practically worthless for cattle and horses. The plant is of little forage value except perhaps on early spring ranges, where it provides succulent green feed for a brief season. It is one of the early spring flowers, blooming from March to July, so that on many of the higher ranges it blossoms, dries up, and disappears before the grazing season.

Small bluebells has erect stems, 3 to 8 inches in height, which are smooth and hairless (glabrous) and unbranched but, like spring-beauty (*Claytonia*), several to many arise from one root. The leaves are alternate, three-fourths of an inch to occasionally 4 inches long, sometimes bluish green, narrow and thickish, glabrous beneath, minutely warty above and rough along the margins. The lower leaves are egg-shaped with the broader end forward, being narrowed at base and short-stalked. The middle and upper leaves are without stalks, somewhat egg-shaped and often half clasping. The azure-blue flowers, borne in close terminal clusters of from 10 to 20, are from three-eighths to three-fourths of an inch long, with a corolla tube from three to four times as long as the outer flower parts (calyx lobes, or sepals). These sepals are united near the base, are oblong lance-shaped, and minutely toothed on the margins. The threadlike stalks (filaments) of the stamens are dilated and as long as the pollen sacs (anthers). The fruit consists of four nutlets, which are gray, finely beset with small, hard dots, and the scar at the base of the calyx where the nutlets are attached is pale and prominent. At maturity the nutlets are enclosed within the greatly enlarged fruiting calyx. The black, tuberous-thickened roots are shallow-seated and either solitary or in clusters.

Piper,[1] whose treatment is followed by some other botanists, recognizes a variety of this species, *M. pulchella glauca*, having more conspicuously bluish (glaucous) herbage, a greater tendency to tuftedness (typical *M. pulchella* has solitary or paired stems from the same root), somewhat narrower leaves, and typically more slender flowers. It probably completely intergrades with the species and has a similar forage status.

[1] Piper, C. V. FLORA OF THE STATE OF WASHINGTON. U. S. Natl. Mus., Contrib. U. S. Natl. Herbarium 11, 637 pp., illus. 1906.

LEWIS MONKEYFLOWER

Mi'mulus lewi'sii

Flowers—rose-pink to purplish, long-stalked, mostly in pairs from the axils of the upper leaves

Outer united flower parts (calyx)—green, symmetrical, neither oblique nor inflated, prismatic, 5-angled, about ¾ in. long, with 5 sharp, nearly equal, linear-lance-shaped teeth

United petals (corolla)—showy, 1 to 2 in. long, funnelform, sparingly bearded in the throat, 2-lipped, with 5 spreading lobes, 2 lobes turned up and the other 3 down

Stamens—4, not conspicuously protruding, attached to corolla but not included in upper "lip"

Seed pod (capsule)—oblong, somewhat papery, enclosed in persistent calyx, 2-celled, splitting down middle back of each cell

Stems—erect, usually 1 or 2 (sometimes up to 4) ft. high, more or less sticky-hairy, often numerous and tufted from a perennial underground rootstock

Leaves—opposite, stalkless, up to about 4 in. long, oblong-egg-shaped to lance-shaped, somewhat sticky-hairy, with several rather prominent and almost parallel veins, remotely wavy-toothed around margins

GAW

The large, showy flowers of this beautiful perennial herb are in evidence from Minnesota to Colorado and Arizona and westward to the Pacific coast from California to British Columbia. Although widely distributed, this species is never very abundant and occurs only in moist places along streams and around springs. It commonly grows in relatively small but dense clumps at the higher elevations (from 5,000 to 10,000 feet), but sometimes is found at lower altitudes, in partial shade on moist sites. Both the common name, Lewis monkeyflower, and the specific name *lewisii* are floral compliments to the famous explorer Captain Meriwether Lewis of the historic Lewis and Clark expedition.

Lewis monkeyflower has but little forage value, usually growing in places too wet for accessibility to livestock. Moreover, its palatability is low—varying from practically worthless to poor for cattle and from poor to fair for sheep. The attractive, pink to rose-red (rarely pure white) flowers of this plant are in demand by wild-flower lovers, and the species is rather widely cultivated.

MONKEYFLOWERS (Mi'mulus spp., syn. *Euna'nus spp.*)

Monkeyflowers are annual or perennial herbs of the figwort family (Scrophulariaceae) or, if one includes the bushmonkeyflowers (*Diplacus* spp.), sometimes shrubs. The common name monkeyflower is an interpretation of the meaning of the scientific name *Mimulus*, which is a diminutive of the Latin *mimus*, mimic, and refers to the grinning mien of the variously colored and spotted, irregular, two-lipped flowers and their resemblance to the masks worn by mimes, or comic actors, on the ancient stage. Members of this fairly large, attractively flowered genus have worldwide distribution, except in the tropical regions. Seventy or more species of the genus occur naturally in western North America, with California the center of distribution. In the West monkeyflowers grow in swampy areas, around springs, along streams, and other moist or wet places in the woods or among rocks and upon cliffs, from the low plains to the high mountains.

Their wide distribution, numerous species, and showiness make monkeyflowers a familiar component of western vegetation, but inferior palatability and usual lack of abundance preclude them from the roster of important forage plants. Sheep nibble the flowers and some of the leaves, but the species are worthless or, at best, poor feed for cattle. Horses dislike these plants; elk and deer graze them but slightly. Any material disturbance of the soil expedites the spread of monkeyflowers, which frequently occur in masses along gullies, washes, and slides in the mountains where the moisture supply is adequate.

Crimson monkeyflower (*M. cardina'lis*) is closely related to Lewis monkeyflower. Its large, velvety, crimson flowers, blended with yellow, are very showy; it has been cultivated to some extent, especially in England, where it was introduced from California by David Douglas. This species grows along streams and ditches from Utah to Oregon, California, New Mexico, and Mexico. It is easily domesticated, if planted in moist situations, and averages from 2 to 4 feet in height; its egg-shaped (ovate) to obovate-lance-shaped, toothed leaves are sticky-hairy.

M. gutta'tus (syn. *M. langsdor'fii*) is one of the most common species of monkeyflower on the western ranges and apparently has no generally accepted English name, although it is sometimes referred to as common monkeyflower. This interesting and very variable species occurs from Alaska and Saskatchewan to New Mexico and California. Its native haunts are chiefly in rich, moist soils along streams from sea level to the higher mountains. The flowers are deep yellow, dotted with purple or brown within; the leaves are coarsely and irregularly toothed, with the upper ones stemless. The early white settlers called this plant wild lettuce and ate the succulent herbage and stems as a salad.[1] This species is so closely related to the cultivated golden monkeyflower (*M. lu'teus*), originally described from Chile, that it has often been confused with that species by botanist and layman alike. Golden monkeyflower and some of its congeners have been subjects of horticultural research because of their natural instability; numerous forms and hybrids show remarkably beautiful and variegated color patterns of the corolla.

Muskplant (*M. moscha'tus*) was discovered and named by David Douglas, who introduced it into England from the Columbia River region of Washington. This spreading or creeping perennial plant soon became a favorite for trellises both in England and in eastern America. The flowers are pale, yellow, dotted with brown, and the densely white-hairy, sticky leaves have a musklike odor. After many years in cultivation this musk odor suddenly disappeared, whereupon the plant immediately lost popularity; the reason for the loss of scent has never been definitely determined.[1] Various authorities report that muskplants found in their native habitat are not always scented.

The species of *Mimulus* have erect or spreading, hairless, or hairy stems with opposite, hairless or hairy (often viscid-hairy), ordinarily toothed leaves. The attractive, generally showy flowers are borne singly on stalks arising from the joint of the leaf and stem or appear as though in clusters (racemes) by the reduction of the upper leaves to bracts. The flowers, slightly resembling those of the cultivated snapdragons, are chiefly yellow, red, or purplish (rarely white), with a pair of bearded or naked ridges extending down the lower side of the interior or along the so-called throat of the flower. In some species, the most striking feature is the brown or other-colored marking in the throat of the corolla. The five united outer flower parts (calyx) form an angled, five-toothed tube; the four anther-bearing stamens occur in pairs. The seed-producing organ (pistil) is an interesting feature of monkeyflowers, the upper portion (stigma) consisting of two flat plates or lobes. When the flower is in bloom, these lobes are expanded, and are very sensitive. They immediately close tightly if touched by a visiting insect, but subsequently open again. Whether this adaptation has any significance in the economy of these plants is a mystery. The fruit, a two-celled capsule containing many small seeds, is enclosed in the calyx tube at maturity.

[1] Saunders, C. F. WESTERN WILD FLOWERS AND THEIR STORIES. 320 pp., illus. Garden City, N. Y. 1933.

MINTLEAF BEEBALM

Monar'da menthaefo'lia, syn. *M. stric'ta*

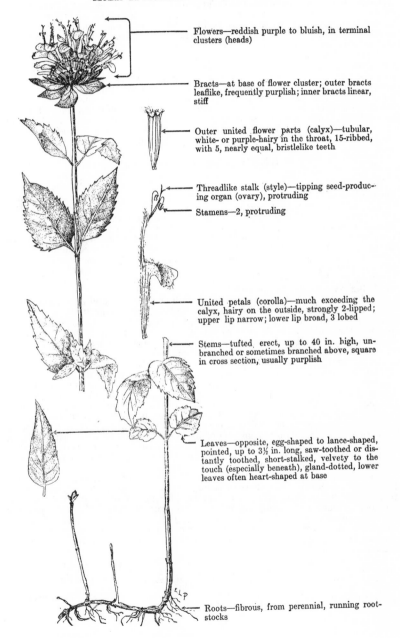

Flowers—reddish purple to bluish, in terminal clusters (heads)

Bracts—at base of flower cluster; outer bracts leaflike, frequently purplish; inner bracts linear, stiff

Outer united flower parts (calyx)—tubular, white- or purple-hairy in the throat, 15-ribbed, with 5, nearly equal, bristlelike teeth

Threadlike stalk (style)—tipping seed-producing organ (ovary), protruding

Stamens—2, protruding

United petals (corolla)—much exceeding the calyx, hairy on the outside, strongly 2-lipped; upper lip narrow; lower lip broad, 3 lobed

Stems—tufted, erect, up to 40 in. high, unbranched or sometimes branched above, square in cross section, usually purplish

Leaves—opposite, egg-shaped to lance-shaped, pointed, up to 3½ in. long, saw-toothed or distantly toothed, short-stalked, velvety to the touch (especially beneath), gland-dotted, lower leaves often heart-shaped at base

Roots—fibrous, from perennial, running rootstocks

The leaves of mintleaf beebalm, a perennial weed have a taste strongly suggestive of sage; in fact, *Monarda* is closely related to the genus *Salvia*, which embraces the true cultivated sages. The specific name, *menthaefolia*, is an adjective derived from the generic name of mint, *Mentha*, and *folium*, leaf— hence mintleaf. Mintleaf beebalm ranges from Illinois and Texas westward to Arizona, Idaho, and Alberta. It occurs over a considerable altitudinal range, from lower elevations in the sagebrush belt to the lower limits of the spruce-fir belt, chiefly on rich, moist soils in weed, brush, and aspen types. This species is common in bottomlands, along streams, and in the vicinity of springs and seeps and is often locally abundant.

Mintleaf beebalm is poor to fair forage for cattle, and fairly good forage for sheep and goats. There is evidence also that it is of some value as deer and elk forage. The wide distribution, common occurrence, and local abundance, combined with the large amount of foliage produced and the reasonably good palatability, make it a fairly valuable range plant. Although not unduly aggressive, this species withstands grazing very well and, on the whole, is one of the more valuable, secondary range weeds. The present tendency of the more conservative botanists is to regard *M. comáta* and *M. scábra* of the western manuals as forms of mintleaf beebalm rather than as distinct species.

BEEBALMS (Monar'da spp.)

Monarda, a member of the mint family (Menthaceae), is a North American genus of about 12 species of annual or perennial herbs. The western and many of the eastern species are perhaps most commonly known as horsemint; this name, however, is widely used for members of the genus *Agastache* and probably should be restricted to that genus. Other names applied to species of *Monarda* are lemon-mint and wildbergamot, the latter being employed chiefly in the East. The true bergamot, source of the commercial oil of bergamot, is *Citrus bergamia*, a species closely related to the orange. *Monarda* is named after Nicolás Monardes, a Spanish physician and botanist. Nine species commonly occur in the West, principally in the Rocky Mountains, the genus apparently not being represented in the Pacific States.

The beebalms are widely distributed within their range, and are common and often locally abundant, chiefly in moist soils. Their palatability apparently varies both with the species, and, to some extent, with local conditions. In general, the palatability is poor to fair for cattle and fair to fairly good for sheep and goats. Horses make only incidental use of these plants and, although game animals undoubtedly crop them, they are not important game feed under normal conditions. Some species are practically worthless as forage.

The beebalms are recognized as members of the mint family by their four-angled stems, opposite leaves, and the fruits, which consist of four small nutlets included within the persistent outer flower parts (calyx). They may be distinguished from other members in this family by the strongly two-lipped corolla, only two anther-bearing, usually exserted stamens, and the fifteen-ribbed, nearly equally five-toothed, elongated calyx usually hairy in the throat. The leaves are gland-dotted and more or less aromatic, and the rather large, usually brightly colored flowers are borne in dense terminal clusters (heads) mostly surrounded by leafy bracts or, in some species, additional flower clusters appear in the upper leaf axils.

The volatile oil present in *Monarda* yields, in the case of both spotted beebalm (*M. puncta'ta*) and Oswego beebalm (*M. di'dyma*), also called Oswego tea, the valuable antiseptic drug, thymol, although *Thymus vulgaris*, also a member of the mint family, is the usual source of supply.[1][2] It is possible that the closely related pony beebalm (*M. pectina'ta*) of the West also contains this drug. Several species are grown commercially as ornamentals, including Oswego beebalm, one of the most brilliant of native American flowers.

---

[1] Wood, H. C., Remington, J. P., and Sadtler, S. P., assisted by Lyons, A. B., and Wood, H. C., Jr. THE DISPENSATORY OF THE UNITED STATES OF AMERICA, BY DR. GEO. B. WOOD AND DR. FRANKLIN BACHE. Ed. 19, thoroughly rev. and largely rewritten . . . . 1,947 pp. Philadelphia and London. 1907.
[2] Hood, S. C. COMMERCIAL PRODUCTION OF THYMOL FROM HORSEMINT (MONARDA PUNCTATA). U. S. Dept. Agr. Bull. 372, 12 pp. 1916.

TUMBLEMUSTARD

Nor'ta altis'sima, syn. *Sisym'brium altis'simum*

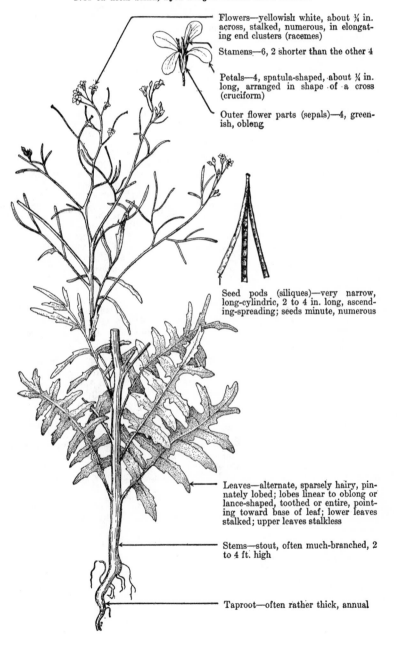

Flowers—yellowish white, about ¼ in. across, stalked, numerous, in elongating end clusters (racemes)

Stamens—6, 2 shorter than the other 4

Petals—4, spatula-shaped, about ¼ in. long, arranged in shape of a cross (cruciform)

Outer flower parts (sepals)—4, greenish, oblong

Seed pods (siliques)—very narrow, long-cylindric, 2 to 4 in. long, ascending-spreading; seeds minute, numerous

Leaves—alternate, sparsely hairy, pinnately lobed; lobes linear to oblong or lance-shaped, toothed or entire, pointing toward base of leaf; lower leaves stalked; upper leaves stalkless

Stems—stout, often much-branched, 2 to 4 ft. high

Taproot—often rather thick, annual

Tumblemustard, also known as hedge mustard, Jim Hill mustard, tall mustard, tall sisymbrium, and tumbling mustard, is a rank, ungainly biennial with tumbleweed proclivities. The specific name *altissima* means very tall. The common name most generally used in the northern part of the United States is Jim Hill mustard, referring to James J. Hill, the late capitalist and railroad builder, whose Great Northern Railroad, transporting the seed of tumblemustard, incidental to the movement of hay, grain, and livestock, greatly assisted in the distribution of this weed pest. Originally from southern Europe, tumblemustard is now distributed throughout Europe, Asia, and much of temperate North America. A specimen in the National Herbarium collected at Philadelphia in 1878 is the earliest authentic record of this species in North America. It was supposedly seen in 1883 near Kansas City, Mo., and was well established in 1892 near Aberdeen, S. Dak. It was observed near Minneapolis in 1894 and was collected the following year at seven different points within a 10-mile radius of that city. The first record of its introduction into Canada was reported in 1885 in Alberta, when specimens were collected on the right-of-way of the Canadian Pacific Railway at the eastern base of the Rocky Mountains.[1] The species is now more or less well established in practically all cultivated portions of North America north of Mexico.

Tumblemustard is a serious weed pest in grain and hay fields as well as in pastures in many localities. It also occurs along railroad right-of-ways and highways, in waste ground, and, to a greater or less extent, on the range in most of the western States. It is especially common in eastern Montana and parts of eastern Colorado, Utah, Nevada, and the Northwest, generally occurring at elevations below the ponderosa-pine belt. Russian-thistle (*Salsola pestifer*) is one of the characteristic associates of tumblemustard in the West.

Tumblemustard, in the main, has a low palatability, although it is grazed by cattle and sheep when the growth is young and tender and during that growth stage probably is of fair palatability, preferred to Russian-thistle.

The only commendable quality of this plant is its ability to revegetate denuded areas quickly and thus provide a measure of soil protection. The plants often produce an enormous amount of seed; it has been estimated that a single large plant will bear 1,500,000 seeds.[2] The seeds, as is true of many of the tumbleweeds, are not easily shed from the tough pods; consequently, one of these plants may be blown about for a whole winter, dropping a few seeds at intervals for many miles. When abundant, the species is a serious nuisance in grain fields, since, in addition to reducing the amount of grain produced, the tumblemustard seed when present in quantity gives such an objectionable flavor to ground grain that livestock, other than sheep, refuse to eat it. A number of experiments have been made looking toward the control of this weed in agricultural lands.[2][3][4] If conservative grazing is practiced on the range, tumblemustard may eventually be supplanted by native perennial species.

Tumblemustard is easily recognized by its erect, much-branched stems; large, deeply divided lower leaves with the upper leaves much reduced; and by the rather small, yellowish white flowers with four separate petals, four narrow spreading sepals, and six stamens, two of which are shorter than the others. The stiff, narrow, many-seeded fruits, or pods are from 2 to 4 inches long. The flowers, which are produced in abundance, are borne in numerous racemes; they mature quickly and only a comparatively small number are in bloom simultaneously. The plants bloom over a long period, and the large, lower leaves commonly dry up and fall without, apparently, retarding flower and seed production.

Norta, a member of the mustard family (Cruciferae), is a small, Old World genus of about 10 species of biennials. In addition to tumblemustard, one other species, *N. irio*, has been naturalized in the United States.

[1] Dewey, L. H. TUMBLING MUSTARD (SISYMBRIUM ALTISSIMUM). U. S. Dept. Agr., Div. Bot. Circ. 7, 8 pp., illus. 1896.
[2] Clark, G. H., and Fletcher, J. FARM WEEDS OF CANADA. Ed. 2, rev. and enl. by G. H. Clark. 192 pp., illus. Ottawa. 1923.
[3] Runnels, H. A., and Schaffner, J. H. MANUAL OF OHIO WEEDS. Ohio Agr. Expt. Sta. Bull. 475, 166 pp., illus. 1931.
[4] Thornton, B. J., and Durrell, L. W. COLORADO WEEDS. Colo. Agr. Expt. Sta. Bull. 403, 115 pp., illus. 1933.

YELLOW OWLCLOVER

Orthocar'pus lu'teus

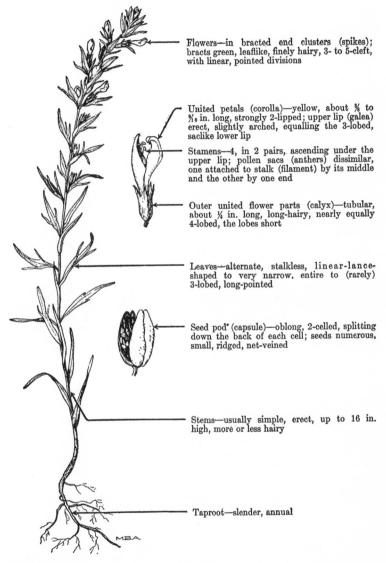

Flowers—in bracted end clusters (spikes); bracts green, leaflike, finely hairy, 3- to 5-cleft, with linear, pointed divisions

United petals (corolla)—yellow, about ⅜ to ⁵⁄₁₆ in. long, strongly 2-lipped; upper lip (galea) erect, slightly arched, equalling the 3-lobed, saclike lower lip

Stamens—4, in 2 pairs, ascending under the upper lip; pollen sacs (anthers) dissimilar, one attached to stalk (filament) by its middle and the other by one end

Outer united flower parts (calyx)—tubular, about ¼ in. long, long-hairy, nearly equally 4-lobed, the lobes short

Leaves—alternate, stalkless, linear-lance-shaped to very narrow. entire to (rarely) 3-lobed, long-pointed

Seed pod* (capsule)—oblong, 2-celled, splitting down the back of each cell; seeds numerous, small, ridged, net-veined

Stems—usually simple, erect, up to 16 in. high, more or less hairy

Taproot—slender, annual

Yellow owlclover, sometimes called yellow orthocarp, is a relatively small annual herb ranging from British Columbia to Saskatchewan, Nebraska, New Mexico, and California. It grows in a wide variety of soils, both dry and moist, from the sagebrush belt upwards to the spruce-fir belt. The species is probably most common on grasslands or in grass-weed types but also grows in brush and timber types. It occurs most abundantly in meadows and parks where the original vegetation has been reduced; consequently yellow owl-clover frequently is abundant on areas where the cover of more palatable plants has been somewhat depleted by overgrazing. The specific name, *luteus*, being Latin for yellow, refers to the color of the flowers.

The species deserves notice because of its commonness and wide distribution, and because it is a representative member of a rather large genus of range species of somewhat unusual appearance. The plants are usually small, produce but little herbage and, in the main, are low in palatability. Accordingly, yellow owlclover is of minor consequence as a forage species. It is practically worthless for cattle and only poor to fair sheep forage.

OWLCLOVERS

Orthocar'pus spp.

Owlclovers, also known as orthocarps, compose a chiefly western North American genus of annual and a few perennial weeds. The genus, including some 30 species in western North America and one in South America, is a member of the figwort family (Scrophulariaceae), being closely related to the paintbrushes and painted-cups (*Castilleja* spp.). The origin and significance of the common name are obscure. The generic name is derived from the Greek words *orthos*, upright, and *karpos*, fruit, and refers to the erect seed pods. There is considerable difference in size, shape, and margins of the leaves between various species of owlclover; their flower colors range from white to yellow, pink, red, and purple; the plants also vary in shape, size, and color of the flower cluster bracts, which are entire, lobed, or divided. In some species they are green and leaflike but in others are more or less petal-like, with about the same range in color as the united petals (corollas). The flowers are borne in terminal spikes; the corolla is strongly two-lipped, with the upper lip erect or arched, and the lower one more or less spreading and usually three-lobed. The four stamens are arranged in two pairs, ascending under the upper lip.

The owlclovers are widely distributed and occur in practically all parts of the West, some species frequently being abundant locally. This is especially true in the California foothills where certain species grow in nearly pure, dense stands, adding brilliancy and characteristic color to the landscape when in flower. The majority of the species occur in California, where the annual species partially resemble winter annuals; the growth starts in February and continues until June, when the plants dry up and disappear. In other parts of the West, however, they often occur as summer annuals in the higher mountains and bloom until the middle of September, or later.

Owlclovers are low in palatability, generally ranking as practically worth-less to poor cattle forage, although fair for sheep; they derive most of their range importance from the fact that they are so widely distributed and frequently abundant.

Throughout the West as a whole, yellow owlclover is the most common and widespread species. Purple-white owlclover (*O. purpureo-al'bus*), with rather open spikes of white flowers which turn rose-purple, is a common plant of the Rocky Mountains. *O. erian'thus*, often called Johnny-tuck, or (less happily) butter-and-eggs, a relatively low species, 4 to 10 inches high, with sulphur-yellow corollas tipped with purple, is often very abundant in the foothills of California, frequently coloring wide stretches during April and May with gold-tinted streamlike bands. Purple owlclover (*O. purpuras'cens*), often called escobita, is another common West Coast species, which occurs in California and Oregon. It averages about 1 foot in height; the leaves are divided into numerous threadlike, often brown-tinged divisions; the bracts of the flower cluster are dilated at the base, and divided into narrow lobes, those of the bracts accompanying the upper flowers having crimson or purple, widended tips; the crimson or purplish corollas are from three-fourths to 1¼ inches long, the lower lip being white-tipped and spotted with yellow or purple dots or markings. This ornamental species is thus far the only member of its genus well established in the horticultural trade.

SWEET-ANISE

Osmorhi′za occidenta′lis, syns. *Glyco′sma occidenta′lis, Washingto′nia occidenta′lis*

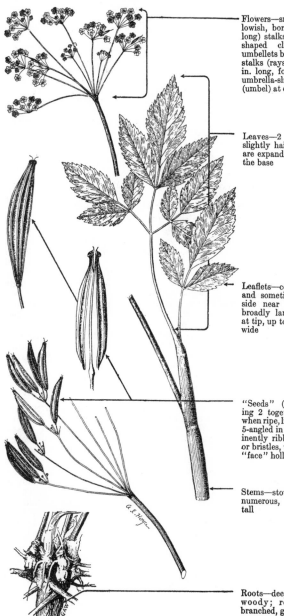

Flowers—small, white or yellowish, borne on short (¼ in. long) stalks in small umbrella-shaped clusters (umbellets); umbellets borne on 5 to 12 erect stalks (rays) which are up to 5 in. long, forming a compound umbrella-shaped inflorescence (umbel) at end of stem

Leaves—2 or 3 times divided, slightly hairy, on stalks which are expanded and sheathing at the base

Leaflets—coarsely saw-toothed and sometimes cut-in on one side near base, narrowly to broadly lance-shaped, pointed at tip, up to 4 in. long and 1 in. wide

"Seeds" (mericarps)— growing 2 together but separating when ripe, linear or club-shaped, 5-angled in cross-section, prominently ribbed, free from hairs or bristles, up to ⅝ in. long, the "face" hollowed-out

Stems—stout, hollow, erect, numerous, leafy, up to 4 ft. tall

Roots—deep-set, thickened and woody; root crown often branched, giving rise to numerous stems

465

Sweet-anise, also known as western aniseroot or sweet cicely, is a stout, erect, and smooth perennial herb of the parsnip or umbellifer family (Pastinaceae, or Umbelliferae). It is by far the most important range plant of the sweetroot (*Osmorhiza*) genus. The appearance and flavor of the seeds are strikingly suggestive of the related anise (*Pimpinella anisum*).

Sweet-anise occurs from Alberta to Colorado, California, and British Columbia. It apparently does not occur in the Southwest but is fairly common elsewhere in the range country. It grows in the mountains from altitudes of approximately 2,000 feet in Washington up to about 9,000 or 10,000 feet in Utah and Colorado, preferring rich, well-drained soils in aspen stands, openings in ponderosa pine and Douglas fir forests, or open or brushy slopes and ridges. This plant is usually associated with grasses and various perennial, broadleaved herbs. It rarely occurs in pure stands but is often an important part of the plant cover, being the key species on many ranges, particularly in the Intermountain region and the central and northern Rocky Mountains.

Sweet-anise is one of the choice range weeds. Its palatability is usually high for all classes of livestock. All of the plant occurring above the ground, except the coarser stems, is often eaten by sheep even when an abundance of other good forage is available. Cattle, horses, deer, and elk also eat the leafage with considerable relish. The plant remains green and palatable throughout the summer grazing season, except on the more dry and exposed sites, but becomes dry and worthless after the first heavy frost in the fall. Reproduction is entirely from seed although the species does not have strong seed habits. Only a relatively few seeds are borne in each flower cluster, but their viability is rather high. Deepset, thickened woody roots, with stored-up food reserves, enable this plant to withstand trampling well and, if given an opportunity to mature seed, it will ordinarily maintain itself or even increase on the range.

SWEETROOTS (Osmorhi′za spp., syns. *Glyco′sma spp., Washingto′nia spp.*)

The English name most commonly used for plants of this genus is probably sweet cicely, although that name is better restricted to the Old World umbellifer genus, *Myrrhis*. Sweetroot is suggested as appropriate and more distinctive for the genus *Osmorhiza*, whose name means fragrant root. Several of the smoothseeded species are segregated by some botanists into a separate genus, *Glycosma*, but the division is not recognized by Coulter and Rose.

On a conservative basis about eleven species of *Osmorhiza*, which is an exclusively North American genus, are known in the western range country. As a group they are widely distributed, at least one species occurring in each of the eleven far Western States. They occur in the mountains, in open woodlands, moist meadows, and in rich, coniferous woods. Some species grow to quite an extent in canyon bottoms; others on well-drained, sandy loam soils in aspen and brush stands.

Although all of the sweetroots are at least fairly palatable to livestock yet, because of their restricted occurrence and abundance, most of them do not generally constitute an important element of the range forage crop. Usually sheep and goats graze them closely while cattle eat most of the species more readily than they do the majority of other weeds. The plants ordinarily remain green and palatable throughout the summer grazing season. They depend wholly on seed for reproduction.

Some botanists adopt the generic name *Washingtonia* for these plants and that name has technical (line) priority under the American Code. There is a growing tendency, however, to use *Washingtonia* for the California palm genus and accept *Osmorhiza* for the sweetroots.

After the sweetroots have set seed, they are easily distinguished from the other range plants of the umbellifer family. The seeds are distinctively long, narrow-ribbed, somewhat club-shaped (clavate), and are often bristly and tipped with a short beak. These herbs have a characteristic, aromatic, licoricelike or aniselike odor and taste, especially in the deepset, thickened, often clustered roots. The small flowers are five-parted, but the teeth of the outer flower parts (calyx) are indistinct. They are usually whitish or yellowish, though occasionally purple in some species, and are borne at the ends of the stems in loosely and openly grouped, umbrella-shaped clusters.

CRAZYWEEDS AND POINTVETCHES

Oxy'tropis spp., syn. *Ara'gallus spp.*

The crazyweeds and pointvetches form a large genus of legumes (pea family, Leguminosae), containing more than 200 species, the majority occurring in the Old World, with Asia the center of distribution. In the United States species of *Oxytropis* are perennial herbs; some of the foreign members are shrubs or undershrubs. On a conservative nomenclatural basis about 35 species are found in the 11 far-western range States. The genus is best represented in the Rocky Mountain States, particularly Montana, Wyoming, and Colorado. The three Pacific States have only about two species each.

The scientific name *Oxytropis* is Latinized from the Greek words *oxus*, sharp, and *tropis*, keel, referring to the sharp beak at the tip of the lowest two united petals (keel) of the flower; this genus is separated from the closely related *Astragalus* genus chiefly on the basis of this character. Any attempt to select a suitable English name for *Oxytropis* is complicated by the fact that it contains both harmless and loco-producing species and by the fact that several species of *Astragalus* are also known to produce locoism. *Oxytropis* species are often called stemless loco, because of the usual absence of leafy stems. The book name, oxytrope, is occasionally applied to them. In the interest of common name standardization, it seems desirable to restrict loco to those species of *Astragalus* which produce locoism. Crazyweed, a name already applied to the best-known species (*O. lambertii*), is also suggested as an appropriate subgeneric name for the loco-producing species of *Oxytropis*. Pointvetch, referring to the characteristic vetchlike aspect and the pointed keel of the flowers, a name suggested by Dr. Frederick V. Coville, has been adopted here for those species of *Oxytropis* not known to be poisonous.

In North America crazyweeds and pointvetches extend from sea level in Alaska to elevations of about 11,000 feet in Colorado and 12,000 feet in California. These plants flourish in sandy soils of grassy plains, and in well-drained, sandy, or gravelly soils of open foothill and montane slopes and ridges. Their deep, woody taproots and frequent dense woolly hairiness enable at least many of these cold-resistive species to grow in rather dry sites, to withstand extended drought, and the bleak environment of wind-swept mountain peaks. It is noteworthy that 11 species are known to occur in Alaska.

In general, the palatability of crazyweeds and pointvetches is poor for cattle and horses and fair for sheep, although sometimes, especially in scarcity of desirable forage, the plants are eaten freely. Although the genus contains harmless species and is widely distributed and plentiful on many western ranges, its relatively low palatability is not disadvantageous considering the livestock losses caused by crazyweeds. From the range standpoint the crazyweeds are more important than the pointvetches.

Extensive grazing of crazyweeds, like similar use of locos, induces a chronic poisoning called locoism. Such plants are habit-formers, their poisonous effects being cumulative, fatalities ensuing only after prolonged use. Addicted animals should be shifted immediately to ranges where the plants are not available, as otherwise the habit will eventuate in their ruination and death. Furthermore, a loco eater is liable to teach other animals the habit.

Among the earliest symptoms of locoism comes loss of weight, followed by gait irregularities, general depression, and such extreme weakness that it is sometimes mistaken for paralysis. Lack of muscular coordination and defects of vision develop, due to the reactions of the plant poison on the central nervous system. Emaciation and weakness increase as the disease progresses, with death often resulting from starvation.

Among domesticated animals probably horses are most seriously affected. In the early stages of loco poisoning, identification of a locoed horse is difficult, as the animal may appear normal except for occasional crazy spells. Locoed horses are usually hard to handle; they cannot be led or backed and can be stopped or turned only with difficulty; occasionally they leap over small pebbles in the road or try to step across a sizable stream. An abnormal growth of mane and tail is another characteristic of loco poisoning.

Cattle display similar symptoms to horses, except that they shake their heads more or less violently, particularly after exertion. At times cattle also tremble markedly, and their eyes become staring.

Locoed sheep do not exhibit such conspicuous symptoms as cattle and horses; their lack of muscular control is not so noticeable, although they display more weakness, stumble, fall easily, and may die from starvation.

According to Marsh[1] the best treatment is to remove locoed animals from the range to good pasture, preferably alfalfa, as all afflicted livestock tend to be constipated, and alfalfa relieves that condition. Where constipation is marked, drenching with Epsom salts is recommended. Once an animal is locoed, subsequently it is unsafe to give the "critter" freedom of the open range, as it will usually become locoed a second time. In the case of valuable horses daily doses of from 4 to 6 teaspoonfuls of Fowler's solution in the drinking water may be administered with benefit. Marsh[1][2] recommends hypodermic doses of about one-fifth of a grain of strychnin for stricken cattle.

No practical method of eradicating crazyweeds from large areas has been devised. Grubbing may prove effective in small, heavily infested patches if the roots are cut 2 or 3 inches below the bud crowns—a practice which prevents subsequent sprouting from those parts. Conservative grazing, which facilitates the reestablishment of perennial grasses and other desirable forage species, is probably the only economic method of reclaiming large areas of range. Seeding to other species may hasten reclamation.

At least three species of *Oxytropis* cause livestock losses from locoism. Among these crazyweed (*O. lamber'tii*) is discussed separately in this handbook. Spike crazyweed (*O. macou'nii*, syns. *O. spica'ta* (Hook.) Standl., *not* (Pall.) O. & B. Fedtsch.; *Ara'gallus spica'tus*), a white-flowered form closely related to *O. lambertii*, growing from Montana to Colorado, is very common in Montana on northern slopes of foothills and mountains at elevations up to about 8,000 feet, and responsible for heavy losses in that State.[3] Rocky Mountain crazyweed (*O. saximonta'na*, syn. *O. albiflo'ra* (A. Nels.) K. Schum., *not* Bunge; *Ara'gallus albiflo'rus*), another white-flowered form closely related to *O. lambertii*, and perhaps only a variety of spike crazyweed, ranges from Montana to Utah and Colorado, mostly at elevations between 4,000 and 10,000 feet, and is frequently abundant and responsible for losses in that area.[4]

Three other species are strongly suspected by stockmen of causing locoism and, tentatively at least, are included in this handbook among the crazyweeds. Whorled crazyweed (*O. richardso'nii*, syn. *O. splen'dens richardso'nii*), which ranges from Yukon to Utah and northern New Mexico, is peculiar in that its leaflets are whorled, or bunched in circles of three or four (or occasionally more). Economically it is a question mark, together with its near relative, showy crazyweed (*O. splen'dens*), sometimes called silvery loco, which ranges from Minnesota to Alaska and Montana.[3] Haresfoot crazyweed (*O. lago'pus*), a silky-hairy, dwarf form in the mountains of Idaho, Montana, and Wyoming, is another species which stockmen consider hazardous.

Bessey pointvetch (*O. bes'seyi*), typical of dry sites in Montana and Wyoming, is rather common in the Yellowstone Valley. It was formerly considered poisonous, but Marsh[2] asserts that it is harmless.

The crazyweeds and pointvetches are similar in general aspect and resemble many of the species of *Astragalus*. When in flower they can easily be distinguished from the latter by both the beak at the tip of the keel and the equal teeth of the outer united flower parts (calyx). Crazyweeds and pointvetches, as a rule, lack leafy stems; their pealike, usually white, yellowish, bluish, or purple flowers are borne in clusters (spikes or racemes) at the ends of leafless flowering stalks. The leaves are basal, usually from the crown of a deep, woody taproot, and are divided (pinnately compound) into paired leaflets arranged along the midrib. Hairiness in varying degree, color, and texture (such as silky or woolly), is characteristic of the leaves, flowering stalks, bracts, calyxes, and pods of all the range species.

The entire genus greatly needs thorough scientific investigation.

---

[1] Marsh, C. D. THE LOCO-WEED DISEASE. U. S. Dept. Agr. Farmers' Bull. 1054, 19 pp., illus. 1919.
[2] Marsh, C. D. STOCK-POISONING PLANTS OF THE RANGE. U. S. Dept. Agr. Bull. 1245, rev., 75 pp., illus. 1929. Supersedes Bull. 575.
[3] Chesnut. V. K., and Wilcox, E. V. THE STOCK-POISONING PLANTS OF MONTANA: A PRELIMINARY REPORT. U. S. Dept. Agr., Div. Bot. Bull. 26, 150 pp., illus. 1901.
[4] Beath, O. A., Draize, J. H., and Gilbert, C. S. PLANTS POISONOUS TO LIVESTOCK. Wyo. Agr. Expt. Sta. Bull. 200, 84 pp., illus. 1934.

CRAZYWEED

Oxy'tropis lamber'tii, syn. *Aro'gallus lamber'tii*

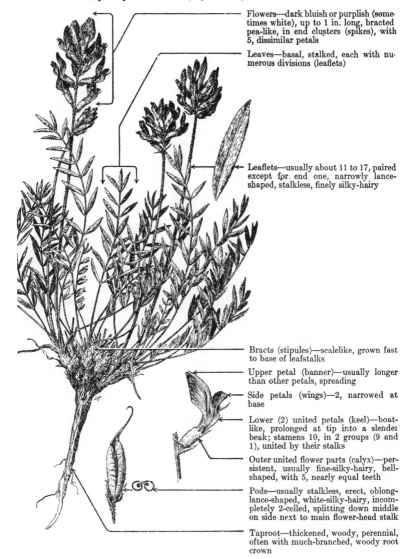

Flowers—dark bluish or purplish (some-times white), up to 1 in. long, bracted pea-like, in end clusters (spikes), with 5, dissimilar petals

Leaves—basal, stalked, each with nu-merous divisions (leaflets)

Leaflets—usually about 11 to 17, paired except for end one, narrowly lance-shaped, stalkless, finely silky-hairy

Bracts (stipules)—scalelike, grown fast to base of leafstalks

Upper petal (banner)—usually longer than other petals, spreading

Side petals (wings)—2, narrowed at base

Lower (2) united petals (keel)—boat-like, prolonged at tip into a slender beak; stamens 10, in 2 groups (9 and 1), united by their stalks

Outer united flower parts (calyx)—per-sistent, usually fine-silky-hairy, bell-shaped, with 5, nearly equal teeth

Pods—usually stalkless, erect, oblong-lance-shaped, white-silky-hairy, incom-pletely 2-celled, splitting down middle on side next to main flower-head stalk

Taproot—thickened, woody, perennial, often with much-branched, woody root crown

Large losses have been attributed (apparently erroneously) to crazyweed under the misnomer, white loco. In this discussion, however, crazyweed is limited to the typically purple-flowered *O. lambertii*, as originally described by Pursh,[1] and does not include the white-flowered species, *O. macounii* (syn. *O. spicata* (Hook.) Standl., *not* (Pall.) O. and B. Fedtsch.) nor the closely

---

[1] See footnote on following page.

469

related *O. saximontana* (syn. *O. albiflora* (A. Nels.) K. Schum., *not* Bunge), for which the term white loco is more appropriate, and which are discussed under W138. More field and laboratory study of these plants is needed, but it seems probable that, even though albino forms of *O. lambertii* occur, they are relatively rare. Furthermore, it seems likely that the typically white-flowered *O. macounii* (of which *O. saximontana* may perhaps prove to be a variety or form) is, to a considerable extent, the *O. lambertii* of range literature, and that it differs from *O. lambertii* not only in color of flowers, but also in characters of calyx, pod, and density of inflorescence.

Crazyweed is also called stemless loco and, less frequently, rattleweed. However, it seems preferable to restrict loco to the genus *Astragalus*. In one of the oldest State lists of poisonous plants published in this country,[2] *Oxytropis lambertii* is called crazyweed, and that name is adopted here. Pursh[1] named this species *lambertii* after the wealthy English botanist, Aylmer Bourke Lambert. He credits (John) Bradbury with having first collected the species along the Missouri River. Aven Nelson,[3] after a study of Bradbury's travels, estimates the type locality as "not far from Yankton", S. Dak.

Owing to the confusion in the manuals and in poisonous-plant literature about union of the typically white-flowered forms with the typically purple-flowered *O. lambertii*, the range of crazyweed cannot be given with precision. It is, without doubt, one of the most common and widely distributed American species of *Oxytropis*, yet probably too wide a range has been ascribed to it. On a conservative basis, the species may be considered to occur from Minnesota to Montana, and southward to Texas and Arizona. It has a wide altitudinal distribution, growing on plains and hillsides up to the aspen and Engelmann spruce-lodgepole pine belts of the high mountains, attaining an elevation of about 10,000 feet in Colorado and the Southwest. It is usually more abundant and characteristic of the higher elevations than the white-flowered species mentioned. Crazyweed seldom appears in pure stands; however, it frequently forms numerous patches over extensive local areas, and often increases rapidly on overgrazed ranges. The deep, thickened, woody taproot enables it to withstand both trampling and drought. This poisonous weed prefers open, well-drained, sandy, or gravelly soils.

Normally, crazyweed is unpalatable to livestock; cattle, horses, and sheep, however, eat it freely when palatable forage is scarce or absent.

Admittedly, crazyweed causes losses of livestock from locoism, but further study is needed to determine the exact extent of the damage since, in most of the loco-poisoning literature, the white-flowered forms are the ones emphasized. Chesnut and Wilcox[4] attribute the majority of the loco losses of livestock in Montana to "white loco weed" (*O. macounii*, syn. *Aragallus spicata*) and, although four other species of the genus are named as causing locoism in that State, they do not include *O. lambertii*. Beath and co-workers[5] affirm that "White loco (*Oxytropis saximontana*) is the plant commonly known in Wyoming as the loco." It is significant that Marsh[6][7] consistently prefers the common name of white loco for *O. lambertii*. Loco symptoms are similar, regardless of the responsible species.

Attempts to isolate and to determine the chemical identity of the poisonous principle in crazyweed have thus far failed.[8]

[1] Pursh, F. FLORAE AMERICAE SEPTENTRIONALIS . . . 2 v., illus. London. 1814.
[2] Bessey, C. E. A PRELIMINARY ACCOUNT OF THE PLANTS OF NEBRASKA WHICH ARE REPUTED TO BE POISONOUS, OR SUSPECTED OF BEING SO. Nebr. State Bd. Agr. Ann. Rept. (1901) 16 : 95–129, illus. 1902.
[3] Nelson, A. TAXONOMIC STUDIES. I. THE LOCO PLANTS. Wyo. Univ. Pubs., Bot. 1 : [109]–121. 1926.
[4] Chesnut, V. K., and Wilcox, E. V. THE STOCK-POISONING PLANTS OF MONTANA : A PRELIMINARY REPORT. U. S. Dept. Agr., Div. Bot. Bull. 26, 150 pp., illus. 1901.
[5] Beath, O. A., Draize, J. H., and Gilbert, C. S. PLANTS POISONOUS TO LIVESTOCK. Wyo. Agr. Expt. Sta. Bull. 200, 84 pp., illus. 1934.
[6] Marsh, C. D. THE LOCO-WEED DISEASE. U. S. Dept. Agr. Farmers' Bull. 1054, 19 pp., illus. 1919.
[7] Marsh, C. D. STOCK-POISONING PLANTS OF THE RANGE. U. S. Dept. Agr. Bull. 1245, rev., 75 pp., illus. 1929. Supersedes Bull. 575.
[8] Couch, J. F. A CONTRIBUTION TO THE STUDY OF LOCOISM. Jour. Pharmacol. and Expt. Ther. 36 (1) : 55–83, illus. 1929.

BROWNS PEONY

Paeo'nia brow'nii

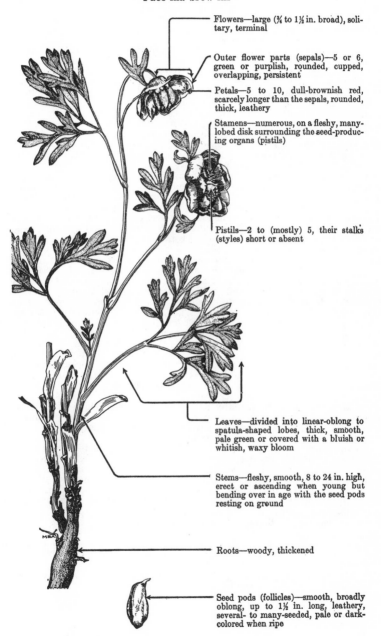

Flowers—large (¾ to 1½ in. broad), solitary, terminal

Outer flower parts (sepals)—5 or 6, green or purplish, rounded, cupped, overlapping, persistent

Petals—5 to 10, dull-brownish red, scarcely longer than the sepals, rounded, thick, leathery

Stamens—numerous, on a fleshy, many-lobed disk surrounding the seed-producing organs (pistils)

Pistils—2 to (mostly) 5, their stalks (styles) short or absent

Leaves—divided into linear-oblong to spatula-shaped lobes, thick, smooth, pale green or covered with a bluish or whitish, waxy bloom

Stems—fleshy, smooth, 8 to 24 in. high, erect or ascending when young but bending over in age with the seed pods resting on ground

Roots—woody, thickened

Seed pods (follicles)—smooth, broadly oblong, up to 1½ in. long, leathery, several- to many-seeded, pale or dark-colored when ripe

Browns peony, also called wild peony and skookumroot, is a robust, somewhat succulent, perennial herb of the buttercup family (Ranunculaceae). It is the only species of *Paeonia* native to North America; the well-known cultivated peonies of this same genus are of Asiatic and European origin. This species was discovered in 1826 by David Douglas, a celebrated Scotch botanist and explorer, near the confines of perpetual snow in the Blue Mountains of Oregon. Douglas presumably named the plant in honor of Robert Brown (1773–1858), an eminent British botanist. The generic name perpetuates that of Apollo in his medical role of *Paeon*.[1]

Browns peony is distributed from British Columbia to Alberta and south to Utah and California. In Oregon and Washington it occurs principally on the east side of the Cascade Mountains, but it extends down the California coast to the southern part of the State, as well as inland in the mountains to the southern Sierras. Although rather common in the Pacific States and in parts of Idaho and Nevada, this species is extremely rare in Utah. This plant grows through a wide range of habitat conditions, varying from the dry hot plains to the cool, moist slopes near the areas of perpetual snow. It ranges from a few hundred feet above sea level to elevations of over 8,000 feet. Browns peony is most typically found on well-drained sites, usually in mixed grass and weed types, but it sometimes appears in sagebrush areas, brushy hillsides, or under open stands of aspen or coniferous timber.

Browns peony generally grows in scattered clumps and seldom, if ever, occurs in pure stands. Unfortunately it ordinarily comprises but a small part of the plant cover. This species starts growth early in the season, customarily being among the first of the flowering plants to appear in the spring. In southern California, it often blooms in January, or even earlier, and is known locally as Christmas-rose. The succulent leafage usually matures early, becoming dry, brittle, and worthless for forage before the close of the summer grazing season. Consequently, this plant is of most value for forage where it occurs on ranges grazed in the spring and early summer. The succulent herbage is usually eaten with great relish by sheep[2] but cattle graze it only lightly.

This plant varies somewhat in palatability, however, as on some ranges it is rated as only fair for sheep and worthless for cattle, and some observers even report that it is never grazed at all in their localities. Browns peony is apparently unable to withstand close cropping for many consecutive seasons.

In preliminary range reseeding trials on the Wasatch Plateau in central Utah,[3] Browns peony became established from the original seeding but failed to reproduce. This plant has been reported locally from northern California as being under suspicion of poisoning sheep, and the leaves are sometimes reputed locally to be poisonous to the touch. However, there is no scientific evidence, whatever, to support these suppositions; in fact, the extensive grazing use of this plant over wide areas seems amply to demonstrate that it is not only harmless, but is actually a good sheep forage. The thick roots of Browns peony have been used medicinally by the Spanish-Californians as a dyspepsia remedy. They have also been used by the Indians in doctoring colds, sore throat, and to give their horses long wind. In certain sections of the West the old settlers prized it as a cure for rheumatism.

The flowers of this herb are large, thick, and leathery in texture, but rather inconspicuous because the dull brownish red petals soon fall off. Moreover, the petals extend but slightly beyond the sepals, which are usually of the same greenish hue as the foliage. The flowers are often fragrant, but the leaves and stems have a peculiar odor. The stems are erect when young but droop as they mature until the seed pods finally rest upon the ground. Ants and possibly other insects manifest a peculiar liking for the tissues of this plant and sometimes destroy the flowers and honeycomb the leaves.

[1] Skinner, C. M. MYTHS AND LEGENDS OF FLOWERS, TREES, FRUITS, AND PLANTS IN ALL AGES AND IN ALL CLIMES. [302] pp., illus. Philadelphia and London. [1925.]
[2] Sampson, A. W. NATIVE AMERICAN FORAGE PLANTS. 435 pp., illus. New York. 1924.
[3] Forsling, C. L., and Dayton, W. A. ARTIFICIAL RESEEDING ON WESTERN MOUNTAIN RANGE LANDS. U. S. Dept. Agr. Circ. 178, 48 pp., illus. 1931.

FERNLEAFS

Pedicula'ris spp.

Flowers—yellowish, irregular, numerous, in bracted end clusters (spikes) 3. to 12 in. or more long; bracts egg-shaped, usually a little shorter than flowers

United petals (corolla)—about ¾ in. long, strongly 2-lipped; upper lip (galea) hooded, with tip slightly produced but not beaked, about twice as long as the 3-lobed lower lip; lobes with round-toothed margins

Outer united flower parts (calyx)—about ⅜ in. long, soft-hairy, 5-lobed; lobes narrowly lanced-shaped

Leaves—alternate, up to 12 in. long, somewhat fernlike, divided (pinnately compound) into leaflets; basal leaves much larger than stem leaves

Leaflets—lance-shaped, with sharply double-toothed margins

Stems—often tufted, stout, up to 40 in. high, hairless

Roots—often with thickened root crown, perennial

Pedicularis bracteosa

Fernleafs compose a genus of 250 or more annual or perennial weeds, mostly natives of the Northern Hemisphere and best represented in the Old World. Although several species of *Pedicularis*, such as elephanthead (*P. groenlan'dica*), Indian-warrior (*P. densiflo'ra*), and sickletop (*P. racemo'sa*), have fairly well-standardized common names, there is a difference of opinion as to the most suitable common name for the genus, although lousewort is frequently used.

The American Joint Committee on Horticultural Nomenclature[1] has approved woodbetony as the English generic name for the cultivated species of *Pedicularis;* however, in the West, woodbetony is very rarely, if ever, used as a name for the native species. We are advised that fernleaf, the English generic name adopted here, will replace woodbetony in the second edition of Standardized Plant Names, now in preparation.

Of the approximately 30 species of fernleaf (all perennial) occurring in the Western States, the majority grown in the mountains from the ponderosa-pine belt to above timber line. They are found in a wide variety of sites, most species being partial to moist soils, although a few occur in relatively dry situations. As a rule, fernleafs are not abundant on the range. These plants vary in palatability from practically worthless to, at best, fair forage for livestock, being more palatable to sheep than to cattle.

The genus belongs to the figwort family (Scrophulariaceae) and is distinguished by the spurless, strongly two-lipped corolla; the upper lip hooded or arched (galeate), sometimes beaked or toothed at the tip; the lower lip erect or ascending, three-lobed with its lobes commonly spreading, the lateral ones being rounded and larger. The calyx is cleft on the lower side and two- to five-lobed. The four stamens, with pollen sacs all alike, are in two pairs, ascending under the upper lip of the corolla. The leaves are alternate, opposite, or whorled (in the western species prevailingly alternate), often tufted at the base of the plant and toothed, lobed, or divided. The flowers are borne in terminal, usually leafy-bracted spikes or racemes.

Elephanthead, which is accorded a separate treatment in this handbook, is well known because of its distinctive reddish-purple, long-beaked flowers.

Meadow fernleaf (*P. crenula'ta*), a species with tufted stems from 4 to 16 inches high, occurs in mountain meadows from Wyoming and Colorado westward to Nevada. The leaves of this species are narrowly oblong to linear, with whitish margins, which are doubly round-toothed. The whitish or purplish flowers are borne in dense, terminal spikes, with the upper lip of the corolla curved, but not beaked. This species is practically worthless as forage and occurs but sparsely on the range. However, it is becoming a pest in some irrigated meadows.

Northern fernleaf (*P. bracteo'sa*), the species pictured at the beginning of this article, is common, widespread, and fairly characteristic of the larger, more palatable species of *Pedicularis*. The specific name of this robust perennial weed refers to the prominent, leaflike bracts of the long clusters of yellowish flowers. This species occurs mainly in moist sites of the ponderosa pine, aspen, and spruce belts; it is not a very common plant and is never abundant. It grows in parks and meadows, along streambanks among willows and other shrubs in both aspen and rather dense coniferous timber, ranging from British Columbia and Alberta to Colorado and California. The palatability of northern fernleaf is poor for cattle and fair for sheep, but is relatively high for this particular genus. Its comparatively low palatability and usually infrequent occurrence locally relegate the species to a position of minor forage importance.

Sickletop (*P. racemo'sa*), one of the most widespread of the western species, occurs chiefly on open mountain sides, and sparsely in lodgepole and spruce timber, from Alberta and British Columbia to California and New Mexico. The flowers of this species are white or pink and borne in a loose, leafy-bracted spike. The upper lip of the corolla is strongly incurving and prolonged into a tapering hooked beak which nearly touches the lower lip. The hairless leaves, not lobed or divided, are minutely and doubly round-toothed (crenate). Many stems, 8 to 20 inches high, with very slender branches, are produced from a woody root crown. Although sometimes cropped by sheep, this species is practically worthless as a forage plant.

Species of fernleaf, especially those with divided leaves, are used horticulturally but are not widely known.[2] Some of the species best known in horticulture are two of the western species, sickletop and Grays fernleaf (*P. gray'i*), the eastern species early fernleaf (*P. canaden'sis*) and swamp fernleaf (*P. lanceola'ta*), and the European fernleaf (*P. palus'tris*).

---

[1] American Joint Committee on Horticultural Nomenclature. STANDARDIZED PLANT NAMES . . . Prepared by F. L. Olmsted, F. V. Coville, and H. P. Kelsey. 546 pp. Salem, Mass., 1923.
[2] Bailey, L. H. THE STANDARD CYCLOPEDIA OF HORTICULTURE . . . New ed., 3 v., illus. New York and London. 1933.

ELEPHANTHEAD

Pedicula'ris groenlan'dica, syns. *Elephantel'la groenlan'dica, P. surrec'ta*

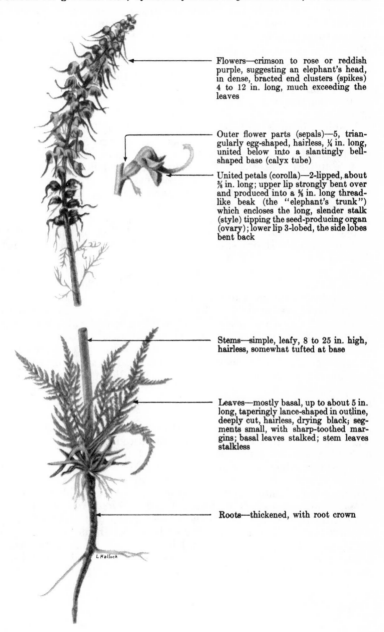

Flowers—crimson to rose or reddish
purple, suggesting an elephant's head,
in dense, bracted end clusters (spikes)
4 to 12 in. long, much exceeding the
leaves

Outer flower parts (sepals)—5, triangularly egg-shaped, hairless, ¼ in. long,
united below into a slantingly bell-
shaped base (calyx tube)

United petals (corolla)—2-lipped, about
⅜ in. long; upper lip strongly bent over
and produced into a ⅝ in. long threadlike beak (the "elephant's trunk")
which encloses the long, slender stalk
(style) tipping the seed-producing organ
(ovary); lower lip 3-lobed, the side lobes
bent back

Stems—simple, leafy, 8 to 25 in. high,
hairless, somewhat tufted at base

Leaves—mostly basal, up to about 5 in.
long, taperingly lance-shaped in outline,
deeply cut, hairless, drying black; segments small, with sharp-toothed margins; basal leaves stalked; stem leaves
stalkless

Roots—thickened, with root crown

L Hallock

Elephanthead, also called elephantflower, elephant-trunk, elephant-weed, Indian-warrior, and little (or little red) elephant, is a smooth, perennial herb with a simple, erect stem, 6 inches to 2 feet tall, and dissected, fernlike leaves which are alternate on the stem and also crowded in a rosette near the base. The specific name *groenlandica* refers to Greenland, where this plant was originally discovered. Most of the common names applied to this plant allude to the resemblance of the reddish or purplish flowers to the head of an elephant, the broad upper lip (galea) of the irregular corolla suggesting the elephant's cranium, its prolonged and strongly curved beak being the trunk, and the lower corolla lip the elephant's lower jaw.

Elephanthead is widely distributed, ranging from Greenland and across the North American continent in the far North from Labrador to Alaska, and south, in the western mountain chains, to California and New Mexico. The showy, terminal flower clusters make it a conspicuous plant in wet meadows and grasslands. In the western United States it is characteristic of the higher mountains, ranging from the ponderosa pine belt to above timber line, but it is also occasionally found at somewhat lower levels, and has been collected at elevations at least as low as 1,500 feet in Idaho and 3,000 feet in Oregon. It prefers moist sites and generally grows in rather rich, clayey, or sandy loam.

The species ordinarily occurs in tufts or bunches and, although it is a common and very well-known plant, it is seldom abundant. On the whole, its forage value is slight. It is grazed, if at all, during the summer. Its utilization by cattle is negligible. It is sometimes cropped by sheep and goats and is rated in some localities as of poor to (at best) fair palatability for those animals.

The curious, very distinctive, long-beaked, brightly colored flowers of this species put in their appearance in late June or early July and flowering continues until about the middle of August. The seeds are produced until about the middle of October. Reproduction is also effected vegetatively by the short creeping underground stems (rhizomes, or rootstocks).

Elephanthead is a member of the figwort family (Scrophulariaceae), a plant family with characteristic irregular or two-lipped flowers, which are often brightly colored and either relatively large and showy or borne in showy clusters. Well-known representatives of the family of common occurrence in the West are the paint-brushes and painted-cups (*Castilleja* spp.) and the pentstemons (*Pentstemon* spp.). The fernleaf genus (*Pedicularis*), to which elephanthead belongs, is distinguished by the distinctly two-lipped, spurless corolla with the margins of its upper lip not recurved; four stamens, in two pairs of unequal length, with their anther sacs all alike; the outer flower parts (calyx) cleft on the lower side; and the ovoid or oblong, oblique, many-seeded fruits (capsules).

RYDBERG PENTSTEMON

Pentste'mon rydber'gii, syn. *P. aggrega'tus*

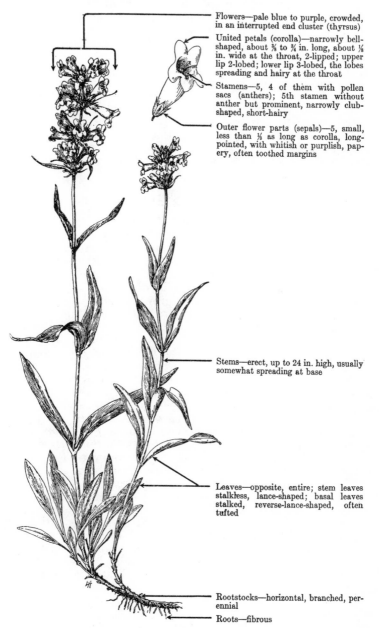

Flowers—pale blue to purple, crowded, in an interrupted end cluster (thyrsus)

United petals (corolla)—narrowly bell-shaped, about ⅜ to ¾ in. long, about ⅛ in. wide at the throat, 2-lipped; upper lip 2-lobed; lower lip 3-lobed, the lobes spreading and hairy at the throat

Stamens—5, 4 of them with pollen sacs (anthers); 5th stamen without anther but prominent, narrowly club-shaped, short-hairy

Outer flower parts (sepals)—5, small, less than ⅓ as long as corolla, long-pointed, with whitish or purplish, papery, often toothed margins

Stems—erect, up to 24 in. high, usually somewhat spreading at base

Leaves—opposite, entire; stem leaves stalkless, lance-shaped; basal leaves stalked, reverse-lance-shaped, often tufted

Rootstocks—horizontal, branched, perennial

Roots—fibrous

Rydberg pentstemon, a perennial with blue or purple flowers and opposite leaves, was named in honor of Dr. P. A. Rydberg (1860–1931), an eminent Swedish-American taxonomic botanist, who contributed greatly to the knowledge of western plants and was the author of many publications on the flora of the West. Rydberg pentstemon occurs in the mountains from Idaho to Montana, Colorado, and Nevada, principally at elevations from 7,000 to 10,000 feet and is common and often locally abundant, chiefly in the grass-weed, sagebrush, and aspen types.

This species is one of the more palatable pentstemons and is fair cattle and sheep forage. It reproduces by means of rootstocks and is able to withstand considerable trampling and, because of these facts and of the relatively light grazing to which it is ordinarily subjected, it often increases on overgrazed ranges. Although not an especially important range plant, this species has been selected for illustration as representative of the large *Pentstemon* genus which, chiefly because of its size, wide distribution, and abundance, constitutes an important group of range weeds.

PENTSTEMONS (Pentste'mon spp.)

Pentstemons, composing a large, chiefly North American genus of about 150 species, are perennial plants with opposite (or occasionally whorled) leaves, and usually showy, often strongly two-lipped flowers. The genus is best represented in the western United States where the bulk of the species occur, constituting one of the common floral elements of the great majority of the vegetative types from sea level to the limits of plant growth, and often being locally abundant.[1] The genus, belonging to the figwort family (Scrophulariaceae), is one of the relatively few genera with five stamens in that very large plant family; it is named rather appropriately, *Pentstemon* being derived from the Greek *pente*, five, and *stemon*, stamen. In most species only four stamens are anther-bearing, the fifth one consisting only of the stalk (filament), which is usually thickened toward the tip and frequently clothed with yellow hairs (bearded). However, in a few species the five stamens are all anther-bearing and produce pollen. Pennell has stressed the point that the original spelling of the generic name is *Penstemon*, and that spelling is now accepted by some authors.[1][2] Some species are occasionally known as foxglove or false-foxglove; those species in which the sterile stamen is bearded are commonly called beardtongue.

The pentstemons vary in palatability from practically worthless to fairly good. Because of the great number and close relationship of species of *Pentstemon* most Forest officers and other observers, other than professional botanists, fail frequently to distinguish the species. As the species undoubtedly vary in palatability there has arisen some confusion as to the palatability of these plants. Until a thorough study can be made of the palatabilities of individual species of *Pentstemon* it is necessary to indicate the forage value of

[1] Dayton, W. A. IMPORTANT WESTERN BROWSE PLANTS. U. S. Dept. Agr. Misc. Pub. 101, 214 pp., illus. 1931.
[2] Pennell, F. W. SCROPHULARIACEAE OF THE CENTRAL ROCKY MOUNTAIN STATES. U. S. Natl. Mus., Contrib. U. S. Natl. Herbarium 20 : 313–381. 1920.

most species only in a general way. As a broad guide to palatability, although numerous exceptions may occur, the species of *Pentstemon* may be separated into four groups: (1) the tall, shrubby species of California and the Southwest, with rather large, relatively thin leaves; (2) low, more or less prostrate or trailing, shrubby or undershrubby species, chiefly of the Northwest, with mostly thick and leathery leaves; (3) herbaceous species, sometimes with woody roots and crown, with somewhat thick foliage covered with a whitish or bluish bloom (glaucous); and (4) the species with green, mostly hairless, delicate foliage.

The larger shrubby species, such as Lemmon pentstemon (*P. lemmon'ii*) and stubflower pentstemon (*P. breviflo'rus*) of the lower elevations in California and littleleaf pentstemon (*P. microphyl'lus*) of central Arizona, are usually much-branched bushes from 1 to 8 feet high. They possess some local browse value for sheep, varying in palatability from poor to fair, or in some localities to fairly good or even higher.

The low shrubby or undershrubby species with small or leathery leaves tend, with a few exceptions, toward low or negligible palatability. Many of these species are low, sprawling plants, growing chiefly on dry, rocky, mountainous soils. Frequently, they are abundant locally, occur in nearly pure stands, and rank among the showiest plants of the high mountains, when in full bloom. Bush pentstemon (*P. frutico'sus*), a woody plant from 6 to 24 (rarely 40) inches high, is characteristic of this group, which includes about 10 species. Bush pentstemon is distributed principally in alpine and subalpine sites from southern British Columbia to Oregon and western Wyoming. Its lower leaves are stalkless, spatula-shaped, finely toothed, about three-fourths of an inch to 1 inch long, with the upper ones smaller and egg-shaped; its purple corollas are about 1 inch long. Colorado pentstemon (*P. coloraden'sis*), firleaf pentstemon (*P. abieti'nus*), Menzies pentstemon (*P. menzie'sii*), rockvine pentstemon (*P. ellip'ticus*), and Scouler pentstemon (*P. scou'leri*) are other closely related and somewhat similar species.

The herbaceous species, with thick, glaucous foliage, many of which have woody roots and root crowns, are often practically worthless to poor in palatability for sheep and practically worthless for other classes of livestock. Blue pentstemon (*P. gla'ber*), eggleaf pentstemon (*P. ova'tus*), Palmer pentstemon (*P. pal'meri*), piñon pentstemon (*P. si'milis*), and Wasatch pentstemon (*P. cyanan'thus*) are some of the most outstanding species in this group.

The herbaceous species, with smooth, green foliage, especially the larger, leafy species, generally rate as fair forage for cattle; occasionally as fairly good forage for sheep. Among the best known of these species are littleflower pentstemon (*P. pro'cerus*), Mancos pentstemon (*P. strictifor'mis*), Rocky Mountain penstemon (*P. stric'tus*), Rydberg pentstemon (*P. rydber'gii*), and slender pentstemon (*P. gra'cilis*). Blueleaf pentstemon (*P. glau'cus*) also belongs in this group, although its blue (glaucous) foliage makes it an exception.

Usually, the pentstemons are weak seeders, although they have strong root systems, reproduce rather vigorously by means of rootstocks, and often show a tendency to increase on overgrazed ranges. An abundance of pentstemon on a range may, hence, be an indication of past overgrazing.

Many of the pentstemons are very attractive and are grown as ornamentals. Among the well-known western species used in horticulture, azure pentstemon (*P. azu'reus*), a California species cultivated at an early date (1849), blue pentstemon, eggleaf pentstemon, Palmer pentstemon, and shell-leaf pentstemon (*P. grandiflo'rus*) are outstanding. Many other species have been domesticated; unquestionably a number of the still untamed species offer promise for ornamental cultivation.

PHLOXES

Phlox spp.

The *Phlox* genus is entirely confined to the North American continent except for Siberian phlox (*P. sibirica*), a species which also occurs in Alaska. A few species in the Southeast are low, more or less trailing shrubs or undershrubs, and many of the species are somewhat woody at the base. Drummond phlox (*P. drummondii*), probably the most commonly cultivated species, and Roemer phlox (*P. roemeriana*), both natives of Texas, are annuals; most of the species are perennial herbs. Genera of the phlox family are found in every State. About 45 species occur in the West, some being diminutive and matlike, others large and bushy. They grow on the plains, in the foothills, and in the high mountains. *Phlox*, meaning flame (alluding to showy, brightly colored flowers), was an old Greek name for campion (*Lychnis*) and was transferred to our American genus by the preeminent Swedish botanist Linnaeus when he wrote his books which revolutionized tl₁e conceptions of the genera and species of plants.

The majority of western pʻiloxes occur in open situations, on rather dry and often gravelly or rocky soils, frequently in grass types in full sunlight. Some species, however, are definitely restricted to the forest and shady sites. Phloxes are very showy plants and often grow in masses, blossoming from midspring to midsummer, and reproducing by seed or creeping rootstocks.

The flowers of phlox are relished by sheep, summer use usually being limited to those parts. The foliage of the species with small and prickly leaves is generally avoided by livestock except, in certain cases, during early spring or when better feed is either unavailable or scarce. The palatability of those species with larger and more tender leaves, which are grazed by sheep and occasionally by cattle and horses, is fair. Their matted growth renders some species valuable as soil binders in retarding erosion. The taller species are popular among wild-flower lovers, and many of the low, cushionlike western species are being introduced into cultivation for rockeries, borders, etc.

Phloxes usually have woody roots or rootstocks and branching stems. Most species have opposite leaves but occasionally the leaves are alternate on the upper stems and, in the case of Roemer phlox, the leaves are regularly alternate. The showy, often fragrant, white, blue, purplish or reddish flowers begin as a slender tube then flare at the top into a five-lobed apex, giving them a salver-shaped structure. The flowers are arranged in clusters (cymes or cymose panicles, the central flowers blooming first), either terminal at the ends of the branches or axillary between the upper leaves and the branch. The five stamens are inserted at different levels on the inside of the showy part of the flower (corolla); the floral cup at the base (calyx) is five-lobed and whitish between the lobes. Usually, only a single seed is produced in each cell of the seed capsule; the wet seeds, unlike those of many plants of this family, do not become mucilaginous nor do they emit small spiral threads.

WOOLLY INDIANWHEAT

Planta'go pursh'ii, syn. _P. patago'nica gnaphalioi'des_

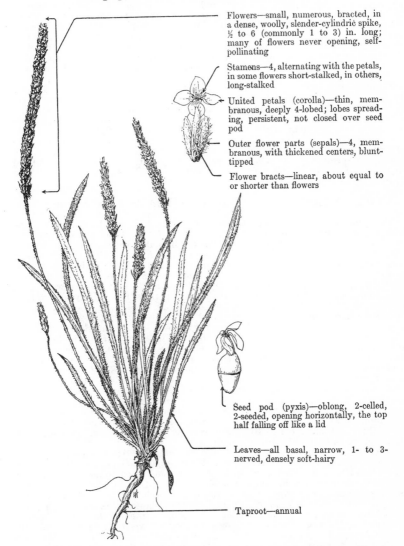

Flowers—small, numerous, bracted, in a dense, woolly, slender-cylindric spike, ½ to 6 (commonly 1 to 3) in. long; many of flowers never opening, self-pollinating

Stamens—4, alternating with the petals, in some flowers short-stalked, in others, long-stalked

United petals (corolla)—thin, membranous, deeply 4-lobed; lobes spreading, persistent, not closed over seed pod

Outer flower parts (sepals)—4, membranous, with thickened centers, blunt-tipped

Flower bracts—linear, about equal to or shorter than flowers

Seed pod (pyxis)—oblong, 2-celled, 2-seeded, opening horizontally, the top half falling off like a lid

Leaves—all basal, narrow, 1- to 3-nerved, densely soft-hairy

Taproot—annual

Woolly Indianwheat is a small, silvery, annual weed from 2 to 15 (commonly 4 to 8) inches high, with small, inconspicuous flowers in a dense, cylindrical spike, which resembles a spike of wheat in general outline.

This small annual occurs from Ontario to Texas and westward to Arizona and British Columbia, growing in all of the western range States except California. It is a light-loving plant, appearing almost invariably in full sunlight on dry, open foothills, mesas, and plains. Its altitudinal occurrence varies from about 1,200 feet in the Northwest to 7,000 or 8,000 feet in the Great

Basin, although it is more common and abundant at low elevations throughout its range. This species grows on a wide variety of soils from heavy clay to nearly pure sand, but apparently prefers loamy soils.

Woolly Indianwheat is most abundant and more important in the Southwest than elsewhere. On some ranges it is considered fairly good or even good spring forage for sheep and cattle, and is one of the most valuable winter annual weeds. It is an outstanding feed on desert lambing grounds about Phoenix, Ariz. Although consⁱderably inferior to alfileria, this plant usually does not dry up as readily, and tends to produce a crop under slightly less favorable conditions. The dense and relatively large seed heads are the most palatable part of the plant, and are reputedly nutritious and fattening. Elsewhere than in the Southwest, woolly Indianwheat ranks as poor forage and is of little or no economic importance.

Because this species is an annual, its abundance depends upon the amount of precipitation and the character and density of the perennial plant cover present. Hence its production varies greatly, and its utility period is naturally short. In view of the uncertainty of this forage crop, livestock population should not be based upon the use of this plant. During favorable years this weed springs up abundantly over large areas and frequently becomes the dominant plant for a short period in the spring on sites supporting sparse perennial vegetation. During dry years, the plant supplies only a limited amount of forage although reproduction during dry years is more certain than that of many other annuals.

PLANTAINS AND INDIANWHEATS (Planta'go spp.)

The plantains, some of the annual species of which are known as Indianwheats, are annual or perennial herbs or half shrubs with usually numerous basal leaves and small, inconspicuous flowers in spikes or heads borne on leafless stems. *Plantago* is the classical Latin name for plantain. *Plantago* is a relatively large genus, consisting of more than 200 species; it belongs to the plantain family (Plantaginaceae). The plantains are chiefly weedy species, found in waste places, maritime, or alpine localities throughout the world, but are especially common in temperate regions; they are widely distributed throughout the United States at low elevations. However, the number of species occurring in the West is relatively few.

A few species of *Plantago*, commonly known as Indianwheats such as *P. purshii* and desert Indianwheat (*P. fastigia'ta*), are fairly high in palatability and are so abundant on some ranges of the Southwest that they class as fairly important spring forage. Thornber[1] ranks the native plantains, or Indianwheats, next in importance to the valuable alfileria (*Erodium cicutarium*) among the winter annuals of southern and western Arizona. Desert Indianwheat, also known as tufted plantain, is listed as a very abundant species of the desert ranges of that region. These Indianwheats produce a large number of seeds, the most palatable part of the plant, which stockmen regard as a good fattening feed for livestock. With the exception of a few species of the Southwest, the plantains occur scatteringly, rate as poor forage for all classes of livestock, and are of little range importance.

Several of the plantains have been used medicinally. The species of greatest present importance is flaxseed plantain (*P. psyl'lium*), native to southern Europe and northern Africa, the seeds of which, sold as psyllium seeds, are used externally or internally in similar manner to flaxseed, which they closely resemble in medicinal properties. Several European species naturalized in America, such as rippleseed plantain, often called common plantain (*P. ma'jor*), a plant with large, broad leaves, and buckhorn plantain, often called lanceleaf plantain and ribwort (*P. lanceola'ta*), are now very common weeds in fields, lawns, and waste places. During pioneer days they were used medicinally.

The plantain genus is characterized by numerous small, bracted, mostly greenish flowers on naked stems; the flower parts are in fours, with the four (rarely two) stamens alternating with the four membranous petals; the seed pod (pyxis) is mainly two-celled and one- to several-seeded, opening transversely so that the top falls off like a lid; the mostly basal leaves have one to several distinct ribs.

---

[1] Thornber, J. J. THE GRAZING RANGES OF ARIZONA. Ariz. Agr. Expt. Sta. Bull. 65: [245]–360. illus. 1910.

WHITE POLEMONIUM

Polemo'nium albiflo'rum

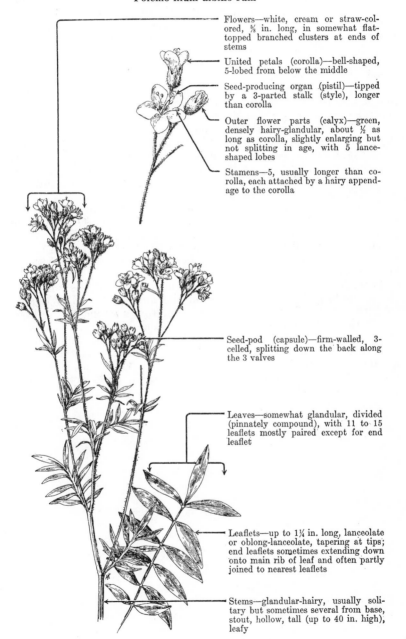

Flowers—white, cream or straw-colored, ⅝ in. long, in somewhat flat-topped branched clusters at ends of stems

United petals (corolla)—bell-shaped, 5-lobed from below the middle

Seed-producing organ (pistil)—tipped by a 3-parted stalk (style), longer than corolla

Outer flower parts (calyx)—green, densely hairy-glandular, about ½ as long as corolla, slightly enlarging but not splitting in age, with 5 lance-shaped lobes

Stamens—5, usually longer than corolla, each attached by a hairy appendage to the corolla

Seed-pod (capsule)—firm-walled, 3-celled, splitting down the back along the 3 valves

Leaves—somewhat glandular, divided (pinnately compound), with 11 to 15 leaflets mostly paired except for end leaflet

Leaflets—up to 1¼ in. long, lanceolate or oblong-lanceolate, tapering at tips; end leaflets sometimes extending down onto main rib of leaf and often partly joined to nearest leaflets

Stems—glandular-hairy, usually solitary but sometimes several from base, stout, hollow, tall (up to 40 in. high), leafy

White polemonium is a leafy, relatively robust, perennial herb of the phlox family. The species name is a Latin adjective meaning white-flowered, derived from *albus*, white, + *flos* (*floris*), flower. The plant is occasionally called white skunkleaf or skunkweed, but the skunklike odor, strong in many species of *Polemonium*, is faint in this species. Jacobs-ladder is another name often applied to plants of this genus because of a fancied resemblance of the leaves to a ladder. The cultivated Greek-valerian (*P. caeru'leum*) is a member of this genus, and the name Greek-valerian is sometimes given to other species.

White polemonium has a restricted range, occurring in southern and southeastern Idaho, extreme western Wyoming, northern and central Utah, and northern Nevada. It is scattered sparsely throughout this range but is abundant on localized areas, sometimes being the dominant or one of the dominant species. The species is largely confined to the aspen and spruce belts and grows in moist to moderately dry, sometimes gravelly, soils, occurring most commonly in aspen stands but also in patches of browse, in moist glades, on open hillsides and with or near willows along streams.

White polemonium varies in palatability from fair to good for sheep and from worthless or poor to fair for cattle. On a few important range areas, especially in central and northern Utah, white polemonium is sufficiently abundant and palatable to rank as one of the five or six choice forage weeds, but ordinarily it is too scattered and not sufficiently relished to merit this rank.

This species averages about 12 to 30 inches high, but is sometimes 40 inches tall, depending chiefly on site and season. The usually solitary or sometimes several stems arise from a strong woody base. The herbage throughout is more or less glandular-hairy. The white or whitish-yellow flowers appear in June and July. The roots of this plant appear never to have been described. As these parts are important in this genus, from a diagnostic viewpoint, it is hoped that field men may be led to make observations on the roots of this species and to collect specimens of those parts.

BLUE SKUNKLEAF

Polemo'nium pulcher'rimum, syns. *P. delica'tum, P. "hu'mile",*[1] *and P. "pulchel'lum",*[1] *P. scopuli'num*

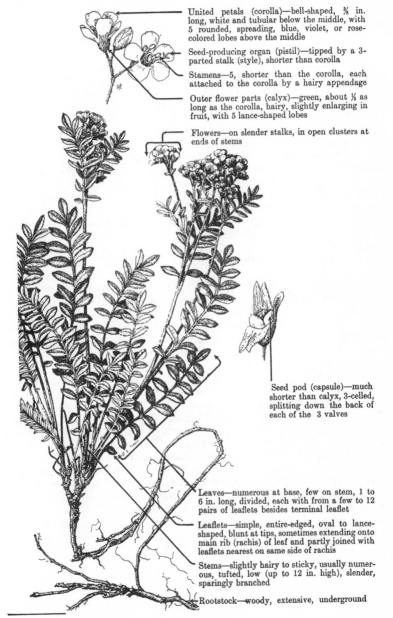

United petals (corolla)—bell-shaped, ⅜ in. long, white and tubular below the middle, with 5 rounded, spreading, blue, violet, or rose-colored lobes above the middle

Seed-producing organ (pistil)—tipped by a 3-parted stalk (style), shorter than corolla

Stamens—5, shorter than the corolla, each attached to the corolla by a hairy appendage

Outer flower parts (calyx)—green, about ½ as long as the corolla, hairy, slightly enlarging in fruit, with 5 lance-shaped lobes

Flowers—on slender stalks, in open clusters at ends of stems

Seed pod (capsule)—much shorter than calyx, 3-celled, splitting down the back of each of the 3 valves

Leaves—numerous at base, few on stem, 1 to 6 in. long, divided, each with from a few to 12 pairs of leaflets besides terminal leaflet

Leaflets—simple, entire-edged, oval to lance-shaped, blunt at tips, sometimes extending onto main rib (rachis) of leaf and partly joined with leaflets nearest on same side of rachis

Stems—slightly hairy to sticky, usually numerous, tufted, low (up to 12 in. high), slender, sparingly branched

Rootstock—woody, extensive, underground

[1] Of United States authors.

Blue skunkleaf is a well-known perennial herb of the phlox family. Together with several other species of *Polemonium*, it is sometimes called Jacobs-ladder because of the imagined resemblance of the paired leaflets to a ladder, and also skunkweed because of the unpleasant odor of the herbage. The specific name *pulcherrimum* is a Latin word which means very fair, or pretty, and was given to this species, to indicate the attractiveness of the flowers, by the distinguished British botanist Sir William J. Hooker (1785–1865), who originally described it.

Blue skunkleaf is a widely spread western species, occurring in all of the 11 far Western States. It is common in eastern Washington and Oregon, western and to some extent eastern Montana, western Wyoming, and throughout Idaho, Utah, and Colorado, but is rare or absent in the southern portions of New Mexico, Nevada, and California. It is typically a high mountain species of the lodgepole pine, aspen, spruce-fir, and alpine belts. In Utah and Colorado it is very common at and above timber line, and is usually found in scattered, small patches in open meadows, canyon bottoms, parks and grassy slopes, or in the diffuse light of open timber stands, mostly in moist, relatively coarse-textured soils, such as rocky or gravelly, occasionally sandy, loam.

This species is of slight forage value, though its importance varies somewhat in different places. It seldom grows in great abundance, and its palatability is usually worthless to poor for cattle and poor to fair, or occasionally fairly good, for sheep. It is most likely to occur on sheep ranges, occupying, as it usually does, areas higher than those ordinarily occupied by cattle. It is best for grazing in midsummer; at the latter part of the season the foliage is frequently frost-bitten and dry.

The rather numerous, slender stems of blue skunkleaf spread out laterally at the base and then become erect, are occasionally branched above, and grow in bunches or tufts. The root starts as a slender or moderately spindle-shaped taproot; later there is an extensive development of lateral rootstocks, and often the crown becomes branched. The root crown is clothed above with the old leaf bases and produces many shallow-growing, fibrous rootlets below. Because of its spreading, often shallow character, most of the root and rootstock system may sometimes be easily pulled from the ground, especially if the soil is loose and moist. The compound leaves, which are finely hairy in some plants and smooth in others, are mostly from the base, those of the stem becoming gradually smaller and with fewer leaflets. The flowers droop while in bud but become erect when they bloom, the outer and lower flowers in each cluster blossoming first. Flowering begins in June or July, or in some sites as early as May, and continues for about 6 to 8 weeks. Seed production starts about July, depending upon the locality, and continues as long as the season is favorable.

DOUGLAS KNOTWEED

Poly'gonum dougla'sii

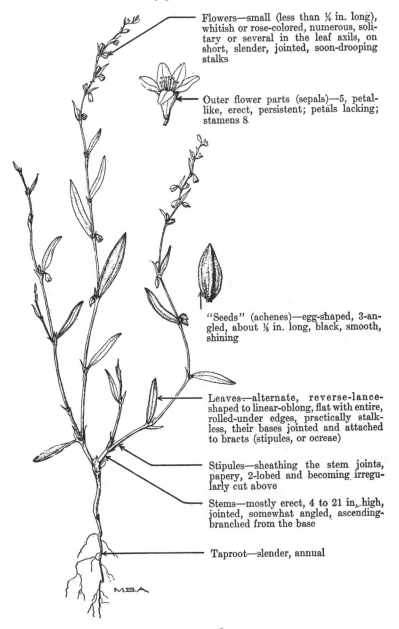

Flowers—small (less than ¼ in. long), whitish or rose-colored, numerous, solitary or several in the leaf axils, on short, slender, jointed, soon-drooping stalks

Outer flower parts (sepals)—5, petal-like, erect, persistent; petals lacking; stamens 8

"Seeds" (achenes)—egg-shaped, 3-angled, about ⅛ in. long, black, smooth, shining

Leaves—alternate, reverse-lance-shaped to linear-oblong, flat with entire, rolled-under edges, practically stalkless, their bases jointed and attached to bracts (stipules, or ocreae)

Stipules—sheathing the stem joints, papery, 2-lobed and becoming irregularly cut above

Stems—mostly erect, 4 to 21 in. high, jointed, somewhat angled, ascending-branched from the base

Taproot—slender, annual

Douglas knotweed, an annual herb with narrow, alternate leaves and erect stems sheathed at the jointed nodes, is widely distributed, ranging from British Columbia and California eastward to Texas, Nebraska, New York, Maine, and Ontario. However, east of the Rocky Mountains it has probably been naturalized, since its distribution is local. Douglas knotweed was named in honor of David Douglas (1799–1834), a distinguished Scotch botanical explorer.

Douglas knotweed abounds on rocky, sandy, or impoverished soils, especially in waste ground and on sites where trampling, excessive grazing, or other destructive influences have largely destroyed the natural, perennial vegetation. Sampson[1] considers this species one of the key plants of the ruderal-early-weed stage, characterized by annuals qualified for the invasion and occupation of lands where the soil has been seriously impaired. These low-value annuals, mostly weeds, with shallow root systems and strong seed habits, are, however, efficient eventually in accumulating sufficient organic matter to support more desirable perennial plants.

This herb is practically worthless as forage for cattle and horses and is only fair feed for sheep, except on severely overgrazed areas, where it dominantly abounds and is moderately cropped by both sheep and cattle. Under such conditions it furnishes an amount of feed equal to that of all the other annual weeds combined.[1] It is of little forage importance on ranges in good condition.

KNOTWEEDS (Poly'gonum spp.)

Knotweeds, also known as doorweeds and knotgrasses, compose a fairly large and widely distributed genus, with some 36 species in the West. The genus belongs to the buckwheat family (Polygonaceae); it includes both annual and perennial plants, a number of the western species being woody at the base (undershrubs). In this discussion the genus *Polygonum* is considered in its more restricted sense, exclusive of the following genera: Fleeceflower (*Acono'-gonum*), cornbind (*Bilderdy'kia*, syn. *Tinia'ria*), bistort (*Bistor'ta*), tovara (*Tovara*), and tearthumb (*Tracaulon*), which are regarded by some authors as too closely related to *Polygonum* to rate generic rank. The generic name *Polygonum* is from the Greek *polus*, many, and *gonu*, knee, referring to the swollen stem joints characteristic of many species. This knotted appearance of the stem is also emphasized in the common name.

This representative group of the buckwheat family is widely distributed throughout the West and occurs in diverse habitats, ranging from extremely dry to very wet or marshy sites. Usually, these plants abound on poor soils, or on areas where such disturbing influences as overgrazing and trampling have depleted the perennial plant cover. On the range they generally grow in greatest abundance in the vicinity of depleted bedgrounds, saltgrounds, and other severely abused sites. Some species are common weeds in cultivated ground; others appear along roadsides. Although generally ranking as undesirable species, knotweeds often mantle denuded areas with a fairly dense cover, which provides some soil protection.

These species are usually low in palatability, being practically worthless as forage for cattle and horses, and only fair for sheep and goats; occasionally, however, they furnish an appreciable amount of sheep forage. Inferior forage quality explains why they are cropped somewhat lightly even on heavily grazed ranges, but as they produce an abundance of seed these plants tend to increase and replace their betters which have succumbed to excessive grazing. Hence, a superfluity of knotweed on a range generally indicates destructive depletion from very severe overgrazing.

In the main, knotweeds are hairless, much-branched, erect, or sprawling herbs, with alternate and somewhat fleshy or leathery, stalkless leaves, jointed to the stipules (ocreae), which sheath the stems at the nodes. The small flowers are borne in clusters in the leaf axils, sometimes bunched near the branch ends in spikes, racemes, or heads. The flowers lack petals; the outer flower parts (calyx) consist of four to six (usually five) nearly separate, petal-like sepals, which are pink, rose, or white, or often greenish and with pale or brightly colored margins. The small, seedlike fruits (achenes) are three-angled, brown or black, and surrounded by the persistent calyx.

---

[1] Sampson, A. W. PLANT SUCCESSION IN RELATION TO RANGE MANAGEMENT. U. S. Dept. Agr. Bull. 791, 76 pp., illus. 1919.

CINQUEFOILS

Potentil'la spp.

Cinquefoil is the name most commonly applied to the large genus *Potentilla* of often rather strawberrylike, mostly perennial (a few species are annual or biennial) herbs [1] belonging to the rose family (Rosaceae). The name cinquefoil is a derivative of the French *cinque*, five, and the Old French or medieval English word *foil*, leaf. It refers to the five, fingerlike (digitate) leaflets characteristic of many species of this genus; the common name fivefinger, also sometimes used, is similarly descriptive of such leaves. The generic noun *Potentilla* is a feminine diminutive derived from the Latin adjective *potens*, meaning powerful, and alludes to the medicinal properties of a number of species which contain relatively large quantities of tannic acid and are notably astringent. This large, variable genus includes about 300 species; it is distributed widely throughout the cooler temperate regions of the Northern Hemisphere and extends even into the Arctic Circle. Cinquefoils also occur in the higher mountains of South America and tropical regions.

Some 110 species of this genus occur on the western ranges, from near sea level in Washington and Oregon to the highest limits of vegetation (about 14,000 feet) in the central Colorado mountains. The species are usually most abundant above the sagebrush belt, occurring principally in scattered stands on the slopes, ridges, glades, parks, and meadows, intermixed with grasses, weeds, and sedges. On many areas they are conspicuous components of the vegetation, particularly in moist, well-drained meadows, open parks of the aspen and spruce belts, and high open ridges above timber line. Many species grow on dry, shallow, sandy, gravelly, or rocky soils, but the majority apparently prefer the rich, deep loams of moist but well-drained sites; they frequently become abundant in the meadows, parks, and better soils of the open hillsides.

In the main, the species of *Potentilla* possess very little forage value, ranking as poor to fair for sheep, and worthless to poor for cattle; horses occasionally crop a few flowers. Deer frequently eat considerable quantities of the foliage, and elk partake lightly of the herbage during the spring, summer, and fall. Apparently, the flowering tops are the most palatable parts of the plant, as the leaves and stems of most, if not all, cinquefoils have an acrid, astringent taste, which evidently is connected with their low palatability and which is probably attributable to their containing tannic acid. As much as 13 percent of tannin has been obtained from the dried leaves of oldfield cinquefoil (*P. canadensis*).[2]

A number of cinquefoils withstand heavy tramping remarkably well, and several even increase abundantly on depleted ranges. For example, Nuttall cinquefoil (*P. nuttal'lii*), blueleaf cinquefoil (*P.*

---

[1] In this work shrubby cinquefoil (*Dasiphora fruticosa*, syn. *P. fruticosa*) is placed in a separate genus.
[2] Peacock, J. C. SOME OF THE UNPUBLISHED RESULTS OF THE INVESTIGATION OF THE TANNINS BY THE LATE PROFESSOR HENRY TRIMBLE. Amer. Jour. Pharm. 72 : 429–433. 1900.

glaucophyl'la), slimstem cinquefoil (*P. fi'lipes*), and Brewer cinquefoil (*P. brew'eri*) have increased conspicuously in meadows, parks,
and open-timbered areas where the more palatable and less resistant
plants have been impaired by excessive grazing and trampling. On
many areas abundance of various species of cinquefoil indicates
range deterioration. Most species produce numerous flowers and
innumerable small seeds, which appear to be of good viability. Once
established, most species, especially the perennials, are very tenacious and are qualified to withstand drought by virtue of their woody
taproots. Although generally erect, they frequently become prostrate and form small mats when subjected to heavy trampling and
abuse. Even under such unsatisfactory conditions, they flower and
produce seed.

Many species of cinquefoil have at various times been employed
medicinally, principally as astringents. All parts of these plants
have seen such service, but particularly the roots. Tormentilla
(*P. tormentil'la*), a native of European meadows, is probably the
only species still used—its roots, under the name of *radix tormentil-
lae*, possess value as a powerful astringent medicine.[3] Various
species, such as the creeping cinquefoil (*P. rep'tans*) of Europe, oldfield cinquefoil, and silver cinquefoil (*P. argen'tea*), a native of Europe and Asia and probably America, have been used as astringents
in the treatment of dysentery, chronic catarrh, and other ailments.[4]
The roots of tormentilla and silver cinquefoil, rich in tannin, are
useful in tanning and also yield a red dye.[3]

Many of the native American species of cinquefoil are rather unattractive because of their small and frequently inconspicuous flowers. However, a large number of the cultivated hardy perennials are
used for border planting. The most valuable forms for garden use
are hybrids (mainly of Himalayan species), which frequently have
double flowers, many having handsome foliage and blooming freely
from June until August, although most profusely during late June
and July. The rather large and showy flowers of these hybrids are
chiefly maroon, scarlet, or orange in color, being frequently banded
attractively with yellow. These plants, which thrive in heavy soil,
are only moderately hardy, being best adapted for planting in the
more southern parts of the country. They rarely attain a height
of over 2 feet and require no staking, as the stems are rigid enough
to remain upright. Choice varieties are propagated by root divisions in the spring; stem cuttings will not root.

The floral characteristics of western cinquefoils are somewhat uniform, but the vegetative aspect of the different species varies considerably. The flowers are usually borne in loose, open clusters at
the ends of the stems, but in a few species are solitary in the leaf
axils. In general, cinquefoil flowers have a cup-shaped, almost hemispheric, base (hypanthium); 5 sepals, alternating with 5 sepallike bractlets; 5, mostly yellow, less frequently purple or white
petals; usually 20 stamens attached in three series to the base of the
hypanthium; and numerous seed-producing organs (pistils). The

[3] Rydberg, P. A. A MONOGRAPH OF THE NORTH AMERICAN POTENTILLEAE. 223 pp., illus.
Lancaster, Pa. 1898.
[4] Schneider, A. PHARMACAL PLANTS AND THEIR CULTURE. Calif. State Bd. Forestry
Bull. 2, 175 pp. 1912.

ripened pistils, or fruit (achenes) are tipped for a while with an often threadlike stalk (persistent style) swollen at the base and attached near the top or somewhat to one side of the "seeds"; the style is eventually deciduous. Most cinquefoils are perennials, having thick, woody taproots and much-branched root crowns; a few species are annuals or biennials, from slender fibrous taproots. Ordinarily, the plants are erect, with simple or branched, leafy or almost leafless, stems. A number are prostrate with runners (like strawberries), and others are even stemless, with only basal leaves from the root crown. The leaves are the most variable character of the genus, ranging from digitate, i. e., with the leaflets arranged like the fingers of a hand, to finely pinnate, i. e., with the leaflets arranged in pairs along a common axis (rachis). The leaves may be densely hairy on either one or both sides, sparingly hairy or hairless, and the 3 to 27 leaflets may be entire, wavy, toothed or deeply cleft on the margins.

Nuttall cinquefoil is deemed of sufficient importance to rate a separate treatment in this handbook. Three other species, representative of the range cinquefoils generally, merit the brief mention below.

Biennial cinquefoil (*P. bien'nis*), a multi-branched, leafy biennial (occasionally annual) herb, with several finely hairy, slender often reddish or purplish stems from a taproot, grows from 8 to 20 inches high. This species is probably the most common biennial cinquefoil on the western ranges. The numerous, small, yellow flowers, which arise from the axils of the upper leaves, produce a multiplicity of small, smooth, whitish "seeds", which insure its perpetuation. The strawberrylike or cloverlike leaves are green on both sides, with three broad, slightly hairy leaflets toothed along the upper half. The lower leaves have long stalks (petioles); the upper, or stem leaves, are almost stalkless. This plant ranges from British Columbia to southern Saskatchewan and southward to Colorado, Arizona, and Lower California, growing commonly on both moist and rather dry sites, although most characteristically on rich, moist, sandy, gravelly, or clay loams. This species frequently inhabits waste places, and is common both in the warmer valleys along ditch banks and in cool moist sites. As a rule it occurs but scatteringly, although in a few sites, especially near cultivated fields, biennial cinquefoil abounds along creeks and irrigation ditches. It has little or no forage value, being seldom grazed, except by sheep, which normally eat small quantities of the foliage at rare intervals. On heavily grazed pastures, these animals may be forced to utilize much of the herbage but, even under such conditions, they consume the plant only as a last resort.

Slimstem cinquefoil (*P. fi'lipes*), a perennial herb ranging from Alberta to Manitoba, northern New Mexico, and Utah, is one of the most common and abundant cinquefoils throughout the Rocky Mountain region. It grows typically in mountain meadows and parks, and on slopes from the ponderosa pine zone up through the spruce-fir belt, occurring up to as high as 12,000 feet in Colorado. This cinquefoil grows most luxuriantly and abundantly in deep, sandy, or clay loams, rich in humus, in association with mountain-dandelion, western yarrow, sedges, needlegrasses, and bluegrasses. At times it is common on drier sites, intermixed with sagebrush and snowberry. Slimstem cinquefoil is grazed by all classes of livestock, as well as by deer and elk. It ranks as one of the more palatable species of cinquefoil, being rated as fair for sheep and goats, poor for cattle, and fair to fairly good for deer and elk. Horses occasionally crop the flower heads but seldom consume much of the foliage. This species withstands heavy trampling and spreads aggressively in moist, rich meadows and parks where heavy grazing has impaired or depleted the better forage. Its abundance on many ranges is beyond doubt indicative of range deterioration.

Slimstem cinquefoil has several simple, few-leaved, erect or decumbent stems arising from the crown (caudex) of a woody taproot. The young leaves emerging from the bud are densely white-hairy. Basal leaves are numerous, principally with seven digitately arranged leaflets about three-fourths to 1¼ inches long, broader above and coarsely toothed on the margins; stem leaves are very limited and almost stalkless. All leaves, when mature, are green and sparingly hairy on the upper surface but silvery beneath with fine, dense whitish hairs. Stems and leafstalks are usually somewhat densely loose-hairy. The two bracts (stipules) at the base of the lower leafstalks are large, thin and brown in color, while those of the stem leaves are large, entire, and leaflike. The yellow to orange flowers, about one-half of an inch wide, are borne in open, few-flowered clusters. The slender flower stalks (pedicels), to which the name *filipes* (from the Latin *filum*, thread, and *pes*, foot or stalk) refers, are silky-hairy and slightly sticky (glandular-hairy).

Blueleaf cinquefoil (*P. glaucophyl'la*), a mostly low, perennial herb with a woody root, extends from British Columbia to Saskatchewan and southward to New Mexico, Arizona, and Nevada. It inhabits mountain valleys and meadows of the aspen-spruce and alpine belts to above timber line and has been collected at an elevation of 13,000 feet in southwestern Colorado. It commonly grows in limestone loams, rich in humus, of moist meadows, parks, and open timber. Its stand is usually scattered, frequently in association with sedges, buttercups, bunchgrass, needlegrasses, and mountain-dandelions. Although fairly common and abundant, this species is not important for forage, being only fair for sheep, and from worthless to poor for cattle and horses. There is evidence that deer and elk graze it lightly. On a number of heavily utilized ranges blueleaf cinquefoil has increased materially, and in most places where its stand is thick, range depletion is probably indicated. This herb, from 6 to 8 (rarely 16) inches in height, is smooth and hairless below but very sparsely hairy above; the white hairs are closely appressed to the stems, leaves, and calyx. The leaves are mainly basal with rather long petioles, although a few small, almost stalkless ones occur along the stem; all have five fingerlike (digitate) leaflets. The leaflets, varying from one-half to 2 inches in length, are wedge-shaped at the base, prominently notched above, and sparingly hairy when young. Soon, however, they become smooth and hairless with a whitish bloom (glaucous); the plant derives its specific name from this character. The yellow flowers are borne in loose, open clusters at the ends of the stems.

NUTTALL CINQUEFOIL

Potentil'la nuttal'lii

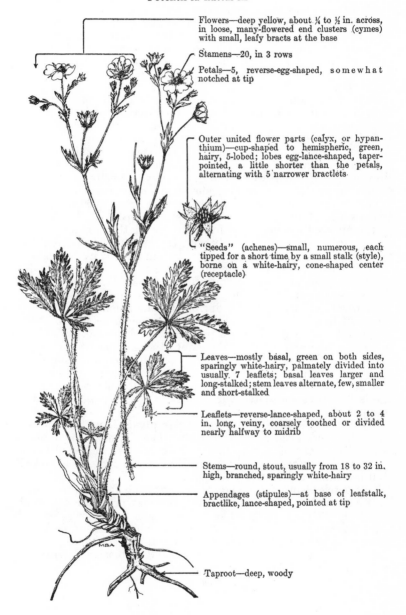

Flowers—deep yellow, about ¼ to ½ in. across, in loose, many-flowered end clusters (cymes) with small, leafy bracts at the base

Stamens—20, in 3 rows

Petals—5, reverse-egg-shaped, somewhat notched at tip

Outer united flower parts (calyx, or hypanthium)—cup-shaped to hemispheric, green, hairy, 5-lobed; lobes egg-lance-shaped, taperpointed, a little shorter than the petals, alternating with 5 narrower bractlets

"Seeds" (achenes)—small, numerous, each tipped for a short time by a small stalk (style), borne on a white-hairy, cone-shaped center (receptacle)

Leaves—mostly basal, green on both sides, sparingly white-hairy, palmately divided into usually 7 leaflets; basal leaves larger and long-stalked; stem leaves alternate, few, smaller and short-stalked

Leaflets—reverse-lance-shaped, about 2 to 4 in. long, veiny, coarsely toothed or divided nearly halfway to midrib

Stems—round, stout, usually from 18 to 32 in. high, branched, sparingly white-hairy

Appendages (stipules)—at base of leafstalk, bractlike, lance-shaped, pointed at tip

Taproot—deep, woody

Nuttall cinquefoil, a herbaceous perennial from a woody taproot, belongs to the rose family (Rosaceae) and was named in remembrance of Nuttall (1786–1859), an Englishman by birth, who developed into a preeminent botanist in this country. Nuttall collected many plants along the Oregon trail and throughout the Northwest. The plant under discussion is characteristic of many species of *Potentilla* and is widely distributed over the western ranges, extending from British Columbia to Saskatchewan and southward to Colorado and California. This plant is most abundant in Utah, Idaho, and western Montana, being found only sparsely in eastern and northern California.

Nuttall cinquefoil grows most abundantly and luxuriantly in the rich, porous loams of meadows and open parks, where it is a conspicuous component of the mixed grass-weed type, being associated with bluegrasses, western yarrow, needlegrasses, sedges, geraniums, and muhly grasses. Occasionally, it becames the dominant species, but seldom occurs in pure stands. Although preferring the better sites, it appears sparsely on the dry, sandy, gravelly, or clay loams of mountain slopes, among sagebrush, in open aspen and Douglas fir, as well as along moist canyon bottoms from 4,500 to 9,000 feet above sea level and from the sagebrush belt up to the lower reaches of the spruce-fir zone. The forage value of this species, although usually low, varies considerably with the locality. In general, however, it is nibbled season long, to a certain extent, by all classes of livestock, except horses, ranking as poor to fair forage for sheep, poor for cattle, and poor to fair for deer and elk. Sheep crop the leaves and flower heads, but tend to discriminate against the somewhat woody stems, especially during the late summer. Cattle graze the plant lightly; horses occasionally crop the flower heads. Nuttall cinquefoil apparently is more palatable on ranges where it occurs in sparse intermixture with abundant other forage. However, this plant, as is the rule in *Potentilla*, presumably contains considerable tannic acid which, almost unquestionably, provides its characteristic acrid-astringent taste. This peculiar bitter flavor of the herbage is doubtless correlated with the rather low palatability of this species.

Nuttall cinquefoil is a very aggressive plant; it withstands heavy trampling and invades ranges readily when the more palatable and less resistant species are weakened by continued heavy utilization. On a number of overgrazed areas this plant has increased markedly, even becoming moderately abundant.

This species is usually an erect herb, growing from 18 to 32 inches high but, on heavily trampled areas, becomes prostrate or creeping and, frequently, almost matlike. Even under severe conditions this plant flowers profusely and produces an abundance of seed which appears to be of high viability. Once established, these plants are very tenacious; their deep taproots and extensive lateral roots enable them to withstand considerable drought.

INDIAN BREADROOT

Psora'lea esculen'ta, syn. *Pediome'lum esculen'tum*

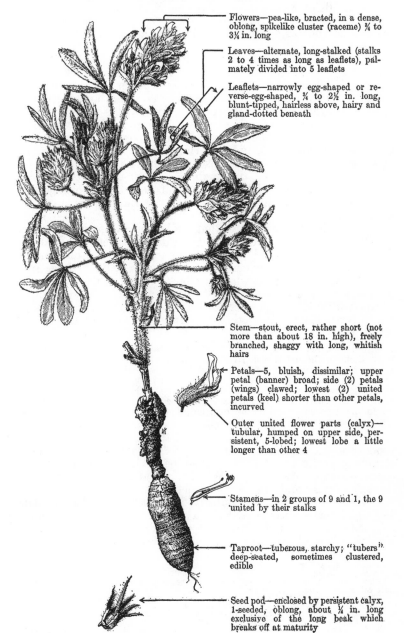

Flowers—pea-like, bracted, in a dense, oblong, spikelike cluster (raceme) ¾ to 3¼ in. long

Leaves—alternate, long-stalked (stalks 2 to 4 times as long as leaflets), palmately divided into 5 leaflets

Leaflets—narrowly egg-shaped or reverse-egg-shaped, ¾ to 2½ in. long, blunt-tipped, hairless above, hairy and gland-dotted beneath

Stem—stout, erect, rather short (not more than about 18 in. high), freely branched, shaggy with long, whitish hairs

Petals—5, bluish, dissimilar; upper petal (banner) broad; side (2) petals (wings) clawed; lowest (2) united petals (keel) shorter than other petals, incurved

Outer united flower parts (calyx)—tubular, humped on upper side, persistent, 5-lobed; lowest lobe a little longer than other 4

Stamens—in 2 groups of 9 and 1, the 9 united by their stalks

Taproot—tuberous, starchy; "tubers" deep-seated, sometimes clustered, edible

Seed pod—enclosed by persistent calyx, 1-seeded, oblong, about ¼ in. long exclusive of the long beak which breaks off at maturity

Indian breadroot, a perennial herb of the pea, or legume family (Leguminosae), is widely distributed from Alberta to New Mexico, Texas, Missouri, and Wisconsin. It is especially well known in the Great Plains region, being most abundant on the dry prairie lands and foothills of Montana, the Dakotas, Nebraska, Kansas, and Missouri. It grows on a variety of soils at fairly low elevations in the open grasslands as scattered individuals; but never occurs in dense stands.

This species, originally collected along the Missouri River by Meriwether Lewis, of the Lewis and Clark expedition (1804–6), was described and named in 1814 by the Saxon-American botanist, Frederick T. Pursh. Both the specific name *esculenta* and the common name breadroot refer to the edible root of this plant; *esculenta* is a Latin adjective, meaning edible. This plant is known under a variety of names as: the pomme blanche or pomme de prairie of the early French voyageurs, Indian turnip, prairie turnip, prairie potato or white apple of the American settlers, the aha or esharusha of the Crow Indians, and the tipsinnah of the Sioux Indians.[1][2] Since Indian breadroot was undoubtedly one of the most important Indian food plants of western North America, the English name is a very appropriate one.

Havard (in Maisch)[1] states that Indian breadroot was mentioned by all the explorers and French-Canadian voyageurs and coureurs de bois who first traded with the Indians of the western prairies, and "is in its best condition when the flowers begin to fade, in the latter part of July." Lewis and Clark[3] reported that the Indians ate both raw and cooked roots of this plant. The dried roots were pulverized into a fine powder for use in soups; the boiled roots were mixed with berries and other materials for puddings. Pursh[4] writes that—

The Indians collected the roots in large quantities, and if for present use they roast them in the ashes, when they give a food similar to yams; if intended for winter use, they are carefully dried and preserved in a dry place in their huts. When wanted for use, they are mashed between two stones, mixed with some water, and baked in cakes over the coals. It is a wholesome and nourishing food, * * *. This root has been frequently found by travelers in the canoes of the Indians, but the plant which produces it has not been known until lately.

Gilmore[5] states that the Indians of the Plains, after peeling the roots, braided them into long strings by their tapering ends, as strings of garlic are braided by the tops. These were then dried in the sunshine or over a fire.[3] When sliced and dried, the roots may be stored for several years without deterioration.[1]

Indian breadroot was reputedly introduced into Europe about 1800 by Lamare-Picquot, a French voyageur, who recommended it as a substitute for the potato. It was cultivated for some time in France, where it was known as *picquotiane;* however, the results

[1] Maisch, J. M. USEFUL PLANTS OF THE GENUS PSORALEA. Amer. Jour. Pharm. 61 : 345–352. 1889.
[2] Blankinship, J. W. NATIVE ECONOMIC PLANTS OF MONTANA. Mont. Agr. Expt. Sta. Bull. 56, 36 pp. 1905.
[3] Thwaites, R. G. (edited by). ORIGINAL JOURNALS OF THE LEWIS AND CLARK EXPEDITION 1804–06 . . . 8 v., illus. New York. 1904–5.
[4] Pursh, F. FLORAE AMERICAE SEPTENTRIONALIS . . . 2 v., illus. London. 1814.
[5] Gilmore, M. R. USES OF PLANTS BY THE INDIANS OF THE MISSOURI RIVER REGION. U. S. Bur. Amer. Ethnol. Rept. (1911–12) 33 : 45–154, illus. 1919. (Reprinted, 1919.)

were discouraging and eventually its production was suspended. Chemical analyses show that the root contains about 70 percent starch and 5 percent sugar.[1]

Indian breadroot is seldom abundant on the range and has little forage value. Some even suspect the herbage of being poisonous, but there seems to be no scientific evidence to substantiate this belief. In general, its palatability is rated worthless to poor for all classes of livestock, although, in some areas, it may occasionally rank as high as fair for sheep. Lewis and Clark[3] stated that this species is a food plant of the brown bear.

This plant dries up soon after blossoming, breaks off near the ground level and is transformed into a tumbleweed, which blows over the prairies, broadcasting its seed. The egg- to spindle-shaped tuberous root (sometimes clustered), encased in a thick, brown, leathery skin which readily peels off, is sometimes as large as a hen's egg, with the stem scars of previous years plainly visible at the upper end. Indian breadroot is sometimes confused with lupines (*Lupinus* spp.), due to the general similarity of leaves and flowers. However, our native lupines do not have tuberous roots, and the leaves of Indian breadroot are glandular, dotted underneath. Usually, these dots are easily discernible by holding a leaf in the light.

SCURFPEAS AND BREADROOTS

Psora'lea spp., syns. *Orbe'xilum spp., Pediome'lum spp., Psorali'dium spp.*

Scurfpeas and breadroots are annual, biennial, or perennial herbs or shrubs of the pea family (Leguminosae) ; our native species, however, are all perennial herbs. The generic name *Psoralea* comes from the Greek *psoraleos*, scabby, or mangy, and alludes to a scurfy or branny indument on some of the species and probably also to the peculiar, dark glandular dots characteristic of the herbage of this genus, which, presumably, reminded the ancients of skin areas affected by some eruption. Approximately 115 species occur, principally in the tropics and subtropics, with some 39 species native to the United States. Some 29 species, most of which are characteristic of the lower, drier vegetative types, occur in the West; they commonly grow on sandy soils of the plains, prairies, and foothills. Although ordinarily not very abundant and usually appearing in scattered clumps, they occasionally grow in dense almost pure stands on favorable sites.

Scurfpeas possess but little forage value, having a palatability of from practically worthless to poor, rarely fair, for sheep and cattle. Some species are distinctly distasteful to grazing animals; chemical analyses have indicated the presence of poisonous compounds in certain species.[1] Slender scurfpea (*P. tenuiflo'ra*), a native western species, erroneously called Indian turnip, is reputedly poisonous to horses and cattle, and is said to have been used by the

---

[1][3] See footnotes on preceding page.

Indians as a fish poison.[6] Such sickness as may have been caused among domestic livestock by certain of the range scurfpeas probably occurred where the animals were forced to eat the plants because of limited forage supply or where these plants contaminated hay. There is a need of further scientific research to ascertain the possible role these species may play in livestock sickness and losses.

The roots of some of the species are tuberous and starchy. Three species—Indian breadroot, Beaverdam breadroot (*P. casto'rea*), and skunktop breadroot (*P. mephi'tica*)—all furnished food for the Indians and early settlers of the Western States.[7] The roots of two plains species, tall breadroot (*P. cuspida'ta*) and little breadroot (*P. hypogae'a*), were also used by them.[8] The leaves of California-tea (*P. physo'des*), common in open spots of wooded slopes in the higher hills and mountains from California north to British Columbia, are aromatic and, when dried, make a pleasant tea which is a satisfactory substitute for Chinese tea and was a popular beverage among the early Californians. Jepson[9] states that the roots of leatherroot (*P. macrosta'chya*) furnished a tough fiber prized by the Pomos and other native Indian tribes. This species is the most common and widely distributed *Psoralea* in California, occurring in rich soils, along streams, and in salt marshes from sea level up to elevations of 3,000 feet. Bauchee seeds, the seeds of Malay-tea (*P. corylifo'lia*), an Asiatic species, have long been used in India in the treatment of such skin diseases as leucoderma, or white leprosy.[10] The roots or leaves of certain other species have been used medicinally, especially in America, for their emetic, astringent, or tonic properties. A case is on record of the poisoning of a child apparently from eating the seeds of silverleaf scurfpea (*P. argophyl'la*).[8]

The North American scurfpeas are rather low, herbaceous perennials, but some of the shrubby forms in other regions attain a height of about 15 feet. A characteristic feature of the genus is the presence of resinous, often black, glandular dots or tubercles on the calyx, leaves, stems, pods, or other parts of the plant; the herbage is often heavy-scented. The alternate leaves are usually cloverlike or lupinelike (digitately, or palmately divided), with one to seven (usually three to five) smooth-edged (in the American species) leaflets. The frequently sweet-scented flowers, mostly white, blue, purple, or pink are arranged in elongated, close, or spreading clusters. The short, thickened, one-seeded, frequently beaked pods of this genus, unlike those of most leguminous plants, do not, as a rule, split open (dehisce) although the pods of some of the breadroot species (section *Pediomelum*) may burst irregularly or break off at the top when mature.

---

[6] Marsh, C. D. STOCK-POISONING PLANTS OF THE RANGE. U. S. Dept. Agr. Bull. 1245, 36 pp., illus. 1924. Supersedes Bull. 575.

[7] Wood, H. C., Remington, J. P., and Sadtler, S. P., assisted by Lyons, A. B., and Wood, H. C., Jr. THE DISPENSATORY OF THE UNITED STATES OF AMERICA, BY DR. GEO. B. WOOD AND DR. FRANKLIN BACHE. Ed. 19, thoroughly rev. and largely rewritten . . . 1,947 pp. Philadelphia and London. 1907.

[8] Pammel, L. H. A MANUAL OF POISONOUS PLANTS CHIEFLY OF EASTERN NORTH AMERICA, WITH BRIEF NOTES ON ECONOMIC AND MEDICINAL PLANTS . . . 2 pts., illus. Cedar Rapids, Iowa. 1910–11.

[9] Jepson, W. L. A MANUAL OF THE FLOWERING PLANTS OF CALIFORNIA. 1,238 pp., illus. Berkeley, Calif. [1925.]

[10] Ghosh, J. C. PSORALIA CORYLIFOLIA. Pharm. Jour. and Pharm. [London] 121 : 54–55. 1928.

WESTERN BRACKEN

Pteri′dium aquili′num pubes′cens, syns. *"Pte′ris aquili′na"*,[1] *Pte′ris aquili′na lanugino′sa*

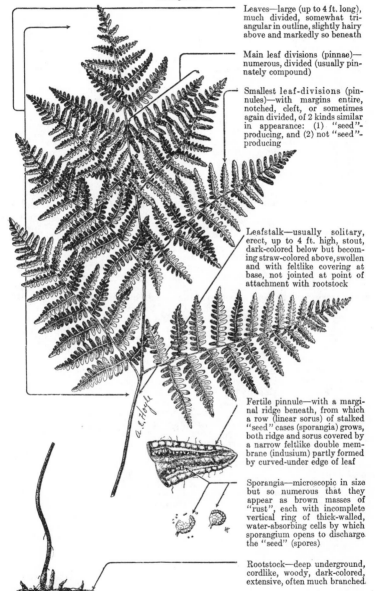

Leaves—large (up to 4 ft. long), much divided, somewhat triangular in outline, slightly hairy above and markedly so beneath

Main leaf divisions (pinnae)—numerous, divided (usually pinnately compound)

Smallest leaf-divisions (pinnules)—with margins entire, notched, cleft, or sometimes again divided, of 2 kinds similar in appearance: (1) "seed"-producing, and (2) not "seed"-producing

Leafstalk—usually solitary, erect, up to 4 ft. high, stout, dark-colored below but becoming straw-colored above, swollen and with feltlike covering at base, not jointed at point of attachment with rootstock

Fertile pinnule—with a marginal ridge beneath, from which a row (linear sorus) of stalked "seed" cases (sporangia) grows, both ridge and sorus covered by a narrow feltlike double membrane (indusium) partly formed by curved-under edge of leaf

Sporangia—microscopic in size but so numerous that they appear as brown masses of "rust", each with incomplete vertical ring of thick-walled, water-absorbing cells by which sporangium opens to discharge the "seed" (spores)

Rootstock—deep underground, cordlike, woody, dark-colored, extensive, often much branched

Roots—numerous, fibrous, wiry, dark-colored

Above ground the plant consists of but a single, very large leaf (frond) which has a leafstalk (stipe) below and a very much divided leaf blade above. As in all ferns, no flowers are produced.

[1] Of western authors.

Bracken (*Pteridium aquilinum*), a perennial fern, is represented in the West only in the variety *pubescens*. That variety, usually known as western bracken, very closely resembles bracken, save for its fine, silky hairs, especially on the under surfaces of the leaves (fronds).

Western bracken is widely distributed, occurring in all the far Western States and ranging from Alaska and British Columbia to Montana and southward to Mexico and California. It probably grows in greatest abundance and attains its maximum development in the Douglas fir regions west of the Cascade Mountains of Washington and Oregon. It is also very abundant in parts of Idaho and California. In altitude it ranges from near sea level in the Pacific Northwest up to about 10,000 feet in Colorado.

Western bracken grows in both moist and fairly dry sites, although it seems to prefer deep, rich, moist soils. It occurs underneath stands of timber such as Douglas fir, aspen, and ponderosa pine and grows in openings and parks among the timbered and wooded areas throughout the western mountains. In places in the Pacific Northwest it occurs in extensive dense patches on burns and cut-over areas, which it quickly invades, and also in openings, and along roadsides and field borders. When the bracken cover dries up during the late summer and fall it often constitutes a very serious fire hazard. The plant invades hay and other cultivated fields and often becomes a serious weed pest, which is difficult to eradicate because of its persistent, wiry, and extensive underground stems, a small portion of which, if left, can give rise to new plants.

As range forage western bracken is usually considered worthless or of distinctly minor importance. Its palatability ordinarily ranges from zero to poor. However, under some circumstances, particularly after frosts in the fall, it is occasionally grazed with as much as fair relish by all classes of livestock.

Lawrence [2] states that horses sometimes acquire a taste for it. When eaten in quantity it is poisonous, at least to cattle and horses. He considers western bracken to be the chief cause of livestock poisoning in western Oregon. He further reports to the effect that, although the plant has been known since pioneer days in western Oregon to be poisonous to horses, causing fern staggers, there is very little good evidence that horses or other livestock are commonly poisoned by this fern on the range or in the pasture. Losses of horses from this disease are, rather, due to feeding them hay which contains about one-third or more of western bracken. These losses are greater in dry seasons, apparently due to shortage of good hay, and are heaviest following the haying season, although, of course, ferny hay may be dangerous at any time of year.

The poison responsible for fern staggers is in the leaves, or fronds, and is not due to the so-called rust (masses of spores) found on the under sides of the leaves. In many parts of the world the young fronds of bracken are boiled and the rootstocks roasted for food. Such poisonous principles as the plant possesses appear to be effectively dissipated by the application of heat. This fern has special astringent properties and is said by some authors to have the property of killing tapeworms.

Western bracken reproduces by two methods, both of which are very effective. As before-mentioned, the widely creeping underground stems (rootstocks, or rhizomes) send up new leaves (fronds) at various places along their length. Thus this fern is able to form dense patches over rather extensive areas. It also reproduces by "seed" (spores), which are produced from July to September in large, brown, powdery masses along the turned-under (revolute, or retrorse) margins of the lower surfaces of the fronds. The individual spore is microscopic in size, and so light that large numbers of them can be borne for great distances by the wind. The young seedling plant, often established far from its parent fern, begins very shortly to produce rootstocks of its own.

The fern genus *Pteridium*, to which western bracken belongs, is included by some botanists in the larger, Old World brake genus (*Pteris*). Bracken is a widely distributed genus of six or eight species, three or four of which occur in North America.

---

[2] Lawrence, W. E. THE PRINCIPAL STOCK-POISONING PLANTS OF OREGON. Oreg. Agr. Expt. Sta. Bull. 187, 42 pp., illus. 1922.

AMERICAN PASQUEFLOWER
Pulsatil la ludovicia'na

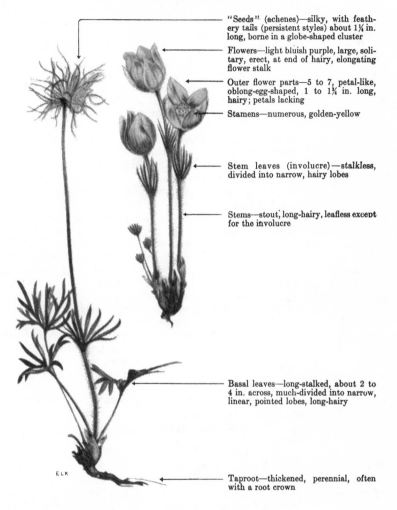

"Seeds" (achenes)—silky, with feathery tails (persistent styles) about 1¼ in. long, borne in a globe-shaped cluster

Flowers—light bluish purple, large, solitary, erect, at end of hairy, elongating flower stalk

Outer flower parts—5 to 7, petal-like, oblong-egg-shaped, 1 to 1¾ in. long, hairy; petals lacking

Stamens—numerous, golden-yellow

Stem leaves (involucre)—stalkless, divided into narrow, hairy lobes

Stems—stout, long-hairy, leafless except for the involucre

Basal leaves—long-stalked, about 2 to 4 in. across, much-divided into narrow, linear, pointed lobes, long-hairy

Taproot—thickened, perennial, often with a root crown

ELK

American pasqueflower, the State flower of South Dakota, is a perennial herb, with attractive, light bluish purple, tuliplike blossoms. It is one of those plants which, due to honest differences of opinion among botanists, has been named and renamed. However, there is a general consensus of opinion among present-day botanists that *Anemo'ne ludovicia'na, A. pa'tens nuttalia'na, A. pa'tens wolfgangia'na, Pulsati'lla hirsutis'sima,* and *P. pa'tens* are all synonyms of *P. ludovicia'na.* This species occurs from Alaska to Washington, Utah, New Mexico, Texas, Illinois, Wisconsin, and Alberta, and has a wide altitudinal range (about 4,000 to 10,000 feet). At the higher elevations, it appears on exposed, sunny slopes, but at lower altitudes, it occurs both in the open and in the shade of trees and shrubs, being especially characteristic of open stands of ponderosa pine.

This species contains the poisonous drug, anemonin,[1] and is listed by Pammel [2] [3] as one of the poisonous range plants. However, there is no record, apparently, of any livestock losses from it. Its palatability is relatively low, and it produces but a small amount of herbage, which matures and largely desiccates by midsummer and ordinarily is only slightly grazed.

The Indians use the crushed leaves of American pasqueflower as a counter-irritant in the treatment of rheumatism and similar diseases; the leaves are applied as a poultice, but if left in contact with the skin long enough will cause blistering.[4] Although the dried herbage of this species is sometimes used as a source of the drug, pulsatilla, the official source of that compound is the dried herbage of Old World species, especially the European pasqueflower (*P. vulgaris,* syn. *Anemone pulsatilla*). The plants are collected shortly after blooming and carefully dried. The material loses its medicinal value if preserved much longer than 1 year. The drug, a violent irritant, causes vomiting and purging with pain, tremors, and collapse, when taken in sufficient quantity. Its chief value is as a counter-irritant. If used internally, it was supposed to exert a powerful effect on the genital organs, but this is somewhat doubtful.[1]

American pasqueflower is one of the first plants to bloom in the spring, which inspired some unknown poet to write:

> When vernal warmth the boreal airs restrain,
> Pasqueflower jewels with gold and Heaven's blue
> The dress, which earth begins to then renew.

The actual time of flowering depends upon location, but, usually, the large hairy buds on their stout, short, furry stems, appear soon after the snow melts. Occasional flowers are produced in the fall. Although the flowering period is short, the plants are readily identifiable until the seed is dropped, as the fruit heads, borne at the top

---

[1] Wood, H. C., Remington, J. P., and Sadtler, S. P., assisted by Lyons, A. B., and Wood, H. C., Jr. THE DISPENSATORY OF THE UNITED STATES OF AMERICA, BY DR. GEO. B. WOOD AND DR. FRANKLIN BACHE. Ed. 19, thoroughly rev. and largely rewritten . . . 1,947 pp. Philadelphia and London. 1907.

[2] Pammel, L. H. A MANUAL OF POISONOUS PLANTS CHIEFLY OF EASTERN NORTH AMERICA, WITH BRIEF NOTES ON ECONOMIC AND MEDICINAL PLANTS . . . 2 pts., illus. Cedar Rapids, Iowa. 1910–11.

[3] Pammel, L. H. POISONOUS PLANTS OF THE RANGE. Ames Forester 1 : 33–[43], illus. 1913.

[4] Gilmore, M. R. USES OF PLANTS BY THE INDIANS OF THE MISSOURI RIVER REGION. U. S. Bur. Amer. Ethnol. Rept. (1911–12) 33 : 45–154, illus. 1919. (Reprinted, 1919.)

of the lengthened stems, are fluffy, feathery balls containing numerous small seeds. American pasqueflower, "elected queen of flower land by the legislature of South Dakota, need never fear to stand in any flower company, however distinguished, however beautiful, however charming." [5]

This plant is the only species of *Pulsatilla* in the eastern and southern part of its range, but from Montana westward to Washington and northward to Alaska, it may be confused with western pasqueflower (*P. occidenta'lis*). Western pasqueflower ranges from Alaska to Montana and California and is the only *Pulsatilla* occurring in the latter State. It differs from American pasqueflower chiefly in having somewhat smaller, lighter-colored (frequently white) flowers. Furthermore, the involucral leaves of western pasqueflower are lobed or divided two or three times into short, narrow lobes, whereas the involucral leaves of American pasqueflower are generally divided into a number of long, narrow lobes. These two species are the only ones in North America, but about 16 other species are found in the north temperate and subarctic regions of Europe and Asia.

Part of the name, pasqueflower, is derived from pasque, the old form of pasch, the feast of the passover, hence Easter. Some authors report that the name was adopted because, before the calendar was revised, these were the most abundant flowers at Easter time; others that a dye for coloring Easter eggs was obtained from them. The generic name, *Pulsatilla*, is the diminutive of the Latin *pulsatio*, meaning, a knocking or beating; its significance is uncertain, although it may refer to the throbbing caused by the irritation of poultices made from these plants.

Although pasqueflower is the common name most widely used, such other appellations as April-fools, Easter-flower, hartshorn, headache-plant, Mayflower, rocklily, wild-crocus, and windflower have variously designated this species. The large downy-hairy buds suggest baby fowl to children who often call them goslings. The Dakota Indians dub the pasqueflower *hakshi-chekpa-walicka*, meaning twin-flower, because usually each plant bears just two flowering stalks.[2] This may be misleading, as although it is possible that two stems are produced more often than any other number, plants with only one stem or with several stems are not uncommon. In Great Britain pasqueflowers are often called Danesblood, due to an early tradition that these plants first appeared on battlefields stained with the blood of invading Danish warriors.

[2] See footnote on preceding page.
[5] [Grosvenor, G. H.] OUR STATE FLOWERS. THE FLORAL EMBLEMS CHOSEN BY THE COMMONWEALTHS. Natl. Geogr. Mag. 31(6) : 481–517, illus. 1917.

COMMON CAMAS

Quama′sia qua′mash, syns. *Camas′sia esculen′ta, C. qua′mash, Q. esculen′ta* [1]

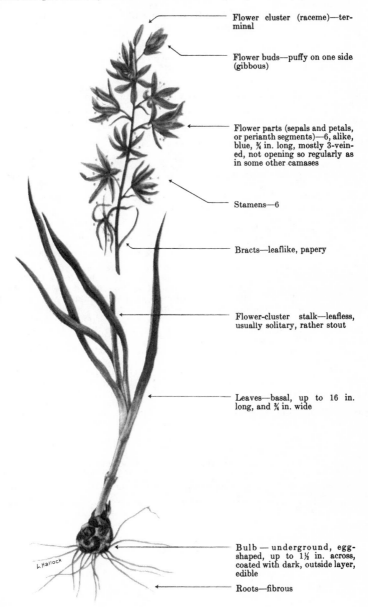

Flower cluster (raceme)—terminal

Flower buds—puffy on one side (gibbous)

Flower parts (sepals and petals, or perianth segments)—6, alike, blue, ¾ in. long, mostly 3-veined, not opening so regularly as in some other camases

Stamens—6

Bracts—leaflike, papery

Flower-cluster stalk—leafless, usually solitary, rather stout

Leaves—basal, up to 16 in. long, and ¾ in. wide

Bulb — underground, egg-shaped, up to 1½ in. across, coated with dark, outside layer, edible

Roots—fibrous

L. Hallock

---

[1] *Q. esculen′ta* Raf., not (Ker) Coville.

Common camas is a perennial, bulbous herb of the lily family, 8 to 24 inches high, ranging from British Columbia to western Montana, Utah, and California. It often occurs in great abundance in moist mountain meadows in the spring but is less common on damp grassy flats and slopes, and in the drier portions of swampy areas.

During the spring the palatability of camas is fair or fairly good, occasionally good, for sheep and cattle. Such game as elk, caribou, and moose, frequently crop camas early in the season. The edible, oval, tuliplike bulbs of common camas were formerly a very important food of the northwestern Indians and are still thus used to some extent. Many of the early western explorers, voyageurs, and missionaries have written interesting accounts about this plant. For example, de Smet[2] reports:

> I cannot pass over in silence the camash root, and the peculiar manner in which it is prepared. It is abundant, and, I may say, is the queen root of this clime. It is a small, white, vapid onion, when removed from the earth, but becomes black and sweet when prepared for food. The women arm themselves with long, crooked sticks, to go in search of the camash. After having procured a certain quantity of these roots, by dint of long and painful labor, they make an excavation in the earth from 12 to 15 inches deep, and of proportional diameter, to contain the roots. They cover the bottom with closely cemented pavement, which they make red hot by means of a fire. After having carefully withdrawn all the coals, they cover the stones with grass or wet hay; then place a layer of camash, another of wet hay, a third of bark overlaid with mold, whereon is kept a glowing fire for 50, 60, and sometimes 70 hours. The camash thus acquires a consistency equal to that of the jujube. It is sometimes made into loaves of various dimensions. It is excellent, especially when boiled with meat; if kept dry, it can be preserved a long time.

Granville Stuart[3] writes that the Snake Indians call this plant *Pah-see-go*, meaning water, or swamp sego, and that the bulb has

> A sweet gummy taste, and is very nutritious. * * * the Indians dig it, cook it in kettles, and dry it, when it becomes very hard, and will keep for years if kept dry. It is also very good boiled when freshly dug. * * * It is very abundant in Oregon, and was an important article of food to the first settlers. Hence, they derive their sobriquet of "camas eaters", "camas" being the name that the root is known by among the whites.

Prof. Blankinship[4] states the Indians made long trips after these bulbs which they stored for winter use; the bulbs were dug after the plants had bloomed; baking improved their flavor. The Flathead Indians called the plant *Etwoi*.

Dr. Frederick V. Coville[5] of the Bureau of Plant Industry, United States Department of Agriculture, has straightened out the complicated synonymy of this plant, the confusion having arisen largely from the fact that the specific name *esculenta* (*-um*) has been applied both to this species and to a very different eastern camas.

Leichtlin camas (*Quama'sia leichtlin'ii*, syn. *Camas'sia leichtlin'ii*), a common species which occurs from Vancouver Island to Sierra County, Calif., is replaced immediately eastward by the very closely related Suksdorf camas (*Q. suksdor'fii*), which represents a different botanical section of the genus, with flowers more regular, often larger, the petallike flower segments twisted together (instead of separately) over the fruit, and the podstalks spreading rather than erect. Its palatability is similar to that of common camas and the bulbs are edible.

---

[2] Smet, P. J. de. OREGON MISSIONS AND TRAVELS OVER THE ROCKY MOUNTAINS, IN 1845–46. 408 pp., illus. New York. 1847.

[3] Stuart, G. MONTANA AS IT IS; BEING A GENERAL DESCRIPTION OF ITS RESOURCES, BOTH MINERAL AND AGRICULTURAL, INCLUDING A COMPLETE DESCRIPTION OF THE FACE OF THE COUNTRY, ITS CLIMATE, ETC. 175 pp. New York. 1865.

[4] Blankinship, J. W. NATIVE ECONOMIC PLANTS OF MONTANA. Mont. Agr. Expt. Sta. Bull. 56, 36 pp. 1905.

[5] Coville, F. V. THE TECHNICAL NAME OF THE CAMAS PLANT. Biol. Soc. Wash. Proc. 11 : 61–65. 1897.

CAMASES

Quama'sia spp., syn. *Camas'sia spp.*

This small North American genus of the lily family is composed of about six species, which with a single exception are confined to the far West. The northwestern Indians are reputed to have named these plants quamash, which later was changed to camash and then camas. The plants are often called blue camas, to distinguish them from the poisonous, greenish- or whitish-flowered deathcamases (*Zygadenus* spp.). Other names include swamp-sego and wild-hyacinth. Certain mountain and foothill ranges which are wet in the spring· are so blue with camas that the distant observer mistakes them for a lake. This optical illusion is apparent only when the flowers are in bloom.

The palatability of camases varies from fair to fairly good, occasionally good for sheep. On the high summer ranges camases are little grazed because they bloom, dry up, and disappear before the sheep are moved to those ranges. Camases occasionally grow on sites too wet for sheep. If given a choice, horses and cattle do not ordinarily graze camas, but they frequently eat these plants along with other meadow forage. Camases are not objectionable when cured in mixed native hay.

The coated bulbs of Cusick camas (*Q. cusickii*) are said to be nauseating, but the bulbs of all the other camases apparently are edible. Several species of *Quamasia* have long been cultivated as ornamentals both in Europe and this country. The long clusters of large, rich blue flowers are beautiful but fade quickly.

The camases are perennial herbs of the lily family, from coated bulbs. Their stalks, leafless or with leaflike bracts, grow up to 2 feet in height. The long narrow leaves rise from the base of the plant. The showy, blue, purplish, or nearly white flowers, which are persistent after withering, are borne in long terminal clusters and appear chiefly from May to early July. Each flower is composed of two series of three similar, separate, and not united parts, or segments (three sepals; three petals). The pollen-sacs of the six stamens are attached by their centers to the supporting stalks and thus are freely swinging; they do not protrude from the flowers. The relatively large (often about three-fourths of an inch long), more or less egg-shaped (ovoid) podlike fruit (capsule) is three-angled, three-celled, and contains several shining black seeds in each cavity.

PLANTAINLEAF BUTTERCUP

Ranun'culus alismaefo'lius, syn. *R. calthaeflo'rus*

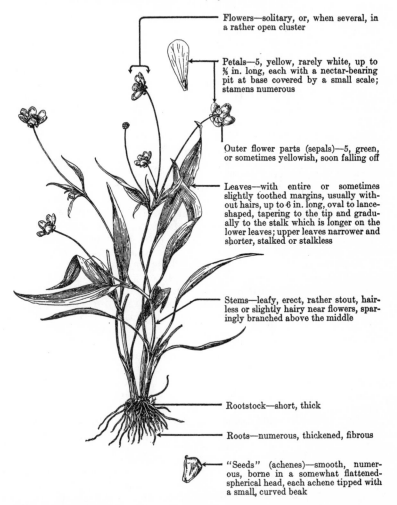

Flowers—solitary, or, when several, in a rather open cluster

Petals—5, yellow, rarely white, up to ⅜ in. long, each with a nectar-bearing pit at base covered by a small scale; stamens numerous

Outer flower parts (sepals)—5, green, or sometimes yellowish, soon falling off

Leaves—with entire or sometimes slightly toothed margins, usually without hairs, up to 6 in. long, oval to lance-shaped, tapering to the tip and gradually to the stalk which is longer on the lower leaves; upper leaves narrower and shorter, stalked or stalkless

Stems—leafy, erect, rather stout, hairless or slightly hairy near flowers, sparingly branched above the middle

Rootstock—short, thick

Roots—numerous, thickened, fibrous

"Seeds" (achenes)—smooth, numerous, borne in a somewhat flattened-spherical head, each achene tipped with a small, curved beak

Plaintainleaf buttercup is one of the more common and widely distributed buttercups in the mountains of the Western States, occurring from British Columbia to western Wyoming, Colorado, Arizona, and northern California. The purport of the common and specific names is practically similar: *alismaefolius* means like the foliage of the aquatic genus *Alisma*, whose species have plantainlike leaves and are known as waterplantains.

Plantainleaf buttercup is one of the first plants to appear in the spring, normally growing very rapidly and maturing by midsummer. It inhabits moist to wet sites, and even exists in shallow water, although the soil may become very dry after the plants complete growth. It is most common in meadows, flats, and parks and on open stream banks, but it also grows on open slopes.

The largest plants and the most dense stands are found in the deep, black loams of flats and meadows; when growing on less fertile and on stony soils, the individual plants are smaller and generally scattered. Mostly it grows in full sunlight, only a few scattered plants occurring in the shade of trees, such as lodgepole pine, which encircle the open sites where the species grows. It is a plant of the mountains, being practically limited to elevations from the ponderosa pine belt to timberline. In the wetter sites it is likely to occur in pure stand; in the better drained areas it is frequently associated with dandelions, clovers, and bluegrasses.

Although plantainleaf buttercup varies in forage value according to locality, it is nowhere in high esteem. Use of this species is limited due to its somewhat acrid taste, which doubtless accounts for its low palatability, and to its extremely early growth, since the plants often mature and practically disappear from the range before the major forage plants are fully developed. It is perhaps most valuable in Colorado, where it is considered fair for cattle and good for sheep. In Utah, the species is fair for cattle and sheep, but in the Northwest and in California it rates as poor for cattle and fair for sheep. However, deer, and possibly elk also, crop plantainleaf buttercup extensively, probably because this species is one of the earliest herbaceous plants available on the range. Studies by one of the authors of this handbook on the Kaibab Plateau, northern Arizona, indicate that this plant is good forage for mule deer.

Throughout its natural range, plantainleaf buttercup often increases appreciably where overgrazing, erosion, or other factors have depleted the original plant cover of good forage species, such as bluegrasses and the better sedges. It is more successfully adapted to invade openings in the plant cover than are most plants, as it makes its growth and matures very early and is sparingly grazed because of its low palatability. Even though erosion may have been prevented, the replacement of the normal cover by plantainleaf buttercup indicates that some remedial action, such as reduction of the numbers of livestock, is necessary.

Plantainleaf buttercup, one of the largest of the entire-leaved buttercups, has stems varying from 6 to 20 inches in height, being much taller than the other entire-leaved western species which are usually less than 8 inches high. The bright and shiny yellow flowers appear in May and June. When the plants are numerous and in blossom, their attractive yellow provides a pleasing landscape effect. However, the petals are soon lost, the achenes mature, and the succulent stems and leaves become dry, brown, and brittle. The plants soon start to disintegrate and by late summer the aerial portions have practically vanished from the range.

BUTTERCUPS (Ranun'culus spp.)

The buttercups, often called crowfoots, compose a large genus of from 275 to 300 species belonging to the buttercup family (Ranunculaceae). The common name buttercup comes from the fancied resemblance of the shiny yellow flowers to a cup of butter. The local name crowfoot alludes to the similarity in leaf shape of some species to the foot of a crow. The generic name *Ranunculus* is a Latin word, diminutive of *rana*, a frog, and means little frog; some species growing in wet places where frogs are found.

Although certain species will survive in moderately dry sites, the buttercups are essentially plants of moist and wet sites, and are widely distributed in the temperate and cool regions of the world. They are annual or perennial herbs, having alternate, lobed, divided, or entire leaves often with a variety of leaf shapes on the same plant. The flower parts are not constant, the outer ones (sepals), which soon fall off, are mostly five. The petals also are commonly 5 in number, but may be up to 15, and rarely as few as 1 or 3. The petals are yellow, or, in a few species, white and at the base are provided with a nectar pit covered by a scale or with a scale only. There are numerous stamens and the many, usually beaked, seeds (achenes) usually form a conspicuous cone or head at the tip of the flower stalk.

Although widespread, the buttercups are seldom important forage plants for domestic livestock. Practically all species are low in palatability, and the majority of them complete growth and disappear from the range before midsummer. However, most species are of considerable value as deer and elk forage, these animals commonly using the range early when buttercups are most palatable. All species have a more or less acrid juice. A few of the more notably acrid species, such as tall buttercup (*R. acris*), and especially rogue buttercup, or cursed crowfoot (*R. sceleratus*), are poisonous.[1] Creeping spearwort (*R. flammula reptans*) may also be poisonous as the species, lesser spearwort (*R. flammula*), which occurs in England, has been shown to be fatal to cattle and horses.[2] Long (*op. cit.*) reports that, in England, the poisonous properties of buttercup vary with the species, the part of the plant, and the season of the year. In the early spring, he states, but little of the poisonous principle is present and some species are not at all poisonous; the flowers are the most poisonous part, then the leaves, and the stem. The toxic principle is volatile and is dissipated in drying, so that buttercups are harmless in hay. The action is chiefly that of an irritant, raising blisters on the skin; when eaten by livestock these species cause inflammation of the mouth and throat and even gastritis, which may prove fatal.

A number of species, chiefly European and Asiatic, have been cultivated as ornamentals. Through breeding and selection, chiefly of

[1] Wood, H. C., Remington, J. P., and Sadtler, S. P., assisted by Lyons, A. B., and Wood, H. C., Jr. THE DISPENSATORY OF THE UNITED STATES OF AMERICA, BY DR. GEO. B. WOOD AND DR. FRANKLIN BACHE. Ed. 19, thoroughly rev. and largely rewritten ... 1,947 pp. Philadelphia and London. 1907.
[2] Long, H. C. PLANTS POISONOUS TO LIVESTOCK. 119 pp., illus. Cambridge. 1917.

Persian buttercup (*R. asiaticus*), double flowers up to 2 inches wide and practically every shade except blue have been developed.

Many buttercups are widely distributed in the mountains of the West. One species with entire leaves, *R. alismellus*, closely resembles plantainleaf buttercup and is sometimes considered a variety of it. Macauley buttercup (*R. macauleyi*), of very high elevations in Colorado and New Mexico, has slightly toothed leaves but is of particular interest because the outer flower parts (sepals) are conspicuously black-hairy, making an interesting contrast to the large, bright yellow petals. The common, sagebrush buttercup (*R. glaberrimus*) and ivy buttercup, or seaside crowfoot (*R. cymbalaria*, syn. *Halerpestes cymbalaria*) have very broad or almost round basal leaves, with the edges indented into few to many shallow lobes. Sagebrush buttercup is 2 to 6 inches high but is such an early plant that it is mostly gone before livestock reach the range. The small ivy buttercup is interesting because it can reproduce by running stems, like the strawberry. The largest of the more common buttercups in the mountains of the West have all the leaves deeply divided. The largest, great buttercup (*R. maximus*) is a stout plant, sometimes reaching a height of 4 feet; Bongard buttercup (*R. bongardi*) and western buttercup (*R. occidentalis*) do not, as a rule, attain a height of over 2 feet. Water buttercup (*R. aquatilis*, syn. *Batrachium aquatile*) has finely dissected leaves and, as the name suggests, lives in the water generally completely submerged except for its floating white flowers. It is perhaps preferable to place it in the related genus *Batrachium*.

NIGGERHEAD

Rudbeck'ia occidenta'lis

Flower heads—short-conic to columnar, usually solitary, on long stalks at ends of stems or stem branches

Inner or upper (disk) flowers of the head—numerous, brownish to purplish, short-tubular, perfect, seed-producing, each with a chaffy bract (palea) loosely clasping it; outer (ray) flowers of the head absent

Bracts—in a series (involucre) surrounding base of flower head, overlapping, usually in 2 rows, leaflike, oblong or lance-shaped, up to nearly 1 in. long, spreading

Leaves—alternate, simple, egg-shaped, tapering at tip, mostly rounded or somewhat heart-shaped at base, entire or irregularly and sparingly toothed, hairless or minutely rough-hairy; lower leaves stalked, the stalks wing-margined; upper leaves stalkless

Stems—stout, occasionally 8 ft. high, nearly hairless, ridged, often clustered at base, usually simple

Roots—coarse, woody, fibrous, from a thickened, often branched and distorted crown

"Seeds" (achenes)—thickened, somewhat angled, each tipped by a white-papery, short but deeply and minutely toothed, persistent crown (pappus)

Niggerhead is a coarse perennial herb of the aster or sunflower (composite) family. It is sometimes called western coneflower, the specific name *occidentalis* meaning western, and the flower heads being conspicuously cone-shaped. The large amount of herbage produced by the individual plant, and its local abundance over relatively extensive areas, together with its wide distribution, occurring in all the western States with the exception of the Southwest, render niggerhead the most important range species of this genus.

Niggerhead grows from the ponderosa pine zone up to and including the spruce zone, usually in moist, but not saturated soil, but sometimes in moderately dry, poor, shallow soil. Open or shaded streambanks, hillsides, and well-drained mountain swales, open parks, and partially shaded slopes in open aspen stands are its favorite sites. One of its most common plant associates is false-hellebore. Throughout most of its range it grows scatteringly, but it occasionally covers a few square rods densely, and in certain localities it is abundant over extensive areas. It is perhaps most common in Utah, where it is fairly prevalent throughout the aspen zone. Before the normal plant cover on certain ranges in the Wasatch Mountains of central Utah was disturbed by continued past overgrazing, with resultant erosion and soil impoverishment, niggerhead was not so extensive or abundant as it is now. These conditions resulted in the decrease in density of the more palatable species, and greatly accelerated the invasion of these lands by niggerhead.

Although niggerhead is low in palatability or even worthless on most ranges, on some sheep or common use areas it is fair or occasionally fairly good. Furthermore, in spite of its usual low palatability, it often supplies considerable forage by virtue of its commonness, large size, and abundant, large leaves. Even when young the stems are too tough and woody for consumption by any class of livestock. Cattle and horses do not relish the flower heads as do sheep, but those parts are often above the reach of sheep. Only where there is a dearth of other forage, as on overstocked ranges, do sheep eat the leaves sufficiently to strip the plants quite bare of them. Niggerhead is most likely to be grazed when growing in mixture with other plants.

In the absence of better plants, niggerhead gives a measure of protection against erosion and floods, although it is not nearly so effective as the normal climax plant cover of bunchgrasses which it has replaced. Whatever protective value it thus affords, is largely due to the deep-growing, coarse, woody, and fibrous roots and to the rapidly formed basal bunches of many-stemmed leafy shoots from the rootcrown, which often attain a diameter up to 1 or 2 feet in the older plants.

The stems of niggerhead are unbranched except occasionally near the top. The leaves vary considerably in size, but average about 2½ inches wide and 5½ inches long on the main body of the plant. The slightly winged leafstalks (petioles) of the basal leaves are several inches long and become increasingly shorter near the top where the leaves become stalkless (sessile). Near the ends of the stems, the leaves are fewer and much reduced in size, making the conelike, dark brown flower heads at the apex very conspicuous. These heads start as small buttons, which gradually elongate until at blossoming time, about the middle of August, they attain full growth and may then become 2 inches long. Marked variations in size of the plant and its parts may occur, due to site conditions.

CONEFLOWERS

Rudbeck'ia spp.

This native North American genus was named *Rudbeckia* by the famous Swedish botanist Linnaeus in honor of the two Professors Rudbeck, father and son, who had been his predecessors at the University of Upsala.

About six or seven species of coneflower grow naturally on western ranges and of these several are cultivated as garden flowers. Among these ornamental species are black-eyed-susan (*R. hirta*), a biennial common in Colorado and eastward, and cutleaf coneflower (*R. laciniata*), a horticultural variety of which is the well-known goldenglow. Cutleaf coneflower naturally extends from Montana south to Arizona and New Mexico and eastward to the Atlantic seaboard. Unlike niggerhead, which has no ray flowers, most of the other species of *Rudbeckia*, including black-eyed-susan and cutleaf coneflower, have conspicuous petallike yellow or orange rays.

With the exception of niggerhead, *Rudbeckia* species are seldom of any importance as forage plants, their palatability usually ranging from worthless to poor. However, in parts of Colorado and Wyoming black-eyed-susan is accounted fair feed for cattle and fairly good for sheep, a condition which is probably directly associated with a paucity of better feed and may indicate locally impoverished soil conditions.

RUSSIAN-THISTLE

Sal'sola pes'tifer, syns. *S. ka'li tenuifo'lia*, "*S. ka'li tra'gus*", and "*S. tra'gus*" [1]

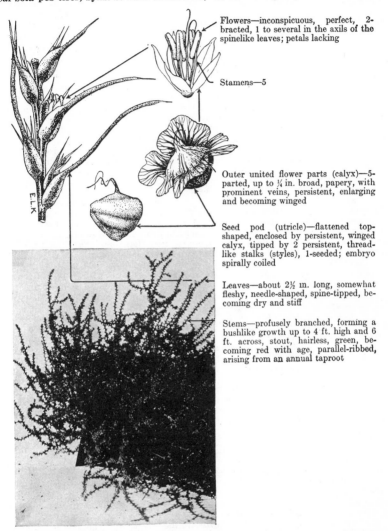

Flowers—inconspicuous, perfect, 2-bracted, 1 to several in the axils of the spinelike leaves; petals lacking

Stamens—5

Outer united flower parts (calyx)—5-parted, up to ¼ in. broad, papery, with prominent veins, persistent, enlarging and becoming winged

Seed pod (utricle)—flattened top-shaped, enclosed by persistent, winged calyx, tipped by 2 persistent, thread-like stalks (styles), 1-seeded; embryo spirally coiled

Leaves—about 2½ in. long, somewhat fleshy, needle-shaped, spine-tipped, becoming dry and stiff

Stems—profusely branched, forming a bushlike growth up to 4 ft. high and 6 ft. across, stout, hairless, green, becoming red with age, parallel-ribbed, arising from an annual taproot

Russian-thistle, one of the numerous annual plants known as tumbleweed, is actually not a thistle but a member of the goosefoot family (Chenopodiaceae), closely related to lambsquarters, saltbushes, and the cultivated beet and spinach. Russian-thistle, a native of Eurasia, was a serious pest in the Russian wheat fields many years before it spread to the United States. This plant was probably introduced into Bon Homme County, S. Dak., in 1886 as an impurity in flaxseed imported from Europe.[2] The few plants produced in-

[1] Of United States authors, not L.
[2] Dewey, L. H. THE RUSSIAN THISTLE AND OTHER TROUBLESOME WEEDS IN THE WHEAT REGION OF MINNESOTA AND NORTH AND SOUTH DAKOTA. U. S. Dept. Agr. Farmers' Bull. 10, 16 pp., illus. 1893.

creased slowly and almost unnoticed for several years, but after becoming acclimated spread rapidly, and now this weed is widely distributed over the western United States and Canada.

Russian-thistle grows from sea level up to 8,500 feet, doing best on high, dry land if not overly crowded by other plants. It does not ordinarily occur in sloughs or lowlands, and makes no progress on the native prairie, except where the sod has been broken by cultivation, overgrazing, prairie-dog holes, etc. Russian-thistle flourishes in rich, moist soils, but does not commonly occur there because it cannot stand crowding by other plants. This weed is a salt-resistant plant, and hence grows well, though not exclusively, on alkali soils. It often forms pure stands on cultivated or overgrazed areas.

On early spring ranges this species rates as fair forage for all classes of livestock. However, after the plant matures and the sharp spines form, it is worthless. It cannot be considered as a desirable forage plant on mountain ranges because livestock will not eat it if other and better forage is obtainable. On winter ranges it is often used by livestock after softening by winter storms. Russian-thistle is quite drought-resistant and is extremely useful in the Western Prairie States during drought years. In many of the drought-stricken areas, this plant has been used successfully as emergency feed to prevent livestock from starving. If cut when in bloom, before the sharp spines form, Russian-thistle makes good emergency hay. Even where cut after the spines have hardened, it may be chopped up and fed as fodder or silage. Russian-thistle is eaten readily when ensiled, especially if mixed with alfalfa or grains. If fed alone, especially during the fall, this plant has a very laxative effect, which may make it a source of danger, particularly to cows in weak condition. This can be overcome by supplemental feeding with grain hay, first-cutting alfalfa, corn fodder, or straw.[3][4][5] According to chemical analyses Russian-thistle contains more protein and carbohydrates than clover and as much or more ash or mineral salts than alfalfa or prairie hay, but it is less palatable and digestible than alfalfa. Feeding tests have shown that Russian-thistle, ground into fodder, was 93.9 percent as valuable as cane fodder for fattening lambs. It is reported[6] that this weed is a favorite host plant upon which the sugar beet webworm lays its eggs. The worms migrate from it to the beets.

Barilla, an impure soda, is obtained from burning plants of *Salsola* and the closely related genera *Salicornia* and *Chenopodium*. It is rather extensively imported into this country from Spain and other Mediterranean countries.

Russian-thistle is an annual, produced from a small seed and growing as high as 4 feet, with profuse branches, often forming a dense bushlike plant from 2 to 6 feet in diameter. When young, the plant is very tender and juicy, with small, narrow, green leaves. After it flowers the small leaves wither and fall off and short, stout, spiny leaves form. The plant then increases rapidly in size and sends out hard stiff branches. In lieu of leaves these branches bear three hard, sharp spines, from one-fourth to one-half of an inch long, at intervals of half an inch or less. A small papery flower, at first green, later pink, grows at the base of each cluster of spines. If this flower is carefully examined, a small, coiled, green seed resembling a minute green snail shell is uncovered. After the first frost the exposed parts of Russian-thistle change from dark green to red. Later the plant breaks off and becomes a tumbleweed.

Kali, or prickly glasswort (*S. ka'li*, syn. *S. tra'gus*), a maritime species of Europe and western Asia, naturalized along the seacoasts of the eastern United States, differs from *S. pestifer* chiefly in its shorter, broader (linear or lance-shaped, rather than filiform) leaves, the upper ones, when old, swollen at the base, and larger fruiting calyxes (one-fourth to three-eighths of an inch, instead of one-eighth to one-fourth of an inch, broad). In western botanical literature *S. kali* and *S. pestifer* are much confused; moreover, some botanists prefer to regard Russian-thistle as a variety of *kali*, under the varietal name *S. kali tenuifolia*.

[3] Dickson, W. F. FEEDS FOR WINTERING CATTLE. Mont. Agr. Expt. Sta. Anim. Husb. Circ. 15 : 30–38. [1932.] [Mimeographed.]
[4] Dominion Agriculture Credit Co., Limited. RUSSIAN THISTLE: ITS USE AND CONTROL. 19 pp. Regina, Sask. [1933.]
[5] [Christensen, F. W., Thompson, E. J., and Briggs, H.] LIVESTOCK FEEDING UNDER DROUGHT CONDITIONS. N. Dak. Agr. Col. Ext. Circ. 126, rev., 16 pp., illus. 1935.
[6] Robbins, W. W., and Boyack, B. THE IDENTIFICATION AND CONTROL OF COLORADO WEEDS. Colo. Agr. Expt. Sta. Bull. 251, [126] pp. 1919.

GROUNDSELS, RAGWORTS, AND BUTTERWEEDS

Sene′cio spp.

The genus *Senecio*, species of which are known as groundsels, ragworts, and butterweeds, belongs to the senecio tribe of the aster, or composite family (Asteraceae, or Compositae) and probably comprises a larger number of species—about 2,600 valid species are known—than any other genus of flowering plants.[1] The genus is of world-wide distribution and, although the species native to the United States are mostly herbs, many species in Australia, Central and South America, and in Africa are climbing vines, shrubs or trees; in New Zealand some species are timberline trees. The name *Senecio* is derived from the Latin *senex*, an old man, and seems to refer to the numerous white hairs (pappus) of the seeds (achenes) or, according to certain writers, to the hoariness of the herbage of some of the better known Old World species. The common name, groundsel, which has been accepted by the American Joint Committee on Horticultural Nomenclature[2] for most of the horticultural species of this genus, and which is undoubtedly the name most often applied to the majority of our range species of *Senecio*, is an old English word whose significance is said to be ground swallower, alluding to the luxuriant growth of some of the British species. Ragwort is a term best restricted to *S. jacobaea* and other species with dissected (ragged) leaves. The term "butterweed" refers to the butter-colored flowers and, in range parlance, best applies to certain palatable species, particularly *S. serra* and *S. triangularis*. For the sake of convenience the term "groundsel" is here used to indicate any species of the genus *Senecio*.

Species of *Senecio* are, as a rule, easily recognized by the character of the bracts (involucre) around the flower heads and by the numerous, soft, white hairs (pappus) which crown the seeds. The comparatively few main involucral bracts are flat, occur in one row, and usually are reinforced at the base by an additional row of very short bractlets. The flower heads (yellow in our species) are, as a rule, comparatively small, mostly erect, and borne in more or less flat-topped clusters, or are solitary in a few species. Petallike ray flowers are present in most of the western species, but usually are not numerous. The heads of a few native western species are comparatively large and nodding; some species lack ray flowers.

Possibly 200 species of *Senecio* occur in this country. The genus is well represented in all the Western States, the various species occurring from sea level up to elevations of about 14,000 feet, under practically all conditions of soil moisture from very dry to wet, and in a wide variety of soil types from rocky gravels to fine clays. Some species prefer the shade; others the direct sunlight. On the more moist sites species of *Senecio* frequently grow in patches and form a fairly dense ground cover. Other species are abundant on moderately dry sites, although they do not ordinarily form pure stands. On the whole, *Senecio* ranks among the most common genera of range weeds, its members occurring in greater or less abundance on practically all ranges.

The great size and diversity of the genus *Senecio* is reflected in the wide variation in economic value existing among its numerous range representatives. There is much still to learn as to the forage worth or possible toxic properties of the individual species. Arrowleaf butterweed (*S. triangularis*), Columbia butterweed (*S. columbianus*), and sawtooth butterweed (*S. serra*), three common range species treated separately in this handbook, are characteristic of the better species and rate from fair to fairly good for cattle and horses and from good to very good for sheep. Quite possibly many of the smooth, succulent species of moist sites deserve similarly high palatability ratings. Usually, the species found in moist sites are more succulent and palatable than those of the drier sites. Many species of moderately dry to dry sites

---

[1] Dayton, W. A. KNOWLEDGE OF PROPERTIES AND USES OF GROUNDSELS INCREASING. U. S. Dept. Agr., Forest Worker 9(2) : 16. 1933.
[2] American Joint Committee on Horticultural Nomenclature. STANDARDIZED PLANT NAMES. . . . Prepared by F. L. Olmsted, F. V. Coville, and H. P. Kelsey. 546 pp. Salem, Mass. 1923.

and some succulent species of moist sites are relatively low in palatability, rating poor for cattle and fair for sheep. However, on some of the semi-desert ranges, especially in the Intermountain region, the native species of the groundsel group are more palatable as fall and winter forage, and are of considerable importance on some of the winter sheep ranges. A great many of the species, especially of the shrubbier sort, have distinctly inferior palatability, rating as practically worthless for cattle and poor for sheep.

In addition to the wide variation in palatability in this genus, the difficulty of evaluating its forage value is increased by the fact that some species are poisonous and have occasionally caused losses of livestock. Broom groundsel (*S. spartioi'des*), Riddell groundsel (*S. riddel'lii*), threadleaf groundsel (*S. longilo'bus*, syn. *S. filifo'lius*), and lambstongue groundsel (*S. integer'rimus*), among the western species, are definitely known as poisonous. Cattle and horses are more susceptible to poisoning by these plants than sheep, although sheep have been killed by corral feeding of threadleaf groundsel.[3] Broom groundsel and threadleaf groundsel are treated elsewhere in this handbook. Clawson (*op. cit.*) has shown that threadleaf groundsel is one of the more poisonous of the American species of *Senecio*, and far more likely to cause trouble on the range than lambstongue groundsel. However, since it is seldom grazed, threadleaf groundsel is hardly a source of danger except on depleted or overstocked range.

The symptoms of *Senecio* poisoning vary somewhat with the class of livestock and the species. Clawson[3] and Van Es and associates[4] have noted that usually there is a tendency for horses and cattle to avoid other animals, and to display marked signs of depression, impaired sensibility, yawning, lack of appetite, weakness, uneasiness, as well as an inclination to chew various articles other than food, the tendency to run into and push against objects, and, in the later stages, to engage in almost constant aimless wandering. In some cases a congestion and yellowish discoloration of the mucous membranes develops, usually accompanied by a peculiar, sweetish, sickening odor emanating from the skin, especially about the head, neck, and shoulders. Cattle exhibit quite similar symptoms; sometimes areas of skin evidently irritate the animal as shown by its attempts to rub the affected spots which, on occasion, literally ooze serum. Some animals are constipated; others evidence a mild diarrhea.[3] Clawson[3] reports that the only visible symptoms observed in affected sheep were "depression, weakness, loss of appetite, a more or less jaundiced condition * * * (and) in some instances, evidences of abdominal pain and spasmodic muscular twitching were noted."

Riddell groundsel (*S. riddel'lii*), a smooth perennial herb with leafy, branched stems about 12 to 40 inches high, occurs chiefly on the plains from Wyoming and Nebraska to Texas and New Mexico. Its hairless leaves are divided into narrow, linear segments, and the numerous hairless flower heads, about three-eighths of an inch high, are borne in somewhat flat-topped clusters. The from 12 to 20 main bracts at the base of the flower head are hairless, narrow, somewhat keeled, and pointed, forming a bell-shaped involucre. A few very short, small bractlets are present at the base of the involucre. Its approximately 12 petallike ray flowers are bright yellow and about three-eighths to one-half of an inch long; the body of the seedlike fruits (achenes) is somewhat hairy. Riddell groundsel is the cause of the so-called walking disease of northwest Nebraska.[4]

Lambstongue groundsel (*S. integer'rimus*, syns. *S. dis'par*, *S. exalta'tus*, *S. lu'gens*, *S. perplex'us*) ranges in the sagebrush, piñon, and ponderosa pine belts, from Minnesota to British Columbia, California, and Colorado. It is a variable species, with leafy stems branched above and 12 to 40 inches high. The lower leaves are stalked and vary in shape from reverse-egg-shaped to reverse-lance-shaped, being hairless or sparsely hairy when young and much larger than the stalkless, lance-shaped to linear stem leaves. The flower heads are numerous, about three-eighths to five-eighths of an inch high and nearly as wide, with those of the terminal cluster borne on shorter stalks than those of the lateral

---

[3] Clawson, A. B. THE AMERICAN GROUNDSELS SPECIES OF SENECIO AS STOCK POISONING PLANTS. Vet. Med. 28 (3) : 105–110, illus. 1933.
[4] Van Es, L., Cantwell, L. R., Martin, H. M., and Kramer, J. ON THE NATURE AND CAUSE OF "THE WALKING DISEASE" OF NORTHWESTERN NEBRASKA. NECROBIOSIS ET CIRRHOSIS HEPATIS ENZOOTICA. Nebr. Agr. Expt. Sta. Research Bull. 43, 47 pp., illus. 1929.

clusters. The bracts at the base of the flower head are narrow, long-taper-pointed, and somewhat thick and fleshy, but not thickened or keeled on the back. The petallike ray flowers are about three-eighths of an inch long. The body of the "seeds" is hairless (glabrous) but crowned with bristlelike hairs (pappus) characteristic of all species of *Senecio*. Clawson [3] reports that this species, although poisonous to cattle and horses, apparently does not affect sheep. Furthermore, he confirms the statements of Van Es and associates [4] that lambstongue groundsel probably never causes trouble on the range or in pastures, possibly because the plants appear only when good forage is fairly abundant, and largely mature, and desiccate before other forage becomes scarce. For practical purposes this *Senecio* appears to be dangerous only when abundant in hay areas.

Ragwort (*S. jacobae'a*), a native of Europe, also known as giant ragwort, staggerwort, stinking willie, and tansy ragwort, has become naturalized in northeastern America and other parts of the world. The distribution of this aggressive plant, a menace to cattle wherever it occurs, is extending and it will probably reach the range country eventually if, in fact, it is not there now. In 1906 Pethick [5] published the results of his feeding experiments, demonstrating that this species was the cause of Pictou cattle disease in Canada. Gilruth's investigation [6] in New Zealand showed that Winton disease, a condition affecting both cattle and horses and very similar to Pictou disease, was caused by rag-wort. This species is a hairless or somewhat woolly, perennial herb, with stout, very leafy stems, 2 to 4 feet high, from short, thick rootstocks. The rather finely divided leaves are 2 to 8 inches long and the short-stalked, very numerous flower heads are about one-half to three-fourths of an inch wide. The bracts of the narrowly bell-shaped involucre are linear-lance-shaped, pointed, green or tipped with black. The body of the seedlike fruits developed from the central (disk) flowers is hairy; the bodies of those of the marginal, petallike flowers (rays) are hairless. Ragwort is a nonofficial drug. Decoctions of it were formerly employed as a mouth wash and throat gargle and in the treatment of catarrh and quinsy. The juice was reputedly very good for healing wounds. Other species of *Senecio*, notably common groundsel (*S. vulga'ris*), useful in the treatment of kidney disorders and as an emetic, were also used by the early herbalists.

It is of interest to note that, with the exception of the genus *Baccharis*, certain species of Senecio are the only members of the immense composite family definitely known to contain well-defined alkaloids in appreciable amounts. These alkaloids are rather toxic and produce cumulative effects. [7]

The native species of *Senecio* are little known horticulturally, although some species are occasionally grown as border plants. Among the species most frequently cultivated are silver cineraria (*S. cinera'ria*), of the Mediterranean region, often called dusty miller; cineraria, familiarly known as florists' cineraria (*S. cruen'tus*), of the Canary Islands, with its numerous hybrids; the South African species, purple groundsel (*S. el'egans*) and ivy groundsel (*S. mikanioi'des*), the latter frequently termed German-ivy; velvet groundsel (*S. peta-sitis*), of Mexico, well known as California-geranium, and Uruguay groundsel (*S. pul'cher*). The genera of gardeners known as *Cineraria*, *Jacobaea*, and *Kleinia* belong to the genus *Senecio*.

[3][4] See footnotes on preceding page.
[5] Pethick, W. H. REPORT [ON PICTOU CATTLE DISEASE]. Canada Dept. Agr. Rept. 1904 : 96–99. 1905.
[6] Gilruth, J. A. HEPATIC CIRRHOSIS AFFECTING HORSES AND CATTLE (SO CALLED "WINTON DISEASE"). New Zeal. Dept. Agr., Div. Vet. Sci. Rept. 1902–3 : 228–278. 1903.
[7] Manske, R. H. F. THE ALKALOIDS OF SENECIO SPECIES. I. THE NECINES AND NECIC ACIDS FROM S. RETRORSUS AND S. JACOBAEA. Canad. Jour. Research 5 : 651–659. 1931.

COLUMBIA BUTTERWEED

Sene'cio columbia'nus, syn. *S. atriapicula'tus*

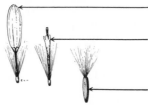

Outside (ray) flowers of head—8 to 12, yellow, petal-like, female, seed-producing

Center (disk) flowers of head—small, yellow, tubular, perfect, seed-producing

"Seed" (achene)—light-colored, the body hairless but tipped by a tuft of numerous, long, soft, white, slender hairs (pappus)

Flower heads—many, erect, usually in a flat-topped end cluster (corymb)

Bracts—in a bell-shaped, 1-rowed series (involucre) around flower head, more than ½ as long as flower head, often with a few small bracts at base; each bract rather thick, lance-shaped, with a triangular, often black tip

Leaves—alternate, thick, usually toothed, variable in shape, shaggy with soft, weak hairs, especially when young; upper leaves smaller than lower leaves, lance-shaped, tapering-pointed, stalkless

Stems—solitary, usually 10 to 24 in. high, white-woolly-hairy especially at base and top and when plant is young

Lower leaves—spatula-shaped, usually rounded at tips, with long, narrowed bases, stalked, with lower part of stalk clasping or sheathing the stem

Roots—numerous, fibrous, rather fleshy, often clustered

Columbia butterweed, sometimes called Columbia groundsel, Columbia senecio, and small butterweed, is a relatively small, leafy, perennial herb. It is fairly characteristic of many of the dry-land species of *Senecio* and, because it is one of the more palatable and common range species, it has been selected for this handbook as illustrative of this group of the large *Senecio* genus. Generally, range men refer to the more palatable species of *Senecio* as butterweeds, apparently alluding to the characteristic butter-colored flowerheads, as well as to the relatively high palatability of such plants for sheep and to their reputed nutritive and fattening properties. The late Dr. E. L. Greene, for many years consulting expert on plant identification for the Forest Service, appears to have named this species *columbianus* after British Columbia, the type locality. As the species is also common in the Columbia River drainage, the English name Columbia butterweed seems appropriate. This species occurs from British Columbia to Saskatchewan, Montana, northern Colorado, Oregon, and possibly also in northern California. It grows chiefly in rather dry soils from the valleys and foothills up to an elevation of approximately 8,000 feet. It is especially characteristic of dry ridges and southern slopes in weed, grass, brush, and ponderosa pine types. Sampson [1] indicates that it occurs up to timberline on the Wallowa National Forest, northeastern Oregon. Although frequently common and sometimes abundant, this plant is generally a secondary species and never grows in dense stands; however, it is an important component of the vegetation of scablands in Oregon.

The average palatability of this weed is fairly good for sheep and poor for cattle. In some localities, particularly in the Pacific Northwest, where Columbia butterweed is often somewhat more succulent than the associated vegetation, it rates as very good sheep forage. Sampson (*op. cit.*) reports that, in the Wallowa region of northeastern Oregon, this species begins growth early and is of value only in the spring, when sheep prefer it to grasses and eat it so ravenously that sometimes opportunity to set seed is lost.

Columbia butterweed is usually from 10 to 24 inches high, but may grow as tall as 3 feet. The leaves on the stem gradually become smaller and more scattered toward the top. Woolly hairs are often prominent at the base and at the top of the young plant. The numerous roots are fibrous, rather fleshy, and often clustered. This species is much smaller and blooms earlier than arrowleaf butterweed (*S. triangularis*).

---

[1] Sampson, A. W. IMPORTANT RANGE PLANTS : THEIR LIFE HISTORY AND FORAGE VALUE. U. S. Dept. Agr. Bull. 545, 63 pp., illus. 1917.

SAWTOOTH BUTTERWEED

Sene'cio ser'ra

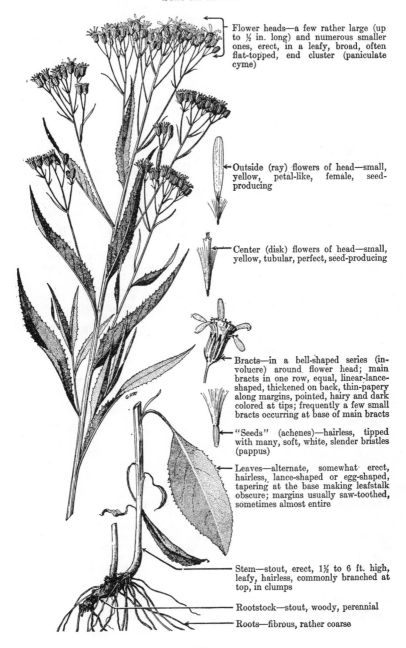

Flower heads—a few rather large (up to ½ in. long) and numerous smaller ones, erect, in a leafy, broad, often flat-topped, end cluster (paniculate cyme)

Outside (ray) flowers of head—small, yellow, petal-like, female, seed-producing

Center (disk) flowers of head—small, yellow, tubular, perfect, seed-producing

Bracts—in a bell-shaped series (involucre) around flower head; main bracts in one row, equal, linear-lance-shaped, thickened on back, thin-papery along margins, pointed, hairy and dark colored at tips; frequently a few small bracts occurring at base of main bracts

"Seeds" (achenes)—hairless, tipped with many, soft, white, slender bristles (pappus)

Leaves—alternate, somewhat erect, hairless, lance-shaped or egg-shaped, tapering at the base making leafstalk obscure; margins usually saw-toothed, sometimes almost entire

Stem—stout, erect, 1½ to 6 ft. high, leafy, hairless, commonly branched at top, in clumps

Rootstock—stout, woody, perennial

Roots—fibrous, rather coarse

Sawtooth butterweed, also known as tall butterweed, and often erroneously called goldenrod, is a tall, leafy perennial of the composite, or sunflower family (Compositae). The specific name *serra* (Latin *serra*, a saw), as well as the common name, refer to the saw-toothed leaves which are characteristic of this plant. Sawtooth butterweed grows in all of the western range States, except possibly Arizona, at altitudes of from 3,000 to 10,000 feet. In the Intermountain region it extends from the sagebrush to the spruce belt, usually being found at elevations between about 5,000 and 9,500 feet; in the central Rocky Mountains it largely occurs between 7,500 and 10,000 feet; in New Mexico it is rare and confined to the highest peaks; in California and the Northwest it chiefly grows between about 3,000 and 7,000 feet. This plant is characteristic of moist but well-drained, rich, sandy, or gravelly loams, but sometimes occurs on drier sites. It occurs on all slopes, apparently without distinction, as well as on level areas. The plant is also common in open-weed types, moist meadows, and in aspen. It may be the dominant element in mixed grass-weed types, where species of bromegrass, wheatgrass, wild-rye, and geranium are its frequent associates.

This species is one of the best forage butterweeds and is probably even more important on the range than the similar and closely related arrowleaf butterweed (*S. triangula′ris*) because it usually grows more abundantly and occurs at somewhat lower elevations. Early in the summer, sheep eat both the stems and leaves but later, as the stems become somewhat woody, only the leaves are consumed. In the Intermountain region, sawtooth butterweed ranks as an excellent forage plant wherever it occurs. It is hardy, leafy, withstands grazing remarkably well, produces a large volume of succulent growth, and is highly palatable to both sheep and cattle, though sheep ordinarily graze it more fully than cattle. Although both sheep and cattle are known to have eaten these plants from the top down one-third or one-half, including the flower heads, the flower and seed heads are, as a rule, left ungrazed; hence, much seed is usually matured. In California and the Pacific Northwest the species is usually regarded as fairly good for sheep but as only a poor to fair cattle weed. Its local abundance and the number of palatable grasses and weeds associated with it are chiefly responsible for the varying esteem in which it is held. Sawtooth butterweed is only rarely touched by horses. It is deemed good forage for deer and elk, especially during the spring and early summer.

In the Intermountain region, where sawtooth butterweed is an important forage plant, it has naturally increased within the past decade, especially on protected ranges. Some of the species' increase in this area, however, is attributable to artificial reseeding which has been conducted on the Uinta [1] and Manti National Forests. The abundant pappus on the copious seeds favors wind dissemination; seed matures from late August to early November.

This species is sometimes confused with goldenrods (*Solidago* spp.) despite that the latter have the bracts of the involucre arranged in several series, in contrast to butterweeds whose bracts are arranged in one series. Sawtooth butterweed differs from the closely related arrowleaf butterweed in that the leaves are lance- or egg-shaped and taper near the base, so that they obscure the leafstalk. Moreover, its leaves are neither square at the base nor triangular- or arrow-shaped as in *S. triangularis*. Typically, the margins of the leaves are sharply saw-toothed, except that the uppermost leaves are occasionally untoothed (entire).

S. ser′ra integrius′cula, a variety of this species with all of the leaves entire or else minutely toothed, and with smaller, narrower, few-flowered heads, is common from eastern Oregon to California, Nevada, and Wyoming, growing along creeks and in other moist places. Kennedy [2] calls it an important forage for sheep in eastern Nevada, where it is grazed from June to August, inclusive. In the early summer, the entire plant is eaten, including the sweet and juicy stems, but later, as they get coarse and woody, the stems are left untouched. The young buds, flowers, and leaves, are eagerly eaten by sheep. The plants are extremely resistive to grazing, and enough seed is produced for natural propagation.

---

[1] Dayton, W. A. KNOWLEDGE OF PROPERTIES AND USES OF GROUNDSELS INCREASING. U. S. Dept. Agr., Forest Worker 9(2) : 16. 1933.
[2] Kennedy, P. B. SUMMER RANGES OF EASTERN NEVADA SHEEP. Nev. Agr. Expt. Sta. Bull. 55, [56] pp., illus. 1903.

ARROWLEAF BUTTERWEED

Sene'cio triangula'ris, syns. *S. sa'liens, S. trigonophyl'lus*

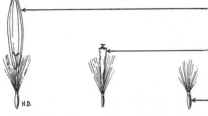

Outside (ray) flowers of head—6 to 12, yellow, petal-like, female, seed-producing

Center (disk) flowers of head—small, yellow, tubular, perfect, seed-producing

"Seeds" (achenes)—hairless except for the tuft at the tip of numerous, long, soft, white, slender hairs (pappus)

Flower heads—several to numerous, erect, about ½ in. high, in an open, often flat-topped, end cluster (cyme)

Bracts—in a bell-shaped, 1-rowed series (involucre) around flower head, equal, broadly linear, thin, with several small bracts at base

Stems—solitary to several, stout, erect, 1 to 6 ft. high, leafy, hairless

Leaves—alternate, triangular or lance-shaped (lower leaves sometimes almost heart-shaped), with usually sharply and evenly toothed margins, abruptly contracted at base, stalked

Rootstock—fleshy, compact, perennial

Roots—fibrous, cordlike

Arrowleaf butterweed, a tall, leafy perennial of the sunflower family (Compositae), is one of the most palatable of the species of groundsels in the western range States. Both the specific and part of the common name allude to the triangular-shaped leaves, and butterweed is appropriate because of the high palatability of the plant whose yellow flowers are the same color as butter. This butterweed is seen from Alaska to Saskatchewan, New Mexico, and California at elevations varying from 1,800 to 11,000 feet, and inhabits areas running from the ponderosa pine belt, through the aspen and spruce belts, to the subalpine zone. Arrowleaf butterweed is particularly abundant at the higher elevations and cooler sites, growing in moist, rich, sandy, or gravelly soils along streams, near springs, or in marshy meadows, where it often forms large, dense patches. In some localities it occurs singly, intermixed with other plants. This plant invariably shuns dry sites. The flowers usually appear during July and August, while the seed ripens in September.

Because of its great succulence, the species is especially relished by sheep, having a palatability rating of from very good to excellent for that class of livestock and from fair to fairly good for cattle. It also ranks as good forage for deer and elk. However, due to the fact that this butterweed grows exclusively in moist or wet sites, and ordinarily is of limited occurrence, its importance is usually limited to those high-mountain ranges where it is locally abundant on the moister sites. During the spring and early summer porcupines commonly feed along the streams, and readily eat the lush leaves of this species.

Sampson[1] found that, on the Wallowa National Forest, northeastern Oregon, the lower portion of the stem is the only part of this plant which sheep will not readily consume up to the first of August, and that the species is one of the most highly relished of the late forage plants of that locality. This investigator noted a rather low seed viability of this species, seed ripened by September 5 having germinated 18 percent in 1908 and 26 percent in 1909, the later maturing seed having a notably lower viability.

Arrowleaf butterweed is confused sometimes with sawtooth butterweed (*S. serra*), as the two plants often occur on similar sites, are of about the same size, and both have large, leafy stems. Differences in leaf form are their chief distinguishing feature, the leaves of arrowleaf butterweed being definitely wedge- or arrow-shaped, in contrast to those of sawtooth butterweed, which are lance- or egg-shaped, and taper at the base to such an extent as to obscure the leafstalk. The leaf margins of both plants are toothed.

---

[1] Sampson, A. W. IMPORTANT RANGE PLANTS: THEIR LIFE HISTORY AND FORAGE VALUE. U. S. Dept. Agr. Bull. 545, 63 pp., illus. 1917.

CREEK GOLDENROD

Solida'go elonga'ta

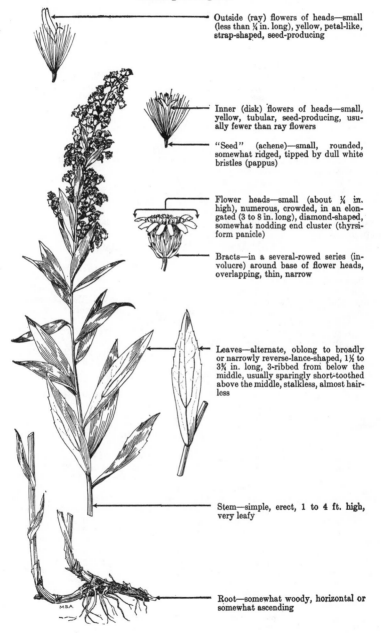

Outside (ray) flowers of heads—small (less than ¼ in. long), yellow, petal-like, strap-shaped, seed-producing

Inner (disk) flowers of heads—small, yellow, tubular, seed-producing, usually fewer than ray flowers

"Seed" (achene)—small, rounded, somewhat ridged, tipped by dull white bristles (pappus)

Flower heads—small (about ¼ in. high), numerous, crowded, in an elongated (3 to 8 in. long), diamond-shaped, somewhat nodding end cluster (thyrsiform panicle)

Bracts—in a several-rowed series (involucre) around base of flower heads, overlapping, thin, narrow

Leaves—alternate, oblong to broadly or narrowly reverse-lance-shaped, 1½ to 3¾ in. long, 3-ribbed from below the middle, usually sparingly short-toothed above the middle, stalkless, almost hairless

Stem—simple, erect, 1 to 4 ft. high, very leafy

Root—somewhat woody, horizontal or somewhat ascending

529

Creek goldenrod, one of the most common goldenrods appearing on the western ranges, is selected for treatment here as in many respects representative of this large and well-known genus. It is widely distributed from British Columbia to Montana, New Mexico, and California. As the common name suggests, this species most frequently grows in moist situations, along streams, and in meadows. However, it is able also to inhabit dry soils, sometimes growing on open ridges and timbered slopes, and in weedy flats, although the individuals in such sites usually lack vigor. In the mountain valleys they are a common sight along fences, roads, and ditches. They usually grow in the full sunlight, but are found in the shade along streams and in timber. The species is most common in the ponderosa pine belt, but extends both above and below that zone. In the Rockies it occurs in the aspen-spruce and in the Sierras reaches the red fir, yet on the coast of California and northward it descends to within a few hundred feet of sea level. Willows, dandelions, and fireweed (*Chamaenerion angustifolium*) are its frequent plant companions.

Creek goldenrod not only ranks as a forage plant but is sometimes regarded as a pest, especially on meadows. However, it is used slightly by livestock as a late season feed. This delayed use is probably due to its low palatability and the fact that it remains green until fall, when most other forage is either exhausted for the season or too dry. In general, this plant rates as poor forage for cattle but fair for sheep.

Healthy and vigorous individuals of the species are attractive plants, the stems being from 1 to 4 feet in height, closely leafy and topped with a long, dense cluster of many yellow flowers, the appearance of the plant bearing witness to the appropriateness of the common name—goldenrod. The flowers are borne for a rather long period, being a commonplace sight from July to September.

GOLDENRODS (Solida'go spp.)

The goldenrods compose a large genus, including some 130 species of the sunflower family (Compositae). The genus is chiefly North American, about 60 species occurring in the eastern part of the country, with about half as many in the West, and a few in Mexico, South America, Europe, and northern Asia. Their wide distribution, abundance, and attractiveness are demonstrated by the fact that Alabama, Kentucky, North Carolina, and Nebraska have selected the genus or some of its species for their respective State flowers.

Several species have been grown as garden plants, as borders, or for mass effects, but such uses have been somewhat limited. The late Thomas A. Edison focused wide attention upon the genus when he discovered it contained rubber. Polhamus,[1] after examining 24 eastern species, found that only the leaves contained appreciable amounts of rubber, and that only two species of the group studied were adapted for commercialization. Since the quantity of rubber varied with individuals of the same species, he suggests the possibility of developing a leafy variety rich in rubber latex by selection. In ancient times certain species of goldenrod were supposed to have wound-healing properties. The generic name *Solidago*, from the Latin *solidus* and *ago*, to unite firmly, comes from this purported use and value.

Most of the many goldenrods on the western ranges are similar to creek goldenrod in general aspect and relatively low forage value. The variations within the genus are interesting. Certain range species, as *S. parryi*, have larger, entire leaves and flowers and somewhat the aspect of arnicas (*Arnica* spp.), except that the leaves are alternate instead of opposite. *S. pumila* is a low, entire-leaved, many-stemmed herb which resembles some species of wild-daisies (*Erigeron* spp.). Still others, at first glance, suggest groundsels (*Senecio* spp.). As a genus, however, they have many constant characters, being perennial herbs, with alternate, mostly toothed, leaves, the basal ones often in conspicuous tufts (rosettes), and few to many small, erect flower heads. Each flower head is surrounded by two or more unequal and overlapping series of bracts and is composed of small, yellow (very rarely white) flowers, the outer ones strap-shaped, the center ones tubular. The "seed" (achene) is crowned by a brush (pappus) of dull white, rough, mostly equal bristles.

---

[1] Polhamus, L. G. RUBBER CONTENT OF VARIOUS SPECIES OF GOLDENROD. Jour. Agr. Research [U. S.] 47 : 149–152. 1933.

WESTERN TANSYMUSTARD

So'phia inci'sa, syn. *Sisym'brium inci'sum*

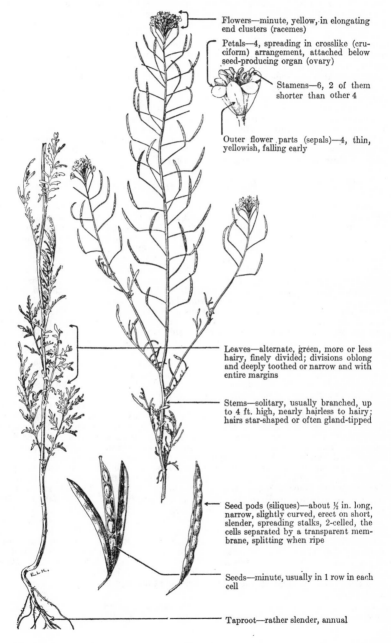

Flowers—minute, yellow, in elongating end clusters (racemes)

Petals—4, spreading in crosslike (cruciform) arrangement, attached below seed-producing organ (ovary)

Stamens—6, 2 of them shorter than other 4

Outer flower parts (sepals)—4, thin, yellowish, falling early

Leaves—alternate, green, more or less hairy, finely divided; divisions oblong and deeply toothed or narrow and with entire margins

Stems—solitary, usually branched, up to 4 ft. high, nearly hairless to hairy; hairs star-shaped or often gland-tipped

Seed pods (siliques)—about ½ in. long, narrow, slightly curved, erect on short, slender, spreading stalks, 2-celled, the cells separated by a transparent membrane, splitting when ripe

Seeds—minute, usually in 1 row in each cell

Taproot—rather slender, annual

Western tansymustard, a green or slightly grayish, slender annual with bright yellow flowers, sometimes bears the book name incised tansymustard, the specific name *incisa*, meaning cut or incised, referring to the sharply cut leaf divisions. However, western tansymustard is an appropriate name for the species since it is probably the most common, abundant, and widespread of the western United States tansymustards. It ranges from Tennessee to Minnesota, British Columbia, California, Texas, and Mexico, but does not occur west of the Cascade and Sierra Nevada Mountains. The species inhabits a wide variety of sites from dry, semidesert areas to moist, rich soils in the mountains, extending upward in Colorado to an elevation of about 10,000 feet and to 11,500 feet in California. It occurs in partial shade under timber, especially aspen, but is usually most abundant in open exposures. It is often conspicuous along ditches, roadsides, and other places where the mineral soil has been exposed.

As regards quality, western tansymustard is a poor forage species, its palatability under normal conditions never being more than fair for sheep and goats and poor for cattle. It is, notwithstanding, of considerable importance on some of the western ranges which have been badly overgrazed, as it occurs rather abundantly and provides soil protection as well as some forage.

This species is variable as to leaves, hairiness, and length of pods. However, the pedicels or stalks of the pods usually stand out from the stem and are shorter than the erect, often somewhat curved pods.

TANSYMUSTARDS (So'phia spp., syn. *Sisym'brium* in part)

Tansymustards, so called because of their more or less tansylike leaves, and because they belong to the large mustard family (Cruciferae, or Brassicaceae), are annual, biennial, or perennial herbs. The most commonly used name of this plant family, Cruciferae, refers to the crosslike arrangement of the four petals of the flowers. *Sophia* is a Greek word meaning wisdom and probably was applied to this genus because the Old World tansymustard, or flixweed (*S. parviflora*, syns. *S. sophia*, *Sisymbrium sophia*) "had a name among the herbalists expressive of some virtues which we in modern days do not discover." [1] The plant was thought serviceable in hysterical cases and as a purgative, but its chief repute was for the healing of wounds.

All the western species of this genus are annuals or biennials. They are distributed throughout the West in a wide variety of soils and plant types but are most abundant in the open, in fields, along roadsides and ditches, and in other places where the mineral soil has been recently exposed. The palatability of tansymustards, in general, is rather low, being seldom better than fair for sheep and goats and poor for cattle. Horses rarely graze these herbs. However, they are sometimes fairly abundant, especially on ranges which have been severely overgrazed, and do provide considerable forage. Like many other annual and biennial species, the tansymustards produce an abundance of seed and are especially adapted quickly to invade areas whose normal plant cover has been reduced. Under similar growth conditions they cannot compete with perennial weeds and grasses, but usually these perennial species are more palatable and are closely cropped and gradually killed out. The shorter-lived plants, thus freed from the competition of the perennials, increase in abundance, and hence constitute an indication of severe past overgrazing.

The tansymustards are definitely identified as belonging to the mustard family by the characteristic sharp, pungent taste; the four separate outer flower parts (sepals); the four separate petals; and the six stamens of which two are shorter than the others. They are further distinguished by the yellow, yellowish, or rarely white flowers born in rather narrow clusters (racemes) which become much lengthened in fruit, and by the pods (siliques) which are seldom over ½ of an inch long, but are several times longer than wide. The pods are 2-celled, with a thin membrane between the cells, and split open at maturity, discharging the minute seeds which are in one or two rows in each cell. The leaves are alternate and usually much divided. Most species are more or less hairy; the hairs, when present, are typically two-branched and attached by the middle or else star-shaped.

---

[1] Pratt, A. THE FLOWERING PLANTS, GRASSES, SEDGES, AND FERNS OF GREAT BRITAIN . . . New ed., rev. by E. Step, 4 v., illus. London and New York. 1899–1900.

FENDLER MEADOWRUE

Thalic'trum fend'leri

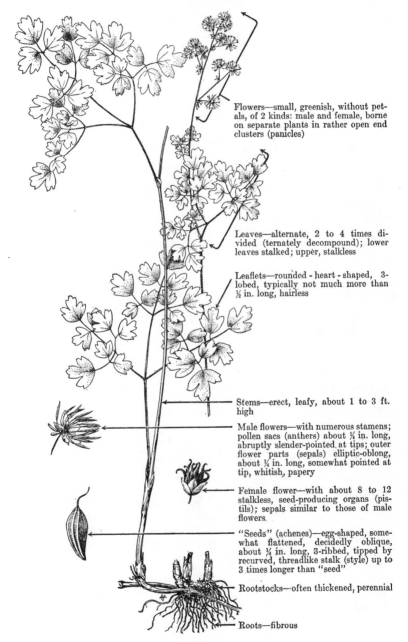

Flowers—small, greenish, without petals, of 2 kinds: male and female, borne on separate plants in rather open end clusters (panicles)

Leaves—alternate, 2 to 4 times divided (ternately decompound); lower leaves stalked; upper, stalkless

Leaflets—rounded - heart - shaped, 3-lobed, typically not much more than ½ in. long, hairless

Stems—erect, leafy, about 1 to 3 ft. high

Male flowers—with numerous stamens; pollen sacs (anthers) about ¼ in. long, abruptly slender-pointed at tips; outer flower parts (sepals) elliptic-oblong, about ¼ in. long, somewhat pointed at tip, whitish, papery

Female flower—with about 8 to 12 stalkless, seed-producing organs (pistils); sepals similar to those of male flowers.

"Seeds" (achenes)—egg-shaped, somewhat flattened, decidedly oblique, about ¼ in. long, 3-ribbed, tipped by recurved, threadlike stalk (style) up to 3 times longer than "seed"

Rootstocks—often thickened, perennial

Roots—fibrous

533

Fendler meadowrue commemorates August Fendler, of St. Louis, who first collected it in the mountains near Santa Fe. Fendler's collections in New Mexico, 1846–47, formed the basis of Dr. Gray's well-known book Plantae Fendlerianae. This erect perennial herb, with divided leaves and small, greenish flowers, is one of the most widely distributed western species of *Thalictrum*, ranging from Montana and Idaho to California and the mountains of western Texas. It is often abundant locally, and occurs chiefly in moist, loam soils in aspen or among shrubs, although also found in open exposures and, to some extent, in ponderosa pine, Engelmann spruce, and other coniferous timber.

On properly grazed ranges Fendler meadowrue is practically worthless to poor in palatability for cattle and poor to fair for sheep. On very heavily grazed ranges it is sometimes almost completely utilized, but ordinarily the close cropping of this species indicates overstocking.

MEADOWRUES (Thalic'trum spp.)

Meadowrues belong to the buttercup family (Ranunculaceae) and compose a genus of about 85 species of erect, perennial herbs with alternate compound leaves. The species are most abundant in temperate regions of the Northern Hemisphere, with only a few occurring in the Andes, in India, and in South Africa. Approximately 13 species grow in the Western States, the majority inhabiting the Rocky Mountains. These western meadowrues prefer rich, moist soils and some shade and appear in greatest abundance in aspen and among shrubs, although they are often found in full sunlight in meadows and parks.

Meadowrues are much alike in general appearance; but besides differing in flower and fruit characters, they are chiefly dissimilar in size, leafiness of stems, shape, size, and texture of leaflets, and color of roots. Field determination of species is not always feasible; fortunately it is seldom, if ever, required for range management purposes, as these plants have practically analogous palatability. They are abundant locally and, despite relatively low palatability, doubtless supply considerable forage. In general, their palatability is practically worthless to poor for cattle and poor to fair for sheep. However, in some instances, they may be utilized rather closely, especially on ranges which are heavily grazed early in the season. Excessive use of meadowrues generally indicates overstocking. Deer crop these species slightly; possibly they are also utilized by elk.

Meadowrue leaves occur both basally and alternately on the plant stem and resemble those of columbine, a closely related genus; they are divided several times and usually in threes (ternately decompound). The leaflets are usually 3-lobed and more or less toothed; and although they vary in size and shape in the different species, the accompanying illustration of Fendler meadowrue is more or less typical of meadowrue leaves. The flowers of meadowrues lack petals and, although individually small, are often showy collectively in terminal clusters (panicles or occasionally racemes); the early-falling, petallike floral bracts (sepals) are greenish, whitish, or purplish. The flowers of a few species are perfect, containing both male (pollen-producing) organs (stamens) and female (seed-producing) organs (pistils); in most species the pistils and stamens are borne in separate flowers on separate plants (dioecious) or occasionally perfect flowers are intermixed with male and female flowers (polygamous). The male flowers are often very attractive with their numerous, delicate, colored stamens.

Meadowrues derive their name from the meadow habitat of the typical Old World species—a habitat which is rather characteristic of the genus as a whole—and from a fancied resemblance of the foliage to that of common rue (*Ruta graveolens*). However, the bitterness of the leaves in meadowrue lacks the peculiarly acrid character of rue. Certain species of meadowrue are sometimes known as poor-man's rhubarb, because their herbage was formerly used as a substitute for rhubarb. *Thalictrum* is Latinized from *thalictron*, a name used by the Greek medical writer, Dioscorides (first century, B. C.), for a plant thought to be the Old World low meadowrue (*T. minus*).

Because of their feathery masses of male flowers, their graceful foliage, often in pleasing contrast to purplish stems, and their hardiness, many of the meadowrues are grown as ornamentals. Some species are suitable for mixed borders and rock gardens; the robust forms are valuable in wild gardens. Such native range species as alpine meadowrue (*T. alpi'num*), early meadowrue (*T. dioi'cum*), Fendler meadowrue, western meadowrue (*T. occidenta'le*), and veiny meadowrue (*T. venulo'sum*) have been used commercially for some time.

There is evidence that some species of meadowrue have active chemical properties; hence a thorough study of the genus from this standpoint would be of interest and value. The roots of bigseed meadowrue (*T. macrocar'pum*) of southern Europe are the source of a crystalline yellow, extremely toxic substance like curare, a plant used by South American Indians for poisoning arrows and darts. This substance consists of thalictrine, an alkaloid insoluble in water, and macrocarpin, a yellow crystalline body soluble in water, representing the coloring principle of *Thalictrum* (roots of some species yield a yellow dye suitable for woolens). The same elements occur in the roots of fen meadowrue (*T. fla'vum*), known also as fenrue and monk's rhubarb, and of dusty meadowrue (*T. glau'cum*) of Europe, as well as in snoutseed meadowrue (*T. rhynchocar'pum*) of north Africa. Thalictrine is a very active cardiac poison, which causes loss of power, convulsive movements, irregularity and depression of the heart beat, and finally death.[1]

Although possibly the American species contain the same toxins, no livestock losses attributable to these plants have been recorded. Domestic animals, to be sure, would hardly be tempted to eat the

[1] Wood, H. C., Remington, J. P., and Sadtler, S. P., assisted by Lyons, A. B., and Wood, H. C., Jr. THE DISPENSATORY OF THE UNITED STATES OF AMERICA, BY DR. GEO. B. WOOD AND DR. FRANKLIN BACHE. Ed. 19, thoroughly rev. and largely rewritten ... 1,947 pp. Philadelphia and London, 1907.

bitter roots even if accessible. Chesnut [2] writes that an Indian once reported a white child as being poisoned by eating the stems of Sierra meadowrue (*T. polycar'pum*), a California species. Chesnut (*op. cit.*) further reports that among some California Indian tribes this plant is known as coyote-angelica, angelica being the universal charm and panacea of the Indian and the coyote symbolizing his ideal of cunning. These Indians believe that coyotes eat this meadowrue without ill effects; and since the species is somewhat aromatic like angelica, they call it coyote-angelica. The Indians also washed their heads with the juice of meadowrue as a cure for headache.[2]

---

[2] Chesnut, V. K. PLANTS USED BY THE INDIANS OF MENDOCINO COUNTY, CALIFORNIA. U. S. Dept. Agr., Div. Bot., Contrib. U. S. Natl. Herbarium 7 : 295–422, illus. 1902.

MOUNTAIN GOLDENPEA

Thermop'sis monta'na

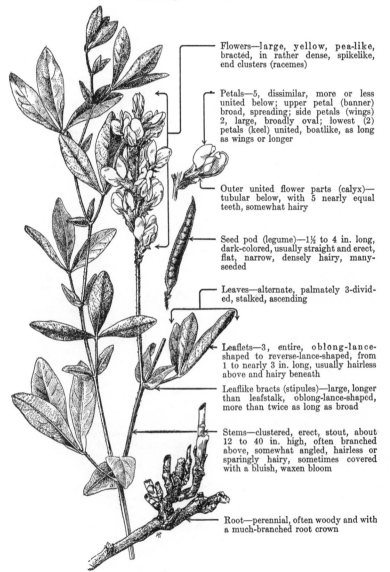

Flowers—large, yellow, pea-like, bracted, in rather dense, spikelike, end clusters (racemes)

Petals—5, dissimilar, more or less united below; upper petal (banner) broad, spreading; side petals (wings) 2, large, broadly oval; lowest (2) petals (keel) united, boatlike, as long as wings or longer

Outer united flower parts (calyx)—tubular below, with 5 nearly equal teeth, somewhat hairy

Seed pod (legume)—1½ to 4 in. long, dark-colored, usually straight and erect, flat, narrow, densely hairy, many-seeded

Leaves—alternate, palmately 3-divided, stalked, ascending

Leaflets—3, entire, oblong-lance-shaped to reverse-lance-shaped, from 1 to nearly 3 in. long, usually hairless above and hairy beneath

Leaflike bracts (stipules)—large, longer than leafstalk, oblong-lance-shaped, more than twice as long as broad

Stems—clustered, erect, stout, about 12 to 40 in. high, often branched above, somewhat angled, hairless or sparingly hairy, sometimes covered with a bluish, waxen bloom

Root—perennial, often woody and with a much-branched root crown

Mountain goldenpea, variously known as buffalo pea, devil's shoestring, Montana-pea, prairie-bean, turkeypea, wild yellow pea, yellow-flowered bitterweed, etc., is a perennial herb with golden-yellow, pealike flowers and belongs to the legume family (Leguminosae). Both the specific and common names refer to the habitat of this plant, *montana* being a Latin adjective which means montane, of or pertaining to mountains. This plant grows from practically sea level in parts of Oregon and Washington up to about 6,500 feet in Montana and about 10,000 feet in Utah and Colorado. It ranges from Montana to New Mexico and westward to eastern Oregon and Washington; it possibly also occurs in northern California. Although mountain goldenpea is able to grow in relatively dry soils, it attains its best development and is most abundant in moist bottomlands and in the fertile, loamy soils of the aspen type; it probably does not grow on acid soils. In the central Rocky Mountains, especially on western slopes in Colorado, this species is one of the most common and abundant weeds of low palatability, occurring in dense, nearly pure stands as undergrowth in aspen on extensive local areas. It is also abundant in parts of Utah and Montana.

Although sheep may occasionally nibble its flowers, mountain goldenpea is worthless as range forage; in fact, there is strong likelihood of severe overgrazing or a serious depletion of palatable forage wherever it is grazed materially. Occasional reports occur,[1,2] which need further substantiation, that it is good hay if cut while young and succulent. Chesnut and Wilcox[3] mention it as having been suspected of poisoning livestock in Montana, but in some feeding experiments with rabbits they were unable to establish any toxic properties.

This species tends to be rather aggressive; when once established, mountain goldenpea is apparently very resistant to drought and its deep-set, extensive root system enables it to withstand considerable trampling. In addition to spreading by perennial underground parts, it usually succeeds (being so little grazed) in producing an annual seed crop. Consequently it often increases on ranges where overgrazing has somewhat depleted the more palatable vegetation. It flowers during late spring and early summer.

GOLDENPEAS (Thermop'sis spp.)

Goldenpeas, also known as buffalo-peas and yellowpeas, compose a small genus of about 20 species, native to North America and northern and eastern Asia. Approximately 12 species occur in the West, being widely distributed from Washington and Saskatchewan to New Mexico and California. They extend from the low plains to the higher mountains, commonly appearing in parks and meadows, in brush types, and in aspen, ponderosa pine, and open Douglas fir and lodgepole pine types. Although goldenpeas occur characteristically as scattered individuals or grow in small patches, some species are very common and often are abundant locally.

The goldenpeas, practically worthless as forage, are important as range plants because of their wide distribution and commonness. Although sheep sometimes nibble the flowers, such use is negligible. These plants have deep-set roots and apparently withstand considerable drought. They spread by means of creeping, underground root branches or rootstocks, and often increase on ranges which have been overgrazed. Some species reputedly contain cytisin, a very poisonous alkaloid found in many leguminous plants; cases of children being poisoned by eating the seeds have been reported.[4] Livestock losses attributed to these plants, although reported, have never been authenticated.

Goldenpeas are attractive, rather low, perennial herbs, with yellow (rarely purple), pealike, odorless flowers borne in usually many-flowered, long, terminal clusters. They are further distinguished by alternate, stalked leaves, divided into three leaflets; large, leaflike bracts (stipules) at the base of the leafstalks; 10 separate stamens; and narrow, flat, 2-valved, many-seeded pods. The generic name *Thermopsis* is a combination of *thermos*, an ancient Greek word for lupine, and *opsis*, resemblance, and refers to the general similarity of these plants to some of the lupines.

Several species, including bean goldenpea (*T. faba'cea*), a Siberian species, and Carolina goldenpea (*T. carolinia'na*) and soft goldenpea (*T. mol'lis*) of the Eastern States, are commonly grown as ornamentals.

[1] Rydberg, P. A. CATALOGUE OF THE FLORA OF MONTANA AND THE YELLOWSTONE NATIONAL PARK. Mem. N. Y. Bot. Gard. 1, 492 pp., illus. 1900.
[2] Smith, J. G. FODDER AND FORAGE PLANTS, EXCLUSIVE OF THE GRASSES. U. S. Dept. Agr., Div. Agrost. Bull. 2, rev., 86 pp., illus. 1900.
[3] Chesnut, V. K., and Wilcox. E. V. THE STOCK-POISONING PLANTS OF MONTANA: A PRELIMINARY REPORT. U. S. Dept. Agr., Div. Bot. Bull. 26, 150 pp., illus. 1901.
[4] Pammel, L. H. A MANUAL OF POISONOUS PLANTS CHIEFLY OF EASTERN NORTH AMERICA, WITH BRIEF NOTES ON ECONOMIC AND MEDICINAL PLANTS . . . 2 pts., illus. Cedar Rapids, Iowa. 1910–11.

MOUNTAIN PENNYCRESS

Thlas'pi alpes'tre, syns. *T. coloraden'se, T. glau'cum, T. purpuras'cens*

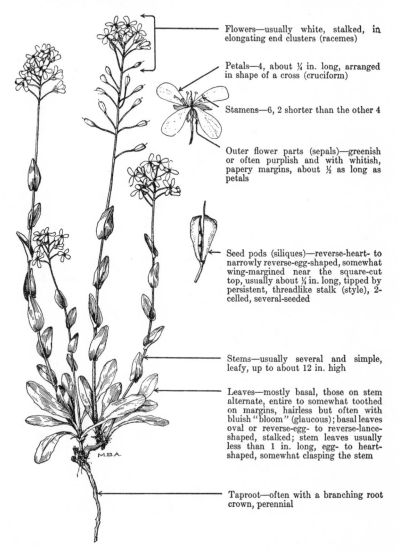

Flowers—usually white, stalked, in elongating end clusters (racemes)

Petals—4, about ¼ in. long, arranged in shape of a cross (cruciform)

Stamens—6, 2 shorter than the other 4

Outer flower parts (sepals)—greenish or often purplish and with whitish, papery margins, about ½ as long as petals

Seed pods (siliques)—reverse-heart- to narrowly reverse-egg-shaped, somewhat wing-margined near the square-cut top, usually about ¼ in. long, tipped by persistent, threadlike stalk (style), 2-celled, several-seeded

Stems—usually several and simple, leafy, up to about 12 in. high

Leaves—mostly basal, those on stem alternate, entire to somewhat toothed on margins, hairless but often with bluish "bloom" (glaucous); basal leaves oval or reverse-egg- to reverse-lance-shaped, stalked; stem leaves usually less than 1 in. long, egg- to heart-shaped, somewhat clasping the stem

Taproot—often with a branching root crown, perennial

Mountain pennycress, a small, usually white-flowered, often short-lived, perennial herb, is common in the mountains from British Columbia to Montana, New Mexico, and California, and probably extends southward, in the highest ranges, into Mexico. It also inhabits Europe and Asia, being originally described from central Europe. It is one of the first plants to appear in the spring, growing while the soil is still moist from melting snow and spring rains. The palatability of this well-known plant is poor to fair for cattle, and fair to fairly good for sheep but it is relatively unimportant on the range, because of small size and the fact that the herbage usually desiccates and disappears early in the grazing season, so that the species actually supplies but little forage for domestic livestock. Mountain pennycress is a representative member of the genus *Thlaspi* as it occurs natively in the West.

The genus *Thlaspi*, usually called pennycress, but also known locally as candytuft, pennygrass, and wild sweet-alyssum, is a member of the crucifer, or mustard family (Cruciferae). *Thlaspi* (from *thlaein*, to crush) is a Greek name for a kind of mustard whose crushed seeds were anciently used as a condiment. It consists of 60 or more species of annual or perennial herbs, widely distributed in temperate, Arctic, and alpine regions, mainly in the Northern Hemisphere, but also occurring in South America, South Africa, and Australia. At least eight perennial species have been described as native in the western United States. However, there is a great deal of intergradation between these species, and botanists differ in opinion as to the exact number which are tenable and valid. There has been a recent tendency to refer most, if not all, of these American species to the old *T. alpestre* of Linnaeus, or else to its varieties. In addition to the perennial species of pennycress, the introduced field pennycress (*T. arven'se*), a weedy annual, native to Europe and Asia, is also common throughout the West.

The native species of pennycress occur chiefly in the mountains in well-drained soils, which often become dry during the summer. These plants make their growth in the spring and early summer, while the soil is still moist, and, as a result, are largely dormant during the dry period. Generally, the western pennycresses are fair or fairly good sheep feed, and poor to fair cattle forage, although they mature so early in the season that the plants are largely dried up on many of the mountain ranges before much of their foliage can be utilized. The range pennycresses, although common, are seldom abundant and are of only secondary importance for forage.

Pennycresses are largely characterized by alternate, usually clasping stem leaves broadened at the base into ear-shaped (auriculate) appendages; by small, white or purplish (rarely rose-colored) flowers, four-parted and with six stamens, two of which are shorter than the other four; and by flattened seed pods (siliques), reverse-wedge-shaped, reverse-heart-shaped or rounded in outline, and mostly crested or winged. The pods are two-celled, each cell containing two to eight seeds. The juice is watery and somewhat acrid.

From an economic standpoint, field pennycress is the most important of the pennycresses in the United States. This plant, known locally as bastard-cress, devilweed, fanweed, Frenchweed, stinkweed, treacle-mustard, and erroneously as Jim Hill mustard, is now well distributed throughout the United States from Maine to Florida and westward to California and Washington. Evidently a very early introduction, it is now abundant in many localities, especially in the northern and northwestern parts of the country, where it grows as a pest in fields, meadows, pastures, and other agricultural holdings, and also abounds along roads and in waste lands. It has also become pestiferous in parts of the Jackson Hole country, Wyoming, but, as yet, seems not to be a problem on western forest ranges as a whole. The species is especially detrimental in fields where dairy cows are pastured because, if grazed, it imparts a disagreeable, somewhat garliclike flavor and odor to the milk. It is a persistent enemy of the wheat grower in the Northwest, the seeds spoiling the flour.[1] Certain farming lands in Montana [2] are no longer used because of the spread of this plant. Both spring and fall cultivations are necessary in the effective combat of this weed because its seed sprouts during both spring and fall, the fall seedlings often surviving the winter. Field pennycress formerly was a popular substitute for mustard.[3]

[1] Beal, W. J. MICHIGAN WEEDS. Mich. Agr. Expt. Sta. Bull. 267, rev., 181 pp., illus. 1915.
[2] Robbins, W. W. FANWEED OR FRENCHWEED. Through the Leaves, Aug. 1920 : 445–447, illus. 1920.
[3] Hulme, F. E. FAMILIAR WILD FLOWERS. 8 v., illus. London, Paris, New York, and Melbourne. 1905.

CLOVERS

Trifo'lium spp.

Clovers, sometimes called trefoils, are annual, biennial or perennial herbs belonging to the large pea family (Leguminosae). The generic name *Trifolium* refers to the characteristic three-divided leaves. The genus, which includes about 300 species, is widely distributed in all north temperate regions, with a few species occurring on the mountains of tropical Africa, on the Andes, and in subtropical South America and in South Africa. A large number of species are native to the far western range States and grow from about sea level to elevations of 14,000 feet. Clovers are relatively common almost everywhere in the western mountains, although most species do best on moist sites—in meadows and along streams. Several species, however, occur abundantly on the open grasslands and in mature timber stands. Some clovers are adapted to grow in poor, dry or poorly drained soils of waste lands. Clovers do best on soils rich in lime and potash. Some of the perennial clovers grow in pure stands and form rather dense sod, which withstands trampling and grazing well.

Clovers have been cultivated since the sixteenth century and are unexcelled for pasturage and hay, their present total acreage in the United States being nearly five times that of alfalfa.[1] Clover has a high feeding value for young and milking animals, being equal to timothy in digestible nutrients, and containing three times as much protein. Most of the native clover species are as palatable as the cultivated forms, but generally they are divided into two groups. Those species which grow on the more moist sites have a palatability of from very good to excellent for all classes of livestock and game animals. On the other hand, those species growing on the drier sites rate from fairly good to good in palatability for sheep, but somewhat lower for cattle and horses. Clovers, including several naturalized species from Europe, are quite abundant and are rather important forage plants on the range.

Cattle and sheep are always liable to bloat from eating green clover, especially if the plants are wet and the animals hungry. However, under normal range conditions, bloating seldom, if ever, occurs. When such animals as horses are pastured upon white clover (*T. repens*) that has gone to seed, the acrid seed often causes the animals to slobber. This condition is not necessarily harmful. Cases are known where alsike clover (*T. hybridum*) has caused severe ulcerations of the mouth, forelegs, and body of horses and mules—a condition known as trifoliosis. There apparently is some evidence that this is caused by a fungus on the clover and not by the plant itself.[2]

Clovers have long been recognized as capable of increasing soil fertility. These plants are able to increase the nitrogen content of the soil from the root tubercles which they bear. Certain bacteria which are able to use free nitrogen of the air live in the root tubercles of the clover plants. After these root tubercles decay this nitrogen becomes available to other plants. The mechanical action of the long, deep root systems of clovers also improves the tilth of the soil. These roots penetrate deeply into the subsoil making plant food, which is inaccessible to most other plants, available to clover.

Several species of clovers have been used successfully in range reseeding projects throughout the West.[3] They produce an abundance of viable seed which germinate well even when several years old. Seeds stored for 9 years had a germination percentage of 71.6 percent.[4] The viability of clover seed containing 15 percent moisture, or less, was unaffected by exposure to tem-

---

[1] Robbins, W. W., and Ramaley, F. PLANTS USEFUL TO MAN. 428 pp., illus. Philadelphia. 1933.

[2] Morgan, H. A., and Jacob, M. I. ALSIKE CLOVER. II. ILL EFFECTS SOMETIMES PRODUCED ON HORSES AND MULES PASTURED EXCLUSIVELY UPON ALSIKE. Tenn. Agr. Expt. Sta. Bull. 18(3) : [22]–30, illus. 1905.

[3] Forsling, C. L., and Dayton, W. A. ARTIFICIAL RESEEDING ON WESTERN MOUNTAIN RANGE LANDS. U. S. Dept. Agr. Circ. 178, 48 pp., illus. 1931.

[4] McRostie, G. P. LONGEVITY OF ALFALFA AND CLOVER SEED. Sci. Agr. 4(8) : 236–238. 1924.

peratures as low as —48° C. for short periods. Most varieties of clover grown in the northern United States are rather resistant to low temperatures.[5]

In various parts of the world, clovers have been used as food by mankind. During famines in Ireland, for example, the dried flowers and seeds of white clover were ground into flour and made into bread. In the Eastern and Southern States the poorer Negro families eat several species raw as a salad with vinegar as a dressing. Clover was also an essential article in the diets of certain Indian tribes. Before the flowers appeared they gathered the fresh green leaves and ate them with relish. Clover eaten green often was a source of bloat among the Indians and sometimes even caused death.[6]

Clovers have trifoliolate leaves and numerous small pealike flowers in a dense head. The flowers bend downward, dry, and turn brown, sometimes remaining on the heads throughout the season. These inflorescence characters, coupled with the absence of coiling and curving of the pods, make it easy to distinguish clovers from medicks (*Medicago spp.*). Clover seed pods invariably are small, usually containing but a single small kidney-shaped seed.

White clover (*T. re'pens*), a perennial with creeping stems which root at the joints, was introduced from Europe but now occurs naturally on fairly moist soils of the mountain ranges at medium to high elevations. It withstands greater temperature extremes than either red or alsike clover and is suited to rather cool, moist regions, being quite tolerant to shade. This clover is relished highly by all livestock. It is extremely nutritious, withstands trampling well, and is stimulated to stronger growth by close grazing. White clover is rich in readily accessible nectar and hence is of considerable economic value to beekeepers.

Alsike clover (*T. hy'bridum*), a perennial introduced from Europe, escaped from cultivation and is now found growing along roads, streams, and meadows in the mountains. It prefers moist soils and will thrive on poorly drained lands or even heavy soils. This clover is not usually grown alone for hay because of its decumbent, spreading habit, but is usually cultivated in mixture with such grasses as timothy and redtop. Alsike clover, although not as palatable as certain other species, is nevertheless highly nutritious and, apparently, does not cause bloat as readily as do some other clovers. This plant is really not a hybrid between red and white clover, as is commonly supposed. The flowers are rose-colored when mature and white when immature, thus the mature lower flowers of the head are rose-colored and the upper immature flowers white. The whole head becomes rose-colored only after all the flowers have matured.

Red clover (*T. praten'se*), because of its shorter life, lack of rootstocks, coarser habit, and greater susceptibility to disease, both from fungi and insects, is not of as much range importance as either white or alsike clovers. Nevertheless it is valuable locally, and its soil-improvement capabilities render it a desirable plant where it occurs. The agricultural significance of this species is, of course, enormous. Westgate and Hillman state:[7] "Red clover may justly be styled the corner stone of agriculture in the North Central and Eastern States." Stebler and Schröter affirm that "Red clover has contributed even more to the progress of agriculture than the potato itself, and has had no inconsiderable influence on European civilization. Its cultivation has led to an increased production of stock as food for man and in this way has fostered and advanced commerce, industry, and science."[8] Bumblebees and a few of the butterflies are the only insects with a proboscis long enough to reach the nectar at the bottom of the flower tube. Since the honeybee brushes past the stigma of the pistil in collecting pollen for bee bread, it is important in the fertilization of the clover flowers. The dried flowers of red clover were formerly reputed to be good for whooping cough and ulcers, but their medicinal use seems to be no longer official.

[5] Steinbauer, G. DIFFERENCES IN RESISTANCE TO LOW TEMPERATURES SHOWN BY CLOVER VARIETIES. Plant Physiol. 1(3) : 281–286, illus. 1926.
[6] Chesnut, V. K. PLANTS USED BY THE INDIANS OF MENDOCINO COUNTY, CALIFORNIA. U. S. Dept. Agr., Div. Bot., Contrib. U. S. Natl. Herbarium 7 : 295–422, illus. 1902.
[7] Westgate, J. M., and Hillman, F. H. RED CLOVER. U. S. Dept. Agr. Farmers' Bull. 455, 48 pp., illus. 1911.
[8] Stebler, F. G., and Schröter, C. THE BEST FORAGE PLANTS FULLY DESCRIBED AND FIGURED . . . Transl. by A. N. McAlpine. 171 pp., illus. London. 1889.

RYDBERG CLOVER

Trifo'lium rydber'gii, syn. *T. confu'sum*

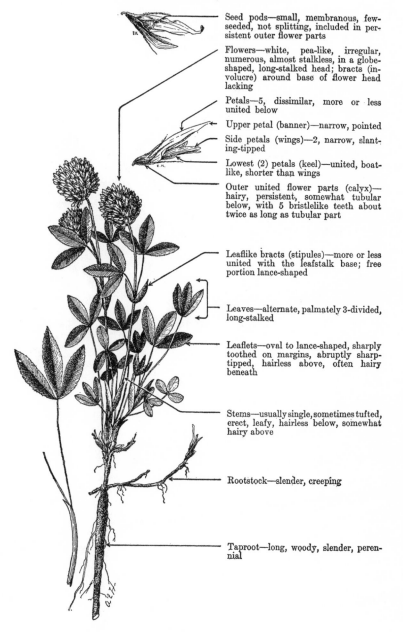

Seed pods—small, membranous, few-seeded, not splitting, included in persistent outer flower parts

Flowers—white, pea-like, irregular, numerous, almost stalkless, in a globe-shaped, long-stalked head; bracts (involucre) around base of flower head lacking

Petals—5, dissimilar, more or less united below

Upper petal (banner)—narrow, pointed

Side petals (wings)—2, narrow, slanting-tipped

Lowest (2) petals (keel)—united, boatlike, shorter than wings

Outer united flower parts (calyx)—hairy, persistent, somewhat tubular below, with 5 bristlelike teeth about twice as long as tubular part

Leaflike bracts (stipules)—more or less united with the leafstalk base; free portion lance-shaped

Leaves—alternate, palmately 3-divided, long-stalked

Leaflets—oval to lance-shaped, sharply toothed on margins, abruptly sharp-tipped, hairless above, often hairy beneath

Stems—usually single, sometimes tufted, erect, leafy, hairless below, somewhat hairy above

Rootstock—slender, creeping

Taproot—long, woody, slender, perennial

Rydberg clover, sometimes called wild white clover, is a characteristic white, perennial, native clover named in honor of Dr. P. A. Rydberg (1860–1931), a well-known American botanist. It occurs in the Rocky Mountains and Wasatch Mountains from Idaho and Montana to northern New Mexico and Arizona, at elevations of from a' out 4,500 feet up to 13,000 feet. Rydberg clover is most abundant along creek bottoms and in moist meadows. Although not very tolerant to shade, it appears commonly in open mature timber at the higher elevations, where it often forms rather dense patches in the openings between the trees.

This leafy clover withstands grazing well and is of considerable forage value, having a palatability rating of from very good to excellent for all classes of livestock. It is reputed to be a favorite food plant of the mule deer on the Kaibab Forest in Arizona and is undoubtedly highly palatable to other game animals. On some of the high mountain ranges in the fir and spruce belt, the rather high grazing capacity is due largely to the abundance of this clover.

Rydberg clover is a smooth, leafy, erect, long-rooted clover, usually about 10 inches high, although sometimes much higher. The numerous white flowers, which bend abruptly downward with age, are arranged in a dense head. The plant usually forms a rather dense sod but sometimes occurs as single or somewhat tufted plants.

VALERIANS

Valeria'na spp.

The valerians, also known in the West as tobacco root and sometimes improperly called sweet anise, belong to the relatively small valerian family (Valerianaceae). A dozen or more species grow on the western ranges. They are perennial herbs, with opposite, simple or divided (compound) leaves, and fleshy strong-scented roots and rootstocks. The valerians can be recognized by the characteristic odor of their roots which, according to a certain old timer, smell "like dirty feet." This comparison gives a vivid and accurate description of the odor. Cats and rats are said to be attracted to valerian roots, which are used on occasion as rat bait.

The name *Valeriana* is derived from the Latin (*valere*, to be strong) and alludes to the medicinal virtues of some species, particularly of common valerian (*V. officinalis*), a native of the Old World, but now cultivated as a drug plant in Europe, New England, and New York. The drug, valerian, a gentle stimulant, devoid of narcotic effects, is extracted from the roots of common valerian. It is used in the treatment of nervous disorders, and has been particularly recommended for hysteria and certain types of fever.[1] The roots of many native species of valerian are reputed to have similar medicinal properties. The chief adulterants and substitutes of commercial valerian are the rhizomes and roots of two Mexican species, Toluca valerian (*V. toluccana*) and Mexican valerian (*V. mexicana*), as well as of *V. phu*, the large garden valerian of southern Europe and western Asia.[2] The latter species has a very suggestive specific name, *phu* being the Grecian equivalent of our phooey, which no doubt refers to the stench of the roots.

The valerians grow in all the Western States, with the fewest species in California. They ordinarily inhabit moist sites in parks, woodlands, and rich, coniferous timberlands, mostly at moderate to high elevations. Their palatability to livestock varies somewhat for the respective species, and in different localities. On the average, however, the valerians are rated as poor to fair for cattle, and fairly good to good for sheep. A few species, such as Scouler valerian (*V. scouleri*) and western valerian (*V. occidentalis*), rank high in palatability for sheep and most of them are grazed with relish by game animals. The valerians, however, rarely are abundant and, therefore, are of only secondary importance in most ranges.

A number of European valerians, as well as several North American species, are grown in gardens as ornamentals. Common valerian, prized for the spicy fragrance of its numerous flowers in the spring, is most widely used for this purpose, being one of the characteristic plants of old gardens in the eastern United States and the Old World.

---

[1] Wood, H. C., Remington, J. P., and Sadtler, S. P., assisted by Lyons, A. B., and Wood, H. C., Jr. THE DISPENSATORY OF THE UNITED STATES OF AMERICA, BY DR. GEO. C. WOOD AND DR. FRANKLIN BACHE. Ed. 19, thoroughly rev. and largely rewritten . . . 1,947 pp. Philadelphia and London. 1907.

[2] Youngken, H. W. A TEXT BOOK OF PHARMACOGNOSY. 538 pp., illus. Philadelphia. 1921.

Edible valerian (*V. e'dulis*, syn. *V. ceratophyl'la* (Hook.) Piper, not H. B. K.), one of the most common and widely distributed western valerians, usually inhabits drier and more open sites than most of its sister species. It grows in open parks, woodlands, and dry meadows from Ontario to Ohio and westward to New Mexico, California, and British Columbia. This species is quite unlike Scouler valerian and western valerian in general appearance, being a tall, erect plant with thick, deepset, fleshy taproots and elongated, loosely branched flower clusters. Its densely tufted basal leaves are rather thick, reverse lance-shaped, mostly entire, and have practically parallel veins. The forage of edible valerian is usually rated poor to fair in palatability for cattle and fair to fairly good for sheep. In some localities, however, it ranks as a distinctly inferior forage plant. Formerly, the thick carrotlike roots of this plant, and possibly the roots of other valerians, were eaten, after prolonged cooking, by various tribes of western Indians.

SCOULER VALERIAN

Valeria'na scou'leri, syns. *"V. sitchen'sis"*,[1] *V. sitchen'sis scou'leri*

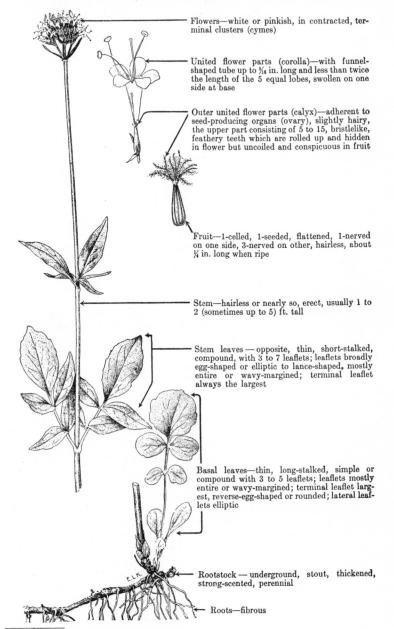

Flowers—white or pinkish, in contracted, terminal clusters (cymes)

United flower parts (corolla)—with funnel-shaped tube up to ⅜ in. long and less than twice the length of the 5 equal lobes, swollen on one side at base

Outer united flower parts (calyx)—adherent to seed-producing organs (ovary), slightly hairy, the upper part consisting of 5 to 15, bristlelike, feathery teeth which are rolled up and hidden in flower but uncoiled and conspicuous in fruit

Fruit—1-celled, 1-seeded, flattened, 1-nerved on one side, 3-nerved on other, hairless, about ¼ in. long when ripe

Stem—hairless or nearly so, erect, usually 1 to 2 (sometimes up to 5) ft. tall

Stem leaves — opposite, thin, short-stalked, compound, with 3 to 7 leaflets; leaflets broadly egg-shaped or elliptic to lance-shaped, mostly entire or wavy-margined; terminal leaflet always the largest

Basal leaves—thin, long-stalked, simple or compound with 3 to 5 leaflets; leaflets mostly entire or wavy-margined; terminal leaflet largest, reverse-egg-shaped or rounded; lateral leaflets elliptic

Rootstock — underground, stout, thickened, strong-scented, perennial

Roots—fibrous

[1] Of United States authors, not Bongard.

Scouler valerian, a smooth perennial herb having densely clustered, white or pinkish flowers and stout, horizontal, strong-scented rootstocks, is characteristic of the more palatable species of *Valeriana*. Because of the pleasing fragrance of its flowers, this species is sometimes referred to as sweet-scented valerian. Some American botanists have confused this plant with Sitka valerian (*V. sitchensis*) of Alaska, but the best present-day botanical opinion is that *V. sitchensis* does not extend southward into the United States, and that the plants so listed by United States authors are actually *V. scouleri*. The latter species was named in honor of Dr. John Scouler, who, with David Douglas, discovered it on moist rocks and islands of the Columbia River.

Scouler valerian is a plant of the Northwest and northern Rockies, being distributed from British Columbia and Alberta to Oregon, Idaho, and Montana. It typically grows in the fertile soils of moist woodlands, aspen stands, and willow patches, under lodgepole pine and Engelmann spruce-alpine fir forests, along stream banks and in mountain parks and meadows. In the Northwest, it is one of the most characteristic plants on old burns of the higher timber types. Although preferring deep, rich, moist soils, this plant also appears on well-drained, relatively dry sites. It ranges from rather low elevations in the humid forests west of the Cascade Mountains in Oregon and Washington up to timber line. Scouler valerian is usually scattered thinly over the range in mixture with other herbaceous vegetation, and but seldom abundant or dominant.

This species is regarded as a valuable forage plant, usually being rated as fair to fairly good for cattle and good to very good for sheep. On burns covered with dead and down timber, sheep seek and graze it with great relish. The foliage is extremely tender and succulent early in the season, when the plants are frequently eaten down to the ground; later in the summer only the leaves and flowers are consumed. Both deer and elk graze this plant.

Scouler valerian reproduces by means of both seed and rootstocks, with the seed crop maturing from approximately mid-August until the end of the growing season. In the higher sites, some individual plants never reach maturity, while those which do mature produce seed of rather low viability. The stout rootstocks with their intertwining mass of fibrous roots enable the plants to survive even heavy grazing fairly well. The roots are reputed to have medicinal properties similar to those of its well-known sister species, common valerian (*V. officina'lis*).

Western valerian (*V. occidenta'lis*, syn. *V. acutilo'ba*) is one of the most important and widespread species on the range. It much resembles Scouler valerian in gross appearance and habitat requirements, but is slightly less palatable, usually being rated as poor for cattle and fairly good for sheep. It differs from Scouler valerian in that its flowers have shorter corolla tubes and its leaves have entire or only very slightly wavy margins. Western valerian is distributed from British Columbia and Montana to New Mexico.

548

WESTERN FALSE-HELLEBORE

Vera'trum califor'nicum, syn. *V. specio'sum*

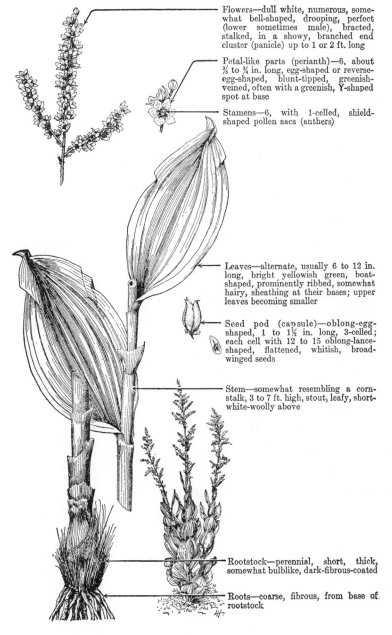

Flowers—dull white, numerous, somewhat bell-shaped, drooping, perfect (lower sometimes male), bracted, stalked, in a showy, branched end cluster (panicle) up to 1 or 2 ft. long

Petal-like parts (perianth)—6, about ⅜ to ¾ in. long, egg-shaped or reverse-egg-shaped, blunt-tipped, greenish-veined, often with a greenish, Y-shaped spot at base

Stamens—6, with 1-celled, shield-shaped pollen sacs (anthers)

Leaves—alternate, usually 6 to 12 in. long, bright yellowish green, boat-shaped, prominently ribbed, somewhat hairy, sheathing at their bases; upper leaves becoming smaller

Seed pod (capsule)—oblong-egg-shaped, 1 to 1½ in. long, 3-celled; each cell with 12 to 15 oblong-lance-shaped, flattened, whitish, broad-winged seeds

Stem—somewhat resembling a corn-stalk, 3 to 7 ft. high, stout, leafy, short-white-woolly above

Rootstock—perennial, short, thick, somewhat bulblike, dark-fibrous-coated

Roots—coarse, fibrous, from base of rootstock

Western false-hellebore, a showy perennial, grows only in the 11 far-western States, where it is one of the largest herbaceous plants of the mountain meadows and moist slopes. The confusion between true hellebores (*Helleborus* spp., of the buttercup family, Ranunculaceae) and false-hellebores (*Veratrum* spp., of the bunchflower tribe, *Melanthieae*, of the lily family, *Liliaceae*), is a very ancient one. Greek physicians used the rootstocks of "hellebore" (*helleboros*) for various purposes, but primarily as a remedy for insanity, and the Greek verb *helleboriao* (literally, "to need hellebore") was applied to a person who was losing his mind. These old-time medical men distinguished two chief types of hellebore, black hellebore (*Helleborus niger*) and white hellebore (*Veratrum album*). It is not altogether unlikely, however, that the *Veratrum* of the ancient Romans was *Helleborus niger*. To avoid confusion, it seems desirable to restrict the English name "hellebore" to the plant genus now known as *Helleborus*, and to call the genus now known as *Veratrum* "false-hellebore." The common name cornlily indicates the similarity of its leaves and their stalk arrangement to corn; the name skunkcabbage, no doubt, alludes to the general resemblance of the young plants of western false-hellebore to the true skunkcabbage (*Spathyema foetida*, syn. *Symplocarpus foetidus*), which is a foul-smelling, broad-leaved herb of the eastern United States. On the Pacific coast the name skunkcabbage more properly applies to the ill-scented, swamp-inhabiting yellow skunkcabbage (*Lysichiton camtschatcensis*), a very close relative of the eastern skunkcabbage.

Western false-hellebore occurs exclusively on moist soils in the mountainous regions. It grows largest and is most abundant on the moist and deep meadow soils, although it also does well on shallow and coarse soils of moist or springy slopes and flats. Not infrequently this herb invades and dominates eroded, but moist, flats and slopes, and in serious cases of depletion is sometimes one of the last perennial plants of the meadow association to disappear. It ordinarily forms small irregular clumps and, as a rule, inhabits open sunny sites. These clumps in some cases grow together to form extensive patches, almost to the exclusion of other herbaceous vegetation. The plant is mainly a native of the higher mountains, being most abundant above 5,000 feet elevation.

The value of western false-hellebore as a forage plant for domestic livestock is of considerable interest, as various early investigators and collectors have reported it either as excellent, unpalatable, or poisonous. However, the consensus of opinion now appears to be that it is poisonous under certain conditions, and that its palatability is highly variable. In Colorado the species is practically worthless for cattle and only poor forage for sheep, but in Montana and northern Idaho it is fairly good for sheep. The herb is little used and rated as poor forage for both cattle and sheep in the Intermountain States and the Southwest. On properly grazed ranges in California and parts of the Northwest it is fairly good for sheep, fair for cattle, and worthless to poor for horses, with the use largely limited to spring and fall. Sheep relish the young shoots, but like other classes of livestock avoid the plant throughout the main growing season, but graze it again after the foliage has been frosted and has become dry and brown. The use of western false-hellebore is very much greater near bed grounds or driveways and where sheep or cattle concentrate. At these areas and on overstocked ranges, the use is frequently so complete that, by midsummer, the entire plant is eaten to within a few inches of the soil. This concentrated use, however, is usually regarded as a sign of serious overstocking. In Montana, and possibly elsewhere, elk and deer graze the plant, especially during the fall and winter.

The poisonous materials are concentrated in the root and the young shoots.[1] As the plant matures, the poison decreases in the aerial portions, so that the species is practically harmless at maturity or when killed by frost. Reports indicate that all classes of livestock are poisoned, but it is generally agreed that the danger is slight where there is plenty of other forage and the animals have normal appetites.

Poisoning usually occurs under some abnormal condition, such as at driveways, bed grounds, overgrazed ranges, or gathering pastures, where hungry animals eat freely of this plant before grazing other forage. Hall and Yates [2] describe the symptoms as including salivation, burning in the throat, weak pulse, and labored respiration, and suggest such stimulants as tannic acid, lard and soda, for treating the sick animals. Poisoned animals usually recover in a few days, although in very serious cases they may die in a few hours. However, on properly grazed ranges, or where western false-hellebore is mainly a fall feed, few animals are poisoned, and deaths are almost unknown. Vansell and Watkins report [3] that blossoms of western false-hellebore sometimes cause heavy losses among honeybees, and that numerous ants, beetles, flies, and other insects are killed by the flowers.

Western false-hellebore is a very distinctive plant, being tall and stout with large, strongly veined, stemless leaves and a long, showy, terminal flower cluster consisting of numerous dull, white flowers. The leaves are frequently punctured by insects and, as the season advances, tend to lose their shape and color. On favorable sites, however, the foliage often remains green until frosted. After frost the plant turns brown and dry so that any such disturbance as wind creates a harsh rustle of the leaves.

FALSE-HELLEBORES (Vera'trum spp.)

The false-hellebores are represented in North America by about eight valid species, of which four are exclusively western. The genus is also represented in Europe and Asia. They are coarse perennial herbs of the bunchflower tribe (Melanthieae) of the lily family (Liliaceae) or, as some authors prefer, a member of the bunchflower family (Melanthaceae) of the lily order (Liliales).

[1] Hanzlik, P. J., and Eds, F. de. PHARMACOLOGY OF VERATRUM CALIFORNICUM. Soc. Expt. Biol. and Med. Proc. 24 : 557–558. 1927.
[2] Hall, H. M., and Yates, H. S. STOCK POISONING PLANTS OF CALIFORNIA. Calif. Agr. Expt. Sta. Bull. 249 : [219]–247, illus. 1915.
[3] Vansell, G. H., and Watkins, W. G. A PLANT POISONOUS TO ADULT BEES. Jour. Econ. Ent. 26 : 168–170. 1933.

The false-hellebores are tall, robust herbs, with unbranched leafy stems arising from a short, thick, brownish or black, poisonous rootstock, which is sometimes covered with a layer of coarse fibrous dead leaf sheaths of previous years. The roots are few, branched, and externally black. The black color of the rootstock may possibly account for the generic name *Veratrum*, as that word is derived from the Latin *vere*, truly, and *ater*, black. The leaves are large, coarse, plaited or folded, and heavily ribbed, stemless or contracted to a broad sheath at the base and are gradually smaller and narrower near the top of the stalk. The flowers are dull white, greenish, or purplish, borne in showy terminal and elongated clusters. These plants have six persistent petallike parts and six stamens; the capsule is three-celled, each cell containing several to many broad-winged seeds. The lower flowers are often male (staminate) only or the staminate and female (pistillate) flowers may occur on separate plants.

The roots of American false-hellebore (*V. viride*) and of the European, or white false-hellebore (*V. album*) yield a powerful poisonous drug, which is used as a heart and arterial sedative.[4] The drug, which contains various related alkaloids, including cevadine, jervine, and veratrine, reduces the pulse power without reducing frequency, but an overdose results in very low pulse, nausea, and muscular prostration. Probably the poisonous effect on livestock is similar, although more marked. There is chemical evidence for believing that similar properties reside in the roots of western species of false-hellebore.

Western false-hellebore is the most common species in the Western States, although American false-hellebore is common in the eastern United States and Canada and has an equally wide distribution. It has much the same characters as western false-hellebore, but is usually recognizable by its drooping clusters of green or yellowish green flowers. The powdered, dried roots of this species are often used as an insecticide, and large quantities are gathered in the Appalachians for that purpose. Fringed false-hellebore (*V. fimbria'-tum*), which grows near the coast in northern California and possibly also in southern Oregon, is interesting because the margins of the petallike parts are fringed, being cleft into many threadlike segments.

[4] Wood, H. C., Remington, J. P., and Sadtler, S. P., assisted by Lyons, A. B., and Wood, H. C. Jr. THE DISPENSATORY OF THE UNITED STATES OF AMERICA, BY DR. GEO. B. WOOD AND DR. FRANKLIN BACHE. Ed. 19. thoroughly rev. and largely rewritten . . . 1,947 pp. Philadelphia and London. 1907.

AMERICAN VETCH

Vi'cia america'na

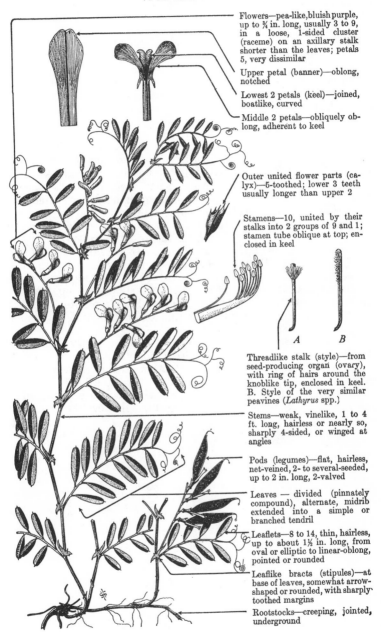

Flowers—pea-like, bluish purple, up to ¾ in. long, usually 3 to 9, in a loose, 1-sided cluster (raceme) on an axillary stalk shorter than the leaves; petals 5, very dissimilar

Upper petal (banner)—oblong, notched

Lowest 2 petals (keel)—joined, boatlike, curved

Middle 2 petals—obliquely oblong, adherent to keel

Outer united flower parts (calyx)—5-toothed; lower 3 teeth usually longer than upper 2

Stamens—10, united by their stalks into 2 groups of 9 and 1; stamen tube oblique at top; enclosed in keel

A   *B*

Threadlike stalk (style)—from seed-producing organ (ovary), with ring of hairs around the knoblike tip, enclosed in keel. B. Style of the very similar peavines (*Lathyrus* spp.)

Stems—weak, vinelike, 1 to 4 ft. long, hairless or nearly so, sharply 4-sided, or winged at angles

Pods (legumes)—flat, hairless, net-veined, 2- to several-seeded, up to 2 in. long, 2-valved

Leaves — divided (pinnately compound), alternate, midrib extended into a simple or branched tendril

Leaflets—8 to 14, thin, hairless, up to about 1½ in. long, from oval or elliptic to linear-oblong, pointed or rounded

Leaflike bracts (stipules)—at base of leaves, somewhat arrow-shaped or rounded, with sharply toothed margins

Rootstocks—creeping, jointed, underground

553

American vetch, a smooth, trailing, or climbing perennial herb, is very common in the range country of the Western States. The specific name, *americana*, given to this plant at the outset of the nineteenth century by the famous Pennsylvania botanist, Gotthilf Muhlenberg (1753–1815), is very apropos, for American vetch is very typical of its genus and is perhaps the most widely distributed and best-known native vetch.

The range of this species extends throughout most of southern Canada, from New Brunswick to British Columbia, and in the United States to Virginia, Kansas, New Mexico, and California. So far as the western range States are concerned, American vetch ordinarily occurs in rather rich, moist, frequently clayey soils from the plains and foothills up to the aspen zone, especially in open, timbered areas or in grass-weed parks and meadows.

American vetch is one of the choice forage weeds, ranking from moderate to high in palatability for all classes of livestock; but because of its delicacy and fragility, and the fact that all its parts above ground are edible—including the flowers and pods—it does not withstand close grazing very well, and it is one of the first plants to decrease under such use. If such close grazing is permitted during the period of rapid development and up to the time for seed to set, the plant makes little or no regrowth from the underground rootstocks, and fails to produce seeds, or to store up a reserve food supply for resuming growth the next season. It may thus be gradually killed out. It usually produces a considerable volume of leafage and tender shoots which are readily eaten throughout the growing season by all classes of livestock but particularly by sheep. American vetch is commonly associated with less palatable plants, such as peavine, geranium, smooth wild-rye, and cinquefoil and, in such mixtures, is frequently very closely cropped.

Wooton and Standley [1] refer to this species as the "common bright blue-flowered vetch of the timbered mountains everywhere in the State" (New Mexico), and call attention to the great variation in width of the leaflets. Flowering begins in June or July and continues through the following month. The seeds are produced until late August or September, depending upon the locality.

---

[1] Wooton, E. O., and Standley, P. C. FLORA OF NEW MEXICO. U. S. Natl. Mus., Contrib. U. S. Natl. Herbarium 19, 794 pp. 1915.

VETCHES (Vi'cia spp.)

The genus *Vicia* belongs to the pea family (Leguminosae, or Fabaceae) and consists of annual or perennial herbs, the majority of which climb by means of tendrils terminating the pinnately divided leaves. *Vicia* is the classical Latin name for vetch. The genus is a large one and has a wide geographical distribution in the Northern Hemisphere, as well as in southern and western South America. About 22 native species and 4 species naturalized from the Old World occur on western ranges. The vetches are of considerable economic importance, since practically all are palatable to domestic livestock; a number of them are grown as fodder plants, others for their edible seeds, and a few (such as scarlet vetch, *V. fulgens*) occasionally are cultivated as ornamentals. Although the native range species occur in only moderate abundance, many of them are widespread, and their herbage is, as a rule, highly palatable throughout the growing season to all classes of livestock, especially sheep. Giant vetch (*V. gigantea*), from Alaska to California, and Modoc vetch (*V. semicincta*), of northern California and southern Oregon, have been limitedly cultivated as forage plants, and it is quite possible that other native vetches are also worthy of trial in cultivation.

Cow vetch (*V. cracca*) is also coming to be considered a valuable species in some parts of the West; Wooton and Standley (*op. cit.*) state that it is not infrequently cultivated in various parts of New Mexico as a fodder or soiling crop. Horsebean, or broadbean (*V. faba*), is used to some extent in Europe for human consumption, but it is grown in the United States mostly for cattle feeding or as a green-manure crop. Bigpod vetch (*V. macrocarpa*) is grown in Algeria as a garden vegetable. The seeds of oneflower vetch (*V. monantha*) are used in France like lentils. Common vetch (*V. sativa*), and hairy vetch (*V. villosa*), which have become naturalized in some parts of the United States, are much cultivated both here and abroad as forage plants. On the whole, the vetches are prized mostly in this country as cover crops and for forage.

Vetches have very dissimilar petals forming the butterflylike flowers characteristic of the pea family. The flowers are borne in rather loose, often 1-sided clusters in the leaf axils and, in the western species, are mostly various shades of blue or purple, though sometimes rose-colored or yellowish white. The trailing or climbing stems are usually angled, often square in cross-section, and are sometimes winged. The alternate leaves are divided (pinnately compound) into (mostly) an even number of leaflets and besides are usually terminated by a simple or branched tendril. In some species, however, these tendrils (which represent morphologically the terminal leaflet of an odd-pinnate leaf) are reduced to a mere rudiment or bristlelike appendage. The rather prominent, leaflike outgrowths (stipules) at the base of the leaves are shaped like half an arrowhead (semi-sagittate). There are 10 stamens arranged in two groups of 9 and 1. The style has an enlarged, rounded tip, or "head" (stigma), with a tuft of hairs more or less encircling it. This character of the style is an important feature, since the vetches greatly resemble the peavines (*Lathyrus* spp.), but in the peavines the style is flattened and hairy along the inner side only.

Like so many of the legumes, vetches possess little swellings (nodules) on their roots. These nodules contain bacteria which are able to take the nitrogen from the soil air and fix it in combination with other elements to form the highly important group of nutritive compounds known as proteins.

SHOWY GOLDENEYE

Viguie'ra multiflo'ra, syn. *Gymnolo'mia multiflo'ra*

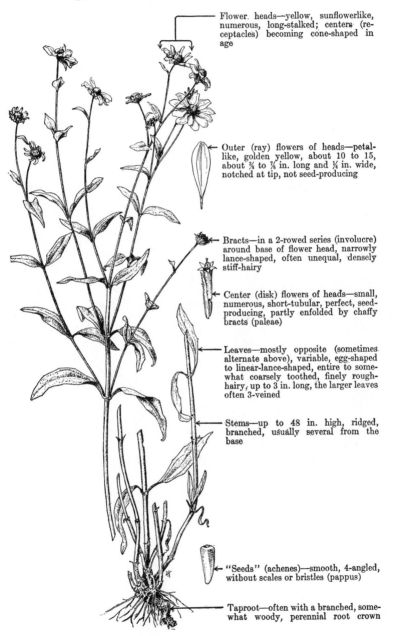

Flower heads—yellow, sunflowerlike, numerous, long-stalked; centers (receptacles) becoming cone-shaped in age

Outer (ray) flowers of heads—petal-like, golden yellow, about 10 to 15, about ⅜ to ⅞ in. long and ¼ in. wide, notched at tip, not seed-producing

Bracts—in a 2-rowed series (involucre) around base of flower head, narrowly lance-shaped, often unequal, densely stiff-hairy

Center (disk) flowers of heads—small, numerous, short-tubular, perfect, seed-producing, partly enfolded by chaffy bracts (paleae)

Leaves—mostly opposite (sometimes alternate above), variable, egg-shaped to linear-lance-shaped, entire to somewhat coarsely toothed, finely rough-hairy, up to 3 in. long, the larger leaves often 3-veined

Stems—up to 48 in. high, ridged, branched, usually several from the base

"Seeds" (achenes)—smooth, 4-angled, without scales or bristles (pappus)

Taproot—often with a branched, somewhat woody, perennial root crown

557

Showy goldeneye, a perennial herb with golden-yellow, sunflower-like flower heads, is sometimes known as rosinweed and as little, small, many-flowered, or mountain sunflower. This species has no well-established common name; showy goldeneye is suggested as a new, appropriate, distinctive, and easily pronounced name in the hope that it will win popular favor. The plant ranges from southern Montana to New Mexico, Mexico, Arizona, California, and Idaho, extending over a considerable altitudinal range in the sagebrush, ponderosa pine, aspen, and spruce belts. It occurs in a wide variety of relatively dry soils, ranging in texture from heavy clays to rocky gravels, and also abounds in grass, weed, brush, woodland, and timber types. However, this plant does not favor dense shade, and in the woodland and timber types ordinarily occurs in openings, where it is usually exposed to direct sunlight for a few hours daily.

Showy goldeneye is common over much of its range and is often locally abundant. Apparently it is an aggressive species, which tends to increase, at least locally, on heavily grazed ranges by supplanting better forage plants. Flowers are produced from July to September; during the late summer and early fall the profuse flower heads of this species are a dominant feature of the floral landscape.

Considerable discrepancy exists in reports as to the palatability of showy goldeneye, and the species merits closer observation on range where it is common. As a rule, it is worthless or at best poor on cattle range, use generally being confined to picking off a few heads. Its value seems to be greatest on browse and grass areas of sheep range where succulent weed feed is scarce, particularly in seasons of drought; in such places and times, its palatability may be rated as fairly good or occasionally even good. In some localities, especially on certain overgrazed cattle ranges of northwestern Colorado, it verges on a pest species, having locally usurped the "place in the sun" formerly enjoyed by its forage betters, decimated by abuse, with marked deterioration of range carrying capacity.

In California the typical form of the species is replaced by a variety, Nevada goldeneye (*V. multiflo'ra nevaden'sis*, syns. *Gymnolo'mia linea'ris, G. nevaden'sis*), which grows in California, Nevada, and southwestern Utah, principally at the lower elevations. It is very similar to showy goldeneye except that the leaves are narrower, linear-lance-shaped, and have rolled-back (revolute) margins. It is not especially abundant, is of low palatability, and relatively unimportant as a range plant.

GOLDENEYES (Viguie'ra spp., syn. *Gymnolo'mia spp.*)

Viguiera is a New World genus, consisting, according to Blake [1] of 143 species and 28 varieties chiefly of Lower California, Mexico, and South America. It is usually composed of perennial herbs or shrubs, although some species are annual; the leaves are opposite, at least below; the numerous small flowers, arranged in mostly yellow heads, have the appearance of a single flower. The genus, named in honor of Dr. L. G. A. Viguier, a physician and botanist of Montpellier, France, is a member of the immense aster, or composite family (Asteraceae, or Compositae). The species are usually called sunflowers, which name is best restricted to the true sunflowers (*Helianthus* spp.) and perhaps to the closely related *Helianthella* genus. Since *Viguiera* has no well-established common name, goldeneye, although never previously applied to this genus, is suggested as an appropriate common name. Blake [1] lists 12 species, involving 7 varieties, which grow in the United States; an annual, Porter goldeneye (*V. por'teri*), is the sole eastern species and occurs in Georgia only. Three of the eleven western species are annuals; four species are shrubby; the others are perennial herbs.

The western annuals, which include annual goldeneye (*V. an'nua*), hairy goldeneye (*V. cilia'ta*), and longleaf goldeneye (*V. longifo'lia*), all extend southward into Mexico. *V. annua* and *V. longifolia* also grow in Arizona, New Mexico, and Texas, *V. annua* extending also into southern Utah; *V. ciliata* in its typical form appears in the United States from Utah to New Mexico, and has, in addition, become naturalized in the neighborhood of Santa Monica, Calif. These three annuals have subsimple or branched, erect stems, yellow flower heads, and are somewhat similar in general aspect to showy goldeneye. Under normal conditions they are practically worthless as forage plants, but may be utilized when other forage is scarce.

The four herbaceous perennial species of the range country include showy goldeneye, annotated at length at the beginning of this discussion, heartleaf goldeneye (*V. cordifo'lia*), which ranges in its typical form from Arizona, New Mexico, and Texas to Mexico; *V. denta'ta*, which grows as var. *lancifo'lia* in Arizona and Mexico and as var. *bre'vipes* in Texas, New Mexico, Arizona, and Mexico; and ovalleaf goldeneye (*V. ova'lis*), occurring in Arizona and New Mexico. In the main, *V. cordifolia, dentata, and ovalis* have egg-shaped leaves, except for *V. dentata lancifolia*, whose leaves are narrowly lance-shaped; some of the leaves of heartleaf goldeneye are also lance-shaped, although all its foliage has a more or less heart-shaped base, as the names heartleaf and *cordifolia* imply. These three species differ materially in habit. Heartleaf goldeneye usually has several stems up to 3 feet tall from a deep root; its flower heads are numerous and borne in panicles, with 6 to 8 ray flowers. *V. dentata* has a slender, much-branched stem from 3 to over 6 feet high,

[1] Blake, S. F. A REVISION OF THE GENUS VIGUIERA. Harvard Univ. Contrib. Gray Herbarium (n. s.) 54, 205 pp., illus. 1918.

with innumerable flower heads bearing 10 to 12 ray flowers. Ovalleaf goldeneye has a moderately stout stem, simple or sometimes branched above, from 12 to 32 inches tall, with only 5 to 11 axillary or terminal flower heads, having 12 ray flowers. Little information is available concerning either the palatability or the abundance of these species. They are probably low in palatability, being utilized as forage only when other feed is scarce. Showy goldeneye and its variety, Nevada goldeneye, are the other two members of this group.

The woody species comprise Death Valley goldeneye (*V. reticula'ta*) limited to the Death Valley region, California; cutleaf goldeneye (*V. lacinia'ta*) found in California and Lower California; Parish goldeneye (*V. deltoi'dea parish'ii*), appearing in California and northern Lower California, Nevada, Arizona, and Sonora; and skeletonleaf goldeneye (*V. stenolo'ba*), which grows in New Mexico and Texas, and in northern Mexico from Chihuahua to Tamaulipas. The flower heads, which are similar to those of showy goldeneye, readily identify these species as members of this genus. Death Valley goldeneye has broadly oval, somewhat heart-shaped, hairy leaves; the leaves of cutleaf goldeneye are all alternate, sometimes in groups at the nodes, and are sharply cut into pronounced lobes; the leaves of Parish goldeneye are triangular in shape, strongly toothed, and conspicuously veined; the leaves of skeletonleaf goldeneye are divided, nearly to the midrib, into 3 to 7 narrow lobes. These shrubby species may have a limited browse value, when other forage is scarce, but otherwise are practically worthless as forage except that livestock will frequently pick off the flowering and fruiting heads or, after frost, nibble the leaves.[2]

[2] Dayton, W. A. IMPORTANT WESTERN BROWSE PLANTS. U. S. Dept. Agr. Misc. Pub. 101, 214 pp., illus. 1931.

MULES-EARS

Wye'thia amplexicau'lis

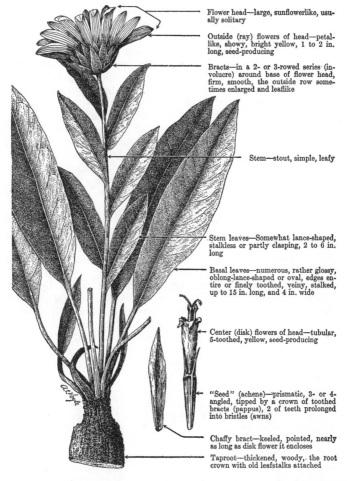

Flower head—large, sunflowerlike, usually solitary

Outside (ray) flowers of head—petal-like, showy, bright yellow, 1 to 2 in. long, seed-producing

Bracts—in a 2- or 3-rowed series (involucre) around base of flower head, firm, smooth, the outside row sometimes enlarged and leaflike

Stem—stout, simple, leafy

Stem leaves—Somewhat lance-shaped, stalkless or partly clasping, 2 to 6 in. long

Basal leaves—numerous, rather glossy, oblong-lance-shaped or oval, edges entire or finely toothed, veiny, stalked, up to 15 in. long, and 4 in. wide

Center (disk) flowers of head—tubular, 5-toothed, yellow, seed-producing

"Seed" (achene)—prismatic, 3- or 4-angled, tipped by a crown of toothed bracts (pappus), 2 of teeth prolonged into bristles (awns)

Chaffy bract—keeled, pointed, nearly as long as disk flower it encloses

Taproot—thickened, woody, the root crown with old leafstalks attached

Mules-ears, also known as green dock, mountain wyethia, black sunflower, and by the Indian name pe-ik, is a smooth, coarse, tufted herb, 1 to 2 feet high, perennial from a thick, woody taproot. It is the commonest and most widespread and one of the most valuable species of the genus *Wyethia*.

These plants were named after Capt. Nathaniel J. Wyeth, an adventurous American traveler, trader, and inventor, with whom Thomas Nuttall, the famous English naturalist, crossed the continent in 1834. Wyeth himself discovered and first collected *Wyethia amplexicaulis*, the first known species. The genus, a member of the aster or sunflower family, is wholly confined to the far-western

States and extreme southwestern Canada, where it is represented by about 15 species, all fairly similar in general appearance and palatability.

Mules-ears is widely distributed, growing from Colorado to Montana, British Columbia, Oregon, and Nevada. It usually occurs in distinct patches averaging from a few square rods to several hundred acres but is also found in small groups and as individual plants intermixed with other weeds, grasses, and browse. It grows on open flats, gentle slopes, and parks from the sagebrush-bluebunch wheatgrass zone through the ponderosa pine and aspen types up into the spruce-fir zones to elevations of about 9,000 feet. This species prefers heavy, compact clay and gumbo soils, and also those with very fine sandy and black topsoil. It often dominates such sites practically to the exclusion of other plants. Its occurrence in distinct patches seems to be thoroughly normal, due to its aggressiveness under certain soil conditions, and not at all necessarily attributable to overgrazing as many believe. However, it is probably true that this plant tends to increase as other less resistant and more palatable plants are killed out by heavy use. The strong, deep-set root system enables the mules-ears plants to resist trampling well. Reproduction is wholly by seed.

Mules-ears leaves, in shape like the ears of a mule, are dark green in color, smooth, somewhat stiff and leathery and are often covered with a resinous or waxy substance.

The flower heads are readily eaten by all classes of livestock as well as by deer and elk, the leaves also being cropped slightly. Sheep prefer the young and tender leaves and will usually seek and crop those in the center of the clumps. Mules-ears has a palatability rating of from 10 to 30 percent for sheep but is usually less palatable for cattle. This species is most important on the spring ranges as well as on areas at medium elevations because growth begins early in the season. The forage becomes tough and harsh and is little eaten after the flowers have matured while the plants brown and dry up during the middle or late summer. Subsequently livestock sometimes eat sparingly of the dry foliage.

The roots of mules-ears were once used by the Indians for food. Nuttall reports [1] that in preparing the roots for consumption the Indians "fermented" them for 1 or 2 days in a ground hole heated with hot stones in order to develop a sweet, agreeable flavor.

Whitehead wyethia (*W. helianthoi'des*) resembles mules-ears both botanically and from a forage standpoint. It differs most conspicuously in having its herbage beset with short stiff hairs, and in having somewhat larger and white or pale yellow flower heads. This species occurs from Montana and northwestern Wyoming to Oregon and Washington.

---

[1] Nuttall, T. A CATALOGUE OF A COLLECTION OF PLANTS MADE CHIEFLY IN THE VALLEYS OF THE ROCKY MOUNTAINS OR NORTHERN ANDES, TOWARD THE SOURCES OF THE COLUMBIA RIVER, BY MR. NATHANIEL B. WYETH. Jour. Acad. Nat. Sci. Phila. 7 : 5–60. 1834.

WOOLLY MULES-EARS

Wye'thia mol'lis

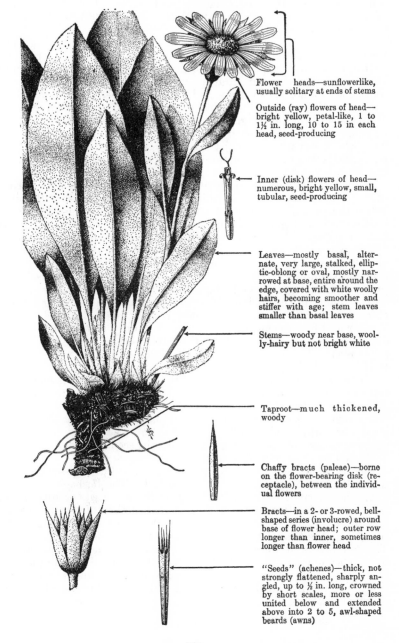

Flower heads—sunflowerlike, usually solitary at ends of stems

Outside (ray) flowers of head— bright yellow, petal-like, 1 to 1½ in. long, 10 to 15 in each head, seed-producing

Inner (disk) flowers of head— numerous, bright yellow, small, tubular, seed-producing

Leaves—mostly basal, alternate, very large, stalked, elliptic-oblong or oval, mostly narrowed at base, entire around the edge, covered with white woolly hairs, becoming smoother and stiffer with age; stem leaves smaller than basal leaves

Stems—woody near base, woolly-hairy but not bright white

Taproot—much thickened, woody

Chaffy bracts (paleae)—borne on the flower-bearing disk (receptacle), between the individual flowers

Bracts—in a 2- or 3-rowed, bell-shaped series (involucre) around base of flower head; outer row longer than inner, sometimes longer than flower head

"Seeds" (achenes)—thick, not strongly flattened, sharply angled, up to ½ in. long, crowned by short scales, more or less united below and extended above into 2 to 5, awl-shaped beards (awns)

Woolly mules-ears, a tufted, perennial herb of the aster or sun-flower family, is also known as woolly wyethia, gray dock, and big sunflower. It is rather similar in general appearance, habitat and forage value to most of the 15 western species of *Wyethia*. Its chief difference is its soft, densely hair-covered leaves. The generic name, *Wyethia*, is in honor of Captain Wyeth (see W206), who appears to have first collected this plant.

Woolly mules-ears is an abundant and common species in California and southern Oregon and also occurs in Nevada. It grows on well-drained soils, exposed ridges, dry open slopes and flats mainly within the ponderosa pine and red fir (*Abies magnifica*) belts and is sometimes found at elevations as high as 9,000 feet. It thrives best under conditions typical of the eastern side of the Sierra Nevada Mountains. The plants grow in dense stands almost to the exclusion of other vegetation in such sites as the red-fir belt, on ridges and flats which have been heavily used and trampled by sheep. Normally, however, they are scattered and appear in mixture with other species.

Woolly mules-ears begins growth soon after the earliest spring plants, and makes its most rapid growth while the soil is still moist. When the plants are young and tender, they are most readily eaten by livestock and game. In general, the species is considered to be low in palatability for cattle and only slightly better for sheep. The flower heads are the most palatable part of the plant and are usually eaten with relish. The close relationship of the plant to the common sunflower (*Helianthus annuus*) suggests that the seeds are probably nutritious. The leafage is but slightly grazed. Deer feed on the plants in the spring when the first shoots appear but general observations indicate that they eat sparingly of the leafage when it is older and less succulent. The plants generally mature and become dry, brittle and worthless during the latter part of August and early September. The roots and fruits of *Wyethia* species were used as food by the Indians.

Their deep-set root systems enable the wyethias to withstand grazing fairly well. In fact, they tend to increase as the more palatable species are killed out by heavy use. Reproduction, except perhaps from vegetative enlargement of the clumps, is entirely from seed which, if uninfested, is of high viability. The plants are rather aggressive despite that a large portion of the seed crop is periodically destroyed by the grubs of an insect.

Woolly mules-ears grows from a thick, woody, deep-set taproot, the stalks attaining a height of 1 to 3 feet. The herbage is silvery and, when young, is thickly covered with soft, white woolly hairs, but with age it often becomes greenish and clothed only with sparse, downy hairs. The leaves in the basal clump are oblong-ovate, pointed at the base, 7 to 19 inches long and are borne on leafstalks. The few leaves produced on the flower stalks are smaller, usually 2 to 5 inches long, and short-stalked. The flower heads are solitary or few, 1 to 3 inches in diameter, with deep yellow ray flowers surrounding a yellow disk made up of small individual flowers set among papery chaff on a flat base.

BEARGRASS

Xerophyl′lum te′nax

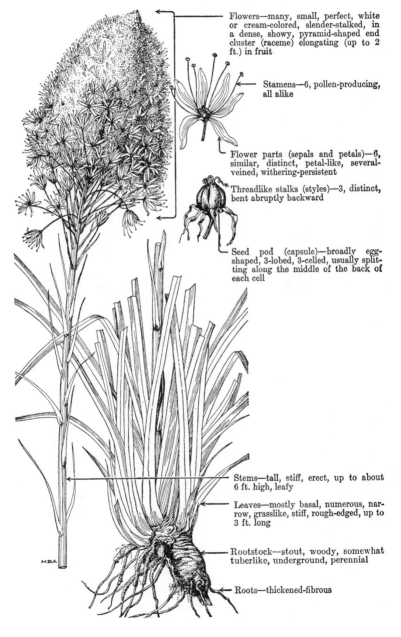

Flowers—many, small, perfect, white or cream-colored, slender-stalked, in a dense, showy, pyramid-shaped end cluster (raceme) elongating (up to 2 ft.) in fruit

Stamens—6, pollen-producing, all alike

Flower parts (sepals and petals)—6, similar, distinct, petal-like, several-veined, withering-persistent

Threadlike stalks (styles)—3, distinct, bent abruptly backward

Seed pod (capsule)—broadly egg-shaped, 3-lobed, 3-celled, usually splitting along the middle of the back of each cell

Stems—tall, stiff, erect, up to about 6 ft. high, leafy

Leaves—mostly basal, numerous, narrow, grasslike, stiff, rough-edged, up to 3 ft. long

Rootstock—stout, woody, somewhat tuberlike, underground, perennial

Roots—thickened-fibrous

Beargrass, sometimes called basketgrass, elkgrass, pinelily, soap-grass, and squawgrass, is a rigid, tufted, evergreen, herbaceous peren-nial plant of the bunchflower family (Melanthiaceae),[1] a group which many botanists prefer to call a subfamily, or tribe (Melan-thieae) of the lily family (Liliaceae). It is said that the name beargrass refers to the fact that bears are reported occasionally to dig up and eat the tuberous rootstocks in the early spring. The generic name is derived from the Greek words *xeros*, dry, and *phyllon*, leaf—dry leaf, and refers to the dry, harsh, rigid leaves. The specific name *tenax* is the Latin for holding fast, which refers possibly to the use of the leaves for binding purposes and for basket making. Beargrass, widely distributed in the mountains from Brit-ish Columbia to California, Nevada, and Montana, is typically a plant of the higher elevations from 3,000 up to about 8,000 feet above sea level. However, strange to say, on the Olympic peninsula in Washington, it appears at sea level, probably because of the cooling effect of the ocean breezes.

This plant grows in all types of soils but best on well-drained slopes and ridges. Beargrass blooms in the spring on the lower slopes and continues until snow falls around the edges of snow banks at high altitudes. Although science does not know definitely, the indications are that this plant does not bloom annually but possibly only once every 5 to 7 years.

Beargrass has very little forage value, although sheep eat the flowers and occasionally nibble at the young leaves. Cattle and some-times sheep pull the leaves and chew off the lower white, tender portion. Deer and elk eat the plant sparingly the year around, es-pecially the more tender leaves. In view of the prevailingly poison-ous character of this plant family, it would not be surprising if scientific research should eventually find toxic properties in bear-grass. Formerly, the Indians bleached and dried the long, fibrous leaves, for weaving and padding. Some roasted the roots for food.

When in bloom, beargrass is one of the most attractive mountain flowers and has appropriately been called The Great White Monarch of the Northwest. The flowers exude a heavy, rather unpleasant fragrance. The flower clusters occur at the top of the stalk, are broad at the base, and taper to a blunt point. Hundreds of cream-white flowers are closely crowded together on slender, white pedicels, their long stamens giving the effect of being solid and appearing feathery. The wiry, grasslike, rough-edged leaves are from 1 to 3 feet long, green on the upper side but a pale gray underneath.

A little known and very closely related species, *X. dougla'sii*, occurs from Oregon to Montana. It differs from *X. tenax* in having a narrower inflorescence, smaller flowers, and more heart-shaped pods. Some botanists regard it as doubtfully separable.

Turkeysbeard (*X. asphodeloi'des*), ranging on sandy pinelands and other acid woods of the eastern United States, from New Jersey to Georgia, North Carolina, and Tennessee, is the third known member of this small, exclusively North American genus.

---

[1] Usually spelled Melanthaceae in the books.

DEATHCAMASES

Zygade'nus spp., syns. *Anticle'a* spp., *Toxicoscor'dion* spp.

Deathcamases, sometimes known as poison-segos, poison-camases, poison-soaproots, and erroneously called lobelias, are herbaceous perennials of the bunchflower family (Melanthiaceae), which many botanists prefer to regard as a tribe or subfamily of the lily family (Liliaceae). These plants are most commonly called deathcamases, to distinguish them from the somewhat similar, edible camases (*Quamasia* spp., syn. *Camassia* spp.) with which they are often confused. The generic name *Zygadenus* is derived from the Greek words *zugon*, a yoke, and *aden*, a gland, and refers to the characteristic, yoked, or paired petal glands of the type species, Atlantic deathcamas (*Z. glaberrimus*) of the Eastern States. In the western species these two glands are united into a single gland found at the base of each flower (perianth) segment. The genus, which is widely distributed from New Brunswick to Alaska and from Florida to northern Mexico, includes approximately 15 species. Deathcamas is represented in all of the eleven far-western States, as well as on range lands in Texas, Kansas, Nebraska, and the Dakotas. The various species occur from slightly above sea level (about 600 feet in California) up to 12,000 feet in Utah. They grow in almost every type of soil and flourish in both dry and moist situations, sometimes actually living in water. Some species grow in clumps or patches, but the majority are mixed with a variety of other herbaceous plants. Usually most species seek full sunlight, but a few prefer shaded sites.

All North American species are poisonous, to a greater or less degree, to both animals and man. Grassy deathcamas (*Z. gramineus*), meadow deathcamas (*Z. venenosus*), foothill deathcamas (*Z. paniculatus*), and mountain deathcamas (*Z. elegans*) are the most common and important species in the West. However, grassy and meadow deathcamases are the most dangerous. *Z. elegans* is only slightly poisonous and probably never is injurious to livestock on the range.[1] The more virulent species of deathcamas cause the majority of sheep losses from poisonous plants on the early spring and summer ranges because they are green and succulent far in advance of most other plants.[2] Plants of this genus are usually dried up before the sheep reach the higher summer ranges, and hence, as a rule, are not then a source of temptation to that class of livestock. Cattle are seldom poisoned unless forced to graze on heavily infested areas, where other forage is scarce. Horses rarely, if ever, eat deathcamas.

Marsh [3] gives the symptoms of deathcamas poisoning as frothing at the mouth, nausea with vomiting, great weakness accompanied sometimes with nervousness and resulting in collapse of the animal, which may lie without food for hours, or even days, before death. While permanganate of potash, aluminum sulphate, and bleeding have been recommended [4] [5] as remedies for deathcamas poisoning, the only practical defense or control, under range conditions, is to prohibit the animals from heavily infested areas.[6] All parts of the plants are toxic; sometimes very small quanties will produce injury. The mature seeds are particularly toxic but, fortunately, the plants are dry and not very palatable at the time of seed dissemination.[6][7]

At certain stages of plant growth, it is very difficult to distinguish deathcamas from such related but harmless plants as camas (*Quamasia*), onion (*Allium*), wild-hyacinth (*Hookera*) and mariposa, including sego-lily (*Calochortus*). Deathcamases often grow in association with onions and wild hya-

[1] Marsh, C. D., and Clawson, A. B. THE DEATH CAMAS SPECIES, ZYGADENUS PANICULATUS AND Z. ELEGANS, AS POISONOUS PLANTS. U. S. Dept. Agr. Bull. 1012, 25 pp., illus. 1922.
[2] Marsh, C. D., Clawson, A. B., and Marsh, H. ZYGADENUS, OR DEATH CAMAS. U. S. Dept. Agr. Bull. 125, 46 pp., illus. 1915.
[3] Marsh, C. D. STOCK-POISONING PLANTS OF THE RANGE. U. S. Dept. Agr. Bull. 1245, rev., 75 pp., illus. 1929. Supersedes Bull. 575.
[4] Chesnut, V. K., and Wilcox, E. V. THE STOCK-POISONING PLANTS OF MONTANA: A PRELIMINARY REPORT. U. S. Dept. Agr., Div. Bot. Bull. 26, 150 pp., illus. 1901.
[5] Talbot, P. R., and Hooper, J. C. WEEDS POISONOUS TO LIVESTOCK. Alberta Dept. Agr. Bull. 1, 40 pp., illus. 1919.
[6] Marsh, C. D., and Clawson, A. B. THE STOCK-POISONING DEATH CAMAS. U. S. Dept. Agr. Farmers' Bull. 1273, 11 pp., illus. 1922.
[7] Niemann, K. W. REPORT OF AN OUTBREAK OF POISONING IN THE DOMESTICATED FOWL, DUE TO DEATH CAMAS. Jour. Amer. Vet. Med. Assoc. 73: 627–630, illus. 1928.

cinths. During the early spring, when these plants are about 3 to 4 inches high, they all look very much alike. Onions can be identified easily by crushing the leaves between the fingers and noting the strong characteristic onion odor, similar to that of the common garden onion. If the onion odor is not present and if, upon cutting a cross section of the leaf, the midrib is distinctly hollow, forming a hollow tube the length of the leaf, the plant is almost certainly a wild-hyacinth. Camas usually is in bloom at this early stage and, because of its blue flowers, is not likely to be mistaken for deathcamas. After the seeds of both camas and deathcamas are mature it is often difficult to distinguish between them. The leaves fold up lengthwise in deathcamas, while camas leaves remain flat. The mature capsules of deathcamas are much smaller, more closely set upon the stem, and split along the partitions separating the three cells, whereas the ripe capsules of camas split down the midrib on the back of the three cells. The mariposas, including sego-lily, are easily distinguished as they have but one or two basal leaves.

Early western explorers frequently mentioned the poisonous deathcamases and their likeness to camases, whose edible bulbs were used extensively as food by the Indians. Despite that the Indians were familiar with the danger in deathcamas, many cases of poisoning occurred among them. The Indians believed that deathcamas bulbs possess medicinal value. Chemical analyses [8] [9] have shown the presence of mixed alkaloids which hasten the heartbeat and make it irregular, slow the respiration, cause convulsions, and have a powerful purgative, emetic, and diuretic action; also of an alkaloid called zygadenine ($C_{39}H_{63}NO_{10}$) which behaves in general very much like the powerful heart-depressant, veratrine ($C_{32}H_{19}NO_{11}$),[9] a poisonous substance (or group of substances) frequently occurring in plants of the bunchflower family, and apparently does not cause convulsions. Additional toxic alkaloids have been isolated from deathcamas by Prof. Jacobson of the Nevada Agricultural College and others and the toxicological chemistry of these plants must still be regarded as in the investigative stage.

Deathcamases have a leafy or leafless stem varying in height from a few inches to 4 feet. The plants are smooth (glabrous) with long, narrow, grasslike leaves arising from the base. Sometimes the leaves and stems are covered with a whitish bloom which rubs off easily. The flowers are greenish white or yellowish in color, being set rather closely in terminal racemes or panicles and are either perfect or have male and female flowers as well (imperfect). The flower heads elongate as the plant matures. The six similar floral segments (perianth) are divided to the base and bear one or two glands. These flower parts wither but persist on the plant until the seed pod (capsule) dehisces and the seeds are dispersed. The six stamens are either free to the base or attached to the petallike floral segments and are about the same length as the segments. The styles are distinct to the base, and the three-lobed and three-celled capsule splits from the top along the three partitions, releasing the numerous angled seeds. The plants have bulbs or sometimes rootstocks (rhizomes). The bulbs have concentric coats like an onion. Rydberg [10] states that, for consistency, *Zygadenus* should be divided into three genera: (1) Plants with a rootstock and two glands (*Zygadenus*); (2) plants with a bulb and single gland, ovary wholly superior (*Toxicoscordion*); (3) plants with a bulb and single gland, ovary partly inferior (*Anticlea*). The majority of botanists, however, prefer to regard these characters as of sectional or subgeneric weight only, and to consider *Anticlea* and *Toxicoscordion* as synonyms of *Zygadenus*.

Some authors deem *Z. venenosus* as synonymous with *Z. gramineus*, but the consensus of opinion among leading botanists of today is that these should be considered separate species. *Z. chloranthus, Z. coloradensis,* and *Z. glaucus* are regarded by most botanists as synonyms of *Z. elegans. Z. douglasii* is a synonym of Frémont deathcamas (*Z. fremontii*) of California.

[8] Heyl, F. W., Loy, S. K., Knight, H. G., and Prien, O. L. THE CHEMICAL EXAMINATION OF DEATH CAMAS. Wyo. Agr. Expt. Sta. Bull. 94, 31 pp., illus. 1912.
[9] Loy, S. K., Heyl, F. W., and Hepner, F. E. ZYGADENINE. THE CRYSTALLIN ALKALOID OF ZYGADENUS INTERMEDIUS. Wyo. Agr. Expt. Sta. Bull. 101 : [89]–98, illus. 1913.
[10] Rydberg, P. A. SOME GENERIC SEGREGATIONS. Bull. Torrey Bot. Club 30 : 271–281, illus. 1903.

MEADOW DEATHCAMAS

Zygade'nus veneno'sus, syn. *Toxicoscor'dion veneno'sum*

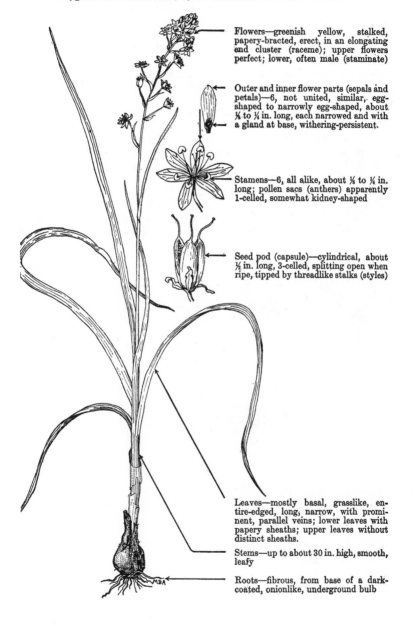

Flowers—greenish yellow, stalked, papery-bracted, erect, in an elongating end cluster (raceme); upper flowers perfect; lower, often male (staminate)

Outer and inner flower parts (sepals and petals)—6, not united, similar, egg-shaped to narrowly egg-shaped, about ⅛ to ¼ in. long, each narrowed and with a gland at base, withering-persistent.

Stamens—6, all alike, about ⅛ to ¼ in. long; pollen sacs (anthers) apparently 1-celled, somewhat kidney-shaped

Seed pod (capsule)—cylindrical, about ½ in. long, 3-celled, splitting open when ripe, tipped by threadlike stalks (styles)

Leaves—mostly basal, grasslike, entire-edged, long, narrow, with prominent, parallel veins; lower leaves with papery sheaths; upper leaves without distinct sheaths.

Stems—up to about 30 in. high, smooth, leafy

Roots—fibrous, from base of a dark-coated, onionlike, underground bulb

This characteristic bulbous herb of the deathcamas genus (*Zyga-denus*) is abundant and widely distributed in the West. The specific name *venenosus* is a Latin word meaning poisonous. The plant is found from British Columbia to California, Utah, Nebraska, and South Dakota, its altitudinal range extending from 1,400 to 8,000 feet. The species prefers rich, moist bottom lands and lower foothills, but sometimes grows on rocky sites. This plant does not ordinarily appear in pure stands, but is very plentiful on some overgrazed ranges.

Meadow deathcamas is one of the most toxic range species,[1] being responsible for the loss of thousands of sheep. It is particularly dangerous, because it furnishes green, succulent feed in advance of many other plants on the early spring ranges. The best way to prevent losses is to herd the sheep away from the areas which are heavily infested. Cultivation will kill meadow deathcamas, but the practice of good range management is probably the most practical method of permanent control, especially if supplemented by the seeding of suitable range grasses to crowd out the meadow deathcamas. Sheep are not likely to eat the plant if plenty of other forage is available. Losses seldom occur on the high summer range, because there is an abundance of other succulent forage, and because the meadow deathcamas plants are dry and unpalatable before the sheep arrive.

The flowers appear during May and June, and the seed is disseminated in July and August. Further information on deathcamas is given in the notes for the genus *Zygadenus*.

---

[1] Marsh, C. D., and Clawson, A. B. THE MEADOW DEATH CAMAS (ZYGADENUS VENENOSUS) AS A POISONOUS PLANT. U. S. Dept. Agr. Bull. 1240, 14 pp., illus. 1924.

ACACIAS

Aca'cia spp.

The acacias belong to the mimosa family (Mimosaceae), which some authors include as a subfamily of the immense legume family (Leguminosae), and are widely distributed throughout the tropics and subtropics and also occur in some temperate regions. Most of the 400 or more species are native to Australia and Africa; about 16 species occur naturally in the West, and the genus is well represented in Mexico. Except for a few herbaceous species, acacias are trees or shrubs; they have either bipinnately compound leaves or apparently simple leaves (the latter are not actually leaves but, rather, leaflike petioles known as phyllodes, no true blade being present). The small, numerous, usually orange-yellow (sometimes lemon-yellow or white) flowers are borne in dense heads, spikes, or axillary racemes.

The acacias are an important source of valuable forest products, including gums, dyes, tannins, medicines, perfumes, lac, fibers, and timber. Many of the species with low tannin content are useful as browse. For example, the leaves and young shoots form the principal browse for goats and camels on African and Asiatic deserts, and certain species in Australia furnish considerable browse for cattle, sheep, and other livestock.[1] Probably all the acacias native to the United States have some forage value, with catclaw, which is written up separately in this handbook, the most important, although the palatability of their herbage is usually low to fair. The pods of acacias are likely to be too bitter, too tough, or both, to be attractive to domestic livestock. In Africa certain species (such as *A. giraffae*) are the favorite food of the giraffe, and Darwin deduced that the development of the elongated neck of this animal was the result of its ancestors' efforts to crop the foliage of these acacia trees. Catechu, the well-known astringent of modern medicine, is obtained from an acacia of Hindustan. A number of species are cultivated as ornamentals. Certain tropical American species, known as bullhorn acacias, are interesting examples of entomophily, the spines being converted into ant chambers, the ants, in turn, protecting the trees from grazing animals and other invaders.[2]

Probably no other semitropical trees of high economic value surpass the acacias in ability to thrive upon and even improve many arid and sterile soils. Although only half hardy to frost, these plants grow well under such restricted precipitation as only a few inches of rainfall annually. The late C. H. Shinn,[1] a former Forest Service supervisor, has called attention to the value of acacias for ocean sand dune and inland sand barren reclamation, under arid and semiarid conditions where the temperature does not fall below 20° F. He states that there are about 40 species well adapted to hedge use and for shelter belts in areas of brisk winds and high

---

[1] Shinn, C. H. AN ECONOMIC STUDY OF ACACIAS. U. S. Dept. Agr. Bull. 9, 38 pp., illus. 1913.
[2] Safford, W. E. ANT ACACIAS AND ACACIA ANTS OF MEXICO AND CENTRAL AMERICA. Smithsn. Inst. Ann. Rept. 1921: 381–394, illus. 1922.

evaporation. He refers to the success of blackwood acacia (*A. melanoxylon*) as a street tree in California near gas works, about copper smelters, in sewage, and in places subjected to overflow, alkali, and sea salt—conditions inimical to the growth of nearly every other species of tree. The propagation of Australian acacias, including many valuable timber species, began about 1850 in California; subsequently, they have been extensively planted. The beautiful plantings at Golden Gate Park, San Francisco, exemplify effective evidence of sand-dune reclamation.[1]

The huisache, or sweet acacia (*A. farnesia'na*), native from western Texas south to northern Chile, is widely cultivated at home and abroad and, under the (unfortunately misleading) names cassie and opopanax, is an aristocrat among commercial perfumery plants. The "wattle" (*Acacia* spp.) is the national emblem of Australia and appears on the coins and postage stamps of that island continent. Many of the acacias, such as koa (*A. koa*) of Hawaii and blackwood acacia, are famous cabinet woods.

Probably no tree has entered into the symbolism of Oriental peoples more than the acacia. The great durability of its wood, resistance to decay, and ability to survive most adverse circumstances have made it an emblem of eternal life and security since earliest time. As such, it enters frequently into Old Testament typology; for example, the altar and the ark of the covenant (containing the tables with the Commandments) were made of acacia (Hebrew *shittah;* plural, *shittim*) wood, probably *A. seyal*. Many authorities believe that the word *gopher* of the Book of Genesis, of which Noah's ark was built, also refers to the acacia and has a similar symbolism.

---

[1] See footnote on preceding page.

CATCLAW

Aca'cia greg'gii

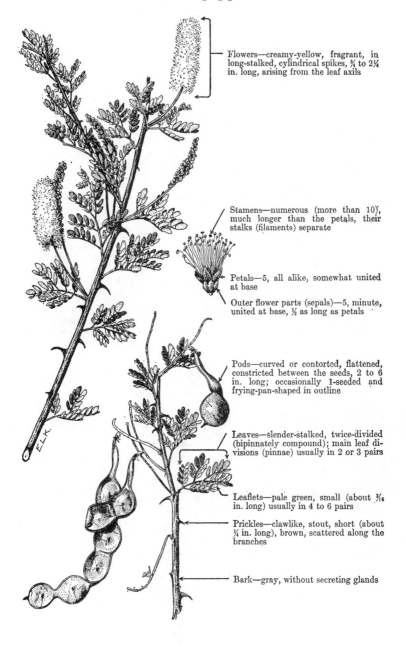

Flowers—creamy-yellow, fragrant, in long-stalked, cylindrical spikes, ¾ to 2¼ in. long, arising from the leaf axils

Stamens—numerous (more than 10), much longer than the petals, their stalks (filaments) separate

Petals—5, all alike, somewhat united at base

Outer flower parts (sepals)—5, minute, united at base, ½ as long as petals

Pods—curved or contorted, flattened, constricted between the seeds, 2 to 6 in. long; occasionally 1-seeded and frying-pan-shaped in outline

Leaves—slender-stalked, twice-divided (bipinnately compound); main leaf divisions (pinnae) usually in 2 or 3 pairs

Leaflets—pale green, small (about ⅜₆ in. long) usually in 4 to 6 pairs

Prickles—clawlike, stout, short (about ¼ in. long), brown, scattered along the branches

Bark—gray, without secreting glands

Catclaw, known also as catclaw acacia, devils-claw, Gregg acacia, paradise-flower, Texas mimosa and uña de gato (claw of cat) is a southwestern species ranging from western Texas to southern Nevada, northern Lower California, and northern Chihuahua, Mexico. It is a typical desert or semidesert species, often occurring in dry valleys and ravines, and on sandy or gravelly, arid mesas, usually in considerable abundance. It is especially characteristic of the creosotebush belt, and is frequently associated with mesquites (*Prosopis* spp.). The flowers usually appear in May or June, and the brown pods mature mainly between July and September.[1]

Acacia (Greek *akakia*) is a name used by the early Greek physician-botanist Dioscorides to describe an Egyptian thorny tree—probably a true acacia. According to some, the word is of Egyptian origin, although others derive it from the Greek *ake*, a point or thorn. This species was named in honor of Dr. Josiah Gregg (1806–1850), explorer and plant collector. Although catclaw grows typically as a prickly shrub 3 to 10 feet high, it frequently develops into an upright tree up to 25 or 30 feet tall, especially on the better soils.

The browse importance of this shrub or small tree varies somewhat, dependent upon associated species, drought, and other local conditions, but, everything considered, it is the most important species of *Acacia* on the southwestern ranges. In general, the species tends to be grazed more in dry than in normal or moist years, and more on ranges where there is little browse than where there is much other palatable browse. On some depleted ranges, catclaw undoubtedly rates as fairly good forage and certain areas have been overstocked as a result of considering such excessive use normal. On conservatively grazed ranges, however, especially when succulent grass is present, this species generally ranks as poor forage. The twigs become green early in the spring, before the new leaves appear, and furnish relatively succulent and fairly palatable forage for a short period at that time. Also, at least in southern Arizona, the new leaves, buds, and flowers are often eaten rather extensively in late spring and until the summer rains begin. In that region there is usually little fresh growth of grass in the spring, and the relative readiness with which catclaw is then grazed is due to its herbage being succulent and green. In drought years, when the dry grass forage of the previous summer has usually been grazed closely by springtime, catclaw, because of its abundance, rather profuse and delicate herbage, and its vigor and ability to withstand heavy grazing, becomes an important feed. Mature leaves and pods, however, are of inferior palatability. Furthermore, sharp prickles render parts of the plant inaccessible to grazing animals.

When of tree habit, catclaw is valued on the range for its shade—a matter of especial importance on arid sites.[1] Goldman notes that catclaw by its shade and thorny protection affords a "favorite hiding place for jack rabbits and other mammals."[2] It is a host plant for several species of lac insects, which produce lac, a material used in varnishes and shellac. When accessible to bee colonies, the fragrant flowers serve as an important source of honey. Standley reports it exudes a gum similar to gum arabic, which is used locally.[3]

Catclaw is readily recognizable by its fragrant yellow flowers, borne in dense cylindrical spikes three-fourths to 2¼ inches long, and by its distinctive flat seed pods. These pods are constricted between the seeds, curved or contorted, one-half to three-fourths of an inch wide, 2 to 6 inches long, and several-seeded (occasionally very short and one-seeded), and are shaped somewhat like a frying pan. Prickles, scattered along the stems, are short (about one-fourth of an inch long), stout, and curved. The leaves are twice divided (bipinnately compound), with very small leaflets. This shrub has rather light gray bark, somewhat furrowed and scaly on the trunk, and very hard, durable wood. Most other acacias growing with catclaw on the range have their flowers in globular clusters, and the majority are either unarmed or have straight thorns.

[1] Dayton, W. A. IMPORTANT WESTERN BROWSE PLANTS. U. S. Dept. Agr. Misc. Pub. 101, 214 pp., illus. 1931.
[2] Goldman, E. A. PLANT RECORDS OF AN EXPEDITION TO LOWER CALIFORNIA. U. S. Natl. Mus., Contrib. U. S. Natl. Herbarium 16 : 309–371, illus. 1916.
[3] Standley, P. C. TREES AND SHRUBS OF NEW MEXICO (FAGACEAE-FABACEAE). U. S. Natl. Mus., Contrib. U. S. Natl. Herbarium 23 : 171–515. 1922.

VINE MAPLE

A'cer circina'tum

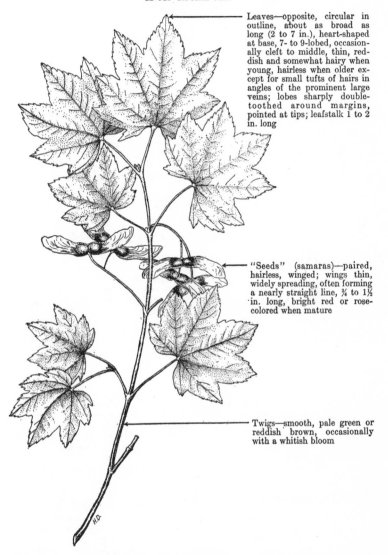

Leaves—opposite, circular in outline, about as broad as long (2 to 7 in.), heart-shaped at base, 7- to 9-lobed, occasionally cleft to middle, thin, reddish and somewhat hairy when young, hairless when older except for small tufts of hairs in angles of the prominent large veins; lobes sharply double-toothed around margins, pointed at tips; leafstalk 1 to 2 in. long

"Seeds" (samaras)—paired, hairless, winged; wings thin, widely spreading, often forming a nearly straight line, ¾ to 1½ in. long, bright red or rose-colored when mature

Twigs—smooth, pale green or reddish brown, occasionally with a whitish bloom

Vine maple gained its name from the straggling, crooked, vinelike appearance of its smooth, slender stems. The specific name *circinatum*, meaning coiled, also alludes to the vinelike habit of growth. This species grows either as a slender shrub or small tree in the forests of the Northwest, ranging from British Columbia to Mendocino County, California. In Washington it occurs mainly on the west side of the Cascade Mountains, but also grows in the canyon bottoms, along drainage lines, and on moist slopes on the eastern side of the mountains. In Oregon this plant apparently is confined almost entirely to the west side of the Cascades; in northeastern California it also occurs under the drier, east side conditions.

Vine maple is exceedingly tolerant of shade and forms an understory in forests of Douglas fir, western hemlock, silver fir, lowland white fir, and on the eastern slope in moist bottoms in the ponderosa pine type. It grows most luxuriantly on the low, alluvial bottom lands where its stems spread in wide curves, sending out long slender branches, which often take root where they contact the ground, forming dense, almost impenetrable, thickets, often many acres in extent, of contorted and intertwined stems. This plant is commonly 5 to 20 feet high, but, on the more favorable sites, it attains treelike proportions up to 30 or 40 feet in height, with main stems up to 10 or 12 inches thick.[1] Vine maple also favors moist, rich soils on flats, benches, depressions, borders of mountain streams, and moist slopes, ranging from near sea level to elevations of about 5,000 feet. After the virgin forests of the Douglas fir region have been logged-off or destroyed by fire, vine maple is usually one of the common species which reappear in the shrub stage of plant succession. When growing under full sunlight in openings, such as clearings, cut-over or burned-over areas, this plant develops into an erect, compact, symmetrical shrub, totally different in appearance from the form it assumes in dense shade.

This species usually rates as fair to good forage for both cattle and sheep, being of greatest significance as a browse plant on the logged-off lands where it furnishes large amounts of palatable herbage. In his studies of grazing use on Douglas fir cut-over lands in Washington, the late Douglas C. Ingram[2] found that utilization of available vine maple herbage by sheep varied from 49 percent to 99 percent over two successive seasons, with averages of about 79 percent and 84 percent. Undoubtedly the higher utilization occurred on the more heavily grazed portions of the range. Ordinarily, large-scale livestock operations are not conducted in the dense virgin forests of the Douglas fir region, although the domestic animals of ranchers and settlers customarily graze in many of the bottoms, usually making moderate use of the vine maple. The twigs are browsed with relish during the winter; it is, in fact, a local practice among settlers in some parts of the Northwest to slash this plant down in the winter to provide emergency feed for their cattle and sheep, when grasses and other natural forage are scarce.

The leaves and twigs of vine maple are also valuable feed of the Columbian blacktail deer and the Roosevelt elk, the important big game species native to the coastal region. These animals browse the leaves in spring and summer, and the leafless twigs often form an important part of their winter diet. The fact that this species grows most abundantly in the lower mountains and bottom lands, where the game animals concentrate during the winter, enhances its importance as a winter game food. Vine maple is one of the key species on the elk ranges of the Olympic Peninsula in Washington, where it is the backbone of the winter range. The elk utilize the herbage and twigs at all seasons of the year and browse many of the plants as high as they can reach. Vine maple is enabled to stand up well under excessive browsing, since many of the branches extend above the reach of grazing animals and the plants, if given a chance, replenish themselves profusely by new shoots and suckers.

The wood of vine maple is heavy, hard, and close-grained but not strong. Although used locally for fuel and for minor domestic purposes, it has no commercial value. The coastal Indians of the Northwest use the slender stems for the bows of their fishing-nets.[1] During autumn, the leaves often dominate the landscape with their brilliant and artistically blended, reddish, yellow, or bright scarlet hues.

A mountain side painted with the autumn foliage of vine maple is a gorgeous and soul-stirring spectacle. Because of its handsome foliage, its slender pale green or reddish brown twigs, and its scarlet flowers with protruding golden stamens, this plant is prized in ornamental cultivation in the Eastern States and in Europe.

[1] Sargent, C. S. MANUAL OF THE TREES OF NORTH AMERICA (EXCLUSIVE OF MEXICO). Ed. 2, reprinted with corrections, 910 pp., illus. Boston and New York. 1926.
[2] Ingram, D. C. VEGETATIVE CHANGES AND GRAZING USE ON DOUGLAS FIR CUT-OVER LAND. Jour. Agr. Research [U. S.] 43 : 387–417, illus. 1931.

ROCKY MOUNTAIN MAPLE

A'cer gla'brum, syns. *A. ne'o-mexica'num, A. triparti'tum*

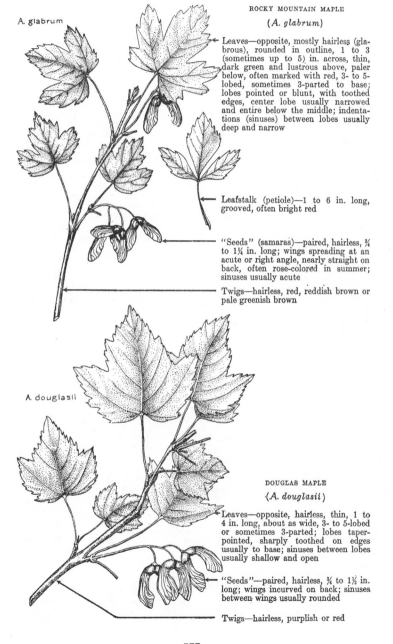

A. glabrum

ROCKY MOUNTAIN MAPLE

(*A. glabrum*)

Leaves—opposite, mostly hairless (glabrous), rounded in outline, 1 to 3 (sometimes up to 5) in. across, thin, dark green and lustrous above, paler below, often marked with red, 3- to 5-lobed, sometimes 3-parted to base; lobes pointed or blunt, with toothed edges, center lobe usually narrowed and entire below the middle; indentations (sinuses) between lobes usually deep and narrow

Leafstalk (petiole)—1 to 6 in. long, grooved, often bright red

"Seeds" (samaras)—paired, hairless, ¾ to 1¼ in. long; wings spreading at an acute or right angle, nearly straight on back, often rose-colored in summer; sinuses usually acute

Twigs—hairless, red, reddish brown or pale greenish brown

A. douglasii

DOUGLAS MAPLE

(*A. douglasii*)

Leaves—opposite, hairless, thin, 1 to 4 in. long, about as wide, 3- to 5-lobed or sometimes 3-parted; lobes taper-pointed, sharply toothed on edges usually to base; sinuses between lobes usually shallow and open

"Seeds"—paired, hairless, ¾ to 1½ in. long; wings incurved on back; sinuses between wings usually rounded

Twigs—hairless, purplish or red

577

Rocky Mountain maple, also called dwarf maple[1] and sometimes known as mountain maple and rock maple, varies in size from a bush about 7 feet high to a small tree. It is one of the most widespread maples on the western ranges, being distributed from South Dakota and Montana to Idaho, Oregon, California, and New Mexico. As the common name indicates, this plant is essentially a Rocky Mountain rather than a Pacific species. It is largely replaced in the Northwest by Douglas maple (*A. douglasii,* syn. *A. glabrum douglasii*). Although these two species are often merged by botanists, typical specimens of each are readily distinguishable, and the best present-day botanical opinion is that they are separate species. Two forms of Rocky Mountain maple have been described as separate species (*A. neo-mexicanum* and *A. tripartitum*), on the basis of their three-parted leaves, but the three-foliate leaf character is not constant, since both compound and simple leaves are often found on the same plants. Most authorities now agree that these variants do not merit specific rank.

Rocky Mountain maple grows on mountain slopes, along streams, moist canyons and gulches, and in moist flats among timber, such as open Douglas fir, aspen, western larch, red fir, and ponderosa pine. It is most characteristic of porous, sandy or gravelly loams, but also appears on cliffs and rocky canyon sides or on dry brushy sites, frequently associated with serviceberry, chokecherry, spirea, and snowberry. Although it thrives best at moderate elevations, it extends from the foothills to altitudes of over 10,000 feet in the southern part of its range. This plant usually appears as a dense low shrub growing as scattered individual clumps, but occasionally occurring in abundance as one of the dominant shrubs on localized range areas. In the most favorable sites it sometimes assumes tree-like proportions, reaching heights of 20 to 30 feet, with a short trunk 6 to 12 inches in diameter.[2]

The forage value of Rocky Mountain maple varies from practically worthless to good. In eastern Montana, Wyoming, Colorado, Utah, much of the Great Basin region and the Southwest, it is considered worthless or poor for all classes of livestock. However, it ranks as fair for sheep and goats and poor for cattle in western Montana, northern Idaho, and parts of Oregon, and is rated fair to good for sheep and fair for cattle in California. Game animals apparently utilize the herbage of this maple extensively. Dixon[3] found that the leaves, twigs, and sprouts are fair in palatability for mule deer in California.

The foliage and twigs of this maple are smooth and mostly hairless (glabrous), hence the specific name *glabrum.* The graceful shining foliage contrasts beautifully with the often red petioles and branches. The leaves are often infested by a blight or fungus which causes portions of the leaves to turn a bright red during the growing season.

DOUGLAS MAPLE (A. dougla'sii, syn. *A. gla'brum dougla'sii*)

Douglas maple, known also as mountain maple or dwarf maple, is a shrub or small tree, very similar in many respects to Rocky Mountain maple. These two species can usually be distinguished by their leaf characters. Douglas maple leaves have 3 to 5 taper-pointed, sharply toothed lobes, the sinuses between the lobes are usually shallow and open, and the lobes are toothed all the way to the base; the wings of the "seeds" of Douglas maple are incurved on the back, and the sinuses between the wings are rounded. In contrast, the leaves of Rocky Mountain maple are rounder in outline, with the three to five lobes usually broader or more obtuse toward the apex.

Douglas maple is essentially a Northwestern species, distributed from Alaska to Vancouver Island, Washington, and Oregon, and extending eastward through the Blue Mountains of Oregon to northwestern Wyoming and Alberta. It is often common on brushy or timber-covered slopes, in fairly heavy shade, about seeps and springs, and along streams, at elevations ranging from sea level to about 6,000 feet. It attains its best development in rich moist loams, where it occasionally grows to tree size, reaching a height of 40 feet and a diameter of from 12 to 18 inches. This plant commemorates David Douglas, the famous Scotch botanical explorer, who discovered this species.

The palatability of Douglas maple is usually fair for cattle and fair to good for sheep and goats. Deer and elk eat freely of the leaves, especially in the spring and early summer, and browse the twigs in the fall and winter.

[1] Sudworth, G. B. CHECK LIST OF THE FOREST TREES OF THE UNITED STATES, THEIR NAMES AND RANGES. U. S. Dept. Agr. Misc. Circ. 92, 295 pp. 1927.
[2] Sargent, C. S. MANUAL OF THE TREES OF NORTH AMERICA (EXCLUSIVE OF MEXICO). Ed. 2, reprinted with corrections, 910 pp., illus. Boston and New York. 1926.
[3] Dixon, J. S. A STUDY OF THE LIFE HISTORY AND FOOD HABITS OF MULE DEER IN CALIFORNIA. PART 2.—FOOD HABITS. Calif. Fish and Game 20(4) : [315]–354, illus. 1934.

CHAMISE

Adeno'stoma fascicula'tum

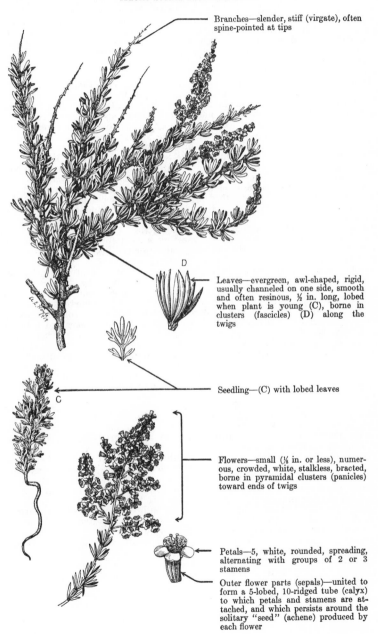

Branches—slender, stiff (virgate), often spine-pointed at tips

Leaves—evergreen, awl-shaped, rigid, usually channeled on one side, smooth and often resinous, ½ in. long, lobed when plant is young (C), borne in clusters (fascicles) (D) along the twigs

Seedling—(C) with lobed leaves

Flowers—small (⅛ in. or less), numerous, crowded, white, stalkless, bracted, borne in pyramidal clusters (panicles) toward ends of twigs

Petals—5, white, rounded, spreading, alternating with groups of 2 or 3 stamens

Outer flower parts (sepals)—united to form a 5-lobed, 10-ridged tube (calyx) to which petals and stamens are attached, and which persists around the solitary "seed" (achene) produced by each flower

Chamise, also known as chamiso and greasewood, is a common, exclusively Californian, evergreen shrub of the rose family, occurring in the foothills of the Sierra Nevadas and the Coast Range from Mendocino and Lake Counties south to Lower California. The generic name, *Adenostoma*, from two Greek words, *adenos* (gland's) + *stoma* (mouth) alludes to the five small glands on the upper inside margin of the calyx tube. The specific name is a Latin adjective derived from *fasciculus* (a little bundle) and refers to the conspicuously clustered (fascicled) arrangement of the small leaves. The common names chamiso and chamise are from the Spanish, *chamiza* (a kind of wild cane, or reed), cognate with the Spanish word *chamizal*, chamise thicket, and appears to refer to the dense thickets formed by this shrub, suggesting an impenetrable stand of cane, or reed.

Chamise inhabits mountain slopes and ridges at elevations of from 500 to 5,000 feet, forming dense brushfields of several thousand acres, occurring either in pure stands or in combination with other chaparral species. Jepson [1] refers to it as the most abundant and characteristic bush in the higher foothills of cismontane California, commonly gregarious and often forming a distinct zone between the lower foothills and the yellow pine belt. Although the species dominates vast areas its belt is discontinuous.

Chamise is one of the most unpalatable shrubs in California, lacks forage value for domestic livestock, and is of but slight importance as a winter browse for deer. Stockmen frequently consider it a pest because of its tendency to crowd out palatable plants over vast areas, and it often constitutes a barrier to the use of isolated feed types and the seasonal migration of livestock. Pursuant to an experimental burn on the Mendocino National Forest, many chamise seedlings came in the first year, and the seedling leaf type was found to be fairly palatable to sheep and cattle. The rather succulent and delicate sprouts produced by chamise the first season following the fire were rather extensively grazed by the livestock but, after the first year, these sprays were largely inedible. Sporadic attempts to replace chamise by burning have thus far proved impractical as an improved permanent type of vegetation has not resulted. The plant quickly reestablishes itself both by vegetative and seed reproduction and rapidly increases both its range and density except possibly where soil fertility has been seriously impaired by recurrent burns.

Chamise is an excellent example of fire-type chaparral. It combines exceptional powers of reproduction with ability to grow on such poor and depleted sites as dry, hot slopes. Hot, rainless summers create a very dangerous situation in areas dominated by dense brushfields of chamise and other chaparral, as this brush type is then highly inflammable and will ignite readily at the crown. Such fires spread rapidly where fanned by high winds accompanied by low humidity. However, when calm weather and high humidity prevail, chamise crown fires drop to the ground and become inactive or greatly subdued.

In southern California, chamise provides protection for very valuable watersheds from erosion as its thick canopy and the numerous roots prevent rapid run-off and soil loss. Very little duff collects under mature chamise stands, since the leaves are small and evergreen, and the infertile soil prohibits the growth of weeds and grasses.

Chamise is a rigid, spreading, leafy shrub from 2 to 10 feet in height, or occasionally somewhat taller. Its slender branches are wandlike and the grayish or reddish brown bark becomes shreddy in age. The bush has a heathlike appearance, principally because it is so densely clothed throughout with clusters of small, green, resinous leaves. It is noteworthy that, although the leaves are characteristically smooth or untoothed (entire) on the margins, those of the seedlings are lobed or divided and are usually arranged singly on the young stems. The open and graceful, pyramidal clusters of small white flowers are borne in June. The calyx tube persists at maturity and surrounds the small, hard, one-seeded fruit.

[1] Jepson, W. L. A MANUAL OF THE FLOWERING PLANTS OF CALIFORNIA. 1,238 pp., illus. Berkeley, Calif. [1925.]

ALDERS

Al'nus spp.

Immature female (pistillate) flower clusters (aments, or catkins)—formed in bud during previous season, opening fully before leaves appear; catkins later developing into woody "cones"

Leaf buds—bright red, slightly hairy, about ¼ in. long, blunt at tip

Mature male (staminate) flower clusters (aments, or catkins)—1½ to 3 in. long and about ¼ in. thick, pendulous, in groups of 3 or 4, fully opening in spring before leaves appear

Male flower clusters—formed in the summer or autumn, naked and erect during winter, up to 1 in. long, light purple, fully expanding in spring

Leaves—alternate, egg-shaped to oblong, pointed at tip, rounded or heart-shaped or sometimes wedge-shaped at base, doubly toothed on edges, dark green and hairless above, pale green and hairless or slightly hairy below, 2 to 4 in. long, prominently veined with the almost parallel main veins running from the midrib to the points of the lobes

Mature female catkins ("cones")—egg-shaped, ½ to ⅝ in. long, woody, persistent; scales thickened, squarish and 3- or 4-lobed at apex

Fruit ("seeds")—small, narrow-thin-bordered nutlets solitary in axil of each "cone" scale

A. tenuifolia

581

The alders, which are widely distributed in the Northern Hemisphere and in the Andes, include about 20 species of shrubs or small to fair-sized trees belonging to the birch family (Betulaceae). *Alnus* is the ancient Latin name for alder. The male (pollenbearing) and female (fruiting) flower clusters are borne separately on different parts of the same branch. The male flower clusters, usually formed during the preceding season, expand in the spring into pendulous, cylindrical catkins, 2 to 6 inches long. The female flower parts are borne in shorter, modified catkins, which develop into distinctive small, woody, persistent cones, bearing numerous very small, flat "seeds" between their thickened bracts. The cones are green at first but become brown when mature and, late in the season or early in the following spring, the scales open and liberate the seedlike nutlets. The leaves, which are shed in autumn and usually while still green, are rather coarse, conspicuously straight-veined, the veins running almost parallel from the midrib to the toothed edges of the leaves. The floral characteristics and foliage of the range species of alder are fairly similar, and mountain alder (*A. tenuifolia*) has been selected as a representative species to illustrate the group.

Alders are widely distributed throughout the western range country, but their occurrence is restricted to moist or wet sites. They commonly grow along streams or inhabit river bottomlands, swamps, wet meadows, bogs, seeps, and moist slopes, ranging from sea level to subalpine situations. In some localities they occur in abundance, occasionally forming dense almost impenetrable thickets in meadows and on mountain sides.

The palatability of alders is generally low or only fair for livestock but, due to their wide distribution and local abundance, they are sometimes an important secondary constituent of the forage crop. In the Rocky Mountain region, the Southwest and Intermountain region, alders are usually rated as poor forage for all classes of livestock, although in California and the Northwest they rank up to fair, or in a few localities fairly good. Alder is usually slightly less palatable for cattle than for sheep and goats. Cattle usually make the greatest use of these plants, however, because they are more apt to concentrate where alders grow; moreover, the leafage is often inaccessible to the smaller animals, but can be more readily reached by cattle.

Game animals utilize the leaves, twigs, and buds of alder with slight to moderate relish, maximum use coming in the fall, winter, and early spring. Both deer and elk prefer the leaves and twigs of the suckers and sapling plants, but often utilize the older plants rather extensively during severe winters. The bark of alder along with that of willows, aspen, and other hardwoods is used by beaver for food; those industrious animals also utilize the stems in building their houses and dams. In Alaska and the far North, the alders are often an important browse for moose and furnish some feed for reindeer.[1]

---

[1] Hadwen, S., and Palmer, L. J. REINDEER IN ALASKA. U. S. Dept. Agr. Bull. 1089, 74 pp., illus. 1922.

The alders propagate profusely by underground rhizomes or suckers as well as by seed. The roots, like those of the legumes, often bear nodules of nitrogen-fixing bacteria and it would seem possible that this would be reflected in a relatively high protein content of the herbage, although this is a matter that needs investigation.

Red alder (*A. ru'bra*) is the only western alder of much commercial value for lumber. The other species are of distinctly minor importance in the production of wood products; they are too small for any purpose except fuel, for which all species are commonly used. They are often a valuable understory in the forest, on account of the protection they afford to the headwaters and lower courses of mountain streams and springy slopes. A number of European, Asiatic and, to a limited extent, several American species are used in this country and abroad as ornamentals.

Mountain alder (*A. tenuifo'lia*) is distributed from Alaska and Yukon Territory to New Mexico and Lower California. It is the most widely distributed and one of the most important of the 7 or 8 species of alder occurring on the western ranges, and is the most common alder of the Rocky Mountains, Sierra Nevadas, and the east side of the Cascades. This shrub or small tree is usually 6 to 15 feet high, but occasionally 30 feet tall and 6 to 8 inches in diameter. It is of only secondary importance as a forage plant, being typical of most of the western alders in palatability for livestock.

Red alder (*A. ru'bra*, syn. *A. orego'na*) often called Oregon alder, is one of the largest of the Pacific coast hardwoods, and from the standpoint of timber production is one of the most important alders in the United States. In fact, it is the leading hardwood of the Pacific coast.[2] It is usually 35 to 40 feet high and from 10 to 15 inches in diameter, but on the best sites it reaches a height of from 60 to 90 feet with the trunk 1½ to 3 feet, or more, in diameter. The stems are straight with thin, smooth-looking, light ashy-gray or whitish bark and, in mature trees, are clear of branches for one-half to two-thirds their length. The roughly toothed, egg-shaped to elliptic leaves are about 3 to 5 inches long, or up to 10 inches long on strong shoots, dark green on the upper surface, but lighter colored and coated with very short, rust-colored hairs below. The wood is light, soft, brittle, and close-grained, being used chiefly for furniture and for smoking salmon.

Red alder ranges from southeastern Alaska southward in the coastal region to southern California. It grows chiefly along streams and in rich, moist bottomlands, but also inhabits springy hillsides and upland swamps. In the Douglas-fir region, red alder is often conspicuous in the shrub stage of plant succession on cut-over and burned-over timberlands. It is especially common on moist sites,

---

[2] Johnson, H. M., Hanzlik, E. J., and Gibbons, W. H. RED ALDER OF THE PACIFIC NORTHWEST, ITS UTILIZATION, WITH NOTES ON GROWTH AND MANAGEMENT. U. S. Dept. Agr. Bull. 1437, 46 pp., illus. 1926.

where it comes in as one of the principal plants to dominate the vegetation until the young Douglas fir trees or other coniferous seedlings become large enough to replace them. The leafage and twigs of red alder sprouts and saplings are grazed by cattle, sheep, and goats, being rated fair or fairly good forage in some localities in the Northwest. Game animals also make use of this browse, especially in the winter.

Sitka alder (*A. sinua'ta*, syns. *A. sitchen'sis, A. vi'ridis sinua'ta*), perhaps more fittingly called thinleaf alder because of its thin, delicate-textured leaves, is one of the most palatable of the native alders, being classed as fair to good sheep browse in some parts of its range. It is generally a slender shrub, usually from 4 to 6 feet high, but occasionally develops into a tree from 20 to 40 feet tall, with a trunk 7 to 8 inches in diameter. The leaves, though thin and membranaceous, are rather large (3 to 6 inches long), green above and pale green and lustrous below with sharply double-toothed edges. The male catkins and immature fruiting cones of Sitka alder open into full flower in the spring with or after the leaves, differing in this respect from all other native species, which produce their flowers in the winter or early spring before the leaves appear. The cones of this species are borne on slender stalks which usually exceed the length of the cones themselves. Sitka alder grows from sea level to about timberline in thickets on wet slopes or along mountain streams, both on the Pacific slope and inland, ranging from the borders of the Arctic Circle in Alaska to Alberta, California, and Colorado.

COMMON SERVICEBERRY

Amelan'chier alnifo'lia, syns. *A. jonesia'na, A. mormo'nica*

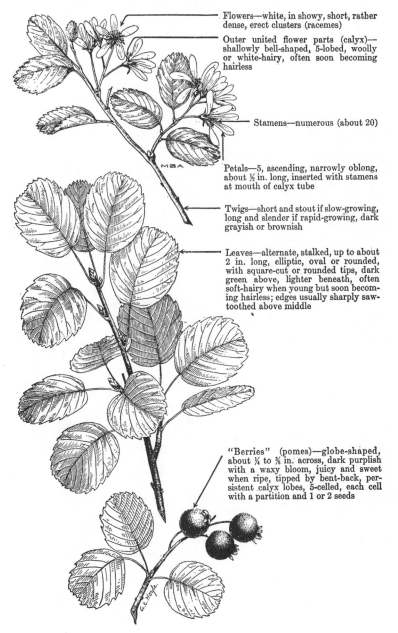

Flowers—white, in showy, short, rather dense, erect clusters (racemes)

Outer united flower parts (calyx)—shallowly bell-shaped, 5-lobed, woolly or white-hairy, often soon becoming hairless

Stamens—numerous (about 20)

Petals—5, ascending, narrowly oblong, about ½ in. long, inserted with stamens at mouth of calyx tube

Twigs—short and stout if slow-growing, long and slender if rapid-growing, dark grayish or brownish

Leaves—alternate, stalked, up to about 2 in. long, elliptic, oval or rounded, with square-cut or rounded tips, dark green above, lighter beneath, often soft-hairy when young but soon becoming hairless; edges usually sharply saw-toothed above middle

"Berries" (pomes)—globe-shaped, about ¼ to ⅜ in. across, dark purplish with a waxy bloom, juicy and sweet when ripe, tipped by bent-back, persistent calyx lobes, 5-celled, each cell with a partition and 1 or 2 seeds

Common serviceberry, without a doubt, is the most widely distributed and best known of the 19 or more species of *Amelanchier* occurring in the West. Locally, and perhaps rather generally, it may be known as saskatoon, alderleaf sarvisberry, western serviceberry, western juneberry, or pigeonberry. It is a low shrub, from 3 to 15 feet in height, or else a small tree up to 20 or more feet tall, with dark grayish twigs and usually dark green foliage. The leaves are generally elliptic or rounded, distinctly toothed above the middle, hairless on the upper side and short-woolly underneath when young, but becoming hairless in age. However, the species is variable, and its exact delimitation has not been determined, especially with reference to the closely related and very similar Pacific serviceberry (*A. florida*). These two forms are so much alike that many authors consider them as one species or regard *A. florida* simply as a variety of *A. alnifolia*. The chief difference is that Pacific serviceberry is more like to be aborescent, the leaves are thinner, narrower, and less hairy underneath, and the flowers tend to be larger and showier. *A. florida* occurs from British Columbia and Alaska to California, Montana, and Colorado, but is most common in the Northwest. *A. alnifolia* extends beyond this range, being found from Alaska south and east to western Ontario, Michigan, the Dakotas, New Mexico, and California. However, they are so much alike that the remainder of this discussion concerning common serviceberry also refers to Pacific serviceberry.

The wide distribution of common serviceberry is largely due to its unusual ability to grow under a great variety of environmental conditions. It is found on dry, rocky slopes in the full sunlight or in the partial shade of coniferous timber; it also occurs on moist deep and fertile soils frequently forming an underbrush in aspen and lodgepole pine. It is probably most common in the upper limits of the ponderosa-pine belt, but it occurs from near sea level in Washington and northward to over 9,000 feet in the Sierras and Rockies. Sometimes this species is locally abundant, but it generally appears more or less scattered along with such other shrubs as manzanita, thimbleberry, Gambel oak, and cherries. In the shrub form, common serviceberry is a low, many-stemmed plant, often having a spread of 6 feet, or more. Under favorable conditions, however, the young plants may be sparsely stemmed and soon assume a tree habit of growth. In many cases, the shrubby specimens also eventually attain treelike proportions by the gradual growth of a few central and erect stems, and the subsequent dying out of the short and bushy growth.

Common serviceberry merits its position among the more valuable browse plants on the western range, due to its wide distribution, palatability, and ready availability to livestock. Throughout most of the West, this plant ranks as fair to fairly good forage for cattle and good for sheep, although in Colorado and on the eastern side of the Rockies generally, it is usually poor to fair feed for cattle and fair to fairly good for sheep. On the average range, it is browsed chiefly after midsummer, when the more palatable grasses and weeds have already been utilized or matured, but on browse ranges, where it constitutes a portion of the more palatable forage, it is usually among the first species grazed. Common serviceberry withstands close use remarkably well. Repeated nipping of the shoot ends induces a rather dense and bushy growth, which tends to protect the inner foliage, and also permits the central stems to grow beyond the grazing height of livestock. After this height is attained, continued close use results in an enlarged or treelike crown and the gradual death of the bushy basal growth. Small shrubs, entirely within grazing range are, of course, killed by continued close use.

Deer and elk are particularly fond of common serviceberry. Dixon,[1] for instance, states that it is one of the several plants considered to be of outstanding importance as a browse for mule deer in California. The juicy fruit is palatable to man and is eagerly devoured by birds, rodents, and such larger wildlife as bears.

SERVICEBERRIES (Amelan'chier. spp.)

The serviceberries, which are also known as sarvisberries, juneberries, shadblows, and shadbushes, constitute a well-known genus of the large and important apple family (Malaceae), or, as some botanists prefer, the apple tribe or subfamily (Maleae) of the rose family (Rosaceae). The genus consists of 25 or more species, which are native to the North Temperate Zone, most of them occurring in North America. The serviceberries are shrubs or small trees, with simple, toothed, or entire leaves, showy flowers having 5 long white petals, and a juicy, usually purplish or bluish black and very palatable, berrylike fruit. The serviceberries are easily recognized and are not likely to be mistaken for any other shrubs or small trees except, perhaps, the hawthorns (*Crataegus* spp.), which are usually spiny and have conspicuously toothed or frequently lobed leaves. Both of these genera have applelike fruits which are somewhat similar superficially; the flesh of the hawthorn fruits is dry and mealy and the seeds large and bony, whereas that of the serviceberries is sweet, usually pulpy, and the seeds are small and hard. The flowers of the hawthorns are borne in more or less flat-topped end clusters, the petals being round in outline; those of the serviceberries are borne in elongate clusters (racemes), the petals being strapshaped or oblong.

The meaning of the generic name *Amelanchier* is not definitely known, but it is probably derived from a Savoy name for the related medlar (*Mespilus germanica*), which has edible fruits. The origin of the common names has been established fairly well. Serviceberry was applied to the genus, because of the similarity of its fruit to that of the European servicetree (*Sorbus domestica*). Juneberry, logically, indicates that the berrylike fruits ripen in June.

[1] Dixon, J. S. A STUDY OF THE LIFE HISTORY AND FOOD HABITS OF MULE DEER IN CALIFORNIA. PART 2—FOOD HABITS. Calif. Fish and Game 20 (4) : [315]–354, illus. 1934.

On the Atlantic coast these shrubs are often called shadblow and shadbush because they bloom when the shad are running.[2]

Besides common serviceberry, three other species of *Amelanchier* are sometimes important on western ranges. Mountain serviceberry (*A. oreo'phila*) is a low, hairy-leaved shrub, growing in clumps on dry situations in the mountains from the Black Hills of South Dakota to New Mexico, Nevada, and Montana. It is sometimes abundant locally, but is rated no higher than fair for sheep and poor for cattle. Redbud serviceberry (*A. rubes'cens*) is sometimes locally abundant in the region from southwestern Colorado to northwestern New Mexico, southern Utah, and Nevada. It has red flower buds, small, narrow, many-toothed leaves, and is most palatable in the spring, being little used in the summer.[3] Utah serviceberry (*A. utahen'sis*), a low bush or small tree, with yellowish or orange-colored fruit, occurs in the foothills and medium elevations from Colorado to New Mexico and Nevada, where it is occasionally common. It is grazed principally in the spring, when it provides fairly good forage for cattle and good to excellent browse for sheep and goats.[4]

Various species, including common serviceberry and the eastern downy shadblow (*A. canaden'sis*), are desirable ornamentals, frequently planted for their showy white flowers and, to some extent, for their attractive and edible fruit. The Indians, who valued the fruit as an important food source, collected and dried the berries for winter use. Explorers and miners also found the fruit a welcome addition to their food supply; the Lewis and Clark party, for example, used it as food in 1804 in the upper Missouri River country.[5]

[2] Parsons, M. E., and Buck, M. W. THE WILD FLOWERS OF CALIFORNIA, THEIR NAMES, HAUNTS, AND HABITS. Rev., 411 pp., illus. San Francisco. 1904.
[3] Forsling, C. L., and Storm, E. V. THE UTILIZATION OF BROWSE FORAGE AS SUMMER RANGE FOR CATTLE IN SOUTHWESTERN UTAH. U. S. Dept. Agr. Circ. 62, 30 pp., illus. 1929.
[4] Dayton, W. A. IMPORTANT WESTERN BROWSE PLANTS. U. S. Dept. Agr. Misc. Pub. 101, 214 pp., illus. 1931.
[5] Thwaites, R. G. (edited by). ORIGINAL JOURNALS OF THE LEWIS AND CLARK EXPEDITION 1804-06 . . . 8 v., illus. New York. 1904-5.

JIMMYWEED

Aplopap′pus heterophyl′lus, syns. *Linosy′ris heterophyl′la, Bigelo′via wrigh′tii, Isoco′ma wrigh′tii*

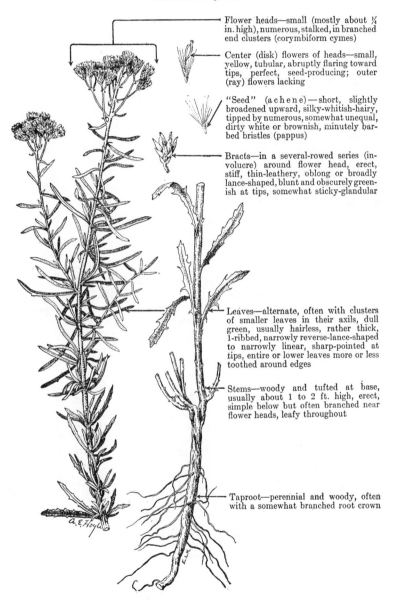

Flower heads—small (mostly about ¼ in. high), numerous, stalked, in branched end clusters (corymbiform cymes)

Center (disk) flowers of heads—small, yellow, tubular, abruptly flaring toward tips, perfect, seed-producing; outer (ray) flowers lacking

"Seed" (a c h e n e)—short, slightly broadened upward, silky-whitish-hairy, tipped by numerous, somewhat unequal, dirty white or brownish, minutely barbed bristles (pappus)

Bracts—in a several-rowed series (involucre) around flower head, erect, stiff, thin-leathery, oblong or broadly lance-shaped, blunt and obscurely greenish at tips, somewhat sticky-glandular

Leaves—alternate, often with clusters of smaller leaves in their axils, dull green, usually hairless, rather thick, 1-ribbed, narrowly reverse-lance-shaped to narrowly linear, sharp-pointed at tips, entire or lower leaves more or less toothed around edges

Stems—woody and tufted at base, usually about 1 to 2 ft. high, erect, simple below but often branched near flower heads, leafy throughout

Taproot—perennial and woody, often with a somewhat branched root crown

Jimmyweed, a dull green, bushy halfshrub growing 1 or 2 (occasionally 4) feet high, is also known as rayless-goldenrod and rosinweed, and sometimes is called rabbitbrush, apparently because of its similarity to some species of rabbitbrush (*Chrysothamnus* spp.). The Greek generic name *Aplopappus* means single or simple pappus, and refers to the single series of unbranched, bristlelike hairs (pappus) surmounting the "seed" (achene). The specific name *heterophyllus* means dissimilar leaves and refers to the variation in the leaves from nearly entire or untoothed to deeply lobed.

This species ranges from Colorado to western Texas, Arizona, and south into Mexico, growing on dry plains, mesas, and foothills from the creosotebush (*Covillea*) belt up to the foothill woodland type. It frequently occurs as the dominant plant over thousands of acres in open savannah woodlands or on open grasslands. It spreads rapidly by seeds during favorable years and often comes in abundantly on overgrazed or depleted ranges. This species seldom grows on ranges well stocked with perennial bunchgrasses, but when this perennial cover is broken and replaced by annual grasses or other short-lived plants, jimmyweed often rapidly invades the grasslands. It sometimes becomes one of the principal plants, even on areas covered by a good stand of secondary grasses. It is a drought-resistant species, largely because of its extensive root system, which penetrates to a depth of 20 feet or more.

Jimmyweed is poisonous to cattle, horses, and sheep and, on closely grazed range, has caused much sickness and high mortality, especially of cattle. It has long been under suspicion as the cause of "milk sickness" or "alkali disease" of domestic animals in the Southwest, and is also thought to be connected with the milk sickness of the human beings who have used milk products from cows feeding upon this plant.[1] Marsh, Roe, and Clawson found, through experimental work, that cattle, horses, and sheep, when given sufficient quantities of rayless goldenrod (i. e., jimmyweed), develop all of the typical symptoms of alkali disease or milk sickness. * * * It has been shown that the toxic substance may be excreted in milk, and that calves and lambs may be poisoned in this manner. It is probable that human cases of milk sickness arise from the consumption of milk or butter from cows feeding on the rayless goldenrod.

The outstanding symptoms[2] in poisoned animals are marked depression and weakness. The animals are inactive and often stand in a humped posture and move with a stiff gait. The weakness is especially pronounced in the forelegs. In the more advanced stages of the disease, the animal is unable to rise. Poisoning can usually be detected by the trembling induced when the animal exercises; it varies from a slight twitching to a violent shaking of the whole body, and stockmen at times call the disease the trembles. Irritation of both the intestines and kidneys is usually noticeable. Poisoned animals should be kept as quiet as possible, since exercise aggravates the trouble. Horses are the most easily poisoned by jimmyweed, and

[1] Marsh, C. D., and Roe, G. C. THE "ALKALI DISEASE" OF LIVESTOCK IN THE PECOS VALLEY. U. S. Dept. Agr. Circ. 180, 8 pp., illus. 1921.

[2] Marsh, C. D., Roe, G. C., and Clawson, A. B. RAYLESS GOLDENROD (APLOPAPPUS HETEROPHYLLUS) AS A POISONOUS PLANT. U. S. Dept. Agr. Bull. 1391, 24 pp., illus. 1926.

sheep are the least susceptible. However, symptoms are readily produced in cattle, horses, and sheep by consumption of small amounts of this plant, especially when it is fed with very little supplemental forage.

Fortunately, jimmyweed normally is unpalatable to all classes of livestock and is not eaten except during scarcity of palatable forage. Losses occur chiefly on overgrazed ranges, especially in winter and spring, when other forage is usually scant. Proper range management, therefore, is the practical expedient for preventing jimmyweed poisoning. Stockmen maintain that it is practical to eliminate this plant from pastures by grubbing.[2] The late Dr. Marsh stated[3] that the closely related burroweed (*A. fruticosus*, syns. *Bigelovia coronopifolia*, *Isocoma coronopifolia*, *I. fruticosa*) of western Texas, southern Arizona, and Sonora, produces the same harmful effects as jimmyweed.

The late Dr. Hall[4] regarded *Aplopappus heterophyllus* as a synonym of *A. pluriflorus*. In view of the uncertainty as to the identity of the obscure eastern Colorado plant, *Linosyris pluriflora* (on which Hall based the combination, *Aplopappus pluriflorus*) Dr. S. F. Blake, composite expert of the Bureau of Plant Industry, recommends continuation of the name *A. heterophyllus* for jimmyweed, pending further study of the matter. Hall recommended the spelling *Haplopappus* for this genus, as better preserving the etymology. The original spelling, *Aplopappus*, is preferred by most botanists and is almost universal in publication.

GOLDENWEEDS AND THEIR CONGENERS
(Aplopap'pus spp.)

Aplopappus is a large and variable genus, greatly confused in botanical literature; groups of what is considered *Aplopappus* (*fide* Blake) in this handbook, have been variously considered under the genera *Chrysoma*, *Ericameria*, *Eriocarpum*, *Isocoma*, *Linosyris*, *Macronema*, *Pyrrocoma*, *Sideranthus*, *Stenotus*, and *Tonestus*. *Bigelovia* is also considered synonymous in part. Many of these plants are often called rayless-goldenrod. The genus is largely herbaceous, although many species are halfshrubs with woody roots and crowns; a considerable number are definitely woody shrubs.

The goldenweeds and their sister species of the genus are common plants and, although usually scattered, are widely distributed over the western ranges. Few of the species have individual common names. They occur mainly on semidesert areas, although a small number of species range into the ponderosa-pine and spruce-fir types. A few herbaceous species, such as *A. falcatus* (syn. *Stenotus falcatus*), furnish fairly good winter sheep feed. However, the genus, as a whole, is very low in palatability, most species being practically

---

[2] See footnote on preceding page.
[3] Marsh, C. D. STOCK-POISONING PLANTS OF THE RANGE. U. S. Dept. Agr. Bull. 1245, rev., 75 pp., illus. 1929. Supersedes Bull. 575.
[4] Hall, H. M. THE GENUS HAPLOPAPPUS. A PHYLOGENETIC STUDY IN THE COMPOSITAE. Carnegie Inst. Wash. Pub. 389, 391 pp., illus. 1928.

worthless as forage for all classes of livestock. Several of the woody western species (*e. g.*, *A. palmeri*, syn. *Ericameria palmeri*, and *A. venetus*, syns. *Bigelovia veneta*, *Isocoma veneta*), have medicinal uses among Indians and Mexicans.[5]

Goldenfleece (*A. arbores'cens*, syns. *Bigelo'via arbores'cens*, *Chryso'ma arbores'cens*, *Ericame'ria arbores'cens*) is a common California species growing from 3 to 15 feet high. Bloomer rabbitbrush (*A. bloo'meri*, syn. *Chrysotham'nus bloo'meri*), whitestem goldenweed (*A. macrone'ma*, syn. *Macrone'ma discoi'deum* Nutt. (1840) not *A. discoi'deus* DC. (1836)), and singlehead goldenweed (*A. suffrutico'sus*, syn. *Macrone'ma suffrutico'sum*) are common, and occasionally abundant, western shrubs. Although their forage value is very low, they are doubtless of some value in erosion control. These species are discussed more fully in "Important western browse plants."[5]

---

[5] Dayton, W. A. IMPORTANT WESTERN BROWSE PLANTS. U. S. Dept. Agr. Misc. Pub. 101, 214 pp., illus. 1931.

MANZANITAS

Arctosta'phylos spp.

The manzanitas compose an important, almost entirely west-American genus of about 40 species, belonging to the large and well known heath family (Ericaceae). The generic name *Arctostaphylos* is from the Greek, *arktos*, a bear, and *staphule*, a bunch of grapes, or berries, hence bearberry. In present usage, bearberry is usually understood to mean the low, prostrate species, *A. uva-ursi*. Most other species are known as manzanita, the Spanish for little apple, as the mature berries strikingly resemble diminutive apples, especially in the larger-fruited species, such as great manzanita (*A. glauca*) and *A. pastillosa*.

These plants are typically found on dry sites. They characteristically grow in the full sunlight on well-drained soils in the openings of coniferous forests and are especially abundant throughout the arid chaparral belts of the California and Oregon foothills. They flourish even in poor soils and, throughout their range, are noted for their ability to invade and make good growth on coarse stony, and frequently shallow soils of low fertility.

With one exception, bearberry, which encircles the Northern Hemisphere, the manzanitas are a North American, essentially western, group of plants. A few other species, for example, pointleaf manzanita (*A. pungens*) and greenleaf manzanita (*A. patula*), grow in most of the mountains of the Western States, and sometimes develop dense stands in the Great Basin region and in the Southwest. However, the members of the genus are well represented and abundant only in California and Oregon, where greenleaf manzanita and whiteleaf manzanita (*A. viscida*) occur profusely in the interior mountains, and woolly manzanita (*A. tomentosa*) and hairy manzanita (*A. columbiana*) are common in the coastal mountains. They form dense brush fields over many thousand acres either in pure stands or intermixed with other shrubs. Such occupancy of large areas results from the gradual spread of manzanita when the less hardy and more useful vegetation is destroyed and the soil depleted by periodic burning or other abuses. Most manzanitas rapidly reseed burned areas, although many species have the obvious advantage of revegetation from root sprouts.[1] The sprouting is from a woody, tuberlike swelling at or near the soil surface. Eastwood manzanita (*A. glandulosa*), greenleaf and woolly manzanitas have this character, but whiteleaf and hairy manzanitas are examples of species that reestablish exclusively by seed.

Most species are upright shrubs about 3 to 7 feet in height, although there are some important exceptions. Pinemat (*A. nevadensis*) and bearberry are low forms with trailing stems that seldom become more than a foot high. Parry manzanita (*A. manzanita*) is probably the largest species, sometimes being over 20 feet in height

---

[1] Jepson, W. L. A MANUAL OF THE FLOWERING PLANTS OF CALIFORNIA. 1,238 pp., illus. Berkeley, Calif. [1925.]

and having a short treelike trunk, although great manzanita, and possibly one or two other species, occasionally attain tree size.[1][2][3]

The genus *Arctostaphylos* is easily identified by distinctive characters of the stems, leaves, flowers, and fruits. The stems and branches, except the weak and shreddy stems of bearberry, are crooked, very rigid, and have a thin, smooth, shiny, dark red or chocolate-colored bark. The alternate, evergreen leaves are leathry, entire-edged (with very rare exceptions), and are usually held in an upright position, apparently to prevent excessive transpiration. The small, white or pink, urn-shaped flowers, borne in small nodding terminal clusters, are five-parted, with 10 (sometimes 8) stamens that have awned anthers and hairy anther stalks. The fruit is a smooth, apple-shaped berry, consisting of several, sometimes united nutlets, surrounded by a mealy pulp.

In the Southwest, manzanitas, and especially pointleaf manzanita, are considered of low forage value for cattle and good for goats,[4] but, otherwise, throughout the West are regarded as waste, except for a temporary and unimportant use of the tender sprouts after a fire. In California and Oregon, goats sometimes browse the leathery leaves and peel and eat the bark,[5] but this only occurs on overstocked ranges. The dense, rigid growth of manzanitas prevents the use of associated forage plants and also constitutes barriers to the movement of livestock over the range.

The manzanitas are of considerable value as a food source for wildlife. The use of the mature berries is not confined to bear, as other wildlife, including grouse and turkey, also feed freely on these fruits. During the fall and winter, deer and elk make some use of the foliage, especially bearberry, and greenleaf manzanita and other species have some value as winter deer feed.[6]

Bearberry leaves were an important component of Indian tobaccos. The tannin in bearberry leaves was formerly valuable for curing pelts. Even today this plant is important as a source of tannin in Russia.[7] Extracts from bearberry, great manzanita and other species have various medicinal uses as astringents, in the treatment of catarrh, and for the alleviation of diseases of the urinary system.[8] The Indians made cider by crushing the ripe berries.[9]

Manzanitas are of greatest importance as a cover for critical watersheds, especially in California. Part of their value rests in the fact that they are often the first plants to come in on burned areas, and thus check soil losses, particularly the sprouting species.

[1] Jepson, W. L. A MANUAL OF THE FLOWERING PLANTS OF CALIFORNIA. 1,238 pp., illus. Berkeley, Calif. [1925.]

[2] Sudworth, G. B. CHECK LIST OF THE FOREST TREES OF THE UNITED STATES, THEIR NAMES AND RANGES. U. S. Dept. Agr. Misc. Circ. 92, 295 pp. 1927.

[3] Saunders, C. F. WESTERN WILD FLOWERS AND THEIR STORIES. 320 pp., illus. Garden City, N. Y. 1933.

[4] Chapline, W. R. PRODUCTION OF GOATS ON FAR WESTERN RANGES. U. S. Dept. Agr. Bull. 749, 35 pp., illus. 1919.

[5] Hatton, J. H. ERADICATION OF CHAPARRAL BY GOAT GRAZING. LASSEN NATIONAL FOREST. U. S. Dept. Agr., Rev. Forest Serv. Invest. 2 : 25–28, illus. 1913.

[6] Dixon, J. S. A STUDY OF THE LIFE HISTORY AND FOOD HABITS OF MULE DEER IN CALIFORNIA. PART 2.—FOOD HABITS. Calif. Fish and Game 20 (4) : [315]–354, illus. 1934.

[7] Wood, H. C., Remington, J. P., and Sadtler, S. P., assisted by Lyons, A. B., and Wood, H. C., Jr. THE DISPENSATORY OF THE UNITED STATES OF AMERICA, BY DR. GEO. B. WOOD AND DR. FRANKLIN BACHE. Ed. 19, thoroughly rev. and largely rewritten . . . 1,947 pp. Philadelphia and London. 1907.

[8] Millspaugh, C. F. AMERICAN MEDICINAL PLANTS. 2 v. New York and Philadelphia. 1887.

[9] Chesnut, V. K. PLANTS USED BY THE INDIANS OF MENDOCINO COUNTY, CALIFORNIA. U. S. Dept. Agr., Div. Bot., Contrib. U. S. Natl. Herbarium 7 : 295–422, illus. 1902.

GREENLEAF MANZANITA

Arctosta'phylos pa'tula, syns. *A. platyphyl'la, A. pun'gens platyphyl'la*

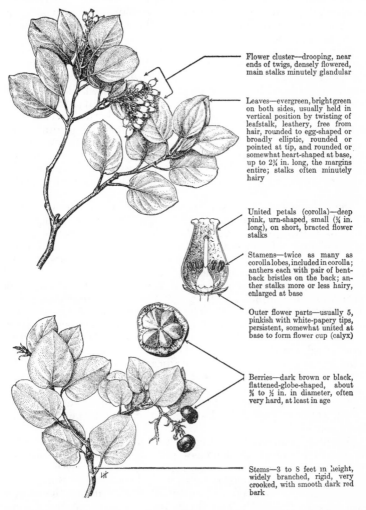

Flower cluster—drooping, near ends of twigs, densely flowered, main stalks minutely glandular

Leaves—evergreen, bright green on both sides, usually held in vertical position by twisting of leafstalk, leathery, free from hair, rounded to egg-shaped or broadly elliptic, rounded or pointed at tip, and rounded or somewhat heart-shaped at base, up to 2¼ in. long, the margins entire; stalks often minutely hairy

United petals (corolla)—deep pink, urn-shaped, small (¼ in. long), on short, bracted flower stalks

Stamens—twice as many as corolla lobes, included in corolla; anthers each with pair of bent-back bristles on the back; anther stalks more or less hairy, enlarged at base

Outer flower parts—usually 5, pinkish with white-papery tips, persistent, somewhat united at base to form flower cup (calyx)

Berries—dark brown or black, flattened-globe-shaped, about ⅜ to ½ in. in diameter, often very hard, at least in age

Stems—3 to 8 feet in height, widely branched, rigid, very crooked, with smooth dark red bark

Greenleaf manzanita, sometimes called buckhorn (or small) manzanita and Indian-tobacco, is a widely branched shrub, 3 to 8 feet high, with crooked, very stout limbs, and smooth, dark red bark. It is so named because its leaves are bright green, in contrast to the dull green or whitish leaves of many manzanitas. The species ranges from Oregon through southwestern Idaho to extreme western Colorado, Utah, and California, and is most plentiful in the ponderosa-pine belt of California, southern Oregon, and the Great

Basin region. In California and Oregon it characteristically forms dense and extensive brush fields on old burns in the pure ponderosa pine and mixed conifer types.

Greenleaf manzanita chiefly inhabits dry slopes and old burns, in full sunlight. It is the commonest manzanita in the Great Basin region and one of the commonest Pacific manzanitas. Jepson [1] refers to it as the dominant and usually the only species of its genus in its area in the Sierra Nevada, where it occurs between 2,500 feet elevation in the north and 9,000 feet in the south. Its zonal distribution is from the piñon-juniper to the aspen belts but it is most characteristic of the ponderosa-pine belt. In western Colorado, where it tends to be rather local and undersized, it occurs mainly between about 7,500 and 9,000 feet. In Utah it is found chieflly between about 6,000 and 9,000 feet. In northern Arizona it occurs about 8,000 feet. It inhabits both limestone and granitic soils, as well as those of sandy, gravelly, rocky, and clayey texture. Its frequent associates are mountain-mahogany, garrya, oaks, and *Ceanothus* spp. The flowering period extends from late March through June, with the berries ripening in late summer and early fall.

The foliage usually has very little or negligible forage value for domestic livestock or deer, except as a utility winter ration or when little or nothing else is available. Goats tend to browse the leaves and peel and eat the bark, especially when there is a shortage of other feed. Most livestock and deer will lightly browse the tender shoots—especially during the first two seasons after a fire. Bear will eat the berries, particularly if the more pulpy fruits of better species are unavailable. The shrub is of chief importance because of its frequent abundance. The extensive brush fields of greenleaf manzanita often prevent the free movement of livestock on the range or the use of isolated feed areas, unless special trails are built and maintained for that purpose. Hatton [2] has reported on an experiment in greenleaf manzanita eradication by goats on the Lassen National Forest, Calif. About 75 percent of the aerial growth of the manzanitas was girdled and killed during the first season where goats were concentrated, but the second year's efforts practically failed. Goats concentrated on the species quit the range in poor condition.

Greenleaf manzanita, being a natural fire hazard, is especially important in forest management plans. The ability of this species to withstand repeated burnings, make rapid new growth and increase its stand density by rootshoots is truly phenomenal. Such sprouting takes place from a woody, often tuberlike swelling of the root crown just beneath the soil. The shrub forms a good ground cover, and through the addition of humus, tends to improve the site. Conifers, especially white fir, will invade and shade out this species and, except for fires, would doubtless tend materially to restrict its range.

---

[1] Jepson, W. L. A MANUAL OF THE FLOWERING PLANTS OF CALIFORNIA. 1,238 pp., illus. Berkeley, Calif. [1925.]
[2] Hatton, J. H. ERADICATION OF CHAPARRAL BY GOAT GRAZING. LASSEN NATIONAL FOREST. U. S. Dept. Agr., Rev. Forest Serv. Invest. 2: 25–28, illus. 1913.

BEARBERRY

Arctosta'phylos uva-ur'si

Flower and fruit stalks—short, scaly-bracted

Fruit (berries)—globose, pink to bright red, smooth on outside, with 1 to 5 hard "seeds" (nutlets) inside, up to almost ½ in. in diameter

Flower clusters—at ends of branches, short, dense, nodding

Leaves — evergreen, leathery, dark green above, lighter below, held in vertical position by twisted leafstalk, spatula-shaped to egg-shaped, rounded at tip, entire, slightly hairy to smooth, up to about 1 in. long

Stems—several from single root, trailing on ground and sending out small roots from under side, each giving rise to erect, branching twigs usually 4 to 6 in. high; bark dark brown or reddish, becoming shreddy with age

United petals (corolla)—white or pink, urn-shaped, small (¼ in. long)

Stamens—twice as many as lobes of corolla (usually 10); anthers each with a pair of bent-back awns on back; anther stalk more or less hairy, enlarged toward base

Outer flower parts—5, often reddish, somewhat united at base to form flower cup (calyx)

Bearberry, or kinnikinnick as it is often called in the Rocky Mountains, is the only manzanita occurring outside western North America. This low, prostrate-trailing, evergreen shrub occurs in northern Europe, Asia, and in North America. It is found from Labrador to Alaska and south to about the southern boundary of New Jersey, Illinois, Nebraska, in the Rocky Mountain chain south to Mexico, and in the Pacific coast ranges and Cascades to California. Bearberry grows under a wide variety of conditions, but prefers coarse, well-drained soils, such as gravelly or sandy loams in partial shade. It is typically associated in the West with open ponderosa pine forests, but also grows in Douglas fir, aspen, and lodgepole-pine stands. Although individual shrubs are from 2 to 6 feet in diameter, stands of them form extensive ground carpets when abundant, often to the exclusion of other shrubby or herbaceous vegetation. On this account bearberry apparently hinders rather than aids timber reproduction in the moister areas where it is abundant, although its open growth on drier sites may encourage timber reproduction through conservation of moisture.

The habit of forming a dense ground cover over rather large local areas makes the species especially valuable for watershed protection. Erosion is prevented and the soil is maintained in a physical condition favorable to the absorption of moisture.

Bearberry is so unpalatable to domestic livestock that it is not even listed as a forage plant for them in grazing-capacity estimates. It, however, supplies considerable food for wildlife. Deer and elk browse the foliage lightly, especially in the winter. These animals, as well as bear, grouse, and wild turkey, relish the mature berries during autumn.

The common name, bearberry, has practically the same meaning as the specific name *uva-ursi*, which comes from the Latin words *uva*, a grape (hence, berry), and *ursi*, bear's, i. e., bear's grape, or bear's berry. The other common name, kinnikinnick, is based on the reported use of bearberry by the Indians in their smoking tobacco.[1] Originally the word referred to the tobacco mixtures of the Indians, but, in present-day usage, it is most often applied either to *Arctostaphylos uva-ursi* or to silky cornel (*Cornus amomum*).

Bearberry stems are trailing, leafy, and slender with dark brown, sometimes reddish, shreddy bark. The leathery, evergreen, spatula-shaped leaves average three-fourths of an inch or less in length. The flowers are small (one-fourth of an inch or less in length), urn-shaped, white or pink, and are borne in small clusters at the ends of the branches during May and June. When mature, the berries are smooth and red or pink with a dry, mealy interior and contain usually five hard, united nutlets.

---

[1] Jones, L. R., and Rand, F. V. VERMONT SHRUBS AND WOODY VINES. Vt. Agr. Expt. Sta. Bull. 145, 199 pp., illus. 1909.

FRINGED SAGEBRUSH

Artemi'sia fri'gida

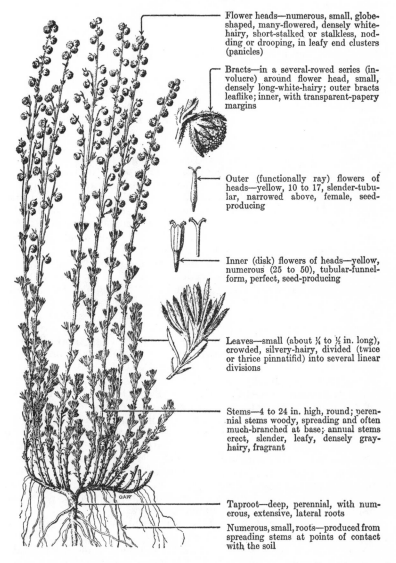

Flower heads—numerous, small, globe-shaped, many-flowered, densely white-hairy, short-stalked or stalkless, nodding or drooping, in leafy end clusters (panicles)

Bracts—in a several-rowed series (involucre) around flower head, small, densely long-white-hairy; outer bracts leaflike; inner, with transparent-papery margins

Outer (functionally ray) flowers of heads—yellow, 10 to 17, slender-tubular, narrowed above, female, seed-producing

Inner (disk) flowers of heads—yellow, numerous (25 to 50), tubular-funnelform, perfect, seed-producing

Leaves—small (about ¼ to ½ in. long), crowded, silvery-hairy, divided (twice or thrice pinnatifid) into several linear divisions

Stems—4 to 24 in. high, round; perennial stems woody, spreading and often much-branched at base; annual stems erect, slender, leafy, densely gray-hairy, fragrant

Taproot—deep, perennial, with numerous, extensive, lateral roots

Numerous, small, roots—produced from spreading stems at points of contact with the soil

Fringed sagebrush, a half-shrub of the Mayweed tribe (Anthemideae) of the huge Composite family (Compositae, or Asteraceae), has a low, perennial, woody base, giving rise to semiherbaceous annual stems. It is almost universally known in the Southwest as estafiata and in the plains, prairies, and northeastern region of the

United States and in southern Canada as pasture sagebrush; it is also locally dubbed arctic, mountain, wild, and worm sage(brush). The species is, of course, not a true sage (*Salvia*). The American Joint Committee on Horticultural Nomenclature[1] has accepted the English name fringed wormwood for this plant in horticulture because of its resemblance and close relationship to wormwood (*A. absin'thium*) of Europe. However, the universal range name for shrubby species of *Artemisia* is sagebrush, a name so descriptive, unequivocal, and usage-sanctioned that it is neither desirable nor advisable to replace it in range literature. The name fringed sagebrush is particularly appropriate, as fringed alludes to the finely dissected leaves; sagebrush is descriptive of the plant's odor and of the perennial character of the stem bases. The flowers have a strong, rather camphorlike odor; and the aromatic herbage, especially when crushed, is reminiscent of the true sages, or salvias, of the mint family (Menthaceae, or Labiatae).

Fringed sagebrush has an enormous range, being probably the most widely distributed and abundant species of the entire *Artemisia* genus. It extends from Mexico northward through the greater portion of the western United States and western Canada, into Alaska, and thence to Siberia, northern Asia, and Europe. It is a common and typical plant of the high plains along the eastern slopes of the Rocky Mountains, and also inhabits valleys, mesas, mountains, and many of the higher grasslands. Although of greatest abundance in the eastern and northern parts of its range, rather extensive local stands occur in southern Colorado, northern New Mexico, and northern Arizona, especially in open parks of the ponderosa pine belt. On the high plains and prairie region from northern Colorado and Nebraska northward throughout Alberta and Saskatchewan, fringed sagebrush is an outstanding species, appearing in mixed grass-weed types, often in association with false tarragon (*A. dracunculoi'des*), cudweed sagewort (*A. gnaphalo'des*), blue grama, needlegrasses, muhly grasses, and wheatgrasses.

Thoughout the Rocky Mountain and Intermountain regions fringed sagebrush ranges from low, semidesert valleys up to elevations of over 11,000 feet. On winter ranges of western Utah and eastern Nevada this plant is dominant in dense stands along the shallow depressions which collect moisture and floodwaters from the summer rains. Its frequent associates in such places include winterfat, shadscale, and rabbitbrushes. Fringed sagebrush also grows scatteringly on slopes, foothills, and mountain sides, intermixed with various weeds, big sagebrush, wheatgrasses, bluegrasses, and eriogonums. Although fairly common in such sites, it seldom abounds save in small or local patches.

All in all, this species inhabits a fairly wide variety of sites, but grows most typically in full sunlight on dry, porous, coarse, gravelly, sandy, or shallow loam soils. However, it tolerates moderate shade well and thrives luxuriantly on ditchbanks and along streams, when it can establish itself in such situations. The plant basks in the

---

[1] American Joint Committee on Horticultural Nomenclature. STANDARDIZED PLANT NAMES. Prepared by F. L. Olmsted, F. V. Coville, and H. P. Kelsey. 546 pp. Salem, Mass., 1923.

glowing sunshine of the southwestern summer, and also withstands the frigid rigors of the Arctic. The specific adjective *frigida* refers to the bleak (frigid) regions of eastern Siberia, where Willdenow (1765–1812), who first named and described this species, procured his type specimen.

As might be at least partly anticipated from its tremendous range and diverse habitats, fringed sagebrush varies considerably in forage value in different places, although generally regarded as one of the better and more important species of *Artemisia*. On western ranges it usually rates as good forage for sheep, fairly good for cattle, and fair for deer and elk, especially for late fall, winter, and early spring use. Macoun,[2] in his explorations of the Northwest, reports that this species is important winter feed for cattle throughout upper British Columbia and the dry Northwest; he adds that local stockmen often prefer it to cured grass or hay because it maintains livestock in sleek and fat condition even in the dead of winter.

The forage value of this plant is highest in the Southwest, where it rates as fairly good in palatability for cattle and very good for sheep and goats, especially during the winter and spring. It is highly prized as a sheep feed during the lambing season. Undoubtedly the greater degree of aridity throughout its southern range, with fewer succulent plant associates, and the longer use of this species on fall, winter, and spring range by sheep and goats, tend to enhance the forage value of fringed sagebrush in that region.[3] On the cattle ranges of the northern plains and prairies, however, this species is considered practically worthless except, as hitherto indicated, during the late fall and winter. In the Northwest, in fact, fringed sagebrush, by rapidly invading deteriorated ranges, may sometimes rank as an indicator of overgrazing. Macoun,[2] in 1875, recognized this fact and stated that, on the benchlands along the lower Thompson River in British Columbia, this species replaced bunchgrass on range depleted by grazing. Thomas P. MacKenzie, Commissioner of Grazing, Department of Lands, British Columbia, also intimates in correspondence with the United States Forest Service that fringed sagebrush becomes an indicator of range depletion in that Province; he even notes a close correlation between range depletion and the number of dry cows, and intimates the possible role of fringed sagebrush in that situation.[3]

In the northern Great Plains near Mandan, N. Dak.,[4] fringed sagebrush has rapidly invaded depleted ranges and has replaced the better forage species along trails, in pastures, and abandoned farm lands, often forming stands of considerable size and sometimes so dense as to exclude all other vegetation. Wherever abundant in this region it is usually indicative of range deterioration. Chemical

---

[2] Macoun, J. REPORT ON THE BOTANICAL FEATURES OF THE COUNTRY TRAVERSED FROM VANCOUVER ISLAND TO CARLETON, ON THE SASKATCHEWAN. Canada Geol. Survey Rept. 1875–76: 110–232, illus. 1877.

[3] Dayton, W. A. IMPORTANT WESTERN BROWSE PLANTS. U. S. Dept. Agr. Misc. Pub. 101, 214 pp., illus. 1931.

[4] Sarvis, J. T. EFFECT OF DIFFERENT SYSTEMS AND INTENSITIES OF GRAZING UPON THE NATIVE VEGETATION AT THE NORTHERN GREAT PLAINS FIELD STATION. U. S. Dept. Agr. Bull. 1170, 46 pp., illus. 1923.

analysis indicates that fringed sagebrush [3] ranks with alfalfa hay in the proportions of crude fiber and carbohydrates, and contains about four times as much fat, one-half as much ash, and two-thirds as much protein as that leguminous forage. Fringed sagebrush is moderately nutritious, being a more important fattening than body-building or energy-producing feed.

Although fringed sagebrush produces an abundance of seed, laboratory germination tests in the Southwest indicate that the viability of fresh seed is low; however, it increases with age up to several years after maturity.[5] The apparent increase of viability of the seed for several years, as well as the tendency to multiply from the rootstocks, enable fringed sagebrush to spread rapidly. The deep, extensive root system qualifies this species to withstand considerable drought and also fortifies the soil against erosion.

Fringed sagebrush is, as stated above, closely related to wormwood of the Old World, the commercial source of medicinal oil of wormwood and absinthe, an intoxicating liquor. Rabak [6] reports that "white sage" (fringed sagebrush) yields a fragrant, essential oil containing a high percentage of borneol camphor and cineol (eucalyptol) which, because of valuable antiseptic qualities, may eventually be used as ingredients in medicinal soaps and scents. He suggests the cultivation of the American plant as a possible commercial source of borneol, used in the manufacture of celluloid. This species seemingly is a far more promising natural source of this material than the plants native to Borneo and the Malay Archipelago, from which the bulk of the present supply of commercial borneol is obtained. Various decoctions of fringed sagebrush were used by the Indians and early western explorers in the treatment of colds, and as a diuretic, mild cathartic, or for bathing. Its pollen, where abundant, causes severe cases of hay fever.[7] Inasmuch as the usual treatment of hay fever cases consists in giving injections of a dilute pollen solution to build up the patient's resistance to the irritant, fringed sagebrush becomes equally important as a preventive and remedy for hay fever caused by its own pollen.

[3] See footnote on preceding page.
[5] Wilson, C. P. THE ARTIFICIAL RESEEDING OF NEW MEXICO RANGES. N. Mex. Agr. Expt. Sta. Bull. 189, 37 pp., illus. 1931.
[6] Rabak, F. WILD VOLATILE-OIL PLANTS AND THEIR ECONOMIC IMPORTANCE: I.—BLACK SAGE; II.—WILD SAGE; III.—SWAMP BAY. U. S. Dept. Agr., Bur. Plant Indus. Bull. 235, 37 pp., illus. 1912.
[7] Hall, H. M., and Clements, F. E. THE PHYLOGENETIC METHOD IN TAXONOMY. THE NORTH AMERICAN SPECIES OF ARTEMISIA, CHRYSOTHAMNUS, AND ATRIPLEX. Carnegie Inst. Wash. Pub. 326, 355 pp., illus. 1923.

BIG SAGEBRUSH

Artemi'sia tridenta'ta

Flower heads—small (about ⅛ in. wide and ¼ in. long), numerous, stalkless, erect, borne in loose, open, leafy-bracted, end clusters (panicles)

Bracts—8 to 18, in a series (involucre) around flower head; outer bracts short, rounded, occasionally narrowed at tip, densely white-hairy; inner somewhat spatula-shaped, white-hairy at least along the middle, with brown, thin-papery margins

Flowers—all alike, 5 to 8 in each head, small, tubular, yellowish or brownish, perfect, seed-producing

"Seeds" (achenes)—small, cylindric-top-shaped, 4- or 5-angled or ribbed, hairless

Leaves—alternate, solitary or in groups, ½ to 1¾ in. long, tapered at base, 3- (rarely 4- to 7-) toothed at tip, silvery-hairy on both sides; upper leaves (especially those of the flower cluster) entire, linear

Stems—woody, 1 to about 16 ft. high, round, much-branched, silvery-white-hairy when young, with gray shreddy bark in age

Big sagebrush, locally known as black sage or blue sage, and often called simply sage or sagebrush, is a large deciduous shrub with silvery green leaves. It is one of the most widespread and most familiar species of *Artemisia*, in addition to being probably the most abundant shrub in western North America.[1] The specific name *tridentata* refers to the three teeth at the apex of the leaf. The species ranges from western Nebraska to Montana, British Columbia, eastern California, Lower California, and northern New Mexico. Big sagebrush occurs as a major part of the plant cover over vast areas of the semiarid lands of the West, ranging in altitude from about 3,000 feet in Oregon and 3,300 feet in Montana to timberline in the mountains of Colorado. However, it grows most abundantly on the valley bottoms, plains, foothills, and mesas up to about 8,000 feet, occupying much of the semidesert lands throughout the Intermountain region and northward through Wyoming, Idaho, eastern Oregon, and eastern Washington. It usually appears in open stands, frequently covering great expanses of country with a dense gray mantle, which is often referred to in ecological literature as the "Northern Desert Shrub Formation." Because of continued overgrazing, with the resultant death or decimation of the valuable perennial bunchgrasses, vast areas of western range contain almost pure stands of this species.

Big sagebrush grows on a variety of soils, from the shallow rocky loams of foothills and slopes to the vast areas of disintegrated lava formations in the Snake River plains of Idaho and eastern Oregon, but seldom occurs abundantly on soils of granitic origin. In northern Nevada and Utah it principally inhabits the rich limestone soils of the valleys and foothills. This species grows most typically and luxuriantly with wheatgrasses, bluegrasses, rabbitbrushes, and snakeweed on the deep, well-drained alluvial clay loams at the foot of the main mountain slopes. In the open ponderosa pine, oak brush, and piñon-juniper belts it ordinarily appears in association with wheatgrasses, snowberries, lanceleaf yellowbrush, serviceberries, and needlegrasses. This plant thrives best on rather light, pervious, well-drained, alkali-free soils having a good water supply, as its deep roots facilitate utilization of water that percolates to considerable depths. Big sagebrush is frequently killed by flooding or by the rise of the water table above the subsoil horizon. Tall, dense stands of the plant are indicative of fertile soil suitable for small grains and adapted for irrigated farming.

Observations by Clements[2] indicate that, although big sagebrush apparently is the dominant plant throughout much of its range, it is now truly climax only on approximately one-fourth (the driest portions) of its present area. Elsewhere it has invaded former grasslands which have been depleted by overuse. The current agricultural lands of the West were developed from the fertile, grassy, big sagebrush areas of former years.

At the outset grazing in the Intermountain region was centralized near settlements. As a direct result the neighboring grassy sage-

[1] Dayton, W. A. IMPORTANT WESTERN BROWSE PLANTS. U. S. Dept. Agr. Misc. Pub. 101, 214 pp., illus. 1931.
[2] Clements, F. E. THE RELICT METHOD IN DYNAMIC ECOLOGY. Jour. Ecology [London] 22 (1) : 1–68, illus. 1934.

brush ranges, which furnished forage for domestic livestock, were soon depleted. Such mismanagement favored the gradual invasion and spread of the relatively unpalatable big sagebrush.[3]

Despite low palatability, this shrub is important to western stockmen, due to its wide distribution and abundance over enormous areas of easily accessible range. On the summer ranges or where succulent forage is plentiful big sagebrush is unimportant and even ranks as a pest in many places. Where abundant this species often furnishes considerable feed for sheep and goats on the lower ranges, particularly those used for winter grazing. Generally speaking, cattle browse the plants only lightly and horses seldom eat more than a few flower heads. Frequently during the late fall, winter, and early spring, especially during periods of heavy snowfall, big sagebrush is utilized by sheep, goats, and cattle. Despite its low palatability, chemical analysis indicates that the leaves of big sagebrush equal alfalfa meal in protein, have a higher carbohydrate content, and yield twelvefold more fat. The high fat content qualifies sagebrush leaves as valuable winter feed, since fat has a high power to produce heat.[4] However, the palatability of the bitter, pungent-tasting leaves is low, due doubtless to the presence of a bitter material and about 3 percent of volatile oil. Notwithstanding that disadvantage, many stockmen find this shrub a valuable forage. On the winter ranges of the Great Basin sheep are frequently confined to big sagebrush areas. At the outset the animals do not readily eat the foliage, but after all other forage is gone they soon acquire an apparent liking for the herbage. Sheep wintered on such areas do well and often remain in excellent condition. In general, the forage value of big sagebrush increases the farther south it grows. Although it rates as poor forage for sheep and practically worthless for cattle in Oregon and Washington, this species ranks as fair forage for sheep and goats and poor for cattle in southern Nevada and Utah, Colorado, and New Mexico. It withstands moderate, but not severe, usage, grows rapidly and vigorously, and produces an abundance of new stems.

Dense stands of big sagebrush have been burned on many areas and occasionally grubbed with the object of opening up the brush so that livestock, particularly sheep, can get at the feed and cover the area more successfully, as well as in the hope of improving the grazing capacity by increasing the more palatable vegetation. Hanson[5] found that when the sagebrush is removed by scraping or grubbing the growth of grass becomes denser and taller. Big sagebrush does not form root sprouts readily and accordingly is easily killed by burning. In view of the profound effects on soil and on vegetative and other biological conditions which fire often makes, care must be used in burning sagebrush areas if damage is not to

[3] Pickford, G. D. THE INFLUENCE OF CONTINUED HEAVY GRAZING AND PROMISCUOUS BURNING ON SPRING-FALL RANGES IN UTAH. Ecology 13 : 159–171. 1932.

[4] McCreary, O. WYOMING FORAGE PLANTS AND THEIR CHEMICAL COMPOSITION—STUDIES NO. 8. Wyo. Agr. Expt. Sta. Bull. 157 : [91]–106. 1927.

[5] Hanson, H. C. IMPROVEMENT OF SAGEBRUSH RANGE IN COLORADO. Colo. Agr. Expt. Sta. Bull. 356, 12 pp., illus. 1929.

be done to the soil and grazing capacity of the area. Pickford[3] reports that on dry, overgrazed, spring-fall Utah ranges, although the big sagebrush cover may be reduced 80 percent or more by burning, the grazing capacity has been lessened over 50 percent. This is due largely to the replacement of highly palatable perennial bunchgrasses by inferior species, particularly downy chess (*Bromus tectorum*), and a notable invasion of such worthless "fireweeds" as certain species of rabbitbrush (*Chrysothamnus*). Undoubtedly the decrease of palatable perennial grasses, after being exposed through the elimination of the sagebrush, was the result of the overgrazing on these ranges. Even on areas promiscuously burned, however, and long protected from grazing, burning tends to deplete the stand of perennial grasses and to allow annual grasses, chiefly downy chess, to increase sharply in density as compared to unburned ranges protected from grazing.

In areas where moisture is relatively good and where there is a remnant of palatable perennial grasses in the sagebrush stand, burning under properly controlled conditions may be effective in eliminating the dense sagebrush and improving the grazing value of the type. Hanson[5] and Morris,[6] at about 8,000 feet elevation in the Laramie River Valley in northern Colorado, on an area with an annual precipitation of about 20 inches, a dense stand of big sagebrush, and a large variety of deep-rooted perennial grasses, obtained an increase in the grazing capacity of experimental plots by burning. The burning was done in early October and with a favorable wind. The area was closed to grazing and on some plots rodents were eliminated. Under such conditions grasses showed an increase in each of the 3 years following burning, although only about half or two-thirds as great as on the area unburned but grubbed of sagebrush.

Recent studies of the burning of sagebrush in southeastern Idaho by the Intermountain Forest and Range Experiment Station indicate that there was slightly less loss in perennial grasses between the good year 1932 and the very severe drought year of 1934 on areas burned to varying degree and protected from grazing than on unburned and ungrazed sagebrush areas. On burns of heavy intensity, however, a very significant decrease in organic matter in the top soil is apparent, as well as a decrease of nitrogen and moisture equivalent.

Big sagebrush produces so much pollen that when the wind blows small yellow clouds of this material are easily discernible in localities where this species occurs. This pollen is the source of many cases of hay fever. Numerous seeds of high viability are produced during September.

This species, although never used officially as a drug, has been much employed locally as a tea substitute, general tonic, a hair and eye wash, in treating colds and diarrhea, and as an antiseptic for wounds. Since the wood ignites easily, burns rapidly, and produces an intense heat, it provided an invaluable fuel for the Indians and early explorers, a use perpetuated by tourists and other visitors to the treeless areas where this plant grows.

[3] See footnote on preceding page.
[5] Hanson, H. C. IMPROVEMENT OF SAGEBRUSH RANGE IN COLORADO. Colo. Agr. Expt. Sta. Bull. 356, 12 pp., illus. 1929.
[6] Morris, M. S. INCREASING FORAGE ON SAGEBRUSH LAND. Colo. Agr. Expt. Sta. Bull. 308-A, 7 pp., illus. 1931.

FOURWING SALTBUSH

A'triplex canes'cens, syns. *A. occidenta'lis, A. tetrap'tera*

In the illustration below, *A* represents a male (staminate) plant and *B* represents a female (pistillate) plant

Flowers—small, of two kinds: male (staminate), and female (pistillate), borne mostly on separate plants (dioecious)

Female flowers—small, inconspicuous, axillary, clustered, stalked, with no flower parts except the 2 small united bracts which enclose the seed-producing organ (pistil) and enlarge as the fruit develops

Male flowers—without petals, not seed-producing, in dense, conspicuous clusters (spikes or spikelike panicles) near the ends of the twigs; flower cup (calyx) usually 5-parted; stamens of same number as calyx lobes

Leaves—alternate or somewhat clustered, stalkless, narrow, linear to linear-oblong or spatula-shaped, up to ⅜ in. wide and 2 in. long, finely scurfy-hairy

Twigs—whitish, scurfy-hairy when young

"Seed", or fruit (utricle)—1-celled, 1-seeded, 4-winged

Fruiting bracts—much enlarged, united nearly to apex, each with 2 broad dorsal wings; wings rounded in outline, up to ⅜ in. wide, thin, net-veined, usually toothed around the edges

Fourwing saltbush is a grayish-white, scurfy shrub, branching freely almost from the surface of the ground, and occasionally attaining a height of 6 to 10 feet, though it is usually lower. In New Mexico it is almost wholly known as chamiza, and that name (or its variants, chamise and chamiso) is in common use elsewhere. The name fourwing saltbush, the suggestion of Dr. Frederick V. Coville of the Bureau of Plant Industry, is a free translation of the Greek synonymous name *tetraptera*. *Atriplex canescens* is often misnamed shadscale, a term properly belonging to the related *A. confertifolia*. Other names sometimes applied to this well-known bush include buckwheat shrub, cenizo (white), greasewood, salt sage, and wafer sagebrush.

Fourwing saltbush is one of the most widely distributed of the west-American species of *Atriplex* and grows, in greater or less abundance, from South Dakota to western Texas, California, Nevada, Utah, and Wyoming. It is characteristic of dry, moderately saline or alkaline situations in the plains, foothills, and intermountain valleys of the creosotebush, sagebrush, and piñon belts, but it is occasionally found up to elevations at least as high as 8,500 feet in southwestern Colorado, and possibly elsewhere. It is sometimes the dominant species over extensive areas, and may occur in pure stands, but generally grows singly and more or less scattered among other shrubs, herbs, and grasses. The species is able to exist on land heavily impregnated with white alkali and also withstands small amounts of black alkali, but it is not entirely restricted to saline or alkaline areas, and is not necessarily an indicator thereof. It prefers deep, sandy soil, occasionally grows on sand dunes, and may be found on gravelly washes, mesas, ridges, and slopes.

Fourwing saltbush is undoubtedly one of the most valuable forage shrubs on arid sites in the Southwest and Intermountain regions. Its importance is due to its abundance, accessibility, size, large volume of forage, evergreen habit, high palatability, and nutritive value. Moreover, it exhibits hardiness to cold and a remarkable ability to withstand drought because of its tremendous root development, sometimes penetrating to depths of about 20 feet.[1] The leaves, stems, flowers, and fruits are cropped by all classes of range livestock except horses, which graze the species only in winter when other forage is sparse. The general palatability of the herbage rates as fairly good to good for cattle and as good for sheep and goats. Deer usually relish it, particularly as winter browse.

The seed crop, when produced, is devoured wholesale, but the high palatability of these parts is naturally a disadvantage to the species from a reproductive standpoint. The stems are very brittle and, on some overgrazed areas, the bushes are so broken down and weakened by grazing that they either fail to produce a viable seed crop or else succumb entirely. If protected in the summer, however, this shrub can successfully withstand reasonably heavy winter use and, under favorable conditions, it reproduces freely from seed and grows rapidly. It does not ordinarily shed its leaves in the winter, and puts out leaves in the spring irrespective of rainfall. Hence it is of especial value as browse when there is a lack of other forage.

Various chemical analyses, as well as feeding tests, have shown that fourwing saltbush has a high nutritive value.[2][3] Because of its nutritive qualities and its ability to grow on poor and salty soils where grain, alfalfa, or tame grasses will not grow, Jared G. Smith[4] recommends it as worthy of cultivation, stressing its superiority to the introduced shrubby Australian saltbushes which lack its ability to withstand the severe winters of our western ranges.

Ordinarily no injury to livestock results from grazing this species under range conditions. There is evidence, however, that it occasionally causes bloat when eaten too liberally, and that too concentrated feeding on this shrub may cause scours in range cattle. It has occasionally proved poisonous to sheep, and is reported as causing a sort of anemia at certain seasons.[5] The marked alkalinity of its herbage, especially when growing in areas highly impregnated with salt, suggests the desirability, wherever possible, of an addition of grasses or other nonsaline feeds in utilizing fourwing saltbush areas.

The grayish woody stems of fourwing saltbush are rigid and somewhat brittle; the bark of the older stems is roughened by small longitudinal fissures. The whitish scurfy twigs bear pale, grayish-green leaves which are often somewhat clustered. The flowers appear in abundance from June to August.

[1] Dayton, W. A. IMPORTANT WESTERN BROWSE PLANTS. U. S. Dept. Agr. Misc. Pub. 101, 214 pp., illus. 1931.
[2] Foster, L., Lantow, J. L., and Wilson, C. P. CHAMIZA AS AN EMERGENCY FEED FOR RANGE CATTLE. N. Mex. Agr. Expt. Sta. Bull. 125, 29 pp., illus. 1921.
[3] Bidwell, G. L., and Wooton, E. O. SALTBUSHES AND THEIR ALLIES IN THE UNITED STATES. U. S. Dept. Agr. Bull. 1345, 40 pp., illus. 1925.
[4] Smith, J. G. FODDER AND FORAGE PLANTS, EXCLUSIVE OF THE GRASSES. U. S. Dept. Agr., Div. Agrost. Bull. 2, rev., 86 pp., illus. 1900.
[5] [Doten, S. B.] PROGRESS MADE DURING THE YEAR ON STATION PROJECTS. PROJECT 22. THE PROBLEM OF POISONOUS RANGE PLANTS. Nev. Agr. Expt. Sta. Ann. Rept. 1921 : 10–12, illus. 1922.

SHADSCALE

A′triplex confertifo′lia

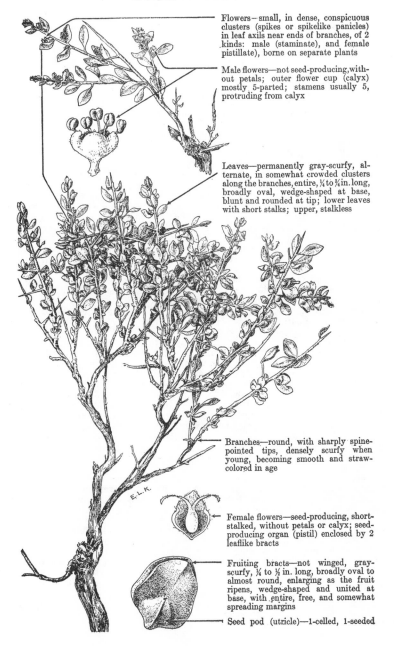

Flowers—small, in dense, conspicuous clusters (spikes or spikelike panicles) in leaf axils near ends of branches, of 2 kinds: male (staminate), and female pistillate), borne on separate plants

Male flowers—not seed-producing, without petals; outer flower cup (calyx) mostly 5-parted; stamens usually 5, protruding from calyx

Leaves—permanently gray-scurfy, alternate, in somewhat crowded clusters along the branches, entire, ¼ to ¾ in. long, broadly oval, wedge-shaped at base, blunt and rounded at tip; lower leaves with short stalks; upper, stalkless

Branches—round, with sharply spine-pointed tips, densely scurfy when young, becoming smooth and straw-colored in age

Female flowers—seed-producing, short-stalked, without petals or calyx; seed-producing organ (pistil) enclosed by 2 leaflike bracts

Fruiting bracts—not winged, gray-scurfy, ¼ to ½ in. long, broadly oval to almost round, enlarging as the fruit ripens, wedge-shaped and united at base, with entire, free, and somewhat spreading margins

Seed pod (utricle)—1-celled, 1-seeded

609

Shadscale, sometimes called spiny saltbush and saltsage. is a compact, spiny shrub growing typically in dense clumps, usually 1 to 2 (occasionally more than 3) feet high. It is one of the most important native species in the *Atriplex* genus, which belongs to the goosefoot family (Chenopodiaceae). The name *confertifolia* literally means crowded leaves.

Shadscale ranges from southern Idaho to Wyoming, Utah, New Mexico, northern Mexico, eastern California, and southeastern Oregon, being most prominent in Utah and Nevada, but abundant also over large areas in other portions of its range. Typically it is a plant of the dry plains and hillsides up to elevations of about 6,000 feet, although it occurs up to 8,000 feet. It is found in the creosotebush, sagebrush, and juniper-piñon belts, associated frequently with sagebrush, rabbitbrush, jointfir (Mormon-tea), winterfat, cactus, and various semidesert bunchgrasses. This shrub is characteristically a dominant species over vast expanses of arid range.

Shadscale frequently grows along the edges of the dry alkaline lake bottoms characteristic of many desert valleys, and extends up the slopes, benches, and dry washes well into the foothills of the surrounding mountains; with greasewood, it often inhabits soils that are strongly impregnated with alkali. It thrives well on moderately alkaline and heavy clay soils, and grows abundantly in sandy and gravelly areas.

Shadscale is grazed chiefly in the fall, winter, and spring and is palatable to all classes of livestock. Although ordinarily less palatable than certain of its plant associates, particularly grasses and black sagebrush (*Artemisia nova*), its abundance on winter ranges makes it very important as forage. The seeds are the most palatable part of the plant and probably the most nutritious; the leaves are also relished. These often fall to the ground during the late autumn, collect in depressions under the bushes, and thus are available to livestock when they enter the winter ranges. After the seeds and leaves are shed the spine-pointed branches become rigid, persisting for several years and affording considerable protection against grazing animals.[1] During moist weather the branches become softened and are moderately cropped.

Overgrazing on much of the winter range has greatly decreased the abundance of highly palatable plants and, consequently, has increased the demands on shadscale and other less desirable species. On excessively grazed ranges shadscale often is browsed to the ground and the rough, coarse forage thus consumed frequently causes sore mouth, especially among young lambs. Weakened, hedged, and dead plants on some overgrazed areas are evidence that shadscale suffers from overuse. Prolonged drought causes heavy mortality.

Although stands of this plant are being maintained fairly well, little or no reproduction is taking place in some areas. A recent range survey conducted under the auspices of the Intermountain Forest and Range Experiment Station, Utah, revealed no shadscale plants younger than 15 years on a heavily grazed area in western Utah. An abundance of good seed is produced by vigorous plants during years of average growth, but the Wyoming Agricultural Experiment Station[2] has failed to secure reproduction under artificial conditions. Shadscale, even though it provides but a partial vegetative cover, aids particularly in alkaline areas, in keeping the soil in place. Where shadscale plants occupy soil hummocks overstocking or range depletion may be suspected.

Shadscale typically grows as lone bushes or clumps of bushes 1 or 2 feet, sometimes as much as 8 feet, in diameter. The stems are woody, round (terete), stiff, rather stout, and most of them end in spiny points. The numerous, rounded or oval, short-stalked, thickish leaves are crowded on the stems. The leaves are one-fourth to three-fourths of an inch long, usually blunt at the apex, and wedge-shaped at the base. Like most saltbushes of the desert regions, shadscale is ash-gray or almost white, due to the scurfy covering on the leaves and young stems. The tiny flowers are borne in small clusters in the leaf axils near the ends of the branches. Male (staminate) and female (pistillate) flowers grow on separate plants. The female flowers have two thick, scurfy bracts united at the base which enlarge from one-fourth to three-eighths of an inch in diameter and tightly enclose the seed. The bracts are not winged or notched, but are broadly oval and rounded at the tips.

---

[1] Jepson, W. L. A FLORA OF CALIFORNIA. 7 pts., illus. San Francisco. 1909–22.
[2] Nelson, E. NATIVE AND INTRODUCED SALTBUSHES. THREE SEASONS' TRIALS. Wyo. Agr. Expt. Sta. Bull. 63, 19 pp., illus. 1904.

WESTERN AZALEA

Aza'lea occidenta'lis, syn. *Rhododen'dron occidenta'le*

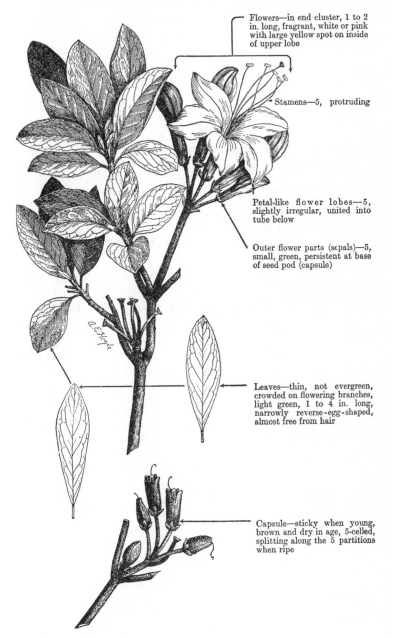

Flowers—in end cluster, 1 to 2 in. long, fragrant, white or pink with large yellow spot on inside of upper lobe

Stamens—5, protruding

Petal-like flower lobes—5, slightly irregular, united into tube below

Outer flower parts (sepals)—5, small, green, persistent at base of seed pod (capsule)

Leaves—thin, not evergreen, crowded on flowering branches, light green, 1 to 4 in. long, narrowly reverse-egg-shaped, almost free from hair

Capsule—sticky when young, brown and dry in age, 5-celled, splitting along the 5 partitions when ripe

Avoided by shepherds because of its poisonous properties but reputed as harmless to cattle, this beautiful flowering shrub is the only true azalea occurring naturally in the West. Western azalea occurs below the 4,000-foot level in the coastal ranges and between 3,000 and 7,500 feet on the western slope of the Sierras, growing in fairly open thickets throughout California and southwestern Oregon. Such thickets are especially prevalent on moist, rich loam soil in the mixed conifer forests, usually along stream banks and in the vicinity of springs and wooded canyons. The most characteristic associates of this species are willows, alders, and other shade- and moisture-loving shrubs.

Some sheepmen and goat producers utilize azalea-infested range without injury to their livestock by denying entrance to flocks until the animals have had several hours fill on good range. Animals poisoned by azalea exhibit such common symptoms of plant poisoning as vomiting, frothing at the mouth, weakness, and depression. They characteristically grind their teeth in a very audible manner.

This azalea is often popularly, although incorrectly, confused with the so-called mountain laurels, but it actually is far removed botanically from the laurel family. Western azalea varies from 2 to 14 feet in height, but is usually about 5 or 6 feet tall. It is readily recognizable because of its showy, fragrant flowers and handsome fall colorings of scarlet and gold; these features have increased its popularity as a cultivated ornamental. Its leaves are deciduous and the new leaves usually appear before other common shrubs start growth in the spring; its flowers are in bloom from May to July. The old bark ordinarily is shreddy and gray in color, while the new shoots vary in hue from green to yellow. Individual stems are close, but not crowded, and vary from 3 to 8 feet or more in height. The regular branching of the upper third of the plant often forms a complete and dense canopy when the leaves are fully out. Its bright green, smooth-edged leaves are thin, approximately 3 inches long, and somewhat boat-shaped. The funnel-shaped blooms, 1 or 2 inches long, are either white or pink with a large yellow blotch on the inside of the upper lobe. The five stamens extend about an inch beyond the five united petals (corolla) which distinguishes the species from the related coast rhododendron (*Rhododendron californicum*) having a similar but smaller flower and 10 short stamens.

FALSE-AZALEA

Azaleas'trum albiflo'rum, syns. *Aza'lea albiflo'ra, Rhododen'dron albiflo'rum*

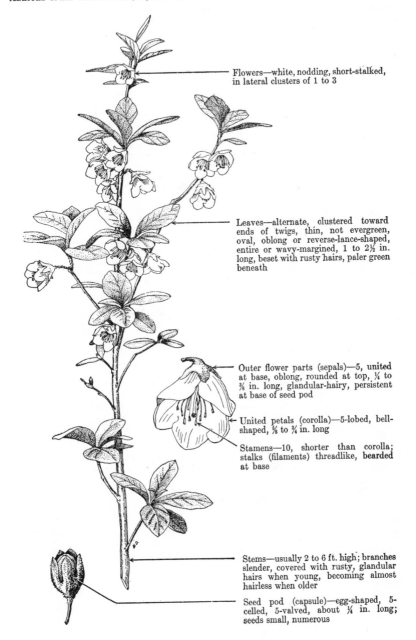

Flowers—white, nodding, short-stalked, in lateral clusters of 1 to 3

Leaves—alternate, clustered toward ends of twigs, thin, not evergreen, oval, oblong or reverse-lance-shaped, entire or wavy-margined, 1 to 2½ in. long, beset with rusty hairs, paler green beneath

Outer flower parts (sepals)—5, united at base, oblong, rounded at top, ¼ to ⅜ in. long, glandular-hairy, persistent at base of seed pod

United petals (corolla)—5-lobed, bell-shaped, ⅝ to ¾ in. long

Stamens—10, shorter than corolla; stalks (filaments) threadlike, bearded at base

Stems—usually 2 to 6 ft. high; branches slender, covered with rusty, glandular hairs when young, becoming almost hairless when older

Seed pod (capsule)—egg-shaped, 5-celled, 5-valved, about ¼ in. long; seeds small, numerous

False-azalea, an erect shrub, 2 to 6 feet high, belonging to the heath family (Ericaceae), has slender branches, deciduous leaves, and white, bell-shaped flowers. It is also variously known as small azalea, white-flowered rhododendron, Rocky Mountain rhododendron, and snowbrush; the latter name, in use by stockmen of the Northwest, is more correctly applied to *Ceanothus velutinus*. The generic name means like the genus *Azalea*, in which this plant is classified by some botanists, and the specific name *albiflorum* is Latin for white-flowered.

False-azalea is distributed from British Columbia to Oregon, northern Idaho, and western Montana. It has also been collected locally in northern Colorado. Presumably it also occurs in the mountains of western Wyoming, but apparently has never been collected there. In the Northwest it is one of the most characteristic shrubs of the Hudsonian life zone, which embraces in that region areas extending from about 5,000 feet to timber line. At the higher elevations it grows under stands of alpine fir (*Abies lasiocarpa*), whitebark pine (*Pinus albicaulis*), and mountain hemlock (*Tsuga mertensiana*), or sometimes occurs in open parks, meadows, or browse stands bordering the timber. In some localities false-azalea also grows at lower elevations in the somber depths of moist forests of western hemlock (*Tsuga heterophylla*) and silver fir (*Abies amabilis*), or occasionally with other coniferous species. In the Rocky Mountains this shrub usually occupies moist, northern slopes, being commonly associated with lodgepole pine (*Pinus contorta*), alpine fir, and Engelmann spruce (*Picea engelmanni*). Although it usually occurs in scattered patches, false-azalea grows in abundance on some mountainous ranges, where it is often one of the dominant undershrubs.

This species is unquestionably poisonous; it has been reliably reported as the source of sheep losses in the Northwest as well as on the Routt National Forest in Colorado. The palatability of false-azalea is usually very low and, under ordinary circumstances, livestock avoid grazing the leafage. On this account, ranges, where it is common, can be grazed without harmful results, if utilized on a conservative basis. Washington sheepmen have learned by costly experience that sickness or even death frequently results if they confine their flocks too closely to areas on which this plant occurs. However, general observations indicate that sheep can eat the leafage of false-azalea in small quantities without harm.

According to Marsh,[1] experiments indicate that this plant is usually more poisonous than the closely related menziesias, or fools'-huckleberries (*Menziesia* spp.), but less dangerous than the deadly blacklaurel (*Leucothoë davisiae*). False-azalea, as well as many other members of the heath family, contains a poisonous substance called andromedotoxin; the symptoms are practically similar in all cases of so-called laurel poisoning. The poisoned animals are depressed and weakened, as shown by a staggering gait, or inability to stand, and irregular breathing; other symptoms including frothing at the mouth, nausea usually accompanied by vomiting and frequently by grinding of the teeth. Prevention is the most practical control as little has been accomplished in the way of remedial treatment. Anything which aids in the elimination of the poison is beneficial and to this end laxatives such as Epsom salts in 4-ounce doses may be given.

False-azalea is the only species of *Azaleastrum* of any significance in the United States. *A. warrenii*, a low nearly hairless plant found in the high mountains of Colorado, is the only other western species which has been described. The genus is poorly defined, however, and many botanists merge it with *Rhododendron* or *Azalea*. False-azalea is rather distinctive, however, and can readily be separated from the western species, at least, of these two genera. It is a smaller shrub, has thin, deciduous leaves, and lateral, few-flowered clusters of small white flowers, usually less than an inch in length; the 10 stamens do not protrude beyond the corolla. In contrast, coast rhododendron (*Rhododendron californicum*), the only true rhododendron growing in the West, has shiny evergreen leaves and large, rose-pink flowers having 10 stamens. Western azalea (*Azalea occidentalis*), the only true azalea native to the West, has deciduous leaves and fragrant white or pink flowers with five exserted stamens.

---

[1] Marsh, C. D. STOCK-POISONING PLANTS OF THE RANGE. U. S. Dept. Agr. Bull. 1245, rev., 75 pp., illus. 1929. Supersedes Bull. 575.

SEEPWILLOW

Bac'charis glutino'sa

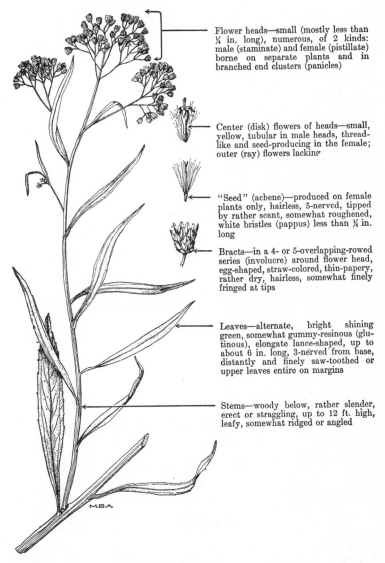

Flower heads—small (mostly less than ¼ in. long), numerous, of 2 kinds: male (staminate) and female (pistillate) borne on separate plants and in branched end clusters (panicles)

Center (disk) flowers of heads—small, yellow, tubular in male heads, thread-like and seed-producing in the female; outer (ray) flowers lacking

"Seed" (achene)—produced on female plants only, hairless, 5-nerved, tipped by rather scant, somewhat roughened, white bristles (pappus) less than ¼ in. long

Bracts—in a 4- or 5-overlapping-rowed series (involucre) around flower head, egg-shaped, straw-colored, thin-papery, rather dry, hairless, somewhat finely fringed at tips

Leaves—alternate, bright shining green, somewhat gummy-resinous (glutinous), elongate lance-shaped, up to about 6 in. long, 3-nerved from base, distantly and finely saw-toothed or upper leaves entire on margins

Stems—woody below, rather slender, erect or straggling, up to 12 ft. high, leafy, somewhat ridged or angled

Seepwillow, known locally as false, Gila, or water willow, and also as groundsel tree, water motie, and water-wally, is a graceful, willowy shrub with many straight, slender stems from 3 to 12 feet high, growing in clumps from a few to 20 feet or more in diameter or sometimes in dense thickets. The current shoots are long and branched toward the top into several straight branchlets, which support a tassel of greenish white flowers. The leaves are lustrous green and willowlike, which explains why willow is frequently incorporated in the various common names. The use of seep and water as part of the local names refers to the common occurrence of this bush around springs and streams. The specific name *glutinosa* refers to the gummy (glutinous) exudations of the branches and leaves.

This shrub ranges from western Texas to Colorado, southern California, and south through Mexico and Central America to Chile. It is an extremely common shrub in the Southwest, but is largely restricted to stream banks, lake margins, flood plains, canyons, and intermittent stream channels where it frequently grows abundantly in nearly pure stands, or as scattered clumps in association with desertwillow (*Chilopsis linearis*), mesquites (*Prosopis* spp.), and other shrubs. It occurs on soils varying from sand to heavy clay, but seems to attain its best development on deep, moist, loamy soils. Its altitudinal range is chiefly between 2,000 and 5,000 feet.

This shrub is important in erosion control because of its abundance along stream and gully channels, and also on account of its deep and extensive root system. Being worthless as forage for all classes of livestock, it is undisturbed by grazing animals and serves efficiently as a soil-binder, when much of the palatable vegetation has been depleted by overuse. The Indians sharpened the pithy stems for use as paint brushes in decorating pottery; they also employed the long, straight stems in building storehouses.[1]

Baccharis [2] is a large (chiefly South American and Mexican) genus of the composite family (Asteraceae, or Compositae), mainly more or less shrubby, and with the sexes distinct (dioecious). Of the 23 species growing naturally in the United States 16 occur in the far West, chiefly in California and the Southwest. The forage value is worthless or poor and some of the species are known to be poisonous. A number of the species are in local repute as medicinal plants; the stiff branches of some of the members are used for home-made brooms. The common explanation of the name *Baccharis* is that it is derived from Bacchus, god of wine, but it was evidently taken by Linnaeus from an old Greek plant name (usually spelled *bakkaris*, or *bakcharis*), said to be of Lydian origin, and which applied to some unknown species (perhaps of the composite genus *Conyza*) whose roots yielded an aromatic oil.

Yerba-de-pasmo, a Spanish term meaning a weed for chills *(B. ramulo'sa*, syn. *B. pteronioi'des*), is a low, resinous, grayish green bush from 1 to 3 feet high, with numerous clustered, variously toothed leaves. It ranges from western Texas to southern Arizona and south into Mexico on dry, gravelly foothills, mesas, and plains in the semidesert shrub, and oak-woodland types. Marsh [3] states that yerba-de-pasmo has been definitely proved poisonous to sheep; he believes it was probably responsible for serious cattle losses in 1918, and later, on the Coronado National Forest of Arizona and the Lincoln National Forest in New Mexico. The species is unpalatable, however, so that losses caused by this plant on the range are normally unknown. Indians and Mexicans make tea, which they use as a remedy for chills, from its leaves; hence the common name.[2]

Broom baccharis (*B. sarothroi'des*), a green, broomlike shrub of the Southwest and Mexico, is suspected of being poisonous in the winter and early spring, when it may sometimes be eaten in the absence of palatable forage. This belief, however, has not yet been sustained by experimental research.

Emory baccharis (*B. emo'ryi*), a somewhat willowlike shrub from 3 to 12 feet high, occurs from Colorado to California and New Mexico. It is a common shrub along washes and flood plains and, to some extent, on dry open ridges. Although its palatability is nil, it is of value in erosion control along intermittent gullies.

Kidneywort (*B. pilula'ris*), a common prostrate-spreading or erect shrub, which ranges from Oregon to southern California, is useful in preventing wind erosion of sand dunes.

[1] Russell, F. THE PIMA INDIANS. U. S. Bur. Amer. Ethnol. Ann. Rept. (1904–5)26: 3–[390], illus. 1908.
[2] Dayton, W. A. IMPORTANT WESTERN BROWSE PLANTS. U. S. Dept. Agr. Misc. Pub. 101, 214 pp., illus. 1931.
[3] Marsh C. D. STOCK-POISONING PLANTS OF THE RANGE. U. S. Dept. Agr. Bull. 1245, rev., 75 pp., illus. 1929. Supersedes Bull. 575.

FALSE-MESQUITE

Callian'dra eriophyl'la

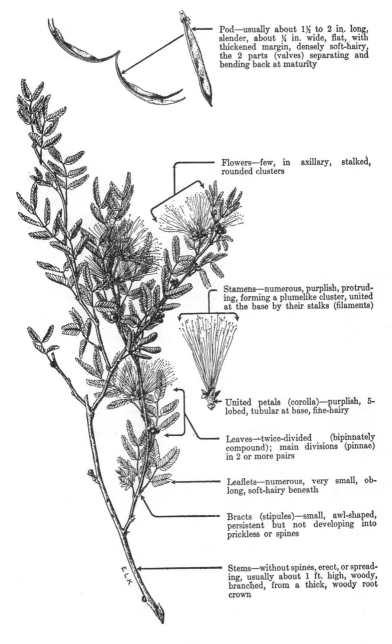

Pod—usually about 1½ to 2 in. long, slender, about ¼ in. wide, flat, with thickened margin, densely soft-hairy, the 2 parts (valves) separating and bending back at maturity

Flowers—few, in axillary, stalked, rounded clusters

Stamens—numerous, purplish, protruding, forming a plumelike cluster, united at the base by their stalks (filaments)

United petals (corolla)—purplish, 5-lobed, tubular at base, fine-hairy

Leaves—twice-divided (bipinnately compound); main divisions (pinnae) in 2 or more pairs

Leaflets—numerous, very small, oblong, soft-hairy beneath

Bracts (stipules)—small, awl-shaped, persistent but not developing into prickless or spines

Stems—without spines, erect, or spreading, usually about 1 ft. high, woody, branched, from a thick, woody root crown

False-mesquite, also known as bastard-mesquite and false-catclaw because of its resemblance to the related mesquites (*Prosopis* spp.) and catclaw (*Acacia greggii*), belongs to the mimosa family (Mimosaceae), which some botanists prefer to regard as a subfamily or tribe of the legume, or pea family (Leguminosae, or Papilionaceae). Yerba bonita (pretty herb), a commonly used Spanish name, is locally applied to this small but showy, purple-flowered, delicate-leaved shrub of the Southwest. The generic name *Calliandra*, translated from the Greek, signifies beautiful stamens, and refers to the conspicuous, brilliant stamens of most species. The specific name *eriophylla* is a Greek adjective meaning woolly-leaved (*erion*, wool + *phullon*, leaf) and, like the common names hairy calliandra and hairy-leaf calliandra, which are occasionally applied to this plant, refers to the hairiness of the leaves of this species. The plant also is sometimes called fairies' duster because the numerous stamens on their long, threadlike stalks form a plumelike cluster resembling a dainty feather duster.

False-mesquite, distributed from western Texas to central Arizona and southward throughout most of Mexico, is the commonest species of *Calliandra* in the West. It grows on the warm, open, sunny exposures of dry mesas and foothills in the desert-shrub and open grassland types, being especially common between elevations of 3,000 and 5,000 feet. This species appears on a wide variety of soils, but is particularly characteristic of sandy gravels of granitic origin and gravelly clay soils. It sometimes constitutes as much as 25 percent of the ground cover over large areas on the more favorable sites. Under less favorable conditions, it grows as scattered individuals and is associated usually with catclaw, mesquite, paloverde, curly-mesquite, three-awns, and with sprucetop, and other lower-range gramas.

This species is a valuable forage plant on many ranges, qualifying wherever it occurs as one of the better yearlong browse plants for all classes of domestic livestock, deer, and possibly other wild animals. The palatability varies, according to plant association, from fairly good to good and is occasionally rated even higher. Generally, on properly grazed range about 40 to 60 percent of the current year's growth of false-mesquite is utilized on a yearlong basis. It is one of the first plants to start growth in the spring if winter and spring rainfall is adequate; at this time, when there is a scarcity of green forage, the succulent shoots, leaves, and flowers are especially palatable. This shrub makes a good second growth and blossoms again with the advent of summer rains and, despite its small size, produces copious foliage which, in the aggregate, provides a relatively large volume of forage. The pods are equal to the flowers and leaves in palatability. False-mesquite, being a low, open-crowned, unarmed shrub, is very accessible to grazing animals and is ordinarily grazed very closely on overgrazed ranges and during drought. Any tendency of the plant to assume a very stubby, stunted appearance indicates that the range is being grazed to excess. False-mesquite, however, withstands heavy grazing, as is evidenced by its persistence on overgrazed areas after the better grasses have practically been exterminated. Heavily browsed plants recover readily under protection or moderate use.

Chemical analyses of leaves and young twigs of false-mesquite from the Prescott National Forest in Arizona, made for the Forest Service by the Bureau of Chemistry and Soils,[1] show that the fats and oils (ether extract) and protein content of this species approximately equals that of alfalfa hay. False-mesquite has a crude fiber content but little more than half that of alfalfa hay; its carbohydrate content (nitrogen-free extract) is also considerably higher.

False-mesquite grows as high as 2 feet and is rather erect when not grazed but, on the open range, it usually varies from 3 to 12 inches in height. The branches are rather stiff and bluish gray in color; the young twigs are soft-hairy. This plant is distinguishable readily from related associates of other genera of the mimosa family by its purple flowers and unarmed branches. Only two other species of *Calliandra*, *C. humilis* and *C. reticulata*, are native to the western United States. They are small (4 to 8 inches tall), substantially herbaceous plants with woody bases, occurring in Arizona, New Mexico, and Mexico, but are not so abundant, widespread, or as high in forage value as false-mesquite.

---

[1] Dayton, W. A. IMPORTANT WESTERN BROWSE PLANTS. U. S. Dept. Agr. Misc. Pub. 101, 214 pp., illus. 1931.

CEANOTHUSES

Ceano'thus spp.

Ceanothus is a large North American genus of about 60 species, occurring mostly in the foothills and mountains of the West, and especially California, where at least 30 species are found. About a dozen species are confined to Mexico. They usually are shrubs, averaging 3 to 8 feet in height; some are deciduous, others are evergreen. Several species, as squawcarpet (*C. prostratus*), are characteristically prostrate; a few others, including island myrtle (*C. arboreus*), probably more accurately known as feltleaf ceanothus, and blue myrtle (*C. thyrsiflorus*), probably better known as blueblossom, become small trees under favorable conditions. The branches of a number of species, such as whitethorn (*C. cordulatus*) and redheart, or spiny myrtle (*C. spinosus*), end in spines, but most species have unarmed branches arranged alternately or oppositely along the several stems arising from the base.

Many species of *Ceanothus* have individual names as, for example, Jersey-tea, or redroot (*C. americanus*), whitethorn, deerbrush, bluebrush, or sweet birch (*C. integerrimus*), muskbush (*C. jepsonii*), squawcarpet, or mahala-mats, and snowbrush (*C. velutinus*). Unfortunately, however, there has never been general agreement as to a generic English name for this important group of woody plants. Probably the names in most general use have been bluebush (or bluebrush), buckbrush, lilac, and myrtle. The first is obviously inappropriate for any but blue-flowered plants and flower color is often variable in the same species. Buckbrush, applied indiscriminately to a host of diverse plants, is trite and indefinite. Lilac and myrtle are quite untenable for species of *Ceanothus*, rightfully applying, as they do, to the very different genera *Syringa* and *Myrtus*, respectively. In United States Department of Agriculture Miscellaneous Publication 101, "Important western browse plants" (1931), at the suggestion of Dr. Frederick V. Coville, of the Bureau of Plant Industry, the name soapbloom was adopted for species of the section *Euceanothus* (which embraces the majority of the species of *Ceanothus*), while hornbrush was adopted for the species of the section *Cerastes*. Soapbloom refers to the soaplike (saponaceous) properties of the flowers of these plants. Hornbrush refers to the typically hard-leaved (horny) species of the *Cerastes* section and, more especially, to the horned pods of that group, which somewhat suggest the head of a viper (*Cerastes*). However, since that publication was issued, experience seems to indicate that there is a greater tendency to use ceanothus as an English name for these shrubs than to adopt soapbloom and hornbrush.

The forage value of *Ceanothus* species varies from worthless to excellent. Squawcarpet, for example, has tough, spiny leaves and its palatability to livestock is negligible or, at best, low, while deerbrush, which has tender, highly palatable foliage and shoots, is a very valuable browse. Some species, notably wedgeleaf ceanothus (*C. cuneatus*), are important constituents of the foothill chaparral. Nearly all species produce abundant seed and some will sprout from the root crown. As a group *Ceanothus* species are quick to invade burned or denuded areas; whitethorn and snowbrush are especially prominent in this regard.

The poisonous glucoside *saponin* has been found in the flowers and fruits of a number of species of *Ceanothus* and it probably occurs in all the species. There is no evidence, however, that *Ceanothus* is a stock-poisoning genus or a source of danger on the range. In fact, it is well known that livestock will often crop the flowers and fruits rather heavily and with evident impunity. The indications are that the *saponin* passes without harm through the digestive tract of the animal unless abrasions or other lesions occur through which the alkaloid can directly enter the bloodstream. The English name soap-bloom for species of *Ceanothus*, and the use of the flowers by Indians and pioneers as a substitute for soap, are reflections of this presence of *saponin* in the inflorescence of these plants.

The leaves of *Ceanothus* species have short leafstalks (petioles) and in many species are prominently three-ribbed or veined on the lower side. The small, usually blue or white flowers are borne in compact or elongated clusters either laterally or terminally on the branches. When in large terminal clusters they are very showy. The five somewhat spoon-shaped petals have very slender, inrolled necks, the arching, hoodlike tips tending to enclose the pollen sacs (anthers). The globose, sometimes three-horned capsules are usually sticky (viscid) when young, becoming dry and separating into three parts when mature.

WHITETHORN

Ceano′thus cordula′tus

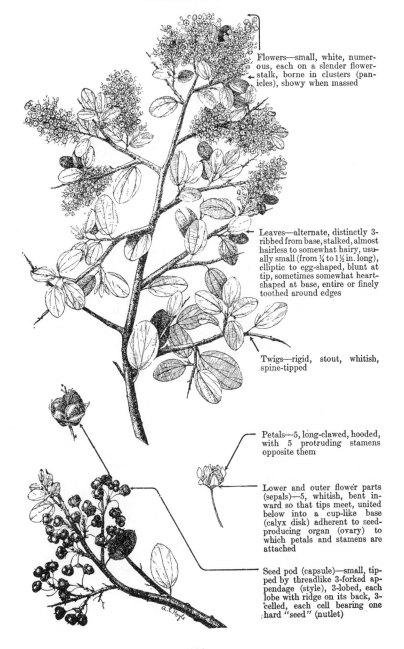

Flowers—small, white, numerous, each on a slender flower-stalk, borne in clusters (panicles), showy when massed

Leaves—alternate, distinctly 3-ribbed from base, stalked, almost hairless to somewhat hairy, usually small (from ¼ to 1½ in. long), elliptic to egg-shaped, blunt at tip, sometimes somewhat heart-shaped at base, entire or finely toothed around edges

Twigs—rigid, stout, whitish, spine-tipped

Petals—5, long-clawed, hooded, with 5 protruding stamens opposite them

Lower and outer flower parts (sepals)—5, whitish, bent inward so that tips meet, united below into a cup-like base (calyx disk) adherent to seed-producing organ (ovary) to which petals and stamens are attached

Seed pod (capsule)—small, tipped by threadlike 3-forked appendage (style), 3-lobed, each lobe with ridge on its back, 3-celled, each cell bearing one hard "seed" (nutlet)

Whitethorn is a deciduous shrub, with spiny-tipped twigs, common in the ponderosa pine, mixed conifer, and red fir stands throughout the Sierra Nevadas of California to southwestern Oregon. It is most abundant in the mixed conifer belt. The species grows on a wide variety of well-drained soils, and is usually found in the open, although it does well in the shade of coniferous timber. Among its most common associates are greenleaf manzanita (*Arctostaphylos patula*) and common serviceberry (*Amelanchier alnifolia*), and, at its upper altitudinal limits snowbrush (*Ceanothus velutinus*) and huckleberry oak (*Quercus vaccinifolia*).

Whitethorn produces abundant seed and like many members of the genus frequently increases after fires or logging, usually in combination with other brush species but sometimes as pure stands. Soil deterioration from repeated fires or other causes apparently does not check the spread of either whitethorn or its companion species, greenleaf manzanita. Under such conditions these two shrubs, either singly or in combination, become dominant plants. Since whitethorn is one of the first plants to become established on denuded soils, it has immediate value in soil protection, and later serves as a nurse crop for coniferous species.

While there is some difference of opinion regarding the forage value of whitethorn, its palatability is distinctly inferior to that of many other *Ceanothus* species. As a rule its browse value ranges from poor to fair for cattle and sheep and from fair to fairly good or occasionally good for goats. Palatabilities as high as very good or even excellent are sometimes reported for whitethorn, especially for goats, but these indicate overgrazed conditions. Usage of whitethorn is often greatly limited because of the general habit of growth in brushfields or dense patches. Plants that are slow-growing, because of age or unfavorable site, are very thorny, have little available forage, and may even be mechanically injurious. On the other hand, vigorous plants have many new tender shoots that provide good forage. However, the maximum use of whitethorn, even when readily accessible, seldom exceeds 20 percent of its foliage. Accordingly stocking must usually be adjusted to facilitate perpetuation of the more palatable species that are grazed in preference to whitethorn.

The numerous, rigid, many-branched, and spreading stems arise from the base, forming a dense, flat-topped bush 1 to 4 feet high and 3 to 9 feet across. The numerous, pale bluish twigs are rigid, sparingly leafy, and commonly terminate in a hard sharp point, or "thorn", a characteristic alluded to in the common name whitethorn. The pale green leaves are usually small and more or less elliptical but vary somewhat in both size and shape. The white flowers are borne in small, dense clusters (panicles) about 1½ inches long and these, in turn, are characteristically massed into larger and very showy flower groups (thyrsiform inflorescence). The small (three-sixteenths of an inch wide) capsule or fruit has three divisions or cells which are easily distinguished when viewed from the top.

WEDGELEAF CEANOTHUS

Ceano'thus cunea'tus

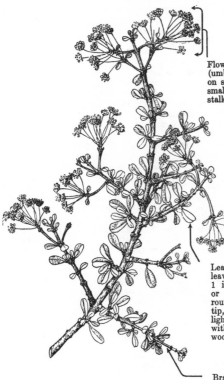

Flower clusters—umbrella-shaped (umbellate), up to 1 in. broad, borne on short, spurlike branchlets; flowers small, numerous, dull white, on slender stalks

Leaves—opposite, often with smaller leaves in the axils, thick, small (up to 1 in. long), oblong or wedge-shaped or reversely egg-shaped, blunt or rounded with a slightly notched tip, entire or, very rarely, few-toothed, light green above, paler green beneath with extremely fine, matted, white-woolly hairs

Branches—widely spreading, mostly in pairs, often unequal in length, almost at right angles to the stems

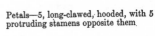

Petals—5, long-clawed, hooded, with 5 protruding stamens opposite them.

Outer flower parts (sepals)—5, somewhat greenish, bent inward so that tips meet, united below into a cuplike disk (calyx disk) to which the base of the seed-producing organ (ovary) and the petals and stamens are attached

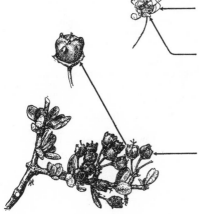

Seed pod (capsule)—globe-shaped or oblong, about ¼ in. across, 3-celled, each cell producing one hard "seed" (nutlet), 3-lobed, each lobe with a conspicuous, erect horn on top

Wedgeleaf ceanothus, known locally as buckbrush, chamise, chaparral, and greasebush, is a rigid, many-branched, thick-leaved, sometimes evergreen shrub, averaging 3 to 12 feet in height, but becomes smaller, more spreading, and densely matlike near the upper limits of its altitudinal range. The specific name *cuneatus* refers to the wedge-shaped bases of the leaves.

The species ranges from Oregon and California to extreme western Nevada and is one of the most widely distributed members of the genus in California, though very rare on the east slopes of the Sierras. It prefers dry, gravelly ridges and slopes and is most common on the interior foothills, but it also occurs locally, and sometimes abundantly, on open rocky sites in the ponderosa pine belt. It frequently forms extensive, impenetrable thickets, which explains the name chaparral applied to this species.

The foothill chaparral belt, where wedgeleaf ceanothus is most abundant, lies between the grasslands of the lower foothills and the ponderosa pine stands of the mountains. This chaparral belt has been subjected to frequent fires and consequently is dominated by such plants as manzanitas, oaks, and wedgeleaf ceanothus. Its vigor, aggressiveness, fire- and drought-resistance, and seed habits equip wedgeleaf ceanothus admirably to endure such conditions.

Cattle and horses seldom eat wedgeleaf ceanothus when other forage is available, although they may browse it rather heavily on poor or depleted ranges. The shrub is fairly palatable to sheep when it is well distributed and can be cropped along with other plants, but apparently it is not relished when it forms most of the ground cover. Chapline [1] has listed it among the foremost species of *Ceanothus* as goat browse. Because goats like the small tough foliage of wedgeleaf ceanothus many foothill farmers have successfully replaced woodland chaparral stands with a superior forage cover of annual grasses. This is usually accomplished by first clearing the land of the trees and most of the brush and then grazing with goats to control the root sprouts and uncut brush. This eradication program, however, is usually feasible only on the better soils which will readily support a grass cover when cleared. Wedgeleaf ceanothus provides the bulk of the winter feed for deer on many areas. In fact, it is so widespread where deer winter—this plant is also used somewhat in their summer dietary—that it ranks as one of the outstanding deer plants of California and Oregon. On the whole, this species is low in palatability except for goats and game. Local stockmen in southern Oregon report that if grazed extensively wedgeleaf ceanothus is injurious to the kidneys of the male livestock. Whether there is anything in the chemistry of this plant which may predispose to the formation of renal and urethral calculi or have other irritant effect can be ascertained only by scientific investigation.

This species occasionally grows as high as 14 feet, though often low and sprawling. Its stiff, moderately leafy, and short to medium long twigs grow almost at right angles to the stem and with age have hard, blunt tips. The bark is usually gray on the younger branches and brownish on the older parts. The sweet-scented flowers are usually white, but in the Coast Range are occasionally light blue to lilac, and appear in the early spring. The leaves, inflorescence, fruit, and to some extent the twigs are beset with glands which exude a balsamlike fragrance. Although wedgeleaf ceanothus is a fairly constant species in most of its range, it is somewhat variable on the margins of its distribution, particularly as to habit and the character of leaves and flowers. The leaves on the young crown shoots are regularly and coarsely toothed (dentate) and commonly occur in threes.

Wedgeleaf ceanothus does not sprout from the rootcrown or roots after fires but produces an abundance of long-lived seeds, which seem to germinate best after heating, thus encouraging its establishment on burns. Chesnut [2] mentions the fondness of squirrels for the seeds of this species and states that its rigid, intricate branches are useful for building fishdams.

---

[1] Chapline, W. R. PRODUCTION OF GOATS ON FAR WESTERN RANGES. U. S. Dept. Agr. Bull. 749, 35 pp., illus. 1919.
[2] Chesnut, V. K. PLANTS USED BY THE INDIANS OF MENDOCINO COUNTY, CALIFORNIA. U. S. Dept. Agr., Div. Bot., Contrib. U. S. Natl. Herbarium 7 : 295–422, illus. 1902.

FENDLER CEANOTHUS

Ceano'thus fend'leri

Seed pod (capsule)—⅜ in. wide, flattened, globe-shaped, somewhat 3-lobed on top, 3-celled, each cell bearing one hard nutlet

Petals—5, clawed, hooded, with 5 protruding stamens opposite them

Outer flower parts (sepals)—5, whitish, bent inward so that tips meet, united below to form cuplike disk (calyx disk), which adheres to seed-producing organ (ovary) and to which petals and stamens are attached

Flowers—small, white, numerous, in rather showy clusters at or near ends of twigs

Twigs—at first greenish, later gray, usually white-hairy but sometimes covered with waxy bloom, rigid, often spine-pointed at tips

Leaves—alternate, 3-ribbed, normally small (½ to 1 in. long), on short leaf-stalks, elliptic, rounded or somewhat pointed at both ends, mostly entire but sometimes finely toothed around edges, green and smooth or somewhat silky above, and pale, white-silky-hairy below

Fendler ceanothus, also known as buckbrush, deerbriar, deerbrush, and mountain ceanothus, is a low, loosely branched, usually deciduous shrub, averaging from 1 to 3 feet in height, with grayish, finely hairy, usually sharp-pointed (spinescent) twigs. It is named in honor of its discoverer, August Fendler, who made the first large collection of New Mexican plants (1847). Asa Gray, a preeminent

American botanist, later discussed those plants comprehensively in his well-known book, Plantae Fendlerianae.

Fendler ceanothus occurs in the foothills and mountains from South Dakota and Wyoming to Arizona and western Texas. While it has been collected at elevations ranging from 4,500 to 11,000 feet, and occurs from the juniper-piñon to the spruce zones, it usually becomes abundant only in the ponderosa pine zone, on open, well-drained slopes in combination with such shrubs as manzanita, mountain-mahogany, and oaks. This shrub tends to form patches or small colonies, which, however, never become dense enough to limit its use by livestock or game.

Its wide distribution, local abundance, small but tender leaves, and delicate twigs, even though spine-tipped, combine to make Fendler ceanothus an important browse plant. Its palatability for livestock generally is greatest in the Southwest, particularly in the Coconino and Prescott regions of northern and western central Arizona, and in the Lincoln region of southern New Mexico. In the Southwest its palatability ranges from fair to good for cattle and from fairly good to good for sheep. Horses also browse it frequently. It is probably of highest value for goats, its palatability for such animals ranging from fairly good to good or even very good. Chapline[1] lists it among the outstanding goat browses of the West, being equaled only by the Pacific species, deerbrush (*C. integerrimus*). In the northern part of its range, especially east and north of Utah, where it is relatively scarce, small, and has but sparse leafage, Fendler ceanothus takes inferior rank, being worthless to poor for cattle and poor to fair for sheep. This species is an important deer feed in many places; on the Kaibab Plateau its palatability for mule deer rates fairly good. Because of its rather small and somewhat scattered leaves the volume of foliage produced per plant is less than that of many other browse species. Hence the shrub may easily be injured by close use, despite that its thorny-tipped twigs protect it somewhat, especially from cattle. Too close utilization of this shrub, particularly where it is abundant, indicates improper range management and should be guarded against. The species is a very desirable one and should not be browsed so closely as to cause complete defoliation. Some of the more protected flower clusters should be permitted to go to seed.

The distinctly three-ribbed, rather small, elliptic, and untoothed leaves, which are silky below and smooth or somewhat silky above, aid in the identification of this species. It flowers from May or June to late July and the fruit ripens in August and September.

Martin ceanothus (*C. mar'tini*), sometimes called small chaparral, is restricted to Utah and Nevada but merits mention, as it is not only a frequent associate in Utah of Fendler ceanothus but is sometimes a locally important browse. It is easily distinguished from Fendler ceanothus by its larger, rounder, toothed, and perfectly hairless (glabrous) leaves and by the fact that the branches are unarmed. Its palatability, ranging from fair to good for all classes of livestock, is about the same as that of Fendler ceanothus, but is more quickly overgrazed because there are no protecting spiny tips on its twigs.

----

[1] Chapline, W. R. PRODUCTION OF GOATS ON FAR WESTERN RANGES. U. S. Dept. Agr. Bull. 749, 35 pp., illus. 1919.

DESERT CEANOTHUS

Ceano'thus greg'gii

Flowers—small, white, in clusters in axils of leaves and toward ends of twigs

Petals—5, long-clawed, hooded, with 5 protruding stamens opposite them

Outer flower parts (sepals)—5, somewhat whitish, bent inward to meet at tips, united below to form calyx disk which adheres to capsule and to which petals and stamens are attached

Seed pod (capsule) — slightly oblong-globe-shaped, about ¼ in. across, 3-lobed (lobes with small, sometimes unequal, spreading horns near middle of back) 3-celled, each cell producing one hard "seed" (nutlet), tipped by slender, threadlike, 3-cleft appendage (style)

Twigs—opposite, grayish or later somewhat brownish, stiff, rigid, rather bluntly spine-tipped, densely white-hairy, especially when young

Leaves—evergreen, opposite or sometimes clustered, thick, leathery, small (¼ to ½ in. long), short-stalked, grayish green, elliptic or oval in shape, usually pointed at both ends, usually entire but sometimes finely toothed around edge, hairy on both sides but more densely white-hairy below, midrib prominent and veins more or less parallel

Desert ceanothus, also known as buckbrush and Gregg hornbrush, is a stout, intricately branched, sometimes evergreen shrub, commonly 2 to 5 feet in height. This shrub commemorates its discoverer, Dr. Josiah Gregg (1806–49), a diligent explorer and collector of the botany of the Southwest, and author of a popular book, The Commerce of the Prairies, concerning the early West. Gregg met a tragic fate, dying of starvation in the Trinity River wilderness in northern California. This species named in his honor inhabits deserts and foothills from western Texas to central Nevada and southeastern California and extends practically to the southern border of Mexico. It grows mainly on slopes in dry, clayey, or sandy soils in semidesert areas of the piñon-juniper and creosotebush belts, chiefly at elevations of 3,500 to 7,000 feet. It is frequently associated with manzanita, oak, and mimosa, and is often abundant enough to form dense stands which lend a characteristic aspect to the landscape.

Although inferior in general palatability to some of its congeners, such as deerbrush (*C. integerrimus*) and Fendler ceanothus (*C. fendleri*), desert ceanothus, when abundant, is an important browse species on many areas, especially as emergency feed, or when growing on winter, spring, or heavily used ranges. It is grazed yearlong in southern Arizona and southern New Mexico. Grazing animals generally prefer the more palatable grasses and weeds and tend to crop such plants closely before turning to this species. Desert ceanothus' palatability is regarded as fair or fairly good for cattle, fair for sheep, and good for goats on forest range in New Mexico. On similar range in Arizona it rates as fair to good for cattle, and fairly good to very good for sheep and goats, particularly the latter. On the Kaibab Plateau of northern Arizona it ranks as fairly good deer feed. Because of their smaller mouths and more flexible lips, sheep, goats, and deer can, if necessary, utilize the foliage of this shrub much more closely than can cattle, which find the numerous short rigid twigs a hindrance. Chapline [1] lists the species as one of the outstanding southwestern goat browses. The more or less evergreen character of the foliage is conducive to prolonged utilization, especially in late fall, winter, and early spring. As a general rule, close use of this species, at least on summer cattle and sheep range, indicates overstocking or possible range deterioration.

The short, stout, rigid twigs, pale and finely woolly when young, are grayish to olive green in color when mature and usually have bluntish but spinelike, mostly leafless tips. The white flowers are likely to be present at almost any time during the growing season, since this species, which usually flowers from March to July, depending upon the rains, frequently has another blossoming period extending from August to October. This species strongly resembles wedgeleaf ceanothus (*C. cuneatus*) of California and Oregon, and a familiarity with either species aids in identifying the other.

---

[1] Chapline, W. R. PRODUCTION OF GOATS ON FAR WESTERN RANGES. U. S. Dept. Agr. Bull. 749, 35 pp., illus. 1919.

DEERBRUSH

Ceano'thus integer'rimus, syn. *C. nevaden'sis*

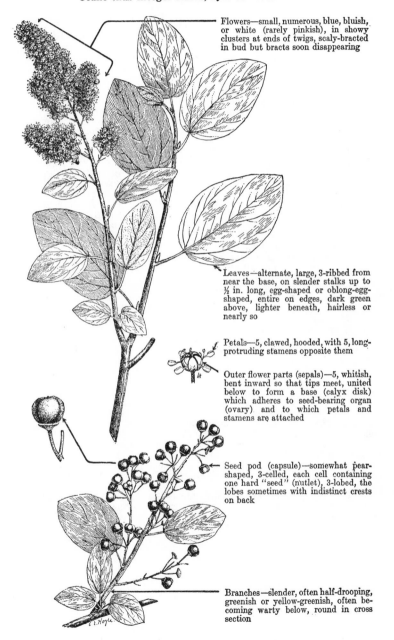

Flowers—small, numerous, blue, bluish, or white (rarely pinkish), in showy clusters at ends of twigs, scaly-bracted in bud but bracts soon disappearing

Leaves—alternate, large, 3-ribbed from near the base, on slender stalks up to ½ in. long, egg-shaped or oblong-egg-shaped, entire on edges, dark green above, lighter beneath, hairless or nearly so

Petals—5, clawed, hooded, with 5, long-protruding stamens opposite them

Outer flower parts (sepals)—5, whitish, bent inward so that tips meet, united below to form a base (calyx disk) which adheres to seed-bearing organ (ovary) and to which petals and stamens are attached

Seed pod (capsule)—somewhat pear-shaped, 3-celled, each cell containing one hard "seed" (nutlet), 3-lobed, the lobes sometimes with indistinct crests on back

Branches—slender, often half-drooping, greenish or yellow-greenish, often becoming warty below, round in cross section

629

Deerbrush, known also as bluebrush, mountain-lilac, and sweetbirch, is a deciduous shrub growing in the mountains from Washington south through California and western Nevada into Arizona. Deerbrush is most commonly found in the ponderosa pine and mixed conifer belts and becomes most abundant on the west slopes of the Cascades of Oregon and of the Sierras in California. It typically grows on well-drained, moderately fertile soils, but is common under many other soil conditions. In fact, there is a great variation between the slow-growing and dwarfed individuals of infertile, shallow soil on exposed sites and the unusually large-leaved and fast-growing individuals in moist, fertile soils. The species grows equally well in the open and half-shade, but quickly dies out under dense shade, as when topped by young conifers.

Reproduction is chiefly by seed, although deerbrush also multiplies by rootstocks after fires or cutting. The seed apparently remains viable for many years, germinating only when favorable conditions develop. Clearing, whether by fire or logging, or both, apparently stimulates germination, as deerbrush often becomes the dominant vegetation following such practices. That is probably why many people believe burning is a logical practice in the management of deerbrush ranges. However, careful study of burns, particularly recurrent burns, has shown that, if forage production benefits, the advantages are only temporary. Burning depreciates forest values, as it destroys timber, watershed protective cover and soil fertility, recreational facilities, and wildlife. Deerbrush may be the dominant browse after a first or second burning, but it rarely survives a third fire. Usually the site deterioration results in the invasion of whitethorn (*Ceanothus cordulatus*) while greenleaf manzanita (*Arctostaphylos patula*) sometimes comes in at its upper range. At the lower growth limits whiteleaf manzanita (*A. viscida*) is a very characteristic associate. Continued burnings almost invariably result in the disappearance of deerbrush and the establishment of dense brush fields of low value.

Deerbrush is one of the most valuable browse plants of the West, and in California it provides more forage than any other browse species. It is considered good to excellent browse for cattle, sheep, goats, and deer, and fair to good for horses. The palatability of leaves and tender young twigs appears to be increased by their wintergreenlike flavor similar to that of true sweet birch (*Betula lenta*). This similarity has led to the frequent use of the common name sweetbirch for deerbrush. Ordinarily cattle use deerbrush ranges more efficiently than sheep, because their greater height enables them to obtain more forage from the older and taller stands.

Deerbrush is so important in the Sierras and southern Cascades that management of many ranges is based on its growth requirements. Deerbrush ranges, for example, are ready for grazing in the spring when the blossoms begin to show. The leaves then are out and the foliage can be partially utilized without apparent injury to the plant. Deerbrush ranges have very high grazing capacities while the plants are young, and produce fat stock. Under average to good growing conditions deerbrush grows rapidly and is often too tall to be browsed when from 6 to 10 years old. Instead of reseeding, a stand of deerbrush becomes dominated by coniferous trees or some other browse species. Under such conditions deerbrush ranges decline rapidly in grazing capacity. Severe grazing to check the most rapidly growing shrubs in order to maintain the deerbrush stand at a satisfactory grazing height is impractical. Under such management the plants become hedgelike and weaken or even die and the forage yield decreases, while timber reproduction, watershed, and other values are impaired.

Research at the University of California (see Forest Worker, vol. 7, no. 6, p. 8, November 1931, and Ecology, vol. 13, no. 4, p. 324, October 1932) has shown that with advancing stages toward seed maturity the relative protein and phosphorus content of bluebrush decline and the percentages of calcium, nitrogen-free extract and fats increase. These chemical changes appear to be closely correlated with the palatability and nutritiousness of deerbrush browse, which tend to decline as the seed matures. August 2–21 was found to be the period on the Tahoe National Forest when cattle tend to leave deerbrush and also when the calcium content of the herbage markedly increased.

Deerbrush is typically a loose and slender branched shrub 4 to 12 feet high. The sweet-scented flowers are borne in showy 2- to 6-inch long terminal clusters from April to July (chiefly May and June).

SQUAWCARPET

Ceano'thus prostra'tus

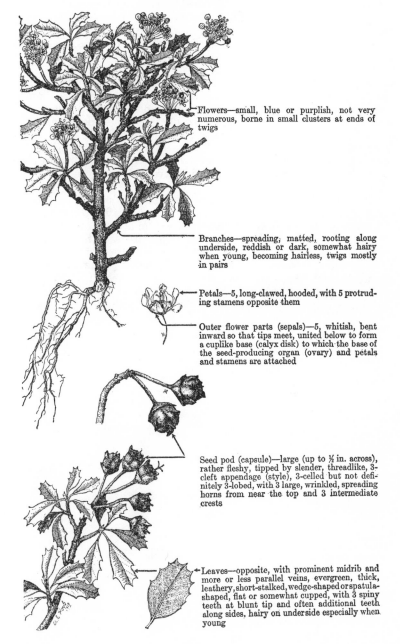

Flowers—small, blue or purplish, not very numerous, borne in small clusters at ends of twigs

Branches—spreading, matted, rooting along underside, reddish or dark, somewhat hairy when young, becoming hairless, twigs mostly in pairs

Petals—5, long-clawed, hooded, with 5 protruding stamens opposite them

Outer flower parts (sepals)—5, whitish, bent inward so that tips meet, united below to form a cuplike base (calyx disk) to which the base of the seed-producing organ (ovary) and petals and stamens are attached

Seed pod (capsule)—large (up to ½ in. across), rather fleshy, tipped by slender, threadlike, 3-cleft appendage (style), 3-celled but not definitely 3-lobed, with 3 large, wrinkled, spreading horns from near the top and 3 intermediate crests

Leaves—opposite, with prominent midrib and more or less parallel veins, evergreen, thick, leathery, short-stalked, wedge-shaped or spatula-shaped, flat or somewhat cupped, with 3 spiny teeth at blunt tip and often additional teeth along sides, hairy on underside especially when young

Squawcarpet, often called mahala-mats, is a prostrate or matlike shrub that ranges from Washington to western Idaho and California. It is probably most abundant in the northern Sierras and southern Cascades. It is limited to ponderosa pine or mixed conifer stands and does best on well-drained soils in partial shade.

Squawcarpet has little, if any, forage value for cattle. Sheep sometimes eat the blossoms, fruit, and new growth, but the volume consumed is too small to warrant consideration of this species in capacity estimates. The buds and the current year's growth have some value as deer feed, especially in winter or early spring when more palatable species are not available. The principal forestry value of squawcarpet rests in its ability to protect the soil against erosion and in its efficiency as a nursecrop for reproduction, a desirable relationship aptly demonstrated by the evident concentration of coniferous reproduction within the colonies of squawcarpet. This aid to forest reproduction is due to a combination of factors, including protection of the seed from rodents and the provision of moisture and light conditions more favorable for germination and growth.

The numerous, leafy, trailing, frequently rooting branches of each squawcarpet plant form a dense mat 2 to 10 feet broad, or in the case of colonies, they intermingle to form a more or less continuous and green ground cover over large areas. The firm, green leaves are from one-half to 1 inch long, 3-toothed at the end, and may be either toothed or smooth on the sides. The rather large, rounded (globose), sometimes sticky capsules are dry and reddish at maturity (summer) and usually by fall have been shed, leaving the empty calyx disk persistent on the stalk (pedicel).

REDSTEM CEANOTHUS

Ceano'thus sangui'neus

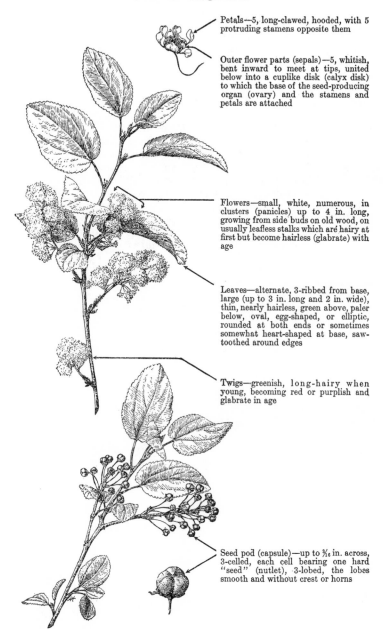

Petals—5, long-clawed, hooded, with 5 protruding stamens opposite them

Outer flower parts (sepals)—5, whitish, bent inward to meet at tips, united below into a cuplike disk (calyx disk) to which the base of the seed-producing organ (ovary) and the stamens and petals are attached

Flowers—small, white, numerous, in clusters (panicles) up to 4 in. long, growing from side buds on old wood, on usually leafless stalks which are hairy at first but become hairless (glabrate) with age

Leaves—alternate, 3-ribbed from base, large (up to 3 in. long and 2 in. wide), thin, nearly hairless, green above, paler below, oval, egg-shaped, or elliptic, rounded at both ends or sometimes somewhat heart-shaped at base, saw-toothed around edges

Twigs—greenish, long-hairy when young, becoming red or purplish and glabrate in age

Seed pod (capsule)—up to ⅝ in. across, 3-celled, each cell bearing one hard "seed" (nutlet), 3-lobed, the lobes smooth and without crest or horns

Redstem ceanothus, also known as red soapbloom and Oregon tree-tea, is usually an erect, open shrub 3 to 10 feet high, which ranges from British Columbia to western Montana and northern California. It is a large-leaved species; the current year's twigs being greenish, but those of the preceding season are commonly reddish, a characteristic which is reflected in most of the common names applied to the species. Redstem ceanothus largely inhabits the ponderosa pine belt, where it grows as scattered shrubs frequently in association with creambush (oceanspray), serviceberry and snowbrush; like those plants it does best on northern and other moist slopes in the open or in partial shade.

The foliage and tender twigs of this shrub are eaten by all classes of livestock, their palatability generally being considered fair to fairly good for cattle and sheep. Palatabilities for this species on some areas are reported as excellent for sheep but this degree of use would probably be reflected in overgrazed conditions. Redstem ceanothus seldom comprises more than a small part of the ground cover. On favorable sites the shrubs tend to be so tall that much of the foliage and edible twigs is out of the reach of livestock. Thus, redstem ceanothus seldom provides a very large amount of forage.

The thin, deciduous leaves of this species are among the largest of the genus. The white flowers are borne in showy clusters, on leafless stalks arising from the sides of the year-old twigs.

SNOWBRUSH

Ceano'thus veluti'nus

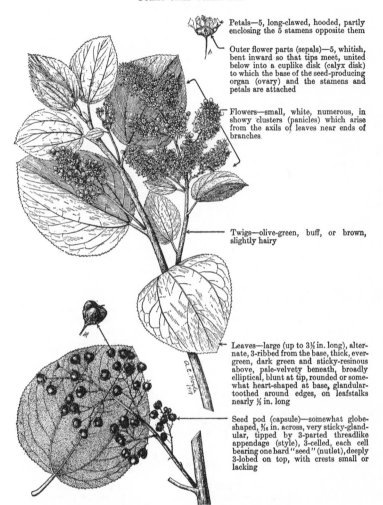

Petals—5, long-clawed, hooded, partly enclosing the 5 stamens opposite them

Outer flower parts (sepals)—5, whitish, bent inward so that tips meet, united below into a cuplike disk (calyx disk) to which the base of the seed-producing organ (ovary) and the stamens and petals are attached

Flowers—small, white, numerous, in showy clusters (panicles) which arise from the axils of leaves near ends of branches.

Twigs—olive-green, buff, or brown, slightly hairy

Leaves—large (up to 3½ in. long), alternate, 3-ribbed from the base, thick, evergreen, dark green and sticky-resinous above, pale-velvety beneath, broadly elliptical, blunt at tip, rounded or somewhat heart-shaped at base, glandular-toothed around edges, on leafstalks nearly ½ in. long

Seed pod (capsule)—somewhat globe-shaped, ⅜₆ in. across, very sticky-glandular, tipped by 3-parted threadlike appendage (style), 3-celled, each cell bearing one hard "seed" (nutlet), deeply 3-lobed on top, with crests small or lacking

Snowbrush is a shiny, smooth, evergreen shrub, commonly diffuse-spreading in habit, with many crooked stems branching from the base. The specific name, *velutinus*, refers to the soft, pale, velvety pubescence on the under surface of the leaves. The common names most frequently applied to this shrub are peculiarly appropriate. Snowbrush refers to the abundant fluffy masses of white flowers; mountain balm to its typically montane habitat and heavy balsamic odor; "sticky laurel" to the sticky and rather glossy character of the upper surface of the leathery leaves; tobacco-brush to the Indians' use of the leaves for tobacco.[1] It is also one of those myriad shrubs called by the unidentifiable name buckbrush.

Snowbrush is one of the most widespread members of the genus, being common in the mountains from British Columbia and Saskatchewan to South Dakota, south into Colorado and California. It is well known in the Rockies, Cascades, and Sierras. Snowbrush has a wide elevational distribution and is found from the piñon-juniper belt up to the aspen type. In Colorado it often occurs at an altitude of 10,000 feet but, according to Professor Jepson,[2] grows up to only 7,000 feet in California. It inhabits a wide variety of sites, and abounds in all exposures and most degrees of sunlight, occurring on practically any soil that is well-drained. It is typically gregarious, commonly growing in small patches or extensive brush fields.

This shrub is well adapted to invade and dominate burns, since the germination of the abundant, long-lived seeds is stimulated by heat and also because numerous sprouts quickly arise from the root crowns of burned individuals. Encouraged by fires, snowbrush has greatly increased its volume, and now sometimes forms dense and inaccessible brush fields especially in California. This rank growth of shrubs, often several thousand acres in size, develops on areas which once supported valuable stands of timber. It provides an excellent soil cover because of its compact growth, and is valuable in the protection of watersheds. Its very density, however, sometimes hinders the reproduction of more valuable timber species, owing to shade and root competition. Natural reproduction and the invasion of timber species is slow. In localities where large dense fields of snowbrush occur, reproduction is often limited to the margins of the stands, where seed trees are present.

The general forage value of snowbrush is very slight, and this plant is worthless for cattle and horses. Goats, sheep, and deer sometimes graze the blossoms slightly as well as the new shoots which spring up after fires, although such utilization is hardly important enough to warrant consideration of this species in range carrying capacity estimates. Ordinarily goats will not browse the species unless they are obliged to do so. Hatton[3] reports that on the Lassen Forest in northeastern California efforts were made to eradicate snowbrush and manzanita from the range by a system of excessive goat grazing, but the results were unsatisfactory, as the goats scarcely browsed snowbrush despite that they were evidently in poorer condition when they came off the range than before. However, L. S. Smith of the United States Forest Service reported in 1931 that for the past 5 years a milk-goat band of about 90 head has been grazed on a brush area near Truckee, Calif., largely under white fir, the dominant local understory species of which type is snowbrush. Smith states that at least 60 percent of the snowbrush "on the slopes for quite a distance each side of their corrals" had been killed by the goats during this period; that the grasses and weeds away from the meadow were trampled but apparently were increasing, that so far no damage to conifer reproduction was noticeable and that the goats were in good condition when removed from the range. Goats sometimes kill shrubs by girdling. Cases are reported where domestic livestock and game animals have browsed snowbrush heavily, but that apparently occurred in winter when a shortage of more palatable feed existed. Elk appear to browse snowbrush only in winter, but deer consume the foliage at any season if better feed is not present. Deer, however, like to bed in snowbrush, which probably accounts for its utlization as browse by those game animals.

Snowbrush averages from 2 to 5 feet in height. On unfavorable sites it may form a lower and more spreading bush, while under favorable conditions it may attain a height of 12 feet in simulation of a small tree. The white, sweet-scented flowers, borne in clusters from 1 to 4 inches long, appear in July and August.

Wahlenberg[4] has called attention to the nitrogen-fixing root-nodules on snowbrush and its value as an aid to ponderosa-pine reproduction.

[1] Schneider, A. PHARMACAL PLANTS AND THEIR CULTURE. Calif. State Bd. Forestry Bull. 2, 175 pp. 1912.
[2] Jepson, W. L. A MANUAL OF THE FLOWERING PLANTS OF CALIFORNIA. 1,238 pp., illus. Berkeley, Calif. [1925.]
[3] Hatton, J. H. ERADICATION OF CHAPARRAL BY GOAT GRAZING. LASSEN NATIONAL FOREST. U. S. Dept. Agr., Rev. Forest Serv. Invest. 2 : 25–28, illus. 1913.
[4] Wahlenberg, W. G. EFFECT OF CEANOTHUS BRUSH ON WESTERN YELLOW PINE PLANTATIONS IN THE NORTHERN ROCKY MOUNTAINS. Jour. Agr. Research [U. S.] 41 : 601–612, illus. 1930.

MOUNTAIN-MAHOGANIES

Cercocar′pus spp.

The genus *Cercocarpus*, which belongs to the rose family (Rosaceae), consists of about 19 species, of which 5 are wholly confined to Mexico, the remaining 14 occurring in the Western States, mainly in the Southwest, the Great Basin, and California. The members of this genus inhabit dry, interior, and mountainous regions. The generic name comes from the Greek *kerkos* (a tail) and *karpos* (a fruit), referring to the peculiar, long-tailed "seeds", which are, perhaps, the most characteristic feature of the genus. The common name, mountain-mahogany, refers to the mountainous habitat characteristic of the genus and to the fact that the wood is very hard and heavy, and often reddish brown in color, suggesting that of true mahogany, a well-known tropical American tree (*Swietenia mahagoni*). Many other names, such as birchleaf mahogany, blackbrush, buckbrush, deerbrush, hardtack, sweetbrush, and tallowbush, are applied to these shrubs in various localities, but most of these names are not particularly distinctive, and some are misleading.

The genus, as a whole, is of considerable importance in the West because it furnishes palatable and, in some cases, yearlong browse for cattle, sheep, and goats. The species with broad leaves are distinctly more palatable, and hence more valuable than are those with narrow, leathery leaves.

Several mountain-mahogany species, which have as yet no well accepted specific English names, in particular *C. breviflorus* and *C. eximius*, possessing rather small, thickish but not leathery leaves, are intermediate in forage value between the *montanus* and *ledifolius* groups. *C. breviflorus* is considered one of the best browse species for all classes of livestock, especially sheep and goats, in southern New Mexico. *C. eximius* is grazed by all classes of livestock and is rated as first-class goat browse in the New Mexico mountains.[1]

The seasoned wood is very hard and, at the same time, brittle. Most of the species are valued for firewood.

The species of mountain-mahogany are half evergreen or evergreen, rather widely branched shrubs or small trees, with furrowed or scaly bark and simple, alternate, or mostly clustered, short-stalked, straight-veined leaves, which are toothed (dentate) or untoothed (entire) on the margin. The short, lateral, spurlike, often spinelike, branchlets are conspicuously roughened for many years by the crowded, narrow, horizontal scars of the fallen leaves. The inconspicuous, greenish-white or reddish flowers occur in groups or are solitary in the axils of the leaves. There are no petals. The elongated, cylindric calyx tube expands abruptly into a five-lobed, petallike portion which falls off (deciduous), and bears the many stamens inserted in two or three rows on its inner rim. This tube surrounds the one-celled ovary, persists in fruit and envelops more

[1] Dayton, W. A. IMPORTANT WESTERN BROWSE PLANTS. U. S. Dept. Agr. Misc. Pub. 101, 214 pp., illus. 1931.

or less closely the single, densely hairy or smoothish, linear-oblong "seed" (achene), which terminates in a long (up to several inches), feathery, variously curved or twisted tail (style).

CURLLEAF MOUNTAIN-MAHOGANY

Cercocar'pus ledifo'lius

Flowers—without petals, solitary or in 2's or 3's, stalkless, borne in the axils of the leaves

Stamens—numerous, in 2 or 3 rows on inside of outer united flower parts (calyx)

Calyx—densely soft-hairy, abruptly flaring above into a soon-falling, somewhat bell- or top-shaped, 5-lobed "limb"; the narrow, cylindric-tubular lower portion usually about ¼ in. long, longer in fruit, persistent

Leaves—alternate or clustered, evergreen, leathery in texture, short-stalked, with rolled-under edges, elliptic to lance-shaped, abruptly sharp-pointed at tip, usually about 1 in. long and less than ½ in. wide, somewhat resinous and hairy (becoming hairless in age) above, pale or rusty-hairy beneath, with prominent midrib

"Seeds" (achenes)—cylindric to spindle-shaped, densely soft-hairy, tipped by a feathery tail 2 to 3 in. long, solitary, enclosed in calyx tube (hypanthium)

E.L.K.

639

Curlleaf mountain-mahogany, also known as curlleaf and desert mahogany, is usually a shrub from 3 to 15 feet high, but it may become a small tree, occasionally becoming 40 feet in height. The specific name *ledifolius* refers to the resemblance of the leaf to that of Labrador-tea (*Ledum*), a genus of the heath family (Ericaceae). The leaves are rolled under (revolute) at the margins which accounts for the common name, curlleaf. Curlleaf mountain-mahogany is by far the commonest, most widely distributed, and best known of the species of *Cercocarpus* which have narrow, leathery leaves, and is the only species of the genus that extends as far north and west as Washington. It ranges geographically from eastern Washington to California, Arizona (north of the Grand Canyon), Colorado, and Montana. Its altitudinal distribution is from the bunchgrass prairie through the piñon and woodland, ponderosa pine, aspen, lodgepole pine, and spruce-fir belts, at elevations of between about 2,000 and 4,500 feet in the northern and northwestern part of its range, where it is often confined to river breaks and the like, and up to 9,000 feet, or perhaps even higher, in the southern part of its range. Tidestrom[1] points out that, in central Nevada, this small tree often takes the place of ponderosa pine and aspen at medium elevations in the mountains, sometimes forming a conspicuous transition type between piñon and white pine.

In the main, curlleaf mountain-mahogany is found on warm, dry, rocky ridges, and chiefly on southern or fairly dry western slopes, or, in the Pacific States, on eastern slopes.[2] However, at lower elevations in the Great Basin at least, it often grows in coarse soils on steep north slopes or among cliffs and ledges. It sometimes occurs on clayey or loamy soils. It characteristically grows in isolated patches of more or less frequent occurrence and is seldom found singly or in continuous, extensive stands. These patches vary from open to rather dense stands, in which curlleaf mountain-mahogany may be practically the only species, or it may occur in association with such low tree or shrubby species as juniper, piñon, oak, serviceberry, bitterbrush, and gooseberry.

As a rule, curlleaf mountain-mahogany has little or no palatability for domestic livestock in the summer but is browsed to some extent by goats, sheep, and cattle in the late fall, winter, and early spring. However, it usually grows at elevations above that of most winter livestock ranges. The leaves are not shed until the end of the second summer, so both leaves and twigs are available throughout the year. It is a good winter game browse, ranking as an outstanding winter forage for deer in northeastern California and for deer and elk in localized areas elsewhere. Ordinarily it is grazed moderately by deer and elk from late fall to early spring. In fact, these animals like to yard up in protected patches of curlleaf mountain-mahogany, and such patches are likely places to jump a buck deer in the hunting season.

Curlleaf mountain-mahogany is perhaps the largest as well as the most typically treelike member of the genus. It is an aromatic, somewhat resinous species of stout, spreading habit with a short trunk and somewhat contorted branches, which form a rather compact, rounded crown. In the larger specimens the lower branches have few twigs or leaves. The trunk measures several inches in diameter in the shrubby forms but may become as much as 2 feet or so in individual specimens of maximum tree size.

Despite the hardness of the wood, the branches are brittle and snap off when submitted to strain. Dead, hanging branches that have been broken because of the snow or other agencies are frequently seen. The red-brown branchlets are covered at first with pale, fine hairs but soon become hairless and frequently have a smooth bloom (glaucous). In their second year, they become silver gray or dark brown and are marked by the conspicuous, elevated leaf scars for many years. The reddish or grayish brown bark is divided by deep broad furrows and broken on the surface into thin, persistent, platelike scales, which are an inch in width on old trunks. The wood of this species is a clear red or rich dark brown color, and strongly suggests the reddish-brown wood of true mahogany. Curlleaf mountain-mahogany wood is dry and extremely hard; it burns for a long time and produces a hot fire, thus making it, when available,

---

[1] Tidestrom, I. FLORA OF UTAH AND NEVADA. U. S. Natl. Mus., Contrib. U. S. Natl. Herbarium 25, 665 pp., illus. 1925.
[2] Dayton, W. A. IMPORTANT WESTERN BROWSE PLANTS. U. S. Dept. Agr. Misc. Pub. 101, 214 pp., illus. 1931.

a favorite fuel of local residents. Standley[3] states that the Gosiute Indians, of Utah, employed the wood of this plant in making their bows. The mature leaves of curlleaf mountain-mahogany are hairless and shiny on the upper surface and are covered with a dense felt of hairs on the lower surface. They vary in length from about one-half to 1¼ inches, and in width from three-sixteenths to seven-sixteenths of an inch, but are usually small (one-sixteenth of an inch wide and one-half of an inch long) in scrub specimens. The upper surface appears to be grooved along the middle because of the thick midrib, which stands out prominently on the lower surface. The nearly triangular bracts (stipules) at the base of the leafstalks are very small and soon fall off (deciduous). The flowering period is from May to July.

Arizona mountain-mahogany (*C. arizo'nicus*), a spiny-twigged shrub which occurs in canyons and on mountain sides of the sagebrush and piñon belts from central Utah and Nevada to Arizona, is closely related to curlleaf mountain-mahogany. It does not attain tree size, has ashy-colored bark, and the leaves, which are about half as long as those of *C. ledifolius*, are so strongly rolled under at the margins as to appear narrowly linear. Although this species is, on the whole, considered inferior from the forage standpoint, it ranks relatively high in some localities as winter feed for game. Littleleaf mountain-mahogany (*C. intrica'tus*), a similar species, extends into southern California but otherwise has a like range and economic status.

---

[3] Standley, P. C. TREES AND SHRUBS OF MEXICO (FAGACEAE-FABACEAE). U. S. Natl. Mus., Contrib. U. S. Natl. Herbarium 23 : 171–515. 1922.

TRUE MOUNTAIN-MAHOGANY

Cercocar'pus monta'nus, syn. *C. parvifo'lius*

Flowers—without petals, solitary or in 2's or 3's, short- and slender-stalked, borne in the axils of the leaves

Outer united flower parts (calyx)—densely soft-hairy, abruptly flaring above into a soon-falling, somewhat bell-shaped or top-shaped, 5-lobed "limb", the narrow, cylindric-tubular portion ("hypanthium" of some authors) about ½ in. long, persistent

Stamens—numerous, in 2 or 3 rows on the flaring part of calyx

Leaves—alternate or somewhat clustered, half evergreen, short-stalked, up to 2 in. long and 1 in. wide, broadly egg-shaped to reverse-egg-shaped, often wedge-shaped at base, triangularly toothed, green and sparingly silky above, pale and densely hairy beneath

"Seed" (achene)—cylindric, soft-hairy, tipped with a feathery tail (style) up to 4 in. long, solitary, enclosed for a time by the persistent calyx tube

True mountain-mahogany is ordinarily a bushy shrub 2 to 10 feet high, rarely becoming a small tree, up to 20 feet tall, with birchlike, thickish, more or less persistent leaves. It bears a number of local names, most of which are indefinite or inaccurate, including alder, blackbrush, deerbrush, sweetbrier, and tallow-brush. The almost universal name for the species in Utah is birchleaf (mountain-) mahogany, which is, however, more fittingly applied to *C. betuloides* (syn. *C. betulaefolius*), a similar species with birchlike leaves.

None of the other species of *Cercocarpus* has a wider distribution than does *C. montanus.* Its range extends from South Dakota and Montana to New Mexico, northeastern California, and Oregon. It ordinarily occurs at elevations between 4,000 and 10,000 feet, either in coarse, sometimes poor, shallow soil on dry slopes and ridges or in the slightly moister, deeper soils of depressions and canyon bottoms. It may also be found on northern slopes at lower elevations. It is frequently associated with Gambel oak, juniper, piñon, ponderosa pine, service-berry, bitterbrush, manzanita, and various species of ceanothus, rabbitbrush, and sagebrush, growing for the most part in distinctly browse types.[1] True mountain-mahogany is sparsely distributed over much of its range but, especially in central and southern Utah and in portions of Colorado and the Southwest, it is often the dominant species of the association and, in localized areas elsewhere, it is common enough to be an important constituent of the forage supply.

Ordinarily this shrub ranks as good, very good, or sometimes even excellent browse for all classes of livestock, being held in higher esteem, on the whole, in Utah and the Southwest than in other parts of its range. It is also one of the most valuable winter feeds for deer.

The leaves of this bush attain full size and the plant is suitable for grazing early in the season but, like those of many other shrubs, they are utilized mostly after midsummer. The leaves normally remain on the plant and are palatable until late fall. In Utah, true mountain-mahogany is practically defoliated by the middle of October. Of course, if an unusual drought occurs or the plants are diseased the leaves dry up early and lose much of their palatability or else drop entirely and prematurely from the bushes. The twigs are palatable yearlong and, wherever available, are grazed with relish. Frequently true mountain-mahogany grows at elevations above the winter range of domestic livestock, which limits its use to some extent. Sheep usually eat all the leaves and only part of the twigs within reach; goats devour both leaves and twigs, while cattle graze the shrub more moderately. Deer and elk eat the leaves and twigs in summer and the twigs in winter.

This species withstands close grazing very well; in fact, the desirability has been suggested of permitting sufficiently close grazing to make the plants bushy and spreading, thus preventing the development of the arborescent habit which would normally occur under the best growth conditions. However, such grazing by any class of livestock, except goats, would result in overgrazing of the herbaceous vegetation and subsequent erosion. Continued overgrazing of true mountain-mahogany seriously affects forage production and may even kill the plants.

The branchlets are sparingly soft-hairy when young and inclined to be reddish in color. The slender, rigid, upright branches and twigs are gray or brownish and become marked with conspicuous ringlike leaf scars. The thickish, conspicuously veined leaves, broadest at the middle and toothed on the margins, are dark green with a tinge of yellow, and somewhat closely resemble those of some birch species. They vary in size in different plants and, to some extent, on the same plant. Lance-shaped, sharp-pointed bracts (stipules) at the base of the leafstalks, from about one-eighth to one-fourth of an inch long, are present for a short time after the appearance of the leaf, but soon drop off. By the time the seed is mature, the calyx tube which partially encloses it has become thin, chestnut-brown, spindle-shaped, only slightly hairy, and deeply cleft from the top down one side. The "seed" is somewhat leathery, grooved on the back, covered with long white hairs, and tipped by a long feathery tail. True mountain-mahogany flowers practically throughout June and most of the seeds mature by mid-August. The seed habits are generally strong.

---

[1] Dayton, W. A. IMPORTANT WESTERN BROWSE PLANTS. U. S. Dept. Agr. Misc. Pub. 101, 214 pp., illus. 1931.

BEARMAT

Chamaeba′tia foliolo′sa

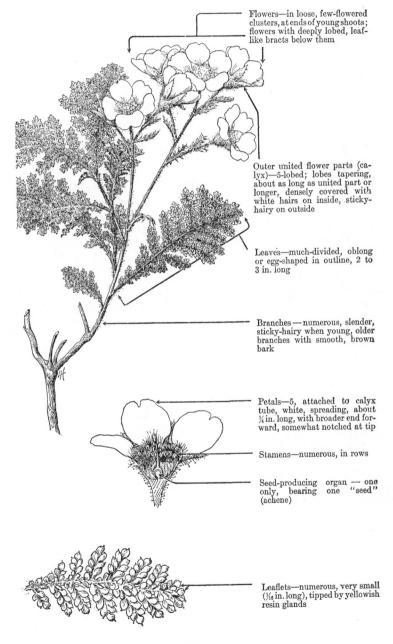

Flowers—in loose, few-flowered clusters, at ends of young shoots; flowers with deeply lobed, leaf-like bracts below them

Outer united flower parts (calyx)—5-lobed; lobes tapering, about as long as united part or longer, densely covered with white hairs on inside, sticky-hairy on outside

Leaves—much-divided, oblong or egg-shaped in outline, 2 to 3 in. long

Branches—numerous, slender, sticky-hairy when young, older branches with smooth, brown bark

Petals—5, attached to calyx tube, white, spreading, about ¼ in. long, with broader end forward, somewhat notched at tip

Stamens—numerous, in rows

Seed-producing organ — one only, bearing one "seed" (achene)

Leaflets—numerous, very small (⅟₁₆ in. long), tipped by yellowish resin glands

645

Bearmat, also known as bear-clover, fernbush, mountain misery, and tarweed, is a low, resinous, heavy-scented, evergreen shrub occurring in the ponderosa pine and mixed conifer types on the west slope of the Sierra Nevadas in California. It most commonly grows in patches or extensive tracts on the dry flats and slopes in the partial shade of coniferous timber species, and often it is the only undergrowth, producing an attractive, parklike effect. Pedestrians are handicapped by the numerous stems of bearmat, while the strong-scented, sticky resin of the leaves damages their clothing, which accounts for the name mountain misery applied to this plant.

The flowers and fruit of bearmat are sometimes eaten by domestic livestock and deer but the quantity consumed is too small to make this species valuable as a forage plant. Generally, areas dominated by bearmat are waste range, but sometimes enough weeds, browse or other palatable plants grow with it to provide fair feed. Bearmat does not seriously obstruct the passage of livestock nor measurably prevent associated palatable plants from being eaten by grazing animals.

Bearmat affects forest relationships either beneficially or harmfully, dependent on the factors under consideration. It has a high value in watershed protection, as it checks run-off, prevents erosion, and maintains the soil in satisfactory condition for moisture absorption. It hinders reproduction of coniferous species, apparently because seed is not properly planted naturally, and such seedlings as do sprout are unable to compete successfully for food and moisture with bearmat's numerous, well-established roots.

Fire fighters probably more than any other group dislike bearmat because its resinous leaves, along with the duff and collection of needles and twigs from the conifers, provide a concentrated fuel that develops a hot, rapid-advancing fire on windy days of low humidity. The presence of this shrub in quantity makes it difficult to construct fire trails, because the numerous, tangled, tough, woody stems and shallow roots must be removed in order to penetrate through the duff to mineral soil.

Bearmat has branched stems, 1 to 2 feet in height, arising at intervals of a few inches from a complicated and sometimes matlike system of roots and underground stems. The strong-scented, resinous leaves, which appear soft and fernlike or tansylike, are divided into very small leaflets, and are borne along the uppermost part of the branches. The white flowers are produced in small, terminal clusters; the petals are soon lost but the five bractlike parts (sepals) immediately beneath them remain and somewhat enclose the one-seeded fruit until fall.

RABBITBRUSHES

Chrysotham'nus spp.

Rabbitbrush is the name most commonly applied to this genus of shrubby plants, including approximately 70 species and about a dozen subspecies, all of which are distinctly confined to western North America. These plants belong to the aster, or composite family (Asteraceae, or Compositae) and are frequently called rabbitsage, rayless-goldenrod, and yellowbrush.

The northern limit of this genus is in British Columbia, Alberta, and Saskatchewan; it extends to South Dakota and western Nebraska on the east; and southward to Texas, southern New Mexico, and southern Arizona, with extensions of a few species into Mexico and Lower California. A few species have been found as far west as the Coast Range Mountains in California. These shrubs are most abundant within the Great Basin, and here they often dominate large tracts. The rabbitbrushes are characteristic shrubs or undershrubs of the open plains and foothills from sea level to 10,000 feet in elevation. They are frequently a conspicuous component of the vegetation on alkaline plains and stream banks throughout the semiarid regions of the West. Most of the species grow at comparatively low altitudes on fairly deep, heavy soils. On moderately alkaline flats, *C. graveolens*, *C. nauseosus* and *C. pinifolius* appear in dense, extensive stands and are often the dominant plants on many areas, associated with saltgrass (*Distichlis spicata*), greasewood (*Sarcobatus vermiculatus*), and povertyweed (*Iva axillaris*). A few members, including *C. lanceolatus*, *C. parryi*, and *C. viscidiflorus serrulatus*, occur in mixed types of the foothills and mountains.

Most species of *Chrysothamnus* have little or no forage value, but a few, such a lanceleaf yellowbrush (*C. lanceolatus*) and twistleaf rabbitbrush (*C. viscidiflorus tortifolius*), rank as fair to good forage for sheep and cattle (see B55). Small rabbitbrush (*C. stenophyllus*) often grows abundantly in desert areas and furnishes considerable forage for sheep during the winter.

Under certain circumstances several of the species are useful indicators of range deterioration. Rubber rabbitbrush (*C. nauseosus*), for example, now grows abundantly on depleted areas that formerly supported a good stand of giant wild-rye (*Elymus condensatus*). Small rabbitbrush has become the dominant plant on many depleted winterfat (*Eurotia lanata*) ranges in western Utah and central Nevada. Sampson[2] states that, in the Wasatch Mountains of Utah, lanceleaf yellowbrush "is the most characteristic forerunner of other aggressive perennial plants which gain a foothold as the wheatgrasses are killed out by overgrazing or other adverse factors." Rabbitbrushes grow profusely over many of the arid lands and stream channels of the West, and by virtue of their deep and extensive root systems serve as impediments to wind and water erosion.

The possibility of utilizing certain species of rabbitbrushes as sources of raw rubber has been investigated by Hall and Goodspeed[3]

---

[2] Sampson, A. W. PLANT SUCCESSION IN RELATION TO RANGE MANAGEMENT. U. S. Dept. Agr. Bull. 791, 76 pp., illus. 1919.
[3] Hall, H. M., and Goodspeed, T. H. A RUBBER PLANT SURVEY OF WESTERN NORTH AMERICA. Calif. Univ. Pubs., Bot. 7: [159]–278, illus. 1919.

who found rubber in *C. nauseosus, turbinatus, teretifolius, paniculatus, linifolius*, with rubber rabbitbrush and its varieties the only feasible source of commercial supply. Not even traces of rubber were found in *C. greenei, howardi, nevadensis, parryi, puberulus*, and *humilis, C. viscidiflorus tortifolius*.

The occurrence of rubber in some rabbitbrushes has long been known to the Indians, who masticated the wood and bark into a crude chewing gum containing rubber. According to Professors Hall and Goodspeed (*op. cit.*), Indians located near St. George, Utah, as early as 1878, showed some Mormon boys how to make the gum. The first samples of rabbitbrush rubber (called chrysil) for scientific work were prepared by Piute Indians at Benton, Calif. Although chrysil vulcanizes readily and yields a product superior to most African or low-grade rubbers, it is inferior to the best grade of Para rubber. The Navaho Indians used a decoction of the flowers of various species of rabbitbrush for dyeing wool yellow [4] and Dr. David P. Barrows reports that the Coahuilla Indians of southern California used a tea made from *C. graveolens* (syn. *C. nauseosus graveolens*) for coughs and pains in the chest.[3]

Most rabbitbrushes have narrow leaves and produce an abundance of showy yellow flower clusters which often literally cover the bushes during the autumn months. Because of these large masses of yellow flowers a number of the species have been used locally for ornamental purposes and offer possibilities for wider cultivation. Tall rabbitbrush (*C. speciosus*, syn. *C. pulcherrimus*) is especially handsome since it produces a greater abundance of golden yellow flowers than any other native shrub within its range.

As a rule, the flower heads are borne in clusters at the ends of the stems, and each head contains from 5 to 30 perfect seed-producing flowers surrounded by several rows of dry, papery or leathery overlapping bracts (involucre) whose tips are often herbaceous. The branches of the seed-producing organ are appendaged and the ripened "seed" (achene) is hairy or smooth, narrow, round or angular, with a crown of soft, white hairs 0.1 to 0.3 inch long.

Many species of the western North American shrubby genus *Chrysothamnus* were originally classified with the Old World cultivated goldilocks (*Linosyris* spp.) or with the South African genus *Chrysocoma*. In 1840 the eminent naturalist, Thomas Nuttall, observed that the shrubs from the West were distinct in aspect and characters from either of the two Old World genera mentioned. This led him to establish his appropriately named genus *Chrysothamnus*. The late Dr. Greene, a distinguished American taxonomist, who for the last 17 years of his life was consulting plant identification expert for the United States Forest Service, apparently was the first American botanist to recognize and use Nuttall's name *Chrysothamnus*. The suppression of this name for 60 years seems to have been due to the enormous prestige and influence of Dr. Asa Gray, who preferred to place the *Chrysothamni* in the genus *Bigelovia* which was established by the Swiss botanist DeCandolle. An examination of De Candolle's original description of *Bigelovia* reveals that it was based on eastern herbs, and that the name *Bigelovia* previously had been used for other genera and accordingly is not tenable for this group. The use of *Chrysothamnus* as a valid genus is now practically universal among botanists.

---

[3] See footnote on preceding page.
[4] Wooton, E. O., and Standley, P. C. FLORA OF NEW MEXICO. U. S. Natl. Mus., Contrib. U. S. Natl. Herbarium 19, 794 pp. 1915.

LANCELEAF YELLOWBRUSH

Chrysotham'nus lanceola'tus

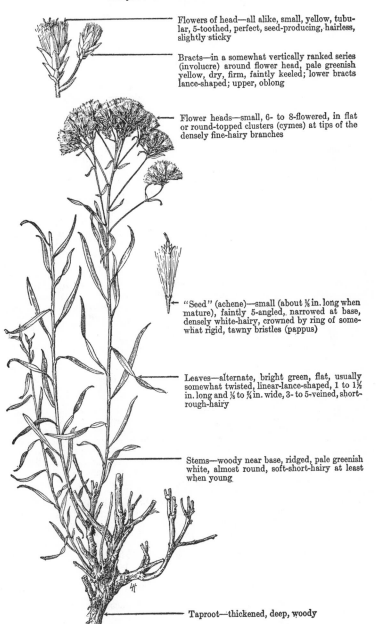

Flowers of head—all alike, small, yellow, tubular, 5-toothed, perfect, seed-producing, hairless, slightly sticky

Bracts—in a somewhat vertically ranked series (involucre) around flower head, pale greenish yellow, dry, firm, faintly keeled; lower bracts lance-shaped; upper, oblong

Flower heads—small, 6- to 8-flowered, in flat or round-topped clusters (cymes) at tips of the densely fine-hairy branches

"Seed" (achene)—small (about ⅛ in. long when mature), faintly 5-angled, narrowed at base, densely white-hairy, crowned by ring of somewhat rigid, tawny bristles (pappus)

Leaves—alternate, bright green, flat, usually somewhat twisted, linear-lance-shaped, 1 to 1½ in. long and ⅛ to ¼ in. wide, 3- to 5-veined, short-rough-hairy

Stems—woody near base, ridged, pale greenish white, almost round, soft-short-hairy at least when young.

Taproot—thickened, deep, woody

Lanceleaf yellowbrush, sometimes called dwarf yellowbrush, is a low woody-based perennial belonging to the rabbitbrush (*Chrysothamnus*) genus of the aster family (Compositae). Although most species of this group are called rabbitbrush, the name "lanceleaf yellowbrush" is so commonly applied to *C. lanceolatus*, because of its lance-shaped leaves, profuse yellow flowers, and yellowish-green herbage, that it is deemed best to adopt it here. The species ranges from Washington to Nevada, Colorado, and Montana at elevations from 5,000 to 10,000 feet in the sagebrush, ponderosa-pine, lodgepole-pine, and aspen belts. It is fairly abundant in southern Idaho, northern Nevada, western Wyoming, Utah, and portions of Colorado. Elsewhere in its range it is scattered over dry plains and foothills, slopes, ridges, valleys, and canyon bottoms. It is frequently one of the dominant species, in the mixed types from the open aspen and ponderosa pine stands down to the upper reaches of the shadscale association, and is often intermixed with wheatgrasses, needlegrasses, serviceberry, snowberry, and lupine. This plant usually occurs, at least sparsely, in most open types of the drier sites within its range, but it is rarely found in pure stands.

Lanceleaf yellowbrush, although not highly palatable, ranks as an important western forage species because of its abundance. It is by far the most important forage species of this genus whose members, in the main, possess little or no value for domestic livestock. Although cattle and sheep graze it lightly early in the spring, it is really little used until the middle of August. During the late fall, this shrub is browsed moderately by cattle and sheep and to a less extent by horses. It occurs on some winter ranges where it is moderately palatable to domestic livestock. Deer browse it lightly both summer and winter, and elk eat it in winter. Its forage value for goats is unknown. The leafage and tender part of the stems together with the flower stalks are utilized by sheep, but the flower heads are discarded and often accumulate around the base of the shrubs.[1]

Lanceleaf yellowbrush increases in abundance as more palatable and less resistant species are depleted by overgrazing and, though it withstands heavy grazing very well, it, in turn, eventually succumbs to continued abuse. Sampson[2] reports that, in the Wasatch Mountains of Utah, this shrub "is the most characteristic forerunner of other aggressive perennial plants which gain a foothold as the wheatgrasses are killed out by overgrazing or other adverse factors." Furthermore, this author states that lanceleaf yellowbrush and needlegrass (*Stipa columbiana*, syn. *S. minor*) are the two primary species of a mixed grass-weed consociation which includes a number of palatable species and usually has as high a carrying capacity as the wheatgrass type, or even higher, at least on sheep or common use ranges.

Lanceleaf yellowbrush, a shrub usually about a foot high (sometimes a little taller), has a stout taproot 4 feet or more in length, from which numerous lateral, secondary roots extend. Usually several woody stalks, which branch into numerous slender, leafy stems, ascend from the base. These leafy stems are densely covered with very fine short hairs. The basal portions of the stalks are grayish brown; the branches are greenish white and somewhat shiny, while the twigs of the current year are pale grayish green. The flat, linear-lance-shaped leaves are from 1 to 1½ inches long and about one-eighth to one-fourth of an inch wide, are usually slightly twisted, rough along the edges, covered with very short hairs, and with three (sometimes five) veins. The flowers are borne in small heads grouped in numerous flat or round-topped clusters at the ends of the stems. The absence of petallike ray flowers in lanceleaf yellowbrush (as in all the species of *Chrysothamnus*) and the straight vertical rows of involucre bracts (phyllaries) at once distinguish these plants from the somewhat similar snakeweeds (*Gutierrezia* spp.) with which they are sometimes confused. Each flower head consists of six to eight small, yellow flowers attached to a common base and surrounded by 3 or 4 rows of loosely overlapping, greenish yellow bracts. The fruits or "seeds" are covered with fine, appressed rigid hairs and are encircled at the top by a row of dense hairs (pappus) about one-eighth of an inch long.

[1] Dayton, W. A. IMPORTANT WESTERN BROWSE PLANTS. U. S. Dept. Agr. Misc. Pub. 101, 214 pp., illus. 1931.
[2] Sampson, A. W. PLANT SUCCESSION IN RELATION TO RANGE MANAGEMENT. U. S. Dept. Agr. Bull. 791, 76 pp., illus. 1919.

RUBBER RABBITBRUSH

Chrysotham'nus nauseo'sus

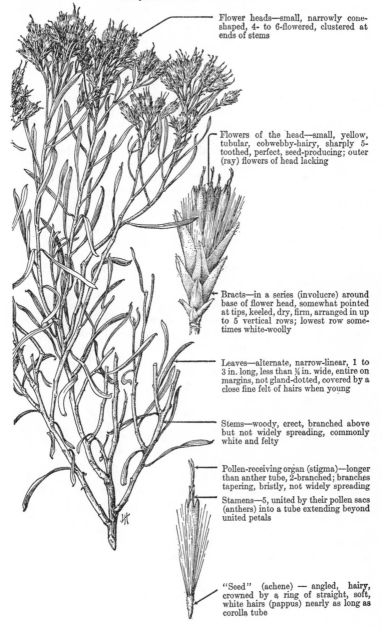

Flower heads—small, narrowly cone-shaped, 4- to 6-flowered, clustered at ends of stems

Flowers of the head—small, yellow, tubular, cobwebby-hairy, sharply 5-toothed, perfect, seed-producing; outer (ray) flowers of head lacking

Bracts—in a series (involucre) around base of flower head, somewhat pointed at tips, keeled, dry, firm, arranged in up to 5 vertical rows; lowest row sometimes white-woolly

Leaves—alternate, narrow-linear, 1 to 3 in. long, less than ⅛ in. wide, entire on margins, not gland-dotted, covered by a close fine felt of hairs when young

Stems—woody, erect, branched above but not widely spreading, commonly white and felty

Pollen-receiving organ (stigma)—longer than anther tube, 2-branched; branches tapering, bristly, not widely spreading

Stamens—5, united by their pollen sacs (anthers) into a tube extending beyond united petals

"Seed" (achene) — angled, hairy, crowned by a ring of straight, soft, white hairs (pappus) nearly as long as corolla tube

Rubber rabbitbrush, a deep-rooted, perennial shrub growing 20 to 40 inches high, is a member of the aster family (Compositae) and is commonly known simply as rabbitbrush. However, the addition of the word rubber to the name is appropriate as this species contains a high grade rubber called chrysil, which vulcanizes readily.[1] *Chrysothamnus* is from the Greek *chrysos* (gold) and *thamnos* (a shrub), referring to shrubby plants with golden-yellow flowers. The specific name *nauseosus* refers to the disagreeable flavor of the herbage. The range of rubber rabbitbrush extends from British Columbia and Alberta south to Wyoming, Utah, Nevada, and eastern California.

Rubber rabbitbrush is very common, and in some localities is one of the most characteristic plants in the plains, foothills, and inter-mountain valleys. It grows on the open sites of the sagebrush, juniper-piñon and ponderosa-pine zones and inhabits dry, sandy, gravelly, or heavy clayey and alkali soils. Rubber rabbitbrush is commonly associated with sagebrush, saltbushes, and various grasses but most frequently grows in dense stands varying in size from a few acres to several square miles. It is often found along roads, fences, and in waste places adjoining farms in arid regions as well as near dry washes and on foothills surrounding semidesert valleys. In the dry bottomlands of many shallow, narrow valleys in parts of the West, rubber rabbitbrush now grows in dense stands where giant wild-rye once grew abundantly but has now been killed out by long-continued overgrazing. Probably rubber rabbitbrush has similarly replaced other forage species that have been unable to withstand disturbing factors to which they were exposed.

Ordinarily under normal conditions the forage value of rubber rabbitbrush is either nil or very low. From September to November all classes of domestic livestock lightly graze the flowertops and occasionally eat meager quantities of the herbage and more tender stems. This shrub is sometimes lightly browsed on the winter range and a few reports indicate localized, moderate to heavy utilization, but this probably represents an overstocked condition.

Rubber rabbitbrush has a very stout woody base from which arise numerous flexible branches. A multitude of slender, erect, semi-herbaceous stems are produced annually. The shreddy-barked basal stalks are hairless, but the branches, and ordinarily the young stems and the leaves, are coated with a more or less dense, matted, woolly covering of fine, short white hairs which give a characteristic whitish color to the bushes. These are often infiltrated with a resinous gum, making the plant sticky and giving a characteristic odor. On some plants the younger stems and the leaves are less densely hairy while occasional older branches lose their hair and become pale or grayish green. The hairy "seeds" (achenes) are slender, angled, and encir-cled at the top by a brushlike row of numerous white, slender bristles which serve to buoy the "seed" as it is disseminated by the wind.

---

[1] Hall, H. M., and Goodspeed, T. H. A RUBBER PLANT SURVEY OF WESTERN NORTH AMERICA. Calif. Univ. Pubs., Bot. 7: [159]–278, illus. 1919.

CLEMATISES

Cle'matis spp., syns. *Atra'gene spp., Vior'na spp.*

The clematis genus includes the plants known as leatherflower, travelers-joy, and virgins-bower and is one of the few genera of the buttercup, or crowfoot family (Ranunculaceae) which have woody stems, but is the only one whose leaves are always opposite. There are about 24 species of clematis native to the West, some of which occur in every State. They all have attractive flowers, and the plumelike tails of the "seeds", which are often produced in masses, are very ornamental. *Clematis*, or rather *Klematis*, is a name used by the old Greek botanist Dioscorides for a climbing plant thought to be clematis. Klematis is a diminutive of the Greek *klema*, a vine branch. This genus includes early spring herbs which commonly appear in open grasslands. Some species are vigorous woody vines which usually occur along streams or in other moist places at lower elevations and form dense clusters in brush and trees or on rocks. Still others are short-stemmed, trailing, herbaceous or woody species common in the high mountains.

Clematis species, when young and tender, provide fair forage for sheep. Cattle occasionally browse the leaves of the climbing species; horses rarely touch them. Some species, notably *C. ligusticifolia*, clamber up supporting objects by means of their twisting, curling leafstalks, and are often used as ornamental vines. The plant was chewed by the Indians as a remedy for colds and sore throats. The early settlers in the West and the Indians sometimes used a decoction of *C. douglasii*, known as headache weed or lions-beard, as a headache cure. An explorer named Geyer reports (London Journ. Bot. 5: 301–302. 1846):

The Saptona Indians use the root of this plant as a stimulant, when horses fall down during their excessive races. They hold a scraped end of the root in the nostrils of the fallen horse. The effect of this is instantaneous, it produces trembling; the animal springs up, and is led to the water to refresh its limbs. I have been told that it never failed, nor produced bad consequences. The scraped root leaves a burning sensation for half a day, if touched with the tongue.

All species of *Clematis* are perennial with mostly enlarged stem joints; large compound opposite leaves; showy flowers, without petals, appearing chiefly in spring and summer, having numerous stamens, and 4 or 5 white, yellow, blue or purple, petallike sepals (calyx lobes), and silky or feathery, tailed "seeds." There are three distinct botanical groups of *Clematis*: (1) True *Clematis*, with large clusters of numerous, small, usually white, fragrant flowers; (2) leatherflowers (genus *Viorna* of some botanists), with usually solitary, thickish, usually pendulous and 4-parted, mostly purplish, bell-like or vaselike flowers; and (3) "virgins-bowers" (genus *Atragene* of some botanists), with very large, solitary, star-shaped, usually bluish flowers.

BLACKBRUSH

Coleo'gyne ramosis'sima

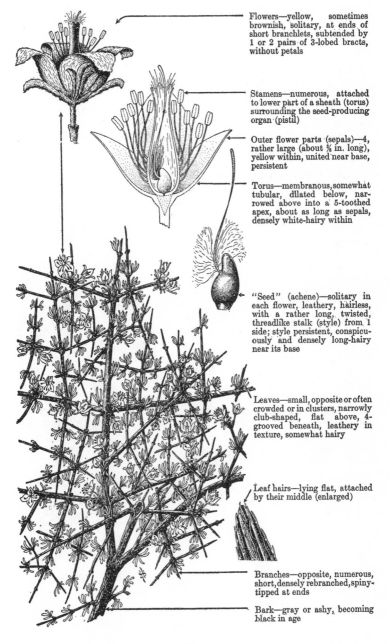

Flowers—yellow, sometimes brownish, solitary, at ends of short branchlets, subtended by 1 or 2 pairs of 3-lobed bracts, without petals

Stamens—numerous, attached to lower part of a sheath (torus) surrounding the seed-producing organ (pistil)

Outer flower parts (sepals)—4, rather large (about ⅜ in. long), yellow within, united near base, persistent

Torus—membranous, somewhat tubular, dilated below, narrowed above into a 5-toothed apex, about as long as sepals, densely white-hairy within

"Seed" (achene)—solitary in each flower, leathery, hairless, with a rather long, twisted, threadlike stalk (style) from 1 side; style persistent, conspicuously and densely long-hairy near its base

Leaves—small, opposite or often crowded or in clusters, narrowly club-shaped, flat above, 4-grooved beneath, leathery in texture, somewhat hairy

Leaf hairs—lying flat, attached by their middle (enlarged)

Branches—opposite, numerous, short, densely rebranched, spiny-tipped at ends

Bark—gray or ashy, becoming black in age

655

Blackbrush, also called Dixie blackb(r)ush and, especially in southern Utah and northern Arizona, burrobrush, is an intricately branched shrub from 1 to 6 feet tall, with numerous, short and rigid, spinelike twigs. It belongs to the rose family (Rosaceae) and is the only species of its genus. The generic name, *Coleogyne*, signifies sheathed ovary (Greek *koleos*, sheath, + *gune*, female) and refers to the peculiar tubular sheath which encloses the ovary, or seed; *ramosissima* is a Latin word meaning very branched, and describes the branched habit of this shrub, with its numerous spinose twigs. The common name, blackbrush, is appropriate, since this bush, when abundant, lends a dark gray or blackish appearance to the landscape.

This species ranges from southern Nevada and southwestern Colorado to Arizona and the Mohave Desert region of California. It is the dominant species of the blackbrush association in the Great Basin and in northern Arizona and inhabits desert mesas and also foothills in the piñon-juniper type. Shantz (in Tidestrom)[1] reports that, in the Intermountain Region, the blackbrush association lies in a broad overlapping belt between the northern and southern desert areas; it accompanies, therefore, both northern and southern desert plants. The species is often associated with spiny hop-sage (*Grayia spinosa*). In southern Utah and northern Arizona it is locally abundant and forms almost pure stands on large areas, typically occurring in sandy or gravelly soils.

The leafage, although small and scanty, is persistent and sometimes evergreen and is available throughout the year. It provides fair forage for cattle and sheep during the winter, especially in the Dixie Forest region of southwestern Utah, where it is abundant. The shrub is self-protected to some extent because of its spiny character and it is apt to survive on heavily used range. Sheep and goats utilize it to better advantage than do cattle. On the Navaho Reservation, where vegetative conditions have been altered by severe overgrazing in the past, it is grazed as closely by goats and sheep as its habit of growth will permit. It also furnishes fair forage for deer, and, possibly for other game animals.

The ashy-gray bark, becoming black in age, has a roughish corrugated appearance. Blackbrush flowers in April and May.

[1] Tidestrom, I. FLORA OF UTAH AND NEVADA. U. S. Natl. Mus., Contrib. U. S. Natl. Herbarium 25, 665 pp., illus. 1925.

PACIFIC DOGWOOD

Cor'nus nuttal'lii

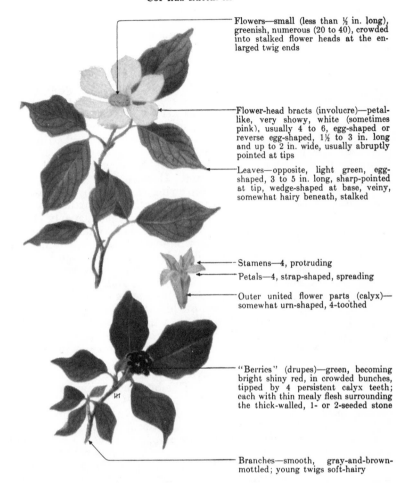

Flowers—small (less than ½ in. long), greenish, numerous (20 to 40), crowded into stalked flower heads at the enlarged twig ends

Flower-head bracts (involucre)—petal-like, very showy, white (sometimes pink), usually 4 to 6, egg-shaped or reverse egg-shaped, 1½ to 3 in. long and up to 2 in. wide, usually abruptly pointed at tips

Leaves—opposite, light green, egg-shaped, 3 to 5 in. long, sharp-pointed at tip, wedge-shaped at base, veiny, somewhat hairy beneath, stalked

Stamens—4, protruding

Petals—4, strap-shaped, spreading

Outer united flower parts (calyx)—somewhat urn-shaped, 4-toothed

"Berries" (drupes)—green, becoming bright shiny red, in crowded bunches, tipped by 4 persistent calyx teeth; each with thin mealy flesh surrounding the thick-walled, 1- or 2-seeded stone

Branches—smooth, gray-and-brown-mottled; young twigs soft-hairy

Of the several species of dogwood in the Western States, Pacific dogwood is by far the showiest in bloom, and the only one that attains genuinely treelike proportions. Its range, as indicated by its common name, extends throughout the Pacific Coast States from the Lower Fraser River and Vancouver Island in British Columbia southward, but west of the summit of the Cascades and Sierras, to southern California. It has also been found in northwestern Idaho. Bailey's Cyclopedia of Horticulture reports that the genus name dogwood was popularized originally in early England, where a solution made by boiling the bark of the bloodtwig dogwood (*C. sanguinea*) in water was used in the treatment of mangy dogs. The generic name *Cornus* is from the Latin *cornu*, a horn, and refers to the hardness of the wood. The famous ornithologist, Audubon, named the plant *nuttallii*, in honor of Thomas Nuttall, the naturalist.

Pacific dogwood is associated intimately with the forest, usually growing singly or in small groups in the shade of some coniferous species. It frequents moist situations on bottoms, coves, near seeps and streams, and on protected mountain slopes. It occurs on a variety of soils, from gravelly to deep loam, making the most satisfactory growth on the fertile forest soils of Oregon and Washington. It grows chiefly at middle altitudes in California, being common in the Sierras in both the ponderosa pine and sugar pine forests. Farther north it is associated closely with Douglas fir. Bigleaf maple (*Acer macrophyllum*), California hazel (*Corylus californica*), and alders (*Alnus* spp.) frequently grow with Pacific dogwood.

Pacific dogwood usually attains a height of from 20 to 30 feet, although trees up to at least 50 feet high, with trunks near 20 inches in diameter, are not unusual. Such heights practically nullify any material use of the foliage as forage. However, much of the foliage of the reproduction, and the slow-growing and shrubby specimens on poor sites occur within the reach of livestock. Furthermore, the tendency of this species to produce many stems, particularly on very moist sites, results in slender growth which is frequently bent near the ground by the weight of the winter snow, and hence made accessible to livestock. However, the volume of this forage is invariably less than it seems to be. Ordinarily, the plants are scattered, compose but a small percentage of the cover, and the branches near the ground are usually not so leafy as the higher ones.

On many ranges the utilization of this plant by livestock is almost negligible, because of other and more palatable browse, or because, as is commonly the case, of light or no use of the timbered portions of the range where it is common. When available under normal use, Pacific dogwood is poor forage for cattle but fair for sheep. The bark and, to some extent, the leaves, have a bitter taste, which may affect livestock use of this species. This bitterness is probably due to quininelike substances, as flowering dogwood (*C. florida*), a closely related eastern species, yields a useful substitute for quinine reputed to possess much the same effect in the treatment of fevers.

Pacific dogwood has gained some importance as an ornamental because its large, white, and showy involucral bracts resemble petals, and with the central, buttonlike head of green flowers, simulate a large, white, and attractive flower. They appear during the spring in the forest; a second flowering in the fall is not uncommon where the species is grown as a cultivated plant. The shiny red fruit and the beautiful autumnal leafage, especially when each leaf contains several colors dominated by reds, are other advantages which adapt it as an ornamental. Pacific dogwood also has its disadvantage, as it is not hardy and, ordinarily, does not thrive outside its native range, although now cultivated successfully in southern England. The wood is dense, fine-grained, and heavy, and is very good for lathe work, although it checks badly if cured rapidly. The wood will probably never be important commercially because the supply is limited.

CALIFORNIA HAZEL

Co'rylus califor'nica, syn. *C. rostra'ta califor'nica*

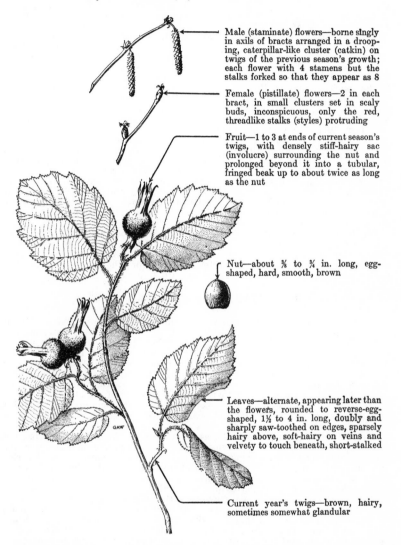

Male (staminate) flowers—borne singly in axils of bracts arranged in a drooping, caterpillar-like cluster (catkin) on twigs of the previous season's growth; each flower with 4 stamens but the stalks forked so that they appear as 8

Female (pistillate) flowers—2 in each bract, in small clusters set in scaly buds, inconspicuous, only the red, threadlike stalks (styles) protruding

Fruit—1 to 3 at ends of current season's twigs, with densely stiff-hairy sac (involucre) surrounding the nut and prolonged beyond it into a tubular, fringed beak up to about twice as long as the nut

Nut—about ⅜ to ¾ in. long, egg-shaped, hard, smooth, brown

Leaves—alternate, appearing later than the flowers, rounded to reverse-egg-shaped, 1½ to 4 in. long, doubly and sharply saw-toothed on edges, sparsely hairy above, soft-hairy on veins and velvety to touch beneath, short-stalked

Current year's twigs—brown, hairy, sometimes somewhat glandular

California hazel is a multistemmed, loosely spreading shrub, mostly 6 to 10 feet high, common in the Pacific coast forested areas. The common name hazel is presumably of north European origin, where it has been variously spelled as haesel, hassel, and hastl. It originally referred to the European hazel, or filbert (*C. avellana*). The species is distributed from central California to British Columbia.

California hazel occurs on a variety of soils, from moist, black loam to dry, stony soils, and even appears in crevices in the rocks. Ordinarily, it becomes most abundant on the moderately fertile but stony soils of slopes and on dry and rocky islands or along stream banks. It prefers cool, shaded sites on northern slopes, along streams, or conifer or oak forests where it forms an understory. It also grows in the open, particularly on burned or cut-over lands. In the coastal mountains, as well as toward the northern extremity of its range, it grows at low elevations, but occurs at increasingly higher situations inland until, at the southern extension of the Sierras, it appears at from 3,000 to 6,000 feet above sea level. Pacific dogwood (*Cornus nuttallii*) and bigleaf maple (*Acer macrophyllum*) are its most common associates.

As a browse plant California hazel is not important, being relatively low in palatability. Its palatability on properly utilized range is usually poor for cattle and only poor to fair for sheep; it is but slightly used by deer. The leaves are somewhat hairy, commonly having an almost velvety feeling to the touch; it may be this character which displeases grazing animals. Unquestionably, California hazel would be an ideal browse if the foliage were more palatable, because it is often abundant, the growth is open, low, and spreading, and the many stems are well clothed with relatively large leaves, thus providing a considerable volume of leafage within reach of livestock.

This species has certain other values and uses, being valuable as a soil binder on steep slopes, both as an understory in the forest and on open, untimbered sites. This value is enhanced by the fact that it sprouts abundantly from the root crown after the tops have been destroyed by fire or other causes. The edible nuts have a sweet flavor and are gathered locally, although a poor crop or early harvest by chipmunks and squirrels often limit the local supply. The Indians formerly used splints for basket manufacture from the slender one- and two-year-old shrubs. The glandular hairs (*spiculae*) on the involucre have been used as a remedy for worms.[1]

The California hazel is a handsome shrub, sometimes attaining a height of over 20 feet but usually grows not over one-half that high. The many stems are sparsely branched, leafy, and slender, and are gracefully disposed to form a full and rounded bush. The catkins appear before the leaves during February and March, but the nuts do not ripen until fall.

HAZELS (Co'rylus spp.)

The hazels, like their near relatives, the alders (*Alnus* spp.) and the birches (*Betula* spp.), belong to the birch family (*Betulaceae*).[2] Tidestrom[3] has shown that the scientific name *Corylus* is related to the Gaelic (Irish) and Celtic names for this genus, and that it stood for the letter C in the tree alphabet of these peoples. The alders and birches are readily distinguishable from hazels because the fruit of the latter is a nut inclosed in a helmetlike involucre, whereas the fruit of alders and birches is a small, winged nutlet not enclosed in an involucre. Approximately 15 species of hazel are native to North America, Europe, and Asia; about half of these occur in North America, but only two, California hazel and beaked hazel (*C. rostra'ta*), occur in the West.

Beaked hazel has taper-pointed leaves, hairless or slightly hairy twigs, and a densely stiff-hairy involucre twice as long as the nut, with the lower portion surrounding the nut. This species is common in eastern North America, extending west to Colorado and the Dakotas, but probably has little or no range significance. Some authorities report beaked hazel as occurring on the Pacific coast, but all herbarium material from this area appears to be California hazel. There is some evidence that the two types tend to merge, and the position taken by some botanists that California hazel is a variety of the beaked hazel, rather than a distinct species, may be sound taxonomically.

The filbert nuts of commerce, fruit of the European species, *C. avellana*, *C. pontica* (syn. *C. avellana pontica*), and *C. maxima*, or the product of crossbreeds of these species, are cultivated extensively in Europe, but are not grown on an extensive scale in North America.

---

[1] Lyons, A. B. PLANT NAMES SCIENTIFIC AND POPULAR . . . Ed. 2, thoroughly rev. and enl., 630 pp. Detroit. 1907.
[2] Because of the involucred fruit, however, some botanists prefer to place the hazels in the family Corylaceae in which are also placed the hornbeams (*Carpinus* spp.) and hophornbeams (*Ostrya* spp.).
[3] Tidestrom, I. THE FLORAL ALPHABET OF THE CELTS. Torreya 23 : 41–49, illus. 1923.

CREOSOTEBUSH

Covil'lea tridenta'ta, syns. *C. glutino'sa, C. mexica'na, Lar'rea tridenta'ta glutino'sa*

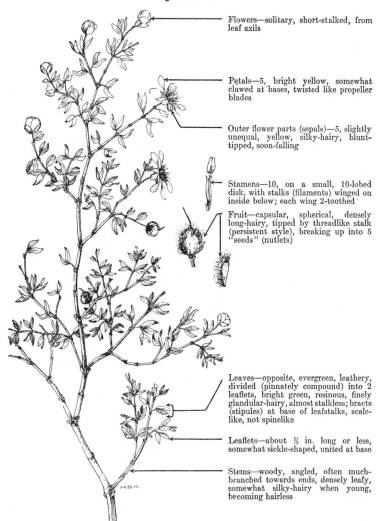

Flowers—solitary, short-stalked, from leaf axils

Petals—5, bright yellow, somewhat clawed at bases, twisted like propeller blades

Outer flower parts (sepals)—5, slightly unequal, yellow, silky-hairy, blunt-tipped, soon-falling

Stamens—10, on a small, 10-lobed disk, with stalks (filaments) winged on inside below; each wing 2-toothed

Fruit—capsular, spherical, densely long-hairy, tipped by threadlike stalk (persistent style), breaking up into 5 "seeds" (nutlets)

Leaves—opposite, evergreen, leathery, divided (pinnately compound) into 2 leaflets, bright green, resinous, finely glandular-hairy, almost stalkless; bracts (stipules) at base of leafstalks, scale-like, not spinelike

Leaflets—about ½ in. long or less, somewhat sickle-shaped, united at base

Stems—woody, angled, often much-branched towards ends, densely leafy, somewhat silky-hairy when young, becoming hairless

Creosotebush, a shapely evergreen shrub, is one of the most characteristic plants of the southwestern deserts. Extensive bright green oases, contrasting sharply with the usual grayish hue of the desert, are formed by pure stands of this shiny-leaved, yellow-flowered shrub. The plant has a creosotelike odor, especially when burned, which accounts for its common name. It is known locally as gobernadora, greasewood, hediondilla, and numerous other common names referring to the strong, pungent odor or to the resinous properties of the plant. The generic name commemorates the eminent botanist, Dr. Frederick V. Coville. The specific name *tridentata* describes the stamen stalk.

This shrub ranges from California eastward through southern Nevada and southwestern Utah, to southern Colorado and western Texas, and south into Mexico. It covers many thousands of square miles in pure stands or in association with bur-sage (*Franseria dumosa*), its very common companion, and various other shrubs. Creosotebush is so characteristic of certain large areas as to constitute a distinctive vegetative unit, called the creosotebush, or *Covillea*, association. Shantz (in Tidestrom [1]) reports that this association is more extensive than any other type of vegetation in the southern desert. This belt, in which creosotebush is so common, is designated by some plant ecologists as the Lower Sonoran Zone. Scientific observers classify the creosotebush association as one of the most permanent types of vegetation. Creosotebush occurs on the sandy or gravelly soils of mesas and hillsides, but attains its maximum development on pervious soils of flats and alluvial fans, where its deep-seated roots obtain adequate moisture. The resinous covering of its stems and leaves minimizes transpiration and protects the plant against drought. The species has long attracted the attention of plant physiologists, and numerous technical papers have been published on its remarkable adaptation to severe climatic and soil conditions. Runyon [2] calls it "the most successful and conspicuous xerophyte (*i. e.*, dry-land plant) in the desert regions of North America." Spalding [3] ascertained that creosotebush has become especially well adapted to dry conditions by the development of numerous root hairs and a very high osmotic pressure within the plant cells, which give it exceptional power in water absorption. He further determined that, although it has acquired capacity for withstanding excessive drought, it attains its best growth where the water supply is favorable.

Creosotebush is important chiefly because of its abundance, as it is the dominant vegetation on large areas, where it serves as an efficient soil protector and stabilizer. However, it is not a good soil builder, and does not facilitate the growth of better plants upon the sites where it occurs abundantly. This species is worthless as forage at all seasons and to all classes of livestock. Usually, very little palatable vegetation grows in a true creosotebush type; hence the carrying capacity of such areas is either very low or nil. Livestock even avoid it during drought, unless absolutely forced to eat it rather than starve. Griffiths [4] reports that sheep are poisoned by this plant when compelled to eat it during years of forage scarcity, and that the greatest mortality occurs among pregnant ewes. Crawford,[5] however, determined that liquid extracted from the leaves of creosotebush and given to sheep and rabbits produced absolutely no undesirable results; he states that the belief among stockmen as to the poisonous effects of this plant is unfounded.

Creosotebush has a prominent place in the mythology of the Pima Indians of the Southwest.[6] The reddish brown resin which is deposited on the branches by the scale insect *Tachardiella* (syn. *Carteria*) *larreae* was used by the Indians for mending pottery, cementing arrow heads, coating baskets, etc. The leaves and twigs were used, in decoction, as a tonic and antiseptic.[5 6 7]

Creosotebush is a much-branched shrub from 3 to 11 feet high. As a rule, it often naturally occurs so widely and uniformly spaced as to convey the impression that the plants have been set out artificially in almost military alinement. The gray stems are banded in black at the nodes and spread out gracefully from the ground, forming a rather broad flat top. The yellow flowers mature rapidly and are soon replaced by the fuzzy, white seed balls.

[1] Tidestrom, I. FLORA OF UTAH AND NEVADA. U. S. Natl. Mus., Contrib. U. S. Natl. Herbarium 25, 665 pp., illus. 1925.
[2] Runyon, E. H. THE ORGANIZATION OF THE CREOSOTE BUSH WITH RESPECT TO DROUGHT. Ecology 15 (2) : 128–138, illus. 1934.
[3] Spalding, V. M. BIOLOGICAL RELATIONS OF CERTAIN DESERT SHRUBS. 1. THE CREOSOTE BUSH (COVILLEA TRIDENTATA) IN ITS RELATION TO WATER SUPPLY. Bot. Gaz. 38 : 122–138, illus. 1904.
[4] Griffiths, D. RANGE INVESTIGATIONS IN ARIZONA. U. S. Dept. Agr., Bur. Plant Indus. Bull. 67, 62 pp., illus. 1904.
[5] Crawford, A. C. NOTES, MAINLY BIBLIOGRAPHICAL, ON TWO AMERICAN PLANTS—SLEEPY GRASS AND CREOSOTE BUSH. Pharm. Rev. 26 : 230–235. 1908.
[6] Russell, F. THE PIMA INDIANS. U. S. Bur. Amer. Ethnol. Ann. Rept. (1904–5) 26 : 3–[390], illus. 1908.
[7] Kunze, R. E. THE DESERT FLORA OF PHOENIX, ARIZONA. Bull. Torrey Bot. Club 30 : 302–307. 1903.

CLIFFROSE

Cowa'nia stansburia'na, syns. *C. al'ba, C. mexica'na stansburia'na,*
"C. mexica'na" [1]

Flowers—solitary, rather large (about
¾ in. across), white to sulphur yellow,
stalked, at ends of short, spurlike twigs

Petals—5, rounded or reverse-egg-
shaped, spreading

Stamens—numerous, in 2 rows, attached to rim of outer flower parts

Outer flower parts (sepals)—5, united
below into a short, top-shaped tube
(hypanthium, or calyx), persistent,
densely white-hairy

Leaves—small, evergreen, crowded at
ends of short, spurlike branchlets,
leathery in texture, usually with 5 to 7,
short, linear lobes, gland-dotted, dark
green above, white-hairy beneath, with
curled-under margins

"Seeds" (achenes)—4 to 10, hairy,
borne on a flat disk in the hypanthium,
each tipped by a long (up to 2 in.)
feathery tail (style)

[1] Of United States authors, not D. Don.

Cliffrose, a leafy evergreen shrub, gets its common name from its rather frequent habitat in the cliffs and from the fact that it is a member of the rose family with fragrant wildrose-shaped flowers. It is often called quinine-bush because its twigs are very bitter. It sometimes appears in literature as *Cowania mexicana*, a distinct and wholly Mexican species.

It occurs from southern Colorado and Utah to California (east of the Sierra Nevada), Sonora, Chihuahua, and New Mexico. It is found chiefly in dry, rocky situations on foothills and mesas up through the woodland type to the lower fringe of the ponderosa pine belt at altitudes ranging from 4,000 to 8,000 feet. Although, perhaps, most characteristic of limestone areas, it grows also on granitic, volcanic, and other igneous formations, often on east and south slopes, and is frequently associated with juniper, piñon, mountain-mahogany, serviceberry, sagebrush, live oak, and other moderately dry site (xerophytic) shrubs and small trees.

Ordinarily, cliffrose is spreading, has many branches, and is 3 to 12 feet high. Under the most favorable circumstances it becomes a small tree from 20 to 25 feet high. The bark on the twigs and of young plants is somewhat roughened with a papery scurf; on the trunks of the larger shrubs, however, it hangs in long shreds somewhat like juniper bark but more loose and papery.

Where abundant, cliffrose is an important and valuable browse for sheep, cattle, and deer, the chief utilization usually being in winter. It is the key species on the winter range of the Kaibab Plateau for both deer and cattle. It is little used by sheep, cattle, or deer during spring and summer if other succulent forage is plentiful. The branches of the shrub are brittle and under abusive grazing are liable to be broken and severely damaged, particularly by cattle. Deer, however, also may break down the branches when there is a shortage of forage. Proper browsing, however, stimulates lateral bud growth which results in the production of a greater number of leafy shoots and more forage than where the plant is protected.

The current growth of shoots, together with their numerous leaves, is the most palatable part of the plant. The growth of the succeeding year arises mainly from the remains of these shoots which are left after grazing. Proper utilization of this browse should be based upon the current shoot growth. The growth habit of the leaves on the older twigs—they are crowded together on the ends of short stubby twigs—makes them readily available.

Although cliffrose usually produces a liberal supply of seed, years of favorable plant increase are sometimes widely separated. The fact that cliffrose plants are unusually long-lived partly counterbalances this shortcoming.

SHRUBBY CINQUEFOIL

Dasi'phora frutico'sa, syn. *Potentil'la frutico'sa*

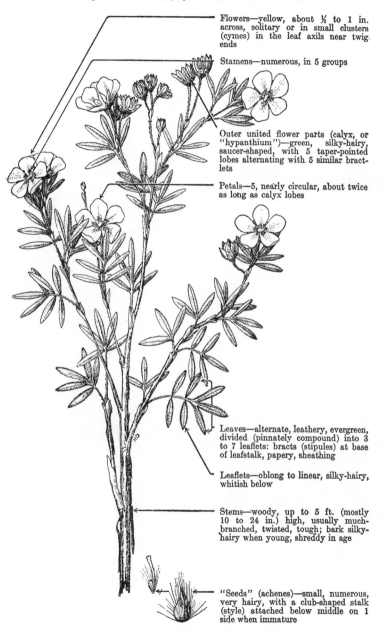

Flowers—yellow, about ½ to 1 in. across, solitary or in small clusters (cymes) in the leaf axils near twig ends

Stamens—numerous, in 5 groups

Outer united flower parts (calyx, or "hypanthium")—green, silky-hairy, saucer-shaped, with 5 taper-pointed lobes alternating with 5 similar bractlets

Petals—5, nearly circular, about twice as long as calyx lobes

Leaves—alternate, leathery, evergreen, divided (pinnately compound) into 3 to 7 leaflets: bracts (stipules) at base of leafstalk, papery, sheathing

Leaflets—oblong to linear, silky-hairy, whitish below

Stems—woody, up to 5 ft. (mostly 10 to 24 in.) high, usually much-branched, twisted, tough; bark silky-hairy when young, shreddy in age

"Seeds" (achenes)—small, numerous, very hairy, with a club-shaped stalk (style) attached below middle on 1 side when immature

Shrubby cinquefoil, a much-branched bush widely distributed in the Northern Hemisphere, is sometimes called bush cinquefoil or shrub cinquefoil and is also known locally as buckbrush, hardhack, ninebark, and yellow rose. It occurs in Europe and Asia and ranges in North America from Greenland and Labrador to Alaska and south to California, New Mexico, Minnesota, Illinois, and New Jersey. This is probably the only species of *Dasiphora* in North America, although the narrow-leaved alpine form, which is commonly gnarled and dwarfed, has been described as a distinct variety or species (*D. fruticosa tenuifolia*, syn. *Potentilla tenuifolia*). However, in view of the variations of the species, it is questionable if this narrow-leaved form is worthy of a separate name.[1]

Dasiphora, a small genus of about eight or nine species belonging to the rose family (*Rosaceae*), is, with the single exception of shrubby cinquefoil, confined to Asia. The name, derived from the Green *dasus*, shaggy, or thick with hairs, and *phoros*, bearing, refers to the densely hairy "seeds". The specific name of shrubby cinquefoil, *fruticosa*, is a Latin adjective which means shrubby or bushy.

Shrubby cinquefoil is mostly from 10 to 24 inches high, but occasionally reaches a height of 5 feet. With its profusion of yellow flowers produced from June until frost, its hairy, grayish-green leaves pinnately divided into from five to seven small, rather narrow, leaflets, and its peculiar reddish-brown, shreddy bark, this shrub is but seldom confused with any other range plant. Shrubby cinquefoil is very common in the West and is often so abundant locally that it is the dominant browse species over small areas. Although essentially a species of cool climates, moisture is apparently a greater limiting factor in its distribution than temperature, since it extends over a wide altitudinal range, occurring from the upper ponderosa pine belt to above timberline. It is characteristic of open exposures, especially moist subalpine meadows and near cold springs and seeps, although it is also commonly found in open timber.

In general, this shrub has a relatively low palatability, usually rating from practically worthless to fairly good for domestic livestock, although deer and elk nibble it. This plant is usually not utilized extensively by game; the leaves have a bitter taste, but are good-sized and evergreen; these desirable characters together with the form of this shrub would, undoubtedly, make it of considerable value on winter range. Unfortunately, however, it occurs chiefly on summer range and is not available for winter use. On some overgrazed ranges, especially in alpine meadows, where shrubby cinquefoil is one of the dominant plants, it had been grazed rather closely, and the plants have assumed a hedgelike appearance. Utilization to such an extent always suggests overstocking and may indicate imminent if not actual depletion of the more palatable plants. Exceptions to the relatively low palatability of shrubby cinquefoil apparently prevail in parts of the Southwest, southwestern Montana, southeastern Idaho, and Utah, where the species is fair to fairly good cattle and fairly good to good sheep forage on closely cropped, but not overgrazed, summer-range meadows. It is also palatable to deer and elk on some of the summer game ranges of Montana, where it is rated eighteenth among the most important browse species.

In New England this species is sometimes an aggressive pest in agricultural lands and, when once established, is difficult to eradicate. In the West, however, the plant does not appear to be especially aggressive either in agricultural lands or on the range. Rydberg[2] reports that the leaves of this species are used as a substitute for tea in Russia. Meehan[3] states that the branches are sometimes used in making brooms in parts of Europe and are equal to heath and birch for such purpose. The plant is also valued for horticultural plantings both in the United States and abroad, because it is easy of cultivation and is one of the few shrubs which produce a profusion of attractive flowers.

---

[1] Dayton, W. A. IMPORTANT WESTERN BROWSE PLANTS. U. S. Dept. Agr. Misc. Pub. 101, 214 pp., illus. 1931.
[2] Rydberg, P. A. A MONOGRAPH OF THE NORTH AMERICAN POTENTILLEAE. Columbia Univ. Dept. Bot. Mem., v. 2, 223 pp., illus. Lancaster, Pa. 1898. (Thesis, Ph. D., Columbia University.)
[3] Meehan, T. THE NATIVE FLOWERS AND FERNS OF THE UNITED STATES IN THEIR BOTANICAL, HORTICULTURAL, AND POPULAR ASPECTS. 2 v., illus. Boston. 1878.

JOINTFIRS [1]

E'phedra spp.[2]

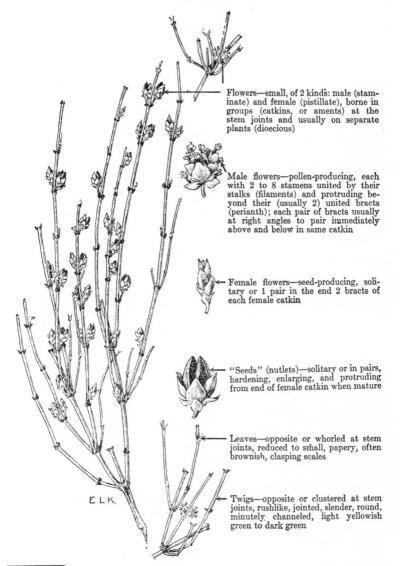

Flowers—small, of 2 kinds: male (staminate) and female (pistillate), borne in groups (catkins, or aments) at the stem joints and usually on separate plants (dioecious)

Male flowers—pollen-producing, each with 2 to 8 stamens united by their stalks (filaments) and protruding beyond their (usually 2) united bracts (perianth); each pair of bracts usually at right angles to pair immediately above and below in same catkin

Female flowers—seed-producing, solitary or 1 pair in the end 2 bracts of each female catkin

"Seeds" (nutlets)—solitary or in pairs, hardening, enlarging, and protruding from end of female catkin when mature

Leaves—opposite or whorled at stem joints, reduced to small, papery, often brownish, clasping scales

Twigs—opposite or clustered at stem joints, rushlike, jointed, slender, round, minutely channeled, light yellowish green to dark green

E.L.K.

---

[1] This is Standardized Plant Names usage. Decision has been reached, since this handbook went to press, by the Forest Service and other bureaus of the Department of Agriculture to adopt ephedra as the English name for these plants, and this usage is shown in the index.

[2] The common pronunciation of this word is e-fee'-dra, putting the accent on the second syllable (penult). The preferred pronunciation, however, is e'-fee-dra, with the accent on the first syllable (antepenult), the second e in the Greek word *ephedra* being the short e (epsilon), so that, under the rules, the stress recedes to the first syllable.

The jointfirs, with jointed branches resembling those of horsetails (*Equisetum* spp.), are distinctive shrubs or small trees belonging to the gnetum family (Gnetaceae), and intermediate between the pine family and the higher flowering plants (angiosperms). Their leaves have degenerated into scales partly ensheathing the joints of the branches. Jointfir, the accepted common name,[3] is rather descriptive, but as yet is only limitedly employed in the range country, where the names Mormon-tea and cañatillo are generally used in references to these plants. Other local names include Brigham-tea, Mexican-tea, jointpine, popotillo, shrubby horsetail, teamsters-tea, and tepopote. *Ephĕdra* is an old Greek plant name, which supposedly refers to some horsetail or to marestail, or water-milfoil (*Hippuris*); it was adopted by Tournefort and later by Linnaeus as the generic name for the jointfirs.

Ephĕdra is a geologically ancient genus, with about 40 species widely distributed throughout the world, chiefly in the warmer desert and mountainous areas of the Northern Hemisphere; 8 to 10 species, however, have been recorded from the Southern Hemisphere, chiefly from South America. The number of species is about equally divided between the Old and New Worlds without any natural interchange of species between these two vast areas. About 10 or 11 species are native to the United States, all confined to the more arid portions of the West, and chiefly in the desert and semidesert areas of the Southwest. Five or six of these species are rather common in the region from southwestern Wyoming to western Texas, eastern and southern California, and southward into Mexico.

Jointfirs grow on dry, open sites in valleys and on slopes, mesas, and foothills, principally in the sagebrush, piñon-juniper, and ponderosa-pine zones, and chiefly in gravelly or sandy soils, but occasionally in clays. Exposed canyon bottoms, dry washes, ridge tops, and breaks with southern exposures are characteristic habitats of these shrubs. The commonly associated plants include gramas, mountain-mahoganies, shadscale and other saltbushes, junipers, and creosotebush. Jointfirs generally occur sparsely as scattered bushes or in clumps but sometimes are the dominant species on limited areas, appearing in almost pure stands in small, localized patches.

Although not equal in palatability to the choicest browse species, the jointfirs are often heavily grazed in such emergency periods as prolonged drought or during scarcity of better forage. At times they are very important elements in winter range carrying capacity due to their moderate palatability, the immense number of stems produced, and the relative abundance of these species on certain areas. Because of the prevalence of overstocking and overgrazing on many western ranges, jointfirs have succumbed to excessive utilization on some areas.

Ever since 2737–2698 B. C., the time of the illustrious, semilegendary Emperor Shen Nung, putative father of Chinese medicine and agriculture and author of its first materia medica, the Chinese have used, both externally and internally, preparations of the

[3] American Joint Committee on Horticultural Nomenclature. STANDARDIZED PLANT NAMES . . . Prepared by F. L. Olmsted, F. V. Coville, and H. P. Kelsey. 546 pp. Salem, Mass. 1923.

dried roots and stems of two species of *Ephedra*,[4] often mixed in prescriptions with the products of other plants. These species are still highly prized in the treatment of coughs, colds, headache, and fever, and are also used as a blood purifier. Even today the stems of these plants are sold in Chinese herb shops throughout the world under the Chinese name ma huang. This Chinese drug plant has for years been referred to a form (var. *helve'tica*) of the Old World common jointfir (*E. dista'chya*, syn. *E. vulga'ris*). Recent investigation, however, has demonstrated that the alkaloid ephedrine, an important drug, is extracted chiefly from Chinese jointfir (*E. si'nica*) and, to a minor extent, from Mongolian jointfir (*E. equiseti'na*). The presence of ephedrine in the Chinese plants led to the investigation of our native species as a possible source of supply; thus far, however, the results of such research have been negative; no ephedrine has yet been found in any American species.[5] Almost all the species of *Ephedra* are easily reproduced from cuttings; considerable propagation work has been conducted in the Southwest in an effort to introduce and cultivate some of the most important Old World species. American Indians and Mexicans have long used decoctions of the stems as an alleged specific for certain ailments of the genitourinary tract, and also as a cooling beverage; in addition, they sometimes roasted and ate the seeds or used them in the preparation of a bitter bread. The pioneers also used the jointfirs for tea and medicine—practices which still prevail among residents of outlying western settlements. Chemical analyses of American jointfirs reveal high percentages of tannin; very little is known about other substances contained in these species, including compounds of possible medicinal or other economic value.

Vine jointfir (*E. antisyphili'tica*), with weak, bright yellow-green, clambering stems, the branches and scales in pairs, is the largest of our range jointfirs, attaining small-tree size (9 to 15 feet) in the Rio Grande Valley. It is found from extreme southwestern Colorado, through Arizona, New Mexico, and western Texas, into northern Mexico. Although of rather limited occurrence, it is grazed to some extent.

California jointfir (*E. califor'nica*) grows naturally in California from the Colorado River and Mohave Deserts north to western Fresno County, west to San Diego, and thence into Lower California.[6] Definite observations are needed concerning its browse value.

Nevada jointfir (*E. nevaden'sis*) and green jointfir (*E. vi'ridis*), probably the most important forage plants among United States species of *Ephedra*, are moderately palatable to all classes of domestic livestock as well as to deer. Frequently these plants are only slightly (if at all) grazed on the summer range, but on the winter

[4] Groff, G. W., and Clark, G. W. THE BOTANY OF EPHEDRA IN RELATION TO YIELD OF PHYSIOLOGICALLY ACTIVE SUBSTANCES. Calif. Univ. Pubs., Bot. 14 (7) : 247–282, illus. 1928.

[5] Black, O. F., and Kelly, J. W. PSEUDO EPHEDRINE FROM EPHEDRA ALATA. Amer. Jour. Pharm. 99 : 748–751. 1927.

[6] Jepson, W. L. A MANUAL OF THE FLOWERING PLANTS OF CALIFORNIA. 1,238 pp., illus. Berkeley, Calif. [1925.]

range, where they chiefly occur, the younger stems are eaten with relish. Green jointfir extends farther north than any of its sister species, occurring from southwestern Wyoming to southeastern California and New Mexico. The range of Nevada jointfir duplicates that of green jointfir except that the former does not grow in Wyoming but extends farther south into Old Mexico. Nevada and green jointfirs are somewhat similar in growth and general appearance, attaining heights of from about 20 to 40 inches, and having numerous, stiff branches, which typically grow in pairs. They also have scales (modified leaves) about one-eighth to three-sixteenths of an inch long, which occur in pairs joined at their base and thus sheathing the stem. However, Nevada jointfir is olive or brownish green and has rather stout, spreading branches; green jointfir is bright yellowish green with its numerous, slender, parallel branches pointing upward like the straws in an upturned broom.

Torrey jointfir (*E. torreya'na*), a low desert bush, ranges from southern Colorado and New Mexico to Arizona, southern Utah, and southern Nevada. Its branches and leafscales are arranged in groups of three instead of in pairs. The leafscales of Torrey jointfir are more or less united around the flexuous branches and very short (one-eighth of an inch long or less). The species occurs from southern Colorado, through southern Utah and Nevada, to Arizona, New Mexico, and northern Mexico; it is an important winter forage, particularly for cattle and sheep.

Longleaf jointfir (*E. trifur'ca*) grows from southern Colorado to the Mohave and Colorado Deserts of southeastern California, western Texas, and northern Mexico. Its branches and leafscales, like those of Torrey jointfir, are paired (opposite). This shrub attains heights of from 2 to $6\frac{1}{2}$ feet and produces an abundance of spine-tipped branches; its leafscales are mostly distinct and are longer (from one-fourth to one-half of an inch long), more tapering, and more persistent than those of Torrey jointfir. Although fairly common in the Southwest, longleaf jointfir, largely no doubt due to its somewhat forbidding growth habit, ranks as valueless for forage, except, perhaps, as an emergency ration.

WRIGHT BUCKWHEATBRUSH

Erio'gonum wrigh'tii

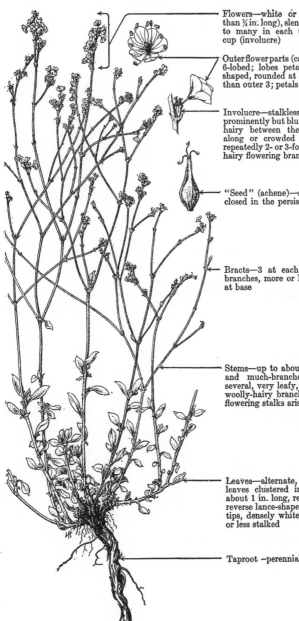

Flowers—white or pink, small (less than ¼ in. long), slender-stalked, several to many in each tubular-bell-shaped cup (involucre)

Outer flower parts (calyx, or perianth)—6-lobed; lobes petal-like, reverse-egg-shaped, rounded at tips, inner 3 longer than outer 3; petals lacking; stamens 9

Involucre—stalkless, erect, 5-toothed, prominently but bluntly angled, woolly-hairy between the angles, scattered along or crowded near ends of the repeatedly 2- or 3-forked, white-woolly-hairy flowering branches

"Seed" (achene)—small, 3-angled, enclosed in the persistent calyx

Bracts—3 at each fork of flowering branches, more or less grown together at base

Stems—up to about 2 ft. high, woody and much-branched at base, with several, very leafy, short, erect, white-woolly-hairy branches from which the flowering stalks arise

Leaves—alternate, often with smaller leaves clustered in the axils, up to about 1 in. long, reverse-egg-shaped or reverse lance-shaped, sharp-pointed at tips, densely white-woolly-hairy, more or less stalked

Taproot—perennial, woody, thickened

Wright buckwheatbrush, known locally as bastard sage, white sage, and wildbuckwheat, and sometimes called bush or white eriogonum, is a low, white-woolly-hairy shrub usually less than 2 feet high, and much branched from the base. This species grows on the more arid plains, in rocky foothills, and in rough mountain canyons; it ranges from California to Colorado, and western Texas, and southward into Mexico. It usually occurs in loose sandy or gravelly soils, and in association with some of the gramas. Although often abundant, it tends to make a scattered rather than a dense stand. The flowers appear from June to November, and the seed is matured and scattered from July to early winter. As might be expected from its rather wide latitudinal and altitudinal range, Wright buckwheatbrush is somewhat variable in aspect, tending to be dwarfed, more matted, woollier, with smaller, rolled leaves, and smaller flowers when growing in the lower, warmer sites, as well as in the higher, colder, and more rocky locations; some of these differences have been made the bases of varietal names.

In parts of the Southwest this shrubby eriogonum is considered fairly good forage for goats and sheep, and fair for cattle. Bidwell and Wooton, who have published [1] a chemical analysis for it, note that cattle and sheep eat the young shoots with relish.

Three other shrubby eriogonums merit brief discussion. Flat-top buckwheatbrush (*E. fascicula'tum*), also called California-buckwheat and flat-top, and the lower growing, closely related rosemary buckwheatbrush (*E. polifo'lium*, syn. *E. fascicula'tum polifo'lium*), have woody, shreddy-barked, clustered-leafy stems and twigs. The white or pinkish flowers are borne in heads at the tips of rather short, leafless flower-head stalks. Flat-top buckwheatbrush is common, sometimes even abundant, in canyons and on dry mountain slopes and mesas in California.

Rosemary buckwheatbrush, hardly specifically distinct from flat-top buckwheatbrush, ranges a little more widely than the latter species, occurring in desert areas and on mountain sides of the creosotebush belt from southern Utah and Arizona to southern California. On some of the semidesert areas of the Tonto National Forest, Arizona, it rates, chiefly due to abundance, as one of the better browse feeds.

Slender buckwheatbrush (*E. microthe'cum*) is a low scattered-leafy bush, usually up to about a foot high, much-branched from the base. It is very widely distributed, occurring from western Nebraska to Montana, Washington, California, Arizona, and Colorado, and prefers dry, open hillsides and the like. Besides being widespread, this species is sometimes locally abundant and valuable. The new growth is grazed on lambing ranges, especially in the Intermountain region, while the foliage is eaten during the winter. Although the forage value of this plant varies with its associates and local abundance, goats, sheep, and cattle eat the flowers, fruits, and tops. It rates as poor to fair spring and summer feed for sheep, and fair to fairly good winter feed.

---

[1] Bidwell, G. L., and Wooton, E. O. SALTBUSHES AND THEIR ALLIES IN THE UNITED STATES. U. S. Dept. Agr. Bull. 1345, 40 pp., illus. 1925.

WINTERFAT

Euro'tia lana'ta

Flowers—small, in dense clusters in the leaf axils, crowded along the stem toward the ends of the branches, of two kinds: male (staminate) clustered above the female (pistillate) ones and borne on the same plant (monoecious). Some plants produce female flowers only

Female flowers—seed-producing; corolla and outer flower cup (calyx) lacking; seed-producing organ (ovary) enclosed by two united bracts (sac) surmounted by two short "ears" and beset with silky, white hairs ⅛ to ¼ in. long arranged in 4 dense, spreading tufts

Male flowers—not seed-producing; no petals; stamens 4, long, slender, extending beyond the hairy, 4-parted calyx

Stems—round, woody at the base, somewhat herbaceous above; twigs and branches silvery-white, densely covered with woolly hairs white at first and becoming pale rust-colored with age

Leaves—alternate, narrowly linear, ¼ to 2 (mostly less than 1) in. long, flat, with rolled-under edges, densely white-hairy

Winterfat, a shrubby perennial, is largely known to western stockmen under the name "white sage", because it resembles many of the herbaceous sagebrushes, or "sages" (*Artemisia* spp.). However, it is not a true sage (*Salvia* spp.) but is closely related to the saltbushes and belongs with them in the goosefoot family (*Chenopodiaceae*). It is also commonly called winter sage, feathersage, and sweetsage. The generic name *Eurotia* is from the Greek *eurōs* (mold), referring to the white, hairy herbage. The specific name *lanata*, from the Latin *lana* (wool or hair), also alludes to the dense, woolly hairs that cover the plant. Winterfat, as the name implies, is chiefly valuable on winter ranges, where it often furnishes an abundance of palatable and nutritious forage highly fattening to sheep and cattle.

This plant is widely distributed from Saskatchewan and Manitoba to western Nebraska, Colorado, western Texas, California, and Washington, growing primarily, and often abundantly, in the lower foothills, plains, and valleys on dry soils that are moderately impregnated with white alkali or salty material. Winterfat is commonly the dominant and most conspicuous plant on vast areas of winter range, growing in distinct patches from several square rods to thousands of acres in area. The species is usually intermixed with various saltbushes, semidesert bunchgrasses, rabbitbrush, sagebrush, and greasewood and, in the higher part of its range, with wheatgrasses and blue grama. It is frequently associated with mesquite in the Southwest. It occurs sparsely at 10,000 feet elevation in the Wasatch Mountains of Utah, growing on dry sandy or shallow clay loams in open grass-weed parks and on ridges.

Winterfat is grazed by all classes of livestock as well as by deer and elk. Bidwell and Wooton[1] state that it is good goat forage. Cotton[2] refers to its value for horses, and it is one of the more important winter-browse species for elk in the Jackson Hole country. The seeds, leafage, and young herbaceous stems are so relished that the plants are often closely cropped. Livestock thrive on winterfat range and are said to be remarkably free from disease because of the tonic properties of this plant.[3] A number of forage analyses of winterfat have been published[1 4] all showing a very high percentage of crude protein. This species is remakably resistant to drought because of its deep taproot and numerous extensive lateral roots. However, during unusually dry years, winterfat produces a very scant, somewhat brittle growth or may appear dead. Its ruggedness is displayed strikingly in its rapid recovery after a devitalizing drought. Even after a winter of minimum snowfall, if satisfactory spring and summer rains occur, this species grows rapidly and often develops 12 inches or more of new stems. Its most luxuriant summer growth depends on the storage of abundant winter moisture.

Persistent and continuous overgrazing has measurably reduced this plant on many ranges and has completely destroyed it on others. In western Utah winterfat has been almost completely replaced on thousands of acres of overgrazed winter ranges by small rabbitbrush (*Chrysothamnus stenophyllus*), and on many of these ranges no winterfat reproduction has occurred during the last 20 years. This shrub responds well to regulated grazing, grows luxuriantly under cultivation, and produces an abundance of viable seed. In New Mexico the germination of fresh seed was found to be almost twice as great as for seed stored 1 year at office-room temperature.

Winterfat has a deep taproot, numerous extensive lateral roots, many erect, herbaceous stems, and a freely branched, woody base which is often congested by the stubbed-off remnants of former stems. Male and female flowers usually occur on the same plant, although a few plants produce only female flowers. The soft, dense, branched, woolly hairs which beset the herbage are first ash-gray and subsequently become a rusty color.

[1] Bidwell, G. L., and Wooton, E. O. SALTBUSHES AND THEIR ALLIES IN THE UNITED STATES. U. S. Dept. Agr. Bull. 1345, 40 pp., illus. 1925.
[2] Cotton, J. S. A REPORT ON THE RANGE CONDITIONS OF CENTRAL WASHINGTON. Wash. Agr. Expt. Sta. Bull. 60, 45 pp., illus. 1904.
[3] Smith, J. G. FODDER AND FORAGE PLANTS, EXCLUSIVE OF THE GRASSES. U. S. Dept. Agr., Div. Agrost. Bull. 2, rev., 86 pp., illus. 1900.
[4] McCreary, O. C. WYOMING FORAGE PLANTS AND THEIR CHEMICAL COMPOSITION. STUDIES NO. 9. Wyo. Agr. Expt. Sta. Bull. 184, 23 pp., illus. 1931.
[5] Wilson, C. P. THE ARTIFICIAL RESEEDING OF NEW MEXICO RANGES. N. Mex. Agr. Expt. Sta. Bull. 189, 37 pp., illus. 1931.

APACHE-PLUME

Fallu'gia paradox'a, syn. *Siever'sia paradox'a*

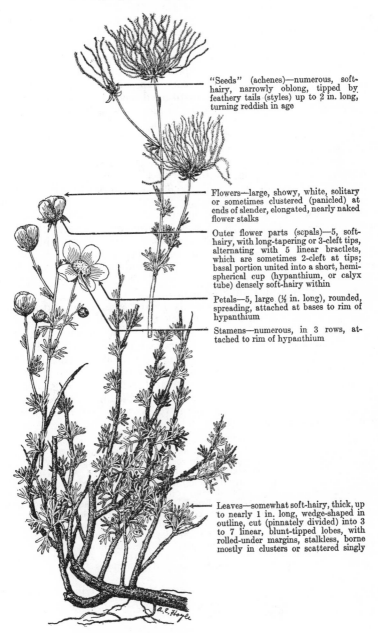

"Seeds" (achenes)—numerous, soft-hairy, narrowly oblong, tipped by feathery tails (styles) up to 2 in. long, turning reddish in age

Flowers—large, showy, white, solitary or sometimes clustered (panicled) at ends of slender, elongated, nearly naked flower stalks

Outer flower parts (sepals)—5, soft-hairy, with long-tapering or 3-cleft tips, alternating with 5 linear bractlets, which are sometimes 2-cleft at tips; basal portion united into a short, hemispherical cup (hypanthium, or calyx tube) densely soft-hairy within

Petals—5, large (½ in. long), rounded, spreading, attached at bases to rim of hypanthium

Stamens—numerous, in 3 rows, attached to rim of hypanthium

Leaves—somewhat soft-hairy, thick, up to nearly 1 in. long, wedge-shaped in outline, cut (pinnately divided) into 3 to 7 linear, blunt-tipped lobes, with rolled-under margins, stalkless, borne mostly in clusters or scattered singly

675

Apache-plume, also known as fallugie and poñil, is a many-branched, often evergreen shrub, typically 2 to 3 feet tall, but attaining 6 or 7 feet in height under the most favorable conditions. The name *Fallugia* commemorates Virgilio Fal(l)ugi, seventeenth century abbot of Vallombrosa, near Florence, Italy, and a writer on botanical subjects. This celebrated monastery in 1870 became the seat of the Italian Royal School of Forestry. The specific name, *paradoxa*, from two Greek words meaning contrary to opinion, was given to this plant because it is a shrub while other members of the genus, *Sieversia*, in which this species was originally placed, are herbaceous perennials. Its common name is derived from the fancied resemblance of its feathery-plumed seed clusters to the eagle-plumed war bonnets of the Apache Indians. Apache-plume belongs to the rose family (*Rosaceae*). The genus *Fallugia* is usually considered by conservative botanists to be "monotypic", consisting of the one species, *paradoxa*, only.

Apache-plume occurs from western Texas and southwestern Colorado to southern Nevada, southeastern California, and south into Mexico. It ordinarily grows at elevations of 5,000 to 7,500 feet in Arizona and New Mexico, although it extends up to 8,500 feet in northern New Mexico. While it attains its best development in deep, moist, rich sites, such as open canyon bottoms and the sides of arroyos, the species occurs in a great variety of soils, including dry, rocky ridges, from the lower brush types through the woodland (piñon-juniper) type to the open ponderosa pine belt. It is most common in the more southerly parts of its range where it usually occurs in sandy or clay loams.

This shrub is common, occasionally locally abundant, and of considerable importance on some ranges. In general, it is fair to low in palatability for cattle, sheep, and goats, but on some ranges it ranks as fairly good or even good forage for both cattle and sheep. Deer nibble at Apache-plume, sometimes to a fair extent, and possibly other game animals. Its chief value is on winter ranges where its small, bunched, evergreen leaves and relatively long, delicate twigs are attractive to grazing animals. It endures close grazing very well, shows excellent recuperative powers, and is a valuable natural aid in erosion control.

The Tewa Indians[1] of New Mexico use the smaller branches tied in bundles as brooms and the larger and straight branches for arrow shafts.

The leaves resemble those of cliffrose (*Cowania stansburiana*) but are neither glandular-dotted nor sticky (viscid). The bark of Apache-plume is white or light-colored and hairy (villous) on the young twigs, becoming hairless (glabrous) and somewhat shreddy on the older branches. The young branchlets of cliffrose are reddish brown and glandular and, before it peels off with age, the bark becomes more conspicuously shreddy or flaky than that of Apache-plume. The showy white flowers of Apache-plume appear as early as May or June. The rather dense plumelike seed clusters, at first greenish and later reddish-tinged, are very distinctive in the autumn.

Wooton and Standley[2] have called attention to the fact that this evergreen shrub is well worthy of cultivation for decorative purposes.

[1] Robbins, W. W., Harrington, J. P., and Freire-Marreco, B. ETHNOBOTANY OF THE TEWA INDIANS. U. S. Bur. Amer. Ethnol. Bull. 55, 124 pp., illus. 1916.
[2] Wooton, E. O., and Standley, P. C. FLORA OF NEW MEXICO. U. S. Natl. Mus., Contrib. U. S. Natl. Herbarium 19, 794 pp. 1915.

YELLOWLEAF SILKTASSEL

Gar'rya flaves'cens

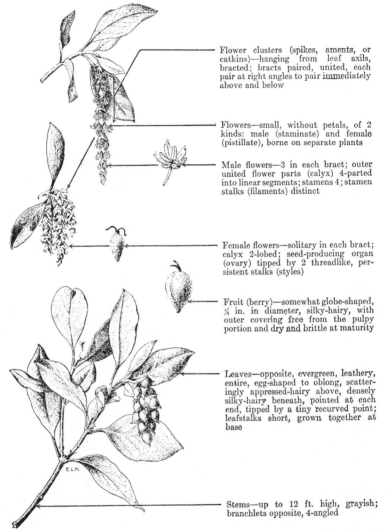

Flower clusters (spikes, aments, or catkins)—hanging from leaf axils, bracted; bracts paired, united, each pair at right angles to pair immediately above and below

Flowers—small, without petals, of 2 kinds: male (staminate) and female (pistillate), borne on separate plants

Male flowers—3 in each bract; outer united flower parts (calyx) 4-parted into linear segments; stamens 4; stamen stalks (filaments) distinct

Female flowers—solitary in each bract; calyx 2-lobed; seed-producing organ (ovary) tipped by 2 threadlike, persistent stalks (styles)

Fruit (berry)—somewhat globe-shaped, ¼ in. in diameter, silky-hairy, with outer covering free from the pulpy portion and dry and brittle at maturity

Leaves—opposite, evergreen, leathery, entire, egg-shaped to oblong, scatteringly appressed-hairy above, densely silky-hairy beneath, pointed at each end, tipped by a tiny recurved point; leafstalks short, grown together at base

Stems—up to 12 ft. high, grayish; branchlets opposite, 4-angled

Although the herbage of this evergreen shrub is beset with a whitish bloom and has a distinct grayish cast, the older leaves are faintly yellowish or golden. Yellowleaf silktassel has a rather restricted range, occurring in the desert-shrub, sagebrush, and piñon belts, chiefly on hillsides and in canyons in rather dry soils, from southeastern California and Arizona to southern Utah and Nevada. It is abundant in parts of Arizona. The leaves and twigs have a bitter flavor and, despite its evergreen habit, the plant is practically worthless as cattle and sheep browse under normal conditions. It is utilized to some extent by goats.

677

SILKTASSELS (Gar'rya spp.)

At least 14 species of silktassel are now recognized in North America; all, except one species of the West Indies, are native to the Western States and Mexico. Silktassels are considered by some authors to be closely related to the dogwoods (*Cornus* spp.) who place them in the dogwood family (Cornaceae). Other botanists regard these plants as forming a distinct plant family (Garryaceae), whose relationship is not certain but probably has closer affinity with the willow family (Salicaceae) than with the dogwoods. These shrubs mostly have a grayish hue and are easily recognized by the short-stalked, opposite, ever-green leaves, the opposite, four-angled branchlets, and the silky, pendent flower and fruit clusters which are (often conspicuously) bracted. As a rule, all parts of the silktassels are permeated with an intensely bitter, quininelike substance, which doubtless accounts for the general low palatability of the genus. The most common species of the western United States are Frémont silktassel (*G. fremon'tii*), Goldman silktassel (*G. goldma'nii*), tasseltree (*G. ellip'tica*), Wright silktassel (*G. wrigh'tii*), and yellowleaf silktassel (*G. flaves'cens*).

Frémont silktassel, locally called bearbrush and California feverbush, ranges from southern California to Washington, mostly on dry ridges and slopes at elevations of from 2,500 to 7,000 feet in the coastal ranges and in the Sierra Nevada Mountains. In California, it grows chiefly as scattered individuals in the chaparral and is largely inaccessible to livestock. In Oregon, the species has come in on burns and it is there generally regarded as fair browse and, in some localities, as one of the principal winter browse species. It is a shrub, mostly from 5 to 10 feet high, with elliptic or oblong, entire-margined leaves, about 1¼ to 2½ inches long, hairless and shining above and grayish hairy beneath or, in age, often very yellow and hairless beneath.

Goldman silktassel, a small species seldom over 3½ feet high, with densely hairy leaves, occurs in western Texas and southern New Mexico and is usually regarded as good goat feed.[1]

Tasseltree, known also as feverbush, quinine-bush, roundleaf silktassel, tree silktassel, and by other local names, ranges from Oregon to California, being common in the chaparral belt of California at elevations of from 100 to 2,500 feet. It is mostly worthless as forage for domestic livestock, although grazed slightly by goats. This is the only treelike species of the genus and the only species grown as an ornamental. It sometimes reaches a height of 20 feet. The leaves are elliptical or somewhat narrowed, with undulate and more or less rolled-back margins, hairless above, densely hairy beneath, and from 1½ to 2½ inches long. The "Forty-niners" used a tea made from a mixture of this species and Frémont silktassel as a substitute for quinine.[2]

Wright silktassel, known by a variety of local names—bearberry, chaparral, coffeeberry, feverbush, grayleaf dogwood, and quinine-bush—is a shrub from 1½ to 10 feet high with thick, evergreen, leathery, sharp-pointed, entire-margined leaves, usually less than twice as long as broad, sparsely hairy and grayish above and principally hairless and yellowish beneath. The male flower clusters, or catkins, are commonly more or less branched. The bark of the branches is smooth and dark red in color; that of the larger stems somewhat furrowed and grayish. This species grows from western Texas to central Arizona and south into Mexico, being found on dry rocky hillsides and in canyons, chiefly in the piñon-juniper belt, at elevations of from 5,000 to 8,000 feet, often in association with oakbrush (*Quercus* spp.), mountain-mahoganies (*Cercocarpus* spp.), manzanitas (*Arctostaphylos* spp.), and sumacs (*Rhus* spp.). Ordinarily, this shrub is regarded as practically worthless as livestock forage, although in southern Arizona it is sometimes grazed to some extent by cattle during the winter.[1] Chapline[3] reports that it has a moderately high palatability as goat browse, especially in summer.

---

[1] Dayton, W. A. IMPORTANT WESTERN BROWSE PLANTS. U. S. Dept. Agr. Misc. Pub. 101, 214 pp., illus. 1931.
[2] Chandler, K. AS CALIFORNIA WILD FLOWERS GROW: SUGGESTIONS TO NATURE LOVERS. 132 pp., illus. San Francisco. 1922.
[3] Chapline, W. R. PRODUCTION OF GOATS ON FAR WESTERN RANGES. U. S. Dept. Agr. Bull. 749, 35 pp., illus. 1919.

SALAL

Gaulthe'ria shal'lon

Flowers—white or pinkish, few to many, stalked, bracted, nodding, in 1-sided, glandular-hairy, axillary or terminal clusters (racemes) 3 to 6 in. long

United petals (corolla)—urn-shaped, ¼ to ⅜ in. long, 5-toothed at narrow opening, hairy; stamens 10, enclosed within corolla, with hairy stalks (filaments)

Outer united flower parts (calyx)—small at first, 5-lobed, hairy, persisting, enlarging and becoming fleshy as it encloses the developing fruit

Leaves — alternate, evergreen, shiny above, 1 to 4 in. long, egg-shaped to oblong, pointed at tip, rounded or heart-shaped at base, finely toothed around the edges

Stems—1 to 8 ft. high, erect or often somewhat spreading, crooked

"Berries"—black or dark purple, ball-shaped, somewhat flattened on top, ¼ to ½ in. in diameter

Salal, an attractive evergreen shrub of the heath family (Ericaceae), is a very common and characteristic undershrub of the luxuriant forests of the Northwest. It occurs on the Pacific slope, west of the Cascade and Sierra Nevada Mountains, ranging from Alaska to central California. Salal is usually one of the dominant species on the floor of the Douglas fir and Sitka spruce forests, being typically associated with such plants as Oregon-grape, vine maple, blueberries, and whortleberries (*Vaccinium* spp.), and western bracken. The floor of the redwood forests in the fog belt of California is often carpeted with this low undershrub. Although salal thrives best on acid soils in the forested areas, where it often forms an extensive evergreen layer it also occurs in openings, burns, and cut-over lands in the Douglas fir region. Under average growing conditions, salal usually appears as a low, spreading shrub, from 1 to 3 feet tall, but in the more favorable sites it grows luxuriantly, forming dense, almost impenetrable thickets sometimes 6 feet or more in height.

This plant is important mainly because of its great abundance, as it is generally rated worthless or low in palatability for all classes of livestock. Moreover, the extensive forested areas where this plant is most abundant are not ordinarily grazed by livestock. However, salal assumes a minor browse importance on cut-over and burned-over lands which are grazed by sheep. In studies of grazing use on Douglas fir cut-over lands in Washington, the late Douglas C. Ingram [1] found that utilization of salal foliage and tender stems by sheep for 2 successive years varied from zero to 55 percent, with yearly averages of 25 and 13 percent. Deer and elk also make light to moderate use of this shrub, especially in the winter, when its utility is enhanced by its evergreen foliage. The berries are eaten by bear and deer, and frequently constitute an important food for such birds as grouse and quail and for other wildlife.

Salal was discovered by Archibald Menzies (1754–1842), surgeon and naturalist for the Vancouver expedition, which explored the northwestern coast in the 1790's. It was later collected near the falls of the Columbia River and at its mouth by Capt. Meriwether Lewis. Lewis and Clark found that salal played an important part in the economy of the Pacific coast Indians.[2] The berries were converted into a delicious syrup used to flavor soups made of various boiled roots; the berries were also used for a kind of bread made by mashing them together and drying in the sun;[3] or were eaten raw. The fruit has a very agreeable flavor and even today is used for food by both the northwestern Indians and white people.

The early explorers understood the Indians to call the fruit sallon, shalal, or shallon. Specimens of salal carried East were identified by the botanist Frederick Pursh as a new species of *Gaultheria*, the genus to which the eastern wintergreen belongs. Pursh, availing himself of the aboriginal word, named the plant *Gaultheria shallon*. Years later, 1824 to 1832, David Douglas, the famous Scotch botanical explorer, found the Oregon Indians calling this plant salal, the name by which it is now best known.[2] Douglas was impressed by the palatability of the berries as well as by the possibilities of this shrub for ornamental plantings. Salal seeds were among the first plant materials which he sent back to England. This plant is now grown commonly as an ornamental in this country as well as in Europe. It is used effectively as an undershrub or border in shady portions of the garden, or in rockeries.

Two other species of *Gaultheria* are native to the West. Bush wintergreen (*G. ovatifo'lia*) is a low, depressed plant from 4 to 8 inches high, with somewhat hairy stems, small, sharp-pointed, egg-shaped leaves, five-eighths to 1½ inches long, small white bell-shaped flowers, and scarlet berries. It grows in the forests of the upper mountain slopes from British Columbia to Oregon and Idaho. It has no value as a forage plant, although the fruit is of excellent quality.

Western wintergreen (*G. humifu'sa*, syn. *G. myrsini'tes*) resembles bush wintergreen, but is much smaller, usually being less than 4 inches high, with leaves less than an inch long. This species is distributed from British Columbia and Alberta to California and Colorado.

The above two species resemble the wintergreen (*G. procumbens*) of northern and eastern North America, from which the commercial oil of wintergreen is distilled. The oil probably does not exist in the leaves, but is formed by a reaction between water and a neutral principle known as *gaultherin*, which is probably present in all three of the western species of *Gaultheria*.[4]

[1] Ingram, D. C. VEGETATIVE CHANGES AND GRAZING USE ON DOUGLAS FIR CUT-OVER LAND. Jour. Agr. Research [U. S.] 43 : 387–417, illus. 1931.

[2] Saunders, C. F. WESTERN WILD FLOWERS AND THEIR STORIES. 320 pp., illus. Garden City, N. Y. 1933.

[3] Lindley, J., and Moore, T. (edited by). THE TREASURY OF BOTANY, A POPULAR DICTIONARY OF THE VEGETABLE KINGDOM . . . 2 pts., illus. London, New York, and Bombay. 1899.

[4] Wood, H. C., Remington, J. P., and Sadtler, S. P., assisted by Lyons, A. B., and Wood, H. C., Jr. THE DISPENSATORY OF THE UNITED STATES OF AMERICA, BY DR. GEO. B. WOOD AND DR. FRANKLIN BACHE. Ed. 19, thoroughly rev. and largely rewritten . . . 1,947 pp. Philadelphia and London. 1907.

WHITESTEM GOOSEBERRY

Grossula′ria iner′mis, syns. *Ri′bes iner′me, R. pur′pusi, R. valli′cola* [1]

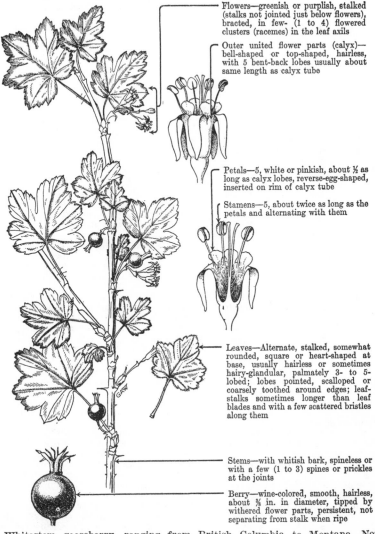

Flowers—greenish or purplish, stalked (stalks not jointed just below flowers), bracted, in few- (1 to 4) flowered clusters (racemes) in the leaf axils

Outer united flower parts (calyx)—bell-shaped or top-shaped, hairless, with 5 bent-back lobes usually about same length as calyx tube

Petals—5, white or pinkish, about ½ as long as calyx lobes, reverse-egg-shaped, inserted on rim of calyx tube

Stamens—5, about twice as long as the petals and alternating with them

Leaves—Alternate, stalked, somewhat rounded, square or heart-shaped at base, usually hairless or sometimes hairy-glandular, palmately 3- to 5-lobed; lobes pointed, scalloped or coarsely toothed around edges; leaf-stalks sometimes longer than leaf blades and with a few scattered bristles along them

Stems—with whitish bark, spineless or with a few (1 to 3) spines or prickles at the joints

Berry—wine-colored, smooth, hairless, about ⅜ in. in diameter, tipped by withered flower parts, persistent, not separating from stalk when ripe

Whitestem gooseberry, ranging from British Columbia to Montana, New Mexico, and California, is probably the most widespread and common of the western gooseberries. It is also known as smooth, wine, or common wild gooseberry. The specific name *inermis* is a Latin adjective meaning unarmed, and refers to the relative freedom of this gooseberry from spines. Whitestem gooseberry is an appropriate common name because the bark of this species is whitish. This shrub varies in height from 1 to 6 feet and is the least prickly of the western species, the stem prickles usually being rather weak and few

---

[1] Syn. *"R. saxosum"* of Coulter and Nelson's manual, not Hook.

in number. Whitestem gooseberry grows in aspen and open coniferous timber stands, in parks and meadows, and occasionally in dry, gravelly, or rocky sites, but attains its best development in rich, moist, alluvial soils such as frequently occur along streams where it is often abundant. This plant usually appears in association with willows. It grows most commonly at elevations of 6,000 to 9,000 feet, but is found as low as about 2,000 feet in the north and as high as about 9,500 feet in the south.[2]

Whitestem gooseberry is one of the better browse species of its genus, due to wide distribution, local abundance, practical freedom from objectionable spines, and numerous relatively large tender leaves, thus providing a considerable bulk of forage. However, the species is relatively low in palatability, being poor for cattle and fair for sheep, goats, deer, and elk.

GOOSEBERRIES (Grossula'ria spp.)

Gooseberries are ordinarily spiny shrubs, belonging to the gooseberry family (Grossulariaceae), a group some conservative botanists prefer to regard as a subfamily or tribe of the saxifrage family (Saxifragaceae). Gooseberries and currants (*Ribes* spp.) are closely related and so much alike that many authors combine them into the one genus *Ribes*. The gooseberries are chiefly distinct from the currants in that: (1) the flower or fruit stalks (pedicels) are not jointed just below the seed-producing organ (ovary), so that the mature fruit does not, as in the currants, break away from its stalk; (2) the stems are usually spiny at the nodes and also often bristly; (3) the flowers are borne in few-flowered clusters (racemes) or, rarely, solitary; (4) the fruits are frequently spiny. Technical differences also occur in the character of the outer united flower parts (calyx tube, or hypanthium) and in the occurrence and position of the bractlets on the pedicel. The presence of spines and bristles is not an entirely reliable distinction, because occasional gooseberry plants have practically smooth stems in contrast to the bristly stems of some of the currants. The flowers, fruits, and leaves of both genera are much alike superficially; the illustration of whitestem gooseberry is characteristic of the genus *Grossularia* as a whole.

The generic name *Grossularia* is from *grossula*, a New Latin name for gooseberry taken from Old French. The gooseberry genus is widespread in the North Temperate Zone and comprises about 60 species, of which approximately 23 species occur in our Western States. Gooseberries are very common and sometimes abundant, especially along streams, where they are frequently associated with alders and willows. However, they are widely distributed on both moist and dry sites, in the open and in rather dense shade from the lower elevations to timber line. These shrubs are usually poor browse plants, their palatability averaging poor for cattle and fair for sheep. Deer and elk browse them lightly. The very spiny species are probably less palatable than the species with few spines. However, despite their low palatability, the gooseberries furnish considerable browse, because of their wide distribution and local abundance.

The fruits of many species are acid, make excellent jelly, and are suitable for sauce and pie; the berries of most of the species are relished by birds and small animals. The gooseberries, as well as their close relatives, the currants, are of particular economic significance throughout the United States wherever white (5-needle) pines are important forest trees, because some species, and perhaps all of them, serve as alternate hosts of the fungus *Cronartium ribicola*, which causes white pine blister rust. The only practical control method is to destroy all gooseberries and currants in the vicinity of white pines.

Gooseberries, especially the European gooseberry (*G. reclina'ta*, syn. *Ribes grossula'ria*), have been cultivated abroad since the sixteenth century for their fruits.[3][4] Wedgeleaf gooseberry (*G. hirtel'la*, syns. *Ri'bes hirtel'lum*, *R. saxo'sum*), ranging from Newfoundland to Manitoba, South Dakota, West Virginia, and Pennsylvania, is the leading native species most commonly cultivated in the United States.

---

[2] Dayton, W. A. IMPORTANT WESTERN BROWSE PLANTS. U. S. Dept. Agr. Misc. Pub. 101, 214 pp., illus. 1931.

[3] Bailey, L. H., and Bailey, E. Z. HORTUS. A CONCISE DICTIONARY OF GARDENING, GENERAL HORTICULTURE AND CULTIVATED PLANTS IN NORTH AMERICA. 652 pp., illus. New York. 1930.

[4] Bailey, L. H. THE STANDARD CYCLOPEDIA OF HORTICULTURE . . . New ed., 3 v., illus. New York and London. 1933.

BROOM SNAKEWEED

Gutierre'zia saro'thrae, syns. *G. diversifo'lia, G. eutha'miae, G. linea'ris, G. longifo'lia, G. te'nuis*

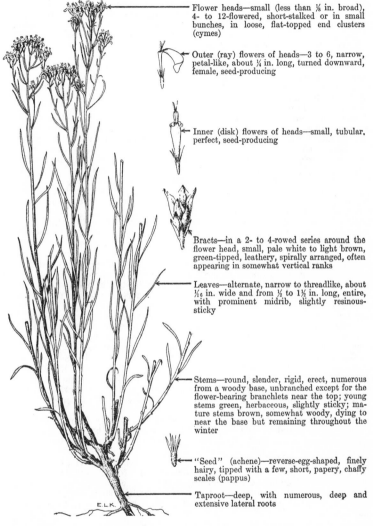

Flower heads—small (less than ⅛ in. broad), 4- to 12-flowered, short-stalked or in small bunches, in loose, flat-topped end clusters (cymes)

Outer (ray) flowers of heads—3 to 6, narrow, petal-like, about ¼ in. long, turned downward, female, seed-producing

Inner (disk) flowers of heads—small, tubular, perfect, seed-producing

Bracts—in a 2- to 4-rowed series around the flower head, small, pale white to light brown, green-tipped, leathery, spirally arranged, often appearing in somewhat vertical ranks

Leaves—alternate, narrow to threadlike, about ¹⁄₁₆ in. wide and from ½ to 1½ in. long, entire, with prominent midrib, slightly resinous-sticky

Stems—round, slender, rigid, erect, numerous from a woody base, unbranched except for the flower-bearing branchlets near the top; young stems green, herbaceous, slightly sticky; mature stems brown, somewhat woody, dying to near the base but remaining throughout the winter

"Seed" (achene)—reverse-egg-shaped, finely hairy, tipped with a few, short, papery, chaffy scales (pappus)

Taproot—deep, with numerous, deep and extensive lateral roots

Broom snakeweed, often known as broomweed, matchweed, turpentine-weed and yellow top, is a half-shrub with woody roots, crowns, and stem bases. The Mexicans often call it yerba-de-vibora and coyaye. In 1816 the genus was named after Piedro Gutierrez, a correspondent of the Madrid Botanical Garden. The specific name, a derivative of the Greek *sarotron* and the new Latin *sarothrum*, meaning broom, refers to the dense, broomlike bunches of dry, herbaceous stems.

On a conservative nomenclatural basis there are about 25 species of *Gutier-rezia*, all confined to the New World. About 10 occur in the United States, all in the West, with broom snakeweed the most common and abundant. It is widely distributed over the Western States, ranging from Alberta to Manitoba, western Texas, southern California, Nevada, and Idaho. It occurs principally on the plains, in semidesert valleys, on low-lying foothills and mountain slopes, at from 4,000 to 8,000 feet above sea level. This species is frequently abundant and conspicuous on desert ranges of the Intermountain Region, in association with shadscale, black sagebrush, dropseeds, gramas, and Indian ricegrass. On the foothills and in the juniper-piñon type, it is commonly associated with big sagebrush, rabbitbrushes, and downy chess; on the plains of western Kansas and Nebraska it is frequently found among gramas and buffalo grass; and in the Southwest it is common in the oak type and also on lower ranges, intermixed with mesquite and soapweed.

Broom snakeweed commonly inhabits dry, well-drained, sandy, gravelly, or clayey loams, but is able to grow on adobe and other heavy clay soils. It flourishes best on the moderately rich limestone clay loams of broad alluvial slopes, but also thrives on shallow, rocky, or sandy soils. It apparently does not occur on saline or alkaline soils.

Throughout most of its range this plant is considered worthless as forage. However, on the winter ranges, notably in western Utah and eastern Nevada, it ranks as fair forage for sheep but poor for horses and cattle during the fall and spring. Horses eat the plant during the winter, while sheep utilize it most directly after growth begins in the spring, presumably because it is one of the first to begin growth, sending out small green shoots at the base of the old dry stems of the previous season. Sheep often relish this young succulent foliage, but usually discard the dry, unpalatable stems. Such usage is unquestionably enhanced by the paucity of better, more palatable forages, which are particularly scarce early in the grazing season.

Broom snakeweed is a very aggressive plant, which rapidly invades areas where the climax vegetation has been depleted by fire, grazing, or drought. On many of the depleted semidesert ranges of western Utah and eastern Nevada, this plant frequently abounds over considerable areas. It occurs with downy chess on burnt-over big sagebrush areas in the Great Salt Lake district of Utah.[1] In eastern Colorado it rapidly invades depleted grama and buffalo grass ranges; in the Southwest, it is an excellent indicator of range deterioration, being one of the first plants to invade ranges where the better forage grasses have been decimated or destroyed by overgrazing.[2]

Although this species is unimportant as forage, being grazed chiefly, if not entirely, for lack of something better, it plays a definitely important role on ranges depleted of better vegetation in protecting the soil against wind and water erosion.[3] Wholesale depletion of the more palatable species, without the invasion of replacements, would result in very serious soil losses. However, this species is a much less valuable soil cover than many of the grasses, as recent studies of the Southwestern Forest and Range Experiment Station show that surface run-off and soil loss are much greater on partially depleted grama ranges invaded by broom snakeweed than on areas where the original grass cover still exists.

Heavy utilization of this plant by livestock probably results in sickness or death, as reported by the late Dr. C. D. Marsh, and by stockmen,[4] but the plant is, without question, frequently grazed by domestic animals without ill effects.

Broom snakeweed is often preyed upon and killed by certain borers and insects, such as species of *Crossidius, Diplotaxis, Mecas,* and *Aphis*.[4] Several species of aphids have been reported as feeding upon broom snakeweed in Utah.[5] This has encouraged the hope that, through them or other agencies, snakeweed may eventually be eradicated from areas where it is now a pest.

[1] Pickford, G. D. THE INFLUENCE OF CONTINUED HEAVY GRAZING AND OF PROMISCUOUS BURNING ON SPRING-FALL RANGES IN UTAH. Ecology 13 : 159–171, illus. 1932.
[2] Jardine, J. T.. and Forsling, C. L. RANGE AND CATTLE MANAGEMENT DURING DROUGHT. U. S. Dept. Agr. Bull. 1031, 84 pp., illus. 1922.
[3] Campbell, R. S., and Bomberger, E. H. THE OCCURRENCE OF GUTIERREZIA SAROTHRAE ON BOUTELOUA ERIOPODA RANGES IN SOUTHERN NEW MEXICO. Ecology 15 (1) : 49–61, illus. 1934.
[4] Dayton, W. A. IMPORTANT WESTERN BROWSE PLANTS. U. S. Dept. Agr. Misc. Pub. 101, 214 pp., illus. 1931.
[5] Pack, H. J., and Knowlton, G. F. A FEW MATCH BRUSH APHIDS FROM UTAH. Canad. Ent. 61: 199–204, illus. 1929.

ALPINE KALMIA

Kal'mia microphyl'la, syns. *K. glau'ca microphyl'la, K. polifo'lia microphyl'la*

"A" in the picture below represents the larger, coarser, longer- and broader-leaved bog kalmia (*K. polifolia,* syn. *K. glauca*), of which some botanists hold alpine kalmia to be a depauperate variety.

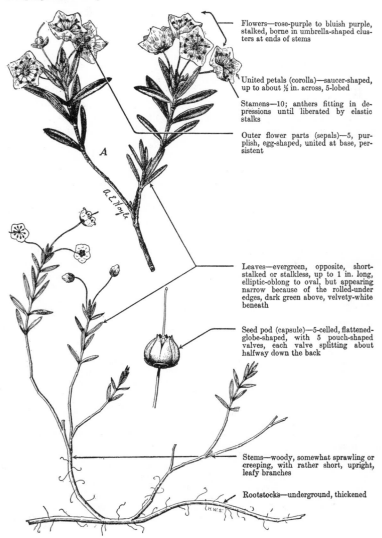

Flowers—rose-purple to bluish purple, stalked, borne in umbrella-shaped clusters at ends of stems

United petals (corolla)—saucer-shaped, up to about ½ in. across, 5-lobed

Stamens—10; anthers fitting in depressions until liberated by elastic stalks

Outer flower parts (sepals)—5, purplish, egg-shaped, united at base, persistent

Leaves—evergreen, opposite, short-stalked or stalkless, up to 1 in. long, elliptic-oblong to oval, but appearing narrow because of the rolled-under edges, dark green above, velvety-white beneath

Seed pod (capsule)—5-celled, flattened-globe-shaped, with 5 pouch-shaped valves, each valve splitting about halfway down the back

Stems—woody, somewhat sprawling or creeping, with rather short, upright, leafy branches

Rootstocks—underground, thickened

Alpine kalmia, often called dwarf or alpine bog kalmia, is a low evergreen shrub, usually 4 to 12 inches high, inhabiting cold, acid, subalpine areas from Alaska to Colorado and California. Despite its wide range, this plant is relatively uncommon, being limited to wet meadows, bogs, and lake and stream banks at high altitudes. It usually grows in full sunlight, frequently forming hummocks or islands in bogs, and clumps or sometimes extensive patches in meadows, where it is interspersed among patches of willows and blueberries. On very moist sites this shrub frequently occurs in mixture with moss, the two forming a complete ground cover.

Fortunately, alpine kalmia, which is poisonous to domestic livestock, is very unpalatable and is seldom grazed unless animals are forced to eat it. Moreover, much of the range where it is found is too wet and boggy to be grazed. These facts, and the short seasonal use of these subalpine areas by livestock, fortunately reduce the possibilities of its being extensively harmful. Clawson [1] and Fleming [2] have proved experimentally that alpine kalmia leaves are poisonous to cattle, sheep, and goats, with sheep the most susceptible. The lethal dose was not determined. However, the various feedings indicated that 0.3 percent of a sheep's weight in green foliage is toxic to that class of livestock, although as much as 2 percent was fed without causing death. Fleming (*op. cit.*) found that as little as 9 ounces sometimes caused poisoning of calves. His experiments indicated that the toxicity varies with the season and locality, but Clawson's work has thus far not supported this conclusion. Clawson describes the symptoms of alpine kalmia poisoning as "principally weakness and nausea, accompanied with salivation and vomiting, (which) may develop within less than 3 hours after a toxic dose has been eaten, or they may not be apparent for 14 hours or more. Poisoned animals may remain ill for more than 2 days and still recover."

The slender, branched, numerous stems of alpine kalmia arise from a rootstock, either singly or in a group. The practically stalkless (sessile) leaves are confined to the upper third of the branches, and are dark green above, whitish below, one-half to 1 inch long, and vary in shape from elliptic-oblong to oval, but appear narrower because the edges tend to roll downwards and inwards. The rose-purple, showy flowers are borne on erect, slender stalks in small terminal clusters. The pollen sacs (anthers) of the stamens are caught in depressions or pouches, giving the stalks (filaments) an elastic bend, so that when disturbed by an insect they spring out and dust its body with pollen. The small, somewhat globe-shaped seed pod (capsule) splits to discharge the seeds and eventually sheds its wall, but the center sometimes persists on the flower stem for another season.

Alpine kalmia is a dwarf shrub, from 4 to 12 (usually 6 to 8) inches high, with small, turned-under (revolute) leaves. It is frequently confused in the books with bog kalmia (*K. polifolia*, syns. *K. glauca*, *K. occidentalis*), which is a low, straggling shrub up to 28 inches in height, extending from Newfoundland and Labrador to Alaska, northern California, Manitoba, the Great Lakes region, and northern New Jersey. In contrast, alpine kalmia has an exclusively western range, and appears to be much more common than bog kalmia on western forest ranges. It was first published by the British botanist Hooker as a variety, *K. glauca microphylla*, and was raised to specific rank by Heller in 1898, under the name *K. microphylla* (Hook.) Heller. Rehder [3] later separated this into two varieties: *K. polifolia microphylla* (Hook.) Rehder, having the leaves mostly elliptical and scarcely revolute, and *K. polifolia rosmarinifolia* Rehd., with linear, strongly revolute leaves. Until

[1] Clawson, A. B. ALPINE KALMIA (KALMIA MICROPHYLLA) AS A STOCK-POISONING PLANT. U. S. Dept. Agr. Tech. Bull. 391, 10 pp., illus. 1933.
[2] Fleming, C. E. PROJECT 22. POISONOUS RANGE PLANTS. Nev. Agr. Expt. Sta. Ann. Rept. 1919 : 39–43. 1920.
[3] Rehder, A. MANUAL OF CULTIVATED TREES AND SHRUBS HARDY IN NORTH AMERICA . . . 930 pp., illus. New York. 1927.

botanical usage crystallizes in a uniform nomenclature for this difficult group, the Forest Service is following Tidestrom[4] in recognizing *K. microphylla* as specifically distinct from *K. polifolia*. The two species, however, if such they are, are very closely related, are apparently identical from a stock-poisoning standpoint, and are undoubtedly often confused with each other not only by stockmen but by scientific investigators.

KALMIAS

Kal'mia spp.

The kalmias compose a small genus of acid-soil plants of the heath family, represented in North America by about 6 species. There are two western species, both of which have been referred to above. Bog kalmia, like alpine kalmia, is also poisonous, a fact which somewhat increases the possibility of livestock losses as it grows under similar conditions but at somewhat lower elevations than alpine kalmia. The longer-leaved eastern species are larger plants, usually over 2 feet in height, with one species, mountain-laurel, or kalmia (*K. latifolia*), a large shrub sometimes becoming a tree over 20 feet high.

Most of the kalmias are desirable as ornamentals, being erect shrubs with attractive evergreen leaves and showy, rose-purple or white flowers. The eastern species, such as mountain-laurel and lambkill (*K. angustifolia*), inhabit wooded areas and, therefore, are more adaptable to cultivation than the western, subalpine species.

The name of the genus honors Peter Kalm, a student of Linnaeus, who collected plants in America during the eighteenth century.

The western kalmias are easily distinguished from most of the other shrubby western genera of the heath family by their small size and their occurrence at high altitudes and in typically moist and boggy sites. The exceptions to this rule are the two genera, mountainheaths (*Phyllodoce* spp.) and cassiopes (*Cassiope* spp.), that also inhabit the subalpine zone. The western representatives of these two genera somewhat resemble alpine kalmia in height, but are easily distinguishable in the field by their smaller and more numerous leaves (in *Cassiope*, scale-like), their more bell-shaped flowers, and their general occurrence on ridges, slopes, and meadow borders, rather than in very wet sites.

---

[4] Tidestrom, I. FLORA OF UTAH AND NEVADA. U. S. Natl. Mus., Contrib. U. S. Natl. Herbarium 25, 665 pp., illus. 1925.

RANGE RATANY

Krame'ria glandulo'sa

Stamens—4, united at the base

Petals—5, purplish, irregular, more or less united; 3 upper petals with narrow blades and long, clawlike bases; 2 lower petals very small, rounded

Outer flower parts (sepals)—5 (or 4), purplish, petal-like, unequal, larger than petals, soft-hairy and glandular on the back

Flowers—axillary, irregular, about ½ in. across, bracted, stalked; stalks densely hairy-glandular

Pods—burlike, 1-seeded, somewhat egg- or heart-shaped, covered with delicate, purple, barbed spines

Leaves—alternate, linear, covered with soft silky hair, stalkless, without bracts (stipules) at the base

Range ratany, also called purple heather because of its purple flowers, and heart-nut on account of its somewhat heart-shaped fruits, is a low, bushy, diffusely branched shrub, 1 to 2 feet high. When this shrub is abundant its bluish green twigs and foliage transmit a dull bluish tint to the landscape, a coloration characteristic of much of the southwestern low, desert-shrub range land. The generic name honors J. G. H. Kramer, an eighteenth century botanist, who was also a physician in the Austrian Army. The specific name *glandulosa* refers to the densely glandular character of the flower stalks and parts of the flower. The genus derives its common name from rhatany, the powerfully astringent root of *Krameria triandra*, of Peru, used in medicine as an astringent and tonic and also for coloring port wine.

This shrub ranges from western Texas to southern Utah, southern California and south into Mexico, being common at altitudes of from 2,000 to 4,500 feet, or higher, and growing on dry, hot foothills and mesas. It occurs on clayey, sandy, or rocky sites, but is most characteristic of gravelly soils. Catclaw, false-mesquite, Wright buckwheat-brush, galleta grass, and grama grasses are the common associates of range ratany. This plant also grows to some extent in the blackbrush (*Coleogyne*) associations of the Southwest, including southern Utah and southern Nevada. It usually occurs as scattered individuals, but is fairly abundant on many ranges and occasionally forms nearly pure stands on localized areas.

Range ratany is an important constituent of the forage supply on many of the lower southwestern ranges. It ranks from fair to fairly good in palatability for cattle and sheep and, on the average, from 25 to 50 percent of its foliage and current growth of stems are utilized on conservatively grazed range, depending upon the association in which it occurs. During dry years it is ordinarily cropped closely and is a good emergency forage. Goats browse it freely. Normally, the new growth is readily available to browsing animals but, under continued close cropping, the shrubs become slightly hedgy with spine-like twigs and thus protect themselves in some degree from excessive use. During favorable years it grows and flowers readily in the spring and again in late summer. The delicately spiny fruit matures rapidly and is disseminated readily by grazing animals, a fact which no doubt aids materially in spreading and maintaining this species.

The rather handsome, purplish, and attractively sweet-scented flowers suggest the possibility of using this shrub as an ornamental. The easily identifiable flowers and spiny, burlike fruit readily distinguish this shrub from other plants. Range ratany can be distinguished from other species of *Krameria* by the conspicuous stipitate glands on its flower stalks, outer flower parts, and occasionally on the leaves. The leaves are tipped by a fine, sharp point which soon drops off. The spines on the fruit of littleleaf ratany (*K. parvifolia*) are barbed throughout their entire length. White ratany (*K. grayi*, syn. *K. canescens* A. Gray (1852) not *K. canescens* Willd. (1825)), has the spines on the fruit barbed only at the tips. These two species, although not so widespread and abundant as range ratany, are relished by all classes of livestock.

SMOOTH LABRADOR-TEA

Le'dum glandulo'sum

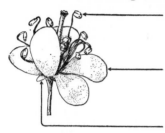

Stamens—usually 10, protruding; anthers opening by end pores

Petals—5, distinct, rounded, spreading

Outer flower parts (sepals)—5, almost distinct, very small, egg-shaped, blunt, persistent

Flowers—small (usually ¼ to ½ in. wide), white, slender-stalked, in clusters arising from large scaly buds usually at ends of branches

Leaves—alternate, evergreen, leathery, oblong to oval, up to 2½ in. long, short-stalked, hairless, dark green above, light and dotted with tiny golden glands beneath, edges entire

Stems—usually 2 to 5 ft. high, branched, mostly smooth, densely leafy towards the ends

Seed pod (capsule)—on recurving stalk, small (about ⅛ in. wide), oval, 5-celled, many-seeded, becoming dry and splitting upward from base along edge of each cell when ripe

There are three species of Labrador-tea in western North America, but smooth Labrador-tea, a leafy, evergreen shrub, is the only species of great importance. It is usually found in or just below the subalpine zones in acid bogs or swamps in the mountains and from British Columbia through the Cascades to the southern Sierras, and through the Rockies to western Wyoming and northern Utah. However, on the moist coastal regions of Washington, Oregon, and northern California it grows at low elevations near the ocean.

In California and in many places elsewhere, smooth Labrador-tea colonizes the edges of bogs, lakes, or streams in company with lodgepole pine or occurs as a shrubby fringe between the lodgepole pine belt and the sea. In the Cascades and the Rockies it is not so closely associated with lodgepole pine, but is commonly found in wet meadows and is often associated with willows along meandering streams. In the highland country, where moisture is abundant, it sometimes grows on slopes and in open timber stands. Smooth Labrador-tea is seldom eaten by domestic livestock, and because it is so little used, considerable difference of opinion regarding its poisonous properties has developed. It is not considered dangerous in the Rockies, and that viewpoint appears to be substantiated by the lack of authentic records of sheep losses from its use in that area. Smooth Labrador-tea is generally considered poisonous in the Pacific Coast States.[1][2] Hence, most sheepmen instruct their herders to avoid localities where this species is present. Marsh,[3] however, on the basis of actual feeding experiments, reports that it is only slightly toxic and probably never causes trouble under range conditions. It is possible that the prevalent Pacific coast opinion respecting the toxicity of this shrub may be due to the habit of certain sheepmen of referring to Labrador-tea and several closely related and poisonous shrubs as "blacklaurels". In California, for example, it is frequently confused with the very poisonous blacklaurel (*Leucothoë davisiae*), with which it is often associated. Although somewhat similar, blacklaurel is easily distinguished by its straight, uniformly leafy stems, larger leaves without resin dots beneath, and by the elongated, open flower or seed clusters, as well as by the more technical flower and fruit characters.

Smooth Labrador-tea is from 2 to 5 or occasionally 6 feet in height and rather stout. The flowers are borne usually during July.

LABRADOR-TEAS (Le'dum spp.)

The Labrador-teas compose a small genus of the heath family (Ericaceae) and are represented in North America by about six species. They characteristically inhabit acid soils of bogs and marshy places, mostly in the subalpine and alpine zones. The common name, Labrador-tea, now applied to the genus, was originally used for the so-called true Labrador-tea (*L. groenlandicum*) because of its use as a substitute for tea in the far North.

The genus is noteworthy in that the extracts of the foliage of the several species have varied uses. Crystal-tea (*L. palustre*) yields the glucoside ericolin, said to be a narcotic and sedative, and smooth Labrador-tea is locally used as an insecticide for cattle vermin and eradicating fleas.

As a group the Labrador-teas are of very low palatability or poisonous, or both, to domestic livestock, although certain species are reported to be important summer reindeer feed in Alaska.[4] Even if palatable, their use would be limited, as they usually inhabit bogs and swamps not readily accessible to domestic livestock.

The Labrador-teas are erect, branching, evergreen shrubs with alternate leaves which are fragrant, especially when crushed. The numerous white flowers are borne in a terminal umbel-like cluster. The petals are 5 and distinct; stamens 4 to 10, longer than the petals; anthers awnless. The fruit is a dry, five-celled capsule that opens from the base. They are further distinguished from the other genera in the heath family by their distinct petals.

---

[1] Jepson, W. L. A MANUAL OF THE FLOWERING PLANTS OF CALIFORNIA. 1,238 pp., illus. Berkeley, Calif. [1925.]

[2] Lawrence, W. E. THE PRINCIPAL STOCK-POISONING PLANTS OF OREGON. Oreg. Agr. Expt. Sta. Bull. 187, 42 pp., illus. 1922.

[3] Marsh, C. D. STOCK-POISONING PLANTS OF THE RANGE. U. S. Dept. Agr. Bull. 1245, rev., 75 pp., illus. 1929. Supersedes Bull. 575.

[4] Hadwen, S., and Palmer, L. J. REINDEER IN ALASKA. U. S. Dept. Agr. Bull. 1089, 74 pp., illus. 1922.

RUSSET BUFFALOBERRY

Lepargyre'a canaden'sis, syn. *Shepher'dia canaden'sis*

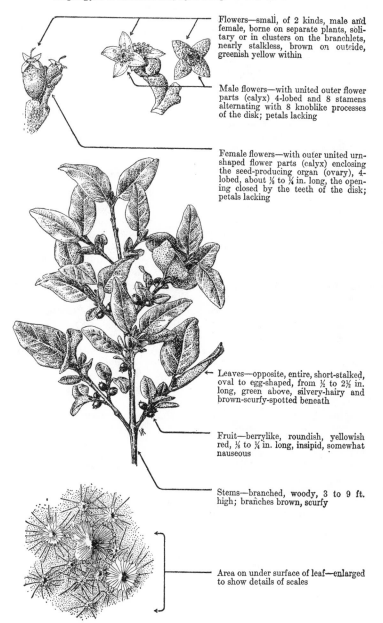

Flowers—small, of 2 kinds, male and female, borne on separate plants, solitary or in clusters on the branchlets, nearly stalkless, brown on outside, greenish yellow within

Male flowers—with united outer flower parts (calyx) 4-lobed and 8 stamens alternating with 8 knoblike processes of the disk; petals lacking

Female flowers—with outer united urn-shaped flower parts (calyx) enclosing the seed-producing organ (ovary), 4-lobed, about ⅛ to ¼ in. long, the opening closed by the teeth of the disk; petals lacking

Leaves—opposite, entire, short-stalked, oval to egg-shaped, from ½ to 2½ in. long, green above, silvery-hairy and brown-scurfy-spotted beneath

Fruit—berrylike, roundish, yellowish red, ⅛ to ¼ in. long, insipid, somewhat nauseous

Stems—branched, woody, 3 to 9 ft. high; branches brown, scurfy

Area on under surface of leaf—enlarged to show details of scales

Russet buffaloberry, a thornless shrub with opposite leaves, is known locally as Canadian or thornless buffaloberry, nannyberry, scurfy shrub, soopoolalia or soopolallie (Indian), wild oleaster, and wild olive. This shrub is widely distributed, ranging from Alaska to eastern Oregon, northern New Mexico, South Dakota, New York, Maine, Newfoundland and Labrador. It occurs chiefly in open, moist woods in the mountains in the ponderosa pine, aspen, and lodgepole pine belts but does not thrive in dense shade. Although usually scattered, this species is sometimes very abundant and even a predominating shrub, often becoming heavily established in old burns especially on north slopes where lodgepole pine is coming in.

This plant has little or no browse value for cattle and is usually considered worthless for sheep, but before frost occurs, in Idaho and Montana, it is regarded as of limited to fair value for sheep.[1] This species is also considered fairly good yearlong forage for deer and elk, especially in the Northwest.

BUFFALOBERRIES (Lepargyre'a spp., syn. *Shepher'dia spp.*)

Lepargyrea, a genus of shrubs with opposite, scurfy leaves, comprising three species, is confined wholly to the western and northern parts of North America. The name *Lepargyrea* is from the Greek *lepis*, a scale, and *arguros*, silver, and refers to the branched, star-shaped scales which beset the leaves. Russet buffaloberry is the most common and widely distributed. Silver buffaloberry (*L. argentea*), also known as redberry and bullberry, is often plentiful on moist hillsides, along streams, and in bottomlands at elevations of from 3,500 to 7,500 feet from Saskatchewan and Alberta to Kansas, New Mexico, and Nevada. Roundleaf buffaloberry (*L. rotundifolia*) is confined to southern Utah and the Grand Canyon region of Arizona, where it inhabits warm, dry, sandy, or rocky slopes.

Russet buffaloberry in Idaho and Montana is considered fair forage for sheep, but elsewhere is practically worthless as forage for domestic livestock. Silver buffaloberry is a thorny shrub, seldom browsed either by domestic livestock or game animals, but in Utah on heavily grazed pastures along the Green and Sevier Rivers, where this plant is fairly abundant, it is eaten by cattle and sheep. Roundleaf buffaloberry, on summer range, generally has little or no browse value for either domestic livestock or game animals and particularly if normal grazing conditions obtain. However, its evergreen character gives it local value on winter ranges where it is abundant.

The buffaloberries are prolific producers of small, berrylike, roundish fruits about one-eighth to one-fourth of an inch long, and, undoubtedly, these fruits are utilized for food by birds and small animals. Fruits of russet buffaloberry are yellowish red and are rather insipid and unpalatable to man, but the reddish (sometimes golden-yellow) sour fruits of silver buffaloberry are excellent for pies, jams, and jellies, and were extensively gathered by Indians and pioneers who preserved them by drying.

Silver buffaloberry is a shrub or small tree 6 to 20 feet high with whitish, somewhat thorny branches. The leaves are oblong, with a rounded apex, and are silvery-scaly on both surfaces. Roundleaf buffaloberry is a low, densely branched shrub with silvery branches and persistent rounded-oval leaves, densely silvery-scurfy on both sides. Its fruits are also scurfy.

[1] Dayton, W. A. IMPORTANT WESTERN BROWSE PLANTS. U. S. Dept. Agr. Misc. Pub. 101, 214 pp., illus. 1931.

BLACKLAUREL

Leuco'thoë davi'siae

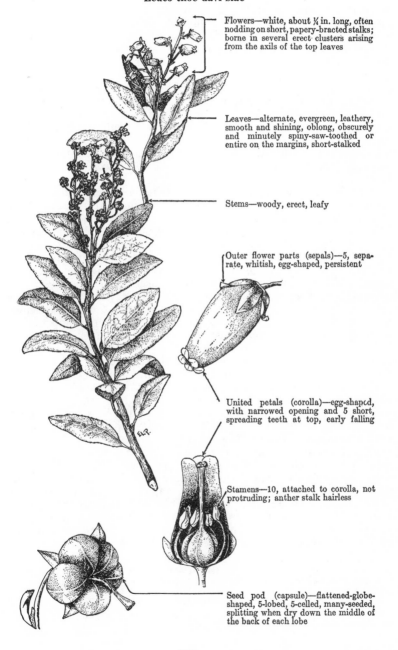

Flowers—white, about ¼ in. long, often nodding on short, papery-bracted stalks; borne in several erect clusters arising from the axils of the top leaves

Leaves—alternate, evergreen, leathery, smooth and shining, oblong, obscurely and minutely spiny-saw-toothed or entire on the margins, short-stalked

Stems—woody, erect, leafy

Outer flower parts (sepals)—5, separate, whitish, egg-shaped, persistent

United petals (corolla)—egg-shaped, with narrowed opening and 5 short, spreading teeth at top, early falling

Stamens—10, attached to corolla, not protruding; anther stalk hairless

Seed pod (capsule)—flattened-globe-shaped, 5-lobed, 5-celled, many-seeded, splitting when dry down the middle of the back of each lobe

Blacklaurel, an evergreen shrub up to 5 feet in height, is the only member of the genus *Leucothoë* of the heath family (Ericaceae) native to western America. The species is limited to California, growing in moist sites in the subalpine zones of the central and northern Sierras, and in the Coast Range in Mendocino and Trinity Counties. The origin of the common name, blacklaurel, is somewhat obscure. The eastern ericaceous shrubs, notably kalmias and rhododendrons, were called laurels by the early settlers because of the superficial resemblance of their leathery, evergreen leaves to those of the laurel tree (*Laurus nobilis*) of southern Europe, crowns of which were worn by the ancient Greeks and Romans as a sign of victory in athletic sports, or other distinction. In North America the term "laurel" is now loosely applied to numerous ericaceous shrubs. The name blacklaurel probably originated because of the black stems or possibly the dark green leaves of this species, which are a decided contrast to the rather paler stems and the light-colored leaves of western azalea (*Azalea occidentalis*), also frequently called laurel.

Blacklaurel is seldom abundant, occurring only in isolated patches, frequently at widely separated points. It characteristically grows in loose colonies. The stems are typically solitary and unbranched, of irregular lengths, and usually bent from the weight of repeated, heavy winter snows. This shrub prefers moist, shady areas, growing under lodgepole pine, along moist meadow and stream borders, and on moist slopes in company with red fir and Jeffrey and white pines. Alders, spireas, and smooth Labrador-tea (*Ledum glandulosum*) are frequently shrubby associates of blacklaurel. Sometimes it is so mixed with smooth Labrador-tea that the two may not be easily distinguishable, except when in flower. Smooth Labrador-tea, however, is more bushlike and has many angular branches that are densely leafy near the summits; the fragrant leaves are glandular-dotted and felty below, and closely subtend the numerous crowded, rather flattened and distinct-petaled flowers.

Blacklaurel is of very low palatability and is probably but rarely grazed by cattle and only occasionally by sheep. Sheep, however, do graze it when hungry, especially when leaving bedgrounds and on long drives. Even this limited use is undesirable, as the foliage is very poisonous. Marsh [1] states that "experimental work shows that very small quantities will poison sheep and that death may be produced by between 1 and 2 ounces" of the green foliage. The symptoms are irregular respiration, frothing at the mouth, vomiting, grinding of the teeth, weakness and a staggering gait, and, in severe cases, inability to stand. Practically the only remedy is to administer some such purgative as Epsom salts to expedite elimination of the poisonous material. The wisest procedure for the sheepman is to instruct his herders to avoid blacklaurel patches.

Blacklaurel plants range from 2 to 5 feet in height. The dark green, oblong leaves vary from 1 to 3 inches in length and are alternately arranged on the straight, leafy stems. The small, white, often drooping flowers are borne during June or July.

---

[1] Marsh, C. D. STOCK-POISONING PLANTS OF THE RANGE. U. S. Dept. Agr. Bull. 1245, rev., 75 pp., illus. 1929. Supersedes Bull. 575.

BEARBERRY HONEYSUCKLE

Loni'cera involucra'ta, syns. *Diste'gia involucra'ta, Xylos'teon involucra'tum*

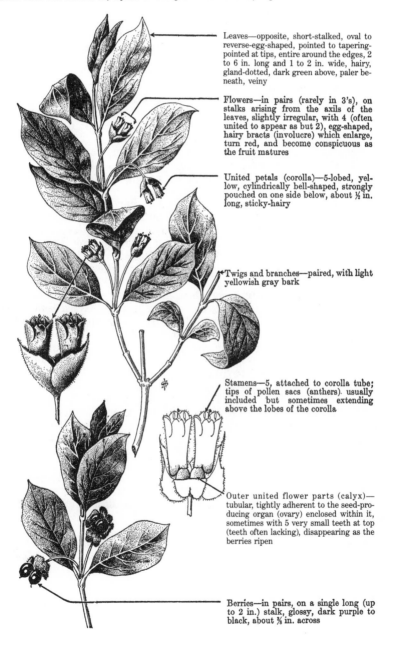

Leaves—opposite, short-stalked, oval to reverse-egg-shaped, pointed to tapering-pointed at tips, entire around the edges, 2 to 6 in. long and 1 to 2 in. wide, hairy, gland-dotted, dark green above, paler beneath, veiny

Flowers—in pairs (rarely in 3's), on stalks arising from the axils of the leaves, slightly irregular, with 4 (often united to appear as but 2), egg-shaped, hairy bracts (involucre) which enlarge, turn red, and become conspicuous as the fruit matures

United petals (corolla)—5-lobed, yellow, cylindrically bell-shaped, strongly pouched on one side below, about ½ in. long, sticky-hairy

Twigs and branches—paired, with light yellowish gray bark

Stamens—5, attached to corolla tube; tips of pollen sacs (anthers) usually included but sometimes extending above the lobes of the corolla

Outer united flower parts (calyx)—tubular, tightly adherent to the seed-producing organ (ovary) enclosed within it, sometimes with 5 very small teeth at top (teeth often lacking), disappearing as the berries ripen

Berries—in pairs, on a single long (up to 2 in.) stalk, glossy, dark purple to black, about ⅜ in. across

Bearberry honeysuckle, also known as bearberry, fly honeysuckle, inkberry, and skunkberry, is a freely branching shrub which is usually erect but sometimes has reclining stems and is more or less vinelike. It is usually 3 to 6 feet high, but occasionally (especially in the Pacific coastal form called by some botanists variety *ledebourii*) attains a height of 9 feet. The glossy, dark, almost black fruits, with their unpleasant taste, give rise to the common names of inkberry and skunkberry. The specific name *involucrata* refers to the bracts (involucre) at the base of the flowers, which enlarge, turn red, and become very conspicuous as the fruit develops.

Bearberry honeysuckle is probably the best known and the commonest of the western honeysuckles. It is widely distributed, ranging from New Brunswick to Alaska, California, Mexico, and the shores of Lake Superior. In the Northwest it is found at elevations up to about 6,500 or 7,000 feet; in Colorado it may grow at altitudes up to 9,000 feet in the lodgepole pine and spruce belts. Moist situations, such as areas contiguous to springs, creek banks, tidelands, and the like, are its favorite haunts. Its common plant associates are willows and alders.

In a few localities, such as in southwestern Montana, southern Idaho, and northern Utah, bearberry honeysuckle is reputed to be fair or fairly good sheep browse, and is also slightly cropped by cattle. Generally, however, it is either poor forage for sheep or worthless for all classes of livestock. Near Yellowstone National Park in Montana elk are reported to graze the young shoots in winter.

Stockmen occasionally report bearberry honeysuckle as poisonous to livestock, especially to cattle, but there is no experimental evidence to support this belief. This species is known to contain saponin, a toxic alkaloid widely distributed in the vegetable kingdom. It seems doubtful, however, that bearberry honeysuckle contains sufficient saponin to endanger livestock on the range. The U. S. Dispensatory,[1] on the authority of "Mérat and De Lens", states that "the fruit of all the species of *Lonicera* is said to be emetic and cathartic."

The lustrous purple-black fruits, with their conspicuous red bracts, give this species of honeysuckle some value as a cultivated ornamental shrub, and several horticultural varieties of it have been developed.

A larger form, Ledebour honeysuckle (*L. ledebourii*, syns. *Distégia ledebourii, Xylosteon ledebourii,* and *L. involucráta ledebourii*), typical of the Pacific coastal region, is regarded as a synonym of bearberry honeysuckle by some botanists and as a variety of it by others.

---

[1] Wood, H. C., Remington, J. P., and Sadtler, S. P., assisted by Lyons, A. B., and Wood, H. C., Jr. THE DISPENSATORY OF THE UNITED STATES OF AMERICA, BY DR. GEO. B. WOOD AND DR. FRANKLIN BACHE. Ed. 19, thoroughly rev. and largely rewritten . . . 1,947 pp. Philadelphia and London, 1907.

HOLLYGRAPES

Odoste'mon spp., syn. *Ber'beris spp.*,[1] *Maho'nia spp.*

About a dozen species of hollygrape are commonly found on the western ranges. They are evergreen shrubs of the barberry family (Berberidaceae) and are merged by many botanists with the barberry genus (*Berberis*). However, certain characters of this group of plants give them an entirely different aspect from the true barberries; for example, the spineless stems; evergreen, pinnately compound leaves with prickly toothed leaflets; terminal flower clusters; and the mostly spherical, blue berries. Some botanists retain the generic name *Mahonia* for the hollygrapes; *Odostemon*, however, is the oldest and therefore has the right of priority. The name *Odostemon* is obviously manufactured from the Greek and appears to mean swollen stamen, referring to the dilated stalks (filaments) of the stamens of many species. The various species are known by such English names as barberry, hollyleaf barberry, mahonia, and Oregon-grape. It seems preferable to use the name Oregon-grape only for the Oregon State flower (*O. aquifolium*) and to designate the other species as hollygrapes.

As a group the hollygrapes are widely distributed throughout all of the far western States and cover a wide range of habitat conditions. Most species are associated with coniferous forests, shady aspen woodlands, or brushy hillsides, yet some thrive on arid slopes and ridges in the juniper-piñon belt of the Southwest. These plants are normally unpalatable to livestock, being, at best, only poor forage plants. However, they merit mention because of their actual or potential economic significance. Several species are grazed with low to moderate relish by game animals, especially during the fall and winter. The hollygrapes often grow on steep, rocky, thin-soiled slopes and on such sites have definite erosion-control value. The fruit of hollygrapes is valued for jelly and preserves and, on occasion, is eaten raw. The bark, roots, and berries of some species are used medicinally; the Indians formerly extracted a yellow dye from the wood and used it in dyeing clothing, baskets, and other articles. In addition, some species are highly valued as ornamentals.

Creeping hollygrape (*O. re'pens*), the most common and widespread of the western species, ranges from southeastern British Columbia, along the east side of the Cascade and Sierra Nevada Mountains, to Arizona, New Mexico, and the Black Hills of South Dakota. This plant is frequently confused in the literature with *O. aquifolium*, with which it is often erroneously merged by authors. Creeping hollygrape is a low, trailing shrub, 4 to 12 inches high, with a few compound leaves made up of two to seven roundish to egg-shaped leaflets margined with numerous teeth, which are armed with weak prickles. Because of its low growth, creeping hollygrape can usually be readily distinguished from the taller, true Oregon-grape. In addition, the leaves of creeping hollygrape have fewer

---

[1] In part.

leaflets, and the teeth usually have weaker spines, although there are many intermediate forms. Differences in leaf surface, however, are most useful in recognizing these plants: The leaflets of Oregon-grape are nearly always shiny above and pale green, but never whitish underneath, whereas those of creeping hollygrape are nearly always dull on top and whitish beneath. Moreover, *O. aquifolium* is chiefly confined to the western side of the Cascades and does not occur in the Rockies; hence there is little possibility of confusing the two species except where their ranges merge on the eastern side of the Cascade Mountains. Creeping hollygrape is also the hardier species, which is of importance in the horticultural use of these plants.

The economic values of creeping hollygrape are similar to those of Oregon-grape and most of the other hollygrapes. It is usually ranked as worthless forage for all classes of livestock, but the leafage is sometimes grazed slightly by sheep and game animals when other browse is scarce. In 1919 the loss of cattle on a driveway of the Tonto National Forest in Arizona was attributed by stockmen to creeping hollygrape. The late Dr. C. D. Marsh of the Bureau of Animal Industry, United States Department of Agriculture, however, emphasized that, although this plant contains certain toxic alkaloids, which have medicinal value, it is only slightly poisonous and, because of its low palatability, is not likely to cause losses.

Longleaf hollygrape (*O. nervo'sus*), also called scaly Oregon-grape, is one of the most common hollygrapes of the Northwest. It ranges from Vancouver Island and British Columbia to California with local occurrence in extreme western Idaho. This plant is closely associated with the Douglas fir forests of the coast region, being one of the abundant undershrubs, especially on the poorer well-drained soils in the uplands of the Douglas fir type. It is usually known as Oregon-grape and is often confused with *O. aquifolium*, with which it is frequently associated. This species is a low plant from 6 to about 18 inches in height, with long, stiff, fernlike foliage clustered at the top of a short woody stem. Each leaf has 11 to 21 lance-shaped to egg-shaped, bristle-toothed leaflets, which have 3 to 5 main veins radiating from near the base. This species is almost worthless as forage, but is browsed lightly during the winter by game animals.

Frémont hollygrape (*O. fremon'tii*) and red hollygrape (*O. haematocar'pus*) are large shrubs characteristic of brush types on dry slopes and ridges of the piñon-juniper belt in the Southwest. Red hollygrape also occurs at lower elevations in the catclaw belt, particularly in southern New Mexico and southern Arizona. Both species are known in the Southwest as algerita, agarita, agrillo, and yellowwood. These bushy shrubs grow from 3 to 10 or 12 feet high, have small, spiny leaves less than 1¼ inches long, and, in general, resemble one another markedly. Frémont hollygrape has dry, inflated dark blue berries, whereas red hollygrape has juicy, blood-red berries. Sometimes cattle, horses, and deer crop the leaves and shoots in the winter or at times when other feed is scarce. The Navaho Indians extracted a yellow dye from the bark and roots.[2]

---

[2] Saunders, C. F. USEFUL WILD PLANTS OF THE UNITED STATES AND CANADA. Ed. 3, rev., 275 pp., illus. New York, 1934.

OREGON-GRAPE

Odoste′mon aquifo′lium, syns. *Ber′beris aquifo′lium, Maho′nia aquifo′lium*

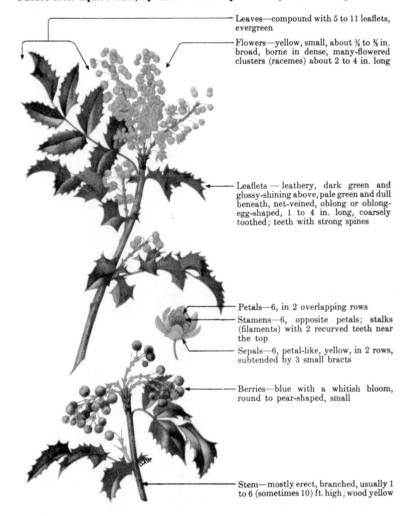

Leaves—compound with 5 to 11 leaflets, evergreen

Flowers—yellow, small, about ⅛ to ⅜ in. broad, borne in dense, many-flowered clusters (racemes) about 2 to 4 in. long

Leaflets — leathery, dark green and glossy-shining above, pale green and dull beneath, net-veined, oblong or oblong-egg-shaped, 1 to 4 in. long, coarsely toothed; teeth with strong spines

Petals—6, in 2 overlapping rows

Stamens—6, opposite petals; stalks (filaments) with 2 recurved teeth near the top

Sepals—6, petal-like, yellow, in 2 rows, subtended by 3 small bracts

Berries—blue with a whitish bloom, round to pear-shaped, small

Stem—mostly erect, branched, usually 1 to 6 (sometimes 10) ft. high; wood yellow

Oregon-grape, the State flower of Oregon, is an attractive evergreen shrub with erect or branched stems usually from 1 to 6 (occasionally up to 10) feet tall. Capt. Meriwether Lewis, of the Lewis and Clark expedition, discovered this handsome plant in April 1806 at the Great Rapids or Cascades of the Columbia River, near what is now Cascade Locks, Oreg. In his journal Lewis referred to Oregon-grape as "mountain holly", probably because of the similarity of its shiny, evergreen, prickly-toothed leaves to those of the common cultivated English holly (*Ilex aquifolium*), a tree whose scientific name traces back to the Roman naturalist Pliny (23–79 A. D.). In fact, *aquifolium* (literally, sharp-leaf) later came to mean holly and, with this significance and resemblance in mind, was adopted by the Saxon botanist Pursh, who spent the years 1799–1811 in botanical travel in North America, as the specific name of Oregon-grape. The English name, hollygrape, now standardized for the genus, in turn refers to the hollylike character of the foliage of these shrubs.

It is fitting that this handsome, conspicuous shrub, which is so intimately associated with the magnificent forests of the Northwest, should be chosen as the floral emblem of the State of Oregon. During the spring the shiny green leaves of Oregon-grape and its fragrant, bright yellow flower clusters form a rare and beautiful combination; the bunches of dark waxy blue berries lend color to the woods in late summer and early autumn, but it is not until winter, when the polished leaves turn bronze and crimson, that this plant is at its best. It is a beautiful shrub in any season.

Oregon-grape is essentially a plant of the Northwest, as it ranges from British Columbia to northern California. It occurs principally in the Douglas fir region west of the Cascade Mountains, but is also common on the eastern slope of the Cascades and, according to Piper,[1] extends eastward to western Idaho. This species usually grows on the floor of coniferous forests in moderately moits, rich, humous soils. It is common on rocky slopes and canyon bottoms in the shade, but also occurs occasionally on drier, openly exposed, rocky slopes, on brushy hillsides, or under stands of aspen, alder, or other hardwoods. Oregon-grape extends from sea level to the summit of the Cascades. It often grows in abundance, being one of the most conspicuous undershrubs in the Douglas fir forests.

Oregon-grape is practically worthless as livestock forage because it is not ordinarily consumed except on overgrazed ranges or areas where palatable vegetation is naturally scarce. However, it is browsed lightly to moderately by both deer and elk, especially in the fall and winter, when deciduous shrubs have lost their leaves, and the herbaceous vegetation has largely disappeared.

This species has been extensively cultivated as an ornamental both in this country and in Europe. Although too large for small rock gardens, it is useful in larger gardens, particularly when pruned regularly to prevent the plant from becoming leggy.[2] The attractive winter foliage is often used for Christmas decorations. The berries are very acid until touched by frost, when they become more palatable. The fruit is often made into jelly, and the juice, reputedly, makes excellent wine. The Indians eat the berries raw. The wood of this plant, as well as of the other western hollygrapes, is a bright golden-yellow and has been utilized by some aboriginal tribes in making yellow dye. The bitter bark of the roots has long been recognized for its valuable medicinal properties; a decoction made from the bark is a favorite tonic of the Indians, being used both as a cure for stomach troubles and as a blood purifier. Extracts of the bark of Oregon-grape are now used in modern medicine as an alterative, laxative, and tonic in the treatment of various diseases.

[1] Piper, C. V. THE IDENTIFICATION OF BERBERIS AQUIFOLIUM AND BERBERIS REPENS. U. S. Natl. Mus., Contrib. U. S. Natl. Herbarium 20 : 437–451, illus. 1922.
[2] Gabrielson, I. N. WESTERN AMERICAN ALPINES. 271 pp., illus. New York, 1932.

MALLOW NINEBARK

Opulas'ter malva'ceus, syns. *O. pauciflo'rus, Physocar'pus malva'ceus, P. pubes'cens*

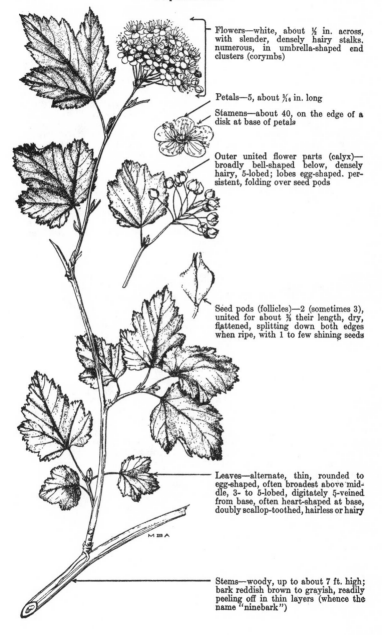

Flowers—white, about ½ in. across, with slender, densely hairy stalks. numerous, in umbrella-shaped end clusters (corymbs)

Petals—5, about ³⁄₁₆ in. long

Stamens—about 40, on the edge of a disk at base of petals

Outer united flower parts (calyx)—broadly bell-shaped below, densely hairy, 5-lobed; lobes egg-shaped. persistent, folding over seed pods

Seed pods (follicles)—2 (sometimes 3), united for about ⅔ their length, dry, flattened, splitting down both edges when ripe, with 1 to few shining seeds

Leaves—alternate, thin, rounded to egg-shaped, often broadest above middle, 3- to 5-lobed, digitately 5-veined from base, often heart-shaped at base, doubly scallop-toothed, hairless or hairy

Stems—woody, up to about 7 ft. high; bark reddish brown to grayish, readily peeling off in thin layers (whence the name "ninebark")

Mallow ninebark, probably the commonest and most widely distributed species of *Opulaster* in the West, is an erect, ornamental shrub, usually from 3 to 7 feet high, with alternate, thin, three- to five-lobed, double-toothed leaves, and numerous white flowers in dense, terminal, somewhat umbrella-shaped clusters. The specific name *malvaceus*, meaning mallowlike, refers to the similarity of the leaves of this species to those of certain species of mallow (*Malva*). Mallow ninebark occurs from British Columbia to Oregon, Nevada, Wyoming, and Montana. It is characteristic of dry rocky slopes, cliffs, and canyon sides in the open and in scattered timber. Its leaves, which turn a deep red brown in the fall, are often a conspicuous feature of the landscape, especially in the Great Basin. This shrub also grows along mountain streams, in canyon bottoms, on north slopes, and in rather heavy timber extending over a wide altitudinal range, from the sagebrush belt into the spruce-fir belt.

This species is abundant in many areas and produces an immense amount of foliage, which is grazed to some extent by cattle, sheep, and goats, generally being poor forage for cattle, fair for sheep, and fairly good for goats. On some ranges it is more valuable, but reports of higher palatability generally represent ranges where better forage plants have been depleted. Ordinarily this shrub has a relatively low, rounded or open growth habit favoring its use as a browse species. It is probably never grazed heavily enough to be seriously damaged, and is of little value on winter range, because it loses its leaves in the fall.

NINEBARKS (Opulas'ter spp., syn. *Physocar'pus spp.*)

The ninebarks, so-called from the supposedly nine layers of thin, exfoliating bark on the stems, compose a relatively small, chiefly North American genus of shrubs belonging to the rose family (Rosaceae). The name *Opulaster* suggests the resemblance of these bushes to *Opulus*, i. e., what is now called the European cranberrybush (*Viburnum opulus*). About 13 species have been distinguished in North America, and one species is native to Manchuria. On a conservative basis, some nine species grow in the West, being recognized by the exfoliating bark, the alternate, three- to five-lobed, toothed leaves, resembling the leaves of currants and gooseberries, and the dense, umbrella-shaped clusters of small, white, or pinkish flowers with five petals and numerous (20 to 40) stamens borne at the edge of a disk at the base of the petals. The fruits consist of from one to five small, dry, somewhat inflated capsules, which when split open discharge the few, small, pear-shaped seeds.

In general, the ninebarks are inferior browse plants, their palatability averaging about poor for cattle and fair for sheep and goats. Their abundance and bushy growth habit, which is conducive to easy utilization, gain considerable importance for the ninebarks as browse species, however.

Mallow ninebark, mountain ninebark (*O. mono'gynus*), and Pacific ninebark (*O. capita'tus*) are probably the most important among western ninebarks. Mountain ninebark occurs in the aspen and spruce belts from the Black Hills in South Dakota to Wyoming, Texas, and New Mexico and is probably the only species growing in the Southwest. It is a rather low shrub, seldom over 40 inches high, and has densely hairy, somewhat inflated fruits with ascending beaks and currantlike, rather deeply three- to five-lobed, sharply toothed leaves about three-fourths of an inch to 1½ inches long. This species is abundant on some New Mexican ranges at middle elevations, but is only a poor to fair browse plant. Pacific ninebark, ranging from California to Idaho and British Columbia, is apparently the only species which grows in California. It is common along streams and is often abundant on steep north slopes in the coast ranges in California at elevations of from 500 to 4,500 feet; elsewhere, it is mostly scattered. This erect or straggly shrub, from 3 to 5 feet high, has roundish, three- to five-lobed, toothed leaves, hairless above and often hairy beneath. The leaves are about 1 to 3 inches long (larger on the sterile shoots), borne on leafstalks from one-half of an inch to 1½ inches long. Each flower usually produces five hairless spreading capsules, which are somewhat longer than the outer flower parts. The palatability of this species is probably about average for the genus.

The ninebarks are rather attractive hardy shrubs and several species are valued as ornamentals.

ENGELMANN PRICKLYPEAR

Opun'tia engelman'ni

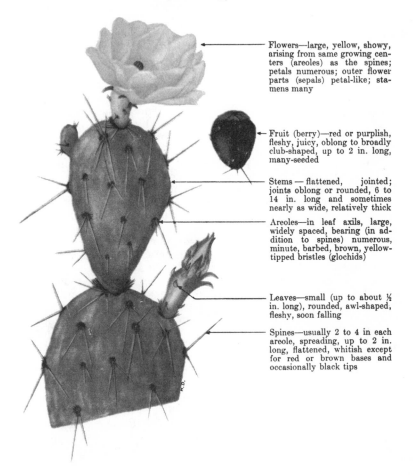

Flowers—large, yellow, showy, arising from same growing centers (areoles) as the spines; petals numerous; outer flower parts (sepals) petal-like; stamens many

Fruit (berry)—red or purplish, fleshy, juicy, oblong to broadly club-shaped, up to 2 in. long, many-seeded

Stems — flattened, jointed; joints oblong or rounded, 6 to 14 in. long and sometimes nearly as wide, relatively thick

Areoles—in leaf axils, large, widely spaced, bearing (in addition to spines) numerous, minute, barbed, brown, yellow-tipped bristles (glochids)

Leaves—small (up to about ½ in. long), rounded, awl-shaped, fleshy, soon falling

Spines—usually 2 to 4 in each areole, spreading, up to 2 in. long, flattened, whitish except for red or brown bases and occasionally black tips

Engelmann pricklypear, a semierect, branched plant commonly growing in dense patches about 3 to 5 (occasionally up to 6 or 7) feet high, or as isolated individuals 1 to 5 feet in diameter, is a characteristic representative of the group of cacti with flattened stem joints commonly known as pricklypears. The flowers of this species are a rich, bright yellow and, as is characteristic of the pricklypear group as a whole, are very showy and beautiful. Patches of Engelmann pricklypear in full bloom present a scene of striking beauty.

The famous French botanist Tournefort, who founded the genus *Opuntia* in 1719, states [1] that his genus is named for a certain small herb (Pliny's "herba Opuntia") which Theophrastus mentions as growing about the town of Opous ("circa Opuntem") in Boeotia, Greece. The species *engelmanni* commemorates Dr. George Engelmann (1809–84), a distinguished German-American physician and botanist, who made extensive studies of cacti, conifers, and other plants, and to whom also Engelmann spruce is dedicated.

Toumey and Rose (in Bailey [2]) state that Engelmann pricklypear, "with its numerous varieties, is the most widely distributed and abundant of the large, flat-stemmed opuntias in the United States." The wide geographic range of the species doubtless is a major factor in its great variability. The species, or some variety of it, occurs from western Texas to California, and practically throughout Mexico—from whence it was first described. The fleshy, flattened stems and the very small size and number of leaves serve to reduce the evaporating surface materially, while the numerous, widespreading, extensive fibrous roots furnish a comparatively large absorbing area. These features combine to make Engelmann pricklypear highly drought-resistant. It is also resistant to heat and, in the United States, attains its best development at low altitudes in the foothills of the southern sectors of the Southwestern States. This plant occasionally forms dense patches on soils of good quality, especially where the grass cover has been depleted.

Engelmann pricklypear attains its greatest forage value as emergency feed for cattle and sheep during extended drought. This and other species of pricklypear have helped to tide many thousands of cattle and sheep over critical periods when the grass crop had failed temporarily. During such emergencies, the spines of pricklypear are singed off in the field to make the fleshy joints accessible to cattle. The spines are sometimes also singed for sheep, but ordinarily the herder cuts off a portion of the joint, which allows the animals to insert their noses into the flesh of the joints and eat the plant without injury from the spines. When thus made available these plants are palatable to cattle and sheep, and good results have been obtained in feeding this species to livestock.[3][4][5] During mod-

[1] Tournefort, J. P. INSTITUTIONES REI HERBARIAE. v. 1, pp. 239–240. Paris. 1719.
[2] Bailey, L. H. THE STANDARD CYCLOPEDIA OF HORTICULTURE . . . New ed., 3 v., illus. New York and London. 1933.
[3] Griffiths, D., and Hare, R. F. PRICKLY PEAR AND OTHER CACTI AS FOOD FOR STOCK II. N. Mex. Agr. Expt. Sta. Bull. 60, 134 pp., illus. 1906.
[4] Hare, R. F. EXPERIMENTS ON THE DIGESTIBILITY OF PRICKLY PEAR BY CATTLE. N. Mex., Agr. Expt. Sta. Bull. 69, 48 pp., illus. 1908.
[5] Griffiths, D. PRICKLY PEAR AS STOCK FEED. U. S. Dept. Agr., Farmers' Bull. 1072, 24 pp., illus. 1920.

erate drought, small amounts of Engelmann pricklypear may be fed straight to supplement other available forage, but when range forage is not available it is necessary to feed larger amounts of this cactus with a pound or two of concentrates for satisfactory results.[5] The plant is a valuable source of water in arid regions. Sheep are said to do well upon it even without water. Various chemical analyses, given in the references cited, show that the water content of the pods or joints of this species is approximately 80 percent. This species also is rich in mineral content and, if eaten too freely, is likely to cause scours. The feed should be prepared only as needed, since it tends to sour readily.

Engelmann pricklypear is grazed but lightly under normal conditions; some of the fruit and very young growth being all that is usually eaten. Even sheep, which can utilize the plant to better advantage than cattle, normally use it but lightly. With the exception of this slight use the plant is of value only as emergency feed. Vorhies and Taylor[6] list pricklypear as an important food of jack rabbits and other rodents.

The fruit of Engelmann pricklypear, though full of seeds, is sweet and edible to human beings, and has been used rather extensively as food by the Indians, being either eaten fresh or dried for winter use. The fruit and young growth of certain varieties are still used locally as food, especially in Mexico where some forms are cultivated for this purpose. This species is frequently grown as an ornamental in cactus gardens.

Some species of pricklypear, although less abundant on the range, are practically spineless and, naturally, are more valuable as forage than the spiny forms, but have difficulty maintaining themselves under heavy grazing. Several spineless species, both native and introduced, are cultivated to some extent as forage plants. The fruit of many species of pricklypear is edible, of good quality and frequently is cultivated for human consumption, especially in Mexico.

The round-stemmed species of *Opuntia* are known as chollas or cane cacti. *Opuntia arborescens*, one of the most common range species of this group, has come in so abundantly on some overgrazed ranges, that it has proved to be a barrier to grazing on rather large areas. This has resulted in efforts to exterminate the plant from such areas. The spines of chollas are sometimes burned off and the plants used as emergency forage, like pricklypears. Several species of cholla produce an abundance of fruit, which is eaten to some extent by cattle. Because of their excessive spininess, however, livestock ordinarily avoid these plants, except for limited utilization of the fruit and very young growth.

---

[5] See footnote on preceding page.
[6] Vorhies, C. T., and Taylor, W. P. THE LIFE HISTORIES AND ECOLOGY OF JACK RABBITS, LEPUS ALLENI AND LEPUS CALIFORNICUS SSP., IN RELATION TO GRAZING IN ARIZONA. Ariz. Agr. Expt. Sta. Tech. Bull. 49: [471]–587, illus. 1933.

MYRTLE BOXLEAF

Pachi'stima myrsini'tes

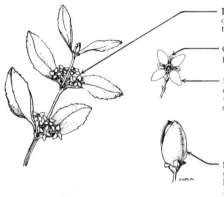

Flowers—greenish or reddish, small, odorless, few, in nearly stalkless clusters (cymes) in the leaf axils

Outer flower parts (sepals)—4, broad, persistent

Petals—4, attached to under edge of disk covering seed-producing organ (ovary) and alternating with the 4 stamens

Seed pod (capsule)—whitish, egg-shaped, small (about ¼ in. long), leathery, opening by 2 valves, 2-celled, 1- or 2-seeded

Leaves—opposite, evergreen, short-stalked, egg-shaped to spatula-shaped, about ½ to 1½ in. long, finely saw-toothed above the middle, with rolled-under margins

Stems—woody, spreading or often prostrate, up to 3 ft. long, usually much-branched; branchlets reddish or brownish, usually 4-ridged

Myrtle boxleaf, known also as false box, goatbrush, mountain-lover, myrtlebush, and Oregon boxwood, is the only species of *Pachistima* native in the West. The only other species of this North American genus of the bittersweet, or staff-tree family (Celastraceae) is Canby boxleaf (*P. can'byi*), which occurs on steep, rocky slopes in the Appalachian Mountains of North Carolina, Virginia, and West Virginia, and in parts of neighboring Ohio. *Pachistima* is the original spelling of the genus name by its founder, the eccentric Constantine Samuel Rafinesque-Schmaltz (1783–1840), and is the form approved by the American Joint Committee on Horticultural Nomenclature.[1] The name is obviously a corruption of the Greek words *pachys* (thick) and *stigma* (mark; hence, stigma).

The specific name *myrsinites*, signifying like myrtle, refers to a resemblance to true myrtle (*Myrtus communis*) of the Old World.

Myrtle boxleaf ranges from British Columbia to California, New Mexico, and Alberta and occurs principally in the ponderosa pine, lodgepole pine, and Engelmann spruce belts. In general, this species is characteristic of moist or fairly moist, sandy or gravelly loam soils on northern slopes in open coniferous timber. However, it is often found in aspen and among shrubs, but rarely in the open; the species also occurs on drier sites, growing on all slopes. In the Northwest, it appears mainly at altitudes between 2,000 and 4,500 feet and is one of the characteristic shrubs of the heavy Douglas fir and mixed coniferous forests of the coast region. It is most common in Utah, Colorado, northern Arizona, and New Mexico at elevations of from 6,000 to 9,000 feet.[2] However, on shady northern slopes, it sometimes grows at much lower elevations.

Myrtle boxleaf is usually unpalatable to livestock and is important chiefly because it is so widely distributed and abundant. Under certain conditions, when a shortage of other forage prevails, as along driveways, this plant may be browsed by cattle and sheep. Deer and elk utilize it extensively on some of the heavily stocked summer and winter game ranges in the Northwest, even the older stems being closely cropped, although heavy use is largely restricted to the winter. Report is to the effect that excessive browsing of this plant by sheep will cause illness. However, no research has been initiated to determine if this species actually contains toxic principles. The plant has some repute in Oregon as a remedy for kidney and rheumatic disorders, and undoubtedly an investigation of its chemical properties would be advantageous.

The boxleafs are hardy, handsome dwarf evergreens suitable for planting in rockeries or on rocky slopes, and as borders for evergreen shrubberies. These plants grow in almost any well-drained soil and may be propagated by seed, layering, or by cuttings.[3]

---

[1] American Joint Committee on Horticultural Nomenclature. STANDARDIZED PLANT NAMES . . . Prepared by F. L. Olmsted, F. V. Coville, and H. P. Kelsey. 546 pp. Salem, Mass. 1923.

[2] Dayton, W. A. IMPORTANT WESTERN BROWSE PLANTS. U. S. Dept. Agr. Misc. Pub. 101, 214 pp., illus. 1931.

[3] Bailey, L. H. THE STANDARD CYCLOPEDIA OF HORTICULTURE . . . New ed., 3 v., illus. New York and London. 1933.

LEWIS MOCKORANGE ("SYRINGA")   (2 leaves)

Philadel'phus lewis'ii

Flowers—white, showy, solitary or in clusters near ends of twigs

Petals—4 or 5, distinct, oval to oblong-egg-shaped, up to about 1 in. long

Stamens—numerous (20 to 60)

Outer united flower parts (calyx)—top-shaped, tubular below, with 4 or 5 lance-shaped to egg-shaped, tapering or sharp-tipped lobes, hairless outside, hairy within, persistent

Threadlike stalk (style)—4-branched above middle, tipping seed-producing organ (inferior ovary), persistent

Seed pods (capsules)—top-shaped, partly enclosed by calyx tube, 4- or 5-celled, 4- or 5-valved, many-seeded, splitting lengthwise along middle of back of each cell

Leaves—opposite, thin, broadly lance-shaped to egg-shaped or oblong, up to 3 in. long, with entire or slightly toothed edges, sharp-pointed, short-stalked, 3- to 5-veined, hairless above, hairy around edges, on veins and at vein axils beneath

Stems—erect or spreading, up to 12 ft. high, with opposite branchlets; twigs red or chestnut-brown, hairless; bark of 2d season with conspicuous cross cracks

711

Lewis mockorange, known almost universally throughout its range as syringa, has been legally adopted as the State flower of Idaho. The name syringa is not satisfactory in this case, since *Syringa* is the generic name of the cultivated lilacs, and also because the name signifies a pipe or trumpet, an application totally inappropriate for mockorange flowers. Indian arrowwood is another name sometimes given to this plant because the Indians used its slender shoots for arrow shafts.[1] The specific name of this attractive shrub is an honorary tribute to Captain Meriwether Lewis of the Lewis and Clark expedition, who discovered and first collected the plant on July 4, 1806, along the Clark Fork River, near Missoula, Mont.[2]

Lewis mockorange, the best known and most outstanding western species of mockorange, is distributed from British Columbia, and the Cascade Mountains of Washington and Oregon, to California and eastward to Montana and northern Utah. The California plants are regarded by some authorities as a variety, *P. lewisii californicus*. Lewis mockorange grows on a variety of sites, but occurs principally on or near canyon bottoms or in other moist, moderately shaded, or open situations. It grows on soils varying from deep, rich, alluvial humic loams to dry, rocky or gravelly loams on open hillsides, usually in typical association with alder, chokecherry, dwarf maple, and willow, or on the drier sites, with bitterbrush, dogbane, mullein, ponderosa pine, serviceberry, and snowbrush. This shrub of the foothills and low mountains extends from near sea level to about 8,000 feet and thrives on all slopes, but favors northerly or easterly exposures. It usually occurs in small, scattered clumps, being common only in restricted localized areas, but is not abundant enough over the range as a whole to form a very important part of the plant cover.

As a forage plant Lewis mockorange is of minor importance and usually is not grazed by domestic livestock on any extensive scale. However, there are exceptions, as in eastern Oregon where it is eaten to a limited extent by cattle, and in central Washington where its palatability is rated as fair for both cattle and sheep. As a game forage Lewis mockorange merits a higher rating. In Montana, deer browse it readily, especially on the winter ranges; in Washington both deer and elk relish this shrub. It is quite likely that game animals utilize this plant elsewhere in its range.

Lewis mockorange, a most attractive shrub when in full bloom, has attained great popularity and is widely cultivated for ornamental purposes. It grows from 3 to 12 feet high and has ascending or spreading branches. The twigs branch oppositely and have red or chestnut-brown bark which during the second season develops conspicuous cross cracks. The showy, white flowers are fragrant and are borne singly on short stems or in loose terminal clusters (cymes).

Lewis mockorange is sometimes confused with Gordon mockorange (*Philadelphus gordonianus*), a popular and showy shrub of the Northwest which grows principally in the coast region from British Columbia to northern California. The leaves of Lewis mockorange have entire or but slightly toothed margins and are hairy around the edges, on the veins, and in the axils of the veins on the lower surface; the blades are three-to five-veined with the inner pair of veins meeting the midrib at some distance from the base of the blade. Gordon mockorange has leaves which are usually toothed, often coarsely, and are fine-hairy over the under surfaces and five-veined, the veins originating at the base of the blade. In Gordon mockorange the styles are united for two-thirds of their length, while those of Lewis mockorange are united for about half their length.

---

[1] Jepson, W. L. A MANUAL OF THE FLOWERING PLANTS OF CALIFORNIA. 1,238 pp., illus. Berkeley, Calif. [1925.]
[2] Piper, C. V. FLORA OF THE STATE OF WASHINGTON. U. S. Natl. Mus., Contrib. U. S. Natl. Herbarium 11, 637 pp., illus. 1906.

MOCKORANGES

Philadel'phus spp.

The mockoranges, attractive flowery shrubs of the hydrangea family (Hydrangeaceae) which is merged by some botanists with the saxifrage family (Saxifragaceae), constitute a widely distributed genus of about 50 species native to North America, Mexico, Central Europe and Asia. Approximately 28 species are native to North America with about 10 of these occurring in the western range States.

The mockoranges appear to have little or no range significance for domestic livestock as they are generally unpalatable or low in palatability for those animals and, furthermore, are usually too scattered to constitute an important part of the range plant cover. These plants are extremely popular shrubs on account of their showy, often fragrant, flowers. Many species are used for ornamentals and numerous hybrids have originated in cultivation, making distinction of the species difficult.

The western mockoranges are mostly erect shrubs with ascending somewhat curving branches. The leaves and branches are opposite. The flowers are showy, white or yellowish white, borne at the ends of short leafy branches, solitary or in loose clusters. The outer flower parts (calyx) are four- or five-parted with the lower portion united to form a persistent tube which is adherent to the seed-producing organ (ovary). The flowers have four or five petals and usually numerous stamens. The ovary is mostly four-celled, with usually four styles which are separated above the middle or more or less united. The ovary ripens into a many-seeded, top-shaped, mostly four-valved seedpod (capsule) which splits down the middle of the back of each cell.

RED MOUNTAINHEATH

Phyllo'doce empetrifor'mis, syn. *Bryan'thus empetrifor'mis*

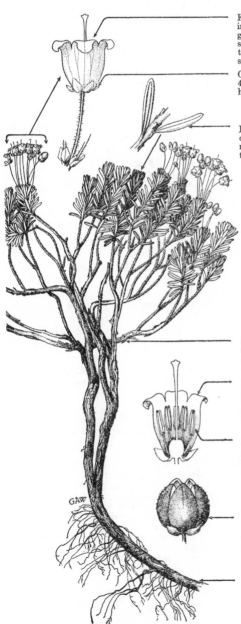

Flowers—pink or red, up to ¼ in. long, each on a slender, glandular stalk, borne in a somewhat flattened or rounded-topped cluster at the top of the stems

Outer flower parts (sepals)—4 or 5, purplish, blunt and hairless

Leaves—evergreen, thickened, crowded on the stems, alternate, narrow, ¼ to ½ in. long, sometimes with rolled-under edges.

Stems—wiry, roughened by leaf scars, often clustered above, and somewhat creeping below

United petals (corolla)—broadly bell-shaped, usually 5-lobed above, the lobes up to ½ as long as united portion, falling off before fruit ripens

Stamens—twice as many as corolla lobes, attached to corolla tube and not protruding; filaments not markedly curved

Seed pod (capsule)—somewhat globe-shaped, 4- or 5-celled, many-seeded, splitting from the top along the partitions

Roots—thickened, woody, extensive

The diminutive heathlike and evergreen shrub, red mountainheath, is the most important of the three species of the genus growing in the mountains of the Western States. The common name, mountainheath, suggests the similarity of its foliage to the small, linear leaves of the true heaths (*Erica* spp.) of the Old World.

Red mountainheath inhabits subalpine and alpine zones from Alaska to northern California, Colorado, and Alberta. Its occurrence throughout this range is variable, being abundant or rare, depending on the local physical conditions and extent of the alpine country. Ordinarily, it inhabits sunny but partially protected sites, such as benches, rim bases and sides of ridges, or fringes the timber surrounding high meadows and lakes. It most commonly grows on coarse-textured, high (and probably always acid) soils, not infrequently among boulders, and sometimes on moist, black, organic, and acid soils of wet meadows. It characteristically grows in relatively small patches, which, however, may, in the aggregate, compose the principal ground cover within the type.

Most observers agree that red mountainheath is valueless as a forage plant for domestic livestock, being avoided by all classes with the possible exception of sheep. Even utilization by sheep is limited to areas of abnormal grazing such as occurs around bedgrounds or along driveways. It has been reported [1] that red mountainheath is poisonous to domestic livestock, but this has not been verified by feeding experiments. There is ample reason to suspect that it may be poisonous, as it belongs to the heath family and is closely related to many plants known to be poisonous, notably the kalmias (*Kalmia* spp.), menziesias (*Menziesia* spp.), and leucothoës (*Leucothoë* spp.). The safest practice for the stockman would be to avoid use of this plant, especially in view of the fact that it often grows near and is sometimes confused with the definitely poisonous kalmias. They are both low, evergreen, patch-forming alpine shrubs, but western kalmias have opposite, fewer, broader, and much larger leaves, and larger, wider, and not bell-like flowers; moreover, they always inhabit bogs or very wet sites. The stamens of kalmias are also quite different, in that the anthers are caught in pouchlike depressions.

Red mountainheath and its two western sister species, Brewer mountainheath (*P. breweri*) and cream mountainheath (*P. glanduliflora*), are characteristic and handsome plants of the alpine zone, and add much to the beauty of this cold region. Green patches of these plants constitute an integral part of the landscape, and when in blossom in July and August have the appearance from a distance of a large bouquet. Brewer and cream mountainheath are much like red mountainheath in aspect and growth requirements. Brewer mountainheath occurs throughout the higher mountains of California, has similarly colored flowers, but with the petals united only half way and the stamens longer than the petals. Cream mountainheath is readily distinguished from these other two by its yellowish or cream-colored flowers. Its range is from Alaska to Oregon, Wyoming, and Montana.

The low, heathlike, alpine shrubs of the mountainheath genus are distinguishable from the other genera of the heath family by their numerous, alternate, small, narrow, inrolled evergreen leaves; rough, leaf-scarred stems; small bell-shaped, five-parted flowers; and by their globe-shaped seedpods (capsules) that split along the partitions from the top down.

---

[1] Dayton, W. A. IMPORTANT WESTERN BROWSE PLANTS. U. S. Dept. Agr. Misc. Pub. 101, 214 pp., illus. 1931.

WESTERN ASPEN

Po'pulus tremuloi'des au'rea, syns. *P. au'rea,* "*P. tremuloi'des*"[1]

Leaves—alternate, somewhat rounded (suborbicular), broadest near the middle, mostly ¾ to 2¼ in. wide, rounded or heart-shaped at base, somewhat shiny and deep yellow-green above, paler beneath, turning golden or orange after frost, somewhat irregularly round-toothed on margins, short-sharp-pointed at tip

Leafstalks—about 1¼ to 3 in. long, flattened

Twigs—smooth and shiny, clear reddish brown at end of first year, becoming pale reddish gray and finally a dull gray

Stems or trunks—up to 90 ft. high and 30 in. in diameter; bark smooth, grayish white, brownish green, pale green, or veined with greenish or yellowish areas, commonly covered with a whitish powder, ridged and furrowed only at base of trunk where, in larger trees, it is blackish and may be from 1 to nearly 2 in. thick

---

[1] In part.

717

Ranging as it does from Alaska to Mexico and from the Pacific coast to western Texas, Colorado, Nebraska, and Manitoba, western aspen is perhaps the best-known tree of the western mountains, where it is a characteristic feature of the landscape. It was in 1911 that the American aspen, previously known solely as *Populus tremuloides*, was definitely separated by Tidestrom [2] into an eastern and a western species. The eastern form retains the name *Populus tremuloides* and the western form is now known as *P. tremuloides aurea*.[3] The species and its varieties are most widely recognized as aspen but less commonly are designated as American aspen, poplar, popple, quaking aspen, quaking asp, trembling aspen, and trembling poplar. The term "aspen", wherever it occurs in this description, refers to the species *tremuloides* as a whole, including its western varieties.

Populus tremuloides, as previously known, ranges from Labrador and Hudson Bay to Alaska, southward through Canada and over most of the United States, except the South Atlantic and Gulf States, and into northern Mexico. As now understood, the American aspen is botanically separated into five closely related forms: (1) American aspen (*P. tremuloides*) in its type form, and (2) kidneyleaf aspen (*P. tremuloi'des renifor'mis*), both mainly eastern forms; (3) western aspen (*P. tremuloi'des au'rea*), the common and widely distributed western form of the species; (4) redbud aspen (*P. tremuloi'des cercidi'phylla*), a locally restricted form of western Wyoming; and (5) Vancouver aspen (*P. tremuloi'des vancouveria'na*), a form confined to the locality of Vancouver Island.[2] From a practical standpoint there is little need for separating the forms, as the ordinary observer will not appreciate the characteristics noted in distinguishing these varieties, because they consist chiefly of relatively trivial differences in flowers, size and shape of leaves, and in autumnal coloration.

Western aspen is naturally a forest-forming variety, which often covers large areas with dense, practically pure stands. It is commonly considered a temporary type, but when it becomes established on fire-denuded areas, where all coniferous seed trees have been killed over extensive areas, thick stands may dominate for many years. In the northern part of its range, western aspen occurs from sea level up to an altitude of from 2,500 or 3,500 feet, and farther south it ranges mostly between elevations of 6,000 and 11,000 feet. It attains its best development on rich, moist, loam soils, but also occurs in wet soils and on dry, gravelly hillsides. On the better sites, it develops into a large tree occasionally 90 feet high and 30 inches or more in diameter.

Western aspen grows typically in open stands and frequently under such favorable soil conditions as to be associated with a varied and luxuriant undergrowth, which is highly palatable to livestock. Furthermore, it is sufficiently palatable to sheep and cattle, which browse extensively on the leaves and twigs, especially during the fall, as to be a material factor in the grazing capacity of many

[2] Tidestrom, I. NOTES ON POPULUS, PLINIUS. Amer. Midland Nat. 2: [29]–35, illus. 1911.
[3] Sudworth, G. B. POPLARS, PRINCIPAL TREE WILLOWS, AND WALNUTS OF THE ROCKY MOUNTAIN REGION. U. S. Dept. Agr. Tech. Bull. 420, 112 pp., illus. 1934.

ranges. On heavily grazed ranges, close cropping may prevent the establishment of aspen reproduction. Some damage may result to reproduction even on moderately grazed areas; wherever aspen stands are desired for timber, protective measures may be necessary. Sampson [4] has shown that cattle will browse this tree to a height of about 70 inches, and that the injury they cause aspen reproduction is slight, except on overgrazed areas. He notes that sheep are more prone than cattle to eat the woody stems of aspen, but that sprouts 45 inches or taller are practically exempt from destruction by sheep. Usually cattle dislike to remain for extended periods in the timber, but tend to congregate in the openings, with the result that aspen ranges thus grazed are ordinarily very unevenly utilized.

Western aspen is generally rated as fair to fairly good or even good forage for cattle and sheep, but usually is more palatable to sheep than cattle. However, in the Northwest it is considered more palatable to cattle than to sheep in the summer (July–August) and equally palatable in the fall (September–October).[5] This plant is also browsed extensively by deer and elk. On the Kaibab National Forest in northern Arizona, western aspen is one of the principal summer deer feeds, being ranked among the key species; in fact, its use reflects closely the utilization of the forage on the summer range as a whole. Deer also eagerly devour and flourish on the nutritious, fallen leaves during the autumn. Deer and, to some extent, elk apparently prefer aspen range, possibly because of the protection and concealment afforded by the thick stands of this species as well as because of its forage.

Not all western aspen stands are desirable range, as frequently on the drier sites the plant is associated with a dense undergrowth of such relatively unpalatable shrubs as bearberry (*Arctostaphylos uva-ursi*), creeping hollygrape (*Odostemon repens*), and snowbrush (*Ceanothus velutinus*), or of unpalatable weeds such as mountain goldenpea (*Thermopsis montana*), or the undergrowth may be very sparse. It is usually impractical to graze livestock on such areas, even though the aspen retains its palatability.

Aspen reproduces vigorously by root shoots, but heavy grazing will keep down practically all reproduction; on closely grazed range, aspen stands frequently assume a parklike aspect, the lack of reproduction, in many instances, indicating an overstocked or improperly grazed range. On such areas, but little aspen foliage is available to livestock, and this may also be true in some of the more mature stands, where reproduction is lacking.

Western aspen, with its smooth, usually whitish bark, and long-petioled, broad, toothed, trembling leaves has no counterpart in the West. The small flowers, borne in hanging clusters (catkins), appear before the leaves, and the small seeds covered with long, silky hairs

---

[4] Sampson, A. W. EFFECT OF GRAZING UPON ASPEN REPRODUCTION. U. S. Dept. Agr. Bull. 741, 30 pp., illus. 1919.
[5] Dayton, W. A. IMPORTANT WESTERN BROWSE PLANTS. U. S. Dept. Agr. Misc. Pub. 101, 214 pp., illus. 1931.

are dispersed early in summer. The male and female flowers are distinct and are borne on separate trees. The Latin varietal name of the western form, *tremuloides aurea*, refers to the leaves, from the Latin *tremulus*, quaking, and *aurea*, for golden.

ASPENS, POPLARS, AND COTTONWOODS (Po'pulus spp.)

Botanically, this genus presents a bewildering and complex group of plants, with a large number of hybrids and other variant forms; in consequence, there is a wide divergence of opinion among botanists as to the number and names of the species. *Populus* is the classical Latin name for these woody plants. This genus is widely distributed in the Northern Hemisphere, principally outside the tropics, and belongs to the willow family (Salicaceae), which includes only one other genus, the willows (*Salix* spp.). Though sometimes stunted and distorted by adverse growth conditions, all the poplars are true trees, with a single main stem, usually having rather broad, often more or less heart-shaped, mostly long-stalked and toothed leaves, and small flowers borne in hanging clusters (catkins). With the exception of the narrowleaf cottonwood (*P. angustifo'lia*, syn. *P. fortis'sima*), which has short leafstalks and narrow leaves and may be mistaken for a tree willow, the western poplars and cottonwoods are unlikely to be confused with other plants. The flower buds of willows are covered by a single scale; those of species of *Populus* are frequently resinous and are covered with several scales. In general, differentiation between members of these two genera is not difficult.

Approximately 15 species and several varieties of *Populus* are native to the West. Based on popular names they may be separated into two groups: (1) Aspens; and (2) poplars and cottonwoods. Poplars and cottonwoods are typical of moist sites and occur mainly along streams, around ponds, and in depressions, where there is plenty of subsurface moisture. They are all palatable to both livestock and game animals, being browsed whenever the foliage is within reach of grazing animals. Generally, however, they are less abundant and, on the whole, are of considerably less forage value than aspen, although they undoubtedly furnish an appreciable amount of feed.

Narrowleaf cottonwood, next to aspen, is probably the most widely distributed western species of *Populus;* it occurs from Alberta to Mexico in all the Western States except California, and is sometimes associated with aspen, growing chiefly along the streams, in small patches or as scattered individuals. Black cottonwood (*P. tricho-car'pa*) is probably the most common species in the Pacific States and extends to Alaska. It ranges inland to Idaho, northwestern Montana, northwestern Wyoming, and Nevada. This is typically a timber tree, the wood being used for apple and sugar barrels and, to a limited extent, for paper pulp. The other species of *Populus* in the West are mostly of local distribution, occurring chiefly along streams at the lower altitudes; from a browse standpoint, they are of limited value.

HONEY MESQUITE

Proso'pis glandulo'sa, syn. *P. juliflo'ra glandulo'sa*

Flowers—in dense, axillary, cylindrical clusters (spikes) 2 to 5 in. long

Flower and seed-pod stalks (peduncles) —conspicuously gland-dotted

Spines—¼ to 1¼ in. long, rigid, nearly straight, usually arising in pairs from swellings in leaf axils

Leaves—twice-divided (bipinnately compound); main leaf divisions (pinnae) 1 or 2 pairs, spreading, short-stalked

Leaflets—numerous, short-stalked or stalkless, hairless, dark green, mostly with abruptly pointed tips

Seed pods—4 to 8 in. long, in drooping clusters, linear, straight or curved, flattened, narrowed between the seeds, not splitting

Stamens—10, distinct, about twice as long as petals; pollen sacs (anthers) gland-tipped

Petals—5, yellowish green, distinct or nearly so

Growth habit—rather spreading

721

Honey mesquite is known also as honeypod, prairie mesquite, or mesquite. When the Spanish conquistadores arrived in Mexico and the Southwest they called the mesquite "algaroba", as it reminded them of the closely related carob tree, algaroba or St. Johnsbread (*Ceratonia siliqua*), of their native land. The name algaroba is often used for mesquite in this country, and is universal in Hawaii, but is a misapplication of a Spanish-Arabic plant name. Honey mesquite is typically a shrub, 5 to 10 feet high, growing in many-stemmed clumps, 3 to 50 feet in diameter. Frequently it develops into a small tree 15 to 20 feet tall but, in some habitats, it may grow only 1 or 2 feet above ground.

This species occurs from eastern Texas and southern Kansas to southern and Lower California and south into Mexico. It inhabits dry, sandy, or gravelly plains, mesas, canyons, and hillsides at elevations between about 2,500 and 5,000 feet. It is very characteristic of sandhills and, over extensive areas, often dominates the landscape either in almost pure stands or in intermixed growth with soaptree yucca (*Yucca elata*), its very common companion.

Honey mesquite provides valuable forage chiefly in its seedpods, which are sweet, rich in protein,[1] and very nutritious. The pods usually are fairly abundant, two crops being produced under favorable conditions. They are relished by cattle, sheep, goats, swine, and especially horses. Deer and other native mammals, as well as some game birds, also seek the pods. However, after lying on the ground during wet periods, the pods soon become sour and unfit for food. Some stockmen claim that horses will occasionally eat these fermented pods with undesirable, or even fatal, results.

The young twigs of honey mesquite become green in the spring before the leaves appear and then are readily grazed by livestock for a short period. The leaves are eaten only slightly when they first appear, and after maturity are usually not cropped except on overgrazed range or during prolonged drought when they are rated as fair emergency forage.

This plant is exceptionally drought-enduring and also withstands excessive grazing; it is very aggressive and invades grasslands readily when the grass cover is broken as a result of overgrazing. Dayton[2] states:

It is all but impossible to kill honey mesquite and its close relative, *Prosopis velutina*, by overgrazing. The fact that many of the seeds pass out of the digestive tract undigested and viable accounts largely for the persistent spread of the plant. The plant is also maintained in spite of overgrazing by reason of its phenomenal root development, which perhaps exceeds that of any other observed plant species. The roots, in addition to a considerable lateral spread, have vertical ground penetration that in many instances reaches 30 feet, and has been reported to reach 60 feet below the surface. The fact that the distribution of honey mesquite is spreading, owing to its natural aggressiveness and the fact that it resists prolonged range overgrazing at the expense of its competitors, have caused some writers to deprecate mesquite as forage. This is especially so on the eastern borders of the species' range, where it is taking possession of grasslands.

---

[1] Forbes, R. H. THE MESQUITE TREE: ITS PRODUCTS AND USES. Ariz. Agr. Expt. Sta. Bull. 13, 26 pp. 1895.
[2] Dayton, W. A. IMPORTANT WESTERN BROWSE PLANTS. U. S. Dept. Agr. Misc. Pub. 101, 214 pp., illus. 1931.

Honey mesquite is a valuable soil binder, especially on sandy areas. Growing in clumps, as it typically does, it catches and holds sand, forming large hummocks. The stems or trunks withstand covering around the base and are not easily killed by drifting sand.

Honey mesquite has many uses. The wood is very hard and makes excellent fence posts, except for the fact that it is the favored food of certain borers.[3] The roots compare favorably with the best hardwoods as fuel. Although the task involves considerable labor, the roots are collected extensively and, in many localities, the roots, together with mesquite stems, constitute the only available native fuel. Honey mesquite lumber is strikingly marked, richly colored, takes a beautiful polish, and is valuable for fine cabinet work. Flawless material is, however, difficult to obtain because of crooks and knots; its use is hence necessarily limited. In San Antonio and Brownsville, Tex., pavement blocks of mesquite were formerly used, both effectively and efficiently, on several streets.[4] A gum similar to gum arabic exudes from the bark or is extracted from wounds in the trunk. Forbes[1] reports that the best grade of gum is used both in the manufacture of gumdrops and mucilage; it is also useful in laundries. He also writes that the gum is highly prized in Mexico for medicinal purposes, while the low-grade material serves well as a dye. Honey mesquite is also suitable for hedges and ornamental purposes.

As the common name indicates, honey mesquite is an important source of nectar, which produces honey of exceptionally fine quality and flavor, being usually marketed as mesquite honey. The pods, ground into a sugary meal, are used by the Mexicans and Indians in making mush or bread. In addition, the natives manufacture atole, a popular drink, from the pods. The Indians also make a weak beer from mesquite pod meal. A purgative drink used by the Mexicans is compounded by making a water extract of the pounded inner bark of the young branches and adding salt to the resulting liquor.[1]

MESQUITES (Proso'pis spp.)

Prosopis, outside of a rather rich development in South America, is a relatively small genus of the warmer parts of the eastern and western hemispheres. It belongs to the mimosa family (Mimosaceae) which some authors prefer to regard as a subfamily of the pea family (Leguminosae). Mesquites are characteristic of warm, mostly dry, subtropical or tropical climates—Central America, the West Indies, Africa, Persia, India, etc.—although they are abundant and important plants in parts of the southern United States, Argentina, Chile, and other countries of similar climate. Three species—honey mesquite (*P. glandulosa*), velvet mesquite (*P. velutina*), and common mesquite (*P. juliflora*)—occur in the United States. The first two

---

[1] See footnote on preceding page.
[3] Craighead, F. C., and Hofer, G. PROTECTION OF MESQUITE CORDWOOD AND POSTS FROM BORERS. U. S. Dept. Agr. Farmers' Bull. 1197, 12 pp., illus. 1921.
[4] Havard, V. THE MESQUIT. Amer. Nat. 18:451–459. 1884.

are native to this country, but there is some difference in opinion as to whether the latter, which occurs in southern and western Texas, eastern New Mexico, and Mexico, is native or introduced—its home being Jamaica and the West Indies. Screwbean (*Strombocarpa odorata*, syns. *S. pubescens*, *Prosopis odorata*, *P. pubescens*) is included in this genus by some authors, but current authorities place it in the genus *Strombocarpa*. All of the mesquites are similar in forage value. The large, sweet, and pulpy pods provide good forage, but the leaves are eaten only slightly except in the absence of better forage. The three aforementioned species supply excellent fence posts and fuel and are useful for many other purposes where a strong, durable wood is desired.

Velvet mesquite, a multibranched tree sometimes attaining 50 feet in height and 2 feet in diameter, occurs in Arizona, Sonora, and Lower California. It often forms open, savanna woodlands over extensive areas and affords essential shade for livestock on hot, arid ranges. Common mesquite is typical of Jamaica and the West Indies, but has been widely introduced and naturalized in many countries where it is considered a very valuable tree for fuel, railroad ties, cabinetmaking, and many other purposes. Wilcox[5] reports that common mesquite ("algaroba") is the most valuable tree which has been introduced into Hawaii, where it now occurs in extensive forests and is highly valued as a forage, fuel, and honey plant. Some authorities classify honey and velvet mesquite as varieties of common mesquite.

---

[5] Wilcox, E. V. THE ALGAROBA IN HAWAII. Hawaii Agr. Expt. Sta. Press Bull. 26, 8 pp. 1910.

WESTERN CHOKECHERRY

Pru'nus demis'sa

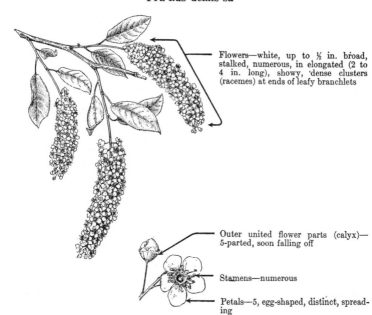

Flowers—white, up to ½ in. broad, stalked, numerous, in elongated (2 to 4 in. long), showy, dense clusters (racemes) at ends of leafy branchlets

Outer united flower parts (calyx)—5-parted, soon falling off

Stamens—numerous

Petals—5, egg-shaped, distinct, spreading

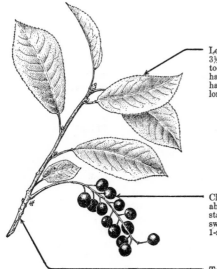

Leaves—alternate, not evergreen, 1 to 3½ in. long, pointed at tips, finely saw-toothed around edges, dark green and hairless above, somewhat lighter and hairy beneath, on stalks about ½ in. long

Chokecherry (drupe)—globe-shaped, about ⅜ in. in diameter, on a hairless stalk, dark purple or black, juicy, sweet, or slightly puckery (astringent), 1-seeded

Twigs—slender and leafy, reddish brown

This erect, leafy shrub or small tree, which attains a height of 30 feet or more, as well as the similar and closely related black chokecherry (*P. melanocar'pa*) are rather common on the western ranges. Unfortunately, there is a diversity of opinion among botanists as to the scientific name which should be applied to these two chokecherries. Two eminent American dendrologists have considered both *P. demissa* and *P. melanocarpa* as varieties of the common chokecherry (*P. virginiana*) of the eastern United States. Western botanists, however, do not agree; some authorities give both *demissa* and *melanocarpa* specific rank; others, composed largely of Pacific coast botanists, recognize *P. demissa* as a valid species and relegate *P. melanocarpa* to varietal rank or suppress it altogether. From a taxonomic standpoint, it is probably preferable to adhere to present usage in the United States Department of Agriculture and recognize both *P. demissa* and *P. melanocarpa* as very closely related, but distinct, species. However, for range-management purposes, they may well be considered identical, because of analogous habits and characters, and similarity in forage value.

Western chokecherry occurs from British Columbia to western Montana and California. Black chokecherry is more midely distributed, occurring in the plains, valleys, and mountains from British Columbia to North Dakota, Kansas, New Mexico, and California. The elevational range is from near sea level at their northern limits and (for black chokecherry) 2,000 feet in the plains east of the Rockies to (for black chokecherry) about 9,000 feet in the mountains of Colorado. These woody plants are generally most abundant from the foothills to the ponderosa-pine belt of the mountains. They grow in sunny, moist, or relatively dry situations, the largest specimens usually being associated with willows, alders, aspen, and dogwood along the streams in open valleys or in sparsely timbered, warm and sunny canyons. They also grow about springs, seeps, and other moist places, but pure and brushy stands are largely limited to moist or well-drained, warm slopes or sandy flats. They usually occur on deep, rather fertile, sandy soils, but frequently do well on rocky talus slopes and about rim rocks.

Although poisonous under some conditions,[1] these two chokecherries are often grazed moderately and in combination with other forage without ill effect. Fortunately, they are not of high palatability, the leaves, twigs, and green bark having a bitter flavor, which is not entirely agreeable to livestock. On the open range they rate as poor to fair forage for both cattle and sheep; and, although losses sometimes occur, they usually are attributable to abnormal use of these chokecherries, as a result of overgrazing or other causes. Most fatalities due to eating these plants occur in areas where livestock are concentrated, such as about water, in corrals and pastures, and along driveways or near bedgrounds.

.The active principle in western chokecherry and black chokecherry, as well as in the closely related common chokecherry of the East, which causes poisoning, is hydrocyanic (prussic) acid (HCN). Strange to say, this acid is not present in the green and healthy

[1] Marsh, C. D. STOCK-POISONING PLANTS OF THE RANGE. U. S. Dept. Agr. Bull. 1245, rev., 75 pp., illus. 1929. Supersedes Bull. 575.

foliage, but develops rapidly from the union of substances released when the leaves are crushed and moistened, as occurs in an animal's stomach during digestion.[2][3][4] The foliage is poisonous over a long period; its virulence does not decrease until the end of August, although the plants are harmless by October. Unfortunately, the leaves of the young shoots, which are the most palatable, are also the most harmful. The Nevada Agricultural Experiment Station[2] determined that a little over one-fourth of a pound of leafage was fatal to sheep and 1½ pounds was sufficient to kill a 500-pound cow. This amount, however, must be consumed at a single feeding, as the animals are able to eliminate the effects of smaller quantities rapidly and to escape harmful results even though total consumption at various periods during the day may exceed the lethal dose. Continued use of chokecherry foliage, however, does not establish immunity against hydrocyanic acid poisoning. Ordinarily, the poisonous acid is released as soon as the foliage is eaten, but sometimes, on dry ranges, lethal quantities are eaten without apparent discomfort, until the animal goes to water. The water consumed moistens the dry food mass in the stomach with resultant formation of the acid, which quickly kills the animal. Fleming and associates[2] report the following symptoms:

The poisoned animal becomes very uneasy, staggers, falls, goes into convulsions, breathes with increasing difficulty with eyes rolling and tongue hanging out. Then it becomes quiet, bloats, and dies, usually within less than an hour after eating the leaves.

Post-mortem examinations easily serve to identify the poison as the stomach contents, when stirred, emit the strong, bitter-almond odor characteristic of hydrocyanic acid.

Various remedies have been suggested, such as administrations of starchy foods or ordinary corn sirup,[3] or a drink composed of freshly mixed sodium carbonate and iron sulphate.[2][5] However, most antidotes have proved of little value, as the poisonous action is usually well advanced before the animal can be treated, particularly on the open range. Furthermore, the convulsions and paralysis of the respiratory system of the poisoned animal make administration of the antidote difficult. Most authorities[1][2][6] believe that livestock losses from chokeberry poisoning can be largely avoided by proper range management, as poisoning usually occurs in areas which are in a depleted condition. The use of overgrazed ranges, or locally overused areas such as watering places, bedgrounds, and along driveways, which are infested with western and black chokecherries, should be

[1] See footnote on preceding page.
[2] Fleming, C. E., Miller, M. R., and Vawter, L. R. THE COMMON CHOKECHERRY (PRUNUS DEMISSA) AS A PLANT POISONOUS TO SHEEP AND CATTLE. Nev. Agr. Expt. Sta. Bull. 109, 30 pp., illus. 1926.
[3] Morse, F. W., and Howard, C. D. POISONOUS PROPERTIES OF WILD CHERRY LEAVES. N. H. Agr. Expt. Sta. Bull. 56: [111]–123, illus. 1898.
[4] Couch, J. F. POISONING OF LIVESTOCK BY PLANTS THAT PRODUCE HYDROCYANIC ACID. U. S. Dept. Agr. Leaflet 88, 4 pp. 1932.
[5] Haring, C. M. PRECAUTIONS AGAINST POISONING BY JOHNSON GRASS AND OTHER SORGHUMS. Calif. Agr. Expt. Sta. [Unnumbered Leaflet], [4] pp. [1917.]
[6] Fleming, C. E., and Dill, R. THE POISONING OF SHEEP ON MOUNTAIN GRAZING RANGES IN NEVADA BY THE WESTERN CHOKECHERRY (PRUNUS DEMISSA). Nev. Agr. Expt. Sta. Bull. 110, 14 pp., illus. 1928.

avoided as much as possible, or else such areas should be grazed in a quiet, conservative manner, so that the livestock will spread out and select a liberal admixture of other feed.[7]

Such wild browsing animals as deer and elk make considerably more use of western and black chokecherries than do livestock. Forest Service observations in Montana, for example, show that these two species are, where abundant, among the most valuable local browse feeds, and that the twigs are often extensively utilized during winter. Western chokecherry, at least, appears to be browsed mainly in the fall and, although generally used, does not seem to poison either deer or elk.[8] The ripe, black cherries rank among the favorite foods of birds.

Western, black, and other chokecherries are well adapted for ornamental use. Their rather handsome form and dark green, shiny foliage is enhanced in the spring by the large, showy flower clusters, and in the fall by the blackish, grapelike clusters of fruit. The cherries are edible, with a sweetish but astringent aftertaste, alluded to in the common name, chokecherry. The fruit is commonly used locally for jellies and jams, and occasionally for wine.

---

[7] Dayton, W. A. IMPORTANT WESTERN BROWSE PLANTS. U. S. Dept. Agr. Misc. Pub. 101, 214 pp., illus. 1931.
[8] Dixon, J. S. A STUDY OF THE LIFE HISTORY AND FOOD HABITS OF MULE DEER IN CALIFORNIA. PART 2—FOOD HABITS. Calif. Fish and Game 20 (4) : [315]–354, illus. 1934.

BITTER CHERRY

Pru'nus emargina'ta

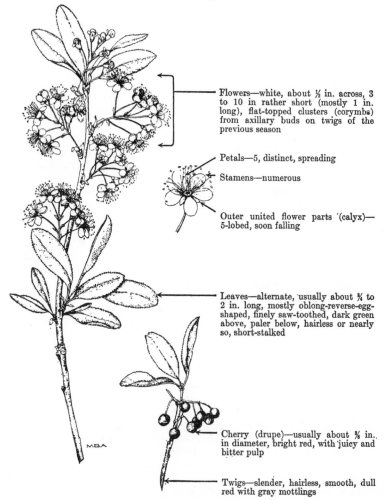

Flowers—white, about ½ in. across, 3 to 10 in rather short (mostly 1 in. long), flat-topped clusters (corymbs) from axillary buds on twigs of the previous season

Petals—5, distinct, spreading

Stamens—numerous

Outer united flower parts (calyx)—5-lobed, soon falling

Leaves—alternate, usually about ¾ to 2 in. long, mostly oblong-reverse-egg-shaped, finely saw-toothed, dark green above, paler below, hairless or nearly so, short-stalked

Cherry (drupe)—usually about ⅜ in. in diameter, bright red, with juicy and bitter pulp

Twigs—slender, hairless, smooth, dull red with gray mottlings

The name bitter cherry is appropriate for this species as the small fruits, or cherries, are intensely bitter even when fully ripe. This cherry may attain the stature of a small tree, 20 feet high or so, having slender upright branches which form a symmetric oblong head; frequently, however, it grows as a spreading shrub, 3 to 10 feet tall, having a rather open growth habit with several crooked stems. The bark, which is bitter and gives off a distinct cherry odor when bruised, is smooth and thin, reddish on the twigs but grayish to dark brown on the stems. Although attractive when in flower, this species is most striking in fall, when the numerous shiny and bright red cherries are displayed. The distribution is limited to the western mountains, occurring from British Columbia to Montana, Arizona, and California.

Bitter cherry grows from near sea level to an altitude of 3,000 feet at its northern extension, but at its southern limits is found chiefly between 5,000 and 9,000 feet. It is generally most abundant in the medium or upper stretches of the ponderosa pine belt, where it frequently occurs in open brush fields as a pure stand or in association with snowbrush, manzanita, silktassels (*Garrya* spp.) and serviceberry. Although it occurs in flats and along streams, it is never abundant in these situations, usually preferring well-drained, moderately fertile but stony sites, on open slopes and ridge tops. Bitter cherry may be rather generally distributed among other browse species, but ordinarily it tends to form patches or extensive tracts, where it is either actually or apparently the dominant plant. These areas are particularly noticeable in the autumn, when the leaves turn yellow after the first frosts.

Bitter cherry is more palatable than would be expected, considering its bitter leaves, twigs, and fruit. The actual use, however, is often much less than sometimes supposed. This is due to the two facts (1) that the tree form and the older and taller shrubby individuals produce most of their foliage beyond the reach of livestock, and (2) that, very often, the thickets, which this species forms either alone or with other shrubs, are so dense as to be inaccessible. On most ranges, the palatability of bitter cherry is poor to fair for cattle and fair to fairly good for sheep. In some cases, actual overgrazing occurs usually where this species is a low but readily available shrub, or along driveways, around watering places, or salt logs, where livestock concentrate. Ordinarily, bitter cherry is a late summer feed, usually untouched by livestock until the herbaceous vegetation and highly palatable browse have been largely consumed.

Apparently, deer and elk outstrip livestock in utilization of bitter cherry, possibly because they frequent the slopes and ridges where it is common. If the species grows on their winter range, these wild animals may even eat the bitter twigs. Birds, squirrels, and bears are only light users of the cherries, probably because of finding them too bitter. Stockmen sometimes claim that bitter cherry is poisonous.[1] However, the species is probably nonpoisonous, at least under range conditions, and there are no authentic records of livestock losses from its use. The closely related, more erect and treelike chokecherries (such as *P. demissa* and *P. melanocarpa*) which have larger leaves, many-flowered showy racemes, and grapelike clusters of black or reddish fruit, are poisonous under some conditions. It seems not unlikely that bitter cherry has been confused with the chokecherries or has undeservedly gained the reputation of being poisonous because of its close relationship to these species.

[1] Dayton, W. A. IMPORTANT WESTERN BROWSE PLANTS. U. S. Dept. Agr. Misc. Pub. 101, 214 pp., illus. 1931.

BITTERBRUSH

Pur'shia tridenta'ta, syn. *Kun'zia tridenta'ta*

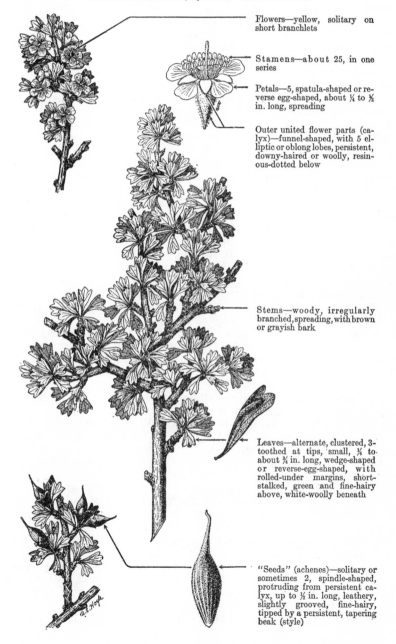

Flowers—yellow, solitary on short branchlets

Stamens—about 25, in one series

Petals—5, spatula-shaped or reverse egg-shaped, about ¼ to ½ in. long, spreading

Outer united flower parts (calyx)—funnel-shaped, with 5 elliptic or oblong lobes, persistent, downy-haired or woolly, resinous-dotted below

Stems—woody, irregularly branched, spreading, with brown or grayish bark

Leaves—alternate, clustered, 3-toothed at tips, small, ¼ to about ¾ in. long, wedge-shaped or reverse-egg-shaped, with rolled-under margins, short-stalked, green and fine-hairy above, white-woolly beneath

"Seeds" (achenes)—solitary or sometimes 2, spindle-shaped, protruding from persistent calyx, up to ½ in. long, leathery, slightly grooved, fine-hairy, tipped by a persistent, tapering beak (style)

Bitterbrush is one of the most important browse plants on western ranges. It is a diffusely branched, semierect, grayish-green shrub of the rose family (Rosaceae). Other common names often applied to this plant are antelope-brush, quinine-brush, black sage and deer-brush. Among stockmen this species, as well as numerous other western shrubs, is frequently called buckbrush. The generic name, *Purshia*, is in honor of Frederick T. Pursh (1774–1820), a distinguished botanical explorer and author. The bush itself, however, was discovered and first collected by the famous explorer, Capt. Meriwether Lewis. The specific name *tridentata* describes the leaves which are three-toothed (tridentate) at the summit. Bitterbrush is a very appropriate common name because of the extremely bitter taste of the herbage. The plant appears in some of the botanical manuals under the name *Kunzia tridentata*, but *Purshia*, being the older generic name, and otherwise tenable, should be universally adopted.

Bitterbrush is one of the most widely distributed of all western shrubs, ranging from Montana to New Mexico, California, and British Columbia. In the Northwest, however, it does not occur west of the crest of the Cascade Mountains. This shrub grows on arid plains, foothills, and mountain slopes within the piñon, ponderosa pine, and aspen belts. It grows mostly in well-drained, sandy, gravelly, or rocky soils on open southerly exposures, at elevations ranging from near sea level in the Columbia Basin of the Northwest to about 9,000 feet in the southern limit of its range. Bitterbrush is generally found growing in association with such dry-land plants as sagebrush, mountain-mahogany, oakbrush, piñon, serviceberry, and wheatgrass. In some of the ponderosa pine stands of eastern Oregon, particularly on the Deschutes and Fremont National Forests, it occurs in dense stands and is one of the principal undershrubs. Idaho fescue is the herbaceous plant most commonly associated with it in these localities. In some areas, such as on the lava flats and benches in northeastern California, bitterbrush often grows in extensive, dense, almost pure stands.

As bitterbrush is usually abundant, sometimes being the chief component of the vegetation, it is an important element of the range carrying capacity. In many places in the West it is regarded as the most important single browse species. The leafage and younger twigs are extensively cropped by sheep, goats, and cattle, but are eaten very little by horses. The palatability of bitterbrush is usually good to very good or excellent for both sheep and cattle throughout most of its range. However, some interesting variations in its palatability occur. Throughout Utah, Colorado, Nevada, northeastern California, and many parts of Idaho, bitterbrush is a highly prized forage plant, but on the Boise, Sawtooth, and Weiser National Forests in Idaho its palatability ranges from worthless to only fair for sheep and poor to fair for cattle, although on adjacent range areas it is regarded as an excellent forage plant. A parallel condition exists in eastern Oregon where, in general, bitterbrush rates as one of the most valuable of all native forage shrubs, being high in palatability for both sheep and cattle. In several localized areas, however, livestock utilize the leafage but very little, even on heavily grazed ranges. In Washington the plant is eaten with only moderate relish, and in Montana it is classed merely as fair forage for cattle and fairly good for sheep. These variations in palatability have not been satisfactorily explained. In part they may be due to fixed feeding habits of the grazing animals in certain localities; to a large extent doubtless the palatability may change with different plant associations or forage combinations; furthermore, there is a possibility that the variation may occasionally be due to the presence of certain chemicals absorbed from the soils which render the plants unpalatable.

Bitterbrush is generally grazed with relish throughout the year but its palatability ordinarily appears to be greatest in spring, winter, and late fall. This species is among the first plants to leaf out in the spring and holds its leaves until early in the winter. Consequently, it is especially important on spring-fall and winter ranges. The forage is of high quality and is said to be a strong feed because it produces solid fat which is not readily lost during inclement weather when feed is scarce or when the animals are shipped long distances.[1] Indicative of the high quality of this forage, fat lambs produced during the spring and summer grazing seasons on the semi-desert bitterbrush ranges of the Deschutes National Forest region of eastern Oregon have equaled or excelled those raised on the neighboring high summer ranges of the Cascades in both weight and quality.

Bitterbrush also withstands heavy grazing remarkably well. On many overgrazed ranges, however, this choice plant is being slowly killed out by excessive use and there is an alarming lack of seedling reproduction over large areas. Forsling and Storm, in their studies of browse utilization in southwestern Utah, determined that continued close utilization of bitterbrush would eventually eliminate it from the range. Under close grazing the upright stems may be killed back to the surface of the ground, whereupon the plant assumes a more or less prostrate, spreading form. It seems resistant to grazing in this shape as the remnant stubs of branches become harsh and serve as a protection against closer grazing. However, continued close grazing of this species in southwestern Utah has proved injurious even in the decumbent form and parts of the plants were found to be dead or in a much weakened condition.[2]

In many parts of the West bitterbrush is one of the chief browse plants for game animals, being especially important as a winter and early spring feed for deer, elk, and antelope. These game animals seek the herbage and eat it with great relish. Dixon[3] lists it as an excellent winter feed of great importance for mule deer in California. This not only holds true in California but elsewhere throughout the range of the plant.

---

[1] Sampson, A. W. NATIVE AMERICAN FORAGE PLANTS. 435 pp., illus. New York. 1924.
[2] Forsling, C. L., and Storm, E. V. THE UTILIZATION OF BROWSE FORAGE AS SUMMER RANGE FOR CATTLE IN SOUTHWESTERN UTAH. U. S. Dept. Agr. Circ. 62, 30 pp., illus. 1929.
[3] Dixon, J. S. A STUDY OF THE LIFE HISTORY AND FOOD HABITS OF MULE DEER IN CALIFORNIA. PART 2.—FOOD HABITS. Calif. Fish and Game 20 (4) : [315]–354, illus. 1934,

Bitterbrush is normally a semierect or low-growing shrub, 1½ to 6 feet high. When growing on exceptionally favorable sites it occasionally attains a height of 9 or 10 feet and assumes the form of a small tree. It is long-lived and exceptionally drought-resistant and thrives under rigorous conditions.

Desert bitterbrush (*P. glandulo'sa*) is the only other species of this genus. The range of this species is restricted to desert areas of southern Nevada and southern California. It resembles *P. tridentata*, but is a dark green shrub with hairless, or practically hairless, evergreen leaves, dotted with impressed glands on the inrolled edges. In contrast, the less persistent leaves of *P. tridentata* are white-woolly underneath and green and fine-hairy on the upper surfaces.

OAKS

Quer'cus spp.

The well-known oak tree has figured prominently in history, verse, and legend from Biblical times, and fragments of its history are also recorded as rock fossils through the geological ages back to the Cretaceous period. *Quercus* is the classical Latin name of the oak tree. This is a very large genus, consisting perhaps of about 500 species, the number varying considerably with the nomenclatural concepts of the individual botanist. It includes trees and shrubs and is almost wholly restricted to the Northern Hemisphere, occurring chiefly in the temperate regions as well as in the tropical mountains.

The religious significance, symbolism, and mythological lore of the oak would require a volume for adequate description. Herodotus, the Greek historian, states that the first oracle was set up in a grove of oak trees at Dodona, Greece; the oaks themselves were thought to inspire the priestess. Some of the familiar Christmas customs cluster around the oak. The festival of Baal (Yiaoul or Yule) was held at Christmastime, and the Yule log, which was burned on that occasion, was always of oak. The mistletoe, because of its close association with the oak, was also held in veneration, particularly at that season of the year. The ancient Druids worshipped in oak groves, and their name commemorates the tree (Greek *drus*, oak tree). Tidestrom [1] has called attention to the fact that *dair* (or *darrach*), the letter D of the Irish (Gaelic) alphabet, is the oak tree. Innumerable personal and place names commemorate the oak, e. g., names with such prefixes as ac-, auch-, auck-, oak-, etc.; and names with such suffixes as -darrach, -darragh, -dare, -derry, etc.

The oak genus is variable with intergradations between the species not uncommon, and hence there are many forms and varieties, which are difficult to distinguish. On a reasonably conservative basis of nomenclature there are approximately 85 species of oak, including well-recognized specific hybrids, occurring natively in the United States. The acorn, a nut set in a scaly cup, is the outstanding character of the genus. Other distinguishing features include: The male and female flowers are borne separately on the same tree (monoecious), the former in drooping, unbranched catkins and the latter solitary or usually a few in a cluster. The leaves are alternate, simple (not compound), and variously lobed, toothed, or entire.

The oaks are most commonly classified into two main groups: (1) The white oaks, with usually light-colored bark, smooth-edged, prickleless leaves, and annual acorns (maturing in 1 year), whose nut shells are hairless on the inner surface; and (2) the black or red oaks, usually having dark-colored bark and more persistent leaves, whose veins frequently extend beyond the leaf margins as short awns or teeth, as well as biennial acorns (maturing in 2 years), whose nut shells are soft-hairy on the inner surface. Dr. William

---

[1] Tidestrom, I. THE FLORAL ALPHABET OF THE CELTS. Torreya 23: 41–49, illus. 1923.

Trelease,[2] an outstanding authority on American oaks, divides them further into a third group, the intermediate oaks (about five species), with gray-brown scaly bark, firm, small, leaves which are entire or have prickly or sharp-pointed teeth, and biennial usually woolly acorns, the acorn shell being woolly within. Other popular oak classifications include live oaks with thick, evergreen, persistent leaves; chestnut oaks with lobed, more or less chestnutlike, leaves; and dwarf, scrubby, shinnery oaks. All of these groups tend to intergrade more or less.

The oaks of the southeastern and eastern States are very important timber trees, especially white oak (*Q. alba*) which produces excellent lumber, being one of the most important hardwood timber species of the East. The hulls of *Old Ironsides* and the other famous early nineteenth century frigates of the United States Navy were made of timber from the eastern live oak (*Q. virginiana*). Eastern oaks are also important because of the tannin contained in the bark, and are used both for fuel and as ornamentals, but are of little economic importance as forage. The western oaks are best represented and of most importance in the Southwest, California, and southern Oregon, although Gambel oak (*Q. gambelii*) and Utah oak (*Q. utahensis*) are very abundant over large areas of the central Rockies. The western oaks are chiefly valued for watershed and soil protection, livestock and wild life forage and protective cover, as well as for cordwood, fence posts, mine props and similar miscellaneous uses. With few exceptions, these species are of little significance in the lumber industry, the trunks of most of them being too crooked or short for suitable saw timber. Many western oaks are shrubs or small trees, and because of their abundance on many ranges are very important range plants. The leaves of a few species furnish fair forage but the foliage of most of them is important only as emergency feed.

The leaves of the deciduous oaks, in general, are more tender, have a higher nutritive value, and are browsed more readily by all classes of livestock than are the leaves of the live oaks. Sheep, and especially goats, utilize the leaves to a greater extent than do either cattle or horses. This is especially true of the live oaks. Mackie[3] made chemical analyses of the leaves of several California oak species and found them relatively high in minerals, protein, crude fiber, ether extract and tannin. He states that oak leaves would probably occupy a high place among forage plants were it not for their excessive content of crude fiber, resins and waxes, and tannin. An exclusive oak leaf diet, because of its tannic acid, sometimes causes sickness, or even death, among cattle and young lambs. The leading symptoms are constipation, emaciation, and inertia. Ill effects are usually avertable by proper management, as oak leaves are not injurious when eaten with a mixture of other forage.

The acorns of many species, especially of the white oak group, constitute an important food of such domestic animals as swine and turkeys, and also of various wild game species, including deer, elk,

[2] Trelease, W. THE AMERICAN OAKS. Natl. Acad. Sci. Mem. 20, 255 pp., illus. 1924.
[3] Mackie, W. W. THE VALUE OF OAK LEAVES FOR FORAGE. Calif. Agr. Expt. Sta. Bull. 150, 21 pp., illus. 1903.

wild hog, bear, and wild turkey, as well as many of the smaller mammals. These particular acorns are high in fats and oils and are very nutritious. In ancient times acorns were a valuable source of food in Greece and France and are still important as food in parts of the Mediterranean region and possibly elsewhere. The acorns of many species were used as food by the Indians, who ground them into a powdery meal and leached out the tannin responsible for the bitter taste with water or wood ash.[4] This meal was subsequently converted into very wholesome and nutritious bread, mush, and soup, and in some localities was the Indian's chief winter food.[5] The Indians also made a decoction by boiling the bark of the oak roots which was used for bowel trouble, especially in children.

Gambel oak with brief notes on closely related species, California black oak (*Q. kelloggii*), and shrub live oak (*Q. turbinella*), are treated separately in this handbook. Other important species deserving mention follow under the three divisions of Trelease's classification of oaks.

White Oaks

Arizona white oak (*Q. arizo'nica*), one of the larger southwestern oaks, is a tree with crooked branches, light gray, ridged bark, and dull, evergreen leaves. It is one of the most common oaks in southern New Mexico, Arizona, and adjacent Mexico in the juniper-piñon and oak-woodland types. The tree is valuable chiefly for its shade, watershed protection, and soil-building properties. The acorns are utilized by livestock and game animals, but the leaves furnish poor forage and are utilized only slightly, except in emergency.

California scrub oak (*Q. dumo'sa*), a shrubby species from 2 to 8 feet high, has dark evergreen leaves with margins varying from entire to sharply toothed. Because of its abundance as chaparral on the dry foothills and slopes of the Coast Range and Sierras of California, it is valuable in watershed protection. The low palatability of this oak is partially attributable to the leathery texture and exceptionally high tannin content[3] of its leaves.

Garry oak (*Q. garrya'na*), the Oregon white oak of the lumber trade and sometimes called Oregon oak, is a Pacific tree or shrub ranging from British Columbia to California, and is the only native oak in the State of Washington. As a tree, it attains a maximum height of about 90 feet and is one of the few important western timber oaks. It is the most palatable of the Pacific oaks, the leaves being poor to fair forage for cattle and fairly good for sheep; the acorns are highly palatable. Brewer oak (*Q. oerstedia'na*, syn. *Q. brew'eri*, *Q. garrya'na brew'eri*) is hardly more than a shrubby form of Garry oak and grows abundantly in almost pure stands—often too dense for effective utilization. It is an important local,

---

[3] See footnote on preceding page.
[4] [Anderson, E.] WHITE-OAK ACORNS AS FOOD. Mo. Bot. Gard. Bull. 12 : 32–33, illus. 1924.
[5] Chesnut, V. K. PLANTS USED BY THE INDIANS OF MENDOCINO COUNTY, CALIFORNIA. U. S. Dept. Agr., Div. Bot., Contrib. U. S. Natl. Herbarium 7 : 295–422, illus. 1902.

erosion-control species in California. Its palatability is slightly inferior to that of Garry oak.

Gray oak (*Q. gri'sea*), a common and abundant tree or shrub of the Southwest, has thickish, gray-green, or bluish green leaves similar to those of Arizona white oak. Its abundance on some ranges makes it an important and valuable drought emergency forage. The foliage is grazed but lightly in the presence of palatable forage, although the mast is eaten readily by livestock and wild animals.

California white oak (*Q. loba'ta*), one of the largest of the American oaks, inhabits the rich bottom lands of the Sacramento and San Joaquin Valleys of California. This is a handsome, exceptionally broad-crowned tree valued for its beauty, shade, and wood, which makes excellent posts and fuel. It produces high-quality acorns, formerly a favorite food of the Indians.[5]

Intermediate Oaks

Canyon live oak (*Q. chryso'lepis*) and huckleberry oak (*Q. vaccinifo'lia*) are common live oaks which grow abundantly in California and southern Oregon. Canyon live oak, a tree from 20 to 60 feet high, with leaves varying from entire to coarsely toothed, is one of the most widely-distributed Pacific Coast oaks, occurring in canyons and on hillsides in the mountains. Huckleberry oak is a shrubby species of the higher mountains, commonly 2 to 6 feet high and, as the name implies, has small, entire leaves which resemble those of "huckleberry" (*Vaccinium* spp.). These two oaks are important as a protective cover but, except for the acorns, are of little or no value as forage.

Red (or Black) Oaks

Emory oak (*Q. emo'ryi*), or blackjack oak, is the commonest forest oak in the foothills and mountains of southern Arizona and New Mexico. It has dark bark, sharp-pointed leaves, and is a more upright tree than most of the Southwestern oaks. Typically, this species has one main trunk with small branches extending at nearly right angles. It provides good watershed protection, satisfactory fuel, posts, and mine props and, for a black oak, the acorns are unusually sweet and palatable. However, the leaves are eaten but little and rate as poor forage even during drought.

---

[5] See footnote on preceding page.

GAMBEL OAK

Quer′cus gambe′lii

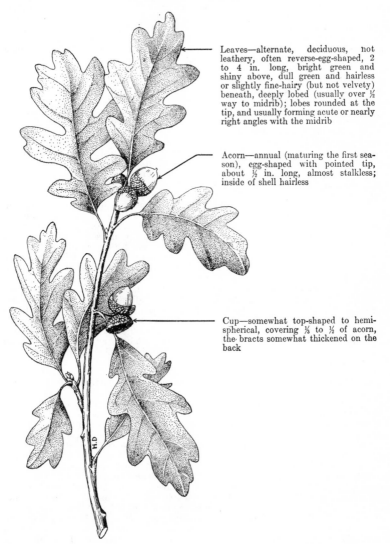

Leaves—alternate, deciduous, not leathery, often reverse-egg-shaped, 2 to 4 in. long, bright green and shiny above, dull green and hairless or slightly fine-hairy (but not velvety) beneath, deeply lobed (usually over ½ way to midrib); lobes rounded at the tip, and usually forming acute or nearly right angles with the midrib

Acorn—annual (maturing the first season), egg-shaped with pointed tip, about ½ in. long, almost stalkless; inside of shell hairless

Cup—somewhat top-shaped to hemispherical, covering ⅓ to ½ of acorn, the bracts somewhat thickened on the back

Gambel oak is best known throughout its range in its autumnal aspect, when its gorgeous leaves color the foothills and mountain slopes.

This species, belonging to the white oak group, is either a small tree or large shrub; it ranges from western Texas to Wyoming, Utah, southern Nevada, and Arizona and south into Mexico. It grows most abundantly in the central and southern Great Basin, where it occurs over large areas of the foothills, canyons, and lower mountain slopes either in dense, pure stands or sometimes in association with chokecherries (*Prunus* spp.), true mountain-mahogany (*Cercocarpus montanus*) and serviceberries (*Amelanchier* spp.). It is also common, and often abundant, in the upper woodland and ponderosa pine types of the Southwest. It is not so drought-enduring as most southwestern oaks, and grows at higher elevations where soil moisture is more plentiful. Although often found on coarse or even rocky sites, it prefers the sandy or gravelly loams, and attains its best development in canyon bottoms and sheltered places in rich loam soils, where its extensive roots receive adequate moisture. This species is a good soil builder, and at least a thin layer of black rich soil is usually found beneath an old-established stand of Gambel oak. As a result, a good understory of palatable, herbaceous vegetation, such as bromegrass, bluegrass, lupine, and geranium, frequently occurs under this oak, especially in the more open stands.

Because of its size, leafiness, and great abundance, Gambel oak produces a vast amount of herbage, which is usually fair in palatability for all classes of livestock, and also for deer. On some grass ranges where there is a scarcity of palatable browse, it is considered fairly good forage. On the other hand, where palatable shrubs are plentiful this species is regarded as having but little forage value. On overgrazed ranges, this oak is usually grazed so closely as to form a grazing line, or "high water mark" below which all of the foliage is stripped annually. This is not an uncommon condition along canyon bottoms where cattle congregate. Gambel oak acorns are relatively sweet and are eaten readily by all classes of livestock, deer, and wild turkeys.

Forsling and Storm [1] found on a controlled area that heavy use of oak resulted in overgrazing the palatable shrubs and herbaceous species; furthermore, the cattle grazed made poor gains and slow growth, and the calf crop was unsatisfactory. These experimenters found that oak and other less palatable shrubs were always utilized to some extent along with the more palatable species.

Experiments by Marsh, Clawson, and Marsh [2] have proven definitely that oak leaves may sometimes produce fatal sickness in cattle. They show, however, that cattle succumb only from an exclusive diet of oak, and that no losses occur where other supplemental forage is available. Gambel oak is an outstanding species in the history of western oak poisoning. Losses are chiefly restricted to cattle, but sheep have also been reported as affected. Oak poisoning has been reported at all seasons where oak leaves are available, but cattle losses have occurred chiefly in the spring and on ranges where grazing was permitted before other forage was available, or on overgrazed range where cattle were forced to subsist on an almost pure diet of oak. There is little or no danger of oak poisoning when the range is grazed properly. The outstanding symptoms of oak-leaf poisoning are constipation, emaciation, and edema; the feces contain mucus and blood.

Gambel oak has been segregated by some modern authorities into a number of species, or forms, based largely on the shape of the acorn and the shape, lobing, color, hairiness, and persistence of the leaves. These characters are so variable, that it is very difficult to distinguish between such species as Utah oak (*Q. utahen'sis*), New Mexican oak (*Q. novomexica'na*), and Vreeland oak (*Q. vreelan'dii*).

Utah oak is very similar to Gambel oak, being segregated chiefly on the basis of the leaf, which is soft-hairy or almost velvety beneath and somewhat reverse egg-shaped in outline. Gambel oak leaves are hairless or only slightly hairy beneath, and usually oblong in outline. The acorns of Utah oak have somewhat thicker scales and are a little larger than those of Gambel oak, being one-half to three-fourths of an inch long; the acorns of Gambel oak are rarely longer than one-half of an inch. Furthermore, Utah oak often grows taller than Gambel oak, occasionally reaching a height of about 30 feet. In economic value these two oaks are practically similar, and hence are seldom differentiated in the field. Sheep losses have been reported in Utah from excessive eating of the acorns of Utah oak.

[1] Forsling, C. L., and Storm, E. V. THE UTILIZATION OF BROWSE FORAGE AS SUMMER RANGE FOR CATTLE IN SOUTHWESTERN UTAH. U. S. Dept. Agr. Circ. 62, 30 pp., illus. 1929.
[2] Marsh, C. D., Clawson, A. B., and Marsh, H. OAK-LEAF POISONING OF DOMESTIC ANIMALS. U. S. Dept. Agr. Bull. 767, 36 pp., illus. 1919.

CALIFORNIA BLACK OAK

Quer'cus kellog'gii, syn. *Q. califor'nica*

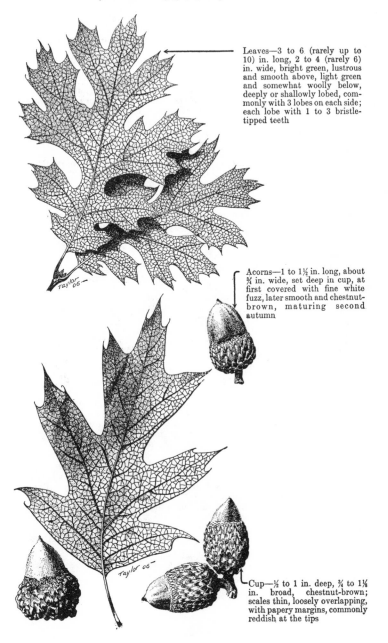

Leaves—3 to 6 (rarely up to 10) in. long, 2 to 4 (rarely 6) in. wide, bright green, lustrous and smooth above, light green and somewhat woolly below, deeply or shallowly lobed, commonly with 3 lobes on each side; each lobe with 1 to 3 bristle-tipped teeth

Acorns—1 to 1½ in. long, about ¾ in. wide, set deep in cup, at first covered with fine white fuzz, later smooth and chestnut-brown, maturing second autumn

Cup—½ to 1 in. deep, ¾ to 1⅛ in. broad, chestnut-brown; scales thin, loosely overlapping, with papery margins, commonly reddish at the tips

California black oak attains the largest size of any of the mountain-inhabiting oaks of Oregon and California. As the common name indicates it is mostly confined to California and belongs to the group of oaks commonly known as the black oaks, which are, as a rule, characterized by dark or black bark, reddish or dark wood, bristle-tipped leaf lobes, and biennial acorns. Its range is from the McKenzie River in western Oregon, south through the Sierras and inner coast ranges, to the high mountains of southern California.

This species is characteristically associated with and reaches its highest development in the mixed conifer belt. Here it commonly becomes a tree 30 to 80 feet in height, but is markedly smaller outside this zone, especially at the upper altitudinal limits. The species is widely distributed within its range, occurring from elevations of several hundred feet in the foothills up to 8,000 feet in the mountains, but it does not occur near the sea or on the plains. It is very adaptable, growing in the shade of coniferous forests, on cold northern slopes, and on exposed and warm southern exposures. It sometimes forms pure stands over extensive areas, especially on canyon slopes and benches. Soils do not seem to be an important limiting factor, as this tree occurs on nearly all types of soils, from fertile valley loams to extremely stony sites or even talus slopes, although its preference is well-drained situations.

Ordinarily California black oak in tree size is wholly beyond the reach of grazing animals. However, the species is abundant, and the reproduction and the dwarf, high-altitude forms provide an important source of browse. Older trees frequently sprout from the trunk base, and fire-killed individuals send forth a profuse new growth. Mackie found that the foliage was high in nutrient value as compared with that of other oaks but believed that the high resin and wax content impaired its palatability.[1] Field observations, however, on California national forests clearly indicate that California black oak is extensively browsed by livestock. It is a very important feed wherever available and abundant, being rated fair forage for cattle and fairly good for sheep. Deer relish its foliage, and are especially fond of the acorns as a fall and winter feed.[2] California black oak is subject to overgrazing as the sprouts, reproduction, or low dwarf forms all have an open growth, thus making the entire foliage within grazing height available. Close use of the large leaves for several seasons causes the stems and branches to die, or where the plant has sufficient height, it results in the production of new growth at a level beyond the reach of browsing livestock.

California black oak is not valuable for lumber as the wood is porous and brittle, and most of the older trees are defective. It is highly prized locally for fuel and is used limitedly in the manufacture of tool handles and wooden mauls. Chemical studies [3] indicate that the yield of acetic acid and alcohol from destructive distillation of this oak equals that obtained from birch and is greater than that obtained from beech and maple; however. little commercial use of the wood for distillation purposes has been made.

California black oak often develops into a handsome broad-crowned tree when growing in the open, but the individuals in dense stands are slender and have few branches. The forms growing at high altitudes are dwarfed, mostly less than 20 feet in height, very irregular in shape, and usually develop their longest branches near the ground. The bark of the young trees and of the limbs is smooth and gray, becoming darker and checked with age until, on the trunks of old trees, it is dark and divided into broad ridges below and oblong plates above. The deciduous leaves vary in color; they emerge from the chestnut-colored, scaly winter buds a dark red or purple and gradually change to a lustrous dark yellow green at maturity. In the fall they turn to various shades of yellow, red, and brown, adding much to the autumnal beauty of their native hills and valleys.

---

[1] Mackie, W. W. THE VALUE OF OAK LEAVES FOR FORAGE. Calif. Agr. Expt. Sta. Bull. 150, 21 pp., illus. 1903.
[2] Dixon, J. S. A STUDY OF THE LIFE HISTORY AND FOOD HABITS OF MULE DEER IN CALIFORNIA. PART 2—FOOD HABITS. Calif. Fish and Game 20 (4) : [315]–354, illus. 1934.
[3] Palmer, R. C. YIELDS FROM THE DESTRUCTIVE DISTILLATION OF CERTAIN HARDWOODS. SECOND PROGRESS REPORT. U. S. Dept. Agr. Bull. 508, 8 pp., illus. 1917.

SHRUB LIVE OAK

Quer′cus turbinel′la, syn. *Q. dumo′sa turbinel′la*

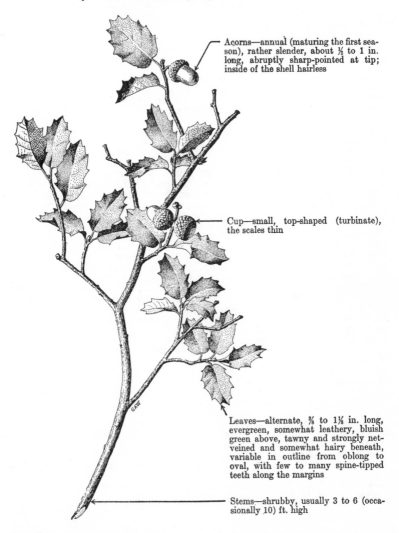

Acorns—annual (maturing the first season), rather slender, about ½ to 1 in. long, abruptly sharp-pointed at tip; inside of the shell hairless

Cup—small, top-shaped (turbinate), the scales thin

Leaves—alternate, ¾ to 1⅛ in. long, evergreen, somewhat leathery, bluish green above, tawny and strongly net-veined and somewhat hairy beneath, variable in outline from oblong to oval, with few to many spine-tipped teeth along the margins

Stems—shrubby, usually 3 to 6 (occasionally 10) ft. high

Shrub live oak, a member of the white-oak group, is also known as chaparral oak, gray oak, and turbinella oak. Chaparral oak alludes to its occurrence as an outstanding chaparral-forming oak of the Southwest. Gray oak refers to the fact that the bark, leaves, and acorn cups of this species frequently have a grayish hue. Turbinella oak, based on the scientific name, is a reminder of the top-shaped acorn cups [1] (Latin *turbinella*, a little top). It is an

---

[1] Greene, E. L. ILLUSTRATIONS OF WEST AMERICAN OAKS. Illus. by A. Kellogg. 84 pp. San Francisco. 1889.

evergreen shrub commonly 3 to 6, but occasionally as much as 10 feet high, and forms dense thickets or large clumps over extensive areas. The species ranges from southern California and northern Lower California through southern Nevada and southern Utah, to New Mexico and possibly also in northern Chihuahua and Sonora. Shrub live oak is a drought-resistant species that inhabits the dry hillsides and mesas on sandy, gravelly, or rocky soils, chiefly at elevations of from 4,000 to 6,500 feet. It is common in the semidesert shrub type and extends up into the juniper-piñon, or woodland type; among its most common associates are catclaw, manzanita, mountain-mahogany, squawberry and silktassel. In southern parts of Utah and Nevada, this species occurs in scattered patches, principally in swales and canyons of the lower winter ranges.

Because of its abundance, its evergreen character, and the fact that it is one of the superior oaks from a palatability standpoint, this species ranks as one of the two or three leading browse oaks of Arizona, [2][3] if not of the Southwest. Its greatest value as forage comes during a drought emergency when all grasses and weeds have withered beyond use. Even in normal seasons, shrub live oak constitutes the chief reserve supply of winter emergency forage on many ranges of central and southern Arizona. In time of stress, livestock will survive on an almost straight diet of this shrub for a period of several months despite that it is not a balanced feed.

During normal years, when grass forage is available, shrub live oak is utilized lightly in the chaparral types. However, on slopes exposed to erosion, wise management doubtless would regard the plant as emergency forage only or, in order to protect the grasses and weeds from overgrazing, permit this shrub to be grazed lightly when those herbaceous plants are practically dormant. On grass ranges where shrub live oak occurs as scattered clumps, it is sometimes rather closely cropped by cattle and sheep and rates as fairly good browse. Goats graze this oak freely, especially in the winter, and use it more than any other class of livestock. This is particularly true in the chaparral types, as shrub live oak, although attaining a height readily accessible to livestock, often occurs in dense clumps or thickets of considerable size, which are practically impenetrable to cattle and sheep, but are partially accessible to goats. Thus, in addition to being more palatable to goats, the foliage is also more available to those animals. Deer consume the foliage on considerable scale; the acorns, or mast, are relished by deer, wild turkey, and possibly other wild game, as well as by many small mammals. The acorns formerly were also used as food by the Indians of the Southwest.

It is probable that large areas of what is now chaparral type were once open brushland which supported a good cover of grasses between scattered brush clumps. As a result of severe and continued overuse, those grasses and other choice forage plants were supplanted by less palatable shrubs, which partly filled in the gaps. In such cases, the brush mantle thus formed, and without the supporting herbaceous cover, although much inferior to the original cover for watershed protection, yet plays an important role as a substitute cover. Proper range management of similar areas should favor the remaining herbaceous plants with the objective of eventually restoring the original, superior vegetative stand (subclimax or climax type).

Shrub live oak differs from most of the oaks of the white oak group (section, or subgenus *Leucobalanus*) in that its leaves have spiny-tipped teeth, in marked contrast to the predominantly prickleless leaves of that group. However, it has rather light-colored bark, rather numerous stamens, short blunt anthers, annual acorns with shells hairless within, and other characteristics of the important white oak group.

---

[2] Griffiths, D. RANGE INVESTIGATIONS IN ARIZONA. U. S. Dept. Agr., Bur. Plant Indus. Bull. 67, 62 pp., illus. 1904.
[3] Thornber, J. J. THE GRAZING RANGES OF ARIZONA. Ariz. Agr. Expt. Sta. Bull. 65: [245]–360, illus. 1910.

CALIFORNIA BUCKTHORN

Rham'nus califor'nica

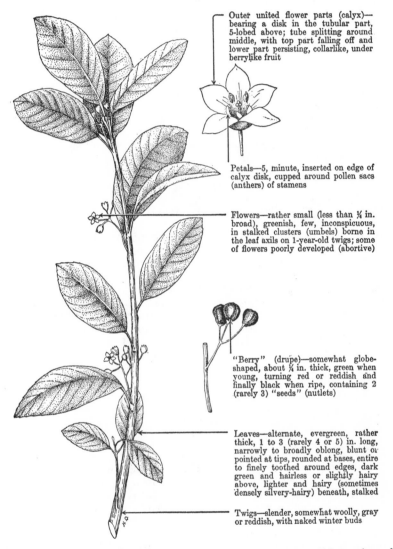

Outer united flower parts (calyx)—bearing a disk in the tubular part, 5-lobed above; tube splitting around middle, with top part falling off and lower part persisting, collarlike, under berrylike fruit

Petals—5, minute, inserted on edge of calyx disk, cupped around pollen sacs (anthers) of stamens

Flowers—rather small (less than ¼ in. broad), greenish, few, inconspicuous, in stalked clusters (umbels) borne in the leaf axils on 1-year-old twigs; some of flowers poorly developed (abortive)

"Berry" (drupe)—somewhat globe-shaped, about ¼ in. thick, green when young, turning red or reddish and finally black when ripe, containing 2 (rarely 3) "seeds" (nutlets)

Leaves—alternate, evergreen, rather thick, 1 to 3 (rarely 4 or 5) in. long, narrowly to broadly oblong, blunt or pointed at tips, rounded at bases, entire to finely toothed around edges, dark green and hairless or slightly hairy above, lighter and hairy (sometimes densely silvery-hairy) beneath, stalked

Twigs—slender, somewhat woolly, gray or reddish, with naked winter buds

This evergreen, olivelike shrub is one of about 14 valid species of *Rhamnus* found in the West. It is variously known as coffeeberry, pigeonberry, yerba-del-oso, and cascara sagrada, although the last name is more applicable to the sister species, cascara buckthorn (*R. purshiana*). California buckthorn is usually several- to many-stemmed, the stems commonly a few inches or a foot apart, slender, leafy, and spreading, the whole forming a rather open, rounded clump 4 to 8 feet high and often much broader than tall. This species is very variable in foliage, fairly distinctive leaf forms having been developed in various climatic areas.[1] Although some authors consider these forms to be of specific rank, more conservative botanists prefer to recognize them simply as varieties or forms of *R. californica*. The fact that the forage utilities of these variations are similar is an additional argument for adhering to the more conservative nomenclatural viewpoint in this treatment.

California buckthorn inhabits foothills and mountain slopes from southern Oregon to southern California. It is most characteristic, common, and abundant in the foothill or lower montane areas at elevations ranging from 1,000 to 3,000 feet, though it frequently descends to near sea level in the valleys or occurs up to 5,000 feet in the Sierras. This shrub is a common component of the foothill woodland chaparral, where it is usually associated with whiteleaf manzanita (*Arctostaphylos viscida*) and wedgeleaf ceanothus (*Ceanothus cuneatus*). Like these and other chaparral species, California buckthorn inhabits warm and dry sites, usually on southern exposures where the soil, generally, is stony, only moderately fertile, and frequently rather shallow. Although very common, this shrub seldom grows in a pure stand, nearly always occurring as large, shrubby individuals, especially in the small openings in the chaparral. The plant is difficult to destroy, especially by fire, as it sprouts freely, the seeds are long-lived, and heat facilitates their germination.

California buckthorn, important chiefly because of its commonness on many ranges, apparently contributes very little to the grazing capacity. Its evergreen leaves are leathery and tough; the twigs and bark are acrid and bitter. On closely grazed or on winter ranges, sheep and goats pick at the foliage but, under more average conditions, the species is usually so unpalatable that it is not used even by goats. The species has local value as ground cover for watershed protection, doubtless serves as a covert for deer, and its edible, juicy fruit is eaten by birds.

BUCKTHORNS

Rham'nus spp.

The buckthorns compose a genus of about 100 species, rather widely distributed throughout the temperate and warm climates of the world, especially of the Northern Hemisphere. The buckthorn family (Rhamnaceae), which takes its name from this genus, contains several other genera, of which the various species of *Ceanothus* are the best known and most valuable from a western range standpoint. The Old World jujube (*Zizyphus jujuba*, syn. *Z. vulgaris*), cultivated for its edible fruits, is also a member of this family. The origin of the common name buckthorn is rather obscure. It may have arisen in Europe, where some of the species are thorny and provide shelter for the male deer, or buck, or it may be a distortion

---

[1] Jepson, W. L. A MANUAL OF THE FLOWERING PLANTS OF CALIFORNIA. 1,238 pp., illus. Berkeley, Calif. [1925.]

of the term boxthorn. *Rhamnus* is the Latinized form of the ancient Greek name for the genus.

The buckthorns are shrubs or (mostly small) trees, with evergreen or deciduous, mostly alternate leaves, and small, usually greenish flowers, borne in axillary clusters. The fruit, which is a fleshy, two- to four-seeded berrylike drupe, serves readily to distinguish the buckthorns from the closely related genus *Ceanothus* in which the fruit is a dry capsule.

Cascara buckthorn (*R. purshia'na*) is probably the most common of the several other species of *Rhamnus* occurring in the West. It is a frequent, but not abundant, shrub or small tree occurring in the forested mountains from British Columbia to western Montana and northern California. It shares its southern range with California buckthorn. However, these two species can usually be distinguished by the typically arborescent habit of cascara buckthorn which, moreover, has larger, thin and deciduous leaves, and prefers moist and shaded sites in the timber. Cascara buckthorn is browsed very lightly by sheep and, to some extent, by deer, but for all practical purposes its forage value is negligible. This plant is important chiefly as the source of cascara sagrada (literally, sacred bark) of commerce, which is used medicinally as a laxative. Most of the bark is collected in Oregon and Washington and is preferable to the California material which is often largely composed of California buckthorn.[2][3][4] However, the name cascara sagrada is also used in the trade for the bark of California buckthorn, "which is a popular remedy in many places in California, especially among the Mexican inhabitants, whose settlements reach not much farther north than San Francisco, and are, therefore, not in the region of typical *Purshiana*." [5]

Alder buckthorn (*R. alnifo'lia*), as the name indicates, has alderlike foliage. It is a low shrub, from 2 to 4 feet high, inhabiting moist situations from Newfoundland to British Columbia, northern California, Idaho, Wyoming, Nebraska, Illinois, and New Jersey. It may have some value as local sheep browse.

Hollyleaf buckthorn (*R. cro'cea*) in its typical form is a low, evergreen, spiny-leaved, short- and stiff-branched shrub, apparently confined to the coast and coastal mountains from central to southern California, and perhaps, also, Lower California. However, in its several varieties it attains tree size (up to 30 feet in height). In the varieties (a) *ilicifo'lia* (syn. *R. ilicifo'lia*), with the leaves often golden beneath, and (b) *pilo'sa* (syn. *R. pilo'sa*), with narrow, revolute, more or less hairy leaves, it extends into Arizona; in the variety (c) *insula'ris* (syn. *R. insula'ris*), a form with larger, almost toothless leaves, it also occurs in the islands off the coast of both southern California and Lower California. The leaves of hollyleaf buckthorn are elliptic in outline; the flowers lack petals; and the fruits are bright red berries, which served as food for the Indians.

The introduced common buckthorn (*R. cathar'tica*), as well as some of the native species, are intermediate hosts for the crown rust disease of oats.[6]

[2] Munger, T. T. THE CASCARA BARK INDUSTRY ON THE SIUSLAW NATIONAL FOREST. Jour. Forestry 17 : 605–607. 1919.
[3] Chicanot, E. L. CASCARA BARK. AN IMPORTANT MINOR FOREST PRODUCT. Empire Forestry Jour. [London] 5 : 102–105. 1926.
[4] Starker, T. J., and Wilcox, A. R. CASCARA. Amer. Jour. Pharm. 103 : 73–97, 147–175, illus. 1931.
[5] Brandegee, K. RHAMNUS CALIFORNICA AND ITS ALLIES. Zoe 1 : 240–244. 1890.
[6] Dietz, S. M., and Leach, L. D. METHODS OF ERADICATING BUCKTHORN (RHAMNUS) SUSCEPTIBLE TO CROWN RUST (PUCCINIA CORONATA) OF OATS. U. S. Dept. Agr. Circ. 133, 16 pp., illus. 1930.

COAST RHODODENDRON

Rhododen'dron califor'nicum

Outer united flower parts (calyx)—bluntly 5-lobed, small and inconspicuous

Stamens—10, colored, shorter than the petals, without appendages

United petals (corolla)—somewhat irregularly 5-lobed, top-shaped or bell-shaped, white at base, shading to rose-purple at the ruffled edges; upper lobe, or "petal" greenish-dotted within

Flowers—1¼ in. long, in showy end clusters, from end buds with thin bracts which soon fall off

Seed pod (capsule)—5-celled, dry, many-seeded, splitting 5 ways from the top and away from the seed-bearing center (placenta)

Leaves—alternate, evergreen, leathery, oblong or elliptic, rich green above, rusty or lighter below, with somewhat inrolled edges, 2½ to 6 in. long, crowded toward ends of flowering branches

Stems—usually 3 to 10 (sometimes, when species treelike, up to 26) ft. high, gray, rather straight and slender (at least in the shrubby plants)

Coast rhododendron, or California rosebay, an erect evergreen shrub, commonly 3 to 10 feet high, occasionally taller and treelike, occurs on the west slope of the Cascades and in the coastal regions from British Columbia into northern California. The generic name *Rhododendron* in this case is also the common name; it is a combination of the Greek *rhodon*, rose, and *dendron*, tree; hence rosetree (or rosebay). It is a very handsome plant, with large, evergreen leaves crowded at the summit of the straight stems. During the spring and early summer the large, showy, terminal, rose-colored flower clusters are attractively displayed above the bright green leaves.

Coast rhododendron inhabits moist, humid woods, both in open and shady sites. It attains maximum development in the shaded forests of the redwood region, where treelike specimens up to as much as 26 feet in height are not uncommon.[1] It does best on moist rich soils, but apparently is unable to survive in extremely wet and boggy places. In the region where coast rhododendron grows, Douglas fir is probably the most common timber species, while salal, western bracken, and hazel are forest floor plants commonly associated with it.

Stockmen consider coast rhododendron negligible to worthless as a forage plant for all classes of livestock. The foliage is definitely unpalatable, but it is not known whether this is due to its thick and leathery character or to some disagreeable taste, possibly resulting from the harmful compound, andromedotoxin.[2] It has been reported as poisonous to sheep,[1] although this has not been substantiated by experimentation. It is highly probable, however, that the plant contains poisonous properties, which are known to be generally present in the eastern and Old World rhododendrons, as well as in the closely related azaleas, including western azalea (*Azalea occidentalis*) of California and southwestern Oregon. However, even if it were definitely known that coast rhododendron is potentially poisonous sickness or losses from it, under range conditions, are probably negligible, as it is unpalatable and, for the most part, grows in regions not grazed by domestic livestock. It is, perhaps, worth while to mention, in this connection, that honey made from rhododendrons has the reputation of producing a violent purgative and emetic effect.

Coast rhododendron is frequently cultivated as an ornamental, evergreen, acid-soil shrub. It is the only true *Rhododendron* growing in the Western States, unless the opinion of certain western botanists is accepted that western azalea and false-azalea (*Azaleastrum albiflorum*) also belong to the genus *Rhododendron*. These last-named two species are actually quite different from coast rhododendron. Western azalea is a deciduous, thin-leaved shrub, having somewhat larger, white, or pink flowers, with the five stamens extending about an inch beyond the corolla (united petals). False-azalea is a smaller shrub, with leafy stems, deciduous leaves, and white, 10-stamened flowers borne in lateral clusters.

---

[1] Jepson, W. L. A MANUAL OF THE FLOWERING PLANTS OF CALIFORNIA. 1,238 pp., illus. Berkeley, Calif. [1925.]
[2] Chesnut, V. K. PRELIMINARY CATALOGUE OF PLANTS POISONOUS TO STOCK. U. S. Dept. Agr., Bur. Anim. Indus. Ann. Rept. (1898) 15 : 387–420, illus. 1899.

SKUNKBUSH

Rhu's triloba'ta, syns. *R. canaden'sis triloba'ta, Schmaltz'ia triloba'ta*

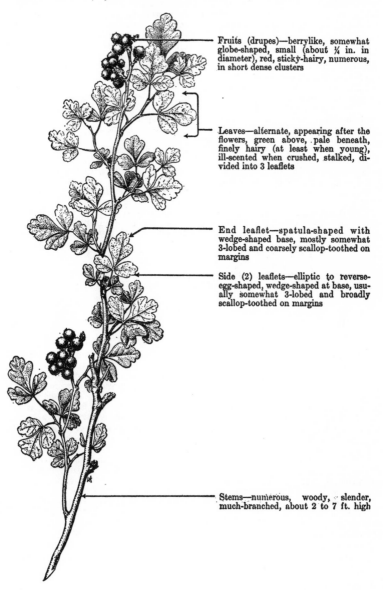

Fruits (drupes)—berrylike, somewhat globe-shaped, small (about ¼ in. in diameter), red, sticky-hairy, numerous, in short dense clusters

Leaves—alternate, appearing after the flowers, green above, pale beneath, finely hairy (at least when young), ill-scented when crushed, stalked, divided into 3 leaflets

End leaflet—spatula-shaped with wedge-shaped base, mostly somewhat 3-lobed and coarsely scallop-toothed on margins

Side (2) leaflets—elliptic to reverse-egg-shaped, wedge-shaped at base, usually somewhat 3-lobed and broadly scallop-toothed on margins

Stems—numerous, woody, slender, much-branched, about 2 to 7 ft. high

Skunkbush, a much-branched shrub from 2 to 7 feet high but which averages about 4 feet, is widely distributed, ranging from Alberta to Illinois, northern Mexico, California, and southern Oregon. It is listed in some of the manuals as occurring in Washington, but the local manuals of that State omit it; hence it is doubtful if skunkbush grows there. This species is often known as squaw-berry, squawbush, and skunkbrush; other common names include lemita, lem-onade sumac, polecat bush, shoneehaw, and three-lobed sumac. Some of these names refer to its disagreeable odor; others to its acid fruits. The specific name is Latin for three-lobed, and refers to the three leaflets. This plant abounds on dry, rocky hillsides, principally at elevations of from 3,500 to 8,000 feet, but also occurs at lower elevations and frequently grows in nearly pure stands. In addition, it appears, to some extent, along streams and in canyon bottoms, specimens in the moister situations being larger and more luxuriant than those of the drier sites. In such locations, this species seldom forms pure stands, but is associated with alders (*Alnus* spp.), serviceberries (*Amelanchier* spp.), chokecherries (*Prunus* spp.), and other shrubs. Skunk-bush inhabits the ponderosa pine and other open coniferous timber stands, as well as oakbrush, typically occupying openings in these types, and does not occur ordinarily in dense shade.

Over most of its range the palatability of this species to domestic livestock is distinctly low. However, in the Southwest and southwestern Colorado the species is usually fair, fairly good, or even good for cattle as well as sheep, depending largely on the local supply of palatable herbaceous vegetation. Chapline[1] reports that "lemita or skunkbush (*Schmaltzia* spp.)" is "of very high palatability" to goats in the Southwest.

The Indians prized the tough, pliable shoots of skunkbush in basketmaking.[2] They also used the dried, powdered fruits as a lotion in the treatment of smallpox.[3] The powder was mixed with water and applied to the unbroken, hard pustules but was used dry on the open sores. These usages are reflected in the English names squawberry and squawbush applied to this species.

In the desert regions of California a variety (*R. triloba'ta anisophyl'la*) occurs, which differs from the typical form of the species chiefly in having smaller leaves with the lateral leaflets unequal in size and the berries bright crimson in color.

SUMACS

Rhu's spp.

Sumacs, under a conservative nomenclatural concept, compose a genus of about 125 species of evergreen or deciduous shrubs or trees containing a milky, usually acrid or resinous sap, and with simple or compound leaves. Besides tannin, they yield waxes, dyes, varnishes, and medicinal compounds. Species of the genus are widely distributed in the temperate and warmer regions of both hemispheres. *Rhus* is the classical name of these plants, which belong to the sumac family (*Anacardiaceae*) that includes various well-known eco-nomic and ornamental trees, such as cashew (*Anacardium occidentale*), mango (*Mangifera indica*), California peppertree (*Schinus molle*), the smoke-trees (*Cotinus* spp.), and pistache (*Pistacia vera*).

As herein discussed, the sumac genus includes the genera *Lithraea*, *Loba-dium*, *Neostyphonia*, *Rhoeidium*, and *Schmaltzia* of some authors, but the poison-ivies, poison-oaks, and poison-sumacs (*Toxicodendron* spp.), merged in the genus *Rhus* by some botanists, are regarded as generically distinct.

On a conservative basis, some 18 species of *Rhus* occur in the West,[4] being separated according to leaf differences into the following well-defined groups:

(1) Three species with undivided, thick, evergreen leaves belonging to the genus *Lobadium* of some authors, are shrubs, or sometimes small trees of the

---

[1] Chapline, W. R. PRODUCTION OF GOATS ON FAR WESTERN RANGES. U. S. Dept. Agr. Bull. 749, 35 pp., illus. 1919.
[2] Wooton, E. O. TREES AND SHRUBS OF NEW MEXICO. N. Mex. Agr. Expt. Sta. Bull. 87, 159 pp., illus. 1913.
[3] Chesnut, V. K. PLANTS USED BY THE INDIANS OF MENDOCINO COUNTY, CALIFORNIA. U. S. Dept. Agr., Div. Bot., Contrib. U. S. Natl. Herbarium 7: 295–422, illus. 1902.
[4] Dayton, W. A. IMPORTANT WESTERN BROWSE PLANTS. U. S. Dept. Agr. Misc. Pub. 101, 214 pp., illus. 1931.

Southwest, and are practically worthless or at least poor browse plants, except occasionally for goats.[4]

(2) Utah sumac (*R. utahen'sis*, syns. *Schmaltz'ia affi'nis, S. simplicifo'lia*), a peculiar species placed by some in the genus *Schmaltzia*, with mostly undivided, rounded, or kidney-shaped leaves, occurs in the sagebrush and piñon-juniper belts from southern Utah to Arizona, possibly extending also into southeastern California. This frequently abundant species, although usually low in palatability, provides local browse for cattle, sheep, and goats, when other forage is either scarce or lacking.[4]

(3) Six or eight species composing the genus *Schmaltzia* of some botanists, of which skunkbush, annotated at length above, is the most familiar example, occur in the West. These shrubs have divided (compound) leaves with mostly three leaflets, and the group as a whole fairly closely resembles *R. trilobata* which is, by far, the commonest and most widely distributed species. They are known by various vernacular names, including lemonade sumacs, sweet sumacs, lemitas (sometimes spelled lametas), and three-lobed sumacs, and are, by all odds, the most valuable species of the genus from a forage standpoint. The palatability of the species of this group varies from practically worthless to fair for cattle and sheep, the higher values prevailing chiefly in the Southwest, where these sumacs also provide very good goat browse. "The acid berries of these shrubs are eaten by Indians and occasionally by whites, and a rather pleasant beverage can be made from at least some of them."[4] The slender, pliable twigs were prized by the Indians for basket work.

(4) About five species of true sumacs, that is, *Rhus* in a restricted sense, are shrubs or small trees characterized by leaves with more than three leaflets (pinnately odd compound), and bearing dense terminal clusters of scarlet, berrylike fruits. Rocky Mountain sumac (*R. cismonta'na*) is typical of this group, whose members are practically worthless as forage plants. Most species of this type contain considerable tannin in the leaves and bark; certain eastern species are employed, to some extent, in the tanning industry. Although somewhat coarse in growth habit, the brilliant autumn foliage and bright-red "berries" of many species are very attractive and give them horticultural value.

CURRANTS

Ri'bes spp.

Some authors classify the currants and the very similar gooseberries in a single genus, *Ribes;* others separate them into four genera: (1) the currants (*Ribes* spp.), (2) the flowering or golden currants (*Chrysobo'trya* spp.), (3) the gooseberries (*Grossula'ria* spp.), and (4) the swamp currants (*Limnobo'trya* spp.). However, the usage is followed here of Dr. Frederick V. Coville, of the United States Department of Agriculture, generally acknowledged to be the foremost living American authority on these plants, who recognizes two genera, *Grossularia* and *Ribes,* the latter genus including the flowering and swamp currants mentioned above. These shrubs are members of the gooseberry family (Grossulariaceae), which some botanists prefer to regard as a tribe or subfamily of the saxifrage family (Saxifragaceae). Under this concept, the genus *Ribes* includes approximately 65 species, natives of the North Temperate Zone, Mexico, and South America, about 56 being native to the western States. The name *Ribes,* variations of which appear in Italian, Spanish, French, Medieval Latin, and other Mediterranean languages, appears to have been derived from *ribas,* the Persian and Arabic name for an Oriental species of rhubarb (*Rheum ribes*). Dr. Coville informs us that "from the juice of the young stems and leaves of this plant was prepared a famous Arabic syrup, of acidulous flavor. For this product there was substituted in western Europe, in later centuries, a syrup of similar taste made from the berries of the European red currants", to which syrup similar names were applied. There is every evidence that Linnaeus, in his "Genera Plantarum" (1737), was led by this word transference in adopting *Ribes* as the generic name for the currant-gooseberry group.

The currants are unarmed or occasionally prickly shrubs with mostly small flowers borne in few- to many-flowered clusters (racemes) or sometimes solitary in the leaf axils. The outer flower part (calyx) is tube- or bell-shaped below and usually 5-lobed above. The five petals are attached to the mouth of the calyx tube, alternate with the five stamens and frequently are smaller than the calyx lobes. The individual flower stalks (pedicels) are jointed just below the seed-producing organ (ovary) and usually bear a pair of more or less conspicuous bracts just below this joint. The leaves are palmately 3- to 5-lobed and usually have toothed margins. The more or less edible fruits are red, black, or yellow berries.

The currants and gooseberries are much alike in general appearance, being separated chiefly on the difference in the flower stalks, or pedicels—jointed in the currants with the berry breaking away from the pedicel; not jointed in the gooseberries, the berry remaining attached to the stalk. Furthermore, the stems (and frequently the berries) of most gooseberries are armed with spines, or prickles, and the flowers (and fruits) are either solitary or in small clusters; most species of currants lack spines on the stems; the fruits are seldom bristly; and the flowers are borne in usually drooping and many-flowered clusters.

Currants are very widely distributed in the West, occurring from the semi-desert areas at lower elevations to the upper limits of the spruce-fir belt in the mountains. Some species favor moist, shaded sites and grow on timbered, north slopes and along streams; others occur on dry, south slopes and ridges in full sunlight. The currants, generally, are mostly scattered, developing as individual bushes or growing in small patches, but seldom forming dense stands of any considerable size. On the whole, however, they are common and in many localities are near the van among the shrubby components of range vegetation.

As browse plants the currants are often a material factor in the carrying capacity of the range because of their common occurrence, the large amount of foliage produced, and the relatively low, rounded, and scattered growth habit, which is conducive to easy utilization. In general, however, their palatability is low, being poor to fair for cattle and poor to fairly good for sheep and goats. Horses rarely crop them, although deer and elk browse the leaves during the summer and fall, and the shoots and twigs during winter, depending upon the amount of other forage available. Although the fruits of all species are edible, certain ones are not pleasing to the human palate; the berries of some native western species are commonly gathered and used by local residents. Undoubtedly the berries are an important source of food for many birds and smaller animals.

The currants are of considerable importance in forestry in all parts of the United States where white (5-needle) pines are important timber trees. These shrubs, as well as the gooseberries, serve as alternate hosts for the fungus (*Cronartium ribicola*) which causes white pine blister rust. This disease, an arch destroyer of white pines, is common over much of the white pine region in the eastern United States and has now become established in many parts of the West. The only practical method of controlling the disease is to eradicate all currants and gooseberries in the vicinity of stands of white pine. Such control methods have been initiated in parts of the country where white pines are important timber trees.[1][2][3]

From a browse standpoint sticky currant (*R. viscosissimum*), wax currant (*R. cereum*)—including the very closely related squaw currant (*R. inebrians*)—and western black currant (*R. petiolare*) are, perhaps, the most important of the western currants and are treated separately in this handbook. A number of other native western currants are also comparatively widespread and common; prominent among these are golden currant, gooseberry currant, citronella currant, prickly currant, and winter currant, brief notes for which species follow:

Golden currant (*R. au'reum*, syn. *Chrysobo'trya au'rea*) is widely distributed throughout the Western States, growing principally along water courses at the lower and medium elevations. The sweet, juicy berries are mostly yellow in color, although some may be red or even black. The stems are without spines or bristles, the calyx tube is very long and slender, and the flowers are yellow. This species rates about average in palatability. It is sometimes grown as an ornamental, although the closely related clove currant (*R. odoratum*, syns. *R. aureum odoratum*, *R. fragrans*, *R. longiflorum*, *Chrysobotrya odorata*) of the gardens, also known as buffalo and Missouri currant, of the Middle West, is perhaps the most extensively cultivated of our native currants. A large-berried form of *R. odoratum* known as Crandall currant is cultivated for its fruit.

Gooseberry currant (*R. monti'genum*, syn. *Limnobo'trya monti'gena*) is a straggling shrub, 1 to 2 feet high, with more or less spiny stems, rather short clusters of only three to seven flowers, and bright red, densely glandular-bristly berries. The 3- to 5-lobed leaves are glandular-hairy and rather small,

[1] Darrow, G. M., and Detwiler, S. B. CURRANTS AND GOOSEBERRIES: THEIR CULTURE AND RELATION TO WHITE-PINE BLISTER RUST. U. S. Dept. Agr. Farmers' Bull. 1398, rev., 43 pp., illus. 1929.
[2] Spaulding, P. WHITE-PINE BLISTER RUST: A COMPARISON OF EUROPEAN WITH NORTH AMERICAN CONDITIONS. U. S. Dept. Agr. Tech. Bull. 87, 58 pp., illus. 1929.
[3] Offord, H. R. THE CHEMICAL ERADICATION OF RIBES. U. S. Dept. Agr. Tech. Bull. 240, 24 pp., illus. 1931.

being mostly less than 1 inch wide. This species occurs chiefly in the high mountains in the spruce-fir belt from British Columbia to Montana, New Mexico, and California; it is also sometimes fairly abundant along the edges of subalpine meadows and parks. It is only fair forage for sheep and poor for cattle. The berries, much sought by grouse and other birds, are also excellent for pie.

Citronella currant (*R. hal'lii*, syn. *R. viscosis'simum hal'lii*), with its light blue, smooth berries and 3- to 5-lobed leaves of variable shape, occurs at medium elevations chiefly in rocky places from southern Oregon to western Nevada and California. The stems are smooth with dark-colored bark, and the leafstalks are coarsely hairy. The fresh leaves have the odor of citronella. This species rates somewhat higher in palatability than the average of the genus, being fairly good browse for cattle, sheep, and goats.

Prickly currant (*R. lacus'tre*, syn. *Limnobo'trya lacus'tris*) grows mostly in swamps and is very widely distributed, ranging from Newfoundland to Alaska and south to Pennsylvania, Colorado, and California. The sharply toothed, mostly 5-lobed, leaves are about three-fourths of an inch to 2 inches long; they are practically hairless, but are borne on hairy leafstalks. The stems are both spiny and bristly, with the spines scarcely longer than the bristles. The small purple-black berries are glandular-hairy. For the most part this species is poor browse.

Winter currant (*R. sangui'neum*), also called redflower currant and blood currant, is one of the most interesting of the western *Ribes*. It is a stout shrub with a balsamic odor and is probably the most robust of the western species, often growing 12 feet high. The flowers are large, spicy-scented, and red, purple-red, rose-colored, or occasionally white. It occurs in dry to moist woods from British Columbia to California. The blue-black berries are globular, rough, glandular-hairy, with a dense, whitish, waxy bloom, and are dry and insipid with a sweetish to bitterish flavor. This species is a very handsome ornamental and is widely cultivated, several horticultural varieties of it having been developed.

Currants, of course, are extensively grown for their fruits. W. T. Macoun (in Bailey)[4] states that currants are not known to have been cultivated prior to the middle of the sixteenth century; that they are not mentioned by any of the ancient authors who wrote about fruit, and that they apparently were unknown to the Romans. Most species cultivated in America for their fruits are derived from two introductions, the European red currant (*R. sativum*) and the European black currant (*R. nigrum*). Swamp red currant (*R. triste*) and American black currant (*R. americanum*) are two native American species which offer promise for cultivation.

Currants are easily cultivated; for the most part they are hardy and well adapted to temperate regions. They reproduce from seed with but little variation. Cuttings of both ripened and green wood may be used for propagation, and the establishment of new plants by layering is comparatively simple. Grafting, however, is not resorted to unless it is desired to propagate some unusual form. A treelike growth habit can be developed by eliminating the root shoots and all the buds except the terminal one on the stem until the stem reaches the desired height.

4 Bailey, L. H. THE STANDARD CYCLOPEDIA OF HORTICULTURE . . . New ed., 3 v., illus. New York and London. 1933.

WAX CURRANT

Ri'bes ce'reum

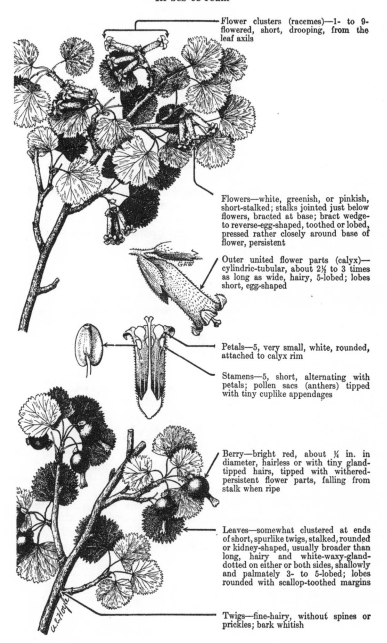

Flower clusters (racemes)—1- to 9-flowered, short, drooping, from the leaf axils

Flowers—white, greenish, or pinkish, short-stalked; stalks jointed just below flowers, bracted at base; bract wedge-to reverse-egg-shaped, toothed or lobed, pressed rather closely around base of flower, persistent

Outer united flower parts (calyx)—cylindric-tubular, about 2½ to 3 times as long as wide, hairy, 5-lobed; lobes short, egg-shaped

Petals—5, very small, white, rounded, attached to calyx rim

Stamens—5, short, alternating with petals; pollen sacs (anthers) tipped with tiny cuplike appendages

Berry—bright red, about ¼ in. in diameter, hairless or with tiny gland-tipped hairs, tipped with withered-persistent flower parts, falling from stalk when ripe

Leaves—somewhat clustered at ends of short, spurlike twigs, stalked, rounded or kidney-shaped, usually broader than long, hairy and white-waxy-gland-dotted on either or both sides, shallowly and palmately 3- to 5-lobed; lobes rounded with scallop-toothed margins

Twigs—fine-hairy, without spines or prickles; bark whitish

Wax currant is an unarmed, much-branched shrub, mostly less than 5 feet high, with numerous rather small (three-eighths to 1¼ inches wide) leaves, borne principally at the ends of short, spurlike twigs. The specific name *cereum* is a Latin adjective meaning waxy, or waxen, and refers to the waxy glands on the leaves. The bush is common on dry, open slopes and ridges, and locally is often the dominant woody plant, although as a rule it does not form dense stands. This species ranges from British Columbia to California, Arizona, and Montana, being one of the most widely distributed of western currants. Its altitudinal range is wide; it occurs in the upper desert, piñon-juniper, ponderosa pine, lodgepole pine, and aspen belts, where it is common in partial shade of these woody plants, although it probably never grows in dense shade. It is frequently associated with such shrubs as big sagebrush (*Artemisia tridentata*), bitterbrush (*Purshia tridentata*), chokecherries (*Prunus* spp.), serviceberries (*Amelanchier* spp.), and rabbitbrushes (*Chrysothamnus* spp.). The bitterbrush–wax currant association is extremely common in the Northwest and in the eastern foothills of the central Rocky Mountains, although in the latter region sagebrush and rabbitbrush usually are also present in greater or less amounts. In the Great Basin and the Southwest, the chokecherries and serviceberries are more commonly associated with wax currant, although by no means its only companions.

The palatability of wax currant, as a rule, is not high, seldom being more than poor or fair, especially during the spring and summer. However, the abundance of this plant and the large amount of herbage produced by this species are sufficient sometimes to class it as a rather important factor in the carrying capacity of the range. Furthermore, its rounded growth habit and freedom from spines and the fact that it usually grows in open stands are conducive to utilization.[1] Chemical analyses tend to indicate that wax currant is nutritious, and has a high protein content.[2] Deer and elk utilize the twigs of this species to some extent for winter forage. The small bright red berries are sometimes utilized by Indians, but are not well flavored; however, they are extensively consumed by birds and rodents.

Squaw currant (*R. ine'brians*), also known as rock currant and wine currant, is a closely related, very similar species, which occurs in the Rocky Mountains and eastward, ranging from South Dakota to western Nebraska, New Mexico, central California, and Idaho. It may be associated with wax currant and appears on similar sites; these two species have about the same palatability. The flowers of squaw currant are usually pinkish, and the oblong or diamond-shaped bracts of the flower stalks are entire- or few-toothed; in contrast, the flowers of wax currant are chiefly whitish and the bracts are wedge-shaped to reverse egg-shaped and usually lobed or toothed near the apex.

---

[1] Dayton, W. A. IMPORTANT WESTERN BROWSE PLANTS. U. S. Dept. Agr. Misc. Pub. 101, 214 pp., illus. 1931.
[2] [Wilson, N. E., Dinsmore, S. C., and Kennedy, P. B.] NATIVE FORAGE PLANTS AND THEIR CHEMICAL COMPOSITION. Nev. Agr. Expt. Sta. Bull. 62, 41 pp., illus. 1906.

WESTERN BLACK CURRANT

Ri'bes petiola're

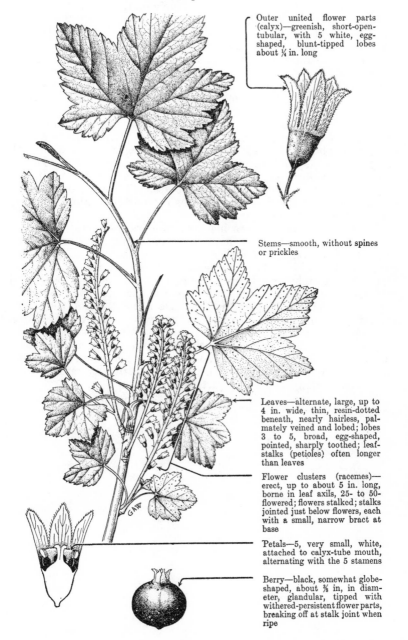

Outer united flower parts (calyx)—greenish, short-open-tubular, with 5 white, egg-shaped, blunt-tipped lobes about ¼ in. long

Stems—smooth, without **spines** or prickles

Leaves—alternate, large, up to 4 in. wide, thin, resin-dotted beneath, nearly hairless, palmately veined and lobed; lobes 3 to 5, broad, egg-shaped, pointed, sharply toothed; leafstalks (petioles) often longer than leaves

Flower clusters (racemes)—erect, up to about 5 in. long, borne in leaf axils, 25- to 50-flowered; flowers stalked; stalks jointed just below flowers, each with a small, narrow bract at base

Petals—5, very small, white, attached to calyx-tube mouth, alternating with the 5 stamens

Berry—black, somewhat globe-shaped, about ⅜ in. in diameter, glandular, tipped with withered-persistent flower parts, breaking off at stalk joint when ripe

Western black currant has been confused with Hudson Bay currant (*R. hudsonia'num*) and, in some of the western botanical manuals, its description has been included under the latter name. The flower clusters of Hudson Bay currant are usually 6- to 12-flowered, and the leaves are firm, and hairy on the lower surface; the flower clusters of western black currant are mostly 25- to 50-flowered and the leaves are thin and essentially hairless. Hudson Bay currant ranges from Alaska, British Columbia, and Montana eastward to Minnesota, Ontario, and Hudson Bay; the range of western black currant is from British Columbia to Oregon (possibly northern California), Nevada, Utah, northern Colorado, and Montana. Western black currant is a mountain species occurring chiefly in the aspen and spruce belts, along streams, and in other moist sites in association with willows, alders, and other shrubs characteristic of such locations. This shrub also grows on drier sites, being in evidence on rocky hillsides in the open in association with other shrubs, as well as in aspen and coniferous timber. In the Northwest, western black currant is a common shrub on cut-over lands at elevations from 4,000 to 6,000 feet. The altitudinal range of this species in the Rocky Mountains extends from approximately 4,000 to 8,500 feet above sea level.

For the most part, western black currant occurs as scattered individuals or in small patches, its distribution being local rather than general. However, it is rather widely distributed, and produces considerable forage. This species is not one of the best browse plants, its palatability seldom being better than poor for cattle and fair for sheep. It is also fair browse for deer and elk. It probably is most utilized during the fall. Deer and elk crop the shoots and twigs of this species on winter ranges, when other feed is scarce.

The berries of this species are utilized by birds and small animals but, because of their peculiar, musky odor, are rarely used by man. This perhaps partly explains why western black currant is sometimes known as dog currant. The species name, *petiolare*, refers to the characteristic long leafstalks (petioles).

STICKY CURRANT

Ri'bes viscosis'simum

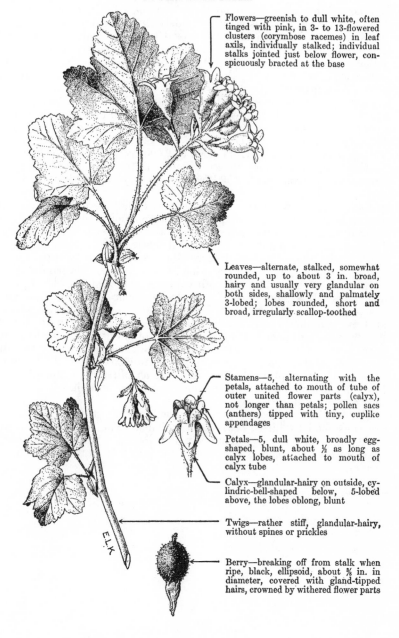

Flowers—greenish to dull white, often tinged with pink, in 3- to 13-flowered clusters (corymbose racemes) in leaf axils, individually stalked; individual stalks jointed just below flower, conspicuously bracted at the base

Leaves—alternate, stalked, somewhat rounded, up to about 3 in. broad, hairy and usually very glandular on both sides, shallowly and palmately 3-lobed; lobes rounded, short and broad, irregularly scallop-toothed

Stamens—5, alternating with the petals, attached to mouth of tube of outer united flower parts (calyx), not longer than petals; pollen sacs (anthers) tipped with tiny, cuplike appendages

Petals—5, dull white, broadly egg-shaped, blunt, about ½ as long as calyx lobes, attached to mouth of calyx tube

Calyx—glandular-hairy on outside, cylindric-bell-shaped below, 5-lobed above, the lobes oblong, blunt

Twigs—rather stiff, glandular-hairy, without spines or prickles

Berry—breaking off from stalk when ripe, black, ellipsoid, about ⅜ in. in diameter, covered with gland-tipped hairs, crowned by withered flower parts

Sticky currant, known also as hairy currant and sandbox currant, is a rather stiff-twigged, bushy, spineless shrub with reddish, shreddy bark and with the leaves, young shoots, flowers, and berries usually densely glandular-hairy. The glandular or viscid nature of the plant is reflected in the specific name *viscosissimum*, a Latin adjective meaning very sticky. This is a rather widely distributed species, ranging from British Columbia to California, Utah, northern Colorado, and Montana. It occurs mostly in the mountains in the ponderosa pine, lodgepole pine, and spruce-fir types, but also grows in aspen and brush types as well as in the open, frequently on rather dry rocky sites. As a general rule, this shrub is of scattered occurrence, but it is common and sometimes locally abundant. In the Northwest this species occurs chiefly between elevations of 1,400 and 5,000 feet, frequently in association with Douglas maple (*Acer douglasii*) and thimbleberry (*Rubus parviflorus*). In California it grows in the mountains at elevations from 8,000 to 9,500 feet, often on rocky sites. In the Great Basin and Rocky Mountains the altitudinal range of this species is from about 2,500 feet (in Idaho) to 9,500 feet (in Utah and Colorado).

As browse, sticky currant is important chiefly because of its local abundance, wide distribution, and the large amount of leafage which it produces. The leaves remain green and are retained until killing frosts occur; the plants form rounded bushes, seldom over 5 feet in height, with the foliage easily accessible to livestock—features which add appreciably to the browse value of this species. Its palatability, however, is, as a rule, low, though varying somewhat with local plant associates. In Colorado it is worthless to poor for both cattle and sheep. In Utah and southern Idaho it is fair or even fairly good—at least for sheep. In Washington, Oregon, and northern Idaho it is worthless to poor for cattle and fair for sheep, and in California it rates as worthless or occasionally poor for cattle and poor to fair for sheep and goats. In general, it is fair deer and elk browse. Sticky currant is probably of most value as fall forage, though it is limitedly browsed during the summer, and deer and elk often nibble the twigs on winter range.

The black, seedy berries, which ripen in August and September, are consumed by birds, bears, and rodents. The ripe berries have little pulp; their flavor, colloquially described as "fuzzy", is peculiar; they are used to some extent locally for jam and as the fruit filling in pies.

NEW MEXICAN LOCUST

Robi′nia neomexica′na

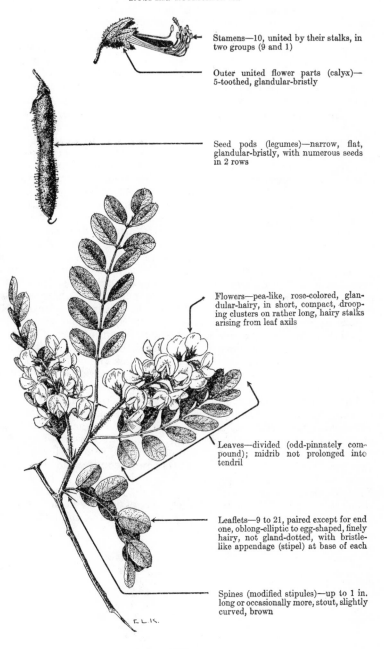

Stamens—10, united by their stalks, in two groups (9 and 1)

Outer united flower parts (calyx)—5-toothed, glandular-bristly

Seed pods (legumes)—narrow, flat, glandular-bristly, with numerous seeds in 2 rows

Flowers—pea-like, rose-colored, glandular-hairy, in short, compact, drooping clusters on rather long, hairy stalks arising from leaf axils

Leaves—divided (odd-pinnately compound); midrib not prolonged into tendril

Leaflets—9 to 21, paired except for end one, oblong-elliptic to egg-shaped, finely hairy, not gland-dotted, with bristle-like appendage (stipel) at base of each

Spines (modified stipules)—up to 1 in. long or occasionally more, stout, slightly curved, brown

E.L.K.

765

New Mexican locust, sometimes (though erroneously) called algaroba or, colloquially, agarroba, is a large, thorny shrub or small tree, varying from several feet up to 20 or 25 feet in height. With the exception of the little known southern New Mexican species *R. rusbyi*, it is the only species of the genus occurring naturally in the Western States. It ranges from western Texas to southern Colorado, southern Nevada, and south into the mountains of northern Sonora. The altitudinal distribution of this species varies from about 4,000 to 9,000 feet. At the lower altitudes it grows chiefly in canyon bottoms and on north slopes, but at the higher elevations the species occurs also on dry ridge tops and rocky slopes. Scattered patches of this shrub are common in open ponderosa pine stands, and also occur, on some small scale, in openings in aspen and spruce-fir types.

This shrub is usually considered as poor to fair forage for cattle and horses. Cattle seem to relish the flowers; both cattle and horses crop the leaves to some extent. The new growth is most palatable and is grazed in early summer before the thorns develop. Chapline [1] designates New Mexican locust as an important browse species of high palatability for goats in the Southwest. Sheep graze it moderately on some ranges, particularly when there is a scarcity of other browse forage. This plant has been heavily grazed and seriously damaged by deer on the Kaibab National Forest. However, such severe use indicates extreme overstocking; under conservative use by deer the species is utilized rather lightly. Black locust (*Robinia pseudoacacia*) of the Eastern States, often cultivated in the West as a common shade tree, is a closely related species and is recognized as poisonous; there are no indications, however, that New Mexican locust produces undesirable effects upon livestock.[2]

New Mexican locust reproduces by both suckers and seed, and recovers rapidly from overgrazing, when given opportunity. It is important in erosion control, as it establishes itself readily on relatively poor sites, and thrives on steep slopes and gully banks. An attractive shrub, easily transplanted, New Mexican locust is sometimes used for ornamental purposes and grows well under cultivation.

This locust, which usually attains a height of from 10 to 15 feet, grows in clumps, frequently forming dense thickets that afford good cover for game birds. The trunk is seldom over 4 inches in diameter, and the top is open and spreading. The leaves resemble those of the common black locust very closely; the large and showy flowers varying from a bright to dark rose-pink, or occasionally nearly white, lack the sweet fragrance of the white flowers of black locust. New Mexican locust is easily distinguished from *R. rusbyi* by the sticky hairs which beset the flowers, seedpods, and flower and fruit stalks. The flowers appear from April to August; the pods are usually fully formed by the middle of September.

---

[1] Chapline, W. R. PRODUCTION OF GOATS ON FAR WESTERN RANGES. U. S. Dept. Agr. Bull. 749, 35 pp., illus. 1919.
[2] Dayton, W. A. IMPORTANT WESTERN BROWSE PLANTS. U. S. Dept. Agr. Misc. Pub. 101, 214 pp., illus. 1931.

ROSES

Ro'sa spp.

FENDLER ROSE (*R. fendleri*)

Flowers—pink or rose, usually clustered

Petals—5, about ½ in. long, reverse-heart-shaped; stamens numerous

Leaves—alternate, divided into leaflets, stalked; bracts (stipules) grown to lower part of leafstalk, flat, winged.

Leaflets—5 or 7 (sometimes 9), elliptic, oval or reverse-egg-shaped, glandular-saw-toothed (or often doubly saw-toothed), green and smooth above, paler and glandular beneath

Rosa fendleri

Fruit (hip)—globe-shaped, about ⅜ in. in diameter, smooth, crowned by 5 persistent, long-taper-pointed outer flower-part lobes (sepals)

BALD-HIP ROSE (*R. gymnocarpa*)

Sepals—rather short, hairless on the back, soon withering and falling

Flowers—pale pink to rose, usually solitary

Leaflets—5 to 9 (sometimes 11), up to a little more than 1 in. long, somewhat round to elliptic, thin, hairless, shiny green above, lighter beneath, with edges doubly saw-toothed; teeth gland-tipped

Hip—orange-red or red, ellipsoid to globe-shaped, about ⅜ in. in diameter, not crowned by persistent sepals

Rosa gymnocarpa

The roses are the best known genus of the large and very important rose family (Rosaceae) ; in fact, they constitute probably one of the most familiar plant groups extant. Originally native to the cooler and temperate climates of the Northern Hemisphere, they have a world-wide distribution through introduction and cultivation. Most peoples of the Northern Hemisphere, and particularly those of Aryan descent, have admired and cultivated roses since practically the dawn of time. Even today, many commonly known words, phrases, and legends reflect this ancient regard for the rose. The legend that Cupid bribed the god of silence with a rose seems to have given birth to the early European custom of suspending a rose from the ceiling when proceedings were to be kept secret; hence the expression, *sub rosa* ("under the rose").[1] The familiar phrase, "bed of roses", originated in Egypt, where mattresses of rose leaves, even today, are especially prepared for people of high rank.[2] The rose gardens and festivals of Persia were, perhaps, the most famous in ancient history. Today, these mostly fragrant and handsome flowers of various hues are almost universal favorites, as is amply demonstrated by their presence in gardens and parks, and also by the elaborate rose pageants and festivals celebrated annually in many cities. The various species of wild rose, although largely neglected in favor of their cultivated relatives, are still held in esteem by many flowerlovers because of their natural, simple, and individual charm. Their popularity is evidenced by the fact that Georgia, Iowa, New York, and North Dakota have selected the wild rose, or a particular species, as their respective State flowers.

Although the genus *Rosa* is a very natural one, distinguished by well-marked characters from allied genera and seldom, if ever, confused with other plants, the taxonomic limits of its individual species are difficult to determine, this being complicated by their tendency to hybridize freely and by the high variability of many of the diagnostic characters. Certain minor characteristics recur in various combinations in each of the sections, or larger groups of species, and are therefore not sufficiently constant to be trustworthy in distinguishing a particular species. This is especially true of the presence or absence of prickles and their form; the texture, hairiness, and glandular character of the leaflets as well as the kind of teeth; the form of the "hips"; and the absence of hairs or the type of glandular hairs present on the sepals.[3] The most conservative estimates recognize well over 100 species. The roses are erect, trailing, or climbing shrubs, usually with prickly stems, that often arise from underground rootstocks. The alternate leaves are odd-pinnate (very rarely simple), with the leaflets commonly saw-toothed; the base of the leafstalk usually appears winged because of the two partly fused (adnate) stipules. Generally, the beautifully colored, and mostly fragrant flowers are attractively displayed, either occurring singly or in clusters at the ends of the branchlets. The five (rarely four, six, seven, or eight) red, pink, or white (also yellow in exotic and cultivated roses) petals are rounded or reverse-heart-shaped, and are in-

[1] Lindley, J. ROSARUM MONOGRAPHIA ; OR, A BOTANICAL HISTORY OF ROSES . . . New ed., 156 pp., illus. London. [1830.]
[2] Clements, E. S. FLOWERS OF COAST AND SIERRA. 226 pp., illus. New York. 1928.
[3] Erlanson, E. W. FIELD OBSERVATIONS ON WILD ROSES OF THE WESTERN UNITED STATES. Mich. Acad. Sci., Arts, and Letters, Papers (1929) 11: 117–135. 1930.

serted with the numerous stamens on a disk lining the throat of the calyx, or hypanthium (tube). The five outer flower parts (sepals) are generally elongated, slender, and simple or variously lobed; they often persist after the fruit has matured, being erect or spreading, or they may be deciduous. The globose or urn-shaped hypanthium is a very characteristic feature of the rose flower; at maturity it becomes fleshy, forming a usually red-colored false fruit, generally known as a hip, containing many hard "seeds" (achenes), which have developed from the numerous, commonly hairy, long-styled immature fruits (carpels) in the base of the hypanthium.

Wild roses are very common on the western ranges, growing under diverse conditions varying from exposed, hot, and dry situations to shaded, cool, and moist places. Ordinarily, they are scattered, and provide a small part of the ground cover, only forming patches or thickets under especially favorable conditions. Most species, however, prefer moist habitats, being found chiefly in the vicinity of seeps, springs, streams, and the sandy banks or flats along streams. A few species extend up to over 9,000 feet elevation in Colorado, but most western roses grow at low and middle elevations. As a group, roses are generally regarded as poor to fair forage for cattle but fairly good for sheep. In the Intermountain region, in Montana, and possibly elsewhere, they are commonly rated as good for sheep. Although browsed season-long, the tendency is to use these plants most heavily in the late summer and fall. Deer and elk consume roses rather generally, sometimes browsing them severely, especially on the winter range. Apparently, the thorny character of the stems does not materially hamper the use of the foliage, as instances of close grazing or overuse are common on heavily grazed ranges.

The two species, Fendler rose (*R. fend'leri*) and bald-hip rose (*R. gymnocar'pa*), shown in the accompanying illustration, as well as several others, are either widely distributed or occur in local abundance, or both, and deserve individual treatment. Fendler rose is commonly a thorny shrub 2 to 3 feet in height, with usually 5 to 7 thin dark green leaflets, and showy pink or rose-colored flowers, which usually are several and clustered. It is widely distributed, growing in the middle and higher elevations in the mountains from Montana and South Dakota to western Texas and Arizona, and south into Mexico. This shrub occurs mainly in open woods, on fertile and moist soils, and is frequently associated with willows, aspen, serviceberry and various oaks. Dayton reports [4] that—

this rose is one of the most important browse species of the genus. Its moderate size is conducive to full utilization and may sometimes subject it to injury. It is ordinarily cropped only moderately, but occasionally closely, by both cattle and sheep.

Bald-hip rose, one of the commonest species in the Northwest, occurs from Vancouver Island and southern British Columbia to western Montana, Idaho, and central California. It is a slender, weak-stemmed shrub up to 10 feet in height and usually has solitary flow-

[4] Dayton, W. A. IMPORTANT WESTERN BROWSE PLANTS. U. S. Dept. Agr. Misc. Pub. 101, 214 pp., illus. 1931

ers; the branches are either smooth or armed with long, slender, straight prickles. This rose is common in the foothills and low to medium elevations of the mountains, growing in the shaded woods and brushy north slopes of the ponderosa pine and Douglas fir belts and commonly associated with hollygrape, salal, oceanspray, and ferns. It is, perhaps, one of the most important of the native roses on the western ranges, and in the Northwest is considered the most palatable species. Maximum use occurs during the late summer and fall. Other than in the Northwest the species rates fair to fairly good in palatability for cattle and good for sheep.

Macoun rose (*R. macou'nii*), Maximilian rose (*R. maximilia'ni*), and Woods rose (*R. wood'sii*) are rather common and similar wild roses which, although of somewhat inferior forage value, are often confused with Fendler rose. Macoun rose, a low, prickly shrub up to 3½ feet high, occurs sparingly in the middle and subalpine elevations from British Columbia to Manitoba and south to Utah and northern New Mexico. The distribution of Maximilian rose is in dispute, owing to differences of taxonomic opinion; it is essentially a northern species ranging from Washington to Saskatchewan and South Dakota and extending southward perhaps as far as New Mexico and Utah. It is a spiny shrub up to 40 inches in height, and is not abundant except possibly locally along canyons at middle elevations. Woods rose is a rather heavily armed shrub from 1 to 6 feet in height; it sometimes is locally abundant on riverbanks, canyons, and in open woods of the ponderosa pine and spruce belts from British Columbia to Nevada and western Kansas.

California wild rose (*R. califor'nica*), a prickly, rather stout shrub 3 to 6 feet high, grows only in California, where it is probably the most common wild rose. It inhabits river and creek flats, and banks and moist or springy places in the low and middle altitudes, and is generally regarded as fairly good browse. Engelmann rose (*R. engelman'nii*), a low shrubby rose seldom over 20 inches high, very bristly, but not spiny, occurs in the open woods from the Dakotas to Montana and Colorado; it is usually considered choice sheep feed.

Nutka rose (*R. nutka'na*), whose large flowers make it one of the most attractive of the western wild roses, is widely distributed from Alaska to California, Colorado, and western Montana. This stout, usually spiny shrub, 2 to 10 feet high, is inferior in palatability to many roses. The ripened fruit, however, is edible by man and beast.[5] Cluster rose (*R. pisocar'pa*), a common, slender, usually prickly-stemmed plant, grows scatteringly along streams and dry ravines from British Columbia to Oregon and Idaho, and possibly also to California and Utah. It is regarded as good sheep browse. Pear-hip rose (*R. pyri'fera*), a rather large shrub up to 4 or more feet in height, is so named because of its pear-shaped fruits, or hips. It inhabits moist, frequently shady situations from Montana to Wyoming, Utah, Nevada, and California, and is regarded as approximately average among the roses in forage value. Spalding rose (*R. spalding'ii*) ranges from British Columbia to Idaho, Wyoming, Utah, northern California, and Oregon, being most common in the ponderosa pine belt, where it grows under a wide variety of soil and moisture conditions. It is an erect, usually spiny shrub about 3 feet high. Spalding rose is one of the more palatable roses, being considered fair for cattle and fairly good to good for sheep.

[5] Rusby, H. H. THE APRIL WILD FOODS OF THE UNITED STATES . . . Country Life in Amer. 9 (6) : 718–719, illus. 1906.

TRAILING BLACKBERRY

Ru'bus macrope'talus

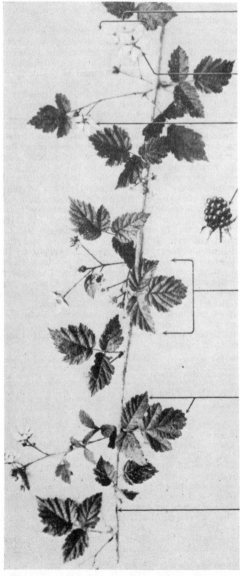

Flowers—white, in few-flowered clusters, of 2 kinds: male (staminate) with numerous stamens, and essentially female (pistillate), borne on separate plants

Outer flower parts (sepals)—5, united at base, egg-shaped, glandular and prickly, usually taper-pointed, persistent

Petals—5, about ⅝ to 1 in. long (longer in male than in female), 1 to 2 times longer than sepals

"Berry" (aggregated druplets)—adherent to central core (receptacle), black or dark purple, cylindric, about ⅝ to 1 in. long, hairless

Leaves—alternate, mostly divided into 3 leaflets

Leaflets—egg-shaped, pointed, roughly toothed, green, somewhat hairy on both sides (especially so beneath); end leaflet broader and longer (2 to 3 in. long) than side leaflets, often somewhat lobed

Stems—trailing, woody, biennial, up to 25 ft. long, usually unbranched the first year but with many, short, flower-bearing branches the second year, hairless or slightly hairy, with short, recurved prickles

Trailing blackberry, also known as creeping blackberry and dewberry, is a common and aggressive trailing shrub of the Pacific Northwest. Although best known because of its delicious fruit, this species is also of considerable range significance, particularly on the cut-over lands in the Douglas fir region. This plant, ranging from British Columbia to northern Idaho and northern California, is by far the most abundant and widely distributed of the Pacific coast species of blackberry. It grows principally on the coastal side of the Cascade Mountains, but also extends over the summit to the eastern slope, where it is confined chiefly to canyon bottoms and moist timbered areas on which site conditions are similar to those prevailing on the west side. This plant is largely replaced in California by a closely related species, California dewberry (*R. ursinus*, listed by some authors as *R. vitifolius*).

Trailing blackberry grows most profusely in cut-over areas and old burns, but also appears commonly in open woods, old fields, and clearings, and along roadsides and fence rows, ranging from sea level to elevations of about 5,000 feet. It is often found in the virgin Douglas fir forests, although it usually does not thrive under dense shade. The cutting and removal of the timber stands and the subsequent broadcast slash burns result in practical elimination of certain species of the original forest and the suppression of other species, due to changes in light, temperature and moisture. However, the profound ecological changes attendant on logging favor the production of trailing blackberry; this species together with fireweed and bracken fern are the principal species to take early possession of the land after cutting and broadcast burning.[1] If the burn is not too severe, the tangled cane growth of trailing blackberry often comprises a principal part of the vegetation for a few years, but gradually disappears as other shrubs and conifer seedlings shade it out.

The extensive cut-over areas in western Washington and Oregon ordinarily produce an abundance of palatable forage during the early stages of plant succession, and large-scale livestock operations are frequently conducted on this temporary ground cover. Under such conditions, trailing blackberry is an important forage plant. The palatability of the leafage is generally fairly good to good for sheep and fair for cattle. In studying grazing use on Douglas fir cut-over lands in Washington, the late Douglas C. Ingram[1] found that utilization of the herbage of trailing blackberry varied from 26 percent on the moderately grazed areas to 91 percent on the heavily utilized portions of the range, with averages of 58 and 62 percent, respectively, during 2 successive years. Deer and elk graze the leaves with moderate relish; deer are exceptionally fond of the ripe berries. The fruit is likewise a favorite food of bear and smaller animals as well as of grouse, quail, and other birds.

Numerous horticultural varieties of blackberries and dewberries have been developed from trailing blackberry.[2][3] Among the outstanding varieties developed from this species are Belle of Washington, Cazadero, Skagit Chief, Washington Climbing, and probably Humboldt.

Trailing blackberry is one of several species of *Rubus* having two kinds of flowers, male (staminate) and female (pistillate), each kind generally being borne on separate plants. The male flowers, having petals up to about 1 inch long, are much larger and showier than the female flowers. The specific name *macropetalus* is an adjective meaning long-petaled (Greek *macros*, long, and *petalon*, petal) and refers to the prominent petals. This species is variable in the form of the leaves and hairiness and prickliness of stems, but apparently is distinct except as it merges into California dewberry.

California dewberry (*R. ursi'nus*) closely resembles trailing blackberry. It differs mainly in its thicker, more hairy, and less sharply and deeply toothed leaves, with a pronounced tendency toward simple or three-lobed leaves. Moreover the stems, sepals, and flower stalks are more hairy but less glandular. California dewberry is a very common plant in the valleys and foothills at low altitudes, growing chiefly along streams or in springy flats from southern Oregon to Lower California. Some botanists prefer to use the older name, *R. vitifolius*, for this species, but according to Bailey,[2] the identity of the plant described as *R. vitifolius* is unknown. This species is of minor importance as a forage plant. Like trailing blackberry, it is prized for its fruit and has been the source of several varieties of cultivated blackberries.

[1] Ingram, D. C. VEGETATIVE CHANGES AND GRAZING USE ON DOUGLAS FIR CUT-OVER LAND. Jour. Agr. Research [U. S.] 43 : 387–417, illus. 1931.
[2] Bailey, L. H. THE BLACKBERRIES OF NORTH AMERICA. Gentes Herbarum 2(6) : [271]–423, illus. 1932.
[3] Darrow, G. M., and Longley, A. E. CYTOLOGY AND BREEDING OF RUBUS MACROPETALUS, THE LOGAN, AND RELATED BLACKBERRIES. Jour. Agr. Research [U. S.] 47 : 315–330, illus. 1933.

THIMBLEBERRY

Ru'bus parviflo'rus, syns. *R. nutka'nus, Bosse'kia nutka'na, B. parviflo'ra, Ruba'cer parviflo'rum*

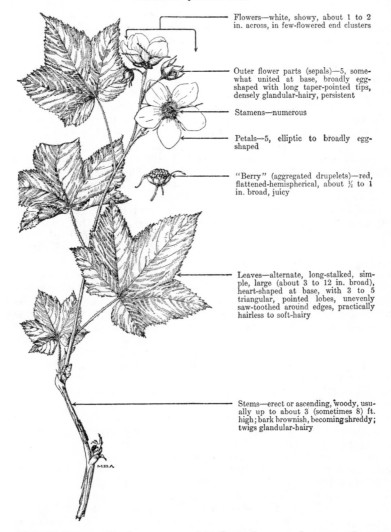

Flowers—white, showy, about 1 to 2 in. across, in few-flowered end clusters

Outer flower parts (sepals)—5, somewhat united at base, broadly egg-shaped with long taper-pointed tips, densely glandular-hairy, persistent

Stamens—numerous

Petals—5, elliptic to broadly egg-shaped

"Berry" (aggregated drupelets)—red, flattened-hemispherical, about ½ to 1 in. broad, juicy

Leaves—alternate, long-stalked, simple, large (about 3 to 12 in. broad), heart-shaped at base, with 3 to 5 triangular, pointed lobes, unevenly saw-toothed around edges, practically hairless to soft-hairy

Stems—erect or ascending, woody, usually up to about 3 (sometimes 8) ft. high; bark brownish, becoming shreddy; twigs glandular-hairy

Thimbleberry, also known as whiteflowering raspberry and sometimes erroneously called salmonberry, is a perennial shrub of the rose family (Rosaceae). It belongs to the group of plants in the blackberry-raspberry genus which have simple but usually lobed leaves, unarmed stems, and flattened fruiting-disks (receptacles), in contrast to the typical *Rubus* group which has usually compound leaves, prickly stems, and convex fruiting-disks. As a result of the great variation in the genus *Rubus*, some botanists have preferred to divide it up into three or more genera, including such segregates as *Bossekia*, *Oreobatus*, and *Rubacer*, but more conservative authorities include all in the one genus *Rubus*. Thomas Nuttall (1786–1859), who first named and described this plant [1] (from the shores of Lake Huron), speaks of the flowers as small, and apparently based his description on a depauperate or otherwise abnormal specimen.

Thimbleberry is, perhaps, the most abundant and widely distributed of the western species of *Rubus*. It occurs in all of the far Western States, and ranges from Alaska to California, Chihuahua, New Mexico, South Dakota, Michigan, and western Ontario. It grows in moist, shaded situations along streams and moist draws, on wooded hillsides under open stands of aspen, ponderosa pine, lodgepole pine, Douglas fir, and western larch, and in partially shaded situations of brushy slopes. This plant favors sandy loam soils, rich in humus, but is also common on rocky, thin-soiled sites.

Thimbleberry, occurring as scattered single plants or often forming dense, almost pure, patches, is a common and conspicuous plant in many localities. It is perhaps less abundant in the mountains of Colorado and the Southwest than elsewhere in its range. On the Pacific coast it is a common undershrub in the humid Douglas fir and western hemlock forests, some patches being so dense that the large leaves form a continuous mosaic on the forest floor. It is also common in the moister situations of the ponderosa pine belt in Washington, Oregon, and California, especially in the upper limits of the zone, or on northern slopes, where Douglas fir or red fir and ponderosa pine grow in mixture. Thimbleberry extends from near sea level to elevations of about 6,000 feet in the Northwest and to 7,000 feet in California; in Colorado it occurs in deep woods, usually between elevations of 6,000 and 9,000 feet, and in the high mountains of New Mexico it appears principally above 9,000 feet.

The palatability of thimbleberry varies considerably in different localities. In the Intermountain region, California, and parts of the Southwest it is generally fair feed for sheep but practically worthless for cattle. It usually rates poor for cattle and fair for sheep in the Northwest, but in some localities is ranked up to fair for cattle and good for sheep. Throughout most of the Rocky Mountain region, from Montana to Colorado, it is ordinarily not grazed by livestock to any material degree. There is marked variation in palatability, however, even in the same region or locality. Under certain specific conditions, as when it occurs under dense stands of timber or with plant associations containing a scarcity of highly palatable vegetation, thimbleberry is sometimes utilized heavily. Both deer and elk graze the leafage of this plant with slight to moderate relish.

The juicy, scarlet berries have an agreeable, tartly sweet flavor. They are often picked and eaten in the woods, but are seldom produced on sufficient scale to be of value for domestic purposes.[2]

[1] Nuttall, T. THE GENERA OF NORTH AMERICAN PLANTS, AND A CATALOGUE OF THE SCECIES TO THE YEAR 1817. 2 v. Philadelphia. 1818.
[2] Hedrick, U. P. (edited by). STURTEVANT'S NOTES ON EDIBLE PLANTS. 686 pp. Albany, N. Y. 1919. [N. Y. Dept. Agr. 27th Ann. Rept. 2(2).]

SALMONBERRY

Ru'bus specta'bilis

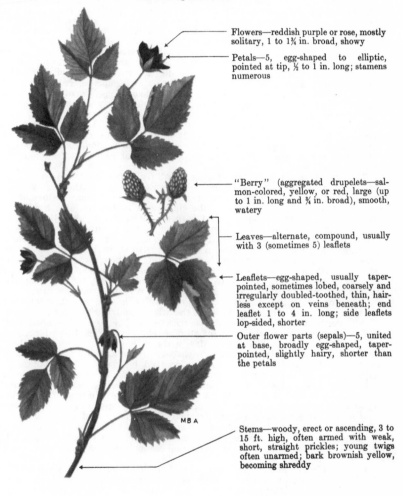

Flowers—reddish purple or rose, mostly solitary, 1 to 1¾ in. broad, showy

Petals—5, egg-shaped to elliptic, pointed at tip, ½ to 1 in. long; stamens numerous

"Berry" (aggregated drupelets—salmon-colored, yellow, or red, large (up to 1 in. long and ¾ in. broad), smooth, watery

Leaves—alternate, compound, usually with 3 (sometimes 5) leaflets

Leaflets—egg-shaped, usually taper-pointed, sometimes lobed, coarsely and irregularly doubled-toothed, thin, hairless except on veins beneath; end leaflet 1 to 4 in. long; side leaflets lop-sided, shorter

Outer flower parts (sepals)—5, united at base, broadly egg-shaped, taper-pointed, slightly hairy, shorter than the petals

Stems—woody, erect or ascending, 3 to 15 ft. high, often armed with weak, short, straight prickles; young twigs often unarmed; bark brownish yellow, becoming shreddy

Salmonberry, so called because of its large, juicy, typically salmon-colored fruit, is an attractive, erect, vigorous-growing shrub, belonging to the same genus as the raspberries and blackberries. The showiness of the distinctive reddish-purple or rose-colored flowers is alluded to by the Latin specific name *spectabilis*, which comes from the same root word as spectacle and spectacular. Salmonberry is a northwestern and Pacific species, being distributed from Alaska to western Montana, northern Idaho and northern California. It is characteristically associated with the humid Douglas fir and Sitka spruce forests of the Pacific coast west of the Cascade Mountains. However, like a number of other typical west-side species, it occurs along drainage lines in moist canyon bottoms on the eastern slope of the Cascades, and also appears on the western slope of the Rocky Mountains in northern Idaho and extreme western Montana. In northern California it is confined chiefly to the coastal strip, reaching as far south as Mendocino County, from whence it extends southward to the Santa Cruz Mountains of the San Francisco Bay region, in the hairy-leaved variety (*R. specta'bilis menzie'sii*).

Salmonberry characteristically grows along streams, in canyon bottoms, moist flats, and swamps in timbered or wooded areas. It occurs in greatest abundance and attains maximum size in the rich, moist soils of alluvial bottom lands, associated with such species as Sitka spruce, red alder, bigleaf maple, western red cedar, vine maple, and various species of willows. This plant is a companion of Sitka spruce throughout nearly all of its range[1] and is common on moist sites in the Douglas fir and western hemlock forests, ranging from near sea level to elevations of over 4,000 feet in the Cascade Mountains and the coast ranges. It is often found on cut-over and burned-over areas, but is apparently less vigorous under such conditions, seldom being abundant except where it borders the virgin forest or occurs in remnants of the original type.

This shrub is an important forage plant for game animals in many parts of the Northwest. Both deer and elk browse freely on the leafage in the summer and utilize the twigs after the leaves have fallen. Salmonberry is one of the key forage species on the elk ranges of the Olympic Peninsula in Washington, where this species has been sought so eagerly by elk that it has been practically eliminated from some of the congested range areas. Its palatability is also fair to good for sheep and fair for cattle. Livestock grazing is not usually practiced on any extensive scale, however, in the areas where salmonberry grows in greatest abundance, although the cattle and sheep of the small ranchers and settlers make considerable use of this plant. Salmonberry propagates rapidly from suckers and, except under conditions of severe overgrazing, generally maintains itself very well on the range.

The large, juicy, salmon-colored or red fruits, having a somewhat insipid, slightly acid taste, are eaten by both the whites and Indians, although not as highly flavored as the native blackberries or raspberries. The northwestern Indians formerly dried the fruit for storage, but the berries, being largely composed of water, are difficult to dry without spoiling. Another method of preparation was to mix the berries with bear grease and boil them into a kind of jam.[2][3] The fruit is highly prized for food by the Alaskan Indians, who gather it in the summer and preserve it for winter use by boiling in salmon oil.[4] The young fleshy shoots of salmonberry are crisp and tender and, because of their sweet, somewhat acid, flavor, were formerly a favorite food of the Indians. They were peeled, tied in bundles, and prepared by steaming over hot stones. The shoots, due to their slight astringency, proved useful as an alterative.[5] They were consumed in large quantities and were evidently in great demand for food, as canoe loads were seen formerly en route to Indian villages. This wild food is often eaten by children and undoubtedly is still used to some extent by Indians.

This handsome shrub has long attracted the attention of gardeners and horticulturists, and a number of attempts have been made to cross salmonberry with raspberry to improve the flavor and keeping qualities of the fruit. This plant is used to some extent both in this country and abroad for ornamental purposes. As early as 1827, David Douglas, the energetic Scotch botanical explorer, introduced salmonberry into England, where it is now successfully cultivated as an ornamental.

[1] Piper, C. V. FLORA OF THE STATE OF WASHINGTON. U. S. Natl. Mus., Contrib. U. S. Natl. Herbarium 11, 637 pp., illus. 1906.
[2] Wilson, T. THE USE OF WILD PLANTS AS FOOD BY INDIANS. Ottawa Nat. 30 : 17–21. 1916.
[3] Evans, W. H. NOTES ON THE EDIBLE BERRIES OF ALASKA. Plant World 3 : 17–19. 1900.
[4] Cooley, G. E. PLANTS COLLECTED IN ALASKA AND NANAIMO, B. C., JULY AND AUGUST, 1891. Bull. Torrey Bot. Club 19 : 239–249. 1892.
[5] [Palmer, E.] FOOD PRODUCTS OF THE NORTH AMERICAN INDIANS. U. S. Dept. Agr. Rept. 1870 : 404–428, illus. 1871.

WILLOWS

Sa'lix spp.

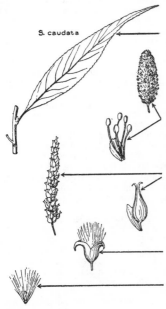

TAIL-LEAF WILLOW (*S. caudata*)

Leaves—appearing with flowers, 2 to 5 in. long, lance-shaped, long-tailed (caudate) at tips, glandular-saw-toothed around margins

Male (staminate) flowers—minute, numerous, with usually 5 stamens protruding from soon hairless, yellowish bracts, in an erect cluster (catkin, or ament) from a single bud scale

Female (pistillate) flowers—small, with short-stalked, seed-producing organs (ovaries) 2-parted at the tip, protruding from small, soon-falling, hairless bracts, in catkins from single bud scales

Seed pod (capsule)—light brown, splitting down from top

Seeds—minute, numerous, with long, soft, white hairs from around base

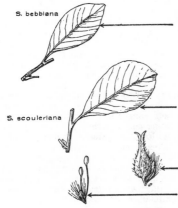

SCOULER WILLOW (*S. scouleriana*)

Leaves—appearing with flowers, up to 2 in. long and 1 in. wide, from narrowly elliptic and pointed at both ends to broadly reverse-lance-shaped and abruptly short-tapering-pointed, entire or somewhat wavy on edges

BEBB WILLOW (*S. bebbiana*)

Leaves—appearing after flowers, up to about 5 in. long, variable in shape (mostly reverse-egg-shaped), thick, entire to faintly toothed on edges, shiny-green above, silvery- to somewhat rusty-hairy or hairless beneath.

Female flowers—hairy

Male flowers—with dark, silky-hairy bracts and 2 stamens

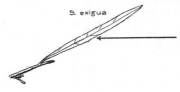

NARROWLEAF WILLOW (*S. exigua*)

Leaves—appearing with flowers, 2 to 5 in. long, less than ½ in. wide, linear

The willows, which compose one of the most familiar groups of woody plants, line the shores of the rivers and streams, grow in dense stands over moist bottom lands, and frequently abound on the mountain meadows and slopes. Because of their prevalence near routes of travel, places of recreation, and in agricultural and grazing areas these plants are familiar to most people.

The willows are represented by about 250 species, practically all native to the north temperate and arctic zones; a few species are confined to the southern hemisphere. The name willow is the present form of the ancient word for the genus, which was variously spelled wilowe, welig, wilge. The scientific name *Salix*, the ancient Latin name of the willow, is probably derived from two Celtic words: *sal*, near, and *lis*, water.

Willows usually grow in moist situations, being commonly associated with fresh water streams and rivers in their natural range. Although they sometimes grow "with their feet in the water", they prefer the moist banks, flats, or slopes bordering the very wet sites. They frequent mountain watercourses, often spreading out and forming dense stands on stream bottoms, meadows and other flat areas. A few species, such as Scouler willow (*S. scouleria'na*, syn. *S. nuttal'lii*) and Bebb willow (*S. bebbia'na*), are sometimes common components of the shrubby vegetation on mountain slopes. The willows seldom grow in the shade; in fact, most species occur only in full sunlight.

Willows are found at practically all elevations. The river forms, such as the large black willow (*S. ni'gra*), frequently thrive on sites only several feet above sea level. A certain few species, including alpine willow (*S. petro'phila*), appear in the mountains above timber line, and dwarf members of the genus extend as far north as any shrubby plants. Most species, however, limit their ranges to medium and low elevations.

The majority of willows prefer deep and fertile soils, as indicated by their abundance on river bottoms and meadow lands. Some species, notably the stream types, e. g., arroyo willow (*S. lasio'lepis*), grow characteristically on rocky stream banks. Scouler willow often inhabits stony soils which, however, are usually fertile enough to support a coniferous forest. Although willows occasionally develop in moist, somewhat acid environments, unlike blueberries (*Vaccinium* spp.), they cannot endure strongly acid soils and are even less tolerant to alkaline or saline conditions.

Willows run the gamut in size from the 100-foot, lumber-producing black willow of the lower Mississippi Valley to the almost herblike, high-altitude, and northern species which are less than 6 inches in height. Several of the common western species, e. g., peachleaf willow (*S. amygdaloi'des*), western black willow (*S. lasian'dra*), and red willow (*S. laeviga'ta*), grow into trees from 40 to 50 feet in height. However, most members of the genus that occur in the mountains, including silverleaf willow (*S. argophyl'la*), narrowleaf willow (*S. exi'gua*), Lemmon willow (*S. lem'moni*), and Bebb willow, are distinctly shrubby in character; they range from 3 to 12 feet high and have numerous, crowded, rather long, slender, and few-branched stems which have extended, nodding, leafy tips.

The deciduous, short-stemmed, alternate, simple leaves of willows are generally long, narrow, or taper-pointed, with the margins entire or weakly toothed. However, there are many variations in leaf shape, size, surface, texture, and color occurring within the genus, and in some cases within the species or even on individual plants. The tendency of willows to produce hybrids, and the fact that they often flower before the leaves appear, causes much confusion. Another complication obtains, because the leaves often vary greatly in shape, color, and pubescence during their development.[1] One peculiarity, for example, hinges on the fact that a leaf may emerge gray and densely soft-hairy, yet at maturity be green and sparingly hairy or bald. An additional difficulty encountered in the determination of critical specimens of willow is the dioeciousness of the genus, i. e., the sexes are distinct, and sometimes it is necessary to have both the male and female plant represented to be positive of the species.

The accompanying illustrations present four of the commonest and most characteristic types of leaf form found in willows. The general outline of the long and taper-tipped leaf of tail-leaf willow (*S. cauda'ta*) is rather characteristic of the larger western willows. The narrowly elliptic leaf of Bebb

---

[1] Ball, C. R. NOTES ON SOME WESTERN WILLOWS. Acad. Sci. St. Louis, Trans. 9: 69–90. 1899.

willow is fairly representative of the leaf form of firmleaf willow (*S. pseudo-myrsini'tes*), blue willow (*S. subcoeru'lea*), Eastwood willow (*S. eastwoo'diae*), and blueback willow (*S. glau'cops*), and of many other shrubby species. The somewhat wedge-shaped leaf of Scouler willow is extraordinary, being found only in the dwarf summit willow (*S. saximonta'na*) and a few other species. The long narrow leaf of narrowleaf willow is also characteristic of dusky willow (*S. melanop'sis*) and silverleaf willows.

Most mature willow leaves are green or dull green with some white hairs, particularly on the under side. However, some species, as the names of satin willow (*S. sitchen'sis*) and silverleaf willow suggest, have light-colored, densely long-hairy leaves. In a few species, such as Lemmon willow, the leaves become hairless, at least when mature.

Willow plants are one-sexed (dioecious); their flowers are in catkins, which usually emerge from the single-scaled buds before the leaves, although they sometimes appear simultaneously. The pussy willow, herald of spring, is the swollen male (staminate) flower bud or catkin, especially if silky and plump. The common cultivated pussy willow of the florists, however, is the native *S. discolor*. The catkins of the male plants become yellow when the pollen matures, falling as a unit and shortly after pollen is shed. The catkins of the female plants emerge green, later becoming white and soft-cottony from the soft hairs attached to the tiny seed; the entire catkin falls intact by midsummer. The tiny seeds are very short-lived, but very plentiful.

The willows are closely related to poplars (*Populus* spp.), the two genera composing the willow family (Salicaceae). The poplars are rather easily distinguished, although they often grow with the willows, particularly in the riparian associations. The western poplars are trees, with long-stemmed, usually heart-shaped, sometimes large, and mostly hairless leaves, although one species, narrowleaf cottonwood (*Populus angustifolia*), has short-stemmed, rather narrow, and lance-shaped leaves, and is sometimes mistaken for a willow. Other differences, less obvious, are that the bracts of poplars subtending the individual flowers are feathery-edged, the flower is on a cup-shaped disk, the stamens 4-12 or numerous, and the buds composed of several overlapping scales. The common *Populus* on the western ranges is aspen, *P. tremuloides aurea* (syn. *P. aurea*).

Willows provide one of the principal sources of browse on many of the western mountain ranges. Although the foliage is most palatable to sheep, cattle probably make greatest use of these plants, because they usually range where willows abound. The palatability varies according to species but, on the average, willows are fair forage for cattle and good for sheep. The willows are most important as a late summer feed because the foliage seemingly increases in palatability as the season advances. At times considerable use is made of the frosted and colored leaves, sheep, in particular, even eating them after they have fallen. The willows are so difficult to differentiate that the field man, unfamiliar with species distinctions, ordinarily fails to determine their individual palatabilities. However, in a limited way, it is apparently possible to place them in broad groups by the use of leaf characters. Thus species, like tail-leaf willow, with relatively large, rather tough and shiny leaves, are of less forage value than the smaller, soft, thin, or pubescent-leaved species, such as Bebb willow. The greensides willow (*S. monochro'ma*) of the Northwest has small, thin, and dark green leaves and rates as an outstanding browse willow in that section. Scouler willow is one of the most widely distributed and most valuable forage willows on the western mountain ranges.[2][3] Its leaves, as shown in the illustration, are unusual in shape for a willow; the species is also distinctive in its habitat as it seldom grows near water courses, usually inhabits open forest slopes, and frequently becomes very abundant on burns. Although it usually occurs as an erect shrub about 15 feet high, occasionally the species develops into a tree 30 feet in height, or taller. Even in the tree forms, however, the growth ordinarily consists of a number of small stems of

---

[2] Sampson, A. W. IMPORTANT RANGE PLANTS: THEIR LIFE HISTORY AND FORAGE VALUE. U. S. Dept. Agr. Bull. 545, 63 pp., illus. 1917.
[3] Dayton, W. A. IMPORTANT WESTERN BROWSE PLANTS. U. S. Dept. Agr. Misc. Pub. 101, 214 pp., illus. 1931.

irregular length. These stems are leafy and, in the main, their growth within grazing height is open and fully available to livestock. Cattle browse Scouler willow freely, but sheep, probably because of its common occurrence on sheep ranges, make heavy use of its foliage. This species withstands close use unusually well; the grazed stems, unless seriously injured, continue to produce leafage for many years.

Livestock tend to browse willows closely on the western ranges. In fact, the taller species commonly show a definite grazing line, and overgrazed, dead, or dying specimens are at times indicators of the former plentifulness of various species. These conditions usually are observable on areas where livestock concentrate, such as sheep bedgrounds, and along driveways, and are particularly noticeable on willows around meadows and draws on cattle ranges. The species of sufficient height and age are usually qualified to resist overgrazing because the numerous stems provide protection for the new shoots. Sometimes their abundance and the density of the stand prevent severe grazing damage. Some species, it is true, are of low palatability and are materially grazed only under abnormal conditions. Ordinarily, however, scattered individuals, low bushes, and even the open stands, which grow where livestock concentrate, are subjected to continued close use and eventual destruction. Generally, wherever willows show serious injury, the herbaceous cover on the meadows is likely to be depleted.

In some areas the willows constitute a very important source of food for wildlife. In the Southwest, where these plants are less abundant than farther north, the willows rank as excellent deer browse. In the Sierra Nevadas, however, willows are apparently not very important in the deer diet.[4] Elk and moose, apparently, pick at the foliage and twig ends during the summer, and utilize the leafless twigs of the 1-year wood during the fall and winter. Alaskan studies show that willows are the chief summer browse of reindeer.[5] With the exception of aspen, willows are probably the most important beaver food in the mountains of the West.

Willows have long been planted to stabilize river banks, and large willow mats, weighted down with rocks, have often been used to protect the levees of the Mississippi and other rivers. Recently, the willows have received special attention in erosion control work in the Western States, the willow boughs being employed largely in the construction of check dams. However, their major value is probably as plantings to stabilize the soil. Willows are particularly adapted for growing on gullies, in meadows, and along streams, as such sites are their natural home. They grow readily from cuttings.

Willows are used in commerce chiefly in the manufacture of wicker baskets and furniture.[6][7] Several species, notably purple willow (*S. purpu'rea*) and almond willow (*S. amygdali'na*), are cultivated in and about New Jersey for that purpose. The black willow, especially in the lower Mississippi Valley, and several other species, such as the white willow (*S. al'ba*), yield lumber on a commercial scale. These two species, as well as other representatives of the genus, are used in the manufacture of artificial limbs, and for juvenile baseball bats and other sport equipment, the tough, light, and elastic wood being well suited for such purposes. Brittle willow (*S. fra'gilis*) is employed in the manufacture of a charcoal, especially valuable for black powder production. Practically all species of willows contain both tannin and salicin.[8]

The common, introduced weeping willow (*S. babylo'nica*) is now widely distributed throughout North America, being planted extensively first as an ornamental.[9] Various species, including white and brittle willows, have been planted widely as windbreaks in the prairie States.

[4] Dixon, J. S. A STUDY OF THE LIFE HISTORY AND FOOD HABITS OF MULE DEER IN CALIFORNIA. PART 2—FOOD HABITS. Calif. Fish and Game 20 (4) : [315]–354, illus. 1934.
[5] Hadwen, S., and Palmer, L. J. REINDEER IN ALASKA. U. S. Dept. Agr. Bull. 1089, 74 pp., illus. 1922.
[6] Lamb, G. N. BASKET WILLOW CULTURE. U. S. Dept. Agr. Farmers' Bull. 622, 34 pp., illus. 1914.
[7] Lamb, G. N. WILLOWS : THEIR GROWTH, USE, AND IMPORTANCE. U. S. Dept. Agr. Bull. 316, 52 pp., illus. 1915.
[8] Detwiler, S. B. THE WILLOWS : IDENTIFICATION AND CHARACTERISTICS. Amer. Forestry 23 : 3–10, illus. 1917.
[9] Bailey, L. H. THE STANDARD CYCLOPEDIA OF HORTICULTURE . . . New ed., 3 v., illus. New York and London. 1933.

BLUEBERRY ELDER

Sambu′cus caeru′lea, syn. *S. glau′ca*

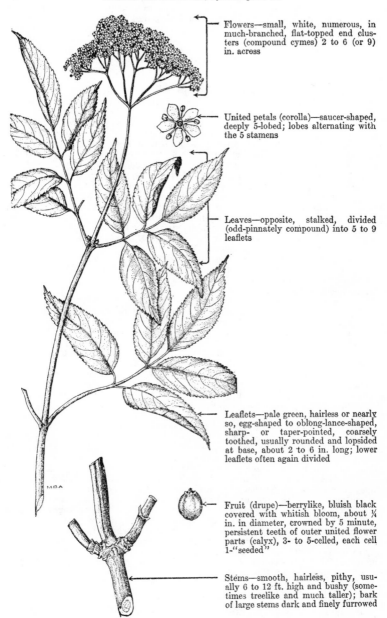

Flowers—small, white, numerous, in much-branched, flat-topped end clusters (compound cymes) 2 to 6 (or 9) in. across

United petals (corolla)—saucer-shaped, deeply 5-lobed; lobes alternating with the 5 stamens

Leaves—opposite, stalked, divided (odd-pinnately compound) into 5 to 9 leaflets

Leaflets—pale green, hairless or nearly so, egg-shaped to oblong-lance-shaped, sharp- or taper-pointed, coarsely toothed, usually rounded and lopsided at base, about 2 to 6 in. long; lower leaflets often again divided

Fruit (drupe)—berrylike, bluish black covered with whitish bloom, about ¼ in. in diameter, crowned by 5 minute, persistent teeth of outer united flower parts (calyx), 3- to 5-celled, each cell 1-"seeded"

Stems—smooth, hairless, pithy, usually 6 to 12 ft. high and bushy (sometimes treelike and much taller); bark of large stems dark and finely furrowed

Blueberry elder, ordinarily a many-stemmed bush from 6 to 12 feet high, sometimes attains treelike proportions, particularly in the southern part of its range, growing to a height of 20 to 25 feet, with a main stem 1 foot in diameter. It ranges from southern British Columbia to California, Arizona, and Alberta in the foothills and piñon-juniper, ponderosa pine, and aspen belts. In California, where it is the common foothill elder, it occurs from sea level up to an elevation of about 5,500 feet; in the Northwest and Idaho, from sea level to about 4,000 feet; and in Utah and Nevada, it appears principally between altitudes of 5,500 and 9,000 feet.[1] In general, this elder occurs scatteringly, although common along streams, in canyons, and on moist flats and slopes in sandy or clayey loam soils. It is frequently associated with bromes (*Bromus* spp.), chokecherries (*Prunus* spp.), serviceberries (*Amelanchier* spp.), and wheatgrasses (*Agropyron* spp.).

The browse value of blueberry elder varies with the season. In the spring it is almost worthless for cattle and practically worthless to poor for sheep; in the summer, sometimes fair to fairly good for both sheep and cattle. In the fall, from the time the fruit ripens until after the first frost, its palatability rises rapidly, the fruit, leaves, and twigs being consumed. The palatability of the frosted herbage is, at least, fairly good for cattle, and good to very good for sheep. However, despite its high fall palatability, this species, because of its usual lack of abundance and the fact that the foliage is frequently beyond the reach of grazing animals, especially sheep, is not a very important browse plant, except possibly in California. Its palatability for goats is probably as good as for sheep; it is good browse for deer and, possibly, also for elk.

The Indians have always made considerable use of blueberry elder, fresh and dried. Decoctions of the dried blossoms are used externally as a lotion and antiseptic wash. This plant is also used internally to check bleeding of the lungs in consumption and is especially valued as an alleviant of stomach troubles. The inner bark yields a strong emetic.

Although the fruits of this species are black, they are covered with a bluish white, waxy bloom, which gives them a cerulean-blue color; whence the common name blueberry elder and the specific name *caerulea;* the latter is a Latin adjective meaning sky blue.

The origin of the name *Sambucus* for the elders, or elderberries, is controversial. The usual explanation is that it is probably derived from the Greek *sambuke*, a musical instrument—perhaps because the pithy stems were used by shepherds and others to fashion rustic pipes, or flutes. Gerard[2] regards this etymology as erroneous. The genus, which embraces about 42 species of shrubs, small trees, or rarely herbs, belongs to the honeysuckle family (*Caprifoliaceae*). It is widely distributed in temperate and subtropical regions. Of about 14 species native to the United States, all but 3 species occur in the West. The characters of elders which permit of easy recognition are: Opposite branches; distinctively pithy young stems; opposite, odd-pinnately divided leaves with toothed leaflets; numerous small, whitish flowers in flat-topped or pyramidal clusters, and small, red, bluish, or black berrylike fruits. Some of the red-fruited species are reputed to have slightly poisonous berries so far as human beings are concerned, but the fruit of the black- or blue-fruited species is edible, at least when cooked. Birds and other wildlife and even domestic livestock relish the berries.

Some authors list Arizona elder (*S. caeru'lea arizo'nica*, syn. *S. glau'ca arizo'nica*), New Mexico elder (*S. neomexica'na*, syns. *S. caeru'lea neomexica'na*, *S. glau'ca neomexica'na*), and velvet elder (*S. velu'tina*, syn. *S. caeru'lea velu'tina*) as varieties of blueberry elder, but majority botanical sentiment seems to be that probably only the first-named should be regarded as a variety, the other two being worthy of specific rank. Arizona elder differs from blueberry elder chiefly in having three to five (mostly three), rather than five to nine leaflets; smaller flower clusters, and smaller fruits. Arizona elder, often occurring as a small tree 30 feet in height with stout spreading branches which form a compact round-topped crown, grows along streams from New Mexico to southern California.

---

[1] Dayton, W. A. IMPORTANT WESTERN BROWSE PLANTS. U. S. Dept. Agr. Misc. Pub. 101, 214 pp., illus. 1931.
[2] Gerard, W. R. ORIGIN OF THE NAME SAMBUCUS. Garden and Forest 8: 368. 1895.

BUNCHBERRY ELDER

Sambu'cus microbo'trys

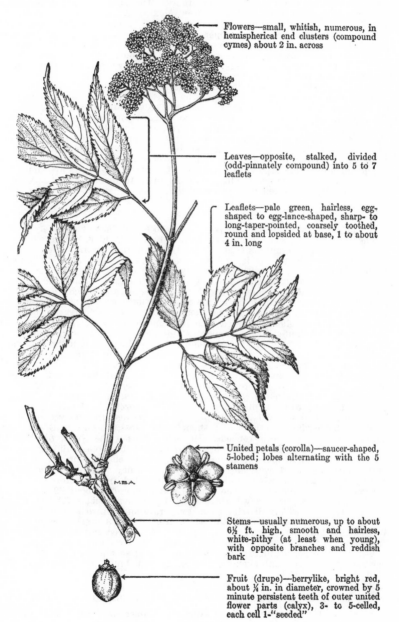

Flowers—small, whitish, numerous, in hemispherical end clusters (compound cymes) about 2 in. across

Leaves—opposite, stalked, divided (odd-pinnately compound) into 5 to 7 leaflets

Leaflets—pale green, hairless, egg-shaped to egg-lance-shaped, sharp- to long-taper-pointed, coarsely toothed, round and lopsided at base, 1 to about 4 in. long

United petals (corolla)—saucer-shaped, 5-lobed; lobes alternating with the 5 stamens

Stems—usually numerous, up to about 6½ ft. high, smooth and hairless, white-pithy (at least when young), with opposite branches and reddish bark

Fruit (drupe)—berrylike, bright red, about ¼ in. in diameter, crowned by 5 minute persistent teeth of outer united flower parts (calyx), 3- to 5-celled, each cell 1-"seeded"

Bunchberry elder, a smooth, many-stemmed shrub, usually 1½ to 6½ feet high, with small, rather compact, rounded clusters of red fruits, is one of the smallest and most common of the western elders in the central Rocky Mountain and Intermountain regions. Both the common and the specific names refer to the compact fruit clusters; *microbotrys* is Latinized from the Greek, *mikro-*, small, and *botrus*, a cluster of grapes. This species ranges from southwestern Montana to South Dakota, New Mexico, Arizona, and Nevada, and possibly extends into northeastern California. It occurs chiefly on moist sites in the mountains of the upper ponderosa pine, aspen, spruce, and subalpine belts. Bunchberry elder grows commonly in meadows and parks, in small openings in timber, and similar sunny situations, but is also occasionally found in scattered aspen. This shrub, although very common, is generally scattered, only rarely occurring in dense, but small, patches.

Bunchberry elder is one of the more palatable elders for use in the summer, when it is browsed rather extensively by cattle, sheep, and goats, as well as by elk and deer. After the first frosts the palatability is somewhat higher than in summer, rating from fairly good to good for cattle and fairly good to very good for sheep. The fruits, leaves, twigs, and sometimes even the large stems are cropped. This shrub is usually low enough so that grazing animals have ready access to the herbage. Ease of procurement combined with its high palatability and common occurrence make the species one of the important browse plants within its range. The bright red fruits are consumed by birds and other animals, but are unpalatable to man. Bunchberry elder is occasionally cultivated as an ornamental.

Blackbead elder (*S. melanocar'pa*), known locally as mountain elder(berry), a smooth shrubby species commonly from 3 to 10 feet high, occurs chiefly in moist sites in the mountains from British Columbia to California, New Mexico, Colorado, and Alberta. It is probably the species of elder most likely to be associated and confused with bunchberry elder. During the fruiting season, however, it is readily distinguished by its black fruits, to which the common name, blackbead elder, alludes. The flower clusters of this species are rounded and slightly larger and more open than those of bunchberry elder. The leaflets, about 2 to 6 inches long, are abruptly long-taper-pointed as contrasted with the somewhat smaller, shorter-pointed leaves of bunchberry elder. Blackbead elder is generally distributed in the ponderosa pine and Engelmann spruce-lodgepole pine belts, and, although fairly abundant, it is seldom the dominant species.[1] For summer use it is poor to fair cattle browse and fair to fairly good sheep browse in some places, but in other localities this species is practically worthless for all classes of livestock. After the advent of frost, however, the palatability is fairly good to good for cattle and good to very good for sheep.[1]

The origin of the name *Sambucus* for the elders, or elderberries, is controversial. The usual explanation is that it is probably derived from the Greek *sambuke*, a musical instrument—perhaps because the pithy stems were used by shepherds and others to fashion rustic pipes, or flutes. Gerard[2] regards this etymology as erroneous. He indicates that the Greek plant name *sampsuchon*, used by Dioscorides, originally applied to a totally different plant (sweet marjoram, *Origanum majorana*), and that some corruption of *sampsuchon* has been used ever since the eleventh century to refer to the elders. *Sambucus* is one of these corruptions and was adopted by Tournefort in 1719 as the generic name for elder. The genus, which embraces about 42 species of shrubs, small trees, or rarely herbs, belongs to the honeysuckle family (*Caprifoliaceae*). It is widely distributed in temperate and subtropical regions. Of about 14 species native to the United States, all but 3 species occur in the West. The characters of elders which permit of easy recognition are: Opposite branches; distinctively pithy young stems; opposite, odd-pinnately divided leaves with toothed leaflets; numerous small, whitish flowers borne in showy flat-topped or pyramidal clusters; and small, red, bluish or black, berrylike fruits.

---

[1] Dayton, W. A. IMPORTANT WESTERN BROWSE PLANTS. U. S. Dept. Agr. Misc. Pub. 101, 214 pp., illus. 1931.
[2] Gerard, W. R. ORIGIN OF THE NAME SAMBUCUS. Garden and Forest 8 : 368. 1895.

THREADLEAF GROUNDSEL

Sene'cio longilo'bus, syn. *S. filifo'lius*

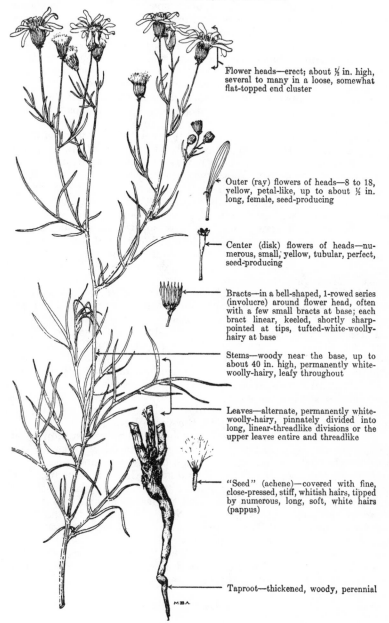

Flower heads—erect; about ½ in. high, several to many in a loose, somewhat flat-topped end cluster

Outer (ray) flowers of heads—8 to 18, yellow, petal-like, up to about ½ in. long, female, seed-producing

Center (disk) flowers of heads—numerous, small, yellow, tubular, perfect, seed-producing

Bracts—in a bell-shaped, 1-rowed series (involucre) around flower head, often with a few small bracts at base; each bract linear, keeled, shortly sharp-pointed at tips, tufted-white-woolly-hairy at base

Stems—woody near the base, up to about 40 in. high, permanently white-woolly-hairy, leafy throughout

Leaves—alternate, permanently white-woolly-hairy, pinnately divided into long, linear-threadlike divisions or the upper leaves entire and threadlike

"Seed" (achene)—covered with fine, close-pressed, stiff, whitish hairs, tipped by numerous, long, soft, white hairs (pappus)

Taproot—thickened, woody, perennial

Threadleaf groundsel is a typical representative of the relatively few shrubby species of this largely herbaceous genus which belongs to the aster family (Asteraceae, or Compositae). The generic name is from the Latin *senex*, an old man, and alludes to the hoary herbage of certain of the Old World species. The specific name *longilobus* and the common name threadleaf refer to the very slender, deeply cut lobes of the leaves. This species ranges from western Texas to Colorado, Utah, Arizona, and south into Mexico. It seldom grows abundantly, but is common and widely distributed from the creosotebush and mesquite types up through the woodland (oak and piñon-juniper types) into the ponderosa pine belt. It is most common on dry open ridges, mesas, and parks throughout the piñon-juniper woodland belt and is not uncommon along roadsides and other waste places. Although occurring on a wide variety of soils, from rocky or sandy to adobe clay, it apparently prefers sandy or gravelly loams. It is drought-resistant by virtue of its deep root system, hoary pubescence, and other xerophytic adaptations.

Threadleaf groundsel, like other shrubby species of *Senecio*, is much inferior to several of the herbaceous species and has little or no forage value. It is eaten slightly by goats and, in cases of dire necessity, sheep will graze the foliage. Recent investigations by Clawson [1] have demonstrated that this species (and especially its young leaves) is poisonous to cattle and horses and, to a lesser extent, to sheep. Mr. Clawson thinks that under range conditions this plant "may, and probably does, cause losses of livestock at times." However, in view of its normally very low palatability, threadleaf groundsel is probably not a source of danger on the range except where serious range depletion obtains, as in periods of prolonged drought or on badly overgrazed or overstocked areas.

Threadleaf groundsel is usually a halfshrub; the stems are largely herbaceous, except at the base, in its northern range, but are often woody, except for the tops, in its southern range. The plant is variable in the form of its leaves and in the hairiness of both its leaves and stems. In some specimens, nearly all leaves are entire; in others, they are dissected to the midrib into narrow lobes. Some individuals, especially those growing at the higher elevations, are only slightly soft-hairy, but those growing on the foothills and mesas are commonly densely covered with soft fine hairs. The yellow flowers are among the first to appear in the spring, and usually bloom all summer; southward they sometimes bloom throughout most of the year.

Broom groundsel (*S. spartioi'des*) is another common halfshrub of this genus. This species is similar to threadleaf groundsel, with the exception that it is hairless and its leaves are entire or rarely lobed at the base. It ranges from Nebraska and Wyoming southward to Arizona and Texas, and grows on dry, open ridges in the sagebrush, oak and piñon-juniper woodlands, and ponderosa-pine belts. The plant is seldom touched by livestock unless other feed is scanty or absent. Preliminary studies by Clawson (*op. cit.*) have demonstrated that it contains toxic properties. (See W168.)

---

[1] Clawson, A. B. THE AMERICAN GROUNDSELS SPECIES OF SENECIO AS STOCK POISONING PLANTS. Vet. Med. 28 (3) : 105–110, illus. 1933.

OCEANSPRAY

Sericothe'ca dis'color, syns. *Holodis'cus dis'color, Schizono'tus dis'color*

Flowers—small (about ⅛ in. long), white or creamy-white, numerous, in large, showy, terminal clusters (panicles) up to 12 in. long

Stamens—about 20, on a ringlike disk

Petals—5, elliptic, about ⅛ in. long

"Seeds" (achenes)—small, usually 5, enclosed by erect sepals, densely hairy with long, silky, white hairs

Outer flower parts (sepals)—5, 3-nerved, pointed, densely short-hairy

Leaves—alternate, somewhat egg-shaped, 1 to 4 in. long, roughly double-toothed along sides and at tips, usually rounded or broadly wedge-shaped at base, not extending very far down along leafstalks, grayish or white-woolly beneath, slightly hairy above

Stems—erect, branching alternately; older bark grayish brown; young twigs fine-hairy

Oceanspray, also known as creambush, is an attractive shrub of the rose family (Rosaceae). It varies from a bushy plant 2½ feet high to practically a tree form, sometimes 20 feet high. These more luxuriant forms grow mostly near the coast west of the Cascade Mountains and are listed by some authors as *S. ariaefolia,* or *S. discolor ariaefolia.* This form apparently is only a robust stage of *S. discolor* with less woolly undersurface of the leaves, and does not seem to merit rank as a separate species.

Oceanspray ranges from British Columbia to western Montana and California. In California it is distributed from Los Angeles northward through the Coast Range, with occasional occurrence in the Sierra Nevada Mountains. This shrub occupies a variety of sites, ranging from the moist shady forests of the coastal plains and mountains to the more arid timbered areas of the interior. It is a very common undershrub in ponderosa pine forests and often appears in moderate abundance on cut-over lands of the Northwest. The plant often is common along creeks and river banks, but also grows in well-drained, sandy, gravelly, or rocky soils of the drier slopes, as well as in the rich, deep, moist soils of canyon bottoms. It extends from near sea level to an elevation of about 7,000 feet.

This shrub is usually regarded as distinctly minor in value for range livestock. Its palatability is rated as zero to fair for cattle and poor to fair for sheep. A few observers have ranked it as good forage for sheep, but the ranges studied were probably not in optimum condition. The leafage and young twigs are generally eaten more readily by livestock in the fall than during the spring and summer. Actually, this species furnishes a greater bulk of forage than is often conceded as the plants occur abundantly on some range areas. In Washington, and perhaps elsewhere throughout its range, oceanspray is grazed readily by both deer and elk. These game animals eat it during all seasons with maximum use in fall and winter. Dixon [1] reports that it is fair forage for mule deer in California.

Oceanspray is normally a symmetrical shrub with erect, somewhat spreading branches. Because it is very handsome in bloom, with large panicles of creamy-white flowers on slender arching branches, this plant has attained wide popularity as a cultivated ornamental. Although the flower buds appear early in the spring, they do not burst into full flower until June or July; the flowering period then continues until late August. The persistent outer flower parts (calyx) become brownish and remain-intact in the broad fruiting clusters long after the petals and seed have fallen; they remain attached until late in the fall and frequently even throughout the winter giving the shrubs a shaggy appearance.

Several other species of *Sericotheca* occur in the West but their forage value is very limited, the foliage normally being of low palatability. Of these, bush rockspirea (*S. dumosa*) is the most widely distributed and best known. It resembles creambush but occurs in drier climates from Wyoming to Oregon, eastern California, New Mexico, and Chihuahua, Mexico. It is usually smaller than oceanspray, being a low compact shrub 16 to 40 inches high, with narrower and less diffuse panicles and with the leaves smaller, long-wedge-shaped at the base, and prolonged along a winged leafstalk, in contrast to the abruptly contracted base of the leaf blade of oceanspray. As its common name indicates, bush rockspirea grows in rocky sites, usually in dry or moderately dry soils in the mountains to elevations of 9,500 feet, frequently in the niches of rocky ledges and cliffs.

---

[1] Dixon, J. S. A STUDY OF THE LIFE HISTORY AND FOOD HABITS OF MULE DEER IN CALIFORNIA. PART 2—FOOD HABITS. Calif. Fish and Game 20(4) : [315]-354, illus. 1934.

JOJOBA

Simmond'sia califor'nica

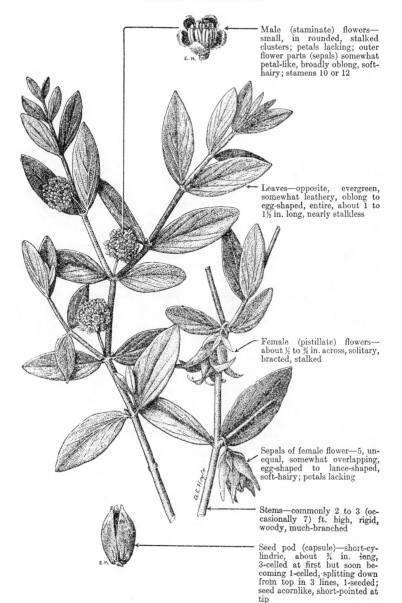

Male (staminate) flowers—small, in rounded, stalked clusters; petals lacking; outer flower parts (sepals) somewhat petal-like, broadly oblong, soft-hairy; stamens 10 or 12

Leaves—opposite, evergreen, somewhat leathery, oblong to egg-shaped, entire, about 1 to 1½ in. long, nearly stalkless

Female (pistillate) flowers—about ½ to ¾ in. across, solitary, bracted, stalked

Sepals of female flower—5, unequal, somewhat overlapping, egg-shaped to lance-shaped, soft-hairy; petals lacking

Stems—commonly 2 to 3 (occasionally 7) ft. high, rigid, woody, much-branched

Seed pod (capsule)—short-cylindric, about ¾ in. long, 3-celled at first but soon becoming 1-celled, splitting down from top in 3 lines, 1-seeded; seed acornlike, short-pointed at tip

Jojoba, a bushy, bluish-green shrub commonly from 2 to 3, but occasionally as much as 6 or 7 feet high, is widely known in the Southwest as coffeeberry and is also locally called bushnut, bucknut, coffeebush, goatberry, and pignut—all such designations alluding to the nutlike fruit. It is the only species of the genus, and belongs to the box family (Buxaceae). The plant was first discovered near San Diego, Calif., apparently in 1835 by Thomas Nuttall, the distinguished British-American botanist-ornithologist. Nuttall named the genus "in memory of Thomas Williams Simmonds, an ardent Botanist and Naturalist, who accompanied Lord Seaforth to Barbadoes about the year 1804, and died soon after, while engaged in exploring the island of Trinidad." The specific name commemorates the type locality.

Jojoba occurs in Arizona, southern California, and Lower California, in sandy or gravelly soils on the dry foothills and mesas, chiefly at elevations of from 2,000 to 4,000 feet. It often occurs locally in nearly pure stands or as one of the principal plants distributed over fairly large areas in association with paloverdes (*Cercidium* spp.), acacias (*Acacia* spp.), and other plants of the desert-shrub type.

Jojoba is an important browse species of the Southwest. Its palatability varies appreciably, depending upon the association in which it occurs, but this species is usually rated as good to very good winter forage and fair summer forage for all classes of livestock. Its presence on dry sites where palatable grasses and other herbaceous species are relatively scarce, enhances its palatability. Its evergreen habit and comparatively large and abundant leafage, which is readily available to livestock, further increase the value of this shrub. Jojoba is very good emergency forage during drought, and on heavily grazed range is sometimes browsed to the point of near-extermination. It withstands heavy browsing well, and recovers rapidly from the effects of overuse, when given protection or grazed conservatively. Jojoba is reported to be the chief source of feed for wild goats and deer on some of the large islands off the California coast.[1] A chemical analysis of the leaves of this shrub made for the Forest Service by the Bureau of Chemistry and Soils of the U. S. Department of Agriculture showed a high percentage of carbohydrates, which tends to confirm the superior browse value of the species.

The large, nutlike seeds of jojoba have an agreeable flavor, somewhat similar to that of filberts, and are a rather important food of both the Indians and Mexicans of the Southwest, California, and Lower California.[2][3] Saunders[2] reports that the Mexicans boil the seeds and extract the oil, which they use as a hair-restorer. He also states that the oil has been used as a substitute for olive oil, and is said never to turn rancid.

Green and Foster[4] report that the average of several chemical analyses of jojoba seeds showed a content of 45.66 percent crude fat. These analyses also showed that the seeds contain a liquid wax very similar to sperm oil, a valuable lubricant. Thornber[5] writes that the plant is spread by squirrels, which collect and store the seed. He also states that the growth of jojoba under cultivation is entirely too slow to merit consideration in artificial range revegetation. The Forest Service, however, with some promise of success, is now conducting tests in transplanting nursery-grown seedlings on the open range for revegetation and soil-erosion control.

Usually, jojoba is easily recognizable by its thick, leathery, bluish-green leaves and dark-brown, nutlike seeds. The male (staminate) and female (pistillate) flowers are borne separately on the same plant; the former in clusters and the latter solitary.

[1] Dayton, W. A. IMPORTANT WESTERN BROWSE PLANTS. U. S. Dept. Agr. Misc. Pub. 101, 214 pp., illus. 1931.
[2] Saunders, C. F. A NEGLECTED NUT OF THE DESERT REGION. Desert 2 : 91, illus. 1930.
[3] Russell, F. THE PIMA INDIANS. U. S. Bur. Amer. Ethnol. Ann. Rept. (1904–05) 26 : 3–[390], illus. 1908.
[4] Green, R. A., and Foster, E. O. THE LIQUID WAX OF SEEDS OF SIMMONDSIA CALIFORNICA. Bot. Gaz. 94 : 826–828. 1933.
[5] Thornber, J. J. THE GRAZING RANGES OF ARIZONA. Ariz. Agr. Expt. Sta. Bull. 65 : [245]–360, illus. 1910.

SPIREAS

Spirae'a spp.

DOUGLAS SPIREA (*S. douglasii*)

Flowers—pink or rose, small, numerous, in rather narrow, elongated, showy end clusters (panicles) 2 to 8 in. long

Seed pods (follicles)—usually 5, small, dry, hairless, shining, each tipped by an erect, threadlike stalk (style), several-seeded; seeds small

Stems and twigs—reddish brown, somewhat woolly-hairy especially when young, striped or ridged

Leaves—alternate, oblong to narrow-oblong, 1 to 4 in. long, rounded or somewhat pointed at both ends, unequally saw-toothed around edges above the middle, green above, short-white-woolly-hairy beneath, short-stalked

S. douglasii

BIRCHLEAF SPIREA (*S. lucida*)

Flowers—white, small, numerous, in rather dense, flat-topped, branched, hairless end clusters (corymbs) up to 4 in. across

Stamens—numerous, longer than the 5 petals, attached to a ringlike disk in the mouth of the bell-shaped outer united flower parts (calyx)

Stems and twigs—straight, not much branched, hairless, yellowish brown to brownish, slender

Seed pods (follicles)—usually 5, small (about ⅛ in. long), dry, hairless, shining, several-seeded; seeds small

Leaves—alternate, larger toward twig ends, broadly egg-shaped or somewhat oblong, usually sharp-pointed (sometimes rounded) at tip, about 1 to 3 in. long, coarsely saw-toothed or cut and doubly saw-toothed along edges of upper ½ or ⅔ of leaves, smooth and shiny above, pale beneath, short-stalked

S. lucida

M.E.A.

The spireas, sometimes called meadowsweet or steeplebush, are attractive shrubs belonging to the large and important rose family (Rosaceae). The 70 or more species are widely distributed in the temperate and cooler climates of the Northern Hemisphere. About 10 species are native to western North America, several being widely scattered through the mountains of most of the Western States. The generic name is derived from *speiraia*, a name used by the Greek philosopher Theophrastus for an Old World species of meadowsweet, or spirea, having spirally twisted (Greek *speira*, a coil or spiral) pods. *Spiraea* is said to have been introduced into more modern botany, as a generic name, by the eminent Belgian physician-botanist Clusius (1526–1609).

The spireas are deciduous shrubs, with slender, erect or spreading, usually scaly-barked stems. Douglas spirea (*S. dougla'sii*) and the other erect species characteristically grow in patches, but with the stems distinct, rarely branched and bushlike. The species with spreading stems, such as subalpine spirea (*S. densiflo'ra*), may also form patches, but more often grow as individual, low and many-stemmed shrubs. Spirea leaves lack bractlike appendages (stipules) at base of the leafstalks; they are alternate, short-stalked, simple (occasionally lobed), strongly veined on the under side, and usually saw-toothed (especially above the middle). The flowers of the native western species are very small (commonly less than one-eighth of an inch long), have five sepals and five petals, and many protruding stamens. They may be white, pink, or rose-colored, but are always numerous and crowded into showy, dense, flat-topped or elongated flower clusters at the ends of the stems or twigs. The fruit consists of a cluster of usually five small pods (follicles), which are not inflated, each containing several seeds.

Most of the spireas prefer deep, fertile, and moist soils, but some species are also common in bogs, on moist rocky slopes, and even in dry sites. They appear on exposures varying from warm and sunny to cool and shaded, nearly all the western species growing under this wide range of conditions. In the West, the genus is most common at middle elevations in the mountains and is most abundant in the moist, Douglas fir region of the Northwest. Common associated shrubs are roses, huckleberries, willows, and snowberries.

Although spireas are low, leafy, and usually accessible to livestock, they are of minor value for forage. Their range importance is primarily due to their wide distribution and abundance. For some reason, possibly because of the presence of a volatile oil containing bitter salicylic aldehyde,[1] the foliage is of low palatability. The leaves remain attached to the plants longer than in most deciduous species, and this may account for the moderate fall use sometimes obtained, but generally the members of this genus are regarded as practically worthless for cattle and poor to fair for sheep. The low value is sometimes shown by the presence of little-used spirea on overgrazed ranges, especially in or bordering depleted meadows where cattle concentrate.

Spireas, as a class, are showy plants when in bloom and add to the beauty and recreational value of woodland areas. Many of the species, both native and introduced, are cultivated as ornamentals, being prized for their attractive foliage and bloom. The species are hardy and flourish under a greater

[1] Wood, H. C., Remington, J. P., and Sadtler, S. P., assisted by Lyons, A. B., and Wood, H. C., Jr. THE DISPENSATORY OF THE UNITED STATES OF AMERICA, BY DR. GEO. B. WOOD AND DR. FRANKLIN BACHE. Ed. 19, thoroughly rev. and largely rewritten . . . 1,947 pp. Philadelphia and London. 1907.

variety of conditions than most cultivated shrubs. Various species are in local repute as medicinal plants; the eastern hardhack (*S. tomento'sa*), for example, which is bitterish and has astringent properties, has been used locally in New England as a tonic, and was undoubtedly similarly employed by the Indians. The spireas have some value in erosion control on the western mountain ranges, especially those species with creeping rootstocks which are able to spread out and thus effectively bind the soil mass.

Subalpine spirea (*S. densiflo'ra*, syns. *S. arbus'cula*, *S. hel'leri*), Douglas spirea (*S. dougla'sii*), birchleaf spirea (*S. lu'cida*, syn. *S. corymbo'sa lu'cida*), and Menzies spirea (*S. menzie'sii*), are probably the most widely distributed and common spireas in the West.

Subalpine spirea, as the name indicates, is most common in the subalpine zone, extending from British Columbia to California, Wyoming, and Montana. This shrub is often associated with western white pine and lodgepole pine, but prefers rocky situations, commonly growing in the soil-filled cracks of the rocks. It is a low (at most, up to 3 feet) much-branched shrub, the stems sometimes being crooked, with dark, red-brown bark. This species ordinarily occurs as individual plants, but sometimes also grows in clumps; it is of negligible forage value. The dense, flat-topped flower clusters are an attractive red in tint.

Douglas spirea, a shrub from 3 to 8 feet in height, with straight, erect stems, is distributed from British Columbia to northern California, chiefly in the coastal region. It occurs characteristically in patches or thickets often covering several acres along creek bottoms, meadow borders, moist flats, and in cut-over Douglas fir lands. The upright, leafy stems grow a few inches to a foot or more apart, and are sparingly branched above the middle; the leaves are woolly beneath. The flowers are rose-colored, and aggregated into dense, pyramid-shaped clusters at the ends of the stems and twigs. Although often abundant on the ranges, it is of negligible value, ordinarily being consumed only where forage is scarce, as on depleted areas, or during the fall.

Birchleaf spirea, a white-flowered species, occurs from British Columbia to Oregon and east to Wyoming, South Dakota, and Saskatchewan. An upright, little-branched shrub, 1 to 3 feet in height, which develops from creeping rootstocks, it differs from the other common western spireas in its relatively large, birchlike leaves, and dense, flat-topped, white flower clusters. On the sterile twigs the smallest leaves are usually at the base and the largest leaves at the tip. On the flowering twigs the same tendency is observed but, as is so often the case, the leaves immediately subtending the flower clusters are reduced in size. It inhabits open hillsides and dry woods, and, although sometimes abundant in the Northwest, its forage value is negligible.

Menzies spirea, which grows from Alaska to Oregon and east to Idaho, resembles Douglas spirea, except that it is smaller (3 to 4 feet high), and has thinner and smooth leaves. The pink or red flower clusters are similarly pyramidal but rather narrow. It usually grows in the sunlight or shade along streams and similar sites, and is sometimes locally abundant. Menzies spirea is perhaps the most palatable of the spireas on the western ranges, rating in the Northwest as fair to good in the fall for both cattle and sheep.[2]

The spireas are closely related to the ninebarks (*Opulaster* spp., syn. *Physocarpus* spp.) and to the rockspireas (*Sericotheca* spp., syn. *Holodiscus* spp.); in fact, many of the species in these two genera were at one time included in the genus *Spiraea*. Like the spireas, they are deciduous shrubs, with simple leaves and usually numerous small flowers crowded into terminal, sometimes very showy, clusters. The chief differences are that the leaves of ninebarks are three-lobed, the bark shreddy, the flowers mostly white, and the pods usually inflated. The rockspireas have toothed or lobed leaves, white flowers, and the "seeds" (achenes) are long-hairy.

---

[2] Dayton, W. A. IMPORTANT WESTERN BROWSE PLANTS. U. S. Dept. Agr. Misc. Pub. 101, 214 pp., illus. 1931.

SNOWBERRIES AND CORALBERRY

Symphoricar'pos spp.

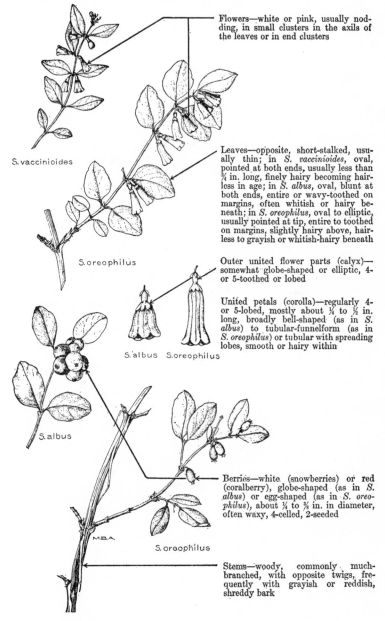

Flowers—white or pink, usually nodding, in small clusters in the axils of the leaves or in end clusters

S. vaccinioides

Leaves—opposite, short-stalked, usually thin; in *S. vaccinioides*, oval, pointed at both ends, usually less than ¾ in. long, finely hairy becoming hairless in age; in *S. albus*, oval, blunt at both ends, entire or wavy-toothed on margins, often whitish or hairy beneath; in *S. oreophilus*, oval to elliptic, usually pointed at tip, entire to toothed on margins, slightly hairy above, hairless to grayish or whitish-hairy beneath

S. oreophilus

Outer united flower parts (calyx)—somewhat globe-shaped or elliptic, 4- or 5-toothed or lobed

United petals (corolla)—regularly 4- or 5-lobed, mostly about ¼ to ½ in. long, broadly bell-shaped (as in *S. albus*) to tubular-funnelform (as in *S. oreophilus*) or tubular with spreading lobes, smooth or hairy within

S. albus   S. oreophilus

S. albus

Berries—white (snowberries) or red (coralberry), globe-shaped (as in *S. albus*) or egg-shaped (as in *S. oreophilus*), about ¼ to ⅜ in. in diameter, often waxy, 4-celled, 2-seeded

S. oreophilus

Stems—woody, commonly much-branched, with opposite twigs, frequently with grayish or reddish, shreddy bark

795

Symphoricarpos, a member of the honeysuckle family (Capri-foliaceae), is a small genus of chiefly North American shrubs, widely distributed in the United States and southern Canada, and also extending into Mexico. Under a conservative nomenclature, there are about 12 species of the genus, 10 of which occur in the western range country; the other 2 are largely eastern in their distribution. One species is confined to Mexico, and one additional species grows in China. The generic name is derived from the Greek verb *symphoreo*, bear together, and *karpos*, fruit, referring to the clustered fruits. These shrubs are frequently known on the range by the indistinctive name buckbrush; other common names include Indian-currant, St. Peterswort, waxberry, and wolfberry. With one exception, all the United States species have white or slightly pink berries. The white-fruited species are most commonly called snowberries, and the single red-fruited species (*S. orbiculatus*) is dubbed coralberry. Many of the American species are closely related and so similar that it is difficult, at least for those unversed in technical botany, to differentiate between some of them. However, for practical range administration, specific determination is probably not essential, since the palatability of the more common and abundant species is almost identical.

Coralberry (*S. orbicula'tus*, syns. *S. symphoricar'pos*, *S. vulga'ris*) is a chiefly eastern species, ranging from New York to Georgia, Texas, Colorado, and Montana. Its range is extending, as a result of escape from cultivation. In the West, this species grows principally along streams at the lower elevations and, from a range standpoint, is neither particularly abundant nor important, although one of the popular species for decorative plantings, because of its hardiness, its prolific, enduring, coral-colored fruit, and almost evergreen foliage.

As a group, the snowberries are most typical of medium elevations in the Rocky Mountain region, being abundant chiefly in the ponderosa-pine, aspen, and spruce belts at elevations of from 6,000 to 9,000 feet. On the Pacific coast, however, several species are common at lower elevations; in fact, some species occur practically at sea level. They grow on dry and moist soils and on all slopes both in shade and in full sunlight. In the Northwest snowberries occur most abundantly along the drainage lines in association with other shrubs, or in parks and openings in the timber. In the Inter-mountain region, central Rocky Mountains, and Southwest they largely prefer relatively dry, southern slopes where they are often the dominant shrubs in small patches. Sampson (in Tidestrom)[1] states that mountain snowberry (*S. oreophilus*) is the most conspicuous shrub of the aspen-fir belt of the Intermountain region.

The palatability of snowberries varies in different localities and with different plant associations. In general there is a tendency for *Symphoricarpos* species to have greater palatability in the Inter-mountain region and on the drier eastern and southern ranges than in the more northern and western areas.[2] However, in the desert

---

[1] Tidestrom, I. FLORA OF UTAH AND NEVADA. U. S. Natl. Mus., Contrib. U. S. Natl. Herbarium 25, 665 pp., illus. 1925.
[2] Dayton, W. A. IMPORTANT WESTERN BROWSE PLANTS. U. S. Dept. Agr. Misc. Pub. 101, 214 pp., illus. 1931.

regions of Utah and Nevada, the local longflower snowberry (*S. longiflo'rus*) is largely unpalatable to livestock. The palatability of the other western species, in general, varies from poor to fair for cattle, except in California, the Intermountain region, and the Southwest, where it is fairly good or perhaps good for sheep and goats but practically worthless for horses. These shrubs are also fair to fairly good forage for deer and elk.

The relatively low, shrubby snowberries, whose foliage is mostly accessible to livestock, withstand grazing very well; often, because of their abundance, they are important factors in the forage supply on many ranges. These plants are especially valuable in the Intermountain region on both cattle and sheep ranges; Chapline[3] regards them as moderately palatable goat browse in the Southwest. These shrubs usually drop their leaves in the fall, and hence are of little value on winter ranges.

Saponin, a poisonous drug, occurs in the leaves (but not the fruit) of common snowberry (*S. al'bus*, syn. *S. racemo'sus*) and of spreading or trailing snowberry (*S. mol'lis*).[4] Poisoning caused by common snowberry has been reported from the Old World; consequently, some authorities include this genus among the plants suspected of being poisonous. However, so far as the Forest Service has knowledge, no case of loss or even sickness has ever been attributed to this genus on the western ranges. It seems probable that, if saponin is present in the western species, it occurs in too small amounts to be important physiologically.[5] No ill effects were produced when the crushed fruits of whortleleaf snowberry (*S. vaccinioides*) were forcibly fed to sheep in experiments at the Salina Experiment Station.[5]

Common snowberry and mountain snowberry are the two most common and widely distributed western snowberries. Common snowberry, an erect shrub 2 to 4 or sometimes 5 feet high, has slender, smooth branches; rather thin, oval, nearly entire to somewhat toothed leaves from three-fourths of an inch to 2 inches long. Its flower clusters are both terminal and axillary, the corollas being about one-fourth of an inch long, broadly bell-shaped, and hairy within. The fruits are white, globose, and from one-fourth to three-eighths of an inch in diameter. This is the most widely distributed species of the genus, ranging from Nova Scotia to Alaska, California, Colorado, South Dakota, Minnesota, Kentucky, and North Carolina. It is an important browse species and one of the most abundant snowberries in the West. In contrast, mountain snowberry, a spreading shrub averaging about 2 to 4 feet in height, is a common species in the mountains from eastern Oregon and Idaho to Colorado, New Mexico, and California. Frequently abundant, it is often the dominant shrub over small areas. In Utah and western Colorado, this shrub frequently abounds in aspen, but elsewhere is usually associated with

[3] Chapline, W. R. PRODUCTION OF GOATS ON FAR WESTERN RANGES. U. S. Dept. Agr. Bull. 749, 35 pp., illus. 1919.
[4] Greshoff, M. PHYTOCHEMICAL INVESTIGATIONS AT KEW. Roy. Bot. Gard. Kew, Bull. Misc. Inform. 1909: [397]–418. 1909.
[5] Marsh, C. D., Clawson, A. B., and Roe, G. C. FOUR SPECIES OF RANGE PLANTS NOT POISONOUS TO LIVESTOCK. U. S. Dept. Agr. Tech. Bull. 93, 10 pp. 1928.

such conifers as ponderosa pine, Engelmann spruce, blue spruce, white fir, and Douglas fir. It is distinguished by its narrow, tubular corolla, hairless within, and from more than one-fourth to over one-half of an inch long; rather thin, oblong to broadly oval, pointed, entire or toothed leaves; and by its white, egg-shaped fruits about three-eighths of an inch long. Snowberries are highly regarded for the beauty of their foliage and fruits, and are widely grown as ornamentals; common snowberry and coralberry are the species most frequently cultivated.

WESTERN POISON-IVY

Toxicoden'dron rydber'gii, syns. *Rhu's rydber'gii, R. toxicoden'dron.*[1] *and T. lon'gipes*

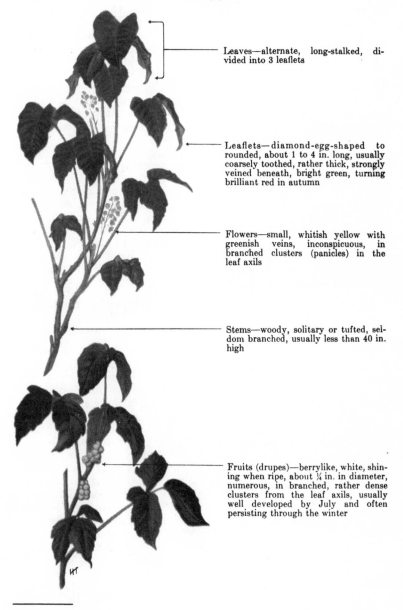

Leaves—alternate, long-stalked, divided into 3 leaflets

Leaflets—diamond-egg-shaped to rounded, about 1 to 4 in. long, usually coarsely toothed, rather thick, strongly veined beneath, bright green, turning brilliant red in autumn

Flowers—small, whitish yellow with greenish veins, inconspicuous, in branched clusters (panicles) in the leaf axils

Stems—woody, solitary or tufted, seldom branched, usually less than 40 in. high

Fruits (drupes)—berrylike, white, shining when ripe, about ¼ in. in diameter, numerous, in branched, rather dense clusters from the leaf axils, usually well developed by July and often persisting through the winter

---

[1] Of western authors.

799

Western poison-ivy is of interest chiefly because of its irritating effect on the human skin. Although some persons are little affected by western poison-ivy few, if any, are entirely immune. Lower animals apparently do not react to the poison; in fact, livestock which crop the plant experience no ill effects. In the past, some of the most conservative botanists have classified this species merely as a western, nonclimbing form of the common poison-ivy (*T. radicans*, syn. *R. radicans*) of the East. However, the geographical distribution of these two species is distinct, and there are well-marked characters of leaves, flowers, and fruit which differentiate them. Western poison-ivy occurs from South Dakota to western Oklahoma, Arizona, Oregon, and British Columbia, growing in a wide variety of situations from the foothills to the ponderosa pine belt, and often being abundant in thickets along streams, in canyons, and on dry, rocky hillsides. Although occasionally nibbled by livestock it is negligible or poor as a browse plant.

It is risky to handle this species, or any members of the genus in studying botanical characters, unless proper precautions are taken to avert poisoning. Fortunately, western poison-ivy is recognizable at a glance, being a relatively low, woody-stemmed plant with long-stalked leaves divided into three, bright green, veiny, rather large, coarse-toothed leaflets. The leaves turn a brilliant red in autumn, and fall from the plants, but the clusters of whitish, shiny, berrylike fruits usually remain attached to the stems throughout the winter. The poisonous properties of this plant are practically the same as those of other species of *Toxicodendron* and are treated in greater detail in the accompanying discussion of the genus.

POISON-IVIES, POISON-OAKS, AND POISON-SUMACS

Toxicoden'dron spp., syn. *Rhu's spp.* in part

Toxicodendron is a genus of small trees, shrubs, or climbing vines having divided (trifoliolately or pinnately compound) leaves and resinous sap; there are approximately 20 species native to North America and Asia, with five occurring in the United States. The more conservative botanists prefer to classify these plants with the true sumacs (*Rhus* spp.). However, the group of species under *Toxicodendron*, whether given generic or sectional rank, has well-marked characters, including a poisonous juice; drooping, loose, and axillary (instead of erect, dense, and terminal) flower clusters; a single and unbranched (instead of three-branched) stalk (style) of the female floral organ (pistil); and white or grayish, wax-producing, smooth or slightly fuzzy, usually shiny (instead of red or reddish, and densely pubescent) fruits, with ridged (instead of smooth) stones. The generic name is a combination of the Greek *toxicon* (pertaining to the bow)[2] and *dendron* (tree), meaning poison tree.

The species of poison-ivy are not, of course, true ivies, *i. e.*, evergreen woody vines or climbing shrubs of the genus *Hedera* of the

---

[2] It is worthy of note that the original poisons of mankind were arrow poisons, used in obtaining food. This explains why our modern science of poisons (toxicology) gets its name from a root word meaning bow. The Greeks used the phrase *toxicon pharmakon* (literally "bow drug") for arrow poisons, and the later Latin word *toxicum* (poison) appears to have been a sort of shorthand derivative from that phase.

ginseng family (Araliaceae). McNair [3] indicates that perhaps the earliest mention of these plants in North America is by the redoubtable Captain John Smith in 1609, who compared their appearance to that of English ivy (*Hedera helix*). Poison-ivies and poison-oaks are shrubs or woody vines having leaves composed of three leaflets, which vary from untoothed (entire) to coarsely toothed or wavy-margined or three- to seven-lobed, and turn a brilliant hue in the fall. The small, greenish, yellowish, or whitish flowers are borne in rather dense clusters (panicles); white or ivory-colored, berrylike fruits (drupes) usually persist on the plant for a considerable period during the fall and early winter.

The typically eastern common poison-ivy (*T. ra'dicans*, syn. *R. toxicoden'dron ra'dicans*), which extends as far west as the eastern edge of the range country, is a woody vine that climbs by means of masses of small aerial rootlets on the stems; it frequently ascends tall trees, sending out branches horizontally in such manner that it is sometimes mistaken for the tree itself. Everything considered, this is probably the most pestiferous plant in the more eastern portions of the United States. Grubbing and the use of various chemicals (such as common salt, crank-case oil, kerosene and sodium chlorate) are the usual methods of eradicating poison-ivy, but success has been obtained in a number of places by allowing goats, sheep, and cattle to graze the plant closely and continuously.[4][5] Sheep and goats are especially efficient in cleaning out areas along walls and fences.

Pacific poison-oak (*T. diversilo'bum*, syn. *R. diversilo'ba*), which either is a many-stemmed, erect bush or climbs by adventitious rootlets, ranges from Washington to California. The three leaflets are variable, roundish to egg-shaped, and diversely lobed or toothed, occasionally resembling an oak leaf. Jepson [6] rates it as the most widely distributed shrub in California. It is often very abundant and ranges from the coastal foothills to central elevations of the ponderosa pine belt. This species produces a large amount of readily accessible foliage of slight to fair palatability for cattle and sheep and, on many ranges, it is an important secondary browse. McNair [7] reports but little apparent variation in the degree of virulence of the poisonous sap of this species throughout the year, and that all parts of the plant are toxic except the anthers and pollen, the true woody tissue (xylem), the cork cells, the epidermis, and the minute hairs (trichomes).

Poison-sumac (*T. ver'nix*, syn. *R. ver'nix*), an erect shrub or small tree common in wet places and lowlands east of the Mississippi

[3] McNair, J. B. RHUS DERMATITIS FROM RHUS TOXICODENDRON, RADICANS AND DIVERSILOBA (POISON IVY): ITS PATHOLOGY AND CHEMOTHERAPY. 298 pp., illus. Chicago. [1923.]
[4] Grant, C. V., and Hansen, A. A. POISON IVY AND POISON SUMAC AND THEIR ERADICATION. U. S. Dept. Agr. Farmers' Bull. 1166, rev., 14 pp., illus. 1929.
[5] Alexander, A. S. SHEEP KILL POISON IVY. Amer. Sheep Breeder and Wool Grower 47: 324–325. 1927.
[6] Jepson, W. L. A MANUAL OF THE FLOWERING PLANTS OF CALIFORNIA. 1,238 pp., illus. Berkeley, Calif. [1925.]
[7] McNair, J. B. A STUDY OF RHUS DIVERSILOBA WITH SPECIAL REFERENCE TO ITS TOXICITY. Amer. Jour. Bot. 8: 127–146, illus. 1921.

River, doubtfully extends into the range country. It has sumac-like (pinnate) leaves, a lacquer-producing sap, and is notorious as a skin-irritant.

One or more of these poisonous species occur in every section of the United States, western poison-ivy and Pacific poison-oak being the far western representatives. Persons unfamiliar with these plants may lessen the danger of contracting "ivy" poisoning by observing the following simple precautions: (1) Avoid shrubs or vines with clusters of white, cream-colored or ivory, berrylike fruits; (2) avoid low, erect and climbing shrubs with the leaves divided into three leaflets, better expressed by the homely saying, "Leaflets three, let it be"; and (3) in the eastern United States, also avoid wet-site shrubs or small trees with smooth, pale bark whose leaves are alternate, divided into more than seven leaflets, and have untoothed margins.

Hill, Mattacotti, and Graham,[8] of the Hall Laboratory of Chemistry, Wesleyan University, isolated and identified urushiol ($C_{21}H_{32}O_2$) as the toxic principle of *Rhus toxicodendron*. Urushiol is a yellow, slightly volatile oil, first obtained by a Japanese scientist, R. Majima, from the Japanese lacquer-tree (*T. vernicifluum*, syns. *R. vernicifera*, *R. verniciflua*), a first cousin to our eastern poison-sumac, and the source of the famous black varnish, or lacquer of the Orient. The three American experimenters mentioned above verified the findings of J. Toyama, another Japanese scientist, that the hydroxyl groups in urushiol are the chief cause of its well-known violently vesicant action. Grant and Hansen[3] state: "All parts of the plant contain the poison, even after long drying, but growth in which the sap is abundant is the most dangerous." Poisoning usually results from touching or brushing against the plants or from handling clothing or other objects which have been in contact with them. Many persons maintain that they have been poisoned merely by being in the vicinity of the plants without actually touching them, although scientific research thus far has not substantiated this contention. Unquestionably, however, numerous severe cases of poisoning have resulted from smoke from the burning plant. Although many persons are practically immune, it is doubtful if anyone is wholly free from susceptibility to the poison, as apparent immunity may disappear at any time.[3] If taken internally in sufficient amount, the poison acts as a violent irritant; cases have been reported of poisoning among children from eating the fruits. The lower animals are not poisoned, apparently, and livestock and game animals consume the leaves, at least, without harmful effects.

Cures for poison-ivy poisoning are legion; practically as numerous as the cases of poisoning. This results from the fact that the dermatitis, or skin rash, is naturally self-limiting, and the eventual cure spontaneous, so that whatever remedy is used is likely to be heralded as a sure cure for "ivy" poisoning. Mild cases usually subside in a few days. However, several fatalities are on record as a result of extensive and severe inflammation; in serious cases it is wise to con-

    [8] See footnote on preceding page.
    [8] Hill, G. A., Mattacotti, V., and Graham, W. D. THE TOXIC PRINCIPLE OF THE POISON IVY. Jour. Amer. Chem. Soc. 56 (12) : 2736-2738. 1934.

sult a physician. The standard external remedies include ferric chloride ($FeCl_3$)—introduced by McNair, sugar of lead (lead acetate), fluid extract of grindelia, and a solution of baking soda or Epsom salts. Couch [9] recommends an oxidizing agent, such as potassium permanganate. Care must be exercised in using sugar of lead not to induce lead poisoning.[10] Zinc oxide and other greasy ointments, which sometimes spread the poison, should be avoided during the early stages of the infection. Prevention is the best remedy. If exposure to these poisonous shrubs is suspected, thorough washing in several changes of water, using a soapy lather, will usually prove effective. Hard scrubbing, which may cause small lesions in the skin and thus facilitate entry of the poison, should be avoided. Soap lather, permitted to dry on the skin, is frequently an effective preventive for susceptible persons obliged to travel in areas infested by these plants.

The literature on poison-ivy, poison-oak, and poison-sumac poisoning (rhus dermatitis) is enormous. In a book published in 1923 McNair [3] gives bibliographies of about 1,100 papers on this subject.

The noisome attributes of these plants are, to some degree, compensated by certain characters of unquestioned beauty. Their handsome foliage, frequently glossy, turns gorgeous colors in the fall. The pale, beadlike fruits, pendent in graceful sprays, often possess a pearl-like luster. These aesthetic values, in fact, are sufficiently pronounced to have led to the horticultural use of about 10 of the species both at home and abroad. It seems likely, however, that no one not the fortunate possessor of a high degree of immunity to urushiol-poisoning would wittingly risk contact with these plants requisite to their planting and nurture.

---

[9] Couch, J. F. POISON IVY AND WHAT TO DO ABOUT IT. Sci. Monthly 33 : 359–362. 1931.
[10] Hansen, A. A. POISON IVY AND TREATMENT FOR IT. Nature Mag. 2 : 147–148, illus. 1923.

BLUEBERRIES AND WHORTLEBERRIES

Vacci'nium spp.

Vaccinium, the classical Latin name for these or related plants, is a large, widely distributed group of shrubs or occasionally small trees, most of which occur in the Old World. The genus belongs to the blueberry family (Vacciniaceae), sometimes considered a sub- family or tribe of the heath family (Ericaceae). As here inter- preted, *Vaccinium* includes the subgenera or sections, true blueberries (*Cyanococ'cus* or *Euvacci'nium*) and cowberries (*Vi'tis-idae'a*), which are designated as separate genera by some authors, but excludes the genera (subgenera or sections of some authors), tree-huckleber- ries, or farkleberries (*Batoden'dron*), dingleberries, or mountain- cranberries (*Huge'ria*, syn. *Oxycoccoi'des*), cranberries (*Oxy- coc'cus*), and deerberries, or "gooseberries" (*Polyco'dium*) of the South.

Species of *Vaccinium* are known throughout the West as huckle- berries, a name more accurately applied to the genus *Gaylussacia* of the Eastern States, whose fruits are the huckleberries of commerce. *Gaylussacia* has firm, often pubescent or resinous leaves, and black berries which are more acid and seedy than those of blueberries. This application of a common plant name from one locality to dif- ferent plants of similar appearance in another region well illustrates the difficulty of selecting and standardizing common names. The name blueberry is well established for the species of *Vaccinium* having bright, waxy-blue (glaucous) berries—and particularly for those species cultivated commercially for their fruit. However, objections to its use for the entire genus are largely based upon the fact that some species of *Vaccinium* have black or red fruits. Con- sequently, whortleberry, a largely British name for these plants, and particularly applied to the black-berried Old World *V. myrtillus* (the botanical type of the genus *Vaccinium*), has been proposed to cover the non-blue-fruited species, and was adopted by the authors of Standardized Plant Names,[1] as well as by the Forest Service in a recent range plant publication.[2] Popularization of the common name blueberries for the blue-fruited species of *Vaccinium*, and of huckleberries for the genus *Gaylussacia*, is recommended as being in accordance with established practice for the cultivated species and to eliminate the confusion in this country concerning the com- mon names of these two closely related genera.

Approximately 18 species of blueberries and whortleberries occur in the Western States, and a few others are native to the region from Alaska to British Columbia. They all inhabit acid soils and are commonly associated with coniferous forests, often forming a dense, almost pure understory in stands of lodgepole pine and Engelmann

[1] American Joint Committee on Horticultural Nomenclature. STANDARDIZED PLANT NAMES . . . Prepared by F. L. Olmsted, F. V. Coville, and H. P. Kelsey. 546 pp., Salem, Mass. 1923.
[2] Dayton, W. A. IMPORTANT WESTERN BROWSE PLANTS. U. S. Dept. Agr. Misc. Pub. 101, 214 pp., illus. 1931.

spruce. These plants are also common shrubs in ponderosa pine, and in the heavy Douglas fir and mixed coniferous forests of Idaho and the Northwest. However, many species apparently succeed in the open, some appearing on northerly, exposed slopes at the lower elevations, with others growing in considerable abundance in alpine meadows and also frequently forming dense stands in burns.

The blueberries and their congeners vary, as browse for sheep, from practically worthless to poor or fair; occasionally they rate as fairly good or, rarely, good. In the main, they are of negligible value for cattle. In general, deer, caribou, and elk crop these plants rather extensively; caribou [3] and elk, in particular, utilize them intensively on closely grazed ranges, and even browse the stems and twigs on winter ranges. The taller species, as a rule, are more palatable than those of low, sprawling growth; the leaves of the former usually are more delicate and succulent. The edible fruits are relished by birds, rodents, and bears. In localities where the larger-fruited species are abundant, the berries are often gathered commercially for human consumption, furnishing seasonal employment to thousands of people.[4]

The species of *Vaccinium* have woody stems, often with somewhat four-angled, greenish branchlets; alternate, deciduous, or evergreen, mostly thin, either entire or finely toothed leaves; and usually drooping, rose-colored, white, or greenish, somewhat bell-like flowers, either solitary or in small clusters. The calyx (outer united flower parts) is small and four- or five-lobed; the corolla is somewhat urn-shaped or bell-shaped, and four- or five-toothed. The pollen sacs (anthers) of the 8 or 10 stamens are awnless, two-awned on the back, or prolonged into tubes opening by pores. The fruit, a four- to five-celled (or 8- to 10-celled by false partitions), blue or black (sometimes red), sweet, edible berry, either with or without bloom (glaucous), is characteristically flattened at one end and crowned by the persistent calyx teeth.

Big whortleberry (*V. membrana'ceum*, syn. *V. macrophyl'lum*), one of the more palatable species, ranks among the important shrubs of Idaho, eastern Washington, and eastern Oregon; it is fully discussed elsewhere in this handbook. Box blueberry (*V. ova'tum*, syn. *Vitis-idae'a ova'ta*), sometimes called "California huckleberry", a tall (4 to 8 feet high), stout species appearing in the humid, coastal forests from California to Vancouver Island, is often the dominant plant in the understory of redwood and Douglas-fir forests. In some places, sheep crop this species fairly well during the fall, winter, and early spring. The oblong-egg-shaped, leathery, evergreen leaves, with toothed margins, are shiny above and from ½ to 1¼ inches long. The flowers are rose color or pink and broadly bell-shaped; the fruits are typically black and lacking in bloom but in one variety are bright blue. Throughout the fog belt in California, this species sometimes forms dense thickets on open ridges, where it fruits abundantly. The Calpella and other Indians often traveled

[3] Murie, O. J. ALASKA-YUKON CARIBOU. North Amer. Fauna 54, 93 pp., illus. 1935.
[4] Dayton, W. A. MINOR BY PRODUCTS OF THE FOREST. A NATIONAL PLAN FOR AMERICAN FORESTRY. 73d Cong., 1st sess., S. Doc. 12, v. 1, pp. 555–562. 1933.

20 or 30 miles to gather the fruits.[5]   Munson [6] quotes the statement of the California horticulturist T. H. Douglas that box blueberry is "one of California's most beautiful hedge-plants and merits greater commercial prominence."

Dwarf blueberry (*V. cespito'sum*), also known as dwarf bilberry, one of the commonest and best known of the western blueberries, ranges from Labrador to Alaska, and south to California, Colorado, and even to the highest peaks of New York and New England.   It is frequently associated with grouse whortleberry (*V. scoparium*) in the coniferous forests of the West.   Dwarf blueberry is a very abundant species but has practically zero palatability.   It is a low, spreading shrub from 3 to 12 inches high (or occasionally 18 inches in the var. *arbus'cula*), with round, not angled, branchlets.   The rather thin, smooth, shining leaves are reverse-egg-shaped or reverse-lance-shaped, narrowed at the base, and have fine-toothed margins. The pink, red, or white, urn-shaped flowers are solitary and pendulous on short stalks in the leaf axils.   The sweet blue berries, about one-fourth of an inch in diameter, have a bloom.

Grouse whortleberry (*V. scopa'rium*, syns. *V. erythrococ'cum*, *V. myrtil'lus microphyl'lum* Hook., 1834, and *V. microphyl'lum* (Hook.) Rydb., not *V. microphyl'lum* Reinw., 1826), ranging from British Columbia to California, northern New Mexico and Alberta, is probably the most abundant and widespread of the western species of *Vaccinium*.[2]   This plant is also known as dwarf, red, small, or littleleaf huckleberry and as red alpine blueberry.   It has a great altitudinal range, growing at elevations of between about 2,500 and 7,500 feet in the Pacific Northwest to between 8,500 and 12,500 feet in Colorado.   It is present on all slopes and appears on both dry and moist sites, but is especially characteristic of sandy or gravelly loams; this plant is practically always a component of the understory of lodgepole-pine stands.   Grouse whortleberry, a distinctly inferior browse, is practically worthless to poor forage.   However, in some localities, it rates as fair or even fairly good forage for sheep, but this is due chiefly to its occurrence where relatively little palatable forage is available.   This species is probably browsed to some extent by deer and other game animals.   The stems of grouse whortleberry average 4 to 8 (sometimes 12) inches in height, with sharply angled, bright green branches.   The thin leaves are mostly less than one-half of an inch long, egg-shaped to lance-egg-shaped, pointed at both ends, and finely toothed.   The small flowers appear in June and July; the bright red berries ripen from late July until September. The berries, although agreeably flavored, are but rarely gathered for human consumption, being small in size (about three-sixteenths of an inch in diameter) and relatively scant in supply; they are utilized by birds and small animals.

[5] Chesnut, V. K.   PLANTS USED BY THE INDIANS OF MENDOCINO COUNTY, CALIFORNIA. U. S. Dept. Agr., Div. Bot., Contrib. U. S. Natl. Herbarium 7 : 295–422, illus.   1902.
[6] Munson, W. M.   THE HORTICULTURAL STATUS OF THE GENUS VACCINIUM.   Maine Agr. Expt. Sta. Ann. Rept. (1901) 17 : [113]–160, illus.   1902.

Ovalleaf whortleberry (*V. ovalifo'lium*), also known as blue whortleberry, and as big, ovalleaf, or tall bilberry, is a large straggling shrub from 3 to 12 feet high, with slender, more or less angled branches and thin, egg-shaped leaves. It grows in both dry and moist woods, in meadows, and in swamps from Quebec to Michigan, Oregon, Alaska, and Japan, from sea level to an elevation of about 5,500 feet. In some places, it furnishes browse for sheep and goats.[2] This shrub abounds in the Northwest; in Alaska, it forms a large part of the forest undergrowth in the low country along the coast, where it averages about 4 feet in height. The large, dark purple berries ripen in September. The late General Funston, the capturer of Aguinaldo, reports them as an important food in Alaska, where they are picked extensively by the natives, who either immediately consume the fresh fruit or preserve and dry it for winter use.[7]

Red whortleberry (*V. parvifo'lium*), the largest of the western "blueberries", sometimes reaching a height of 18 feet, ranges from sea level to an elevation of about 5,000 feet, from Alaska to California, west of the Cascade and Sierra Nevada Mountains. It occurs most commonly in moist, coniferous woods, chiefly in stands of Sitka spruce, Douglas fir, and redwood; it attains its best development on moist sites in the spruce type, where both duff and humus have accumulated. The thin, moderately palatable leaves and slender, delicate twigs of this shrub, which is frequently abundant amidst plants of low forage utility, make it of some local value for sheep and, occasionally, for cattle; the species is also an important game browse in certain localities. The green branches of this plant are sharply angled; the rather sparse leaves are oblong or egg-shaped, entire, more or less rounded at both ends, an inch or less in length, dull green in color, and pale beneath; the greenish white flowers are globe-shaped; the berries are light red, rather dry, and, although acid, have a pleasant flavor.

Blueberries are now cultivated comercially both in the eastern United States and in the Pacific Northwest, but less commonly in the Southeast. Their culture is not difficult, although they require an acid soil (especially one composed of peat and sand), plenty of moisture, and satisfactory drainage and aeration.[8] When once established, the plants survive indefinitely. The cultivated blueberries are chiefly improved varieties of highbush blueberry (*V. corymbo'sum*), also known as swamp blueberry, a native of the United States, growing in acid bogs, meadows, and moist or rocky woods from Newfoundland to Minnesota and southward to Louisiana and Georgia. The cultivated varieties, which outyield and produce larger berries than the wild species, were developed largely by Dr. Frederick V. Coville, of the United States Department of Agriculture. Dr. Coville's experimental work in the improvement and technical breeding of blueberries paved the way for their commercial production. He was assisted ably in this work by Miss Elizabeth C. White, of New Lisbon, N. J., who supplied much of the foundation stock for the plant breeding experiments and later pioneered the commercialization of the new domesticated varieties.[9] These improved horticultural varieties do not breed true because they are crosses or hybrids; hence, seedlings should not be used in the establishment of commercial blueberry patches.[6] The expansion of commercial plantings throughout the areas where blueberries are grown apparently depends primarily upon the development of successful, quick methods of propagation.[10] Improvement in propagation by cuttings offers the greatest possibilities.

Lowbush blueberry (*V. angustifo'lium*, syn. *V. pennsylva'nicum* Lam., not Mill.), present in dry hills and woods from Newfoundland to Saskatchewan, Wisconsin, Illinois, and Virginia, produces a sweet bluish-black berry, the earliest maturer in the North, and furnishes the bulk of the blueberries for the eastern markets. Improved sorts, however, have not been developed to any extent.

Commercial blueberry plantings from the eastern highbush blueberry in the Northwest, especially in Washington, were begun in 1917 by Henry C. Gane, with plants secured from Dr. Coville.[11] Some attempt has also been made there to

[7] Funston, F. BOTANY OF YAKUTAT BAY, ALASKA. (BOTANICAL REPORT BY F. V. COVILLE.) U. S. Dept. Agr., Div. Bot., Contrib. U. S. Natl. Herbarium 3(6) : 325–351. 1896.
[8] Coville, F. V. DIRECTIONS FOR BLUEBERRY CULTURE, 1921. U. S. Dept. Agr. Bull. 974, 24 pp., illus. 1921.
[9] Bailey, J. S., and Franklin, H. J. BLUEBERRY CULTURE IN MASSACHUSETTS. Mass. Agr. Expt. Sta. Bull. 317, 19 pp., illus. 1935.
[10] Ware, L. M. PROPAGATION STUDIES WITH THE SOUTHERN BLUEBERRY. Miss. Agr. Expt. Sta. Bull. 280, 40 pp., illus. 1930.
[11] Crowley, D. J. OBSERVATIONS AND EXPERIMENTS WITH BLUEBERRIES IN WESTERN WASHINGTON. Wash. Agr. Expt. Sta. Bull. 276, 19 pp., illus. 1933.

test rabbiteye blueberry (*V. virga'tum*), also called southern blueberry, now cultivated commercially in the Southeastern States where it is native. This species, closely related to highbush blueberry, has proved hardy in Washington, but its economic importance there is as yet undetermined. Thus far no attempts have been made to improve any of the western blueberries or to cross them with the cultivated highbush blueberry. The western ovalleaf blueberry, which produces exceptionally large berries and is a vigorous grower, apparently offers promising commercial potentialities, particularly for crossing with low-growing species, such as lowbush blueberry.[6] Some of the western highbush species mature their fruits so uniformly that one picking harvests the entire crop. On the other hand, the cultivated blueberries ripen rather unevenly and require 4 or 5 pickings. Although uneven ripening probably best satisfies the fresh fruit trade and is desirable for home use, the canning industry prefers berries harvested in one or two pickings.[11] Hybrids of native species and the cultivated blueberries may eventually rank high in the blueberry industry of the Northwest. Box blueberry, big whortleberry, ovalleaf whortleberry, and delicious blueberry (*V. delicio'sum*), are the native commercial blueberries of Washington.[11]

---

[6] Munson, W. M. THE HORTICULTURAL STATUS OF THE GENUS VACCINIUM. Maine Agr. Expt. Sta. Ann. Rept. (1901) 17 : [113]–160, illus. 1902.
[11] See footnote on preceding page.

BIG WHORTLEBERRY

Vacci'nium membrana'ceum, syn. *V. macrophyl'lum*

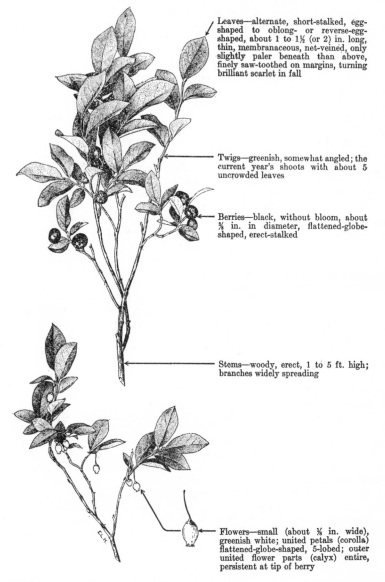

Leaves—alternate, short-stalked, egg-shaped to oblong- or reverse-egg-shaped, about 1 to 1½ (or 2) in. long, thin, membranaceous, net-veined, only slightly paler beneath than above, finely saw-toothed on margins, turning brilliant scarlet in fall

Twigs—greenish, somewhat angled; the current year's shoots with about 5 uncrowded leaves

Berries—black, without bloom, about ⅜ in. in diameter, flattened-globe-shaped, erect-stalked

Stems—woody, erect, 1 to 5 ft. high; branches widely spreading

Flowers—small (about ⅙ in. wide), greenish white; united petals (corolla) flattened-globe-shaped, 5-lobed; outer united flower parts (calyx) entire, persistent at tip of berry

Big whortleberry is a fairly large shrub, ranging chiefly in the mountains, from Alaska to the northern peninsula of Michigan, northern Wyoming, Idaho, and northern California. Its local names include big, high(bush), large, and thinleaf huckleberry, bilberry, or blueberry. Although this and other species of *Vaccinium* which belong to the blueberry family (Vacciniaceae) are commonly referred to in the West as huckleberries, that name is preferably restricted to the genus *Gaylussacia*, and blueberry to the blue-fruited members of the genus *Vaccinium*. The specific name of this species refers to its thin (membranaceous) leaves. Big whortleberry, although not found in the humid coastal country of Washington and Oregon, is very abundant in the more arid regions farther east at elevations of from 2,500 to 7,000 feet. It grows on all slopes, although probably most commonly on northern exposures, and in both wet and dry sites, especially in sandy or gravelly loams, both in the open and in the dense shade of white fir, hemlock, and other coniferous trees. This species often forms the dominant undergrowth in coniferous woods over extensive areas and is one of the chief shrubs in old burns, frequently being associated with such woody plants as honeysuckles (*Lonicera* spp.), mountain-ashes (*Sorbus* spp.), serviceberries (*Amelanchier* spp.), snowbrush (*Ceanothus velutinus*), thimbleberry (*Rubus parviflorus*), and roses (*Rosa* spp.). The flowers usually appear from about the middle of May to June, occasionally lasting into July.[1] The sizable, agreeably flavored, sweetish berries, red at first but black when mature, begin to ripen about the middle of July to the middle of August, the major portion of the fruit crop being produced before September 20.[1]

Big whortleberry is practically worthless to poor browse for cattle and horses. Its palatability varies from poor to about fair on the average for sheep, although under some conditions it may be fairly good or even good. It is generally utilized more extensively on ranges where it occurs in mixture with palatable weeds and grasses. The maximum palatability periods of this species vary measurably; but generally it is used most extensively either early or late in the season, when the sheep are entering or leaving the range. Big whortleberry is chiefly important as browse in eastern Oregon, eastern Washington, and the Snake River Valley of Idaho, where it rates as fair to fairly good sheep feed. It is also an important game feed, especially on the winter elk ranges of those States. Although this shrub loses its leaves in the fall, elk crop the twigs on the winter range, and at times utilize the plant so closely, especially when other forage is scarce, that the bushes may be destroyed.

The fruits of big whortleberry are picked extensively for local consumption, and are even marketed on some scale. Customarily, the Klamath Indians of Oregon cross the Cascade Mountains about the third week in August for a several weeks' picnic and to gather and dry their winter's supply of these berries.[2] The shrubs growing in burns are the most prolific fruit producers and, due to this fact, the plant has been the innocent cause of numerous man-made forest fires. The berries, an important food of birds and rodents, are also highly relished by bears.

---

[1] Dayton, W. A. IMPORTANT WESTERN BROWSE PLANTS. U. S. Dept. Agr. Misc. Pub. 101, 214 pp., illus. 1931.
[2] Coville, F. V. NOTES ON THE PLANTS USED BY THE KLAMATH INDIANS OF OREGON. U. S. Dept. Agr., Div. Bot., Contrib. U. S. Natl. Herbarium 5 : 87–108. 1897.

SOAPTREE YUCCA [1]

Yuc'ca ela'ta, syn. *Y. radio'sa*

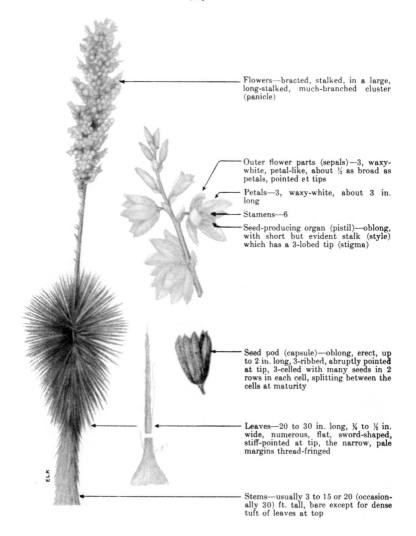

Flowers—bracted, stalked, in a large, long-stalked, much-branched cluster (panicle)

Outer flower parts (sepals)—3, waxy-white, petal-like, about ½ as broad as petals, pointed et tips

Petals—3, waxy-white, about 3 in. long

Stamens—6

Seed-producing organ (pistil)—oblong, with short but evident stalk (style) which has a 3-lobed tip (stigma)

Seed pod (capsule)—oblong, erect, up to 2 in. long, 3-ribbed, abruptly pointed at tip, 3-celled with many seeds in 2 rows in each cell, splitting between the cells at maturity

Leaves—20 to 30 in. long, ¼ to ½ in. wide, numerous, flat, sword-shaped, stiff-pointed at tip, the narrow, pale margins thread-fringed

Stems—usually 3 to 15 or 20 (occasionally 30) ft. tall, bare except for dense tuft of leaves at top

ELK

---

[1] This name is adopted from a suggestion contained in IMPORTANT WESTERN BROWSE PLANTS (U. S. Dept. Agr. Misc. Pub. 101), footnote 5, p. 14. Soapweed has been in almost universal use for this species but the name is applied to other species of *Yucca* as well and is obviously inappropriate for arborescent plants.

Soaptree yucca, more often known simply as soapweed or palmilla (Mexican for little palm), is a somewhat palmlike plant, crowned with a dense tuft of swordlike leaves; the naked, treelike stems are from 3 to 20 feet high or, under the most favorable conditions, occasionally even 30 feet high. The species is one of the most common and conspicuous desert shrubs or trees of the Southwest, being particularly picturesque when the large, beautiful clusters of waxy-white flowers appear in May and June. It is then often reproduced both on canvas and film by artists and photographers. Because this species is symbolic of the Southwestern deserts, its selection as the State flower of New Mexico is very appropriate. Yucca, usually spelled yuca, was the Carib name for cassava (*Manihot utilissima*), a well-known tropical food plant of the spurge family. Linnaeus is said to have selected the name *Yucca* for this American liliaceous genus as a result of a misapplication of the name to it by the seventeenth century British botanist John Gerard. The specific name *elata* means tall, and refers to the height and stately appearance of the more luxuriant individuals of this species.

Soaptree yucca occurs from western Texas, through southern New Mexico and southern Arizona, south into Mexico, preferring dry, sandy plains and mesas, although it is able to grow on clayey or gravelly soils. In its chosen habitat it is frequently the dominant plant over extensive areas. Black grama (*Bouteloua eriopoda*) is one of its most common associates, but on some ranges, where black grama has almost or entirely disappeared due to overgrazing, soaptree yucca still persists in association with honey mesquite (*Prosopis glandulosa*), snakeweed (*Gutierrezia sarothrae*), and other plants of low palatability.

The flowers of soaptree yucca, borne in large clusters during May and June, are succulent and, if within reach, are eagerly sought by cattle. The growing tips in the center of the upper circle of leaves are also grazed to some extent while young and fleshy, especially during a dearth of other forage. The greatest value of this species is as a maintenance food for range cattle in time of prolonged drought. The leaves, except for the growing tips, are harsh, tough, and sharp-pointed, and livestock have difficulty in utilizing them on the range. However, special chopping and shredding machines have been devised for converting the green leaves and stalks of such plants into emergency feed. Wooton [2] reports that "if fed alone it may be expected to keep stock from starving; if fed with concentrates a properly balanced ration may be worked out." Forsling [3] found that "from 15 to 20 pounds of chopped soapweed with 1 to 1⅓ pounds of cottonseed meal daily will maintain the average breeding cow and may improve her condition slowly." He noted that feeding chopped soaptree yucca without a supplemental concentrate like cottonseed meal was not entirely satisfactory. The chopped feed is palatable to livestock as the juices of the plant are sweet. The slight danger of cattle choking or bloating can be overcome by use of machinery which will chop the plant into small pieces, and by

---

[2] Wooton, E. O. CERTAIN DESERT PLANTS AS EMERGENCY STOCK FEED. U. S. Dept. Agr. Bull. 728, 31 pp., illus. 1918.
[3] Forsling, C. L. CHOPPED SOAPWEED AS EMERGENCY FEED FOR CATTLE ON SOUTHWESTERN RANGES. U. S. Dept. Agr. Bull. 745, 20 pp., illus. 1919.

feeding in moderation during the first few days. Otherwise, this feed has a very good effect upon livestock. Experiments show that cattle can be fattened if fed freely on a mixture of 1 pound of meal to 15 pounds of "soapweed." Economically, however, the use of this plant should be restricted to drought emergencies. The feeding of chopped soaptree yucca in 1918 saved many thousands of southwestern cattle from starvation.[3] Fortunately, this plant is not killed by cutting, as it sprouts readily from the roots. Growth, however, is very slow and a rotation of from 10 to 15 years is necessary to insure a perpetual supply.[2][3]

The roots of soaptree yucca are used locally (under the name amole) as soap by both Indians and white men. This use is reflected in the common names soaptree yucca and soapweed. The soap has a particularly high reputation for shampooing the hair and, as such, is marketed commercially on a limited scale. The Indians also use the remarkably tough leaf fibers in making baskets, ropes, and mats. During the World War emergency, the fiber was used as a substitute for jute in the manufacture of bagging, but has never attained commercial importance in peace times.

Soaptree yucca has a local utility in checking wind erosion and also is esteemed for the shade which it provides in regions where shade is at a premium.[4][5] It is a valuable and beautiful ornamental plant, especially on ranches where the water supply is not sufficient to enable introduced shade trees and shrubs to survive. The wood, as in other arborescent yuccas, is light and flexible, yet tough and porous—hence very desirable as splints for broken limbs. Campbell and Keller [5] report that mature *Yucca elata* plants show an annual growth of one-half of an inch to two inches, depending largely on the amount of summer rainfall, the average annual growth being about an inch. These authors also observed the growth and longevity of the leaves of this species, and give a list of the insects, reptiles, and mammals associated with it.

The yuccas, numbering about 30 species, are confined to North and Central America, Bermuda, and the West Indies, most of them being native to the arid regions of the Southwest and the tablelands of Mexico. Together with a number of other genera belonging to the lily family (Liliaceae), the yuccas are distinctive in this largely herbaceous family because of their frequent arborescent habit of growth, large size, and the bold, rather palmlike effect which they lend to the landscape. Although some of the species of yucca are acaulescent, i. e., do not produce an erect stem except for the flower stalk, the majority develop a trunk, often treelike, which may be branched or unbranched. The long, stiff, sword-shaped or linear, needle-pointed leaves, which are usually fiber-bearing and sometimes toothed on the margins, are characteristic of this genus; the leaves form a dense basal tuft in the stemless species or clothe the trunk or ends of the branches in the arborescent forms. The huge,

[4] Dayton, W. A. IMPORTANT WESTERN BROWSE PLANTS. U. S. Dept. Agr. Misc. Pub. 101, 214 pp., illus. 1931.
[5] Campbell, R. S., and Keller, J. G. GROWTH AND REPRODUCTION OF YUCCA ELATA. Ecology 13 : 364–374, illus. 1932.

mostly erect clusters of large, waxy, whitish, and usually pendent flowers are striking in appearance. The flowers are perfect (i. e., containing both male and female parts) and the evident stalk (style) of the seed-producing organ (ovary) is stout. The rather thickish perianth parts are separate or only slightly united, the inner three usually being white or cream-colored and more delicate in texture than the outer three, which are sometimes tinged with purple or pink; the six stamens are inserted at the base. The fruit is a three-celled or imperfectly six-celled capsule, either dry or somewhat fleshy and berrylike. Soaptree yucca is distinguished among its treelike sister species of the United States largely by having the flower cluster raised on a conspicuously long (about 3 to 7 feet), naked stalk, by its slender, thread-fringed leaves, pale or white on the margins, and by its dry, erect, splitting (dehiscent) fruit.

Yucca flowers are not self-pollinated, but depend upon the agency of certain small moths (*Tegeticula* spp., syn. *Pronuba* spp.) ; in fact, both the yuccas and the moths are interdependent for perpetuation of their respective species.[6][7] *T. alba* (syn. *Pronuba alba*) pollinates *Yucca elata* and datil (*Y. baccata*).[6][7] The female moth, working at night, collects pollen from one flower, then flies to another, lays her eggs in the seed-producing organ, and "in a manner which corresponds to actions full of purpose and deliberation climbs to the style (*i. e.*, the stalk of the pistil, or seed-producing organ) and thrusts the pollen ball down the stigmatic tube." [8]

Small soapweed (*Y. glau'ca*), also called soapweed yucca, is a short-stalked, narrow-leaved species with small flowers about 1½ inches long. The datil, meaning little date, often called banana yucca, is similar, but the leaves are much broader and more rigid and the flowers larger (2 to 3 inches long) ; its somewhat banana-like fruits have a sweet, edible pulp surrounding the seeds. The Datil National Forest of New Mexico was named after this species. The flower clusters of both of the above species are palatable to cattle and sheep, and the young leaves are eaten to some extent, especially during drought. Cattle and deer, attracted by their succulence and palatable juices, sometimes pull the leaves and chew the lower portions of these plants. These species lack the pulpy stem of soaptree yucca, being much inferior as chopped emergency feed. The Indians used the fruit of the datil as food; the roots of both of the above species as soap; and the leaves as fiber in weaving.

[6] Trelease, W. FURTHER STUDIES OF YUCCAS AND THEIR POLLINATION. Mo. Bot. Gard. Ann. Rept. 4: [181]–226, illus. 1893.
[7] Comstock, J. H. AN INTRODUCTION TO ENTOMOLOGY. Rev., 1,044 pp., illus. Ithaca, N. Y. 1933.
[8] Jepson, W. L. A MANUAL OF THE FLOWERING PLANTS OF CALIFORNIA. 1,238 pp., illus. Berkeley, Calif. [1925.]

INDEX

This index has been arranged to serve also as a check list of the genera, species, and varieties of plants discussed in the body of the publication. Accepted plant names, both English and Latin, appear in heavy type. Synonyms are shown in ordinary type. Where the Latin and English generic names are identical (*e. g.*, Acacia, Geranium) the name is not repeated.

Since the publication is not paged, the symbols adopted for the respective generic, specific, and varietal discussions (arranged in the order G, GL, W, and B) are given in lieu of pagination. Italicization of a symbol indicates that the genus, species, or variety referred to is not written up separately but is given subordinate treatment under another heading.

[5] Since this handbook went to press, a movement has been started to adopt podgrass as the English name for **Triglochin**, shore (or seaside) podgrass for **T. maritima**, and American (or short) podgrass for **T. striata**. **T. maritima**, the only species with arrowlike fruit, would be called arrowpod or arrow podgrass.

---

[7] Dock is the name of large-leaved species of **Rumex.**

[8] The English name, jointfir, was adopted for these plants in the text, in accordance with Standardized Plant Names usage. Since the handbook went to press, the Forest Service and other bureaus of the Department of Agriculture have adopted **ephedra** as the English name for these plants.

---

[9] True foxglove is **Digitalis.**

[10] Old World genus. American species are preferably placed in the genus **Pteridium.**

---

[11] True sage is **Salvia.**   [12] The medicinal bark of **Rhamnus purshiana.**

[13] A cultivated Old World climber. Range species of **Clematis** are sometimes called by this name.
[14] Since this handbook went to press, a movement has been started to adopt podgrass as the English name for **Triglochin**, shore (or seaside) podgrass for **T. maritima**, and American (or short) podgrass for **T. striata**. T. maritima, the only species with arrowlike fruit, would be called arrowpod or arrow podgrass.

[15] Viorna, recognized by some botanists as a separate genus is, by most authorities, held to be only a subgenus or section of **Clematis.**

[16] **Virgins-bower** is frequently applied to other species of **Clematis.**

A CATALOG OF SELECTED
DOVER BOOKS
IN ALL FIELDS OF INTEREST

A CATALOG OF SELECTED DOVER
BOOKS IN ALL FIELDS OF INTEREST

DRAWINGS OF REMBRANDT, edited by Seymour Slive. Updated Lippmann, Hofstede de Groot edition, with definitive scholarly apparatus. All portraits, biblical sketches, landscapes, nudes. Oriental figures, classical studies, together with selection of work by followers. 550 illustrations. Total of 630pp. 9⅛ × 12¼.
21485-0, 21486-9 Pa., Two-vol. set $25.00

GHOST AND HORROR STORIES OF AMBROSE BIERCE, Ambrose Bierce. 24 tales vividly imagined, strangely prophetic, and decades ahead of their time in technical skill: "The Damned Thing," "An Inhabitant of Carcosa," "The Eyes of the Panther," "Moxon's Master," and 20 more. 199pp. 5⅜ × 8½. 20767-6 Pa. $3.95

ETHICAL WRITINGS OF MAIMONIDES, Maimonides. Most significant ethical works of great medieval sage, newly translated for utmost precision, readability. Laws Concerning Character Traits, Eight Chapters, more. 192pp. 5⅜ × 8½.
24522-5 Pa. $4.50

THE EXPLORATION OF THE COLORADO RIVER AND ITS CANYONS, J. W. Powell. Full text of Powell's 1,000-mile expedition down the fabled Colorado in 1869. Superb account of terrain, geology, vegetation, Indians, famine, mutiny, treacherous rapids, mighty canyons, during exploration of last unknown part of continental U.S. 400pp. 5⅜ × 8½. 20094-9 Pa. $6.95

HISTORY OF PHILOSOPHY, Julián Marías. Clearest one-volume history on the market. Every major philosopher and dozens of others, to Existentialism and later. 505pp. 5⅜ × 8½. 21739-6 Pa. $8.50

ALL ABOUT LIGHTNING, Martin A. Uman. Highly readable non-technical survey of nature and causes of lightning, thunderstorms, ball lightning, St. Elmo's Fire, much more. Illustrated. 192pp. 5⅜ × 8½. 25237-X Pa. $5.95

SAILING ALONE AROUND THE WORLD, Captain Joshua Slocum. First man to sail around the world, alone, in small boat. One of great feats of seamanship told in delightful manner. 67 illustrations. 294pp. 5⅜ × 8½. 20326-3 Pa. $4.50

LETTERS AND NOTES ON THE MANNERS, CUSTOMS AND CONDITIONS OF THE NORTH AMERICAN INDIANS, George Catlin. Classic account of life among Plains Indians: ceremonies, hunt, warfare, etc. 312 plates. 572pp. of text. 6⅛ × 9¼. 22118-0, 22119-9 Pa. Two-vol. set $15.90

ALASKA: The Harriman Expedition, 1899, John Burroughs, John Muir, et al. Informative, engrossing accounts of two-month, 9,000-mile expedition. Native peoples, wildlife, forests, geography, salmon industry, glaciers, more. Profusely illustrated. 240 black-and-white line drawings. 124 black-and-white photographs. 3 maps. Index. 576pp. 5⅜ × 8½. 25109-8 Pa. $11.95

THE BOOK OF BEASTS: Being a Translation from a Latin Bestiary of the Twelfth Century, T. H. White. Wonderful catalog real and fanciful beasts: manticore, griffin, phoenix, amphivius, jaculus, many more. White's witty erudite commentary on scientific, historical aspects. Fascinating glimpse of medieval mind. Illustrated. 296pp. 5⅜ × 8¼. (Available in U.S. only) 24609-4 Pa. $5.95

FRANK LLOYD WRIGHT: ARCHITECTURE AND NATURE With 160 Illustrations, Donald Hoffmann. Profusely illustrated study of influence of nature—especially prairie—on Wright's designs for Fallingwater, Robie House, Guggenheim Museum, other masterpieces. 96pp. 9¼ × 10¾. 25098-9 Pa. $7.95

FRANK LLOYD WRIGHT'S FALLINGWATER, Donald Hoffmann. Wright's famous waterfall house: planning and construction of organic idea. History of site, owners, Wright's personal involvement. Photographs of various stages of building. Preface by Edgar Kaufmann, Jr. 100 illustrations. 112pp. 9¼ × 10.
23671-4 Pa. $7.95

YEARS WITH FRANK LLOYD WRIGHT: Apprentice to Genius, Edgar Tafel. Insightful memoir by a former apprentice presents a revealing portrait of Wright the man, the inspired teacher, the greatest American architect. 372 black-and-white illustrations. Preface. Index. vi + 228pp. 8¼ × 11. 24801-1 Pa. $9.95

THE STORY OF KING ARTHUR AND HIS KNIGHTS, Howard Pyle. Enchanting version of King Arthur fable has delighted generations with imaginative narratives of exciting adventures and unforgettable illustrations by the author. 41 illustrations. xviii + 313pp. 6⅛ × 9¼. 21445-1 Pa. $5.95

THE GODS OF THE EGYPTIANS, E. A. Wallis Budge. Thorough coverage of numerous gods of ancient Egypt by foremost Egyptologist. Information on evolution of cults, rites and gods; the cult of Osiris; the Book of the Dead and its rites; the sacred animals and birds; Heaven and Hell; and more. 956pp. 6⅛ × 9¼.
22055-9, 22056-7 Pa., Two-vol. set $21.90

A THEOLOGICO-POLITICAL TREATISE, Benedict Spinoza. Also contains unfinished *Political Treatise*. Great classic on religious liberty, theory of government on common consent. R. Elwes translation. Total of 421pp. 5⅜ × 8½.
20249-6 Pa. $6.95

INCIDENTS OF TRAVEL IN CENTRAL AMERICA, CHIAPAS, AND YU-CATAN, John L. Stephens. Almost single-handed discovery of Maya culture; exploration of ruined cities, monuments, temples; customs of Indians. 115 drawings. 892pp. 5⅜ × 8½. 22404-X, 22405-8 Pa., Two-vol. set $15.90

LOS CAPRICHOS, Francisco Goya. 80 plates of wild, grotesque monsters and caricatures. Prado manuscript included. 183pp. 6⅜ × 9⅜. 22384-1 Pa. $4.95

AUTOBIOGRAPHY: The Story of My Experiments with Truth, Mohandas K. Gandhi. Not hagiography, but Gandhi in his own words. Boyhood, legal studies, purification, the growth of the Satyagraha (nonviolent protest) movement. Critical, inspiring work of the man who freed India. 480pp. 5⅜ × 8½. (Available in U.S. only)
24593-4 Pa. $6.95

ILLUSTRATED DICTIONARY OF HISTORIC ARCHITECTURE, edited by Cyril M. Harris. Extraordinary compendium of clear, concise definitions for over 5,000 important architectural terms complemented by over 2,000 line drawings. Covers full spectrum of architecture from ancient ruins to 20th-century Modernism. Preface. 592pp. 7½ × 9⅝. 24444-X Pa. $14.95

THE NIGHT BEFORE CHRISTMAS, Clement Moore. Full text, and woodcuts from original 1848 book. Also critical, historical material. 19 illustrations. 40pp. 4⅝ × 6. 22797-9 Pa. $2.50

THE LESSON OF JAPANESE ARCHITECTURE: 165 Photographs, Jiro Harada. Memorable gallery of 165 photographs taken in the 1930's of exquisite Japanese homes of the well-to-do and historic buildings. 13 line diagrams. 192pp. 8⅝ × 11¼. 24778-3 Pa. $8.95

THE AUTOBIOGRAPHY OF CHARLES DARWIN AND SELECTED LETTERS, edited by Francis Darwin. The fascinating life of eccentric genius composed of an intimate memoir by Darwin (intended for his children); commentary by his son, Francis; hundreds of fragments from notebooks, journals, papers; and letters to and from Lyell, Hooker, Huxley, Wallace and Henslow. xi + 365pp. 5⅜ × 8. 20479-0 Pa. $5.95

WONDERS OF THE SKY: Observing Rainbows, Comets, Eclipses, the Stars and Other Phenomena, Fred Schaaf. Charming, easy-to-read poetic guide to all manner of celestial events visible to the naked eye. Mock suns, glories, Belt of Venus, more. Illustrated. 299pp. 5¼ × 8¼. 24402-4 Pa. $7.95

BURNHAM'S CELESTIAL HANDBOOK, Robert Burnham, Jr. Thorough guide to the stars beyond our solar system. Exhaustive treatment. Alphabetical by constellation: Andromeda to Cetus in Vol. 1; Chamaeleon to Orion in Vol. 2; and Pavo to Vulpecula in Vol. 3. Hundreds of illustrations. Index in Vol. 3. 2,000pp. 6⅛ × 9¼. 23567-X, 23568-8, 23673-0 Pa., Three-vol. set $37.85

STAR NAMES: Their Lore and Meaning, Richard Hinckley Allen. Fascinating history of names various cultures have given to constellations and literary and folkloristic uses that have been made of stars. Indexes to subjects. Arabic and Greek names. Biblical references. Bibliography. 563pp. 5⅜ × 8½. 21079-0 Pa. $7.95

THIRTY YEARS THAT SHOOK PHYSICS: The Story of Quantum Theory, George Gamow. Lucid, accessible introduction to influential theory of energy and matter. Careful explanations of Dirac's anti-particles, Bohr's model of the atom, much more. 12 plates. Numerous drawings. 240pp. 5⅜ × 8½. 24895-X Pa. $4.95

CHINESE DOMESTIC FURNITURE IN PHOTOGRAPHS AND MEASURED DRAWINGS, Gustav Ecke. A rare volume, now affordably priced for antique collectors, furniture buffs and art historians. Detailed review of styles ranging from early Shang to late Ming. Unabridged republication. 161 black-and-white drawings, photos. Total of 224pp. 8⅜ × 11¼. (Available in U.S. only) 25171-3 Pa. $12.95

VINCENT VAN GOGH: A Biography, Julius Meier-Graefe. Dynamic, penetrating study of artist's life, relationship with brother, Theo, painting techniques, travels, more. Readable, engrossing. 160pp. 5⅜ × 8½. (Available in U.S. only) 25253-1 Pa. $3.95

HOW TO WRITE, Gertrude Stein. Gertrude Stein claimed anyone could understand her unconventional writing—here are clues to help. Fascinating improvisations, language experiments, explanations illuminate Stein's craft and the art of writing. Total of 414pp. 4⅝ × 6⅜.   23144-5 Pa. $5.95

ADVENTURES AT SEA IN THE GREAT AGE OF SAIL: Five Firsthand Narratives, edited by Elliot Snow. Rare true accounts of exploration, whaling, shipwreck, fierce natives, trade, shipboard life, more. 33 illustrations. Introduction. 353pp. 5⅜ × 8½.   25177-2 Pa. $7.95

THE HERBAL OR GENERAL HISTORY OF PLANTS, John Gerard. Classic descriptions of about 2,850 plants—with over 2,700 illustrations—includes Latin and English names, physical descriptions, varieties, time and place of growth, more. 2,706 illustrations. xlv + 1,678pp. 8½ × 12¼.   23147-X Cloth. $75.00

DOROTHY AND THE WIZARD IN OZ, L. Frank Baum. Dorothy and the Wizard visit the center of the Earth, where people are vegetables, glass houses grow and Oz characters reappear. Classic sequel to *Wizard of Oz*. 256pp. 5⅜ × 8.
         24714-7 Pa. $4.95

SONGS OF EXPERIENCE: Facsimile Reproduction with 26 Plates in Full Color, William Blake. This facsimile of Blake's original "Illuminated Book" reproduces 26 full-color plates from a rare 1826 edition. Includes "The Tyger," "London," "Holy Thursday," and other immortal poems. 26 color plates. Printed text of poems. 48pp. 5¼ × 7.   24636-1 Pa. $3.50

SONGS OF INNOCENCE, William Blake. The first and most popular of Blake's famous "Illuminated Books," in a facsimile edition reproducing all 31 brightly colored plates. Additional printed text of each poem. 64pp. 5¼ × 7.
         22764-2 Pa. $3.50

PRECIOUS STONES, Max Bauer. Classic, thorough study of diamonds, rubies, emeralds, garnets, etc.: physical character, occurrence, properties, use, similar topics. 20 plates, 8 in color. 94 figures. 659pp. 6⅛ × 9¼.
         21910-0, 21911-9 Pa., Two-vol. set $15.90

ENCYCLOPEDIA OF VICTORIAN NEEDLEWORK, S. F. A. Caulfeild and Blanche Saward. Full, precise descriptions of stitches, techniques for dozens of needlecrafts—most exhaustive reference of its kind. Over 800 figures. Total of 679pp. 8⅛ × 11. Two volumes.   Vol. 1 22800-2 Pa. $11.95
                                   Vol. 2 22801-0 Pa. $11.95

THE MARVELOUS LAND OF OZ, L. Frank Baum. Second Oz book, the Scarecrow and Tin Woodman are back with hero named Tip, Oz magic. 136 illustrations. 287pp. 5⅜ × 8½.   20692-0 Pa. $5.95

WILD FOWL DECOYS, Joel Barber. Basic book on the subject, by foremost authority and collector. Reveals history of decoy making and rigging, place in American culture, different kinds of decoys, how to make them, and how to use them. 140 plates. 156pp. 7⅞ × 10¾.   20011-6 Pa. $8.95

HISTORY OF LACE, Mrs. Bury Palliser. Definitive, profusely illustrated chronicle of lace from earliest times to late 19th century. Laces of Italy, Greece, England, France, Belgium, etc. Landmark of needlework scholarship. 266 illustrations. 672pp. 6⅛ × 9¼.   24742-2 Pa. $14.95

ILLUSTRATED GUIDE TO SHAKER FURNITURE, Robert Meader. All furniture and appurtenances, with much on unknown local styles. 235 photos. 146pp. 9 × 12. 22819-3 Pa. $7.95

WHALE SHIPS AND WHALING: A Pictorial Survey, George Francis Dow. Over 200 vintage engravings, drawings, photographs of barks, brigs, cutters, other vessels. Also harpoons, lances, whaling guns, many other artifacts. Comprehensive text by foremost authority. 207 black-and-white illustrations. 288pp. 6 × 9. 24808-9 Pa. $8.95

THE BERTRAMS, Anthony Trollope. Powerful portrayal of blind self-will and thwarted ambition includes one of Trollope's most heartrending love stories. 497pp. 5⅜ × 8½. 25119-5 Pa. $8.95

ADVENTURES WITH A HAND LENS, Richard Headstrom. Clearly written guide to observing and studying flowers and grasses, fish scales, moth and insect wings, egg cases, buds, feathers, seeds, leaf scars, moss, molds, ferns, common crystals, etc.—all with an ordinary, inexpensive magnifying glass. 209 exact line drawings aid in your discoveries. 220pp. 5⅜ × 8½. 23330-8 Pa. $4.50

RODIN ON ART AND ARTISTS, Auguste Rodin. Great sculptor's candid, wide-ranging comments on meaning of art; great artists; relation of sculpture to poetry, painting, music; philosophy of life, more. 76 superb black-and-white illustrations of Rodin's sculpture, drawings and prints. 119pp. 8⅜ × 11¼. 24487-3 Pa. $6.95

FIFTY CLASSIC FRENCH FILMS, 1912–1982: A Pictorial Record, Anthony Slide. Memorable stills from Grand Illusion, Beauty and the Beast, Hiroshima, Mon Amour, many more. Credits, plot synopses, reviews, etc. 160pp. 8¼ × 11. 25256-6 Pa. $11.95

THE PRINCIPLES OF PSYCHOLOGY, William James. Famous long course complete, unabridged. Stream of thought, time perception, memory, experimental methods; great work decades ahead of its time. 94 figures. 1,391pp. 5⅜ × 8½. 20381-6, 20382-4 Pa., Two-vol. set $19.90

BODIES IN A BOOKSHOP, R. T. Campbell. Challenging mystery of blackmail and murder with ingenious plot and superbly drawn characters. In the best tradition of British suspense fiction. 192pp. 5⅜ × 8½. 24720-1 Pa. $3.95

CALLAS: PORTRAIT OF A PRIMA DONNA, George Jellinek. Renowned commentator on the musical scene chronicles incredible career and life of the most controversial, fascinating, influential operatic personality of our time. 64 black-and-white photographs. 416pp. 5⅜ × 8¼. 25047-4 Pa. $7.95

GEOMETRY, RELATIVITY AND THE FOURTH DIMENSION, Rudolph Rucker. Exposition of fourth dimension, concepts of relativity as Flatland characters continue adventures. Popular, easily followed yet accurate, profound. 141 illustrations. 133pp. 5⅜ × 8½. 23400-2 Pa. $3.50

HOUSEHOLD STORIES BY THE BROTHERS GRIMM, with pictures by Walter Crane. 53 classic stories—Rumpelstiltskin, Rapunzel, Hansel and Gretel, the Fisherman and his Wife, Snow White, Tom Thumb, Sleeping Beauty, Cinderella, and so much more—lavishly illustrated with original 19th century drawings. 114 illustrations. x + 269pp. 5⅜ × 8½. 21080-4 Pa. $4.50

SUNDIALS, Albert Waugh. Far and away the best, most thorough coverage of ideas, mathematics concerned, types, construction, adjusting anywhere. Over 100 illustrations. 230pp. 5⅜ × 8½. 22947-5 Pa. $4.00

PICTURE HISTORY OF THE NORMANDIE: With 190 Illustrations, Frank O. Braynard. Full story of legendary French ocean liner: Art Deco interiors, design innovations, furnishings, celebrities, maiden voyage, tragic fire, much more. Extensive text. 144pp. 8⅞ × 11¾. 25257-4 Pa. $9.95

THE FIRST AMERICAN COOKBOOK: A Facsimile of "American Cookery," 1796, Amelia Simmons. Facsimile of the first American-written cookbook published in the United States contains authentic recipes for colonial favorites—pumpkin pudding, winter squash pudding, spruce beer, Indian slapjacks, and more. Introductory Essay and Glossary of colonial cooking terms. 80pp. 5⅜ × 8½. 24710-4 Pa. $3.50

101 PUZZLES IN THOUGHT AND LOGIC, C. R. Wylie, Jr. Solve murders and robberies, find out which fishermen are liars, how a blind man could possibly identify a color—purely by your own reasoning! 107pp. 5⅜ × 8½. 20367-0 Pa. $2.00

THE BOOK OF WORLD-FAMOUS MUSIC—CLASSICAL, POPULAR AND FOLK, James J. Fuld. Revised and enlarged republication of landmark work in musico-bibliography. Full information about nearly 1,000 songs and compositions including first lines of music and lyrics. New supplement. Index. 800pp. 5⅜ × 8¼. 24857-7 Pa. $14.95

ANTHROPOLOGY AND MODERN LIFE, Franz Boas. Great anthropologist's classic treatise on race and culture. Introduction by Ruth Bunzel. Only inexpensive paperback edition. 255pp. 5⅜ × 8½. 25245-0 Pa. $5.95

THE TALE OF PETER RABBIT, Beatrix Potter. The inimitable Peter's terrifying adventure in Mr. McGregor's garden, with all 27 wonderful, full-color Potter illustrations. 55pp. 4¼ × 5½. (Available in U.S. only) 22827-4 Pa. $1.75

THREE PROPHETIC SCIENCE FICTION NOVELS, H. G. Wells. *When the Sleeper Wakes, A Story of the Days to Come* and *The Time Machine* (full version). 335pp. 5⅜ × 8½. (Available in U.S. only) 20605-X Pa. $5.95

APICIUS COOKERY AND DINING IN IMPERIAL ROME, edited and translated by Joseph Dommers Vehling. Oldest known cookbook in existence offers readers a clear picture of what foods Romans ate, how they prepared them, etc. 49 illustrations. 301pp. 6⅛ × 9¼. 23563-7 Pa. $6.00

SHAKESPEARE LEXICON AND QUOTATION DICTIONARY, Alexander Schmidt. Full definitions, locations, shades of meaning of every word in plays and poems. More than 50,000 exact quotations. 1,485pp. 6½ × 9¼. 22726-X, 22727-8 Pa., Two-vol. set $27.90

THE WORLD'S GREAT SPEECHES, edited by Lewis Copeland and Lawrence W. Lamm. Vast collection of 278 speeches from Greeks to 1970. Powerful and effective models; unique look at history. 842pp. 5⅜ × 8½. 20468-5 Pa. $10.95

THE BLUE FAIRY BOOK, Andrew Lang. The first, most famous collection, with many familiar tales: Little Red Riding Hood, Aladdin and the Wonderful Lamp, Puss in Boots, Sleeping Beauty, Hansel and Gretel, Rumpelstiltskin; 37 in all. 138 illustrations. 390pp. 5⅜ × 8½. 21437-0 Pa. $5.95

THE STORY OF THE CHAMPIONS OF THE ROUND TABLE, Howard Pyle. Sir Launcelot, Sir Tristram and Sir Percival in spirited adventures of love and triumph retold in Pyle's inimitable style. 50 drawings, 31 full-page. xviii + 329pp. 6½ × 9¼. 21883-X Pa. $6.95

AUDUBON AND HIS JOURNALS, Maria Audubon. Unmatched two-volume portrait of the great artist, naturalist and author contains his journals, an excellent biography by his granddaughter, expert annotations by the noted ornithologist, Dr. Elliott Coues, and 37 superb illustrations. Total of 1,200pp. 5⅜ × 8.
Vol. I 25143-8 Pa. $8.95
Vol. II 25144-6 Pa. $8.95

GREAT DINOSAUR HUNTERS AND THEIR DISCOVERIES, Edwin H. Colbert. Fascinating, lavishly illustrated chronicle of dinosaur research, 1820's to 1960. Achievements of Cope, Marsh, Brown, Buckland, Mantell, Huxley, many others. 384pp. 5¼ × 8¼. 24701-5 Pa. $6.95

THE TASTEMAKERS, Russell Lynes. Informal, illustrated social history of American taste 1850's–1950's. First popularized categories Highbrow, Lowbrow, Middlebrow. 129 illustrations. New (1979) afterword. 384pp. 6 × 9.
23993-4 Pa. $6.95

DOUBLE CROSS PURPOSES, Ronald A. Knox. A treasure hunt in the Scottish Highlands, an old map, unidentified corpse, surprise discoveries keep reader guessing in this cleverly intricate tale of financial skullduggery. 2 black-and-white maps. 320pp. 5⅜ × 8½. (Available in U.S. only) 25032-6 Pa. $5.95

AUTHENTIC VICTORIAN DECORATION AND ORNAMENTATION IN FULL COLOR: 46 Plates from "Studies in Design," Christopher Dresser. Superb full-color lithographs reproduced from rare original portfolio of a major Victorian designer. 48pp. 9¼ × 12¼. 25083-0 Pa. $7.95

PRIMITIVE ART, Franz Boas. Remains the best text ever prepared on subject, thoroughly discussing Indian, African, Asian, Australian, and, especially, Northern American primitive art. Over 950 illustrations show ceramics, masks, totem poles, weapons, textiles, paintings, much more. 376pp. 5⅜ × 8. 20025-6 Pa. $6.95

SIDELIGHTS ON RELATIVITY, Albert Einstein. Unabridged republication of two lectures delivered by the great physicist in 1920–21. *Ether and Relativity* and *Geometry and Experience*. Elegant ideas in non-mathematical form, accessible to intelligent layman. vi + 56pp. 5⅜ × 8½. 24511-X Pa. $2.95

THE WIT AND HUMOR OF OSCAR WILDE, edited by Alvin Redman. More than 1,000 ripostes, paradoxes, wisecracks: Work is the curse of the drinking classes, I can resist everything except temptation, etc. 258pp. 5⅜ × 8½. 20602-5 Pa. $4.50

ADVENTURES WITH A MICROSCOPE, Richard Headstrom. 59 adventures with clothing fibers, protozoa, ferns and lichens, roots and leaves, much more. 142 illustrations. 232pp. 5⅜ × 8½. 23471-1 Pa. $3.95

PLANTS OF THE BIBLE, Harold N. Moldenke and Alma L. Moldenke. Standard reference to all 230 plants mentioned in Scriptures. Latin name, biblical reference, uses, modern identity, much more. Unsurpassed encyclopedic resource for scholars, botanists, nature lovers, students of Bible. Bibliography. Indexes. 123 black-and-white illustrations. 384pp. 6 × 9. 25069-5 Pa. $8.95

FAMOUS AMERICAN WOMEN: A Biographical Dictionary from Colonial Times to the Present, Robert McHenry, ed. From Pocahontas to Rosa Parks, 1,035 distinguished American women documented in separate biographical entries. Accurate, up-to-date data, numerous categories, spans 400 years. Indices. 493pp. 6½ × 9¼. 24523-3 Pa. $9.95

THE FABULOUS INTERIORS OF THE GREAT OCEAN LINERS IN HISTORIC PHOTOGRAPHS, William H. Miller, Jr. Some 200 superb photographs capture exquisite interiors of world's great "floating palaces"—1890's to 1980's: *Titanic, Ile de France, Queen Elizabeth, United States, Europa,* more. Approx. 200 black-and-white photographs. Captions. Text. Introduction. 160pp. 8⅜ × 11¾. 24756-2 Pa. $9.95

THE GREAT LUXURY LINERS, 1927-1954: A Photographic Record, William H. Miller, Jr. Nostalgic tribute to heyday of ocean liners. 186 photos of Ile de France, Normandie, Leviathan, Queen Elizabeth, United States, many others. Interior and exterior views. Introduction. Captions. 160pp. 9 × 12. 24056-8 Pa. $9.95

A NATURAL HISTORY OF THE DUCKS, John Charles Phillips. Great landmark of ornithology offers complete detailed coverage of nearly 200 species and subspecies of ducks: gadwall, sheldrake, merganser, pintail, many more. 74 full-color plates, 102 black-and-white. Bibliography. Total of 1,920pp. 8⅜ × 11¼. 25141-1, 25142-X Cloth. Two-vol. set $100.00

THE SEAWEED HANDBOOK: An Illustrated Guide to Seaweeds from North Carolina to Canada, Thomas F. Lee. Concise reference covers 78 species. Scientific and common names, habitat, distribution, more. Finding keys for easy identification. 224pp. 5⅜ × 8½. 25215-9 Pa. $5.95

THE TEN BOOKS OF ARCHITECTURE: The 1755 Leoni Edition, Leon Battista Alberti. Rare classic helped introduce the glories of ancient architecture to the Renaissance. 68 black-and-white plates. 336pp. 8⅜ × 11¼. 25239-6 Pa. $14.95

MISS MACKENZIE, Anthony Trollope. Minor masterpieces by Victorian master unmasks many truths about life in 19th-century England. First inexpensive edition in years. 392pp. 5⅜ × 8½. 25201-9 Pa. $7.95

THE RIME OF THE ANCIENT MARINER, Gustave Doré, Samuel Taylor Coleridge. Dramatic engravings considered by many to be his greatest work. The terrifying space of the open sea, the storms and whirlpools of an unknown ocean, the ice of Antarctica, more—all rendered in a powerful, chilling manner. Full text. 38 plates. 77pp. 9¼ × 12. 22305-1 Pa. $4.95

THE EXPEDITIONS OF ZEBULON MONTGOMERY PIKE, Zebulon Montgomery Pike. Fascinating first-hand accounts (1805-6) of exploration of Mississippi River, Indian wars, capture by Spanish dragoons, much more. 1,088pp. 5⅜ × 8½. 25254-X, 25255-8 Pa. Two-vol. set $23.90

A CONCISE HISTORY OF PHOTOGRAPHY: Third Revised Edition, Helmut Gernsheim. Best one-volume history—camera obscura, photochemistry, daguerreotypes, evolution of cameras, film, more. Also artistic aspects—landscape, portraits, fine art, etc. 281 black-and-white photographs. 26 in color. 176pp. 8⅜ × 11¼.
25128-4 Pa. $12.95

THE DORÉ BIBLE ILLUSTRATIONS, Gustave Doré. 241 detailed plates from the Bible: the Creation scenes, Adam and Eve, Flood, Babylon, battle sequences, life of Jesus, etc. Each plate is accompanied by the verses from the King James version of the Bible. 241pp. 9 × 12.
23004-X Pa. $8.95

HUGGER-MUGGER IN THE LOUVRE, Elliot Paul. Second Homer Evans mystery-comedy. Theft at the Louvre involves sleuth in hilarious, madcap caper. "A knockout."—Books. 336pp. 5⅜ × 8½.
25185-3 Pa. $5.95

FLATLAND, E. A. Abbott. Intriguing and enormously popular science-fiction classic explores the complexities of trying to survive as a two-dimensional being in a three-dimensional world. Amusingly illustrated by the author. 16 illustrations. 103pp. 5⅜ × 8½.
20001-9 Pa. $2.25

THE HISTORY OF THE LEWIS AND CLARK EXPEDITION, Meriwether Lewis and William Clark, edited by Elliott Coues. Classic edition of Lewis and Clark's day-by-day journals that later became the basis for U.S. claims to Oregon and the West. Accurate and invaluable geographical, botanical, biological, meteorological and anthropological material. Total of 1,508pp. 5⅜ × 8½.
21268-8, 21269-6, 21270-X Pa. Three-vol. set $25.50

LANGUAGE, TRUTH AND LOGIC, Alfred J. Ayer. Famous, clear introduction to Vienna, Cambridge schools of Logical Positivism. Role of philosophy, elimination of metaphysics, nature of analysis, etc. 160pp. 5⅜ × 8½. (Available in U.S. and Canada only)
20010-8 Pa. $2.95

MATHEMATICS FOR THE NONMATHEMATICIAN, Morris Kline. Detailed, college-level treatment of mathematics in cultural and historical context, with numerous exercises. For liberal arts students. Preface. Recommended Reading Lists. Tables. Index. Numerous black-and-white figures. xvi + 641pp. 5⅜ × 8½.
24823-2 Pa. $11.95

28 SCIENCE FICTION STORIES, H. G. Wells. Novels, *Star Begotten* and *Men Like Gods,* plus 26 short stories: "Empire of the Ants," "A Story of the Stone Age," "The Stolen Bacillus," "In the Abyss," etc. 915pp. 5⅜ × 8½. (Available in U.S. only)
20265-8 Cloth. $10.95

HANDBOOK OF PICTORIAL SYMBOLS, Rudolph Modley. 3,250 signs and symbols, many systems in full; official or heavy commercial use. Arranged by subject. Most in Pictorial Archive series. 143pp. 8⅛ × 11.
23357-X Pa. $5.95

INCIDENTS OF TRAVEL IN YUCATAN, John L. Stephens. Classic (1843) exploration of jungles of Yucatan, looking for evidences of Maya civilization. Travel adventures, Mexican and Indian culture, etc. Total of 669pp. 5⅜ × 8½.
20926-1, 20927-X Pa., Two-vol. set $9.90

DEGAS: An Intimate Portrait, Ambroise Vollard. Charming, anecdotal memoir by famous art dealer of one of the greatest 19th-century French painters. 14 black-and-white illustrations. Introduction by Harold L. Van Doren. 96pp. 5⅜ × 8½.
25131-4 Pa. $3.95

PERSONAL NARRATIVE OF A PILGRIMAGE TO ALMANDINAH AND MECCAH, Richard Burton. Great travel classic by remarkably colorful personality. Burton, disguised as a Moroccan, visited sacred shrines of Islam, narrowly escaping death. 47 illustrations. 959pp. 5⅜ × 8½. 21217-3, 21218-1 Pa., Two-vol. set $17.90

PHRASE AND WORD ORIGINS, A. H. Holt. Entertaining, reliable, modern study of more than 1,200 colorful words, phrases, origins and histories. Much unexpected information. 254pp. 5⅜ × 8½. 20758-7 Pa. $5.95

THE RED THUMB MARK, R. Austin Freeman. In this first Dr. Thorndyke case, the great scientific detective draws fascinating conclusions from the nature of a single fingerprint. Exciting story, authentic science. 320pp. 5⅜ × 8½. (Available in U.S. only) 25210-8 Pa. $5.95

AN EGYPTIAN HIEROGLYPHIC DICTIONARY, E. A. Wallis Budge. Monumental work containing about 25,000 words or terms that occur in texts ranging from 3000 B.C. to 600 A.D. Each entry consists of a transliteration of the word, the word in hieroglyphs, and the meaning in English. 1,314pp. 6⅜ × 10.
23615-3, 23616-1 Pa., Two-vol. set $27.90

THE COMPLEAT STRATEGYST: Being a Primer on the Theory of Games of Strategy, J. D. Williams. Highly entertaining classic describes, with many illustrated examples, how to select best strategies in conflict situations. Prefaces. Appendices. xvi + 268pp. 5⅜ × 8½. 25101-2 Pa. $5.95

THE ROAD TO OZ, L. Frank Baum. Dorothy meets the Shaggy Man, little Button-Bright and the Rainbow's beautiful daughter in this delightful trip to the magical Land of Oz. 272pp. 5⅜ × 8. 25208-6 Pa. $4.95

POINT AND LINE TO PLANE, Wassily Kandinsky. Seminal exposition of role of point, line, other elements in non-objective painting. Essential to understanding 20th-century art. 127 illustrations. 192pp. 6½ × 9¼. 23808-3 Pa. $4.50

LADY ANNA, Anthony Trollope. Moving chronicle of Countess Lovel's bitter struggle to win for herself and daughter Anna their rightful rank and fortune—perhaps at cost of sanity itself. 384pp. 5⅜ × 8½. 24669-8 Pa. $6.95

EGYPTIAN MAGIC, E. A. Wallis Budge. Sums up all that is known about magic in Ancient Egypt: the role of magic in controlling the gods, powerful amulets that warded off evil spirits, scarabs of immortality, use of wax images, formulas and spells, the secret name, much more. 253pp. 5⅜ × 8½. 22681-6 Pa. $4.50

THE DANCE OF SIVA, Ananda Coomaraswamy. Preeminent authority unfolds the vast metaphysic of India: the revelation of her art, conception of the universe, social organization, etc. 27 reproductions of art masterpieces. 192pp. 5⅜ × 8½.
24817-8 Pa. $5.95

CHRISTMAS CUSTOMS AND TRADITIONS, Clement A. Miles. Origin, evolution, significance of religious, secular practices. Caroling, gifts, yule logs, much more. Full, scholarly yet fascinating; non-sectarian. 400pp. 5⅜ × 8½.
23354-5 Pa. $6.50

THE HUMAN FIGURE IN MOTION, Eadweard Muybridge. More than 4,500 stopped-action photos, in action series, showing undraped men, women, children jumping, lying down, throwing, sitting, wrestling, carrying, etc. 390pp. 7⅞ × 10⅝.
20204-6 Cloth. $19.95

THE MAN WHO WAS THURSDAY, Gilbert Keith Chesterton. Witty, fast-paced novel about a club of anarchists in turn-of-the-century London. Brilliant social, religious, philosophical speculations. 128pp. 5⅜ × 8½.
25121-7 Pa. $3.95

A CEZANNE SKETCHBOOK: Figures, Portraits, Landscapes and Still Lifes, Paul Cezanne. Great artist experiments with tonal effects, light, mass, other qualities in over 100 drawings. A revealing view of developing master painter, precursor of Cubism. 102 black-and-white illustrations. 144pp. 8¾ × 6⅜.
24790-2 Pa. $5.95

AN ENCYCLOPEDIA OF BATTLES: Accounts of Over 1,560 Battles from 1479 b.c. to the Present, David Eggenberger. Presents essential details of every major battle in recorded history, from the first battle of Megiddo in 1479 b.c. to Grenada in 1984. List of Battle Maps. New Appendix covering the years 1967–1984. Index. 99 illustrations. 544pp. 6½ × 9¼.
24913-1 Pa. $14.95

AN ETYMOLOGICAL DICTIONARY OF MODERN ENGLISH, Ernest Weekley. Richest, fullest work, by foremost British lexicographer. Detailed word histories. Inexhaustible. Total of 856pp. 6½ × 9¼.
21873-2, 21874-0 Pa., Two-vol. set $17.00

WEBSTER'S AMERICAN MILITARY BIOGRAPHIES, edited by Robert McHenry. Over 1,000 figures who shaped 3 centuries of American military history. Detailed biographies of Nathan Hale, Douglas MacArthur, Mary Hallaren, others. Chronologies of engagements, more. Introduction. Addenda. 1,033 entries in alphabetical order. xi + 548pp. 6½ × 9¼. (Available in U.S. only)
24758-9 Pa. $11.95

LIFE IN ANCIENT EGYPT, Adolf Erman. Detailed older account, with much not in more recent books: domestic life, religion, magic, medicine, commerce, and whatever else needed for complete picture. Many illustrations. 597pp. 5⅜ × 8½.
22632-8 Pa. $8.95

HISTORIC COSTUME IN PICTURES, Braun & Schneider. Over 1,450 costumed figures shown, covering a wide variety of peoples: kings, emperors, nobles, priests, servants, soldiers, scholars, townsfolk, peasants, merchants, courtiers, cavaliers, and more. 256pp. 8⅜ × 11¼.
23150-X Pa. $7.95

THE NOTEBOOKS OF LEONARDO DA VINCI, edited by J. P. Richter. Extracts from manuscripts reveal great genius; on painting, sculpture, anatomy, sciences, geography, etc. Both Italian and English. 186 ms. pages reproduced, plus 500 additional drawings, including studies for *Last Supper, Sforza* monument, etc. 860pp. 7⅞ × 10¾. (Available in U.S. only) 22572-0, 22573-9 Pa., Two-vol. set $25.90

THE ART NOUVEAU STYLE BOOK OF ALPHONSE MUCHA: All 72 Plates from "Documents Decoratifs" in Original Color, Alphonse Mucha. Rare copyright-free design portfolio by high priest of Art Nouveau. Jewelry, wallpaper, stained glass, furniture, figure studies, plant and animal motifs, etc. Only complete one-volume edition. 80pp. 9⅜ × 12¼. 24044-4 Pa. $8.95

ANIMALS: 1,419 COPYRIGHT-FREE ILLUSTRATIONS OF MAMMALS, BIRDS, FISH, INSECTS, ETC., edited by Jim Harter. Clear wood engravings present, in extremely lifelike poses, over 1,000 species of animals. One of the most extensive pictorial sourcebooks of its kind. Captions. Index. 284pp. 9 × 12. 23766-5 Pa. $9.95

OBELISTS FLY HIGH, C. Daly King. Masterpiece of American detective fiction, long out of print, involves murder on a 1935 transcontinental flight—"a very thrilling story"—NY Times. Unabridged and unaltered republication of the edition published by William Collins Sons & Co. Ltd., London, 1935. 288pp. 5⅜ × 8½. (Available in U.S. only) 25036-9 Pa. $4.95

VICTORIAN AND EDWARDIAN FASHION: A Photographic Survey, Alison Gernsheim. First fashion history completely illustrated by contemporary photographs. Full text plus 235 photos, 1840–1914, in which many celebrities appear. 240pp. 6½ × 9¼. 24205-6 Pa. $6.00

THE ART OF THE FRENCH ILLUSTRATED BOOK, 1700–1914, Gordon N. Ray. Over 630 superb book illustrations by Fragonard, Delacroix, Daumier, Doré, Grandville, Manet, Mucha, Steinlen, Toulouse-Lautrec and many others. Preface. Introduction. 633 halftones. Indices of artists, authors & titles, binders and provenances. Appendices. Bibliography. 608pp. 8⅜ × 11¼. 25086-5 Pa. $24.95

THE WONDERFUL WIZARD OF OZ, L. Frank Baum. Facsimile in full color of America's finest children's classic. 143 illustrations by W. W. Denslow. 267pp. 5⅜ × 8½. 20691-2 Pa. $5.95

FRONTIERS OF MODERN PHYSICS: New Perspectives on Cosmology, Relativity, Black Holes and Extraterrestrial Intelligence, Tony Rothman, et al. For the intelligent layman. Subjects include: cosmological models of the universe; black holes; the neutrino; the search for extraterrestrial intelligence. Introduction. 46 black-and-white illustrations. 192pp. 5⅜ × 8½. 24587-X Pa. $6.95

THE FRIENDLY STARS, Martha Evans Martin & Donald Howard Menzel. Classic text marshalls the stars together in an engaging, non-technical survey, presenting them as sources of beauty in night sky. 23 illustrations. Foreword. 2 star charts. Index. 147pp. 5⅜ × 8½. 21099-5 Pa. $3.50

FADS AND FALLACIES IN THE NAME OF SCIENCE, Martin Gardner. Fair, witty appraisal of cranks, quacks, and quackeries of science and pseudoscience: hollow earth, Velikovsky, orgone energy, Dianetics, flying saucers, Bridey Murphy, food and medical fads, etc. Revised, expanded In the Name of Science. "A very able and even-tempered presentation."—The New Yorker. 363pp. 5⅜ × 8. 20394-8 Pa. $5.95

ANCIENT EGYPT: ITS CULTURE AND HISTORY, J. E Manchip White. From pre-dynastics through Ptolemies: society, history, political structure, religion, daily life, literature, cultural heritage. 48 plates. 217pp. 5⅜ × 8½. 22548-8 Pa. $4.95

SIR HARRY HOTSPUR OF HUMBLETHWAITE, Anthony Trollope. Incisive, unconventional psychological study of a conflict between a wealthy baronet, his idealistic daughter, and their scapegrace cousin. The 1870 novel in its first inexpensive edition in years. 250pp. 5⅜ × 8½. 24953-0 Pa. $4.95

LASERS AND HOLOGRAPHY, Winston E. Kock. Sound introduction to burgeoning field, expanded (1981) for second edition. Wave patterns, coherence, lasers, diffraction, zone plates, properties of holograms, recent advances. 84 illustrations. 160pp. 5⅜ × 8¼. (Except in United Kingdom) 24041-X Pa. $3.50

INTRODUCTION TO ARTIFICIAL INTELLIGENCE: SECOND, EN-LARGED EDITION, Philip C. Jackson, Jr. Comprehensive survey of artificial intelligence—the study of how machines (computers) can be made to act intelligently. Includes introductory and advanced material. Extensive notes updating the main text. 132 black-and-white illustrations. 512pp. 5⅜ × 8½. 24864-X Pa. $8.95

HISTORY OF INDIAN AND INDONESIAN ART, Ananda K. Coomaraswamy. Over 400 illustrations illuminate classic study of Indian art from earliest Harappa finds to early 20th century. Provides philosophical, religious and social insights. 304pp. 6⅜ × 9⅜. 25005-9 Pa. $8.95

THE GOLEM, Gustav Meyrink. Most famous supernatural novel in modern European literature, set in Ghetto of Old Prague around 1890. Compelling story of mystical experiences, strange transformations, profound terror. 13 black-and-white illustrations. 224pp. 5⅜ × 8½. (Available in U.S. only) 25025-3 Pa. $5.95

ARMADALE, Wilkie Collins. Third great mystery novel by the author of *The Woman in White* and *The Moonstone*. Original magazine version with 40 illustrations. 597pp. 5⅜ × 8½. 23429-0 Pa. $7.95

PICTORIAL ENCYCLOPEDIA OF HISTORIC ARCHITECTURAL PLANS, DETAILS AND ELEMENTS: With 1,880 Line Drawings of Arches, Domes, Doorways, Facades, Gables, Windows, etc., John Theodore Haneman. Sourcebook of inspiration for architects, designers, others. Bibliography. Captions. 141pp. 9 × 12. 24605-1 Pa. $6.95

BENCHLEY LOST AND FOUND, Robert Benchley. Finest humor from early 30's, about pet peeves, child psychologists, post office and others. Mostly unavailable elsewhere. 73 illustrations by Peter Arno and others. 183pp. 5⅜ × 8½. 22410-4 Pa. $3.95

ERTÉ GRAPHICS, Erté. Collection of striking color graphics: *Seasons, Alphabet, Numerals, Aces* and *Precious Stones*. 50 plates, including 4 on covers. 48pp. 9⅜ × 12¼. 23580-7 Pa. $6.95

THE JOURNAL OF HENRY D. THOREAU, edited by Bradford Torrey, F. H. Allen. Complete reprinting of 14 volumes, 1837–61, over two million words; the sourcebooks for *Walden*, etc. Definitive. All original sketches, plus 75 photographs. 1,804pp. 8½ × 12¼. 20312-3, 20313-1 Cloth., Two-vol. set $80.00

CASTLES: THEIR CONSTRUCTION AND HISTORY, Sidney Toy. Traces castle development from ancient roots. Nearly 200 photographs and drawings illustrate moats, keeps, baileys, many other features. Caernarvon, Dover Castles, Hadrian's Wall, Tower of London, dozens more. 256pp. 5⅜ × 8¼. 24898-4 Pa. $5.95

AMERICAN CLIPPER SHIPS: 1833–1858, Octavius T. Howe & Frederick C. Matthews. Fully-illustrated, encyclopedic review of 352 clipper ships from the period of America's greatest maritime supremacy. Introduction. 109 halftones. 5 black-and-white line illustrations. Index. Total of 928pp. 5⅜ × 8½.
25115-2, 25116-0 Pa., Two-vol. set $17.90

TOWARDS A NEW ARCHITECTURE, Le Corbusier. Pioneering manifesto by great architect, near legendary founder of "International School." Technical and aesthetic theories, views on industry, economics, relation of form to function, "mass-production spirit," much more. Profusely illustrated. Unabridged translation of 13th French edition. Introduction by Frederick Etchells. 320pp. 6⅛ × 9¼. (Available in U.S. only)
25023-7 Pa. $8.95

THE BOOK OF KELLS, edited by Blanche Cirker. Inexpensive collection of 32 full-color, full-page plates from the greatest illuminated manuscript of the Middle Ages, painstakingly reproduced from rare facsimile edition. Publisher's Note. Captions. 32pp. 9⅜ × 12¼.
24345-1 Pa. $4.95

BEST SCIENCE FICTION STORIES OF H. G. WELLS, H. G. Wells. Full novel *The Invisible Man*, plus 17 short stories: "The Crystal Egg," "Aepyornis Island," "The Strange Orchid," etc. 303pp. 5⅜ × 8½. (Available in U.S. only)
21531-8 Pa. $4.95

AMERICAN SAILING SHIPS: Their Plans and History, Charles G. Davis. Photos, construction details of schooners, frigates, clippers, other sailcraft of 18th to early 20th centuries—plus entertaining discourse on design, rigging, nautical lore, much more. 137 black-and-white illustrations. 240pp. 6⅛ × 9¼.
24658-2 Pa. $5.95

ENTERTAINING MATHEMATICAL PUZZLES, Martin Gardner. Selection of author's favorite conundrums involving arithmetic, money, speed, etc., with lively commentary. Complete solutions. 112pp. 5⅜ × 8½.
25211-6 Pa. $2.95

THE WILL TO BELIEVE, HUMAN IMMORTALITY, William James. Two books bound together. Effect of irrational on logical, and arguments for human immortality. 402pp. 5⅜ × 8½.
20291-7 Pa. $7.50

THE HAUNTED MONASTERY and THE CHINESE MAZE MURDERS, Robert Van Gulik. 2 full novels by Van Gulik continue adventures of Judge Dee and his companions. An evil Taoist monastery, seemingly supernatural events; overgrown topiary maze that hides strange crimes. Set in 7th-century China. 27 illustrations. 328pp. 5⅜ × 8½.
23502-5 Pa. $5.95

CELEBRATED CASES OF JUDGE DEE (DEE GOONG AN), translated by Robert Van Gulik. Authentic 18th-century Chinese detective novel; Dee and associates solve three interlocked cases. Led to Van Gulik's own stories with same characters. Extensive introduction. 9 illustrations. 237pp. 5⅜ × 8½.
23337-5 Pa. $4.95

Prices subject to change without notice.

Available at your book dealer or write for free catalog to Dept. GI, Dover Publications, Inc., 31 East 2nd St., Mineola, N.Y. 11501. Dover publishes more than 175 books each year on science, elementary and advanced mathematics, biology, music, art, literary history, social sciences and other areas.